The SAGE Handbook of
Rhetorical
Studies

The SAGE Handbook of
Rhetorical
Studies

Edited by
Andrea A. Lunsford
Stanford University

Associate Editors
Kirt H. Wilson
University of Minnesota, Twin Cities

Rosa A. Eberly
Pennsylvania State University, University Park

Los Angeles • London • New Delhi • Singapore • Washington DC

For information:

SAGE Publications, Inc.
2455 Teller Road
Thousand Oaks, California 91320
E-mail: order@sagepub.com

SAGE Publications Ltd.
1 Oliver's Yard
55 City Road
London EC1Y 1SP
United Kingdom

SAGE Publications India Pvt. Ltd.
B 1/I 1 Mohan Cooperative Industrial Area
Mathura Road, New Delhi 110 044
India

SAGE Publications Asia-Pacific Pte. Ltd.
33 Pekin Street #02-01
Far East Square
Singapore 048763

Printed in the United States of America

Library of Congress Cataloging-in-Publication Data

The SAGE handbook of rhetorical studies/Editor[s], Andrea A. Lunsford, Kirt H. Wilson, Rosa A. Eberly.
   p. cm.
Includes bibliographical references and index.
ISBN 978-1-4129-0950-1 (cloth)
  1. Rhetoric. I. Lunsford, Andrea A., 1942- II. Wilson, Kirt H., 1967- III. Eberly, Rosa A.
IV. Title: Handbook of rhetorical studies.

PN175.S15 2009
808—dc22   2008019321

Printed on acid-free paper

08 09 10 11 12   10 9 8 7 6 5 4 3 2 1

Acquiring Editor:	Todd R. Armstrong
Associate Editor:	Deya Saoud
Editorial Assistant:	Aja Baker
Production Editor:	Sarah K. Quesenberry
Copy Editor:	QuADS Prepress (P) Ltd.
Proofreader:	Jenifer Kooiman
Indexer:	Rick Hurd
Typesetter:	C&M Digitals (P) Ltd.
Cover Designer:	Gail Buschman
Marketing Manager:	Carmel Schrire

Contents

Acknowledgments

Producing a collection of distinguished essays for *The SAGE Handbook of Rhetorical Studies* has been a rare privilege, but it has also been a challenge. What good fortune, then, to have had the support and assistance of so many colleagues and friends. To Todd Armstrong, who first broached the idea of this book and whose wisdom has guided us throughout the long writing and editing process, we owe a great debt of gratitude. In addition, SAGE's Deya Saoud has answered more questions and attended to more details than anyone should ever have been required to do, and she has done so with the greatest generosity and good humor. We are also grateful to Aja Baker and Sarah Quesenberry for their meticulous attention to detail.

Without the remarkable work of a brilliant group of section editors, this book would not have been possible: The contributions of C. Jan Swearingen, Edward Schiappa, Cheryl Glenn, Martín Carcasson, Carolyn Miller, John Lyne, Rosa Eberly, and Kirt Wilson are apparent in every page of this volume. Their work was of course made possible by the contributors to this book, all of whom took on the task of writing new and deeply sourced overview essays on key topics in rhetorical studies on top of already crowded schedules and overextended lives. Enduring thanks to them as well.

Special thanks also go to the scholars who provided insightful and critically helpful reviews of this work-in-progress: Mark Lawrence McPhail of the Department of Corporate Communication and Public Affairs at Southern Methodist University; Alisse Portnoy of the Department of English Language and Literature at the University of Michigan; Patricia A. Sullivan of the Department of Communication and Media at the State University of New York, New Paltz; Jeffrey Walker of the Division of Rhetoric and Composition at the University of Texas; and David Zarefsky of the Department of Communication Studies at Northwestern University.

Introduction

Rhetorics and Roadmaps

ANDREA A. LUNSFORD

KIRT H. WILSON

ROSA A. EBERLY

Language is a place of struggle.

—bell hooks (1990)

Rhetoric appears as the connective tissue peculiar to civil society and to its proper finalities, happiness and political peace.

—Marc Fumaroli (1983)

Some speech for another history.

—Peter Dimock (1998)

The idea of a *SAGE Handbook of Rhetorical Studies* emerged in 2004 during conversations among the SAGE editor Todd Armstrong and Professors Andrea Lunsford and Jim Aune. It seemed like a *good* idea, one whose time had come: This *Handbook* would join a long list of other distinguished handbooks published by SAGE, volumes designed to provide overviews of the best scholarship in important fields, to serve not only as an introduction for advanced undergraduate and graduate students but also as a reference text for established scholars. Moreover, this *Handbook* would come at a time when rhetoricians in departments of communication—under siege from both empirical-social scientists and university administrators—were building alliances to maintain their disciplinary legitimacy and when rhetoricians in English departments were increasingly joining ranks with their colleagues in writing studies to form new departments, occasionally with *rhetoric* in their titles. On the national scene, the dangerously misguided bumbling of the second Bush administration pointed to the urgency of making a shared space for critique, resistance, and alternative rhetorical visions of viable 21st-century democracy. Internationally, scholars in English and communication were making serious efforts to include and study the rhetorical theories and practices of Europe, Africa, and Asia.

That was nearly 4 years ago, before we had any idea of how difficult it would be to bring out this volume. The conceptualization, after all, had come easily enough: This volume would be written and edited by scholars in both English and communication studies. A multidisciplinary perspective would extend the project's scope and bring together voices that could articulate the complex roadmaps of interdisciplinary rhetoric. The editorial team was chosen with these principles in mind. Jim Aune, Kirt Wilson, Martin Carcasson, John Lyne, and Ed Schiappa were trained primarily in communication departments; Andrea Lunsford, Cheryl Glenn, Carolyn Miller, and Jan Swearingen were trained primarily in English studies; Rosa Eberly was trained in English, writing studies, and speech communication and holds faculty appointments in both communication and English. We paired scholars from each field around topics of common concern (noting, not to put too fine a point on it, that all the scholars from one discipline were men and all those from the other were women). Why then did we encounter significant difficulties? In a nutshell, despite the proximity of our fields, working collaboratively across English and communication turned out to be even more complicated than we had imagined it would be.

Nearly 25 years earlier, scholars in communication and in English also had worked together to honor Edward P. J. Corbett in a volume called *Essays on Classical Rhetoric and Modern Discourse* (Connors, Ede, & Lunsford, 1984). The introduction to

that volume attributes the "decline" of rhetoric after its momentary revival in 18th-century America to three forces: (1) the tendency to equate rhetoric with Hugh Blair's concept of *belles lettres* rather than to focus on classical rhetoric as the productive art of public discourse, (2) increased specialization of disciplines and the rise of English, and (3) the growing emphasis on written discourse rather than oral performance in college and university curricula. Particularly important, in hindsight, was the series of disciplinary divorces that transpired as groups broke away from the Modern Language Association (MLA), founded in 1883. The first to establish its own identity was the group that began the National Council of Teachers of English (NCTE) in 1911, taking rhetoricians such as Fred Newton Scott and other scholars of oral communication with them. Scholars such as James Winans and James O'Neill worked to create an organization of their own, and in 1914 the National Association of Academic Teachers of Public Speaking (later the Speech Communication Association and now the National Communication Association [NCA]) was born, effectively severing the ties between speaking and writing, which remained in English. Addressing the history of communication studies in his 1998 Arnold Lecture, Bruce Gronbeck (1999) noted the gendered nature and consequences of these disciplinary changes. In the United States at the turn of the 20th century, "female elocutionists were associated with fine arts, and male rhetoricians with the socio-political arts. . . . [R]hetoric and elocution were largely gendered, and the women were sent home when rhetorical studies came to dominate collegiate and university instruction" (p. 8).

In 1924, the Linguistic Society of America took as its mission advancing "the scientific study of language." This disciplinary narrowing and fragmenting was not good for rhetoric, an interdisciplinary and synthetic art capable of bringing together knowledge and ability in various fields with audiences and exigencies of various kinds. Thus, those who studied and professed rhetoric found themselves—often for practical or quotidian rather than theoretical or ideological reasons—housed in very different departments or schools or both. Ironically, the events that fragmented the study of rhetoric revealed a cross-disciplinary anxiety: how to legitimize the study and practice of human rhetorical interaction as the central concern of education and not simply as an ancillary interest and how to do so in the context of a field of study and practice denominated a nondiscipline at the very moment of its literal founding, when Plato put the *-ic* in rhetoric (*rhetor-ike*).

Several additional 20th-century developments—theoretical, methodological, and practical—also returned attention to rhetoric. An educational shift toward communication as a fundamental skill brought publicity and occasionally controversy to the arts of speaking and writing and, particularly, the relationship between the quality of instruction and the proper functioning of workplaces and polities. The influence of the University of Chicago teachers and critics Richard McKeon, Ronald Crane, and Richard Weaver, as well as Kenneth Burke (associated, though never officially affiliated, with Chicago), generated attention to pluralist "ideas and methods" and the theoretical, critical, and practical consequences of different points of departure. Daniel Fogarty's (1959) *Roots for a New Rhetoric* paved the way for still another "new rhetoric" that would emerge as European scholars encountered Anglo-American rhetoric; and, most notably in Perelman and Olbrechts-Tyteca's (1969) *The New Rhetoric* and in the founding of the journal *Philosophy and Rhetoric*, some philosophers moved their foci from formal and informal logic to rhetorical inquiry.

In 1949, the Conference on College Composition and Communication (CCCC) provided an opportunity to bring those in

English and in communication together. Despite this effort, teachers of writing and of speaking were nearly entirely unaware of each others' work, as they have remained until very recently. In the 1960s, however, more cross-fertilization seemed possible with the founding of The Rhetoric Society of America (RSA), whose first newsletter (December 1968) lists as members of its founding board of directors Edward P. J. Corbett, Wayne C. Booth, John Rycenga, William Irmscher, Ross Winterowd, Henry Johnstone, Richard Larson, Robert Gorrell, Joseph Schwartz, Richard Hughes, Harry Crosby, Owen Thomas, and Donald C. Bryant. These scholars came from English, speech, philosophy, and linguistics, a virtual reuniting of the groups that had splintered in the early 20th century. While this august board of intellectuals reflected the creative spirit of inquiry that marked the 1960s, it failed to represent what was, perhaps, the most enduring challenge to the post–World War II academy, the inclusion of women and minorities. This group was diverse in some ways but not in others: As was all too common at the time, no women or people of color appeared among the leaders.

Thus, at the end of the tumultuous 1960s, rhetoric stood at an important crossroads. In communication, the methods of Neo-Aristotelian criticism were no longer viable, and administrators and department chairs began to wonder whether rhetoric might benefit from the methodologies that their colleagues in the social sciences had embraced. In English, scholars expressed a renewed interest in rhetoric not only as a forgotten tradition but also as a potential resource for intellectual inquiry. Simultaneously, students across the academy challenged their professors to explain how two and a half millennia of rhetorical history mattered to the political issues that animated their private and public lives. Within these contexts, an interdisciplinary group of scholars assembled, in 1970, at the Wingspread Conference Center in Racine, Wisconsin. The rationale for the conference, as expressed to the National Endowment for the Humanities by the Speech Communication Association, was fourfold: (1) Unrest at home and abroad necessitated a reevaluation of traditional theories of persuasion; (2) technological change had created new problems that required new methods of analysis; (3) scholars needed to consider the new perspectives suggested by shifts in psychology, linguistics, philosophy, English, and anthropology; and (4) rhetoric required a new formulation to reach its scholarly and pedagogical potential ("Rhetoric Project Assured," 1969). In their 1971 book, Bitzer and Black modestly summarized the purpose of Wingspread and its accompanying conference, Pheasant Run, as an effort to "outline and amplify a theory of rhetoric suitable to 20th-century concepts and needs" (p. v).

Even a partial list of those who attended Wingspread gave one reason for hope. The presence of Carroll Arnold, Edwin Black, Henry Johnstone, Wayne Booth, Chaim Perelman, Lloyd Bitzer, Edward P. J. Corbett, Samuel Becker, and Richard McKeon suggested that a truly cross-disciplinary approach to the study of rhetoric was imminent. Again, however, the absence of even a single woman or person of color, despite the conference's extensive attention to the era's political issues, reveals the dissociations that sustained this particular intellectual community. Regardless, the Wingspread and Pheasant Run conferences did play a role in rhetoric's evolution across the academy, largely because the scholars who attended these conferences legitimized a kind of methodological pluralism. They had reoriented theoretical development, first, toward the "new rhetorics" and, eventually, toward critical theory and philosophy. Most important, conference participants had broadened the object domain of rhetorical inquiry. "It is imperative," they concluded, "that rhetorical studies be broadened to explore communicative procedures and practices not traditionally covered" (Bitzer & Black, 1971,

p. 238). The impact of this expansion was both disciplinary and personal.

Roadmap #1

Institutional and disciplinary histories are often personal histories as well. I (Andrea Lunsford speaking/writing here) began work toward the PhD at Ohio State in 1972. As a teacher of high school and community college students in the late 1960s with only an MA in English literature, I realized that while I had a fair idea of how to teach reading of literary works, I had almost no idea how to teach writing. (I wasn't even thinking of speaking at the time, though I had been fortunate to have some good speech classes during my undergraduate career at the University of Florida.) When I received a copy of Edward P. J. Corbett's Classical Rhetoric for the Modern Student, *I read it with amazement: What I had been trying to teach myself how to do was here described in detail and related to a 2,000-year-old tradition. As soon as I could, I quit my job and applied to graduate school, arriving in Columbus in the fall of 1972 to find that Corbett was teaching not rhetoric but 18th-century literature and the Bible. He was also, however, editing* College Composition and Communication— *which he invited me to help out with, and he was willing to do a series of independent study courses with me on the history of rhetoric. In addition, he introduced me to his colleagues in speech communication, including James Golden and Goodwin Berquist. In a correspondence with Jim Golden a few years ago, he said, "It is quite clear that English and Speech came together through the relationship we created and sustained [at Ohio State]." Indeed, Corbett and Golden had both arrived at Ohio State in 1966; in 1968, they edited a volume on the rhetoric of Blair, Campbell, and Whately, and they regularly visited each other's classes and encouraged their graduate students to do "crossover" work. I was fortunate, then, to take a number of courses taught in the Department of Speech. I completed my degree in 1977 and joined the English faculty at the University of British Columbia, unaware of how remarkable my training* had been and how fortunate I had been to learn across these disciplinary boundaries.

When I returned to Ohio State as a professor of English in 1986, I joined a small but thriving group of rhetoric and writing specialists in English and in speech communication. In addition to Ed Corbett, the English faculty included Frank O'Hare, Kitty Locker, Sara Garnes, Ann Dobyns, and Louis Ulman. Josina Makau was in speech communication, along with Sonia Foss, and soon Mary Garrett, James Darsey, and Jim Hikins rounded out the speech communication community. We began holding quarterly rhetoric colloquia between English and speech communication faculty and graduate students, and our students moved back and forth across departments, taking courses in both; we regularly served on each other's dissertation committees. But like other speech communication departments around the country, Ohio State's was to take an antirhetorical turn, led by a dean who valued only quantitative research. In an amazingly short time, this dean and her successor eliminated rhetoric as a serious field of study in speech communication. Golden and Berquist retired, and hiring in rhetoric ground to a halt. In 1994, Makau left for another position, as did Jim Darsey a little later and, soon after Darsey's departure, Mary Garrett. By the time Garrett left in 1999, the speech communication rhetoric group was effectively dissolved, and several graduate students who had been pursuing PhDs in speech communication moved over to English, where the rhetoric and writing group then stood at 14 tenure-line faculty members.

Before Makau left, she and I talked together and with colleagues about trying to establish a new department of rhetoric and writing at Ohio State. Eventually, we faced too many obstacles at both the departmental and college levels, and in retrospect I simply didn't have the vision and ability to create this change. I am still asking myself, "What if . . . ?"

Today, dozens of new departments and programs exist, dotting the academic landscape. Yet most of these departments and programs deal primarily in writing studies; few focus intensely on rhetorical history and theory, and fewer still bring together scholars of rhetoric from communication and English.

Since I have spent my long career entirely in departments of English, I still see writing, reading, and speaking (and increasingly listening and viewing) as arts that English can and should encompass. But as my narrative roadmap indicates, I also appreciate—and often embrace—the desire to create new alliances, new ways to move beyond the strictures of the all too often narrow disciplinarity of English.

* * * * *

This reflection provides one concrete example of disciplinary identifications and divisions, of one scholar's journey that in some ways reflects the status of rhetoric and rhetorical education in the United States in the mid- to late 20th century. What had seemed so promising in the 1970s as a matter of theoretical expansion and again in the 1980s as a revival of classical rhetoric, which increasingly informed writing (and rhetoric) programs, began to wane as the emphasis shifted strongly to composition theory and practice in English and prescriptive methods of rhetorical criticism in communication. The CCCC program, long a bellwether for shifts in the English discipline, featured fewer and fewer sessions on rhetoric, and composition journals reflected the same shift. In the meantime, communication departments continued the emphasis on empirical studies and on social science methodologies, leaving many humanist rhetoricians on the fringes of these departments. These trends, along with the pressing sense of fragmentation, denied rhetoric a chance to inform university curricula or national discussions of educational priorities and reform.

Roadmap #2

My (Kirt Wilson speaking/writing here) graduate education began at Purdue University in 1989. Purdue was the only program to which I applied, and I considered myself fortunate to be considered, let alone employed, as a graduate instructor of public speaking. I came to speech communication *late in my undergraduate career. As a freshman, I was convinced that my future field would be clinical psychology. This certainty began to crumble when, after a class in oral interpretation, the professor insisted that I try out for the collegiate forensic team. I had participated in team sports since elementary school, and I was intrigued by the idea that I could combine two things that I loved—competition and oral performance. Traveling to a wide variety of small midwestern colleges, I dutifully competed in Prose, Poetry, Duo, and Impromptu Speaking, and many of the tournaments and events I entered still persist in my memory with startling clarity.*

Before long, I realized that my coach hoped that I would play a very specific role for the team. I was to be the black orator, the speaker who would breathe life into James Weldon Johnson's The Creation *and then shift gears in the next round to offer a rhetorical critique of South Africa's apartheid policy. Initially, this expectation bothered me, but my long history in athletics had conditioned me well—success for a team means that everyone must play a part; one must leverage every opportunity for the good of the whole. Eventually, I reconciled myself to this situation when I realized that my race could be important, but its significance would not be defined by the occasional insult I endured. It would be important to me as a strategic category—a means to victory and a rhetorical and political problem to be analyzed before public audiences. What began as an expectation based solely on the color of my skin became, at least in my mind, a strategic decision to embrace an identity from which others and I might learn. I was never the team's star—others would go to nationals while I remained at state; nevertheless, the experience was exhilarating. I had found an intellectual community that I understood and in which my contributions were valued. The "veil of race" was omnipresent, of course, but it did not preclude the generous friendships I developed with my white teammates. Needless to say, I changed my major from psychology to speech communication.*

Although it is less common than it once was, a great many professors in communication studies encountered rhetoric through exposure to forensics and collegiate debate. I began my PhD at
Northwestern *in 1991, an institution with a storied debate tradition. Most of my professors—David Zarefsky, Michael Leff, G. Thomas Goodnight, and Tom Farrell—had first competed on the debate circuit and later coached debate teams. The scholars we read in class—Edwin Black, Robert L. Scott, Michael McGee, Steven Lucas, David Frank, Phil Wander, Edward Schiappa, Charlie Willard, Bob Craig, Craig Smith, Karlyn Kohrs Campbell, Kathleen Hall Jamieson—were debaters and coaches before they became published scholars. The graduate students with whom I studied, Gordon Mitchell and Erik Doxtader, would disappear on Thursday or Friday to accompany Northwestern's undergraduate team as it secured yet another victory. When I accepted my current position at the University of Minnesota, I was the only rhetoric scholar without a debate pedigree. One retirement (Robert L. Scott) and a hire (Ronald Greene) later, and my status as the exception remains intact. Today, few rhetoric graduate students in communication programs believe that coaching debate is a desirable career choice; nevertheless, the argumentative skills of those who once held a national ranking are respected still. You have to be very confident or very foolhardy to challenge some of my colleagues either in the classroom or at a national convention.*

The influence of forensics and collegiate debate on the field of communication studies during the 20th century was profound. As speech-communication departments solidified their identity and moved with confidence away from the traditions of English and composition, debate and forensics functioned as a kind of "minor league," a proving ground for young talent and a recruiting resource for departments. Forensics and debate attracted bright young minds that were articulate and interested in the interconnections among rhetorical theory, philosophy, and public policy. Debate and forensics rewarded both aggression and obsession; consequently, these future professors possessed an amazing knowledge of both history and the details of domestic and foreign policy. The penchant among communication scholars to read widely and borrow, sometimes shamelessly, from other fields reflected the practices of debate and individual events. An intense interest in political conflict meant that the discipline quickly recognized the cultural transformations that reshaped the United States in the 1960s and 1970s; but, at the same time, this recognition did not include a welcoming of women and African Americans. Debate, in particular, was a decidedly masculine enterprise. Women who succeeded in that space (e.g., Karlyn Kohrs Campbell and Kathleen Hall Jamieson) earned the respect of many, but the process of earning that respect was taxing and the norms of the debate culture were inherently agonistic. Most important, debate and forensics helped reinforce values and practices that defined the communication discipline in the 20th century: a restless desire to discover the next important topic, a belief that the quality of one's scholarship was determined by its argumentative force, an emphasis on oral rather than written forms of communication, a presumption of individual and disciplinary self-sufficiency, and an implicit assumption that a single scholar could know everything that mattered and answer any question that was relevant.

* * * * *

In 2000, at the biennial meeting of the RSA, a large group of rhetoric scholars met in open session to talk about how better to coordinate our scholarly and political efforts for the good of rhetorical studies and our shared worlds. During 2001 and 2002, conversations at national meetings brought scholars of rhetoric in English and in communication together once again to address their related interests. In particular, the creation of the Alliance of Rhetoric Societies (ARS) constituted a community of scholars from existing academic societies devoted entirely or in some part to rhetorical studies, including American Forensic Association, American Society for the History of Rhetoric, Coalition of Women Scholars in the History of Rhetoric, Canadian Society for the History of Rhetoric, Conference on College Composition and Communication, International

Society for the History of Rhetoric (ISHR), International Society for the Study of Argumentation, Kenneth Burke Society, National Communication Association, and Rhetoric Society of America. In inviting members of these organizations to join the ARS Board, Gerard A. Hauser (a contributor to this volume) wrote that ARS would "seek to regularize dialogue among rhetoricians and, thereby, promote a comprehensive intellectual community of rhetoricians who share in the common labor of scholarship" (personal communication, 2001). Today, ARS is chaired by the University of Minnesota's Art Walzer (a contributor to this volume), and the group includes representatives from most professional societies interested in rhetoric, writing, and argumentation.

In September 2003, the ARS held the "Conference on the Status and Future of Rhetorical Studies" at Northwestern University; addressing four major issues: (1) How ought we understand the concept of rhetorical agency? (2) Do we have a "rhetorical tradition," or are we better advised to think of "traditions"? If we do recognize a tradition or several traditions, how do we identify and characterize it (or them)? (3) What should be the institutional and social goals for academic rhetoric in the 21st century? How can rhetoric best contribute to the social, political, and cultural environment that extends beyond the university? (4) What does it mean to teach rhetoric? What does it mean to teach composition and performance seriously? What is the relationship between rhetoric and composition? Should they be distinguished? Four plenary speakers and respondents kicked off this working conference, which resulted in a set of reports/position papers later published in Rhetoric Society Quarterly (Summer 2004). Since then, ARS has continued to explore these issues and to sponsor workshops during RSA meetings; the 2007 workshop devoted much of its time to probing the relationship between rhetoric in communication and rhetoric in writing and English programs; to working toward making rhetoric more visible in places such as the American Council of Learned Societies, the Survey of Earned Doctorates, and the National Research Council; and to developing model undergraduate major programs (within both disciplines) that could encourage the founding of more such majors. In 2008, ARS will hold a workshop as part of RSA's biennial institute.

Roadmap #3

"I wake to sleep and take my waking slow. I learn by going where I have to go." I (Rosa Eberly speaking/ writing here) fell in love with that villanelle by Theodore Roethke (1953) when I took my first American literature class at Penn State, with Ron Maxwell, then a tenured assistant professor and soon to become the director of the Writing Center. Back in 1980, my first year at Penn State (a first-generation college student, I was allowed to apply to only one college), I was not a "lit major" or even an English major: I was a "journ major," a 17-year-old cub reporter, soon promoted to desk editor, of Penn State's superlative student daily. I was a debater and extemporizer in high school—went to the state finals in extemp; but "the paper" seduced my soul in college, and for much of my under-graduate career I skipped classes and worked at The Daily Collegian *50 to 60 hours a week. I changed my major to English, writing option, my second year because the journalism major—at the time still housed in the College of the Liberal Arts—felt redundant, given what I was learning at one of the top three student dailies in the country. When one of my journ professors learned that I had changed my major, he refused to sign the paperwork for my Newspaper Fund Scholarship and accused me of "wanting to write the Great American novel." Well, no, actually. . . . In any case, I was fortunate to learn early that there are consequences to changing paths, or helping forge new ones, . . . "and learn by going where I have to go." In short, the various strands of rhetorical theory and practice—of the language arts—threaded, sometimes knotted,* sometimes knitted, through my educational history and my life.

I became a serious student at Penn State after courses with Jim Rambeau, Gus Kolich, Bob Hudspeth, and Wilma Ebbitt. Wilma—Mrs. Ebbitt, who, I learned much later, not only taught at the University of Chicago but also taught the likes of Phillip Roth and Wayne Booth how to teach writing there—introduced me to rhetoric and composition in my last year of undergraduate study. My senior honors thesis was on William Faulkner's narrative strategies, and I was hired by a local Knight-Ridder newspaper as assistant news editor on the "bulldog" edition, where I stayed for 2 years, as planned, before going to graduate school.

While I had the great fortune to study with Wayne Booth at Chicago and to complete my MA with him as my advisor, I escaped Hyde Park as soon as I could. My parents couldn't quite get their heads around why I was going to college again, so I thought I'd return to Centre County and maybe get my teaching certification. One education course extinguished that desire. Meanwhile, I had started teaching as a lecturer in English: rhetoric and composition. I learned how to teach from Nancy Lowe, Marie Secor, and Jack Selzer; I learned about the mysteriously powerful enthymeme from Jeff Walker; I encountered collaborative learning through Ron Maxwell in the Writing Center. Though I applied to other graduate programs, the pull of central Pennsylvania and the quality of the PhD program Penn State was building gave me no good reason to leave. My PhD was in both English and speech communication: major in English (at least three times as many lit classes as rhetoric classes) and minor in speech (all history and theory of rhetoric). Studying rhet-comp in English and the history and theory of rhetoric with Jerry Hauser in speech-com helped me finally understand why I had left Chicago. In staying at Penn State for the PhD, I had chosen to become a scholar of rhetoric.

Attending my first RSA meeting in 1992 in Minneapolis persuaded me that I would have a professional home, despite the necessity of MLA, CCCC, NCA, and a few other conferences each year. In taking my first job at the University of Texas at

Austin, arriving in the second year of existence of the Division of Rhetoric and Composition (DRC), my good fortune continued. Though I took a good deal of guff from folks whose jobs I did not accept ("She wants to work in a DIVISION. Get it? It's not English: it's a DIVISION."), I again felt I was forging, with superlative collaborators, some kind of new path for the study and practice of interdisciplinary rhetoric; furthermore, the DRC's Computer Writing and Research Lab and Undergraduate Writing Center enabled rhetoric to make its powerful presence known across and beyond campus. Several of my colleagues in communication at Utah also became important allies in work and friends for life. I remain passionate about the connections among rhetoric, public education, and sustainable democracies. I have been blessed by so many of rhetoric's road trips, and I look forward to the wakings and wanderings to come.

---

* * * * *

The efforts of ARS demonstrate that we continue to try to learn, think, and work collaboratively. Yet in spite of ARS, fragmentation continues; as our three narrative accounts of the roadmaps we consulted (and stumbled on) in coming to rhetoric suggest, scholars in rhetoric reside in several different departments—now not only Communication and English but also newer departments of Writing Studies; Communication, Rhetoric, and Digital Media; Writing, Rhetoric, and American Cultures; Composition and Cultural Rhetoric, and so on. Such an array of disciplinary homes is not unique to rhetoric; indeed, it may indicate, in part, the decline of disciplines as we have known them for the past 100 years. Consider the many homes of scholars who study media, for example, or cognition: While interdisciplinarity is still very, very hard to do, the experiences of women's or gender studies departments or ethnic studies departments are instructive; traditional disciplinarity is clearly fraying at the edges. If there is to be a sustainable 21st-century

revival of rhetoric, we will need to think well beyond old boundaries; furthermore, we will have to work productively together to discredit and defeat reactionary attacks on any and all disciplines ending with "studies" and to explain rhetoric—pluralistically and pragmatically and well—to a variety of academic and public audiences. *The SAGE Handbook of Rhetorical Studies* hopes to participate in just such a revival by mapping the territory of rhetoric today and by laying solid groundwork on which scholars can build something new. Coming together to create a rhetoric capable of moving beyond disciplinarity means, among other things, coming to grips with a series of key problematics.

THE NATURE, SCOPE, AND FUNCTION OF RHETORIC

Among the many issues facing our field of study, the long-standing debate over the nature, function, and scope of rhetoric continues to loom large. Rhetoric has been viewed as the "counterpart" of dialectic (Aristotle), as the art of speaking well (Quintilian), as the purview of elocution and pronunciation alone (Ramus), as the study of misunderstandings (Richards), as the "symbolic means of inducing cooperation in beings that by nature respond to symbols" (Burke, 1969, p. 43), and as "hot air" or deceptive practices (Plato, Chaucer, Locke, and a host of others). As a plastic art that molds itself to varying times, places, and situations, rhetoric is notoriously hard to pin down, and arguments about how to define rhetoric and what its scope should be characterize the long history of Western rhetoric.

The earliest U.S. colleges and universities defined rhetoric narrowly, in Ramistic terms, but as the works of Cicero and Quintilian became more widely available in the 18th century, rhetorical education in the United States began to adopt broader definitions; books such as John Ward's (1759) *A System of Oratory* considered invention and arrangement as within the scope of rhetoric, along with style and delivery. Yet as writing took on more and more importance in higher education and as college student populations doubled and tripled and new students flooded the campuses, this broader definition of rhetoric began to give way to restricted conceptions of rhetorical and grammatical correctness rather than to a more expansive Ciceronian understanding of the arts of rhetoric.

In addition, and very important, during the 19th and early 20th centuries, the curriculum shifted its primary focus from the production to the consumption of discourse: Whereas students in earlier times had opportunities to practice rhetoric—in speeches, debates, dramatic performances, and other aspects of the old *progymnasmata*—they were now made increasingly to focus on reading (consuming writing by others), while they themselves wrote, sometimes daily, perfunctory "themes" that were graded primarily for correctness. If we take the long view, we can see that the rise of writing (from before the time of the printing press well into the 20th century) goes hand in hand not only with the decline of robust oral traditions and the production of discourse but with capitalist commodification of value as well. What can be commodified, of course, can be owned and protected; hence, the regime of copyright launched in the early 18th century grew to control texts, to allow for only certain kinds of circulation, and to grant rights of production to a few while denying them to many. Such protected and valuable texts were to be consumed by students and the general public alike; any writing that students did would be in response to these commodified and protected great works. And rhetoric, previously understood as a culturally productive and practical art, was left to focus in its most legitimate forms on the arts of effective oral persuasion or hermeneutics. During the same time period, literature came to define itself as imaginative literature—"high" forms of fiction and poetry, thus excluding much that

had been within the grasp of rhetoric but was now excluded from it.

THE STATUS OF RHETORICAL KNOWLEDGE

Such limited definitions of rhetoric clearly affect the status of rhetorical knowledge as well. In the Western tradition, the argument between philosophy and sophistry perfectly captures competing conceptions of rhetorical knowledge, with philosophy linking Truth to dialectic and logic and the sophists linking contingent truth to rhetoric. In the *Phaedrus* and *Gorgias*, Plato makes his case clear: The way to knowledge, truth, and wisdom comes through the application of rigorous logical principles. Rhetoric, more akin to cooking or ornamentation, could create the appearance of truth but not truth itself. While Plato does sketch in what a noble rhetoric might look like toward the end of the *Phaedrus,* it is clear that he doesn't expect such an art to be probable, or even possible.

In the debate between philosophy and rhetoric, philosophy long held the upper hand. But 20th-century challenges to Platonic notions of truth and knowledge began to mount as thinkers across a range of fields (from physics and history to literature, sociology, economics, and even law) began to build more relational, contingent, social theories of knowledge. In 1967, the influential *Central States Speech Journal* published Robert L. Scott's "On Viewing Rhetoric as Epistemic," effectively launching a debate over the nature of knowledge within rhetorical circles. Drawing on the work of Stephen Toulmin, Douglas Ehninger, and Wayne Brockriede, Scott argues that humans "must consider truth not as something fixed and final but as something to be created moment by moment in the circumstances in which [they find themselves] and with which [they] must cope." Scott concludes by saying, "In human affairs, then, rhetoric, perceived in the frame herein discussed, is a way of knowing; it is epistemic" (p. 17). Scott's essay drew response and criticism from several quarters, which Scott answered in three additional essays (1976, 1990, 1994). But in spite of Barry Brummett's (1990) declaration that epistemic rhetoric was dead (a declaration vehemently denied by Richard Cherwitz & James Hikins, 1995, 1998), scholars continue to acknowledge rhetoric's ability to make knowledge and define contingent truths.

This social turn in rhetorical studies is paralleled in composition, especially in the early work of Janet Emig, whose *The Composing Processes of Twelfth Graders* (1971) laid the groundwork for her influential essay "Writing as a Mode of Learning" (1977), in which she argued that writing is a means of creating knowledge. During the next decade, James Berlin (1987) developed the concept of "social epistemic rhetoric," which he defined as "the study and critique of signifying practices in relation to subject formation within the framework of economic, social, and political conditions" (p. 77). For Berlin, this form of rhetoric views knowledge as produced through the relationship among writers, communities, and contexts. Thus, there can be no Truth but only the kinds of contingent truths rhetors struggle to create. Berlin's goal was to engage student writers in the kind of cultural and political critique that could lead to transformative change.

It is beyond the scope of this introduction to trace the myriad paths of the social turn in communication, rhetoric, and writing and the ways in which that turn has led to an understanding of rhetoric and writing as capable of both creating and shaping knowledge—epistemic, doxastic, material. Suffice it to say that, in terms of a theory of knowledge, rhetorical scholarship today is much closer to sophistic than Platonic concepts of knowledge: In the absence of absolute certainty, rhetoric is the art (and theory and practice) that can guide humans to make the best decisions possible in any given circumstance. Furthermore, as Kenneth Burke (1969) reminds us, rhetoric is

perhaps the primary means through which humans overcome their physical separation to create communities, affiliations, and networks of collective meaning. What kind of contingent truths rhetoric can produce and what status those truths should enjoy, however, remain as fraught as ever: A viable and sustainable 21st-century rhetorical turn will need to build a strong case for rhetoric as seeing, making, and doing.

Future scholarship also must make room for theories that view rhetoric as something more than an epistemology and an instrument of persuasion. In communication studies, the work of critical cultural scholars such as Raymie McKerrow (1989), Maurice Charland (1987), Dana Cloud (1994), and Ronald Greene (1998) resists easy distinction between rhetoric and its circulation or its consequences. To understand rhetoric materially is to consider, first, that existing structures, institutions, and modes of distribution are technologies of communication not unlike words and symbols. The print technologies that so interest cultural historians and many scholars in English are more than just vehicles for knowledge or its formulation. They also are material elements that constitute and sustain print cultures; consequently, these technologies have an impact on meaning *and* communal relations and systems of social power. What distinguishes a speech text from a printing press is, from this perspective, a complex question. Both are simultaneously the means and the products of rhetoric. In recent years, critical perspectives on rhetoric have had a profound and often controversial impact on both communication and English. Their influence is evident especially in the study of agency and identity.

RHETORICAL AGENTS AND AGENCY

What we have been calling the social turn in rhetoric leads to a careful consideration of participants in rhetorical situations and, more particularly, the nature of those participants.

No challenge has been greater for rhetoric in postmodern times than that of accounting for rhetorical agents and their agency. Concerns with subjectivity and agency, of course, grew out of the Enlightenment, with its emphasis on originality and on the individual, words that came to have very different meanings than they had held in the past. For instance, prior to the 18th century, "originality" meant not uniqueness but a return to origins; indeed, an individual was most often understood as one from among a series of types as set forth by Plato, Aristotle, Theophrastus, and other historically distant sacred and secular writers. As theorists reacted against the Enlightenment, they inevitably turned to the teleology and individualism of that period, declaring the (decidedly individual, autonomous) author to be dead and illustrating the degree to which "individuals" are rather constituted in and through discourse, at best occupying "subject positions." In reflecting on the problem of agency at the ARS conference, Karlyn Kohrs Campbell (2005) commented wryly,

> The term "agency" is polysemic and ambiguous, a term that can refer to invention, strategies, authorship, institutional power, identity, subjectivity, and subject positions, among others. I imagine myself in my speech writer persona rafting down a river filled with rapids named Barthes, Derrida, and Foucault at the end of which I must navigate a vortex of feminist controversy with Judith Butler, Seyla Benhabib, Nancy Fraser, and Michelle Ballif as sirens luring me seductively toward disaster as I consider whether the phoenix of female agency can emerge out of the ashes of the dead male author. (p. 1)

Indeed, feminist theorists have resisted the post-structuralist challenge to individual autonomy and agency, often noting with irony the fact that no sooner had women established claims to autonomy and agentive power than those concepts were declared "dead." Most

certainly, Maria Stewart, W. E. B. Du Bois, Julia Cooper, Ralph Ellison, and Richard Wright did not need a critique of subjectivity to understand the contingent nature of Black identity, but they chose not to abandon agency either. Similarly, buoyed by end-of-philosophy pragmatism, scholars such as Fraser and Gayatri Chakravorty Spivak have helped articulate notions of strategic essentialism that bracket insoluble theoretical questions in favor of positive social change in actually existing communities. In short, notions of agency, particularly in material practice, do not necessarily reify the Cartesian dualism.

Rhetoricians too had a hard time giving up on agency: After all, despite differences in linguistic and cultural traditions, the concept of the rhetor as a person who could and did do things with language has been a hallmark of Western rhetorical theory. In her ARS talk, a version of which was later published in *Communication and Critical/Cultural Studies*, Campbell (2005) offered a series of propositions about rhetorical agency today:

> [Agency is] communal and participatory, hence, both constituted and constrained by externals that are material and symbolic; is "invented" by authors who are points of articulation; emerges in artistry or craft; is effected through form; and is perverse, that is, inherently, protean, ambiguous, open to reversal. (p. 2)

Like many of their colleagues in communication, scholars of rhetoric and writing in English also have worked to posit a sense of agency that would reject Enlightenment norms while providing for the possibility of meaningful symbolic action. A long-standing but now somewhat dated joke in the field features graduate students, deep into post-structuralist theory in their seminars, learning that all the world is a text and that meaning is infinitely deferred, and then going to teach their (usually required) writing classes in which they mentor young students in shaping voices and messages to which others can and will respond. In fact, composition and rhetoric have long resisted the attacks on agency, working rather to build a sense of empowerment and authority in student writers. It is not unusual for students to coauthor scholarly articles in the field (see, e.g., Anderson et al., 1990); and for the past 5 years, *Young Scholars in Writing: Undergraduate Research in Writing and Rhetoric* has served as a venue for student writers to publish their work, offering them another means of exerting a form of agency.

Among the many scholars of writing who have addressed issues of agency, we point particularly to Lester Faigley (1992), Susan Miller (1998), Cheryl Glenn (1997, 2004), and Jacqueline Jones Royster (1996, 2000). Writing from within the intellectual traditions of African American women, Royster provides an eloquent rationale for the kinds of agency practiced and passed down from one generation of Black women to another. Karlyn Kohrs Campbell's (1973, 1986; Campbell & Jerry, 1988) groundbreaking work on 19th- and 20th-century feminist rhetoric recognizes both the traditional and the nontraditional forms of agency employed by women orators. Likewise, Michael Leff's (1986, 1992; Leff & Sachs, 1990) invitation to critics to consider the artistry of exemplary texts not only helped start the close textual movement in communication studies, but also reintroduced the speaker's inventional power as an important consideration of the rhetorical situation.

If rhetoric has needed to retain some possibility of rhetorical agents and agency, it seems imprudent to lean too far in that direction today, especially given what we know about the relationship between agency and the traditional concept of Western individualism—the belief that human beings can act in purely autonomous ways. This sense of agency, after all, can be seen as deeply ethnocentric, suggesting that all of culture and society are simply the accumulated results of radically individual actions. In the case of

enabling student writers to take on authorship and agency, the danger is overt: As Don Kraemer (1991) says, "Asking students to be like us" is "simultaneously oppressive and emancipatory: oppressive because the students are enjoined, emancipatory because the students' and teachers' discourse communities change as they join" (p. 54). As a result, we need to take special care in constructing occasions for students to engage with rhetorical agency. Yet in spite of these very real dangers, most contemporary theorists make room for at least some form of agency, with thinkers such as William Sewell (1992) describing a "capacity for agency" in all people and arguing, moreover, that agency is both individual and collective (pp. 20–21) and Charles Taylor (1985a, 1985b) arguing that all people have the potential to act as agents. In communication studies, Michael Leff writes of the work of rhetoricians who are "seeking to discover a more intricate relationship between rhetorical performance and the social and cultural milieu," particularly noting James Crosswhite's argument that rhetorical agency results from an "interplay between individual action and the cultural environment in which individuals speak and act" (Leff & Lunsford, 2004, p. 63). Rhetorical scholars trained and practiced in public as well as academic scholarship will be more able, pragmatically and pluralistically, to explain rhetorical agency to—and practice rhetorical agency with—a wide variety of audiences across and beyond their campuses and communities.

Campbell (2005) sums up her meditation on agency, which includes a memorable exploration of the works, person, and responses to Sojourner Truth, by saying,

> What needs to be resisted is a simplistic, humanistic view of agency rooted in the theory of George Campbell and his contemporaries, and the simplistic approaches to cause and effect that arose out of some social scientific approaches to the study of

mass communication, for example. What is needed are synthetic, complex views of authorship as articulation, of the power of form as it emerges in texts of all sorts, of the role of audiences in appropriating and reinterpreting texts when they emerge and through time, and of the links of all these to the cultural context, material and symbolic, in which discourse circulates. (p. 17)

RHETORIC AND PUBLIC ENGAGEMENT

If rhetoricians have sought a space for rhetorical agency, they have done so in some sense by claiming agency—the power to take efficacious actions—for rhetoric itself. As the discussion above suggests, rhetoricians in both communication and English believe that the work of rhetoric should and does make a difference in the world. Indeed, the concept of rhetorical agency demands a realm within which its agency is manifest, and thus rhetoric has long sought to encourage civic engagement, to create public spaces for deliberation and debate, and to help develop a robust theory of the public sphere. In particular, rhetoricians have worked to provide a means of moving beyond Habermas's (1962/1989) view of public life as a form of spectator sport dominated by corporate media and consumerism. A subfield within communication has focused on public discourse studies as scholars explore the relationships among "public," "public sphere," and "public discourse." Among many we could name, Gerard Hauser (2003, 2004) has articulated a sphere of rhetorical action in which rhetors can identify and resist what Wayne Booth (2004) calls "rhetrickery" and take action to establish and maintain civic life. Within English, rhetoricians such as Selfe and Hawisher (2000) have helped characterize and explore the way new media create civic and public spheres that writers and speakers can shape as well as participate actively within. The debate over whether or not such a rhetorical public sphere

can be developed and maintained, either virtually or materially, will not be settled anytime soon, since we have much to learn about how discourse arises and circulates in digital contexts. In fact, today the very concepts of public and private have been called into question by the explosion of social networking sites, with the argument that such sites constitute the most important arena for public discourse today. The spectacular growth of social networking sites began in earnest with Six-Degrees.com in 1997 and hit the mainstream in 2003 with MySpace, followed by Facebook (2004) and YouTube (2005). Scholars, teachers, and parents were quick to note that such sites privileged the public over the private; in fact, users of the sites seemed not to feel a need for what many older people consider the right to privacy. As a result, privacy concerns have arisen, especially in terms of younger users (George, 2006). Whatever the eventual effect of social networking sites, the public is unlikely to abandon them, and the public sphere likely cannot do without their millions of users.

RHETORIC AND PEDAGOGY

For scholars of rhetoric, the opening up of new publics and new arenas for public discourse presents a welcome challenge, an opportunity to test our theories of the epistemic capacity of rhetoric as well as theories of rhetorical agency and civic engagement. They also offer the opportunity for revisiting rhetoric's relationship to pedagogy, since so much of what we teach is affected by new and highly mediated environments. Of the issues we have discussed that face rhetoric today, pedagogy is the one that in some ways has most clearly separated scholars in communication from those in English/rhetoric and composition. Attention to teaching and to pedagogy has been central to the work of scholars in rhetoric and writing: Indeed, an insistent attention to pedagogy has been said—often pejoratively—to define the field. In contrast, communication has deem-phasized pedagogy; it has not been a promi-nent aspect of the discipline's most public and celebrated scholarship. To be sure, teachers of speech founded the discipline, and *The Speech Teacher*, now *Communication Education*, has 80 years of published history and many dedi-cated readers. Nevertheless, conference panels on the basic speech course and theories of ped-agogy do not receive the attention of panels devoted to public address, rhetorical theory, or critical/cultural communication. Furthermore, although the accepted histories of rhetoric in communication begin with affirmations about the public-speaking course, they quickly move on to disputes over research methodology and theory. The International Society for the History of Rhetoric exemplifies this stance in its dismissal of pedagogy: "We do not accept papers on pedagogy," they have said. The dismissal of pedagogy is not unique to com-munication or ISHR, of course; MLA has only reluctantly yielded pedagogy a place at the dis-ciplinary table. Even in the CCCC, which was founded on pedagogical concerns, a some-times bitter conflict has sprung up between theory and practice, with those advocating for the crucial role of theory arguing that studies in composition/rhetoric will not prosper or mature unless the field gives up its attachment to practice, to pedagogy.

This teaching-based distinction between communication and composition may, however, be resolving itself. The ARS conference, for example, kicked off with both Jerzy Axer and Jeffrey Walker sounding a similar theme: Rhetoric, they both argued, is a *teaching* tradition (see Walker, 2003). In his address, Walker sketched in two distinct impetuses in rhetoric: one toward production of theoretical knowledge and the other toward development of the communicative capacities necessary to civic life in a democracy. This second impetus is what Walker sees as rhetoric's teaching tradition, one that offers "a gymnastic for the mind" as well as a habitus for life.

Scholars in rhetoric and composition would agree with Walker's and Axer's view of rhetoric as a teaching tradition and with the importance of our working proactively to put rhetoric at the center of the educational enterprise (Walker, 2003). In addition, they would agree on the need to focus on a range of communicative abilities—including writing, reading, speaking, and listening. It has been instructive to see renewed attention to spea-king, especially; as speech departments morphed into communication departments, the often-required speech courses began to disappear, yet students' need to "stand and deliver" in various media continued to grow. As a result, many rhetoric and writing pro-grams began incorporating speaking into the curriculum, sometimes working with their colleagues in communication to teach multimodal communication most effectively.

RHETORIC(S) AND TRADITION(S)

As Walker (2003) suggests, whether the goal of rhetoric is to theorize or to teach depends in large part on how the rhetorical tradition is defined. And certainly this issue of traditions is at the heart of many debates among rhetori-cians today. While scholars acknowledge that rhetoric is a universal art in the sense that every language will carry with it theories and modes of persuasion and communication, it is still the Western tradition of rhetoric that speaks most loudly and that still makes claim to being "the" rhetorical tradition." In point of fact, the focus on Western rhetorical tradi-tions is evident in major resources such as the *Encyclopedia of Rhetoric and Composition* (Enos, 1996), the *Encyclopedia of Rhetoric* (Sloane, 2001), Bizzell and Herzberg's *The Rhetorical Tradition* (2001), and most stan-dard histories of the field (see, e.g., Howell, 1975; Kennedy, 1980)—and in this volume as well. In addition, most graduate courses on rhetorical history lean heavily toward the West. But the dominance of Western rhetoric has come under increasing scrutiny as scholars have explored other rhetorical traditions and, within the Western tradition, have sought to recover or redefine a rhetorical tradition that would include women, people of color, and those who practiced as well as theorized about rhetoric.

At the ARS conference, two groups spent 3 days debating the question of rhetorical tradition/traditions. In reporting on these discussions, Pat Bizzell and Susan Jarratt (2004) say,

> Although some wanted to emphasize that even the traditional tradition is not monolithic, others, the majority, wanted to emphasize that we must talk of multiple histories and must encourage much more study of figures and texts never before included in "traditional" studies of rhetorical traditions. (p. 20)

Participants in these discussions tried out a number of different terms, metaphors, and models, concluding (not a little ironically), "Do we have a rhetorical tradition then? Well, the answer seems to be yes, as long as we don't conceptualize it as a 'tradition' and don't restrict it to only one, traditional-tradition, history" (p. 21). Throughout, participants wrestled with the practicalities—and the ethics—of how to teach the history of rhetoric in ways that honor such multiple histories, how "responsibly to meet the obligation to move out of a narrow sphere of established scholarship (Western, elite, male-dominated)—to 'world-travel'—without becoming a tourist" (p. 21).

The editors of the forthcoming *Norton Anthology of Rhetoric and Writing* have struggled for several years with how best to meet such a challenge. Declaring in a prospectus for the volume that it would attempt to

> re-shape the field of rhetoric and writing, first by refusing a separation of the language arts (reading, writing, speaking, and listening),

second by refusing a separation of theory and practice, and finally by refusing to define rhetoric as a western phenomenon only. By focusing on rhetorics rather than rhetoric, this anthology will acknowledge and value the existence of many different rhetorics across time and culture. Such a focus will also broaden and complicate our understanding of Western rhetorical traditions and enable us to become more critical and skeptical when the categories of these Western traditions are being applied to the study of speech in, for example, China, India, Africa, or elsewhere in the world. Finally, a focus on practice as well as theory will allow us to include powerful performances of rhetoric, again across time and cultures. (Lunsford, 2004)

These were bold words. As the editors (LuMing Mao, Jacqueline Jones Royster, Susan Jarratt, Thomas Miller, Robert Hariman, and Andrea Lunsford) have found—and as those at the ARS conference would have predicted—they have been hard to deliver on. But not impossible. As this book goes to press, *The Norton Anthology of Rhetoric and Writing* is slowly but surely taking shape, and while it will certainly fail to achieve its goals fully, it hopes to make a strong start in that direction. In any event, this anthology will join a growing body of work on rhetorical traditions in Africa, China, Japan, Mexico, India, Sweden, and many other places as well.

While some essays in *The SAGE Handbook of Rhetorical Studies* focus primarily on scholarship related to the Western tradition, a number push in new directions, beyond Greece and Rome and the Western tradition. Certainly the voices of women and other marginalized groups are now part of the history of rhetoric as well as part of the discussions of disciplinary discourse, pedagogy, and the public arena. As C. Jan Swearingen and Edward Schiappa point out in their introduction to Part I of this volume, some new transcultural rhetorical studies reveal that practices "regarded as 'feminine' in the West are in other cultures regarded as elegant, elite, and educated." Readers of this volume will find women's voices, and their work, present in each part.

Balancing views from the fields of communication and English, *The SAGE Handbook of Rhetorical Studies* aims to contribute to the debates outlined in this introduction—on how to locate rhetoric institutionally; to define the nature, function, and scope of rhetoric; to assess the status of rhetorical knowledge; to characterize rhetorical agency; to encourage civic engagement and develop a theory of the public sphere; and to reexamine the relationship between rhetoric and pedagogy. In attempting to survey the territory of rhetorical scholarship today, we have divided the book into four parts: Historical Studies in Rhetoric; Rhetoric Across the Disciplines; Rhetoric and Pedagogy; and Rhetoric and Public Discourse. The first part comprises nine essays that treat major periods in rhetorical history as well as specialized topics within that history, such as historiography, argumentation, religion, feminist perspectives, and comparative rhetorics. The essays in Part II, on rhetoric across the disciplines, provide intensive surveys of work on rhetoric and the natural sciences, literary criticism and theory, health and medicine, international relations, and economics; this part concludes with a look at the rhetoric of interdisciplinarity. The part on pedagogy and rhetoric takes up the question of whether or not rhetoric has always been a teaching tradition in essays that explore pedagogical issues related to introductory courses in composition and in communication, in upper-division courses, and in larger communities of practice, concluding with a meditation on "Challenges to a Rapprochement Between Speech Communication and English." Finally, the fourth part—on rhetoric and public discourse—focuses on historical, critical, and theoretical approaches to rhetoric as it engages, participates, and helps shape (mostly U.S.) publics and public spheres. Together, the essays across these four parts aim to provide roadmaps to rhetoric's disciplinary, interdisciplinary, and occasionally postdisciplinary guises, maps useful not only to students at the advanced undergraduate and graduate levels who want a strong introduction to the field but also to scholars of rhetoric (in English, communication, and related fields such as classics, law, or history) who will use the *Handbook* and its extensive bibliographies in their scholarly work and lives. It is this work—and these lives—that will create rhetoric's future and draw new maps for helping us see how to get there.

REFERENCES

Anderson, W., Best, C., Black, A., Hurst, J., Miller, B., & Miller, S. (1990). Cross-curricular underlife: A collaborative report on ways with academic words. *College Composition and Communication, 41*(1), 11–36.

Berlin, J. A. (1987). *Rhetoric and reality: Writing instruction in American colleges, 1900–1985.* Carbondale: Southern Illinois University Press.

Bitzer, L. F., & Black, E. (1971). *The prospects of rhetoric.* Englewood Cliffs, NJ: Prentice Hall.

Bizzell, P., & Herzberg, B. (2001). *The rhetorical tradition* (2nd ed.). New York: Bedford.

Bizzell, P., & Jarratt, S. (2004). Rhetorical traditions, pluralized canons, relevant history, and other disputed terms: A report from the history of rhetoric discussion groups at the ARS Conference. *Rhetoric Society Quarterly, 34,* 19–25.

Booth, W. (2004). *The rhetoric of rhetoric: The quest for effective communication.* Oxford, UK: Wiley/Blackwell.

Brummett, B. (1990). The reported demise of epistemic rhetoric: A eulogy for epistemic rhetoric. *Quarterly Journal of Speech, 76,* 69–72.

Burke, K. (1969). *A grammar of motives.* Berkeley: University of California Press.

Campbell, K. K. (1973). The rhetoric of women's liberation: An oxymoron. *Quarterly Journal of Speech, 59,* 74–86.

Campbell, K. K. (1986). Style and content in the rhetoric of early Afro-American feminists. *Quarterly Journal of Speech, 72,* 434–455.

Campbell, K. K. (2005). Agency: Promiscuous and protean. *Communication and Critical/Cultural Studies, 2,* 1–19.

Campbell, K. K., & Jerry, E. C. (1988). Woman and speaker: A conflict in roles. In S. S. Brehm (Ed.), *Seeing female: Social roles and personal lives* (pp. 123–133). New York: Crewed Press.

Charland, M. (1987). Constitutive rhetoric: The case of the "Peuple Quebecois." *Quarterly Journal of Speech, 73,* 133–150.

Cherwitz, R. A., & Hikins, J. W. (1995). Burying the undertaker: A eulogy for the eulogists of rhetorical epistemology. *Quarterly Journal of Speech, 76,* 73–77.

Cherwitz, R. A., & Hikins, J. W. (1998). Why the epistemic in epistemic rhetoric? The paradox of rhetoric as performance. *Text and Performance Quarterly, 15,* 189–205.

Cloud, D. L. (1994). The materiality of discourse as oxymoron: A challenge to critical rhetoric. *Western Journal of Communication, 58,* 141–163.

Connors, R., Ede, L., & Lunsford, A. A. (1984). *Essays on classical rhetoric and modern discourse.* Carbondale: Southern Illinois University Press.

Dimock, P. (1998). *A short rhetoric for leaving the family.* Normal, IL: Dalkey Archive Press.

Emig, J. (1971). Writing as a mode of learning. *College Composition and Communication, 28,* 122–128.

Emig, J. (1977). The *composing processes of twelfth graders.* Urbana, IL: National Council of Teachers of English.

Enos, T. J. (Ed.). (1996). *Encyclopedia of rhetoric and composition.* New York: Garland.

Faigley, L. (1992). *Fragments of rationality.* Pittsburgh, PA: University of Pittsburgh Press.

Fogarty, D. (1959). *Roots for a new rhetoric.* New York: Teachers' College Press.

Fumaroli, M. (1983). Rhetoric, politics, and society: From Italian Ciceronianism to French classicism. In James J. Murphy (Ed.), *Renaissance eloquence* (pp. 253–273). Berkeley: University of California Press.

George, A. (2006). Living online: The end of privacy? *New Scientist,* 2569. Retrieved August 29, 2007, from www.newscientist.com/ channel/tech/mg19125691.700-living-online-the-end-of-privacy.html

Glenn, C. (1997). *Rhetoric retold: Regendering the tradition from antiquity through the renaissance.* Carbondale: Southern Illinois University Press.

Glenn, C. (2004). *Unspoken: A rhetoric of silence.* Carbondale: Southern Illinois University Press.

Greene, R. W. (1998). Another materialist rhetoric. *Critical Studies in Mass Communication, 15,* 21–41.

Gronbeck, B. E. (1999). *Paradigms of speech communication studies: Looking back toward the future* (1998 Carroll C. Arnold Distinguished Lecture). Boston: Allyn & Bacon.

Habermas, J. (1989). *The structural transformation of the public sphere: An inquiry into a category of bourgeois society* (T. Burgur & F. Lawrence, Trans.). Cambridge, UK: Polity Press. (Original work published 1962)

Hauser, G. (2003). *Rhetorical democracy: Discursive practices of civic engagement.* Mahwah, NJ: Lawrence Erlbaum.

Hauser, G. (2004). Teaching rhetoric: Or why rhetoric isn't just another kind of philosophy or literary criticism. *Rhetoric Society Quarterly, 34,* 39–53.

hooks, b. (1990). *Yearning: Race, gender, and cultural politics.* Boston: South Bend Press.

Howell, W. S. (1975). *Poetics, rhetoric, and logic.* Ithaca, NY: Cornell University Press.

Kennedy, G. A. (1980). *Classical rhetoric and its Christian and secular tradition from ancient to modern times.* Chapel Hill: University of North Carolina Press.

Kraemer, D. (1991). Abstracting the bodies of/in academic discourse. *Rhetoric Review, 10,* 52–69.

Leff, M. C. (1986). Textual criticism: The legacy of G. P. Mohrmann. *Quarterly Journal of Speech, 72,* 377–389.

Leff, M. C. (1992). Things made by words: Reflections on textual criticism. *Quarterly Journal of Speech, 78,* 223–231.

Leff, M., & Lunsford, A. A. (2004). Afterword: A dialogue. *Rhetoric Society Quarterly, 34,* 55–69.

Leff, M. C., & Sachs, A. (1990). Words the most like things: Iconicity and the rhetorical text. *Western Journal of Communication, 54,* 252–273.

Lunsford, A. A. (2004). *Prospectus for the Norton Anthology of rhetoric and writing.* Unpublished manuscript.

McKerrow, R. E. (1989). Critical rhetoric: Theory and praxis. *Communication Monographs, 56,* 91–111.

Miller, S. (1998). *Assuming the positions: Cultural pedagogy and the politics of ordinary writing in early America.* Pittsburgh, PA: University of Pittsburgh Press.

Perelman, C., & Olbrechts-Tyteca, L. (1969). *The new rhetoric: A treatise on argumentation* (J. Wilkinson & P. Weaver, Trans.). Notre Dame, IN: University of Notre Dame Press.

Rhetoric project assured. (1969). *Spectra, 4,* 1–2.

Roethke, T. (1953). *The Waking: Poems, 1933–1953.* Garden City, NY: Doubleday Press.

Royster, J. J. (1996). When the first voice you hear is not your own. *College Composition and Communication, 47,* 29–40.

Royster, J. J. (2000). *Traces of a stream.* Pittsburgh, PA: University of Pittsburgh Press.

Scott, R. L. (1967). On viewing rhetoric as epistemic. *Central States Speech Journal, 18,* 9–17.

Scott, R. L. (1976). On viewing rhetoric as epistemic: Ten years later. *Central States Speech Journal, 27,* 258–266.

Scott, R. L. (1990). Epistemic rhetoric and criticism: Where Barry Brummett goes wrong. *Quarterly Journal of Speech, 76,* 300–303.

Scott, R. L. (1994). Rhetoric as epistemic: What difference does that make? In T. J. Enos & S. C. Brown (Eds.), *Defining the new rhetorics* (pp. 120–136). Englewood Cliffs, NJ: Prentice Hall.

Selfe, C., & Hawisher, G. (2000). *Global literacies and the World-Wide Web.* London: Routledge.

Sewell, W. H. (1992). A theory of structure: Duality, agency, and transformation. *American Journal of Sociology, 98,* 1–29.

Sloane, T. (Ed.). (2001). *Encyclopedia of rhetoric.* New York: Oxford University Press.

Taylor, C. (1985a). The concept of a person. *Human Language and Agency: Philosophical Papers, 1,* 97–114.

Taylor, C. (1985b). What is human agency? *Human Language and Agency: Philosophical Papers, 1,* 1–44.

Walker, J. (2003). *On rhetorical traditions: A response to Jerzy Axer.* Retrieved January 6, 2008, from https://webspace.utexas.edu/jw2893/www/RhetoricalTraditions.htm

Ward, J. (1759). *A system of oratory.* A series of lectures publicly read at Gresham College.

PART I

Historical Studies in Rhetoric

Historical and Comparative Rhetorical Studies

Revisionist Methods and New Directions

C. JAN SWEARINGEN

EDWARD SCHIAPPA

One of the most significant recent developments in historical studies in rhetoric has been the increasing attention given in every field and period to comparative studies. Whether addressing the modern rhetorics of Perelman and Olbrechts-Tyteca, I. A. Richards, and Kenneth Burke, or the continuing influence of classical models on many contemporary and international practices of rhetoric, scholars increasingly attend to the presence of multiple rhetorical models and cultures throughout the world. The past 15 years have seen the emergence of new societies for the study of rhetoric in Scandinavia, Latin America, and China, with pan-Asian and East-West rhetorical studies now more prominently represented in the meetings of the International Society for the History of Rhetoric and the Rhetoric Society of America (Koeneke, 2004; Lu, 1998; Mao, 2006; Sen, 2005; Wang, 2004; You, 2006). A rich new diversity and revisionism among research methods has accompanied the movement toward inclusion and comparison. Different communities of interpretation have formed around the new methods used to define and study rhetoric, so much so that examining the formation of contemporary interpretive communities has itself become a part of the historical study of rhetoric. Whether the primary subject is gender, genre, class, ethnicity, or national identity and history, historical studies in rhetoric have become necessarily comparative (Fahnestock & Secor, 2003; Horner, 1990; Lipson & Binkley, 2004). The continuing use of a Greco-Roman rhetorical home base is now energetically debated (Kennedy, 1998; Lipson & Binkley, 2004; Sutherland, Chapter 3, this volume). Simple comparisons with a classical paradigm are long gone, replaced by more nuanced definitions and redefinitions of what rhetoric is, how it is used, and how it may best be observed and studied. The classical concept of "audience" has long since been widened to include readerships, communities of discourse, and the formation of voluntary political and religious communities. Concepts of ethos, rhetor, and author, similarly, now examine the mutual shaping of rhetoric by its speakers and hearers, its writers and readers, working in concert with one another (Baumlin & Baumlin, 1994; Swearingen, 1991). At the same time, and in sharp contrast to communitarian models, some modern studies of rhetoric past and present question the very notion of community as a remnant of Western hegemonic enlightenment rhetorical canons and focus their attention instead on the dismantling of that legacy, with various purposes (Aune, Chapter 5, this volume).

A starting point for most inquiries remains the word *rhetoric*, from the Greek word *rhêtorikê*, coined by Plato to not-so-flatteringly denote the "Art of the Rhetor" (Schiappa, 1990). But today the term can be used to refer to various phenomena, including individual acts of suasion (such as traditional oratory), literary works and other aesthetic genres with rhetorical puposes, the teaching of written and spoken discourse, or analytical frameworks for the evaluation and critique of efforts at persuasion. Philosophies or theories of rhetoric attempt to define and explain "rhetoric" as a frequent if not ubiquitous human activity with important ontological, epistemological, and/or ethical implications. As noted in Chapter 5, theories of rhetoric grew in scope in the 20th century to the point that everything, or virtually everything, can be described as "rhetorical." Such accounts can be called theories of "Big Rhetoric" and are credited with popularizing or at least rationalizing what Herbert W. Simons (1990) calls the "rhetorical turn" in a variety of disciplines. Within the journals and conventions of rhetoric scholars, popularization is often characterized by studies of the form "the rhetoric of X," where X could literally be anything. Outside the discipline of communication studies, popularization is evidenced by the apparently ever-increasing ranks of scholars who use "rhetoric" as a relevant and important term of art within their scholarship. By any measure, it can be argued fairly convincingly that "rhetoric" has become a widely used construct in scholarship in many fields. For better or worse, its very nature as a scholarly discipline continues to change as it crosses and includes more and more disciplines, regions, periods, genres, and topics.

Expansive definitions or theories of rhetoric have changed what counts as appropriate objects of analysis. Whereas the Greco-Roman origins of the term *rhetoric* previously limited what scholars analyzed *as* rhetoric, Big Rhetoric made it possible for scholars to describe a far broader range of phenomena as rhetorical, as long as important and interesting insights could be gained through such descriptions (Kennedy, 1998; Schiappa, Scott, Gross, & McKerrow, 2002).

There are a number of narratives on the rise of Big Rhetoric already in print in communication studies (Gaonkar, 1990; Simons, 1990), rhetoric and composition (Berlin, 1987; Young & Goggin, 1993), and interdisciplinary publications (Mailloux, 2000; Nelson, Megill, & McCloskey, 1987; Roberts & Good, 1993). Aune in Chapter 5 provides a rich narrative as well, but one more cannot hurt. Many accounts identify the 1960s as a turning point, a period that brought, for better or worse, a confluence of changing rhetorical practices, expanding rhetorical theories, and opportunities for rhetorical criticism. The cultural clashes of the 1960s were felt perhaps most acutely on college campuses. The sufficiency of deliberative argument and public address can be said to have been called into question whether one was an antiwar activist who hated Lyndon B. Johnson's war in Vietnam, or if one was a proestablishment stalwart trying to make sense of the rhetoric of protest and demonstration. Years later, scholars would characterize war itself as rhetorical. What *counts* as rhetorical practice was up for grabs.

At about the same time, our understanding of rhetorical theory was being expanded. Here we can identify two main strands of thought. For ease of reference, we can call one the symbolic interactionist rationale and the other the epistemological rationale. The symbolic interactionist rationale can be boiled down to a syllogism:

All persuasive actions are rhetorical.

All symbol/language-use is persuasive, therefore

All symbol/language-use is rhetorical.

Perhaps the two most significant pronouncements of this approach—for one generation of rhetoric scholars, at any rate—are by Richard Weaver and Kenneth Burke. Weaver (1970) claims that "language is sermonic" in the sense that whenever we offer a description or label a phenomenon we are "preaching" a particular way of making sense of it (pp. 201–225). And, of course, Burke (1950) has two famous (or infamous) statements in *Rhetoric of Motives*: First, that rhetoric is "the use of language as a symbolic means of inducing cooperation in beings that by nature respond to symbols" (p. 43); and second, that "something of the rhetorical motive comes to lurk in every 'meaning,' however purely 'scientific' its pretensions. Wherever there is persuasion, there is rhetoric. And wherever there is 'meaning,' there is 'persuasion'" (p. 172). Obviously, such pronouncements serve as encouragement to those who would define rhetoric broadly and arguably fueled the popularization of rhetorical studies.

The epistemological rationale is fueled by the argument that the philosophical criteria used traditionally to separate "higher" ways of knowing, such as "science" (as *epistêmê*), from "rhetoric" (as *doxa*) have been critiqued persuasively. Again, at least for the post–World War II generation, the key writers here are Chaim Perelman, Stephen Toulmin, Robert L. Scott, and Thomas S. Kuhn. In 1958, Perelman and Lucie Olbrechts-Tyteca published *The New Rhetoric* in which they argue, in effect, that everything outside of scientific demonstration and mathematical logic was the province of rhetoric and argumentation (Perelman & Olbrechts-Tyteca, 1969/1958). Also in 1958, Toulmin critiqued the "analytic ideal" and, borrowing a page from Hume, argues that all substantive claims are contingent. Enter Robert L. Scott, who took Toulmin's case the next step in 1967 by arguing, in effect, that since the "certain" or "absolute" side of binaries such as certain/contingent, absolute/probable are unavailable, we are left to dwell in the historicized land of contingency and probability, which means that cultural knowledge is the product of rhetorical activity. Rhetoric thus can be viewed as epistemic. Kuhn (1970) provides the historical evidence to apply these insights to the hitherto forbidden land of Science; a bushel full of articles and books written in the past 40 years attests to the efforts by rhetorical scholars to identify various rhetorical aspects of the practices of scientists. In a similar vein, continuing efforts to define rhetoric as a scientific linguistic inquiry expand I. A. Richards' and Perelman and Olbrechts-Tyteca's efforts after each of the 20th century's World Wars (Koeneke, 2004; van Eemeren, Chapter 6, this volume).

The preceding narrative suggests that broad definitions of rhetoric and the popularization of rhetorical studies is partly due to scholarly attention begun in the rhetorical practices of the 1960s, partly due to specific positions advanced by influential theorists and partly due to the understandable desires of members of a discipline to see what they are doing as important. No matter which explanation one might prefer, popularization proceeded apace. The broadening of the scope of rhetoric has facilitated the recognition and appreciation of "the rhetorical" in a variety of historical and cultural contexts previously neglected by rhetoric scholars—understudied and undervalued social groups (including women and minorities), neglected genres of communicative practice throughout history (diaries, poetry, theatre, scientific discourse, and various forms of art), and whole cultures previously ignored by rhetoric scholars. As George A. Kennedy (1998) has argued, practices describable as rhetoric can be identified even among animal species.

Why scholars engaged in historical and comparative studies is a question that generates answers as diverse as the scholars doing such research. *What* one studies and *how* one goes about the study of rhetoric ultimately are decisions fueled by the values, interests, and purposes one brings to the table. It may be worth noting, however, that the collective motivations of historians and comparativists involve a dialectic between *similarity* and *difference*. It can be argued that the more one studies rhetoric, the more one finds a common human impulse to influence each other and to produce shared meaning and understanding. But it is also the case that the historical and comparative work produce accounts of rhetoric that are amazingly diverse. What a particular rhetorical scholar finds most *salient* will be a function of his or her own interests (Schiappa, 2003, pp. 206–212), but we all benefit from the study of the splendid banquet of scholarship that this set of chapters charts.

Alluding to all these contexts, Richard Enos (Chapter 2) reviews traditional and revisionist approaches to classical rhetorics that have widened the domain of rhetorical objects of study. He provides a rich history of the many recent and not-so-recent historical studies in rhetoric that have reconstituted the field beginning in the 1960s. Two streams, one pedagogical and one historical and scholarly, began to converge in a variety of ways, not the least of which was a shared interest in the study of rhetoric in contexts. Enos defines the primary task of the historian of rhetoric as the reconstruction of how meaning is made and shared through discourse. Moving away from simply narrating a historical account of rhetoric in Rhodes or stele inscriptions in Egypt, rhetorical studies of all times and places should reconstruct an entire rhetorical situation, providing an argument that offers evidence to a reader, a way of validating an interpretation. In his chapter, Enos provides many examples of a two-stage process. The first stage, which he compares with archaeology, is represented by finding new artifacts, new rhetorical objects of study, in the vast fields of inquiry that have opened up in the past 30 years. The second stage Enos defines is the reconstruction of the artifact by employing the heuristics of rhetorical layering. The benefits of rhetorical archaeology are evident in each of the chapters in this section and far beyond as well. An especially vivid example of the process Enos describes is Antoinette Wire's (1995) study *The Corinthian Women Prophets: A Reconstruction Through Paul's Rhetoric*. Both biblical and classical rhetorical studies now debate and define new methods of contextual reconstruction (Swearingen, 2002; Zulick, Chapter 7, this volume). Indeed, throughout rhetorical history, and evident in the methods now available to the historian, heated debates also surround the issue of proper objects for study.

Christine Mason Sutherland (in Chapter 3) takes up directly the matter of inclusion and exclusion, the questions of what figures and what uses of language should be counted as rhetoric. She begins her consideration of Early Modern women rhetoricians with the question of period boundaries: Should these be drawn by date, by language, by genre, or by a combination of factors? She locates those women rhetoricians who lived before the 16th century as belonging to the Middle Ages, based on the traditional dating of Modern English to 1485. In this context, Julian of Norwich becomes even more important as the first author writing in (Middle) English, but also problematic as a woman rhetorician because she so clearly renounces her own author-ship, for the complicated reasons Sutherland explains and explores. On the other end of the Early Modern period, Sutherland observes, Margaret Fell continues to be located as a Renaissance figure, even though she was writing up to the end of the 17th century and did not die until the early 18th century. Nonetheless, Sutherland suggests, 1688 presents a reasonable end date for the Renaissance because on several fronts the reign of William and Mary may be said to inaugurate the Enlightenment.

Concerning the inclusion and exclusion of individual figures and genres, Sutherland forges a middle ground somewhere between including everything written by women in the Middle Ages and Renaissance, and restricting the choices to women who clearly and self-consciously identify themselves as rhetorical, either in practice or theory. In the first section, dealing with public discourse, she includes women whose works have been studied from a rhetorical point of view by historians of rhetoric today, even when the women studied did not at the time identify themselves or their writings as rhetorical. They may have simply taken it for granted in an oral/rhetorical age. They may have declined the title or role for any of a number of reasons. Nonetheless, they are now regularly studied from a rhetorical point of view by historians of rhetoric. Similarly, in the second section, on semiprivate and private discourses, Sutherland selects figures based on those already studied from rhetorical perspectives today. The third section, an examination of social practices, provides additional examinations of rhetorical actions, spaces, and contexts shaped by new understandings of women as rhetorical in the Early Modern period. As to genres, within each section, Sutherland has decided to exclude historical fiction, drama, verse, and works of translation—even though women were active translators during these periods. Nonetheless, she proposes that in our studies of women's rhetorics we extend the genre boundaries of what has been considered rhetoric to include polythetic and enthymematic forms of reasoning recognized as early as Aristotle as "inartistic" modes of rhetoric, as well as Cicero's distinction between *contentio* and *sermo*: public adversarial debate versus "conversational," informal, colloquial dialogue: the paradigm after all, for sermons. Sutherland's rich and ample examination of a bounty of new figures, as well as of contemporary studies of those figures, provides a valuable guide to the newly recovered women of the Middle Ages and Renaissance.

In Chapter 4, Lynée Lewis Gaillet and Elizabeth Tasker's study of rhetorics in the 18th and 19th centuries begins where Sutherland leaves us, with the modernization of rhetoric during the Enlightenment, beginning in the late 17th century. Along with the question of what, exactly, was modernized, Gaillet and Tasker examine the push and pull of successive waves of neoclassicism during these periods and after, providing further evidence that rhetoric has always had a hard time giving up or shaking off its classical beginnings. They identify four movements that developed within Enlightenment rhetoric: neoclassical, belletristic, elocutionary, and psychological-epistemological (often called "the new rhetoric"). Like Enos and Sutherland, Gaillet and Tasker propose improved, multilayered methodologies for studying rhetorics in these periods: (1) further *recovery* of primary texts, (2) *interpretation*, analysis, and rereading, and (3) *conversation* and scholarly debate about the rhetoric of the period (Horner, 1990, pp. 138–139). When this threefold method is extended to encompass the traditional fourfold division of the 18th century rhetorics, we begin to see new patterns, particularly when works by women and nonelite, marginalized groups are thrown into the mix. Thomas Miller's (1997) work *The Formation of College English: Rhetoric and Belles Lettres in the British Cultural Provinces* provides particularly good examples of the multiple enlightenments, neoclassicisms, and vernacular rhetorics that were shaping both the theory and the practice of rhetoric in the period. Regarding the 19th century,

Gaillet and Tasker emphasize the goldmines yet to be explored in this century that has so often been written off as a rhetorical dead end, somewhere between the brilliant innovations of the Enlightenment and the new sciences of 20th-century rhetoric and linguistics. At the same time, they note, 19th-century rhetorical studies have formed one of the headwaters for recent feminist studies in rhetoric because so many women activists became public rhetorical figures in the 19th century, in both Britain and America, advancing the abolitionist, social reform, and women's suffrage causes (Campbell, 1989). Nineteenth-century rhetorical pedagogy, particularly in the United States, provides an additional object of recovered study as we begin to observe more keenly the roots of current-traditional rhetoric in the 20th century (Johnson, 1991). An unexpected bonus in Gaillet and Tasker's discussion is the consideration of Native American and non-Western traditions whose study is providing rich new understandings by comparing different cultures' understandings of the public sphere, community, eloquence, and gendered aspects of rhetoric. The fruits of these comparative rhetorical studies are yet to be fully defined, but their movement beyond "recovery-of-lost-figures" mode and into the processes of interpretation and contextualization has begun. We can now see that just as the Enlightenment did not happen solely among the elites of Europe, rhetorical practices and innovations developed, were taught, and were practiced far from the rhetorical textbooks and classrooms of Western universities.

The past 15 years have produced directions for studies in historical and comparative rhetoric comprising new knowledge and new definitions based on recovered individuals and communities. As such studies developed innovations in methodology for studying earlier periods; they began to include debates about how and how much to approach marginalized and non-Western rhetorical traditions. The debates surrounding these new inclusions are as interesting as the inclusions themselves. Early modern vernacular rhetoric now includes the speech and writing of women and nonelite males whose rhetoric until recently was not studied as rhetoric at all. Paradoxically, in literary studies, this reunion of early modern vernaculars with rhetorical studies has returned both rhetoric and literature to a union that they held for a very long time in the curricula of the late medieval and early modern periods: rhetoric as an art of stylistics and early modern vernacular literature as one of its often playful products. Although some of these studies are no news to scholars in comparative literature, they are new to historians of rhetoric who have focused at times too singularly on the curriculum of the late medieval schools and too little on the contrapuntal relationships among schooled Latin rhetoric and burgeoning oral—and then written—vernaculars. Conversely, medieval and early modern comparative literature scholars are often unfamiliar with rhetorical history and theory, and have increasingly learned from these fields how to read for the text within the oral word, and the oral word within the text. Early Modern and 18th-century studies of rhetorical figures and practices now range widely among traditional and recently incorporated materials, allowing for better understandings of rhetorical practices among nonelite communities.

As nontraditional rhetorics are incorporated into the rhetorical canon, the aims of rhetorical research have changed to accommodate the new materials. The Early Modern and 18th-century studies, reviewed here by Sutherland, and Gaillet and Tasker, now allow us to see not one but several enlightenments tied to not one but several rhetorical traditions. Julian of Norwich, Sutherland emphasizes, was not only the first vernacular English author, but also a very early Enlightenment figure in her emphasis on the capacities of the human mind and spirit.

Spanning all periods, Kate Ronald's chapter (Chapter 8) on feminist rhetorical scholarship identifies studies of Early Modern women, who, alongside their sisters in the 18th and 19th centuries, developed a number of distinctive tropes and strategies, which they shared, and shared with one another, forming a new tradition that has only recently begun to be mapped out and explored. In remote rural colonial Mexico, Sor Juana Ines de la Cruz, illegitimate criola, nun, and courtesan, became an acclaimed writer on two continents. Her *Respuesta*, rich in ironic uses of the feminine trope of self-abnegation, recites a litany of learned and rhetorical women of the past and present, going back to the Bible, which most women then and subsequently knew and could quote from. Yet the list was repeatedly rebuked and suppressed outside women's communities, for reasons that are now being documented and studied. Ronald's chapter compasses the numerous recent studies that have extended these examinations into the past and across the present. Kate Ronald's history of feminist rhetorical studies picks up the thread of reclamation and reinterpretation that has shaped so much recent historical scholarship in rhetoric. "Reclaiming," "rereading," and "regendering" became beacons for many feminist scholars as they worked on reworking the definitions of the field and its objects of study. Always in concert with their surrounding cultures and dominant communities, marginalized groups found inventive ways to appropriate and employ what Frederick Douglass called "the master's voice."

That process continues and is now being extended to the study of emerging democracies and related political reforms throughout the world (Hum and Lyon, Chapter 9, this volume; Salazar, 2002). Just as feminist scholars have studied feminist rhetorics, gendered rhetorics, and rhetorics about gender, scholars from diverse minority cultures have also taken up the study of their rhetorics, alongside the rhetoric about them. A noteworthy parallel between feminist and comparative cultural rhetorics has been the recognition that rhetorical practices regarded as "feminine" in the West are in other cultures regarded as elegant, elite, and educated (Lu, 1998; Lyon, 2004). Chinese protocols regarding silence, understatement, and deference, for example, resemble Western feminine practices that in the West are often encoded as weak or negative.

Sue Hum and Arabella Lyon review the often-contentious contours of international and particularly East-West studies in rhetoric. The rejection of the Western paradigm is often emphatic and liberationist. Some of these studies want to avoid the term *rhetoric* entirely because of its Western origins, agonistic traditions, and bad fit with the understandings of language and persuasion practiced in China and Asia more generally.

Hum and Lyon identify four practices currently in play that suggest different solutions to these problems. Some scholars, at least sometimes, are committed to an Athenian or a Burkean rhetoric and use it as the position from which they see the rhetorical world. Others import perspicuous methods, but they are anxious about what those methods impose. A third group carefully works within a particular framework, minimizing the comparative nature of their work. Finally, a few use non-Western tools on Western texts. One particularly vivid example of this last method is presented in the recent work of Hui Wu, who, like Bo Wang, has been working on 20th-century Chinese women writers' rhetorical practices. Wu's work exemplifies the use of new methodologies, and insights from non-Western cultures applied to canonical Western texts, resulting in very different renderings of rhetorical language. Such readings can reshape Western knowledge and self-perception and avoid the colonialist concern with importing Western methodologies into other cultures. Since the political and academic power structure still lies within the West, the primary goal of such studies is to create knowledge, not oppression. In "The Paradigm of Margaret Cavendish: Reading Women's Alternative Rhetorics in a Global Context," Wu reads Margaret Cavendish not in comparison with, but through the lens of contemporary Chinese women's discourse. In examining the material conditions of women, she is able to argue for a broader definition of what constitutes rhetoric. Wu's work gives hope that, just as Aristotle has become the subject of feminist readings, someday soon he may be interpreted through a Confucian tradition (Wu, 2005; You, 2006).

Regarding comparative rhetorical studies more generally, Hum and Lyon observe that a significant obstacle has been the lack of publication of analysis and theory by scholars in and from non-Western cultures. A small but established body of work that compares European rhetorics and Chinese rhetorical studies has just begun to accumulate a body of scholarship large enough for response, dialogue, and engagement with other cultures. Too much non-Western scholarship, when it does appear, has been subsumed to Western rhetoric. Very little has been examined in its own terms until recently. If one wanted to develop a project, for example, on South Asia, one would have trouble finding a starting point. The dearth of South Asian, Southeast Asian, or East Asian (outside China) research is illustrated by Bo Wang's 2004 survey of research in Asian rhetoric: All the scholars interviewed were sinologists. There are some studies of Gandhi, but Gandhi's rhetoric has too often been analyzed, Hum and Lyon propose, because his impeccable English allows him to be seen as a "stand-in Euro." They conclude,

> We compare rhetorics so that we may understand the limits of the term and our own conceptual frame for it. As we denationalize and denormalize our notions of rhetoric, we search for understanding the power of communication in an era defined by new communication technologies, increased mobility, displacements of people, and cultural clashes. To that end, comparative rhetoric is a vital enterprise, but it can only be such if it offers more than a repeat of colonial tendencies. (Hum & Lyon, Chapter 9, this volume)

Like new studies of early and not-so-early vernacular rhetorics, recent studies in religious rhetoric have amplified understandings of how oral and literate, homiletic and scriptural attitudes toward the spoken and the written word are shaped by rhetorical understandings only recently included in some areas of biblical and religious studies (Glenn, 1997; Schussler-Fiorenza, 1999; Sutherland & Sutcliffe, 1999). Zulick's discussion here explains both ancient and modern approaches to religious rhetorical topics and materials, as well as their future directions. Augustine has long been a central figure for understanding the intersection of religious and classical rhetoric and the long transition from rhetorical models of composition to hermeneutic models of interpretation (Swearingen, 1991). Recent New Testament rhetorical studies focus on the intersections between Hellenistic rhetorical schools and the composition practices of Paul and the gospel writers. Among the newest of approaches in religious rhetoric have been studies of the Hebrew scriptures, and Jewish hermeneutics, especially within Hellenistic rhetorical culture, that provide new understandings of the interactions among Greek, Jew, and Gentile in the richly multicultural world that Paul addressed explicitly as a mixed audience, adapting classical models to a religious purpose (Stowers, 1994; Wire, 1995). Studies of Paul's letters, of the genre of the gospels, and of the Hebrew scriptures provide enriched understandings not only of religious rhetorics in different traditions, but also of the relationships between rhetorical persuasion and religious faith, both encoded as *pistis* in the lexicon of Hellenistic rhetoric and early Greek Christianity (Eriksson, Olbricht, & Ubelacker, 2002; Swearingen, 2002).

Van Eemeren's discussion of recent argumentation theory and scholarship in Chapter 6 provides a welcome cross-referencing of European rhetorical studies since the new rhetoric with developments in British and American philosophy, communication studies, and rhetoric. His analysis reminds us of the many strands that link but also become tangled in relationships among linguistics, discourse analysis, the new rhetoric, and argumentation theory in the various fields where they are studied. Toulmin and Perelman and Olbrechts-Tyteca develop approaches that are strikingly similar, not only to one another, but also to some of Aristotle's earliest explorations of *enthymemata* and *paradigmata*, the informal logics structured by premise and conclusion. To these models, van Eemeren introduces the newer field of pragma-dialectics, an attempt to reconcile analytical dialectical models of rhetoric with the practical and pragmatic aims of rhetorical argumentation. Like several other chapters in this section, van Eemeren notes methods of reconstruction that are being developed specifically for examining and understanding various modes of implicitly argumentative discourse. Like Enos's "archaeology" and the "rereading" models that Ronald describes, reconstruction models of argumentation allow for examining beneath the surface and between the lines modes of argument and rhetoric. In studying nontraditional and non-Western rhetorics, this methodology should prove particularly valuable in making the case that there is more argumentation and rhetoric than there at first seems to be in the discourses of women or Chinese. At the same time, tables can be turned to point out that new attention to models of argumentation and rhetorical practices outside Western paradigms of logic and rhetoric are beginning to give us a newly pragmatic approach to our own traditions.

Van Eemeren provides a European perspective, observing that in the United States the study of rhetoric has survived more robustly during the 19th and 20th centuries, both in the academic curriculum and in contributions to new rhetorical theories and methods. He particularly applauds Burke's stunning revisionism in considering many aspects of persuasion, and Toulmin's attention to the long-standing tradition of *phronesis*, another reminder of the pragmatic aims of rhetorical theory and practice.

Van Eemeren concludes with a reprise of Goodnight's concerns that the public sphere is being eroded by the technical and the personal in rhetorical studies and awareness. Here again we see the concerns about models of community and shared values that are addressed by Aune and by Walzer and Beale. Van Eemeren notes the two-edged sword of community and group models:

> If it is only the powerful interests in a group that have defined communal standards, the goal of argument-as-critique is to expose this practice and to suggest alternatives, so that those who were excluded or marginalized can be brought into the process of deliberation. (van Eemeren, Chapter 6, this volume)

Like Hum and Lyons' discussion of the two-edged sword of even a Habermasian notion of community, van Eemeren emphasizes the ongoing need for dialectical critique from outside the community of values and shared discourses, alongside a continuing refinement of models of dialectic, rhetoric, and argumentation in relationship to one another. Despite the recent revival of both dialectics and rhetoric in several fields, "there is a wide conceptual gap between the two perspectives on argumentation, which have been mutually isolated since their ideological separation in the 16th and 17th centuries and were viewed as incompatible paradigms" (van Eemeren, Chapter 6, this volume). But recently, scholars in argumentation theory, as well as scholars working cross-culturally, have begun to explore approaches to argumentation that do not so resolutely segregate rhetorical and dialectical understandings.

Comparative and historical studies of rhetoric's history and theory increasingly take into account the philosophical and disciplinary backgrounds of current rhetorical scholars. Ranging across the several fields represented within Communication and English, as well as work being done in comparative literature, classics, and biblical studies, historical studies of rhetoric have become increasingly conscious of their historiographical methods, assumptions, and purposes. Similarly, comparative rhetorical studies increasingly move beyond the classical Greek and Roman models that for so long defined the beginning of the rhetorical time line and the identification of rhetorical forms and genres (Hum & Lyon, Chapter 9, this volume; Walzer & Beard, Chapter 1, this volume). Walzer and Beard examine the history of rhetorical theory in light of the need for a historiography of rhetorical theory. Aune reviews the several schools of rhetorical theory and interpretation that have emerged in the 20th century, defining both goals and challenges for the 21st century. Van Eemeren's chapter encourages us to examine how the modern linguistic study of argumentation, among other genres, has once again called into question the relationship between rhetoric and linguistics, and between rhetoric and discourse as models of human language and communication. Aune, Walzer, and Beale conclude by emphasizing that we have entered the new century with the divisions and debates clearly redefined and ready for further deliberation. In developing new self-definitions, the scholarship represented here includes histories and theories of historiography alongside examinations of how recent rhetorical scholarship represents a response to larger movements in 20th-century philosophy and political science (Aune, Chapter 2, this volume). Debates about communitarian and anticommunitarian rhetorical models continue, inviting reflection on how society, as distinct from culture, has been conceived of in different intellectual traditions during the 20th century (Aune, Chapter 2, this volume). The time line, the cultural domain, and the frame of analysis are addressed more and more explicitly in most contemporary discussions of the history of rhetoric. Time and place are no longer taken for granted as cultural givens, whether talking about the medieval period or Chinese uses of parallelism. We can no longer assume or impose any uniform definition of rhetoric. As a result, its very nature is being reconceived in ways that are troubling to some and exciting to others. Various uses of tropes, metaphor and chiasmus, narrative and persuasion, and all the tools of rhetoric and objects of rhetorical scrutiny are increasingly seen as local and global, with care to distinguish the two through comparison. At the same time, as Aune reminds us, the purposes and the rhetoric of our scholarship about rhetoric, the audiences and communities it addresses, have also become renewed imperatives as we consider the ethics of rhetoric, the ethics of interpretation, and our rhetoric about both.

REFERENCES

Baumlin, J., & Baumlin, T. F. (Eds.). (1994). *Ethos: New essays in rhetorical and cultural theory.* Dallas, TX: Southern Methodist University Press.

Berlin, J. A. (1987). *Rhetoric and reality: Writing instruction in American Colleges, 1900–1985.* Carbondale: Southern Illinois University Press.

Burke, K. (1950). *A rhetoric of motives.* New York: Prentice Hall.

Campbell, K. K. (1989). *Man cannot speak for her: Critical study of early feminist rhetoric 1830–1925.* Westport, CT: Greenwood Press.

Eriksson, A., Olbricht, T. H., & Ubelacker, W. (Eds.). (2002). *Rhetorical argumentation in biblical texts.* Harrisburg, PA: Trinity Press.

Fahnestock, J., & Secor, M. (2003). *A rhetoric of argument.* New York: McGraw-Hill.

Gaonkar, D. P. (1990). Rhetoric and its double: Reflections on the rhetorical turn in the human sciences. In H. W. Simons (Ed.), *The rhetorical turn* (pp. 341–366). Chicago: University of Chicago Press.

Glenn, C. (1997). *Rhetoric retold: Regendering the tradition from antiquity through the renaissance.* Carbondale: Southern Illinois University Press.

Horner, W. B. (1990). *The present state of scholarship in historical and contemporary rhetoric.* Columbia: University of Missouri Press.

Johnson, N. (1991). *Nineteenth century rhetoric in North America.* Carbondale: Southern Illinois University Press.

Kennedy, G. A. (1998). *Comparative rhetoric: An historical and cross-cultural introduction.* Oxford, UK: Oxford University Press.

Koeneke, R. (2004). *Empires of the mind: I.A. Richards and Basic English in China 1929–1979.* Stanford, CA: Stanford University Press.

Kuhn, T. S. (1970). *The structure of scientific revolutions* (2nd ed). Chicago: University of Chicago Press.

Lipson, C. S., & Binkley, R. (2004). *Rhetoric before and beyond the Greeks.* Albany: State University of New York Press.

Lu, X. (1998). *Rhetoric in ancient China, fifth to third century B.C.: A comparison with classical Greek rhetoric.* Columbia: University of South Carolina Press.

Lyon, A. (2004). Confucian silence and remonstration: A basis for deliberation? In C. Lipson & R. Binkley (Eds.), *Rhetoric before and beyond the Greeks* (pp. 131–146). Albany: State University of New York Press.

Mailloux, S. (2000). Disciplinary identities: On the rhetorical paths between English and speech. *Rhetoric Society Quarterly, 30,* 5–29.

Mao, L. (2006). *Reading Chinese fortune cookie: The making of Chinese American rhetoric.* Logan: University of Utah Press.

Miller, T. P. (1997). *The formation of college English, rhetoric and belles lettres in the British cultural provinces.* Pittsburgh, PA: University of Pittsburgh Press.

Nelson, J. S., Megill, A., & McCloskey, D. N. (1987). *The rhetoric of the human sciences.* Madison: University of Wisconsin Press.

Perelman, C., & Olbrechts-Tyteca, L. (1969). *The new rhetoric* (J. Wilkinson & P. Weaver, Trans.). Notre Dame, IN: Notre Dame University Press. (Original work published 1958 as *La Nouvelle Rhétorique: Traité de l'Argumentation.* Paris: Presses Universitaires de France)

Roberts, R. H., & Good, J. M. M. (1993). *The recovery of rhetoric.* Charlottesville: University of Virginia Press.

Salazar, P.-J. (2002). *An African Athens: Rhetoric and the shaping of democracy in South Africa.* Mahwah, NJ: Erlbaum.

Schiappa, E. (1990). Did Plato coin Rhetorike? *American Journal of Philology, 111*(4), 457–470.

Schiappa, E. (2003). *Protagoras and Logos* (2nd ed.). Columbia: University of South Carolina Press.

Schiappa, E., Scott, R. L., Gross, A. G., & McKerrow, R. (2002). Rhetorical studies as reduction or redescription? A response to Cherwitz and Hikins. *Quarterly Journal of Speech, 88,* 112–120.

Schussler-Fiorenza, E. (1999). *Ethic and rhetoric: The politics of biblical studies.* Minneapolis, MN: Augsburg Fortress.

Scott, R. L. (1967). On viewing rhetoric as epistemic. *Central States Speech Journal, 18,* 9–17.

Sen, A. (2005). *The argumentative Indian.* New York: Farrar-Strauss-Giroux.

Simons, H. W. (Ed.). (1990). *The rhetorical turn.* Chicago: University of Chicago Press.

Stowers, S. (1994). *A rereading of Romans.* New Haven, CT: Yale University Press.

Sutherland, C. M., & Sutcliffe, R. (Eds.). (1999). *The changing tradition: Women in the history of rhetoric.* Calgary, Alberta, Canada: University of Calgary Press.

Swearingen, C. J. (1991). *Rhetoric and irony: Western literacy and Western lies.* New York: Oxford University Press.

Swearingen, C. J. (2002). The tongues of men: Understanding the Greek rhetorical sources of Paul's letters to the Romans and Corinthians. In A. Eriksson, T. H. Olbricht, & W. Ubelacker (Eds.), *Rhetorical argumentation in biblical texts* (pp. 232–243). Harrisburg, PA: Trinity Press.

Toulmin, S. (1958). *The uses of argument.* Cambridge, UK: Cambridge University Press.

Wang, B. (2004). A survey of research in Asian rhetoric. *Rhetoric Review, 23,* 171–181.

Weaver, R. M. (1970). *Language is sermonic.* Baton Rouge: Louisiana State University Press.

Wire, A. (1995). *The Corinthian women prophets: A reconstruction through Paul's rhetoric.* Minneapolis, MN: Fortress.

Wu, H. (2005). The paradigm of Margaret Cavendish: Reading women's alternative rhetorics in a global context. In J. J. Royster & A. M. M. Simpkins (Eds.), *Calling cards: Theory and practice in the study of race, gender, and culture* (pp. 171–188). Albany: State University of New York Press.

You, X. (2006). The way, multimodality of ritual symbols, and social change: Reading Confucius's *Analects* as a rhetoric. *Rhetoric Society Quarterly, 36*(4), 425–448.

Young, R., & Goggin, M. D. (1993). Some issues in dating the birth of the new rhetoric in departments of English: A contribution to a developing historiography. In T. Enos & S. C. Brown (Eds.), *Defining the new rhetorics* (pp. 22–43). Newbury Park, CA: Sage.

1

Historiography and the Study of Rhetoric

ARTHUR E. WALZER

DAVID BEARD

Historiography is the critical study of the assumptions, principles, and purposes that have informed a historical account—in our case here, of rhetoric. A good description of the methods that a historian might use to create a history of rhetoric was offered by Stephen M. North, who drew on descriptions Robert J. Connors provided of his own work writing the histories of 19th-century rhetoric and writing instruction in North America. North presented the process in linear stages, though he recognized that actual research is always recursive. First is the empirical stage, where relevant texts are identified, found, and validated. In the validation stage, the historian practices "internal criticism": that is, examines the text in context to ensure that the historian understands the vocabulary employed—what "invention" or "correctness" means, for example. This is really a check to

prevent the researcher from inadvertently imposing a modern meaning on an older text. After finding the text and coming to understand it in context, the historian puts the text in relationship to other texts to detect a pattern. The pattern found always depends on what the historian is looking to find, often related to a disciplinary exigency. For example, in the (then) subfield of rhetoric-composition in English departments during the 1970s, there was dissatisfaction with the shape rhetoric had taken in the 20th century—how impoverished it seemed relative to its earlier formations—and so historians attempted to identify when classical concepts were replaced and why. Then, the historian hypothesizes causes for the change; here again subjective choices would abound. One historian might seek immediate causes within the community creating and using a textbook, for example, while another might seek more distant but powerful causes in the political economy. The final stage would be the dialectic stage where the historian would engage others in the disciplinary community in a discussion about the plausibility of the history written (North, 1987, pp. 63–90; see also Connors, 1991, 1992).

But even in the idealized version of the process that North described, there are many subjective choices that historians make—some that precede even the first visit to a library. For example, what should the history of rhetoric be—a history of theories of rhetoric, the teaching of rhetoric, or the practice of oratory? How should that history be constituted—as a continuing tradition of influence from an originary classical period or as radically distinct periods shaped by local historical conditions? What stance should the historian take toward the history related—sympathetic and accepting of ancient suppositions or critical of practices that today seem unjust or unfounded? These questions have been the subject of intense debate in the past 25 years within rhetoric studies.

BACKGROUND

Historiographic debates in rhetoric studies cannot be completely understood in the absence of knowledge of the disciplinary contexts in which they occurred. The rising status of rhetoric in the 20th century in both the disciplines primarily concerned with rhetoric—speech communication and, in English, rhetoric-composition—bear on the nature of the debates over the historiography of rhetoric.

The classical tradition of rhetoric, so important to education in the West through the Renaissance, began to decline in influence during the Enlightenment, a decline that continued until rhetoric's revival in the 20th century. The initial revival occurred in 1900, with a survey taken by the Modern Language Association (MLA) Pedagogical Section querying whether graduate study in rhetoric

was possible. Respondents argued for study of "the history of rhetoric and the development of rhetorical theory from Aristotle down to the present" (Mead, 1900, p. xxv). As a result of this MLA initiative and Fred Newton Scott's intellectual energy, Michigan divided its department of English into separate departments of English and rhetoric in 1903. Scott's "Seminary in the History and Theory of Rhetoric" and monograph series *Contributions to Rhetorical Theory* (1899) mark a short-lived beginning of advanced rhetorical study in the 20th century. But Scott's revival did not take root. The more significant revivals took place later and separately in programs that today we would recognize as speech communication and rhetoric-composition.

In 1914, a group of speech teachers left the National Council of Teachers of English (NCTE) to establish their own professional identity as teachers of public speaking. They founded the National Association of Academic Teachers of Public Speaking, which subsequently evolved into the National Communication Association, and created a journal, the *Quarterly Journal of Public Speaking,* which subsequently became the *Quarterly Journal of Speech* (Windt, 2001, p. 5; see also Keith, 2007). But while the rebels agreed that speech teachers needed a distinct identity, the nature of that identity was the subject of internal debate in the early issues of the *Quarterly Journal.* Some sought to establish the new speech discipline as a science or social science; others, equally committed to establishing speech as a distinct discipline, wanted it rooted in the humanities (Windt, 2001, pp. 5–7). This latter group has come to be identified as the "Cornell School of Rhetoric" because most of the prime movers subsequently had contact as faculty members or graduate students with Cornell. The "Cornell School" began to form in the 1920s and 1930s, when a group of scholars from a number of departments on the Cornell faculty—including Everett Lee Hunt and

Herbert Wichelns in Speech, Alexander Drummond and Lane Cooper in English, and Harry Caplan in Classics—cooperated in creating and offering the first seminar on classical rhetoric. Most were proficient in Greek and Latin. The seminar focused on Plato's *Phaedrus*, Aristotle's *Rhetoric*, Cicero's *On the Orator*, and Quintilian's *Institutes*. Hunt was the primary force (Windt, 2001, pp. 10–11). His "Plato and Aristotle on Rhetoric and Rhetoricians," published in 1925 in *Studies in Rhetoric and Public Speaking in Honor of James Albert Winans* (the first chair of the speech department), was a product of the seminar; it was still being assigned in graduate seminars in classical rhetoric in communication departments in the 1970s. The work of the "Cornell School," which went on to include Hoyt Hudson and Wilbur Samuel Howell, is a model of how a new discipline can be shaped by a relatively small group of scholars who work in concert to establish a curriculum, train graduate students, and publish widely (Kuypers, 2001; see also Benson, 2003).

As Robert Connors, Lisa Ede, and Andrea Lunsford (1984) observe, the renascence of rhetoric studies in speech departments was not felt by those teaching writing in English departments (p. 8). At first, isolated seeds of interest did not flower: Alfred Kitzhaber's 1953 dissertation on *Rhetoric in American Colleges, 1850–1900* was not published in Kitzhaber's lifetime, its influence felt only through photocopies decades later (Kitzhaber, 1990). There was an interest in the value of classical rhetoric as a way to teach writing at the University of Chicago beginning in the 1940s; Richard Weaver (1948) actively taught composition and published articles through the NCTE while completing his own research in classical rhetoric there. But composition in its formative years was, like the field of speech in its early years, open to both humanistic and social scientific paradigms (Strain, 2005).

In the 1960s, a more substantial revival in English began. In 1962, Albert Duhamel, who studied under Richard McKeon at Chicago, published a textbook that drew on classical concepts, such as *topoi*. Workshops and sessions on classical rhetoric began to appear on the program of the College Composition and Communication Conferences during this period (Connors et al., 1984, p. 10). Then, in 1965, Edward P. J. Corbett published *Classical Rhetoric for the Modern Student*, which created "a bombshell effect" for teachers of composition when it appeared (Bizzell, 2003, p. 112). Programs in rhetoric were started in the English department at the University of Iowa in 1967, at Rensselaer in 1969, and at the University of Southern California in 1972 (Corbett, 1993, p. 69). This was also the time when those who identified as teachers of rhetoric or composition (subsequently, "rhetoric-composition") were seeking to identify themselves as a distinct field within English, to be seen not merely as teachers performing pedagogical task in a service course but as scholars within a humanistic discipline. These scholars embraced the history of rhetoric as their own in part to claim a humanistic ground for new graduate programs in an emerging, distinct field of rhetoric-composition. Scholars of literary theory had the *Poetics;* scholars of rhetoric-composition had the *Rhetoric*. A number of histories of rhetoric became influential—some written by Classicists, such as George Kennedy (1963, 1980), some written by scholars in English, such as Corbett (1965) and Brian Vickers (1988), and some by scholars in communication, including Tom Conley (1990). Proudly classical in orientation, these pioneering histories shaped the revival of rhetoric in the context of teaching the practical arts of writing and public speaking in the second half of the 20th century and established rhetoric as a discipline within the humanities.

From a historiographic perspective, this period of 1960 to 1985 seems to be an age of innocence. Both communication scholars and scholars of rhetoric-composition wanted to locate their disciplines within the galaxy of the traditional humanities and cited rhetoric's 2,500-year history and its central place in the creation of the liberal arts curriculum proudly and unproblematically as a foundation for that claim. The idea that this tradition might be subject to a radical critique *within* the humanities was not anticipated, was perhaps unimaginable. In the 1980s, however, the traditional humanities collectively became subject to a critique that challenged the way histories had been written since the Enlightenment, a critique that denied that a history could be an objective account of the past and denied humanists' claim to Matthew Arnold's disinterested criticism. While some of these criticisms had been made earlier (by Nietzsche, for instance), in the 1980s this revisionist position for the first time became dominant. Scholars working within the several paradigms related to "postmodernism" insisted not only that all histories are necessarily partial in the sense of incomplete but also that they are all partial in the sense of working on behalf of some interests to the disadvantage of other interests. These scholars rejected as illusions the "grand narratives" that presented history as a continuous story of development; they rejected too the ideal of the timeless classic that transcended its historical and political contexts to speak to people, regardless of time or culture (Lyotard, 1983). The orthodox history of rhetoric that had emerged by 1980, consisting of a canon of philosophical texts concerned with the epistemological and ethical status of rhetoric, written by white males from within the Western tradition, was an inviting target for these critics. It also was a history that failed to explain the depressed state of rhetoric within English departments, where the teaching of writing was overseen by a composition theory that seemed impoverished relative to the scope and vitality of classical theory. These concerns gave rise both to criticisms of the historiography of the orthodox history of rhetoric and to efforts to create new

histories on completely different historiographic assumptions from those that had informed the orthodox history of the rhetorical tradition.

Before we begin to tell the story of the debates of the past 25 years, a disclaimer: The recent work in historiography has made scholars in rhetoric increasingly aware of the inherent bias in all historical accounts and, therefore, of the obligation of scholars to make their own commitments available to the reader. In the spirit of transparency, we offer these descriptions of our own positions. Arthur E. Walzer's historiographic positions are clear from his *George Campbell: Rhetoric in the Age of the Enlightenment* (2003). Walzer took a "great man," "great work" approach to Campbell. In this book, he assumed that the *Philosophy of Rhetoric* is a significant work in the rhetorical tradition, posited that it is challenging and difficult, in need of explication, and maintained that it is the historian's job to place Campbell's work in historical contexts that would bring its meanings to light. He acknowledged that his work was, therefore, one of historical reconstruction (p. 2). To this end, he placed the *Philosophy of Rhetoric* in two contexts. Since Campbell acknowledged being influenced by other rhetorical theorists (Cicero and Quintilian especially), Walzer read Campbell's work in relationship to what he unproblematically called the "rhetorical tradition"; and since Campbell's work, including the *Philosophy of Rhetoric*, was permeated with references to important 18th-century Scottish philosophers, Walzer also interpreted Campbell with reference to 18th-century empiricist philosophy. It is clear from other scholars' work on Campbell that all Walzer's historiographic assumptions were open to challenge. Some scholars doubted that the *Philosophy of Rhetoric* was inherently important as Walzer assumed; rather, its "importance" was constructed by appeal to certain elitist assumptions about the importance of "the rhetorical tradition," itself a problematic notion, these critics claimed. If Campbell has been influential, the task of the historian is critical—to take the measure of Campbell's influence. These scholars, therefore, looked back on the 18th century from the perspective of our time and traced some of their current discontents to Campbell's influence. Walzer has learned much from these other historians and critics, and while he has not abandoned the historiography that informed his book on Campbell, he respects these other positions and believes that he can fairly discuss assumptions different from his own.

David Beard began his graduate study of rhetoric in the 1990s, a time when articles engaging historiographical debates outnumbered articles in traditional history in rhetoric-centered journals—when historical narratives and metanarratives were hotly contested. At the same time, rhetorical criticism was opening itself to new objects of analysis and new bodies of theory. The study of the rhetoric of inquiry enabled the study of rhetorical practices in different disciplines; the study of the rhetoric of popular culture enabled rhetorical criticism of a quickly multiplying body of texts; the projects for critical rhetoric (piloted by Berlin in composition and McKerrow in communication) opened rhetoric to new bodies of theory. At the same time that rhetoric has flowered, under these intellectual conditions, it remained constrained by historical and material conditions of the disciplines that teach it. As discussed in "Out of the Aerie Firmament" in the *Quarterly Journal of Speech*, Beard (2007) insists on the importance of grounding a history of rhetoric in a history of disciplines and institutions. The history and historiography of rhetoric must be triangulated against the histories of the disciplines of communication and of composition. In some sense, conditioned by the debates of the 1980s and 1990s about the history of the intellectual field called rhetoric, Beard is impatient for the next kind of history of rhetoric as a material and institutional complex.

ISSUE 1: A HISTORY OF PHILOSOPHIC RHETORIC AND THE PROBLEM OF THE CANON

The orthodox history of rhetoric that had emerged by 1980, comprising a canon of philosophical texts concerned with the epistemological and ethical status of rhetoric, was challenged by a new generation of scholars on three grounds. The orthodox history was ahistorical (inadequately grounded in the study of the political and social history of its times) and incomplete (leaving unvoiced some potential contributions to the understanding of rhetorical theory) and was intellectually limited by its selection of texts from Euro-American male authors exclusively.

James Berlin was one of the first to argue that the histories written by Kennedy (1980), Corbett (1965), Vickers (1988), and Howell (1971) are ahistorical—a history of a transcendent, eternal rhetoric, detached from political and economic conditions in which rhetoric is in fact rooted. Berlin (1994) parodied this history as "Plato speaks to Aristotle and Aristotle to Cicero and Cicero to Quintilian and Quintilian to Augustine and Augustine to himself" (p. 112). Rhetoric is on this account a "march of ideas" that is "unified, coherent, rational" (p. 112). Thomas Miller (1993) characterized this historiographic practice as elitist, based on a "history of ideas" model considered outmoded by historians who no longer accept the history of *intellectuals* as equivalent to a history of a *discipline*. According to Miller (1993), the rhetorical tradition is a "fiction"; presenting the tradition as history fosters misinterpretation and misunderstanding of the way rhetoric actually works in history. Such a historiography forces the historian to "to pretend that when figures like Isocrates and Ramus talk about rhetoric, they are talking about the same thing," which Miller claimed is not the case (p. 27).[1] Much more than a stable term skipping across the waves of time, "rhetoric is a product of the economic, social, and political, and conditions of a specific historical moment" (Berlin, 1994, p. 115). Its historical study should begin from that claim.

Critics also argued that the current history was incomplete, with century-long gaps (Gross, 2005). A most glaring omission is the 19th century, a period that was especially important for the history of writing instruction. Robert J. Connors (1991), one of the most important historians in the revival of rhetoric in English departments, observed,

> The traditional rhetorical histories end abruptly with Whately, and the rest of the nineteenth century is an echoing tomb. The story picks up again in the 1920s, with I. A. Richards and Kenneth Burke. . . . What we see in these books is an intentional excision of a hundred years of rhetorical history, a wiping out of most of the nineteenth century as if it had never existed. (p. 50)

But, Connors insisted, there is a great deal of rhetorical praxis in the 19th century—courses being taught in universities, textbooks sold, administrative and faculty rationales promulgated, classroom materials created, and, of course, student themes written. A history that excluded textbooks and featured only philosophical and theoretical publications was too narrow.

In two works on the history of rhetoric—one on the 19th century and one on the 20th century—James Berlin attempted to address the problems of a history based on a putatively ahistorical rhetorical tradition and the failure of current histories to account for the 19th-century textbook tradition. First, Berlin conceived 19th-century rhetoric not as part of monologic, unchanging tradition but as a response to forces within the 19th century: Rhetoric, he posited, changes to reflect the ontological and epistemological presuppositions of a given period. Furthermore, he constituted his history of rhetoric in the 19th

century as a history of the teaching of writing. Within the 19th century, three versions of rhetoric are evident: a moribund classical rhetoric that declined as the Aristotelian epistemological premises on which it was based came to seem untenable; an 18th-century theory based on the theories of Campbell, Blair, and Whately that was "overwhelmingly dominant in American colleges" because it was "compatible with the social and intellectual climate of the time," specifically Scottish Common Sense Realism (Berlin, 1984, pp. 32–33); and a "Romantic rhetoric" that "had little effect" because the college curriculum was imbued with the assumptions of Scottish Commonsense realism that could not accommodate the assumptions of Emersonian Romantic rhetoric (p. 56). Berlin then constituted a history of rhetoric in 19th-century North America based on analysis of representative textbooks in each of these distinct traditions.

But Berlin's historiography itself became subject to criticism. Susan Miller (1982) objected to the assumption, made by Berlin but also by other, earlier histories, that one could write a history of writing instruction by focusing on textbooks exclusively. We need access to other classroom materials and student work, she maintained. This objection was partly addressed subsequently by Brereton's (1995) documentary history. Nan Johnson (1991) offered a more fundamental criticism, arguing that equating the history of rhetoric with the history of writing instruction reflected a "praxis bias" that fallaciously assumed that a history of how writing was taught constituted a history of rhetoric as a discipline (p. 13). Johnson called for and wrote a more comprehensive history that included expanded coverage of much that Berlin and others had done—an analysis of the philosophical assumptions of rhetoric during the period and how these assumptions influenced pedagogical principles and prescriptions in textbooks—but also analyzed how oratory was taught, what genres were most important, and what civic and cultural function rhetoric was assigned in the culture at large during the period (p. 3).

A second criticism of traditional histories is its exclusivity—a limited canon of texts, all written by white males. Although canons often seem inseparable from the idea of a discipline and are practically useful, postmodernists maintained that canons always reflect bias and stifle innovation. Rhetoric's canon of authors characterized by Graff and Leff (2005, p. 20) as reflecting an exclusively "white male, European demographic," seemed to confirm the critics' suspicions. Following their counterparts in English literature, revisionist historians in rhetoric attacked the canon. Debates followed on whether the canon should simply be expanded to include contributions from women, from African Americans, from non-Europeans, or whether these "others" should reject invitations to what had been a white male club and create a different basis for constituting the discipline. Perhaps the desire of a canon is inherently misguided.

Particularly interesting from a historiographic perspective is the debate among feminist scholars on the appropriate response to the sexism that has characterized the rhetorical tradition and its canon. The public nature of rhetorical speech has contributed to making rhetoric especially a preserve of powerful males; women have historically been denied the right to participate in politics and the law courts, and therefore in rhetoric. Historians of rhetoric have typically assumed that their responsibility was to regret but reflect this history in their accounts. To many historians today, this complacency is unacceptable. But intervening into this history is not unproblematic.

The response to Karlyn Kohrs Campbell's (1989) landmark work *Man Cannot Speak for Her* is a good site to explore the complexities inherent in efforts to recover the voices of women. Campbell's work analyzed and anthologized women's speeches that were part of the women's rights movement beginning in 1830. Her multiple criteria for determining what to emphasize and what to ignore included the inherent quality of the speeches in addition to their influence on the movement. She treated some speeches as classics of public address—in her words, as "enduring monuments of human thought and creativity" and therefore worthy of inclusion in the canon of public address (p. 15). It is this last historiographic principle of selection that prompted criticism because it suggested that the purpose of feminist works of recovery should be to discover "great speeches" by women to include in the traditional canon.

Barbara Biesecker was an influential critic. Biesecker (1992) welcomed Campbell's recovery of women orators but criticized the notion that the goal of such recovery is to include women in a canon that, she maintained, was formed on patriarchal values. In selecting and explicating the speeches in terms of their artistic quality, Campbell had presented the history of women orators as a "series of cameo appearances by extraordinary women," an approach that Biesecker claimed mimicked and affirmed the ideology of individualism that characterizes the male-dominated canon of the received tradition (p. 144). Michelle Ballif (1992), writing at about the same time as Biesecker, argued that "efforts to make women legitimate by situating them in patronymic narratives does nothing to enfranchise them—because it does nothing to the phallogocentric economy which disenfranchised them." If, Biesecker (1992) wrote, feminists want

> to produce something more than the story of a battle over the right to individualism between men and women, we might begin by taking seriously post-structuralist objections to the mode of human subjectivity that has served as the cognitive starting point of our practices and our histories. (p. 147)

Jan Swearingen (1999) described well the position Biesecker espouses: Women should reject being included in a history of rhetoric "based on a linear, male, venerate-the-great-ones model that feminists, as proponents of egalitarian, collective and collaborative models of knowing, speaking and writing, should want to repudiate" (p. 35). But Swearingen did not like the alternative either: a status quo that excluded women on the (circular) grounds that what women write and speak is not, by definition, rhetoric because women have been excluded from rhetoric's public forums. If the history of rhetoric or the rhetorical tradition cannot include women, Swearingen maintained, then our definition of what constitutes the history of rhetoric will have to change. Historians should intervene to broaden the definition of rhetoric to include the kinds of writing that women have done. For example, the work of women mystics, who contributed to the Medieval tradition of *poetria nova*, and the contributions of women to mourning and religious rituals throughout the ancient Near East are rhetoric (p. 36). The responsibility of the feminist historian is not merely to fit women's contribution into the status quo but to disrupt the received tradition and redefine "rhetoric" in a way that ensures that the contributions of women are included. "When the history of a field is changed, its definition and subjects change—all to the better," Swearingen insisted (p. 36).

A more radical response to the challenge of accommodation was advocated and practiced by Cheryl Glenn in *Rhetoric Retold: Regendering the Tradition From Antiquity Through the Renaissance* (1997). Glenn's historiographic principles combine a feminist perspective that would deliberately and creatively seek out ways to write women into the history of rhetoric with ideological critique (p. 4). The feminist historian must expose the ways in which gender has functioned as an ideology in the history and received tradition. Only after this ideology is exposed can we understand the existing record and begin to see women's reactions to it as strategic responses to oppression. In this way Glenn would "regender" the history: analyze it from a woman's point of view. What were the silencing mechanisms? How were women excluded? And, especially, how was rhetoric complicit in this history of oppression and exclusion? The result (she maintained) will not be merely a feminist history that fits women into the landscape but a change in the landscape itself (p. 6). Glenn's historiography is self-consciously interventionist and political. For Glenn, history *does* something and is always partisan. The purpose of her history is libratory on behalf of women.

Christine Mason Sutherland (1999) argued that the more radical approach of "postfeminist" historiography went too far. She regretted a history that excluded women from rhetoric's public forums. The strategies for inclusion that she would adopt, however, evidenced a conservative historiography deeply respectful for the idea of "tradition." She drew on the work of John Tinkler (1987) to point out that in *De Officiis*, Cicero distinguished the official genres of public rhetoric, which he called *contentio* from *sermo*, a second type that included genres such as letters that women have a history of working in. Sutherland's model, then, was a conservative historiography that would seek warrants in the words of an authoritative figure in a canonical work to expand the meaning of rhetoric and include women. Sutherland explicitly warned against engaged historiography that overtly pursues libratory agendas. That absolute objectivity is impossible is not a sufficient reason for historians to give up trying to achieve it, she maintained. Furthermore, "reading the literature of the past according to the protocols of the present" will result in a silencing of its own: We will fail to allow the women of the past to speak their own message (p. 15).

Similar challenges to the basic historiographical assumptions in the analysis of

African American rhetoric were also made. There has been a long tradition of analysis of African American rhetoric (in the context of abolitionist movement, the Harlem Renaissance, and the civil rights movement of the 1960s and 1970s). This recovery work continues to this day in the analysis of major African American women authors and orators such as Ida B. Wells (Royster, 1995), Marie Stewart, and Frances E. W. Harper (Logan, 1999), in the analysis of the central role that women played in the abolitionist movement (Bacon, 2002); and in studies of the contributions of African American pedagogues, such as elocutionists like Hallie Quinn Brown, and the variety of 19th- and early 20th-century African American educators discussed by Gilyard (2004), Kates (2001), Royster and Williams (1999), and Zaluda (1998). No one challenges the worth of these texts for analysis. But there has been debate about the proper historiographic assumptions with which to approach these African American texts.

Traditional rhetorical criticism has approached African American discourse with the same tools as it has approached the discourse of its white contemporaries. The assumption was that the Western rhetorical tradition has infused our shared culture so that analytic tools that were brought to bear on Edmund Burke were adequate to an analysis of the discourse of Martin Luther King, Jr., and W. E. B. DuBois. That assumption has been contested. As Molefi Asante (1987) noted, "Cicero's *De Inventione* and Aristotle's *Rhetoric* create a special Western perspective on discourse that in and of itself is no problem. The problem arises when those products are seen as standards for the rest of the world" (p. 74). The orthodox tradition may face its limit conditions when approaching discourses from non-Euro-American sources. Such challenges have led many scholars to look to new sources for rhetorical theory (Afrocentric, Mesopotamian, and Egyptian sources, for example).

Asante has advanced an "Afrocentric" theory of rhetoric, thus constructing an alternative

rhetorical tradition that better unpacks African and African American discourse. It supplants classical Greek and Roman terms and tools for the analysis of African American discourse, replacing it with a conceptual field derived from "ancient Meroe, Kemet, and Abyssinia" (Asante, 1987, p. 71). Terms such as "*logos*," with its complex of meanings in Western rhetoric, are replaced with "*nommo*," a term that grounds rhetoric in vocal expression and attributes "a speaker's power" to "the generation and transformation of sounds" (Asante, 1987, p. 60). The Afrocentric perspective decenters the speaker: "Separateness of speaker or artist from audience in Euro-American society is based upon the degree of participation. But in African society the coherence among persons and things accords, so that music, dance, or *nommo* must be a collective activity" (Asante, 1987, p. 78). Asante crafted a parallel rhetorical tradition, free from the assumptions of the classical tradition and rooted instead in African linguistics, social structures, and performing and traditional arts.

To understand that African American rhetoric, Asante insisted that we need to understand the continuity between African and African American cultural life. Asante claimed that "the recognizable modalities of black Americans constitute a continuum from Africa to the New World" (Asante, 1988, p. 65). We must see principles such as "nommo" visible in Booker T. Washington and in Duke Ellington. A younger generation of scholars, for example, Adetokunbo F. Knowles-Borishade (1991), applied these Afrocentric perspectives to a variety of rhetorical texts, analyzing them in ways that could not be accomplished using classical rhetorical tools. Asante and the scholars who have followed his path work within a completely different paradigm of rhetorical tradition.

Asante was not the only scholar to look to other cultural traditions for rhetorical insight. Jacqueline Jones Royster, for example, insisted that our historiography permits us to see only a small part of a much richer rhetorical tradition. Royster (2003) used the metaphor of landscape to make her point. The Western tradition in rhetoric, though it extends for 2,500 years and covers two continents, is, in Royster's view, only a small garden in a landscape that is the size of our globe and as old as recorded history. She analyzed the work of Enheduanna, a Mesopotamian priestess whose writings date from 2300 to 2225 BCE, to make her point. Similarly, Lipson and Binkley's *Rhetoric Before and Beyond the Greeks* (2004) explored Mesopotamian, Egyptian, and other Near Eastern rhetorics.

The challenge these texts have offered to the task of writing the history of rhetoric remains unanswered. While Richard Marback (1998) yokes debates over the sophists to debates about Bernal's *Black Athena*, his point is the value of the postcolonial critique, not that Bernal gives license to integrate Semitic texts into the rhetorical tradition. Archaeological evidence for relationships between African and Egyptian and Greek culture may not be adequate to justify writing these texts into the orthodox histories of rhetoric. Additionally, the conceptual fields developed may simply be too distinct to synthesize. As a result, it seems that this line of inquiry must develop as a separate rhetorical tradition rather than be incorporated into the current tradition.

The criticisms of the traditional canon created *canonoia*, a term coined by John Schilb (1994, p. 131) to indicate a period of anxiety about rhetoric's canon. The most drastic antidote was prescribed by Robert Gaines (2005), who proposed replacing the idea of a canon with a "corpus" consisting of "all known texts, artifacts, and discourse venues that represent the theory, pedagogy, practice, criticism, and cultural apprehension of rhetoric in ancient times" (p. 62). But are bias and acrimony sufficient reasons for dismissing the notion of a canon altogether? Steven Mailloux (2005) took issue with Gaines's position. Mailloux argued that

replacing a canon with a corpus is not practical. Furthermore, such a proposal assumes that all works are of equal importance or equal value. Some works necessarily do and should become the attention of a disciplinary community's "interpretive focus"—a canon (p. 184). Furthermore, while Mailloux did not deny that rhetoric's canon reflects the racism and sexism of the West, he rejected Thomas Miller's (1993) conclusion that the rhetorical tradition has, therefore, "just about outlived its usefulness" (p. 27). For Mailloux (2005), this would be true "only if the tradition is seen as a closed canon privileging the classical narrowly defined" (p. 183). But, according to Maurice Charland (2003), the canon and the rhetorical tradition should be seen as disciplinary constitutions and, therefore, able to be amended as the scholarly work of recovery and expansion proceeds.

ISSUE 2: THE IDEA OF "TRADITION"

In addition to mounting attacks on the current canon of male-authored, philosophical texts, critics have also argued that the idea of a *tradition* itself creates historiographic problems. Critics claimed that the notion of "tradition" carries with it certain interpretative presuppositions that limit what the historian sees, and while a partial view is characteristic of all histories, the notion of "tradition" is particularly invidious because it honors bias, makes it part of something sacred—*the* tradition. Foucault's criticism of the "unities" in the *Archaeology of Knowledge* (1971) is relevant here. The notion of "origin" and the assumption of continuity inherent in the idea of "tradition" have fostered monologic, teleological histories, Foucault maintained. We "must rid ourselves of a whole mass of notions" that "diversifies the theme of continuity" (p. 21), including "tradition." He would have the historian question and suspend the assumption of continuity and sameness and seek instead for sudden breaks with the past in tracing history (pp. 25–26).

Revisionist historians have identified two discrete problematic historiographic assumptions inherent in the notion of tradition that have characterized and (they argue) limited our understanding of the history of rhetoric. First, the revisionists complain that the idea of tradition fosters an assumption that an originary period (the Classical period) and a particular early work (Aristotle's *Rhetoric*) are normative for the history of rhetoric. All subsequent, and even prior, periods and contributions are then measured against these norms; what is treasured is what leads to and develops from the norm; what departs from the norm or the tradition is missed or less valued. Second, histories of a tradition are generally histories of influence. Historians see their task as tracing the influence of works on each other; the originary period or a single theory becomes normative. It is not only that our histories have conceived of the history of rhetoric in a way analogous to the way philosophy has conceptualized its history—as a series of transcendent texts that address each other within a tradition—but also that some of these texts dominate that history. Whitehead's remark that the history of philosophy can be seen as a footnote to Plato applies as well to the traditional histories of rhetoric since Plato's critique in the *Gorgias* set the agenda, and Aristotle's *Rhetoric*, written in response to the *Gorgias* and the *Phaedrus*, served as the culminating model.

Aristotle's dominance in our traditional histories is the subject of Jane Sutton's (1994) "Structuring the Narrative for the Canon of Rhetoric: The Principles of Traditional Historiography (an Essay) With the Dead's *Differend* (a Collage)." Sutton targeted George Kennedy's histories, which she said naively accept Aristotle's own account of his contribution as bringing the fledgling, incomplete, and flawed previous work to completion; his

work would then render prior theory irrelevant. Along the same lines, James Berlin (1994) accused the traditional histories of valorizing certain figures, including primarily Aristotle. Aristotle's influence in the traditional historians was criticized by Jasper Neel (1994) in *Aristotle's Voice*. Neel claimed that Aristotle's rhetorical theory, which has become dominant in the discipline, cannot be distilled out from his political views, which are incompatible with our own. By linking our discipline so closely with Aristotle, we unavoidably embrace the racism and sexism inherent in Aristotle's hierarchical habit of thought, according to Neel.

The most self-conscious and comprehensive revisionist history written as an effort to displace Plato and Aristotle as originary sources of rhetoric's tradition and to insert the Sophists as paradigmatic for rhetoric is Susan C. Jarratt's *Rereading the Sophists: Classical Rhetoric Refigured* (1991). Jarratt maintained that the "exclusion of the Sophists has operated not only historically but historiographically; that is, the domination of Platonic and Aristotelian judgments on the sophists have determined the ways histories about them have been written" (p. 3). Furthermore, Jarratt identified a specifically *sophistic historiography* and called for new histories of rhetoric based on these principles. She then modeled this historiography in her *Rereading*. According to Jarratt (1991), rhetoric permeated every topic for the sophists: "Sophistic rhetoric collided and interbred with literature, science, and philosophy before such interests were bracketed by Aristotle as disciplines" (p. 13). Accordingly, a history of rhetoric based on sophistic historiography would not confine itself to canonical theoretical texts but would find its landmarks in "any literary artifact as it operates to shape knowledge and effect social action" (p. 13). Second, a sophistic historiography would guard against the assumptions of continuity and progress that characterize the pioneering histories because the sophists, in challenging conventional wisdom, often critically disrupt establishment narratives, as Gorgias modeled in his defense of the notorious Helen (pp. 16–17). Third, histories of rhetoric should imitate the antithesis, associational parataxis, and other stylistic and epistemological practices that characterize the sophists. According to Jarratt, a history written on sophistic historiographical principles would criticize its own assumptions and acknowledge its conclusions as tentative (pp. 21–27), would not favor "empirical data" over "imaginative reconstructions," and would measure its value by how well it "served social needs" (p. 28). With an overt political agenda in mind, Jarratt not only offered a critical reinterpretation of classical rhetoric but also made the sophists our contemporaries. She found in their rhetoric-centered philosophy a feminist alternative to a patriarchal politics and in their theory of education a model for critical pedagogy for today's composition curriculum.

The second objection to the historiographical practice of the traditional histories—that they tend to feature and honor influence—was registered by Carole Blair and Mary Kahl (1990) and separately by Blair (1992) in articles that seemed to have been written with Foucault's (1971) *Archaeology* at hand. Blair's criticism was similar to Sutton's: Our histories, Blair wrote, "typically treat ancient Greek and Roman works with an uncritical reverence" and treat "later rhetorics as derivations on versions of ancient rhetoric, thus privileging the ancient writers" (p. 404). But she went further in claiming that this historiography of influence fosters a number of "questionable argumentative strategies" (p. 405), including reducing the discussion of subsequent theories to their similarity to their putative classical forebears and ignoring theories entirely that are marked departures from classical rhetoric. Identifying the classical as the ideal and tracing its influence causes the historians who adopt this model to "overlook vital aspects of theories

or reduce them to adumbrations of their predecessors" (p. 406). George Kennedy's *Classical Rhetoric and Its Christian and Secular Tradition From Ancient to Modern Times* (1980) was her principal example, and she cited complaints from Renaissance scholar John Ward and 18th-century scholar Lloyd Bitzer that Kennedy's bias toward the Classical paradigm blinded him to what is most interesting in Renaissance and 18th-century rhetoric (p. 406). Blair pointed to the ideological implications of equating history with tradition and valuing works that reference that tradition by calling this approach a "politics of preservation."

Takis Poulakos (1990) undertook to offer a specific alternative to Kennedy's historiography of influence. Poulakos both criticized the historiography of the traditional approach and advanced his own historiography as an alternative. Poulakos focused on Kennedy's analysis of the surviving funerary orations performed from 431 to 322 BCE. He argued that Kennedy's historiographic assumptions led him to see the history of rhetoric as a continuous tradition maintained by imitation and manifest in conventions that particular practitioners honored, creating a tradition. These assumptions led Kennedy to focus on the formal features of funeral orations, features that recur as formulas of the genre. Poulakos offered an alternative analysis of the same body of work that emphasized differences within the funerary oration—differences that he claimed resulted from changes in political ideology as Athens's imperialism evolved in response to geopolitical realities. For Poulakos, funerary orations in Ancient Greece are interesting because of the political role they played. They are exemplary of Althusser "ideological state apparatus," and they are noteworthy because they interpellate subjects. Thus, a history of rhetoric could be constructed as a history of the way the state constitutes subjects during a given period. Poulakos claimed that he advanced his historiography not as a replacement for Kennedy's approach but as a second, parallel history: Our responsibility as historians of rhetoric is to "produce alternative versions of our tradition, to admit the limitations and biases of our peculiar viewpoints, and to leave behind us various and divergent histories of rhetoric" (p. 186).

The criticisms of the historiography of the pioneering histories of the rhetorical tradition and the alternatives advanced can be questioned and have been subject to rebuttal. Though the critics made us aware that there are many ways of conceptualizing the history of rhetoric, from a historiographic perspective there is nothing inherently wrong with constituting a history of a discipline as a history of a tradition. Nor is it necessarily wrong to structure that history as one of influence. In the case of rhetoric, this approach seems warranted since the theorists in rhetoric's traditional pantheon—beginning, at least, with Aristotle, continuing to Cicero and Quintilian, on down to Campbell, Blair, and Whately, Perelman, and Burke—all consciously wrote within a tradition, acknowledging the influence of past theorists on their work. To write as if Quintilian had not been influenced by Cicero, or that Quintilian did not influence Campbell and Blair, or that Burke and Perelman were not influenced by Aristotle, would be strange history indeed. At least in regard to the rhetorical tradition, influence is not the historian's invention, not an illusion. Nor is it necessarily true (as Carole Blair maintained) that searching for influence and assuming that a theorist is writing within a tradition prevents the historian from seeing what is new. Tradition is not stultifying for the artist and need not be for the historian tracing influence. As Maurice Charland (2003) wrote, citing Lyotard, the performer who references previous work, perhaps by ringing changes on it or exaggerating it, is often recognized as the most innovative (p. 128). Similarly, from the point of view of the critic or historian,

comparisons are just as likely to highlight innovation by casting difference into relief as they are to blind—especially when the theorist or artist analyzed is consciously working within a tradition. Even Foucault, whose *Archaeology* (1971) has clearly inspired Carole Blair, only warned of the danger of assuming influence uncritically. If George Kennedy, a classicist by training, has emphasized classical rhetoric more than subsequent developments in rhetoric, this limitation of Kennedy's history does not prove that all influence studies are inherently biased or flawed. Even in the case of *Classical Rhetoric and its Christian and Secular Tradition* (1980) the critics did not prove that the influence Kennedy assumed to be important was not present or not significant. And to Jane Sutton's complaint (1994) that the traditional histories of rhetoric have taken Aristotle's *Rhetoric* as normative, this is not *de facto* evidence of bias. Not only is the *Rhetoric* widely acknowledged to be the most complete and original treatment of the subject we have, it is also true that it negotiates the disconnect between the *techne* tradition of rhetoric and the need of moderns for a theoretical account of persuasion: The *Rhetoric* is a handbook, but the most philosophical handbook ever written. It has served as a bridge between rhetoric as a productive art and as a theoretical one.

ISSUE 3: THE INTENTIONS OF HISTORIES

Revisionist historians often called for new and different histories not because existing histories were inaccurate (since "accuracy" is a relative concept for postmodernists and, in any case, no history is complete) but for pragmatic reasons: Existing histories defined the discipline in a way that limited it—by excluding too much or by grounding the discipline ontologically and epistemologically in ways that could not accommodate contemporary perspectives. A history always *does* something, and postmodernists wanted the histories to do something other than what existing histories did. This pragmatic justification would not readily be accepted by a traditional historian, who would likely claim that the goal of his or her history was to record the story as accurately as possible. It is doubtful that, for example, George Kennedy and Susan Jarratt would agree on what an adequate history of rhetoric would be. To understand, if not to resolve, these differences between traditional and revisionist histories, some scholars appealed to a taxonomy of purposes that Richard Rorty created in an analysis of the historiography in philosophy.

Rorty identified four genres of history writing that differ according to the historian's purpose. *Historical reconstruction* is concerned with understanding a text according to its own intentions and within its historical context. The historian writing a historical reconstruction intends to interpret the text in a way consistent with the original author's purposes and using a terminology that the author and the author's contemporaries would understand. George Kennedy's *The Art of Persuasion in Greece* is an example of what Rorty terms *rational reconstruction* and what subsequent historians in rhetoric have called *modern appropriation*: attempts to understand an original text in modern terms and for modern purposes while remaining true to the general spirit of the original. A text is analyzed in terms meaningful to the historian and the historian's contemporaries, even if those purposes and terms were not used or anticipated by the original author. Jarratt's *Rereading the Sophists* is an example of contemporary appropriation since Jarratt purposefully and openly used the sophists to develop a historiography that she argues better accommodates feminist perspectives on the history of rhetoric—a perspective that she acknowledged the original sophists did not anticipate. Rorty's distinctions[2] were imported into rhetoric studies by Edward Schiappa, especially in

exchanges with John Poulakos over the possibility of offering a rhetorical reconstruction of a sophistic rhetoric. In "Toward a Sophistic Definition of Rhetoric" (1983) and subsequently also in his *Sophistical Rhetoric in Classical Greece* (1995), Poulakos identified a collective sophistic definition of rhetoric that he attributed to 5th-century sophists. According to Schiappa (1990b, 1991), Poulakos had confusedly presented a modern appropriation as a historical reconstruction. According to Schiappa, the "sophists" from whom Poulakos had claimed to derive a shared view of rhetoric did not have a common view of rhetoric or share much else in common as far as we can tell from the very limited samples of their work that survives. There could be no historical reconstruction of a sophist philosophy. What Poulakos (and some others) identified as a sophists' perspective was a "mirage," an imagined creation of their own desire for an alternative to Plato's idealistic metaphysics and epistemology—one that was more accommodating to the constructivist views of rhetoric that Poulakos and other scholars in rhetoric preferred (Schiappa, 1991). Poulakos and the other advocates for the sophists were appropriating the sophists for their own purposes but presenting their work as if it were a historical reconstruction of the sophists' views.

In his response to Schiappa, Poulakos (1990) did not deny that he was appropriating the sophists—did not deny that he was presenting their work in modern terms and using ancient concepts for his own purposes:

> This project has been driven not by the wish to make more things known about [the sophists] but by the conviction that our effort to make sense of our postmodern condition needs a postPlatonic [*sic*] and a postAristotelian [*sic*] rhetoric, the kind that enables us to say that there is more to our understanding of ourselves than eternal Truth and the fixed categories of Logic. (p. 226)

In one sense, then, this debate turned out to be no debate at all: Schiappa accused Poulakos of appropriating the sophists and Poulakos (1995) proudly stated that he was appropriating the sophists in order "to stimulate some new thinking on our own rhetorics" (p. 3). Or if there is a debate it is over whether or not there is an alternative to modern appropriation. Poulakos claimed that there is not. Schiappa, he writes,

> suggests that the interpreter can escape his/her present horizon and retrieve the past as it was. Such retrieval, Schiappa maintains, includes getting into the "mindset" of past authors so as to recreate how they and their contemporaries understood a given text. In effect, he claims that he can escape the conditions that determine his present life . . . and transpose himself to fifth century B.C. Athens. (J. Poulakos, 1990, p. 220)

It is this claim of objectivity that is an illusion; it is Schiappa who has summoned up a mirage, Poulakos maintained.

If Poulakos had shifted the burden of proof to Schiappa, Schiappa was prepared to meet it, proposing hermeneutic practices for interpreting ancient texts. He proposed a historiography that features three methods that can enable an interpreter to enter into the meaning of an ancient text as a basis for a genuine historical reconstruction of its meaning: First, that the original words of an ancient writer have priority over subsequent reports of the writer's work or intentions; second, that a lexicon of key terms be identified and examined in myriad contexts as a reliable way to comprehend how a concept or theory was understood by an ancient writer and his audience; third, that the researcher of Ancient Greece take seriously the transition that Greece underwent in transitioning from a predominately oral culture to a literate culture (Schiappa, 1999, p. 12). Schiappa demonstrated the power of this method in support of his groundbreaking claim that a consciousness of

rhetoric as an art probably did not exist before the 4th century. Relying on this method, Schiappa discovered through a keyword search of Liddell and Scott's *Greek-English Lexicon* that the first use of the term *rhetorike* in a surviving Ancient text appears in Plato's *Gorgias* in the 4th century. He concluded that, therefore, prior to this, while there was of course oratorical practice, there could have been no genuine theorizing of rhetoric (1990a, 1999, pp. 14–29). The implications of this argument are not only that referring to a 5th-century sophist "theory of rhetoric" is an anachronism but that much of the "standard account" of the origins of rhetoric found in works such as George Kennedy's *Classical Rhetoric and Its Christian and Secular Tradition From Ancient to Modern Times* (1980) needs significant revision. In identifying a 5th-century taxonomy of rhetorics—a handbook tradition, tradition of imitation, and a critical tradition—Kennedy implied an awareness of theory that, Schiappa maintained, was misleading. Rhetoric was not "invented" by Corax, by the "sophists," or by any other writer in the 5th century. Schiappa (1999) concluded that while interpreting the past is always problematic and that no account can claim to be either final or absolutely objective, texts themselves do set in place some interpretative limits that allow us to identify some interpretations as outside those bounds and others as far more likely, especially if widely accepted by other experts (pp. 57–60).

Fortunately, it does not fall to us to arbitrate between Poulakos and Schiappa. We can say, however, that while most revisionist historians foreground their assumptions, they do not set forth the limits that guide their interpretations of ancient texts. Typically, revisionist historians state that while they assume that many interpretations of ancient texts are valid and that none is definitive, they also believe that not all interpretations are equal; yet lacking confidence in methods, they do not state limits on interpretative freedom, relying only on a belated test of acceptance by the relevant interpretive community. Schiappa too embraces this pragmatic test but he also proposed a method to serve as a set of rails to limit the universe of possible acceptable interpretations.

A related historiographic problem involving historians' intentions emerged in the rhetoric-composition community. The problem was a consequence of the dual purposes that motivated their project. On the one hand, scholars wanted to create a historical narrative where none existed—to tell the story of writing instruction in 19th-century America. But these historians also saw themselves as reformers who intended to guide present practice and to direct and shape an incipient "rhetoric-composition" discipline. In this second role, they were addressing not only those interested in history but all writing teachers. Robert J. Connors (1997) acknowledged this second purpose when he wrote that his "agenda" was "reforming current practice through reviewing the genesis of a pedagogy" (p. 19).

The purposes of the reformer and the historian are in tension in much of this early work. James Berlin's landmark histories of rhetoric and writing instruction in the 19th and 20th centuries can serve as an illustration. As historian Berlin maintained, rhetoric is not monologic; it changes to reflect the ontological and epistemological presuppositions of a given period, and he identified three different rhetorics in the 19th century—classical, 18th-century, and Romantic. He attributed the dominance of the 18th-century version not to its superiority—he judged it inferior to classical rhetoric—but to its compatibility with the dominant intellectual climate of 19th-century America (Berlin, 1984, pp. 32–33). But Berlin as a reformer and teacher had additional items on his agenda. He wanted to persuade teachers that teaching writing is not merely a matter of developing students' skills but instilling a philosophy because rhetoric is derived from epistemological and ontological

assumptions: "Regardless of one's approach to writing instruction, it is impossible to deny that in teaching students about the way they ought to use language we are teaching them something about how to conduct their lives" (p. 92). Different writing theories have different philosophical assumptions, as his history of 19th-century rhetoric showed. Moreover, the theory that reigned in the classrooms of the 20th century, called by Berlin and others "current traditional rhetoric," was, in Berlin's view, an impoverished theory that should be abandoned. But the "obtuseness" of English teachers makes them embrace this theory as inevitable (1987, p. 6). He would change that. But this reformist program sits uneasily with the historian's claim that the salient theory of rhetoric is the one that is most consistent with the dominant epistemological assumptions. Berlin had argued that John Quincy Adams's *Lectures* based on classical rhetoric, though impressive, failed, not because his theory was inferior as a theory of writing to what replaced it, but because it was incompatible with the period's assumptions. But as a reformer, he judged theories on his own absolute terms and recommends accordingly.

A second related historiographic problem that resulted from marrying a reformist agenda to a historian's is the tendency to promote what Stephen North called "chrono-centricism." In the context of tracing the history of 19th-century writing instruction, chrono-centricism is the fallacy of *assuming* that present practice is superior to that of the past. North's target was not Berlin but Robert J. Connors's (1981) award-winning article, "The Rise and Fall of the Modes of Discourse." North (1987) quoted this sentence from Connors' history: "For years the fact that this schema did not help students learn to write better was not a concern, and even today the modes are accepted by some teachers despite their lack of basis in useful reality" (p. 454). North then asks,

On what basis has the supposition that the scheme was a failure become "the fact"? By means of what unmentioned textual evidence is [Connors] able to say whether this purported failure was or was not "a concern," and to whom, or for how long? Or that teachers who use the modes today are so misguided, operating with schema founded in a useless (?) reality? What can a Historical [*sic*] inquiry tell us about what constitutes a "useful" reality or how writing is "actually done"? (p. 89)

Connors subsequently reflected on his early practice, agreeing essentially with North's critique. Connors (1997) wrote that when he began writing about the history of composition teaching in America,

the foundation of composition studies as a discipline was in full swing; and criticizing the older methods of teaching writing that had been handed down to us was an almost automatic task for one beginning historical study. . . . It was a simple theme: our composition predecessors were fools, and we now see through their mediocre work and can transcend it, thus ushering in the millennium. . . .

But, unfortunately for the purity of my Manichaean vision, I kept reading. I began to read the old journal articles and professional books; I began to know the voices, and I began to see the outlines of what our disciplinary ancestors were trying to understand and were up against. By the middle 1980s I knew more about the cultures, and the societal pressures and the conditions under which people often worked, and the struggle that teaching writing has always been. And, to tell the truth, my earlier mode of critical dismissal, which was based on a shallow reading of one kind of source [textbooks], became something I could no longer maintain. (pp. 19–20)

Connors's account of his experience has a ring of familiarity and truth to it. Attempting to read a work in context, attempting to see it as its author saw it, does change one's perspective. And even if historians can never entirely move outside of their own perspectives, they can move in that direction if that is their purpose.

CONCLUSION

The debates about historiography, painful as they sometimes have been, have had the good effect of making all more aware of the need to articulate the politics and methods that have shaped their work. Even unapologetic traditionalists such as Tom Conley, Laurent Pernot, and, in his most recent history, George Kennedy, have acknowledged the subjectivity of their own approaches—Conley (1990) by acknowledging that what he writes is "my version of the rhetorical tradition" and explaining what that is (p. viii), Pernot (2005) by interrupting his narrative with excursuses that often address historiographic controversies, and Kennedy (1994) by granting the validity of an alternative approach, the history of rhetoric as ideology (p. 11). But the revisionists, who needed no prodding to acknowledge the subjectivity of their work, sometimes write as if one approach to the writing of history is as valid as any other; they seem to allow the fact that no history can claim complete objectivity to function as excuse for not trying to achieve impartiality. In any case, they fail to state what restraints guide even their own interpretations.

Still, it is true that the claim for the importance of methods often goes too far. There is a potential material explanation for these intellectual debates about historiography, an explanation that is prior to any concern about methods—the changing demographic of the professoriate. According to the reports in *Rhetoric Review*, which surveys the state of graduate education in rhetoric and composition, by the year 2000, women occupied 50% of the faculty positions, a marked increase from the

1970s, when they occupied fewer than a third of the positions (Brown, Jackson, & Enos, 2000). Similar changes are visible across the university: According to the National Center for Education Statistics' study of New Entrants to the Full-Time Faculty of Higher Education Institutions, by 1993, women constituted 41% of junior faculty across the university but only 28% of the senior faculty (Department of Education, 1998). Similarly, the number of ethnic minorities in untenured positions in 1993 was one sixth of the total against one ninth of the senior faculty. The junior faculty of the 1990s were demographically different from the tenured colleagues who hired them, and that difference prompted a more critical look at the tradition and at the nature of discipline itself.

Furthermore, we need to acknowledge the reality that these debates were less about methods or historiography than they were about disciplinary identity. Robert Gaines (2005) observed, wisely we think, that the "dispute over the ancient rhetorical canon is essentially a tug-of-war between contemporary scholarly factions whose chief interests are not in the comprehension of rhetoric in ancient times but rather the exploitation or imposition of disciplinary authority" (p. 62). Janet Atwill (1994) similarly argued that calls for revisionist histories are often not grounded in a dissatisfaction with current methodology or in providing an accurate account of the past. "Histories," Atwill wrote, "do not simply provide windows into the past; rather they perform signifying functions in the present" (p. 109).

NOTES

1. This line of argument has persisted; whether the key terms of the rhetorical tradition can be understood as persistent across historical contexts has been raised in the recent work by Gerry Philipsen (2007). Philipsen has made persuasive arguments that Departments of Public Speaking, Speech, Speech-Communication, and Communication used a fairly homogeneous set of terms to describe an evolving and changing set of disciplinary constructs (p. 353). The use of those closely related terms effaces real intellectual differences across time in the history of rhetoric.

2. Rorty (1984) identifies two other genres of history writing—doxography (the historian analyzes an original theory in terms of a modern theory but on the presumption that the purposes of the original author and the interpreter are the same) and *Geistesgeschichte* (the historian attempts to reconstruct an original theory but to show its flaws and to argue for the superiority of a modern theory)—but the discussion in rhetoric focused only on the distinction between historical reconstruction and modern appropriation.

REFERENCES

Asante, M. K. (1987). *The Afrocentric idea.* Philadelphia: Temple University Press.

Asante, M. K. (1988). *Afrocentricity.* Trenton, NJ: Africa World Press.

Atwill, J. M. (1994). Contingencies of historical representation. In V. J. Vitanza (Ed.), *Writing histories of rhetoric* (pp. 98–111). Carbondale: Southern Illinois University Press.

Bacon, J. (2002). *The humblest may stand forth: rhetoric, empowerment, and abolition.* Columbia: South Carolina Press.

Ballif, M. (1992). Re/dressing histories; or, on re/covering figures who have been laid bare by our gaze. *Rhetoric Society Quarterly, 22,* 91–97.

Beard, D. (2007). Out of the aerie realm of the intellectual firmament. *Quarterly Journal of Speech, 93,* 349–351.

Benson, T. (2003). The Cornell School of rhetoric: Institution and idiom. *Communication Quarterly, 51,* 1–56.

Berlin, J. A. (1984). *Writing instruction in nineteenth-century American colleges.* Carbondale: Southern Illinois University Press.

Berlin, J. A. (1987). *Rhetoric and reality: Writing instruction in American colleges, 1900–1985.* Carbondale: Southern Illinois University Press.

Berlin, J. A. (1994). Revisionary histories of rhetoric: Politics, power, and plurality. In V. J. Vitanza (Ed.), *Writing histories of rhetoric* (pp. 112–127). Carbondale: Southern Illinois University Press.

Biesecker, B. (1992). Coming to terms with recent attempts to write women into the history of rhetoric. *Philosophy and Rhetoric, 25,* 141–161.

Bizzell, P. (2003). Editing the rhetorical tradition. *Philosophy and Rhetoric, 36,* 109–118.

Blair, C. (1992). Contested histories of rhetoric: The politics of preservation, progress, and change. *Quarterly Journal of Speech, 78,* 403–428.

Blair, C., & Kahl, M. L. (1990). Introduction: Revising the history of rhetorical theory. *Western Journal of Speech Communication, 54,* 148–159.

Brereton, J. C. (1995). *The origins of composition studies in the American college, 1975–1925: A documentary history.* Pittsburgh, PA: University of Pittsburgh Press.

Brown, S. C., Jackson, R., & Enos, T. (2000). The arrival of rhetoric in the twenty-first century: The 1999 survey of doctoral programs in rhetoric. *Rhetoric Review, 18,* 233–242.

Campbell, K. K. (1989). *Man cannot speak for her: A critical study of early feminist rhetoric* (Vols. 1–2). New York: Greenwood Press.

Charland, M. (2003). The constitution of rhetoric's tradition. *Philosophy and Rhetoric, 36,* 119–134.

Conley, T. M. (1990). *Rhetoric in the European tradition.* New York: Longman.

Connors, R. J. (1981). The rise and fall of the modes of discourse. *College Composition and Communication, 32,* 444–463.

Connors, R. J. (1991). Writing the histories of our discipline. In G. Tate & E. C. Lindemann (Eds.), *An introduction to composition studies* (pp. 49–71). New York: Oxford University Press.

Connors, R. J. (1992). Dreams and play: Historical method and methodology. In G. Kirsch & P. A. Sullivan (Eds.), *Methods and methodology in composition research* (pp. 15–36). Carbondale: Southern Illinois University Press.

Connors, R. J. (1997). *Composition-rhetoric: Backgrounds, theory, pedagogy.* Pittsburgh, PA: University of Pittsburgh Press.

Connors, R. J., Ede, L. S., & Lunsford, A. A. (1984). The revival of rhetoric in America. In R. J. Connors, L. S. Ede, & A. A. Lunsford (Eds.), *Essays on classical rhetoric and modern discourse* (pp. 1–15). Carbondale: Southern Illinois University Press.

Corbett, E. P. J. (1965). *Classical rhetoric for the modern student.* New York: Oxford University Press.

Corbett, E. P. J. (1993). A history of writing program administration. In T. Enos (Ed.), *Learning from the histories of rhetoric: Essays in honor of Winifred Bryan Horner* (pp. 60–71). Carbondale: Southern Illinois University Press.

Department of Education. National Center for Education Statistics. (1998). *New entrants to the full-time faculty of higher education institutions* (NCES 98–252). Washington, DC: Government Printing Office.

Foucault, M. (1971). *The archaeology of knowledge and discourse on language* (A. M. Sheridan Smith, Trans.). New York: Pantheon Books.

Gaines, R. N. (2005). De-canonizing ancient rhetoric. In R. Graff, A. E. Walzer, & J. M. Atwill (Eds.), *The viability of the rhetorical tradition* (pp. 61–73). Albany: State University of New York Press.

Gilyard, K. (2004). Aspects of African American rhetoric as a field. In E. Richardson & R. Jackson (Eds.), *African American rhetoric(s): Interdisciplinary perspectives* (pp. 1–18). Carbondale: Southern Illinois University Press.

Glenn, C. (1997). *Rhetoric retold: Regendering the tradition from antiquity through the renaissance.* Carbondale: Southern Illinois University Press.

Graff, R., & Leff, M. (2005). Revisionist historiography and rhetorical tradition(s). In R. Graff, A. E. Walzer, & J. M. Atwill (Eds.), *The viability of the rhetorical tradition* (pp. 11–30). Albany: State University of New York Press.

Gross, A. G. (2005). The rhetorical tradition. In R. Graff, A. E. Walzer, & J. M. Atwill (Eds.), *The viability of the rhetorical tradition* (pp. 31–45). Albany: State University of New York Press.

Howell, W. S. (1971). *Eighteenth century British logic and rhetoric.* Princeton, NJ: Princeton University Press.

Hunt, E. L. (1925). Plato and Aristotle on rhetoric and rhetoricians. In A. M. Drummond (Ed.), *Studies in rhetoric and public speaking in honor of James Albert Winans.* New York: Century.

Jarratt, S. C. (1991). *Rereading the sophists: Classical rhetoric refigured.* Carbondale: Southern Illinois University Press.

Johnson, N. (1991). *Nineteenth-century rhetoric in North America.* Carbondale: Southern Illinois University Press.

Kates, S. (2001). *Activist rhetorics and American higher education 1885-1937.* Carbondale: Southern Illinois University Press.

Keith, W. (2007). *Democracy as discussion: Civic education and the American Forum Movement.* Lanham, MD: Lexington Books.

Kennedy, G. A. (1963). *The art of persuasion in Greece.* Princeton, NJ: Princeton University Press.

Kennedy, G. A. (1980). *Classical rhetoric and its Christian and secular tradition from ancient to modern times.* Chapel Hill: University of North Carolina Press.

Kennedy, G. A. (1994). *A new history of classical rhetoric.* Princeton, NJ: Princeton University Press.

Kitzhaber, A. R. (1990). *Rhetoric in American colleges 1850–1900.* Dallas, TX: Southern Methodist University Press.

Knowles-Borishade, A. F. (1991). Paradigm for classical African orature: Instrument for a scientific revolution? *Journal of Black Studies, 21,* 488–500.

Kuypers, J. A. (2001). Hoyt Hopewell Hudson's nuclear rhetoric. In J. Kuypers & A. King (Eds.), *Twentieth-century roots of rhetorical studies* (pp. 70–102). Westport, CT: Praeger.

Lipson, C. S., & Binkley, R. A. (2004). *Rhetoric before and beyond the Greeks.* Albany: State University of New York Press.

Logan, S. W. (1999). *We are coming: The persuasive discourse of nineteenth-century Black women.* Carbondale: Southern Illinois University Press.

Lyotard, J.-F. (1983). *The postmodern condition: A report on knowledge* (G. Bennington & B. Massumi, Trans.). Minneapolis: University of Minnesota Press.

Mailloux, S. (2005). Afterword: Using traditions: A Gadamerian reflection on canons, contexts, and rhetoric. In R. Graff, A. E. Walzer, & J. M. Atwill (Eds.), *The viability of the rhetorical tradition* (pp. 181–194). Albany: State University of New York Press.

Marback, R. (1998). Rhetoric at the end of history: Post-colonial theory and writing histories of rhetoric. *Journal of Advanced Composition, 18*(1), 77–89.

Mead, W. E. (1900). The graduate study of rhetoric. *Proceedings of the eighteenth annual meeting of the Modern Language Association of America, 1900,* xix–xxxii.

Miller, S. (1982). Is there a text in this class? *Freshman English News, 11,* 22–33.

Miller, T. P. (1993). Reinventing rhetorical traditions. In T. Enos (Ed.), *Learning from the histories of rhetoric: Essays in honor of Winifred Bryan Horner* (pp. 24–41). Carbondale: Southern Illinois University Press.

Neel, J. (1994). *Aristotle's voice: Rhetoric, theory and writing in America.* Carbondale: Southern Illinois University Press.

North, S. M. (1987). *The making of knowledge in composition: Portrait of an emerging field.* Portsmouth, NH: Boynton/Cook.

Pernot, L. (2005). *Rhetoric in antiquity* (W. E. Higgins, Trans.). Washington, DC: Catholic University Press.

Philipsen, G. (2007). The early career rise of "speech" in some disciplinary discourse, 1914–1946. *Quarterly Journal of Speech, 93,* 352–354.

Poulakos, J. (1983). Toward a sophistic definition of rhetoric. *Philosophy and Rhetoric, 16,* 35–48.

Poulakos, J. (1990). Interpreting sophistical rhetoric: A response to Schiappa. *Philosophy and Rhetoric, 23,* 218–228.

Poulakos, J. (1995). *Sophistical rhetoric in classical Greece.* Columbia: South Carolina Press.

Poulakos, T. (1990). Historiographies of the tradition of rhetoric: A brief history of classical funeral orations. *Western Journal of Speech Communication, 54,* 172–188.

Rorty, R. (1984). The historiography of philosophy: Four genres. In R. Rorty, J. B. Schneewind, & Q. Skinner (Eds.), *Philosophy in history* (pp. 49–75). Cambridge, UK: Cambridge University Press.

Royster, J. J. (1995). To call a thing by its true name: The rhetoric of Ida B. Wells. In A. Lunsford (Ed.), *Reclaiming rhetorica: Women in the rhetorical tradition* (pp. 167–184). Pittsburgh, PA: University of Pittsburgh Press.

Royster, J. J. (2003). Disciplinary landscaping, or contemporary challenges in the history of rhetoric. *Philosophy and Rhetoric, 36,* 148–167.

Royster, J. J., & Williams, J. C. (1999). History in the spaces left: African-American presence and narratives of composition studies. *College Composition and Communication, 50,* 563–584.

Schiappa, E. (1990a). Did Plato coin *rhetorike? American Journal of Philology, 111,* 457–470.

Schiappa, E. (1990b). Neo-sophistic rhetorical criticism or the historical reconstruction of sophistic doctrine? *Philosophy and Rhetoric, 23,* 192–217.

Schiappa, E. (1991). Sophistic rhetoric: Oasis or mirage? *Rhetoric Review, 10,* 5–18.

Schiappa, E. (1999). *The beginnings of rhetorical theory in classical Greece.* New Haven, CT: Yale University Press.

Schilb, J. (1994). Future historiographies of rhetoric and the present age of anxiety. In V. J. Vitanza (Ed.), *Writing histories of rhetoric* (pp. 128–138). Carbondale: Southern Illinois University Press.

Scott, F. N. (1899). *References on the teaching of rhetoric and composition* (Contributions to Rhetorical Theory Series No. 4.) Ann Arbor: University of Michigan Press.

Strain, M. M. (2005). In defense of a nation: The National Defense Education Act, Project English, and the origins of empirical research in composition. *Journal of Advanced Composition, 25,* 513–542.

Sutherland, C. M. (1999). Women in the history of rhetoric: The past and future. In C. M. Sutherland & R. Sutcliffe (Eds.), *The changing tradition: Women in the history of rhetoric* (pp. 9–31). Calgary, Alberta, Canada: University of Calgary Press.

Sutton, J. (1994). Structuring the narrative for the canon of rhetoric: The principles of traditional historiography (an essay) with the dead's *differend* (a collage). In V. J. Vitanza (Ed.), *Writing histories of rhetoric* (pp. 156–179). Carbondale: Southern Illinois University Press.

Swearingen, C. J. (1999). Plato's women: Alternative embodiments of rhetoric. In C. M. Sutherland & R. Sutcliffe (Eds.), *The changing tradition: Women in the history of rhetoric* (pp. 35–45). Calgary, Alberta, Canada: University of Calgary Press.

Tinkler, J. (1987). Renaissance humanism and the *genera eloquentiae. Rhetorica, 5,* 279–309.

Vickers, B. (1988). *In defence of rhetoric.* Oxford, UK: Clarendon Press.

Walzer, A. E. (2003). *George Campbell: Rhetoric in the age of enlightenment.* Albany: State University of New York Press.

Weaver, R. M. (1948). To write the truth. *College English, 10,* 25–30.

Windt, T. O., Jr. (2001). Everett Lee Hunt and the humanistic spirit of rhetoric. In J. Kuypers & A. King (Eds.), *Twentieth-century roots of rhetorical studies* (pp. 1–30). Westport, CT: Praeger.

Zaluda, S. (1998). Lost voices of the Harlem Renaissance: Writing assigned at Howard University, 1919–31. *College Composition and Communication, 50,* 232–257.

2

Rhetorical Archaeology

Established Resources, Methodological Tools, and Basic Research Methods

RICHARD LEO ENOS

Understanding the relationship between established resources, methodological tools, and basic research methods is essential for those who wish to do advanced work in rhetoric. This relationship is best explained by an archaeological analogy. If, as rhetoricians, we consider our mission to be not only to teach but also to discover and create new knowledge for teaching, then we may envision the discovery of new knowledge as an uncharted, unmapped jungle at the center of which lies buried treasure. Leading up to the edge of the jungle are areas that have already been cleared. The path in these established areas is straight and direct at the outset but becomes rougher and less traveled as we approach the jungle. This established path stops at the fringe of the jungle. To cut a new path that will take us deeper into the jungle, we must develop new tools, because our old tools were not designed for the challenges that we now face.

This archaeological analogy parallels the relationship that I wish to establish between resources, research, and methods. Discovering new knowledge in rhetoric is akin to the task of cutting back a jungle frontier. First, we must travel the well-worn path of research done by others so that we can benefit from their

Author's Note: Portions of this essay are developed from earlier work published by the author. The author thanks Sarah L. Yoder and Amy K. Hermanson for their careful reading of this essay and their insightful suggestions for its improvement.

knowledge, but also see what needs to be explored and (in some cases) to correct or adjust earlier work. In short, we must become familiar with established resources. The knowledge of earlier work will, in turn, help us navigate our own orientation. More important, this knowledge of resources will help us see if existing research tools and methods can continue to help us excavate our uncharted terrain. If our old tools fail, the development of tools becomes important, because the instruments for research are driven by our objectives. These tools may be borrowed and modified from other disciplines to meet our own needs, as will be discussed here, or they may need to be created, since existing tools may not provide the required instrumental demands of our task.

Ultimately, our knowledge of existing resources and methodological tools, as well as the development or refinement of new tools, will help us engage in primary research. Such exploration will culminate in the discovery of "treasure"—in this case, new knowledge about rhetoric's history. Other parts of this volume will focus on different aspects of this mission, but the orientation of our journey in this essay is the treasure that awaits us in the discovery of lost artifacts from the history of rhetoric. To that end, select examples of existing resources will be provided as a way of moving toward the development of methodological tools and the procedures for basic, primary fieldwork. It is important to underscore that the discussion of resources appearing below is only a sampling, intended to illustrate (but by no means exhaust) the types of resources that are available. In the space devoted to this discussion, it would be impossible to develop a thorough listing for all periods and cultures in the history of rhetoric. The emphasis here is based on my own research concentration, classical rhetoric, but the examples offered are intended to serve as paradigms for other periods in our discipline's rich history.

ESTABLISHED HISTORIES

Those beginning to study the history of rhetoric will be pleased to know that we already have a number of well-established histories of rhetoric. All histories, however, are interpretations, and those interpretations are driven by the objectives of the historian. For some, the objective is coverage—that is, to lay out the panorama of this discipline in one coherent overview. For other historians, the goal may be a particular thematic emphasis or comparison. For example, the history of rhetoric may be done to illustrate the relationship of rhetoric to other disciplines, such as philosophy, poetry, or religion. Still other historians may write "recovery" histories to bring to light long-neglected topics, such as women in the history of rhetoric. All these perspectives are important, and knowledge of such work is critical for mastering existing information as well as revealing the need for future work. Notably, many historians will end their accounts by pointing out related areas of study where further work is needed.

General works on the history of rhetoric provide broad, foundational perspectives. Such expansive treatments of rhetoric's history include George Kennedy's *Classical Rhetoric & Its Christian & Secular Tradition From Antiquity to Modern Times* (1999), Thomas M. Conley's *Rhetoric in the European Tradition* (1990), Brian Vickers's *In Defence of Rhetoric* (1988), and James J. Murphy's *A Short History of Writing Instruction: From Ancient Greece to Modern America* (2001). Without question, however, the most important of all such works to date is Patricia Bizzell and Bruce Herzberg's *The Rhetorical Tradition: Readings from Classical Times to the Present* (2001). With more than 1,600 pages, this voluminous work provides not only historical accounts and helpful bibliographical references of rhetors and rhetoricians but also a convenient and coherent collection of primary sources.

George Kennedy's work in the history of rhetoric is a good example of resources that provide period coverage. Kennedy's studies of classical rhetoric include *The Art of Persuasion in Greece* (1963), *The Art of Rhetoric in the Roman World* (1972), and *Greek Rhetoric Under Roman Emperors* (1983), as well as his revision and abridgment of these three works, *A New History of Classical Rhetoric* (1994). All these works are excellent illustrations of resources that lay a solid foundation on the topics, issues, and individuals of their respective periods of rhetoric. Scholarship prompted by Kennedy's histories include James J. Murphy et al.'s *A Synoptic History of Classical Rhetoric* (1995), Edward Schiappa's *The Beginnings of Rhetorical Theory in Classical Greece* (1999), and Laurent Pernot's *Rhetoric in Antiquity* (2005). All these works illustrate the value of resources that coherently account for a particular period of rhetoric.

In addition to resources on classical rhetoric, there are other period studies that help establish a foundational knowledge of the field. Such works include George L. Kustas's *Studies in Byzantine Rhetoric* (1973), James J. Murphy's *Rhetoric in the Middle Ages* (1974), Wilbur Samuel Howell's *Logic and Rhetoric in England: 1500–1700* (1961) and *Eighteenth-Century British Logic and Rhetoric* (1971), Thomas Miller's *The Formation of College English: Rhetoric and Belles Lettres in the British Cultural Provinces* (1997), Winifred B. Horner's *Nineteenth-Century Scottish Rhetoric: The American Connection* (1993), and James Berlin's *Writing Instruction in Nineteenth-Century American Colleges* (1984). Of course, there are many other fine works devoted to period study than can be offered here, and such works also illustrate a periodic approach to the history of rhetoric.

SPECIALTY AND THEMATIC STUDIES

In addition to general and period studies of rhetoric's history, there are resources devoted to special topics. That is, these works examine a topic, issue, individual, or group in depth and weave that theme into the broader tapestry of our history. Studies of the relationship between orality and literacy, pioneered by Walter Ong (e.g., *Orality and Literacy,* [1993]) and Eric Havelock (e.g., *The Muse Learns to Write,* [1986]), illustrate the powerful epistemic relationship between oral and written expression. These works have demonstrated that one cannot study the history of rhetoric without becoming sensitive to how mentalities operate differently in nonliterate and literate cultures. The same sort of benefits can be yielded from other topical orientations, such as Andrea Lunsford's edited volume, *Reclaiming Rhetorica: Women in the Rhetorical Tradition* (1995), and Cheryl Glenn's work on women in the history of rhetoric, *Rhetoric Retold: Regendering the Tradition From Antiquity Through the Renaissance* (1997). Similarly, detailed treatment of prominent figures is a valuable resource for study, as is readily apparent in works such as Ekaterina V. Haskins's *Logos and Power in Isocrates and Aristotle* (2004) and John D. Schaeffer's brilliant study of Giambattista Vico, *Sensus Communis: Vico, Rhetoric, and the Limits of Relativism* (1990). Finally, thematic studies are valuable resources for understanding the relationships that exist between disciplines, such as George Kennedy's *New Testament Interpretation Through Rhetorical Criticism* (1984), Jeffrey Walker's *Rhetoric and Poetics in Antiquity* (2000), and Debra Hawhee's *Bodily Arts: Rhetoric and Athletics in Ancient Greece* (2004). Such scholarly studies are strong examples illustrating the interaction of rhetoric with disciplines such as religion, poetics, and athletics.

REFERENCE WORKS AND JOURNALS

Reference works that provide clearly stated descriptions are an essential resource for advanced study in the history of rhetoric. Such works are intended to provide coherent starting points and representative bibliographies for continued study. There are two dominant reference works in rhetoric that serve as such resources: Theresa J. Enos's *Encyclopedia of Rhetoric and Composition* (1996) and Thomas O. Sloane's *Encyclopedia of Rhetoric* (2001). Additionally, we have reference works that evaluate research, such as Winifred B. Horner's *Historical Rhetoric: An Annotated Bibliography of Selected Sources in English* (1980) and her other edited work, *The Present State of Scholarship in Historical and Contemporary Rhetoric* (1983/1990). Recently, more specialized reference works have contributed to our field, such as Michelle Ballif and Michael G. Moran's excellent resource, *Classical Rhetoric and Rhetoricians: Critical Studies and Sources* (2005).

Of course, academic journals provide the most current resource for work in rhetoric. Our field has five major journals devoted to historical rhetoric: *Rhetoric Society Quarterly, Rhetorica, Rhetoric Review, Philosophy & Rhetoric,* and *Advances in the History of Rhetoric.* Other academic journals—such as the *Quarterly Journal of Speech, College Composition and Communication, Journal of Advanced Composition,* and *Written Communication*—regularly include work on historical rhetoric. Occasionally there are edited collections that gather the best article-length works in historical rhetoric. For example, Lawrence Erlbaum Associates publishes the Landmark Essays Series, offering 15 specialized collections of essays on rhetoric.

PRIMARY SOURCES, RESOURCES, AND NEEDS

Primary sources, unlike the resources mentioned above, are artifacts that are the direct objects of study. The above sections treat secondary sources, but advanced work in rhetoric's history requires the researcher to examine primary material directly and, as will be discussed later in this chapter, to discover new primary sources—the treasures buried at the center of our jungle! The impressive advances of the Internet have now brought much of the known primary source material within reach, and these resources will be treated in detail in other parts of this volume. This essay provides a sampling of the existing print resources that enable us to access what other researchers have discovered and retrieved for study.

There are several traditional resources for primary work. As mentioned above, works such as Bizzell and Herzberg's *The Rhetorical Tradition* (2001) provide students with samples of primary materials that are presented along with introductory material and bibliographical sources for further study. Other primary resource collections are often organized by specific periods, such as Rosamond Kent Sprague's *The Older Sophists* (1990); Patricia P. Matsen, Philip Rollinson, and Marion Sousa's *Readings From Classical Rhetoric* (1990); and James L. Golden and Edward P. J. Corbett's *The Rhetoric of Blair, Campbell, and Whately: With Selected Bibliographies* (1990).

There are, however, resources that provide complete editions of primary works in the history of rhetoric. There are two established series of particular interest for historians of rhetoric. *The Landmarks in Rhetoric and Public Address Series* by Southern Illinois University Press provides a number of primary texts ranging from Antiquity through British Rhetorical Theory (especially the 18th and 19th centuries) into the early American period. Readers should note that the editors' introductions to these primary works are themselves invaluable; a vivid example is Linda Ferreira-Buckley and S. Michael Halloran's (2005) critical introduction to the work of Hugh Blair (pp. xv–liv). Other facsimile series, less accessible, include *English Linguistics 1500–1700* (see Enos & Lentz, 1976) and the microfilm collection *British and Continental Rhetoric and Elocution* (n.d.). As mentioned earlier, several such collections of primary resources are now online and available for retrieval.

Many of the editions of the *Loeb Classical Library Series* offered by Harvard University Press are excellent resources for primary material on ancient rhetoric. These editions include the text in its original language (Greek or Latin) with an opposite-facing English translation. In addition to the *Loeb Series*, there are individual treatments of important primary resources; the best example of such works is George Kennedy's *Aristotle on Rhetoric: A Theory of Civic Discourse* (Aristotle, trans. 2007). Kennedy's introduction and notes are excellent. For the benefits of this essential primary work to be fully realized, however, Kennedy's edition is best accompanied by William M. A. Grimaldi's brilliant commentaries on Aristotle's *Rhetoric* (1980, 1988).

Two points should become evident in this sampling of secondary and primary resources. The first point is that much secondary scholarship is readily available for study. The second point is that there is a body of primary material that has already been prepared and distributed as a resource for study. Although this discussion has treated only samples of primary and secondary materials, it is obvious that much more research needs to be done. Under every rubric in this discussion, we could rightly state that both our secondary research and the retrieval of new, primary resources is incomplete! To that end, and to continue our archaeological analogy, our trek into the jungle seeking treasures of rhetoric must continue. The remainder of this essay will build on what we have learned from the resources discussed to guide us in the development of methodological tools and discovery procedures for acquiring new primary resources for the history of rhetoric.

METHODOLOGICAL TOOLS

New approaches to contemporary rhetoric have prompted us to reflect on the very activity of historical research and ask a very basic but important question: Is research in the history of rhetoric nothing more than the discovery and assimilation of new facts? Of course, sensitivity leading to a better understanding of our discipline's rich history is predicated on the gathering of artifacts, but without a view to the methods, mission, and value of such work, the task of doing history can become reduced to the assimilation of trivia without purpose. As historians of rhetoric, we would do well to reflect on our mission. Of course, on one level, our mission is clear: to provide the most thorough and accurate history of rhetoric possible. But we should ask ourselves further, "What are the boundaries and ends of our historical research?" The argument advanced in this essay is that our mission in the history of rhetoric should be extended to include not only a thorough history but to do so in order to understand the heuristics that operated in past cultures, seeking to understand their mentalities as well as the skills that they mastered so well. I fully appreciate the argument that history is valuable for its own sake, but history has a great potential to help us today, and that resource should not be squandered. It is wasted, however, because traditional methods of research simply cannot—and were not designed to—do historical research that rediscovers and reconstructs powerful heuristics that were once employed but are now lost. To attain this mission, we must seek to apply new methods of research. This chapter discusses the implications of that view and offers an example (through the analogy of archaeology) to illustrate the merits of this directive.

New Mentality Toward Historiography

Realizing the importance of situated discourse led to an obvious challenge to historians of rhetoric. Any historical research, as with contemporary writing practices, needs to be no less attentive to situational constraints and the mentalities of culture. To fully appreciate and be sensitive to rhetoric, one must understand context—in this case, historical context. Modern researchers of rhetoric, informed by cognitive psychology, indirectly have challenged historians of rhetoric to find methods to understand discourse with the same sensitivity to the social and cultural construction of thought and expression that they have exhibited in their studies. For example, reading Aristotle's *Rhetoric* independent of an understanding of the civic functions of classical Athens inherently limits an understanding of the work itself. In short, the willingness to apply current research methods to historical rhetoric and its contexts prompts an inclusive mentality that makes historical research a site for innovative inquiry.

It should be noted that many historians of rhetoric did indeed recognize the need for extending the range, methods, and application of historical research. The bond between thought and expression—particularly when examined through the methods of historical empiricism—have become increasingly apparent. In the late decades of the 20th century, Edward P. J. Corbett (1970), James L. Kinneavy (1970), and other experts in historical rhetoric established that the principles of classical rhetoric form a powerful paradigm of heuristics for the teaching of writing. In a similar respect, historians of rhetoric such as George Kennedy (1963) and Wilbur Samuel Howell (1961) established that a study of the history of rhetoric was a vast treasure chest for the theory and practice of oral and written expression and, more important, that many of these treasures were still to be discovered. More recently, historians of rhetoric such as Cheryl Glenn (1997) have shown that the composing processes of women in the rhetorical tradition are best understood in situated contexts. These works illustrate that the study of rhetoric gave us not only our history but also a vast resource for applying heuristics of composition and communication.

In sum, this period was one in which scholars of rhetoric did much more than solidify a humanistic perspective; there was also a quest for appropriating more systematic methodologies for teaching oral and written communication. Earlier scholars of rhetoric had explicated principal heuristics of classical rhetoric—and readily acknowledged the inextricable bond that existed between oral and written expression—but few historians of rhetoric had delved deeply into the complex epistemic processes that served to shape meaning in historical context. The monumental challenge such work raises is clear: If the route to studying written communication passes through orality, how can we study oral rhetoric, which is inherently fluid and momentary, historically? Responding to this challenge, scholars argued that the route to the historical study of orality lay in examining the artifacts of literacy, since orality was inextricably bonded to literacy in ancient societies. This orientation, fueled by the work of Eric Havelock (1982a, 1982b, 1986) and Walter Ong (1993), exposed the importance, the complexity, and the relationship of oral and written composition in both historical and contemporary studies.

The new direction shown by Havelock, Ong, and others led scholars to focus on rhetorical theory anew. Similarly, the early research of Lloyd Bitzer (1968) and the later writings of James Berlin (1996) stressed the importance of situated learning and contextual meaning. All these, and certainly other factors outlined in this synoptic overview of the past few decades, led to a new orientation based on three evolving views. First, as elegantly and succinctly captured by Janice Lauer (1993, 1999), composition became a manifestation of a "new rhetoric." Second, orality and literacy are, and have been for most of our history, inextricably bound together, and even when not so tightly paired, nonetheless warranted (at the least) comparative study. Third, the heuristics of classical rhetoric continue to offer powerful paradigms for composition, particularly when these heuristics are situated within their historical context, or *kairos,* in order to be fully understood. What emerged over the years was a fruitful and symbiotic interaction among historical research, situated learning, and empirical studies that would result in methods that reconstruct the historical context so that it can be diachronically observed and studied. The results of this symbiotic approach have reshaped the historical study of rhetoric. Not the least of this reshaping entails a reconsideration of the (re)sources of our evidence.

An Alternative Approach to the Book-Tradition Monopoly on Rhetoric

As is readily apparent from the first section of this essay, our discipline enjoys one of the longest "book" traditions in Western thought. The volumes of works on rhetorical theory and the artifacts of oral and written discourse have left us with an abundance of material for study. Yet for all the wealth of material, our tradition is still largely a book tradition. Imagining the study of rhetoric without texts of inscribed discourse is almost unthinkable. Whether oral or written, whether theory or practice, our resources for the study of rhetoric have been monopolized by the medium of the book. Current technological developments have made it clear that this book tradition is now being challenged and certainly will be contested in the future. Recently, electronic media have expanded the province of rhetoric to assimilate present and future developments in cyberliteracy. Breaking the monopoly of the book tradition is something that should be recognized as valuable not only for future research in rhetoric, but also for examining the study of our past.

Although technological developments will continue to challenge our current mentality

toward, and reliance on, the book tradition of rhetoric, we also need to recognize a challenge to the book tradition that comes from our past. We are so acculturated to thinking of the artifacts of rhetoric as being imprinted on bound volumes of paper that we have frequently overlooked other ways that the history of rhetoric has been preserved for our study. To cite one example, the very foundations of our printed tradition have been challenged by oralists of the preceding generation such as Milman Parry (1980), Albert B. Lord (1976), Eric A. Havelock (1986), and Walter J. Ong (1993). From a historical perspective, the studies of these scholars have shown the strong, endemic relationship between orality and literacy. Yet in this area, too, we have (by default) been limited to those specimens of orality that have been textually inscribed. Paper literacy has, for all practical purposes, maintained its monopoly on the resources used for the historical study of rhetoric, both in terms of orality and literacy. Nonetheless, the body of research on orality and literacy has, if nothing else, influenced us to reconsider not only the nature of literacy but also how printed texts ought not possess exclusive rights on resources for study.

Our myopic view of historical evidence carries a high cost with limited options. First, we can seek to discover new literacy sources for the history of rhetoric. Two fairly recent, and prominent, examples illustrate this point. The works of Margery Kempe are a good illustration of a recorded oral composition that was discovered and is now assimilated into our history (Glenn, 1997). Kempe is now part of the book tradition of rhetoric. The late-19th-century discovery of Aristotle's *Constitution of Athens* is another illustration of a discovery of a primary source that tells us much about the context of rhetorical discourse. This work by Aristotle also has been assimilated into the book tradition. Such examples from this first option are rare, not only because discoveries are very labor intensive but also because we tend to make these discoveries by accident; that is, such works are not systematically sought after but often are stumbled on during other projects. The second option, and by far the more popular and conventional, is to "fine-tune" long-standing works that have descended for centuries through a chain of transmitters with the hope that we can find new and insightful things to say about canonical works. In some respects, the entire "New Criticism" movement in literature was a macroscopic illustration of endlessly refining meaning to the point of triviality.

The two prevailing options mentioned above do not provide us with many alternatives or opportunities for innovative research in rhetoric. There is, however, a third option that can resolve this apparent dilemma: We can choose to expand our perspective toward available sources of evidence beyond the "book" tradition. That is, we can dilate the repository of our resources to include nontraditional literary sources of the history of rhetoric and, in so doing, exponentially increase our repository of evidence. This chapter argues that epigraphical resources—writing done on durable material such as marble, metal, or wood—illustrate the potential for just such an expansive view of the history of rhetoric. By examining epigraphical evidence that, for the most part, has been made available for study only recently, we can provide a broader, more representative, and more sensitive view of our field than currently exists. This is not to say that the only nontraditional resources for further study of the history of rhetoric are epigraphical, for equally strong arguments could be advanced to show that the resources from architecture, the plastic arts, and other aspects of archaeology could also expand our insights. Rather, the intent here is to establish a paradigm for this third option by showing how epigraphy can enhance the knowledge of our discipline's history enormously and that other nontraditional sources may well do the same. What will also become apparent, however, is

that this new research option also requires new research methods, methods that differ from the conventional forms of rhetorical and literary analysis.

BASIC RESEARCH METHODS FOR ARCHAEOLOGICAL FIELDWORK IN RHETORIC

Roughly 100 years ago, archaeology moved from being a fashionable way that the rich could rob ancient statuary and priceless treasures to a serious academic study of the past. That is, about 100 years ago, archaeologists began to complement the study of ancient texts with physical evidence. If this marking of time is accepted for the sake of argument, then our research sophistication in rhetoric in this area—in seeing nontextual artifacts as historical evidence—lags behind archaeology by about a century. As did our colleagues in classical studies, we also need to dilate the range of primary sources to include nonliterary evidence.

I first came to realize the unexamined resources available to us in epigraphy in 1972 when I saw an inscription outside Rome that recorded matter-of-factly that a youth named Horace had won a poetry contest! At the time I thought that this was an interesting curiosity—I even showed a slide of this inscription to my graduate students at the University of Michigan—but I never saw it as more than a sideshow anecdote. In 1974, while studying at the summer program of the American School of Classical Studies at Athens, the potential for studying archaeological and epigraphical sources for historical rhetoric was dramatically—but casually—brought home to me by my late professor, Fordyce Mitchell. I was especially impressed when he pointed out inscriptions that recorded rhetorical and literary contests that (to this day) remained stored at archaeological sites in remote locations. On our trip to Boetia, we stopped at a small sanctuary about 30 miles outside Athens called the Amphiareion of Oropos. Knowing my interest in rhetoric, Mitch (as he liked to be called) pointed out a marble inscription that listed victors at rhetorical and literary contests that were regularly held at this small site. That moment was an epiphany! At once the possibility of new sources for rhetoric was made literally visible to me.

In the summer of 1977, I was able, with the cooperation of the Greek Government and the American School of Classical Studies at Athens, to examine Greek inscriptions at Amphiareion. I discovered that inscriptions at this site, which once was a center for oratorical, literary, and dramatic contests, provided evidence of ancient oral interpreters, or rhapsodes, practicing an art that most contemporary scholars had thought perished three centuries earlier. These findings brought the role of the Hellenic rhapsode in the history of rhetoric into much sharper focus, while at the same time illustrating vividly the endemic ties of oral and literate composition that persisted over centuries. More important, my 2 months of fieldwork made it apparent that a vast resource of evidence was awaiting study by historians of rhetoric.

Over the years, I returned to Greece and that small sanctuary, eventually publishing the study in 1985 (see also Enos, 1993). In a similar vein, I was encouraged when Christopher Johnstone (1996), a professor in the Communication Department at Penn State University, did a study of acoustics in Athens's general assembly, the Pnyx (*Theory, Text, Context: Issues in Greek Rhetoric and Oratory*). Johnstone, along with student assistants, traveled to Greece and did on-site testing of speaking conditions. His research provides many valuable observations about the physical conditions and acoustical constraints of Greek oratory (see my review in *Rhetoric Review*, Enos, 1998). Similarly, James Fredal makes a compelling argument in his 2006 book, *Rhetorical Action in Ancient Athens: Persuasive Artistry From Solon to Demosthenes*, that "rhetorical action" in Athens is best understood not only by what can be determined from speeches and textbooks but also by examining the resources of Athenian archaeology, anthropology, and architecture (24ff.). My hope is that such research will promote both fieldwork and the creation of new research methods needed for such study—if you will, an archaeology of rhetoric.

To engage in rhetorical archaeology, we must reconstruct not only the discourse and the cultural context but also the mentalities that are indigenous to the period. One of the first facts that I point out to beginning students of classical rhetoric is that most Greeks and Romans could not read silently (Stanford, 1967, p. 2). Students are startled to learn that reading without saying the words aloud is not "natural" but an acquired skill, a talent so rare that it was noted as a curiosity in Antiquity. My point in making such an observation is not merely to shock students, but rather to make them aware of the tacit assumptions that we make at even the most basic levels of communication. That is, even the most basic presumptions—such as reading silently—must be verified.

My belief about the importance of being sensitive to the most basic components of our discipline in scholarly studies is in harmony with Janice M. Lauer and Andrea Lunsford's (1989) view about the training of our doctoral students. "Very much at issue in current historical work," Lauer and Lunsford argue, "are several deceptively simple questions: What has it meant to be a reader or a writer in, say classical Athens or Medieval London?" (p. 107). The archaeological motif proposed here requires that we reflect on the most fundamental of notions. Both grammar and rhetoric seek to co-create meaning between rhetor and auditors or readers. To be successful, such a process requires a sensitive understanding of the heuristics by which others structure their thoughts and sentiments, what they see as powerful arguments, and their hierarchies of values. As researchers, our job in reconstructing this process is to recreate this joint effort between rhetor and auditors or readers. In brief, we seek to reconstruct discourse as the medium by which meaning is created and adjudicated.

To do this reconstruction well, we must understand both a particular culture and the mentalities of the participants operating in that culture. For example, the uniquely Roman creation of satire as a high literary art (Quintilian, 10.1.93) is also a sign of their mentality and worldview. My favorite illustration of this sort of reconstruction is Dante. There is little doubt that when Italy decided to select one of her many dialects as the national language (Italian), the choice of the Florentine dialect was due, in large part, to the literary genius of Dante, whose work in the vernacular helped create Italian literature. Dante, like Homer, Virgil, and Shakespeare, had supreme control over his language, to the extent that he could express whatever he wished in the most poignant way possible. Yet I suspect that if you asked Dante how he composed these literary masterpieces, he would not be aware of his own epistemic rhetorical process. We may say in exasperation, "Well, if Dante could not understand how he expressed himself, what hope do we have of revealing his genius?" Here is our great challenge. If we can somehow reconstruct the rhetorical processes of luminaries such as Dante, we will unlock heuristics that could be invaluable in refining our own systems of expression, as well as capture the high art of Renaissance eloquence in Italy.

Nontraditional Resources and Their Value for the Historical Study of Rhetoric

For those not familiar with epigraphical research, its procedures need to be understood before its benefits to the study of rhetoric can be appreciated. Within the past few decades, archaeological excavations in Greece have brought forth information critical to the understanding of ancient rhetoric. A great number of inscriptions have been recorded and are available for study. Such examinations, however, present obvious limitations. Those recordings of inscriptions that manage to reach library shelves in the form of published volumes do so years, sometimes decades, after discovery. Even the most comprehensive of collections, such as *Inscriptiones Graecae*, cover holdings only up to a certain date. Yearly reporting of epigraphical discoveries have been offered in *Revue des éstdues grecques*, but these often are little more than critical summaries of epigraphical findings. In brief, not all inscriptions reach publication in a form suitable for study. A vast number of inscriptions are simply catalogued and left at archaeological sites. Moreover, as Donald William Bradeen and Malcolm Francis McGregor (1973) reveal in *Studies in Fifth-Century Attic Epigraphy*, there is a benefit to fieldwork that cannot be matched by merely examining an inscription that has been recorded in a book by someone else: "Our studies in Athens taught us much. In particular, we learned once again the lesson that in epigraphical study there is no substitute for autopsy." Bradeen and McGregor went on to argue that "arm-chair" epigraphy is a "profitable exercise" but that "the stone itself . . . is the final witness. This was brought home to us in those tragic years when Athens was inaccessible to scholars" (p. viii). Efforts were made to assimilate epigraphical works into the book tradition but, as Bradeen and McGregor point out, this has its natural limitations and inevitable delays. While it is obvious that recent technological developments make the recording of epigraphical sources much more available, what is still desperately needed is fieldwork in rhetoric and composition so that new sources can be available for study. Pursuing this line of study means that we need to complement our office research by walking from the aisles of bookshelves and going into the field for on-site research. That is, historians of rhetoric need to make on-site visits to repository centers and to discover firsthand new resources for the history of our discipline. Much of my academic life has been devoted to making these resources available through direct observation and in encouraging other historians of rhetoric to engage in fieldwork for the discovery of new primary sources.

Since taking my first classical rhetoric course in 1968, I have learned that an oral tradition preceded and paralleled a manuscript tradition. From these two early experiences in Italy and Greece, I realized that an epigraphical tradition had also existed and that a rhetorical and literary tradition had been inscribed. Thanks to recent archaeological excavations, this invaluable historical source now lay before our eyes for study. Since those early experiences, it has become apparent to me that a great deal of information about rhetoric comes directly from Antiquity and, in this sense, is a true primary source; that is, the information was not transmitted and interpreted over the centuries from scribe to scribe, but comes directly to us from the period. Preserved on these ancient artifacts are orations of political and social importance, educational information, and records of literary and rhetorical contests. In short, an entire history could be significantly advanced if such data were available to scholars for study. In the years that followed, I have had occasion to return to Italy and Greece and to study these sources. This chapter provides an overview synthesizing these experiences so that others may see this as an attractive area of study, one that will complement our book tradition of rhetoric. While the procedures listed below are specific to securing permission to examine epigraphical sources, it is obvious that the same basic protocol exists for other primary material.

Securing Archival Permission for Fieldwork: A Case Study

As mentioned above, on-site research requires fieldwork. The procedure of this research consists of four components: (1) isolating research sites, (2) securing permission prior to investigation, (3) collecting on-site data, and (4) determining research objectives after returning from fieldwork.

1. *Isolating research sites:* One of the earliest and most obvious problems for discovering new primary sources for the history of rhetoric is isolating research sites. Our knowledge of the history of rhetoric serves as a staring point, for from our history we can identify established locations for the study of rhetoric. We know, for example, that Gorgias of Leontini (Sicily) traveled to Athens and stayed to teach for an extended period of time. We also know that the famous Attic orator, Aeschines, left Athens and went to the island of Rhodes, where he established a school of rhetoric. Centuries later, we can read the accounts of Cicero and see that his own education took him from his home in Arpinum to Rome and later to Athens and Rhodes for study. This generally known information on the history of rhetoric signals active locations for the study and practice of rhetoric over an extended period of time. Other sites, admittedly less obvious, can be brought to light when we review the history of rhetoric. It is clear, however, that such early preparation is a critical factor for success in the field. Previous investigations while in Greece, coupled with subsequent investigations while in the United States, are helpful in identifying and isolating likely sites for study. Such preliminary work has, for example, revealed (at least) 10 major locations:

1. The Athens Epigraphical Museum
2. The Ancient Corinth Museum
3. The Delphi Archaeological Museum
4. The Chios Archaeological Museum

5. The Mytilene Archaeological Collection
6. The Olympia Archaeological Museum
7. The Isthmia Archaeological Collection
8. The Nemea Archaeological Museum
9. The Thebes Museum
10. The Epidauros Archaeological Museum

Current directories indicate extensive holdings of inscriptions available for examination at these sites. It is also important to note that many of these museums are in the vicinity of the original archaeological sites and that additional inscriptions remain available for observation and study on-site. Many of these locations, especially Athens, were known educational centers for rhetorical and literary training, while other locations were also centers for oratorical and literary contests. However, there are also numerous lesser-known sites that now house evidence. Part of the reason for this condition is that the transportation and storage of stone inscriptions to major educational centers and museums is both expensive and difficult. The Epigraphical Museum at Athens, for example, has an impressive variety of inscriptions, yet its collection represents only a fraction of what remains in the field. As a result, many of the inscriptions are left on-site, often at remote locations. This condition is different from other primary sources. Manuscripts, in contrast, are often available at central repositories. In Florence, the Biblioteca Medicea Laurenziana is housed in the Church of San Lorenzo. The same availability for primary material, in this case a rare edition of the *Rhetorica ad Herennium,* is available at the Biblioteca Reale in Torino. At these particular sites, rare editions of Cicero's orations, as well as his rhetorical treatises, are available for study. What is even more helpful is that such libraries can be often accessed by e-mail, so permission can be acquired in a matter of days and material can be ready for study on arrival in Florence or Torino. However, because epigraphical material is not easily transported for storage and collection, and because cataloguing is both expensive and difficult, it is essential that fieldwork be a part of our research agenda as a discipline.

2. *Securing permission prior to investigation:* Excluding inscriptions that are on public display, the study of epigraphical sources requires permission. As with most European countries, Greece has a well-established custom of protocol and proper procedures. Normally, permission to study epigraphical sources is secured through an established and identifiable entity. The American School of Classical Studies at Athens is an invaluable resource and aid in securing permission for sources prior to investigation. Through the American School of Classical Studies at Athens, permission is granted from the Greek Ministry of Science and Culture or the Greek Archaeological Service. Likewise, the official photograph of important inscriptions, especially those that are intended for publication, must also be obtained from these sources with permission to publish explicitly granted. In my experience, the Greek Ministry will review permission requests and provide a statement of authorization, which can be shown either to the regional directors of Antiquity (Ephors) or to the officials who are supervising the archaeological site. Although, as mentioned above, the services of e-mail have greatly enhanced the speed of this process, it is essential to understand that all such material must be approved well in advance of the fieldwork and can often take up to several months.

3. *Collecting on-site data:* Actual investigation at the site consists of recording and interpreting epigraphical data. Normally, the recording of such data takes place outside, under the hot Greek sun and at remote locations that require extensive walking over steep terrain. Under such conditions, it is very difficult to actually study inscriptions that deal with rhetoric. The primary task on-site is to

photograph, draw, and record these inscriptions for later, more detailed study. In short, evidence gathering is the primary objective during fieldwork.

4. *Determining research objectives after returning from fieldwork:* Subsequent to the fieldwork, new information relevant to the history of rhetoric can now be assimilated in a manner that is suitable for study. The objective is to return home with an accurate representation of primary material that is suitable for detailed examination. Initially, the findings of such work are presented in journals. In the past, epigraphical sources have been cited in published articles on rhapsodes, sites for the study and performance of rhetoric during the Second Sophistic, contest winners in oratorical and literary events, and research on the origins of the formal study of rhetoric. Eventually, these individual studies were synthesized in my 1993 volume, *Greek Rhetoric Before Aristotle* (Enos, 1993).

Illustrations of the Array of Evidence From Fieldwork in Greece

What are the benefits of such fieldwork? Through the procedures that are outlined above, I have been able to acquire a variety of new evidence on our discipline's history. The spectrum of this evidence is best realized by both breadth and depth. That is, my hope is that demonstrating the possibilities from such fieldwork should become evident by citing an array of findings.

1. *Visiting the site of rhetorical situations:* One of the first axioms that we learn in rhetoric is that it must be studied in context. While this principle is obvious in contemporary rhetoric, it is equally true in ancient rhetoric. In many instances, the physical evidence still remains and can be an enormous help in reconstructing the *kairos,* or situational context, of the rhetoric under examination. In addition, we have ancient commentary that

serves as a guide for our analysis. For example, the ancient geographer Pausanias traveled throughout Greece and wrote descriptions of many of the buildings that he saw. From Pausanias's accounts, we have a frame of reference that will help us in reconstructing the environment. Some of the obvious examples of interest are the Athenian Agora, which contains not only the Bema, or rhetor's platform, but also the Boule, where citizens assembled to deliberate. Large public meetings were held at the Pnyx. As mentioned earlier, Christopher Johnstone (1996) has done pioneering work on acoustics at the Pnyx that has helped us better understand the constraints facing Athenian orators. Archaeological excavations done by the American School of Classical Studies at Athens have provided a thorough knowledge of the Odeion, the ancient theater that Pausanias tells us was a site for both declamations and sophistic teaching. Museums often accompany such archaeological sites and often contain valuable artifacts for historians of rhetoric. In Athens, water clocks and writing instruments give us direct evidence of oral and literate practices (Enos, 2002). The Acropolis Museum, for example, has a statue of a writer that captures, for a moment in time, the actual act of composing.

2. *Statuary:* The physical appearance of prominent rhetors and rhetoricians has been a major interest in our discipline. This source of evidence is often available for examination. Busts of Demosthenes, for example, are on display in both the British Museum and in Greece's National Archaeological Museum. It is not uncommon, moreover, for an inscription to be carved at the base of the bust, as is the case with a dedication to Plutarch at Chaironeia. These visual representations help complement the narratives that we have compiled in our verbal "book" tradition of rhetoric.

3. *Inscriptions:* Perhaps the most prevalent and obvious source for study is, as mentioned earlier in this essay, the numerous on-site

inscriptions. In my travels throughout Greece, I have noticed a number of ancient inscriptions that merit detailed study. Some of these are as follows. Ancient Greeks complemented athletic contests with rhetorical, literary, and dramatic contests. Lists of victors, such as those mentioned at the Amphiareion of Oropos, tell us a great deal about individuals, cities, events, and (in short) their cultural heritage. Many inscriptions, particularly those at the Epigraphical Museum in Athens, explicitly mention rhetoric (EM 2959), *rhetores* (EM 10606), philosophers (EM 9684), and Sophists (EM 446). On some occasions, entire speeches are recorded on stone, as is the case of an address by Nero that is preserved at the Thebes Museum. Other inscriptions record decrees that provide insights to the political climate of the time and the formal role of ambassadors or *rhetores*. There is little question why epigraphist Fergus Millar (1985) claimed that inscriptions "are by far the most important surviving products of the political processes of the period" (p. 99). Still other inscriptions further help paint a vivid picture of rhetoric in the ancient work. One inscription in the Athenian Agora lists library rules for readers. Another inscription in the Museum at Delphi actually records musical notations for a hymn to Apollo, thereby providing a source for understanding better the euphony and phonology of the Greek tongue. All these examples, however, are only presented as an overview to establish the much more important principle that a wealth of nontraditional, primary material awaits those scholars who wish to extend the knowledge of our discipline by assimilating this evidence into the rhetorical tradition. This principle, of course, is intended to apply beyond epigraphy and classical rhetoric; it should be clear that for each period in the history of rhetoric, nontraditional sources of primary evidence are awaiting discovery and analysis.

Research Heuristics

Our work in historical empiricism is a parallel to an archaeological motif. Imagine, as discussed in the last section, that we have gone to Greece and discovered one of Aristotle's lost works on rhetoric, or perhaps a speech of Demosthenes, or a dialogue of Plato. How do we "display" our historical treasure when it is not one of the plastic arts but rather one of the verbal arts? The very simple research heuristic proposed here will provide a structure for archaeologically reconstructing our verbal artifact, what I have termed *rhetorical layering*. It involves four layers that must be done in sequence but, after reconstruction, can then be analyzed for their dynamic interaction: discovery, reconstruction, analysis, and display. In the first layer, discovery, we must realize the social and cultural conditions by identifying the political structure, the social patterns, and cultural hierarchies of values. All these will help us understand the mentalities in operation. For the second layer, reconstruction, we must model or recreate what Lloyd Bitzer (1968) calls the *rhetorical situation* or what James Kinneavy (1986) terms *kairos*. That is, we must reconstruct the conditions that induce and explain why rhetoric and composition were brought into existence. By isolating the exigencies, audience, and constraints (in Bitzer's terms), we will be able to reconstruct the context within the social dynamics of the culture. The third layer, analysis, requires that we examine the actual discourse. There are several rhetorical theories that provide schemes for analysis, but the most appropriate one will have to be determined by how sensitive it is to the context. For example, in an agonistic situation, theoretical explanations of argument offered in Aristotle's *Rhetoric* or in Chaim Perelman and L. Olbrechts-Tyteca's *The New Rhetoric: A Treatise on Argumentation* (1969) may be most sensitive. In other situations, such as in Christian discourse, an Augustinian perspective on education and charity might be the most appropriate approach. Issues that focus on cooperative discourse may be best understood through Kenneth Burke's theories. Capturing the expression of women may require approaches recently advocated by historians of rhetoric such as Cheryl Glenn. The point is that the archaeological motif allows historians of rhetoric to reconstruct the meaning of discourse by reconstructing the social and cultural context within which thoughts and sentiments are expressed. Such a reconstruction will reveal the interaction among the dynamics of mentality, expression, and social conditions. At the fourth layer, display, results are presented in a manner by which we "exhibit" our artifact in a reconstructed context that will help readers grasp the utterance at the moment of *kairos,* much as we do an exhibit at a museum.

CONCLUSION: THE BENEFITS OF RHETORICAL ARCHAEOLOGY

Reconstructing how meaning is made and shared through discourse is the primary task of the historian of rhetoric. Far from merely chronicling an event or weaving a tale, this reconstruction is an "argument" that offers evidence to the reader as a way of validating an interpretation. Two important phases in the process are treated here. The first phase is the need for fieldwork akin to, and in collaboration with, archaeological research methods. The second phase is the reconstruction of the artifact by employing the heuristics of rhetorical layering. These two phases will enable us to add to and amend the rhetorical tradition. That is, these two phases will serve as both normative and regulatory methods for adjudicating the validity of our historiography. In the process, our historiography will continually

prompt inclusive, representative, and thorough accounts that reconstruct the dynamic and complex ways that we have sought to express our thoughts and sentiments across time and within cultures. We enhance our research skills and expertise by limiting unwarranted presumptions and by grounding observations within the context from which the discourse emanated. Rhetorical layering consists of four interactive strata of analysis: discovering the social, political, and cultural conditions; reconstructing the rhetorical situation or *kairos* that induces discourse; analyzing the actual discourse; and finally, displaying of this work in a manner that reconstructs the dynamic interaction of these layers. Reconstructing this event will then help in choosing the most sensitive heuristics to analyze discourse or theory and, consequently, explicate the event for public display.

The intent of this chapter is to make a convincing argument for a general principle through a specific topic. The general principle is that advances in the history of rhetoric will occur if we extend the range of our primary resources as well as the depth. That is, we need to recognize that nontraditional sources of evidence exist outside the "book" tradition, and we need to discover this evidence through fieldwork. This work may involve visiting remote archaeological sites, but it may also require searching in obscure libraries and private collections throughout the world. My illustration is also intended to point out that new research methods need to be acquired, ones that will provide sensitive ways of evaluating nontraditional evidence. The benefits of adopting this view will mean that we will be able to complement our valuable "book" tradition with a new orientation; together, both approaches will help provide a more thorough and representative understanding of rhetoric and truly result in advances in the history of rhetoric.

REFERENCES

Aristotle. (2007). *On rhetoric: A theory of civic discourse* (2nd ed., G. A. Kennedy, Trans.). Oxford, UK: Oxford University Press.

Ballif, M., & Moran, M. (Eds.). (2005). *Classical rhetorics and rhetoricians: Critical studies and sources.* Westport, CT: Praeger.

Berlin, J. A. (1984). *Writing instruction in nineteenth-century American colleges.* Carbondale: Southern Illinois University Press.

Berlin, J. A. (1996). *Rhetorics, poetics, and cultures: Refiguring college English studies.* Urbana, IL: NCTE.

Bitzer, L. (1968). The rhetorical situation. *Philosophy and Rhetoric, 1,* 1–14.

Bizzell, P., & Herzberg, B. (Eds.). (2001). *The rhetorical tradition: Readings from classical times to the present* (2nd ed.). Boston: Bedford.

Bradeen, D. W., & McGregor, M. F. (1973). *Studies in fifth-century Attic epigraphy.* Norman: University of Oklahoma Press, for the University of Cincinnati.

British and Continental Rhetoric and Elocution. (n.d.). A microfilm series of 120 entries sponsored by the Speech Communication (now National Communication Association). Ann Arbor, MI: University Microfilms International.

Conley, T. M. (1990). *Rhetoric in the European tradition.* New York: Longman.

Corbett, E. P. J. (1970). *Classical rhetoric and the modern student.* Oxford, UK: Oxford University Press.

Enos, R. L. (1993). *Greek rhetoric before Aristotle.* Prospect Heights, IL: Waveland Press.

Enos, R. L. (1998). *Theory, text, context: Issues in Greek rhetoric and oratory* (C. L. Johnstone, Ed.). Albany: State University of New York Press, 1996. Reviewed in *Rhetoric Review, 16,* 327–334.

Enos, R. L. (2002). Inventional constraints on the technographers of ancient Athens: A study of *kairos.* In P. Sipiora & J. Baumlin (Eds.), *Rhetoric and kairos: Essays in history, theory and praxis* (pp. 77–88). Albany: State University of New York Press.

Enos, R. L., & Lentz, T. M. (Eds.). (1976, Winter). A bibliographical guide to English Linguistics: 1500–1800. *Rhetoric Society Quarterly, 6,* 68–79.

Enos, T. (Ed.). (1996). *Encyclopedia of rhetoric and composition: Communication from ancient times to the information age.* New York: Garland Press.

Ferreira-Buckley, L., & Halloran, S. M. (Eds.). (2005). Editors' introduction. In *Hugh Blair: Lectures on rhetoric and belles lettres* (pp. xv–liv). Carbondale: Southern Illinois University Press.

Fredal, J. (2006). *Rhetorical action in ancient Athens: Persuasive artistry from Solon to Demosthenes.* Carbondale: Southern Illinois University Press.

Glenn, C. (1997). *Rhetoric retold: Regendering the tradition from Antiquity through the Renaissance.* Carbondale: Southern Illinois University Press.

Golden, J. L., & Corbett, E. P. J. (Eds.). (1990). *The rhetoric of Blair, Campbell, and Whately: With Selected Bibliographies.* Carbondale: Southern Illinois University Press.

Grimaldi, W. M. A. (1980). *Aristotle, Rhetoric I: A commentary.* New York: Fordham University Press.

Grimaldi, W. M. A. (1988). *Aristotle, Rhetoric II: A commentary.* New York: Fordham University Press.

Haskins, E. V. (2004). *Logos and power in Isocrates and Aristotle.* Columbia: University of South Carolina Press.

Havelock, E. A. (1982a). *The literate revolution in Greece and its cultural consequences.* Princeton, NJ: Princeton University Press.

Havelock, E. A. (1982b). *Preface to Plato.* Cambridge, MA: Belknap Press of Harvard University Press. (Original work published 1963)

Havelock, E. A. (1986). *The muse learns to write: Reflections on orality and literacy from Antiquity to the present.* New Haven, CT: Yale University Press.

Hawhee, D. (2004). *Bodily arts: Rhetoric and athletics in ancient Greece.* Austin: University of Texas Press.

Horner, W. B. (Ed.). (1980). *Historical rhetoric: An annotated bibliography of selected sources in English.* Boston: G. K. Hall.

Horner, W. B. (Ed.). (1990). *The present state of scholarship in historical and contemporary rhetoric* (Rev. ed.). Columbia: University of Missouri Press. (Original work published 1983)

Horner, W. B. (Ed.). (1993). *Nineteenth-century Scottish rhetoric: The American connection.* Carbondale: Southern Illinois University Press.

Howell, W. S. (1961). *Logic and rhetoric in England: 1500–1700.* New York: Russell & Russell.

Howell, W. S. (1971). *Eighteenth-century British logic and rhetoric.* Princeton, NJ: Princeton University Press.

Johnstone, C. L. (1996). Greek oratorical settings and the problem of the Pnyx: Rethinking the Athenian political process. In C. L. Johnstone (Ed.), *Theory, text, context: Issues in Greek rhetoric and oratory* (pp. 97–127). Albany: State University of New York Press.

Kennedy, G. A. (1963). *The art of persuasion in Greece.* Princeton, NJ: Princeton University Press.

Kennedy, G. A. (1972). *The art of rhetoric in the roman world: 300 B.C.–A.D. 300.* Princeton, NJ: Princeton University Press.

Kennedy, G. A. (1983). *Greek rhetoric under Christian emperors.* Princeton, NJ: Princeton University Press.

Kennedy, G. A. (1984). *New Testament interpretation through rhetorical criticism.* Chapel Hill: University of North Carolina Press.

Kennedy, G. A. (1994). *A new history of classical rhetoric.* Princeton, NJ: Princeton University Press.

Kennedy, G. A. (1999). *Classical rhetoric & its Christian & secular tradition from ancient to modern times* (2nd ed.). Chapel Hill: University of North Carolina Press.

Kinneavy, J. L. (1970). *A theory of discourse.* New York: W. W. Norton.

Kinneavy, J. L. (1986). *Kairos:* A neglected concept in classical rhetoric. In J. D. Moss (Ed.), *Rhetoric and praxis: The contribution of classical rhetoric to practical reasoning* (pp. 79–105). Washington, DC: Catholic University of America Press.

Kustas, G. L. (1973). *Studies in Byzantine rhetoric* (Analekta Vlatadon 17). Thessaloniki, Greece: Patriarchal Institute for Patristic Studies.

Lauer, J. L. (1993). Rhetoric and composition studies: A multimodal discipline. In T. Enos & S. C. Brown (Eds.), *Defining the new rhetorics: Written communication* (Vol. 7, pp. 44–54). Newbury Park, CA: Sage.

Lauer, J. L. (1999). *Acceptance speech for the exemplar award.* Atlanta, GA: CCCC.

Lauer, J. L., & Lunsford, A. (1989). The place of rhetoric and composition in doctoral studies. In A. Lunsford, H. Moglen, & J. Slevin (Eds.), *The future of doctoral studies in English* (pp. 106–110). New York: Modern Language Association of America.

Lord, A. B. (1976). *The singer of tales.* New York: Atheneum.

Lunsford, A. (Ed.). (1995). *Reclaiming rhetorica: Women in the rhetorical tradition.* Pittsburgh, PA: University of Pittsburgh Press.

Matsen, P. P., Rollinson, P., & Sousa, M. (Eds.). (1990). *Readings from classical rhetoric.* Carbondale: Southern Illinois University Press.

Millar, F. (1985). Epigraphy. In M. Crawford (Ed.). *Sources for ancient history* (pp. 80–136). Cambridge, UK: Cambridge University Press.

Miller, T. P. (1997). *The formation of college English: Rhetoric and belles letters in the British cultural provinces.* Pittsburgh, PA: University of Pittsburgh Press.

Murphy, J. J. (1974). *Rhetoric in the middle ages: A history of rhetorical theory from St. Augustine to the Renaissance.* Los Angeles: University of California Press.

Murphy, J. J. (Ed.). (2001). *A short history of writing instruction: From ancient Greece to modern America* (2nd ed.). Mahwah, NJ: Hermagoras Press, an imprint of Lawrence Erlbaum.

Murphy, J. J., Katula, R. A., Hill, F. I., Ochs, D. J., & Meador, P. A. (Eds.). (1995). *A synoptic history of classical rhetoric* (2nd ed.). Davis, CA: Hermagoras Press.

Ong, W. J. (1993). *Orality and literacy: The technologizing of the word.* New York: Routledge.

Parry, M. (1980). *The making of Homeric verse* (A. Parry, Ed.). New York: Arno Press.

Perelman, C., & Olbrechts-Tyteca, L. (1969). *The new rhetoric: A treatise on argumentation* (J. Wilkinson & P. Weaver, Trans.). Notre Dame, IN: University of Notre Dame Press.

Pernot, L. (2005). *Rhetoric in Antiquity* (W. E. Higgins, Trans.). Washington, DC: Catholic University of America Press.

Quintilian. *Institutio oratoria.*

Schaeffer, J. D. (1990). *Sensus communis: Vico, rhetoric, and the limits of relativism.* Durham, NC: Duke University Press.

Schiappa, E. (1999). *The beginnings of rhetorical theory in classical Greece.* New Haven, CT: Yale University Press.

Sloane, T. O. (Ed.). (2001). *Encyclopedia of rhetoric.* Oxford, UK: Oxford University Press.

Sprague, R. K. (Ed.). (1990). *The older sophists* (Rev. ed.). Columbia: University of South Carolina Press.

Stanford, W. B. (1967). *The sound of Greek: Studies in the Greek theory and practice of euphony.* Los Angeles: University of California Press.

Vickers, B. (1988). *In defence of rhetoric.* Oxford, UK: Clarendon Press.

Walker, J. (2000). *Rhetoric and poetics in Antiquity.* Oxford, UK: Oxford University Press.

3

Medieval and Renaissance Rhetorical Studies of Women

CHRISTINE MASON SUTHERLAND

Until the past two decades or so, it was assumed that women had no place in the history of rhetoric. Rhetoric was assumed to be the province of men, and when scholars such as Ivor Richards and Kenneth Burke revived the study of rhetoric as an academic discipline in the 1920s and 1930s, they did not question this approach. Neither did Edward Corbett, George Kennedy, and J. J. Murphy, when in the 1960s and 1970s they led American scholarship back to a serious study of classical rhetoric. Corbett, indeed, described rhetoric as "one of the most patriarchal of academic disciplines" (Glenn, 1997, p. 9). Since then, some of these scholars have contributed vitally to the inclusion of women in the history of rhetoric, but at the time—the mid-20th century—it was not even a question: Rhetoric was public, concerned with matters of state, which for most of history meant that women

played no part in it. Indeed, for a very long time—over a thousand years—the study of rhetoric was linked to the study of Latin, a language that nobody learned from his mother. As Walter Ong (1982) has said, "It was a sex-linked language, written and spoken only by males, learned outside the home in a tribal setting, which was in effect a male puberty rite setting, complete with physical punishment and other kinds of deliberately imposed hardships" (p. 113). It was therefore taken as axiomatic that women had no place at all in rhetoric until the beginning of the women's liberation movements in the 19th century.

Any consideration of women's place in Medieval and Renaissance rhetoric must begin, then, with an appraisal of what has changed in recent years to allow us to raise the question at all. In what follows I will give some account of the progress that has been made and the challenges that face historians of women's rhetoric, addressing two important questions: what can be included as among the rhetorical works of Medieval and Renaissance women, and by what methods should this material be studied?

Let me begin by setting some parameters: First, as concerns time. Since the Medieval period in rhetoric is dated from the time of Augustine—some scholars include him with Classical and some with Medieval rhetoricians—there is no problem, since the earliest woman I shall discuss lived in the 9th century. However, the distinction between the Medieval period and the Renaissance is more difficult to determine, as is the date at which the Renaissance may be said to be over. I have decided that women rhetoricians who lived before the 16th century shall be considered as belonging to the Middle Ages. This is consistent—or nearly so—with the traditional dating of Modern English to 1485. So far as the end of the Renaissance is concerned, I have been guided by the practice of Patricia Bizzell and Bruce Herzberg (2001) in the second edition of *The Rhetorical Tradition*: They place Margaret Fell, who published *Women's Speaking Justified* in 1666, in the Renaissance period. I shall therefore make 1688 the cut-off date for the Renaissance: The reign of William and Mary may be said to inaugurate the Enlightenment.

There remains the question of what to exclude from studies of rhetoric. I shall take up this matter in detail later, but a few preliminary remarks are in order here. Should one include everything written by women in the Middle Ages and the Renaissance? Or should one include only the works by women who were conscious of engaging in rhetorical theory or practice? The first criterion is perhaps too broad, the second too narrow. I have reached a compromise. In the first section, which deals with public discourse, I have discussed, with a very few exceptions,

only those works that have been studied from a rhetorical point of view by historians of rhetoric. Not all the women studied were necessarily aware that they were practicing rhetoric, though many of them may simply have taken it for granted. However, the fact that they have been recognized as rhetoricians by scholars in rhetoric justifies their inclusion: that is, I have, to some extent, assigned the question of what is to be counted as rhetoric to my colleagues in the field. That this is an ongoing project should be obvious: There remain other public documents that have not yet received such study, and some of these I allude to as possibilities for the future. In the second section, which deals with semipublic or private discourse, I have included, in addition to those texts which have been discussed by historians of rhetoric, a selection of writers whose work might well be considered as rhetoric. Since they wrote outside the then accepted rhetorical tradition, they may not have even considered the question. Nevertheless, it seems to me that they should be included under an earlier definition of rhetoric given by Cicero. I shall argue this point below. The third section deals not so much with texts as with social practice and the question therefore hardly arises.

Next, the question of what genres count as rhetoric: This is a challenging question for all historians of rhetoric, if only because the boundaries of genres shift over time. Some efferent discourse—history, for example—was in earlier times written in verse. Although in general I prefer to use approaches that would have made sense to the women whose work I study, in this instance I propose to use modern definitions more familiar to my readers. Therefore, although I shall argue below for radical extensions to what has traditionally been considered as rhetoric, some boundaries must be set. Accordingly— perhaps controversially—I have excluded works of fiction from this account, even historical fiction or drama, likewise anything written in verse. I have also excluded, rather reluctantly, works of translation: reluctantly, because much of the work of Renaissance women rhetoricians lay in translation. However, considerations far beyond rhetorical theories and methods must be brought to bear on studies of translation, and I have therefore excluded it.

To return to our question: What has happened in recent years to promote the study of women in the history of rhetoric? At this point, it is appropriate to note certain highlights, key publications by notable scholars in the field who have stimulated research and discussion and made available avenues of publication for other historians or rhetoric. A foundational document is Jane Donawerth's "Bibliography of Women and the History of Rhetorical Theory," published in the *Rhetoric Society Quarterly* in 1990, the forerunner of her book *Rhetorical Theory by Women Before 1900*, published in 2002. Works of this kind are invaluable to other scholars who benefit from such fundamental research in defining the field. In discussions of methods of research, Patricia Bizzell's special issue of the *Rhetoric Society Quarterly* in 2002 is of the greatest importance. A more detailed discussion of the questions raised in this issue will be given below. Bizzell and Bruce Herzberg have also contributed by making available the texts by a number of Medieval and Renaissance women in *The Rhetorical Tradition*, especially in the second edition (2001).

In recognizing those who have provided a publishing opportunity for historians of women's rhetoric, we must note the pioneering work of Andrea Lunsford, whose *Reclaiming Rhetorica: Women in the Rhetorical Tradition* led the way in 1995. Also published in 1995, Carole Levin and Patricia A. Sullivan's *Political Rhetoric, Power, and Renaissance Women*, with a rather different focus, presents essays on a number of important women writers of the Middle Ages and the Renaissance. The next significant publication is *Listening to Their Voices: Rhetorical Activities of Historical*

Women, edited by Molly Meijer Wertheimer (1997). The collection makes available research on six notable figures in the Medieval and Renaissance periods, as well as on many others.

In 1997, a notable contribution was made to the history of women's rhetoric by Judith Rice Henderson of the University of Saskatchewan, then President of the International Society for the History of Rhetoric. Henderson identified women in the history of rhetoric as one of the key themes of the conference, and one of the plenary lectures was devoted to it. Even more important was Henderson's decision to fund the publication of a *Proceedings* on this topic, and to build its cost into the conference fee. This meant that the volume was received by everyone who attended the conference, thus extending the knowledge of the field to historians of rhetoric who might previously have known little about it. The *Proceedings* was upgraded to full scholarly status by undergoing peer review. Edited by Christine Mason Sutherland and Rebecca Sutcliffe, it was published in 1999 by the University of Calgary Press under the title *The Changing Tradition: Women in the History of Rhetoric*.

At the outset, then, we see that much of the progress in the study of women's rhetoric may be attributed to the endeavors of scholars, both female and male, to rediscover writers forgotten or ignored by traditional scholarship. I will deal with some of these below. However, to some degree what has changed has been definitions of rhetoric. Here is what Thomas P. Miller has to say in his essay, "Reinventing Rhetorical Traditions," published in 1993: "The rhetorical tradition is a fiction that has just about outlived its usefulness" (p. 26). He continues,

Given the constitution of the canon, one must conclude that for a couple of thousand years the only people who used rhetoric were white male Europeans, a state of affairs that is at odds with our belief that every community uses rhetoric to put shared assumptions and values into social practice. (p. 26)

Miller suggests that instead of studying the tradition of rhetoric, we study "the rhetoric of traditions. . . . If we adopt this more broadly engaged approach we can begin to make the discursive practices of marginalized traditions a central part of the history of rhetoric" (p. 26). This is in fact what has happened: Since Miller wrote in 1993, traditional definitions of rhetoric have been radically challenged.[1]

Since these definitions are now usefully in flux, what I propose to do is to look for women in the history of rhetoric in the Medieval and Renaissance periods through three different lenses—what Kenneth Burke calls terministic screens—to see what different perspectives we get by using each of them (1966, p. 45). First, I will take one used by the historians of rhetoric until fairly recently, as given by George Kennedy in *Comparative Rhetoric: An Historical and Cross-Cultural Introduction:* "A structured system of teaching public speaking and written composition" (1998, p. 2). The key characteristics of rhetoric were, then, that it concerned public discourse and that it was formally taught, typically only to young males to prepare them for service in the public world. As the title of his book suggests, Kennedy himself is no longer satisfied with this definition, but nonetheless it can stand as the traditional definition used by historians of rhetoric in the earlier part of the 20th century.

Even using this extremely restricted viewpoint, we can find a number of women in the Middle Ages who participated in the rhetorical tradition as writers and teachers, and whose contributions have been assessed in recent years by scholars in the history of rhetoric. I cannot give an exhaustive account of them, but I will briefly mention some of the most important. Prominent among these are Hildegard of Bingen (1098–1179), visionary

and mystic, artist, musician, and rhetorician. She was highly regarded in her own time by such important figures as Bernard of Clairvaux, and she brought her arguments to bear even on the Pope. Julia Dietrich gives an account of her as a rhetorical figure in "The Visionary Rhetoric of Hildegard of Bingen" (1997). Another public figure who engaged in powerful dispute with the higher clergy, addressing even the Pope, was Catherine of Siena (1347–1380). Margo Husby Scheelar discusses her work and influence in "Ethos Over Time: The Ongoing Appeal of St. Catherine of Siena" (1999). On a lower level were the wife and daughters of the 11th-century Manegold, learned women who helped him in his profession of teaching rhetoric. John Ward considers the contributions of these women in "Women and Latin Rhetoric from Hrosvit to Hildegard" (1999). Toward the end of the Middle Ages, we have the important work of Christine de Pisan (1364–1430), who defended women against the particularly vicious attacks on them that characterized the time.[2] Excerpts from her work have been included in the second edition of Bizzell and Herzberg's *The Rhetorical Tradition* (2001), and her significance as a rhetorician is discussed by Jenny R. Redfern (1995) in "Christine de Pisan and The Treasures of the City of Ladies: A Medieval Rhetorician and her Rhetoric" and by Daniel Kempton (1997) in "Christine de Pizan's Cité des Dames and Tresor de la Cité: Towards a Feminist Scriptural Practice." Christine's rhetorical theory is excerpted in Donawerth's *Rhetorical Theory by Women Before 1900* (2002).

A particularly important figure in the Middle Ages is the first woman writer in English, Julian of Norwich (1343–after 1416). Julian was an anchoress, an urban hermit. Anchorites lived enclosed, never going out into the world. Julian's cell had three windows: One gave on to the interior of the church of St. Julian (from which she took her name in religion), one allowed her to communicate with the servant who saw to her needs, and one gave on to the street. Through this window she could offer counsel to those who came to ask her advice. At the age of 30, Julian received a series of visions or "showings" as she called them. They are regarded as one of the most important records of medieval mysticism. Her knowledge and use of rhetoric have been identified by Colledge and Walsh (1978) in their definitive edition of her work, and she is also discussed by Cheryl Glenn in *Rhetoric Retold* (1997). Julian is known to have counseled Margery Kempe (1373–1439), another important writer of the late Middle Ages. Like Julian, she was an East Anglian, the wife of a burgess of Kings Lynn. Between 1432 and 1436, her autobiography, *The Book of Margery Kempe*, was dictated to scribes, she herself being illiterate. Glenn gives an account of her both in *Reclaiming Rhetorica* (1995) and in *Rhetoric Retold* (1997).

The number of women engaged with the tradition at this public level increases during the Renaissance. With its strong emphasis on rigorous and demanding scholarship grounded in familiarity with Latin, the Renaissance tradition might be expected to be particularly unfavorable to women. Yet there were a significant number of practicing women rhetoricians in this period, and even more who by their support encouraged learning in others. Notable among these are Queen Isabella of Castile, who employed a woman professor of rhetoric, Beatrix Gelinda, at her court (Glenn, 1997, p. 205). Her daughter, Katharine of Aragon, was the first queen of Henry VIII. It was Katharine who made learning respectable, even fashionable for women of the nobility in England; she invited the Renaissance scholar Juan Vives to England to assist in the education of her daughter, the Princess Mary (Kersey, 1981, p. 35). Vives and Erasmus and Sir Thomas More, the most prominent humanist scholars of the time, did not object to women's learning; they stipulated only that their

practice of rhetoric should be confined to the family.

Yet there were some women, nonetheless, whose work was made public: Foremost among them was Elizabeth I of England (1533–1603). According to the cultural values of the time, as head of state she counted as an honorary man, and was therefore free of the restrictive conventions applied to women. A superb scholar and rhetorician, as monarch she exploited to the full her paradoxical status as both male and female, becoming not only one of the few women public speakers of the time but also, according to Cheryl Glenn, one of the most powerful women of any time (1997, pp. 118ff.). Ilona Bell (1995) and Lena Cowen Orlin (1995) have also discussed her importance in the history of rhetoric. Another woman of the 16th century whose work should be considered here is Anne Askew (1521–1546), forced from a private to a public role by her trials for heresy. Her *Examinations* gives a record of these trials later made public by Bishop Bale and by John Foxe (Mazzola, 1995, p. 158).

The number of women rhetoricians who published their work increases significantly in the 17th century. One of the most interesting is Margaret Cavendish, Duchess of Newcastle (1623–1673). A prolific writer in almost every known genre, including oratory, she was a notable figure of her time, drawing a great deal of attention to herself and publishing—with her husband's full support—under her own name. This was highly unusual: Most women of the time, if they published at all, did so anonymously. But not for her the discreet retirement advocated by the bourgeois moralists of her era: She gloried in her notoriety. Her rhetorical practice, in particular her *Orations of Divers Sorts* (1662) and her *Description of a New World Called the Blazing World* (1666/1992), is discussed by Christine Mason Sutherland in "Aspiring to the Rhetorical Tradition: A Study of Margaret Cavendish (1997). Cavendish also produced rhetorical theory of a kind. Sutherland deals with this in an essay in the *Dictionary of Literary Biography* (2003), and Donawerth includes excerpts from it in *Rhetorical Theory by Women Before 1900* (2002). Influenced by her brother-in-law, Charles Cavendish, and her husband, William, who later became a founding member of The Royal Society, Margaret also attempted to engage in scientific writing. Richard Nate discusses Cavendish's work in this genre in an essay published in *Rhetorica* in 2001.

Roughly contemporary with Cavendish was a woman just as bold but in a different cause: Margaret Fell (1614–1702), the cofounder with George Fox (whom she later married) of the Society of Friends, better known as Quakers. Her *Women's Speaking Justified* (1666) is included in the second edition of Bizzell and Herzberg's *The Rhetorical Tradition* (2001) and also in Donawerth's *Rhetorical Theory by Women Before 1900* (2002). Fell challenges accepted interpretations of Scripture in order to justify women's rhetorical practice. Sutherland (2006) has addressed her importance as a woman rhetorician in "Margaret Fell and the Problem of Women's Ethos."

Another 17th-century woman who promoted women's involvement with rhetoric was Bathsua Makin (fl. 1673). She was influenced by the notable Dutch woman scholar, Anna Maria van Schurman, whose Latin treatise on the education of women was translated into English and published in 1673 as *The Learned Maid*. Makin is especially important for her work, *An Essay to Revive the Ancient Education of Gentlewomen*, in which she looks back to Tudor times when, she believes, the learned woman was more socially acceptable than she became during the 17th century. At one time governess to Princess Elizabeth, daughter of Charles I, later in life she opened a school for girls. It was to promote this educational establishment attempt that she wrote her essay, using a masculine persona to bolster her ethos and deflect adverse criticism (Miller, 1997).

It is obvious that much has been done by historians of women's rhetoric in recent years to bring some of these marginalized figures into prominence. Much, however, remains to be done. For example, there is the gifted and eloquent polemicist, Rachel Speght (ca. 1597–?), whose engagement in the notorious Querelle de Femmes has been discussed by Linda Woodbridge in *Women and the English Renaissance* (1986) and by Barbara Kiefer Lewalski in *Writing Women in Jacobean England* (1993); so far as I know, however, she has not been studied by historians of women's rhetoric. A particularly interesting project would be the study of works of biography and autobiography by women. Early in her writing career, Margaret Cavendish wrote her autobiography, *A True Account of My Birth and Breeding* (1656), and one of her most successful later works was her biography of her husband, William Cavendish, Duke of Newcastle, who engaged in the Civil War on the Royalist side. It would be especially interesting to compare this work with one by Lucy Hutchinson: *Memoirs of the Life of Colonel Hutchinson* (1973), an account of her husband's activities on the side of the Parliamentarians (Fraser, 1984, p. 135). Even by this most narrow of definitions, then, women were not entirely absent from the rhetorical tradition during the Middle Ages and the Renaissance.

Let us now use another lens, or terministic screen, and see what that reveals. The one I am going to use was given by Cicero, and carries all the credibility of its source. Cicero makes a distinction between two kinds of rhetoric: *contentio* and *sermo*. *Contentio* is public and adversarial. *Sermo* is not. Of the two, it is *contentio* that has been central to the understanding of rhetoric, while *sermo* has been marginalized. Yet according to Cicero, both are or should be within the scope of rhetoric. Here is what he says about it in *De Officiis*:

Sermo should find its natural place in social gatherings, in informal discussions, and in intercourse with friends; it should also seek admission at dinners. There are rules for *contentio* laid down by rhetoricians; there are none for *sermo*, yet I do not know why there should not be. (Tinkler, 1987, p. 284)

Adopting this broader—and incidentally earlier—definition from Cicero enormously extends our scope. Relatively few women participated in the tradition of public rhetoric, though they were by no means entirely absent from it. A great many more engaged in *sermo*. There is, for example, the domestic literature, instructions written by mothers for the guidance of their children, according to Clella I. Jaffe, "the principal genre of laywomen" in the medieval period (1997, p. 177). So far as I have been able to discover, the earliest text in this genre to have been researched by historians of rhetoric is Dhuoda's *Handbook for William* (Jaffe, 1997). William (826–850) had been sent to the court of Charles the Bald. His mother wrote a manual of moral instruction for him, a work surviving in fragments dating from the 10th to 11th century, which has been discussed by Clella I. Jaffe (1997). Under *sermo* we can include Heloise, daughter of Hersindis, whose letters to Abelard have become famous since her time (Ward, 1999); we can also include Marguerite d'Alencon (1492–1549) and her correspondence with the Bishop of Meaux, a work discussed by Laurel Carrington (1997).

Particularly important to *sermo* is the rhetoric of conversation that developed so strongly in 17th-century France. Madeleine de Scudery (1608–1701) is the most important figure here, and the selection from her rhetorical works published (with introduction) in 2004 by Jane Donawerth and Julie Strongson is especially welcome. Donawerth (1998) has also contributed a useful essay on women's conversational rhetoric, in which she discusses Cavendish and Fell as well as de Scudery. A Swedish woman who was brought up in this French tradition is considered by Stine Hansson, who shows that the preparation for

conversation in the salons of the time was long, thorough, and based on the principles of classical rhetoric (Hansson, 1994).

But beyond these women whose work has received attention from historians of rhetoric are many more who so far have not. For example, there are the writers of letters. According to Alison Truelove, in the 15th century "men both tolerated and positively expected women to partake in letter-writing" (2001, p. 44). Some such letter writers are famous, for example, the Paston women of Norfolk, who defended Caister Castle against attack in the 15th century and wrote letters to their menfolk in London to keep them up to date with events at home (King, 1991, p. 167). Others are less well-known. All could profitably be included as producers of *sermo*. Then there is the huge category of religious writing, prayers, and reflections, for example, *The Lamentations of a Sinner* by Queen Katherine Parr (1514?–1548), the last wife of Henry VIII, and the letters of Lady Jane Grey (1537–1554), the Nine Days Queen (King, 1991, p. 209). Also to be included are personal records, such as the 17th-century diaries of Lady Anne Clifford (1590–1676), which record the progress of a law case that lasted for more than 40 years (Clifford, 1989, pp. 35–53). Excerpts from this work are included in an excellent anthology of women's autobiographical writings (edited by Elspeth Graham, Hilary Hinds, Elaine Hobby, & Helen Wilcox, 1989), which offers a rich variety of documents for study by historians of rhetoric.

Finally, let us take a definition even earlier than Cicero's: In the *Phaedrus*, Plato (trans. 1973) defines rhetoric as "a method of moving [people's] minds by means of words, whether the words are spoken in a court of law or before some other public body or in private conversation" (p. 73). This extraordinarily wide definition opens up a whole area of discourse in which women can be seen not in the margins so much as in the matrix. As Quintilian (trans. 1989) observes, it is women—mothers and other female caregivers—who provide children with their first experience of language, and he himself stresses how important such early experience is:

> As regards parents, I should like to see them as highly educated as possible, and I do not restrict this remark to fathers alone. We are told that the eloquence of the Gracchi owed much to their mother Cornelia, whose letters even today testify to the cultivation of her style. (I.1.6, p. 23)

The use of this definition opens the field alarmingly wide; arguably it belongs more to the study of social history than to that of rhetoric. Yet rhetoric is embedded in social contexts, and to ignore the contribution of women to the very foundations of rhetoric is to do them and ourselves a disservice. As rhetoric has traditionally contributed to all the disciplines, so too it has drawn from them all, and this fruitful exchange should be continued and extended.

Furthermore, as Richard Enos (2002) has argued, we cannot confine our studies to texts: "One of our first obligations is to realize that understanding better the place of women in the history of rhetoric can only be accomplished by expanding our range beyond extant literary sources" (p. 68). Further support for such expansion is given by Barbara Biesecker, who, according to Carol Mattingly, fears that "the emphasis on individual figures reproduces problems in the 'old order' because by validating token women, we promote the notion that few women can participate in the rhetorical game" (2002, p. 100). If we thus extend our sphere of interest, we can include many more women in the history of rhetoric.

Extension of the kind thus envisaged by Enos and Biesecker would allow us to study the rhetorical contributions of women who throughout the ages in the Western world have educated their children. The educational achievements of most of these women we shall never know, but there are records of some of

them. Interestingly, the work of one of them at least has been addressed by a historian of rhetoric. In his essay in the winter 2004 number of *Rhetorica*, Jeffrey Walker gives an account of Psellos's "Encomium of His Mother." Psellos, an 11th-century Byzantine rhetorician, used this work to make a number of points that Walker examines in great detail. Obviously, Walker is primarily interested in Psellos rather than Thoedota, his mother. However, some details of her own standing in rhetoric emerge: The son gives his mother credit for establishing him as a scholar, and for teaching him about "the intellectual equality of women with men" (2004, p. 52). Psellos records her capacity for eloquence and argument and her devotion to learning (p. 75). Astonishingly gifted intellectually and "a paragon of natural eloquence" (p. 77), she managed to educate herself with a little help from a nearby monastery. This she passed on to her son, supervising his education until he was 8 years old, when she prevailed on the family to send him away to school. There have been many such women: Juan Luis Vives, the notable Renaissance scholar, for example, already noted, "received an early education from his gifted mother" (Kersey, 1981, p. 19). Another like her is Lady Bacon (née Cooke) who educated her brilliant young son Francis until at the age of 12 he proceeded to Cambridge. According to George Ballard (1985), "it was to the great abilities and tender care of so accomplished a parent that her two sons owed the early part of their education" (p. 195). A study of the practices of such women from a rhetorical point of view could significantly extend our recognition of the importance of women to the whole rhetorical tradition.

Depending on which of these definitions we use, the field of study can be seen as relatively restricted or very wide indeed. I believe that if we are to do justice to what women have actually achieved in the field of rhetoric, we must make it as wide as possible. In doing so, we shall need to develop new approaches to research methods: New fields of study require new ways of analyzing and discussing them. As Karlyn Kohrs Campbell (2002) has said, we need to "challenge the suitability of traditional theory to analyze or evaluate women's discourse" (p. 45). In recent years, there has been extensive discussion of this question in several issues of the *Rhetoric Society Quarterly*. The discussion was inaugurated by Richard Leo Enos in 1999. In "Rediscovering the Lost Art of Researching the History of Rhetoric," he asks if it would be "unthinkable for us, like our colleagues who have done such a good job in the social sciences, to develop new methodologies to try to account for the evidence they present in the formulation of their theories?" (1999, p. 16). Patricia Bizzell (2000) takes up the discussion in "Feminist Methods of Research in the History of Rhetoric: What Difference Do They Make?" Here she too recognizes the necessity of developing new approaches:

> Feminist research in the history of rhetoric presents the most trenchant challenges to traditional scholarly practices, opening up exciting new paths not only in the material scholars can study but also, and perhaps ultimately more significantly, in the methods whereby we study it. (p. 5)

In this essay, Bizzell gives an extended analysis of a controversy among feminist rhetoricians. She identifies the heart of the dispute as the question of the place of the emotions in feminist research in rhetoric—not the emotions of the audience, as in pathos, but those of the researcher. This question of feminist epistemology was raised as long ago as the mid-1980s by the writers of *Women's Ways of Knowing* (1986), who make a distinction between the typically masculine mode of "separate" knowing—the objective, impersonal, dispassionate approach of traditional scholarship—and the "connected" knowing preferred by women: Women see the contestants as persons, not positions, and are afraid that

"someone will get hurt" (Belenky, Clinchy, Goldberger, & Tarule, 1986, p. 105). This question is pursued from a different angle by Lisa Ede and Andrea Lunsford. In *Singular Texts/Plural Authors: Perspectives on Collaborative Writing* (1990), they make the point that women tend to value and enjoy cooperation more than competition.

A special issue was devoted to this subject in the *Rhetoric Society Quarterly* in 2002: *Feminist Historiography in Rhetoric*, edited by Patricia Bizzell. This issue takes up some of the questions raised earlier and revisits some old disputes as well as supplying new arguments and points of view. Karlyn Kohrs Campbell discusses the topic from the point of view of consciousness raising. Richard Leo Enos uses a metaphor from archeology to clarify what is involved in all rhetorical research, applying it particularly to women's rhetoric. Susan Jarratt considers the question of memory and its connection to the emotions in the work of women rhetoricians. Carol Mattingly and Hui Wu (2002) both discuss the ways in which political fashions and allegiances can deflect and distort feminist research.

I too deal to some extent with this question of ideology in my own essay, which concludes the issue. Particularly urgent for me is the problem of anachronism, which I discuss at length in an earlier essay, "Women in the History of Rhetoric: The Past and the Future" (Sutherland & Sutcliffe, 1999, pp. 19–27). It is a temptation, perhaps for any historian, to apply, consciously or unconsciously, the values of her own era to the study of the past and thus to misunderstand and misrepresent writers of earlier times. It is a particular temptation for feminist historians of rhetoric: They are driven by the quest for literary grandmothers referred to by Virginia Woolf, and their identification on an emotional level with these women, though an important element in this kind of research, can sometimes lead them to project on to earlier writers values that those writers would have repudiated. The point is well made by Juliet Fleming in a review of a book on Renaissance drama:

> Today literature is the domain of the individual; . . . But the intellectual economy of early modern England was based on notions of authorship that were collective, aphoristic and non-subjective; excellence in the field of letters was understood, in the first instance, as skilled imitation, and not as the utterance of a distinctive voice. The writing by women that is being recovered from the archive reminds us that Renaissance literature differs from our own, and differs precisely over the question of modern subjectivity and its values. To read early modern women's writing according to the protocols of a liberal feminist search for women's "oppositional voice" (or where that fails, for the "speaking silence") has its feminist point. But it has yet to give us serious critical purchase on the texts in question. (Fleming, 1996, p. 12)

I have found that the best way to deal with this ongoing problem is to try by any available means to enter the world of the writer I am studying, to immerse myself as much as possible in her culture, her values—what Aristotle (trans. 1984) calls the premises of enthymemes (I.2.25, p. 28). And this, of course, involves a holistic approach that includes the emotions: In a way what I am attempting is equivalent to the participatory research now used by anthropologists. This is not to say that I have abandoned the traditional humanist scholarship in which I was trained: respect for the author, fairness, completeness, consistency, and meticulous attention to detail. Rather, I add to these principles deriving from the rhetoric in general and from feminist rhetoric in particular: the importance of context and the necessity of including both ethos and pathos. That this holism is typical not only of rhetoric but also of feminism is a point forcefully made by Lisa Ede, Cheryl Glenn, and Andrea Lunsford in "Border Crossings: Intersections of Rhetoric and Feminism" (1995). I have also been strongly influenced by the caring tradition in feminist practice, drawing on the work of Carol Gilligan (1982). Where I diverge from the principles of traditional scholarship most radically, however, is in stressing the importance of the connection between researcher and researched and of starting from one's own experience. That this approach is typical of feminist research methods is confirmed by women's studies theorists Gloria Bowles and Renate Duelli Klein (1983): Feminist researchers, they believe, wish to establish "a link between researcher and researched" (p. 15).

Recently, I have found this approach theorized in another field. Wes Folkerth (2002) makes this distinction:

> Monothetic meaning is a function of the semantic component of sign systems such as a natural language. . . . Polythetic meaning, on the other hand, is a "time-immanent" mode of experiential meaning, meaning that is embodied in experience in time. (p. 21)[3]

Polythetic meaning is derived from experience, in this case that shared experience which can bring us closer to the person whose writings we study, informing and illuminating our research.

Obviously, then, in recent years a great deal of progress has been made toward including women in the history of rhetoric: Much remains to be done, but at least some foundations have been laid. Opening up the tradition in this way to what Hans Kellner (1994) calls "the unschooled practice of communication" (p. 23) rather than confining it to the conscious practice of schooled public discourse allows us to observe the considerable extent to which women have always been participants in rhetoric and to celebrate what they have done. The expansion of the field of study has made necessary an equivalent extension of methods of study that has enabled us to offer a more sensitive and authentic interpretation of what these earlier women have achieved.

NOTES

1. See, for example, Victor J. Vitanza (1994) and George Kennedy (1998).

2. For an account of the rise of misogyny in the late Middle Ages, see Enders (1999).

3. Folkerth gives credit for this distinction to Alfred Schutz (Folkerth, 2002, p. 21).

REFERENCES

Aristotle. (1984). *The rhetoric and the poetics of Aristotle* (W. Rhys Roberts & I. Bywater, Trans. Introduction by Edward P. J. Corbett). New York: Modern Library.

Ballard, G. (1985). *Memoirs of several ladies of Great Britain who have been celebrated for their writings or skill in the learned languages, arts and sciences.* (Ruth Perry, Ed.). Detroit, MI: Wayne State University Press.

Bell, I. (1995). Elizabeth I: Always her own free woman. In C. Levin & P. A. Sullivan (Eds.), *Political rhetoric, power, and renaissance women* (pp. 57–82). New York: State University of New York Press.

Belenky, M. F., Clinchy, B. M., Goldberger, N. R., & Tarule, J. M. (1986). *Women's ways of knowing: The development of self, voice, and mind.* New York: Basic Books.

Bizzell, P. (2000). Feminist methods of research in the history of rhetoric: What difference do they make? *Rhetoric Society Quarterly, 30*(4), 5–17.

Bizzell, P. (2002). Feminist historiography in rhetoric. *Rhetoric Society Quarterly, 32*(1), 7–10.

Bizzell, P., & Herzberg, B. (Eds.). (2001). *The rhetorical tradition: Readings from classical times to the present* (2nd ed.). Boston: Bedford St. Martin's Press.

Bowles, G., & Klein, R. D. (Eds.). (1983). *Theories of women's studies.* London: Routledge & Kegan Paul.

Burke, K. (1966). *Language as symbolic action.* Los Angeles: University of California Press.

Campbell, K. K. (2002). Consciousness raising: Linking theory, criticism and practice. *Rhetoric Society Quarterly, 32*(1), 45–64.

Carrington, L. (1997). Women, rhetoric and letter writing: Marguerite d'Alençon's correspondence with Bishop Briconnet of Meaux. In M. M. Wertheimer (Ed.), *Listening to their voices: The rhetorical activities of historical women* (pp. 215–232). Columbia: University of South Carolina Press.

Cavendish, M. (1656). *A true account of my birth and breeding.* London: James Allestree.

Cavendish, M. (1662). *Orations of divers sorts.* London.

Cavendish, M. (1666/1992). *The description of a new world called the blazing world and other writings* (K. Lilley, Ed.). London: Pickering & Chatto.

Clifford, A. (1989). The diary of Anne, Countess of Dorset, Pembroke and Montgomery, daughter and heiress of George Clifford, Earl of Cumberland (1616–1617). In E. Graham, H. Hinds, E. Hobby, & H. Wilcox (Eds.), *Her own life: Autobiographical writings by seventeenth-century Englishwomen* (pp. 35–53). London: Routledge.

Colledge, E., O. S. A., & Walsh, J., S. J. (Eds.). (1978). *A book of showings to the Anchoress Julian of Norwich.* Toronto, Ontario, Canada: Pontifical Institute of Mediaeval Studies.

Dietrich, J. (1997). The visionary rhetoric of Hildegard of Bingen. In M. M. Wertheimer (Ed.), *Listening to their voices: The rhetorical activities of historical women* (pp. 199–214). Columbia: University of South Carolina Press.

Donawerth, J. (1990). Bibliography of women and the history of rhetorical theory. *Rhetoric Society Quarterly, 20*(4), 403–414.

Donawerth, J. (1998). Conversation and the boundaries of public discourse in rhetorical theory by Renaissance women. *Rhetorica, 16*(1), 181–199.

Donawerth, J. (Ed.). (2002). *Rhetorical theory by women before 1900: An anthology.* Oxford, UK: Rowman & Littlefield.

Donawerth, J., & Strongson, J. (Eds. and Trans.). (2004). *Madeleine de Scudery: Selected letters, orations and rhetorical dialogues.* Chicago: University of Chicago Press.

Ede, L., & Lunsford, A. (1990). *Singular texts/plural authors: Perspectives on collaborative writing*. Carbondale: Southern Illinois University Press.

Ede, L., Lunsford, A., & Glenn, C. (1995). Border crossings: Intersections of rhetoric and feminism. *Rhetorica, 13,* 401–442.

Enders, J. (1999). Cutting off the memory of women. In C. M. Sutherland & R. Sutcliffe (Eds.), *The changing tradition: Women in the history of rhetoric* (pp. 47–55). Calgary: University of Calgary Press.

Enos, R. (1999). Rediscovering the lost art of researching the history of rhetoric. *Rhetoric Society Quarterly, 29*(4), 7–20.

Enos, R. (2002). The archeology of women in rhetoric: Rhetorical sequence as a research method for historical scholarship. *Rhetoric Society Quarterly, 32*(1), 65–79.

Fleming, J. (1996, August 23). Absent Elizabethans. Review of renaissance drama by women. S. P. Cerasano and Marion Wynne Davies. *Times Literary Supplement,* p. 12.

Folkerth, W. (2002). *The sound of Shakespeare.* London: Routledge.

Fraser, A. (1984). *The weaker vessel.* New York: Knopf.

Gilligan, C. (1982). *In a different voice: Psychological theory and women's development.* Cambridge, MA: Harvard University Press.

Glenn, C. (1995). Reexamining *The Book of Margery Kempe: A rhetoric of autobiography.* In A. Lunsford (Ed.), *Reclaiming rhetorica: Women in the rhetorical tradition* (pp. 53–71). Pittsburgh: University of Pittsburgh Press.

Glenn, C. (1997). *Rhetoric Retold: Regendering the tradition from antiquity through the Renaissance.* Carbondale: Southern Illinois University Press.

Graham, E., Hinds, H., Hobby, E., & Wilcox, H. (Eds.). (1989). *Her own life: Autobiographical writings by seventeenth-century Englishwomen.* London: Routledge.

Hansson, S. (1994). Rhetoric for seventeenth-century salons: Beata Rosenhane's exercise books and classical rhetoric. *Rhetorica, 10*(1), 43–65.

Hutchinson, L. (1973). *Memoirs of the life of Colonel Hutchinson with fragments of an autobiography of Mrs Hutchinson.* (J. Sutherland, Ed.). London: Oxford University Press.

Jaffe, C. I. (1997). Dhuoda's *Handbook for William* and the mother's manual tradition. In M. M. Wertheimer (Ed.), *Listening to their voices: The rhetorical activities of historical women* (pp. 177–198). Columbia: University of South Carolina Press.

Jarratt, S. (2002). Sappho's memory. *Rhetoric Society Quarterly, 32*(1), 11–43.

Kellner, H. (1994). After the fall: October reflections on the histories of rhetoric. In V. J. Vitanza (Ed.), *Writing histories of rhetoric* (pp. 20–37). Carbondale: Southern Illinois University Press.

Kempton, D. (1997). Christine de Pizan's Cité des Dames and Tresor de la Cité: Towards a feminist scriptural practice. In C. Levin & P. A. Sullivan (Eds.), *Political rhetoric, power, and renaissance women* (pp. 15–37). New York: State University of New York Press.

Kennedy, G. A. (1998). *Comparative rhetoric: An historical and cross-cultural introduction.* Oxford, UK: Oxford University Press.

Kersey, S. N. (1981). *Classics in the education of girls and women.* London, UK: Scarecrow Press.

King, M. L. (1991). *Women of the Renaissance.* Chicago: University of Chicago Press.

Levin, C., & Sullivan P. A. (Eds.). (1995). *Political rhetoric, power, and renaissance women.* New York: State University of New York Press.

Lewalski, B. K. (1993). *Writing women in Jacobean England.* Cambridge, MA: Harvard University Press.

Lunsford, A. (Ed.). (1995). *Reclaiming rhetorica: Women in the rhetorical tradition.* Pittsburgh: University of Pittsburgh Press.

Mattingly, C. (2002). Telling evidence: Rethinking what counts in rhetoric. *Rhetoric Society Quarterly, 32*(1), 99–108.

Mazzola, E. (1995). Expert witnesses and secret subjects: Anne Askew's examinations and renaissance self-incrimination. In C. Levin & P. A. Sullivan (Eds.), *Political rhetoric, power, and renaissance women* (pp. 157–171). New York: State University of New York Press.

Miller, N. W. (1997). Ethos, authority and virtue for seventeenth-century women writers: The case of Bathsua Makin's *An essay to revive the ancient education of gentlewomen* (1673). In M. M. Wertheimer (Ed.), *Listening to their* voices: The rhetorical activities of historical women (pp. 272–287). Columbia: University of South Carolina Press.

Miller, T. P. (1993). Reinventing rhetorical traditions. In T. Enos (Ed.), *Learning from the histories of rhetoric: Essays in honour of Winifred Bryan Horner* (pp. 26–41). Carbondale: Southern Illinois University Press.

Nate, R. (2001). Plain and vulgarly express'd: Margaret Cavendish and the discourse of the new science. *Rhetorica, 19*(4), 403–417.

Ong, W. J. (1982). *Orality and literacy: The technologizing of the word.* New York: Routledge.

Orlin, L. C. (1995). The fictional families of Elizabeth I. In C. Levin & P. A. Sullivan (Eds.), *Political rhetoric, power, and renaissance women* (pp. 85–110). New York: State University of New York Press.

Plato. (1973). *Phaedrus and Letters VII and VIII* (W. Hamilton, Trans.). Harmondsworth, UK: Penguin Books.

Quintilian. (1989). *Institutio Oratoria* (H. E. Butler, Trans.). Cambridge, MA: Harvard University Press.

Redfern, J. R. (1995). Christine de Pisan and *The Treasure of the City of Ladies*: A Medieval Rhetorician and her rhetoric. In A. Lunsford (Ed.), *Reclaiming rhetorica: Women in the rhetorical tradition* (pp. 73–92). Pittsburgh: University of Pittsburgh Press.

Scheelar, M. H. (1999). Ethos over time: The ongoing appeal of St. Catherine of Siena. In C. M. Sutherland & R. Sutcliffe (Eds.), *The changing tradition: Women in the history of rhetoric* (pp. 59–71). Calgary: University of Calgary Press.

Sutherland, C. M. (1997). Aspiring to the rhetorical tradition: A study of Margaret Cavendish. In M. M. Wertheimer (Ed.), *Listening to their voices: The rhetorical activities of historical women* (pp. 255–271). Columbia: University of South Carolina Press.

Sutherland, C. M. (2003). Margaret Cavendish, Duchess of Newcastle. In E. A. Malone (Ed.), *Dictionary of literary biography. Vol. 281: British rhetoricians and logicians, second series* (pp. 36–47). Farmington Hills, MI: Gale.

Sutherland, C. M. (2006). Margaret Fell and the problem of women's ethos. In P. Bizzell (Ed.), *Rhetorical agendas: Political, ethical, spiritual* (pp. 351–356). Mahwah, NJ: Lawrence Erlbaum.

Sutherland, C. M., & Sutcliffe, R. (Eds.). (1999). *The changing tradition: Women in the history of rhetoric.* Calgary: University of Calgary Press.

Tinkler, J. F. (1987). Renaissance humanism and the genera eloquentiae. *Rhetorica, 5*(3), 279–309.

Truelove, A. (2001). Commanding communications: The fifteenth century letters of the Stonor women. In J. Daybell (Ed.), *Early modern women's letter writing 1450–1700* (pp. 42–58). Basingstoke, UK: Palgrave.

Vitanza, V. J. (Ed.). (1994). *Writing histories of rhetoric.* Carbondale: Southern Illinois University Press.

Walker, J. (2004). These things have I not betrayed: Michael Psellos' encomium of his mother as a defense of rhetoric. *Rhetorica, 22*(1), 49–101.

Ward, J. (1999). Women and Latin rhetoric from Hrosvit to Hildegard. In C. M. Sutherland & R. Sutcliffe (Eds.), *The changing tradition: Women in the history of rhetoric* (pp. 121–132). Calgary: University of Calgary Press.

Wertheimer, M. M. (Ed.). (1997). *Listening to their voices: The rhetorical activities of historical women.* Columbia: University of South Carolina Press.

Woodbridge, L. (1986). *Women and the English Renaissance.* Urbana: University of Illinois Press.

Wu, H. (2002). Historical studies of women here and there: Methodological challenges to dominant interpretive frameworks. *Rhetoric Society Quarterly, 32*(1), 81–97.

4

Recovering, Revisioning, and Regendering the History of 18th- and 19th-Century Rhetorical Theory and Practice

LYNÉE LEWIS GAILLET

ELIZABETH TASKER

Scholars generally agree that the modernization of rhetoric commenced in the late 17th century, coalesced in the 18th century, and was largely abandoned by the late 19th century. Winifred Bryan Horner explains that 18th- and 19th-century curricula and pedagogy paved the way for new academic disciplines, including composition, literary criticism, and speech communication—disciplines that quickly eclipsed the newly modernized rhetoric. Not until after the mid-20th century did rhetoric experience a resurgence when scholar/teachers searching for modern models of writing instruction embraced the theories and teaching practices of rhetors such as Blair and Campbell (Horner, 1990a). This reclamation of 18th- and 19th-century rhetorics fueled a "Renaissance of Rhetoric," which George Kennedy (1999) identifies as beginning in the last third of the 20th century (p. 293). As part of this renaissance, new interest in historiography and criticism of 18th- and 19th-century rhetoric reshaped perspectives of the period. Enlightenment rhetoric quickly became codified into four distinct movements: neoclassical, belletristic, elocutionary, and psychological-epistemological (often called "the new rhetoric"). Subsequently, these trends, canonized as part of the mainstream rhetorical tradition, became the rubric for understanding and studying rhetorical history of the periods. (For detailed discussions of primary and secondary scholarship addressing British Enlightenment rhetoric published pre-1990, see Enos, 1996; Horner, 1990a; Sloane, 2001.)

Yet despite the enduring usefulness of the fourfold view of the 18th- and 19th-century rhetoric, this rubric has proven restrictive in its pigeonholing of figures and texts. Even more problematic is its exclusion of important rhetorics and rhetorical venues falling outside the scope of the pulpit, the law court, and the podium—the dominant and predominantly masculine discourse communities of Western civilization. This exclusion is of prime concern to historians interested in postmodern, feminist, and global rhetorics. Thus, a remapping of 18th- and 19th-century rhetoric is underway. Adopting recovery and revisionist research methodologies, historians are unearthing unexamined archives, revisiting primary and canonical materials, and making use of new technologies to extend the scope and possibilities inherent in 18th- and 19th-century rhetorical theory and practice. The terrain of these periods within the rhetorical tradition has shifted considerably in the past decade. This chapter explores the emerging scholarship characterizing this protean ground.

BROAD WORKS AND OVERVIEWS

In recent years, general works tracing the rhetorical tradition have broadened coverage of the 18th and 19th centuries to reflect the expanding canon. However, representation still primarily concentrates on the Western rhetorical tradition—a natural starting place given rhetoric's classical roots and sphere of influence during the period. The importance of 18th- and 19th-century rhetoric to the history of Western rhetoric is well documented in Parts 4 and 5 of Patricia Bizzell and Bruce Herzberg's *The Rhetorical Tradition: Readings From Classical Times to the Present* (2001). Part 4 presents Enlightenment Rhetoric and includes primary excerpts from mostly British, Scottish, and Irish authors (John Locke, David Hume, Mary Astell, Thomas Sheridan, Gilbert Austin, George Campbell, and Hugh Blair), many of whom epitomize the fourfold view of 18th-century rhetoric, and one Italian, Giambattista Vico. Part 5 of *The Rhetorical Tradition,* dedicated to 19th-century rhetoric, demonstrates how this period comes into its own. Initially dominated by the "new rhetoric" of the 18th century, later 19th-century rhetorical history includes American adaptations of writing instruction, women's rhetorics, rhetorics of men of color, and the relationship of rhetoric to romanticism and modern philosophy. The editors have selected excerpts of primary works from three British authors (Richard Whatley, Alexander Bain, and Herbert Spencer), six Americans (Maria Stewart, Sarah Grimké, Frederick Douglass, Phoebe Palmer, Frances Willard, and Adams Sherman Hill), and one Swiss (Friedrich Nietzsche). Although Bizzell and Herzberg's (2001) anthology has been criticized for its narrow selection of excerpts, overall, its thorough introductions, numerous bibliographical references, and inclusion of sizable, representative excerpts recommend it as one of the most helpful introductory reference works currently available on rhetoric from the period. Notably, this text initiates the practice of anthologizing works from the rhetorical tradition and paves the way for future collections mentioned below.

The *Encyclopedia of Rhetoric and Composition: Communication From Ancient Times to the Information Age* (Enos, 1996) and the *Encyclopedia of Rhetoric* (Sloane,

2001) include excellent discussion of both periods. Full-length essays by experts, Winifred Bryan Horner (1990a, 1990b) and Thomas Miller (1997) on 18th-century rhetoric and Linda Ferreira-Buckley (1996) and Nan Johnson (2001) on 19th-century rhetoric and offer superb introductions and analyses of the developments of rhetorical theory. Both encyclopedias also include shorter entries detailing historical movements, trends, and figures of the periods. Another broad work that elucidates the period is George Kennedy's *Classical Rhetoric and Christian and Secular Tradition* (1999). Citing earlier work by Howell, Kennedy's chapter on the 18th century explains the critical role of 17th- and 18th-century French theorists, such as Lamy, Boileau, Fenelon, and Rollins, in conveying tenets of neoclassical rhetoric to 18th-century English and Scottish rhetorical theorists. James Murphy's edited collection, *A Short History of Writing Instruction: From Ancient Greece to Modern America* (2001), offers a systematic overview of both British (Ferreira-Buckley & Horner, 2001) and American (Wright & Halloran, 2001) composition instruction from the two periods. These chapters not only describe pedagogical practices but also connect writing instruction to social and technical developments, issues of empowerment and democratization, and the integration of vernacular language within academic curricula. The discipline needs more works like this one: thoughtful, intellectual treatises dedicated to the study of specialized issues within the field.

Detailed, specialized research is found in the surge in feminist scholarship in rhetoric shaping the last decade as evidenced by the publication of five ground-breaking anthologies of women's rhetorics. First, Andrea Lunsford's *Reclaiming Rhetorica: Women in the Rhetorical Tradition* (1995) includes contemporary essays on Mary Astell, Mary Wollstonecraft, Margaret Fuller, Ida B. Wells, and Sojourner Truth and also explores issues of women's suffrage and higher education in the 19th century. Similarly,

collected essays in Molly Meijer Wertheimer's *Listening to Their Voices: The Rhetorical Activities of Historical Women* (1997) examine female rhetoric associated with patriarchy, religion, mother's manuals, letter writing, and other "feminine" rhetorical strategies. Christine Sutherland and Rebecca Sutcliffe's *The Changing Tradition: Women in the History of Rhetoric* (1999), a compilation of 17 feminist essays originally presented at the 1997 Conference of the International Society for the History of Rhetoric at the University of Saskatchewan, include analyses of the treatises of Mary Astell and the journals of Methodist mystic Hester Anne Rogers. In Joy Ritchie and Kate Ronald's ambitious *Available Means: An Anthology of Women's Rhetoric(s)* (2001), 22 of the 67 excerpts of female writing are from the long 18th and the 19th centuries, beginning with Margaret Fell's "Women's Speaking Justified" from 1666 and ending with an excerpt of Gertrude Buck's "The Present Status of Rhetorical Theory" in 1900. Last, Jane Donawerth's *Rhetorical Theory by Women Before 1900* (2002b) expands traditional definitions of rhetoric by including a wide range of genres under-examined female-authored rhetorical and a global view of the pre-20th century rhetorical map.

THE 18TH CENTURY

Golden and Corbett (1990) call the 18th century "one of the most prolific eras in rhetorical history" (p. 7). Yet, after the publication of the first edition of *The Rhetoric of Blair, Campbell, and Whately* (1968) and Wilbur Samuel Howell's *Eighteenth-Century British Logic and Rhetoric* (1971), secondary scholarship on 18th century rhetoric declined for several decades. In 1990, Winifred Horner concluded her 18th-century chapter of *The Present State of Scholarship in Historical and Contemporary Rhetoric* by noting the "paucity" and "narrow approach" in scholarship for the period and called for more work on three levels: (1) further *recovery* of primary texts, (2) *interpretation*, analysis, and rereading, and (3) *conversation* and scholarly debate about the rhetoric of the period (pp. 138–139). Following Horner's calls, the discipline witnessed a rejuvenation of research into 18th-century rhetoric, including new editions of primary texts by Hugh Blair, Mary Astell, and Madeleine de Scudery; a slew of secondary texts covering a wide variety of European rhetoricians, theorists, and rhetorical venues; and significant scholarly conversation and debate about received definitions and boundaries of the period, especially in the form of feminist and postmodern critiques of Enlightenment rhetoric.

Recent scholarship reexamines the relationship between Enlightenment philosophy and the traditional four-pronged view of neoclassical, elocutionary, belletristic, and epistemological rhetoric. Bizzell and Herzberg (2001) cite the collective influence of early Enlightenment thinkers, including Ramus, Descartes, Bacon, and, later, Locke and Hume, who advocated learning in the vernacular and emphasized common sense, individual reasoning, and inductive logic—all primary characteristics of the new rhetoric of the 18th century (pp. 791–810). Thomas Miller in Sloane's (2001) *Encyclopedia of Rhetoric* states that the theories of these Enlightenment philosophers, along with the continental neoclassic rhetoric of the 17th century, serve to explain the four-pronged expansion of rhetoric in the 18th-century to consider altogether "logic, speech, composition, and modern concepts of literature and psychology" (p. 228). Yet H. Lewis Ulman (1994), in *Things, Thoughts, Words and Actions: The Problem of Language in Late Eighteenth Century British Rhetorical Theory*, notes that the four movements "do not serve well as fixed categories into which we can unambiguously place individual treatises" (p. 5). Miller (cited in Sloane, 2001) also reminds us that even though the 18th century was a time of turbulent social, political, and economic change, which required

skillful practitioners of rhetoric in civic arenas, "the major rhetorical theorists of the Enlightenment remained aloof from the impassioned orations and pamphlets of their time and turned instead to philosophers of the new learning" (p. 278). He suggests that popular rhetorics went unnoticed by the rhetorical theorists of the day, who were busy conceiving of a new rhetoric from a cognitive ivory tower concerned primarily with science, literature, aesthetics, and taste.

Feminist scholars have also critiqued Enlightenment rhetoric as another historical privileging of masculine discourse. In a 1992 *Rhetoric Society Quarterly* volume dedicated to feminist rereadings of canonical works, Catherine Hobbs Peaden, for example, describes Locke as following Bacon in the creation of a gender-based dichotomy of language, which values "a 'good' masculine scientific discourse," devalues "a 'bad' feminized rhetoric," and negatively personifies rhetoric itself as feminine (p. 81). Two years later, Adam Potkay (1994) provides a similar, yet less dire, reading of 18th-century rhetoric as gendered; he sees the midcentury British and Scottish rhetoric as characterized by the tension between the feminized movements of sensibility and polite style and the period's fascination with the masculine eloquence of classical rhetoric.

In addition to critiques of traditional categorization recent conversations productively adopt a range of research methods to trace the influence of rhetorical theories of the mid- to late-18th-century rhetoric on 19th- and 20th-century developments. For example, contributors to Lynée Lewis Gaillet's *Scottish Rhetoric and Its Influences* (1998a) use comparative and archival methods to point out the influences of Blair, Whatley, Jardine, and Bain on 19th-century American higher education. Ulman's *Things, Thoughts, Words and Actions* (1994) documents the influence of the psychological-philosophical, belletristic, and elocutionary movements on theories of 20th-century rhetoric. Generally, recent scholarship on 18th-century rhetoric applies two major categories of research methodology: the first and most common is the study of specific historical figures—men and women who theorized or practiced rhetoric in the 18th century; the second concerns thematic research encompassing cultural, literary, or other language-based hegemonies and signs. In explaining the thematic approach, Horner cites Stephen Browne, who has characterized this type of methodology as an exploration of "the 'voices' that express this age" (p. 119). Recent methodologies taking thematic approaches to voice and venue reflect both a maturing of conversations about the period and a growing postmodern approach to research. Yet traditional research methods centering on historical figures continue to yield variable contributions to the field.

New Research on Historical Figures

Over the past decade, scholarship on individual rhetors of the eighteenth century has not only expanded current thinking about traditional canonical figures but has also updated the canon with previously unrecognized or understudied rhetors and rhetorical theorists. The recent work on historical figures runs the methodological gamut of traditional, feminist, and postmodern approaches involving rereading, recovery, and revision. Variety in researcher perspectives has enriched and complicated the eighteenth-century rhetorical landscape by examining heretofore overlooked rhetorical practices, traditions, and biases, as well as new connections between rhetoric and other disciplines. In multiple works, Jane Donaworth (1997, 1998) introduces Madeleine de Scudery as an important figure in historical rhetoric and associates her with "a new rhetoric of conversation" (1998, p. 184), which in the past 5 years has come to be called salon rhetoric (Craveri, 2005). In *Rhetoric on the Margins of Modernity: Vico, Condillac, Monboddo* (2002), Catherine Hobbs delivers a postmodern reading of "the relationship of rhetoric and the culture of modernity" in which she covers the theories of

three "impure figures often considered marginal in rhetoric and philosophy as a way to develop a more complex account of eighteenth-century rhetorics" (p. 3). Arthur Walzer in *George Campbell: Rhetoric in the Age of Enlightenment* (2003), argues that Campbell's aim in the *Philosophy of Rhetoric* was not to reject or even reformulate classical rhetoric, but, in fact, to theorize more fully its operations using Enlightenment methods. Christina Mason Sutherland in *The Eloquence of Mary Astell* (2005) provides a detailed discussion of Astell's rhetoric and her reaction to the works of Locke, Descartes, Lamy, and the French school of Port Royal Logic. Sutherland's discussion of Astell's appropriation and adaptation of Bernard de Lamy's *The Art of Speaking* is particularly compelling (pp. 137–152), as is Sutherland's recognition that Astell builds indirectly on the rhetoric of conversation elaborated by Scudery (p. 158). Also in 2005, David Holmes's article "Say What? Rediscovering Hugh Blair and the Racialization of Language, Culture, and Pedagogy in Eighteenth-Century Rhetoric" describes what Holmes sees as Blair's "ethnocentric standardization of taste" and participation in the "widely accepted racialized discourses of his time" (p. 204). Stephen McKenna in *Adam Smith: The Rhetoric of Propriety* (2006) challenges readers to reassess the connections between Smith's theories of rhetoric and economics and examines the influence of rhetorical propriety's influence on 18th-century developments in science, epistemology, and aesthetics.

Two collections, Michael Moran's *Eighteenth-Century British and American Rhetorics and Rhetoricians* (1753/1994) and Lynée Lewis Gaillet's *Scottish Rhetoric and Its Influences* (1998a), offer focused (but briefer) readings of a larger number of theorists and practitioners of rhetoric in the 18th century. Valuable for its diverse representations, Moran's collection includes introductory biographical/interpretative essays on 34 figures, mostly from Britain and Scotland, but including a few French and American figures as well, presented alphabetically from Anthony Blackwell to Mary

Wollstonecraft. This reference work profiles well-known theorists from the four movements of rhetoric, as well as other unique figures ranging from the gifted orator and theorist Edmund Burke, to miscelleanous writer Charles Gildon, to American grammarian and dictionary author Noah Webster, to Princeton University president John Witherspoon. Moran (1753/1994) also includes a summary of one anonymous work of elocutionary theory titled "An Essay on the Action Proper for the Pulpit." Intended for an audience familiar with 18th-century rhetorical theory, Gaillet's (1998a) collection covers fewer figures in greater depth. Contributors explore the ways in which Scottish rhetoricians shaped present-day studies in psychology, philosophy, science, literary criticism, oral communication, English literature, and composition. The essays are presented in two groups: Part I rereads influential figures, such as Hume, Smith, Blair, Campbell, and Reid, against backdrops of various rhetorical, philosophical, ethical, and pedagogical theories; Part II furthers the conversation about the influences of Scottish rhetoric on 19th-century America and British education.

The past decade also witnessed the publication of major scholarly editions of several primary texts from the long 18th century: Patricia Springborg's edition of Mary Astell's *A Serious Proposal to the Ladies, Parts I & II* (1997), Karen Newman's translated edition of Madeleine de Scudery's *The Story of Sapho* (2003), Jane Donawerth and Julie Strongson's translated edition of Scudery's *Selected Letters, Orations, and Rhetorical Dialogues* (2004), and Linda Ferreira-Buckley and S. Michael Halloran's complete edition of Hugh Blair's *Lectures on Rhetoric and Belles Lettres* (2005). This latest edition of Blair's texts goes a step beyond the substantial excerpts provided in Golden and Corbett's *The Rhetoric of Blair, Campbell, and Whatley* (1990) by providing all Blair's lectures,

including his last 12—Lectures XXXV through XLVII—which are remarkable for Blair's comparison of ancient, French neo-classical, and British 18th-century historical writing, poetics, and literary forms. The primary editions of Scudery and Astell also detailed fascinating statements of rhetorical theory especially valuable to feminist scholars of rhetoric interested in the late-17th-century female intellectual thought.

Still missing from research on figures of the period are studies of significant theorists or practitioners outside Great Britain or France. With the exception of Italian Vico Giambattista, study of 18th-century continental rhetoricians is scarce. We have no sustained investigations of specific Eastern, Asian, and African rhetors of the period and very few in-depth studies of American historical figures as rhetoricians—although popular culture and interdisciplinary studies have paid close attention to American forefathers and mothers in recent years (Olson, 2004; Roberts-Miller, 2006). Also, while scholarship on mid- to late-18th-century rhetoric in Great Britain is thorough, early-18th-century rhetoric of the British Isles is underexamined. An exploration of significant figures who came after Locke and Astell and before the midcentury Scottish rhetorics, particularly anyone who might connect Astell to later movements, would prove valuable. Comparisons could be made of Astell's use of logic, persuasive argument, common sense philosophy, and delineations of styles for composition to the work of Campbell and Whatley, whom she precedes by 70 years. Investigation is also required to fully understand the influence of Scudery as a rhetorical theorist, social role model, and an icon for female authorship. Despite the recovery of Astell, Scudery, Fell, and Wollstonecraft, research into 18th-century female rhetoric lags behind all other periods. The texts of Aphra Behn, Susannah Centilivre, and other female authors of the period need to be culled for contributions to rhetorical theory, and a closer examination of female monarchs, intellectuals, preachers, and actresses as public speakers is warranted. Finally, the work of the Bluestockings, who were avid practitioners of letter writing, poetry, rhetoric, and literary criticism, should be reread for its potential contribution to female and belletristic rhetorics, and the rhetoric of conversation.

Cultural Voices of the 18th Century

In addition to new critical works on historical figures of rhetoric, the field now has a number of excellent rhetorical studies centered on thematic aspects of 18th-century culture. In the foreword to Adam Potkay's *The Fate of Eloquence in the Age of Hume* (1994), published by Cornell University in the *Rhetoric and Society* series, general editor Wayne E. Rebhorn states the purpose of the series: "to study rhetoric in all the varied forms . . . by situating it in the social and political contexts to which it is inextricably bound" and that

> rhetoric is . . . a necessary cultural practice . . . that is profoundly implicated in a large array of other disciplines and practices . . . [R]hetoric constitutes a response to historical developments in a given society . . . [,] crystallizes cultural tensions and conflicts . . . [,] defines key concepts, and . . . affects and shapes the social order. (1994, p. vii)

Rebhorn's description is apt, not just for characterizing this series, but also the burgeoning body of culturally based research in historical rhetoric.

Examples of the cultural approach within recent scholarship include Jon Thomas Rowland's *Swords in Myrtle Dress'D": Towards a Rhetoric of Sodom: Gay Readings of Homosexual Politics and Poetics in the* *Eighteenth Century* (1998), Christopher Grasso's *A Speaking Aristocracy: Transforming Public Discourse in Eighteenth-Century Connecticut* (1999), Peter Walmsley's *Locke's Essay and the Rhetoric of Science* (2003), Paul Goring's *The Rhetoric of Sensibility in Eighteenth-Century Culture* (2004), Clement Hawes's *Mania and Literary Style: The Rhetoric of Enthusiasm From the Ranters to Christopher Smart* (2005), and Cynthia Sundberg Wall's *The Prose of Things: Transformations of Description in the Eighteenth Century* (2006). Eighteenth-century homosexual politics and poetics, early New England political oratory, discourse on modern science, religious enthusiasm, and changes in prose style represent cultural objects for rhetorical study. These author's cultural readings of rhetoric unearth aspects of the 18th century that traditional studies of historical figures overlook. For example, both Potkay's and Goring's studies characterize how the cult of sensibility and polite style both influence and are influenced by the rhetoric of the period. Goring's (2004) study also ties the rhetoric of 18th-century sensibility to Habermasian notions of the public sphere and to body studies, performance theory, and literary and theater history. Another economically influenced study, Wall's *The Prose of Things* (2006), details how lifestyle changes and the availability of goods in the 18th century transformed readers' perceptions of the material world and caused writers to give objects and descriptions a psychological dimension previously not seen in prose, either fiction or nonfiction.

Within cultural studies, the research opportunities for historians of rhetoric are endless. Scholars might take a closer look at rhetoric and popular culture in England, especially with a consideration of Habermas's theories of the public sphere. The rhetoric of conversation is also a promising topic and one that crosses/includes cultures and figures; Hugh Blair, George Campbell, Mary Astell, Madeleine de Scudery, and Bernard Lamy all address conversation, a commonality that has not been addressed in secondary scholarship. Also, scholars interested in material culture, body studies, and performance theory might find an examination of the belletristic and elocutionary traditions of both Scottish and French rhetoricians to be fruitful.

THE 19TH CENTURY

Often considered an uninteresting and uneventful period in rhetorical history, the 19th century, until recently, was routinely dismissed as a rhetorical wasteland, a period defined only by its current-traditional approach to writing instruction. In the revised edition of *The Present State of Scholarship in Historical and Contemporary Rhetoric* (Horner, 1990a), Donald Stewart appropriates categories from 18th-century scholarship to discuss 19th-century rhetoric. However, these categories alone—classical, elocutionary, psychological-epistemological, belletristic, and practical—can no longer contain or describe 19th-century rhetorical scholarship. Defined by both recovery and revisionist methodologies, recent research on the period explores the interdisciplinary relationship among education, religion, social practices, and technological developments; revisits the reputation of the field's heroes and villains, aligning these figures' work with cultural practices and events of their time; and adds previously overlooked voices to the rhetorical tradition.

Linda Ferreira-Buckley's excellent overview of 19th-century rhetoric in the *Encyclopedia of Rhetoric and Composition* (1996) identifies important emerging rhetorical trends influenced by "empiricism, Scottish common-sense philosophy, associational and faculty psychology, Romanticism, scientism, and phrenology" that contest this sterile, stereotypical view of the period. Citing recent scholarship, Ferreira-Buckley demonstrates ways in which the field was beginning in 1996 to understand how 19th-century rhetoric

addressed "the public (civic life), the professional (individual expertise), or the private (individual self-improvement)" (p. 468). The past 10 years of scholarship concerning 19th-century rhetoric supports Ferreira-Buckley's claim. The appended bibliography lists diverse and interdisciplinary scholarship published in the past decade—the bulk of which addresses American rhetoric. Falling within the categories of public, professional, and private rhetoric, the list of entries offered herein, which is extensive but by no means exhaustive, proves that the 19th century was indeed a vital period in the development of rhetorical history.

The Shift in Composition Studies

Until the 1980s, speech departments generated the majority of research about 19th-century rhetoric. English department scholars up to this time looked to rhetoric primarily as an intellectual grounding for composition theory and pedagogy. Not until the early 1990s did widespread definitions and conceptions of 19th-century rhetoric shift to include a politicized understanding of historical developments and institutional constraints that define composition. No longer is the 19th century viewed as a little-studied extension of the 18th-century in the area of rhetoric or as a period within composition history defined simply by what was omitted—invention, ethos, audience consideration, etc. In 1990, Stewart acknowledged that rhetoric needs to be studied against the specific historical conditions that gave it meaning and power. At that point, the field moved away from constructing a linear trajectory of 19th-century developments in writing instruction toward more complicated analyses of coexisting, layered histories of the discipline.

As scholars began researching historical and institutional contexts for writing instruction, archival research addressing new venues and little-known figures emerged. Notably, John Brereton's award-winning

Origins of Composition Studies in the American College, 1875–1925: A Documentary History (1995) made a rich archive of papers, assignments, and reports readily available. Other works, including Lucille Schultz's *The Young Composers: Composition's Beginnings in Nineteenth-Century Schools* (1999); Carr, Carr, and Shultz's *Archives of Instruction* (2005), and Sharon M. Harris's edited collection *Blue Pencils and Hidden Hands: Women Editing Periodicals, 1830–1910* (2004), gave primacy to student essays, textbooks, journals, letters, and published articles. Adopting historiographical methodologies, Russell M. Wyland's *An Archival Study of Rhetoric Texts and Teaching at the University of Oxford, 1785–1820* (2003) revisits elite education. He examines institutional records and personal papers to determine not only which classical rhetoric texts Oxford students read but also how those works were taught during a time of curriculum reform.

To date one of the most interesting archival projects addressing student writing is Erika Lindemann's *True and Candid Compositions: The Lives and Writings of Antebellum Students at the University of North Carolina* (2005). A collection of 121 archival documents (including 108 student writings) from 1795 to 1869, this digital resource provides an exceptional view into relationships between students and their local communities. Each of the six chapters includes an introductory essay that contextualizes the accompanying primary documents (letters, compositions, speeches, creative work, diary entries, and digital images). Drawing from published histories of the University, minutes of faculty and trustees meetings, newspapers, catalogues and directories, alumni records, and writings by relatives and friends of the students, the introductory essays analyze both locale and exigencies prompting students' varied uses of written and spoken language. Comprehensive attention to writer, document, era, and place define this rich archival

resource. Similarly nuanced projects are in process at other colleges and universities and, it is hoped, will be broadly accessible soon, preferably as digital (searchable) documents.

Another emerging area of archival research concerns the reexamination of historical figures associated with the birth of composition studies. Works such as Charles Paine's *The Resistant Writer: Rhetoric as Immunity, 1850 to the Present* (1999) advocate revisionist histories that provide a more nuanced assessment of such traditional "villains" of composition history as Edward T. Channing and Adams Sherman Hill in an effort to understand their work as a response to the cultural contingencies of their periods. In analyzing the "young tradition of composition historiography," Paine encourages scholars to produce "histories that read compositionists and their theories *through* competing institutions of their eras" in an effort to "helpfully complicate" historiography (p. xi). Recent scholarship in that vein includes investigations such as JoAnn Campbell's *Toward a Feminist Rhetoric: The Writing of Gertrude Buck* (1996), Donald and Patricia Stewart's posthumously published biography of Fred Newton Scott (1997), many of the "figure" essays collected in Lynée Lewis Gaillet's *Scottish Rhetoric and Its Influences* (1998a; see also Gaillet, 1998b; Gaillet & Miller, 2001), and Sherry Booth's "A Moment for Reform: Rhetoric and Literature at the University of Glasgow, 1862–1877" (2003). Composition historiography is now a firmly established line of enquiry in composition studies (Russell, 2002), as brilliantly illustrated in Barb L'Eplattenier and Lisa Mastrangelo's collection *Historical Studies of Writing Program Administration: Individuals, Communities, and the Formation of a Discipline* (2004). Accessible, engaging, and intellectual, this collection of stories—based on archival research dating back to 1774—provides a rich history and (re)view of the work currently defining writing program administration.

In the past decade, scholars of 19th-century rhetoric have also challenged existing assumptions about the history of rhetoric and composition. As scholars began examining relationships between culture and writing instruction, conceptions of the 19th century as a period of stagnant, current-traditional pedagogy divorced from rhetorical theory and culture exploded. The following highly acclaimed works indicate the range of emerging perspectives: Thomas Miller's *The Formation of College English: Rhetoric and Belles Letters in the British Cultural Provinces* (1997) examines the civic concerns of rhetoric and the politics associated with the adoption of belle lettres in the nonelite British colleges and universities. Sharon Crowley's *Composition in the University: Historical and Polemical Essays* (1998) questions the primacy that has historically been given to first-year composition courses in the field of rhetoric and composition by critiquing the limitations of our institutional systems. Mariolina Rizzi Salvatori in *Pedagogy: Disturbing History, 1819–1929* (1996) presents a documentary history of the contested key term *pedagogy* in which she examines how and questions why pedagogy came to be viewed subservient to research by both institutions and the academic culture. And pointedly avoiding the study of academic prose, Susan Miller's *Assuming the Positions: Cultural Pedagogy and the Politics of Commonplace Writing* (1998) analyzes "commonplace" writings (diaries, letters, journals, travel notes, recipes, remedies) dating from 1650 to 1880. She argues that these writings from daily life in Virginia capture the humanity of writers in ways academic writing cannot and contends that by ignoring such "commonplace writing" historians are distorting the past.

This recent scholarship opens many avenues for future examinations of 19th-century educational theories and practices,

influences and borrowings. Study of 19th-century instruction in rhetoric and writing is critical to understanding the origins of contemporary educational practices; yet, the period remains understudied. Archival resources from the period—including institutional data, school-reform reports, lecture notes, student writings, class plans, society minutes, committee reports, local school legislation, teachers' diaries and journals, commencement addresses, and so forth—await discovery and analysis.

Regendering and Recovering 19th-Century Rhetoric

The most important development in recent scholarship on 19th-century rhetoric concerns the positions of authority that Western female orators and writers claimed for themselves within public and private spaces. The past decade's proliferation of feminist readings of the history of rhetoric essentially redefines 19th-century rhetorical theory. Nan Johnson's excellent introduction, "The Feminist Analysis of Rhetoric as a Cultural Site," to her groundbreaking *Gender and Rhetorical Space in American Life, 1866–1910* (2002) traces the "remapping" of 19th-century rhetoric and succinctly chronicles current avenues of feminist research. Johnson argues that

> during the postbellum era, we see the rise of nonacademic pedagogies of rhetoric and popular constructions of rhetorical propriety that became implicated in a cultural program of gender politics that sought to control negotiations about the boundaries of *rhetorical space* as well as the debate about who was allowed to occupy it. (p. 2)

Labeling nonacademic rhetorical traditions and spaces "parlor rhetoric," Johnson offers a brilliant analysis in *Gender and Rhetorical Space* of the cultural conventions and constructions of rhetorical performance that conspired to maintain the status quo of postbellum white women.

The power to speak, access to education, race, cultural gender expectations, and silencing characterize 19th-century women's struggle to find a public voice (Buchanan, 2005). Feminist scholars attempt to rescue the voices of 19th-century women activists from obscurity, reminding us of the diverse careers and roles female rhetors adopted in the 19th-century society despite cultural boundaries that limited women's access to public rhetorical spaces. We now have scholarship portraying 19th-century women as abolitionists (Bacon, 1998; Logan, 1999; Royster, 1997), preachers (Brekus, 1998; Collins, 1997; Mountford, 2003), suffragettes (Conway, 1995; Gifford, 1995; Zaeske, 1995), physicians (Wells, 1996, 2001), educators (Adams, 2001; Donawerth, 2002; Fitzgerald, 2002; Hobbs, 1995; Johnson, 2002; Kates, 2001), and social reformers (Connors, 1997, 1999; Knight, 1998; Mattingly, 2001, 2002; Tonn, 1996; Watson, 1999).

Scholars exploring the rhetorical engagement of abolitionists analyze the powerful cultural circumstances—slavery, lynching, oppression of women—that motivated 19th-century African American women to engage in civic rhetorical practices aimed at both black and white audiences. In their search for artifacts, scholars such as McHenry (2002), Logan (1995), and Royster (2000) are forced to redefine both archival research methodologies and positions/roles of researchers, as Royster eloquently explains,

> Because of the "marginality" of what I do, I have had to create proactive spaces rather than reactive spaces from which to speak and interpret. The task of creating new space, rather than occupying existing space, has encouraged in me the shaping of a scholarly ethos that holds both sound scholarly practices and ethical behavior in balance and harmony and that consistently projects this balancing in research and writing. (p. 252)

Logan's *With Pen and Voice* (1995) examines how 19th-century African American

women claimed the authority of Christian beliefs to engage in civic rhetoric. Religious traditions figure prominently in other recent histories as well, including Mattingly's *Well-Tempered Women: Nineteenth-Century Temperance Rhetoric* (1998), J. H. Hobbs's "*I Sing for I Cannot Be Silent": The Feminization of American Hymnody 1870–1920* (1997), Brekus's *Strangers and Pilgrims: Female Preaching in America 1740–1845* (1998), Collins's "Women's Voices and Women's Silence in the Tradition of Early Methodism" (1997), Mattingly's *Well-Tempered Women* (1998), and Mountford's *The Gendered Pulpit: Preaching in American Protestant Spaces* (2003). Logan wonders if the silencing of these women rhetors, who were enormously influential during their own time, is due in part to their religious fervor. The rhetorical dynamics of the silencing of both voices and traditions is a key component of current investigations of rhetorical history. Although many of the subjects of these investigations spoke with authority to contemporary publics, not many have been remembered. As Gere (1997) reminds us, "the last stage in any cultural project is forgetting" (p. 16).

Thanks to recent attempts to "remember" lost voices and regender the canon, we now have fascinating (although often brief) accounts of important and influential women rhetors. The list is impressive: Browne's (1999) study of Angelina Grimké, Connors's (1999) analysis of Frances Wright, Donawerth's (1999) treatment of Hannah More and Lydia Sigourney, Gifford's (1995) study of Frances Willard, and Kates's (1997a, 1997b) investigations of Hallie Quinn Brown and Mary Augusta Jordan, along with the long list of female rhetors profiled in the three collections edited by Sutherland and Sutcliffe (1999), Watson (1999), and Wertheimer (1997). However, definitive and accessible editions of many 19th-century rhetors' works—studies that model Thomas Miller's treatment of John Witherspoon—are still absent from the scholarship. For example, we have no definitive edition or comprehensive treatment of Bain—although he is perhaps the best known figure from this period. Most telling, Greenwood Press has published *Eighteenth-Century British and American Rhetorics and Rhetoricians* (Moran, 1753/1994) and *Twentieth-Century Rhetorics and Rhetoricians* (Moran & Ballif, 2000), but *Nineteenth-Century Rhetorics and Rhetoricians* is conspicuously absent.

Other Voices

The emergence of First Nations histories and examinations of the rhetorical uses of language by indigenous peoples in North America is a welcome addition to recent 19th-century scholarship. Works such as Deborah Miranda's (2000) examination of composition pedagogy in "Indian" boarding schools, and Malea Powell's treatment of "survival rhetoric" (2002) and study of the "Indian" reform movement (2004) present fascinating accounts and suggest avenues for possible study. Although the field has witnessed emerging scholarship addressing what Rebecca Moore Howard (2006) has collected and labeled "Native American Languages, Discourses, and Rhetorics" (http://wrt-howard .syr.edu/Bibs/NativeAm.htm), still too few historical/archival projects concerned with both education and language use are available.

N. Krishnaswamy's (2001) entry for continental "Indian Rhetoric" in the *Encyclopedia of Rhetoric* (Sloane, 2001) offers only a passing reference to the 19th century—but one pregnant with possibilities for research. During this period, the continent was introduced to Western rhetoric by travelers, missionaries, British colonial rule, the introduction of science and technologies, and the adoption of English as the language of commerce and education. One wonders what changes occurred to the continent's rich oral tradition, subcontinent styles and poetics,

Islamic notions of aesthetics, and Indic literature when faced with Western notions and definitions of a unified rhetorical tradition. These areas are ripe for enquiry.

Bo Wang's (2004) survey of research in Eastern rhetoric is perhaps the best recent source for understanding the current status of Asian rhetorical traditions. She interviews leading scholars of Eastern rhetoric, posing questions about the status of the field, methodology, and comparative rhetorics. The discipline needs scholarship that builds on investigations by researchers such as Wang (2004), Garrett (1999, 2001), and Liu (1996)—scholars who revisit the Western rhetorical tradition from non-Western perspectives, who encourage dialogue between East and West, who don't impose Western models on investigations of Eastern traditions and practices. Wang characterizes cutting-edge research in Eastern rhetoric as scholarship that "is mindful of the logic of Orientalism, that studies Asian rhetoric in its own cultural and political contexts, that appropriates Asian rhetoric for Western contexts, and that applies Asian rhetorical traditions to the study of pedagogical issues" (p. 173). Unfortunately, few works fitting this description address either 18th- or 19th-century rhetorical traditions, evidenced by the gaps in Benjamin Elman's overview of Eastern rhetoric in the *Encyclopedia of Rhetoric* (Sloane, 2001; see also Elman, 2008). Clearly many other 19th-century voices are awaiting discovery.

IMPLICATIONS

Recent scholarship changes the face of 18th- and 19th-century rhetorical study. No longer is the visage solely white, European, male, and middle class. Scholars have expanded the canon to include the voices of women, people of color, civic rhetors, and activists—people who speak and write not only in the traditional classroom or from the pulpit but also on stage, in newspapers, and flyers, from the parlor, at grassroot meetings, in public squares, on reservations, in letters and essays, from recovered diaries and journals, in commission reports, and in autobiographies, etc. These recovered voices no longer represent addenda, codicils, and asides to the tradition but are in fact so richly integrated into the fabric of the periods that the retextured definitions and representations of rhetorical theory and practice are hardly recognizable by earlier standards as 18th- and 19th-century constructs.

In many ways, researchers working in these periods are still in recovery mode, but in the past 15 years enough foundational work has become available that scholars can now enter into rich Burkean parlor conversations. Although many critics dismiss figure studies, our review of recent literature from these two periods indicates the complexities and richness inherent in current treatments of sole rhetors. At every turn, figures are viewed as products of their own local cultures, moored to the exigencies of their times. In addition, recent studies centering on voice, venue, and language show us the great value of approaching historic research in rhetoric through postmodern methods, tying studies of language and persuasive acts to cultural practices, movements, and ideologies. The discipline still needs detailed bibliographies addressing both figures and cultural issues— similar to the comprehensive and diverse bibliographies Howard has collected within composition studies—and these references need to be available online.

To attract new students and scholars to both periods, the field must make both primary and secondary works accessible to undergraduates as well as graduate students and professional scholars. Works such as James Herrick's *The History and Theory of Rhetoric* (2005) and Bizzell and Herzberg's *The Rhetorical Tradition* (2001) provide introductory essays to the periods targeted to both undergraduate and graduate students, but *The Norton Anthology of Rhetoric and*

Composition (Lunsford, Hariman, Jarratt, Mao, & Royster, in press) holds the greatest promise for widespread dissemination of rhetorical theory and practice. Perhaps once this textbook is published with the blessing of Norton, the number of undergraduate survey courses in the history of rhetoric will increase. And Horner and Gaillet are in the process of editing a new edition of the *Present State of Research in the History of Rhetoric*—a much anticipated update. All these works, along with the two encyclopedias of rhetoric and this SAGE *Handbook*, provide an impressive arsenal for studying the field.

We applaud recent rereadings of the traditional Western canon through critical foci: historiographic, cultural, feminist, and political. However, in all areas, even the traditional, much work remains for scholars of both 18th- and 19th-century rhetoric. While the monolith of the rhetorical canon remains intact, new formations are always visible in its silhouette. Not many years ago, the rhetorical landscape of the 18th and 19th centuries appeared to be shaped only by the mainstream reaction of modern Western intellectuals to classical rhetoric. Thanks to scholars committed to intensive archival research, that view no longer dominates scholarship from the period. As more archival and library holdings are made available electronically, we anticipate an increase in scholarship that locates lost figures of all periods, examines the impact of popular culture on rhetoric, and views intersections of diverse (and multiple) rhetorics. Still needed are studies that not only expand and balance the rhetorical canon with non-Western perspectives but also teach us about diverse value systems, alternative forms of persuasion and rhetorical purposes, and reveal rhetorical features that appear common across culture during the 18th and 19th centuries.

The range, depth, and sheer number of recent publications addressing the history of 18th-and 19th-century rhetorical theory are unprecedented and impressive indeed. The door to investigation is wide open, inviting researchers to enter the conversations.

REFERENCES

Adams, K. H. (2001). *A group of their own: College writing courses and American women Writers, 1880–1940.* Albany: State University of New York Press.

Astell, M. (1997). *A serious proposal to the ladies, Parts I & II* (P. Springborg, Ed.). Brookfield, VT: Pickering & Chatto.

Bacon, J. (1998). Do you understand your own language? Revolutionary Topoi in the rhetoric of African-American abolitionists. *Rhetoric Society Quarterly, 28*(2), 55–76.

Bizzell, P., & Herzberg, B. (Eds.). (2001). *The rhetorical tradition: Readings from classical times to the present* (2nd ed.). Boston: Bedford/St. Martin's.

Blair, H. (2005). *Lectures on rhetoric and belles lettres* (L. Ferreira-Buckley & S. M. Halloran, Eds.). Carbondale: Southern Illinois University Press. (Original work published 1783)

Booth, S. (2003). A moment for reform: Rhetoric and literature at the University of Glasgow, 1862–1877. *Rhetoric Review, 22,* 374–395.

Brekus, C. A. (1998). *Strangers and pilgrims: Female preaching in America, 1740–1845.* Chapel Hill: University of North Carolina Press.

Brereton, J. C. (1995). *The origins of composition studies in the American college, 1875–1925: A documentary history.* Pittsburgh, PA: University of Pittsburgh Press.

Browne, S. H. (1999). *Angelina Grimké: Rhetoric, identity, and the radical imagination.* East Lansing: Michigan State University Press.

Buchanan, L. (2005). *Regendering delivery: The fifth canon and antebellum women rhetors.* Carbondale: Southern Illinois University Press.

Campbell, J. (1996). *Toward a feminist rhetoric: The writings of Gertrude Buck.* Pittsburgh, PA: University of Pittsburgh Press.

Carr, J. F., Carr, S., & Schultz, L. M. (2005). *Archives of instruction: Nineteenth-century rhetorics, readers, and composition books in the United States.* Carbondale: Southern Illinois University Press.

Collins, V. T. (1997). Women's voices and women's silence in the tradition of early methodism. In M. M. Wertheimer (Ed.), *Listening to their voices: The rhetorical activities of historical women* (pp. 233–254). Columbia: University of South Carolina Press.

Connors, R. J. (1997). *Composition-rhetoric: Backgrounds, theory, and pedagogy.* Pittsburgh, PA: University of Pittsburgh Press.

Connors, R. J. (1999). Frances Wright: First female civic rhetor. *College English, 62,* 30–57.

Conway, K. M. (1995). Woman suffrage and the history of rhetoric at the Seven Sisters Colleges, 1865–1919. In A. Lunsford (Ed.), *Reclaiming rhetorica: Women in the rhetorical tradition* (pp. 203–226). Pittsburgh, PA: Pittsburgh University Press.

Craveri, B. (2005). *The age of conversation* (T. Waugh, Trans.). New York: New York Book Reviews.

Crowley, S. (1997). *Composition in the university: Historical and Polemical essays.* Pittsburgh, PA: University of Pittsburgh Press.

de Scudery, M. (2003). *The story of Sapho* (K. Newman, Trans. & Ed.). Chicago: University of Chicago Press.

de Scudery, M. (2004). *Selected letters, orations, and rhetorical dialogues* (J. Donawerth & J. Strongson, Trans. & Eds.). Chicago: University of Chicago Press.

Donawerth, J. (1997). As becomes a rational woman to speak: Madeleine de Scudery's rhetoric of conversation. In M. M. Wertheimer (Ed.), *Listening to their voices: The rhetorical activities of historical women* (pp. 305–319). Columbia: University of South Carolina Press.

Donawerth, J. (1998). Conversation and the boundaries of public discourse in rhetorical theory by Renaissance women. *Rhetorica, 16,* 181–199.

Donawerth, J. (1999). Hannah More, Lydia Sigourney, and the creation of woman's tradition of rhetoric. In C. J. Swearingen & D. Pruett (Eds.), *Rhetoric, the polis, and the global village* (pp. 155–161). Mahwah, NJ: Erlbaum.

Donawerth, J. (2002a). Nineteenth-century United States conduct book rhetoric by women. *Rhetoric Review, 21,* 5–21.

Donawerth, J. (Ed.). (2002b). *Rhetorical theory by women before 1900*. New York: Rowman & Littlefield.

Elman, B. (2008). *Classical historiography for Chinese history*. Retrieved May 14, 2008, from www.princeton.edu/~classbib

Enos, T. (Ed.). (1996). *Encyclopedia of rhetoric and composition: Communication from ancient times to the information age*. New York: Garland Press.

Ferreira-Buckley, L. (1996). Nineteenth-century rhetoric. In T. Enos (Ed.), *Encyclopedia of rhetoric and composition: Communication from ancient times to the information age* (pp. 468–473). New York: Garland Press.

Ferreira-Buckley, L., & Horner, W. B. (2001). Writing instruction in Great Britain: The eighteenth and nineteenth centuries. In J. J. Murphy (Ed.), *A short history of writing instruction: From ancient Greece to modern America* (pp. 173–212). Mahwah, NJ: Lawrence Erlbaum.

Fitzgerald, K. (2002). A rediscovered tradition: European pedagogy and composition in nineteenth-century normal schools. *College Composition and Communication, 3,* 224–250.

Gaillet, L. L. (Ed.). (1998a). *Scottish rhetoric and its influences*. Mahwah, NJ: Lawrence Erlbaum.

Gaillet, L. L. (1998b). George Jardine: The champion of the Scottish Commonsense School of Philosophy. *Rhetoric Society Quarterly, 28*(2), 37–53.

Gaillet, L. L., & Miller, T. P. (2001). Making use of the nineteenth century: The writings of Robert Connors and recent histories of rhetoric and composition. *Rhetoric Review, 31,* 147–157.

Garrett, M. (1999). Some elementary methodological reflections on the study of the Chinese rhetorical tradition. *International and Intercultural Communication Annual, 22,* 53–63.

Garrett, M. (2001). Chinese rhetoric. In T. O. Sloane (Ed.), *Encyclopedia of rhetoric* (pp. 89–92). Oxford, UK: Oxford University Press.

Gere, A. R. (1997). *Intimate practices: Literacy and cultural work in U.S. Women's Clubs, 1880–1920*. Urbana: University of Illinois Press.

Gifford, C. D. (1995). Frances Willard and the Woman's Christian Temperance Union's conversion to woman suffrage. In M. S. Wheeler (Ed.), *One woman, one vote: Rediscovering the Woman's Suffrage Movement* (pp. 117–133). Troutdale, OR: New Sage Press.

Golden, J., & Corbett, E. P. J. (1990). *The rhetoric of Blair, Campbell, and Whately*. Carbondale: Southern Illinois University Press.

Golden, J., & Corbett, E. P. J. (1968). *The rhetoric of Blair, Campbell, and Whately* (1st ed.). New York: Holt, Rinehart & Winston.

Goring, P. (2004). *The rhetoric of sensibility in eighteenth-century culture*. Cambridge, UK: Cambridge University Press.

Grasso, C. (1999). *A speaking aristocracy: Transforming public discourse in eighteenth-century Connecticut*. Chapel Hill: University of North Carolina Press.

Harris, S. (Ed.). (2004). *Blue pencils and hidden hands: Women editing periodicals, 1830-1910*. Boston: Northeastern University Press.

Hawes, C. (2005). *Mania and literary style: The rhetoric of enthusiasm from the Ranters to Christopher Smart*. Cambridge, UK: Cambridge University Press.

Herrick, J. (2005). *The history and theory of rhetoric* (3rd ed.). Boston: Allyn & Bacon.

Hobbs, C. (2002). *Rhetoric on the margins of modernity: Vico, Condillac, Monboddo*. Carbondale: Southern Illinois University Press.

Hobbs, C. (Ed.). (1995). *Nineteenth-century women learn to write*. Charlottesville: University Press of Virginia.

Hobbs, J. H. (1997). *"I sing for I cannot be silent": The feminization of American Hymnody, 1870–1920*. Pittsburgh, PA: University of Pittsburgh Press.

Holmes, D. G. (2005). Say what? Rediscovering Hugh Blair and the racialization of language, culture, and pedagogy in eighteenth-century rhetoric. In J. J. Royster & A. M. M. Simpkins (Eds.), *Calling cards: Theory and practice in the study of race, gender, and culture* (pp. 203–214). Albany: State University of New York Press.

Horner, W. B. (1990a). *The present state of scholarship in historical and contemporary rhetoric*. Columbia: University of Missouri Press.

Horner, W. B. (1990b). The roots of modern writing instruction: Eighteenth and nineteenth century Britain. *Rhetoric Review, 8,* 322–345.

Howard, R. M. (2006). *Native American languages, discourses, and rhetorics.* Retrieved June 25, 2006, from http://wrt-howard.syr.edu/Bibs/NativeAm.htm

Howell, W. S. (1971). *Eighteenth-century British logic and rhetoric.* Princeton, NJ: Princeton University Press.

Johnson, N. (2001). Nineteenth-century rhetoric. In T. O. Sloane (Ed.), *Encyclopedia of rhetoric* (pp. 518–527). Oxford, UK: Oxford University Press.

Johnson, N. (2002). *Gender and rhetorical space in American Life, 1866–1910.* Carbondale: Southern Illinois University Press.

Kates, S. (1997a). The embodied rhetoric of Hallie Quinn Brown. *College English, 59*(1), 59–71.

Kates, S. (1997b). Subversive feminism: The politics of correctness in Mary Augusta Jordan's correct writing and speaking (1904). *College Composition and Communication, 48*(4), 501–517.

Kates, S. (2001). *Activist rhetorics and American higher education, 1885–1937.* Carbondale: Southern Illinois University Press.

Kennedy, G. A. (1999). *Classical rhetoric & its Christian and secular tradition from ancient to modern times* (2nd ed.). Chapel Hill: University of North Carolina Press.

Knight, L. W. (1998). An authoritative voice: Jane Addams and the oratorical tradition. *Gender & History, 10,* 217.

Krishnaswamy, N. (2001). Indian rhetoric. In T. O. Sloane (Ed.), *Encyclopedia of rhetoric* (pp. 384–387). Oxford, UK: Oxford University Press.

L'Eplattenier, B., & Mastrangelo, L. (Eds.). (2004). *Historical studies of writing program administration: Individuals, communities, and the formation of a discipline.* West Lafayette, IN: Parlor Press.

Lindemann, E. (2005). *True and candid compositions: The lives and writings of Antebellum students at the University of North Carolina.* Retrieved June 25, 2006, from http://docsouth.unc.edu/true/intro/overview.html

Liu, Y. (1996). To capture the essence of Chinese rhetoric: An anatomy of a paradigm in comparative rhetoric. *Rhetoric Review, 14,* 318–335.

Logan, S. W. (Ed.). (1995). *With pen and voice: A critical anthology of nineteenth-century African-American women.* Carbondale: Southern Illinois University Press.

Logan, S. W. (1999). *"We are coming": The persuasive discourse of nineteenth-century black Women.* Carbondale: Southern Illinois University Press.

Lunsford, A. (Ed.). (1995). *Reclaiming rhetorica: Women in the rhetorical tradition.* Pittsburgh, PA: University of Pittsburg Press.

Lunsford, A., Hariman, R., Jarratt, S., Mao, L. M., & Royster, J. (Eds.). (in press). *Norton anthology of rhetoric and composition.*

Mattingly, C. (1998). *Well-tempered women: Nineteenth-century temperance rhetoric.* Carbondale: Southern Illinois University Press.

Mattingly, C. (2002). *Appropriate[ing] dress: Women's rhetorical style in nineteenth-century America.* Carbondale: Southern Illinois University Press.

Mattingly, C. (Ed.). (2001). *Water drops from women writers: A temperance reader.* Carbondale: Southern Illinois University Press.

McHenry, E. (2002). *Forgotten readers: Rediscovering the lost history of African American literary societies.* Durham, NC: Duke University Press.

McKenna, S. J. (2006). *Adam Smith: The rhetoric of propriety.* Albany: State University of New York Press.

Miller, S. (1998). *Assuming the positions: Cultural pedagogy and the politics of commonplace writing.* Pittsburgh, PA: University of Pittsburgh.

Miller, T. P. (1997). *The formation of college English: Rhetoric and belles lettres in the British cultural provinces.* Pittsburgh, PA: University of Pittsburgh Press.

Miranda, D. A. (2000). "A string of textbooks": Artifacts of composition pedagogy in Indian boarding schools. *Journal of Teaching Writing, 16*(2), 213–232.

Moran, M. G. (1994). *Eighteenth-century British and American rhetorics and rhetoricians.* Westport, CT: Greenwood Press. (Original work published 1753)

Moran, M. G., & Ballif, M. (2000). *Twentieth-century rhetorics and rhetoricians: critical studies and sources.* Westport, CT: Greenwood Press.

Mountford, R. (2003). *The gendered pulpit: Preaching in American Protestant spaces.* Carbondale: Southern Illinois University Press.

Murphy, J. J. (2001). (Ed.). *A short history of writing instruction: From ancient Greece to modern America.* Mahwah, NJ: Lawrence Erlbaum.

Olson, L. (2004). *Benjamin Franklin's vision of American community: A study of rhetorical iconology.* Columbia: University of South Carolina Press.

Paine, C. (1999). *The resistant writer: Rhetoric as immunity, 1850 to the present.* Albany: State University of New York Press.

Peaden, C. (1992). Understanding differently: Rereading Locke's essay concerning human understanding. *Rhetoric Society Quarterly, 22*(1), 75–90.

Potkay, A. (1994). *The fate of eloquence in the age of Hume.* Ithaca, NY: Cornell University Press.

Powell, M. (2002). Rhetorics of survivance: How American Indians use writing. *College Composition and Communication, 53,* 396–434.

Powell, M. (2004). Extending the hand of empire: American Indians and the Indian Reform Movement, a beginning. In K. Gilyard & V. Nunley (Eds.), *Rhetoric and ethnicity* (pp. 37–45). Portsmouth, NH: Boynton/Cook.

Ritchie, J., & Ronald, K. (Eds.). (2001). *Available means: An anthology of women's rhetoric(s).* Pittsburgh, PA: University of Pittsburgh Press.

Roberts-Miller, P. (2006). Agonism, wrangling, and John Quincy Adams. *Rhetoric Review, 25,* 141–161.

Rowland, J. T. (1998). *Swords in "myrtle dress'd": Towards a rhetoric of Sodom: Gay readings of homosexual politics and poetics in the eighteenth century.* Madison, NJ: Fairleigh Dickenson University Press.

Royster, J. J. (2000). *Traces of a stream: Literacy and social change among African-American women.* Pittsburgh, PA: University of Pittsburgh Press.

Royster, J. J. (Ed.). (1997). *Southern horrors and other writings: The anti-lynching campaign of Ida B. Wells, 1892–1900.* Boston: Bedford Books.

Russell, D. R. (2002). *Writing in the academic disciplines: A curricular history* (2nd ed.). Carbondale: Southern Illinois University Press.

Salvatori, M. R. (Ed.). (1996). *Pedagogy: Disturbing history, 1819–1929.* Pittsburgh, PA: University of Pittsburgh Press.

Schultz, L. M. (1999). *The young composers: Composition's beginnings in nineteenth-century schools.* Carbondale: Southern Illinois University Press.

Sloane, T. O. (2001). *Encyclopedia of rhetoric.* Oxford, UK: Oxford University Press.

Stewart, D. C. (1990). The nineteenth century. In W. B. Horner (Ed.), *The present state of historical and contemporary rhetoric* (pp. 151–186). Columbia: University of Missouri Press.

Stewart, D., & Stewart, P. L. (1997). *The life and legacy of Fred Newton Scott.* Pittsburgh, PA: University of Pittsburgh Press.

Sutherland, C. M. (2005). *The eloquence of Mary Astell.* Calgary, Alberta, Canada: University of Calgary Press.

Sutherland, C. M., & Sutcliffe, R. (Eds.). (1999). *The changing tradition: Women in the history of rhetoric.* Calgary, Alberta, Canada: University of Calgary Press.

Tonn, M. B. (1996). Militant motherhood: Labor's Mary Harris "Mother" Jones. *Quarterly Journal of Speech, 82,* 1–21.

Ulman, H. L. (1994). *Things, thoughts, words and actions: The problem of language in late eighteenth century British rhetorical theory.* Carbondale: Southern Illinois University Press.

Wall, C. S. (2006). *The prose of things: Transformations of description in the eighteenth century.* Chicago: University of Chicago Press.

Walmsley, P. (2003). *Locke's essay and the rhetoric of science.* London: Bucknell University Press.

Walzer, A. E. (2003). *George Campbell: Rhetoric in the age of Enlightenment.* Albany: State University of New York Press.

Wang, B. (2004). A survey of research in Asian rhetoric. *Rhetoric Review, 23,* 171–181.

Watson, M. (Ed.). (1999). *Lives of their own: Rhetorical dimensions in autobiographies of women activists.* Columbia: University of South Carolina Press.

Wells, S. (1996). Women write science: The case of Hannah Longshore. *College English, 58*(2), 176–191.

Wells, S. (2001). *Out of the dead house: Nineteenth-century women physicians and the writing of medicine.* Madison: University of Wisconsin Press.

Wertheimer, M. M. (Ed.). (1997). *Listening to their voices: The rhetorical activities of historical women.* Columbia: University of South Carolina Press.

Wright, E. A., & Halloran, S. M. (2001). From rhetoric to composition: The teaching of writing in America to 1900. In J. J. Murphy (Ed.), *A short history of writing instruction: From ancient Greece to modern America* (pp. 213–246). Mahwah, NJ: Lawrence Erlbaum.

Wyland, R. M. (2003). An archival study of rhetoric texts and teaching at the University of Oxford, 1785–1820. *Rhetorica, 21,* 175–195.

Zaeske, S. (1995). "The promiscuous audience": Controversy and emergence of the early woman's rights movement. *Quarterly Journal of Speech, 81,* 191–207.

5

Coping With Modernity

Strategies of 20th-Century Rhetorical Theory

JAMES ARNT AUNE

The problem for rhetorical theory after the birth of Enlightenment liberalism lies in the central role of moral autonomy in the emerging view of the liberal self. The very philosophy of liberal democracy itself was based on a fundamental distrust of persuasion. Once the autonomous individual rather than the family or community became the fundamental building block of politics, any effort to subvert that autonomy, whether through rhetoric or violence, came to be viewed as a "heteronomous imposition," as Immanuel Kant put it. For Kant, perhaps the most influential theorist of liberalism in the Western democracies, a normal adult is capable of full self-government in moral matters: "No authority external to ourselves is needed to constitute or inform us of the demands of morality. We can each know without being told what we ought

to do because moral requirements are requirements we impose on ourselves" (Schneewind, 1992, p. 309). "The starry heavens above me and the moral law within me" are fundamental anchors for the liberal self (Kant, 1788/1956, pp. 161–163). Any effort to persuade another to adopt a different moral path is likely to appeal to the human capacity for rationalization—exempting oneself from the plain, internally revealed universal law.

The rejection of rhetoric is implicit in Kant's ethical writings, but it becomes explicit in his work on aesthetics. In his *Critique of Judgment* (1790/1987), a major influence on the developing Romantic view of language and literature, Kant had condemned oratory for treating intellectual understanding as a kind of mere play (p. 190), and even a "dialectic that borrows from poetry only as much as the speaker needs in order to win over people's minds for his own advantage before they judge for themselves, and so make their judgment unfree" (p. 197). Kant's view of oratory was thus inextricably linked with his creation of a new idea of the liberal self as European societies were emerging from both stifling religious orthodoxy and absolutist political regimes. Kant put freedom at the heart of his theory of knowledge (*Critique of Pure Reason*), of ethics (*Critique of Practical Reason, Groundwork of the Metaphysics of Morals*), and of aesthetics (*Critique of Judgment*). Freedom, for Kant, above all means being free from outside influences—avoiding "heteronomy," the *nomos* or rule of the "other." The free autonomous subject must rationally choose the universal moral laws he gives to himself, carefully avoiding any rationalizations that might lead him to create exceptions or treat the other person as a means rather than an end. From Kant's universalizing deontological (emphasizing "duty," *deon*) ethics, then, the art of rhetoric was not only immoral but politically dangerous. As Bryan Garsten (2006) has argued recently, Kant, like Rousseau and Hobbes, crafted modern liberalism as a response to the rhetorical power of religious demagogues and revolutionary orators, seeking institutional means to contain the most dangerous political vice: "enthusiasm."

It may seem strange to begin a chapter on 20th-century rhetorical theory with Kant. The reason for my choice is that, painting with a broad brush, the differing projects of 20th-century theory can be categorized in terms of their reaction to the problem of rhetoric and autonomy identified by Kant, projects that I will identify as *modernist, antimodernist,* and *postmodernist.* One possible reaction to Kant's argument is to reject the notion of the self as autonomous and thus return to a communitarian view of ethics and politics (Tönnies, 2001), as advocated by Alasdair MacIntyre, Michael Sandel, and Charles Taylor in political philosophy, and most prominently in rhetorical studies by Richard Weaver (Young, 1995). The

antimodernist temptation is inherent in present-day theory, given the continuity of the rhetorical "tradition" between Athens and the present. The effort to construct a coherent narrative of rhetoric's birth, death, and resurrection is central to the antimodernist view. Preeminent *modernists* in the 20th-century tradition include Kenneth Burke, I. A. Richards, Chaim Perelman, and Lucie Olbrechts-Tyteca, all of whom sought a "new rhetoric" adapted to modernity and its economic, cultural, and political institutions. For these writers, the study of rhetoric furthers the goal of personal autonomy by freeing citizens from the bewitchments of language and ideology (Richards and Burke) and by enabling practical reasoning under conditions of uncertainty (Perelman and Olbrechts-Tyteca).

The Modernist intellectual revolution, then, had cast permanent suspicion on orators' "heteronomous impositions" on audiences' minds. But the Modernist revolution, as Robert Pippin (1999) has argued in his pathbreaking *Modernism as a Philosophical Problem,* generated its own reaction in the form of the unease of European intellectuals with scientific development, the new mass culture, and the autonomous self. Four "Masters of Suspicion"—Freud, Marx, Nietzsche, and Darwin—apparently dismantled the ego boundaries and rationality of the self, contending that the libido, the mode of production, the will to power, or the relentlessly selfish desire of genes to reproduce themselves were doing their work beneath the surface of the self-satisfied bourgeois consciousness. If Freud, Marx, and Darwin were committed to the development of rational, naturalistic morality, Nietzsche undercut the very prospect of rationality itself, with his view of knowledge as inevitably perspectival and driven by power (Ricoeur, 1970, p. 20). Kenneth Burke certainly took Marx and Freud seriously (and sparred with Darwinians on the full extent of our "motion"-based, animal natures), but by the century's end it was

Nietzsche who had emerged as the patron saint of a new *postmodernist* view of rhetoric energized by new technologies that promised not only new forms of argument and persuasion but also the end of the autonomous "humanist" self, as the human-machine interface promises to yield multiple species or multiple selves.

This chapter will unfold in the following way: First, I will discuss the problem of the historiography of rhetorical theory, suggesting that all we have at present is a set of competing narratives about the rhetorical tradition. Adding to my focus on the Kantian autonomous self, I propose a more sociologically driven account of changes in theorizing about rhetoric. The second section of the chapter provides an advanced introduction to the semantic, dramatistic, and argumentation traditions as exemplary of the modernist perspective. The third section identifies the development of an antimodernist rhetorical theory that imitates the communitarian turn in political theory. Finally, I identify both the main themes in postmodernist theory and engage in the risky practice of predicting where rhetorical theory might go from here. A few caveats to the reader: Rhetorical theory is a huge subject, so I have limited my focus to those writers who have created a systematic view of rhetoric. Also, although my own modernist sympathies are perhaps already apparent, this is a work of exposition and, perhaps, immanent critique rather than an effort at advocacy. If I do have a theoretical agenda, it is to persuade students of rhetoric to take the problem of historiography more seriously, especially as historiography interacts with social theory. As I suggest in my criticism of the antimodernists, the current rush to connect rhetoric to "culture" and "cultural studies" ignores the fact that culture is not exactly the same as society, and that we need to pay attention to sociological forces such as marketization, globalization, and secularization that lead to social strain—social strain that both constrains public argument and opens up new rhetorical spaces and new rhetorical agents.[1]

SEARCHING FOR RHETORIC: MOURNING AND MELANCHOLIA

The journal *Philosophy and Rhetoric* was founded at Penn State in the annus mirabilis 1968. Two articles from the first volume represent ongoing preoccupations of rhetorical theorists: the definition of "rhetoric" and "rhetorical studies" and the issue of the ongoing "viability" of the rhetorical tradition itself.

Lloyd F. Bitzer's (1968) "The Rhetorical Situation" defined the nature and scope of rhetoric as an art of framing messages in response to specific exigences (states of imperfection marked by urgency) in the public world. Like Aristotle, however, Bitzer emphasized the notion of "available" means of persuasion: material and ideological-emotional factors (corresponding to Aristotle's nonartistic and artistic proofs, respectively) constrained the audience's potential response. Richard Vatz (1973) responded to Bitzer in an equally classic article, "The Myth of the Rhetorical Situation," in which he contended that Bitzer underestimated the power of the rhetor to create the very meaning of the situation itself. Scott Consigny (1974) continued the debate by trying to split the difference between what might now be called the "realism" of Bitzer and the "postmodernism" of Vatz by proposing a more dialectical view of the interaction of rhetor and context and by recovering the classical rhetorical tool of "topical" invention as a way for rhetors to manage indeterminate contexts. Another important essay, published the year before Bitzer's, was Robert L. Scott's "On Viewing Rhetoric as Epistemic" (1967). Scott's essay approached the world-creating power of rhetoric in a manner different from Vatz, grounding it in a uniquely modernist-existentialist vision of the autonomous self whose god terms are tolerance, will, and responsibility (p. 16).

The Bitzer-Vatz antinomy of rhetor and situation proved to have considerable staying power as a sort of "essentially contested" problem in rhetorical theory. Richard Cherwitz and James Hikins (1985) continued to defend a realist epistemology for rhetoric against Barry Brummett's (1981) strong relativism. The postmodern turn of rhetorical studies added Nietzsche's perspectivism to the debate on rhetorical epistemology (Whitson & Poulakos, 1993). A mutation of the dispute continued with the Big Rhetoric/Little Rhetoric distinction developed by Edward Schiappa (2001). The "cash value" of the ongoing debate seems to lie in competing institutional implications: Should researchers narrow the scope of rhetorical analysis to public deliberation such as political and legal rhetoric? Is rhetorical analysis simply one more tool in the arsenal of cultural studies? How do English "rhet-comp" scholars define the nature and scope of their work in relation to Communication (and occasionally political science) scholars? Will we ever have a new systematic theory of rhetoric comparable with those of Aristotle, Cicero/Quintilian, or George Campbell, or should we continue to pursue "middle-range" theories of the rhetoric of science, of political rhetoric, or visual rhetoric?

A second essay in the 1968 volume of *Philosophy and Rhetoric* pursued the problem of the historiography of rhetoric in terms of "systems of rhetoric" closely related to the dominant problems of their historical periods. Douglas Ehninger (1968) called the classical period of rhetoric "grammatical," an act of naming the parts of rhetoric as a social practice. The 18th century (George Campbell, Hugh Blair) created a "psychological" system in response to changing views of the human mind. Finally, the 20th-century system of rhetoric was "sociological," concerned with problems of the social order, identifying barriers to social harmony and proposing

better communication as an ameliorative strategy. Ehninger's argument clearly was intended as a brief sketch of a historical method; in other work, he identified four patterns or "dominant trends" in 18th-century theory: classicism, psychological-epistemological theory, elocutionism, and belles lettres. As Carole Blair (1992), the primary critic of Ehninger's work, contended, the warrant for singling out these specific historical periods— even if intuitively persuasive—was never spelled out by Ehninger (p. 412). I am less interested at the moment in Ehninger's method than in what is not stated in the essay. Ehninger, one of the most influential rhetoricians of his time, *did not consider classical rhetorical theory in any sense normative for rhetorical theorizing in the 20th century.* The same is true of Scott's work on rhetoric-as-epistemic. Ernest Bormann (1972), another influential theorist of the time, developed "fantasy-theme analysis," and, later, "symbolic convergence" theory from current psychological theory and from sociological work on small groups and not from classical rhetoric. While I was a "speech" major in college during 1971–1975, and an occasional visitor to department colloquia on rhetoric at the University of Minnesota during that time, the heritage of classical rhetoric was viewed as something a knowledgeable rhetorical scholar should know about, but it was about as relevant to contemporary theorizing and rhetorical criticism as, say, Aristotle's *Poetics* is to the analysis of Faulkner or Joyce in a department of English. The next generation of rhetorical theorists, including figures as diverse as Thomas B. Farrell (1993), Michael Leff (1998), Robert Hariman (2003), C. Jan Swearingen (1991), Edward Schiappa (2001), and Michael McGee (1985) placed classical rhetorical theory at the center of their work. Something had clearly stalled in the development of rhetorical theory after 1969 that required a return to historical foundations. This change reflected the collapse of the

Deweyan-progressive and Modernist vision of the earlier generation. It also reflected growing disillusion with the liberal view of the autonomous self. The rhetorical tradition's connection to an earlier view of the self as embedded in communal practice made it a likely place to look for scholarly and practical alternatives to a discredited liberalism.

THE ANTIMODERNIST MOMENT

Ehninger argued that 20th-century rhetorical theory responded to an overwhelming sense of crisis. Western Imperialism, Fascism, and Communism led to two World Wars and one long Cold War. New communication technologies, first radio and then television, appeared to create both new democratic possibilities and more powerful demagogues. Class struggle in the Western democracies yielded the post–World War II "social democratic compromise," which brought prosperity to millions and yet seemed to burn itself out in unresponsive bureaucracies and fiscal crisis by the 1970s. What was once called the "Third World" erupted first in movements for national liberation and then in genocidal wars, unimaginable human misery, and the battle for control of petroleum. The Western Left, formerly unified around questions of class inequality, fragmented into various forms of identity politics. Race and ethnicity, gender, and sexual orientation defined the battlegrounds of both electoral politics and academic inquiry. Meanwhile, radical libertarian views of government and neoconservative views of foreign policy passed from well-funded think tanks to the halls of power (Aune, 2001). Increases in infant mortality, like the new legitimacy of torture, appeared simply as collateral damage in the inevitable march of the "Washington Consensus" to world domination and as, perhaps, the only realistic alternative to "Islamo-fascism." Radical academic inquiry outside the policy sciences proceeded in its quest to capture the commanding heights of literature departments, but was never more irrelevant in its actual public influence. Not only was the center not holding, but the very notion of a center seemed to be a dangerous Western invention.

At various points in this grim narrative, rhetorical theorists proposed historical accounts of the causes of current malaise and, perhaps for the first time since the Renaissance, proposed that a return to the centrality of rhetoric in education and public life would go a long way toward improving that malaise. Whether the slender reed of rhetorical theory could bear such social, political, and cultural weight was another issue. Wayne Booth (1974) traced the twin forces of scientism and irrationalism back to Descartes's emphasis on systematic doubt and self-evidence (pp. 133–134). Perelman (1982) added the capitalist demand for quantitative evidence, Peter Ramus, and the Protestant emphasis on individual salvation to the list of causes of the decline of rhetoric and of the modern crisis (pp. 3–7). Richard Weaver (1948) argued that the cultural cohesiveness of the West was dealt a fatal blow from realism's defeat by nominalism in the 12th century (pp. 3–17). Richard McKeon (1971) blamed the Church (p. 49). W. S. Howell (1965) blamed the displacement of artistic proof by the inartistic proof valued by scientific argument (p. 292). Thomas B. Farrell (1993) blamed the loss of the Aristotelian political-moral-rhetorical vision.

The list could go on. All these writers shared a sense that modernity suffers from a split of cultural visions: between a scientific and technological worldview reluctant to discuss problems of ethics and value and a romantic worldview in which individual self-expression seems to undercut the possibility of rational public argument. Political thinkers as diverse as Hannah Arendt, Leo Strauss, Alasdair MacIntyre, and Ronald Beiner tell a similar story. It is, as Terry Eagleton (1990) puts it, a story about a time when

the three great questions of philosophy—
what can we know? what ought we to do?
what do we find attractive?—were not as
yet fully distinguishable from one another. A
society, that is to say, where the three mighty
regions of the cognitive, the ethico-political,
and the libidinal-aesthetic were still to a
large degree intermeshed. (p. 366)

Although Eagleton fails to connect his story
to rhetoric (as he did in his earlier work on
Walter Benjamin), it doesn't take much intellectual labor to see that his three mighty
regions were once unified in the classical
rhetorical tradition. The Modernist emphasis
on the autonomous self or the "self-defining
subject," had displaced the classical figure of
the orator-statesman from the center of public
life (Taylor, 1975, pp. 17–18).

Classical rhetorical theory constructed a
vision of its audience as participating in the
crafting of civic virtue under the guidance of
the orator-statesman. Rhetorical theory was
not so much a distinct form of intellectual
inquiry as it was the practical part of a
political-legal education. Politics, in turn, was
not conceived as a separate "sphere" from the
social or familial, but as the place where the
human *telos* was to be achieved.

The ideal orator was conceived as the
person of such broad knowledge and

> general competency that he could apply the
> accumulated wisdom of the culture to any
> particular case in a sufficiently logic fashion
> to move his hearers' minds (*logos*), and with
> enough emotional force to engage their pas-
> sions (*pathos*). The name given to the third
> of the traditional modes of rhetorical
> appeal, *ethos,* underlines the importance of
> the orator's mastery of the cultural heritage;
> through the power of his logical and emo-
> tional appeals, he became a kind of living
> embodiment of the cultural heritage, a voice
> of such apparent authority that the word
> spoken by this person was the word of com-
> munal wisdom, a word to be trusted for the
> weight of the person who spoke it and the

> tradition he spoke for. (Halloran, 1976,
> pp. 235–236)

American education was designed to fulfill
this cultural vision (Halloran, 1982). It placed
debate at the heart of the curriculum, both in
the classroom and in extracurricular activity,
enabling not only civic leaders but also ordinary citizens to argue about matters of considerable complexity, as illustrated by widespread
newspaper coverage of the constitutional ratification debate, pored over in taverns and
other public settings across the early republic,
and by the high eloquence of Webster,
Calhoun, Clay, Douglas, and Lincoln over
states' rights and slavery. The rise of the
research university, the land-grant emphasis
on useful arts, and, eventually, the massive
increase in the size of undergraduate enroll-
ments throughout the United States after
World War II made the older civic education
seem both quaint and fiscally inconceivable.

The shift to individual needs as the focus of
higher education paralleled the Enlightenment
and Modernist emphasis on the self-defining
subject. "Man comes to know himself by
expressing and hence clarifying what he is and
recognizing himself in this expression. The
specific property of human life is to culminate
in self-awareness through expression" (Taylor,
1975, p. 17). If self-expression rather than
clear communication or deliberation on public
questions is the highest purpose of language,
then rhetoric must yield to poetics as the chief
focus of education in language: "The human
center of gravity is on the point of shifting from
logos to poeisis" (p. 18). Art becomes the
primary means of survival in a disenchanted
world. "Literature" becomes exclusively
imaginative literature, which in turn is the
expression of a "people's" soul. Paradoxically,
then, the seeming antinomy between scientism
and modern aestheticism disappears in their
similar view of public discourse: Truth consists
of perfect transparency, whether of scientific
results, poetic vision, or the general will.

Rhetoric, in the classical sense, has to disappear, replaced either by Gouldner's (1979) culture of critical discourse (CCD) or by the largely visual and emotional language of mass democracy.

University of Chicago English professor Richard Weaver (1910–1963) crafted his rhetorical theory as response to mass democracy. He viewed the study of rhetoric as a cure for the cultural crisis engendered by science, industrial capitalism, and "mass" education and communication. Weaver taught at Texas A&M University from 1937 to 1939, where he

> encountered a rampant philistinism, abetted by technology, large-scale organization, and a complacent acceptance of success as the goal of life. Moreover, I was here forced to see that the lion of applied science and the lamb of the humanities were not going to lie down together in peace, but that the lion was going to devour the lamb unless there was a very stern keeper of order. (Foss, Foss, & Trapp, 2003, p. 157)

As he drove back to College Station in the fall of 1939, he realized he didn't have to go back and instead turned around and enrolled at Louisiana State University, another outpost of Southern Agrarianism, for his Ph.D. Weaver worked for the rest of his life at the University of Chicago, teaching primarily lower-level writing courses (for which he enthusiastically volunteered).

A key phrase in his defense of rhetoric is "Language Is Sermonic" (Weaver, 2001). Weaver criticizes the social-scientific, journalistic, and general semantics view that you can have neutral, "objective," "scientific" communication. All acts of communication take a point of view and attempt to persuade. Before the invention of the modern, "objective" press (see Schudson, 1980), newspapers were openly partisan, reinforcing a notion of the citizen as part of a community, a good party member rather than the individual, autonomous

"informed citizen" that became the ideal of 20th-century liberalism (Schudson, 1998). Weaver shows here an odd sympathy with what would come to be called post-structuralism. Weaver, following Plato or Aristotle, would contend that post-structuralists are on a dangerous path when they provide a rhetoric without an accompanying dialectic.

Healthy cultures have a balance of dialectic and rhetoric.

> Dialectic is abstract reasoning on the basis of propositions; rhetoric is the relation of the terms of these to the existential world in which facts are regarded with sympathy and are treated with that kind of historical understanding and appreciation which lie outside the dialectical process. (Weaver, 1995, p. 56)

Education or journalism that is only negative, always questioning assumptions is destructive. Ruthless philosophical criticism can undermine a culture, so, for example, Athens was justified in putting Socrates to death. One influential theme in American conservative rhetoric since Weaver's death has been the concept of the "adversary culture," identified first by Spiro Agnew as a northeastern elite that controls the universities and the press. Perhaps, at the highest level of abstraction, one causal explanation for conservative political success since Reagan has been that "Red" states continue to speak the language of rhetoric while "Blue" states are dominated by a CCD. CCD, unfortunately, functions as pure dialectic, in Weaver's terms, lacking a strong sense of rhetoric.

Weaver's insistence on the availability of a nonperspectival truth and on the need for a homogeneous traditional community have made him an outlier among 20th-century rhetoricians, yet similar arguments—less tainted by Southern racism—can be found in those influenced by Alasdair MacIntyre, Charles Taylor, Michael Sandel, Mary Ann Glendon, and other currently popular "communitarians" who reject liberalism's focus on the autonomous self. No matter what one thinks of Weaver's politics, his definition of rhetoric from his essay on the *Phaedrus* remains inspiring in an age of negative attack ads and unprecedented mendacity by our political leaders:

> So rhetoric at its truest seeks to perfect men by showing them better versions of themselves, links in that chain leading up to the ideal, which only the intellect can apprehend and only the soul have affection for. This is the truly justified affection of which no one can be ashamed, and he who feels no influence of it is truly outside the communion of minds. Rhetoric appears, finally, as a means by which the impulse of the soul to be ever moving is redeemed. (Weaver, 1953, p. 25)

The perennial appeal of the antimodernist view, like traditionalist conservatism or communitarianism, is that the autonomous self is prone to loneliness. The paradox of the antimodernist position is that it can only be defended from within a modernist society— Richard Weaver praised the values of the Old South from his urban, Northern setting at the University of Chicago. Alasdair MacIntyre (1984) looks back to St. Benedict in hopes of restoring community (chap. 18). Even if the communal virtues of such past or presently isolated communities were retrievable in any institutional way, the antimodernist arguments themselves speak to the modernist autonomous self. How, other than putting everyone under a massive "veil of ignorance," might we prevent the autonomous self from criticizing the heteronomy of a restored community? A way out of modernist loneliness is the act of civic participation, extending one's own act of self-government to a larger community of autonomous selves who respect the force of the better argument.

MODERNISM I: THE ARGUMENTATION TRADITION

It would be inaccurate to say that one cannot construct a rhetorical theory on the basis of modernist assumptions. In the next two sections of this chapter, I will discuss the works of Chaim Perelman/Lucie Olbrechts-Tyteca (hereafter P/O-T) and Kenneth Burke, respectively. P/O-T and Burke both accept the value of individual autonomy and seek to preserve it against uniquely 20th-century threats: the positivist assault on values and rational argument, totalitarian politics, and, at least in Burke's case, the dominance of technology over traditional work and communicative practices. P/O-T preserve the Kantian emphasis on the rational subject, while Burke identifies with Marx, Freud, and Darwin by identifying unconscious threats to rationality, coming from ideological rationalizations of class power, unconscious drives toward sex and death, and the remainders of our primate heritage encoded in our bodies. Unlike the post-structuralists, however, Burke does agree with Freud's phrase "*Wo Es war, Soll Ich werden*"—Where It (the Id) was, there shall the Ego develop, meaning that by understanding unconscious threats to rationality, as well as their exploitation in literary and political rhetoric, we can become less prone to ideological manipulation and set about the task of purifying our societies from war (*ad bellum purificandum*). Both Burke and P/O-T, however, remain solidly grounded in the CCD by shifting the focus of their rhetorical theories away from the orator-statesman and toward the informed citizen as rhetorical critic.

The quest to create the "informed citizen" was the main project of the field of "Speech" as it was created in the United States in the early 20th century. Although scholarship on the history of rhetorical theory appeared in the main speech journals such as the *Quarterly Journal of Speech* from early on, the average Speech department in the United States was grounded in practice, specifically the practice of oral communication. Students majoring in Speech would take courses in voice and articulation, acting, speech correction, public speaking, drama, debate, and public address. In the late 1920s, under the influence of the Progressive movement generally and John Dewey in particular, Speech departments began emphasizing "discussion" as a complement to debate as a tool for public inquiry. Speech teachers took on a larger role in creating community forums, often on the radio, to enhance civic dialogue (Keith, 2007, pp. 157–164). By the 1970s, however, courses in discussion were supplanted by sociologically based courses in small group communication, while debate remained an important activity in American high schools and colleges. Some elite universities, such as Harvard or Dartmouth, have kept lavishly funded debate programs down to the present day, even though they have largely eliminated any faculty positions in speech or communication. It was the dominant association of rhetoric in speech departments with debate as a practical skill that connected American rhetoricians in that tradition with the work of Stephen Toulmin, as well as P/O-T. Toulmin (1958), like P/O-T, sought an alternative to logical positivism in identifying the nature of rationality in practical contexts such as the courtroom, the legislative assembly, or even academic discussion.

The key question the argumentation theorists faced was this: In a pluralistic democracy with differing religious and moral traditions among the citizenry, what would constitute reasonable standards for public argument? In Aristotelian terms, what set of beliefs, values, and goals might serve as major premises for enthymemes about public action (from welfare reform to war against Iraq)? What is the nature of "public reason"? P/O-T (1969) define the study of argumentation as "the study of the discursive techniques allowing us to induce or to increase the mind's adherence to the theses presented for its assent" (p. 4).

P/O-T (1969) contend that a standard for rational and ethical argument can be found in the interplay between the Universal and Particular Audiences for a message. The Universal Audience consists of those who are competent and reasonable, yet each speaker has a different conception of the universal audience, as do different cultures and time periods (p. 33). A rational argument is what the audience happens to accept as reasonable at any given time. It is still debatable whether or not P/O-T present a culturally relativistic view of rationality or if their notion of a universal audience implies the Kantian principle of universalizability as a basis for the ethical evaluation of rhetorical practices. A modernist liberal like myself would probably try to split the difference between these two arguments by contending that a liberal society—a society with free (yet regulated) markets, freedom of speech and press, free elections, and the rule of law has a built-in recovery mechanism for bad decisions. As the Nobel-prize-winning development economist Amartya Sen writes in *Development as Freedom* (2000), after studying the history of famines throughout the world, no society with free speech, a free press, and free elections has ever experienced a famine—because famines are caused not so much by lack of food as by the concentration of political power in the hands of an elite.

More specifically, argumentation theorists such as P/O-T and Toulmin reacted against three trends in 20th-century philosophy: *scientism* or *positivism*—the idea that only scientifically or empirically verifiable statements are true; *emotivism*—the idea that value judgments are mere assertions of "taste" or "power" rather than "good reasons"; and *motivism*—the idea (from Marx and Freud) that there is always a "hidden motive" behind what we say (Booth, 1974).

Argumentation requires studying the relationship among logic (the internal structural validity of formal or informal arguments, without reference to an audience), dialectic (the structuring of the argumentative process), and rhetoric (ways of relating a controversy to a particular audience in a particular social and political setting) (Wenzel, 1990). Whereas classical and Renaissance theorists of reasoning had radically separated logic, dialectic, and rhetoric, P/O-T's radical move was to unify them under the broader theory of argumentation, contending, for example, that a philosophical text could just as easily be studied rhetorically as a political speech. They argue that philosophy emerged out of the epideictic genre of oratory, which seeks to strengthen a consensus around certain values (P/O-T, 1969, pp. 48–51).

Other recurring topics of argumentation research included a study of argument patterns or strategies that cut across many controversies. For example, Douglas Walton (1992a, 1992b) has devoted books to specific appeals, such as "slippery slope" arguments, emotional appeals, appeals to authority, and so on, trying to identify the logical structure of the arguments and their potential weaknesses, rather than simply labeling them as fallacies, which traditional logic texts did. Argumentation as a subfield of rhetoric also includes a number of empirical qualitative or even quantitative studies of how couples, groups, and organizations engage in reason giving and decision making (see O'Keefe, 2003).

A common thread in argumentation theory is the effort to make the dialectical (procedural) aspects of controversy more explicit, helping advocates identify exactly where and how disagreement takes place. At the heart of the *New Rhetoric*, for example, is this scheme identifying key parts of a debate. One reason why many American students have found it difficult to follow the *New Rhetoric* is that its examples of practical argument are either dated or, more often, so limited to European politics and culture that they are difficult to understand. I have used the contemporary abortion controversy to illustrate P/O-T's method.

The starting point for analyzing argumentation is in locating the "agreements" that serve as premises (P/O-T, 1969, pp. 65–74). Agreements are about the following:

1. *Facts:* When established, they are by definition withdrawn from argumentation. "When does life begin?" (fertilization, "ensoulment" or "quickening," brain waves?)

2. *Truths:* Complex relations among facts (a theory of causation, for instance). Would a total abortion ban increase unsafe, 'back alley' abortions? Do parental notification laws simply postpone abortions to the third trimester?

3. *Presumptions:*

   a. What counts as "normal" behavior or expectations? Default rules in software programs are a kind of presumption.

   b. What is likely to be true in the absence of proof to the contrary?

   c. Institutional rules, for example, "innocent until proven guilty" under an adversarial justice system (the United States), or the way Congress has determined that the burden of proof falls on the employer in race/sex discrimination cases.

   d. Unwarranted burden shifting or inability to agree on where to set presumption creates unresolvable controversies. Burden shifting, or the fallacy of ignorance ("I'm right because you can't prove I'm not") is a major problem in public discourse. One silly example is the following statement by the Rev. Jerry Falwell: Jesus Christ favored the death penalty. On the cross, Falwell says, He could have spoken up: "If there ever was a platform for our Lord to condemn capital punishment, that was it. He did not" (Andersen, 1983, p. 36). To return to the example of abortion, Justice Blackmun's majority opinion in *Roe v. Wade* is a remarkable example of how an advocate can seize presumption. After listing a number of groups opposed to or supporting abortion rights, Blackmun concludes, "We need not resolve the difficult question of when life begins. When those trained in the respective disciplines of medicine, philosophy, and theology are unable to arrive at any consensus, the judiciary, at this point in the development of man's knowledge, is not in a position to speculate as to the answer" (*Roe v. Wade*, p. 160). In other words, the burden of proof is on those who would define life as beginning at conception. Blackmun may have chosen an effective strategy for his strictly legal argument, but it is clear that this particular problem of burden of proof and presumption is what continues to dog the controversy some 35 years later.

In addition to identifying the structure of the "real" for both sides, P/O-T then suggest identifying common or differing values or value hierarchies in play in the debate. Values may be abstract or concrete (P/O-T, 1969, pp. 77–79). Edmund Burke famously contended, in *Reflections on the Revolution in France*, that the French revolutionaries espoused the meaningless abstraction of Liberty, Equality, Fraternity, while all England knows what "the rights of Englishmen" are, as embodied in traditional texts, rituals, and legal practices. Proabortion advocates may argue at both the abstract and concrete levels: the defense of "reproductive freedom" or the health risks associated with illegal abortions ("No More Coat Hangers!"). Antiabortion advocates tend to avoid abstract "rights talk," and focus instead on the humanity of the fetus, often as illustrated by close-up color photographs. Some moderates on both sides have argued that the constitutional value of federalism or states' rights means that the controversy should have been decided by the individual states (Ely, 1973).

Finally, the analyst of a controversy can identify *Loci* (highly general preferences that serve as guides to choice, or recurrent argument patterns) (P/O-T, 1969, pp. 83–99):

1. A locus is often a condensed *maxim*—an embodiment of common sense: "Least said, soonest mended" (but also "Nothing ventured, nothing gained"). Love maxims are often interestingly contradictory: "Absence makes the heart grow fonder," yet "Out of sight, out of mind" is true as well.

2. The locus of *quantity* is a utilitarian, "greatest good of the greatest number" argument: A recent global study of women's health has demonstrated that the actual rate of abortions remains constant worldwide, even when comparing countries where abortion is illegal to where abortion is legal (Sedgh, Henshaw, Singh, Aahman, & Shah, 2007).

3. The locus of *quality* often is used to combat quantitative arguments, emphasizing the uniqueness and irreplaceability of a single thing: "Thank God my Mom didn't abort me" is a popular T-shirt among conservative college students. A related locus is the locus of *the person*: the importance of the autonomy, dignity, and self-worth of the individual. Massachusetts congressman Barney Frank has effectively countered the antiabortion movement's use of the locus of quality and the person by arguing, "Republican respect for life begins at conception and ends at birth."

4. The locus of the *existent* is used to contend that what is possible is better—"A bird in the hand is worth two in the bush." Some moderate pro-life activists have argued for a compromise between the two sides of the controversy by allowing abortions only in the first trimester.

Other applications of the loci in the analysis of public policy argument include J. Robert Cox's (1982) discussion of the "locus of the irreparable," or James Arnt Aune's discussion of the "locus of the inevitable" in current discussions of technology. Jean Goodwin (2007) has identified 13 major loci in the U.S. Supreme Court decisions on free speech in the 20th century, including the "slippery slope" and "chilling effect" loci.

In general, then, P/O-T, like other members of the argumentation tradition in 20th-century rhetorical theory, are committed to the modernist principle of preserving autonomy by enabling both audiences and advocates to develop a clearer view of what is happening in a public controversy. This focus on procedural rationality fits well within the tradition of classical political liberalism, contending that no agreement on ultimate ends is possible in a democratic society, yet an overlapping consensus on facts and values may enable rational decision making across different communities (Rawls, 1993). As I noted earlier, following Robert Pippin (1999), another strain in philosophical modernism displayed discontent with liberalism, contending that it was unaware of its own status as an ideology (pp. 40–41). Marx, Freud, and Darwin came along to unsettle the liberal, autonomous self by discovering a political, sexual, and animal unconscious in human beings. Kenneth Burke attempted to preserve the practical insights of classical rhetoric while integrating the works of these Masters of Suspicion into a late modernist rhetorical theory.

MODERNISM II: KENNETH BURKE AND THE DRAMATIC SELF

One major critique of the argumentation tradition in rhetorical studies is that even though it bases rationality on society and culture, it is unable to account for many features of modern mass politics. It presumes common ground among participants (agreement on facts, truths, presumptions) of the sort you might have in an appellate court or the Senate rather than the take-no-prisoners negative campaigning of the sort that was common in 19th-century America and has reached its highest development in the age of Fox News and Karl Rove. Henry Adams's famous comment that politics is "the systematic organization of hatreds" has never seemed more true. Although the abortion controversy can be analyzed in argumentation terms, as I did above, the argumentation perspective does not quite capture the meaning of the deep-seated

emotions a discussion of abortion evokes. A successful political campaign, whether in a democratic or totalitarian society, requires two skills: an ability to manipulate deep-seated irrationalities in the public and the ability to construct a simple, coherent political narrative with readily identifiable heroes and villains. The prominent political psychologists Solomon, Greenberg, and Pyszczynski have performed a series of studies demonstrating that audience members who have thoughts of their own death, especially if triggered unconsciously, are more likely to find what the psychologists call "worldview defense" persuasive. Even subtle reminders of 9/11 awakened unconscious thoughts in audience members that later affected their willingness to endorse Bush Administration policy. They concluded that Bush's popularity was sustained by mortality reminders. As John Judis (2007) summarizes,

> The psychologists concluded in a paper published after the election that the government terror warnings, the release of Osama bin Laden's video on October 29, and the Bush campaign's reiteration of the terrorist threat (Cheney on election eve: "If we make the wrong choice, then the danger is that we'll get hit again") were integral to Bush's victory over Kerry. "From a terror management perspective," they wrote, "the United States" electorate was exposed to a wide-ranging multidimensional mortality salience induction. (p. 19)

If a gripping drama associated with strong emotions such as fear and anger can trump a reasoned argument, what is the role of rhetoric? Cicero or Richard Weaver would have had no trouble with Bush administration rhetoric about the war on terror because of their rejection of the autonomous self as the basis of politics. As William Lewis (1987) has written, the success of Ronald Reagan can be explained by his mastery of a simple core narrative: "America is a chosen nation, grounded in its families and neighborhoods, and driven inevitably forward by its heroic working people toward a world of freedom and economic progress unless blocked by moral or military weakness" (p. 297). Like any "myth" it is "widely believed, generally unquestioned, and clearly pedagogical." The modernist liberal, however, seems to have nowhere to go. Kenneth Burke's theory of dramatism seems to provide a way out for the liberal modernist, provided that the study of rhetoric includes unconscious appeals as well as argument.

Kenneth Burke (1897–1994) grew up in Pittsburgh, Pennsylvania, where he was the boyhood friend of Malcolm Cowley, the noted American literary critic. Burke briefly attended Columbia and Ohio State but never earned a college degree. He was part of the Greenwich Village bohemian literary scene in the 1920s, where he worked as a journalist and wrote poetry and short stories (*The Complete White Oxen*, 1968a) as well as one novel, *Towards a Better Life*. In the late 1920s, he bought a farm in Andover, New Jersey, where he continued to live, without electricity or other modern amenities, for the rest of his life, a sign of his later emphasis on technology rather than capitalism as the main destroyer of modern civilization (Selzer, 1997).

Like many American writers of the 1930s, Burke was a Communist fellow traveler. He attended the Communist Writer's Congress in 1935, where he delivered an interesting paper titled "Revolutionary Symbolism in America," proposing a "red rhetoric," and discussing the limited rhetorical appeal for Americans in being called "workers" (Burke, 1997). He was booed but remained sympathetic to Communism well into the 1950s. Almost all his key works are now available in paperback from the University of California Press, but as Edward Schiappa and Mary Keehner (1991) have painstakingly demonstrated, many are Burke's "edited" versions from the 1950s, with some interesting pro-Communist parts left out. His major works of the 1930s are *Counter-Statement*

(1931/1968b), important for its discussion of poetic form and his introduction of rhetoric as a means of cultural analysis; *Permanence and Change* (1935/1984b), a critique of positivist social science, and an introduction to his method of "perspective by incongruity," a classically "modernist" use of juxtaposition of opposing concepts to create new meaning, for example, "the bureaucratization of the imaginative" or "trained incapacity"; and *Attitudes Toward History* (1937/1984a), his most explicitly Marxist work, which takes a rhetorical view of historical development, introducing his concepts of the tragic and comic frames. *The Philosophy of Literary Form* (1941/1973), still one of his most widely read works, contains the influential essay on the rhetoric of Hitler's *Mein Kampf*.

After working as a drug addiction researcher and teaching briefly at the University of Chicago, Burke took a teaching position at Bennington College, where he taught from 1943 to 1961. He was denied a teaching position at the University of Washington in 1953, because of academic McCarthyism. Burke's interest in rhetoric and in history led him to be marginalized in the academic climate of the 1950s, which was dominated by the "New Criticism," the idea that literature should be studied as autonomous objects, independent of historical context. His two most important works are *A Grammar of Motives* (1945/1969a) and *A Rhetoric of Motives* (1950/1969b). During this time, he received his greatest recognition in the fields of Speech and Sociology. He never published the third volume of his trilogy, *A Symbolic of Motives*, although *The Rhetoric of Religion* (1961/1970) and *Language as Symbolic Action* (1966) continued to develop his thought. A minor and rather incoherent work, *Dramatism and Development*, appeared in 1972. The Parlor Press has recently published his *Symbolic of Motives* (2007b) as well as *Burke on Shakespeare* (2007a). As literary studies became more theoretically oriented in the 1980s, Burke was recognized belatedly as an important figure. "Reader-response" criticism and the

New Historicism, perhaps the most enduring of the new movements in literary studies, claimed him as an important precursor. He was even awarded the National Medal of Arts and Letters by President Reagan in 1981.

It is difficult to pigeonhole Burke in terms of any overarching -ism, but there are some clear, if conflicting, influences on his work. Burke is above all an American thinker, in the tradition of Emerson, William James, John Dewey, and Thorstein Veblen. His fascination with problems of communication in a pluralistic society continues a distinctively American preoccupation. He is influenced by Marx, in that he is critical of capitalism, and of the various devices capitalism uses to make our social order appear "natural," but as time goes on he sees "technology" as the chief culprit for social disorder. His insistence that hierarchy and "social mystery" are inevitable, given our natures as symbol-using animals, is a persuasive refutation of classical Marxism. He is influenced by Freud, in his interest in the unconscious, "identification," "projection," and the bodily roots of consciousness. He is influenced by Aristotle, especially Aristotle's *Rhetoric* and the notion of the "entelechy." It could be argued, however, that he is really a Platonist at heart, concerned with unmasking rhetoric and directing his readers' eyes to a transcendent realm of "tolerance and contemplation." There is a common tendency at the present time to turn Burke into a poststructuralist, but his Aristotelianism and Freudo-Marxist insistence on the importance of "matter" (what he calls "recalcitrance") suggest otherwise.

Burke's hope is to expand the traditional realm of literary criticism into a sociorhetorical analysis of the sources of conflict in modern society. A representative Burkean argument is this one, from *Permanence and Change:*

> In these troublesome antics, we may even find it wise on occasion to adopt incongruous perspectives for the dwarfing of our impatience. We in cities rightly grow shrewd at

appraising man-made institutions—but beyond these tiny concentration points of rhetoric and traffic, there lies the eternally unsolvable Enigma, the preposterous fact that both existence and nothingness are equally unthinkable. Our speculations may run the whole qualitative gamut, from play, through reverence, even to an occasional shiver of cold metaphysical dread—for always the Eternal Enigma is there, right on the edges of our metropolitan bickerings, stretching outward to interstellar infinity and inward to the depths of the mind. And in this staggering disproportion between man and noman, there is no place for purely human boasts of grandeur, or for forgetting that men build their cultures by huddling together, nervously loquacious, at the edge of an abyss. (1935/1984b, p. 272)

The "purification of war" (the motto of Burke's trilogy) requires a thoroughly ironic stance toward the bickerings of the "symbol-using animal," equipping "citizen-critics" (Eberly, 2000) with the tools for analyzing public discourse and literature.

While a thorough introduction to Burke is beyond the scope of this chapter, here are some key analytic concepts from his work. First, *identification analysis.* Burke uses the Freudian term to enlarge the scope of rhetoric from its classical conception. A classical theorist might have asked, How does the rhetor "identify" with the audience? "I was a farm boy myself." "I feel your pain." The modernist rhetorician, however, asks whether there are "unconscious" identifications: the President as Father, the German people as a weak woman "wooed" by powerful, masculine Hitler. In general, does the rhetor create a sense of "consubstantiality" between herself and her audience, or is the rhetor somehow "above" the audience, making for "social mystery"? (e.g., the Pope, your doctor) (1950/1969b, pp. 20–23; pp. 114–116). Is there "mystification" in the rhetoric—"eulogistic" covering of less attractive motives (p. 178)?

Second, analyze what Burke calls the "archetypal drama" of human relations (or what we now, following Lyotard, might call "master narratives"). Much political discourse, especially the rhetoric of radical movements, attempts to enlist the audience in a larger social drama, a drama that mimics the Christian narrative. How does the discourse operate as a rhetoric of rebirth for the speaker? How does the speaker take the audience through the drama of pollution, guilt, purification, and redemption? Does the speaker advocate scapegoating or mortification as purification strategies? (1941/1973, pp. 199–220). Much like Reagan's telling of "America's Story," or Adolf Hitler's rhetoric of rebirth of the German *Reich* by expelling the Jews and other elements that threaten community, major ideological shifts in a mass audience appear to require a new narrative of a nation's progress or decline, identifying key heroes and villains as well as a new savior to bring about complete rebirth.

Third, in dissecting a rhetorical narrative, one may identify its basic structure: What follows what, and why? Identify all progressions—key terms, images, ideas, emotions, attitudes, places, people, and things. Identify the overall form of the discourse— syllogistic (like a detective novel, which is appealing because it ties up all its narrative loose ends), conventional (a ritual repetition, like the Passover Seder or the Catholic Mass), qualitative (the use of foreshadowing, as in the use of train imagery in Tolstoy's *Anna Karenina*), and incidental form (tropes or schemes, which play with the meaning and structure of the word or sentence). Burke (1931/1968b) writes, "Form . . . is an arousing and fulfillment of desires. A work has form in so far as one part of it leads a reader to anticipate another part, to be gratified by the sequence" (p. 124).

Fourth, identify how terms cluster both with and against each other. In a cluster analysis, one asks what goes with what, and

why? Make an index of significant terms— terms of high intensity or frequency: god terms, devil terms, ultimate terms, "terministic screens." Make a concordance of significant terms—that is, identify the context in which terms appear, as a way of finding out what they mean by finding out what the speaker associates them with. After identifying the significant terms, ask what goes against what, and why? Identify dramatic alignments: what terms, images, ideas, emotions, attitudes, places, people, things are opposed to each other (Burke, 1964, pp. 145–172).

Finally, at the most abstract level of rhetorical analysis, one can ask about the fundamental metaphysical or metarhetorical account of human motives that underlies the philosophy of the text being analyzed. Here Burke introduces one of his most famous, yet often misused, concepts: the Pentad. *A Grammar of Motives* (Burke, 1945/1969a) is organized around the key nodal points of a drama: Act, Scene, Agent, Agency, and Purpose. While a well-rounded philosophy would focus on the Act as containing all the other parts of the drama, as in Burke's preferred Aristotelian philosophy, other philosophies can be characterized in terms of the key term in the human drama that they emphasize. The key question here for the critic is, What is the author's basic mode of framing reality? What terms constitute the author's "terministic screen," a fundamental perspective that works simultaneously as a "selection, reflection, and deflection of reality"? (Burke, 1966, p. 45). Here is a relatively simple example (not Burke's) of how different ways of framing reality affect audience judgment of an action. Let us imagine that a 12-year-old boy, from a poor section of town and a member of a historically oppressed group, shoots a 75-year-old grandmother on the street while stealing her purse. If our philosophical frame emphasizes Scene, one might judge the Act like this: While the act was wrong, we need to take into account and ameliorate the bad social conditions that drive a boy to this kind of deed (what Burke calls *determinism*). In response, a conservative might frame the act in (idealist, individualist) terms of the Agent: "I don't care if he was poor or a victim of discrimination; he's still responsible. My father was poor and oppressed, but he didn't go around killing grandmothers. He lifted himself up by his own bootstraps." A liberal pragmatist, however, might respond in turn by focusing on Agency: "Look, it was a bad action, but we need to ask what we can do to keep guns out of the hands of children." Finally, a religious mystic might respond in terms of cosmic Purpose (as I once heard two women in a doctor's office frame a similar violent event in our town): "It just goes to show the hand of Satan in our lives."

Burke's goal in the *Grammar* is to promote pluralism by identifying the internal logic and rhetoric of major philosophies and by proposing an alternative "representative anecdote" to the then-influential behaviorist psychology by contending that human relations is better interpreted as drama rather than in terms of stimulus and response (Burke, 1945/1969a, pp. 59–61). The goal of pluralism fits in well with a modernist philosophy of the Agent, as first formulated in Kantian Idealism, by identifying rhetorical strategies that might subvert the autonomous self's rational self-consciousness. Unlike classical rhetoric or antimodernist rhetorics in the 20th century, Burke's *Rhetoric of Motives* (1950/1969b) ends on an oddly mystical and contemplative note (the last page is 333, perhaps symbolizing the Trinity?), suggesting that Burke agrees with Plato's and Aristotle's contention that the philosophic life is the highest life for human beings, not that of the citizen-orator:

> But since, for better or worse, the mystery of the hierarchic is forever with us, let us, as students of rhetoric, scrutinize its range of entrancements, both with dismay and delight. And finally let us observe, all about us, forever goading us, though it be in

fragments, the motive that attains its ultimate identification in the thought, not of the universal holocaust but of the universal order—as with the rhetorical and dialectic symmetry of the Aristotelian metaphysics, whereby all classes of beings are hierarchically arranged in a chain or ladder or pyramid of mounting worth, each kind striving towards the perfection of its kind, and so towards the kind next above it, while the strivings of the entire series head in God as the beloved cynosure and sinecure, the end of all desire. (1969b, p. 333)

Earlier in the *Rhetoric* (1950/1969b), Burke had introduced the image of the ego as a parliamentary orator, contending with the competing factions of the Superego and the Id (p. 23). The final 20th-century approach to rhetorical theory, *postmodernism*, attacks the modernist project of preserving the autonomous self by destroying the idea of a conscious, responsible self.

POSTMODERNISM AND THE JOY OF NIHILISM

Postmodernism is a puzzling term, in part because of the implied question: "What comes after Postmodernism?" Although popularized by Jean-François Lyotard (1984) in the early 1980s, it was originally used by American poet Charles Olson and literary critic Ihab Hassan to refer to a new style in architecture, literature, and music, characterized by a playful quality, as opposed to the high seriousness of much modernist art (compare Magritte with Picasso, for example, or Frank Gehry's Bilbao Museum with Mies van der Rohe's Seagram's Building); an erosion of boundaries between high and popular culture; and, finally, a celebration of "mere" style, surface, the free play of signifiers without a signified.

Philosophically, across the human sciences, postmodernism has become synonymous with post-structuralism, the French philosophical reaction against both Sartrean existentialism and Levi-Strauss's structuralism associated primarily with Jacques Derrida, Michel Foucault, Gilles Deleuze, and Felix Guattari. As a philosophic stance (perhaps illustrating a mystical view of language as Purpose, in Burkeian terms) post-structuralism, while never easy to pin down in a series of propositions, consists of incredulity toward master narratives—*"grands récits"* (Lyotard, 1984)—meaning that the "directionality" of history as promised by Enlightenment liberalism or by Marxism has collapsed; the rejection of "foundationalism"—the modern scientific quest (following Descartes) to establish knowledge on absolutely certain premises—in favor of what Clifford Geertz (1983) has called "local knowledge," fragments rather than theories or systems; a critique of Eurocentrism, with a preference for marginalized voices and a rejection of the traditional canon or core curriculum; a shift in the role of the academic intellectual from scholar/critic to "performer"; and, finally, a contention that all is rhetorical—or, as Derrida wrote, "there is nothing outside the text"— because we can never escape the prison house of language. Above all, the modernist autonomous self has been replaced by a "subject-position" spoken into existence by rhetorical/ideological practices. Postmodernism, one could say, is the final revenge of the Sophists against Plato.

In this section of the chapter, I briefly introduce the main implications for rhetorical theory of four figures essential to the postmodern turn in rhetorical studies: Nietzsche, Heidegger, Foucault, and Derrida. Friedrich Nietzsche (1844–1900) is the universally acknowledged patron saint of postmodernism. His rhetorical definition of "truth" is widely quoted. Truth is

> a mobile army of metaphors, metonymies, anthropomorphisms: in short a sum of human relations which have been poetically and rhetorically intensified, transposed, adorned, and after long usage seem to a

> nation fixed, canonical, and binding; truths are illusions of which one has forgotten that this is what they are; metaphors which have become worn out and have lost their sensual power; coins which have lost their pictures and now are no longer of account as coins but merely as metal. (Nietzsche, 1989, p. 250)

Since truth and values are rhetorically constructed, what matters most to human beings is the will to power, the will to affirm life by creating saving illusions for ourselves. He proposed, as Deleuze (1988) writes, "not the ambivalent joy of hatred, but the joy of wanting to destroy whatever mutilates life" (p. 23). In political terms, Nietzsche is perhaps best viewed as a sort of aristocratic libertarian who hated democracy, feminism, and socialism. Somehow, heavily filtered through French post-structuralism, he has displaced Marx as the chief emancipatory theorist on the academic Left.

Another equally antidemocratic influence on post-structuralism is Martin Heidegger (1889–1976), known primarily for *Being and Time* (1962) and for his more poetic later writings, especially *Poetry, Language, and Thought* (1971). His pro-Nazi speeches as Rector of the University of Freiburg in 1933 (for which he never apologized) continue to tarnish his reputation in the larger academic community, although his central themes are popular among postmodern rhetorical theorists. Above all, he contends, Western thought is at an "end" or "crisis," brought on by its "forgetfulness of Being." Perhaps we can go back to the pre-Socratics, or listen to the voices of the great mad poets, notably Hölderlin, in whom Being speaks to us. In a famous analysis of Van Gogh's painting of a peasant's shoes, Heidegger praises Van Gogh because he just lets the shoes be, a stance we should share: patient waiting, listening to the voice of Being (Heidegger, 1971, pp. 15–86). Heidegger also has some interesting things to say about the Sophists and about rhetoric (he calls Aristotle's discussion of the emotions "the first systematic hermeneutic of the everydayness of being with one another" in *Being and Time* [p. 178]). He condemns Plato and Aristotle for having brought about a rationalist stance toward Being that leads to the dominance of technology over human beings. His defense of the pre-Socratics has had considerable influence on contemporary efforts to retrieve and defend the Sophists as significant theorists of rhetoric. His most distinctively postmodern themes are the rejection of reason as "control," and his insistence that "language speaks us," rather than the other way around.

The idea that "language speaks us" is stripped of its mystical connotations by Michel Foucault (1926–1984) in his analysis of the construction of knowledge and subjects by social institutions such as medicine, psychiatry, the human sciences, and penology. Foucault, with the exception of his one theoretical statement, *The Archaeology of Knowledge* (2002), concentrated on empirical, even positivist, historical descriptions of what he called "discursive formations." A discursive formation is known through the discovery of rules or procedures that make the production of "knowledge" possible, often authorized by particular institutional bodies. It authorizes who may speak or not speak, the style of communication or argument, and where speaking takes place. Unlike Marxism, which based its arguments on the centrality of class power and economic domination, Foucault sees "power" everywhere, most notably in the helping professions and in the University. His followers in rhetorical studies, notably Carole Blair, have been interested in demonstrating how academic conventions "discipline" subjects or create the phenomena they profess to study (Blair, Brown, & Baxter, 1994). In an influential historiographical essay on rhetorical theory, Blair (1992) contends that it is impossible to create a coherent history of rhetoric, and that rhetoric itself is bound to

disappear into the more general problematic of cultural studies (Blair, 1997).

Like Nietzsche, the implications of Foucault's beliefs for political practice are highly ambiguous. His politics were essentially anarchistic, devoted to overturning power in all its modes. He was especially active in prison reform and in gay liberation; late in life he became convinced that the United States was the greatest country on earth because of the way it allowed multiple lifestyles and subjectivities. Whether one can reconcile his early writings, which emphasize the constructed character of the self, with his later writings on Greco-Roman ethics, which emphasize an ethic of self-care, remains an open issue in Foucault scholarship (Paras, 2006).

The implications of Derrida's (1930–2004) philosophy for rhetorical studies center on the axiom of structural linguistics that signs only refer to other signs, not to the thing itself. Western thought has been based on the idea that knowledge should be like the immediacy of speech rather than exhibiting the constructed character of writing. Derrida contends that in this sense "writing" is prior to speech, meaning that Western thought is based on the idea of full seeing or presence (Derrida, 1976). The idea of a poster session at a convention is the best illustration of the idea that "science" should become as "transparent" as possible.

Literary works, philosophical texts, political ideologies are all constructed on the basis of "binary oppositions" in which the second term is seen as an inferior thing: philosophy/rhetoric, male/female, literal/figurative. This idea parallels Perelman's concept of dissociation, although dissociation is a strategy in Perelman while it occurs unconsciously in Derrida. The process of deconstruction works by showing how texts are self-contradictory, depending on the concepts they marginalize; perhaps the most obvious deconstruction in the history of rhetoric is to demonstrate how Plato uses rhetoric to attack rhetoric (Aune, 1990).

Derrida was much influenced by Emmanuel Levinas, the French-Israeli philosopher who condemns Western philosophy for being more concerned with Knowledge than with Ethics, making it deaf to the voice of the "Other":

> It all happens as though the multiplicity of persons . . . were the condition for the fullness of "absolute truth," as though each person, through his uniqueness, ensured the revelation of a unique aspect of the truth, and that certain sides of it would never reveal themselves if certain people were missing from mankind. (Levinas, trans. 1994, p. 133)

In Jewish terms, we know God only through the *mitzvot,* or divine commandments, ordering us to turn toward the Other and his or her claims on us (Levinas, trans. 1994, pp. 133–134). Deconstruction as an attack on absolute truth can be seen as continuing the Jewish attack on idolatry, or as the ongoing war being "Athens and Jerusalem" that is perhaps the constitutive debate of Western culture.

The post-structuralist themes of the power of language, the replacing of individual autonomy with fluid subject positions, and the attack on institutional authority have been the most influential on contemporary rhetorical studies. There is as yet no central text for postmodern rhetorical studies, in the way that Burke's *Rhetoric of Motives* and P/O-T's *New Rhetoric* are for modernist rhetoric. Some key figures include Victor Vitanza, Carole Blair, and Bradford Vivian. Raymie McKerrow's (1989) essay on "Critical Rhetoric," however, has been particularly influential, emphasizing Foucault's work.

McKerrow (1989) defines critical rhetoric as the critique of domination, especially as that domination is created through discursive construction of "common sense." We must recognize that Power is everywhere, not just concentrated in capitalist economic power. Like Foucault, we need a never-ending skepticism,

permanent criticism (p. 96). A critical rhetoric emphasizes that there is no "truth." "Truth" is an instrument of power. We must, McKerrow writes, "embrace Sophism" (p. 99).

From these post-structuralist axioms, McKerrow (1989) derives the following implications for rhetorical studies. First, critical practice is invention. We need to forget the idea of studying "public address" because we now only have "fragments" that the critic must assemble. It is more important to study "The Facts of Life" than "great speeches by long-dead great speakers" (p. 101). Second, Communication is "polysemous." There are multiple ways to decode texts; we must read popular texts for their liberatory possibilities (e.g., Madonna as empowering women). Finally, critical rhetoric is a political performance, not a detached scholarly pursuit; it is a fight against all forms of repression or oppression.

Another representative post-structuralist approach to rhetoric is Bradford Vivian's (2004) impressive recent book, *Being Made Strange: Rhetoric Beyond Representation.* He argues for a conception of ethos that is no longer based on character or custom but "generated by the discursive practices that engender such categories and infuse them with meaning and value in social, political, and ethical contexts." This new version of ethos is defined "in terms of difference rather than identity, multiplicity instead of unity, and mutation instead of essential continuity" (p. 15). The view of subjectivity and ethos in this *new* new rhetoric is to "diagnose how the ethos, the accepted sense and value of common truths, ideals, and relations, determines who, quite literally, is allowed to speak in our culture and how one is authorized to do so" (p. 192). Like the modernist rhetorics of Burke and P/OT, McKerrow and Vivian develop a critical practice designed to understand rhetorical strategies that might undermine individual autonomy and liberty— *yet without the autonomous subject.*

Just as the antimodernist rhetorical stance can be criticized for its nostalgia for a unified culture that perhaps never existed (or "Salem without the witches," as Amy Gutmann puts it, 1985, p. 319), and modernist rhetoric can be criticized for valorizing critique over educating citizen-orators, postmodernist rhetoric has some severe problems. It remains unclear how critical or postmodern rhetoric can assist radical or reform social movements in altering the existing order. Traditional radical rhetoric, such as the speeches of Eugene Debs or Elizabeth Cady Stanton or Frederick Douglass, mediated between radical ideology and popular audiences by appealing to traditional community values and by modeling great orators of the past. Douglass learned to speak by imitating those great dead white males Edmund Burke and, especially, Charles James Fox (Lasch, 1996, pp. 185–186). One searches in vain throughout the texts of postmodernist rhetoricians for any examples of effective postmodernist rhetoric. Also, by exaggerating the role of academic knowledge and language in creating human subjects, it may be that postmodernist rhetoricians are exhibiting their own "occupational psychosis" or "trained incapacity," in Kenneth Burke's terms (1935/1984b, p. 48). Are they projecting the sense of political powerlessness felt by the American Left since the 1980s, displacing political struggle into the realm of symbols and culture rather than of law and public policy? Are they projecting their own social location, which thrives on endless talk, into a universal position from which to create culture as a whole? If there is no truth, but only power, how different is postmodernist rhetoric from the emotivism of earlier 20th-century logical positivism? If, say, an invocation of universal human rights against torture at Abu Ghraib relies on a Western, imperialist, logocentric, liberal subject position, are there any good reasons for preferring a liberal system of human rights over American imperialism or Islamic fundamentalism? Despite their current distaste for the liberal autonomous subject, perhaps postmodernists might be shocked back into reality (and truth) by the recognition that it is not "subject positions" that can be tortured, but rather lonely, vulnerable, autonomous human beings.

CONCLUSION

As I said in the introduction to this chapter, no one would have predicted a bright future for rhetoric in the 20th century. No one would have predicted the sheer volume of scholarly study of rhetoric or of the tremendous growth in the number of courses and departments devoted to its study. It is difficult to predict what comes "after postmodernism," but there are a number of encouraging developments. Most strikingly, it has been postmodernist rhetoricians who have been most skillful in integrating the teaching of rhetoric with the new technologies, especially the Internet (Haynes, 2003). The internationalization of American rhetoric and communication departments has led to an interest in comparative rhetorics; we need no longer view rhetoric as a theoretical practice limited to Europe and North America. An emerging theme across the human sciences is the importance of evolutionary biology for the understanding of human behavior. George Kennedy (1992) made an important start for this line of research with his essay "A Hoot in the Dark," which compared epideictic rhetoric to the "display" behaviors of birds and animals during courtship. A renewed interest in the biology of human nature, communication, and politics would be a useful antidote to the postmodernist overemphasis on the malleability of the human subject, assuming it can escape its historic association with scientific racism.

Yet the study of rhetoric has not fully hit the mainstream of American or European academic life. Nurtured largely in land-grant universities and mostly banned from elite private universities, rhetorical studies can reach its full promise as an academic field only if it displaces current practices in the language arts. Public speaking and debate remain crucial skills for citizens, whether in the workplace, politics, or in religious institutions. Writing about public issues is a more worthwhile practice for high school and college students than doing literary criticism. A focus on citizenship skills at the heart of general distribution requirements across the university, not just in writing and communication, might help improve the dialogue of the deaf that characterizes American democracy. Paradoxically, then, those who study persuasion must themselves become better persuaders, making a case for rhetoric as a central practice in education at all levels—not because of rhetoric's all-constituting power, as the postmodernists would have it, but because rhetoric's more modest focus on effective communication is needed now more than ever. As John Dewey, that central figure for modernist rhetoricians of all varieties, wrote in 1929,

> No government by experts in which the masses do not have the chance to inform the experts as to their needs can be anything but an oligarchy managed in the interests of the few. . . . The essential need . . . is the improvement of the methods and conditions of debate, discussion, and persuasion. That is *the* problem of the public. (Dewey, 1929/1980, p. 208)

The original Kantian error at the beginning of the modern period was to assume that the autonomous liberal subject could do without the art of rhetoric. Any effort to restore liberal democracy in an age of torture, systematic lying by political leaders, and religious fundamentalism must begin with the effort of autonomous subjects to persuade other autonomous subjects. That is *the* problem of rhetoric.

NOTE

1. A list of works this chapter omits probably would be longer than the chapter itself, but here are some important threads I have left out for reasons of space. I. A. Richards's influence has been greater in literary criticism, but he did write an important short work on rhetoric, *The Philosophy of Rhetoric* (1936), which provided a new definition of "rhetoric" as a discipline: "the study of misunderstanding and its remedies" (p. 3). The work is most famous for its discussion of metaphor in terms of "tenor" and "vehicle." Richards develops the modernist view of rhetoric, as I define it in this chapter, by using rhetorical analysis to eliminate barriers to the decision making of the autonomous self. A similarly "semantic" approach to rhetoric, now virtually forgotten but once very influential in language arts curricula, was the movement of General Semantics, developed by Count Alfred Korzybski in *Science and Sanity* (1933). His most frequently quoted phrase from that work is "The map is not the territory." General Semantics was a popularized version of logical positivism, and proposed careful attention to the abstracting character of language as a means of improving mental and social "hygiene." I have also left out more middle-range theories of rhetoric, including the rhetoric of science, the rhetoric of inquiry, theories of rhetorical criticism, and emerging discussions of feminist rhetoric and comparative rhetoric. As the 20th century ended, the question of the centrality of classical rhetoric to rhetorical studies surfaced again. For an important debate on this issue, see Graff, Walzer, and Atwill's (2005) *The Viability of the Rhetorical Tradition*. I have also left out a serious consideration of the relationship between rhetorical studies and what has come to be called "critical-cultural studies." The National Communication Association's journal *Communication and Critical-Cultural Studies* (founded in 2004) is a good example of the blending of critical rhetoric with media studies. It remains to be seen whether scholars of critical-cultural studies in communication will retain any connection to rhetorical studies as it was practiced in the second half of the 20th century.

REFERENCES

Andersen, K. (1983, January 24). An eye for an eye. *Time*, 36.

Aune, J. A. (1990). Rhetoric after deconstruction. In R. Cherwitz (Ed.), *Rhetoric and philosophy* (pp. 253–272). Hillsdale, NJ: Lawrence Erlbaum.

Aune, J. A. (2001). *Selling the free market: The rhetoric of economic correctness*. New York: Guilford Press.

Blair, C. (1992). Contested histories of rhetoric: The politics of preservation, progress, and change. *Quarterly Journal of Speech, 78*, 403–428.

Blair, C. (1997). "We are all just prisoners here of our own device": Rhetoric in speech communication after Wingspread. In T. Enos, R. McNabb, C. Miller, & R. Mountford (Eds.), *Making and unmaking the prospects for rhetoric* (pp. 29–36). Hillsdale, NJ: Lawrence Erlbaum.

Blair, C., Brown, J. R., & Baxter, L. A. (1994). Disciplining the feminine. *Quarterly Journal of Speech, 80*, 383–409.

Bitzer, L. (1968). The rhetorical situation. *Philosophy and Rhetoric, 1*, 1–14.

Booth, W. (1974). *Modern dogma and the rhetoric of assent*. Notre Dame, IN: University of Notre Dame Press.

Bormann, E. (1972). Fantasy and rhetorical vision: The rhetorical criticism of social reality. *Quarterly Journal of Speech, 58*, 396–407.

Brummett, B. (1981). A defense of ethical relativism as rhetorically grounded. *Western Journal of Speech Communication, 45*, 286–298.

Burke, K. (1964). *Terms for order*. Bloomington: Indiana University Press.

Burke, K. (1966). *Language as symbolic action: Essays on life, literature, and method*. Berkeley: University of California Press.

Burke, K. (1968a). *The complete white oxen: Collected short fiction of Kenneth Burke*. Berkeley: University of California Press.

Burke, K. (1968b). *Counter-statement*. Berkeley: University of California Press. (Original work published 1931)

Burke, K. (1969a). *A grammar of motives*. Berkeley: University of California Press. (Original work published 1945)

Burke, K. (1969b). *A rhetoric of motives*. Berkeley: University of California Press. (Original work published 1950)

Burke, K. (1970). *The rhetoric of religion: Studies in logology*. Berkeley: University of California Press. (Original work published 1961)

Burke, K. (1972). *Dramatism and development*. Worcester, MA: Clark University Press.

Burke, K. (1973). *The philosophy of literary form: Studies in symbolic action*. Berkeley: University of California Press. (Original work published 1941)

Burke, K. (1984a). *Attitudes toward history*. Berkeley: University of California Press. (Original work published 1937)

Burke, K. (1984b). *Permanence and change: An anatomy of purpose*. Berkeley: University of California Press. (Original work published 1935)

Burke, K. (1997). Revolutionary symbolism in America. In A. Fried (Ed.), *Communism in America: A history in documents* (pp. 278–280). New York: Columbia University Press.

Burke, K. (2007a). *Burke on Shakespeare*. West Lafayette, IN: Parlor Press.

Burke, K. (2007b). *Essays toward a symbolic of motives*. West Lafayette, IN: Parlor Press.

Cherwitz, R. & Hikins, J. (1985). *Communication and knowledge: An investigation in rhetorical epistemology*. Columbia: University of South Carolina Press.

Consigny, S. (1974). Rhetoric and its situations. *Philosophy and Rhetoric, 7*, 175–186.

Cox, J. R. (1982). The die is cast: Topical and ontological dimensions of the locus of the irreparable. *Quarterly Journal of Speech, 68*, 227–239.

Deleuze, G. (1988). *Foucault* (S. Hand, Trans.). Minneapolis: University of Minnesota Press.

Derrida, J. (1976). *Of grammatology* (G. C. Spivak, Trans.). Baltimore: Johns Hopkins University Press.

Dewey, J. (1980). *The public and its problems*. Athens, OH: Swallow Press. (Original work published 1929)

Eagleton, T. (1990). *The ideology of the aesthetic*. Oxford, UK: Basil Blackwell.

Eberly, R. (2000). *Citizen-critics: Literary public spheres*. Urbana: University of Illinois Press.

Ehninger, D. (1968). On systems of rhetoric. *Philosophy and Rhetoric, 1*, 131–144.

Ely, J. H. (1973). The wages of crying wolf: A comment on *Roe v. Wade. Yale Law Journal, 82,* 920–949.

Farrell, T. B. (1993). *Norms of rhetorical culture.* New Haven, CT: Yale University Press.

Foss, S., Foss, K., & Trapp, R. (2003). *Contemporary perspectives on rhetoric* (3rd ed.). Arlington Heights, IL: Waveland Press.

Foucault, M. (2002). *The archaeology of knowledge.* London: Routledge.

Garsten, B. (2006). *Saving persuasion: A defense of rhetoric and judgment.* Cambridge: Harvard University Press.

Geertz, C. (1983). *Local knowledge: Further essays in interpretive anthropology.* New York: Basic Books.

Goodwin, J. (2007, December 14). *Free speech topoi.* Retrieved May 17, 2008, from http://faculty-web.at.northwestern.edu/comm stud/freespeech/course/topoi.html

Gouldner, A. P. (1979). *The future of intellectuals and the rise of the new class.* New York: Oxford University Press.

Graff, R., Walzer, A. E., & Atwill, J. (2005). *The viability of the rhetorical tradition.* Albany: State University of New York Press.

Gutmann, A. (1985). Communitarian critics of liberalism. *Philosophy and Public Affairs, 14,* 308–322.

Halloran, S. M. (1976). Tradition and theory in rhetoric. *Quarterly Journal of Speech, 62,* 234–241.

Halloran, S. M. (1982). Rhetoric in the American college curriculum: The decline of public discourse. *Pre/Text, 3,* 245–270.

Hariman, R. (2003). *Prudence: Classical virtue, postmodern politics.* University Park: Pennsylvania State University Press.

Haynes, C. (2003). Writing offshore: The disappearing coastline of composition. *JAC, 23.4,* 667–724.

Heidegger, M. (1962). *Being and time* (J. Macquarrie & E. Robinson, Trans.). New York: Harper & Row.

Heidegger, M. (1971). *Poetry, language, and thought* (A. Hofstadter, Trans.). New York: Harper & Row.

Howell, W. S. (1965). Renaissance and modern rhetoric: A study in change. In J. Schwartz & J. A. Rycenga (Eds.), *The province of rhetoric* (pp. 292–308). New York: Ronald Press.

Judis, J. (2007, August 27). Death grip: How political psychology explains Bush's ghastly success. *New Republic,* pp. 17–20.

Kant, I. (1956). *Critique of practical reason* (L. W. Beck, Trans.). Indianapolis: Bobbs-Merrill. (Original work published 1788)

Kant, I. (1987). *Critique of judgment* (W. S. Pluhar, Trans.). Indianapolis, IN: Hackett. (Original work published 1790)

Keith, W. M. (2007). *Democracy as discussion: Civic education and the American forum movement.* Lexington, KY: Lexington Books.

Kennedy, G. (1992). A hoot in the dark: The evolution of general rhetoric. *Philosophy and Rhetoric, 25,* 1–21.

Korzybski, A. (1933). *Science and sanity.* New York: International Non-Aristotelian Publishing.

Lasch, C. (1996). *The revolt of the elites and the betrayal of democracy* (New ed.). New York: W. W. Norton.

Leff, M. (1998). Cicero's Pro Murena and the strong case for rhetoric. *Rhetoric and Public Affairs, 1,* 63–65.

Levinas, E. (1994). *Beyond the verse: Talmudic readings and lectures* (G. D. Mole, Trans.). Bloomington: Indiana University Press.

Lewis, W. F. (1987). Telling America's story: Narrative form and the Reagan presidency. *Quarterly Journal of Speech, 73,* 280–303.

Lyotard, J. (1984). *The postmodern condition: A report on knowledge* (B. Massumi, Trans.). Minneapolis: University of Minnesota Press.

MacIntyre, A. (1984). *After virtue* (2nd ed.). Notre Dame, IN: University of Notre Dame Press.

McGee, M. C. (1985). The moral problem of argumentum per argumentum. In R. Cox, M. Sillars, & G. Walker (Eds.), *Argument and social practice: Proceedings of the fourth SCA/AFA conference on argumentation* (pp. 1–15). Annandale, VA: SCA.

McKeon, R. (1971). The use of rhetoric in a technological age: Architectonic productive arts. In L. F. Bitzer & E. Black (Eds.), *The prospect of rhetoric* (pp. 44–63). Englewood Cliffs, NJ: Prentice Hall.

McKerrow, R. (1989). Critical rhetoric: Theory and praxis. *Communication Monographs, 56,* 91–111.

Nietzsche, F. (1989). On truth and lying in an extramoral sense. In S. L. Gilman, C. Blair, &

D. J. Parent (Eds. and Trans.), *Friedrich Nietzsche on rhetoric and language* (pp. 246–257). New York: Oxford University Press.

O'Keefe, D. J. (2003). The potential conflict between normatively-good argumentative practice and persuasive success: Evidence from persuasion effects research. In F. H. van Eemeren, J. A. Blair, C. A. Willard, & A. F. Snoeck Henkemans (Eds.), *Anyone who has a view: Theoretical contributions to the study of argumentation* (pp. 309–318). Amsterdam: Kluwer.

Paras, E. (2006). *Foucault 2.0: Beyond power and knowledge.* New York: Other Press.

Perelman, C. (1982). *The realm of rhetoric.* Notre Dame, IN: Notre Dame University Press.

Perelman, C., & Olbrechts-Tyteca, L. (1969). *The new rhetoric: A treatise on argumentation* (J. Wilkinson & P. Weaver, Trans.). Notre Dame, IN: Notre Dame University Press.

Pippin, R. (1999). *Modernism as a philosophical problem* (2nd ed.). Oxford, UK: Basil Blackwell.

Rawls, J. (1993). *Political liberalism.* New York: Columbia University Press.

Richards, I. A. (1936). *The philosophy of rhetoric.* New York: Oxford University Press.

Ricoeur, P. (1970). *Freud and philosophy* (D. Savage, Trans.). New Haven: Yale University Press.

Roe v. Wade, 410 U.S. 113 (1973).

Schiappa, E. (2001). Second thoughts on the critiques of big rhetoric. *Philosophy and Rhetoric, 34,* 260–274.

Schiappa, E., & Keehner, M. F. (1991). The "lost" passages of *Permanence and change. Communication Studies, 42,* 191–199.

Schneewind, J. B. (1992). Autonomy, obligation, and virtue: An overview of Kant's moral philosophy. In P. Guyer (Ed.), *The Cambridge companion to Kant* (pp. 309–341). Cambridge, UK: Cambridge University Press.

Schudson, M. (1980). *Discovering the news.* New York: Basic Books.

Schudson, M. (1998). *The good citizen: A history of American public life.* New York: Free Press.

Scott, R. L. (1967). On viewing rhetoric as epistemic. *Central States Speech Journal, 18,* 9–16.

Sedgh, G., Henshaw, S. K., Singh, S., Aahman, E., & Shah, I. H. (2007). Induced abortion: Estimated rates and trends worldwide. *The Lancet, 370,* 1338–1345.

Selzer, J. (1997). *Kenneth Burke in Greenwich Village.* Madison: University of Wisconsin Press.

Sen, A. (2000). *Development as freedom.* New York: Anchor Books.

Swearingen, C. Jan. (1991). *Rhetoric and irony: Western literacy and Western lies.* New York: Oxford University Press.

Taylor, C. (1975). *Hegel.* Cambridge, UK: Cambridge University Press.

Tönnies, F. (2001). *Community and civil society* (J. Harris & M. Hollis, Trans.). Cambridge, UK: Cambridge University Press.

Toulmin, S. (1958). *The uses of argument.* Cambridge, UK: Cambridge University Press.

Vatz, R. (1973). The myth of the rhetorical situation. *Philosophy and Rhetoric, 6,* 154–161.

Vivian, B. (2004). *Being made strange: Rhetoric beyond representation.* Albany: State University of New York Press.

Walton, D. N. (1992a). *The place of emotion in argument.* University Park: Pennsylvania State University Press.

Walton, D. N. (1992b). *Slippery slope arguments.* Oxford, UK: Clarendon Press.

Weaver, R. (1948). *Ideas have consequences.* Chicago: University of Chicago Press.

Weaver, R. (1953). *The ethics of rhetoric.* Chicago: Henry Regnery.

Weaver, R. (1995). *Visions of order.* Philadelphia: Intercollegiate Studies Institute.

Weaver, R. (2001). Language is sermonic. In P. Bizzell & B. Herzberg (Eds.), *The rhetorical tradition* (2nd ed., pp. 1351–1360). New York: Bedford Press.

Wenzel, J. W. (1990). Three perspectives on argument: Rhetoric, dialectic, logic. In J. Schuetz & R. Trapp (Eds.), *Perspectives on argumentation: Essays in honor of Wayne Brockriede* (pp. 9–26). Prospect Heights, IL: Waveland Press.

Whitson, S., & Poulakos, J. (1993). Nietzsche and the aesthetics of rhetoric. *Quarterly Journal of Speech, 79,* 131–145.

Young, F. D. (1995). *Richard Weaver: A life of the mind.* Columbia: University of Missouri Press.

6

The Study of Argumentation

FRANS H. VAN EEMEREN

"Argumentation" is a word from ordinary language that has been given a more precise and technical meaning in the study of argumentation. According to the handbook *Fundamentals of Argumentation Theory*, which was coauthored by a prominent group of argumentation scholars, *argumentation* can be defined as a verbal, social, and rational activity aimed at convincing a reasonable critic of the acceptability of a standpoint by advancing a constellation of propositions justifying or refuting the proposition expressed in the standpoint (van Eemeren et al., 1996). This definition does justice to the "process-product ambiguity" of the word *argumentation*: It not only refers to the activity of advancing reasons but also to the shorter or longer stretches of discourse or text resulting from it. Furthermore, it emphasizes that argumentation is prototypically a linguistic activity that takes place between two or more people and is inspired by reason. This does not imply that nonlinguistic acts and emotions cannot play a role or that people cannot argue with themselves, but then there is some additional feature that in argumentation is not always there.

It is a sine qua non of argumentation that it pertains to a *standpoint*, a point of view with regard to a certain issue. Speakers or writers who advance argumentation defend their standpoint to listeners or readers who (are assumed to) doubt its acceptability or have a different standpoint of their own. Argumentation is aimed at convincing these listeners or readers of the acceptability of the standpoint. By advancing argumentation, arguers make an appeal to reasonableness: They silently assume that the listeners or readers will act as reasonable critics when evaluating the justifications or refutations they have offered. Otherwise, it would not make sense to advance argumentation.

The study of argumentation is broad and varied. It is undertaken by scholars of diverse disciplinary backgrounds—from communication and discourse analysis to linguistics, logic, and law—and includes an abundance of subjects—from premise acceptability and argumentation by analogy to the argumentative use of questions in mediation and Edward Kennedy's argumentative manipulations in the Chappaquiddick speech. Among the types of research that have been carried out are philosophical studies of the concepts of rationality and reasonableness, theoretical studies in which models of argumentation are developed that are based on such concepts, qualitative as well as quantitative empirical research of various aspects of argumentative reality, analytic studies aimed at a theoretical reconstruction of argumentative discourse and texts, and—last but not least—practical studies of specific kinds of argumentative practices, possibly leading to a critical appreciation and the development of methods or proposals for improvement. Together, these five types of studies represent the constitutive components of a comprehensive research program for argumentation scholars. In carrying out some specific part of such a program, they tend to concentrate in the first place on three problem areas: the analysis, evaluation, and production of argumentative discourse and texts.

One of the problems argumentation theorists are jointly concerned with is the identification of *standpoints*, *argumentation*, and other argumentative moves that are pertinent to analysis, evaluation, and production. Linguistic utterances only convey a standpoint or some other argumentative move if they have a specific function in the communication process. To convey a standpoint, for instance, an utterance must express a positive or a negative position with respect to a certain proposition. In ordinary discourse, however, explicitness of the communicative function is the exception rather than the rule. Nevertheless, in most languages there are some indicators that refer specifically to standpoints and argumentation, such as the words "therefore," "hence," "so,"

"thus," "ergo," "since," "for," and "because" in English. Sometimes the communicative function becomes clear after the event, when it is identified or indicated by one of the participants ("You have now heard my major arguments," "So, that is your standpoint then, eh?"). More often than not, however, no clear identification of the function of an argumentative move will be given and the propositional content may also remain unclear. The fewer the number of verbal pointers that are present, the more it will be necessary to make use of contextual clues, verbal as well as nonverbal. To detect such clues and put them to good use, some knowledge of the type of speech event involved is usually required as well as some background knowledge or some general or specific knowledge of the world.

Another vital problem is the identification of elements that remain unexpressed in the discourse but are often the pivotal points of an argument. This holds in particular for *unexpressed premises*. In the arguments composing ordinary argumentation, usually one of the premises is left unexpressed. In some cases, their identification is quite simple. There are also cases, however, in which the identification of unexpressed premises causes more problems—usually, because there are several possibilities. To determine what the commitments of an arguer are, the analyst must not only carry out a logical analysis, based on a formal validity criterion, but also a pragmatic analysis, based on standards for constructive communication. The logical analysis is thus instrumental to the achievement of a satisfactory pragmatic analysis. In the logical analysis, an attempt is made to reconstruct the argument as one having a valid argument form; in the pragmatic analysis, the unexpressed premise is then more precisely defined on the basis of contextual information, background knowledge, and pertinent knowledge of the world.

Arguers who put forward an argument are not automatically involved in an attempt to logically derive the conclusion from the premises but, in some way or other, they must be aiming at achieving a transfer of acceptance from the explicit premise to the standpoint. Hence, they attempt to design the argument in such a fashion that it will convince the listener. In this endeavor, they rely on more or less readymade *argument schemes*. Argument schemes are conventionalized ways of relating a premise to a standpoint. Because such argument schemes characterize the type of justification or refutation the explicit premise gives of the standpoint, an analysis of the argument schemes used in argumentative discourse provides information as to the principles, standards, criteria, or assumptions involved in argumentative attempts to defend a standpoint, that is, about the *topoi* on which the arguments rest. The problem of identifying argument schemes is another problem that is crucial to argumentation theory and, again, pragmatic insight must be brought to bear in the identification.

A central problem in the analysis of argumentative discourse is the determination of the structure of the argumentation. The *argumentation structure* of a discourse or text is determined by the way in which the reasons advanced in defense of a standpoint hang together and jointly support the standpoint. Argumentation for or against a standpoint can be "single argumentation" consisting of one reason for or against the standpoint (and an unexpressed premise), but argumentation can also have a more complex structure, depending on the way in which the defense of the standpoint has been organized to respond to (anticipated) doubt or criticism. In more complexly structured argumentation, the reasons put forward for or against a standpoint can be alternative defenses of the standpoint that are unrelated. They can also be interdependent because the individual arguments strengthen or complement each other, so that they constitute a "parallel chain" of reasons, or because the one argument supports the other, so that they constitute a "serial chain" of

reasons. Identifying the contextual and other pragmatic factors that must be taken into account to identify the various argumentation structures is an important problem to argumentation theory because an adequate evaluation of argumentative discourse cannot be made as long as the argumentation structure is not clear.

Another problem argumentation theorists are interested in is the identification of *fallacies*. In his groundbreaking study *Fallacies* (1970), Charles A. Hamblin showed that the prevailing "logical standard definition" of fallacies as arguments that seem valid but are not, does not cover a great number of generally recognized fallacies. Some fallacies are not invalid arguments, some are not arguments, and some are fallacious for some other reason. If the logical standard definition is dropped, however, as many modern argumentation theorists have done, and fallacies are more broadly conceived as discussion moves that damage the quality of argumentative discourse in some way, it is easier to bring to the light what is fallacious about them. Because in that case a more "situated" view of the fallacies is generally taken, a pragmatic approach is required that makes allowances for the context of communication and interaction in which the fallacies occur. All the same, there are still some argumentation theorists who maintain a more formal approach to the fallacies.

A last problem to be mentioned here is the reconstruction of argumentation in *special fields*, such as law and politics, which to some extent depends on more or less institutionally determined conventions. In modern Western society, juridical proceedings have become the argumentative practice par excellence because all kinds of disputes that cannot be resolved without recourse to specific procedures and the judgment of disinterested outsiders are delegated to lawyers and similarly trained professionals. Argumentation theorists therefore pay special attention to argumentation in the field of law, concentrating on the soundness criteria that prevail, the conceptions of reasonableness underlying them, and the rationale of the differences between legal argumentation and argumentation in other fields.

THE VARIETY OF THEORETICAL APPROACHES

The state of the art in the study of argumentation is characterized by the coexistence of a great variety of approaches, which differ considerably in conceptualization, scope, and theoretical refinement. Some argumentation scholars, especially those having a background in rhetoric and discourse analysis, have a primarily (and sometimes exclusively) descriptive goal. They are interested in finding out how speakers and writers use argumentation, with varying degrees of success, to convince or persuade others. Other argumentation scholars, often inspired by logic and philosophy, study argumentation for normative purposes. They are interested in developing soundness criteria that must be satisfied for the argumentation to be reasonable. Although in the study of argumentation both extremes are represented, many argumentation scholars take a middle position and assume that the study of argumentation has a normative as well as a descriptive dimension.

The analysis, evaluation, and production of argumentation are viewed differently in the various theoretical approaches to argumentation. Although this is not always acknowledged, it is clear that most of these approaches are strongly affected by either the dialectical perspective or the rhetorical perspective on argumentation developed in Antiquity. Approaches that are rhetorically oriented tend to put an emphasis on factors influencing the effectiveness of argumentation, viewing effectiveness as a matter of a "right" that speakers or writers are entitled to on the basis of the qualities of their argumentation rather than as a matter of fact. If the factual effectiveness of argumentation, in the sense of its actual persuasiveness, is the primary interest, then empirical "persuasion research" is required that amounts to empirical testing of attitude change. Approaches that are dialectically oriented focus primarily on the quality of argumentation in defending standpoints in regulated critical dialogues. They tend to put an emphasis on finding ways of guarding the reasonableness of argumentation by regimentation.

Together, but independently of each other, Chaim Perelman and Stephen E. Toulmin have revived the theoretical study of argumentation by publishing, in the same year (1958), two highly influential studies of argumentation. Perelman published, together with Lucie Olbrecht-Tyteca, the impressive volume *La Nouvelle Rhétorique*, which appeared in 1969 in English as *The New Rhetoric*, and Toulmin (1958) published *The Uses of Argument*. There are two different reasons for describing both contributions to the study of argumentation as "neoclassical." First, they have had an impact on the study of argumentation since the 1950s that is almost as big as the impact a classical scholar such as Aristotle has had since Antiquity. Second, these scholars have started a revaluation of insights that has led to the study of argumentation back to its classical roots. These neoclassical contributions have been the cradle of modern argumentation theory.

A new start was called for, because it had become clear in the 1950s that, unlike what many had thought, for studying argumentation logic alone is not enough. A great many linguistic, contextual, situational, and other pragmatic factors, which play a crucial part in argumentative communication, are left outside consideration in logic: who speaks to whom, in what argumentative situation, what has happened before that, what happens next, in what way exactly are the argumentative utterances phrased, which discourse conventions are followed in the process, and so on. In practice, logicians deal with formal derivations from abstract—and in some sense even empty—premises. In order to be able to make an unequivocal distinction between the "valid" and the "invalid" *argument forms* underlying such reasoning, they put some vital aspects of argumentative reality in brackets. Both Perelman and Toulmin were not only fully aware that logicians act like this, but they also pointed out why this is not right and offered an alternative.

PERELMAN AND OLBRECHTS-TYTECA'S NEW RHETORIC

Perelman and Olbrechts-Tyteca's conception of reasonableness goes, just as Toulmin's, against formal logic; they associate formal logic without any further ado with a reasonableness conception *more geometrico*. Because of this formal—"geometrical"—conception of reasonableness, logic is in their opinion neither sufficient nor relevant for the study of argumentation, if not both. The new rhetoric is meant to create an alternative framework for all forms of "nonanalytic thinking." In the new rhetoric, argumentation aimed at justification is considered complementary to formal proof, and it is urgent that a theory of argumentation be developed that is complementary to formal logic. Perelman views the new rhetoric as a reaction to "positivistic empiricism" and "rationalistic idealism," in which important areas of rational thinking, such as legal reasoning, are in his opinion simply passed by. By using the term *positivistic empiricism*, Perelman very probably refers to the analytic school of thought generally called logical empiricism or—disregarding any differences—logical positivism or neopositivism. And *rationalism* refers to the philosophy that regards reason ("ratio") as the only reliable source of knowledge, not experience (as empiricism claims). Perelman reacts to a rationalism based on "idealism," that is, one in which reality is reduced to ideas—to "consciousness contents."

According to the new rhetoricians, argumentation theory must pertain to differences of opinion in which *values* play a part and neither empirical verification nor formal proof, nor even a combination of the two, offers a way out. The theory of argumentation should show how choices that are made and decisions that are taken could be justified on rational (and reasonable) grounds. As Frege (1879/1967) analyzed mathematical thinking to develop a theory of logical reasoning, Perelman and Olbrechts-Tyteca examined philosophical, juridical, and other sorts of argumentation, according to Perelman (1970, p. 281) to develop a theory about arguing with values. Perelman and Olbrechts-Tyteca (1958/1969) define their new rhetoric as "the study of the discursive techniques allowing us *to induce or to increase the mind's adherence to the theses presented for its assent*" (p. 4).

In the description Perelman and Olbrechts-Tyteca give of the premises that can be used as the starting point of an argumentation, of special interest are the values, which relate to an audience's preferences for the one over the other, the value hierarchies, which vary as a rule more strongly per audience and are often more important than the values themselves, and the *loci* (or *topoi*), which are preferences that an audience endorses just like that so that they can be used as an immediate justification. In argumentation, certain argument schemes are used in connection with the point of departure that is chosen. These schemes rest on the principles of association. Every association puts a proposition in a particular argumentative relationship with the proposition contained in a standpoint. Perelman and Olbrechts-Tyteca's typology of argument schemes is an attempt at making an inventory of the various kinds of associations that can be made in the practice of argumentation. They distinguish three main categories: quasilogical relations, relations based on the structure of reality, and relations establishing the structure of reality. These distinctions are made analytically; in practice, relations can be combined and strengthen or weaken each other. Some critics have observed that the categories distinguished in Perelman and Olbrechts-Tyteca's catalog are neither well-defined and systematic nor mutually exclusive. These, and other, infirmities prevent unequivocal application of their theory in the analysis of argumentation.

Rather than a normative argumentation theory, the new rhetoric is a descriptive catalog of types of argumentation that can be successful in practice. Besides the technique of association, Perelman and Olbrecht-Tyteca also distinguish the technique of "dissociation," which involves splitting an existing concept into the old concept and a new concept that allows the arguer to avoid a contradiction by assigning a different value to the new concept and the old concept. Whether it concerns an association or dissociation, in the new rhetoric the soundness of argumentation is always linked to its success with an audience. Argumentation is sound if it adduces assent, or more assent with a standpoint among the audience. Thus, the soundness of argumentation is measured against its effect on a target group, which may be a "particular audience," but can also be the "universal audience" consisting of those whom the speaker or writer views as the embodiment of reasonableness. Everyone can imagine the universal audience in the way he or she prefers it to be, with all the norms of reasonableness that go with it. This means that the universal audience is ultimately a construction of the speaker or writer and provides a standard of reasonableness that is in some sense arbitrary. Because the audience is decisive in determining which argument schemes are supposed to be active and determining their validity, it is impossible to achieve an unequivocal and unanimous analysis of argumentative discourse that is based on Perelman and Olbrechts-Tyteca's typology.

TOULMIN'S MODEL OF ARGUMENTATION

Toulmin was interested in the way in which ideas and claims can be justified. He took a special interest in the norms that must be used when giving a rational assessment of argumentation put forward in support of views and assertions. Is there one universal system of norms that can be used to evaluate all kinds of argumentation in all areas or should each type of argumentation be judged in accordance with its own norms? In *The Uses of Argument*, Toulmin (1958) explains for the first time systematically what his views are with regard to answering these questions. He explained his ideas concerning rationality and reasonableness later in *Human Understanding* (1972) and *Knowing and Acting* (1976).

Gradually, Toulmin had come to the conclusion that formal logic cannot offer any further insight in the problems he was concerned with. In his opinion, more could be learned from observing the juridical process of argumentation. Analogously with the procedural way of acting in law, a model could be sketched of the various steps that must be made in argumentation. In a court of law, just as in argumentation, propositions are to be justified and the nature of these propositions can also vary considerably. The proofs that are put forward in a legal case are in the one case, and in the one kind of case, different from the other, but in all cases there are general similarities in the procedure that was followed.

In *The Uses of Argument*, Toulmin (1958) presents a model that represents the "procedural form" of argumentation: the functional steps that can be distinguished in the defense of a standpoint or *claim*. According to Toulmin, the soundness of argumentation is primarily determined by the degree to which the *warrant*, which connects the *data* adduced in the argumentation with the claim that is defended, is made acceptable by a *backing*. In Toulmin's basic model, it is assumed that the warrant is a rule without any exceptions and that the correctness of the warrant itself is not doubted. If there are exceptions to the rule, the force of the warrant is weakened and a *rebuttal* needs to be added. Then, the claim must be weakened by means of a modal term that involves a qualification of the claim and is therefore called a *qualifier*. A *backing* is required if the authority of the warrant is not immediately accepted. To account for such complications, the basic model must be extended on the points that are mentioned.

However inspiring Toulmin's ideas about argumentation and his model may have been, some argumentation scholars have brought forward a number of theoretical objections and it has also been noted that in some cases it is difficult to apply the model in practice. Toulmin's definitions of the data and the warrant make it often difficult, as Toulmin concedes, to keep them apart. This problem stems partly from the fact that Toulmin introduces the data and the warrant by means of two different descriptions. According to the first description, data provide specific information of a factual nature whereas warrants are general, hypothetical, rule-like statements that serve as a bridge between data and claim and justify the step from the data to the claim (1958, p. 98). According to the second description, data are called on explicitly and warrants implicitly (1958, p. 100). Because, depending on the prior knowledge the audience is supposed to have, factual information can just as well be left implicit whereas the relevant rule is made explicit, it can be difficult to determine in practice which statements serve as data and which statements serve as warrants.

Toulmin claims that the procedural form of argumentation is "field independent": The various steps that are taken—and are represented in the model—are always the same, irrespective of the kind of subject argumentation pertains to. What kind of backing is required, however, depends on the field to which the standpoint at issue belongs. An ethical justification, for instance, requires a different kind of backing than a legal justification. Toulmin concludes from this that the evaluation criteria for determining the soundness of argumentation are "field dependent." In this way, he puts argumentation in the rhetorical context of normative expectations prevailing in a specific field of argumentation. This means that the criteria for judging argumentation are historically determined and must be established empirically. According to Toulmin, the notion of "validity of argumentation"—validity in a broader sense than logical validity—is an "intraterritorial" notion, not an "interterritorial" one. Argumentation must therefore be evaluated with norms that are relevant and adequate for the field the standpoint that is defended belongs to, and the assessment criteria for argumentation may not automatically be transferred from the one field to the other. The conception of reasonableness Toulmin adheres to here is relativistic in a special way.

COMMONALITIES AND DIFFERENCES BETWEEN PERELMAN AND TOULMIN

There are some striking commonalities between the approach to argumentation taken in the new rhetoric and Toulmin's approach in developing his model. Both started from a broad philosophical background and a strong interest in the justification of views by argumentation in ordinary language. Both emphasized that argumentation can pertain to a great variety of topics and that value judgments may play a part. Neither Perelman nor Toulmin regarded modern formal logic as an adequate tool for dealing with argumentation. Both turned to the juridical procedures of law for finding an alternative model and developed their own theoretical framework for analyzing argumentation. Both gained broad recognition, but both not immediately. In Perelman's case, this was probably also due to the fact that his work was not published in English until 1969.

In fact, neither Perelman nor Toulmin received recognition straight from their fellow philosophers but both only through the recognition of the practical potential of their theories in the field of speech communication. Even theoretically there is a connection between the new rhetoric and Toulmin's model because Perelman's points of departure can be viewed as types of data and his argument schemes as types of warrants or backings.

Both neoclassical approaches are imbued with notions and distinctions that can already be found in the works of their classical predecessors. In Toulmin's case, this applies, for instance, to the similarity between the roles the warrant and the backing play in his model and the classical topoi or loci. Even more striking is the resemblance between the Toulmin model and the classical epicheirema as described by Cicero (see the bottom of the page).

In Perelman's case, his goals fit in well with those of Aristotle in the *Rhetoric,* albeit that Aristotle's system is primarily heuristic and Perelman's analytic. Just as in classical rhetoric, in the new rhetoric it is postulated that argumentation is always designed to achieve a particular effect on those for whom it is intended. Thus, in both classical rhetoric and the new rhetoric, the audience plays a crucial part. Among the other similarities is the classification of premises. Also, this

classification is in both cases connected with the degree to which premises are acceptable for an audience. Other notable similarities can be found in the argument schemes. The major part of the types of arguments that Perelman characterizes as based on the structure of reality were already represented in Book III of the *Topics.* And the argument schemes establishing the structure of reality offer the same possibilities for generalizing with respect to reality as classical rhetorical induction. In principle, the distinction between the argument schemes based on the structure of reality and those establishing the structure of reality runs parallel with Aristotle's more precise distinction between rhetorical syllogisms (*enthymemata*) and rhetorical induction (*paradigmata*).

In spite of the commonalities between Toulmin and Perelman, the differences prevail. Oxbridge-bred Toulmin is much more analytic in the way in which he develops and writes down his ideas. Continental Perelman's intellectual proceeding comes closer to practicing phenomenology. And although both argumentation scholars turn to the juridical model, for Toulmin the context of law was nothing more than a fitting example, whereas for Perelman it was a genuine area of interest. Among the evidence of this special interest are *The Idea of*

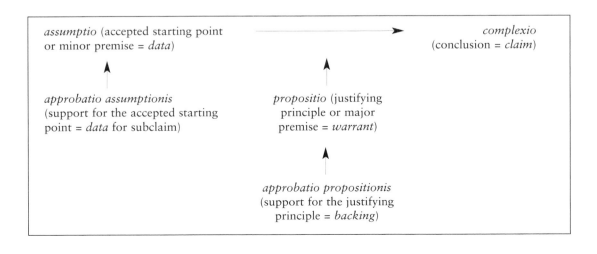

Justice and the Problem of Argument (1963), *Logique Juridique* (1976), and *Justice, Law and Argument* (1980). Still more important are the ensuing differences between the two theories. While Toulmin presents an analytic model that is ready for practical application, the new rhetoric offers an overview of elements playing a part in the process of convincing or persuading an audience that stimulates further reflection. These differences explain why Perelman has acquired more followers among fellow rhetoricians and philosophers of law whereas Toulmin's work has had a greater impact on students of communication and authors of practical textbooks.

INFORMAL LOGIC

Out of dissatisfaction with the treatment of argumentation in logical textbooks, inspired by Toulmin and to a lesser extent Perelman, since the 1970s an approach to argumentation has been propagated by a group of philosophers in Canada and the United States that is known as "informal logic." The label *informal logic* covers a collection of normative approaches to the study of reasoning in ordinary language that remain closer to the practice of argumentation than formal logic. Since 1978 the journal *Informal Logic*, started by J. Anthony Blair and Ralph H. Johnson, has been the speaking voice of informal logic and the educational reform movement concentrating on "critical thinking" that is connected with it.

Johnson and Blair (1977/1993) have indicated what they have in mind when they speak of an informal logical alternative. In *Logical Self-Defense,* they explain that the premises of an argument have to meet the criteria of "relevance," "sufficiency," and "acceptability." In the case of relevance, the question is whether there is an adequate substantial relation between the premises and

the conclusion of an argument; in the case of sufficiency, whether the premises provide enough evidence for the conclusion; in the case of acceptability, whether the premises themselves are true, probable, or in some other way trustworthy. Other informal logicians have adopted these three criteria, albeit sometimes under slightly different names (e.g., Govier, 1987). In *Acceptable Premises,* James B. Freeman (2005) provides the first comprehensive theory of the problem of premise acceptability from an epistemological perspective on informal logic.

Informal logicians remain primarily interested in the premise-conclusion relations in arguments. Although they maintain that argumentation should be sound in a logical sense, most of them do not stick to the formal criterion of deductive validity. In their studies of the fallacies, which are collected in *Fallacies,* John Woods and Douglas Walton (1989) choose a logical approach that is formal in a more general sense. Each fallacy requires in their view its own theoretical treatment, and this leads them to apply a variety of logical systems to the fallacies. A more outspoken informal logician, Ralph Johnson (2000), takes a predominantly logical approach but complements it in *Manifest Rationality* with a "dialectical tier." Other informal logicians are searching for appropriate alternatives in other directions. In this endeavor, the Toulmin model is probably their first source. Perelman's views and the rhetorical approach in general have received less attention. An exception is Christopher Tindale (1999), who turns in *Acts of Arguing* emphatically to rhetorical insights.

THE FORMAL DIALECTICAL APPROACH

Of all prominent modern approaches, the formal dialectical approach to argumentation, which was coined and introduced by Hamblin (1970), is probably furthest removed from

Perelman's and Toulmin's approaches. The scholars who are responsible for the revival of dialectics in the second part of the 20th century view argumentation as part of a procedure to resolve a difference of opinion by testing the tenability of the "thesis" at issue in a discussion that is formally regulated. In designing such a procedure, they make use of ideas developed by Rupert Crawshay-Williams (1957), Arne Naess (1966), and the Erlangen School of dialogue logic led by Paul Lorenzen and Kuno Lorenz (1978). The most completely worked out proposal for a theory of "formal dialectics" was presented by Else M. Barth and Erik C. W. Krabbe (1982). In *From Axiom to Dialogue*, they described a formal-dialectical procedure for determining by means of a regimented dialogue game between the "proponent" of a thesis and an "opponent" whether the thesis can be maintained in light of the opponent's "concessions" (propositions that the opponent has accepted). The proponent attempts to bring the opponent in a contradictory position by skillfully exploiting the concessions. If the proponent succeeds, the thesis has been successfully defended *ex concessis*, that is, given the concessions.

The quintessence of Barth and Krabbe's formal dialectics is a translation of formal logical systems into formal rules of dialogue that build on the Erlangen School dialogue logic. In *Commitment and Dialogue*, Walton and Krabbe (1995) integrate the approach of the Erlangen School with the more permissive kind of dialogues promoted in Hamblin's dialectical systems. They provide a classification of the major types of dialogue and discuss the conditions under which commitments should be held or may be retracted in an argument without violating any rules of the dialogue. Commitments are in this approach defined in such a way that in some cases an arguer can be held to his or her commitments, but not in others.

THE PRAGMA-DIALECTICAL APPROACH

In *Speech Acts in Argumentative Discussions* (1984), Frans H. van Eemeren and Rob Grootendorst developed the pragma-dialectical approach to argumentation, which connects with formal dialectics, but is also fundamentally different. The agreement is expressed in the term "dialectic," the difference in the replacement of the term "formal" by "pragma" (for "pragmatic"). In pragma-dialectics argumentation is viewed as a communicative and interactional discourse phenomenon that is to be studied from a normative as well as a descriptive perspective. The dialectical dimension is inspired by normative insights from "critical rationalism" and formal dialectics, the pragmatic dimension by descriptive insights from speech act theory, Gricean language philosophy, and discourse analysis.

Pragma-dialectics starts from four metatheoretical principles: "functionalization," "socialization," "externalization," and "dialectification" of argumentation, in which pragmatic and dialectical starting points are systematically combined. Functionalization is achieved by recognizing that argumentative discourse occurs through—and in response to—speech act performances. Socialization is achieved by extending the speech act perspective to the level of interaction, so that the ways in which positions with regard to standpoints and criticisms and defenses of standpoints are mutually conveyed can be accounted for. Externalization is achieved by capturing the propositional and interactional commitments created by the speech acts performed. Finally, dialectification is achieved by regimenting the exchange of speech acts in an ideal model of a critical discussion.

In the pragma-dialectical model of a critical discussion, the stages are analytically distinguished that argumentative discourse must pass through to resolve a difference of opinion about the standpoint at issue by putting the tenability of this standpoint to the test: the "confrontation stage," in which the difference of opinion comes about; the "opening stage," in which the procedural and material point of departure of the discussion is determined; the "argumentation stage," in which the standpoints are defended against any criticism that is advanced; and the "concluding stage," in which the result of the discussion is determined. The model also defines the nature and distribution of the speech acts that play a constructive part in the various stages of the resolution process.

In pragma-dialectics, the critical norms of reasonableness authorizing the speech acts performed in the various stages of a critical discussion are accounted for in a set of dialectical rules, ranging from the prohibition to prevent each other from expressing any position one wishes to assume in the confrontation stage, to the prohibition to misrepresent the result of the discussion in the concluding stage (van Eemeren & Grootendorst, 2004). Any violation of any of the rules, in whatever stage it occurs, amounts to making an argumentative move that is an impediment to the resolution of a difference of opinion and is therefore, and in this sense, considered fallacious (van Eemeren & Grootendorst, 1992). The use of the term *fallacy* is thus systematically connected with the rules for critical discussion.

For various reasons, argumentative reality does not always resemble the ideal of a critical discussion. A pragma-dialectical analysis is aimed at reconstructing from the theoretical perspective of a critical discussion all those, and only those, speech acts that play a potential part in resolving a difference of opinion on the merits, so that an adequate starting point is achieved for a fair evaluation. In *Reconstructing Argumentative Discourse*, van Eemeren, Grootendorst, Sally Jackson, and Scott Jacobs (1993) emphasize that the reconstruction should be faithful to the commitments that may be ascribed to the

participants on the basis of their contributions to the discourse. To go beyond a "naïve" reading of the discourse, the analyst's intuitions must be augmented by textual and contextual evidence, background knowledge, and relevant knowledge of the world, including knowledge about the results of (qualitative as well as quantitative) empirical research of argumentative reality.

RADICAL ARGUMENTATIVISM

Starting in the 1970s, Oswald Ducrot and Jean-Claude Anscombre have developed in a number of publications (almost exclusively in French) a descriptive linguistic approach to language use and argumentation. Because in their view almost all verbal utterances—often implicitly—lead the listener or reader to a certain conclusion and are therefore crucially argumentative in their meaning, they refer in *L'argumentation dans la langue* (Anscombre & Ducrot, 1983) to their theoretical position as "radical argumentativism." Ducrot and Anscombre's descriptive approach is characterized by a great interest in words such as "only," "no less than," "but," "even," "still," "because," and "so," which can serve as argumentative "operators" or "connectors" and give the linguistic utterances a specific "argumentative force" and "argumentative direction." In a certain context, the sentence "The ring costs only one hundred euros" points in the direction of a conclusion such as "Buy that ring" and the sentence "The ring costs no less than one hundred euros" in the direction of a conclusion such as "Do not buy that ring."

Another kind of observation made by Ducrot and Anscombre is that a word such as "but" only determines the direction of the conclusion that is suggested by the sentence and not the content of this conclusion. Whatever conclusion may be drawn in a specific context, in all cases, the presence of the word "but" causes this conclusion to be the opposite of, and also stronger than, the conclusion that has to be drawn from the part of the sentence preceding "but." According to Ducrot and Anscombre, the opposite standpoints suggested by "but" in a sentence such as "Paul is rich, but he is married" select two different "argumentative principles" that are on a par with the *topoi* from classical rhetoric (Anscombre, 1994). In the context assumed by Henning Nølke (1992), these are in this example: "The more someone has the property of being rich, the more attractive it is for a woman to get to know him better" and "The more someone is tied to another woman, the less attractive it is for a woman to get to know him better." In this case, the latter *topos* has a bigger argumentative force than the first, which is as it were put aside—"overruled"—by the latter. Thereby, the last *topos* determines the eventual argumentative direction of the sentence, which leads to an implicit conclusion such as "It is no use trying to get to know Paul better."

THE REVIVAL OF RHETORIC

In the United States, the study of rhetoric has survived remarkably better than in Europe. Not only was classical rhetoric already in the 19th century more strongly represented in the academic curriculum but the development of modern rhetorical approaches has also been more prolific. Among the most important 20th-century rhetoricians are I. A. Richards, Richard Weaver, and Kenneth Burke, whose broad aims and ambitions vary from developing a culture based on the ideal and the truth to helpful insights for correcting misunderstandings. Burke's (1950) definition of rhetoric as "the use of words by human agents to form attitudes or to induce actions in other human agents" comes close to the traditional definitions concentrating on "persuasion." Because he views persuasion as a result of "identification," he considers identification as a necessary complement. The argumentative angle of rhetoric, connecting rhetoric with the ability to find the appropriate means of persuasion and to use of them in a speech, has been predominant for a long time and has even been considered paradigmatic.

In the last decades of the 20th century, a powerful revaluation of rhetoric has taken place in the study of argumentation that revised the irrational and even antirational image of rhetoric that had come into being during the past centuries. It is remarkable that the rehabilitation of rhetoric started at about the same time in various countries. A considerable time after Perelman and Olbrechts-Tyteca's pioneering work, in the United States several argumentation scholars defended the rational qualities of rhetoric. Joseph W. Wenzel (1980), for one, would like to give rhetoric full credit, but then emphatically in relation with logic and more in particular dialectics. In France, Olivier Reboul (1990) argued in favor of giving rhetoric a satisfactory position in the study of argumentation beside dialectics. He regarded rhetoric and dialectic as different disciplines, which display some overlap: Rhetoric applies dialectic to public discussions while dialectic is at the same time a part of rhetoric because dialectic provides rhetoric with intellectual tools. In Germany, Josef Kopperschmidt (1989) took the reappraisal of rhetoric a considerable step further: He argued that, viewed from a historical perspective, rhetoric is the central concern of argumentation theorists. Such examples of revaluing rhetoric can be noticed on a much broader scale. In many cases, tribute is paid to Perelman, and more in particular to Perelman and Olbrecht-Tyteca's book, *The New Rhetoric*.

AMERICAN COMMUNICATION AND RHETORIC

The scholars currently engaged in the study of argumentation in American (speech) communication do not share the same perspective. Their most obvious common feature is their insistence that argumentation relates to audiences and fits within the rhetorical tradition. Most of the literature is concerned with the connection between claims and people in some kind of rhetorical practice, which David Zarefsky (1993) defines in broad terms as "the practice of justifying decisions under conditions of uncertainty."

The view of argumentation as practice contrasts sharply with the analytic view of argumentation as a logical structure. This different outlook was to a great extent inspired by the American debate tradition, which started in colleges and universities in the late 19th century. In the early and middle years of the 20th century, connections were made with classical rhetorical theory, which led to a debate tradition dominated by the paradigm of "stock issues." An influential departure from this tradition was *Decision by Debate* (1963) by Douglas Ehninger and Wayne Brockriede, which offered a broader perspective. Making use of the Toulmin model, debate was viewed as a means of making decisions critically and described as fundamentally a cooperative rather than competitive enterprise. This started an exploration of alternatives to the received tradition that resulted in the late 1970s and early 1980s in different paradigms or models of debate—the traditional perspective on debate known as "the stock-issues model" took its place among these alternatives. The debate tradition has greatly influenced American argumentation studies. Even Dale Hample's *Arguing* (2005), dealing for the most part with argument production, can be seen as a descendant of the debate tradition.

Besides the debate tradition there has always been a considerable group of scholars who continued to study argumentation from the perspective of classical rhetoric. Among the contemporary examples of such scholars are Michael Leff (2003) and Edward Schiappa, who have contributed to the study of argumentation by profound rhetorical analyses. Although the influence of Perelman's new rhetoric has been more limited than in Europe, some of his ideas have permeated American argumentation scholarship. The concept of loci, akin to the "topics" in classical rhetoric, has been used as a way to understand sources of argument. The treatment of *figures* and *tropes* has made clear that they have the argumentative function of strengthening or weakening presence, that is, the salience of an idea or topic. The concept of dissociation has proven to be important to definitions and stipulations when advancing or retarding arguments (Schiappa, 2002).

The "social science approach" to communication, which emphasizes descriptive and empirical, rather than normative, studies and seeks to produce testable statements about communication in general rather than shedding insight on particular significant cases, received a significant boost from World War II studies of persuasion and attitude change. It was brought to bear on argumentation studies in the 1970s, predominantly by a group of scholars united by their commitment to "constructivism." Charles A. Willard, for one, who defined argumentation as an interaction of people who maintain what they construe to be incompatible claims, started to develop a constructivist theory of argumentation (Willard, 1983). If argumentation is indeed, as Zarefsky says, the practice of justifying decisions, then the focus of attention is on justifications, that is, on public acts. Lloyd Bitzer was among the scholars who came to see the enthymeme as a communicative act—rhetorical proof being a joint creation of speaker and listener. Starting from the idea of communicative acts as public features of conversational argument, Jacobs and Jackson (1982) initiated a program for studying argumentation in informal conversations. They tried to understand the reasoning processes individuals actually use to make inferences and resolve disputes in ordinary talk. A related direction in empirical argumentation research is studying argument in natural settings such as school board meetings, counseling sessions, and public relations campaigns, to produce "grounded theory"—a theory of the specific case.

Another trend affecting argumentation studies in American communication and rhetoric is the recovery of practical philosophy, harking back to the classical concept of *phronesis*—practical wisdom in a given case—that was recovered by Toulmin and Perelman. Another Toulmin concept that has strongly influenced American argumentation scholarship is that of "field." In *Human Understanding* (1972), Toulmin described fields as "rational enterprises," which he equates with intellectual disciplines, and explored how the nature of reasoning differed. This treatment led to vigorous discussion about what defined a "field of argument": subject matter, general perspective or worldview, or the arguer's purpose, to mention a few of the possibilities. The concept of fields of argument, however defined, encouraged recognition that the soundness of arguments is not universal and certain, but field specific and contingent. This belief was another step in resituating argument within the rhetorical tradition. Instead of asking whether an argument was sound, the questions became "Sound for whom?" and "Sound in what context?" The core idea is that the grounds for knowledge claims lie in the epistemic practices and states of consensus in knowledge domains. In the late 1960s, Robert Scott contributed further to the emerging belief that truth is relative to argument and to audience and stimulated studies of what sorts of knowledge are rhetorically constructed and how arguing produces knowledge.

Thomas Goodnight (1982) has preferred the term *spheres* to the term *fields*, emphasizing more general and all-encompassing categories. By sphere he means "the grounds upon which arguments are built and the authorities to which arguers appeal" (p. 216). Goodnight uses "argument" to mean interaction based on dissensus, so the *grounds* of arguments lie in doubts and uncertainties. He distinguishes

three spheres of argument: "the personal," "the technical," and "the public." His triad stresses differences between arguments whose relevance is confined to the arguers themselves, arguments whose pertinence extends to a specialized or limited community, and arguments that are meaningful for people in general. Goodnight's first concern is that the public sphere is being "steadily eroded by the elevation of the personal and technical groundings of argument" (p. 223).

Another force that has shaped the nature of argumentation studies within communication and rhetoric is social and cultural critique. The intellectual underpinning of argument-as-critique is "postmodernism." There are many varieties of postmodernism. The more extreme variety is the denial that there can be any such thing as communal norms or standards for argument and the claim that what passes for such standards is socially constructed. If it is only the powerful interests in a group that have defined communal standards, the goal of argument-as-critique is to expose this practice and to suggest alternatives, so that those who were excluded or marginalized can be brought into the process of deliberation.

ESTABLISHING A LINK BETWEEN DIALECTICS AND RHETORIC

In spite of the recent revival of both dialectics and rhetoric, there is a wide conceptual gap between the two perspectives on argumentation, which have been mutually isolated since their ideological separation in the 16th and 17th centuries and were viewed as incompatible paradigms (Toulmin, 2001). Recently, some argumentation scholars have come to the conclusion that this sharp division requires weakening because the dialectical and the rhetorical perspective on argumentation do not necessarily exclude each other. An argument has even been made for establishing a link between rhetoric and dialectics: The two perspectives on argumentation lead to different kinds of insights and the analysis and evaluation of argumentative discourse would be enriched if they could be combined.

In the Netherlands, van Eemeren aims with Peter Houtlosser for an integration of insights from rhetoric into the pragma-dialectical theory of argumentation (van Eemeren & Houtlosser, 2002). In their view, the parties involved in a difference of opinion "maneuver strategically" to realize at the same time their dialectical and their rhetorical aims, thus trying to combine effectiveness with observing the critical standards for argumentative discourse. They claim that in each of the dialectical stages of the process of resolving a difference of opinion on the merits there is a rhetorical goal that corresponds with the dialectical goal. In the strategic maneuvering to reconcile the simultaneous pursuit of these goals, three aspects can be analytically distinguished: making an opportune selection from the topical potential available at the stage concerned, approaching the audience effectively, and carefully exploiting presentational means. These three aspects correspond with some focal points of rhetorical study—topics, audience adaptation, and presentational devices—so that insights acquired in rhetoric are brought to bear in explaining how rhetorical and dialectical considerations play a part in the various ways of strategic maneuvering.

REFERENCES

Anscombre, J.-C. (1994). La nature des topoï. In J. C. Anscombre (Ed.), *La théorie des topoï* (pp. 49–84). Paris: Kimé.

Anscombre, J.-C., & Ducrot, O. (1983). *L'argumentation dans la langue*. Liège, Belgium: Pierre Mardaga.

Barth, E. M., & Krabbe, E. C. W. (1982). *From axiom to dialogue: A philosophical study of logics and argumentation*. New York: Walter de Gruyter.

Burke, K. (1950). *A rhetoric of motives*. Berkeley: University of California Press.

Crawshay-Williams, R. (1957). *Methods and criteria of reasoning: An inquiry into the structure of controversy*. London: Routledge & Kegan Paul.

Ehninger, D., & Brockreide, W. (1963). *Decision by debate*. New York: Harper Collins.

Freeman, J. B. (2005). *Acceptable premises: An informal approach to an informal logic problem*. Cambridge, UK: Cambridge University Press.

Frege, G. (1967). Begriffsschrift: eine der arithmetischen nachgebildete Formelsprache des reinen Denkens [Bergiffsschrift: A formula language, modelled upon that of arithmetic, for pure thought]. In J. van Heijenoort (Ed.), *From Frege to Gödel: A sourcebook in mathematical logic, 1879-1931*. Cambridge, MA: Harvard University Press. (Original work published 1879)

Goodnight, G. T. (1982). The personal, technical, and public spheres of argument: A speculative inquiry into the art of public deliberation. *Journal of the American Forensic Association, 18*, 214–227.

Govier, T. (1987). *Problems in argument analysis and evaluation*. Dordrecht, The Netherlands: Foris.

Hamblin, C. L. (1970). *Fallacies*. London: Methuen. (Reprinted with a preface by J. Plecnik & J. Hoaglund.) Newport News, VA: Vale Press.

Hample, D. (2005). *Arguing: Exchanging reasons face to face*. Mahwah, NJ: Lawrence Erlbaum.

Jacobs, S., & Jackson, S. (1982). Conversational argument: A discourse analytic approach. In J. R. Cox & C. A. Willard (Eds.), *Advances in argumentation theory and research* (pp. 205–237). Carbondale: Southern Illinois University Press.

Johnson, R. H. (2000). *Manifest rationality: A pragmatic theory of argument*. Mahwah, NJ: Lawrence Erlbaum.

Johnson, R. H., & Blair, J. A. (1993). *Logical self-defense* (3rd ed.). Toronto, Ontario, Canada: McGraw-Hill Ryerson. (Original work published 1977)

Kopperschmidt, J. (1989). *Methodik der Argumentationsanalyse*. Stuttgart, Germany: Fromann-Holzboog.

Leff, M. (2003). Tradition and agency in humanistic rhetoric. *Philosophy and Rhetoric, 36*, 135–147.

Lorenzen, P., & Lorenz, K. (1978). *Dialogische Logik*. Darmstadt, Germany: Wissenschaftliche Buchgesellschaft.

Naess, A. (1966). *Communication and argument: Elements of applied semantics*. London: Allen & Unwin.

Nølke, H. (1992). Semantic constraints on argumentation: From polyphonic micro-structure to argumentative macro-structure. In F. H. van Eemeren, R. Grootendorst, J. A. Blair, & C. A. Willard (Eds.), *Argumentation illuminated* (pp. 189–200). Amsterdam: Sic Sat.

Perelman, C. (1963). *The idea of justice and the problem of argument*. New York: Humanities Press.

Perelman, C. (1970). The new rhetoric: A theory of practical reasoning. *The Great Ideas Today. Part 3: The contemporary status of a great idea* (pp. 273–312). Chicago: Encyclopedia Britannica.

Perelman, C. (1976). *Logique juridique: Nouvelle rhétorique*. Paris: Dalloz.

Perelman, C. (1980). *Justice, law and argument: Essays on moral and legal reasoning*. Dordrecht, The Netherlands: Reidel.

Perelman, C., & Olbrechts-Tyteca, L. (1958). *La nouvelle rhétorique: Traité de l'argumentation*. Paris: Presses Universitaires de France. (English translation [1969] as *The new rhetoric: A treatise on argumentation*. Notre Dame, IN/London: University of Notre Dame Press)

Reboul, O. (1990). Rhétorique et dialectique chez Aristotle. *Argumentation, 4,* 35–52.

Schiappa, E. (2002). Evaluating argumentative discourse from a rhetorical perspective: Defining "person" and "human life" in constitutional disputes over abortion. In F. H. van Eemeren & P. Houtlosser (Eds.), *Dialectic and rhetoric: The warp and woof of argumentation analysis* (pp. 65–80). Dordrecht, The Netherlands: Kluwer Academic.

Tindale, C. W. (1999). *Acts of arguing: A rhetorical model of argument*. New York: State University of New York Press.

Toulmin, S. E. (1958). *The uses of argument*. Cambridge, MA: Cambridge University Press.

Toulmin, S. E. (1972). *Human understanding*. Princeton, NJ: Princeton University Press.

Toulmin, S. E. (1976). *Knowing and acting: An invitation to philosophy*. New York: Macmillan.

Toulmin, S. E. (2001). *Return to reason*. Cambridge, MA: Harvard University Press.

van Eemeren, F. H., & Grootendorst, R. (1984). *Speech acts in argumentative discussions. A theoretical model for the analysis of discussions directed towards solving conflicts of opinion*. Berlin, Germany: De Gruyter.

van Eemeren, F. H., & Grootendorst, R. (1992). *Argumentation, communication, and fallacies: A pragma-dialectical perspective*. Hillsdale, NJ: Lawrence Erlbaum.

van Eemeren, F. H., & Grootendorst, R. (2004). *A systematic theory of argumentation: The pragma-dialectical approach*. Cambridge, UK: Cambridge University Press.

van Eemeren, F. H., Grootendorst, R., Jackson, S., & Jacobs, S. (1993). *Reconstructing argumentative discourse*. Tuscaloosa: University of Alabama Press.

van Eemeren, F. H., Grootendorst, R., Snoeck Henkemans, A. F., Blair, J. A., Johnson, R. H., Krabbe, E. C. W. et al. (1996). *Fundamentals of argumentation theory*. Mahwah, NJ: Lawrence Erlbaum.

van Eemeren, F. H., & Houtlosser, P. (2002). Strategic maneuvering: Maintaining a delicate balance. In F. H. van Eemeren & P. Houtlosser (Eds.), *Dialectic and rhetoric: The warp and woof of argumentation analysis* (pp. 131–159). Dordrecht, The Netherlands: Kluwer Academic.

Walton, D. N., & Krabbe, E. C. W. (1995). *Commitment and dialogue: Basic concepts of interpersonal reasoning*. Albany: State University of New York Press.

Wenzel, J. W. (1980). Perspectives on argument. In J. Rhodes & S. E. Newell (Eds.), *Dimensions of argument: Proceedings of the Summer Conference on Argumentation* (pp. 112–133). Annandale, VA: Speech Communication Association.

Willard, C. A. (1983). *A theory of argumentation*. Tuscaloosa: University of Alabama Press.

Woods, J., & Walton, D. N. (1989). *Fallacies: Selected papers, 1972–1982*. Dordrecht, The Netherlands: Foris.

Zarefsky, D. (1993). Argumentation in the tradition of speech communication studies. In F. H. van Eemeren, R. Grootendorst, J. A. Blair, & C. A. Willard (Eds.), *Perspectives and approaches: Proceedings of the Third International Conference on Argumentation* (Vol. 1, pp. 32–52). Amsterdam: Sic Sat.

7

Rhetoric of Religion

A Map of the Territory

MARGARET D. ZULICK

The connection between rhetoric and religion goes back, at least in emblem, to the Goddess Peitho herself, the personification of persuasion and receiver of supplicants who wish to win over their lovers with words (Stafford, 2000). Both rhetoric and religion appear to be universal to the human condition. Yet rarely are they correlated in the course of human inquiry. Thus, the rhetoric of religion is an immense undiscovered country, necessitating multiple critical and theoretical approaches and different hermeneutical stances and forms of knowledge. It can be approached from either coast, whether from religious scholars seeking insight into language use or from rhetoricians looking at religious motives in rhetoric. It has been done from a faith perspective as well as from a purely humanistic mode of inquiry.[1] Only a few of these possibilities have yet been realized in existing research.

And even while the number of studies of specific cases begins to grow, there is still little attempt to organize them into a systematic treatment.

I began my own foray into the rhetoric of religion as a student of the Hebrew Bible, in search of a humanistic critical approach. From that standpoint I encountered the tradition of rhetoric. Through its lens I began to see the Hebrew Bible not only as a consummate rhetorical text but also as a formative moment in the history and theory of rhetoric. The inquiry into religious language led me to further question the nature of rhetorical consciousness. I found a theoretical fellow traveler in the writings of Kenneth Burke and a second great field of religious influence in American public discourse. Since I can shine a small spotlight over the vast territory of religious rhetoric, I offer in this essay

125

exploratory sections on each of these areas: interactionism and religious discourse, biblical rhetoric, and American rhetorics of religion. By so doing, I hope to present others with the opportunity to trace the larger outlines of the rhetoric of religion, showing where the interconnections lie between religious discourse, rhetorical theory, biblical exegesis, and public discourse and where are the lacunae that remain to be filled in by further research.

In reviewing the history and current state of research in these three active areas, I will seek out avenues of systematic theoretical inquiry. Therefore, I will focus on research that advances theories of rhetoric, with only incidental mention of often very worthy and useful research that uses rhetoric primarily as a tool to explore religious texts and cases, without problematizing the relationship between rhetoric and religion. Since it is possible to ask how rhetoric informs religious history and theology as well as to ask how religion informs the history and theory of rhetoric, the rhetoric of religion must be interdisciplinary in scope. Indeed, one recent volume of distinguished essays, *Rhetorical Invention and Religious Inquiry,* is exemplary of such a direction (Jost & Olmsted, 2000). This essay will, I hope, function to introduce some key literature in religion and biblical studies to rhetoricians and introduce some of the work in rhetoric to scholars of religion and biblical literature. Necessarily, each field may discover that their own area is covered at a very introductory level. Nonetheless, I hope that a general guide to past and prospective scholarship in the rhetoric of religion will prove useful to many.

KENNETH BURKE, RHETORICAL CONSCIOUSNESS, AND THE IDEA OF THE TRANSCENDENT

In 1928, Owen Barfield, Oxford don and theosophist, argued for a different view of the development of consciousness, imagination,

and language. Rather than an abstract idea of "spirit," for instance, arising by analogy from the more concrete cognate "breath," he suggested that instead the abstract and the concrete meanings had become divided from an initial seamless whole, stemming from a world in which the imagination of spirit and the matter of breath were concrete and indissoluble (Barfield, 1973, pp. 81–89).

Mary Douglas (1966) seems to echo this notion when she argues that the mythical worldview is not merely superstition, an incomplete knowledge of the laws of nature, but a different way of responding to the environment, an address to the universe in a way that expects a response, that imparts consciousness and intention to the world of nature: "Physical forces are thought of as interwoven with the lives of persons . . . The universe responds to speech and mime" (pp. 87–88).

Myth and religion, the very idea of the transcendent, are so universal to the human condition that they seem to require more than accident or cultural influence to explain. This is not to argue for or against deism or suggest any empirical claim to the existence of God. We do not need an objective God to understand the function of God-language. But the universality of God-language does suggest that something about what makes us human also gives rise to the idea of transcendent consciousness. As rhetoricians, perhaps we may speculate that the "idea of the holy," as Rudolf Otto once coined the phrase, is a natural byproduct of the invention of language (Otto, 1923). It is Bakhtin's "loophole addressee," a sort of placeholder for the logical necessity of address, which projects for every thought a respondent who would understand it completely. So the desire to communicate with a transcendent other consciousness can in itself give rise to the active projection of such a consciousness. If all this is the case, then there also would be more than an accidental connection between religious consciousness and rhetorical consciousness, the awareness of language in its aspect as addressed.

Characteristically, Kenneth Burke was interested in religion not as a critical subject but as a pure analog to his interactive theory of language, or "logology." In other words, as he put it in one review essay, of an author who made claims for innate transcendence in certain figurative poetic effects, "All told, we are asking the question whether a survey of the structural resources inherent in language might not account for the poetic manifestations ... Might the conditions of language itself be enough to account for the 'origin' of any poem?"(Burke, 1982, pp. 333–334; Carter, 1996).

For Burke, the realm of the transcendent is neither beyond language not prior to it, but it is a logical extension of language as such. In other words, he is looking at the other side of the usual corollary between language and transcendence. Instead of using language to express an ontological transcendent that is somehow beyond language, Burke uses theology as a trope for logology, the reflexive and self-transcending linguistic hierarchy. In *Rhetoric of Religion,* he outlines six analogies by which language not only partakes of, but in some sense invents the transcendent simply by its own fact of being: "There is a sense in which language is *not* just 'natural,' but really *does* add a 'new dimension' to the things of nature" (Burke, 1970, p. 8). His explanation for this involves the necessary fact that we can easily perform transformations on the words for things that we cannot do easily, or at all, with the things themselves.

> There is a sense in which the *word* for tree "transcends" the thing as thoroughly as does the Platonic idea of the tree's perfect "archetype" in heaven. It is the sense in which the name for a class of objects "transcends" any particular member of that class. (p. 10)

Burke's six analogies must be studied at length, and not in this essay,[2] but suffice it to say that the first analogy, between words and The Word of the Gospel of John, encompasses a hierarchy of terms for things, terms for social relations, terms for words as such (grammar and rhetoric), and finally terms for the supernatural, which is at the top of the tree because only in this realm do the ideas exist solely by means of the words that describe them and exclusively as analogies borrowed from the other categories. The divine must be imagined before it can be experienced. The supernatural transcendent arises as an extension of the linguistic transcendent.

Several rhetoricians have discussed whether Kenneth Burke was himself a theologian (Appel, 1993; Feehan, 2001; Maddux, 2006). Burke himself may not have known and certainly didn't say when asked (Booth, 2001). At any rate, it seems not in the purview of the rhetoric of religion either to raise or attempt to answer ontological questions about divinity. It is the *idea* of divinity, its constraints and its inventional possibilities, that should concern us. Here it does seem there is much to be gained from looking at the reciprocal transference between religious and rhetorical transcendence.

There are two lessons to be gained from Burke's rhetoric of religion that will bear on the rest of this article. First, the structural reflexivity of using words about words to describe words about God means that, where the idea of the divine or of any transcendent is concerned, the words we use to describe it cannot be distinguished from the words we use to invent it. Second, rhetorical forms, like all forms, are structurally interactive, because they are co-constructed by the audience. They "conjure," interact with and reproduce prior patterns of experience and prior rhetorical forms. When successive layers of reflexive words about God, authority claims legitimating them, responses to them, and further justifications adapting them to new contexts are aggregated over time into a multivocal sacred text, we get a rhetorical document like the Bible.

BIBLICAL RHETORIC

The connection between rhetoric and the Bible goes back to ancient times, in all probability as far back as Hellenistic Judaism and the writing of the New Testament itself. But the conscious theorizing of rhetoric in the Judeo-Christian context could only begin once there was an existing canon of Judeo-Christian scripture. Perhaps, the foremost landmark of early Christian rhetoric has been Augustine of Hippo.[3] This great Christian theologian spans the transition between the classical and the medieval world, bringing a Roman rhetorical education with him into the Christian fold. His treatise *De doctrina Christiana* (*On Christian Doctrine*) wrestles with the problem set for anyone attempting to translate the classical tradition of rhetoric into the Christian context (Augustine, trans. 1958). The problem for rhetoric is threefold. First, Christian rhetoric relies on divine revelation rather than invention for the discovery of arguments. Therefore, Augustine replaces the invention section of a traditional handbook with a treatise on the interpretation of signs.[4] Second, given this divine source of knowledge, the teaching of argument must be justified as more than mere deception. Third, the phenomenon of human freedom of will arises as a rhetorical issue for the first time in Augustine. The last two questions are addressed together in Book Four, which is at once a defense of biblical eloquence and a discussion of levels of style. Augustine magisterially queries, "Who would dare to say that truth should stand in the person of its defenders unarmed against lying" (IV.3) and quite plaintively argues for the continuing necessity of persuasion, the third level of style: "How do these [teaching and delight] help a man who both confesses the truth and praises the eloquence but still does not give his assent?" (IV.29). This particular dilemma could rarely pertain in Aristotle's rhetorical situation, where each audience comes to the speech already mandated to act, one way or the other, as a result of the speech. But in the case of Christian homiletic, the audience may walk away uncommitted, even against their own intellectual agreement, because Christian persuasion has no external mandate, but engages the interior will directly and without third party authorization. This theme of the mystery of the human will is more developed in the *Confessions*, but it defines the rhetorical situation in *De Doctrina* as well.

The theory of signs devised by Augustine builds on Aristotle but creates a hermeneutic worldview of its own, one that has gone on to influence all modern semiotics as well as rhetoric. By first distinguishing between enjoyment and use, then between love of God on the one hand and love of one's neighbor as a means to the love of God on the other, Augustine establishes a hierarchy of values in which a framework for the interpretation of signs can be laid. The most important result of this framework is the rule of charity, which establishes a theological parallel to a reasonable doubt standard for accommodating error and distinguishing error from sin. The rule of charity speaks to the most important use of Augustine's rhetoric for his own religious situation, one in which the major controversies that resulted in catholic orthodoxy as we know it were still being fought out. According to the rule of charity, while mistakes in interpretation can occur, the place of scripture in the hierarchy of values is not as an end to be enjoyed for its own sake but as a means to further the love of God and one's neighbor. Therefore, any interpretation that is mistaken but does have the same purpose of charity is simply mistaken and not sinful. Thus, Augustine clears a path for plural approaches to interpretation amid the dreadful heat of religious controversy.

Augustine's dilemma, to establish a rhetoric for an authoritative discourse, sets the stage not merely for exegesis but for all religious rhetoric. If, in Aristotelian terms, rhetoric deals only with things that "seem to admit of issuing in more than one possible way," then authoritative texts and the theological doctrines based on them cannot be addressed as rhetoric without demoting their status as divinely ordained truth. Yet the eloquence of these texts can and should be defended, and to do that their adherents must treat them in and on the terms of rhetoric.

The tradition of demonstrating the eloquence of biblical literature through identifying rhetorical and poetic features of its style continues.[5] It could be said that the entire medieval tradition of rhetoric owes its existence to this primary marriage of rhetoric and hermeneutics in Augustine. One fascinating example, however, raises a distinct counterpoint. That is *The Book of the Honeycomb's Flow,* a Jewish treatise on biblical eloquence in the Italian humanist tradition. Written by Judah Messer Leon, an Italian Jew in the 15th century, it quotes Cicero at length and makes high claims for the power of biblical persuasion while at the same time defending the art of rhetoric (Messer Leon, trans. 1983). This volume demonstrates the continuity of biblical rhetoric in the Renaissance resurgence of classical humanism, as once again the Bible's eloquence must be defended in the terms of Cicero.

The English Enlightenment embraced the humanist rhetorical tradition (Wilson, 1553) and with it brought us Bishop Lowth's treatise on biblical rhetoric. Lowth's *Lectures on the Sacred Poetry of the Hebrews (De sacra poesi Hebraeorum)* of 1753 is traditionally cited as marking the beginnings of literary-historical criticism of the Bible (e.g., Cheyne, 1893). In that work the name of rhetoric is conspicuously absent; but "poetry" occupies the position of principal opposite to philosophy in the introduction. Lowth (1787) argues that poetry achieves through eloquence the same truth that philosophy arrives at more directly, but less pleasantly, through reason. His analysis of Hebrew poetics includes levels of style, especially the sublime, and employs

devices and tropes such as allegory, comparison, metaphor, and personification. Thus, the rhetorical tradition under a substitute name was present at the beginnings of modern "higher criticism" (Buss, 1974; Lowth, 1787; compare Meynet, 1990). As historicism began to predominate in the German academy during the 19th century, however, the rhetorical tradition as a critical method receded in favor of form and tradition criticism.

The contemporary map of biblical rhetoric is dominated by New Testament rhetorical criticism. Even before George Kennedy's window-opening *New Testament Interpretation Through Rhetorical Criticism* (1984), Amos Wilder wrote the now classic *Early Christian Rhetoric: The Language of the Gospel* (1971), in which he laid out the gap created by the absence of rhetoric in biblical criticism, which left to us the choice of historical or literary or theological readings but not a union of the three. Form criticism sought out the generic origins of biblical forms in a posited oral prehistory. Literary criticism admires the beauty of the Bible but cannot grapple with its insistent persona of proclamation (pp. xviii–xx). Wilder argues that early Christian rhetoric brought with it a new language, whose content cannot be separated from the way in which it is communicated (p. 118).

Amos Wilder's (1971) treatment of the Greek New Testament as both an extension and transformation of Hellenistic Greek literature would not have been possible without his deep knowledge of Greco-Roman literature and rhetoric. But it was George Kennedy, 20 years later, who brought the full toolbox of rhetorical *techne* to bear on New Testament rhetorical criticism, including modern rhetorical theory. This book has led to an entire new field of New Testament studies as New Testament scholars begin to take note of and incorporate the parallels between the Greek of the New Testament and its antecedents in Greek rhetoric. The most robust trend in this scholarship has taken full advantage of concepts such as Bitzer's rhetorical audience to restore a sociopolitical voice to the rhetoric of the New Testament. This trend was enunciated by Elisabeth Schussler Fiorenza as early as 1987, in essays now incorporated in her book *Rhetoric and Ethic: The Politics of Biblical Studies* (Schussler Fiorenza, 1999b). In the same year, Wilhelm Wuellner published "Where Is Rhetorical Criticism Taking Us?" in which he thoroughly established the larger sense of text and context demanded by reference to the rhetorical tradition (Wuellner, 1987). Also in the same year, George Kinneavy made a major contribution to both rhetoric of religion and New Testament studies in his work *The Greek Rhetorical Origins of Christian Faith*. In an extended word study of *pistis* in the New Testament, he makes the convincing argument that the specific content of *pistis*, "faith," in the New Testament owes its origins to the Greek rhetorical concept of *pistis*, "belief, proof" rather than to the Hebrew Bible cognate, *emunah*, "faithfulness" (Kinneavy, 1987).

Such connections may seem obvious to rhetoricians not familiar with the world of New Testament studies. In fact, however, rhetoric exists at the interstices of several different disciplines. Even classicists may be less familiar with the history of rhetoric than with the high literature of Homer and Euripides, while traditionally New Testament studies have focused on the distinctiveness of the Christian revolution and its radical difference from surrounding Greek culture. Add to this the fact that most students of New Testament Greek had a background in theology rather than classics, and it becomes more understandable why until relatively recently the rhetorical milieu of the New Testament, the rich culture of Judeo-Hellenism, was virtually unexplored. An early and still irreplaceable exception to this situation is David Daube's monograph, "Rabbinic Methods of Interpretation and Hellenistic Rhetoric" (1949).

In recent years, however, New Testament scholarship has been rapidly filling this gap. Rhetorical criticism is now a mainstream part of New Testament studies, and even if I were to write exclusively on New Testament rhetorical criticism, the many excellent works it has produced could not be comprehensively covered in this space. I would like to focus on one trend that takes up the lead of Schussler Fiorenza and Wilhelm Wuellner, in exploring the implications of social context and taking contemporary rhetorical theory fully into account. This trend has been called socio-rhetorical criticism, as represented in the writings of Burton L. Mack and Vernon Robbins (Mack, 1990; Mack & Robbins, 1989; Robbins, 1996a, 1996b).

Socio-rhetorical criticism restores argument to the vocabulary of biblical rhetoric, but only to be challenged on ideological grounds. In an essay originally delivered to the 1994 Pretoria Conference on Rhetoric and Religion (Porter & Olbricht, 1996), Schussler Fiorenza (1999a) challenged socio-rhetorical analysis in a way that illuminates once more the reflexive power of rhetoric. For her, the "rhetorical half-turn" does not rise above "empiricist-positivist scientism" and mere antiquarianism if it does not engage as well a full rhetoric of inquiry, a journey into suspicion of the disciplinary constraints of criticism. It is not enough to critique the language of the Bible, in other words, without an accompanying critique of one's own standpoint. Vernon Robbins (2002) gives a cogent rebuttal in a response to Schussler-Fiorenza, defining his own approach as "interactionism."

By this stage in the debate, we have at issue three rhetorics of New Testament analysis: the "antiquarian" (read Aristotelian) style that applies the stylistic *techne* of Greco-Roman rhetoric to the composition of the New Testament; the "interactionist" style that goes on to incorporate the sociopolitical motives (in the Burkean sense) of the New Testament; and the ideological stance that completes the turn by submitting the analysis itself to a hermeneutic of suspicion that seeks to examine the motives of criticism.

HEBREW BIBLE

The rhetoric of the Hebrew Bible presents a different critical horizon than the New Testament. Until very recently, it had to be assumed that there could have been very little if any influence on the writing of the Hebrew Bible from the Greco-Roman tradition.

Modern rhetorical criticism of the Hebrew Bible began at about the same time as that of the New Testament, as an extension of and corrective to form criticism. James Muilenburg's (1969) essay illustrates a central divide in the theorizing of rhetoric that still creates gaps in research between fields. Form criticism had attended exclusively to historical context, to the detriment of internal structure or literary design. In reintroducing rhetoric, Muilenburg repaired to a European conception of rhetoric as limited to the study of style. Many rhetorical critics continue in this vein, aligning rhetorical criticism of the Hebrew Bible with canonical and narrative criticism and using the technical terms of rhetoric as tools of analysis.

Phyllis Trible is the best known rhetorical critic of the Muilenburg school and her feminist counter-readings make the transition from style to ideological reading (Trible, 1978, 1984). Her more recent book on rhetorical criticism includes a thorough summary of modern rhetorical theory as applied to biblical criticism, and also traces the entire history of Hebrew rhetoric, including the Muilenburg school and its descendants (Trible, 1994).

But the question of what if any rhetorical theory of its own may be found in the Hebrew Bible remains unanswered in this tradition. The absence of a direct cultural link between the *techne* of rhetoric and the composition of biblical Hebrew is reflected in the fact that Kennedy in his *Comparative Rhetoric* treats the Old Testament as part of a chapter on rhetoric in the Ancient Near East, three chapters distant from rhetoric in Greece and Rome (Kennedy, 1998). This very fact, in a way, licenses rhetoricians of the Hebrew Bible to appropriate other rhetorics besides the classical *techne*, as well as to seek for an implicit rhetorical theory in the Bible itself (Zulick, 1992a, 1992b).

With the rise of "minimalist" theories of the composition of the Hebrew Bible, a whole new field is opened up for rhetorical criticism. Recently, a group of scholars has questioned some of the basic assumptions of the documentary hypothesis that assigned large portions of the composition of the Hebrew Bible to preexilic antecedent documents, known as the Yahwist, the Elohist, the Priestly source, and the Deuteronomist, as well as the Deuteronomistic History. If in fact much of this material is the product of Hellenistic Judaism rather than preexilic Hebrew, the question of direct influence from the rhetorical tradition is once again reopened. This trend is collected, represented, and responded to in the essays from the volume *Did Moses Speak Attic? Jewish Historiography and Scripture in the Hellenistic Period* (Grabbe, 2001).

There are of course many ways of approaching a rhetoric of the Hebrew Bible, and while rhetoricians without a deep background in the history and languages of this text may never be able to address such technical issues as mentioned above, they can certainly build on the work of others in that area. This circumstance invites further collaborative work of the sort produced by Scult, McGee, and Kuntz (1986). Building on the double account of Genesis created by the twinning of two separate sources, J (Yahwist) and P (Priestly), they went on to bring out not only the difference between the two accounts but also the rhetorical dialectic between them and the resulting complementary discourse of power and sacred legitimation (Scult et al., 1986).

Until quite recently, the only overview of speech as a phenomenon in the Hebrew Bible was Walter Zimmerli's (1959) essay "Die Weisung des Alten Testamentes zum Geschäft der Sprache." This essay is mainly concerned with speech as a theological problem. In an earlier essay, I attempted a different kind of overview by studying the available Hebrew terms for speech, eloquence, argument, and persuasion (Zulick, 1992a). But another way to build toward a rhetoric of the Hebrew Bible is to examine its incorporated oratorical genres. Although there are represented speeches in the narratives of the Hebrew Bible as well as the New Testament, the primary form of recorded direct address found in the Hebrew Bible is prophecy.

The difficulties are formidable for any rhetorician addressing Hebrew prophecy as a rhetorical genre. There are few critics who possess the historical and linguistic *techne* required for study of the Hebrew Bible.[6] Some biblical scholars have experimented with rhetoric and used communication models to describe biblical prophecy. Yehoshua Gitay (1981, 2001) has pioneered rhetorical criticism of the prophets, although for him rhetoric is the aspect of literary criticism most concerned with style, along the lines of the Muilenburg school. Both Robert Carroll (1980) and Thomas Overholt (1989) have used communication models to describe the prophetic experience.

Furthermore, prophetic rhetoric is perhaps the crucial form of speech in connecting the rhetoric of the Hebrew Bible to American public discourse. Sectarian America read the direct address and the narratives of the prophets as their own rhetorical universe, as if it spoke to them directly, and their response to it shaped the myth of America. In the next section, we will look at the literature of prophetism in American public discourse.

RHETORIC OF AMERICAN RELIGIOUS DISCOURSE

If we were to tackle in this article a complete review of American religious discourse, there would be no end to it. The sermonic tradition in America is a major genre of American literature and a key to its heart and soul. The field of homiletics is sadly overlooked by almost everyone outside its several denominational homes. The recent publication in the Library of America of a volume of sermons only shows how far we have to go even to establish a set of compass points as to what counts as significant in this area, let alone to have enough of a canon to begin the process of challenging it (Warner, 1999).

Yet interest in the influence of religion on American political speech has rarely been higher. This has made itself felt in several high-profile books on the subject (e.g., Albright, 2006; Dionne & DiIulio, 2000; Phillips, 2006) and also in criticism of Bush administration rhetoric (e.g., Dean, 2005; Milich, 2006). Sharon Crowley offers an engaging and dialogic foray into evangelical religion in her book *Toward a Civil Discourse: Rhetoric and Fundamentalism* (2006).

Nevertheless, rhetorical criticism of religious discourse in the American situation has to date largely concentrated on prophetism and apocalyptic rhetoric. Most of the literature on rhetoric of religion published in journals of rhetoric and communication has been in this area. Yet though much has been written, much still needs to be done. Two American protestant discursive traditions, Quakerism and Puritanism, have received the largest share of interest from rhetoricians. This is not without reason, since the two traditions taken together provided the main spiritual conduits that led from the English Revolution to the American Revolution. In a direct comparison of the two traditions, Baltzell (1979) significantly undervalued Quakerism.

Disproportionate to its numbers, and distinctly more politically radical than Puritanism, Quakerism continued to guide progress toward human liberty in the agitation for the abolition of slavery, for women's rights, and in the late 19th and 20th centuries for labor, pacifism, and civil rights. For this reason, it has attracted attention in rhetorical theory and criticism (Andrews, 1967; Bauman, 1983; Graves, 2004; Lippard, 1988; Mechling & Mechling, 1992).

In the case of both Quakerism and Puritanism, scholars have addressed the specific topic of prophetism. Sacvan Bercovitch (1978) took up the genre of American prophetism in his influential *The American Jeremiad.* He took a common expression, dating back to the 18th century and often used satirically as a synonym for a diatribe on manners and mores, and redefined it in opposition to Perry Miller's (1956) use of the same term to describe the Puritan diatribe against corruption in their "new society." Miller used the term in the tragic frame to characterize Puritan anxiety at the failed vision of the new society. Bercovitch (1978) noted the affirmative aspect of Puritan rhetoric on America, in the fact that they never lost the vision of perfection against which they measured the sins of their contemporaries. Thus, Bercovitch opened up the world of Puritan religion, a world in which America figured as the landscape of promise as prefigured by the prophets. But the concept now transcends the strict oratorical genre of the jeremiad to become a mode of discourse, a style of speech grounded in an entire worldview. This mode is better termed *prophetic.*

Bercovitch (1978) was more interested in the Puritan appropriation of biblical rhetoric than in the biblical genre of prophecy as such. Even less attention to the specific characters of biblical prophecy has been paid since by scholars of American public address. A group of essays published mostly in communication journals since the 1980s has used the terms *prophetic* and *apocalyptic* virtually interchangeably. These studies were thoroughly collected and reviewed in Stephen O'Leary's book *Arguing the Apocalypse* (1994). O'Leary has produced by far the best book-length work on apocalyptic rhetoric, and he does "recognize the distinction between prophetic and interpretive discourse" (p. 13), but the profound epistemological differences between them are obscured when he goes on to treat apocalypticism as an expression of prophecy (p. 72). James Darsey takes a giant step in the right direction with his *The Prophetic Tradition and Radical Rhetoric in America* (1997). Unlike many earlier rhetorical studies, Darsey treats the Old Testament tradition in an earlier chapter and establishes the prophetic character of a certain strand in American dissent rhetoric. But the problems do not end there. Like Bercovitch and O'Leary, Darsey interprets prophetism broadly. In a fascinating section on the failure of prophetic discourse, the demagoguery of Joseph McCarthy is termed *prophetic.* It is not so much the secularity of McCarthy's rhetoric as the lack of distinct markers of the prophetic genre that makes this a difficult extension of the idea of prophetism. Among the strongest of these markers is the presence of a claim to divine authorization of words and actions, either explicitly through the inclusion of a call or conversion narrative, as in the case of Nat Turner's confession (Turner, 1831, p. 133) or implicitly through the use of paraphrase, the use of vision and dream as metaphors, and the theological passive, as in the case of Angelina Grimké's Address in Pennsylvania Hall, among many others (Grimké [1838] as cited in Campbell [1989]).

To what extent, however, do the markers of prophecy as a genre in the Hebrew Bible carry over to the genre of prophetism in American public discourse? For a people steeped in biblical speech, it seems likely that were we to look for them we would find many examples of direct appropriation and imitation of prophetic discourse. After all, new prophecy must be heard as prophecy by its audience, and therefore it must resemble earlier prophecy. Generic markers make it possible for new prophecy to be understood immediately as prophetic.

Unlike the primary audience of American prophetism, rhetorical critics are not as familiar as they should be with the generic characters of prophetic discourse. One of these misunderstandings points out the necessity for more rigorous interdisciplinary application. Unlike many rhetoricians, most scholars of the Hebrew Bible accept a generic and historic distinction between prophecy and apocalypticism (Collins, 1984). This distinction is not just a formal one, but is derived from different patterns of experience as the composition history of biblical text unfolds. Apocalypticism such as the discourse of the Books of Daniel and Revelation occurs late in the tradition and relies on a canon of reading earlier prophecy. On behalf of a persecuted community, it projects a *forensic future*, in which the calamities and persecutions of the present day (the persecution under Antiochus Epiphanes and the Roman occupation, respectively) can all be comprehended as part of a divine plan laid out to the prophets in the past. Thus, it relies on pseudepigraphic texts placed in the mouths of known past prophets. Prophetic rhetoric, as I have argued elsewhere (Zulick, 2003), projects a *deliberative future*, one in which oral performance has been translated into written text. This future always takes the form of an indeterminate warning to persevere in faith, and it always serves the reflexive function of justifying God as well as authorizing divine speech. The vernacular understanding of "prophecy" identifies its central speech act as that of predicting the future. A closer look at biblical literary prophecy—such as the books of Isaiah, Jeremiah, Hosea, and Amos—shows the central speech act of prophecy to be delivering God's will and judgments to the people. Prophetic call narratives preface collections of

literary prophecy with a story that in one way or another shows the prophet to be touched by God and the words to be those of God and not the prophet's own invention. Some of these call narratives, and other narratives of prophets such as Moses, Samuel, Elijah, Micaiah, Amos, and Jeremiah, show the prophet actively opposing or bypassing the authority of the state and king.

What does this mean for prophetism in American public discourse? If we take into account the interactive and reproductive powers of genre, much indeed. Different Protestant denominations possess different epistemologies regarding prophecy. The two traditions referenced above are cardinal examples. Evangelical and fundamentalist groups are often dispensationalists, for instance, deriving from Puritanism and Calvinism and holding that the canon of Scripture is closed and God no longer speaks directly to the people through the medium of prophecy but only through the written word. Quakers, on the other hand, can be grouped among strands of American protestantism that derive from the dissenting sects of the English Revolution and to some extent the Anabaptists. To these we must add, in at least this one respect, the later developments of Mormonism and Pentecostalism. These groups do believe in direct inspiration and continuing revelation.

Each ideological position paints a different landscape of prophecy onto the landscape of America as the Promised Land. While the first group interprets American history as the fulfillment of prophecy, the second group in addition to this produces new prophecies in direct imitation of Hebrew prophetic narratives. It is this spirit of "new light" that gave religious authority to American dissenters, from the abolition of slavery to the Vietnam War.

Apocalypticism is also mapped onto the landscape of America as the Promised Land. But apocalypticism rarely speaks a word of warning or divine judgment to the people. Instead, it justifies and reinforces the sense of a righteous community surrounded by the enemies of God, yet destined to prevail in the end. Prophetic diatribes call nations to account and supply transcendent authorization on behalf of those who must speak but who lack a political mandate. Apocalyptic rhetoric in its proper situation is a liminal discourse. It performs a transcendent narrative to justify the outsiders' experience of suffering and alienation and gives comfort to the marginalized and oppressed. Out of its liminal situation, however, it can be and has been adapted to authorize triumphalism and manifest destiny.

Both prophetic and apocalyptic discourses intervene in customary authority structure by generating a transcendent authority that trumps all others. "God told me so" is not a claim that can be countered or overruled by a community that shares such a belief structure. In generating transcendence, the prophetic discourses invent for others the world in which they themselves believe so passionately. Yet different hermeneutics of prophecy can profoundly affect the ways in which prophetic discourse is distributed and appropriated in American public discourse.

CONCLUSIONS

The Protestant revolution rejected Church authority and chose instead the Word, whether written in Scripture or inscribed in the heart, as sole arbiter of faith and reason. We have been struggling with words and the Word ever since. Clearly, we need to inquire further into the ways in which different solutions to the problem of the word yield different stances toward the word and the world. Rhetoric offers a methodological means of comparison for assessing the influence of biblical discourse on American public discourse. And attention to the distinct tradents within American religious discourse will yield a better understanding of how religious rhetoric functions. None of this has as yet been done in a systematic way. Instead, we have had articles scattered throughout the discipline looking at particular

examples of prophetic and biblical rhetoric without pursuing the connections between them or systematically contextualizing them in religious as well as American history and ideology. To do this will take collaborative effort since no one scholar could possess the tools to do it all. Such an effort is not only worthwhile but urgent, if we are to move toward a deeper understanding of the possibilities and risks of the ongoing role of religious discourse in a pluralistic society.

For those of us who believe that rhetoric is more than merely a toolset but is beyond that a statement and a question about the relationship between language and human existence, the territory of religious discourse offers much to ponder.

NOTES

1. In a recent special issue of *Rhetoric and Public Affairs*, several scholars were invited to discuss the relationship between their various faith perspectives and their scholarly research (Medhurst, 2004).

2. See Maddux for a discussion of the six analogies (Maddux, 2006).

3. For key essays on Augustine's *De doctrina*, see articles by James Murphy (1960), Mark Jordan (1980), Marjorie Boyle (1990), Kathy Eden (1990), Arnold and Bright (1995), and Patton (1977).

4. This observation gives insight into the question whether *De doctrina* is primarily about rhetoric. When compared with the highly conventional arrangement of the traditional rhetorical handbook, one can see that Books 1 to 3 are alternative to a discussion of invention.

5. See for instance Classen's (2002) recent discussion of Melanchthon's rhetoric.

6. For my own efforts in this direction, see Zulick (1992b, 1998, 2003).

REFERENCES

Albright, M. (2006). *The mighty and the almighty: Reflections on America, God, and world affairs*. New York: HarperCollins.

Andrews, J. R. (1967). The Ethos of Pacifism: The Problem of Image in the Early British Peace Movement. *Quarterly Journal of Speech, 53,* 28–33.

Appel, E. C. (1993). Kenneth Burke: Coy theologian. *Journal of Communication and Religion, 16*(2), 99–110.

Arnold, D. W. H., & Bright, P. (Eds.). (1995). *De doctrina christiana: A classic of Western culture.* Notre Dame, IN: University of Notre Dame Press.

Augustine. (1958). *On Christian doctrine* (D. W. Robertson, Trans.). New York: Liberal Arts Press.

Baltzell, E. D. (1979). *Puritan Boston and Quaker Philadelphia: Two Protestant ethics and the spirit of class authority and leadership.* New York: Macmillan.

Barfield, O. (1973). *Poetic diction: A study in meaning* (2nd ed.). Hanover, NH: Wesleyan University Press.

Bauman, R. (1983). *Let your words be few: Symbolism and silence among seventeenth-century Quakers.* Cambridge, UK: Cambridge University Press.

Bercovitch, S. (1978). *The American jeremiad.* Madison: University of Wisconsin Press.

Booth, W. C. (2001). The many voices of Kenneth Burke, theologian and prophet, as revealed in his letters to me. In C. Henderson & D. C. Williams (Eds.), *Unending conversations: New writings by and about Kenneth Burke* (pp. 179–201). Carbondale, IL: Southern Illinois University Press.

Boyle, M. O. R. (1990). Augustine in the garden of Zeus: Lust, love and language. *Harvard Theological Review, 83,* 117–139.

Burke, K. (1970). *The rhetoric of religion: Studies in logology.* Berkeley: University of California Press.

Burke, K. (1982). Towards a transcendent immanence. *Cross Currents, 32*(3), 329–336.

Buss, M. (1974). The study of forms. In J. H. Hayes (Ed.), *Old Testament form criticism* (pp. 1–56). San Antonio: Trinity University Press.

Campbell, K. K. (Ed.). (1989). *Man cannot speak for her: Key texts of the early feminists.* New York: Praeger.

Carroll, R. P. (1980). Prophecy and dissonance: A theoretical approach to the prophetic tradition. *Zeitschrift für die Alttestamentliche Wissenschaft, 92,* 108–119.

Carter, C. A. (1996). *Kenneth Burke and the scapegoat process.* Norman: University of Oklahoma Press.

Cheyne, T. K. (1893). *Founders of Old Testament criticism.* New York: Scribner.

Classen, C. J. (2002). *Rhetorical criticism of the New Testament.* Boston: Brill.

Collins, J. J. (1984). *The apocalyptic imagination.* New York: Crossroad.

Crowley, S. (2006). *Toward a civil discourse: Rhetoric and fundamentalism.* Pittsburgh, PA: University of Pittsburgh Press.

Darsey, J. (1997). *The prophetic tradition and radical rhetoric in America.* New York: New York University Press.

Daube, D. (1949). Rabbinic methods of interpretation and Hellenistic Rhetoric. *Hebrew Union College Annual, 22,* 239–264.

Dean, J. (2005). Evil's political habitats. *Theory & Event, 8*(2).

Dionne, E. J., & DiIulio, J. J. (2000). *What's God got to do with the American experiment?* Washington, DC: Brookings Institution Press.

Douglas, M. (1966). *Purity and danger: An analysis of the concepts of pollution and taboo.* London: Routledge & Kegan Paul.

Eden, K. (1990). The rhetorical tradition and Augustinian hermeneutics in de doctrina christiana. *Rhetorica, 8,* 45–64.

Feehan, M. (2001). Kenneth Burke and Mary Baker Eddy. In C. Henderson & D. C. Williams (Eds.), *Unending conversations: New writings by and about Kenneth Burke* (pp. 206–226). Carbondale: Southern Illinois University Press.

Gitay, Y. (1981). *Prophecy and persuasion.* Bonn, Germany: Linguistica Biblica.

Gitay, Y. (2001). Prophetic criticism: "What are they doing?" The case of Isaiah: A methodological assessment. *Journal for the Study of the Old Testament, 96,* 101–127.

Grabbe, L. L. (Ed.). (2001). *Did Moses speak Attic? Jewish historiography and scripture in the Hellenistic period.* Sheffield, UK: Sheffield Academic Press.

Graves, M. P. (2004). One Friend's Journey. *Rhetoric & Public Affairs, 7,* 513–523.

Jordan, M. D. (1980). Words and word: Incarnation and signification in Augustine's de doctrina christiana. *Augustinian Studies, 11,* 177–196.

Jost, W., & Olmsted, W. (Eds.). (2000). *Rhetorical invention and religious inquiry: New perspectives.* New Haven: Yale University Press.

Kennedy, G. A. (1984). *New Testament interpretation through rhetorical criticism.* Chapel Hill: University of North Carolina Press.

Kennedy, G. A. (1998). *Comparative rhetoric: An historical and cross-cultural introduction.* New York: Oxford University Press.

Kinneavy, J. L. (1987). *The Greek rhetorical origins of Christian faith: An inquiry.* New York: Oxford University Press.

Lippard, P. V. (1988). The rhetoric of silence: The Society of Friends' unprogrammed meeting for worship. *Communication Quarterly, 36,* 145–156.

Lowth, R. (1787). *Lectures on the sacred poetry of the Hebrews* (Vols. 1 and 2). Retrieved October 17, 2006, from http://galenet .galegroup.com.ezproxy.wfu.edu:3000/servlet /ECCO

Mack, B. L. (1990). *Rhetoric and the New Testament.* Minneapolis, MN: Fortress Press.

Mack, B. L., & Robbins, V. K. (1989). *Patterns of persuasion in the gospels.* Sonoma, CA: Polebridge Press.

Maddux, K. (2006). Finding comedy in theology: A hopeful supplement to Kenneth Burke's logology. *Philosophy & Rhetoric, 39*(3), 208–232.

Mechling, E. W., & Mechling, J. (1992). Hot Pacifism and Cold War: The American Friends Service Committee's witness for peace in 1950s America. *Quarterly Journal of Speech, 78,* 173–195.

Medhurst, M. J. (Ed.). (2004). Religious and theological traditions as sources of rhetorical invention [Special issue]. *Rhetoric and Public Affairs, 7*(4).

Messer Leon, J. (1983). *The book of the honeycomb's flow/Sepher Nopheth Suphim* (I. Rabinowitz, Trans.). Ithaca, NY: Cornell University Press.

Meynet, R. (1990). Histoire de "L'analyse Rhetorique" en Exégèse Biblique. *Rhetorica, 8,* 291–320.

Milich, K. J. (2006). Fundamentalism Hot and Cold: George W. Bush and the "Return of the Sacred." *Cultural Critique, 62,* 92–125.

Miller, P. (1956). *Errand into the wilderness.* Cambridge, MA: Harvard University Press.

Muilenburg, J. (1969). Form criticism and beyond. *Journal of Biblical Literature, 88,* 1–18.

Murphy, J. J. (1960). St. Augustine and the debate about Christian rhetoric. *Quarterly Journal of Speech, 46,* 400–410.

O'Leary, S. (1994). *Arguing the apocalypse: A theory of millennial rhetoric.* New York: Oxford University Press.

Otto, R. (1923). *The idea of the holy: An inquiry into the non-rational factor in the idea of the divine and its relation to the rational* (J. W. Harvey, Trans.). London: Oxford University Press.

Overholt, T. (1989). *Channels of prophecy: The social dynamics of prophetic activity.* Minneapolis, MN: Fortress Press.

Patton, J. H. (1977). Wisdom and eloquence: The alliance of exegesis and rhetoric in Augustine. *Central States Speech Journal, 28,* 96–105.

Phillips, K. P. (2006). *American theocracy: The peril and politics of radical religion, oil, and borrowed money in the 21st century.* New York: Viking.

Porter, S. E., & Olbricht, T. H. (Eds.). (1996). *Rhetoric, scripture and theology: Essays from the 1994 Pretoria conference.* Sheffield, UK: Sheffield Academic Press.

Robbins, V. K. (1996a). *Exploring the texture of texts: A guide to socio-rhetorical interpretation.* Valley Forge, PA: Trinity Press International.

Robbins, V. K. (1996b). *The tapestry of early Christian discourse: Rhetoric, society and ideology.* Valley Forge, PA: Trinity Press International.

Robbins, V. K. (2002). The rhetorical full-turn in biblical interpretation: Reconfiguring rhetorical-political analysis. In F. D. Watson & A. J. Hauser (Eds.), *Rhetorical criticism and the Bible* (pp. 48–60). Sheffield, UK: Sheffield Academic Press.

Schussler Fiorenza, E. (1999a). Challenging the rhetorical half-turn: Feminist and rhetorical Biblical criticism. In Schussler Fiorenza (Ed.), *Rhetoric and ethic: The politics of biblical studies* (pp. 83–104). Minneapolis, MN: Fortress Press.

Schussler Fiorenza, E. (1999b). *Rhetoric and ethic: The politics of biblical studies.* Minneapolis, MN: Fortress Press.

Scult, A., McGee, M. C., & Kuntz, J. K. (1986). Genesis and power: An analysis of the biblical story of creation. *Quarterly Journal of Speech, 72*(2), 113–131.

Stafford, E. (2000). Peitho: The seductive power of rhetoric. In E. Stafford (Ed.), *Worshipping virtues: Personification and the divine in ancient Greece* (pp. 111–146). London: Duckworth.

Trible, P. (1978). *God and the rhetoric of sexuality.* Philadelphia: Fortress Press.

Trible, P. (1984). *Texts of terror: Literary-feminist readings of biblical narratives.* Philadelphia: Fortress Press.

Trible, P. (1994). *Rhetorical criticism: Context, method, and the book of Jonah.* Minneapolis, MN: Fortress Press.

Turner, N. (1831). *The confessions of Nat Turner, leader of the late insurrection in Southampton, Virginia, as fully and voluntarily made to Thomas R. Gray.* Baltimore: Thomas R. Gray.

Warner, M. (Ed.). (1999). *American sermons: The pilgrims to Martin Luther King, Jr.* New York: Library of America/Penguin Putnam.

Wilder, A. N. (1971). *Early Christian rhetoric: The language of the gospel.* Cambridge, MA: Harvard University Press.

Wilson, T. (1553). *The art of rhetoric* (P. E. Medine, Ed.). University Park: Pennsylvania State University Press.

Wuellner, W. (1987). Where is rhetorical criticism taking us? *Catholic Biblical Quarterly, 49*(3), 448–463.

Zimmerli, W. (1959). Die Weisung des Alten Testamentes zum Geschäft der Sprache. In W. Schneemelcher (Ed.), *Das Problem der Sprache in Theologie und Kirche: Referate vom Deutschen Evangelischen Theologentag 27–31 Mai 1958 in Berlin* (pp. 1–20). Berlin: Alfred Topelmann.

Zulick, M. D. (1992a). The active force of hearing: The ancient Hebrew language of persuasion. *Rhetorica, 10,* 367–380.

Zulick, M. D. (1992b). The Agon of Jeremiah: On the dialogic invention of prophetic ethos. *Quarterly Journal of Speech, 78,* 125–148.

Zulick, M. D. (1998). The normative, the proper, and the sublime: Notes on the use of figure and emotion in public argument. *Argumentation, 12,* 481–492.

Zulick, M. D. (2003). Prophecy and providence: The anxiety over prophetic authority. *Journal of Communication and Religion, 26*(2), 195–207.

8

Feminist Perspectives on the History of Rhetoric

KATE RONALD

In 1990, when I decided to teach a graduate course devoted solely to women's rhetoric, I had to scramble to find the texts for the course. I put books on reserve, I copied madly, and I stretched to make connections between primary historical material—acts of women's rhetorics—and secondary current works of feminist rhetorical theory. At that point, including women in historical overviews of the rhetorical tradition required making what often seemed like arbitrary and isolated choices. Should students read Aspasia alongside Plato? Virginia Woolf with I. A. Richards? Could Toni Morrison replace Bakhtin? Should one prefer Mary Wollstonecraft to George Campbell? Making the primary texts of women's rhetorics accessible to students required a great deal of effort, and I still worried that my selections were haphazard, my choices arbitrary.

As of 2006, I had taught that course at the graduate and undergraduate levels at least 10 times. When I ordered books for its latest version I realized that I was still scrambling and stretching—not to find appropriate or accessible, affordable texts, but rather to pare down the possibilities and to make thematic, theoretical, and methodological choices. I could have chosen from among at least eight collections of primary material, as well as works that focus on one or a group of particular women rhetors; I could have ranged throughout the past 2,000 years of women in Western rhetorical history; I could have chosen from at least five works that present or "extrapolate" women's rhetorical theory. In other words, my problems in designing the course are now pedagogical, theoretical, and rhetorical—not bibliographic.

In this essay, I hope to offer a guided tour of that explosion of research in women's rhetoric over the last decade and a half. Fifteen years ago, we were just beginning to name "women's rhetoric" as a subfield of rhetoric and composition; today, it boasts its own conference, its own journals, its own evening at the Conference on College Composition and Communication (the Coalition of Women Scholars in the History of Rhetoric meeting), and its own series from Southern Illinois University Press.[1] Perhaps one central example most clearly makes my point about the influence of feminist rhetoric on the field overall: When Patricia Bizzell and Bruce Herzberg's *The Rhetorical Tradition: Readings from Classical Times to the Present* (2001) first appeared in 1990, it immediately became the "standard" text for teaching the history of rhetoric. A sweeping run from the sophists to the 20th century, this huge collection of primary work contained exactly 6 works by women, out of 35 entries. When the second edition appeared in 2000, women authored 13 out of 55 entries.

What happened in the 10 years in between illustrates the changing perspectives on what counts as rhetoric. In 1992, Bizzell explained the lack of women in the first edition as a result of the overwhelmingly "traditional" research being conducted in rhetoric and composition. She also said that there were many works by women that they "could not find a way to excerpt" for this anthology (p. 53). Much more than a justification for the male-dominated *Rhetorical Tradition*, Bizzell's essay could serve as a map through the territory I'm proposing to tour here. In "Opportunities for Feminist Research in the History of Rhetoric," she outlines three strands of scholarship that would help rewrite the rhetorical canon and rhetorical theory. First, becoming a "resistant reader" of the rhetorical canon would be to "notice" (or to "listen hard") for aspects that a reader is "not supposed to notice, but that disturb," and to

"appropriate canonical works to feminist uses" (pp. 50–51). Or scholars could look for rhetoric by women in history that could be read as "similar" to the rhetorical work of canonical, male authors (p. 53). In other words, she calls for finding more rhetorical women. Bizzell's final call is for research that would "redefine rhetoric so as to make it inclusive of work by women that would not be construed as rhetorical under traditional paradigms" (p. 54).

Bizzell was either outrageously prescient or a darn good leader, probably both, for these suggestions represent almost exactly what the readers of her 1992 essay have accomplished in the past 16 years. Feminist scholars in rhetoric have "reread" the canonical texts (Jarratt, 1991), "reclaimed" women rhetors in history (Lunsford, 1995), and "regendered" the rhetorical tradition (Glenn, 1997). Women scholars in the history of rhetoric have also recovered an amazing amount of rhetoric by women, reimagined our rhetorical heritage, and redefined rhetorical theory, creating a wholly new tradition, complete with new theories and, as I hope to argue, new practices of writing, reading, teaching, and feminist activism.

Rather than lead this tour chronologically, I will stop at some signposts along the way, including historical markers spaced 10 years apart—in 1995 and 2005—to spotlight the diversity and the movement of research in feminist rhetoric. In between, I'll try to offer a taxonomy of research subjects, snapshots of issues in research methodologies and, finally, some directions for future scholars.[2]

BEFORE 1990

Although Bizzell claimed in 1992 that it was difficult to find women's rhetoric to excerpt for *The Rhetorical Tradition*, at least two collections of primary rhetoric by women had appeared before 1990. Karlyn Kohrs Campbell's *Man Cannot Speak for Her* (1989) is often viewed as the first collection of primary work by women public speakers. (It's also been the catalyst for heated debates about methodology in feminist rhetoric, as I will discuss below.) Collecting "key rhetorical acts" from the women's rights movement (from Maria Stewart in 1832 to Crystal Eastman in 1920), Campbell also included a second volume of analysis that "calls into question what has become the canon of public address in the United States" (p. 9). There's no doubt that Campbell's anthology and analysis set the stage for the renaissance of research in feminist rhetoric. Yet, 20 years earlier, Miriam Schneir had also published a collection of feminist rhetoric. *Feminism: The Essential Historical Writings*, published in 1972 (and revised in 1994, along with the second volume, *Feminism in Our Time: The Essential Writings, World War II to the Present*), does not have the rhetorical focus of Campbell's work, but it was available to scholars of rhetoric nonetheless. Just to add one more example of work before 1990, Gerda Lerner's *The Creation of Patriarchy* (1986; followed by *The Creation of Feminist Consciousness* in 1993) argued that the largest impediment to women's progress was the "absence of a tradition . . . . Women had no history—so they were told; so they believed" (p. 219). Both of Lerner's volumes aim to show, first, how women have been kept from knowing and interpreting their history and, second, how women subverted male hegemony in their struggle for voice. Again, although not a strictly rhetorical analysis, Lerner's work seems essential to any regendering of the rhetorical tradition.

REREADING THE RHETORICAL TRADITION

Susan Jarratt's *Rereading the Sophists: Classical Rhetoric Refigured* and C. Jan Swearingen's *Rhetoric and Irony: Western Literacy and Western Lies*, both published in 1991, were among the first works by women to question the received rhetorical history that

filled the pages of the first edition of *The Rhetorical Tradition* and to suggest alternative, feminist readings of the "history of rhetoric" that was taught in graduate programs in rhetoric and composition around the country, starting with Plato (or the sophists) and running through Kenneth Burke and Wayne Booth. Jarratt (1991), in what was considered a radical rereading of the sophists that Plato so thoroughly denigrated, offers a critique of rhetoric as verbal combat, arguing that instead of seeing *logos* as triumphant over *mythos* in the classical arena, we might regard *nomos*, or practical, social context, as the key term in rhetorical history. She connects the contingent, contextual rhetoric of the sophists with contemporary feminist theory and practice. Swearingen (1991) also rereads the classical rhetorical tradition up through Augustine as deceptive and agonistic, arguing that we might more usefully read rhetorical history not as oral combat but as the beginning of our assumptions about literacy. She too connects her rereading to contemporary feminist studies. These two "early" books in feminist rhetoric, then, represented the vanguard of what Bizzell (1992) called "resistant readings" of the rhetorical tradition (p. 52). Into this category also falls Miriam Brody's *Manly Writing* (1993), an exploration of the metaphors historically used in writing instruction and a wonderful exposé of the gendered nature of rhetorical education.

Cheryl Glenn's *Rhetoric Retold: Regendering the Tradition From Antiquity Through the Renaissance* (1997) answered Bizzell's call for scholars to find women in rhetorical history whose writings parallel and complement the male tradition. "Re-mapping" women into rhetorical history, however, Glenn goes much further than adding women to rhetorical history. While she identifies "women who found access to education and rhetorical accomplishments" and concludes that they were "indeed supporting, complementing, and enhancing the contributions of their male counterparts to the development of the male dominated rhetorical art," Glenn also maps a "new rhetorical territory," defining the rhetoric of devotion, autobiography, the body, and silence. This groundbreaking work served as a model for much of the more particularized research I describe below.

SIGNPOST NUMBER 1: 1995

Anthologies dominated the first wave of the renaissance in women's/feminist rhetoric. Three notable books, each appearing in 1995, will serve to illustrate the range of rhetorical sites and methodologies that marked this emerging field. Catherine Hobbs edited *Nineteenth Century Women Learn to Write*, Andrea Lunsford published *Reclaiming Rhetorica: Women in the Rhetorical Tradition*, and Shirley Wilson Logan presented *With Pen and Voice: A Critical Anthology of Nineteenth-Century African-American Women*.

Hobbs (1995) gathers together essays that trace U.S. women's acquisition of literacy during the Victorian era, exploring rhetorical sites as diverse as women's clubs and conduct manuals, state Normal schools, Ratcliffe College, and a Cherokee female seminary, with a postscript that includes primary rhetoric from Jerusha Jones in 1875. Together, these essays chart the ways in which gender complicates historical and theoretical definitions of literacy, as well as conceptions of public and private voice. Lunsford's (1995) anthology ranges much more widely, from essays on Aspasia and Diotima to Langer and Kristeva. The goal of *Reclaiming Rhetorica*, as Lunsford states in the introduction, is to "reconfigure" woman's place in the rhetorical tradition; its underlying principle was "diversity and inclusivity," as well as "rich and intense collaboration" between the authors themselves and their historical and contemporary subjects (p. 6). Logan's (1995) anthology, unlike the first two in my arbitrary category, collects primary work by 19th-century African American

women. In her introduction, Logan describes the seven rhetors within, ranging from Maria Stewart in 1832 to Victoria Earle Mattthews in 1897, as offering "unique rhetorical strategies from women wrestling with unique problems" (p. xv).

"Listening" becomes a key term in this body of work. Lunsford (1995), in referring to the "archeological investigations" necessary to reclaiming women's rhetoric, says, "Most particularly, the essays in this volume aim to contribute to that work first of all by *listening*—and listening hard—to and for the voices of women in the history of rhetoric," because "the tradition has never recognized the forms, strategies, and goals used by many women as 'rhetorical'" (p. 6). Logan (1995) ends her introduction by simply stating that she wanted little editorial tinkering with the women's speeches; instead, she says that she wanted to "reconstruct the rhetorical context and to let the women speak" (p. xvi). In both senses of the term, then, these anthologies taught readers to hear rhetoric differently, both by recovering primary acts of public persuasion by women and by theorizing rhetoric and literacy differently.

These three books conveniently (if not overly neatly) represent several major strands of scholarship in feminist/women's rhetoric(s) during this 10-year period: (1) collections of primary rhetorical acts by women; (2) collections of essays about women's rhetorical acts; (3) studies of individual women, groups of women, and particular time periods; (4) studies of particular rhetorical sites or strategies in women's rhetoric; and (5) new forms and topics of rhetorical theory. My categories here might be a bit arbitrary: Glenn's *Rhetoric Retold* (1997), for example, covers the classical era to the Renaissance and so would fit under Strand 3; and it suggests new forms of rhetorical theory (Strand 5) but also exemplifies a "resistant reading" of the rhetorical tradition (Strand 1). Krista Ratcliffe's *Anglo-American Feminist Challenges to the*

Rhetorical Tradition (1996) studies three particular women and so might fall under Strand 3, but it also creates new rhetorical theory (Strand 5). Nevertheless, these categories will help me (and, I hope, my readers) navigate the impressive and diverse scholarship during this important decade.

RECOVERING PRIMARY RHETORIC BY WOMEN

Since Campbell's volume *Man Cannot Speak for Her* (1989), feminist scholars have provided the field with many collections of primary rhetorical acts by women. To my mind, this work is the most central to the field. It is the material I was scrambling to find when I taught that first seminar in women's rhetoric(s). Following Logan's 1995 anthology of 19th-century African American women's public address, we now have collections such as Jane Donawerth's *Rhetorical Theory by Women before 1900* (2002), ranging from Ran Chao's first-century *Lessons for Women* to Mary Augusta Jordan's *Correct Writing and Speaking* in 1904. A more wide-ranging anthology is *Women Imagine Change: A Global Anthology of Women's Resistance from 600 B.C.E. to Present*, edited by Eugenia Delamotte, Natania Meeker, and Jean O'Barr in 1997. In 2001, Joy Ritchie and I edited *Available Means: An Anthology of Women's Rhetoric(s)*, a collection of 70 women rhetors from Aspasia to Gloria Steinem (Ritchie & Ronald, 2001). In that anthology, which we published to "gather" women's rhetorics for our graduate and under-graduate courses, we wanted to make available the texts that have been the subjects of so much exciting recovery and retelling of women's rhetorical history (e.g., Aspasia, Mary Wollstonecraft, Margaret Fuller, Susan B. Anthony, Adrienne Rich). But we also wanted to continue to unsettle this emerging canon with other works that may cause us to examine our assumptions about what constitutes feminist rhetorical practice and theory (works by

Dorothy Allison, Toni Morrison, or St. Catherine of Sienna, for example).

Other scholars have provided the field with the primary texts of particular women in the rhetorical tradition. In 1996, Joann Campbell published *Toward a Feminist Rhetoric: The Writing of Gertrude Buck*, a collection of Buck's writings from 1899 to 1922 while she was teaching at Vassar. Campbell chronicles Buck's efforts to "rethink a patriarchal rhetorical tradition, reshape teacher-centered classrooms, and revise intellectual and social issues of concern to women" (p. ix). In 1997, Jackie Royster published *Southern Horrors and Other Writings: The Anti-Lynching Campaign of Ida. B. Wells, 1892–1900*, which provides the primary texts of Wells's rhetoric as well as an introductory analysis of her persuasive techniques in the context of Reconstruction and the development of the "women's sphere" of influence.

In feminist and women's rhetoric courses during this time, teachers have used a variety of primary texts for the study of feminist rhetorical strategies. Among the most frequently taught rhetors are Christine de Pisan, Margaret Fuller, Sarah and Angelina Grimké, Virginia Woolf, Mary Daly, Gloria Anzaldúa (1987), bell hooks (1989, 1994), and Adrienne Rich (1979, 1986). For a relatively full list of such possibilities, please see Appendix B in Ritchie and Ronald's *Available Means* (2001). Most recently, we're beginning to see combinations of primary texts and full rhetorical analysis, as in Christine Mason Sutherland's *The Eloquence of Mary Astell* (2005), which includes the full texts of her work as well as chapters on her "problem of ethos" and her rhetorical theory.

COLLECTIONS OF RHETORICAL ANALYSIS AND CRITIQUE

Anthologies have been a staple of the resurgence of feminist studies in rhetoric and com-position, beginning, of course, with Lunsford's

Reclaiming Rhetorica in 1995. Since then, Molly Wertheimer has published *Listening to Their Voices: The Rhetorical Activities of Historical Women* (1997), which includes essays on Aspasia, Lucie Olbrechts-Tyteca, Mary Wollstonecraft, and women's voice and silence in Early Methodism. In 1999, Christine Mason Sutherland and Rebecca Sutcliffe presented *The Changing Tradition: Women in the History of Rhetoric*, a collection of individual essays organized around the themes of women as "excluded," "alongside," "participating," "emerging into," and "engaging" the rhetorical tradition. In 2005, Hildy Miller and Lillian Bridwell-Bowles edited *Rhetorical Women: Roles and Representations*, a wide-ranging volume (including work on Frances Wright by Karlyn Campbell, on Sarah Winnemuca Hopkins by Malea Powell, and on "The Reality of Our Work" by Dorothy Allison) that hopes to "outline some of the major rhetorical patterns that are at work in this complicated business of representation—from describing the rhetorical perspective of self, to the positions of individual rhetors, to whole groups of women in various periods" (p. 1). Another expansive volume is *Fractured Feminisms: Rhetoric, Context, and Contestation* (Gray-Rosendale & Harootunian, 2003), which treats feminist perspectives on topics ranging from writing across the curriculum to program administration, pedagogy, and global perspectives.[3]

STUDIES OF INDIVIDUAL WOMEN, GROUPS OF WOMEN, AND PARTICULAR TIME PERIODS

Other scholars have focused on particular groups, or groupings, of women. To my mind, Krista Ratcliffe's *Anglo-American Feminist Challenges to the Rhetorical Traditions: Virginia Woolf, Mary Daly, and Adrienne Rich* (1996) represents the height of work in feminist rhetorics. Carefully analyzing each 20th-century woman's rhetorical context and choices, Ratcliffe "extrapolates" their rhetorical theories and then offers implications for teaching rhetoric and writing based on that revised rhetorical theory. But I want to use Ratcliffe in another category (rewriting rhetorical theory), just as I want to use Jacqueline Jones Royster's *Traces of a Stream: Literacy and Social Change Among African American Women* (2000) to discuss methodology, although she focuses primarily on the period from the colonial to 19th-century United States. Sutherland's (2005) study of Mary Astell could fit here as well, although she includes the primary texts as well as her own rhetorical analysis.

Two examples of the kind of study I'm putting in this category are Shirley Wilson Logan's *"We Are Coming": The Persuasive Discourse of Nineteenth-Century Black Women* (1999) and Janet Eldred and Peter Mortensen's *Imagining Rhetoric: Composing Women of the Early United States* (2002). Both books are primarily rhetorical analyses, but both append some primary material as well, making them especially useful for the classroom. Building on her earlier anthology of primary work, Logan (1999) explores the ways in which "the persuasive discourse of nineteenth century black women adapted itself to its multiple audiences and multilayered exigencies" (p. xvi). Eldred and Mortensen (2002) devote chapters to five 18th- and 19th-century women teachers, analyzing fiction, composition textbooks, journals, and anthologies for young writers, following Bizzell's call to look for rhetorical theory in places other than the academy. They "recover what women in the early U.S. imagined instruction and practice in composition should be, and show how this imagination shaped their awareness of female civic rhetoric—its possibilities and limitations" (p. 32).

Certainly these two studies represent the best of the field's focus on particular women in particular time periods. Just as surely, they illustrate the ways in which the 19th-century

United States has dominated feminist rhetorical studies (see Buchanan, 2005; Cobb, 2000; Eldred & Mortensen, 2002; Gere, 1997; Johnson, 2002; Kates, 1999; Logan, 1995, 1999; Mattingly, 1999, 2002; Mountford, 2003; Royster, 1997). I believe that much more work needs to be done on the 20th century, especially, it seems to me, in political rhetoric; certainly more work needs to be done on women's rhetorics before 1800; and clearly the field needs to think beyond North American borders.[4]

STUDIES OF PARTICULAR RHETORICAL SITES AND STRATEGIES

This category overlaps the previous one in many, perhaps arbitrary, ways. Here, as with the previous section, 19th-century North American rhetoric predominates. But I think it's important to note the ways in which scholars in feminist rhetoric have focused on particular sites and strategies of women's rhetorics, expanding what counts as a rhetorical space and rereading traditional rhetorical strategies through a gendered lens. Nan Johnson (2002), for example, looks at the ways in which the "parlor" served as a powerful rhetorical space in 19th-century middle-class U.S. culture. In *Gender and Rhetorical Space in American Life, 1866-1910* (2002), she rereads the history of rhetoric as a "drama about how convention is inscribed and redefined within rhetorical space" (p. 2). She explores "how nonacademic or parlor traditions of rhetoric and popular constructions of rhetorical performance after the Civil War . . . promote[d] a code of rhetorical behavior for women that required the performance of conventional femininity" (p. 2). In this sense, Johnson's work also functions as a "resistant" reading of the rhetorical tradition, just as does Lindal Buchanan's recent *Regendering Delivery: The Fifth Canon and Antebellum Women Rhetors* (2005). Tracing the performances, styles, and

constraints of "pioneering" women's rhetorics, Buchanan argues that a "re-gendered fifth canon addresses far more than the speaker's manipulation of voice and body on a public platform and instead views rhetorical performance as the moment when dominant cultural values are enacted and, sometimes, are resisted and revised" (p. 160).

Other researchers have focused on even more specific sites. Anne Ruggles Gere's (1997) *Intimate Practices: Literacy and Cultural Work in U.S. Women's Clubs: 1890–1920* uses extensive archival research to show how diverse groups of women's clubs, including Jewish, Mormon, white middle-class, working class, and African American, redefined literacy as a shared, collaborative project that influenced the developing concept of American-ness and nation. Carol Mattingly's (1999) *Well-Tempered Women: Nineteenth-Century Temperance Rhetoric* shows how the Woman's Christian Temperance Union, by presenting their arguments and themselves in familiar language and dress, extended the "women's sphere" into politics and mobilized public support for women's causes, including suffrage. Beth Daniell's (2003) *A Communion of Friendship: Literacy, Spiritual Practice, and Women in Recovery* studies the ways in which women in Al-Anon use reading, writing, and speaking to develop and understand their spirituality. Based on interviews and analysis, Daniell's study argues that our field should turn attention to the "little narratives" of rhetoric rather than the "grand" narratives of the rhetorical tradition (pp. 4–7). Roxanne Mountford focused on the highly gendered space of preaching in *The Gendered Pulpit: Preaching in American Protestant Spaces*. First published in 2003, with a new edition in 2005, Mountford's book combines personal experience and case studies of contemporary women preachers with a thorough historical analysis of *ars praedicandi* in order to illuminate the role of physicality and oral performance in assumptions about what counts as rhetoric.

I will simply list a few other rhetorical sites and strategies that feminist scholars in rhetoric have explored. Cinthia Gannett's (1992) *Gender and the Journal: Diaries and Academic Discourse* centers on the gendered private/ public tension in rhetorical studies. Marguerite Helmers focuses on women's home altars in "Objects, Memory, and Narrative: New Notes Toward Materialist Rhetoric" (Ronald & Ritchie, 2006). Carol Mattingly's (2002) fascinating *Appropriate(ing) Dress: Women's Rhetorical Style in Nineteenth Century America* explores how 19th-century women public speakers used dress and appearance to claim the authority of the platform. And Wendy Hesford's work on rape and the violence of genocide points our discipline beyond our own borders into global rhetorics and conflicts—see *Haunting Violations* (2001) coedited with Kozol, "Documenting Violations" (2006), and "Reading Rape" (1999).

After her groundbreaking *Rhetoric Retold* (1997), Cheryl Glenn has turned her attention to the rhetorical strategy of silence. *Unspoken: A Rhetoric of Silence* (2004) ranges from treatments of current political women like Anita Hill and Lani Guinier to Southwest Native American tribes to current theories of collaboration as it explores the ways "silence can be as powerful as speech, the ways that silence and silencing deliver meaning" (p. xi). Surely Glenn's latest project signals the accomplishments of our field's feminist rhetorical project: From recovery of silenced voices to an examination of silence as rhetorical force seems to me a very long way to come.

REWRITING RHETORICAL THEORY

All these categories, of course, include theory and theorizing. In their introductions to anthologies, and in their studies of particular groups and time periods, all the authors I've mentioned here write, and rewrite, rhetorical theory. And, in *Traces of a Stream*, Royster (2000) notes how African American women

rhetors redefine the relationships among audience, writers, and message; her reading rewrites traditional appeals to logic, emotion, and character into a focus on context, the ethos of material experience, and an insistence on rhetorical action (p. 32).

But two particular works, it seems to me, deserve individual attention in this category. Krista Ratcliffe, in *Anglo-American Feminist Challenges to the Rhetorical Traditions* (1996), overtly seeks to "extrapolate" theories of rhetoric from "women's and/or feminist critiques of language as well as from the textual strategies of such critiques" (p. 4). Ratcliffe reads Virginia Woolf, Mary Daly, and Adrienne Rich in order to

> contribute to the continuing conversation about feminisms and the rhetorical tradition by inviting teachers not only to question how Woman, women, and feminists have been located as part of, and apart from, these [canonical, rhetorical] traditions but also to explore the implication of such locations for rhetorical history, theory, and pedagogy. (p. 6)

Reading these three 20th-century women writers both within and against categories such as location, material conditions, invention, style, arrangement, memory, and audience, Ratcliffe (1996) also offers models for reading other primary texts and imagining "new texts of rhetorical history, theory and pedagogy" (p. 28). Moreover, in a concluding chapter, she extrapolates rhetorical concepts that should inform our teaching of rhetoric and writing. In other words, the theory she writes is both rhetorical and pedagogical.

Foss, Foss, and Griffin (1999) use the word *explicate* to describe their work in *Feminist Rhetorical Theories*. They overtly label the work of nine 20th-century women (including bell hooks, Gloria Anzaldúa, and Paula Gunn Allen) as theory, as "ways of organizing communication that are distinct, insightful, and important to rhetorical studies" (p. 10).

Analyzing how each woman sees the "nature of the world," "the definition of feminism," "the nature of the rhetor," her "rhetorical options," and the ways in which each woman represents "transformations of rhetorical theory," this ambitious project, like Ratcliffe's, offers methods for reading—and using—women's rhetorics not only to find new theory but also to enact changed practice.

SIGNPOST NUMBER 2: 2005

A small detour here. Krista Ratcliffe has recently published *Rhetorical Listening: Identification, Gender, Whiteness* (2005), and although this project could be described as a parallel to Glenn's study of silence, I believe it's taking the field of feminist rhetoric to a new place. While not specifically about women's historical rhetoric, this feminist rhetorical project seeks to define rhetorical listening as a "trope for interpretive invention and as a code for cross-cultural conduct" (p. 17). Arguing that perhaps we can "hear things we cannot see," Ratcliffe offers a "stance of openness that a person may choose to assume in relation to any person, text, or culture"; the purpose of rhetorical listening is "to negotiate troubled identifications in order to facilitate productive communication" (p. 25). Focusing chapters on "listening" to public debates, to scholarly discourses, and to classroom resistance, Ratcliffe indeed writes new rhetorical theory here, taking the feminist rhetorical project from resistance and subversion to new strategies of communication not based on the agonistic rhetorical tradition that Brody, Glenn, Jarratt, and Swearingen critiqued. Ratcliffe also takes her project from theory to practice, including in an appendix materials for teaching. (In another new book published in 2005, Julie Jung explores the concept of listening in pedagogical contexts. See *Revisionary Rhetoric, Feminist Pedagogy and Multi-Genre Texts*.)

Also in 2005, Wendy Hesford and Wendy Kozol edited *Just Advocacy? Women's Human Rights, Transnational Feminisms, and the Politics of Representation*, another important signpost, I think, in the expansion of feminist rhetorical projects. Bringing together some of the most respected scholars in international women's studies and set in the context of global crisis, this collection explores the often overlooked ways in which women and children are further subjugated when political or humanitarian groups represent them solely as victims and portray the individuals who are helping them as paternal saviors.

METHODOLOGICAL ISSUES

The methods of research represented in my categories range from archival study to interviews to historical archeology. The field has proven, no doubt, that texts by women rhetors can be recovered and reclaimed and that, therefore, theory and history can be redefined. Over all this research hangs a spirit of collaboration, not only among scholars but also with the subjects of research. The prefaces to every work I've cited include acknowledgements to other women scholars in the field. Indeed, as Ede, Glen, and Lunsford (1990) showed in *Singular Texts/Plural Authors*, acknowledging the shared work of scholarship is part of a feminist practice.

Two notable rifts in this spirit of collaboration might illustrate more fully the issues debated about methodology. In 1992–1993, Barbara Biesecker and Karlyn Campbell debated the inclusion of women in the rhetorical tradition in a rather heated exchange in *Philosophy and Rhetoric*. In "Coming to Terms With Recent Attempts to Write Women into the History of Rhetoric," Biesecker (1992) worried that Campbell's *Man Cannot Speak for Her* (1989) might represent "female tokenism," and cautioned scholars in women's rhetoric to "write the story not only of the differences between women's and men's subject (re)formation, but, also, to write into that account the differences between women"

(p. 157). Campbell (1993), in "Biesecker Cannot Speak for Her Either," replied that Biesecker's argument simply worked to "silence women once more" (p. 157). The debate, to my mind, directly connects to the diversity of work in women's rhetoric since then.

Another methodological debate took place in the pages of *College English* in 2000. Responding to Susan Jarratt and Ong's (1995) and Cheryl Glenn's (1994) work on Aspasia, Xin Liu Gale (2000) raised questions about whether scholars can treat this figure (whose rhetorical work exists only in male texts) both as a rhetorical construct and as a historical figure; she asks a series of methodological questions:

> How can we write radical alternative histories of rhetoric without compromising our credibility as historians and scholars? How can we do primary scholarship without having to submit slavishly to the authority of the traditional male perspective and method? How can we foreground our research in postmodern and antifoundational theory without resorting to rhetorical ploy? (p. 383)

Jarratt (2000) responded that "new histories" should be evaluated by "rhetorical criteria: Does this history instruct, delight, and move the reader? Is the historical data probable? Does it fit with other accounts or provide a convincing alternative? Is it taken up by the community and used?" (p. 391). Glenn (2000) countered,

> Historiography's central question is not "true" or "false." Instead, historiography asks us to consider questions of knowledge (in what context is it produced and normalized? whom does it benefit?), ethics (to what/whom are these practices accountable? what/whom do they privilege?), and power (what practices might produce historical remembrances? what are the effects of such representation)? (p. 389)

I use these debates to illustrate the growing sophistication of feminist research in the history of rhetoric. However, to my mind, Jackie Royster provides the most cogent answer to these series of questions in *Traces of a Stream* (2000), where she insists that recovery work demands a different measure of evidence, a different perspective on history. Using the Swahili concepts of *sasa* and *zamani* time, Royster insists that scholars must take the "long view, a view in which the focus is not expected to be fine-tuned" (p. 83). *Sasa* means the time in which a person lives and also the time in which that person is remembered by the living; *zamani* means the time when that person passes out of anyone's living memory. Studying the literate lives of African American women before 1600 from the perspective of *sasa* time is, Royster argues, problematic. But, she says, using a *zamani* perspective, "We can acknowledge our own ignorance of individual stories as a significant factor and not assume so arrogantly that our not knowing predetermines that they and their experiences were absent, deficient, or unimportant" (p. 80). Then, she says, "imagination becomes a critical skill, that is, the ability to see the possibility of certain experiences even if we cannot know the specificity of them" (p. 83). In other words, looking for "traces" leads to seeing a "stream"—and that's the goal of the body of work I've been cataloging here. Royster's concept of imagination as a research tool seems to me the most promising and generous tool we have.

A CAUTIONARY WORD AND SOME IMPLICATIONS FOR FUTURE STUDY

I realize that the tone of this essay is celebratory, as it should be. The amount and quality of work in feminist rhetorical history and theory over the last 16 years deserves much praise. But I caution against the field becoming too self-congratulatory. Let's remember that in

1673, Bathsua Makin published *An Essay to Revive the Ancient Education of Gentlewoman in Religion, Manners, Arts and Tongues. With An Answer to the Objections Against This Way of Education* (see Teague, 1998). Makin's subheadings include the arguments that "women educated in the arts and tongues have been eminent in them," "women have been good linguists," and "women have been good orators" (Teague, 1998, pp. 112–115). This tract includes a long, detailed catalog of women rhetors that our field has only recently "recovered." In other words, we're recovering what was lost, found, and then lost again. We should take Lerner's advice about creating a "usable past" seriously; in *Why History Matters* (1998), she says,

> We learn from our construction of the past what possibilities and choices once existed. . . . [W]e then draw conclusions about the consequences of our present-day choices. This, in turn enables us to project a vision of the future. It is through history-making that the present is freed from necessity and the past becomes usable. (p. 117)

All the work I've outlined here points toward a usable past.

But Lerner (1998) also argues that an idea depends "for its spread and impact on the interaction of theory and practice" (p. 67). Therefore, besides expanding the sites and subjects of research in feminist rhetoric, I believe that some central next questions should ask the following questions: What difference does this emerging canon of women's rhetorics make to our teaching of writing and rhetoric? How is the recovery of women's rhetorics translating into revised, reexamined theories, practices, and pedagogies of writing, rhetoric, and discourse? Toward that end, Joy Ritchie and I have edited *Teaching Rhetorica: Theory, Practice, Pedagogy* (Ronald & Ritchie, 2006), a collection that asks leading scholars in feminist rhetoric to answer

questions about how this new and expanding body of rhetoric is changing conceptions of theory, pedagogy, and professional practice. As Ann Berthoff (1987), a woman rhetorician perhaps overlooked in this revival, tells us, "How your theory works and what it changes will best tell you what your theory is" (p. xxiii). The collaborative and hopeful spirit of this body of scholarship in feminist rhetorical history should lead us to "think about our thinking," as teachers, scholars, administrators, and as citizens.

NOTES

1. I am simply not able to cover, or even touch on, all the work on feminist rhetoric that I know, much less what I don't. I especially regret not being able to deal in more detail with individual chapters in collections or articles in journals. My advice to scholars is simply to put the words *woman*, *feminist*, and *rhetoric* into your search engine and stand back. The bibliographies of many of the works I've cited here are also excellent and far more extensive than mine.

2. But before I've even gotten to my third page, I realize I already have some new rhetorical problems. Do I call this new field "women's rhetoric"? Or "feminist rhetoric"? Do I use the plural *rhetorics*—to indicate the expansive diversity of women writers and to avoid the elitist homogenizing tendencies of defining any field? Or do I put that "s" in parentheses—*rhetoric(s)*—to celebrate both the field's openness and its claim to legitimacy? I've made each of these choices at various times, sometimes using all six options in the course of a 20-minute talk. Some of the women rhetors studied here are decidedly not feminist; most of the authors of the studies decidedly claim feminist identities. Hildy Miller and Lillian Bridwell-Bowles (2005) make a strong case for the term *woman* in their introduction to *Rhetorical Women*, arguing that "in order to conduct postmodern feminist analysis of historical and contemporary rhetors and their rhetorics, we must hold at least one term constant—and that term is 'woman'" (p. 8). But my point at the outset is that the debate itself illustrates the vibrancy of this area of research, especially its growth in the last decade.

3. Other anthologies, although not focused specifically on rhetorical history, have influenced the field's thinking about gender and rhetoric and composition. See especially Jarratt and Worsham's *Feminism and Composition* (1998) and Phelps and Emig's *Feminine Principles* (1995). For a discussion of the role of anthologies in feminist rhetorical studies, see Kathleen Ryan's "Recasting Recovery and Gender Critique as Inventive Arts" (2006).

4. Wendy Hesford provides an example of work that takes the field into this last direction. See especially her work on transnational feminisms and women's rights.

REFERENCES

Anzaldúa, G. (1987). *Borderlands/La frontera: The new mestiza.* San Francisco: Aunt Lute Books.

Berthoff, A. E. (1987). Preface. In P. Friere & D. Macedo (Eds.), *Literacy: Reading the word and the world.* South Hadley, MA: Bergin & Garvey.

Biesecker, B. (1992). Coming to terms with recent attempts to write women into the history of rhetoric. *Philosophy and Rhetoric, 25*(2), 140–161.

Bizzell, P. (1992, Fall). Opportunities for feminist research in the history of rhetoric. *Rhetoric Review, 11,* 50–58.

Bizzell, P., & Herzberg, B. (2001). *The rhetorical tradition: Readings from classical times to the present.* Boston: Bedford. (Original work published 1990)

Brody, M. (1993). *Manly writing: Gender, rhetoric, and the rise of composition.* Carbondale: Southern Illinois University Press.

Buchanan, L. (2005). *Regendering delivery: The fifth canon and antebellum women rhetors.* Carbondale: Southern Illinois University Press.

Campbell, J. (Ed.). (1996). *Toward a feminist rhetoric: The writing of Gertrude Buck.* Pittsburgh, PA: University of Pittsburgh Press.

Campbell, K. K. (1989). *Man cannot speak for her: A critical study of early feminist rhetoric* (Vols. 1 and 2). New York: Greenwood Press.

Campbell, K. K. (1993). Biesecker cannot speak for her either. *Philosophy and Rhetoric, 26*(2), 153–159.

Cobb, A. (2000). *Listening to our grandmother's stories: The Bloomfield Academy for Chickasaw females, 1852–1949.* Lincoln: University of Nebraska Press.

Daniell, B. (2003). *A communion of friendship: Literacy, spiritual practice, and women in recovery.* Carbondale: Southern Illinois University Press.

Delamotte, E., Meeker, N., & O'Barr, J. (Eds.). (1997). *Women imagine change: A global anthology of women's resistance from 600 B.C.E. to present.* New York: Routledge.

Donawerth, J. (Ed.). (2002). *Rhetorical theory by women before 1900.* Lanham, MD: Rowman & Littlefield.

Ede, L., Glenn, C., & Lunsford, A. (1990). *Singular texts/Plural authors.* Carbondale: Southern Illinois University Press.

Eldred, J. C., & Mortensen, P. (2002). *Imagining rhetoric: Composing women of the early United States.* Pittsburgh, PA: University of Pittsburgh Press.

Foss, K., Foss, S., & Griffin, C. L. (1999). *Feminist rhetorical theories.* Thousand Oaks, CA: Sage.

Gale, X. L. (2000). Historical studies and postmodernism: Rereading Aspasia of Miletus. *College English, 62*(3), 361–386.

Gannett, C. (1992). *Gender and the journal: Diaries and academic discourse.* Albany: State University of New York Press.

Gere, A. (1997). *Intimate practices: Literacy and cultural work in U.S. women's clubs: 1890–1920.* Urbana: University of Illinois.

Glenn, C. (1994). Sex, lies, manuscript: Refiguring Aspasia in the history of rhetoric. *College Composition and Communication, 45,* 180–199.

Glenn, C. (1997). *Rhetoric retold: Regendering the tradition from antiquity through the Renaissance.* Carbondale: Southern Illinois University Press.

Glenn, C. (2000). Truth, lies, and method: Revisiting feminist historiography. *College English, 62*(3), 387–389.

Glenn, C. (2004). *Unspoken: A rhetoric of silence.* Carbondale: Southern Illinois University Press.

Gray-Rosendale, L., & Harootunian, G. (Eds.). (2003). *Fractured feminisms: Rhetoric, context, and contestation.* Albany: State University of New York Press.

Hesford, W. (1999). Reading rape stories: Material rhetoric and the trauma of representation. *College English, 62*(2), 192–221.

Hesford, W. (2006). Documenting violations: Rhetorical witnessing and the spectacle of distant suffering. In K. Ronald & J. Ritchie (Eds.), *Teaching rhetorica: Theory, pedagogy, practice* (pp. 161–197). Portsmouth, NH: Heinemann.

Hesford, W. S., & Kozol, W. (Eds.). (2001). *Haunting violations: Feminist criticism and the crisis of the real.* Urbana: University of Illinois Press.

Hesford, W. S., & Kozol, W. (Eds.). (2005). *Just advocacy? Women's human rights, transnational feminisms, and the politics of representation.* Piscataway, NJ: Rutgers University Press.

Hobbs, C. (1995). *Nineteenth century women learn to write.* Charlottesville: University Press of Virginia.

hooks, b. (1989). *Talking back: Thinking feminist, thinking black.* Boston: Southend Press.

hooks, b. (1994). *Teaching to transgress: Education as the practice of freedom.* New York: Routledge.

Jarratt, S. (1991). *Rereading the sophists: Classical rhetoric refigured.* Carbondale: Southern Illinois University Press.

Jarratt, S. (2000). Rhetoric and feminism: Together again. *College English, 62*(3), 390–393.

Jarratt, S., & Ong, R. (1995). Aspasia: Rhetoric, gender, and colonial ideology. In A. Lunsford (Ed.), *Reclaiming rhetorica: Women in the history of rhetoric* (pp. 9–24). Pittsburgh, PA: University of Pittsburgh Press.

Jarratt, S., & Worsham, L. (Eds.). (1998). *Feminism and composition: In other words.* New York: Modern Language Association.

Johnson, N. (2002). *Gender and rhetorical space in American life: 1866–1910.* Carbondale: Southern Illinois University Press.

Jung, J. (2005). *Revisionary rhetoric, feminist pedagogy and multi-genre texts.* Carbondale: Southern Illinois University Press.

Kates, S. (1999). *Activist rhetorics and American higher education: 1885–1937.* Carbondale: Southern Illinois University Press.

Lerner, G. (1986). *The creation of patriarchy.* New York: Oxford University Press.

Lerner, G. (1993). *The creation of feminist consciousness: From the Middle Ages to eighteen-seventy.* New York: Oxford University Press.

Lerner, G. (1998). *Why history matters: Life and thought.* New York: Oxford University Press.

Logan, S. W. (Ed.). (1995). *With pen and voice: A critical anthology of nineteenth-century African American women.* Carbondale: Southern Illinois University Press.

Logan, S. W. (1999). *"We are coming": The persuasive discourse of nineteenth-century black women.* Carbondale: Southern Illinois University Press.

Lunsford, A. (Ed.). (1995). *Reclaiming rhetorica: Women in the history of rhetoric.* Pittsburgh, PA: University of Pittsburgh Press.

Mattingly, C. (1999). *Well-tempered women: Nineteenth-century temperance rhetoric.* Carbondale: Southern Illinois University Press.

Mattingly, C. (2002). *Appropriate(ing) dress: Women's rhetorical style in nineteenth century America.* Carbondale: Southern Illinois University Press.

Miller, H., & Bridwell-Bowles, L. (2005). *Rhetorical women: Roles and representations.* Tuscaloosa: University of Alabama Press.

Mountford, R. (2003). *The gendered pulpit: Preaching in American Protestant spaces.* Carbondale: Southern Illinois University Press.

Phelps, L. W., & Emig, J. (Eds.). (1995). *Feminine principles and women's experience in American composition and rhetoric.* Pittsburgh, PA: University of Pittsburgh Press.

Ratcliffe, K. (1996). *Anglo-American feminist challenges to the rhetorical traditions: Virginia Woolf, Mary Daly, Adrienne Rich.* Carbondale: Southern Illinois University Press.

Ratcliffe, K. (2005). *Rhetorical listening: Identification, gender, whiteness.* Carbdondale: Southern Illinois University Press.

Rich, A. (1979). When we dead awaken: Writing as revision. In *On lies, secrets, and silence: Selected prose 1966–1978* (pp. 33–68). New York: Norton.

Rich, A. (1986). Notes toward a politics of vocation. In *Blood, bread, and poetry: Selected prose, 1979–1985* (pp. 210–232). New York. Norton.

Ritchie, J., & Ronald, K. (Eds.). (2001). *Available means: An anthology of women's rhetoric(s).*

Pittsburgh, PA: University of Pittsburgh Press.

Ronald, K., & Ritchie, J. (Eds.). (2006). *Teaching rhetorica: Theory, pedagogy, practice.* Portsmouth, NH: Heinemann.

Royster, J. J. (Ed.). (1997). *Southern horrors and other writings: The anti-lynching campaign of Ida B. Wells, 1892–1900.* Boston: Bedford Books.

Royster, J. J. (2000). *Traces of a stream: Literacy and social change among African American women.* Pittsburgh, PA: University of Pittsburgh Press.

Ryan, K. J. (2006). Recasting recovery and gender critique as inventive arts: Constructing edited collections in feminist rhetorical studies. *Rhetoric Review, 25*(1), 22–40.

Schneir, M. (Ed.). (1972). *Feminism: The essential historical writings.* New York: Vintage.

Schneir, M. (Ed.). (1994). *Feminism in our time: The essential writings, World War II to the present.* New York: Vintage Books.

Sutherland, C. M. (2005). *The eloquence of Mary Astell.* Calgary, Alberta, Canada: University of Calgary Press.

Sutherland, C. M., & Sutcliffe, R. (Eds.). (1999). *The changing tradition: Women in the history of rhetoric.* Calgary, Alberta, Canada: University of Calgary Press.

Swearingen, J. (1991). *Rhetoric and irony: Western literacy and Western lies.* New York: Oxford University Press.

Teague, F. (1998). *Bathsua Makin, woman of learning.* London: Associated University Press.

Wertheimer, M. M. (Ed.). (1997). *Listening to their voices: The rhetorical activities of historical women.* Columbia: University of South Carolina Press.

9

Recent Advances in Comparative Rhetoric

SUE HUM

ARABELLA LYON

I hope to have identified a few things Indians do not want from writing: stereotypes, cultural appropriations, exclusion, ignorance, irrelevance, rhetorical imperialism.

—Lyons (2000)

Because rhetoric itself is such a problematic concept—one defined differently within every culture, epoch, and motive and then located so randomly across the disciplines, comparative rhetoric has proven even more problematic to define. When scholars consider comparative rhetoric, they must ask familiar questions: What definition of rhetoric is in use? What is ethical rhetorical practice? To these have been added new questions: If cultures do not share the concept of rhetoric, what are we comparing? By what method and means do we come to know a culture different from our own? If cultures and discourses are differently empowered, and if they do not share the same definitions of ethics and rhetoric, then can we ethically practice or study rhetoric across differences?

Comparative rhetoric has developed over the past few decades in response to globalization, transnational politics, and the American empire.[1] The following survey will examine (1) concerns with definitions of comparative and rhetoric, (2) the nature of appropriate methodology, (3) the significance of the scholar's reflection on her practice and immersion in culture(s), and (4) the representation of other people's rhetoric. To illustrate some of the directions comparative rhetoric is taking, we examine the contours of recent work on Eastern and Chinese rhetoric.

DEFINITIONS

In comparative rhetorical studies, scholars have moved beyond the models of Aristotle's (trans. 2007) persuasion and Burke's (1950) identification in looking for theoretical bases for analysis. Most cultures do not share even that broad field for discussing metalinguistic awareness.[2] In assuming that the world's traditions of political discourse can be contained between these two poles—the Athenian and North American democrat, both highly concerned with rationality and deliberation—scholars constrict their insights at the outset and too often condemn themselves to colonialist and Orientalist readings.[3] On the other hand, overly copious definitions of rhetoric limit the precision of viewing particular details in the rhetorics of unfamiliar cultures. While Schiappa's (2001) pragmatic argument in favor of big or broadly defined rhetoric is politically useful, even necessary, for recognizing and examining diverse language practices and the contested nature of the term *rhetoric*, surely the discipline cannot study all symbol systems and still produce nuanced, careful scholarship across cultures, scholarship that reveals the differences in assumptions about the practices of rhetoric. Pretending that a discipline can study all of writing, speech, movement, music, image, and film diminishes its ability to engage with the other without "stereotypes, cultural appropriations, exclusion, ignorance, irrelevance, rhetorical imperialism" (Lyons, 2000, p. 462). Kennedy's (1998) definition of rhetoric as all "effective expression" from bird to human (p. 3) diminishes recognition of culture, *human culture*, as a defining aspect of rhetoric. His definition becomes even more problematic with its "evolutionary" organization from animal through oral to literate (Mao, 2003, p. 410).

In work that depends on cross-cultural sensitivity, it is appropriate to apply broad but culturally based definitions of rhetoric. While big definitions, such as Garrett's (1999) "symbolic inducement" (p. 55), can work to open up the study of alternative rhetorics, we find such definitions problematic in their inclusion of poetry, literature, and song to the diminishment of politics, the connection that makes rhetoric vital to the understanding of power. Using broad definitions, comparative rhetoric can become comparative literature, comparative philosophy, and comparative anthropology. A middle way is offered by Mailloux's (1998) "rhetoric as the political effectivity of trope and argument in culture" (p. xii), a definition that emphasizes the political nature of rhetoric while acknowledging both its discursive nature and cultural base. Broader definitions of rhetoric are useful in comparative rhetoric because they force scholars outside disciplinary assumptions and habits of reading and force engagement with alterity. The work of comparative rhetoric, however, is not simply transcendence of universals and affirmation of the prevailing "tradition" but also an attempt to define the cultural bases of discursive power and the ways it privileges some statements and strategies in the production of knowledge and reproduction of power (Foucault, 1972). Comparative rhetoric now is seen by some scholars as a strategy for engaging other cultures, knowledges, and discourses rather than a discovery of commonplaces and universals.

Just as defining rhetoric presents problems for the comparatist, *comparative* itself has come to be seen as a more fluid term, if not in definition, then in terms of ethical practices. What is it that we compare? To what purpose? With what motive? Are similarities or uniqueness more telling discoveries? What might constitute a valid or an interesting comparison or contrast? What kinds of methods constitute comparison? What are the accepted ethics of comparative work? Are they adequate? What qualifies one to write about another culture, and who are the appropriate practitioners of comparative rhetorics? While the most common understanding of comparative rhetoric is comparison across nationalities or nation states, comparative rhetoric might examine gender, race, ethnicity, and religion as sites of potential revelation. Comparison reads texts across and through cultures as it also reads across time and space. Aristotle's persuasion and Burke's identification exemplify a method for comparing rhetorics across culture, space, and time, and in this sense, all study of texts is comparative. No rhetorical situation or text is truly understood except in relationship to other situations and texts. Even so, focus on the comparative nature of all texts, many believe, diminishes the primary motives for the evolving field of comparative rhetoric at the start of the 21st century. Given globalization in the wake of decolonization, currently most comparative work is concerned with the development of global consciousness and communication in the battle between McWorld and Jihad (Barber, 1996).

In seeking an ethical definition of comparative rhetoric, some scholars now avoid references to and assumptions about tradition. They resist the temptations of Kennedy's (1998) definition of comparative rhetoric as "the cross-cultural study of rhetorical traditions as they exist or have existed in different societies around the world" (p. 1), because the nature of a rhetorical tradition—whether one means a textual canon or a historical, cultural context—is very problematic.[4] Jarratt (2005) argues that there are basic questions about "*the* tradition, multiple traditions, or the lack of continuous traditions" (p. 95). Any tradition is a politically motivated construct, and given the forces that make Western rhetoric a set of complex, heterogeneous practices, how does one approach the heterogeneous linguistic and cultural practices of another culture and then compare their tradition(s) with the tradition(s) of the West? If the tradition of Western rhetoric

is problematic and difficult to trace or define, then what does it mean to carry the concept of tradition and those scholarly assumptions to other cultures?

These problems of definition can be clarified by a case study. Recent work on classical Chinese rhetoric demonstrates that like many other cultures, the Chinese do not share our rhetorical "tradition" and have different assumptions about language, communication, and the individual.[5] It is true that one will find metaphors and topoi in Chinese speeches, but identifying corresponding structures bypass any project of engaging Chinese culture as an equal other. While there are texts on style and writing and essays on speaking in ancient China, there is little *systemic* grammar, linguistics, rhetoric, poetics, or literary theory; there is no evidence of an epic.[6] Systemic work appears later, but what exists is often viewed by the Chinese as marginal and/or immoral and sophistic.[7] Against these difficulties, we know that rhetorics live in China's long, deep, and rich traditions of public discourse, education, and political action. If Western scholars only look at similarities and the differences of omission, they miss the opportunity to understand what metalinguistic awareness means outside the West. China's philosophical concern with process, cycle, and movement over Being, creation, and permanence is congenial with many aspects of Western rhetoric (and apart from Western philosophy), but prior understandings of what is rhetoric may focus us on the wrong aspects of Chinese culture and filter out what is significant.[8] One may erase what is uniquely Chinese by foregrounding Western assumptions. One may distort and colonize an alternative understanding revolutionary to Western rhetoric. This is not simply the dilemma and tragedy of interpretation; it is the destruction of the other's voice by reading nonreflectively from the standpoint of one's training.

To interpret and translate reflectively is to identify words, grammars, and concepts that allow one to move between locations, to traverse the divide, to understand both the Athenian and the Han writer and speaker. No reflective scholar approached the field with immediate understanding; rather, over time, appropriate terms were developed. In an early article, for example, Lu and Frank (1993) suggest that *bian* (argue, debate) is the term that most closely approximates *rhetoric* between 500 and 200 BCE, but the longing for a one-to-one correspondence is no longer part of the discussion. Many more terms are now seen as indicating rhetorical theory: *shuo* (speak, explain, make clear), *shui* (speak effectively, convince, persuade), *quan* (urge), *jian* (remonstrate), *ming* (naming, dialectics), *yue* (speaking), *ci* (speech), and *yan* (say, language). These terms together allow one to glimpse both the broad and the heterogeneous nature of Chinese rhetoric, and the process by which scholars come to them reflects the development of "a language of ambiguous similarity," that reveals the particular and the universal (Lu, 1998, pp. 91–92). As Mao (2003) warns us, this language of similarity may focus us on the commonality between cultures and not allow us to interrogate both cultures, their rhetorics, and their assumptions (pp. 416–419). In understanding the conceptual space of Chinese public discourse, in using Chinese concepts that reference more actions than simply argument and persuasion, a scholar gives up the specificity of a disciplined and Western definition of rhetoric and develops the potential to see the resources of language more complexly. Finding appropriate culture-specific definitions is a significant task in comparative work.

METHODOLOGY

A comparatist faces at least two significant methodological problems in approaching texts: translation and the question of an appropriate methodology as the usual rhetorical tools may not be appropriate. While there exists a large

literature on translation in general, outside of some work on the classics, it has not been addressed significantly in rhetoric's literature. What has received significant attention is the problem of reading a text comparatively and ethically. Should one simply address a culture in grounded analysis through close readings, avoiding established (Western) rhetorical tools, immerse oneself in one culture, and perhaps not even compare, as Shuter (2000) suggests? Or can one use a method such as the pentad or speech act theory outside of its culture? What are the consequences of importing a method into a culture in which that method is not indigenous?

Mao (2003) points out that cross-cultural study faces the challenges of avoiding a "deficiency model," where a non-Western culture is defined and judged against a Western norm (ideal). He elaborates what Garrett (1999) calls "the methodological paradox," where one must start with a method external to the culture but based in the researcher's rhetorical training.[9] This paradox makes it impossible to approach the other's culture on its own terms within its own assumptions. Just as Heisenberg's Uncertainty Principle (1927) taught 20th-century scientists the necessity and flaw of a standpoint for viewing a phenomenon, so the methodological paradox should teach rhetoricians the necessity and flaw of their training and research. Even with an awareness of the challenges of both "the deficiency model" and "the methodological paradox," self-reflective Western scholars often fail to find new understandings of discursive hegemonies (Garrett, 1999). Difference has a specificity that is hard to describe in ways that truly acknowledge without exoticizing it. An accurate comparative rhetoric requires the creation of new vocabularies indicative of those new concepts. Translation and method intertwine.

When one acquires the words and concepts of another culture's rhetorical tradition, one is not translating the word in any simple sense.[10]

Just as *logos, pathos,* or *ethos* may not be translated to English so as to preserve their connotations, the preservation of the original meaning—as in our earlier discussion of China—creates a significant vocabulary necessary for intercultural discourse. One cannot take critical vocabularies and indigenous forms as givens, easily transferred between cultures. Vocabularies and forms may need to be preserved if a comparative approach is to have meaning. Translation can diminish necessary differences and hide methodological assumptions.

Earlier, we raised the issue of defining comparison and understanding the questions of the ethical implications of comparing and what might be compared. In this section, we more fully explore the ethical implications of comparison as embedded in the selection of methods. Obviously, a paper analyzing Chinese or Scottish rhetoric alone and using the tools of those cultures is minimally comparative. For a rhetorical study to be truly comparative, it has to engage the texts of at least two cultures. This claim creates two problems: the problem of how to see across cultures, for it is impossible to view without a standpoint and that standpoint is never fully in both places, and the problem of what constitutes a separate culture.

When Kastely (1997) defines rhetoric as "the art of position," he foregrounds the work of resisting ideologies, epistemological closures, and hierarchies of persuasion (p. 217). While this definition may be too broad for analyzing discourses across cultures, when Kastely grounds rhetorical action in "the play of positions," not "the will of individual agents," he asks scholars to understand how they have been figured and positioned (p. 218). This theory of position defines a historical concern of comparative rhetoricians. In 1932, Richards wrote,

> Can we in attempting to understand and translate a work which belongs to a very

different tradition from our own do more than read our own conceptions into it? Can we make it more than a mirror of our minds, or are we inevitably in this undertaking trying to be on both sides of the looking-glass at once? (p. 86)

Thirty-nine years later, Oliver (1971) advocated for the recognition of Chinese and Indian rhetoric on their own terms as "rhetoric always is authentic only in its cultural matrix" (p. ix). He writes,

> The most likely distortion is to seek to depict the rhetoric thus extracted in Western terms. It is tempting to look in the philosophy for what appear to us to be rhetorical universals, such as invention, disposition, style, delivery and memory, and the three Aristotelian modes of proof—ethos, pathos, and logos. In effect unless we find a Western rhetoric, it is a temptation to conclude there is no rhetoric there at all. And, equally lamentably, whatever rhetoric is found is very likely to be labeled and described in Western rhetorical terms—since, otherwise, we would scarcely be aware that rhetoric is what we are in fact dealing with. (p. 261)

Oliver's focus on rhetoric outside of Western terms holds out the hope of finding something more than Western rhetoric. He hopes that we can find a new position from which to see both the familiar and the other. Given Richards's and Oliver's early admonitions (though problematic execution of the practice), why do we find Western rhetoric constantly used as the methodological approach to others' texts? Why are we, and others, still making this point 75 years after Richards?

At the moment, there are four practices in play that suggest different answers to these questions. Some scholars, at least sometimes, are committed to an Athenian or a Burkean rhetoric and use it as the position from which they see the rhetorical world. Others import perspicuous methods, but they are anxious about what those methods impose. A third group carefully works within a particular framework, minimizing the comparative nature of their work. Finally, a few use non-Western tools on Western texts.

Many comparatists have applied Western methods to the analysis of non-Western rhetorics. Blinn and Garrett (1993) respond to scholarly claims that the Chinese are not analytical and logical. They read *Intrigues of the Warring States*, a volume of 500 early Chinese speeches, to find Aristotle's topoi.[11] From that finding, they then argue that the Chinese are rational; in doing so, they tend to bypass engagement with cultural differences, but their purpose is to correct Orientalism and to help scholars understand Chinese speeches. The effect is to provide a necessary argument, not to subsume other cultures under Western terms and approaches. Alternatively, using Anglo-American ordinary-language philosophy to read closely particular classical Chinese texts, Lyon (2004, 2008) is concerned with understanding how early Chinese political argument is different from contemporary Western rhetoric. In this case, the limits of the method are acknowledged, but Western theory functions not as (a) truth, but as a lens (Richards's "speculative instrument"): a lens that critiques Western rhetoric.

Many see the third approach, indwelling in the culture and text, as the best approach for comparative work. In the study of Chinese rhetoric, Lu (2004) describes the discipline's progress as "moving from a superficial understanding of Chinese rhetorical practices through the Western lens, to an in depth exploration of original texts in search of rhetorical senses and meanings in ancient Chinese contexts" (p. 3).[12] In effect, she sees the field as moving from a less-than-engaged comparative rhetoric to a more sinocentric rhetoric. Her exemplar of a comparative rhetoric text is sinocentric rhetoric without being straight sinology: *Rhetoric of the Chinese Cultural Revolution: The Impact on Chinese Thought, Culture, and Communication*.[13] In this book,

while she draws on Western rhetorical theory, Lu also uses personal experience and classical Chinese rhetorical and cultural traditions to analyze the political discourse of the Cultural Revolution.

The examination of a text within its cultural context seems to be the most revealing of political insight, and the most useful to political and cultural rhetorical studies. This is particularly clear when one reads two different types of analyses of the rhetoric of contemporary Hindu nationalism.[14] When Roy and Rowland (2003) use Burke's (1941) work on Hitler and mythic narrative to analyze Hindu nationalism and the rhetoric of Bal Thackeray, they are forced to discuss repeatedly the Nazis as a nationalist movement. Their Burkean dependence brings historical and cultural connotations that they must repeatedly deny (Roy & Rowland, 2003, pp. 226, 230). Yet despite some claims to a different meaning, the effect of their analogy leads readers to see the rhetoric of Hindu nationalism as "Nazi-like," a blaspheme in most vocabularies. In the end, Roy and Rowland (2003) do claim that the narrative pattern of *Mein Kampf* "is at the core of nationalist/religious identity movements" (p. 243), lumping all such movements as based in good-evil dichotomies and scapegoating with threats of emasculation. When one compares their unfortunate analogy and analysis of Hindu nationalist rhetoric with those of the Nobel prize–winning economist Sen (2005) or the Indian social historian Thapar (2000), one is struck by their lack of generalization, the focus of their claims and evidence, and their careful analysis, which might actually lead to intervention. In their culturally based studies of Hindu nationalist discourse, both Sen (2005) and Thapar (2000) focus on the great Hindu epics *Mahabharata* and *Ramayana*, narratives never mentioned in Roy and Rowland's (2003) mythic analysis.[15] These great epics help demonstrate Indian argumentative traditions and the role of Hindu deities, such as Rama, in politics. The end result of Roy and Rowland's work is a claim to a universal place of myth in nationalism, while the end result of Sen's (2005) and Thapar's (2000) insights is political understanding of the sources of discord with the attendant possibility of remedy.

New methodologies and insights from non-Western cultures are now being applied to Western texts. These very different renderings of rhetorical language reshape Western knowledge and self-perception without the same colonial concerns of importing Western methodologies into other cultures. Since the political and academic power structure still lies within the West, the primary goal of such studies is to create knowledge, not oppression. Wu (2005) reads Margaret Cavendish through the lens of contemporary Chinese women's discourse. In examining the material conditions of women, she is able to argue for a broader definition of what constitutes rhetoric. Wu's work gives hope that just as Aristotle has been subjected to feminist readings, someday soon he may be interpreted through a Confucian tradition.[16]

These four methodological approaches are still being discussed and developed within comparative rhetoric, but at the core of the discussion is the third contemporary issue of whether one can or should make claims of universalism if one is always positioned from a partial view. If for a moment, we work with Kastely's (1997) definition of rhetoric as "the art of positioning," then what does it mean to position one's self as omniscient?

ACKNOWLEDGING STANDPOINT, OR THE PROBLEM OF UNIVERSALISM

The critique of universalism or Platonism is a commonplace for rhetorical scholars. Most see the critique of universalism and the focus on situation as the basis of rhetoric. Beginning with studies by and of Gorgias, Isocrates, or Aristotle, critiques of universalism consistently have been made by rhetoricians throughout

the last quarter of the 20th century as a response to earlier structuralism and positivism.[17] Nevertheless, many rhetoricians continue to subsume the discourses of other cultures (all discourses of all cultures) under the rubric of Western rhetorical theory. What is the basis or drive behind the claim of universal insight (Kennedy, 1998; Roy & Rowland, 2003)?

Many comparatists now find that the answer is embedded in the paradoxical box of Western discourse, understood as a colonialist discourse that sets scholars up to claim its values as ideal, both as the best and as the most transcendent. Struggling to escape the trap of idealism, Western rhetoric makes small progress. Take, for example, Blinn and Garrett's (1993) response to scholars who claim that Chinese rhetoric lacks logic and consequently is less ideal or complete than Western modes of rhetoric. When they respond to the flawed insight and dangerous hierarchy, their recourse, given their training and their audience, is to turn to Aristotelian topoi. Although sensitive to cultural differences, Blinn and Garrett willingly accept a soft universalism (pp. 94–95) and seek "to determine" if the argumentation of the *Intrigues of the Warring States* "utilizes the Aristotelian *topoi.*" Speakers in third- and fourth-century China had never heard of topoi, let alone used them, but the discursive patterns of rhetorical scholarship lead even the best of scholars into the problematic acceptance of the centrality of Aristotle.

The roots of the discipline's conceptual paradox are in the patriarchal and colonialist ideologies that pervade discussions of the other. As Royster (2005) tells us, "we have positioned academic discourses in the realm of public discourses, highlighting abstracted, objectified, and dispassionate voices as most valuable" (p. 3). This means that scholars are most rewarded for work that silences the specifics of the other's cultures, meanings, and intentions. Despite the critiques made again and again,[18] rhetorical scholars are not respected for narrow claims based on specific texts and authors. For insights from other cultures and noncanonical texts to enter disciplinary rhetoric, scholars must look at the specific texts within a methodological frame and develop a vocabulary based in those cultures. The most important work, at this stage in comparative rhetoric, is the focused study, one conscious of its standpoint.

SPEAKING FOR/ABOUT OTHERS

Given the partiality of any standpoint, the centrality of a researcher's voice, and the difficulty of grasping a culture or a text as a whole (even one's own culture), the ethics of representing has deep problems.[19] These problems, the current crisis in representation, are especially true when scholars begin to work outside their areas of training. While we have been discussing issues of method and representation throughout the chapter there are particular criteria for representing and claiming insights for and about others fairly. Alcoff (1991) argues that, while some say "that speaking for others is arrogant, vain, unethical, and politically illegitimate" (p. 6), sometimes it is appropriate to speak for them. A retreat from speaking for others supports the individualistic, autonomous ideology of the West and sets the desire to avoid criticism and error before the needs of dialogue. As Alcoff writes, "Often the possibility of dialogue is left unexplored or inadequately pursued by more privileged persons" (p. 23). Given the mediated nature of all representation, given the political need for some representing of others, she offers a less dangerous approach to speaking for others—a four-step program. First, the impetus to speak must be interrogated, even resisted. Rather than teach, one must develop skills of listening. Second, our location or standpoint and context should be analyzed, preferably collectively. Third, the speaker must embrace accountability and be open to criticism.

Fourth and most important, one must weigh and understand the effects of one's claims. Alcoff offers an example of complex effect: When a First World person speaks about the Third World, the effect may be to reinscribe the dominance of the First World. When a rhetorician applies Aristotelian vocabulary to South African liberatory rhetoric, the effect may be to subsume contemporary South African rhetoric under that of classical Athens, thereby ignoring its own inventions.[20] The effects of writing or not writing, both, should be considered by any scholar undertaking a comparative study.

To minimize the dangers of speaking from privilege, one approach would be to provide accurate descriptions rather than judgments, thus preventing the reduction of the other's texts to an object that is consumed by Western traditions. Unjudged, other cultures are better understood and offer more knowledge when the gaze of ethnocentrisms (Eurocentrism) has been dulled through self-reflection, openness to difference and critique, and consciousness of effect. If one only describes, even though description has a standpoint, one minimizes the dangers of colonizing the other's rhetoric. This approach, however ethical, does limit the production of knowledge.

In a quest for insight into all that rhetoric might be—reflective, examined, respectful, located insight—we argue that sometimes a scholar trained in Western rhetoric can speak of other cultures' rhetorics. While potentially exploitative, an external standpoint can reveal hidden assumptions and create new understandings. In a collection of essays on early China and Greece, the philosopher Hall (2002) discusses the appropriate role of amateur sinologists, or what we might consider cultural outsiders. Just as rhetoricians argue about the productivity of revisionist and reconstructive historiography,[21] Hall argues that the tension between speculation and scholarship is necessary for recovering meaningful texts. He argues for a full collaboration between Western philosophy and sinology if texts are to be teachable. We would expand on his philosophical orientation to translation to say that rhetorical interpretation of texts benefits from a comparative approach that allows for speculation with respect for and grounding in the other's history as well as reflection on the outsider's motive and assumptions. Revisionist or speculative readings without consideration of standpoint, accountability, and effect are less than scholarship. The quest of meaning, however, cannot be limited to the standpoints within each disparate culture; pragmatically, they must be in dialogue. If comparative rhetoric is a method of analyzing different discourses, a means of discovering common grounds of engagement, and a strategy for revealing cultural assumptions, then revisionist readings and the recovery of lost perspectives cannot be separated without the loss of inventive power.

FUTURE DIRECTIONS

The primary difficulty for comparative rhetoric is the lack of publication of analysis and theory by scholars in non-Western cultures. There exists a small but established body of work that compares European rhetorics, and Chinese rhetoric has just begun to have a body of literature large enough for response, dialogue, and engagement with other cultures. Much of non-Western scholarship still has had little development. When it does appear, often it is simply subsumed to Western rhetoric, never examined for its own worth, let alone compared. If one wanted to develop a project, say on South Asia, for example, one would have trouble finding a starting point. There is such a dearth of South Asian, Southeast Asian, or East Asian rhetoric outside of China that when Wang did her 2004 survey of research in Asian rhetoric, all the scholars interviewed were sinologists. There are some articles that focus on Gandhi, but as Gorsevski (2004) warns us, Gandhi's rhetoric is often analyzed because of his impeccable

English, which allowed him to be seen as a "stand-in Euro" (p. xxi).[22] While there is a growing body of literature comparing dominant Anglo-American and African American rhetorics,[23] for the most part, Afrocentric comparative rhetorics—comparisons in which at least one text or theory is informed by an African worldview—are underdeveloped unless one includes African American rhetoric.[24] Even when one finds Afrocentric rhetorical research, it is likely to deal globally while ignoring the diversity that is Africa. This approach, taken by scholars such as Collins (2001) and Asante (1998), is problematic in its generalization of time, space, and nation. Afrocentrism offers a theoretical umbrella, a vast model, to cover perhaps the specificity needed to develop fully a conversation about the relationships among various African rhetorics, cultures, and traditions as well as their relationships with the rest of the world.

One area that has seen some development is early Egypt, and it might provide us a clearer understanding of what is ultimately needed. Since the first volume of *Rhetorica* (1983), when Fox wrote about ancient Egyptian rhetoric, it has been posited as a counterpoint to Athenian rhetoric. While the literature is not copious, the serious engagement of half a dozen scholars has produced kingdom-specific analyses of rhetorical canons, tropes, rhetors, gender, court procedures, class, and genre.[25] While the scholarship covers a 1,500-year period, as a body, it begins to nuance the specifics of Egyptian dynastic rhetoric within its own cultural frame. These kinds of analyses would facilitate international understanding of the successes and failures of the current rhetoric of African nations, nongovernment agencies, and people. For us to make sense of Native American, South American, and Middle Eastern rhetorics, we need sufficient scholarship to have conversations about the specifics of each cultural inflection, especially its contemporary inflection.

Perhaps one of the best hopes for comparative rhetoric, one that truly engages difference, is in some of the very fine anthologies appearing in recent years. Collections such as Gray-Rosendale and Gruber (2001) and Lipson and Binkley (2004) introduce a wide range of scholars to a variety of cultures and provide a variety of comparative methods. The growing literature on non-Western rhetoric offers significant possibilities for understanding other cultures and for reflecting on Western rhetoric.

CONCLUSIONS

We compare rhetorics so that we may understand the limits of the term and our own conceptual frame for it. As we denationalize and denormalize our notions of rhetoric, we search for understanding of the power of communication in an era defined by new communication technologies, increased mobility, displacements of people, and cultural clashes. To that end, comparative rhetoric is a vital enterprise, but it can only be such if it offers more than a repeat of colonial tendencies. A comparative historical approach, focused on moments, texts, and political situations within cultures, would allow us to develop the "shared, interlocutionary dialogic modes of thought and language" that Swearingen (1991) proposes (p. 18). In looking at particular texts in particular moments, scholars show the interplay of diverse factions within a culture as well as across cultures. Openness to new definitions, methods, and understandings of ourselves and our cultures, critical awareness of the ethics of speaking, and dialogic engagement with other rhetorics will make rhetorical studies a more powerful speculative instrument in the 21st century.

NOTES

1. Hesford (2006) reviews the recent rhetoric and composition literature in this "global turn."

2. At the risk of being seen as Orientalists, we do think it is important to acknowledge both difference and similarity between cultures. For discussions of Orientalism in rhetoric, see our discussion below of Liu (1996). Or one might look at the discussion of contact zones in Mao (2006).

3. See Garrett (1999), Liu (1996), Lu (2000), Lyon (2004), Mao (2006), Oliver (1971), Richards (1932), Sen (2005), and Shuter (2000).

4. In addition to Graff, Walzer, and Atwill (2005), see Bizzell (2000), Glenn (1997), Kastely (1997), Lipson and Binkley (2004), Lunsford (1995), and Miller (1993).

5. Lloyd (1990) provides an excellent overview of the similarities and differences between classical Greece and China. His most telling point reminds us that cultures are never monolithic and broad claims are troublesome.

6. Without a doubt, there are interesting rhetorical texts in China, but their place in the culture and their relationship to the Western concept of rhetoric are problematic. Liu (1996) very articulately presents what rhetorical theory is available in China. His difficulty in separating Chinese philosophy and poetry from Chinese rhetoric is emblematic of the point we are making about comparative rhetorical work needing to struggle with definitional boundaries. Recently, Kirkpatrick (2005) argues that Kui's *Wen ze* is the first systemic rhetoric (1170 AD), though Wu (2006) is developing the claim for an earlier text, *Guiguzi* (400–300 BCE), and Oliver (1971) claims that the Han Feizi (~289–233 BCE) is a systemic treatment.

7. Wu (2006) raises the issue of the marginalization of *Guiguzi* by both Western and Chinese classicists, emphasizing its exclusion from a canon dominated by Confucian ethics.

8. The Western desire to see Chinese thought as a mirror image of the West is not without problems. Much as rhetoric is posited as the feminine and suspect other to philosophy, the "rhetorical" nature of Chinese thought may well be simply its casting as different. Clearly a civilization as vast as China's cannot be so simply described. See Saussy (2002) for a careful discussion of this inclination.

9. Garrett (1999) provides an early consideration of appropriate methodologies for comparative rhetoric.

10. Hum (2005–2006) provides a discussion of idiomatic sayings in Hokkien, an oral Chinese dialect.

11. Goldin (2005) presents a very interesting review of the literature considering whether

Strategems of the Warring States can be considered a rhetoric. He argues that it is not.

12. Jia (2000) provides a brief historical survey
of this literature.

13. Wu (2001) also achieves such a progressive
balance.

14. Examinations of Indian rhetoric are
underdeveloped. Good examples of early comparative work are found in Oliver (1971) and Gangal
and Hosterman (1982).

15. Roy and Rowland (2003) orientalize
Hindu narratives, calling them "pacific" and "contemplative" (p. 232) even though the great epics
are full of quests and battles.

16. See Freeland (1998) or Lyon (2004) for a
reading of Confucius that offers an alternative
model of deliberation as a correction to Aristotle.

17. For a good history, see Kimball (1986).

18. Among the many are Liu (1996), Lu
(1998, 2000), Mao (2006), and Shome (1999).

19. Hum (2006) highlights the problematic of
identity politics in an age of diaspora.

20. While the scarcity of African rhetoric
makes criticism of any serious project thorny, the
repeated use of classical Greek vocabulary to
describe South African democracy in Salazar
(2002) undercuts his project.

21. See Lyon's review (1998).

22. For examples of Western co-option of
Gandhi, see Hendrick (1956) and Murti (1968).

23. Royster (2005) provides a concise discussion of this concept and its contemporary implications (pp. 1–3).

24. Our definition is an adaptation of Collins
(2001, p. 185).

25. Fox's (1983) early work was followed by
Lesko (1997, 1999) and Lipson (1990, 2004).
Hutto (2002), Kennedy (1998), and Sweeney
(2004) have also written on early Egypt.

REFERENCES

Alcoff, L. (1991, Winter). The problem of speaking
for others. *Cultural Critique, 20,* 5–32.

Aristotle. (2007). *On rhetoric* (2nd ed., G. A. Kennedy,
Trans.). New York: Oxford University Press.

Asante, M. K. (1998). *The Afrocentric idea* (Rev.
ed.). Philadelphia: Temple University Press.

Barber, B. (1996). *Jihad vs. Mcworld: How global-
ism and tribalism are reshaping the world.*
New York: Ballantine Books.

Bizzell, P. (2000). Feminist methods of research in
the history of rhetoric: What differences do they
make? *Rhetoric Society Quarterly, 30,* 5–17.

Blinn, S. B., & Garrett, M. (1993). Aristotelian
topoi as a cross-cultural analytic tool.
Philosophy and Rhetoric, 26, 93–112.

Burke, K. (1941). *The philosophy of literary form:
Studies in symbolic action.* Baton Rouge:
Louisiana State University Press.

Burke, K. (1950). *A rhetoric of motives.* New York:
Braziller.

Collins, D. F. (2001). Audience in Afrocentric
rhetoric: Promoting human agency and social
change. In L. Grey-Rosendale & S. Gruber
(Eds.), *Alternative rhetorics* (pp. 185–200).
Albany: State University of New York Press.

Foucault, M. (1972). *Power/Knowledge: Selected
interviews and other writings, 1972–1977*
(C. Gordon, Ed.). New York: Pantheon Books.

Fox, M. V. (1983). Ancient Egyptian rhetoric.
Rhetorica, 1, 9–22.

Freeland, C. (Ed.). (1998). *Feminist interpretations
of Aristotle (re-reading the canon).* University
Park: Pennsylvania State University Press.

Gangal, A., & Hosterman, C. (1982). Toward an
examination of the rhetoric of ancient India.
Southern Speech Communication Journal, 47,
277–291.

Garrett, M. M. (1999). Some elementary methodological reflections on the study of the Chinese
rhetorical tradition. *International and Intercultural Communication Annual, 22,* 53–63.

Glenn, C. (1997). *Rhetoric retold: Regendering the
tradition from antiquity through the
Renaissance.* Carbondale: Southern Illinois
University Press.

Goldin, P. R. (2005). *After Confucius: Studies in
early Chinese philosophy.* Honolulu:
University of Hawaii Press.

Gorsevski, E. W. (2004). *Peaceful persuasion: The
geopolitics of nonviolent rhetoric.* Albany:
State University of New York Press.

Graff, R., Walzer, A. E., & Atwill, J. M. (2005). *The
viability of the rhetorical tradition.* Albany:
State University of New York Press.

Gray-Rosendale, L., & Gruber, S. (2001).
*Alternative rhetorics: Challenges to the rhetor-
ical tradition.* Albany: State University of New
York Press.

Hall, D. L. (2002). What has Athens to do with
Alexandria? Or why sinologists can't get along

with(out) philosophers. In S. Shankman & S. W. Durrant (Eds.), *Early China/ancient Greece: Thinking through comparisons* (pp. 15–34). Albany: State University of New York Press.

Hendrick, G. (1956). The influence of Thoreau's "Civil Disobedience" on Gandhi's Satyagraha. *New England Quarterly, 29*(4), 462–471.

Hesford, W. S. (2006). Global turns and cautions in rhetoric and composition studies. *PMLA, 121,* 787–801.

Hum, S. (2005–2006, Winter). Idioms as cultural commonplaces: Corporeal lessons from Hokkien idioms. *JAEPL: Journal for the Assembly of Expanded Perspectives on Learning, 11,* 42–51.

Hum, S. (2006). Articulating authentic Chineseness: The politics of reading race and ethnicity aesthetically. In P. Vandenberg, S. Hum, & J. Clary-Lemon (Eds.), *Relations, locations, positions: Composition theory for writing teachers* (pp. 442–470). Urbana, IL: National Council of Teachers of English. (Reprinted from *Readerly/Writerly Texts, 9*(1/2), 61–82, 2001, Spring/Summer and Fall/Winter)

Hutto, D. (2002). Ancient Egyptian rhetoric in the old and middle kingdom. *Rhetorica, 20,* 213–233.

Jarratt, S. C. (2005). A human measure: Ancient rhetoric, twenty-first-century loss. In R. Graff, A. E. Walzer, & J. M. Atwill (Eds.), *The viability of the rhetorical tradition* (pp. 95–112). Albany: State University of New York Press.

Jia, W. (2000). Chinese communication scholarship as an expansion of the communication and culture paradigm. In D. R. Heisey (Ed.), *Chinese perspectives in rhetoric and communication* (pp. 139–161). Stamford, CT: Ablex.

Kastely, J. L. (1997). *Rethinking the rhetorical tradition: From Plato to postmodernism.* New Haven, CT: Yale University Press.

Kennedy, G. A. (1998). *Comparative rhetoric: An historical and cross-cultural introduction.* New York: Oxford University Press.

Kimball, B. A. (1986). *Orators and philosophers: A history of the idea of liberal education.* New York: Teachers College.

Kirkpatrick, A. (2005). China's first systemic account of rhetoric: An introduction to Chen Kui's Wen Ze. *Rhetorica, 223,* 103–152.

Lesko, B. (1997). Women's rhetoric from ancient Egypt. In M. M. Wertheimer (Ed.), *Listening to their voices: The rhetorical activities of historical women* (pp. 89–111). Columbia: University of South Carolina Press.

Lesko, B. (1999). "Listening" to the ancient Egyptian woman: Letters, testimonials and other expressions of self. In E. Teeter & J. A. Larson (Eds.), *Gold of praise: Studies on ancient Egypt in honor of Edward F. Wente* (Studies in Ancient Oriental Civilization, No. 58, pp. 247–254). Chicago: University of Chicago Press.

Lipson, C. (1990). Ancient Egyptian medical texts. *Journal of Technical Writing and Communication, 20,* 391–409.

Lipson, C. (2004). Ancient Egyptian rhetoric: It all comes down to *Maat.* In C. Lipson & R. Binkley (Eds.), *Rhetoric before and beyond the Greeks* (pp. 79–97). Albany: State University of New York Press.

Lipson, C., & Binkley, R. (Eds.). (2004). *Rhetoric before and beyond the Greeks.* Albany: State University of New York Press.

Liu, Y. (1996). To capture the essence of Chinese rhetoric: An anatomy of a paradigm in Comparative Rhetoric. *Rhetoric Review, 14,* 318–335.

Lloyd, G. E. R. (1990). *Demystifying mentalities.* New York: Cambridge University Press.

Lu, X. (1998). *Rhetoric in ancient China, fifth to third century B.C.E.: A comparison with classical Greek rhetoric.* Columbia: University of South Carolina Press.

Lu, X. (2000). The influence of classical Chinese Rhetoric on contemporary Chinese political communication and social relations. In D. R. Heisey (Ed.), *Chinese perspectives in rhetoric and communication* (pp. 45–56). Stamford, CT: Ablex.

Lu, X. (2004). *Rhetoric of the Chinese cultural revolution: The impact on Chinese thought, culture, and communication.* Columbia: University of South Carolina Press.

Lu, X., & Frank, D. (1993). On the study of ancient Chinese rhetoric/bian. *Western Journal of Communications, 57,* 445–463.

Lunsford, A. (Ed.). (1995). *Reclaiming rhetorica: Women in the rhetorical tradition.* Pittsburgh, PA: University of Pittsburgh Press.

Lyon, A. (1998). Sources of non-canonical readings, or doing history from prejudice. *Rhetoric Review, 16*, 226–241.

Lyon, A. (2004). Confucian silence and remonstration: A basis for deliberation. In C. Lipson & R. A. Brinkley (Eds.), *Rhetoric before the Greeks* (pp. 131–145). Albany: State University of New York Press.

Lyon, A. (2008). Rhetorical authority in Athenian democracy and the Chinese legalism of Han Fei. *Philosophy and Rhetoric, 41*, 51–71.

Lyons, S. R. (2000). Rhetorical sovereignty: What do American Indians want from writing? *College Composition and Communication, 51*, 447–468.

Mao, L. (2003). Reflective encounters: Illustrating comparative rhetoric. *Style, 37*, 401–425.

Mao, L. (2006). *Reading Chinese fortune cookie: The making of Chinese American rhetoric.* Logan: Utah State University Press.

Mailloux, S. (1998). *Receptive histories: Rhetoric, pragmatism, and American cultural politics.* Ithaca, NY: Cornell University Press.

Miller, T. P. (1993). Reinventing rhetorical traditions. In T. Enos (Ed.), *Learning from the histories of rhetoric: Essays in honor of Winifred Bryan Horner* (pp. 25–41). Carbondale: Southern Illinois University Press.

Murti, V. V. R. (1968). Influence of the Western tradition on Gandhian doctrine. *Philosophy East and West, 18*, 55–65.

Oliver, R. T. (1971). *Communication and culture in ancient India and China.* Syracuse, NY: Syracuse University Press.

Richards, I. A. (1932). *Mencius on the mind: Experiments in multiple definition.* London: Kegan Paul.

Roy, A., & Rowland, R. C. (2003). The rhetoric of Hindu nationalism: A narrative of mythic redefinition. *Western Journal of Communication, 67*, 225–248.

Royster, J. J. (2005). Marking trails in studies of race, gender, and culture. In J. J. Royster & A. M. M. Simpkins (Eds.), *Calling cards: Theory and practice in the study of race, gender, and culture* (pp. 1–14). Albany: State University of New York Press.

Salazar, P. (2002). *An Athenian Athens: Rhetoric and the shaping of democracy in South Africa.* Mahwah, NJ: Lawrence Erlbaum.

Saussy, H. (2002). No time like the present: The category of contemporaneity in Chinese studies. In S. Shankman & S. Durrant (Eds.), *Early China/ancient Greece: Thinking through comparisons* (pp. 35–54). Albany: State University of New York Press.

Schiappa, E. (2001). Second thoughts on the critiques of big rhetoric. *Philosophy and Rhetoric, 34*, 260–274.

Sen, A. (2005). *The argumentative Indian: Writings on Indian history, culture and identity.* New York: Farrar, Straus, & Giroux.

Shome, R. (1999). Postcolonial interventions in the rhetorical canon: An "other" view. In J. L. Lucaites, C. M. Condit, & S. Caudill (Eds.), *Contemporary rhetorical theory* (pp. 591–608). New York: Guilford Press.

Shuter, R. (2000). The culture of rhetoric. In A. Gonzalez & D. V. Tanno (Eds.), *Rhetoric in intercultural contexts* (pp. 11–17). Thousand Oaks, CA: Sage.

Swearingen, C. J. (1991). *Rhetoric and irony: Western literacy and western lies.* New York: Oxford University Press.

Sweeney, D. (2004). Law, rhetoric, and gender in Ramesside Egypt. In C. Lipson & R. Binkley (Eds.), *Rhetoric before and beyond the Greeks* (pp. 99–113). Albany: State University of New York Press.

Thapar, R. (2000). *Cultural past: Essays in early Indian history.* New Delhi, India: Oxford University Press.

Wang, B. (2004). A survey of research in Asian rhetoric. *Rhetoric Review, 23*, 171–181.

Wu, H. (2001). The alternative feminist discourse of post-Mao Chinese writers: A perspective from the rhetorical situation. In L. Grey-Rosendale & S. Gruber (Eds.), *Alternative Rhetorics* (pp. 219–234). Albany: State University of New York Press.

Wu, H. (2005). The paradigm of Margaret Cavendish: Reading women's alternative rhetorics in a global context. In J. J. Royster & A. M. M. Simpkins (Eds.), *Calling cards: Theory and practice in the study of race, gender, and culture* (pp. 171–188). Albany: State University of New York Press.

Wu, H. (2006, May). *China's first treatise on persuasion.* Paper presented at the Rhetoric Society of America meeting, Memphis, TN.

PART II

Rhetoric Across the Disciplines

Rhetoric, Disciplinarity, and Fields of Knowledge

JOHN LYNE

CAROLYN R. MILLER

Does rhetoric, as Plato had Gorgias claim, have other areas of knowledge under its control? Or, as his Socrates claimed, does rhetoric have no use for knowledge at all? Gorgias seems to concede the point but counts it an advantage rather than a deficiency of rhetoric: "But is this not a great comfort, Socrates, to be able without learning any other arts but this one to prove in no way inferior to the specialists?" (Plato, trans. 1961, p. 459c). This critique of rhetoric mounted in the early part of the *Gorgias* relies on a sharp distinction between knowledge and opinion, holding that those who are learned about medicine, say, or about music or numbers, can produce knowledge in others through the use of persuasion but that those who are learned only about rhetoric can produce only opinion, or belief.

We begin with this well-known (if artificially staged) altercation to emphasize that the relationship between rhetoric and knowledge has been under question for quite some time. Plato's representation of this issue in the *Gorgias* is apparently the beginning of the conceptualization of rhetoric in relation to other bodies of knowledge (Schiappa, 1991). As such, it also marks the beginning of the notion of "disciplinarity"—of the conviction that knowledge must be systematic, methodical, and self-conscious and that such knowledge is shared among those who devote themselves to its acquisition and testing, that is, among experts. Thus, according to Edward Schiappa, Plato's apparent coining of the term *rhetorikê* in the *Gorgias* indicates that the verbal art of political speakers in the assembly and the law courts had emerged as a practice that aimed to be a "discipline" (p. 40). Plato's brief was that rhetoric could never measure up to the requirements of a true discipline.

Plato's effort to restrain the Gorgianic ambitions of rhetoric, to make of it at best a supplement, a secondary handmaid to knowledge, and at worst a practice with reckless disregard for knowledge, has been enormously persuasive to subsequent thinkers. The verbal arts are contained by the insistence on the distinction between opinion and knowledge, a distinction that posits rhetoric-free pathways to knowledge. Michael Leff (1987) puts the distinction as a metonymy: The historically prevailing view has been that rhetoric is "a thing contained . . . an art domiciled within the territory of politics and domesticated by this political confinement"(p. 1). The view that Gorgias defended so inadequately in Plato's dialogue, a view that has come around again in the neo-Sophistic movement, is that rhetoric is a container, or "a containing force." "Unfettered by any particular subject matter, rhetoric becomes a power that ranges across the entire domain of human discourse, containing whatever matter it encounters" (p. 1). Leff calls these two versions of rhetoric the restrained and the liberated. They have elsewhere been called simply Little and Big rhetoric (Schiappa, 2001), or traditional and "globalized" rhetoric (Gaonkar, 1997).

The contemporary movement that helped to liberate rhetoric and has made it possible to include in this *Handbook* a section on rhetoric and the disciplines holds that rhetoric is "epistemic," a claim first made by Robert Scott (1967). This line of thought challenges the Platonic distinction between knowledge and opinion (and thus the general classical distinction between rhetoric and dialectic). Scott's thesis has been the subject of much debate: Harpine (2004) points out that it has been taken to mean anything from the ontological claim that rhetoric creates reality to the minimally controversial notion that knowledge is posited, tested, and modified through rhetorical interactions among interested parties. Although Barry Brummett (1990) declared the epistemic thesis dead in 1990 and Scott (1990) himself acknowledged that it was not the heart of the point he had been trying to make, Schiappa (2001) observes that in one form or another it has become embedded in the general assumptions of many rhetorical scholars who came of age after the 1960s, part of the intellectual background that has "liberated" or "globalized" rhetoric.

Two additional developments that serve as premises to this line of work were enabled by viewing rhetoric as epistemic: the appearances of "rhetoric of inquiry" and of "rhetoric of science." The notion of a rhetoric of inquiry developed in the 1980s at the University of Iowa as a rubric under which denizens of different specialized fields could talk about the modes of arguments and persuasion within their respective fields as well as explore rhetorical strategies that different communities of inquiry may have in common. The terrain of interest would include but not be limited to the sciences. It would also include the humanities, the social sciences, and professional fields such as law. Broadly speaking, it undertook to explore the discourses of knowledge, particularly their generative dimensions—in philosophical terms; they were more interested in the context of discovery than in the context of justification (Nelson, Megill, & McCloskey, 1987; Simons, 1990). The rhetoric of science shares many of the same concerns, but with a focus on the internal practices of the sciences as well as their public manifestations. For many, rhetorical engagement with science was licensed by Thomas Kuhn's (1962) *The Structure of Scientific Revolutions,* which argued that the historical development of scientific disciplines was not governed by logic but influenced by psychology and argumentation. The rhetoric of science was seen by its early practitioners as the interesting "hard case" for epistemic rhetoric that paved the way for inquiry into other less epistemically privileged disciplines (Gross, 1990). Many of the contributions to this literature are discussed in Jeanne Fahnestock's chapter in this volume (Chapter 10). As with any significant development in the field, the rhetoric of science has stirred controversy. A lively discussion of what happens to the idea of rhetoric once it is "globalized" to cover bodies of specialized knowledge occurs in the set of essays edited by Gross and Keith (1997). Among the themes taken up by the various authors in that volume is that the commitment of traditional rhetoricians to civic discourse, and the possibility that using rhetoric as a hermeneutic for exploring the sciences, would be at the cost not only of that commitment but of a robust conception of rhetoric itself. Dilip Gaonkar (1997) triggers this extended debate by maintaining that the rhetoric that is everywhere is a "thin" and less useful rhetoric.

The relationship between rhetoric and the disciplines must take account not only of knowledge but also of the other term of the power-knowledge pair. Foucault has taught us that power constitutes knowledge; and long before that, Bacon argued that knowledge should be in the service of power. Rational enterprises, as Toulmin (1972) characterized them, have both cognitive and social dimensions; that is, disciplines are political arenas. Thus, our understanding of the relationship between rhetoric and knowledge must include not only rhetoric's epistemic qualities but also the social, historical, and political dimensions of knowledge and its construction and dissemination. These dimensions are both internal, as knowledge experts vie with one another for priority, allies, and influence on the intellectual content of the discipline, and external, as disciplines and subdisciplines compete for public attention, resources, and influence.

Before turning to the chapters themselves, we need to call attention to four general issues that seem especially pertinent to the relationship between rhetoric and special fields of knowledge and provide part of the relevant background. One cluster of issues that arises concerns the relative incommensurability of different disciplinary discourses. The issue of incommensurability, famously articulated by Kuhn (1962), was extensively examined by rhetoricians in a very useful volume edited by Randy Allen Harris (2005) titled *Rhetoric and Incommensurability*. This issue is always part of the tacit understanding of those who study rhetoric within specialized disciplines. Rhetoric trades on the lingua franca of interpretive communities. For there to be any communication between disciplinary communities, some such common language must either be antecedently available or constructed on the job. This is equally true of any disciplinary inquiry that aspires to influence public discourse. Such linguistic intercourse is not without its risks.

A second general issue concerns the role of expertise. In thinking about how specific fields of knowledge intersect with public discourse, it should be recognized that a pivotal role is often played by the expert. The familiar rhetorical genres in which expertise goes public, so to speak, would include testimony before political or regulative bodies, published letters to the public from concerned scientists, and consultation and advice to filmmakers and novelists. Thinking about expertise within a rhetorical frame makes it clear that experts should be defined not just by what they know but by what they do in the name of their own expertise. On this model, expertise would be thought of, not just as a relationship between a specialist and a field of knowledge, but also as a relationship between the specialist and different audiences, in terms of shared linguistic resources, availability, and rhetorical ethos. It would also include what Collins and Evans (2007) call interactional expertise, a capacity to deploy the language of a specialty—a capacity not closely tied to expertise in the specialized field. This, of course, is a kind of rhetorical expertise.

There is no doubt that scientific claims can enter many, if not most, of the areas within which public deliberation occurs. To the extent that this occurs, one could simply relegate them to the category of "inartistic proofs," in the Aristotelian sense—something like introducing a knife in a murder trial. But what this ignores is the ways in which the rhetoric of science intermingles with public discourse. Bringing scientific "evidence" to bear on a matter of public interest is not so simple as producing a knife. In fact, very often the contribution of science is to establish by disciplinary criteria whether the object before us is what it appears to be. This becomes problematic, and rhetorically interesting, when the assumptions of the relevant science differ from those of the audience that is trying to incorporate the expert knowledge. For instance, there are neuroscientists who, as expert witnesses, can testify that the idea that people act on the basis of intentions is an illusion, a claim that runs counter to our common sense about human action. This means that our relationship to experts, who not infrequently contradict common sense, is a complicated one.

Generally speaking, we want experts to be "on tap but not on top" when expertise is brought to bear on matters of public concern, which implies that expertise plays a subordinate role in matters of public deliberation (McGee & Lyne, 1987). But it can also play a subordinating role, sometimes to the point of closing down public deliberation. In addition, experts often have the opportunity to affect public discourse through nonpublic or semipublic means through activity in "backstage" areas that occupy a middle ground between the public forums and the expert journals and laboratories. For example, expert influence is exerted on congressional staffers, on the selection process of review committees, on the construction of executive summaries to government reports. These roles and forums are less visible and less available to the public (and to rhetorical scholars) but affect how specialized knowledge and expertise are brought to bear on public issues (Miller, 2005).

A third set of issues concerns the way in which scientific language and scientific claims chain out across disciplines and across cultures. As science seeks public "understanding," it also runs the risk of becoming captive to a popular rhetoric, that is to say, to the politically inflected deployments of scientific terms and concepts beyond their contexts of origin. This risk is sometimes welcomed, as for instance when scientists warn the public about "catastrophic" climate change in hopes that a prudent response might be forthcoming. Once available to a wider public, however, the rhetoric of a given science is no longer under the control of the scientists. And, it seems fair to say, unintended consequences can surprise even the brightest minds. Because any terministic development within a discipline can in principle become the inspiration for public discourse, the relationship between disciplinary and nondisciplinary (or interdisciplinary) usage warrants the attention of civic-minded rhetoricians.

Rhetoricians usually feel most comfortable in the spaces of civic and cultural life and may be reluctant to take on the internal discourse of a natural science or other discipline outside their own. This is quite understandable. They may also find it difficult to locate, access, and interpret backstage material. Yet those who do go looking there have found that the rhetorical strategies and tropes in the disciplines are not in principle different from those found in any other context. Some training in the relevant field is no doubt useful to those who want to cast light on their discursive practices. But one does not necessarily have to "go native" to find promising points of entry. We know, after all, that for all the specificity of disciplines, they draw on the shared pools of language and imagery and argumentative strategy that are available to members of the more general culture. The semiotic flow goes in both directions, and the tropes traverse the walls of disciplinarity. Notions from evolutionary biology, such as "fitness" or "selfish gene," gain wide currency. Terms used by physicists, such as "Big Bang" or "string theory," originate in ordinary language, are adopted for specialized use, and then become popular metaphors for the public. The story is similar for many terms from psychology and postmodern literary theory. It would be misleading to say that such terms mean the same thing in the context of the discipline as in the context of public debate; they can be bearers of meaning, nonetheless, and this means that they can have rhetorical significance. In this sense, the language of disciplines is both wide, insofar as it presupposes the broader culture, and narrow, insofar as it is carefully marshaled in support of disciplinary understandings.

A fourth issue is the contested disciplinary status of rhetoric itself. Some, following Protagoras, prefer to see rhetoric as a "virtue" or native human capacity that, while it may be improved and developed, cannot be a form of expertise. Others have suggested that the globalization of rhetoric, including significantly the rhetorical critique of science and other disciplines, has so attenuated rhetoric as to prevent it from making distinctive or effective contributions to understanding our discursive universe. In this view, if rhetoric aims to be a metadiscipline, able to describe and critique all other disciplines, it becomes less of a discipline itself, losing both its identity and its intellectual content. Without its content, rhetoric is a sham discipline, much as Plato charged. Without its distinct identity, rhetoric can't say anything that can't be (and hasn't been) said by psychology, sociology, philosophy, or perhaps literary criticism. More practically, rhetoric as a discipline has been damaged by the material conditions of its academic existence, divided between departments of Communication and English and often also wedged into departments of Classics or History, but at the center of none of these.

Rhetoric's difficulties as a discipline are reflected in its teaching, one of the most basic responsibilities of any discipline. In English departments, rhetoric was for a long while relegated to introductory courses in writing, which some even regarded as remedial. In Communication departments, where rhetoric has been taught by scholars to advanced students, theory and criticism are commonly disconnected from practice. Courses in practical rhetoric, at both introductory and advanced levels and in both departments, have long been taught primarily by marginal faculty, many of them not scholars, or scholars of rhetoric. The recent pedagogical movements that have disseminated rhetoric across the disciplines—Writing in the Disciplines, Writing Across the Curriculum, Communication Across the Curriculum—reprise the debate between Gorgias and Socrates: Does rhetoric have a subject matter? Can the rhetorician have sufficient subject-matter knowledge to be effective? Must rhetoric be a supplement to the other disciplines?

The six chapters presented in this part vary considerably with respect to the metaphors they use and the direction of their interests. We selected authors and topics to represent a range of disciplines, from the traditional academic areas, such as the natural sciences, the humanities, and the social sciences, to the more open range of interdisciplinary fields, to the discourses of public policy and medicine, in which the specialized and the nonspecialized are in constant contact. Disciplines have their own rhetorical idioms and practices, and these may be studied in their own right. Additionally, disciplines are brought by relations of power or by rhetorical invention into contact with other discourse communities, be they other disciplines or a broader public. The authors represented here consider these various possibilities, ranging from the internal discourse of physics to the application-oriented rhetoric of foreign policy studies.

Jeanne Fahnestock's chapter (Chapter 10) on rhetoric in the natural sciences could be seen as a sort of a fortiori argument; that is to say, if a rhetorical perspective can be of value even within the natural sciences, then it follows that it will be of value in the humanities and social sciences. Fahnestock sketches out the case for taking seriously the notion of rhetoric in the natural sciences. In the course of doing so, she has admirably organized various strands of scholarship. Her overview of the literature is enriched by her own work on "figures of thought" in the sciences, a phrase that creates a bridge between rhetorical invention and cognition. Moreover, it constructs that bridge within the context of the natural sciences.

Don Bialostosky (Chapter 12) turns our attention to recent historical trends within the field of literary theory and criticism, where "rhetoric" was a rubric favored by two very different schools of thought. In looking for a fresh way to think of rhetoric as method, he wants to get beyond the "vertiginous irony" of deconstructive criticism and, like Wayne Booth, longs for a more stable but perhaps more modest footing. Specifically, he wants to find a way of doing literary criticism that captures the most basic forms of human interaction. And he finds an answer in a modification of Bakhtin's dialogic approach to action. This comports with Fahnestock's move to characterize the "figures of thought" as "interactional devices," and turns attention toward the repertoire of interactive performance. He draws the radical conclusion that what follows from this redefinition of figures of thought is that all secondary genres, including all literary genres, are composed of a more basic set of primary genres. Thus, he offers us a limited number of building blocks that are nevertheless capable of capturing the panoply of human interactions. And in the course of it he absolves those of us whose eyes glaze over when exotically named "figures" are catalogued. Contesting the very meaning of rhetoric and the nature of its methods is a perennial part of the rhetorical tradition. If Bialostosky is right, the use of rhetoric in literary criticism and theory has passed through a period of "confident monism" and now has an opening for something that is at once more elemental and more compatible with the performative strand of the rhetorical tradition. It would also become more conversant with the range of human interaction generally, and would rely less on obscure terminology.

Whereas Bialostosky's focus is on interaction, Edward Clift's is on its economic counterpart, exchange. Clift's chapter (Chapter 11) on the rhetoric of economics argues that the body of work that looks at the field of economics through a rhetorical lens has reached a kind of critical mass, such that it invites reconsideration of the basic category of the economic. In *The Rhetoric of Economics*, Deirdre McCloskey (1985), first looked at the discipline of economics as a field of argument and persuasion, and this very notion has inspired subsequent rhetorical readings of "the dismal science." McCloskey's original position was that economists who better understand their own rhetoric will become better at their own discipline. But she has also held that a large portion of the real economy is composed of linguistic exchanges that are, in a broad sense, processes of persuasion. Taking the latter point seriously, Clift makes an unexpected move between the world of neoclassical economics and post-structural notions of exchange and allocation, and then cashes it out by doing an economic/rhetorical reading of *The Sopranos*. This move provides a kind of "perspective by incongruity" that in effect treats the fields of rhetoric and economics as interchangeable. And at that point, the rubric might be "rhetoric as economics."

Julie Thompson Klein (Chapter 15) has provided an account of how rhetoric operates in interdisciplinary exchange and development. Examining Women's Studies as a case example of an interdisciplinary field, she explores its relationship to antecedent fields and to "boundary objects" that facilitate interaction among established fields in the construction of a new field. Her remarks apply as well to other examples of interdisciplinary fields, such as American studies and composition studies. Moving beyond examples, Klein examines the rhetoric of the self-conscious literature on interdisciplinarity itself: the recurrent metaphors and topoi, the "terministic screens" that have been used in understanding how new knowledge and new modes of knowledge production emerge and how they become organized into what we recognize as disciplines, or protodisciplines. In following the discussions about disciplinarity, multidisciplinarity, interdisciplinarity, and transdisciplinarity, she illustrates the operations of power in the domain of intellectual relations: the search for status and legitimation, the construction of boundaries, the claims for innovation or system.

Gordon Mitchell (Chapter 14) has concentrated on how the field of foreign policy studies might be reshaped by the mounting evidence that rhetorical efforts can pay off mightily in facilitating changes in international relations. Thus, his focus is less on the internal rhetorical operations of a discipline than on its topicalization of rhetoric as a matter that affects the conduct of foreign policy and its relations among nations. By examining the underappreciated role that rhetorical interventions played in ending the Cold War, Mitchell finds evidence that the academic field's orientation toward policy "realism" is in need of correction. He argues that foreign policy studies will have more relevance and explanatory power if they embrace the substantive role that rhetoric plays in shaping international relations.

Judy Segal (Chapter 13) helps us see the general shape of the emerging field of the rhetoric of medicine. With health care and medicine taking on a rapidly increasing share of the economy, the increasing stakes involved in "selling" medical products and services, the reorientation of many social and personal issues toward medicalization, and the escalating demands of the aging baby boomers, there is an increasing need to understand the rhetoric attending and facilitating these changes. Segal shows us how medicine as a professional discipline can be interrogated rhetorically: what kinds of texts and objects are of interest, what methods of inquiry are used, and what kinds of scholars are doing this work and why. Health is both a personal and a public policy concern, and medicine is both a multidiscipline and a powerful professional practice. Inquiry in these areas thus encounters multiple issues of power, interaction, value, privacy, expertise, and the like—all rich territory for the rhetorician.

Together, these six chapters present multiple ways of thinking about the relationship between the universe of public discourse that rhetoric traditionally explores and the specialized discourses represented by the disciplines. To think about this general theme metaphorically, we can envision the latter as islands, each providing habitat for its own ecology and evolution, and each capable of being understood only in its own terms. Given such a picture, it would make sense for rhetoricians to visit these habitats and record the inhabitants' ways of arguing and persuading, their use of tropes and figures, and their configuration of audiences to be addressed. Or maybe, instead, disciplines should be conceptualized as specific locales on a continent, each with its own "dialect" or terminology and ways of doing business, but still a reflection of a more expansive social reality. Viewing the matter that way, it would make sense to begin with generally familiar rhetorical forms and track down the variations that occur within specific locales. Or perhaps we could think of the inhabitants of disciplines as ethnicities among the discourse of knowledge, not confined to particular locales but having a recognizable style. By shifting our metaphor, we shift the nature of the rhetorician's task. There is no default position in approaching the matter, and the chapters that follow bear this out.

REFERENCES

Brummett, B. (1990). A eulogy for epistemic rhetoric. *Quarterly Journal of Speech, 76,* 69–72.

Collins, H., & Evans, R. (2007). *Rethinking expertise.* Chicago: University of Chicago Press.

Gaonkar, D. P. (1997). The idea of rhetoric in the rhetoric of science. In A. G. Gross & W. M. Keith (Eds.), *Rhetorical hermeneutics: Invention and interpretation in the age of science* (pp. 25–85). Albany: State University of New York Press.

Gross, A. G. (1990). Rhetoric of science is epistemic rhetoric. *Quarterly Journal of Speech, 76,* 304–306.

Gross, A. G., & Keith, W. M. (Eds.). (1997). *Rhetorical hermeneutics: Invention and interpretation in the age of science.* Albany: State University of New York Press.

Harpine, W. D. (2004). What do you mean, rhetoric is epistemic? *Philosophy and Rhetoric, 37*(4), 335–352.

Harris, R. A. (Ed.). (2005). *Rhetoric and incommensurability*. West Lafayette, IN: Parlor Press.

Kuhn, T. S. (1962). *The structure of scientific revolutions*. Chicago: University of Chicago Press.

Leff, M. (1987). The habitation of rhetoric. In J. W. Wenzel (Ed.), *Argument and critical practices: Proceedings of the fifth SCA/AFA conference on argumentation*. Annandale, VA: Speech Communication Association.

McCloskey, D. N. (1985). *The rhetoric of economics*. Madison: University of Wisconsin Press.

McGee, M. C., & Lyne, J. R. (1987). What are nice folks like you doing in a place like this? Some entailments of treating knowledge claims rhetorically. In J. S. Nelson, A. Megill, & D. N. McCloskey (Eds.), *The rhetoric of the human sciences: Language and argument in scholarship and public affairs* (pp. 381–406). Madison: University of Wisconsin Press.

Miller, C. R. (2005). Risk, controversy, and rhetoric: Response to Goodnight. *Argumentation and Advocacy, 42*(1), 34–37.

Nelson, J. S., Megill, A., & McCloskey, D. N. (Eds.). (1987). *The rhetoric of the human sciences*. Madison: University of Wisconsin Press.

Plato. (1961). *Plato: The collected dialogues* (E. Hamilton & H. Cairns, Eds., L. Cooper, Trans.). Princeton, NJ: Princeton University Press.

Schiappa, E. (1991). *Protagoras and logos: A study in Greek philosophy and rhetoric*. Columbia: University of South Carolina Press.

Schiappa, E. (2001). Second thoughts on the critiques of big rhetoric. *Philosophy and Rhetoric, 34*(3), 260–274.

Scott, R. L. (1967). On viewing rhetoric as epistemic. *Central States Speech Journal, 18*, 9–17.

Scott, R. L. (1990). Epistemic rhetoric and criticism: Where Barry Brummett goes wrong. *Quarterly Journal of Speech, 76*, 300–303.

Simons, H. W. (Ed.). (1990). *The rhetorical turn: Invention and persuasion in the conduct of inquiry*. Chicago: University of Chicago Press.

Toulmin, S. (1972). *Human understanding: The collective use and evolution of concepts*. Princeton, NJ: Princeton University Press.

10

The Rhetoric of the Natural Sciences

JEANNE FAHNESTOCK

The body of knowledge called the "natural sciences" includes all those disciplines that construct a world beyond human agency: astronomy, physics, chemistry, biology, geology. Rhetoric, from its classical roots, is the art of constructing discourse that influences beliefs and actions through human agency. Discourse cannot persuade ion channels or archebacteria or black holes, but it can persuade humans to have certain beliefs about such entities and to construct experiments and technologies based on those beliefs. Studying human persuasion about the natural world would seem then to be a normal continuation of the rhetorical studies of any other type of discourse. After all, scientists engage in controversy, they produce arguments in all modalities (oral, written, visual), they group themselves into specialized audiences with constitutive standards of judgment, they respond to influence by altering their beliefs and practices over time, they acknowledge the authority of individuals and texts, and they invest their practices and disagreements with considerable affective energy. All these features also would describe political or legal or ceremonial discourse, which have long been subjects of rhetorical analysis.

Yet examining the enterprises of science (its institutions, audiences, texts, and other practices) from a self-consciously rhetorical perspective is a fairly new enterprise. The eventual "license" to investigate the rhetoric of science was granted by several intellectual movements post–World War II. Karl Popper's doctrine of falsification (that scientific theories are never "proved" but simply resist refutation) inevitably draws attention to argumentation, even to potential self-refutation as a constraint, and so legitimates a rhetorical approach. More influential has been Thomas Kuhn's version of historical change in science that depicts normal versus revolutionary shifts from one paradigm to another, bringing persuasion in as a factor in changing scientific allegiances. But even without Popper or Kuhn, a rhetoric of science could have grown from developments internal to the discipline. For also in the 1960s, Robert L. Scott extended the territory of rhetoric from political/social discourse to "epistemic" discourse, pointing out that knowledge in any field, including the sciences, is constituted by the argumentative practices of that field (see the introduction to this part). In the 1970s, the work of Michel Foucault authorized an examination of the "discursive practices" that create institutional power in a culture, and Foucault himself modeled his methods by examining, among other cases, 17th- and 18th-century systematics (Foucault, 1970, pp. 125–165). In the 1980s, writing teachers, placed in classrooms for students in science and engineering disciplines, inevitably began examining the genres they were preparing students to write. Given these motivations, in the late 1980s and 1990s, rhetoricians began to look at scientific movements and texts in greater numbers. But applying rhetorical methods to this area still creates discomfort and even resistance.

A difficulty in applying rhetoric to texts in the natural sciences is that in some ways the object of study is more stable than the method of study. Contemporary rhetoric is a highly eclectic discipline, allied on one side with a historical and sociological focus on people, events, trends, movements, group practices, and cultural context, and allied on the other side with a humanist focus on texts of all kinds, oral and written, involving close attention to language and to structures in discourse that only come into view with methods of analysis established in rhetorical theory (with a different rhetorical theory, a different method, different elements come into view). Of course, these two broad approaches, the contextual and textual, inevitably interact; in fact, this interaction could be said to constitute a distinctly rhetorical approach. But the range of methods that can be applied in the study of persuasion is vividly on display in an anthology

compiled by Jack Selzer, *Understanding Scientific Prose* (1993), in which contributors respond to an article on evolutionary theory by Richard Lewontin and Stephen Jay Gould, doing so in ways that variously pay attention to the writers' and subject's intellectual and cultural milieu, to readers' practices and responses, and to argumentative features in the text.

With its double focus on texts and contexts, rhetoric as the study of persuasion overlaps with history, sociology, philosophy, linguistics, literary studies, cultural studies, and journalism, and, not surprisingly, work in these other fields also overlaps with rhetoric. The two sociologists, Bruno Latour and Steve Woolgar (1986), for example, who studied interactions in a contemporary science lab as though it were an exotic culture, nevertheless had to come up with a taxonomy of statement types to characterize how their subjects negotiated the degree of certainty in the claims they were willing to support (pp. 75–81).

Hence the work of many scholars, such as Latour and Woolgar, who do not identify themselves as rhetoricians, could be included in an overview of rhetorical studies of natural science. The rhetorical study of science is therefore at the crossroads of several disciplines: It engages the philosophy of science in what counts as evidence and proof and to what extent knowledge is constructed symbolically; the sociology of science in how groups constitute themselves, communicate, and reach intersubjective agreement on particular beliefs and overall standards of belief; and the history of science on how cases are made, successfully or unsuccessfully, and how beliefs about and actions on nature change over time.[1] This chapter, therefore, will not eliminate work in "science studies" that is not explicitly rhetorical, but it will highlight the work of those who identify themselves as rhetoricians. After a discussion of Groundbreaking Work, the field is sampled below beginning with areas that have drawn the greatest attention (Scientific Genres, Scientific Language, Cases and Reception Studies) and ending with areas that deserve greater attention (Individual Rhetors, Marginalized Rhetors, Accommodations, Visual Rhetoric, Science and Religion, Science and Mathematics). A final section considers the lingering resistance to rhetorical studies of science.

GROUNDBREAKING WORK IN THE RHETORIC OF SCIENCE

In his introduction to the collection *Landmark Essays in the Rhetoric of Science* (1997) Randy Allen Harris traces the origins and early work in the discipline and provides a thorough and eclectic bibliography of the field up through 1997. Harris, however, highlights contributions from those whose primary disciplinary affiliation is in rhetoric and composition. Among the groundbreaking monographs he cites are Charles Bazerman's *Shaping Written Knowledge* (1988; see discussion below), Lawrence J. Prelli's *A Rhetoric of Science* (1989), Alan Gross's *The Rhetoric of Science* (1990), and Greg Myers's *Writing Biology* (1990; see discussion below). Given their titles, both Prelli's and Gross's texts clearly invest in a distinctly rhetorical approach. Both open with reviews of primarily classical rhetorical constructs, which are then applied in subsequent chapters in the analysis of various scientific texts and cases to demonstrate, as Gross puts it, "how the sciences construct their specialized rhetorics from a common heritage of persuasion" (1990, p. 206). Prelli applies stasis theory and the inventional *topoi* with useful clarity to cases involving primate language, chemical memory transfer, parapsychology, and creationism, among others. Gross offers short, separate studies ranging from the importance of first-person testimony of conversion in the initial acceptance of Copernicus to the role of descriptive presence and narrative persona in

Watson and Crick's 1953 paper on DNA and Watson's subsequent autobiography. Gross is more eclectic than Prelli in his tools of analysis (noting rhetorical figures, finding the familiar "tensions" of the close-reading new critic and using the story grammars of the Proppian analyst), and he initially adopted a strong position on the constructive role of rhetoric in scientific knowledge. A new version of this work (*Starring the Text: The Place of Rhetoric in Science Studies*, Gross, 2006), drops some chapters and contains new ones on the cold fusion debacle, the Bohr-Einstein debate, and occupational medicine. Attentive throughout to philosophical issues, Gross organizes his cases in a sequence moving from discovery to the dissemination and institutionalization of scientific claims. A new first chapter offers an overview of the scholarship and places rhetoric as a valuable partner among the disciplines studying science. Because of their explicitness in rhetorical method and their applications to various cases, both Prelli and Gross are useful introductions to the field.

SCIENTIFIC GENRES

Though the nature and extent of a 17th-century "scientific revolution" can provoke disagreement, two institutions did come into existence in the 1660s: the scientific society and the scientific journal, the latter sponsored by the former. Rhetoricians and linguists have studied the genre of the scientific article itself, emphasizing its evolution into a conventional form constraining its content. In the late 1980s, Charles Bazerman's highly influential *Shaping Written Knowledge* (1988) focused, in the words of its subtitle, on "The Genre and Activity of the Experimental Article in Science." In separate chapters, Bazerman sampled articles in the first science journal, the *Philosophical Transactions of the Royal Society*, noting the increasing proportion of experimental reports and their changing standards of arrangement. In another chapter, he compared articles on spectroscopy in the *Physical Review*, connecting changes in length to agreements on theoretical perspectives and noting significant increases in the number of citations as the field matured. Bazerman's pioneering work was followed by linguist Dwight Atkinson's (1999) concentrated study of the *Philosophical Transactions* from 1675 to 1975, which includes data on the sciences represented, the arrangement strategies used, and measurable language features.

By the second half of the 20th century, the scientific research report became a highly formulaic genre, its structure conveniently described by the acronym IMRAD (introduction, materials and methods, results and discussion). The most detailed analysis of the conventional moves of this genre is again the work of a linguist, John Swales (1990), who minutely analyzed what rhetoricians would call the exigence-forming moves of the typical introduction to a research report. The most ambitious study of the scientific article is Gross, Harmon, and Reidy's *Communicating Science* (2002). These authors sampled hundreds of articles in English, French, German, and American periodicals across four centuries and documented the changing language features, argument forms, and use of visuals, among other features, in a sweeping overview. Their statistical picture is enriched by analyses of representative articles chosen from every science.

The study of research reports is augmented by work in "citation studies" tracing the connections among articles based on their references to other works. Driven in part by the mechanism created by the Institute for Scientific Information (ISI) for ranking journals according to their "impact factor" (a measure of how often work appearing in one journal is cited elsewhere), quantified citation patterns have been used as evidence of the dissemination of ideas and the impact of reputation (Latour, 1987; Merton, 1988; Seglen, 1997). New trends in web publication (including the accessibility of preprints electronically) are changing the nature and pace of citation and dissemination. New methods of searching by citation, available on Web browsers, will facilitate the study of dissemination beyond quantification.

The reviewing of articles before publication, and of the grant proposals that make research possible, is also of interest to rhetoricians; the back and forth in reviewing shows the negotiation of acceptable arguments and the pressure of a disciplinary audience's otherwise unselfconscious standards for what counts as a persuasive case (see Zuckerman & Merton, 1971, for a brief history). Exemplary work on such negotiations came in groundbreaking work from Greg Myers, primarily a discourse analyst, whose *Writing Biology* (1990) is organized around scientific genres. Myers studies the successive drafts of two biologists' grant proposals as they change under criticism from reviewers (see also Gross, 2006, pp. 98–110; works by Blakeslee and Graves, cited below). Another chapter follows two articles through draft versions from submission to final acceptance, showing how the authors had to revise to make their work acceptable. Myers's subsequent chapters continue with exemplary comparative studies on differing sides of two controversies, one on lizard reproductive behavior and one on the much more public debates over sociobiology. In between is a chapter comparing popularizations. The sites of rhetorical negotiation covered by Myers—especially granting agencies' (study section) responses to proposals and reviewers' responses to papers—could use much more study, despite the difficulty of accessing the materials involved. Examining peer review practices for what actually "disqualifies" would be interesting especially in light of scandals of faulty and even fraudulent research reaching publication in respectable journals.[2]

Other genres influential in the natural sciences have not been studied extensively, especially what is arguably the most influential genre of all, the review article. These pieces, usually written by people of stature in a field, periodically assess progress, assign credit, and identify the key research problems. Review articles usually begin the official history of a research area, and those who receive credit in a review are more likely to receive later recognition when prizes are awarded. Those whose work is not cited in a widely recognized review outlet are effectively silenced and have less chance of funding and later access to publication. The processes by which mainstream science excludes certain lines of research (especially those that later prove successful) has been of interest to historians but again begs for a rhetorical approach. Still other genres largely ignored by rhetoricians, and by others, are the scientific textbook (though there is some linguistic work on this genre, see below), progress reports of sponsored research in institutional settings, patent applications, and the verbal/visual poster, now a major vehicle for presenting research at meetings.

THE LANGUAGE OF SCIENCE

In addition to work on scientific genres, a great deal of attention has been invested in the language of science by scholars from different disciplinary perspectives. Sociolinguists and stylisticians routinely characterize the languages of science as technical or specialist *registers*. In English, scientific language is a recognized variant, with characteristic vocabularies and even syntactic practices. The impenetrability of this language to nonspecialist audiences is a frequent (though arguably exaggerated) complaint. Influential work on the language of science can be found in Halliday and Martin's *Writing Science* (1993) and Martin and Veel's *Reading Science: Critical and Functional Perspectives on Discourses of Science* (1998). Though grounded in a functional systemic linguistics that is unfamiliar to most U.S. readers, the features of scientific writing identified in the separately authored essays of these collections are readily understood and the emphasis on complexities in textbook language from a student's perspective is useful. Especially noteworthy is Chapter 4 in *Writing Science* on "Some Grammatical Problems in Scientific English," which explains the distinctive noun clusters (e.g., *glass crack growth rate* as a single term), the condensation of clauses, and the migration of concepts into nominals. Chapter 10, "Technicality and Abstraction: Language for the Creation of Specialized Texts," compares the roots and uses of abstract terms in the sciences and the humanities. In Halliday and Martin's 1998 collection, Halliday revisits his characterization of what he calls the typical clause structure used in science that connects two large nominal groups with some relatively weak "relational" verb such as "to be" or "have" or a handful of others ("Things and Relations" in *Reading Science*). This structure is blamed for the impenetrability of much science writing and for its reifying tendencies and what might be called argumentative "strong-arming." Some of the most meticulous work on scientific style has come from William Vande Kopple, both on grammatical subjects (1994) and changes over time (2002).

Several recent monographs have addressed the pressures on and features of contemporary scientific language. Scott L. Montgomery, a geologist by training, analyzes difficulties in professional science writing and offers a historical perspective on its formation, including a fascinating chapter on naming features on the moon, in *The Scientific Voice* (1996). Ann Blakeslee (2001) records the process of cross-disciplinary language adjustment by physicists attempting to address biologists and chemists in *Interacting With Audiences*. Steven Darian's *Understanding the Language of Science* (2003), based in part on textbook examples, examines scientific language at the service of the modes (defining, classifying, comparing, etc.). Carol Reeves's *The Language of Science* (2005) is a teaching text on scientific language, emphasizing features such as metaphor and hedging, and referencing her earlier articles on language practices in controversies surrounding AIDS research (1996, 1998) and the linguistic practices involving prions (2002).

Some of the work on scientific language, such as Halliday and Martin's, has been done from the perspective of repairing practice, not just documenting it: So George Gopen and Judith Swan (1990) argue that it is not the lexicon or the clause density that creates the difficulties of some science writing, but rather the failure to observe given/new information organization from sentence to sentence. Further insight into the language of science (and its genres) can be found in textbooks on science writing (Katz & Penrose, 2003; Montgomery, 2005), which, in addition to the many manuals sponsored by different scientific associations, attempt to instill best practices.

One special feature of scientific writing has received considerable attention: the practice of hedging or qualifying claims. Indeed, scientists are usually more modest about the degree of their claims in light of their available evidence than are their humanist colleagues. Scientific articles routinely end with *it seems likely that* or *x cannot be ruled out* (see Crismore & Vande Kopple, 1997; Hyland, 1998).

One would assume that a rhetoric of science would address issues in the language of science that have been raised by philosophers who have focused especially on problems of reference, on the relationship between naming and creating entities for purposes of theorizing. There are after all many cases in the history of science where entities are speculatively sketched into place—the electron, the gene, brown dwarfs, the ion channel in the cell wall—which later evidence brings out of the realm of speculation. There are other entities, such as the black hole, that seem to acquire increasing degrees of certainty with repeated use, even in the absence of widely accepted verification. Yet another problem occurs for

philosophers when a term persists but seems to radically change its meaning as it is used in two different theoretical systems: for example, the electron of Rutherford and the electron of quantum theory. The problems of reference raised in these examples are, however, less of a problem to rhetoricians who tend to see meaning as defined in context (Lyne, 1995) or who adopt a speech act perspective and see all statements or assertions as utterances made in certain contexts (specified time, place, and participants).

Historians of science have also tackled language issues. So Steven Shapin (1984) discussed what he calls "virtual witnessing" in the language of Robert Boyle. Noting that the early practices of the Royal Society required the performance of experiments/demonstrations before assembled witnesses as the standard of verification, Shapin describes how Boyle creates an overparticularized or what would now be called "thick" descriptive style to convey to readers the experience of witnessing. Rhetoricians might point out, however, that in the 17th century (Boyle's time), everyone with Boyle's education would have been specifically trained in grammar and rhetoric to write detailed descriptions (hypotyposis) in the service of argument.

FIGURATION AND SCIENTIFIC LANGUAGE

When people think of the rhetorical dimensions of language per se, they often think of the figures of speech, and for many "figure of speech" equals metaphor. Metaphors have acquired a special interest in the rhetoric of science because of their frequently documented role in scientific discourse, both in expert publications and in pedagogical and popularizing texts. Metaphors are a node for the intersecting interests of philosophers, historians, and students of the language and rhetoric of science. In work done several decades ago, two philosophers, Max Black (1962) and Mary

Hesse (1966) sketched in the role of metaphorical thinking in the sciences, but the attention has, if anything, increased in the past few years with Ken Baake's study of scientific language in the making at the Santa Fe Institute, *Metaphor and Knowledge* (2003) and chemistry professor emeritus Theodore L. Brown's *Making Truth: Metaphor in Science* (2003), a survey of the constitutive metaphors in cases from atomic models to global warming. A recent work by Heather Graves (2005), also based on ethnographic methods (see above on Myers), argues for the constitutive power of metaphor and of the often conflated but distinct trope of metonymy in knowledge formation in solid-state physics. Works dedicated to metaphor in biology and specifically to the gene have come from Evelyn Fox Keller (1995, 2001) and Elizabeth Shea (in press), while Ceccarelli (2004) has studied the mixed metaphors surrounding the humane genome project.

A complication in treatments of figuration in the sciences is the nature of figuration itself. Are there really two domains of language, the literal and the figural? Are the presumed figural uses of language ruled out of court in expert discourse of science? The many studies of metaphor in science, mentioned above, would certainly answer no to the second question. My own work has also investigated the heuristic and explanatory power of figures of speech, but it has concerned figures other than metaphor, including those "schemes" that meet both semantic and syntactic criteria (e.g., *antithesis, antimetabole, incrementum, gradatio*) and figures of word formation and repetition (e.g., *agnominatio, polyptoton,* and *ploche*). As defined in this study, figures are "epitomes," succinct and yet complete expressions of certain lines of argument explicated in the topics (both in rhetorical manuals, and, in the early modern period, in dialectical treatises). Given their epitomizing force, the figures can prompt invention and they can persist across texts of different genres addressed to different audiences (Fahnestock, 2004).

INDIVIDUAL RHETORS AND WORKS

While scientific research is now disseminated primarily in journal articles, increasingly online, monographs of varying lengths still appear, and in previous centuries they were the key works for disseminating science. One could easily compile a canon of scientific classics written by famous figures in scientific history (e.g., Gjertsen, 1984). Among major scientists and works, few have received sustained treatment from rhetoricians. But one exception is Darwin, thanks primarily to the work of John Angus Campbell over the past 25 years. Campbell's exemplary scholarship covers multiple aspects of Darwin's rhetoric, from his large-scale strategies using the cultural "grammar" of natural theology (1975, 1986, 1987), to his inventional sources (1990a, 1990b), to his textual strategies (1989, 1995).

While there is no book-length study of Darwin as a rhetor, there are two of Galileo. Both these works carefully place Galileo in the context of the discourse arts of his age and grant a limited role to the rhetorical dimensions of his texts. A study demonstrating this division comes from a philosopher and scholar of Galileo, Maurice A. Finocchiaro, whose *Galileo and the Art of Reasoning: Rhetorical Foundations of Logic and Scientific Method* (1980) makes a continuous division between those parts of Galileo's *Dialogue Concerning the Two Chief World Systems* that represent the logical core of his argument and those parts that, in Finocchiaro's view, are rhetorical accommodations to his potentially hostile audience. He believes that "in addition to argument, rhetoric is sometimes crucial in science: and hence, rhetoric has an important role to play in scientific rationality and the rhetorical aspects of science should not be neglected" (Finocchiaro, 1980, p. 5). Much of Jean Dietz Moss's *Novelties in the Heavens* (1993) also concentrates on Galileo's works, not only the *Dialogue* but also *The Starry Messenger,* the *Assayer,* and others (for more on Moss, see below). Isaac Newton also has received some "rhetorical" attention. The historian and Newton biographer, Richard Westfall (1991), contributed a piece comparing Galileo and Newton as rhetors; though he modestly prefaces his piece with a disclaimer that he had never studied rhetoric, he nevertheless offers interesting observations on how the former had to construct his audience, while the latter did not.

The relative paucity of work by rhetoricians on the great scientific rhetors and on individual works is to some extent repaired by the attention to individual scientists available in the work of historians. Biographies of key figures in the history of science abound and many offer overviews of the productivity, if not necessarily of the rhetorical methods, of individual scientists. The historian Frederick Holmes (1987), for instance, has paid attention to Lavoisier's methods when, in working with successive drafts, he discovered how thoroughly Lavoisier revised his writing and how the process of textual revision served as a tool of theoretical clarification (see also Holmes, 1991). Robert Boyle has also garnered attention from historians for his presumably innovative rhetorical practices in establishing an appropriate language of science (e.g., Golinski, 1987; Shapin, 1984). But while historians often concentrate on individual researchers, just as scholars in literary studies focus intently on the work of individual authors and mainstream rhetoricians attend to the discourse of individual political figures, a concentration on individual scientists has not been as attractive to rhetoricians.

CASE STUDIES AND RECEPTION STUDIES

What has been more attractive to rhetorical scholars is attention to reception studies and case studies, especially surrounding controversies. This attention seems obviously central to a *rhetorical* approach that should be interested in whether a persuasive text persuaded. Not surprisingly, many studies have been published on the reception history of scientific works and on scientific controversies that are, in effect, histories of competing receptions. There have been studies of the controversial program of sociobiology (Journet, 1984; Howe & Lyne, 1992; Lyne & Howe, 1990), on punctuated equilibrium (Lyne, 1986), and on the dramatic fall of the chemists who claimed to discover cold fusion (Pinch, 1996).

An exemplary reception study is Leah Ceccarelli's *Shaping Science With Rhetoric: The Cases of Dobzhansky, Schrödinger, and Wilson* (2001). Ceccarelli first of all creates a new genre, the "interdisciplinary inspirational monograph," an attempt by a researcher in one field to enlist/recruit the cooperation of researchers from other disciplinary backgrounds on a new frontier. She next compares the successes of three works in this genre, primarily by an examination of reviews. She traces the success of physicist Erwin Schrödinger's *What Is Life?* to his use of polysemous terms that could be read by biologists and physicists in ways compatible with their own, nonoverlapping understanding of a key term in his argument, the "laws of physics." According to Ceccarelli, E. O. Wilson has been comparatively unsuccessful since his recruiting of other disciplinary workers comes across as a desire for dominating. Ceccarelli's work has been exemplary in its comparative approach, its use of reception evidence, and of what she calls "microstructures of textual strategy" (2005, p. 263).

Reception studies invite more empirical or social scientific methods of analysis as surveyed in an article by Danette Paul, Davida Charney, and Aimee Kendall, "Moving Beyond the Moment" (2001). This piece expresses considerable impatience with rhetorical studies of science that focus on classical texts and their features, exclusive of any evidence that those features had any effect on readers. The authors recommend four techniques for pursuing the "actual effects" of texts on readers over time: quantitative assessments of the reach of a piece based on its citation history; peer commentary where accessible from reviewers (now sometimes available on journal Web sites); observational studies of readers' responses using think-aloud protocols (readers verbalizing their reactions into a tape recorder as they read); and studies of diachronic responses to a text or program assessed in various ways, such as by matching the introductions of early and later papers in a field. Paul and Charney's own work (1995) on the dissemination and maturing of chaos theory as a field models this last approach. However, despite its opening exigence-setting polemics against standard text analysis, Paul et al.'s (2001) multimethod approach inevitably returns to theories about potentially significant formal features.

The problem of reception has another dimension from the perspective of Kuhn. A corollary of his "paradigm" view seemed, to many, to be an *incommensurability* between theories that amount to different worldviews. Like languages from radically different language groups under the Sapir-Whorf hypothesis that carve up the universe in different ways, so radically different theories are held to be mutually unintelligible and even without transformation parameters. Randy Allen Harris (2005) assembled an anthology of pieces on this issue with contributions from Bazerman and De los Santos, Prelli, Miller, Gross, Lessl, and others. Most of the pieces in this anthology favor a view of incommensurability as rhetorically repairable.

SCIENTIFIC ACCOMMODATION: ADDRESSING NONDISCIPLINARY AUDIENCES

Implicit in the program of reception studies has been the reception of theories, ideas, and methods among members of the scientific community as the most critical and interested audience concerned. But there are many other publics interested in science, and scientific ideas have had large-scale social repercussions, the link between the study of variation and heredity in the late 19th century and the subsequent eugenics movement being one of many examples. The widespread cultural effects of scientific beliefs have received the attention of "science studies" specialists whose work in the history of ideas can be especially important to rhetoricians studying the deployment of scientific ideas in policy arguments.

Contemporary rhetoricians have abandoned any simple notion of the "public" in favor of a view of intersecting "publics." Rhetoricians of science are similarly aware of many stratified publics who may be the addressees of "scientific" discourse of different types serving different functions. For example, the two most influential weekly science publications, *Science* in the United States and *Nature* in the United Kingdom, have modularized formats, carrying pieces in the front of an issue that introduce or explain the expert-addressed research reports appearing later in the same issue. Other publics for accommodated science can almost be defined, operationally, as the readerships of various publications that are devoted to science (e.g., *Scientific American, American Scientist, Science News, Discover, Natural History*) and of mass media outlets that routinely carry science reporting (e.g., the major newspapers and news weeklies). These publications, especially the latter, are often blamed for misrepresentations leading to public fears and pressure for policies that may restrict or decrease funding for scientific enterprises. Hence the role of these outlets in shaping public attitudes in countries where there is widespread government funding of science is crucial. Ultimately, public pressure, though usually wielded by special interest groups, drives science in democracies.

Responsive to criticisms of science communication, science journalists, and the academic specialists who train them, have studied and criticized their own practices.

These practitioners of accommodation have the almost daily responsibility of creating the interface between expert scientific communities and various publics, and their self-conscious reflections about their own practice also constitute an important dimension of the rhetoric of science. A special journal (and supporting program) in the United Kingdom has been devoted to *The Public Understanding of Science.* Using social science methods of tracking opinion dynamics, this journal features articles examining media coverage and its results in attitude surveys. A similar journal in the United States is *Science Communication.* An excellent introduction to this area is Gregory and Miller's *Science in Public: Communication, Culture and Credibility* (1998). This work gives a brief history of science popularization, examines the construction of scientific publics, investigates newspaper reporting practices, offers case studies (especially of stories involving public risks such as the alar scare), and makes recommendations for improved practices. One chapter also deals with the important role of science museums in the public's understanding of and attitude toward science.

Many individual studies have focused on the dissemination of scientific claims in various public forums (see Fahnestock, 1986; Myers, 2003; Paul, 2004; Shinn, 1985). An exemplary work covering the history of the public understanding of genetics is Celeste M. Condit's *The Meaning of the Gene* (1999). Based on a quantitatively rigorous sampling and coding of popular periodicals, this work follows public attitudes on genetic determinism from the eugenics movement in the beginning of the century to the current era of gene testing and the promise of genetic therapies and finds that the discourse has more positive egalitarian and ethical features than critics have suggested. (For a study of prevailing public metaphors for the genome see Condit et al., 2002.)

Another area of study pays attention to high-profile writers, often scientists with literary ambitions, who have addressed the public: for example, Oliver Sacks, Loren Eiseley, Stephen Jay Gould, Carl Sagan, and James Trefil (see McRae, 1993). The role of popularizing works from scientists themselves is, however, an area that deserves far more attention. These works are not always derivative from expert discourse. In a new and somewhat anarchic field such as cognitive studies, for example, an astonishing number of books setting out conceptions of consciousness have been addressed to a nonexpert if not uninformed public (e.g., by Antonio Damasio, Terence Deacon, Daniel Dennett, Roger Penrose).

A SPECIFICALLY RHETORICAL HISTORY OF SCIENCE

While there has been substantial work on high-profile scientific genres, scientific language, and some reception and case studies, several areas, such as that of the scientist-popularizers just mentioned, deserve further attention. One area would combine the history of rhetoric with the history of science. The rhetorical theory of any period can of course be applied to the scientific discourse of any era. Carolyn Miller (1992) productively applies the classical rhetorical concept of "kairos" to rhetorical studies of science, and Joseph Little (2000) uses a late 20th-century theory of analogy to interpret the work of an early 20th-century scientist. But a historical approach within the rhetoric of science would look specifically for the influence of contemporary rhetorical theory on the practices of scientists *and the expectations of their audiences* who were trained in that theory, and that would include most of the scientists and audience members born before the 20th century. (As an index of the possibilities here it is worth remembering that Boyle wrote a treatise on figures of speech, Priestley wrote a rhetoric text, Lavoisier was a lawyer, and Pasteur won oratorical prizes.)

An exemplary work paying attention to contemporary discourse arts in the analysis of scientific arguments is Jean Dietz Moss's *Novelties in the Heavens* (1993), mentioned above. This study looks at key texts in the "Copernican Controversy," beginning with *De Revolutionibus*, and following with those who promoted and resisted his new cosmology, including Kepler, Galileo, the Jesuit Christopher Scheiner, and others. Moss pays careful attention to the roles of the then distinct arts of demonstration, dialectic and rhetoric among Italian academics and argues that rhetoric, newly energized, was distinctively brought into the campaigns for new scientific views that could be defended with only probable arguments. The project of understanding the controversy over Galileo's work from the Church's perspective is clarified by understanding contemporary theories of argumentation. A recent contribution to that understanding from Moss and William A. Wallace (2003) is an anthology of translations from sections of 16th-century rhetorical and dialectical treatises.

Not surprisingly, the early modern origins of the "scientific revolution" are an important site for examining the role of rhetoric in scientific argument, and Francis Bacon is a key figure (Stephens, 1975; Zappen, 1989). For the most part, however, though a certain rhetoricized attention to historical cases has flourished (e.g., Dear, 1991; Pera & Shea, 1991), the rhetorical history of science is a blank slate.

MARGINALIZED RHETORS

The study of race, class, and gender is a feature of the history and sociology of science, and so justifiably it is a feature of rhetorical studies of science. Indeed, one could say that it is more justifiably a matter for rhetoricians since the race, class, and gender of rhetors and audiences, and the institutionalization of these factors, are key elements in perceived personae

and in access to training, sites of practice, and forums for dissemination.

An enormous historical enterprise is well underway recovering the contributions of women to the sciences and examining the effects of gender on science itself. Barbara T. Gates has been an extraordinarily productive scholar in recovering and interpreting writing about nature in various genres by women in the 19th and early 20th centuries in her study *Kindred Nature* (1999), the edited collection of scholarly articles on individual women, *Natural Eloquence* (Gates & Shteir, 1997), and the anthology *In Nature's Name* (Gates, 2002). Margaret Rossiter has surveyed women with more mainstream careers in American science (1984, 1995; see also Kohlstedt's anthology on women in science, 1999), and Jack (2009). Most of this recovery work comes from historians, but inevitably some attention has been given to the rhetorical/textual practices of women in the sciences as a result of reconstructing their careers. A key interpretive work of particular interest to rhetoricians is Londa Schiebinger's *The Mind Has No Sex? Women in the Origins of Modern Science* (1989), which argues that the rise of scientific societies and the demise of convent schools actually diminished the opportunities for women to pursue scientific learning.

Much of the recovery work has (and will) involve the work of women artists whose subject matter was natural history. The most widely studied of these women has been Maria Merian, the 17th-century German painter, active in the Netherlands, who became a student of insects, producing accurate portrayals of developmental stages and associated plants (Wettengl, 1998). The market for albums illustrating collections of flowers, birds, and the like from the 17th into the 20th centuries was in fact met by a host of women artist/naturalists only now being identified, including figures such as Anna Comstock, an illustrator of insect manuals who became a professor of entomology at Cornell (Sheffield, 2001).

Among the individual women scientists who have attracted significant attention are the following: Margaret Cavendish, late-17th-century writer, the first and only woman admitted to meetings of the Royal Society until its membership was opened to women in 1945; Emile du Châtelet, Voltaire's collaborator in the popularization of Newton; Caroline Herschel, an observational astronomer, discoverer of four comets; Maria Mitchell, American astronomer; Sofia Kovalevsky, Russian mathematician. These women, and many others whose activities need recovery, were initiated to the exclusively male world of science through the activities of their husbands, fathers, and brothers. In the 20th century, the number of women in science increased dramatically; the following have received significant historical/biographical though not rhetorical attention: Marie Curie, Lise Meitner, Irene Joliot-Curie, Barbara McClintock, Margaret Mead, Rachel Carson, Rosalind Franklin, Jane Goodall. Evelyn Fox Keller's biography of the geneticist Barbara McClintock (1983) deserves singling out since it depicts a scientist, ignored by the mainstream for much of her career, who worked with a unique and perhaps gendered perspective on her subject.

The thriving school of feminist science studies has been of particular interest to rhetoricians since scholars in this field emphasize the social construction of knowledge as they detail male bias in scientific theorizing. Key works in this area include Evelyn Fox Keller's *Reflections on Gender in Science* (1996), which begins from her own experiences as a mathematician; Sandra Harding's *The Science Question in Feminism* (1986), which deconstructs "objectivity"; Donna Haraway's *Primate Visions* (1989), which traces gendered theories of evolution through the history of primatology; and Londa Schiebinger's *Has Feminism Changed Science?* (2001), which answers the title question in the affirmative. Several anthologies of work from feminist

philosophers and historians of science are available (Lederman & Bartsch, 2001; Mayberry, 2001; Myers, 2001). Especially useful is the 1996 anthology edited by Keller and Longino, which has articles addressing issues of representation and language. Feminists have uncovered blind spots in the work of male theorists whenever the subject of study itself involves gender. But unaddressed issues from a rhetorical perspective abound, most notably whether there is a detectable gendered mode of language or arguing per se in science.

Attention to African Americans' participation in science and its institutions has come, once again, largely from historians in recovery work. The contributions of several outstanding figures have received considerable attention, including Benjamin Banneker, a colonial era astronomer and almanac compiler; Ernest Everett Just, the mathematician (Manning, 1983); Charles Drew, the developer of blood plasma transfusions, and George Washington Carver, the premier U.S. agricultural chemist (McMurry, 1981). Biographical dictionaries are available listing hundreds of other African American scientists and inventors (see Kessler, Kidd, Kidd, & Morin, 1996; Krapp, 1999; Warren, 1991; the Library of Congress has also compiled a list of reference sources and biographical dictionaries on African American science: www.loc.gov/rr/scitech/SciRefGuides/africanamericans.html). None of these figures in African American science or their individual works has received any sustained rhetorical attention. One of the few studies from a larger perspective is Pearson's *Black Scientists, White Society, and Colorless Science: A Study of Universalism in American Science* (1985).

Scholars interested in institutionalized science have given some attention to the context and activities of science education and research in historically black colleges, universities, and medical schools. The second Morrill Act of 1890 led to the creation of land grant schools for African Americans in 17 southern states under the "separate but equal" provision. These schools were required to emphasize agriculture and the mechanical arts, as were the schools endowed by the 1862 Morrill Act, but their intended emphasis on "industrial education" was discredited by W. E. B. DuBois in his polemics against Booker T. Washington. Eventually, these schools developed into first-rate research institutions (see issues of *Agricultural History* for Spring 1991 and *Agriculture and Human Values* for Winter, 1992, devoted to these schools; see also Mays, Smith, & Helms, 2002; Neyland, 1990), but a notable early exception to their early struggles was the success of the Tuskegee Institute in developing a viable tradition of agricultural chemistry in the early 20th century under the direction of Carver (Mayberry, 1992). The rhetorical dimensions of the Tuskegee group's contributions and sustained activity from a doubly marginalized position (as outliers to both the dominant scientific community and to the avant-garde of African American thinkers like DuBois) deserve a great deal more study.

THE VISUAL RHETORIC OF SCIENCE

Science texts have pictures, graphs, diagrams, and tables. Contemporary articles in molecular biology and astronomy have lurid illustrations in highly saturated false colors; a recent article on the rediscovery of the Ivory-billed woodpecker included a link to the few seconds of video depicting a blurry bird flitting through a wintry swamp. This visual dimension of scientific persuasion has increased dramatically with recent digital technologies, but it has in fact been present since the first notable works in the tradition; Vesalius's *De Humani Corporis Fabrica* used a revived art of wood cutting, which, in the case of Brunsfel's *Botanica*, made it possible to replicate undistorted images of plants (see Ivins and Blunt, *The Art of Botanical Illustration*). One hundred years later, the third number of the first scientific journal, *The Transactions of the Royal Society,* included a

sheet of engraved images ineptly correlated to the journal's contents and employing conventions of visualization variously adopted from geometry, mechanical diagrams, architecture, mapmaking, and portraiture.

With the exception of Brian Ford's popularized *Images of Science* (1993), no single history of scientific visualization traces the changing technologies of seeing, the means of their reproduction, or the conceptual breakthroughs in their use, though there have been important works on various epochs or practices of visualization in the sciences. An exemplary study is geologist Martin Rudwick's on the new "visual language", which enabled the science of geology to develop in the late 18th and early 19th centuries (1976). A recent work from art historian David Freedberg, *The Eye of Lynx* (2002), records the visualization project of the early-17th-century "Academy of Linceans" to document types in all the kingdoms of nature into a vast visual archive that would constitute, for its time, a virtual "cabinet of curiosities." Both Rudwick and Freedberg, a geologist and art historian, are innocent of rhetorical theory but their works push the persuasiveness of visuals in science.

Four anthologies are particularly useful in demonstrating the range of visual imagery in the sciences as well as means of analysis. Art and cultural historians contributed to the studies in Ellenius's *The Natural Sciences and the Arts: Aspects of Interaction From the Renaissance to the Twentieth Century* (1985). Highlights in this collection include Harms's exploration of the sources of natural history illustrations in the 16th-century emblem tradition, where images of animals were associated with moral lessons, and Ellenius's study of late 19th-century wildlife painting as a source for a new ecological perspective on habitat. Another anthology offering a four-century overview of visualization practices in the sciences is Brian S. Baigre's *Picturing Knowledge: Historical and Philosophical Problems Concerning the Use of Art in Science*

(1996), ranging from Bert Hall's study of anatomical illustrations in the Middle Ages to Michael Ruse's examination of Sewall Wright's odd diagrams of adaptive fitness used in his arguments for population size and genetic drift. Valuable essays include historian of chemistry David Knight's review of chemical illustrations (liberally defined to include portraits of chemists and depictions of laboratories) and Robert J. O'Hara's demonstration of the various 19th-century techniques for visualizing taxonomic systems. The documentation and discussion of visual practices in these pieces again illustrates the impossibility of distinguishing a particularly rhetorical disciplinary approach from that of an art historian who considers the context in which visuals appeared.

Concentrating primarily on contemporary practices, the sociologists Michael Lynch and Steve Woolgar edited *Representation in Scientific Practice* (1990), which among its interesting pieces includes Lynch's criticism of the selection and mathematization involved in scientific depiction, Myers's analysis of the reifying illustrations in E. O. Wilson's *Sociobiology*, Law and Lynch's analysis of field guides for bird watching, and F. Bastide's very useful overview of visual types in an article about crystal structure contested as fraudulent. Luc Pauwels's recent collection *Visual Cultures of Science* (2006), with its valuable introductory essays, extends the subjects of analysis to X-rays, wall charts, and filmmaking.

One would expect rhetoricians of science to examine the persuasive effects of visuals since they are so important in the effectiveness of scientific arguments, and in this attention to visuals, the rhetoric of science is following the current interest in visuals so notable among scholars in communication and the humanities. There is, however, a key difference in the visual rhetoric of science since so many of its visuals are noniconic and since so many involve instrumentation for creating visible traces of invisible phenomena. The images of concern here are not visuals used to clarify or highlight

(the way a schematic drawing does) or to take a body of data and render it in visual form (the way graphs and bar charts do). Instead, these are visuals that count as evidence, often the only evidence, of a phenomenon: the printout of a scintillation counter measuring radioactivity in samples; the diffraction patterns produced by X-ray crystallography; the video of reactions occurring in real time with fluorescing proteins; the images of ion pores produced by atomic force microscopy. Such visualizations are difficult to check for accuracy since there may be no other ways of "seeing" the phenomena they realize. Furthermore, many of these images are generated and manipulated digitally, creating special anxieties about image veracity. In the wake of several retraction scandals involving images in the past few years, the editors of the *Journal of Cell Biology* proposed stringent new rules for digital image manipulation (Rossner & Yamada, 2004).

A visual rhetoric of science faces the same theoretical shortcomings plaguing those who want to analyze scientific argumentation or language: the fragmentary nature of the available theory or its disjunction from rhetoric. The only relatively complete theory of visual representation that includes scientific images in the context of all visual practices is Gunther Kress and Theo van Leeuwen's *Reading Images: The Grammar of Visual Design* (2006), though it does not address the unique problem of evidence-generating visualization. How disciplinary communities come to accept and police new technologies of seeing and to accord them the status of direct evidence needs much more examination, as does the relatively untouched area of how visuals perform in popularizations.

RELIGION AND THE NATURAL SCIENCES

The relationship of these two "magisteria," as Stephen Jay Gould called them, is an important issue in the history of science and in public polemics about science. Recently, the presumed antagonism between religion and science has been "historicized," traced in one case to the concerted effort of some late-19th-century scientist-polemicists struggling for academic hegemony. Thomas Lessl (1985) has argued that the "representative anecdote" of Galileo versus the Church was blown up dramatically during this time as a cautionary tale. Also in reaction to earlier themes in the history of science (the so-called Whig history that constructed a story of continuous progress of science over religion) a newer generation of historians has not dismissed the role of religious beliefs in the motivations of many scientists, including John Ray, Robert Boyle, Isaac Newton, Michael Faraday, Asa Gray, and so on. Tracing the direct influence of religious ideas on scientific research has been the result. Michael Faraday, for example, believed on theistic grounds in the ultimate unity of all phenomena and, having established the connection between electricity and magnetism (and incidentally inventing the electric motor), he continually searched for a relationship between magnetism and light.

The current decline in the cultural power of science is traced by many in the science community to the rise of a new "dark ages" and a return to religious superstition. But it can be more credibly traced to a post–World War II backlash against atomic energy and to the successes of the environmental movement inaugurated by Rachel Carson. At any rate, in the beginning of the 21st century, neither science nor religion can compete for cultural dominance with the "mass distractions," the incessant media presence, of the sports, movie, and music industries. (As a general index of the relative cultural importance of science, consider the amount of print space given by the *New York Times* to science—once a week plus the odd article—compared with the amount given to the arts in a daily section. Religion has even less presence.) To continue to talk about the cultural hegemony of the sciences in the twenty-first century, or its vulnerability to religion, seems naïve.

RHETORIC OF MATHEMATICS

If religion represents one end of a spectrum where science ceases, at the other end would be mathematics, a purely logical language of proof beyond the vagaries of persuasion. Yet even mathematics has been reexamined from a rhetorical perspective. In 1987, two mathematicians, Philip J. Davis and Reuben Hersh, claimed that even mathematical proofs had a rhetorical dimension in that their typical form, the "standard proof," was usually written not in complete, logical form, but in forms accommodated to mathematical audiences. In an intriguing recent article, Alain Bernard (2003) recommended that historians of ancient mathematics consider rhetorical theory as the informing context, with its doctrines of issue formation and a repertory of techniques (*topoi*) to be drawn on in solving a particular case. Giovanna Cifoletti (2006) has traced the surprising relationships between early modern algebra and the revised discourse arts of the 16th century. And G. Mitchell Reyes (2004) has argued that the development of calculus in the late 17th century relied on an essentially rhetorical justification of the method of infinitesimals (see also Fahnestock, 1999, p. 101). To add to these promising isolated publications, and to fill the need for a specific rhetorical history of science (Wynn, 2009), the role of mathematics as a persuasive language in itself and a source of perhaps unique *topoi* deserves more rhetorical investigation.

RESISTANCE TO A RHETORIC OF THE NATURAL SCIENCES

Publishing an essay on the "science wars" in 2000, Stephen Jay Gould praised historians and sociologists of science, but explicitly excepted certain "self-promoting and cynical rhetoricians" (p. 259), associating them with an extreme relativism that undercut the notion of progress in science. No sooner had the first full-length monographs in the rhetoric of science appeared in the early 1990s, than criticism came from the ranks of speech communication rhetoricians in the work of Dilip Gaonkar, who dismissed the application of rhetorical constructs to scientific cases as providing no distinct insight. His work was answered in a volume of responses in 1997 (Gross & Keith, 1997) and in an exchange over a review of this work in the *Quarterly Journal of Speech* by Herbert Simons (1999). Leah Ceccarelli's (2005) analysis of responses to her own *Shaping Science With Rhetoric* shows that disciplinary huffiness against rhetoric applied to science is alive and well.

Another outspoken critic of existing approaches in the rhetoric of science has been Steve Fuller. Fuller's (1995) dismissal of much of the scholarship has been based on his own desire to see what he calls a "strong program in the rhetoric of science," imitating the Edinburgh School's "strong programme in the sociology of knowledge." He has found fault with the history and sociology of science as well, but he has been especially dismissive of what he calls "textualism" or "literary" approaches to scientific texts (2001). Fuller's main criticism is that scholars produce "close readings" of texts that are in no way relevant to the kinds of reading practices employed by most working scientists. In this criticism, that scientists do not read articles the way humanists read poems, Fuller is certainly on solid ground as the work of Charney and others has shown. However, Fuller's criticisms in no way dismiss the importance of close analysis of texts, in whatever modality. For even if scientists are sometimes selective readers, it is not only the *readers* of science texts who are of interest to rhetoricians, important as they may be in studies of influence and reception. It is also the writers and the texts themselves that represent normative practices, the public versions of scientific arguments, produced with a disciplinary audience's standards in mind.

Despite (or perhaps because of) the criticisms, the rhetoric of the natural sciences is an area of intense scholarly activity. Indeed, none of the areas discussed above is sampled

exhaustively and the pace of contributions is increasing. The field also has an institutional presence in the American Association for the Rhetoric of Science and Technology and the Association of Teachers of Technical Writing, and though it could use its own journal, pieces under a rhetorical rubric routinely appear in general rhetoric and communication journals. Scientists themselves, when they have been involved in studies, are receptive to investigations of their persuasive practices. The net result of the scholarship on the rhetoric of science is, arguably, a deep appreciation for the human effort and creativity that produces enduring knowledge in the natural sciences.

NOTES

1. Historians of science (in a subdiscipline itself only 80 years old) are perhaps the most important enablers of a rhetorical perspective of science. They construct the accounts and identify the texts that rhetoricians then examine; alternatively, in their own works they often paraphrase or analyze styles of writing and argument. And for those who take a more "social movement" perspective, they provide accounts of originators and lines of influence, and so on. But they do not reciprocally pay attention to the rhetoric of science. The Bibliography of the History of Science Society, for example, does not survey articles in any rhetoric or communication journals.

2. One famous case concerns a paper appearing in the British medical journal *The Lancet*, which incorrectly established a connection between autism and the vaccine against measles, mumps, and rubella, leading many parents to refuse vaccination for their children (see Oldstone, 2004). What is interesting about this case is the agreement, in hindsight, on the published paper's faults just a few years of its publication. A second and far more dramatic case concerns the apparent falsification of results by the first scientist (Hwang) to claim to have successfully cloned human embryos in order to harvest embryonic stem cells with the patients' DNA. This research had important consequences for a ballot initiative in California and the 2004 presidential election. Here is indeed a test case of the influence of

politics on the presumption in favor of a line of research. Cases like this one also raise the interesting issue of whether the review process can detect outright fraud.

REFERENCES

Atkinson, D. (1999). *Scientific discourse in sociohistorical context: The Philosophical Transactions of the Royal Society of London, 1675–1975.* Mahwah, NJ: Lawrence Erlbaum.

Baake, K. (2003). *Metaphor and knowledge: The challenges of writing science.* Albany: State University of New York Press.

Baigre, B. S. (Ed.). (1996). *Picturing knowledge: Historical and philosophical problems concerning the use of art in science.* Toronto, Ontario, Canada: University of Toronto Press.

Bazerman, C. (1988). *Shaping written knowledge.* Madison: University of Wisconsin Press.

Bernard, A. (2003). Ancient rhetoric and Greek mathematics: A response to a modern historiographical dilemma. *Science in Context, 16*(3), 391–412.

Black, M. (1962). *Models and metaphors.* Ithaca, NY: Cornell University Press.

Blakeslee, A. M. (2001). *Interacting with audiences: Social influences on the production of scientific writing.* Mahwah, NJ: Erlbaum.

Blunt, W. (1994). *The art of botanical illustration: An illustrated history.* New York: Dover Publications.

Brown, T. L. (2003). *Making truth: Metaphor in science.* Champaign: University of Illinois Press.

Campbell, J. A. (1975). The polemical Mr. Darwin. *Quarterly Journal of Speech, 60,* 442–449.

Campbell, J. A. (1986). Scientific revolution and the grammar of culture: The case of Darwin's *Origin. Quarterly Journal of Speech, 72,* 351–376.

Campbell, J. A. (1987). Charles Darwin: Rhetorician of science. In J. S. Nelson, A. Megill, & D. N. McCloskey (Eds.), *The rhetoric of the human sciences* (pp. 69–86). Madison: University of Wisconsin Press.

Campbell, J. A. (1989). The invisible rhetorician: Charles Darwin's third party strategy. *Rhetorica, 7,* 55–85.

Campbell, J. A. (1990a). Scientific discovery and rhetorical invention: Darwin's path to natural selection. In H. W. Simons (Ed.), *The rhetorical turn* (pp. 58–89). Chicago: University of Chicago Press.

Campbell, J. A. (1990b). On the way to the *Origin:* Darwin's evolutionary insight and its rhetorical transformation. *The Van Zelst lecture in communication.* Northwestern University School of Speech, Evanston, IL.

Campbell, J. A. (1995). Topics, tropes, and tradition: Darwin's reinvention and subversion of the argument from design. In H. Krips, J. E. McGuire, & T. Melia (Eds.), *Science, reason and rhetoric* (pp. 211–236). Pittsburgh, PA: University of Pittsburgh Press.

Ceccarelli, L. (2001). *Shaping science with rhetoric: The cases of Dobzhansky, Schrödinger, and Wilson.* Chicago: University of Chicago Press.

Ceccarelli, L. (2004). Neither confusing cacophony nor culinary complements: A case study of mixed metaphors for genomic science. *Written Communication, 21*(1), 92–105.

Ceccarelli, L. (2005). A hard look at ourselves: A reception study of the rhetoric of science. *Technical Communication Quarterly, 14*(3), 257–265.

Cifoletti, G. (2006). From Valla to Viète: The rhetorical reform of logic and its use in early modern algebra. *Early Science and Medicine, 11*(4), 390–423.

Condit, C. M. (1999). *The meanings of the gene: Public debates about human heredity.* Madison: University of Wisconsin Press.

Condit, C. M., Bates, B. R., Galloway, R., Brown Givens, S., Haynie, C. K., Jordan, J. W., et al. (2002). Recipes or blueprints for our genes? How contexts selectively activate the multiple meanings of metaphors. *Quarterly Journal of Speech, 88*(3), 303–325.

Crismore, A., & Vande Kopple, W. J. (1997). Hedges and readers: Effects on attitudes and learning. In R. Markkanen & H. Schröder (Eds.), *Hedging and discourse: Approaches to the analysis of pragmatic phenomenon in academic texts* (pp. 83–114). New York: de Gruyter.

Darian, S. G. (2003). *Understanding the language of science.* Austin: University of Texas Press.

Davis, P. J., & Reuben H. (1987). Rhetoric and mathematics. In J. S. Nelson, A. Megill, & D. McCloskey (Eds.), *The rhetoric of the human sciences: Language and argument in scholarship and public affairs.* Madison: University of Wisconsin Press.

Dear, P. (Ed.). (1991). *The literary structure of scientific argument: Historical studies.* Philadelphia: University of Pennsylvania Press.

Ellenius, A. (Ed.). (1985). *The natural sciences and the arts: Aspects of interaction from the renaissance to the twentieth century.* Stockholm: Almquist & Wiksell.

Fahnestock, J. (1986). Accommodating science: The rhetorical life of scientific facts. *Written Communication, 3,* 275–296.

Fahnestock, J. (1999). *Rhetorical figures in science.* New York: Oxford University Press.

Fahnestock, J. (2004). Preserving the figure: Consistency in the presentation of scientific arguments. *Written Communication, 21*(1), 6–31.

Finocchiaro, M. A. (1980). *Galileo and the art of reasoning: Rhetorical foundations of logic and scientific method.* Dordrecht, Netherlands: Reidel.

Ford, B. (1993). *Images of science: A history of scientific illustration.* New York: Oxford University Press.

Foucault, M. (1970). *The order of things: An archaeology of the human sciences.* New York: Vintage Books.

Fuller, S. (1995). The strong program in the rhetoric of science. In H. Krips, J. E. McGuire, & T. Melia (Eds.), *Science, reason, and rhetoric* (pp. 95–118). Pittsburgh, PA: University of Pittsburgh Press.

Fuller, S. (2001). Science. In T. O. Sloane (Ed.), *Encyclopedia of rhetoric.* New York: Oxford University Press.

Freedberg, D. (2002). *The eye of the lynx. Galileo, his friends, and the beginnings of modern natural history.* Chicago: University of Chicago Press.

Gates, B. T. (1999). *Kindred nature: Victorian and Edwardian women embrace the living world.* Chicago: University of Chicago Press.

Gates, B. T. (Ed.). (2002). *In nature's name: An anthology of women's writing and illustration, 1780–1930.* Chicago: University of Chicago Press.

Gates, B. T., & Shteir, A. B. (Eds.). (1997). *Natural eloquence: Women reinscribe science.* Madison: University of Wisconsin Press.

Gjertsen, D. (1984). *The classics of science. A study of twelve enduring scientific works.* New York: Lilian Barber Press.

Golinski, J. (1987). Robert Boyle: Skepticism and authority in seventeenth-century chemical discourse. In A. Benjamin, G. Cantor, & J. R. R.

Christie (Eds.), *The figural and the literal* (pp. 58–82). Manchester, UK: Manchester University Press.

Gopen, G. D., & Swan, J. (1990). The science of scientific writing. *American Scientist, 78,* 550–558.

Gould, S. J. (2000). Deconstructing the "science wars" by reconstructing an old mold. *Science, 287,* 253–261.

Graves, H. (2005). *Rhetoric in(to) Science: Style as invention in inquiry.* Cresskill, NJ: Hampton Press.

Gregory, J., & Miller, S. (1998). *Science in public: Communication, culture, and credibility.* New York: Plenum Press.

Gross, A. (1990). *The rhetoric of science.* Cambridge, MA: Harvard University Press.

Gross, A. (2006). *Starring the text: The place of rhetoric in science studies.* Carbondale: Southern Illinois University Press.

Gross, A., Harmon, J. E., & Reidy, M. (2002). *Communicating science: The scientific article from the 17th century to the present.* New York: Oxford University Press.

Gross, A., & Keith, W. M. (1997). *Rhetorical hermeneutics: Invention and interpretation in the age of science.* Albany: State University of New York Press.

Halliday, M. A. K. & Martin, J. R. (1993). *Writing science: Literacy and discursive power.* Pittsburgh, PA: University of Pittsburgh Press.

Haraway, D. J. (1989). *Primate visions: Gender, race, and nature in the world of modern science.* New York: Routledge.

Harding, S. (1986). *The science question in feminism.* Ithaca, NY: Cornell University Press.

Harris, R. A. (Ed.). (1997). Introduction. In *Landmark essays in the rhetoric of science* (p. xiii). Mahwah, NJ: Lawrence Erlbaum.

Harris, R. A. (Ed.). (2005). *The rhetoric of incommensurability.* Lafayette, IN: Parlor Press.

Hesse, M. (1966). *Models and analogies in science.* South Bend, IN: Notre Dame University Press.

Holmes, F. L. (1987). Writing and discovery. *Isis, 78,* 220–235.

Holmes, F. L. (1991). Argument and narrative in scientific writing. In P. Dear (Ed.), *The literary structure of scientific argument: historical studies* (pp. 164–181). Philadelphia: University of Pennsylvania Press.

Hyland, K. (1998). *Hedging in scientific research articles*. Amsterdam: Benjamins.

Howe, H., & Lyne, J. (1992). Gene talk in sociobiology. *Social Epistemology, 6*, 1–54.

Ivins, W. M. (1969). *Prints and visual communication*. New York: Da Capo Press.

Jack, J. (2009). *Science on the home front: The rhetoric of women scientists in World War II*. Urbana: University of Illinois Press.

Journet, D. (1984). Rhetoric and sociobiology. *Journal of Technical Writing and Communication, 14*, 339–350.

Katz, S., & Penrose, N. (2003). *Writing in the sciences: Exploring conventions of scientific discourse* (2nd ed.). Boston: Allyn Bacon.

Keller, E. F. (1983). *A feeling for the organism: The life and work of Barbara McClintock*. New York: Holt.

Keller, E. F. (1995). *Refiguring life: Metaphors of twentieth-century biology*. New York: Columbia University Press.

Keller, E. F. (1996). *Reflections on gender in science*. New Haven, CT: Yale University Press.

Keller, E. F. (2001). *The century of the gene*. Cambridge, MA: Harvard University Press.

Keller, E. F., & Longino, H. E. (Eds.). (1996). *Feminism and science*. New York: Oxford University Press.

Kessler, J. H., Kidd, J. S., Kidd, R., & Morin, K. (1996). *Distinguished African-American scientists in the twentieth century*. Phoenix, AZ: Oryx Press.

Kohlstedt, S. G. (Ed.). (1999). *History of women in the sciences: Readings from Isis*. Chicago: University of Chicago Press.

Krapp, K. M. (Ed.). (1999). *Notable black American scientists*. Detroit, MI: Gale Research.

Kress, G., & van Leeuwen, T. (2006). *Reading images: The grammar of visual design* (2nd ed.). London: Routledge.

Latour, B. (1987). *Science in action: How to follow scientists and engineers through society*. Cambridge, MA: Harvard University Press.

Latour, B., & Woolgar, S. (1986). *Laboratory life: The construction of scientific facts*. Princeton, NJ: Princeton University Press.

Lederman, M., & Bartsch, I. (Eds). (2001). *The gender and science reader*. London: Routledge.

Lessl, T. M. (1985). Heresy, orthodoxy, and the politics of science. *Quarterly Journal of Speech, 74*, 18–34.

Little, J. (2000). Analogy in science: Where do we go from here? *Rhetoric Society Quarterly, 30*(1), 69–92.

Lynch, M., & Woolgar, S. (1990). *Representation in scientific practice*. Cambridge, MA: MIT Press.

Lyne, J. (1986). Punctuated equilibria: Rhetorical dynamics of a scientific controversy. *Quarterly Journal of Speech, 72*, 132–147.

Lyne, J. (1995). Rhetoric in the context of scientific rationality. In H. Krips, J. E. McGuire, & T. Melia (Eds.), *Science, reason and rhetoric* (pp. 245–267). Pittsburgh, PA: University of Pittsburgh Press.

Lyne, J., & Howe, H. F. (1990). Rhetorics of expertise: E. O. Wilson and sociobiology. *Quarterly Journal of Speech, 76*, 134–151.

Manning, K. (1983). *Black Apollo of science: The life of Ernest Everett Just*. New York: Oxford University Press.

Martin, J. R., & Veel, R. (1998). *Reading science: Critical and functional perspectives on discourses of science*. New York: Routledge.

Mayberry, B. D. (1992). *A century of agriculture in the 1890 land grant institutions and Tuskegee University. 1890–1990*. New York: Vantage Press.

Mayberry, M. (Ed.). (2001). *Feminist science studies. A new generation*. London: Routledge.

Mays, M. D., Smith, H., & Helms, D. (2002). Contributions of African-Americans and the 1890 land-grant universities to soil science and the soil survey. In D. Helms, A. B. W. Effland, & P. J. Durana (Eds.), *Profiles in the history of the U.S. soil survey* (pp. 169–190). Ames: Iowa State University Press.

McMurry, L. O. (1981). *George Washington Carver: Scientist and symbol*. Oxford, UK: Oxford University Press.

McRae, M. W. (1993). *The literature of science: Perspectives on popular scientific writing*. Athens: University of Georgia Press.

Merton, R. K. (1988). The Matthew effect in science II: Cumulative advantage and the symbolism of intellectual property. *Isis, 79.4*, 606–623.

Miller, C. (1992). Kairos in the rhetoric of science. In S. P. Witte, N. Nakadate, & R. Cherry (Eds.), *A rhetoric of doing* (pp. 310–327). Carbondale: Southern Illinois University Press.

Montgomery, S. L. (1996). *The scientific voice.* New York: Guilford Press.

Montgomery, S. L. (2005). *The Chicago guide to communicating science.* Chicago: University of Chicago Press.

Moss, J. D. (1993). *Novelties in the heavens: Rhetoric and science in the Copernican controversy.* Chicago: University of Chicago Press.

Moss, J. D., & Wallace, W. A. (2003). *Rhetoric and dialectic in the time of Galileo.* Washington, DC: Catholic University of America Press.

Myers, G. (1990). *Writing biology: Texts in the social construction of scientific knowledge.* Madison: University of Wisconsin Press.

Myers, G. (2003). Discourse studies of scientific popularization: Questioning the boundaries. *Discourse Studies, 5*(2), 265–279.

Neyland, L. W. (1990). *Historically black land-grant institutions and the development of home economics: 1890–1990.* Tallahassee: Florida A&M University Foundation.

Oldstone, M. B. A. (2004). Immune to the facts. *Nature, 432,* 275–276.

Paul, D. (2004). Spreading chaos: The role of popularizations in the diffusion of scientific ideas. *Written Communication, 21*(1), 32–68.

Paul, D., & Charney, D. (1995). Introducing chaos (theory) into science and engineering: Effects of rhetorical strategies on scientific readers. *Written Communication, 12*(4), 396–438.

Paul, D., Charney, D., & Kendall, A. (2001). Moving beyond the moment: Reception studies in the rhetoric of science. *Journal of Business and Technical Communication, 15*(3), 372–399.

Pauwels, L. (Ed.) (2006). *Visual cultures of science.* Dartmouth, NH: University Press of New England.

Pearson, W. (1985). *Black scientists, white society, and colorless science: A study of universalism in American science.* Millwood, NY: Associated Faculty Press.

Pera, M., & Shea, W. R. (1991). *Persuading science: The art of scientific rhetoric.* Canton, MA: Science History.

Pinch, T. (1996). Rhetoric and the cold fusion controversy. In H. Krips, J. E. McGuire & T. Melia (Eds.), *Science, reason, and rhetoric* (pp. 153-176). Pittsburgh, PA: University of Pittsburgh Press.

Prelli, L. J. (1989). *A rhetoric of science: Inventing scientific discourse.* Columbia: University of South Carolina Press.

Reeves, C. (1996). Language, rhetoric and AIDS. *Written Communication, 13*(1), 130–157.

Reeves, C. (1998). Rhetoric and the AIDS virus hunt. *Quarterly Journal of Speech, 84*(1), 1–22.

Reeves, C. (2002). An orthodox heresy: Scientific rhetoric and the science of prions. *Science Communication, 24*(1), 98–122.

Reeves, C. (2005). *The language of science.* London: Routledge.

Reyes, G. M. (2004). The rhetoric in mathematics: Newton, Leibniz, their calculus and the rhetoric of the infinitesimal. *Quarterly Journal of Speech, 90,* 163–188.

Rossiter, M. (1984). *Women scientists in America: Struggles and strategies to 1940.* Baltimore: Johns Hopkins University Press.

Rossiter, M. (1995). *Women scientists in America: Before affirmative action, 1940–1972.* Baltimore: Johns Hopkins University Press.

Rossner, M., & Yamada, K. M. (2004). What's in a picture? The temptation of image manipulation. *Journal of Cell Biology, 166*(1), 11–15.

Rudwick, M. J. S. (1976). The emergence of a visual language for geological science 1760–1840. *History of Science, 14,* 149–195.

Schiebinger, L. (1989). *The mind has no sex? Women in the origins of modern science.* Cambridge, MA: Harvard University Press.

Schiebinger, L. (2001). *Has feminism changed science?* Cambridge, MA: Harvard University Press.

Seglen, P. O. (1997). Why the impact factor of journals should not be used for evaluating research. *British Medical Journal, 314*(7079), 498–502.

Selzer, J. (Ed.). (1993). *Understanding scientific prose.* Madison: University of Wisconsin Press.

Shapin, S. (1984). Pump and circumstance: Robert Boyle's literary technology. *Social Studies of Science, 14,* 481–520.

Shea, E. (2008). *How the gene got its groove.* Albany: State University of New York Press.

Sheffield, S. L.-M. (2001). *Revealing new worlds: Three Victorian women naturalists.* London: Routledge.

Shinn, T., & Whitley, R. (1985). *Expository science: Forms and functions of popularisation.* Dordrecht, the Netherlands: Reidel.

Simons, H. W. (1999). Rhetorical hermeneutics and the project of globalization. *Quarterly Journal of Speech, 85*, 86–109.

Stephens, J. (1975). *Francis Bacon and the style of science*. Chicago: University of Chicago Press.

Swales, J. (1990). *Genre analysis: English in academic and research settings*. Cambridge, UK: Cambridge University Press.

Vande Kopple, W. (1994). Some characteristics and functions of grammatical subjects in scientific discourse. *Written Communication, 11*(4), 534–564.

Vande Kopple, W. (2002). From the dynamic to the synoptic style in spectroscopic articles in the *Physical Review:* Beginnings and 1980. *Written Communication, 19*(2), 227–264.

Warren, W. (1991). *Black women scientists in the US*. Bloomington: Inidana University Press.

Westfall, R. S. (1991). Galileo and Newton: Different rhetorical strategies. In M. Pera & W. R. Shea (Eds.), *Persuading science: The art of scientific rhetoric*. Canton, MA: Science History.

Wettengl, K. (Ed.). (1998). *Maria Sibylla Merian, 1647–1717: Artist and naturalist*. Frankfurt am Main, Germany: Verlag Gerd Hatje.

Wynn, J. (2009). Arithmetic of the species: Darwin and the role of mathematics in his argumentation. *Rhetorica 27*(2), forthcoming.

Zappen, J. (1989). Francis Bacon and the historiography of scientific rhetoric. *Rhetoric Review, 8*, 74–90.

Zuckerman, H., & Merton, R. K. (1971). Patterns of evaluation in science: Institutionalisation, structure and functions of the referee system. *Minerva, 9*(1), 66–100.

11

The Rhetoric of Economics

EDWARD M. CLIFT

Invisible hand:

Mother of inflated hope,

Mistress of despair.

—Ziliak (2002)

Heads or tails? How many of us have made important decisions after resorting to this familiar method? Flipping a coin dematerializes its monetary value but raises its symbolic significance to the realm of human action. A quarter, in this case, can be much more meaningful than the 25 cents it represents. Only the willing suspension of one's rationality can endow the result with individual and collective decision-making power. The moment of suspense that adheres to the act typically unites observers in a rhetorical matrix of personal desire and communal agreement. Rarely is the toss of a coin considered a mere game. As with other abstract economic forces, the outcomes of this kind of intentionally random participation in the universe's game of chance can mean serious business in the destiny of a life.

The rhetoric of economics is a nascent field that seeks to understand the economic manifestations of persuasion. It exists on the edges of mainstream economic theory and has yet to transform either the core practices or educational parameters of professional practice in that discipline. Marginal spaces can be fertile, however, and the rhetoric of economics has proven to be no exception. It has inspired a small cadre of researchers to seek critical insights about our economic lives and about the academic discourse of economics.

Two decades of research into the rhetoric of economics has yielded a wide range of studies that are beginning to cohere into a narrative of their own. They tell the story of a somewhat fractious disciplinary engagement between a social science field (economics) and a humanities field (rhetoric). Although it may seem odd to juxtapose these two fields, doing so highlights their shared concern with the various types of exchange that take place between people as they actualize their motivations. Thus, for example, credit is a cousin to character, as it relies on markers of ethos to predict behavioral probabilities. The rhetoric of economics began as a challenge to the scientific facade of economics. Its concerns now range from the demarcation of new types of goods, such as carbon credits, to the development of materialist perspectives on identity and human values. Turning one discipline's critical lens on another has led to a number of surprising results.

This essay aims to explicate the profound connections that exist between rhetoric and economics. It seeks to show how their combined explanatory power may lead us to critical insight regarding the global flows of finance and social discourse in the general economy. Recent inroads in the field have led some scholars such as Klinger (2008), Salvo (2008), and Zuidhof (2008) to posit a more generative connection between the two disciplines, shifting the attention toward the role rhetoric plays in the production and reproduction of economic realities. This newfound emphasis on the economy as cultural discourse has resulted in a promising new direction of research in the rhetoric of economics. Centered on what might be described as "productive rhetoric" (Carter, 2008), it encourages the entry of cultural studies and post-structuralist perspectives into the field.

One persistent thread in the rhetoric of economics has been a concern for the types of subjectivities that seem to accompany economic systems. The Protestant ethic,

class consciousness, and bourgeois morality can all be characterized as manifestations of the economic in our consciousness and self-identity (McCloskey, 2006). Kenneth Burke was among those who have noted the fluid relationship between one's occupation and one's preoccupations, observing that "occupation and morality are integrally intermingled" (Burke, 1954/1984, p. 284). Pursuant to this insight, I will devote the last part of the essay to a post-structuralist analysis of *The Sopranos*, reading it as a narrative of an anxious prototypical subjectivity exhibiting the logic of capitalism.

Metal coins, as described above, change their very nature when tossed into the air. How much more flexible in their meaning are the dollar bills and other paper notes made possible by the printing press, once characterized by Daniel Defoe as "air money" (Sherman, 1996)? Or the green-, blue-, gold-, platinum-, and even plum-colored virtual transactions of plastic credit cards with evocative names such as Discover, American Express, and MasterCard Maestro? Raising questions about the social semiotic meanings of economic life challenges the traditional neoclassical view of the economy as a general equilibrium of supply and demand arrived at through the orderly interactions of self-interested rational actors (Arrow & Debreau, 1954). Such inquiries lead to concerns that a fearsome irrationality of sorts might persist in the marketplace and perhaps even at the heart of a discipline that is arguably the most consequential of the social sciences in terms of its impact on daily life.

Competing economic perspectives continually clash over theoretical constructs and their application, reflective of the close association of the discipline with vital issues of survival and prosperity. From its earliest beginnings, economics sought to clarify and encourage processes that might provide more resources to more people. It is of no small significance that Adam Smith, its founder, was also a moral philosopher and teacher of rhetoric (Aune, 2001, p. 15). Smith argued in *The Wealth of*

Nations (published in the emblematic year of 1776) that individuals acting in their own self-interest would benefit the community over time through the metaphorical force of "the invisible hand." The classical economics of Smith, David Ricardo, Thomas Malthus, and John Stuart Mill sought to improve the general welfare by understanding and managing the costs and distribution of goods. Policies aimed at improving the general welfare, such as the promotion of free trade and the restraint of monopolistic practices, are among the concrete manifestations of classical economics.

Mainstream economics has taken on the trappings of a full-fledged science, but it presumes certain ideological tenets. It is based on a century-old neoclassical synthesis of rational-choice models and macroeconomic factors in the form of its general equilibrium model. Perfect information and reasoned deliberation are seen to combine in ways that set prices allowing individuals to maximize their utility and firms to maximize their profit. Mathematics and statistical analysis have been predominant in neoclassical methodology since the publication of Paul Samuelson's *Foundation of Economic Analysis* in 1947. Thus, neoclassical economics presents itself as a scientific enterprise whose objective discoveries regarding the economy can help predict and control markets for the betterment of all.

Other economic theories have had a difficult time penetrating the edifice of the neoclassical model, with its celebration of the scientific method and the rationality of the individual. Notable among these is Marxism, which takes a much more critical stance in its characterization of profit as the systematic class-based exploitation of surplus labor value. Differential ownership of modes of production and the ideological manipulation of class interests are seen to usurp the efficient allocation of scarce resources envisioned by the neoclassical model. Amariglio, Cullenberg, and Ruccio (2001) provide recent examples of a neo-Marxist approach combined with a postmodern perspective. Feminist approaches, as summarized by Woolley (1998), challenge the gender inequalities that exist in the economy and the androcentric bias of neoclassical research.

Another influential model, that of the Austrian School, applauds the methodological individualism and subjectivism often identified with libertarian political philosophy. It can be traced back to the publication of Carl Menger's *Principles of Economics* in 1871 and has long been associated with the economists Friedrich Hayek and Ludwig von Mises. These writers drew attention to the innovating activities of the entrepreneur rather than price equilibrium as the key hermeneutic component of a necessarily creative capitalism (Rothbard, 1989).

During its heyday in the early part of the 20th century, economists identified with the Austrian School emphasized the psychic relationship between individuals and the social systems in which they act. They took systematic coherence as a standard for understanding behavior rather than fixed axioms of rationality and the assumption of perfect information, while endorsing the acceptance of uncertainty rather than certainty as the source of profits in risk-based economies. Shackle's *Epistemics and Economics* (1972/1992) outlines the primary philosophical differences between this approach and the neoclassical one. It is interesting to note that epistemics had entered the field of rhetoric just a few years before Shackle's study (see Scott, 1967). A growing concern with the problem of knowledge in both fields laid the groundwork for the interdisciplinary connections that developed a decade later. As McCloskey (1994) states,

> If the economy depends on the faculty of speech, then the economy will require verbal interpretation . . . [and] can be listened to and read like a text. . . . The conclusion is that of Austrian and hermeneutical economists . . . The neoclassical division of objective and subjective, preference and constraints, should give way to the conjective. (pp. 377–378)

Rhetoric entered the critical debate surrounding mainstream economics in 1986 with the publication of Deirdre (formerly Donald) McCloskey's landmark study, *The Rhetoric of Economics*. Written by a former faculty member of the economics department at the University of Chicago, a bastion of traditional neoclassical theory, this book carried an ethos that was hard for establishment economists to ignore. Trained at Harvard as an economic historian, McCloskey had been an associate professor of economics and history in Chicago from the early 1970s until she left in 1980. Later, as a professor with a chaired position in the economics department at the University of Iowa, she initiated a research agenda that brought to light the critical role of persuasive speech in all facets of economic scholarship.

McCloskey's "rhetorical turn," manifest in her work at the University of Iowa, challenged the aura of objective neutrality advanced by economics and other fields reliant on mathematical or statistical description. In association with John Lyne, Alan Megill, John Nelson, N. Katherine Hayles, and other faculty members at the University of Iowa, McCloskey's interests expanded to include the knowledge practices found in other disciplines. Starting with an interdisciplinary seminar on rhetoric in the disciplines, their efforts converged in the creation of the Project on Rhetoric of Inquiry (POROI), now an interdisciplinary program at the University of Iowa, which explores the rhetorical aspects of the various fields of knowledge. Nelson, Megill, and McCloskey (1987) characterize their mission in this passage:

> Rhetoric of inquiry rests on two assertions. It maintains that argument is more unified than is commonly understood, and far more unified than the fragmentation of academic fields might imply. Every scientist or scholar, regardless of field, relies on common devices of rhetoric: on metaphors, invocations of authority, and appeals to audiences—themselves creatures of rhetoric. But rhetoric of inquiry also insists that argument is more

diverse than is commonly understood and far more diverse than the official philosophies of science or art allow. Every field is defined by its own special devices and patterns of rhetoric—by existence theorems, arguments from invisible hands, and appeals to textual possibilities or archives—themselves textures of rhetoric. (pp. 4–5)

McCloskey makes the controversial claim that her own discipline of economics had lost sight of its origins in philosophical questions relating to the general moral and material well-being of human populations. It had fallen victim, in her view, to statistical charades and nonempirical theorizing, with the consequence that its claims were rendered far less generalizable to real-world cases. She argues in later books (1990, 1994, 1998) that economists had veered off course by investing too much descriptive authority in abstract mathematics and the search for statistical significance as opposed to empirical observation and the search for social significance. Economics, McCloskey argued, shortchanges itself when it relies too heavily on scientific methodologies and chooses to restrict its research to the elucidation of prudence and thrift alone (McCloskey, 1997). She diagnosed a shortsightedness and lack of self-awareness regarding the way rhetoric is used to define, and create, economic realities.

McCloskey was not alone in being suspicious of economic doctrines. Coming from the field of rhetoric to economics, James Aune, in *Rhetoric and Marxism* (1994), would make what could be seen as a parallel argument concerning Marxism, that is, that its demise was hastened by its own objectification of economic processes and failure to engage rhetoric in a meaningful way. Motivation, in his view, can never be reduced to economic logic whether it takes the form of class struggle or the rational maximization of utility (Aune, 2001, p. xiv). It is more about contingent human understandings and representations, which would be an opening to rhetoric.

McCloskey tries to uncover the human dimension of economics by exposing its rhetoric. Mainstream economists, she clearly states, use rhetorical strategies to make persuasive claims about reality despite their attestations of scientific objectivity. She describes in copious detail how economic scholarship relies on rhetorical appeals to authority and scientific tradition, statements of belief, hypothetical thought experiments, and even abstract aesthetic principles (McCloskey, 1998, p. 25). The law of supply, for example, is matched by a symmetrical law of demand in the general theory of equilibrium even though it is nowhere near as easily or objectively measured.

According to McCloskey (1986), analogy functions as a sort of "master trope" for economics owing to its ability to transfer meaning from one domain to another. She finds that economic reasoning is often applied to noneconomic spheres of life on the basis of the mistaken assumption that it provides a universal explanatory framework. Movies in popular culture provide a clear example since they are so often reviewed as if their quality were identical to their box office receipts. By articulating the salience of rhetoric to economic reasoning, McCloskey hopes to expand the parameters of the field and thereby increase both its accuracy and relevance. She argues thus:

> Economics is not a matter solely of syllogism, regression, or experiment. It is also analogy and authority. We should accept this fact, broadening and thereby improving the conversation of economists. The conversation would be more open; it would be more productive; and it would be more to the point. (p. 102)

These efforts can be seen as expanding the rhetorical work of Wayne Booth (1974) and Chaim Perelman (1982) as well as the literary theories of narrativity. A more "literary" approach to economics, in this view, offers to "bring economics back into the conversation of mankind" (McCloskey, 1994/2000, p. 382). In McCloskey's view, economists are storytellers who are as dependent on the establishment of ethos and other rhetorical qualities as any

other professional persuader. Monetarism, Keynesianism, and other economic schools of thought tell different stories about reality, but none of them can offer a full description in her estimation.

The early stages of the rhetoric of economics movement thus focused on the discourse of economics as a discipline to uncover its distinctive tools of persuasion (Klamer, 1987). Highlighting the numerous methods of argumentation employed by economists, it aspired to open up intellectual spaces where questions of human import could once again be asked. This effort paralleled research trends of the 1980s in the history of science and rhetoric of inquiry movements (Lyne, 1985). It also reflected the ethical concerns of communication theorists who believe scholarship is always imbricated in the reality it seeks to describe (Krippendorff, 1989).

The field soon shifted to include the impact of language itself on the overall economy. A decade after the publication of her groundbreaking book, McCloskey, both independently and in collaboration with the Dutch economist Arjo Klamer, produced a comprehensive accounting of that portion of the GDP that might be linked to persuasive rhetoric (Klamer & McCloskey, 1995; McCloskey, 1994). Their analysis was not limited to the advertising, media, and public relations industries. It included occupational categories such as managers, lawyers, financial planners, educators, editors, publishers, and entrepreneurs. They argued for the importance to economics of understanding huge swaths of the economy as forums of "sweet talk"—a far cry from the rational equilibrium models of neoclassical economics.

McCloskey's work reflects the theoretical arc of the rhetoric of economics as it evolved from a fairly straightforward critical stance to recognition of its own embeddedness in economic phenomena. After demonstrating the use of rhetoric within the discipline and the relative importance of sweet talk (Klamer & McCloskey, 1995) in the economy, McCloskey has most recently shifted her focus to a study of how the economy itself contributes to the formation of cultural attitudes though the language use and communication practices that sustain it. This turn to a constitutive view of rhetoric makes the invisible hand of Adam Smith visible once more and by doing so provides a point of access for scholars seeking to understand the particular nature of today's global economy.

An implication of this work was that economics should not rely solely on the presumed existence of rational expectations or the supposed relevance of statistical models to build neutral objective models of economic activity (Ziliak & McCloskey, 2004, 2007). The revelation of their discipline's rhetorical nature makes it a bit more difficult for economists to avoid recognizing their own evaluative judgments, a point repeatedly made clear in Klamer's (1984) *Conversations with Economists*. Rhetoric has surfaced in the discipline of economics as a self-conscious element where it was once invisible and constrained by strict rules of narrow argumentative logic. The result is a growing recognition that the economy and rhetoric are paired enterprises, mutually involved in the creation and reflective understanding of patterned, highly motivated relational exchanges between people. McCloskey's (2006) more recent work argues that certain character traits, which she identifies as the seven bourgeois virtues, will typically accompany trade-based economies of exchange. These include prudence, temperance, justice, courage, love, hope, and faith. An overemphasis on prudence, in her view, has left mainstream economics without a full and complete picture of the human agent (McCloskey, 2008, p. x).

The introduction of rhetoric into economics extends the relevance of rhetoric in a world fractured by globalization, new technologies, and international free-flowing capital. From this perspective, neoclassical models do not always have the flexibility to deal with these present-day realities in line with which the orderly production of goods is secondary to the ephemeral consumption of meaning. The rhetorical perspective challenges the vision of the economy that concentrates on price points and prudence to the exclusion of all else. A related approach now on the horizon, cultural economics, calls for academic study of the intersections between an individual's economic activity, the subjective values and identity attached to it, and the social system in which it is enacted (see Du Gay & Pryke, 2002).

Researchers from diverse disciplines including anthropology, economics, and communication studies have been drawn to the empirical examination of how people rhetorically perform their economic identities within the abstract social body. In this framework, words and arguments are no longer the only focus; images and other visual paraphernalia are interrogated as well for their role in the representation of the economic. This picture of the economy appears less rational on the surface, but it may be more in tune with our individual and social selves. Just as neoclassical economics was sustained by the general equilibrium model, cultural economics or productive rhetoric will need to develop its own broad-based understanding of the general economy going forward.

In *Selling the Free Market: The Rhetoric of Economic Correctness* (2001), Aune suggests that rhetoric should explore the political potential of redefining itself as a social science. He argues that rhetoric must move past its heritage in the humanities if it is to deal adequately with the unique and novel persuasive characteristics of pervasive disembodied discourses such as economics. Detachment from the humanities would allow rhetoric to absorb elements of cultural studies that are currently neglected owing to the field's historic interest in the persuasive speech of discrete individuals. Instead of assailing the methodological and theoretical justifications of mainstream economics, Aune critiques the process that led to its widespread acceptance.

Economic correctness is Aune's (2001) term for the discursive expectations established by political forces seeking to naturalize their class base. It leads to the disempowering notion that there is only one politically correct way of speaking about the market and economic complex. Preferred meanings get established for concepts such as the free market, globalization, deregulation, and privatization that support political realities over economic ones. The conservative right, he argues, actively constructs and exploits a "sense of victimhood on the part of ordinary hard-working taxpayers" to stay in power (Aune, 2001, p. 91). Aune's approach would lead the rhetoric of economics to take a much different course from the one charted by McCloskey (1997) in her work on the bourgeois virtues. He criticizes McCloskey for restricting her analysis to problems of method while defending and even expanding the values of what he believes to be a maleficent capitalism. Rhetoric, for Aune, is a powerful tool and should be more usefully deployed in exposing the discursive sociopolitical dimensions of economic argument.

Aune is not alone in his efforts to push the boundaries of the rhetoric of economics. New scholarship reaches far beyond McCloskey's original project to examine the myriad productive influences that economics and rhetoric, and thus the manifold structures of survival and identity, have on each other. McCloskey herself has joined the trend, noting that she has been called "out of [her] comfortable 'criticism' of economics as an academic field and into the actual, daily, fruit-selling, labor-buying economy" (McCloskey, 2008, p. vii). Two important motifs recur regularly in the contemporary literature of rhetoric and economics, one of which moves toward a transdisciplinary mode of thinking while the other gravitates toward a recovery and critique of the dynamic subjectivism associated with the Austrian School.

The transdisciplinary aspect emphasized the human being as both the cause and effect of economic activity. The exchange of goods, in this view, is a symbolic conversation of needs

and desires forged in the first instance by the rhetorical processes of society and especially by its construction of the individual as consumer. It is characterized as a phenomenon that results from the interface with others and as a consequence cannot help but overlap with other rhetorical processes found throughout the discursive network. As the rhetoric of economics has evolved, rhetoric, too, must change to meet its new agendas. A promising focus, advocated by Brad Vivian (2004), is "rhetoric in the middle voice" (p. 81), about which he writes,

> In the most general terms, rhetoric in the middle voice connotes the formation and dissemination of meanings prior to individual intentions or utterances . . . Rhetoric in the middle voice connotes the capacity of discourse itself to engender and transform meanings and values, to lend priority to discursive difference, rather than to maintain an identity between speech governed by intention and the transcendent meanings or values it represents. Rhetoric in the middle voice cannot be suppressed or domesticated by appeals to essential truth, knowledge, virtue, or being. (p. 87)

A recent series of essays by emerging scholars shows how profitable the middle voice can be when applied to our contemporary economic landscape. Carter (2008) argues that it is imperative to develop "productive rhetoric" as a research orientation to keep rhetoric alive as an academic enterprise. He proposes that textual analysis should shift its focus toward productive and form-giving functions and away from its historical emphasis on critical and instrumental dimensions. A productive rhetoric, in his view, supplies knowledge of the context in which the economy and its salient processes have to function. The price discovery mechanism in markets, for example, depends on the kind of information that circulates and to whom it is made available. He notes,

> While such a mechanism is astounding, it does not work in a vacuum. Market participants rely on communication, persuasion,

argumentation, and information in order to arrive at a price point or an exchange point. Market players make use of as much information as is available in order to make decisions. Markets themselves create valuable information that, in turn, reveals aggregate price points for producers to consider as they decide whether or not to create more or less of what they make. Free markets rely on rhetoric to work. Rhetoric helps to define goods and services. It makes the persuasive case for value and conveys the ethos, pathos, and **logos** of market participants. (pp. 16)

Düppe (2008) and Gore (2008) extend this theme of productive rhetoric, with the former broadening its scope to include McCloskey's own rhetoric of conversational humanism and the latter tracing its route back to the origins of liberal thought. Economists, Düppe claims, use metaphors to make statements about the world. This fact alone creates a plurality of discourses that reveal the unavoidably human, and hermeneutic, nature of the discipline in his mind. It is increasingly difficult to separate economics from rhetoric as a result, which leads him to the conclusion that both fields should fall under the purview of a conversational humanism. Gore (2008), in his analysis of J. S. Mill's *System of Logic* and *Principles of Political Economy*, deftly shows how life and liberty, and politics, came to be separated from business despite the fact that they share strong commonalities. The contrast between the two works creates an opening for scholarship to explore. He observes,

> For all our social science, data mining, and fact checking we come, finally, to the reality of human minds engaged in processes of understanding and misunderstanding. Human beings in *this* world cannot escape rhetoric. Strong, sensible, and true general maxims often have subtle, weaker, but no less true counter maxims. Liberty includes the freedom to trade free from government intervention, but it also requires the enforcement of equality—especially in education. The key is finding a balance between general

maxims like freedom from government interference and counter-maxims like social and government intervention in education. An economy that achieves such a balance is one that serves human interest. Mill's liberalism respects the limits of life. It calls for an economic inquiry that acknowledges the full spectrum of humanity. Humility, like honesty, is the best policy in this regard for our scholarly endeavors since the business of living is, in its own way, as important as the art of life. (pp. 51–52)

Other essayists in the rhetoric of economists have chosen to spotlight firsthand accounts of how economics and rhetoric work together in practice. Fotros (2008) and Paulani (2008) offer their readers intriguing narratives of how social scientific disciplines such as economics are reinterpreted when they leave their academic home and enter the messy realities of global culture. Fotros and Paulani, for example, explore the ways economic methodology and philosophies come to involve themselves with the educational and government institutions, respectively, of Iran and Brazil. They provide intriguing accounts of how the disciplinary knowledge of economics migrates around the globe and comes to be translated or repurposed in its new contexts.

Active reinterpretation of economics can be derived from institutional features such as those associated with education or the judicial system. Baake (2008) reflects on his own activities, for example, as a writing teacher to consider the influence of words on social scientific efforts to provide objective descriptions of the world. His story is a moving account of how the writings of a single student named Shanna about economics sparked a series of internal dialogues on the power of rhetoric to define what it is we know. Balak and Lave (2008) take an epistemic approach to their understanding of the impact that the Chicago School's theory of antitrust had on the judicial review system overseeing corporate activity. They argue that the breakup of a purely rationalistic model for economic activity will eventually lead to a reevaluation of the entire antitrust system by the courts.

A few researchers have conducted extensive empirical studies that support McCloskey's claims and reach interesting conclusions regarding scholarship in economics. Three of them, Pessali and Fernandez (2008), Szmrecsanyi and Goldschmidt (2008), and Monasterio and Fernandez (2008), have recently provided quantitative data that illustrate the methodical use of narrative and other rhetorical strategies by economists. Pessali and Fernandez examine changes in the style of argumentation employed by the economist Oliver Williamson over the course of his career. They analyze citation data to support the claim that he changed his discourse style to reach receptive interdisciplinary audiences located outside mainstream economics. The empirical study conducted by Szmrecsanyi and Goldschmidt uses citation data drawn from academic journals to describe narrative elements favored by classical economic theory. They conclude that the rich variety of stories told within the sphere of economic discourse and the rhetorical aspects of their construction contradict the discipline's austere image of itself. In the same manner, Monasterio and Fernandez uncover the rhetorical processes that were responsible for the widespread success of Robert Putnam's book *Bowling Alone* (2000) and his concept of social capital.

Cyphert (2008) breaks new ground by investigating commercial behavior itself as a genre of productive rhetoric. The art and business of life, from her perspective, do not simply overlap as they do with Mill but actively produce one another in a creative fashion. She presents an emerging model wherein commerce is accompanied by many of the tenets familiar to rhetoric, including "product ethos," the "epistemology of pleasure," and "decency/decorum in exchange." Shilts (2008) explores similar relationships between rhetoric and corporate forms in a

historical study of company law in 19th-century Britain. He demonstrates the critical importance of rhetorical coherence to the establishment of the common sense needed for economies to operate effectively. It is an important insight supported by an extensive examination of the historical record leading to the development of limited liability.

Salvo (2008), Siry (2008), and Zuidhof (2008) explore the speculative formation of derivative markets that are made possible by the kind of rhetorical coherence advanced by Shilts. Salvo seeks to integrate rhetoric and economics by illustrating how much the two fields can accomplish if they work together. As a case in point, he examines the creation of sulfur dioxide (SO_2) markets in the late 1980s and the positive impact such trading had on the control of acid rain. Siry, too, focuses on carbon trading and the way that rhetoric can help economics address market failures. He believes rhetoric can redefine the meaning of externalities by bringing the ecological impact of pollution and other transboundary problems to the fore. Zuidhof deals with the consequences of such a theoretical move in his study of market metaphors at four prominent think tanks. He argues that economics and rhetoric have already merged in enough ways for the key question now to be to determine how economic rhetoric relates to other discourses such as those in politics. The market is a priori a political concept for the policy think tanks he examines.

Economic action and understanding take place within a larger framework of rhetorical motivation that does not always follow the ordered world of rational expectations. Emotions such as greed and fear are known, for example, to periodically roil the world's stock markets far beyond their hypothetical equilibrium points. Instead of letting such circumstances befuddle us as violations of neoclassical principles, we can turn to rhetoric for useful insights. The rhetoric of economics has opened the door to a productive understanding of cultural economics and is now confronted with a plethora of economic discourses struggling for attention. Rich dialogue can emerge only when the economic conversation is not limited to the strict rigidities of neoclassical economics or its critical naysayers. Deleuze & Guattari's (1987) *A Thousand Plateaus: Capitalism and Schizophrenia* achieved an element of this dialogic integration by capturing some of the possibilities inherent in an understanding of capitalism linked to identity formation.

In keeping with this post-structuralist approach, Klinger (2008) interrogates the growing reliance of rhetoric and economics on each other to perform their labor in the social system. His close reading of Alan Greenspan's rhetoric during his tenure as Chairman of the Federal Reserve (1987–2006) illustrates how much markets were influenced by his ethos and calculated presentation of self. Many observers, Klinger recalls, would make prognostications regarding the monetary policies of the Fed by parsing every word of Greenspan's public announcements or trying to gauge the thickness of his briefcase on the way to meetings. His analysis makes it abundantly clear that seemingly minute differences in the speech acts of Greenspan could cause huge swings in market valuations worldwide. The dramatism of Greenspan's public utterances made him the locus of attention within the larger macroeconomic narrative. His words became endowed with the metonymical function of providing direction to the markets.

The fact is we may all be the heroes of our economic dramas, albeit with less fanfare than that which accompanied Greenspan. Du Gay (1997) claims that hybrid work identities increasingly blur distinctions between production and consumption and are rhetorically managed to be consistent with abstract features of economic life. Adkins and Lury suggest, too, that the self-identity of workers has in fact become a "key resource" in the "mutual interdependence of the performance of identity and the performativity

of economies" (1999, p. 599). Not only does management try increasingly to intervene in the emotional lives of workers, but also workers seek to manage the impressions they generate by patching together identities through the stylization and citation of accommodating personality traits. As Salaman (1997) notes, identities are already actively managed by organizations under the rubric of *corporate culture* to promote the efficiency of the economic unit.

Psychic and social systems attach their own particular meanings to the commodified objects that suture them together. The double perspective on the object combines to unify the meaning of signs as monads, or "pleats of matter," in Deleuze's terms (1993). Direct communication between these perspectives is most prevalent during periods of radical social change when new couplings between the two systems—micro and macro—are being formed. Wallerstein (2000) describes three logistic waves, or *trends seculaire* (p. 207), in the history of capitalism according to the way in which primary commodities are exchanged and lifetimes traded. The first was based on agriculture, the second on industrialism, and the third on service and information. He believes each of the three stages reflects fundamental shifts in the social processing of human labor and rhetorical identification.

Mooers (2001) bemoans the loss of rationalism found in the third stage, contending,

> What is being suggested here is that with the ascendancy of finance capital, the ideological verities of an older form of capitalism have been scrambled and reconfigured. Notions of human beings as "rational self-seekers" whose actions result in broad social benefits have been overtaken by a conception which views human actions as essentially unpatterned, chaotic, and unregulated. In this context, rational forms of behavior make less sense; risk-taking or "purposive-nonrational action" becomes more common. (p. 70)

Each stage of the capitalist economy brings with it a corresponding expansion of risk and reward. Despite their seeming rationalism, all instruments for the management of risk soon come up against an unpredictable element that cannot be quantified. It is at this point of contingency that risk becomes an intimate article of faith for the social system. As a result, collectivities must engage subjectivities in an experimental dialogic conversation regarding their intimate consumptions and risk tolerance. These sumptuary exchanges result in distinctly postmodernist patterns of communication and social interaction that, in keeping with the progress of Wallerstein's tertiary stage, are speculative in nature. In place of its traditional focus on the achievement of adherence to established beliefs within the terms of *dissoi logoi*, the rhetoric accompanying this transition is dramatistic, experimental, and itself constitutive of the new realities that it seeks to describe (see Lyne, 1985; Shotter, 1993, for a complete discussion of constitutive rhetoric).

A strong conception of rhetoric makes it responsible for much more than the technical operations of persuasive appeal. It is also involved in the cultivation of expectations about the world and the containment of its contingencies. This understanding leads to a weightier critique that recognizes the complicity of rhetoric in the realities derived from its constructive faculties. In light of this expanded role for rhetoric, McCloskey (2001) recalls Hayek's Leibnizian discovery that the "division of persuasion" is as critical to the functioning of the economy as the division of labor. Instead of being ignorant of its persuasive modalities, economic activity makes full use of rhetoric to mine the capabilities of subjectivities. Increases in gross domestic product (GDP) have long been a function of productivity enhancements at the level of the individual worker and their subjectivity. The industrial revolution was accompanied by media campaigns, for example, that encouraged workers to combat their own "sloth and ignorance."

Following a "strong rhetoric of economics," one should be as interested in subjectivity as much as in methodology. One should be able to account for the formative structures of feeling that reproduce economic conditions from day to day. Since subjectivity is largely constructed over time through interactions with others, economic exchange can be considered a function of a larger set of self-other relations. Accordingly, economic relations should be evident in the cultural texts of the times.

In television shows such as *The Sopranos* and *Sex and the City,* HBO has recently produced what might be described as a new cycle of the Old English morality play designed to give shape to experimental subjectivities. These two shows in particular neatly divide the abstract social body into its productive and reproductive problematics. They can be read as an extended meditation on the proper and improper ways of consuming others and forming subjectivity given the civilizing constraints of city life.

The Sopranos provides an interesting case study for the examination of strong rhetoric in action. The protagonist, Tony Soprano, is an everyman figure who is driven to therapy by an overwhelming sense of dread regarding the economic changes affecting his mafia-related business enterprises. This program is emblematic of the modern subject's troubled search for self in an era of rapid economic change and uncertainty. It portrays a subject at his or her "boiling point," as Bataille (1967/1991; see also 1991/1993) defines this type of intense psychological zone (*ebullition*, p. 10). Tony's surname designates a similarly unsettled mental terrain since it is derived from the Italian *sopra,* meaning "over the top," and not from the term applied to a high female singing voice. In his role as a crime boss coming to terms with shifting economic conditions, he is desperate to quell his turpitude with the balm of an objective, and even religious, certitude.

Weber (1968) explains how the charisma of leaders can be used to resolve contradictions in a social system. Tony's description of himself in season four as the "sad clown, laughing on the outside and crying on the inside" sums up the sentiments of subjects trying to balance the demands of competing expectations. Psychological imbalance is also represented by the body's instability at critical junctures in the narrative. Tony labors under a social, and even transcendent, microscope. He is repeatedly felled by panic attacks that seemingly come from nowhere. By cultivating anxiety and staging contingent imbalances, the morality play artificially creates the conditions of its own becoming.

The marketing of cultural crisis as individual uncertainty dislocates identity and reverses the ideological direction of power in which "alimentary and sexual regimes" regulate "obligatory, necessary or permitted interminglings of bodies" (Deleuze & Guattari, 1987, p. 90). Bodies, in the morality play, are invested with the power to experimentally design their own productive and reproductive regimes. The responsibility and high level of scrutiny attached to these lifetime projects is the source of their generalized anxiety. In both premodern and postmodern contexts, morality plays have inundated popular culture with expressions of anxiety that eventually serve as a prelude to new transcendental justifications.

Morality plays are able to facilitate the development of this increasingly speculative system owing to their skilled manipulation of the sovereignty of the subject. In this respect, Tony Soprano can be thought of as a modern version of the figure of "Humanum Genus" in the medieval play *Everyman*. After being figuratively "born" into the social plethora of signs through the Lincoln Tunnel, his charge is to salvage the productive body metaphorically housed in a restaurant belonging to his friend Artie. The violent episodes found in the series can be thought of as sacrifices made to collective forms of economic calculation, which are then balanced and recalculated by his internal processes of conscience.

The portrayal of a universal hero engaged in an epistemological quest for certainty allows morality plays to create ideologies that follow Therborn's (1980) account of subjection as acceptance of representations of "what is, what is good, and what is possible" (p. 94). The anxiety of the subject in disposing its desires creates opportunities for power to design itself. As strange as it sounds, Tony becomes a priest of the everyday through his power to kill. He is an executioner of appearances. Like a Japanese samurai, or any "made man," he has the metaphysical authority to sacrifice others as objects to a collective ideal of silence.

Economic actors frequently behave in ways that are not rational precisely because entrepreneurial profit is so closely tied to the uncertainties of risk. Weber (1974) identified the "Protestant ethic" as the spirit of industrial capitalism because of its ability to rationalize wage labor in a bureaucratic economy. Bataille (2001), in contrast, sought to define an ethic of irrational secular theology, or "atheology," which could potentially adapt market theory to the excessive base materialism characteristic of other raw exchanges in human desire such as those that take shape as love or hate. As perspectives on the meaning of human labor, Weber's vision applies to a world of factories and large corporations, while Bataille's applies to a world of fledgling Internet companies and mafia turf battles. In the latter model, consumption of information and of each other in the way of "services" is the backbone of production itself, and its influence is felt far beyond the efficiency of "just-in-time" manufacturing.

Unlike other economic systems that wait too long for certainty or become overly dependent on their own traditions, capitalism innovates on itself by eagerly traversing the uncoded terrain from nostalgia to novelty. Its embrace of anxiety allows it to continually refresh itself in the nether regions of cultural unconscious and autopoietic self-observation. The culture it creates is not based on the inertia of a mythical past but rather the containment of contingency across random futures. Morality plays, by cultivating anxiety, are the key ingredient of a rhetorical apparatus aimed at the reification of premonition instead of tradition. Modern capitalism, with its derivatives and forward contracts, is periodically refreshed by texts such as *The Sopranos* that convey new ways of interacting with the abstract economic body.

The strength of a speculative capitalism is found in the advantages generated by the early recognition of adaptive beliefs before they are discovered or verified by other epistemological strategies. Why else would anxiety, as a nonrational matching engine, be used to create a unified subject? Is premonition—a faith in and for the future—the crucial feature of modernism's success at muscling out competing cultural stances? The problematic of the productive body found in *The Sopranos* can thus be considered as an allegorical aporia to be discussed ad infinitum without resolution. Its true purpose is to generate the movement of thought by which the capitalist social system maintains itself and fends off its rivals.

Staying true to its genre, the modern morality play places faith over reason by transforming Tony's conscience into beliefs about the future. Anxiety and uncertainty regarding the future of the capitalist world-system explains the resurgence of faith all over the world as cultures battle for continued memetic presence. Western culture has not escaped this whirlwind; on the contrary, it has intensified faith through the radical twist of mandating belief in the future instead of the past. The rhetoric described in this chapter illustrates how the deepest aspects of the soul are now regularly machined and retooled to meet new challenges that lie ahead rather than old ones left behind. Secular faith makes productive use of contingency to solve the contradictions of capitalism and meet the temporal mandates of premonition. The cultural cycle of innovation is rapid and

complete once the meaning of life itself becomes subject to the manufacturing process.

The interdisciplinary study of rhetoric and economics addresses persistent questions regarding the general purpose of communication processes. It responds to the challenge of "rethinking communication systems as unevenly organized and structurally dispersed cybernetic minds—dialogic networks—of corporeal bodies producing subjects as embodiments of cultural-political instabilities and identities" (Hawes, 1999, p. 256). Rhetoric in capitalism is conceived as a way of encountering the challenges of unknown futures when the precedent of tradition fails. Thus capitalism excels at the symbolic containment of chance, which Bataille calls the "last demon" (1954/1988, p. 172). Its rationality is a guise maintained by the fact that its beliefs are contractually assigned to the future instead of the past. Power, in such a world, resides in the rhetorical "art" of defining contingency (Pottage, 1998).

I have outlined the early features of rhetoric's critique of economics and explored their evolving relationship as two parallel theories of exchange. The recent resurgence of interest in the rhetoric of economics derives in large part from the growing overlap between the two fields in academia and in everyday life. Information, a shorthand description for the rhetorical flow of meaning in society, is now widely recognized as a key resource in capitalism, on par with land, capital, and labor. Appadurai's (1986) edited book on the social life of commodities was prescient for its use of conceptual distinctions such as *mediascape* and *technoscape* in an attempt to break down the barriers between rhetoric and things. "Commodities," he wrote, "are things with a particular type of social potential" (p. 6). McGee and Lyne (1987), writing from a rhetorical perspective around the same time, also recommend a closer scholarly engagement between human sciences such as rhetoric and the more material concerns found in the social sciences. They conclude,

In sum, rhetoric must operate in the context of pervasive power structures, normative commitments, and practical needs; and the rhetoric of the human sciences should take note of that as its starting point. The problem is not finding with Michel Foucault that power/knowledge is a unity, and hoping that unmasking this connection is a liberation from power and passion. Rather, the human sciences should be seeking ways of managing the inevitable integration of power/knowledge within discourses that give life direction. This is what it must mean to treat knowledge claims rhetorically, if rhetoric is not to slide into sophistry, on the one hand, or become a new mode of academic self-perpetuation on the other. (p. 400)

The transdisciplinary perspectives of emerging scholars are bringing fresh voices to the economic conversation and elaborating the collaborative involvement of rhetoric in economic processes. New markets like carbon-trading credits have to be defined and perceived as valuable before they can be traded (Salvo, 2008). Rhetoric is productive of economics in a multitude of ways. Yet economic activity can also be considered a persuasive force in its own right on the rhetorical landscapes of psychic and social systems. McCloskey's (2006) comprehensive examination of the bourgeois virtues and their origin in the mercantile economy is a case in point. In sympathy with this general approach, I have tried to show how the rhetorical play of messages in *The Sopranos* derives from the need of contemporary capitalism to cultivate anxiety among its constituents if it is to continue to grow and find new markets.

It is too soon to determine whether the rhetoric of economics will have its desired impact on mainstream economics. Measuring its success in this way may be too linear an approach. Perhaps the field is destined to develop more autonomously or in closer coordination with rhetorical studies. Its greatest impact may even be in disparate fields as the POROI program seems to indicate (Aune, 2001, p. 173). There are certainly areas where the leading approaches to the rhetoric of economics feel incomplete, which should be expected from such a fledgling interdisciplinary field of study. Does the emphasis on capitalist values, for instance, gloss over political realities? How will it resolve the inner tension between analytic and normative approaches to its subject matter? Will it incorporate cultural studies and its accompanying metanarratives of identity, discourse, and power?

The uncertainties behind these questions add an element of zest to the entire project. There is plenty of rich unexplored material for rhetoricians in an era of globalization and extreme capitalism. The market news in early 2008 is filled with reports of the worst housing crisis in decades, a result of "subprime" lending and the repackaging of mortgages into "jumbo collateralized debt obligations." Complex financial concepts such as that of moral hazard suddenly seem to be on everyone's lips as the whole world tries to come to grips with the consequences of substantial write-downs in the value of economic assets and plunging stock markets worldwide. The economy sometimes feels as if it is less concerned with the efficient production and distribution of goods than it is with the early discovery of the next asset or credit bubble.

Within this tumultuous context, rhetoric usefully recasts the economic sphere as a representational space where human contact and transformation occurs. Life, so to speak, is another way of making marks on a page. Economics and rhetoric share a common concern for how those marks are made and distributed in competitive landscapes of meaning. The rhetoric of economics provides insight into the ways economic logic relates to context at both the abstract and individual levels. It reveals a world of exchange based on the establishment and circulation of rhetorical preferences rather than purely rational ones. The distance, in sum, between the rough-and-tumble marketplace and the comfortable home of our subjectivity may be shorter and more thoroughly rhetorical than we currently realize.

REFERENCES

Adkins, L., & Lury, C. (1999). The labor of identity: Performing identities, performing economies. *Economy and Society, 28*(4), 598–614.

Amariglio, J., Cullenberg, S., & Ruccio, D. F. (Eds.). (2001). *Post-Modernism, economics, and knowledge.* New York: Routledge.

Appadurai, A. (1986). *The social life of things: Commodities in cultural perspective.* Cambridge, UK: Cambridge University Press.

Arrow, K., & Debreau, G. (1954). Existence of a competitive equilibrium for a competitive economy. *Econometrica, 22*(3), 265–290.

Aune, J. (1994). *Rhetoric and Marxism.* Boulder, CO: Westview Press.

Aune, J. (2001). *Selling the free market: The rhetoric of economic correctness.* New York: Guilford Press.

Baake, K. (2008). Teaching rhetoric with economics: A canon of eloquence, truth, lies, or all of the above? In E. Clift (Ed.), *How language is used to do business: Essays on the rhetoric of economics* (pp. 113–138). New York: Edwin Mellen Press.

Balak, B., & Lave, J. (2008). The Devil and the Angel whispering in the spouse's ear: Protecting the sanctity of the marriage between antitrust and economics. In E. Clift (Ed.), *How language is used to do business: Essays on the rhetoric of economics* (pp. 267–330). New York: Edwin Mellen Press.

Bataille, G. (1988). *Inner experience.* Albany, NY: State University of New York Press. (Original work published 1954)

Bataille, G. (1991). *The accursed share: An essay on general economy: Vol. 1. Consumption.* New York: Zone Books. (Original work published 1967)

Bataille, G. (1993). *The accursed share* (Vols. 2 and 3; R. Hurley, Trans.). New York: Zone Books. (Original work published 1991)

Bataille, G. (2001). *The unfinished system of non-knowledge.* Minneapolis: University of Minnesota Press

Booth, W. (1974). *Modern dogma and the rhetoric of assent.* Chicago: University of Chicago Press.

Burke, K. (1984). *Permanence and change: An anatomy of purpose* (3rd ed.). Berkeley: University of California Press. (Original work published 1954)

Carter, L. (2008). Rhetoric, markets, and value creation. In E. Clift (Ed.), *How language is used to do business: Essays on the rhetoric of economics* (pp. 7–34). New York: Edwin Mellen Press.

Cyphert, D. (2008). The rhetoricity of enterprise. In E. Clift (Ed.), *How language is used to do business: Essays on the rhetoric of economics* (pp. 209–226). New York: Edwin Mellen Press.

Deleuze, G. (1993). *The fold: Liebniz and the Baroque* (T. Conley, Trans.). Minneapolis: University of Minnesota Press.

Deleuze, G., & Guattari, F. (1987). *A thousand plateaus: Capitalism and schizophrenia* (B. Massumi, Trans.). Minneapolis: University of Minnesota.

Du Gay, P. (1997). Organizing identity: Making up people at work. In P. Du Gay (Ed.), *Production of culture/Cultures of production* (pp. 285–322). Thousand Oaks, CA: Sage.

Du Gay, P., & Pryke, M. (Eds.). (2002). *Cultural economy.* Thousand Oaks, CA: Sage.

Düppe, T. (2008). The meaning-surplus of rhetoric and hermeneutics: Metaphor and humanism in economics. In E. Clift (Ed.), *How language is used to do business: Essays on the rhetoric of economics* (pp. 53–86). New York: Edwin Mellen Press.

Fotros, M. (2008). The state of economic methodology in the education of economics in Iran. In E. Clift (Ed.), *How language is used to do business: Essays on the rhetoric of economics* (pp. 87–90). New York: Edwin Mellen Press.

Gore, D. (2008). J. S. Mill's Art and Business of Life and the humility of bona fide scholarship. In E. Clift (Ed.), *How language is used to do business: Essays on the rhetoric of economics* (pp. 35–52). New York: Edwin Mellen Press.

Hawes, L. C. (1999). The dialogics of conversation: Power, control, vulnerability. *Communication Theory, 9*(3), 229–264.

Hayek, F. A. (1980). *Individualism and economic order.* Chicago: University of Chicago Press. (Original work published 1948)

Klamer, A. (1984). *Conversations with economists.* Lanham, MD: Rowman & Littlefield.

Klamer, A. (1987). As if economists and their subjects were rational. In J. S. Nelson, A. Megill, & D. N. McCloskey (Eds.), *The rhetoric of the human sciences: Language and argument in scholarship and public affairs* (pp. 163–183). Madison: University of Wisconsin Press.

Klamer, A., & McCloskey, D. (1995, May). One quarter of GDP is persuasion. *American Economic Review, 85*(2), 191–195.

Klinger, G. (2008). Money talks: Alan Greenspan and the voice of capital. In E. Clift (Ed.), *How language is used to do business: Essays on the rhetoric of economics* (pp. 407–434). New York: Edwin Mellen Press.

Krippendorff, K. (1989). On the ethics of constructing communication. In B. Dervin, L. Grossberg, B. J. O'Keefe, & E. Wartella (Eds.), *Rethinking communication: Paradigm issues, I* (pp. 66–96). Newbury Park, CA: Sage.

Lyne, J. (1985). Rhetorics of inquiry. *Quarterly Journal of Speech, 71*, 65–73.

McCloskey, D. (1986, Fall). The rhetoric of economics. *Social Science, 71*(97), 102.

McCloskey, D. (1990). *If you're so smart: The narrative of economic expertise.* Chicago: University of Chicago Press.

McCloskey, D. (1994). *Knowledge and persuasion in economics.* Cambridge, UK: Cambridge University Press.

McCloskey, D. (1997). The vices of economists; the virtues of the bourgeoisie. Ann Arbor: University of Michigan Press.

McCloskey, D. (1998). *The rhetoric of economics* (2nd ed.). Madison: University of Wisconsin Press.

McCloskey, D. (2000). *Knowledge and persuasion in economics.* Cambridge, UK: Cambridge University Press. (Original work published 1994)

McCloskey, D. (2001). Persuade and be free: A new road to Friedrich Hayek [Review of the book *Friedrich Hayek* by A. Ebenstein]. *Reason Online.* Retrieved January 18, 2008, from www.reason.com

McCloskey, D. (2006). *The bourgeois virtues: Ethics for an age of commerce.* Chicago: University of Chicago Press.

McCloskey, D. (2008). How to buy, sell, make, manage, produce, transact, consume with words. In E. Clift (Ed.), *How language is used to do business: Essays on the rhetoric of economics* (pp. v–xxxix). New York: Edwin Mellen Press.

McGee, M. C., & Lyne, J. R. (1987). What are nice folks like you doing in a place like this? Some entailments of treating knowledge claims rhetorically. In J. S. Nelson, A. Megill, & D. N. McCloskey (Eds.). *The rhetoric of the human sciences: Language and argument in scholar-*

ship and public affairs (pp. 381–406). Madison: University of Wisconsin Press.

Mooers, C. (Autumn, 2001). The new fetishism: Citizenship and finance capital. *Studies in Political Economy, 66*, 59–84.

Monasterio, L., & Fernandez, R. (2008). Making rhetoric work: An analysis of the work of Robert Putnam. In E. Clift (Ed.), *How language is used to do business: Essays on the rhetoric of economics* (pp. 187–208). New York: Edwin Mellen Press.

Nelson, J. S., Megill, A., & McCloskey, D. N. (1987). Rhetoric of inquiry. In J. S. Nelson, A. Megill, & D. N. McCloskey (Eds.). *The rhetoric of the human sciences: Language and argument in scholarship and public affairs* (pp. 3–18). Madison: University of Wisconsin Press.

Paulani, L. (2008). Neoliberalism and rhetoric: The Brazilian chapter. In E. Clift (Ed.), *How language is used to do business: Essays on the rhetoric of economics* (pp. 91–112). New York: Edwin Mellen Press.

Perelman, C. (1982). *The realm of rhetoric.* Notre Dame, IN: University of Notre Dame Press.

Pessali, H., & Fernandez, R. (2008). Negotiating transaction cost economics: Oliver Williamson and his audiences. In E. Clift (Ed.), *How language is used to do business: Essays on the rhetoric of economics* (pp. 139–166). New York: Edwin Mellen Press.

Pottage, A. (1998). Power as an art of contingency: Luhmann, Deleuze, Foucault. *Economy and Society, 27*(1), 1–27.

Putnam, R. (2000). *Bowling alone: The collapse and revival of American community.* New York: Simon & Schuster.

Rothbard, M. N. (1989). The hermeneutical invasion of philosophy and economics. *Review of Austrian Economics, 3*, 45–59.

Salaman, G. (1997). Culturing production. In P. Du Gay (Ed.), *Production of culture/Cultures of production* (pp. 232–275). Thousand Oaks, CA: Sage.

Salvo, M. (2008). Inventing markets: Limits of construction, limits of fact. In E. Clift (Ed.), *How language is used to do business: Essays on the rhetoric of economics* (pp. 331–340). New York: Edwin Mellen Press.

Samuelson, P. A. (1947). *The foundations of economic analysis.* Cambridge, UK: Harvard University Press.

Scott, R. L. (1967). On viewing rhetoric as epistemic. *Central States Speech Journal, 18*, 9–17.

Shackle, G. (1992). *Epistemics and economics: A critique of economic doctrines*. Edison, NJ: Transaction Books. (Original work published 1972)

Sherman, S. (1996). *Finance and fictionality in early eighteenth century accounting*. Cambridge, UK: Cambridge University Press.

Shilts, W. (2008). Making McCloskey's rhetoric empirical: Company law and tragedies of the commons in nineteenth-century Britain. In E. Clift (Ed.), *How language is used to do business: Essays on the rhetoric of economics* (pp. 227–266). New York: Edwin Mellen Press.

Shotter, J. (1993). *Conversational realities: Constructing life through language*. London: Sage.

Siry, J. (2008). Economic externalities and ecologies: Opportunities to solve market failures that cause air pollution. In E. Clift (Ed.), *How language is used to do business: Essays on the rhetoric of economics* (pp. 341–348). New York: Edwin Mellen Press.

Szmrecsanyi, B., & Goldschmidt, N. (2008). The cameelious hump and 'just-so stories' in economic literature—A linguistic analysis. In E. Clift (Ed.), *How language is used to do business: Essays on the rhetoric of economics* (pp. 167–186). New York: Edwin Mellen Press.

Therborn, G. (1980). *The ideology of power and the power of ideology*. London: NLB.

Vivian, B. (2004). *Being made strange: Rhetoric beyond representation*. Albany: State University of New York Press.

Wallerstein, I. (2000). *The essential Wallerstein*. New York: New Press.

Weber, M. (1968). *On charisma and institution building* (S. Eisenstadt, Ed.). Chicago: Chicago University Press.

Weber, M. (1974). *The Protestant ethic and the spirit of capitalism*. London: Allen & Unwin.

Woolley, F. R. (1998). The feminist challenge to neoclassical economics. In D. L. Prychitko (Ed.), *Why economists disagree: An introduction to the alternative schools of thought* (pp. 309–332). Albany: State University of New York Press.

Ziliak, S. T. (2002, September). Haiku economics, No. 1. *Rethinking Marxism: A Journal of Economics, Culture, and Society, 14*(3), 111–112.

Ziliak, S. T., & McCloskey, D. (2004). Size matters: The standard error of regressions in the *American Economic Review. Journal of Socio-Economics, 33*(5), 528–554.

Ziliak, S. T., & McCloskey, D. (2007). *The cult of statistical significance: How the standard error is costing jobs, justice, and lives*. Ann Arbor: University of Michigan Press.

Zuidhof, P.-W. (2008). The market as metaphor: Four stories of the market at U.S. policy think tanks. In E. Clift (Ed.), *How language is used to do business: Essays on the rhetoric of economics* (pp. 349–406). New York: Edwin Mellen Press.

12

Rhetoric in Literary Criticism and Theory

DON BIALOSTOSKY

I remember the day in 1972 or 1973 when the young man with an M.A. from Yale presented his deconstructive reading in Wayne Booth's seminar in rhetorical criticism at the University of Chicago. Although we seminar members were disciplined in pluralism and in understanding before what Booth came to call "overstanding," our aggressive incredulity was palpable. In what sense was this rhetorical criticism at all? How could a rhetorical criticism, in which we had learned to read for implied authors guiding our decisions about characters, issue in indecision, with authors out of play and language working its inevitable aporetic effects? What was this stuff, and where did it come from? We roughed him up pretty badly, but little did we realize how thoroughly his school would take its revenge on us. We would find ourselves dated, marginalized, left behind nearly as completely as our Chicago School Aristotelian predecessors had been outflanked and obscured by the deconstructionists' New Critical forebears. This time, though, instead of winning poetry and poetics, they would carry off rhetoric. Like our Chicago forebears, most of us would remain convinced that we were right, but that would not stop the world from passing us by and adopting the radically simplified, easily reproduced, language-centered, impersonal and sublime rhetoric deconstruction would offer. We had our day in that seminar, but we were going to be had. Almost. If the winners always get to tell the history, and I'm presenting myself as one of the losers, how is it that I am getting the floor in this handbook to tell it as I see it? How did one of the losers get authorized to say where rhetoric in literary criticism and theory are today, how they got here, and where they might go from here? Perhaps it is simply because the editors of this section are not in the field of literary criticism and theory and knew me from interdisciplinary rhetorical organizations where, if I were to be uncharitable to them and myself, the losers of disciplinary battles gather to lick their wounds and reassure one another that all is not lost. Perhaps, though, I have exaggerated both the victory of deconstruction and the defeat of my Chicago School. Everyone knows that deconstruction suffered a severe setback with the scandals surrounding the revelation of Paul de Man's wartime journalism, although its principal practitioners have survived that defeat and continue to invest de Man's legacy. And we know that "theory," which was for many in the 1970s and 1980s the same as deconstruction, which was for many the same as rhetoric, is now talked about in the past tense, having been at least twice supplanted by New Historicism and Cultural Studies, though it is still widely discussed and taught.

It is less widely known but still discoverable that some Chicago-trained rhetorical critics, most notably James Phelan (1981, 1996, 2005) and Peter Rabinowitz (1987) and Phelan and Rabinowitz (1994, 2005), fled the center of "theory" thus understood to take over narrative theory from the flagging structuralist narratologists, while others (actually maybe just one of us—myself) engaged deconstructive rhetorical criticism on its flank, where it had appropriated Wordsworth's poetry, and simultaneously tried to outflank it by assimilating what had been Chicago School rhetorical interests into Bakhtinian dialogic terms—a move with which some of my Chicago colleagues, including David Richter (1986, 1990) and Booth himself, also flirted but did not finally make. The rule of deconstruction was never so complete that it shut out all opportunities to practice rhetorical theory and criticism of other kinds; it never dominated all the journals, presses, and hiring committees in a field where dominant critical fashions in a few key institutional sites change much more rapidly than faculty, curricula, editors, and readers across the field as a whole. So I'm here to tell the tale more than 30 years into a career professing rhetoric in literary

theory and criticism (and in composition) and aware that the graduate student I helped assault in that seminar represented something more powerful than any of us then knew but not something so powerful that its later revenge was the end of me.

In terms of the well-known opposition that de Man (1979) posited between trope and persuasion, deconstruction concerned itself with the former and Chicago with the latter, and both could easily dismiss what the other school was doing as not rhetorical criticism at all. The rhetoric of trope treated rhetoric as that figurative capacity of language that produces undecidable possible meanings that cannot be reduced to grammatical univocality or determined one way or another without violence; the rhetoric of persuasion treated it as a transaction between language user and receiver, implied author or narrator, and implied reader or reader, usually concerned to affect the latter's epideictic evaluation of characters, subordinated, in good Aristotelian terms, to their poetic function in plots.

The deconstructive critics drew on what Genette (1982) called a restrained rhetoric, derived from the French tradition of Fontanier and grounded in a few passages of Nietzsche's, outside his lectures on rhetoric, that concentrated on tropes and figures. In these terms, they could find persuasion irrelevant to rhetoric and see rhetoric in all language. The Chicago critics never talked about tropes and figures as such (it was a topic Aristotle's rhetoric didn't explicitly broach), though it has recently become clear that the "authorial intrusions" Booth (1961, 1983) sought to justify were, as Fahnestock (1999) has suggested, figures of thought. The first edition of *The Rhetoric of Fiction* calls attention to these figures without ever naming them or identifying their provenance in Quintilian (the second edition makes a blanket gesture in his direction). Booth (1974) recognizes that provenance for the trope/figure irony to which he devoted a whole book in the hope of stabilizing the vertiginous irony of deconstructive reading, but deconstructive readers limited themselves to what Quintilian recognized as irony as a way of life, or at least a way of reading, without returning to classical sources or taking an interest in any of the trope/figure's more limited uses.

Both schools drew selectively from rhetorical theory to develop reading practices that offer distinctive satisfactions to those who participate in them, and as pedagogies of reading they are likely to continue. Chicago readers can account for how they are affected by representations of characters and actions in narrative; deconstructive readers can be impressed by the sublime workings of language that their readings reveal. But like New Criticism, in relation to which both these projects in different ways developed, both schools generate readings that exemplify their practices and produce arguments that elaborate and justify them, but neither could be said to foster a research program. Chicago inquirers have already constructed more and more finely distinguished accounts of narrators, authors, implied authors, and readers, and though there are more books to read closely in these terms, there are not new problems to be addressed by those readings. Deconstructive readings will continue to appeal to those who find the allegories they generate compelling, but, like all allegorical readings, they have their interest only for the sect or church that is pleased to find its beliefs repeatedly confirmed by making unlikely texts turn out to bespeak already expected allegorical results; such readings have little appeal to nonbelievers.

Looking back on both these projects as in some sense finished, I see them both as rhetorical in a stipulative sense, not in a traditional or a fully theorized one. Let rhetoric be those "figural" features of language that trouble univocality or let rhetoric be those features of narratives that orient readers to the moral qualities of characters relevant to their

fulfilling their roles in plots, and we will generate these kinds of rhetorical criticism. There is little point in quarreling with such stipulations as such, for they simply underwrite projects and direct attention to the features they have named. The appropriation of the term *rhetorical* by both schools sets them in apparent conflict with one another, but they were good examples of the pluralist alternatives the Chicago School sometimes tried to treat as equally valid alternatives. The two critical modes consciously and deliberately defined their key term differently and so did different work with it. The deconstructionists may have been wiser on this point than their Chicago counterparts, for the latter felt compelled to argue with actual or hypothetical versions of deconstructive rhetorical criticism, but the deconstructionists just ignored them and went on thinking the way they had set out to do. It was their confident monism that kept provoking the Chicago critics, who would have let them alone to play out the implications of their definition if they had just been pluralistically willing to admit it was one definition among many.

The term *rhetorical* is not, however, a neologism that is simply available for any school to define as it pleases; it is, and was when these schools appropriated it, already a word in wide circulation with a long history, various authoritative instantiations, and quite a few current institutional claimants. It is not surprising that some of those claimants were indignant at what seemed to them to be misappropriations of a term of which they had some claim to ownership and understanding. Brian Vickers (1988), for example, waxed wroth at De Man's claim to the term (and ignored the Chicago School's work altogether even with a whole chapter on rhetoric and the modern novel, the sad fate of the losing side). His *In Defence of Rhetoric* limns what could be a fruitful line of inquiry that links the rhetorical practices of authors with what they learned in their rhetorical educations—a correlation that brings us down as far as James Joyce and Randall Jarrell and applies with equal or greater aptness to writers of the Renaissance and the 18th century (and, as I have helped show, to the Romantics, who are somehow supposed to have left this education behind) and touches, too, on the writing of colonized people who were subjected to rhetorical training in their Western educations. It would be a project that turned away from the opposition between historical knowledge and criticism that has been with us since the New Critics (and is still with us in the Chicago and deconstructive projects) and instead historicized critical appreciation in part through the teaching of how past writers learned to write and read by studying rhetorical treatises and exemplars.

Vickers (1988) revives the lore of the figures not as a generalized troping undistinguished from a generalized figurality but as a historically catalogued repertoire of numerous figures of speech and thought as well as tropes distinct from them that writers learned to use to a variety of salient effects. He goes a considerable way to meet the call Jonathan Arac (1987) issued in *Critical Genealogies* to "repluralize the figures"—a call that recalled the philological knowledge that Auerbach (2003) and Curtius and some of their followers brought to their criticism (see Curtius & Trask, 1990). But in his zeal to show the deniers of rhetoric how much it has to bring to the critical task, Vickers (1988) falls into the scholarly habits that have made the task of recovering the rhetorical tradition as a live working tradition a difficult one. He cites too many variations in too many classical and modern sources of definitions of the figures, names too many figures in their Greek and Latin variants, and illustrates their presence in too many works, none of which he reads to the level of a serious contribution to its criticism. He leaves his readers—few of whom would have considered themselves critics or theorists anyway, for he is mainly preaching to the

rhetorical choir—with the impression that defensive pedantry rather than functional criticism can issue from recovery of the resources that the rhetorical tradition supplied to the writers we have subsequently separated into the literary tradition.

Here, it seems to me, there is still room for a significant project of historical and theoretical inquiry into rhetorical criticism and for a rhetorical inquiry, too, into how best to make the fruits of that project widely recognized and used. What Vickers (1988) has somewhat hastily and polemically adumbrated is a potentially rich and relatively underexplored area of investigation. It has not yet been pursued widely as a shared project, in part at least because rhetoric as a field of inquiry has been twice separated from literary criticism in the United States—once through the formation of speech departments that abandoned literature departments to focus on the art in its civic, political manifestations and again by the appropriation of rhetoric to composition studies within English departments, where the focus on production rather than reception has often exploited rhetoric for only half its potential. Literary criticism has been othered in both these appropriations of rhetoric, just as rhetoric has been removed from and othered in the literary part of English studies, while literary study itself has to some degree recently been superseded by cultural inquiries, some of which bring back civic rhetorics close to those used in departments of communication. This institutional history has meant that a full-scale inquiry into the rhetorical underpinnings of what only recently has been fractioned off as "literature" has not yet been undertaken, even though most writers marked as "literary" in all but the last century or so were schooled in rhetoric and saw what we take as their literary work within a rhetorical frame of reference. There have been specialized studies of particular writers and particular periods—especially the medieval and early modern (e.g., Armstrong, 2006; Miriam, 1947, 1962;

Payne, 1963; Tuve, 1947)—in relation to their rhetorical educations, and there have been gestures toward writers in other periods (e.g., Bialostosky, 1992; Bialostosky & Needham, 1995), but the problem of learning to read earlier literary writers with critical terms and expectations informed by the rhetorical habits and understandings they wrote with has not been comprehensively addressed or recognized as a theoretical resource across the boundaries of literary periods. Neither has the question of whether or how rhetorical criticism informed by the long tradition of rhetorical theory and rhetorical writing might transfer to those writing and reading in the wake of that tradition (but see Bender & Wellbery, 1990).

To address this unfinished business, let me raise some of the questions that might be fruitful to ask, mention some of the recent work that might be called on to help answer them, and note some of the cautions that might be observed in addressing them.

What difference does it make to literary criticism that most of the writers for most of the Western literary tradition were schooled, directly or indirectly, in rhetoric and wrote what we have come to call literary texts in a context of rhetorical ends and rhetorical resources? What aspects of their work should we look to as evidence of their learning of rhetoric, and given that they learned it, what kinds of appreciation of their work would our recognition of it enable? It is not enough to point to their use of tropes and figures or their conformity to a pattern of arrangement to say, yes, indeed, they were rhetorically trained and rhetoric is therefore important. What otherwise anomalous features could we account for by recognizing their rhetorical provenance? What points could we take, what turns could we follow, what discoveries could we make about what they expected their readers to know and value that we might otherwise have missed? What can we learn about rhetoric when we find it poetically embodied, and what

do we make of poetry, and literature more generally, when we recognize it as an embodiment of rhetoric?

What difference does it make if we understand the rhetorical tradition itself, as Jeffrey Walker (2000) teaches us to do, as more fundamentally literary than its earlier historians have taken it to be? A literary scholar writing the history of rhetoric, Walker has found epideictic rhetoric, which has closest affinities with poetic utterance, more fundamental and continuous in the history of rhetoric than the deliberative rhetoric that has been the center of the art for historians concerned with its civic praxis. Starting from Walker's history, rhetoricians with literary-critical interests need not see themselves poaching on poetic territory owned by others but can boldly venture into a province of rhetoric where poetic works are and always have been and where much rhetoric has much in common with those works. How might this epideictic provenance orient the reading of literature?

How much common ground is there among the rhetorical training writers through the ages received, and where is that common ground best represented? What parts of that training, what terms and distinctions and notions of their use were most consequential in shaping writing over time? How could those parts be most fruitfully represented and acquired in contemporary criticism as a repertoire of critical terms and expectations? These are crucial questions if the history of rhetoric is to become a functional resource for rhetorical criticism of literature. Though the place and shape of rhetoric have varied significantly through time, though different rhetorical treatises shaped to different purposes have been available to writers at different times, though rhetorical terms have been variously defined, is it possible to construct a nontrivial (or perhaps we might better call it "posttrivial") version of rhetorical functions and participants, patterns and moves, that could serve contemporary readers as a rhetorical toolkit for reading literary works across time? Such a toolkit would not have tools to fit every particular work, shaped as they were under various versions of rhetoric. It can't have so many varied tools that one doesn't know where to look for one that fits the case, nor can the toolkit be reduced to a one-size-fits-all tool that lacks the capacity to discriminate interesting functional features across a sufficient range. The art of rhetoric itself has considerable experience in organizing itself within parameters such as this, sorting topics and figures and argumentative patterns to address the likely situations to which orators using them might be called, but scholarship on the art has tended to accumulate variants, multiply entities, and lose touch with functional delimiters. It may be helpful to think of the rhetorical critic of literature we are arming as a rhetorician who draws from the history of rhetoric rather than as a scholar of that history; then we can set out to shape an account of the commonplaces of rhetorical criticism to that rhetorician-critic's task of discriminating and appreciating a wide array of literary works.

How can we name, define, and mobilize the resources of the rhetorical tradition—not just tropes and figures but also other stylistic distinctions and other kinds of distinctions, including topics, modes of argument, patterns of arrangement, issues of delivery in written texts—for the use of contemporary literary critics and students of literature? Perhaps the best example we have of a successful attempt to do this—concerned, however, not with literary criticism but with critical-rhetorical appreciation of scientific argument—is Jeanne Fahnestock's *Rhetorical Figures in Science* (1999). Fahnestock's introduction provides a thoughtfully reduced history of rhetoric aimed at deriving some functional definitions of figures that can be of service in appreciating their use in both the invention and the presentation of scientific arguments. She reviews traditional definitions of tropes and figures and related enthymemes (though not all of

them) and criticizes them with an eye to clarifying the features they can discriminate in use. She suggests alternative ways of thinking about the troubling and interesting category of figures of thought and offers analogs from contemporary speech-act theory and pragmatic linguistics for thinking about them. She delimits a subset of figures appropriate for her critical task and devotes the remainder of her book to examining their working in specific writers and writings. Although she goes further into the history of rhetoric than she needs to for the purposes of her work in rhetoric of science, she treats the extra history she provides in a way that makes it functionally available for other rhetoricians of science and even for rhetorical critics of other genres. My own mobilization of traditional distinctions concerning arrangement and figures of thought to address some anomalies in the interpretation of Wordsworth's *Prelude* moves in a parallel direction, governed by similar critical rather than historical priorities (Bialostosky, 1992).

Are there contemporary vocabularies available in other inquiries into language and argument that offer ways not only to redescribe but also to rethink these rhetorical resources? Fahnestock's (1999) brief considerations of the vocabularies of speech-act theory and pragmatics open lines of inquiry that might issue in fruitful redescriptions, even reconceptualizations, of traditional rhetorical terms and distinctions in contemporary theoretical vocabularies. In evaluating these vocabularies, we need to be careful, as we have already been with historical scholarship, to rein in theoretical overelaborations of categories and definitions. The point of seeking more recent vocabularies is to make traditional rhetorical distinctions more readily available for current use and perhaps to articulate their relations in memorable frames of reference that might let us understand them better and deploy them more thoughtfully.

This is a question to which I would like to propose an answer by pursuing a possible line of redescription drawn from the Bakhtin School, contrasting it to an elaboration of Fahnestock's undeveloped suggestion that we think of figures of thought in terms of speech-act theory, and showing that Bakhtin's terms capture her insights better than J. L. Austin's. Fahnestock (1999) finds the rubric "figures of thought" misleading, because the paradigmatic instances Quintilian cites "have less to do with the content than with the context." She suggestively renames figures of thought "interactional devices" and says that such moves are "more like gestures, ways of marking in speech or constructing in written texts the intentions, interactions, and attitudes among participants." The "energy of interaction," she goes on, "resembles the twentieth-century notion of the speech act either intended or accomplished by an utterance." Elaborating further in a long note, Fahnestock concludes that "many of the figures of thought . . . specify interactions between speaker and audience and reciprocal intentions and effects" (p. 197).

Fahnestock's (1999) emphasis on the way figures of thought embody or imitate the interactions among participants in the discursive situation fits the terms of the Bakhtinian rereading of the figures I will elaborate subsequently, but first, I want to consider her suggestion that figures of thought might be understood in terms of speech-act theory.

The basic distinction in speech-act theory between constative and performative utterances parallels Quintilian's distinction between unfigured discourse that directs attention to the matter and figures of thought that artfully enact or act out some transaction among the participants in the discursive situation. It does help to think of the figures of thought as performative and to recognize that even straightforward narration and proof directed toward the matter—included on Cicero's list of figures but not on Quintilian's—are kinds of performance, just as, it turns out for Austin (1962), constative utterances are kinds of performance. It may also help to

recognize that figures of thought may bring into being the discursive interactions they enact, just as performative utterances may result in new relationships among the parties to them.

Austin's positing of the categories constative and performative is part of what J. Hillis Miller (2001) recognizes as the primarily grammatical or logical rather than rhetorical bent of his thought (pp. 39–40), and the interests he has in classifying verbs of discursive action or clearly distinguishing performative from constative utterances are not the interests of a pragmatic pedagogically oriented rhetorical criticism concerned with modeling what happens in literary discourse for the sake of reading it better. So speech-act theory may offer the performative as a helpful way of thinking about figures of thought in general, but a contemporary rhetoric of the figures of thought could be diverted from its purposes if it let itself get caught up—as rhetorical theorists repeatedly have done in the past—in logical or grammatical disputes over mutually exclusive definitions of categories, the classification of the figures in those categories, or even the ultimate collapse of the distinction between them.

Bakhtin's dialogic theory offers a more rhetorically useful way to capture Fahnestock's (1999) "interactional" insight and resituate the classical figures of thought in currently available terms, because it has a comprehensive account of the *participants* interacting in discourse that helps organize the figures of thought and a powerful account of speech genres that helps reinterpret them. The Bakhtin School's account of discourse from its earliest essays posits that "any locution actually said aloud or written down for intelligible communication . . . is the interaction of three participants: the speaker (author), the listener (reader), and the topic (the who or what) of speech (the hero)" (Voloshinov & Bruss, 1987), and it adds in later work the additional premise that the topic or hero or object of discourse is always "a focal point for heteroglot voices among which [the speaker or writer's own voice] must sound; these voices create the background necessary for his own voice" (Bakhtin, Holquist, & Emerson, 1981). That is, the hero has always already been spoken of and spoken for so that the current speaker's voice must always find its place among those that have already had their say about it. This model of the participants interacting in a discursive event permits us to see the figures of thought as foregrounding or acting out the current writer's or speaker's relations to all participants—to precedent speakers or writers on the subject, to the hero as evaluated object or potential speaker, to the listener's or reader's previous or potential utterances, or to the speaker's own utterance in progress.

For example, the paradigmatic figure of response to precedent utterance is the prosopopoeia or attribution of words to another of which quotation is a literal species; the model figure of address to the hero is the apostrophe that turns from the listener to speak to, sometimes to personify, the topic of discourse; the representative figure of address to the reader is the anticipation of his or her objection or concurrence with the speaker; the figure of the speaker's reference to himself or herself as producer of the utterance currently in progress that brings such gestures into view is the self-interruption, but any first-person enacting of discursive actions, from announcing the sequence of topics to saying "in conclusion, I . . . " to apologizing for going on at too great length, brings the speaker figuratively to the fore. The Bakhtin School's account of interactions among discursive participants thus permits us to stabilize and enlarge Fahnestock's (1999) insights to recognize figures of thought as four main types of interactions among four discursive participants, not just relations of speaker and audience, as Fahnestock says, though her examples go further, and not just relations of speaker and topic, as the term *figures of thought* might seem to suggest.

Bakhtin's account of speech genres (Bakhtin, Holquist, & Emerson, 1986) enables another fruitful rethinking of the figures of thought not just in literary genres but also in written genres across the board. He defines primary speech genres—typifiable utterances that bespeak typifiable relations among the participants in discursive interactions in everyday exchanges—as the constituents of secondary speech genres—the more elaborate, usually written, utterances that characterize the disciplinary discourses of scientific, business, political, military, and literary communication in institutionally organized spheres of communication. Figures of thought in these secondary genres "play out," as Bakhtin puts it, "various forms of primary speech communication" (p. 98). He elaborates,

> Quite frequently, within the boundaries of his own utterance the speaker (or writer) raises questions, answers them himself, raises objections to his own ideas, responds to his own objections, and so on. But these phenomena are nothing other than the playing out of speech communication and primary genres. This kind of playing out is typical of rhetorical genres . . . but other secondary genres (artistic and scholarly) also use various forms such as this to introduce primary speech genres and relations among them into the construction of the utterance (and here they are altered to a greater or lesser degree for the speaking subject does not change). Such is the nature of secondary genres. (Bakhtin et al., 1986, pp. 72–73)

Although Bakhtin does not use the rhetorical term *figures of thought* in this discussion, he has both enumerated key figures and redefined them fruitfully as the incorporation of primary speech genres, which stand on their own in everyday discourse, into secondary genres, where they function as the parts of more complex utterances that interrelate to one another in some ways as the primary genres interrelate in everyday dialogic exchange (Bakhtin et al., 1986).

The radical conclusion that follows from this redefinition of figures of thought is that all secondary genres, including all literary genres, are composed of them; such figures, understood as primary genres enacted within the compass of more highly elaborated utterances, are the building blocks of those genres. Any text, therefore, should be analyzable into a sequence of such figures; we should be able to resolve it into a series of interactions with precedent utterances, its topic or hero, its audience, and the utterance in progress. Every text, in these terms, can be understood as built up as a sequence of figures of thought, and our effort to appreciate critically complex secondary utterances such as literary works should attend to their sequencing and their interactions.

Let me illustrate how we follow in a challenging poem the sequence of interacting internalized speech genres—or figures of thought—involving several discursive participants by describing in these terms a piece of Milton's "Lycidas" that unfolds as a series of internal questions, answers, self-corrections, and corrections from others. Milton's speaker at line 50 first asks a question that functions as an accusation—"Where were ye, Nymphs, when the remorseless deep/Closed o'er the head of your loved Lycidas?" He then builds his case against the nymphs, enumerating the places where they weren't, places from which he imagines they might have been able to prevent Lycidas's drowning. But then he catches himself, responds to his own words, and withdraws his own accusation: "Ay me, I fondly dream had ye been there!" For he realizes and explains that if the Muse herself couldn't save that first poet Orpheus from his pursuers, how could he imagine that these lesser nymphs could have done anything for Lycidas? But their failure and the Muse's failure to help prompts another question from him: What good does it do to serve the thankless Muse and tend the trade of poetry? If the Muse can't save you, why not, he goes on, give up the discipline of learning to write and instead enjoy dallying with pastoral maids? Again, he answers himself that fame is the reason why, but then objects to his own answer that just when you are hoping to achieve fame, you die, and what then? This time another voice intervenes to correct him—Phoebus, who reminds him that fame is not a worldly good but a heavenly one, judged by Jove and not subject to mortal terminations. The speaker invokes pastoral waters to bring his song back from the "higher mood" of Phoebus's song to his own pastoral note and next begins an account of a coroner's inquest in which he listens to the representatives of the sea deny responsibility for the shipwreck in which Lycidas died and blame it on his boat. I think I have gone far enough to illustrate the way the poem internalizes a series of familiar types of utterances, enacts interactions among several participants, and builds one figure on another as answer to question, question prompted by conclusion, objection prompted by the next conclusion, or self-reflexive fresh start taken after another voice has put in its oar in the internalized conversation. And this has taken us far enough to see how classical rhetorical categories like the figures of thought might be made critically functional redescribed in the contemporary critical idiom of Bakhtin's theories.

One consequence of reinterpreting figures of thought within Bakhtin's account of speech genres is that the figures become recognizable as an artificial technical specification of a universal vernacular phenomenon. The art of rhetoric as Quintilian elaborated it may have initially codified figures of thought and tried to set apart their deliberate, even insincere, use as a mark of art, but Quintilian recognized in Cicero's account a broader understanding of the figures of thought as a set of noticeable discursive moves, and Fahnestock (1999) has driven that point home, calling figures "better but not unique ways to achieve certain discourse functions" (p. 23). If we use Bakhtin's account of speech genres to articulate a derivation of figures of thought from primary types of utterance, then the use of those "figures" need not be a sign of knowledge of the art. The discursive moves to which the art has given technical names can be used by writers innocent of those names and innocent of the art itself. Although artistic practice might highlight and cultivate and direct the use of figures of thought, it has no monopoly on their use. This resituating of the figures (and potentially of other rhetorical terms and distinctions) as artificial selections from a natural discursive repertoire raises further questions that a fresh inquiry into rhetorical criticism might address. Just how technical are the resources that the art of rhetoric has codified? Have the technical names by which rhetoricians have learned and taught them obscured their vernacular origin and their pervasiveness in ordinary language use? Which, if any, of them are strictly artificial, available only to the rhetorically schooled, and what is the relation of these artificial resources to the workings of ordinary language? How has schooling in them affected their deployment? What are the most important artificial practices contingent on specific rhetorical sources that shaped the work of particular authors or periods, genres or spheres or communication? How can they best be discovered and made available to critics focused on those specialties? On the other hand, to what extent can technically named rhetorical devices and patterns be recognized in practices of unschooled discourse or discourse schooled without formal rhetorical training? What implications do our answers to this last question have for criticism of writers of the past century or so who learned to write without reference to formal rhetorical training, or at least to formal rhetorical training linked to classical education? And to writers from all centuries, women, and others not given access to such formal training? To what extent have they, nonetheless, learned what we can call rhetorical moves, from their everyday availability, from study of earlier authors who were formally schooled in them, or from modern versions of rhetorical education conducted under other names? To what extent can the historically

underwritten rhetorical criticism we have been imagining here fruitfully address itself to that part of the history of literary production, "posttrivial" or "extratrivial" literature, as it were, that was not shaped by formal rhetorical training? To what extent can we draw on rhetorical formalizations of discourse moves as an open-ended generic vocabulary that can help us notice moves that preexisted their formalization and that exist whether or not those formalizations are explicitly taught? If the extent is considerable, we will have opened the way to articulating a rhetorical criticism grounded in what can be learned from the history of rhetorical theory and practice but not restricted to seeking explicit correlations between literary productions and historically specific rhetorical educations.

I hope I have raised enough questions to prompt others to consider further elaborating and contributing to the project of historical and theoretical inquiry into rhetorical literary criticism that I am proposing. Consequential critical projects are not the work of single critics but of groups engaged with deploying the same critical resources and advocating for their program under a recognizable banner. New Criticism and Deconstruction both represented collective projects, however internally diversified, and both achieved a proper nominalization that made them objects of adherence, opposition, and representation. There are introductions to, bibliographies of, and anthologies on them. There are books exemplifying their practices for wider audiences. They have afterlives in histories of criticism, which my Chicago School, metonymically identified with its institution of origin, does not.

As rhetoricians, we should be well prepared to undertake the advocacy required. What would we call the criticism I have been desiderating? Just "Rhetorical," hoping to recapture the word? "New Rhetorical," hoping to try the well-worn gambit that has served New Critics and New Historicists alike, though Howell (1971) has already used the phrase otherwise in the history of rhetoric? "Interactive," perhaps, to highlight our Bakhtin-school insights? Or is there a neologism like "deconstruction" waiting to be recovered from rhetoric's great storehouse of Latin and Greek technical terms? Whatever we call our toolbox of rhetorical terms, we will have to present the acquisition of it as an attractive project, not dry-as-dust or lifetime-consuming antiquarian work but work functional from the start in improving our understanding and enjoyment of literary works and in discovering their affinities with everyday discourse and the written texts of other spheres of communication. It needs to come not just with good name recognition and advertising but with an effective user's manual, a pedagogical sequence that helps new users get immediate use from the toolkit and build toward more complicated, less scripted uses. The New Critics did not neglect this part of their program; indeed, they attended to it more assiduously than to theoretical defense, while my Chicago predecessors published an enormous tome of rigorous scholarly argument, polemical critique, and theoretical elaboration that persuaded few beyond the Midway (see Crane, 1952). Booth's (1961) intervention into the discussion of fiction, less formidably written and focused on a genre not well developed in New Criticism, found a wider following. Deconstruction's advocates took an interesting tack, professing rigor and courting difficulty but also building an aura of sublimity, inevitability, and European sophistication around their work. Their following did not spread as far or go as deeply into the educational system as New Criticism (and it depended in part on New Criticism for its appeal), but though it was practiced by a relatively small coterie, it achieved a prestige out of proportion to its size.

I have come back to the earlier critical schools from which I started these reflections and inventions. No one, I hope, will have mistaken them for an attempt at a comprehensive survey of all the work that could be called

rhetoric in literary criticism and theory now or in the recent past; I offer an apology to any and all who feel that their consequential work in this kind was neglected—Burkeans, rhetorical hermeneuts, feminist rhetoricians, to name a few at the risk of omitting others even from this list of omissions. I have written from what I think I know after many years of interest in this topic, which, of course, means that I have also written from considerable ignorance. As I have said, it is the story of one who found himself on the losing side but lived to tell the tale.

As I have not yet said, it is also the work of one who is fond of Francis Bacon's survey of the state of learning and the learned in his time, interested in what appears cultivated and what lies fallow and aware of the need to promote collective labors to bring fallow fields under the plow. I have produced a small, idio-syncratic piece of what Bacon and Kitchin (1973) might have called recent literary history, a story of a branch of learning, told at least partly from outside the self-serving stories of its sects, attending to "their inventions, their traditions, their diverse administrations and managings, their flourishings, their oppo-sitions, decays, depressions, oblivions and removes, with the causes and occasions of them," with the goal of making us better at managing these affairs of learning and perhaps enabling us deliberately to intervene to improve them (p. 70). I have found rhetorical criticism and theory of literature "deficient," as Bacon would have put it, but not without some suggestive and hopeful resources and possibilities. Such surveys of the state of learning are inescapably presumptuous and quixotic, but they are also occasionally fruitful. If you have indulged me in reading this far, I hope you will help make this one so.

REFERENCES

Arac, J. (1987). *Critical genealogies: Historical situations for postmodern literary studies.* New York: Columbia University Press.

Armstrong, E. (2006). *A Ciceronian sunburn: A Tudor dialogue on humanistic rhetoric and civic poetics.* Columbia: University of South Carolina.

Auerbach, E. (2003). *Mimesis: The representation of reality in Western literature* (50th anniversary ed.). Princeton, NJ: Princeton University Press.

Austin, J. L. (1962). *How to do things with words.* Cambridge, MA: Harvard University Press.

Bacon, F., & Kitchin, G. W. (1973). *The advancement of learning.* London: J. M. Dent.

Bakhtin, M. M., Holquist, M., & Emerson, C. (1981). *The dialogic imagination.* Austin: University of Texas Press.

Bakhtin, M. M., Holquist, M., & Emerson, C. (1986). *Speech genres and other late essays* (1st ed.). Austin: University of Texas Press.

Bender, J. B., & Wellbery, D. E. (1990). *The ends of rhetoric: History, theory, practice.* Stanford, CA: Stanford University Press.

Bialostosky, D. H. (1992). *Wordsworth, dialogics, and the practice of criticism.* Cambridge, UK: Cambridge University Press.

Bialostosky, D. H., & Needham, L. D. (Eds.). (1995). *Rhetorical traditions and British romantic literature.* Bloomington: Indiana University Press.

Booth, W. C. (1961). *The rhetoric of fiction.* Chicago: University of Chicago Press.

Booth, W. C. (1974). *A rhetoric of irony.* Chicago: University of Chicago Press.

Booth, W. C. (1983). *The rhetoric of fiction* (2nd ed.). Chicago: University of Chicago Press.

Crane, R. S. (1952). *Critics and criticism, ancient and modern.* Chicago: University of Chicago Press.

Curtius, E. R., & Trask, W. R. (1990). *European literature and the Latin Middle Ages.* Princeton, NJ: Princeton University Press.

de Man, P. (1979). *Allegories of reading: Figural language in Rousseau, Nietzsche, Rilke, and Proust.* New Haven, CT: Yale University Press.

Fahnestock, J. (1999). *Rhetorical figures in science.* New York: Oxford University Press.

Genette, G. (1982). *Figures of literary discourse.* New York: Columbia University Press.

Howell, W. S. (1971). *Eighteenth-century British logic and rhetoric.* Princeton, NJ: Princeton University Press.

Miller, J. H. (2001). *Speech acts in literature.* Stanford, CA: Stanford University Press.

Miriam, J. (1947). *Shakespeare's use of the arts of language.* New York: Columbia University Press.

Miriam, J. (1962). *Rhetoric in Shakespeare's time: Literary theory of Renaissance Europe.* New York: Harcourt.

Payne, R. O. (1963). *The key of remembrance, a study of Chaucer's poetics.* New Haven, CT: Yale University Press. (Published for the University of Cincinnati)

Phelan, J. (1981). *Worlds from words: A theory of language in fiction.* Chicago: University of Chicago Press.

Phelan, J. (1996). *Narrative as rhetoric: Technique, audiences, ethics, ideology.* Columbus, OH: Ohio State University Press.

Phelan, J. (2005). *Living to tell about it: A rhetoric and ethics of character narration.* Ithaca, NY: Cornell University Press.

Phelan, J., & Rabinowitz, P. J. (1994). *Understanding narrative.* Columbus, OH: Ohio State University Press.

Phelan, J., & Rabinowitz, P. J. (2005). *A companion to narrative theory.* Malden, MA: Blackwell.

Rabinowitz, P. J. (1987). *Before reading: Narrative conventions and the politics of interpretation.* Ithaca, NY: Cornell University Press.

Richter, D. H. (1986). Bakhtin in life and in art. *Style, 20,* 411–419.

Richter, D. H. (1990). Dialogism and poetry. *Studies in the Literary Imagination, 23,* 9–27.

Tuve, R. (1947). *Elizabethan and metaphysical imagery: Renaissance poetic and twentieth-century critics.* Chicago: University of Chicago Press.

Vickers, B. (1988). *In defence of rhetoric.* New York: Oxford University Press.

Voloshinov, V. N., & Bruss, N. H. (1987). Discourse in life and discourse in art. In *Freudianism: A critical sketch* (pp. 94–116). Bloomington: Indiana University Press.

Walker, J. (2000). *Rhetoric and poetics in antiquity.* New York: Oxford University Press.

13

Rhetoric of Health and Medicine

JUDY Z. SEGAL

The very idea of a rhetoric of science enabled the study of a rhetoric of medicine, and that, in turn, enabled a more encompassing study, not only of medicine as an object of investigation, but also of health and illness more generally. What began in the 1980s as the analysis of texts of biomedicine (see, e.g., Anderson, 1989; Solomon, 1985) became, over time, a study of health and medicine, broadly defined, according to rhetorical principles, also broadly defined.

The realm of health and medicine itself is structured by, and, in a sense, *is,* a set of texts (e.g., medical journal articles, regulatory documents, prescriptions), genres (e.g., professional talks, hospital case presentations, doctor-patient interviews), and discourses (e.g., pharmaceutical discourse, end-of-life discourse, health policy discourse). Texts are bounded discursive objects; genres are the repeated means of structuring texts to accomplish particular actions; discourses are sets of cultural habits exhibited in a range of texts and genres. The defining feature of rhetorical study is that it isolates the persuasive element in these texts, genres, and discourses, and seeks to understand something about what they do, how they act in professional and public settings.

This essay approaches work in rhetoric of health and medicine with two things, primarily, in mind: topic/theme, on the one hand, and theory/methodology on the other. What do practitioners of rhetoric of health and medicine work on—and how do they work on it? The *what* of the field will emerge in examples of the *how* of it, but the character of the field can be

Author's Note: For helpful discussions about drafts of this essay, I thank Colleen Derkatch and Alan Richardson. Thanks to Katja Thieme for invaluable research assistance.

drawn, initially, in sample research questions: What are the means of persuasion routinely deployed in the debate on the regulation of midwifery (Lay, 2003; Spoel & James, 2006)? How does the "charter document in psychiatry," the *Diagnostic and Statistical Manual of Mental Disorders*, constrain the production of texts that then derive from clinical encounters (Berkenkotter, 2001; McCarthy, 1991)? In the absence of positive diagnostic tests, how do patients persuade physicians that they are ill and in need of care (Segal, 2007a)? What are the conventional features of the hospital case presentation, and how is the genre reproduced in the course of medical training (Lingard & Haber, 2002)? What are the terms of influence in the discourse of decision making about the end of life (Hyde & McSpiritt, 2007; Keränen, 2007; Segal 2005b)?[1] These are some of the questions that occupy scholars in rhetoric of health and medicine.

Projects in rhetoric of health and medicine, in general, aim to be useful. Their usefulness often lies in their ability simply to pose questions that are prior to the questions typically posed by health researchers. In the case of cosmetic surgery, for example, before we ask the more obvious medical/health questions—for example, "How can it be performed most safely?" and "Should it be covered by health insurance plans?"—we might ask, "How are people persuaded to see themselves as improvable by cosmetic surgery in the first place?" That is a question for research in rhetoric of health and medicine. (See, e.g., John W. Jordan [2004] on the "plastic body"; in the broader sphere, including rhetoric as rendered in bioethics, see Carl Elliott [2003].)[2]

Research in rhetoric of health and medicine is also, typically, "motivated," in the sense of Kenneth Burke's (1969) use of that term: The criticism itself is a form of symbolic action. Rhetorical critics, overall, often proceed with what Richard Weaver (1970) called a "sense

of the *ought*" (p. 211), even if they can say only that things ought to be better (but not how); the ameliorative urge is a feature of their criticism.[3] This may be especially true for rhetorical critics of health and medicine. Not that we who do the work are Michael Moore (2007) crafting *Sicko*—shaming for change—but, even when our work is essentially descriptive, it often arises from a moral purpose. It may begin with a sense of a problem, perceived as discursive in nature, that might, if properly described, bend to a solution also discursive in nature. James C. Wilson and Cynthia Lewiecki-Wilson (2001) claim that rhetoricians are concerned with "issues of justice" (p. 2), and that they "extend rhetorical analyses beyond an immediate text to investigate the interconnections of language and material practices" (p. 3).

The following section describes work in rhetoric of health and medicine primarily according to its theories and methodologies. The description is done by exhibiting examples of research projects with a range of approaches.[4] In each case, any claim made about theoretical/methodological orientation pertains only to the work discussed, and not to other work by the same author, which may take a different approach. Following this section is an account of the sociology of rhetoric of health and medicine: its research culture(s). The essay ends with a brief reflection on rhetoric after disciplinarity.

THEORY AND METHODOLOGY IN RHETORIC OF HEALTH AND MEDICINE

Arguably, work that most obviously counts as rhetoric of health and medicine is criticism of the texts, genres, and discourses of health and medicine, *as performed by a rhetorical critic*. The statement may seem tautological at first, but it seeks to characterize analysis performed by a person trained within a scholarly tradition on public discourse into a subjectivity suggesting particular lines of inquiry and procedures for thinking. (Rhetorical theory can be learned in a course or two, but a rhetorical frame of mind takes years to develop.) Persons so trained will typically have studied Plato; Aristotle; Cicero; Quintilian; major figures in medieval, Renaissance, Enlightenment, and 19th-century rhetorics; as well as Kenneth Burke, Richard Weaver, Chaim Perelman, and Wayne Booth (and, probably, Michel Foucault and Jacques Derrida); they will also have studied works of rhetorical criticism by some of those authors, as well as by, for example, E. P. J. Corbett (1969), Donald Cross Bryant (1973), and Edwin Black (1992).[5] While there is not field unanimity about what constitutes rhetorical training (or, indeed, rhetorical theory), there is some consensus currently in rhetoric of health and medicine that the body of rhetorical theory is, at least, continuous, however variegated the theory is. In their introduction to a collection of essays on the rhetoric of disability, Wilson and Lewiecki-Wilson (2001) write, for example, that "from a postmodern perspective, classical and postmodern rhetorics really are not separable (p. 3).[6] And, so, while it is difficult, it is not impossible to say that there is a rhetoric of health and medicine based on a rhetorical canon.

Some work in rhetoric of health and medicine is part canon-based criticism and part something else (I would say my own work is part canon-based criticism and part cultural studies, for example). Certainly, some work is both *noncanonical* and importantly rhetorical. I mentioned two studies on the influence of the *Diagnostic and Statistical Manual of Mental Disorders* in clinical settings (Berkenkotter, 2001; McCarthy, 1991); these studies are noncanonical and rhetorical. In its broad definition, rhetoric of health and medicine is theoretically and methodologically diverse. Finally, a full description of rhetoric of health and medicine includes work, across a range of disciplines, that takes a keen interest in discourse and persuasion, while it is, for the most part, not well informed on matters of rhetorical history and theory. Many sociologists, anthropologists, historians, and others write books and articles that anyone interested in rhetoric of health and medicine ought to read; we know this is true not least because of the routine presence of authors who would not count themselves as rhetoricians on the reading lists of rhetoric-of-health-and-medicine courses taught by scholars who very much are rhetoricians.[7]

I begin with a description of my own work and move to a characterization of other work based on the rhetorical canon. I then survey projects in other, more broadly rhetorical, areas of theory and methodology; I then describe rhetorically interested work across disciplines. The description of the first of my own projects identifies my work as being rhetorical analysis of a particular type (canon based, as I've said); the description of the second locates my work in relation to rhetorically interested research on its topic across disciplines. Both descriptions specify my claim that rhetoric of health and medicine aims to be useful and is ameliorative in motive.

Rhetorical Criticism Based on Canonical Rhetorical Theory

The first project (part of a book in progress) is a study of persuasive strategies in pharmaceutical marketing. The premise of the research is that pharmaceutical advertising operates not only as a deliberative rhetoric, exhorting an audience to acquire a drug, it is also an epideictic rhetoric, exhorting an audience to acquire a drug *according to a hierarchy of values*. That is, a central goal of pharmaceutical advertising is to persuade people that they can take drugs and be good people at the same time; indeed, they may have an obligation to take drugs.

Once pharmaceutical advertising is described as an epideictic rhetoric, and once advertisements and the values that underpin them are described, then public debate can proceed on those values themselves. (This is how the project aims to be useful.) For example, is sociality so desirable a value that we ought to medicate shyness with drugs (for social anxiety disorder)? While we demonize users of steroids, is productivity so desirable that we ought to prescribe antidepressants, sleeping pills, amphetamines, and pain medications, all in the name of enhancing performance at work? Arguments on these points include in their warrants an analysis of persuasive strategies in pharmaceutical advertisements.

This project, then, isolates persuasive appeals in direct-to-consumer advertising for prescription pharmaceuticals, with an eye on strategy. It notes, for example, that a primary strategy of pharmaceutical advertisers is not to *dissociate* illicit drugs and prescription pharmaceuticals (by identifying the first with pleasure and the second not with pleasure but with an earnest effort to maintain good health); rather, a strategy of pharmaceutical advertisers is to *split pleasure*. That is, while the pleasures of illicit drugs are represented in public discourse as largely solitary, fantastical, and unproductive pleasures,[8] the pleasures of prescription pharmaceuticals are represented in pharmaceutical advertisements as social, authentic, and productive. The antidepressant Paxil invites you to "let the world say hello to the real you," while, with Effexor, another antidepressant, you can "be involved with family and friends the way you used to be." Moreover, it is not only psychotropic drugs that reinsert the user into the social scene. The migraine drug Relpax restores to the family picture a mother whose headache has removed her violently from it (in a magazine advertisement, Mom appears in the family vacation photo crushed by a boulder); Ambien not only lets you sleep but also lets you sleep so that you can be productively at work the next morning.[9]

My analysis depends entirely on rhetorical theory to exist. It relies, in the first instance, on classical rhetoric—in particular, the understanding that a rhetorical occasion best

realized in the genre of the funeral oration (Aristotle's epideictic rhetoric) also functions as an everyday rhetoric of values. My analysis is indebted also to the 20th-century rhetorical theory of Chaim Perelman and Lucie Olbrechts-Tyteca (1969), who specify the idea of a public audience (they suggest how rhetors answer the anticipated but unvoiced objections of audience members), offer a theory of liaisons and dissociations (they describe how rhetors structure reality for audiences by creating and destroying conceptual alliances), and explain, for a theory of argumentation, the idea of philosophical pairs (they enable my observation that a key strategy of pharmaceutical advertising in general is *splitting* pleasure[10]).

My second project (forthcoming) concerns the public function of breast cancer narratives. It explores questions of the permissible and the impermissible in widely circulating breast cancer narratives, such as those published in newspapers and popular magazines, and argues that the genre itself of the personal narrative acts, in part, to regulate the experience of breast cancer. The project was inspired by an idea introduced by historians of science Robert Proctor and Londa Schiebinger: agnotology, the study of ignorance.[11] I investigate the extent to which ignorance about cancer is maintained by the rehearsal of stories that have standard plots and features and suppress or displace other accounts.

Like the pharmaceuticals project, this one is rooted in the notion of epideictic rhetoric, a rhetoric in which we affirm what is praiseworthy by praising individuals for embodying it and affirm what is blameworthy by blaming individuals for embodying that. The breast cancer project is classical also by virtue of its interest in how discourse functions in a public forum. Its approach to breast cancer narratives is both Aristotelian and Burkean: It asks what breast cancer narratives *do*.[12] What do they do *for* us and what do they do *to* us? It suggests that, inter alia, they advise people on how to be ill.

The central questions for rhetorical criticism are "Who is persuading whom of what?" and "What are the means of persuasion?" In the case of breast cancer narratives, these questions prompt other ones that productively can be inserted into conversations women have about their health.[13] How is breast cancer knowledge shaped for us, and by whom? Is breast cancer primarily a disease of individuals, survived (and storied) individually—or is it, as importantly, a disease of complex and less personal etiology, enacted and reenacted in individual bodies? What does it mean really to "fight" breast cancer, and what would it mean to prevent it? How does the proliferation of breast cancer products and breast cancer walks and runs and climbs influence the experience of women who have breast cancer? Shall women with breast cancer find common ground with other people who are ill or disabled, or shall they establish for themselves a new normal, where "normal" is still the ideal, but it includes one-breasted women, perhaps bald or nauseated—while ill and disabled people are still the less fortunate others? The usefulness of this rhetorical analysis is in the way it irritates widely circulating values of breast cancer "survival." (The Breast Cancer Foundation, e.g., weighs in on the matter of how one should be ill by "salut[ing] women . . . who not only have the courage to battle breast cancer, but are able to do it with . . . unflagging optimism, creativity, and humour."[14]) Like much rhetorical criticism, mine subjects unexamined terms to examination.

My research on breast cancer narratives has taken me to a range of sources across disciplines. Most of the authors I consulted did not self-identify as rhetoricians, but all attended to the ways in which, and the ends to which, breast cancer stories are persuasive. Cultural critic Barbara Ehrenreich (2001) comments on the policing of stories by community forces sponsoring a "cult of pink kitsch" (p. 50). Sociologist Samantha King (2006) writes about the shift from "activism" to "activity," and the

selling of the idea that women are themselves responsible for preventing breast cancer, one case at a time. Authors across disciplines cite authors across disciplines. Frequent sources are Susan Sontag, literary and cultural critic (1978); Audre Lorde, poet (1980); G. Thomas Couser, literature specialist (1997); Arthur Frank, sociologist (1995); Mike Bury, political scientist (2001); and Cheryl Mattingly, anthropologist (1998). Some of the most rhetorically minded nonrhetoricians I discovered in my research were Victoria Pitts, sociologist (2004); Dorothy Broom, epidemiologist (2001); Laura Potts, health educator (2000); and Diane Price Herndl, literature specialist (2006).[15] Two of the authors I consulted would, I think, count themselves as rhetoricians and count their own analyses as, *in the first instance,* rhetorical. Phaedra Pezzullo (2003) specifies ways that public debates over breast cancer are constrained in ways linked to environmental and gendered discourses; Cynthia Ryan (2005) uses both fieldwork and textual analysis to examine patterns of editorial decisions at *MAMM* Magazine; she focuses on the presentation of medical information in *MAMM* and the portrayal of survivors' identities.

Let me continue my description of a canonically based rhetoric of health and medicine by describing a piece of criticism that is itself canonical. Martha Solomon wrote "The Rhetoric of Dehumanization: An Analysis of Medical Reports of the Tuskegee Syphilis Project" in 1985 and followed, in 1994, with a second essay in which she reflects on the process of writing the first one. "The Rhetoric of Dehumanization" takes as its subject about 40 years of journal articles published during the conduct of the Tuskegee Syphilis Project. As Solomon says, in the name of knowledge production, a population of African American men was observed through the course of their syphilis infections; the men were left untreated while researchers documented the progress of the disease. Solomon's project was to explain how reports could continue to appear in mainstream medical journals without creating outrage among journal readers, who knew, after all, that antibiotic treatments existed of which the "research subjects" were deprived.

Solomon herself is dispassionate; her work is descriptive; her approach is analytical. Her theory is Burkean, and what she argues, finally (using Burke's [1969] pentad of terms of dramatism: act, agent, agency, scene, and purpose), is that the genre itself of the medical journal article created the conditions in which the research subjects, objects of study, were configured not as human beings, agents, but as agencies of research, and scenes upon which the disease was performed. I have, from time to time, wondered if Solomon (1985) herself, while indicting indirectly the scientific genre of the medical journal article was not herself too quasi-scientific in her analysis. By her own admission, she refuses to be outraged: "I make an earnest effort," she says, "to show how texts work rather than judge whether it is just that they should have worked at all" (1994, p. 306). In many ways, however, Solomon's essay is almost perfect as an essay in canonical rhetoric of health and medicine, because it takes a uniquely rhetorical perspective to reveal what might be otherwise invisible (a generic habit that shifts the ground of symbolic action) and her description itself is utterly persuasive; her own outrage would have been extraneous.

Solomon's essay uses rhetorical theory to both formulate and answer questions about persuasion and dehumanization in biomedicine—and her essay fulfils Burke's (1973) own ideal for criticism: his purpose, when he analyzed *Mein Kampf,* was "to find all available ways of making the Hitlerite distortions of religion apparent, in order that politicians of his kind in America be unable to perform a similar swindle" (pp. 219–220). Solomon's criticism illuminated the potential for atrocities in generic features themselves endogenous to medical writing; her analysis might make others less able to "perform a similar

swindle." Following are three other rhetoricians of health and medicine who have undertaken analyses that are, like Solomon's, based in canonical rhetorical theory.

Celeste Condit (2000) offers a rhetorical analysis of a speech by geneticist Paul Berg in which he seeks public ratification of an essentially genetic model of health. Using principles of rhetorical analysis, Condit describes the strategies by which the speech, and the model it advances, are rendered persuasive. Then, Condit directs her attention to a material and public space—the clinic, where women are asked to make decisions about prenatal testing according to the model Berg advances. Condit writes about clinics (plural), where the choices that genetic medicine suggests are represented differently for women of different classes, education, and means. Condit not only observes, but also contributes to, debate on the problematics of genetic medicine.

In a recent issue of *Quarterly Journal of Speech,* Lisa Keränen (2007) takes a canonical rhetorical approach to questions of decision making at the end of life. Focusing on the "'Patient' Preferences Worksheet" in use in U.S. hospitals, Keränen says her goal is to "lay bare the underlying rhetorical dynamics of end-of-life decision making in an institutional context" (p. 180). Like Michael Hyde and Sarah McSpiritt (2007), who write in the same journal issue about euthanasia, moral exigencies, and the "rhetoric of perfection," Keränen moves among sources in philosophy, literature, medicine, and rhetorical theory. For Keränen, as for Hyde and McSpiritt, central issues for critical consideration are authority, ethics, influence, and judgment, and rhetorical study focuses those issues.

J. Blake Scott (2002) combines readings of Aristotelian rhetorical theory and contemporary Foucauldian discourse theory to examine the public policy debate over mandatory HIV testing of newborns in the United States. The central structure Scott uncovers is what he calls a "knowledge enthymeme," in which, for example, failure to acquire knowledge—in this case, by HIV testing of newborns—is a dereliction of maternal duty. He demonstrates how the knowledge enthymeme deflects attention away from any harmful effects of testing and away from the contexts of the lives of affected women. He invites other rhetorical critics to consider the play of the knowledge enthymeme in other AIDS-related discourses, health discourses more generally, and other power-knowledge regimes. This, according to Scott, is how rhetoricians intervene in public policy (p. 78).

The following authors, in the particular work I am citing, do their analysis with special recourse, not to canonical rhetorical theory, but, respectively, to discourse analysis, genre theory, and principles of professional communication. Good descriptions of these theoretical approaches are readily available (see sources mentioned, for example), but, for a point of reference, I offer these few sentences. *Discourse analysis* is a catholic set of practices used by linguists, sociologists, anthropologists, and others interested in language and culture. Many discourse analysts refer for methodology to Deborah Lupton (1992), who suggests a set of procedures to foreground the interplay of language and ideology, revealing power relations as they are encoded in texts (their lexicon, syntax, style, and pragmatics). *Genre theory* attends first to conventional features of texts (again, lexical to pragmatic, but rhetorical, as well: It attends to conventional structures of argumentation). It focuses on repeated textual elements as they constitute social action. In genre approaches, an oft-cited theorist is Carolyn Miller (1984), for the idea that we ought to identify genres not, in the first instance, by their formal elements but rather by the social work, in part through those elements, they perform. *Professional communication* is better characterized by its objects of inquiry (texts used in the conduct of life in the professions) than by its modes of analysis,

which are various and include canonical-rhetorical, discourse-analytic, and genre-analytic approaches, among others. Professional communication may be characterized also by its genealogy. As a field of study, with its own journals, conferences, and essential texts, it began in the union of scholarship on technical writing on the one hand, and, on the other, composition research and pedagogy reinvented as writing across the curriculum, and, then, writing in the disciplines and writing in the professions. A good source on methods of research in professional communication is Lay and Gurak (2002).

Rhetoricians of health and medicine may cross categories in a single work. It is easy to imagine a canonically rhetorical discourse analysis of a genre of professional communication. See, for example, an essay by Linn Bekins, Thomas Huckin, and Laura Kijak (2004) that describes rhetorical moves characterizing the genre of the personal statement in medical school applications.

Rhetorical Criticism Based on Discourse Analysis

Mary Lay[16] is author and coauthor of a body of work that traverses topics in health and medicine, feminist criticism, and professional communication. An essay that covers all these areas of research also has special recourse to discourse analysis. "Midwifery on Trial" (2003) examines questions of power and resistance in five court cases involving traditional midwives. At issue is who, in the world after *Roe v. Wade*, will count as a medical caregiver for pregnant women. The essay's focus is on argumentation in cases where courts are challenged to resolve conflicts among state interests (as regards health and life), individual privacy rights, and medical authority.

More examples of rhetorical work in a discourse-analytic mode are two of Amy Koerber's essays that examine questions of the discourse of breast-feeding advocacy as set against more scientific, institutionalized discourse on infant feeding. Koerber (2005, 2006) analyzes interviews with nonphysician breast-feeding advocates and their clients and sets their discourse against the discourse of "high-profile" physicians. By engaging with transcripts and texts, Koerber plumbs questions of rhetorical agency, resistance, and change.

In an essay on the discourse of prognosis in medicine, Ellen Barton (2004) mobilizes Erving Goffman's (1959) distinction between "front-stage" and "back-stage" discourse to formulate an argument about the presentation of prognoses in doctor-patient encounters in oncology. Part of the announced purpose of Barton's essay (her work is often meta-methodological) is to suggest that "discourse-based methods have the potential to become the basis for productive critical engagement between practitioners and researchers in professional communication" (p. 67).

Rhetorical Criticism Based on Genre Theory

Carol Berkenkotter (2001) gathers evidence to demonstrate that "professions are organized by genre systems and their work is carried out through genre systems" (p. 327) and that "genre systems play an intermediate role between institutional structural properties and individual communicative action" (p. 329). Berkenkotter's case for the play of genre systems in psychiatry is made in reference to the paperwork generated in the therapeutic encounter and the expression in that paperwork of the suasive force of the "meta-genre," the *Diagnostic and Statistical Manual of Mental Disorders (DSM)*. (For the term *meta-genre*, Berkenkotter cites Giltrow, 1998.)

The *DSM* is the subject also of Lucille McCarthy's (1991) account of the rhetorical pressure that one genre—the "charter document," *DSM-III*—exerts on another: the clinical interview in psychiatry. McCarthy describes a case in which the diagnostic

interview itself is shaped by what the practitioner has internalized about diagnostic criteria as listed in the *Manual*. According to McCarthy's description, possibilities for diagnosis and treatment are importantly constrained by the *DSM*, and norms and values are then replicated in documents that follow from the clinical interview.

Lorelei Lingard, Kim Garwood, Catherine Schryer, and Marlee Spafford (2003) focus their attention on the clinical genre of the medical case presentation. The primary purpose of their essay is to illustrate how the genre itself is a conventionalized structure for professionalization. In the course of learning case presentations, novice physicians also learn how certainty is represented as a quality of the *ethos* or character of the profession.

The genre theory authors whom I have mentioned have all engaged in research collaborations with health/medical practitioners (see, in addition, Berkenkotter & Ravotas, 2002; McCarthy & Gerring, 1994). While any rhetorician of health and medicine might collaborate productively with health researchers and practitioners, it is telling that genre analysts do so especially. One reason is that genres are always genres in use, and the experts in their use are always the professionals who use them. Rhetoricians with a special interest in professional communication for the same reason frequently collaborate with practitioners.

Rhetorical Criticism Based on Theories of Professional Communication

In a collaborative project, rhetorician Philippa Spoel and midwife/midwife educator Susan James (2006) examine submissions from health care groups concerning the debate in Ontario, Canada about the regulation of midwifery in that province. Their essay analyzes the arguments made by various professional interest groups when the problem is an essential conflict between models of care:

an established (biomedical) model of health care, on the one hand, and "midwifery's alternative, women-centered model of childbirth care" (p. 167), on the other. Spoel and James demonstrate that interest groups each appeal strategically, and differently, to the value of the "public interest" in order to advance their own positions.

In one of her recent projects, Carol Reeves (2005) looks at argumentative strategies used by Nobel Prize winner, Stan Prusiner, in his account of transmissible spongiform encephalopathies (diseases such as "mad cow disease"). Analyzing texts by Prusiner, Reeves is able to offer observations about medico-scientific argumentation more generally. She focuses on linguistic elements of the texts in question (clause types, lexical shifts, etc.) and the rhetorical work that language does.

In a recent essay using a professional communication approach, Barbara Heifferon (2006) turns to the history of smallpox and smallpox vaccinations in order to derive a set of guidelines for contemporary public health education. Heifferon suggests ways to reform the public message on smallpox vaccination, on the idea that deliberately level-headed messages are necessary if we are not to repeat public health disasters of the past.

While an inward-looking taxonomy of work done by rhetoricians of health and medicine emphasizes heterogeneity in the field, the view outward, to other disciplines, suggests the homogeneity of rhetoricians' analyses compared with analyses less centrally rhetorical. The boundary exercise adds breadth and depth to a description of the field and adds a problem too for mapping: Work done by sociologists and others is both rhetoric and not rhetoric at the same time.

Rhetorically Interested Work Across Disciplines

In their Introduction to *Body Talk: Rhetoric, Technology, Reproduction,* the authors—Mary Lay, Laura Gurak, Clare Gravon, and Cynthia Myntti (2000)—ask, "What exactly are the components and methods of rhetorical analysis?" (p. 8). They answer in part by offering examples of feminist rhetorical criticism in matters of science and medicine. Among their first examples are analyses by Emily Martin, an anthropologist, and Carol Cohn, a psychologist. Martin's work and Cohn's work indeed address persuasive elements in discourse (Martin writes about gender stereotypes informing biological accounts of human reproduction; Cohn writes about terms that shape thinking about technoscience and nuclear strategy), but Martin and Cohn are not, by self-identification or by discipline, rhetorical analysts, and neither one deploys the conceptual frameworks and the terms of rhetorical history and theory. Other "rhetorical critics" named in the Introduction to *Body Talk* include Evelyn Fox Keller (a physicist and philosopher of science), Londa Schiebinger (a historian of science), and Paula Treichler (a psycholinguist working in cultural studies of science and medicine).[17]

Randy Allen Harris points out in his Introduction to *Landmark Essays on Rhetoric of Science* (1997) that some of the most notable work in rhetoric of science has been done by nonrhetoricians. Rhetoric of health and medicine is similarly indebted to work outside its own disciplinary range, and perhaps, because it is a younger field, more so. Work in sociology, anthropology, and so on may be essential to research and scholarship in rhetoric of health and medicine, but it is worth noting that, as Harris says, "Sociologists speak another, closely related language to ours in which *rhetoric* is a vaguer, shallower, though decidedly similar term" (p. xxvii).

The disciplines and the researchers/scholars most relevant to any project in rhetoric of health and medicine will depend very much on the project itself. It is difficult to name authors across disciplines, absent topics. Here, however, is a brief survey of cross-disciplinary books and articles of interest in rhetoric of health and medicine, by authors whose other work may or may not take up rhetorical matters.

Sociologists have a well-established interest in the persuasive element of health and medical discourse. Peter Conrad's *The Medicalization of Society* (2007) collects, and adds to, work Conrad has been doing for years on conditions that move into the medical realm from elsewhere (as, e.g., shyness has become "social anxiety disorder"). "Biomedicalization" itself is a term indispensable to rhetorical studies in health and medicine, and we are indebted for it, especially to Adele Clarke (see, e.g., Clarke, Shim, Mamo, Fosket, & Fishman, 2003). Sociologist Steve Epstein (1996) is often cited by rhetoricians of health and medicine.

Anthropologist Margaret Lock takes up questions of language and persuasion in much of her work. Researchers on the rhetoric of breast cancer find invaluable Lock's (1998) essay on predictive genetic testing as a kind of divination. "Rhetoric," moreover, is invoked by some anthropologists as a term of art. Susan Greenhalgh's (2001) autoethnography is a study of herself as a patient with fibromyalgia; as Greenhalgh tries to discover the forces behind her worsening condition postdiagnosis, she offers what she calls a "rhetorical" explanation, and lists six "rhetorical devices" she considers central to biomedicine itself.[18] For his part, anthropologist Joseph Dumit (2004) relies on Kenneth Burke (1969)—in particular, Burke's ideas about ambiguity—to write about imaging technologies in medical settings and "how brain images are put to persuasive use in specific contexts" (Dumit, 2004, p. 10).

Without using the term *rhetoric* itself, bioethicist Carl Elliott (2003) writes about enhancement technologies in a rhetorical mode: They depend, he argues, on a persuadable public. Of further interest to rhetoricians is Elliott's exchange with psychiatrist Peter Kramer (see Elliott, 1998; Kramer, 2004), in which Elliott describes a cultural turn to a "tyranny of happiness," implicated, he says, in the public acceptance of pharmaceutical mood enhancers, while Kramer argues against "the valorization of sadness." The debate centers on the relations of culture, identity, and persuasion.

Kramer is one of several rhetorically inclined medical practitioners. Physician Eric Cassell (2004) is often cited by rhetoricians for his special attention to the language of medicine and experience. Jonathan Metzl is a psychiatrist, as well as professor of psychiatry and women's studies; in *Prozac on the Couch: Prescribing Gender in the Era of Wonder Drugs* (2003), his "pharmacokinetics of narrative form" (p. 166) is what a rhetorician might see as a rhetorical construction of self in first-person depression accounts. Metzl's analysis of advertising of psychopharmaceuticals is rhetorical absolutely.

Other disciplinary homes of work broadly understood as rhetoric of health and medicine are in history and literature, and in several fields of health research (health economics and epidemiology, among others). Historians of rhetorical interest include Andrea Tone (2005), Jeremy Greene (2004), and Edward Shorter (2005). Rhetorically inclined literature specialists include Elaine Scarry (1985), Diane Price Herndl (2006), and Susan Squier (2004). In health fields, Joel Lexchin and Barbara Mintzes (2002) have insiders' looks at public persuasion in a pharmaceutical age.

One of the features of research in rhetoric of health and medicine is that it defies disciplinary boundaries; at least, it blurs them. With the rise of interdisciplinary programs in women's studies, cultural studies, science and technology studies, and so on, researchers in general are identifying less with traditional disciplines and more with fields of inquiry and transdisciplinary methodologies. With a nod, then, to *post*disciplinarity in rhetoric of health and medicine, here is an excerpt from the web biography of a researcher whom I described earlier as an anthropologist with an interest in Burke:

> Professor Dumit received his B.A. from Rice University (Anthropology and Philosophy, 1989) and his Ph.D. from the University of California, Santa Cruz (History of Consciousness, 1995). He was an NIMH Research Fellow in the Department of Social Medicine at Harvard Medical School (1995–1997), and a Postdoctoral Fellow at the Dibner Institute (1997–1998). . . . He is . . . Director of Science and Technology Studies at UC Davis. (Dumit, 2007)

That is a 21st-century research profile, suggesting, for one thing, the availability of research questions, including some rhetorical ones, that heretofore lacked the ability to be asked.

RESEARCH CULTURE(S) IN RHETORIC OF HEALTH AND MEDICINE

I have surveyed disciplines and interdisciplines to indicate the range of work that might count as rhetorical studies of health and medicine, in its widest definition, and I have explained as well that there is quite a range of work that makes up a (loosely) disciplinary rhetoric of health and medicine. Given the variety of work on health and medicine done by researchers who identify their work as rhetorical, and given the different locations (departments, journals, conferences, etc.) where that work is performed, a description of the field should include a sociology of it—a look at the community identities of, and interactions among, rhetoricians of health and medicine.

Even such a limited sociology (i.e., one that leaves out rhetorical work done by historians and psychiatrists, for example) will be Janus faced: It will look inward to different research communities within rhetorical studies, and it will look outward to research communities where the work of rhetoricians intersects with

the work of other scholars, much of it in novel gatherings that may not even have existed 30 years ago. While (internally) rhetoricians of health and medicine present their work through the Association for Rhetoric of Science and Technology (if they identify their work as rhetoric of science) and through the Medical Rhetoric caucus of the Conference on College Composition and Communication (if they identify their work as composition studies)—more on this in a moment—they also branch in several directions, presenting their work at meetings in, for example, health communication, narrative studies, disability studies, and science and technology studies. Janus's second view, the branching view, is where I begin, with rhetoricians of health and medicine who bring rhetorical studies to these research communities and bring the scholarship of these research communities to rhetorical studies.

Health communication is a field that shares interests with, but is separate from, rhetoric of health and medicine. Research in health communication is typically more applied and more empirical than most rhetorical research, and it is performed by, for example, experts in professional communication, as well as nurses and other health professionals. But rhetoricians travel easily here. In an essay in the journal *Health Communication,* rhetoricians Amanda Young and Linda Flower (2002) report on the development of a health care communication model called, "collaborative interpretation"— a rhetorical practice, they explain, designed to reduce misunderstanding between patients and care providers, and to structure their interaction toward a more complete diagnostic story and a collaborative treatment plan.

Experts in narrative studies are typically communication and literature specialists (see, respectively, Harter, Japp, & Beck, 2005; Hunter, 1991), but researchers using narrative analysis are often physicians or psychologists (see, respectively, Charon, 2006; Pennebaker, 2004) or other health practitioners.[19] Rhetoricians make a special contribution to the field. In an essay in *Literature and Medicine*, Charles M. Anderson (1998) uses rhetorical theory to study stories, but he takes as material for analysis not patients' stories, rather stories of medical students. Anderson identifies four narrative patterns constituting what he calls a "rhetoric of healing," a "set of symbolic processes that provide the complex discursive conditions of health, wholeness, and a sense of identity" (p. 281).

A third research community welcoming rhetoricians of health and medicine is disability studies. In "Deafness, Literacy, Rhetoric" (2001), rhetorician Brenda Jo Brueggemann seeks to "redraw, rhetorically, the territory of deafness as a disability in the nexus of literacy" (p. 117). Breuggemann explains how an education system that sets language against communication, and emphasizes the former, leaves deaf students "linguistically lacking, audiologically disabled, civically crippled, culturally deprived" (p. 130). The essay follows Brueggemann's (1999) book-length treatment of "rhetorical constructions of deafness."

The central disciplines of science and technology studies are history, philosophy, and sociology of science. Increasingly, rhetoric of science has taken its place in science and technology studies scholarship, and the work of rhetoricians of health and medicine is presented at meetings of, for example, the Society for Social Studies of Science. Joan Leach's (in press) examination of rhetorical theories of testimony is a contribution to both rhetoric of health and medicine and research in science and technology studies. In a forthcoming essay, Leach compares contemporary trauma narratives and scientific rhetoric of biomedicine. She argues that the discourses which seem at first oppositional to each other are, in fact, complementary, and not, finally, so dissimilar. Both, for example, rely on forms of mediation, and both act rhetorically as Aristotle's "inartistic proof": testimony.

Janus faces in. Scholars working in rhetoric reside, we know, in different departments;

a premise of this book is that there are, minimally, two departmental homes for rhetoricians: English and Communication. Scholars working in rhetoric of health and medicine importantly have no single research community. They attend different conferences and publish in different journals. Their professional identifications are not incidental to the work these scholars do; rather they often define it.

In 2000, a special issue appeared of *Technical Communication Quarterly* (*TCQ*) on "medical rhetoric"; editors were Barbara Heifferon (English, Clemson University) and Stuart Brown (English, New Mexico State University). In 2001, a special issue of *Journal of Medical Humanities* (*JMH*) appeared, on "rhetoric and biomedicine"; the editor was John Lyne (Communication, University of Pittsburgh). The *TCQ* issue features essays by scholars from, primarily, departments of English, and most of the contributors are affiliated with the Conference on College Composition and Communication, in particular its special interest group on medical rhetoric. The context of this research is composition studies and professional writing. In contrast, the *JMH* issue features essays by scholars from, primarily, departments of Communication, and most of the contributors are affiliated with the Association for Rhetoric of Science and Technology, which meets, and sponsors panels, at the conference of the National Communication Association. The context of research is rhetoric of science.[20] Lyne's editor's introduction, subtitled, "How Rhetoric Matters to Biomedicine," marks the collected essays as allied to canonical rhetorical theory (the *TCQ* issue has no editor's introduction).[21]

A third collection of essays, this one under the heading "Discourses of Medicine," was published as a special issue of the *Journal of Business and Technical Communication* in 2005; the editor was Ellen Barton (English, Wayne State University). In this special issue, rhetorical analysis is taken to be one way of doing discourse studies of medicine; Barton writes, "Theoretically, the field of technical and professional communication draws on a generative variety of rhetorical and critical frameworks, especially genre theory" (p. 248). Barton's system of classification, in which professional communication is the highest order category (and rhetoric is an approach) is interesting to the project of mapping the field in question—as, in my system of classification, rhetoric is the highest order category (and professional communication is an approach). The inversion of hierarchies is evidence of an appealing latitude in describing a still emerging field.[22]

The three special journal issues suggest different constituencies of rhetoric of health and medicine as it is occupied by (those whom I have called) rhetoricians. The different sorts of work done within each correspond—loosely, and with overlaps and exceptions—with theoretical/methodological categories that I introduced earlier (*JMH* = canonical rhetorical theory; *JBTC* and *TCQ* = discourse theory, genre theory, and professional communication). Differences within the scholarship will either become more entrenched with time, as researchers become more specialized, or they will blend out, as rhetoric of health and medicine establishes itself as a single field embracing a range of approaches. It is too soon to know how things will go.[23]

CONCLUSION

The first cut I made in describing rhetoric of health and medicine was between scholars who are trained in the history and theory of rhetoric (rhetoricians), and other researchers, who may be sociologists, philosophers, or psychiatrists but have a research interest in discourse and persuasion. A second cut was within the first category of scholars; I identified a range of theories and methodologies in rhetorical study, broadly conceived. I also specified rhetoric of health and medicine done by critics trained in rhetorical history and theory as what might be the center of a series

of concentric circles of work subsumed under the name of rhetoric of health and medicine. I located my own work in that center section, although I added that my work is not, typically, wholly based on canonical rhetorical theory. Moreover, my work branches out of rhetorical studies in interdisciplinary directions. The pharmaceuticals project I described, for example, is also research in science and technology studies; my breast cancer project is also research in narrative studies.

I hope that, at every point in this description, readers have accepted my disclaimers and inferred still more. As I have said, theories/methodologies overlap; categories are unbound; hierarchies impart information about structure and not value. Throughout, I have sought to make the case that we are in a postdisciplinary world of research and scholarship; my description was not then intended as a boundary project.[24]

But inter- and postdisciplinary work are not, for that reason, undisciplined, and I do not mean to give up the idea of rhetoric itself. It may be that rhetorical analysis is a transdisciplinary method, available for use in the service of any research project, but it is not *only* that. An anthropologist may talk about "rhetorical devices" of biomedicine, sociologists may lay claim to Kenneth Burke—and students with a single course in rhetorical criticism will undertake rhetorical analysis (of course they will). Rhetoric, however, delivers more, the more it is studied. Whatever researchers in the broadest realm of rhetoric of health and medicine choose to emphasize in their work (in topic, theory, or method), to the extent that their work is focused on questions of persuasion, it will be better when it is done with more knowledge of rhetorical history and theory.

I said earlier that rhetorical theory can be taught in a course or two, but a rhetorical frame of mind takes years to develop. Perhaps we may seek the opportunity to use graduate student training as a framework for thinking about what rhetoric of health and medicine is. We might, in other words, begin to know what rhetoric of health and medicine is by figuring out what it would take to prepare to do it well.

NOTES

1. A description of rhetorical projects, thematically, on a continuum from local (material texts in the everyday practice of medicine) to global (say, metaphors of medical models) is in Derkatch and Segal (2005), an essay written for medical students and physicians.

2. Research in health and medicine can be useful without being applied—although some rhetorical research is applied. Here are two examples of the contrast. Using rhetorical principles, Lorelei Lingard (2006) seeks to decrease surgical error by designing interventions aimed at improving communication in operating rooms; her work is applied. But Charles M. Anderson's (1989) groundbreaking work in rhetoric of surgery is not applied. It explains how human beings are framed when they are objects and subjects of surgery, and, because it illuminates the culture of biomedicine, it may help improve the conditions of surgical practice over time. Richard M. Perloff's project of applied research in *Persuading People to Have Safer Sex* (2001) is aimed at making safer-sex messages more persuasive to the public. In contrast, J. Blake Scott (2003) scrutinizes the very notion of safe(r) sex and examines its discursive force. His work is useful because the better HIV/AIDS discourse is understood, the more the disease can be contained.

3. Much has been written in rhetorical theory about the motives of rhetorical critics (see, e.g., Hart, 1994, on the obligations of the critic). Robert L. Ivie (2001) talks about "productive criticism," where "rhetoric" is a generative term for social critique. Productive criticism "bridge[s] the divide between *rhetorica utens* [rhetoric for use] and *rhetorica docens* [rhetoric for study] within a framework of scholarship that engages public issues. The thoroughly rhetorical critic . . . is a productive scholar who enriches the social imaginary for the purpose of enhancing human relations."

4. Much work will be omitted in the account—for space reasons, but also because scholarship in rhetoric of health and medicine can be hard to find. It might appear in *Rhetoric Society Quarterly* or *Quarterly Journal of Speech*—or in *Technical Communication Quarterly* or *Journal of Business and Technical Communication*, journals that have been mentioned in other chapters of this book. The scholarship, however, might also be found in *Literature and Medicine* or the *Journal of Medical Humanities*. A rhetorically focused article might turn up in interdisciplinary health journals such as *Social Science and Medicine* and *Health: An Interdisciplinary Journal for the Social Study of Health, Illness and Medicine*. Science and Technology Studies journals, such as *Social Studies of Science* and *Science as Culture* publish some essays in anthropology and sociology that look a great deal like rhetoric, and they publish essays by self-identified rhetoricians too. The bibliographer, moreover, should not overlook the *British Medical Journal* or *The Lancet*. A rhetorical analysis might turn up in the pages of a book on feminist approaches to medical ethics or a book on ideologies of breast cancer. As is the case for some other rhetorical fields, bibliography is a key challenge for research in this one. On interdisciplinarity and bibliography in rhetoric of health and medicine, see Segal (2005a).

5. This is a rough list; for more authors, and for titles and dates, see, for example, Bizzell and Herzberg (2001).

6. For a further discussion of questions of rhetorical theory and method as they pertain to rhetoric of health and medicine, see Segal (2005b), Introduction.

7. For example, for a senior seminar called "Rhetorics of Health and Medicine" at the University of Colorado, Lisa Keränen includes on her reading list works by sociologists Deborah Lupton, Paul Starr, and Arthur Frank; literature specialists Susan Sontag and Elaine Scarry; and scholars in other disciplines.

8. Derrida (1993) details these pleasures of illicit drugs.

9. These ads for Paxil (GlaxoSmithKline, 2004), Effexor (Wyeth, 2003), Relpax (Pfizer, 2004), and Ambien (Sanofi-Aventis, 2004) appeared in wide-circulation magazines, including,

respectively, *People,* for the first three and the *New York Times Magazine* for the fourth.

10. Splitting is also suggested by a rhetorical notion—*dissoi logoi*—dating back to the sophists.

11. In a widely posted call for proposals, leading to a conference at Stanford University, October 2005, Proctor and Schiebinger introduced into interdisciplinary science studies a new theoretical perspective and methodology: agnotology, the study of the cultural production of ignorance. Proctor and Schiebinger's idea was that we deploy resources of research and scholarship to investigate how we know what we know (epistemology), but we do not marshal the same resources to investigate how, and why, we don't know what we don't know.

12. Writing about rhetorical criticism based on Aristotle, E. P. J. Corbett (1969) says that the rhetorician is "more interested in a literary work for what it *does* than for what it *is*" (p. xxii; emphasis in original). Donald Bryant (1973) writes that the rhetorical critic distinguishes between "the treatment of artifacts as significant primarily for what they *are* and the treatment of them as primarily significant for what they *do*" (p. 27; emphasis in original).

13. About 1% of people with breast cancer are men.

14. This quotation is from a review excerpted in an advertisement for *Cancer Vixen* by Marisa Acocello Marchetto (2006), an illustrated story of breast cancer from discovery of a lump through treatment.

15. This is what I mean by "rhetorically minded" here: Pitts hypothesizes that she will find a "cyber agency" in Internet narratives; Broom describes conventional and hegemonic features in breast cancer narratives; Potts takes up the idea of "counternarrative" in breast cancer accounts—the relation of stories to the dominant social order; Herndl asks to whom and for whom breast cancer stories are told.

16. See also publications under the name Mary Lay Schuster.

17. A version of the foregoing paragraph and part of the next one is in Segal (2005a, p. 311).

18. These are scientism (biomedicine is rational, objective, and logical); reification (things in medicine that seem unknowable are knowable);

domination (medicine masters nature); biomedical infallibility (medicine itself does not usually make mistakes); physician heroism (the doctor conquers illness); and patient benefit (everything done in medicine is done for the patient) (p. 33).

19. For a discussion of narrative analysis as a transdisciplinary method in health studies, see Segal (2007b).

20. In North America, English department appointments often come with teaching and administrative responsibilities in writing, so it is not surprising that the more practically and pedagogically inclined rhetoric of health and medicine is housed in departments of English.

21. *Journal of Medical Humanities* (*JMH*) is not a "rhetoric" journal, and so these essays could be seen, like contributions to *Health Communication* or *Social Studies of Science,* to be ones that branch out from any core research community in rhetoric of health and medicine. The *JMH* issue, however, functioned for rhetoricians as a means of gathering research in the field; it had an internal function as well as being an account of rhetoric for the interdiscipline, medical humanities.

22. In 2007, Barton, with Susan Wells, led a "medical rhetoric" seminar of the Rhetoric Society of America's second biennial summer institute. In the seminar's bibliographies, one master list was for "Medical Communication," with sublists for Discourse Analysis, Conversational Analysis, Health Communication, Narrative and Medicine (Traditional), Medical Ethnography, Composition Studies and Professional/Technical Communication; the other master list was for "Medical Rhetoric," with a unified bibliography including readings by rhetoricians and nonrhetoricians, on both health and medical topics and on topics in rhetoric of science and science studies more generally.

23. One ambiguous indication of direction is a forthcoming collection of essays with contributors across constituencies: *Rhetoric of Healthcare: Essays Toward a New Disciplinary Inquiry,* edited by Barbara Heifferon and Stuart Brown. The title positions the volume as "rhetoric[al]," "new," "disciplinary," and in the mode of "inquiry"; on the other hand, "healthcare" announces an interest in topics at the border of rhetoric of health and medicine and health communication (i.e., with interest skewed to professional communication).

24. For a discussion of boundary work, see Gieryn (1983).

REFERENCES

Anderson, C. M. (1989). *Richard Selzer and the rhetoric of surgery*. Carbondale: Southern Illinois University Press.

Anderson, C. M. (1998). 'Forty acres of cotton waiting to be picked': Medical students, storytelling, and the rhetoric of healing. *Literature and Medicine, 17*(2), 280–297.

Barton, E. (2004). Discourse methods and critical practice in professional communication: The front-stage and back-stage discourse of prognosis in medicine. *Journal of Business and Technical Communication, 18*(1), 67–111.

Barton, E. (2005). Introduction. Special issue: The discourses of medicine. *Journal of Business and Technical Communication, 19*(3), 245–248.

Bekins, L. K., Huckin, T. N., & Kijak, L. (2004). The personal statement in medical school applications: Rhetorical structure in a diverse and unstable context. *Issues in Writing, 15*(1), 56–75.

Berkenkotter, C. (2001). Genre systems at work: *DSM-IV* and rhetorical recontextualization in psychotherapy paperwork. *Written Communication, 18*(3), 326–349.

Berkenkotter, C., & Ravotas, D. (2002). New research strategies in genre analysis: Reported speech as recontextualization in a psychotherapist's notes and initial assessment. In E. Barton, G. Stygall, & R. Gundlach (Eds.), *Discourse studies in composition* (pp. 229–255). Cresskill, NJ: Hampton.

Bizzell, P., & Herzberg, B. (Eds.). (2001). *The rhetorical tradition: Readings from classical times to the present*. Boston: Bedford/St. Martin's.

Black, E. (1992). *Rhetorical questions: Studies of public discourse*. Chicago: University of Chicago Press.

Broom, D. (2001). Reading breast cancer: Reflections on a dangerous intersection. *Health: An Interdisciplinary Journal for the Social Study of Health, Illness and Medicine, 5*(2), 249–268.

Brueggemann, B. J. (1999). *Lend me your ear: Rhetorical constructions of deafness*. Washington, DC: Gallaudet University Press.

Brueggemann, B. J. (2001). Deafness, literacy, rhetoric: Legacies of language and communication. In J. C. Wilson & C. Lewiecki-Wilson (Eds.), *Embodied rhetorics: Disability in language and culture* (pp. 115–134). Carbondale: Southern Illinois University Press.

Bryant, D. C. (1973). *Rhetorical dimensions in criticism*. Baton Rouge: Louisiana State University Press.

Burke, K. (1969). *A grammar of motives*. Berkeley: University of California Press.

Burke, K. (1973). The rhetoric of Hitler's 'battle.' In *Philosophy of literary form: Studies in symbolic action* (3rd ed., pp. 191–220). Berkeley: University of California Press.

Bury, M. (2001). Illness narratives: fact or fiction? *Sociology of Health and Illness, 23*(3), 263–285.

Cassell, E. J. (2004). *The nature of suffering and the goals of medicine* (2nd ed.). New York: Oxford University Press.

Charon, R. (2006). *Narrative medicine: Honoring the stories of illness*. Oxford, UK: Oxford University Press.

Clarke, A. E., Shim, J. K., Mamo, L., Fosket, J. R., & Fishman, J. R. (2003). Biomedicalization: Technoscientific Transformations of Health, Illness, and U.S. Biomedicine. *American Sociological Review, 86*, 161–194.

Condit, C. M. (2000). Women's reproductive choices and the genetic model of medicine. In M. M. Lay, L. J. Gurak, C. Gravon, & C. Myntti (Eds.), *Body talk: Rhetoric, technology, reproduction* (pp. 125–141). Madison, WI: University of Wisconsin Press.

Conrad, P. (2007). *The medicalization of society: On the transformation of human conditions into treatable disorders*. Baltimore: Johns Hopkins University Press.

Corbett, E. P. J. (Ed.). (1969). *Rhetorical analyses of literary works*. New York: Oxford University Press.

Couser, G. T. (1997). *Recovering bodies: Illness, disability, and life writing*. Madison: University of Wisconsin Press.

Derkatch, C., & Segal, J. Z. (2005). Realms of rhetoric in health and medicine. *University of Toronto Medical Journal, 82*(2), 138–142.

Derrida, J. (1993). The rhetoric of drugs. An interview. *Differences, 5*(1), 1–25.

Dumit, J. (2004). *Picturing personhood: Brain scans and biomedical identity*. Princeton, NJ: Princeton University Press.

Dumit, J. (2007). *Faculty biography*. Retrieved July 18, 2007, from http://web.mit.edu/STS/faculty/info/Dumit_Joseph-css.html

Ehrenreich, B. (2001). Welcome to cancerland: A mammogram leads to a cult of pink kitsch. *Harper's Magazine, 302*(1818), 43–53.

Elliott, C. (1998). The tyranny of happiness: Ethics and cosmetic psychopharmacology. In E. Parens (Ed.), *Enhancing human traits: Ethical and social implications* (pp. 177–188). Washington, DC: Georgetown University Press.

Elliott, C. (2003). *Better than well: American medicine meets the American dream*. New York: W. W. Norton.

Epstein, S. (1996). *Impure science: AIDS, activism, and the politics of knowledge*. Berkeley: University of California Press.

Frank, A. (1995). *The wounded storyteller: Body, illness, and ethics*. Chicago: University of Chicago Press.

Gieryn, T. F. (1983). Boundary-work and the demarcation of science from non-science: Strains and interests in professional ideologies of scientists. *American Sociological Review, 48*(6), 781–795.

Giltrow, J. (1998, January). *Meta-genre*. Paper presented at the 2nd International Symposium on Genre, Vancouver, British Columbia, Canada.

Goffman, E. (1959). *The presentation of self in everyday life*. Garden City, NY: Doubleday.

Greene, J. (2004). Therapeutic infidelities: 'Noncompliance' enters the medical literature, 1955–1975. *Social History of Medicine, 17*(3), 327–343.

Greenhalgh, S. (2001). *Under the medical gaze: Facts and fictions of chronic pain*. Berkeley: University of California Press.

Harris, R. A. (1997). Introduction. In R. A. Harris (Ed.), *Landmark essays on rhetoric of science: Case studies*. Mahwah, NJ: Hermagoras.

Hart, R. (1994). Wandering with rhetorical criticism. In W. L. Nothstine, C. Blair, & G. Copeland (Eds.), *Critical questions: Invention, creativity, and the criticism of discourse and media* (pp. 71–81). New York: St. Martin's Press.

Harter, L. M., Japp, P. M., & Beck, C. (Eds.). (2005). *Narratives, health, and healing:*

Communication theory, research, and practice. Mahwah, NJ: Lawrence Erlbaum.

Heifferon, B. A. (2006). The new smallpox: An epidemic of words? *Rhetoric Review, 25*(1), 76–93.

Heifferon, B., & Brown, S. C. (Eds.). (in press). *Rhetoric of healthcare: Essays toward a new disciplinary inquiry*. Cresskill, NJ: Hampton Press.

Herndl, D. P. (2006). Our breasts, our selves: Identity, community, and ethics in cancer autobiographies. *Signs, 32*(1), 221–245.

Hunter, K. M. (1991). *Doctors' stories: The narrative structure of medical knowledge*. Princeton, NJ: Princeton University Press.

Hyde, M. J., & McSpiritt, S. (2007). Coming to terms with perfection: The case of Terri Schiavo. *Quarterly Journal of Speech, 93*(2), 150–178.

Ivie, R. L. (2001). Productive criticism then and now. *American Communication Journal, 4*(3). Retrieved July 24, 2007, from www.acjournal.org/holdings/vol4/iss3/special/ivie.htm

Jordan, J. W. (2004). The rhetorical limits of the "plastic body." *Quarterly Journal of Speech, 90*(3), 327–358.

Keränen, L. (2007). "Cause someday we all die": Rhetoric, agency, and the case of the "patient" preferences worksheet. *Quarterly Journal of Speech, 93*(2), 179–210.

King, S. (2006). *Pink ribbons, inc.: Breast cancer and the politics of philanthropy*. Minneapolis: University of Minnesota Press.

Koerber, A. (2005). "You just don't see enough normal": Critical perspectives on infant-feeding discourse and practice. *Journal of Business and Technical Communication, 19*(3), 304–327.

Koerber, A. (2006). From folklore to fact: The rhetorical history of breastfeeding and immunity, 1950–1997. *Journal of Medical Humanities, 27*(3), 151–166.

Kramer, P. D. (2004). The valorization of sadness: Alienation and the melancholic treatment. In C. Elliott & T. Chambers (Eds.), *Prozac as a way of life* (pp. 48–58). Chapel Hill: University of North Carolina Press.

Lay, M. M. (2003). Midwifery on trial: Balancing privacy rights and health concerns after *Roe v. Wade*. *Quarterly Journal of Speech, 89*(1), 60.

Lay, M. M., & Gurak, L. J. (Eds.). (2002). *Research in technical communication*. Westport, CT: Praeger.

Lay, M. M., Gurak, L., Gravon, C., & Myntti, C. (Eds.). (2000). *Body talk: Rhetoric, technology, reproduction.* Madison: University of Wisconsin Press.

Leach, J. (in press). Hi-tech testimony and low-tech rhetoric. In A. Pinchevsky (Ed.), *Media witness.*

Lexchin, J., & Mintzes, B. (2002). Direct-to-consumer advertising of prescription drugs: The evidence says no. *Journal of Public Policy & Marketing, 21*(2), 194–201.

Lingard, L. (2006, October). *Advancing patient safety through a rhetorical approach to communication.* Paper presented at Health Humanities conference, Vancouver, British Columbia, Canada.

Lingard, L., & Haber, R. (2002). Learning medical talk: How the apprenticeship complicates current explicit/tacit debates in genre instruction. In R. Coe, L. Lingard, & T. Teslenko (Eds.), *The rhetoric and ideology of genre: Strategies for stability and change* (pp. 155–170). Cresskill, NJ: Hampton Press.

Lingard, L., K. Garwood, K., Schryer, C. F., & Spafford, M. M. (2003). A certain art of uncertainty: Case presentation and the development of professional identity. *Social Science & Medicine, 56*(3), 603–616.

Lock, M. (1998). Breast cancer: Reading the omens. *Anthropology Today, 14*(4), 7–16.

Lorde, A. (1980). *The cancer journals.* San Francisco: Aunt Lute Books.

Lupton, D. (1992). Discourse analysis: A new methodology for understanding the ideologies of health and illness. *Australian Journal of Public Health, 16*(2), 145–150.

Lyne, J. (2001). Contours of intervention: How rhetoric matters to biomedicine. *Journal of Medical Humanities, 22*(1), 3–13.

Marchetto, M. A. (2006). *Cancer Vixen: A true story.* New York: Alfred A. Knopf.

Mattingly, C. (1998). In search of the good: Narrative reasoning in clinical practice. *Medical Anthropology Quarterly, 12*(3), 273–297.

McCarthy, L. (1991). A psychiatrist using *DSM-III.* In C. Bazerman & J. Paradis (Eds.), *Textual dynamics of the professions* (pp. 358–378). Madison: University of Wisconsin Press.

McCarthy, L. P., & Gerring, J. P. (1994). Revising psychiatry's charter document *DSM-IV. Written Communication, 11*(2), 147–192.

Metzl, J. M. (2003). *Prozac on the couch: Prescribing gender in the era of wonder drugs.* Durham, NC: Duke University Press.

Miller, C. (1984). Genre as social action. *Quarterly Journal of Speech, 70,* 151–167.

Moore, M. (2007). *Sicko* [Documentary film]. United States: Weinstein Company.

Pennebaker, J. W. (2004). *Writing to heal: A guided journal for recovering from trauma and emotional upheaval.* Oakland, CA: New Harbinger Press.

Perelman, C., & Olbrechts-Tyteca, L. (1969). *The new rhetoric: A treatise on argumentation* (J. Wilkinson & P. Weaver, Trans.). Notre Dame, IN: Notre Dame University Press.

Perloff, R. M. (2001). *Persuading people to have safer sex: Applications of social science to the AIDS crisis.* Mahwah, NJ: Lawrence Erlbaum.

Pezzullo, P. C. (2003). Resisting "National Breast Cancer Awareness Month": The rhetoric of counterpublics and their cultural performances. *Quarterly Journal of Speech, 89*(4), 345–365.

Pitts, V. (2004). Illness and Internet empowerment: Writing and reading breast cancer in cyberspace. *Health: An Interdisciplinary Journal for the Social Study of Health, Illness and Medicine, 8*(1), 33–59.

Potts, L. K. (2000). Publishing the personal: Autobiographical narratives of breast cancer and the self. In L. K. Potts (Ed.), *Ideologies of breast cancer: Feminist perspectives* (pp. 98–127). New York: St. Martin's.

Reeves, C. (2005). "I knew there was something wrong with that paper": Scientific rhetorical styles and scientific misunderstandings. *Technical Communication Quarterly, 14*(3), 267–275.

Ryan, C. (2005). Struggling to survive: A study of editorial decision-making strategies at *MAMM* magazine. *Journal of Business and Technical Communication, 19*(3), 353–376.

Scarry, E. (1985). *The body in pain: The making and unmaking of the world.* New York: Oxford University Press.

Scott, J. B. (2002). The public policy debate over newborn HIV testing: A case study of the knowledge enthymeme. *Rhetoric Society Quarterly, 32*(2), 57–83.

Scott, J. B. (2003). *Risky rhetoric: AIDS and the cultural practices of HIV testing.* Carbondale: Southern Illinois University Press.

Segal, J. Z. (2005a). Interdisciplinarity and bibliography in rhetoric of health and medicine. *Technical Communication Quarterly, 14*(3), 311–318.

Segal, J. Z. (2005b). *Health and the rhetoric of medicine.* Carbondale: Southern Illinois University Press.

Segal, J. Z. (2007a). Illness as argumentation: A prolegomenon to the rhetorical study of contestable complaints. *Health: An Interdisciplinary Journal for the Social Study of Health, Illness and Medicine, 11*(2), 227–244.

Segal, J. Z. (2007b). Interdisciplinarity and postdisciplinarity in health research in Canada. In V. Raoul, C. Canam, A. D. Henderson, & C. Paterson (Eds.), *Unfitting stories: Narrative approaches to disease, disability, and trauma* (pp. 11–22). Waterloo, Ontario, Canada: Wilfred Laurier University Press.

Segal, J. Z. (in press). Breast cancer narratives as public rhetoric: Genre itself and the maintenance of ignorance. *Linguistics and the Human Sciences, 3*(1).

Shorter, E. (2005). *Written in the flesh: A history of desire.* Toronto, Ontario, Canada: University of Toronto Press.

Solomon, M. (1985). The rhetoric of dehumanization: An analysis of medical reports of the Tuskegee syphilis project. *Western Journal of Speech Communication, 49*(4), 233–247.

Solomon, M. (1994). Commentary. In W. L. Nothstine, C. Blair, & G. A. Copeland (Eds.), *Critical questions: Invention, creativity, and the criticism of discourse and media* (pp. 301–306). New York: St. Martin's.

Sontag, S. (1978). *Illness as metaphor.* New York: Farrar, Straus and Giroux.

Spoel, P., & James, S. (2006). Negotiating public and professional interests: A rhetorical analysis of the debate concerning the regulation of midwifery in Ontario, Canada. *Journal of Medical Humanities, 27*(3), 167–186.

Squier, S. M. (2004). *Liminal lives: Imagining the human at the frontiers of biomedicine.* Durham, NC: Duke University Press.

Tone, A. (2005). Listening to the past: History, psychiatry, and anxiety. *Canadian Journal of Psychiatry, 50*(7), 373–380.

Weaver, R. M. (1970). *Language is sermonic: Richard M. Weaver on the nature of rhetoric.* Baton Rouge: Louisiana State University Press.

Wilson, J. C., & Lewiecki-Wilson, C. (Eds.). (2001). *Embodied rhetorics: Disability in language and culture.* Carbondale: Southern Illinois University Press.

Young, A., & Flower, L. (2002). Patients as partners, patients as problem-solvers. *Health Communication, 14*(1), 69–97.

14

Rhetoric and International Relations

More Than "Cheap Talk"

GORDON R. MITCHELL

On September 26, 2002, 33 international relations (IR) scholars placed an advertisement in the Op-Ed page of the *New York Times* titled "War With Iraq is Not in America's National Interest" (Art et al. 2002). As signatory Jack Snyder (2003) explained, most of the scholars in the group were "realists"—subscribers to a theory of IR holding that the behavior of states can be explained and predicted by analyzing how national interests determine foreign policy. That such a group of scholars would take stock of the situation in the fall of 2002 and conclude that war with Iraq would be an unwise policy is not remarkable. However, the fact that these particular academics were making the case presents a conundrum, one that speaks to the relation between the field of rhetoric and IR.

In their long-running and frequently intense disciplinary argument with "social constructivists," realists assert that since the national interests of states are relatively stable and overriding factors driving foreign policy, analysis of these interests should take priority in scholarship. This commitment runs counter to the research program of social constructivism, which looks to communicative factors such as domestic politics and public debates to discern precisely how particular state interests emerge and evolve (e.g., Haacke, 1996; Lynch, 1999; Payne & Samhat, 2004). If the realist notion that social processes have little impact on the formation of national interests and foreign policy is accurate, why then would a group of realist scholars invest such time and effort into the expensive enterprise of taking out an advertisement in the *New York Times*?

The realists' foray invites questions regarding audience, evidence, source credibility, and argument—typically key issues in the study of rhetoric. For the political scientist Rodger Payne (2007), this performative tension cues the need for a particular strain of IR scholarship that foregrounds communicative action as a key element of analysis.

> Neorealist theory is not a critical theory, but many of the scholars who have helped develop this theory in the field of international relations behave very much as critical theorists when they partake in foreign policy debates. The neorealists implicitly and explicitly embrace presuppositions about the importance of public debate and political communication that are almost entirely consistent with the premises of critical theory. In the Iraq debate and in other examples, the neorealists are revealing lies, political spin, and other distortions of the debate promulgated by government elites and their allies. They challenge the legitimacy of established policies and critique what they see as excessive secrecy. Most importantly, these neorealists seek to transform public and elite consciousness so as to produce social pressures for alternative outcomes. For critical theorists, this contradiction between realist theorizing and policy action is logically unsustainable and suggests an opening for alternative outcomes. It would strongly imply the significant need for an understanding of foreign policy, and likely a theory of international relations, that accounts for communicative action. (p. 510)

Fresh impetus for a communication-based approach to IR also comes from recent trends in world affairs. IR scholarship conducted under the banner of realism has traditionally deployed "realpolitik" nomenclature to explain and predict events. IR realists tend to view the world as a place where the behavior of nation-states can be explained with reference to the relatively fixed parameters of stable national interests and identities (Morgenthau, 1948; Waltz, 1979). Yet defense analysts John

Arquilla and David Ronfeldt, inventors of the term *cyberwar* (1993), now argue that the advent of a new mode of international politics they term *noöpolitik* presents difficult anomalies for the realist paradigm.

The rise of a networked global society characterized by asymmetrical conflicts and the heightened efficacy of transnational, nongovernmental actors, say Arquilla and Ronfeldt (2000, 2007), has yielded the "noosphere," a backdrop for international politics that resembles prognostications sketched by the futurist Pierre Teilhard de Chardin (1965; see also Cobb, 1998). In the noosphere, a global "realm of the mind" links actors together in ways that complicate the exercise of traditional modes of state power, hence a new form of political action, "noöpolitik":

> By noöpolitik we mean an approach to statecraft, to be undertaken as much by non–state as by state actors, that emphasizes the role of informational soft power in expressing ideas, values, norms, and ethics through all manner of media. This makes it distinct from realpolitik, which stresses the hard, material dimensions of power and treats states as the determinants of world order. Noöpolitik makes sense because knowledge is fast becoming an ever stronger source of power and strategy, in ways that classic realpolitik and internationalism cannot absorb. (Arquilla & Ronfeldt, 2007)

Both of these trends—IR realists' performative embrace of public argument practice, on the one hand, and the dawn of noöpolitik, on the other—highlight how the nexus between rhetoric and foreign policy studies is becoming fertile ground for intellectual interchange, with a growing number of IR scholars drawing on the concept of argumentation to explain global events that resist snapping snugly into the tidy templates of Cold War power politics. This moment of intellectual convergence suggests that the field of communication may be working as what Leah Ceccarelli (2001, p. 5) calls a "conceptual chiasmus"—an interdisciplinary bridge connecting different scholarly communities working on overlapping subject matter.

The rhetoric-as-bridge possibility is intriguing in light of the fact that realism and social constructivism—the two intellectual land masses being connected—have developed for decades as isolated islands. The moat separating the communities was the prevailing realist view that discounted communication as mere "cheap talk" that does little more than carry (often unreliable) diplomatic signals from one state to another. As the process of human communication rises in salience to transcend "cheap talk" models, scholars of rhetoric and argumentation emerge as interlocutors capable of contributing a conceptual apparatus to analysis of world affairs that charts a third course, transcending the realism-social constructivism deadlock in IR.

The North Carolina–based Triangle Institute for Security Studies (TISS) has facilitated academic interchange along these lines through its scholarly conferences and publications.[1] For example, a 1998 TISS conference on Bridging Gaps in the Study of Public Opinion and American Foreign Policy featured a roundtable discussion that put the political scientist Ole Holsti in conversation with the public argument scholars David Cheshier and Erik Doxtader (Cheshier, Doxtader, & Holsti, 1998). This dialogue, which centered on Holsti's (1996) groundbreaking book, *Public Opinion and American Foreign Policy*, hints at how the lens of rhetoric can bring sharp focus to foreign policy studies that treat public opinion and deliberative practice as constitutive dimensions of global politics.

The overlap between rhetoric and IR scholarship becomes clearer when one compares Thomas Goodnight's (1998) call for study of "argument formation[s]" in world affairs with Thomas Risse's (2000) insight that by attending to "arguing in the international public sphere" (p. 21), IR scholars can effectively combine realism and social constructivism. Such a focus highlights human communication as a "site of invention from

which arguments can be drawn forward and discourse fashioned to explain, justify and support policy" (Goodnight, 2006, p. 95). Reinforcing Goodnight's view and echoing Risse's suggestion, Cori Dauber and David Cheshier (1998) locate the rhetorically informed study of foreign policy in a conceptual middle space that foregrounds the iterative relationship between material conditions and discursive practices:

> The political scene in any polity will be shaped by complex interactions between public arguers, where the realities of geopolitics and culture will shape both arguer and audience and in turn be made the topoi and evidence of their claims. (p. 40)

It is notable that Dauber and Cheshier (1998) position their public argument approach to security studies as an alternative to Samuel Huntington's (1993) realpolitik "clash of civilizations" thesis, much the same way that the IR scholar Marc Lynch (2000, pp. 309–316) uses public sphere theory to ground his critique of Huntington. This overlapping emphasis on argumentation challenges the deterministic underpinnings of Huntington's pessimistic worldview by illustrating how the global milieu is marked by moments of rhetorical exigence—opportunities to color with words and images what some paint as the inexorable march of history toward cataclysmic conflict. It also responds to two of IR realism's explanatory weaknesses—difficulty in accounting for the heightened efficacy of nongovernmental organizations (NGOs) as actors on the world stage (Keck & Sikkink, 1998; Payne, 2000; Payne & Samhat, 2004; Samhat, 1997, pp. 350–356) and descriptive myopia resulting from reductive formulations of communicative action in global affairs (Risse, 1999; Risse-Kappen, 1995). On a normative level, the public argument approach opens a critical aperture for commentators to articulate visions of world affairs where international disputes are resolved and complex problems solved through border-crossing dialogue oriented toward mutual understanding rather than strategic deployment of force via power, money, or arms (Association of German Scientists, 2000; Bohman, 1999; Bohman & Lutz-Bachmann, 1998; Linklater, 1998; Payne, 1996).

The value of such theoretical orientation is demonstrated by recent books in rhetoric that use democratic deliberation as a normative point of departure to ground analysis of foreign affairs (e.g., Hartnett & Stengrim, 2006; Ivie, 2005; Taylor, Kinsella, Depoe, & Metzler, 2007; Winkler, 2006). Can this line of research chart a path that transcends IR's realism/constructivism divide in a way that parallels Richard Bernstein's (1983) famous "beyond relativism and objectivism" formulation? The following pages explore this hypothesis, by considering in turn three topical areas that present rich opportunities for understanding how human communication shapes IR and simultaneously informs study of the same phenomena.

Part I examines how the proposed globalization of public sphere theory plays out in a study on Cold War superpower relations. Part II pursues a similar vector of analysis in the context of Jordanian foreign policy from 1988 to 1998. Part III considers how recent technological developments and political trends complicate efforts to cultivate critical public discussion on security matters in entertainment-saturated spheres of public deliberation.

TRANSNATIONAL ACTIVISM AND THE COLD WAR ENDGAME

Barry Buzan (2000) traces the roughly 20-year history of the IR subfield called "critical security studies" and situates it vis-à-vis realism, IR's dominant paradigm. For Buzan, a defining feature of the critical security studies research program is that instead of accepting realism's theoretical categories (such as threat, security, and state interest) at face value, it shows how these categories are "socially constructed" through various security discourses (p. 3). Here, the way rhetors represent

material conditions in the world becomes as important, if not more important, than the material conditions themselves. As Buzan points out, this emphasis on discourse and representation simultaneously opens up security studies to diverse research methodologies and places a host of new normative questions on the table. These questions include "what should and shouldn't be constructed as threats" and "whose interests are served or damaged by particular processes of securitization and desecuritization" (p. 3).

During the Cold War, talk of the socially constructed nature of security threats was often dismissed in the academy and beyond as little more than Pollyanish bluster. However, as Edward Kolodziej (2000) observes, "The sudden and unexpected implosion of the Soviet Union and the abrupt end of the Cold War prompted a probing, if not always fruitful, debate about what is—or what should be—security studies" (p. 18). Part of this debate played out in the context of discussion about what caused the Cold War to end. Commentators partial to the realist paradigm of power politics explained the Soviet Union's demise as an act of capitulation to overwhelming U.S. military superiority (Brzezinski, 1992; Kirkpatrick, 1990).

Kolodziej (2000), echoing many other voices in critical security studies, disputes this account: "The military dimension of the East-West competition does not appear to have been determinative in explaining either the timing, speed and wholesale unraveling of the Soviet state and empire" (p. 24; see also Deudney & Ikenberry, 1992, p. 124; Pike, Blair, & Schwartz, 1998, pp. 295–297; Powaski, 1998, p. 260; Reiss, 1992, pp. 192–193).

So if the mighty steel of U.S. military strength did not tame the Russian bear, what did? Matthew Evangelista's (1989) answer to this question should pique the interest of rhetoricians. He posits that the sharing of "information, arguments, [and] ideas" between networks of Soviet and American transnational activists constituted a major factor that influenced superpower policy and eventually brought about a peaceful end to the Cold War (p. 7). Turning to the case studies of debates concerning nuclear testing, antiballistic missile defense, and conventional force deployments, Evangelista literally pries open what he calls the "black box" (p. 7) of Soviet policy, documenting previously obscured aspects of Cold War history through exhaustive study of Soviet-era archives, numerous interviews of key Soviet-era officials, review of recent memoir accounts, and inspection of newly declassified U.S. and British archival documents.

Many of these resources chronicle cooperative efforts by Soviet and American scientists, doctors, and activists to create independent channels of communication that kept accurate and reliable information about military intentions and deployments flowing in both directions. Such lines of communication also galvanized an interlocking pattern of peace movement activism that steered Soviet and American leaders toward more moderate postures and policies. Evangelista (1989) cites the early "Pugwash" meetings between U.S. and Soviet scientists as the "birth" of such transnational activism (pp. 31–35). During the 1950s, such meetings helped dramatize the danger of nuclear fallout in the respective public spheres, creating a political momentum that eventually produced a nuclear test ban agreement.

Following a chronological pattern, Evangelista (1989) proceeds to track the entry of a new class of players to the stage of transnational activism in the 1970s—medical doctors. Taking advantage of the opportunity to treat aging Soviet leaders, American physicians such as Bernard Lown visited the Soviet Union and formed lasting relationships with Soviet counterparts such as Evgenii Chazov. The Lown-Chazov connection paved the way for the Boston-based Physicians for Social Responsibility (PSR) to evolve into a transnational network that eventually became

the International Physicians for the Prevention of Nuclear War (IPPNW). Comprising some 200,000 members from 80 countries, the IPPNW won the Nobel Peace Prize in 1985.

In 1981, Lown traveled to the USSR with Carl Sagan, under IPPNW auspices, to make a remarkable series of public appearances designed to educate Soviet audiences about the nuclear arms race. At the time, Lown and Sagan were vilified in the United States by Cold War hawks, who felt that such discussion would compromise American military credibility and bolster Soviet resolve to win a nuclear war. Evangelista's research shows that such transnational activism had the reverse effect. Accurate reportage of IPPNW meetings appeared in Soviet newspapers such as *Pravda* (circulation 10 million), *Izvestiia* (more than 8 million), *Komsomol'skaia pravda* (10 million), and *Literaturnia gazeta* (more than 2.5 million). Soviet national television broadcast nine IPPNW congresses, reaching additional millions. According to Evangelista (1989), these efforts "set a precedent for public discussion—'glasnost'—on nuclear issues, well before Mikhail Gorbachev came into office and began using the term" (p. 155). Evangelista documents how Gorbachev later acknowledged the significance of IPPNW activism by presenting to Lown a copy of the 1987 Intermediate-Range Nuclear Forces Treaty bearing the following inscription:

> Dear Bernard! I want to thank you for your enormous contribution to preventing nuclear war. Without it and other powerful antinuclear initiatives, it is unlikely that this Treaty would have come about. I wish you all the best. Mikhail Gorbachev. (p. 876)

Evangelista's (1989) most convincing analysis shows how transnational linkages shaped the course of Gorbachev's presidency. He tracks the way that physicists and doctors, working alongside peace activists such as Randall Forsberg of the Institute for Defense and Disarmament Studies (IDDS), were able to create the "breathing room" necessary for

Gorbachev and U.S. President Ronald Reagan to engineer a peaceful Cold War endgame:

> In addition to coordination of specific policy initiatives, the transnational network of US and Soviet disarmament supporters also worked together to create an overall atmosphere conducive to restraint on each side. In order for Gorbachev to succeed in cutting back Soviet military programs and military spending, he had to make a plausible case that the United States did not pose a serious threat to Soviet security . . . As the Nuclear Freeze movement sought to persuade Ronald Reagan that he had to tone down his harsh rhetoric about the Soviet Union and careless comments about nuclear war, Soviet reformers pushed initiatives that would diminish the 'enemy image' of the USSR in Reagan's eyes. . . . The warming of US-Soviet relations would not have been possible had Reagan not been pushed by the US peace movement to address the threat of nuclear war. . . . American transnational activists, while trying to constrain US military programs, also considered it important to persuade the Soviet government that it did not pose a threat so grave that Soviet unilateral restraint or even negotiated settlements would be dangerous. . . . They managed to persuade Gorbachev, sometimes in direct discussion, that the Soviet Union should 'unlink' the signing of a strategic weapons reduction treaty from US pursuit of SDI. Star Wars, they argued, would eventually fade away, especially if the Soviet Union continued to pursue its reformist course in defense and disarmament, not to mention internal democratization. (pp. 383–384)

Evangelista's (1989) findings raised serious questions about realpolitik models of IR that explain U.S. Cold War victory over the Soviet Union in terms of one mammoth billiard ball smashing into and destroying its more fragile counterpart. His impressive empirical research illustrates how threats, policies, and norms were constructed and deconstructed by argumentation conducted in transnational channels of communication. If the significance of

this finding for students of argumentation is not already apparent, it becomes obvious in Evangelista's final case study, which examines the influence of transnational activism on post-Soviet policy.

In 1989, the renowned poet Olzhas Suleimenov founded a movement to halt nuclear testing in the Soviet republic of Kazakhstan. As Evangelista (1989) explains, this movement was transnational from inception: By naming their group "Nevada," Suleimenov and his fellow activists attempted to "attract the attention of grassroots antinuclear activists ('downwinders') working to shut down the U.S. test site in Nevada" (p. 352). These efforts succeeded in galvanizing quickly a transnational movement that brought some 50,000 protesters to a demonstration in Kazakhstan on August 6, 1989 (Hiroshima day). Evangelista was present at another important event in the Kazakh village of Karaul in May 1990, when Lown and Suleimenov dedicated a monument to victims of nuclear testing. According to Evangelista,

> the impact was direct and powerful. An official in the Soviet foreign ministry admitted in early 1990 that the movement was responsible for forcing the Soviet military to cancel eleven of its eighteen scheduled nuclear tests for 1989 . . . In December 1990, the Kazakhstan parliament banned nuclear weapons testing on the republic's territory. (p. 354)

Evangelista notes that eventually, this decision worked as "a key prerequisite for the United States, Britain, France, and China to cease their tests" (p. 9).

Rhetorical scholars steeped in knowledge of how naming produces powerful bonds of identification will appreciate the way in which Suleimenov's decision to call the Kazakh antinuclear testing movement "Nevada" played an important role in fomenting the transnational activism chronicled by Evangelista (1989). Future studies might explore how similar patterns of rhetorical invention shape efforts to forge transnational social movements in the security realm. This work would find theoretical support in a burgeoning corpus of literature focusing on the transnational dimensions of social movement activity (see, e.g., Cohen & Shim, 2000; Khagram, Riker, & Sikkink, 2002; Smith, Chatfield, & Pagnucco, 1997), as well as rhetorical studies of foreign policy anchored in concepts such as the "representative anecdote" (Carpenter, 2004). One challenge facing scholars pursuing this line of investigation is that the frequently episodic nature of transnational activism complicates its categorization as social movement activity. For example, Sidney Tarrow (1998, pp. 184–188) stipulates that sustained, rather than temporary or sporadic, contact is necessary for transnational activism to reach the status of a social movement.

Another aspect of Evangelista's work that hints at future lines of research in rhetoric lies on a theoretical level. In developing his theory of transnational activism, Evangelista (1989) acknowledges a significant debt to Risse's "pathbreaking" work on transnational public spheres (p. 17; see also Risse-Kappen, 1995). Recently, Risse (2000) refined his theory of "communicative action in world politics." Scholars of argumentation and rhetoric may be curious to note that in this explication, Risse relies heavily on a distinction between "arguing" and "rhetorical behavior" to explain precisely how his approach differs from neorealist IR perspectives that purport to account for communicative action in world affairs (see also Schimmelfennig, 1999, 2001). According to Risse (2000), neorealist approaches tend to rely on a "cheap talk" model of communication, where international actors engage in communication strategically to persuade interlocutors but are not really willing to change their positions based on outcomes of deliberation: "Actors engaging in rhetoric are not prepared to change their own beliefs or to be persuaded themselves by the 'better argument'" (p. 8). This form of international communication stands in sharp contrast to what Risse calls the "arguing mode," where

parties attempt to approximate Habermasian dialogues geared toward mutual understanding: "In contrast to rhetorical behavior, they are themselves prepared to be persuaded" (p. 9).

Risse's (2000) distinction between rhetoric and argument does not find much support in rhetorical theory, where reductive approaches that treat rhetoric as strategic manipulation are criticized roundly for their conceptual thinness. Thicker descriptions position rhetoric as a practical art of using dialogue to coordinate action when interlocutors at loggerheads are forced to act in situations marked by uncertainty or when collective decisions must be made before all the relevant facts are in (Doxtader, 1991; Farrell, 1993; Ivie, 2005). Public argument-driven security studies might fruitfully explore how these insights could help differentiate bargaining (purely strategic communication undertaken for instrumental purposes), arguing (dialogue oriented toward mutual understanding), and rhetoric (the communicative search for joint agreement on necessary actions in light of imperfect conditions). Such differentiation could enhance the descriptive power of IR theories by adding texture to the argument/ rhetoric binary some approaches use to explain communicative action in international politics.

SECURITY DEBATES IN ARAB PUBLIC SPHERES

In 1988, the Hashemite Kingdom of Jordan surprised the world by relinquishing its claim to the West Bank, effectively severing ties with thousands of Palestinians living on territory that was once part of Jordan. During the 1990 Gulf crisis, Jordan bucked world expectations again by refusing to join the U.S.-led military coalition against Iraq. In signing a 1994 peace treaty with Israel, the Jordanian leadership made yet another unanticipated foreign policy move that was difficult to explain from within the realist IR framework. Realism holds that IR can be described accurately and predicted reliably by examining how state interests and

national identities animate foreign policy decisions. Yet in each of the instances listed above,
Jordanian foreign policy appeared to diverge
from, and even to contradict, long-standing
interests of the Jordanian state and identities
of the Jordanian people.

Marc Lynch (1999) develops a theory of IR
designed to sharpen accounts of Jordanian
behavior from 1988 to 1998. At the center of
Lynch's approach is the notion that shifts in
state interests and national identity can occur
when public spheres of deliberation enable the
airing of competing viewpoints in episodes of
argumentation: "State identity and interests . . .
become subject to change at those points
when an open public sphere permits the
appearance of public deliberation oriented
toward questioning consensus norms" (p. 255).
In a move that globalizes this theory, Lynch
stipulates that public spheres of deliberation
need not map cleanly onto the predetermined
boundaries of state borders:

> Instead of conceptualizing the public sphere
> as a single, unified arena in which a unified
> public debates the affairs of a single state, it
> is possible to think about public sphere
> structure as a network of overlapping and
> competing publics, which are not necessar-
> ily bounded by state borders. (p. 47)

Lynch (1999) draws on field research conducted in Jordan, Egypt, and the West Bank,
along with analysis of Arabic media publications and documents from official archives, to
show how public spheres of deliberation developed in Jordanian society and the Arab world
from 1988 to 1998. He documents how the
Jordanian norm of *hiwar* (dialogue) was nurtured during this period through spikes in newspaper circulation, spread of radio transmitters,
relaxation of state control over media outlets,
and greater participation of editorial commentators from across the political spectrum.

Lynch's (1999) theory is not presented as a
brand of full-blown constructivism designed
to undermine completely the rationalist
explanations yielded by IR's realist paradigm.

Rather, Lynch argues, "a public sphere
approach can bridge constructivist and
rationalist arguments" (p. 11). A temporal
distinction sets up this bridging maneuver. In
periods of "normal politics," when "an
effective public sphere does not exist," Lynch
says that the rationalist tools of IR realism
work well, because "actor identity and
interests are likely to be relatively stable"
(p. 11). Echoing Thomas Kuhn (1970), Lynch
(1999) adds, "Identities and interests change
primarily during moments of crisis, when they
lose their 'taken for granted' quality and
become the subject of explicit public debate"
(p. 12). The key moments of change in
Jordanian foreign policy described by Lynch
are all preceded by episodes of crisis when
state identities and interests are thrown into
flux and thematized as topics of public debate.

Lynch's (1999) case studies describe how these
nascent public spheres influenced Jordanian
security policy by enabling fundamental
transformations in interests and identities. For
example, Lynch suggests that Jordan's "severing
of ties" with the West Bank was made possible
by a two-tiered process of public deliberation.
On one level, Jordanian diplomats persuaded
skeptical Arab colleagues that disengagement
would fortify the Palestinian identity and further
the interests of an emergent Arab consensus
by enhancing the collective security of all Arab
nations. With such a tentative consensus secured,
King Hussein announced the severing of ties
with the West Bank in 1988, an act that
inaugurated commencement of a second phase
of deliberation in Jordan's domestic public
sphere. In the ensuing debate, vigorous argumentation prompted calcified norms to shift in
the key sites of Jordan's nascent public sphere:
professional associations, political parties, the
press, the Islamist movement, and public opinion
surveys. In Lynch's view,

> change in Jordanian identity and interests—
> a change in preferences over outcomes—
> could only be produced by a domestic
> dialogue and the reconfiguration of domestic

institutions. The emergence of the Jordanian public sphere in the 1990s provided a site for such deliberation. (p. 100)

Similar patterns of public sphere activity are isolated as pertinent agents of change in Lynch's two other case studies: Jordan's boycott of the U.S. Gulf War coalition and its signing of a 1994 peace treaty with Israel.

While Lynch (1999) is keen to highlight the constitutive role of public participation in influencing Jordan's security policy from 1988 to 1998, he is quick to distinguish his approach from realist accounts that fill explanatory gaps on an "ad hoc basis" by citing public opinion as a factor "constraining" policy making:

> It is important to distinguish between public opinion, as conventionally employed by foreign policy analysts, and the public sphere. . . . Rather than simply being a question of the extent to which public opinion constrains state policy, the issue is the extent to which public sphere discourse constitutes the state's articulation of interests. (p. 21)

Lynch reveals his Habermasian affinities here, insisting that public sphere dialogue is more than just "cheap talk"—in his view, such dialogue has the power to reconstitute the fundamental building blocks on which foreign policy rests.

If Lynch (1999) is correct about the strong function of public sphere deliberation in constituting state identities and interests, policymakers (especially those in the United States) would do well to heed his concluding remarks, which suggest that public sphere theory "has important implications for the debates over the appropriate response to 'rogue' regimes in the international society" (p. 269). In a world where state interests and identities have roots that go all the way down to civil society, cosmetic regime changes are unlikely, in the long run, to produce more moderate policies in so-called rogue states.

Lynch (1999) hints at a more promising approach for dealing with Iran, one of the nations branded as part of the Bush administration's "axis of evil." A policy of engagement and dialogue, Lynch suggests, "can offer the potential for changing preferences and for identifying common identities and interests" (p. 269). Elsewhere, Lynch (2000) expounds on this idea, blending Iranian President Mohammed Khatami's prescription for a "dialogue of civilizations" with international public sphere theory to craft a vision of global affairs where the persuasive cachet of argumentation supplants coercion and manipulation as primary modes of communication (see also Association of German Scientists, 2000).

Lynch (1999) is hopeful that his account of the "Arabist public sphere" will have enduring salience and "inform a generalizable international public sphere theory" (p. 34). Some readers may not share Lynch's sanguine outlook on this point, given that his approach draws heavily from Jurgen Habermas, whose work focuses primarily on the role of deliberation in highly developed capitalist societies. The question of whether Habermasian theory has sufficient flexibility and explanatory scope to elucidate the dynamics of a putative global public sphere (which includes many nations and peoples who do not openly embrace Western norms of political deliberation) has been the focus of recent debate in critical theory (Calhoun, 2002; Dallmayr, 2001; Habermas, 1998, 2001; McCarthy, 2002).

Rhetorical scholars are well positioned to contribute to this debate, perhaps by using their expertise in argumentation to identify and address the theoretical anomalies present in public-sphere-based accounts of IR. For example, Lynch's (1999, p. 11) notion that "an effective public sphere does not exist" when identities and interests remain stable during periods of "normal politics" sounds much like Thomas Farrell and Thomas Goodnight's (1981) description of "accidental publics" that only come into being during catastrophic episodes. However, it seems untenable to maintain that public sphere structures disappear when crises subside and "normal politics" resume. In fact, many case studies in argumentation document precisely how public sphere activity plays a significant role in will formation during periods of normal politics (see Palczewski, 2001; Rowland & Jones, 2002; Zarefsky, 1986).

Perhaps Lynch's (2000) international public sphere theory could be modified to account for this anomaly by including the concept of "controversy." In the parlance of argumentation studies, controversy is a phenomenon that occurs when underlying norms of communication are contested through "oppositional arguments" levied in public spheres of deliberation (see Goodnight, 1991, 1999; Mitchell, 2000; Olson & Goodnight, 1994; Phillips, 1999). If Lynch (2000) described periods of international deliberation when state interests and identities are contested as episodes of international public controversy, he might position himself better to articulate how public sphere structures persist during periods of normal politics that follow the resolution of controversy.

THE MIME-NET AND SPECTATOR SPORT WARFARE

The U.S. Marine Corp Modeling and Simulation Office recently acquired and modified the popular video game Doom for training exercises, altering the software to replace monsters with realistic simulations of enemy forces that young soldiers might encounter during actual combat. In Kosovo, NATO bombardiers wielded handheld "wizzos," Nintendo-like devices that helped pilots guide precision weaponry to their targets from 40,000 feet. For UN coalition soldiers, the battlefield experience of the Gulf War similarly recalled childhood visits to the video arcade.

James Der Derian (2001) explores these phenomena as part of what he calls the Military-Industrial-Media-Entertainment Network

(MIME-NET). Der Derian sees the MIME-NET as an extension of the "Revolution in Military Affairs" (RMA), a trend in arms procurement and military doctrine that favors the development and deployment of sophisticated, high-tech weaponry (Freedman, 1998; Laird & Mey, 1999). As a latter-day incarnation of President Dwight D. Eisenhower's Military Industrial Complex, the MIME-NET represents an interlocking constellation of organizations and interests that controls the tenor of public debate on security policy (increasingly by exploiting interfaces between warfare and media entertainment networks): "The new MIME-NET runs on video-game imagery, twenty-four hour news cycles, multiple nodes of military, corporate, university, and media power, and microchips, embedded in everything but human flesh (so far)" (Der Derian, 2001, p. 126).

While Der Derian (2001) seems genuinely impressed by the futuristic military technology he encounters, this sense of awe only redoubles the moral and political qualms he harbors about the MIME-NET. Specifically, he finds the virtualization of the warfare troubling because of its tendency to produce phenomenological detachment from battlefield violence: "Through the MIME-NET, the enemy can be reduced to an icon in a target-rich environment, perhaps even efficiently vilified and destroyed at a distance" (p. 147). The sense of alienation created by the conflation of entertainment technology and actual combat, Der Derian says, numbs soldiers and the public alike to the brutality of warfare: "In this high-tech rehearsal for war, one learns how to kill but not to take responsibility for it, one experiences 'death' but not the tragic consequences of it" (p. 10). On a political level, Der Derian asserts that this process results in a hollowing out of political discourse, with virtual pyrotechnics substituting for collective deliberation about matters of war and peace:

Something is lost in virtuality: not only the possibility but the very concept of political difference is hollowed out. It stops being a site of negotiation and becomes a screen for the display of dazzling virtual effects, from digital war games to national party conventions to video-camera bombing. (p. 202)

Der Derian warns that with the direct experience of battlefield carnage emptied from media representations of actual conflict, it becomes much easier for war hawks to take the moral high ground and justify the use of force by packaging risk-free humanitarian missions as virtuous campaigns.

A recent TISS report surveys how the values, opinions, and perspectives of military leaders differ from those of their civilian counterparts (Kohn & Feaver, 1999). Part of this report features Cori Dauber's (2001) public argument analysis of how differing views of "casualty shyness" structure public deliberation and steer policy making. Der Derian (2001, p. 171) cites the casualty shyness portion of the TISS study (he calls it "casualty aversion") to help explain why organizations such as the Institute for Creative Technologies craft virtuous war narratives that resonate in the MIME-NET framework of public debate. Here is one instance of intellectual traffic crossing the Ceccarellian "conceptual chiasmus" that bridges argumentation studies and IR scholarship. When the TISS scholar Peter Feaver was appointed to the Bush administration's National Security Council staff in June 2005, the mobility of rhetorically informed foreign policy studies was illustrated again. It was widely reported that Dauber's (2001) and Kohn and Feaver's (1999) casualty shyness thesis served as the rationale for President Bush's emphasis on "victory" as the rhetorical strategy to sell the Iraq war in a series of four speeches (Shane, 2005).

Another potential chiasmus can be found in the work of Craig Demchak (2000), who describes how rapid advances in military technology portend sea changes in war doctrine and political discourse. The military's traditional reliance on lethality, reach, and resupply as force multipliers has shifted to an emphasis on tools that maximize accuracy, speed, and legitimacy. In this "watershed" period of transition, Demchak argues that new military preferences are bound to emerge regarding technologies, doctrines, and tactics.

In a similar vein, Colin McInnes (2000) shows how high-tech weaponry blurs the boundaries between sport and war. McInnes describes how the "major wars" of the early 20th century have given way to more localized conflicts that unfold far from the capitols of Western democracies. With the sense of war's direct risk diluted by physical distance, McInnes says, citizens come to experience warfare as spectators, "located out of harm's way but engaged courtesy of the media" (p. 160). McInnes suggests that in this condition, public discourse on security matters comes to resemble a commentary on sporting events.

The suicide hijackings of September 2001, cast fresh light on the analysis provided by Demchak (2000) and McInnes (2000). At face value, McInnes's proposition that war has become a spectator sport for Western publics seems to have crumbled along with the World Trade Center. Yet closer inspection of his argument reveals a nuance—McInnes treats spectator sport warfare less as a naturalized condition and more of a calculated strategy pursued by military leaders to enhance the legitimacy of their actions. As such, he anticipates that technologically disadvantaged adversaries will resort increasingly to asymmetric strategies of attack that are designed to puncture the veneer of virtuality by drawing Western spectators directly into the field of violence:

The West's lead in RMA technologies might lead enemies to adopt "asymmetric strategies." These strategies are generally aimed not at winning battles but at drawing Western societies more directly into a war, through attacks on infrastructure or populations. In other words the concern about asymmetric strategies is not related to their direct impact on the battlefield but to their ability to prevent war from being a spectator sport. (p. 160)

Demchak's (2000) analysis also contains elements that deserve a second look in the post-9/11 milieu. According to Demchak, as the RMA prepares Western military forces to fight futuristic conflicts that bear little resemblance to the "great wars" of the early 20th century, the concept of war itself is likely to undergo transformation. Here, traditional views of wars as contests between state armies are likely to give way to models where Western militaries use technological wizardry to target specific organizations and even individual persons:

> This "repersonalization of war" harkens back to military conflicts of several centuries ago when the battle goal was to kill the king or the general . . . the battle ended as soon as someone made it up there [on the mountain] to kill the major lord. (p. 188)

While the current U.S. "war on terror" is unlikely to end with the capture or "liquidation" of Osama bin Laden, Demchak's observations about the protean nature of warfare certainly seem to have added salience in the midst of a conflict where American forces have targeted a terrorist organization reputed to have havens in over 60 nations (see also Stahl, 2006). One political complication that Demchak (2000) sees in a world where military missions increasingly take on the character of police actions is that such actions become harder to track and control via political instruments:

> Under these new definitions, preventive and highly personalized military actions which are only possible with information warfare technologies then become social corrections of possible unwanted severe behaviours, not war by other means. As such, such military

operations will become more ubiquitous and more difficult to control by treaties. (p. 189)

CONCLUSION

As the interlocking trends of economic globalization and political interdependence gather momentum, stresses on the state-centric system of world politics are likely to mount. It is a safe bet that leaders of national governments will find options for effective unilateral action increasingly scarce in a 21st-century milieu where policy challenges such as environmental protection, global security, and economic stability demand new forms of political cooperation.

> With regard to the political means and ends of traditional grand strategy, the realist and neorealist days of state-monopolized 'high politics' (see Morgenthau 1948; Waltz 1979) are likely numbered, as the rise of nonstate actors and the emergence of a global civil society bring the social dimension of world politics to the fore. (Arquilla & Ronfeldt, 1999, p. 56)

As Arquilla and Ronfeldt (1999) explain further, these new conditions warrant a shift away from the dominant realpolitik framework of IR, toward a noöpolitik approach that locates the engine of world politics in globally linked communication networks where competing ideas shape the course of events.

Although Arquilla and Ronfeldt (2000) suggest that these trends portend a "revolution in diplomatic affairs," such a communicative approach to IR is less revolutionary than might appear at first glance. Evangelista's (1989) work shows how Soviet and U.S. transnational activists forged communicative links outside established channels of interstate diplomacy to shape the Cold War endgame. More recent examples of such policy-relevant international public sphere activity are documented in Lynch's (2000) scholarship, which details the role of popular dialogue in constituting Jordanian security policy. In the field of rhetoric, Francis Beer and Robert Hariman's (1994) work shows how the very concept of foreign policy realism itself is usefully understood as a social construction that has been cultivated strategically by interlocutors fashioning rhetoric to portray the paradigm as a stable, naturalized phenomenon.

These analyses exhibit the heuristic value of viewing public argument as a constitutive dimension of security policy. Such public-argument-driven security studies might be enriched by interdisciplinary dialogue that turns overlapping concepts into productive points of theoretical synergy. For example, Risse (1999, 2000) and Schimmelfennig's (1999, 2001) strand of IR constructivism, which is notable for its emphasis on the role played by rhetoric in shaping foreign policy, draws on Habermas's (1998, 2001) theory of communicative action for support. Yet in the field of argumentation studies, Habermas's view of rhetoric has been subjected to vigorous criticism. The notion that rhetoric is little more than strategic manipulation of audience preferences has been widely discredited, displaced by thicker accounts that position rhetoric as the practical art of using dialogue to reach collective decisions in moments of uncertainty. Theoretical conversation about the dynamics of rhetorical action in international affairs might take this conceptual divergence as a promising point of departure.

Another potential point of interfield synergy converges around the notion of the "public sphere." Evangelista (1989) and Lynch (2000) rely heavily on public sphere analysis in their respective projects, and their expansive international vision demonstrates the considerable potential of a public-argument-driven IR approach. Perhaps cross-pollinating this critical strategy with public sphere concepts developed elsewhere could be useful. For instance, the idea of "counter-public spheres" has received significant attention recently in the field of communication (Asen & Brouwer, 2001; see also Felski, 1989;

Fraser, 1989). The notion of "international counter-public spheres" has not yet been thematized in IR circles. However, it is not difficult to imagine how this theoretical construct could augment public-argument-driven accounts of IR. Consider that much of the transnational political debate featured on the Internet not only challenges official state policies but also calls into question the explicit and tacit norms of communication governing debate in formalized international public spheres of deliberation. To the extent that such communicative behavior bears a resemblance to domestic "counter-public sphere" activity designed to carve out independent spaces for discussion in polities where the official public sphere is insufficiently inclusive, such transnational dialogue might be perspicuously elucidated using counter-public sphere theory.

Ever since Immanuel Kant (1795/1957) proposed that a global association of republics linked by a common commitment to free speech and deliberation might bring "perpetual peace," leaders, citizens, and scholars have wondered about the prospect of a world ordered more by words than weapons. Kant's universalist musings seem naively utopian in the present milieu, where the dangers of apparently intractable conflicts are heightened daily by the spread of advanced weapons geared toward mass destruction. But while Kant's vision of perpetual peace may remain an ever-elusive fiction, the growing salience of transnational deliberation in world politics is an inescapable fact. The erosion of nation-state sovereignty, spread of global communication technology, and rapid development of economic and political interdependence are factors that have combined to change the global landscape dramatically. This chapter has explored how public argumentation can have a powerful political cachet in this new landscape and how technological trends give rise to new forms of rhetoric with potential to shape events in ways that are only beginning to be understood.

NOTE

1. The Triangle Institute for Security Studies (TISS) is an interdisciplinary consortium of Duke University, The University of North Carolina at Chapel Hill, and North Carolina State University. The object of TISS is to promote communication and cooperation among faculty, graduate students, and the public across disciplines and beyond the confines of each university to advance research and education concerning national and international security, broadly defined. Originally established in 1958, TISS has benefited from private foundation funding, most notably from the Ford Foundation, in addition to its university backing, and from help from other agencies such as the National Strategy Information Center and the Army War College (see the TISS Web site at www.pubpol.duke.edu/centers/tiss).

REFERENCES

Arquilla, J., & Ronfeldt, D. (1993). Cyberwar is coming! *Comparative Strategies, 12*(2), 141–165.

Arquilla, J., & Ronfeldt, D. (1999). *Noöpolitik: Toward an American information strategy.* Santa Monica, CA: RAND.

Arquilla, J., & Ronfeldt, D. (2000). *What if there is a revolution in diplomatic affairs?* (U.S. Institute of Peace Virtual Diplomacy Series Publication No. 6). Retrieved May 25, 2008, from www.usip.org/virtualdiplomacy/publications/reports/ronarqISA99.html

Arquilla, J., & Ronfeldt, D. (2007). The promise of noöpolitik. *First Monday, 12*(8). Retrieved May 25, 2008, from www.firstmonday.org/issues/issue12_8/ronfeldt/index.html

Art, R., Betts, R., Copeland, D., Desch, M., Ganguly, S., & Glaser, C., et al. (2002, September 26). War with Iraq is not in America's national interest [Advertisement]. *New York Times,* p. A29.

Asen, R., & Brouwer, D. C. (Eds.). (2001). *Counterpublics and the state.* New York: State University of New York Press.

Association of German Scientists. (2000, November 16). *A warning against the USA's missile defense plans: A plea for a European "Diplomacy First!" approach* (Peace Research Institute Frankfurt Briefing). Retrieved May 25, 2008, from www.hsfk.de/abm/forum/vdweng.htm

Beer, F. A., & Hariman, R. (Eds.). (1994). *Postrealism: The rhetorical turn in international relations.* East Lansing: Michigan State University Press.

Bernstein, R. J. (1983). *Beyond objectivism and relativism: Science, hermeneutics, and praxis.* Philadelphia: University of Pennsylvania Press.

Bohman, J. (1999). Citizenship and norms of publicity: Wide public reason in cosmopolitan societies. *Political Theory, 27*(2), 176–202.

Bohman, J., & Lutz-Bachmann, M. (1998). *Perpetual peace: Essays on Kant's cosmopolitan ideal.* Cambridge: MIT Press.

Brzezinski, Z. (1992). The Cold War and its aftermath. *Foreign Affairs, 71*(4), 31–49.

Buzan, B. (2000). Change and "insecurity" reconsidered. In S. Croft & T. Terriff (Eds.), *Critical reflections on security and change* (pp. 1–17). London: Frank Cass.

Calhoun, C. (2002). Constitutional patriotism and the public sphere: Interests, identity, and solidarity in the integration of Europe. In P. DeGreiff & C. Cronin (Eds.), *Global justice and transnational politics* (pp. 275–312). Cambridge: MIT Press.

Carpenter, R. H. (2004). *Rhetoric in martial deliberations and decision making.* Columbia: University of South Carolina Press.

Ceccarelli, L. (2001). *Shaping science with rhetoric: The cases of Dobzhansky, Schrodinger, and Wilson.* Chicago: University of Chicago Press.

Cheshier, D., Doxtader, E., & Holsti, O. (1998). Round table panel: Bridging gaps in the study of public opinion and American foreign policy. *American Diplomacy, 3*(2). Retrieved May 25, 2008, from www.unc.edu/depts/diplomat/AD_Issues/amdipl_7/public1.html

Cobb, J. (1998). *Cybergrace: The search for god in the digital world.* New York: Crown.

Cohen, R., & Shim, M. R. (Eds.). (2000). *Global social movements.* London: Athlone Press.

Dallmayr, F. (2001). Conversation across boundaries: Political theory and global diversity. *Millennium: Journal of International Studies, 30*(2), 331–347.

Dauber, C. (2001). Image as argument: The impact of Mogadishu on U.S. military intervention. *Armed Forces and Society, 27*(2), 205–230.

Dauber, C., & Cheshier, D. (1998). The place and power of civic space: Reading globalization and social geography through the lens of civilizational conflict. *Security Studies, 8*(2/3), 35–70.

Demchak, G. (2000). Watersheds in perception and knowledge. In S. Croft & T. Terriff (Eds.), *Critical reflections on security and change* (pp. 166–197). London: Frank Cass.

Der Derian, J. (2001). *Virtuous war: Mapping the military-industrial-media-entertainment network.* Boulder, CO: Westview Press.

Deudney, D. C., & Ikenberry, G. J. (1992). Who won the Cold War? *Foreign Policy, 87,* 123–138.

Doxtader, E. (1991). The entwinement of argument and rhetoric: A dialectical reading of Habermas' theory of communicative action. *Argumentation and Advocacy, 28*(2), 51–64.

Evangelista, M. (1989). *Unarmed forces: The transnational movement to end the Cold War.* Ithaca, NY: Cornell University Press.

Farrell, T. B. (1993). *The norms of rhetorical culture.* New Haven, CT: Yale University Press.

Farrell, T. B., & Goodnight, G. T. (1981). Accidental rhetoric: The root metaphors of Three Mile Island. *Communication Monographs, 48*(3), 270–300.

Felski, R. (1989). *Beyond feminist aesthetics: Feminist literature and social change.* Cambridge, MA: Harvard University Press.

Fraser, N. (1989). *Unruly practices: Power, discourse and gender in contemporary social theory.* Minneapolis: University of Minnesota Press.

Freedman, L. (1998). *The revolution in strategic affairs.* Adelphi Paper No. 318. Oxford, UK: Oxford University Press/International Institute for Strategic Studies.

Goodnight, G. T. (1991). Controversy. In D. Parson (Ed.), *Argument in controversy: Proceedings of the seventh SCA/AFA conference on argumentation* (pp. 1–13). Annandale, VA: Speech Communication Association.

Goodnight, G. T. (1998). Public argument and the study of foreign policy. *American Diplomacy, 3*(3). Retrieved May 25, 2008, from www.unc.edu/depts/diplomat/AD_Issues/amdipl_8/goodnight.html

Goodnight, G. T. (1999). Messrs. Dinkins, Rangel, and Savage in colloquy on the African Burial Ground: A companion reading. *Western Journal of Communication, 63*(4), 511–525.

Goodnight, G. T. (2006). Strategic doctrine, public debate and the terror war. In W. W. Keller &

G. R. Mitchell (Eds.), *Hitting first: Preventive war in U.S. security strategy* (pp. 93–114). Pittsburgh, PA: University of Pittsburgh Press.

Haacke, J. (1996). Theory and praxis in international relations: Habermas, self-reflection, rational argumentation. *Millennium: Journal of International Studies, 25*(2), 255–289.

Habermas, J. (1998). *The inclusion of the Other: Studies in political theory* (C. Cronin & P. De Greiff, Eds.). Cambridge, MA: MIT Press.

Habermas, J. (2001). *The postnational constellation* (M. Pensky, Ed.). Cambridge, MA: MIT Press.

Hartnett, S. J., & Stengrim, L. A. (2006). *Globalization and empire: The U.S. invasion of Iraq, free markets, and the twilight of democracy.* Tuscaloosa: University of Alabama Press.

Holsti, O. (1996). *Public opinion and American foreign policy.* Ann Arbor: University of Michigan Press.

Huntington, S. P. (1993). A clash of civilizations? *Foreign Affairs, 72*(3), 22–49.

Ivie, R. L. (2005). *Democracy and America's war on terror.* Tuscaloosa: University of Alabama Press.

Kant, I. (1957). *Perpetual peace* (L. W. Beck, Trans.). New York: Bobbs-Merrill. (Original work published 1795)

Keck, M., & Sikkink, K. (1998). *Activists beyond borders: Advocacy networks in international politics.* Ithaca, NY: Cornell University Press.

Khagram, S., Riker, J. V., & Sikkink, K. (2002). From Santiago to Seattle: Transnational advocacy groups restructuring world politics. In S. Khagram, J. V. Riker, & K. Sikkink (Eds.), *Restructuring world politics: Transnational social movements, networks, and norms* (pp. 3–23). Minneapolis: University of Minnesota Press.

Kirkpatrick, J. J. (1990). Beyond the Cold War. *Foreign Affairs, 69*(1), 1–16.

Kohn, R., & Feaver, P. (Eds.). (1999, October 28–29). Triangle Institute for Security Studies project on the gap between the military and civilian society. In *Digest of findings and studies presented at the conference on the military and civilian society,* Cantigny Conference Center, Wheaton, IL. Retrieved May 25, 2008, from www.poli.duke.edu/civmil

Kolodziej, E. (2000). Security studies for the next millennium. In S. Croft & T. Terriff (Eds.), *Critical reflections on security and change* (pp. 18–38). London: Frank Cass.

Kuhn, T. (1970). *The structure of scientific revolutions*. Chicago: University of Chicago Press.

Laird, R. F., & Mey, H. H. (1999). *The revolution in military affairs*. Washington, DC: Institute for National Strategic Studies.

Linklater, A. (1998). *The transformation of political community*. Columbia: University of South Carolina Press.

Lynch, M. (1999). *State interests and public spheres*. New York: Columbia University Press.

Lynch, M. (2000). The dialogue of civilizations and international public spheres. *Millennium: Journal of International Studies, 29*(20), 307–330.

McCarthy, T. (2002). On reconciling cosmopolitan unity and national diversity. In P. DeGreiff & C. Cronin (Eds.), *Global justice and transnational politics* (pp. 235–274). Cambridge, MA: MIT Press.

McInnes, C. (2000). Spectator sport warfare. In S. Croft & T. Terriff (Eds.), *Critical reflections on security and change* (pp. 142–165). London: Frank Cass.

Mitchell, G. R. (2000). *Strategic deception: Rhetoric, science and politics in missile defense advocacy*. East Lansing: Michigan State University Press.

Morgenthau, H. (1948). *Politics among nations: The struggle for power and peace*. New York: Alfred A. Knopf.

Olson, K., & Goodnight, G. T. (1994). Entanglements of consumption, cruelty, privacy, and fashion: The social controversy over fur. *Quarterly Journal of Speech, 80*(3), 249–276.

Palczewski, C. H. (2001). Contesting pornography: Terministic catharthis and definitional argument. *Argumentation and Advocacy, 38*(1), 1–17.

Payne, R. A. (1996). Deliberating global environmental politics. *Journal of Peace Research, 33*(2), 129–136.

Payne, R. A. (2000, March 14–18). *Habermas, discourse norms, and the prospects for global deliberation*. Paper presented at the 41st International Studies Association convention, Los Angeles. (Published by Columbia International Affairs, Online at www.ciaonet.org/isa/par01)

Payne, R. A. (2007). Neorealists as critical theorists: The purpose of foreign policy debate. *Perspectives on Politics, 5*(3), 503–514.

Payne, R. A., & Samhat, N. H. (2004). *Democratizing global politics: Discourse norms, international regimes and political community*. Albany: State University of New York Press.

Phillips, K. (1999). A rhetoric of controversy. *Western Journal of Speech Communication, 63*(4), 488–510.

Pike, J. E., Blair, B. C., & Schwartz, S. I. (1998). Defending against the bomb. In S. I. Schwartz (Ed.), *Atomic audit: The cost and consequences of US nuclear weapons since 1940* (pp. 269–325). Washington, DC: Brookings Institution Press.

Powaski, R. E. (1998). *The Cold War*. New York: Oxford University Press.

Reiss, E. (1992). *The strategic defense initiative*. Cambridge, UK: Cambridge University Press.

Risse, T. (1999). International norms and domestic change: Arguing and communicative behavior in the human rights area. *Politics and Society, 27*(4), 529–559.

Risse, T. (2000). "Let's argue!" Communicative action in world politics. *International Organization, 54*(1), 1–39.

Risse-Kappen, T. (1995). *Cooperation among democracies: The European influence on US foreign policy*. Princeton, NJ: Princeton University Press.

Rowland, R. C., & Jones, J. M. (2002). "Until next week": The Saturday radio addresses of Ronald Reagan. *Presidential Studies Quarterly, 32*(1), 84–111.

Samhat, N. H. (1997). International regimes as political community. *Millennium: Journal of International Studies, 26*(2), 349–378.

Schimmelfennig, F. (1999). *The double puzzle of EU enlargement: Liberal norms, rhetorical action, and the decision to expand to the east* (ARENA Working Paper No. WP 99/15). Retrieved May 25, 2008, from www.arena.uio.no/publications/wp99_15.htm

Schimmelfennig, F. (2001). The community trap: Liberal norms, rhetorical action, and the eastern enlargement of the European Union. *International Organization, 55*(1), 47–80.

Shane, S. (2005, December 4). Bush's speech on Iraq echoes voice of an analyst. *New York Times,* p. 1.

Smith, J., Chatfield, C., & Pagnucco, R. (Eds.). (1997). *Transnational social movements and global politics.* Syracuse, NY: Syracuse University Press.

Snyder, J. (Spring, 2003). Imperial temptations. *The National Interest, 71,* p. 37.

Stahl, R. (2006). Have you played the war on terror? *Critical Studies in Media Communication, 23*(2), 112–130.

Tarrow, S. (1998). *Power in movement: Social movements and contentious politics* (2nd ed.). Cambridge, UK: Cambridge University Press.

Taylor, B. C., Kinsella, W. J., Depoe, S. P., & Metzler, M. S. (Eds.). (2007). *Nuclear legacies: Communication, controversy, and the U.S. nuclear weapons complex.* Lanham, MD: Lexington Books.

Teilhard de Chardin, P. (1965). *The phenomenon of man* (B. Wall, Trans.). New York: Harper & Row.

Waltz, K. (1979). *Theory of international politics.* New York: McGraw-Hill.

Winkler, C. K. (2006). *In the name of terrorism: Presidents on political violence in the post-World War II era.* Albany: State University of New York Press.

Zarefsky, D. (1986). *President Johnson's war on poverty: Rhetoric and history.* Tuscaloosa: University of Alabama Press.

15

The Rhetoric of Interdisciplinarity

Boundary Work in the Construction of New Knowledge

JULIE THOMPSON KLEIN

The relationship of rhetoric and interdisciplinarity may be construed in two ways. The concepts and methods of rhetoric have a widening presence beyond its traditional academic domain, infusing new approaches into many disciplines and interdisciplinary fields. At the same time, they have transformed knowledge studies. Grounded traditionally in epistemology and the history of ideas, knowledge studies have expanded to include a growing body of rhetorics of inquiry, revealing the ways in which persuasive discourses construct, order, legitimate, and institutionalize disciplinary formations. These formations govern the objects we study, the methods we use, and the "economies of value" that manufacture discourse in professional cultures (Messer-Davidow, Shumway, & Sylvan, 1993, p. vii). Few studies, however, have examined the rhetoric of interdisciplinary inquiry.

In the case of interdisciplinarity, the task is compounded by the diversity of activities. The word *interdisciplinary* appears across all knowledge domains: in natural sciences, social sciences, humanities, the professions, and interdisciplinary fields. A rhetoric of interdisciplinary inquiry might be conducted in several ways. Explanatory styles of research and teaching might be identified and patterns of claims making revealed. Scholars could investigate the linguistic dynamics of collaboration and other work modes or the ways genres of scholarship institutionalize practices. The narrative knowledge of personal stories, institutional case studies, and field histories might be analyzed. Or shifting patterns of language might be traced to identify the emergence of new networks at the interface of disciplines. This chapter focuses on yet another strategy: examining figurative language and nomenclature. The figurative history of a word, Thomas McLaughlin (1990) observes, is part of its meaning, whether talking about poetry, gender identity, or concepts (pp. 83–85). Nomenclature is more technical, codifying practices into Kenneth Burke's (1966) notion of a "terministic screen" that filters, directs, and redirects attention in certain directions rather than in others (pp. 45–46).

In choosing this particular focus, the chapter bridges two gaps. The claim of interdisciplinarity is often advanced in rhetorical studies. However, few rhetoricians draw deeply on the published scholarship on interdisciplinarity, relying instead on a few favored references closer to their immediate academic sphere. And vice versa: Rhetorical scholarship is not familiar to many interdisciplinary scholars and teachers, even though figurative language and nomenclature populate their descriptions of theory and practice. The one dimension of rhetoric that has received the most attention is the persuasive role of language in the dynamics of communication. It is a major theme in studies of collaborative research and team teaching. Yet even that discussion is rarely informed by rhetorical scholarship. This chapter bridges the two gaps by bringing together concepts from both spheres to understand figuration and nomenclature in the discourse of interdisciplinarity.

The first and overriding concept—boundary work—arose in science studies, giving a single label to the composite set of claims, activities, and institutional structures that define and protect knowledge practices. Individuals and groups work directly and through institutions to create, maintain, break down, and reformulate boundaries between domains. In science studies, the focus has been primarily on disciplinary formations, though several studies have focused on interdisciplinary formations and practices (see especially Fisher, 1993, pp. 13–14; Klein, 1996, pp. 1–2, 36–37, 57–84). Boundary work is an especially fruitful concept for thinking about the relationship of rhetoric and interdisciplinarity because it complements two powerful concepts in rhetorical scholarship—Richard McKeon's (1987) notion of rhetoric as an architectonic art and Kenneth Burke's (1966) notion of terministic screens. The chapter triangulates the three concepts—boundary work, architectonic arts, and terministic screens—in a discussion of the interdisciplinary fields and the broader discourse of interdisciplinarity, followed by the technical nomenclature used to schematize and legitimate different types of interdisciplinary work.

INTERDISCIPLINARY FIELDS

In 1971, in his essay "The Uses of Rhetoric in a Technological Age," Richard McKeon reminded us that rhetoric has a long historical connection with the development of theory, practice, and methods to create and use outcomes of knowledge production and action. Technical languages of distinction have schematized knowledge throughout Western intellectual history, from Aristotle's typology of forms to the rise of modern disciplinary fields in the late 19th and 20th centuries. Yet, McKeon exhorted, subject matters are not readymade to respond to all the questions and issues we encounter. "We make subject-matters to fit the examination and resolution of problems, and the solution of problems brings to our attention further, consequent problems, which frequently require the setting up and examination of new fields" (p. 18). The productive arts of constructing new interdisciplinary fields challenge conventional priorities.

McKeon's essay appeared at a significant turning point. In 1971, increased outputs in all areas were being heralded, but McKeon found interdisciplinary connections to be noticeably absent. Viewed on a longer timescale, however, the growth of interdisciplinary fields was accelerating at that point. The history of interdisciplinary fields and hybrid specializations dates to the 1930s and 1940s, in the development of comparative literature, area studies, and American studies. In the 1950s and 1960s, social psychology, molecular biology, radio astronomy, cognitive science, materials science, and biochemistry gained recognition. In the 1960s and 1970s, black studies, women's studies, and ethnic studies emerged, as well as environmental studies, urban studies, and science, technology, and society studies. By the early 21st century, a host of examples appeared across the academy, including new formations of cultural studies, media studies, and clinical and translational science. Today, the rise of new disciplines, interdisciplines, and paradisciplines is no longer regarded as an unusual event. In the wake of anti-, cross-, and interdisciplinary studies, Marjorie Garber (2001) adds, some traditional disciplines have even been renamed, becoming English studies, literary studies, and romance studies (p. 78).

Raymond Miller (1982) identified three major impetuses for new fields that produce new subject matters and methods for addressing problems and questions not accommodated in conventional taxonomies. *Topics* are associated with problem areas. "Crime," for instance, is a social concern that appears in multiple social science disciplines and in criminal justice and criminology programs. "Area," "labor," "urban," and "environment" also led to new programs. Study of the "aged" led to the development of gerontology, and new subject matters were formed in "peace" and "conflict" studies. The category of *life experience* became prominent in the late 1960s and 1970s with the development of fields such as black studies, ethnic studies, and women's studies. *Hybrids* gave rise to "interstitial crossdisciplines," such as social psychology, economic anthropology, political sociology, biogeography, culture and personality, and economic history (pp. 11–15, 19).

New fields have implications for the rhetorical practice of schematization. When a committee was charged with examining the methodology used in the 1995 National Research Council's study of research-doctorate programs in the United States, it faulted the study for its outdated or inappropriate taxonomy of fields. In proposing a new taxonomy, the committee recommended an overall increase in the number of recognized fields from 41 to 57. Among their detailed recommendations, they called for greater recognition of emerging fields of knowledge production. They singled out feminist, gender, and sexuality studies as well as nanoscience, bioinformatics, and computational biology. The new and expanding category of "global area studies," they also urged, should include subfields of New Eastern, East Asian, South Asian, Latin American, African, and Slavic studies (Ostriker & Kuh, 2003).

Even as they enter taxonomic codes, however, new fields are confronted by a nagging question. Where do they fit? The metaphor of fit, Lynton Caldwell (1983) replied in the context of environmental studies, prejudges the epistemological problem at stake in their emergence. Many fields arose for the very reason McKeon identified—a perceived misfit among need, experience, information, and the structuring of knowledge and curriculum embodied in disciplinary organization. If the structure of the academy must be changed to accommodate them, Caldwell asserted, then perhaps the structure itself is part of the problem. Interdisciplinary studies represent a latent restructuring of knowledge. The political economy of the academy, Stanley Katz (1996) acknowledged, forces institutions to play the traditional power game of seeking resources and securing institutional space. Yet the formation of interdisciplinary fields marks the possibility of a more flexible design. Identity fields in particular, Douglas Bennett (1997) adds, constitute a "sacred edge" in the reopened battle over inclusion and exclusion (p. 144). Women's studies is a major case in point.

THE CASE OF WOMEN'S STUDIES

McKeon (1971) described new fields as architectonic arts that reorganize existing categories and subject matters by exploring new topics in new conceptual vocabularies. Their demonstrative rhetoric develops grounds for discovery and invention beyond conventional boundaries. The challenge was signified by pervasive spatial metaphors depicting women's studies as the "outside within" a "fortress" or "citadel" from which women were "barred" entry. Annette Kolodny (1980) described literary criticism as a "minefield." Feminist critics had the choice of being "camped" on the edge or working to defuse the minefield, to avoid marginalization as a "tributary" in the "backwater" or being confined to a "ghetto." At the same time, the conditions of marginality are conditions of strength. The field's epistemological power depends on its location in spaces where conventional boundaries are blurred (Women's Studies, 1990, pp. 210–211).

Over time, women's studies shifted the terms of relationship from the conventional dichotomy of being "either/or" to the more complex mediation of being "both/and." Feminist boundary work transformed traditional institutional practices and intellectual categories that excluded "women" and "gender." Cross-cutting topoi functioned as "boundary objects" that facilitated heterogeneous interactions among different professional groups with a common purpose. In a classic definition, Star and Griesemer (1989) described boundary objects as negotiable entities that simultaneously delimit and connect. Concrete conceptual objects such as the history of women, philosophy of gender, knowledge construction, and biologies of sexuality fostered unity across fields, but they were still plastic enough to allow for separately located meanings. Ellen Messer-Davidow (2002) recalled the architectonic process in her study *Disciplining Feminism*. Research frameworks and analytic concepts such as "family," "class," "race," "community," "socialization," "social control," and "social conflict" needed to be reformulated, traditional categories of "women" and "men"

reconstructed, "sex-gender systems" denaturalized, "identities" and "oppressions" multiplied, and all categories problematized (pp. 101–111, 165–166). Even as this transformation was occurring, though, women's studies did not exist separately from the disciplines.

The forging of a new cognitive and social architecture occurred as much within the disciplines as outside them. To change the disciplines, one program coordinator remarked, women's studies had to be "of them, in them, and about them." Scholars and teachers worked simultaneously within and in opposition to disciplines, wielding their forms of power and authority for feminist purposes (cited in Boxer, 1982, pp. 671, 693). As a result, women's studies is both disciplinary and interdisciplinary (Wiegman, 2002, p. 3). Diane Elam defines its space as both a "discipline of difference" and an "interdisciplinary discipline." Reconstituting disciplinarity as cross-disciplinarity does not elevate feminism to a theoretical metalanguage or totalizing master narrative. Borders are crossed through continuous inter- and intradisciplinary cross-fertilization (Elam, 1990, pp. 294–298; 2002). The field offers an intellectual community and an institutional site for feminists who do most of their work in disciplines, legitimating gender as a category of analysis (Addelson & Potter, 1991, p. 271). Within their disciplinary locations, they disperse centripetally into specializations. Within the shared space of women's studies, they move centrifugally to "cross-disciplinary" research and teaching (Hartman & Messer-Davidow, 1991, p. 5).

The formation of new fields has been likened to producing a new creole, a concept borrowed from linguistics to indicate a new language culture. "Creolized disciplines," Cornwall and Stoddard (2001) observe, can be alternative, resistant, or emergent. Women's studies may be viewed as an emergent discipline with its own canons, methods, and issues. At the same time, it is alternative or resistant to the traditional discursive practices of disciplines (p. 162). Susan Stanford Friedman's (2001) description of working in two locations accentuates the dynamic movement of feminist boundary work. Her academic home base—literary studies— provides an intellectual anchoring and a substantive platform of knowledge of literature, narrative and figuration, and representation, and a methodological base for strategies of reading texts in varied cultural contexts. Her political home base—feminism—provides an approach to asking questions about gender, power relations, and other systems of stratification, and an ethical commitment to social justice and change. From these two homes, Friedman travels to other (inter)dis- ciplinary homes, bringing back what she learned and what is useful for her projects. Travel stimulates new ways of thinking, exposing the constructedness of what is taken for granted, dislodging unquestioned assump- tions, and producing new insights, questions, and solutions to intellectual impasses at home.

The tensions of "home" and "abroad" appear in all interdisciplinary fields. Recalling her awkward beginning as a graduate student in another major interdisciplinary field— American studies—Patricia Limerick (1997) remembers feeling "homeless," even though American studies has been a place of refuge for those who cannot find a home in more conventional neighborhoods. One of the advantages of the field is its permeable borders, but expansive borders require adapting to disorientation (pp. 451–454). "The broad rubric of American studies," George Lipsitz (2002) reported in a review of the current state of the field, "now conceals more from us than it reveals." Being inclusive, open minded, and interdisciplinary carries the responsibility to define the conditions that bring members of a field together, the historical trajectories they inherit, and the forces that connect their work as researchers and teachers to broader social formations (p. 441).

Naming is a concrete rhetorical strategy of defining location. Naming, Armstrong and Fontaine (1989) found when reviewing names used in the field of composition studies, entails a process of sorting and gathering, comparing and contrasting within an individual's evolving view of reality, and demarcating territorial relationships in political-semantic webs (pp. 7–8). Scholars and teachers who study American culture call themselves Americanists, literary critics, historians, art historians, musicologists, and film and media critics, as well as feminists, African Americanists, and members of other ethnic and national groups. Many also see themselves as members of the field of cultural studies or, at least, as "doing cultural studies" in some way. The names people choose in women's studies, Sandra Coyner (1991) found in sorting through that field, typically identify them with another community, as historians, literary critics, psychologists, or social workers. Naming tends to designate a position within a program—as women's studies faculty, student, or director—more than the kind of work performed (pp. 349–351).

FIGURING NEW KNOWLEDGE

Over the course of the 20th century, a major shift in the figurative language of knowledge description occurred, away from static images of a foundation and a structure to the dynamic properties of a network, a web, a system, and a field. The rhetoric of teaching and learning shifted in kind from metaphors of accumula- tion and discrete inputs of information and facts to acts of constructing knowledge and problem posing. Following suit, metaphors of production, prescription, control, perfor- mance, mastery, and expertise were supplanted by dialogue, process, inquiry, transformation, interaction, construction, and negotiation. Older tropes of unity, universality, and cer- tainty were replaced in turn by tropes of plu- rality, heterogeneity, and complexity. And the image of the curriculum shifted from vertically stacked silos to horizontal pathways, clusters, connections, matrixes, and communities.

Interdisciplinarity was implicated in all these shifts, fostering a parallel redescription of the work of research and teaching. At first glance, the images are predictable. A physicist describes knowledge in terms of elements and particles, fission and fusion. A mathematician speaks of subsets, vectors, and the frontiers of convexity. An engineer talks of through-flow, a biologist of symbiosis and fecundity, an economist of market strategies, an anthropologist of disciplinary ethnocentrism and tribal rivalries, a systems theorist of feedback and cybernetic relations, and so on. Two sets of figurations, though, cut across the dispersed discourse of interdisciplinarity—geopolitics and boundaries, and organicism and ecology.

Geopolitics and Boundaries

Michel Foucault's archaeological studies of knowledge fostered a "topographical discourse" that figures prominently in studies of both disciplinarity and interdisciplinarity. Topographical discourse, Jeffrey Peck (1989) summarized, draws attention to intellectual *surfaces,* academic *contours,* and scholarly fields of *demarcated* interests. Spatial metaphors—turf, territory, boundary, and domain—highlight boundary formation and maintenance. The argument strategies of description, explanation, analysis, interpretation, and legitimation constitute the categories, taxonomies, and statements governing rules of organization in intellectual territories. Geopolitics is especially central to the conception of interdisciplinarity because, as Robert L. Scott (1979) put it, there is a "distinctly political face to the circumstances in which interdisciplinary efforts must thrive or not" (p. 312).

The political character of interdisciplinary boundary work is accentuated in descriptions of disciplines (see Klein, 1990, pp. 77–84). A discipline is portrayed as a "domain," "private property," and an "island fortress" staked off by "patrolled boundaries" and "no trespassing notices." A field is an "empire" and an "oligarchy," a graduate division a "territory," and a scientific domain a "mandarin culture" or "balkanized region of research principalities." Territories are "feudalized" into separate "fiefdoms." Specialists nurture "academic nationalism," keeping "domain assumptions" intact. Even in medical care, the patient becomes the "turf" of specialists. The dominant policy is "protectionism" carried out with a "tariff mentality." The local mission is a "territorial imperative," and disciplinary jargon is "the shibboleth of adequate professional training by the in group."

Efforts to construct new interdisciplinary subject matters and conceptual vocabularies cut horizontally across the vertical "silos" and "mine shafts" of disciplines in a "third-party challenge," "breaching" boundaries and promoting excursions to the "frontiers" of knowledge. Where once "no interdisciplinary interlopers invaded" and no "intellectual scavengers" pilfered, "alien intrusion" is detected. Interdisciplinary scholars are warned to "stay out . . . or pay the price" for "fishing in a posted pond." Undaunted, researchers, teachers, and practitioners engage in "border traffic" and "intellectual migration," traversing the "no man's land" between disciplines in the "academic Demilitarized Zone." The hazards are well-known, likened to straying from the beaten path, mucking around in uncharted swamps, and standing on the edge of a cliff. Educators who embark on the "poorly charted waters of non-disciplinary or interdisciplinary study" are accused of succumbing to the beguiling "siren songs" of values, problem solving, simplicity, usefulness, modernism, skills, and subject coverage.

Some come to rest in the "bureaucratic foothills of interdepartmental cooperation" or in designated interdisciplinary programs, the "Switzerland of academia." Others form "little islands" of "transdisciplinary cosmopolitanism," practice a "global strategy," or forge a "common-law marriage" of allied disciplines. "[E]nvoys are sent and occasional temporary alliances formed" between "warring fortresses." "Truce and synthesis" are required. The "annexing" of "satellite disciplines," though, does not go unnoticed. No discipline willingly abdicates its "mandated sovereignty." "Foreign policy" and "complex boundary readjustments" are formulated. "Bilateral treaties" may be in order and the beginnings of a "common market" sketched out.

A parallel language of belief reinforces the geopolitical dynamics of interdisciplinary work. Propelled by the "sheer force of orthodoxy," disciplinarians "sing out of the same prayer book" and seek "right doctrine" in their journals. To experiment with disciplinary knowledge is to "meddle" with the "preordained," to disturb the "intellectual idols," to tear off the "labels which still decorate the pediments of the university temples," and to challenge the "awe-inspiring pontiffs." Disciplinarians are exhorted to "stop whoring after strange gods," and interdisciplinarity is cast as a "hedonic calculus," a "black art kept in check by disciplinary Luddites" who are members of a lost tribe cast adrift. Disciplinarians talk about the value of interdisciplinarity, but their words are condemned as "pious but ritualized obeisances." Undeterred, interdisciplinarians attempt to "convert" specialists into generalists, as they themselves were once "baptize[d]" into specialization. They stage their own "revivals," dispatch their own "missionaries," and have their own "frequent strain" of "millennial interdisciplinarity" advanced by a "scornful prophetic minority" with a corner on "some special Truth." Yet an individual researcher does not veer too far from "home," lest she risk "excommunication." Likening heresy to disease, the "dreaded poison" of specialization can only be expunged with the "antidote" of interdisciplinarity, lest the university succumb to "hardening of the arteries."

The duality of boundaries repeats. A boundary, Mae Henderson (1995) reflected in a collection of essays on the field of border studies, is both a dividing line and a zone of crossing. Within interstitial spaces, new questions blur and merge older distinctions, contributing to the larger project of rethinking culture, canon, and disciplinarity (pp. 2, 5, 27). Like the disciplines that study it, Michael Kearney (1991) cautions, the geographical border is riddled with holes and contradictions. It is a zone of contested space, capital, and meanings. Classical constructions of anthropology and history have been challenged and reordered by new studies of the border area and its cultural politics. Many of these studies are "antidisciplinary." They work to transcend the domains of standard disciplines and have formed outside the official institutional body of the state. Alternative formations are not without risk, however. The rise and institutionalization of border studies may create an academic counterpart of the border patrol, controlling transnational ethnic minorities as objects of study (pp. 61–62). The impact is not limited to border studies. Recalling an earlier example, American studies illustrates the porosity of both disciplinary and interdisciplinary categories.

Since its emergence in the 1930s and 1940s from intersecting interests in the disciplines of history and literary studies, the field has reconstructed its own boundaries. Interdisciplinarity, Paul Lauter (2001) suggests, now does double duty. Boundaries of genre, audience, and discipline intersect in new forms of borderland scholarship, art, and everyday culture, challenging the processes by which differences are naturalized, installed, and maintained (pp. 127–128, 133–134). The changing demographics of the United States have accelerated this process. An interdisciplinary notion of America, Campbell and Kean (1997) propose, is a meeting place of many cultures and knowledges where identity, language, and space are constantly interchanged, contested, and crossed over (p. 10). To the north and south of the U.S. borders lie other Americas that move beyond biculturality to new conditions of multiculturality, multilinguality, and crossing of class lines (Allen, 1992, p. 305). On the southern tier, New Mixtec identities have emerged, as well as new hybrid forms of art, media, and popular culture, and scholarly discourse (DeSoto, 2001, p. 304). The concept of *mestiza* consciousness has had a particularly powerful impact on border theory and the parameters of American studies, sociological studies of immigration, and scholarship on gender (Elliott, 2001a, pp. 307–308; 2001b, pp. 106–107).

The architectonics of forming new knowledge communities is a threefold process. Interdisciplinary fields detach a category as subject and object from existing disciplinary frameworks, loosening boundaries and stimulating trading zones. They fill gaps in knowledge from lack of attention to a category, creating new interim pidgin tongues and creole language cultures. And if the communities attain critical mass, they constitute new social and cognitive structures that reconfigure the space of the academy. The knowledge produced in interdisciplinary research enters the curriculum in three ways: as the intellectual foundation for interdisciplinary programs, as new topics in core curricula and general education, and as new foci in traditional subjects and disciplines. Interests are not isolated to the boundary lines of newly formulated subject matters, though. Facilitating movement beyond their own boundaries is part of the raison d'être of new fields. Gender is not confined to women's studies. Culture is not the sole property of anthropology or traditional humanities disciplines. Globalization is not isolated to programs of international studies. Sustainability is not the sole province of environmental studies. Conflict, justice, and democratic participation in decision-making are present outside policy studies. And health, wellness, and the body are not restricted to medicine.

Organicism and Ecology

Other images also appear in the discourses of interdisciplinary fields and interdisciplinarity itself. Physical and topological or architectural metaphors that accentuate relations among elements call attention to joints, points of connection, overlaps, interconnections, interpenetrations, breaks, and cracks (Goldman, 1995, pp. 222–223). In the context of social sciences, Donald Campbell (1969) portrays the structure of knowledge as clusters of specialties represented by fish scales. The redundant piling up of specialties leaves gaps that may be filled with novel specialties, ranges of competence, and administrative arrangements. In describing the interdisciplinary study of American culture, Gene Wise (1978, 1979) speaks of a journey and concentric circles. The scholar locates connecting links while traveling through fields of experience in an open process of acquiring knowledge. Scholarship is not a series of discrete and linear contributions—"like building blocks in a pyramid." It is a series of dialogues in what will always be an unfinished experience.

Interdisciplinary work is also likened to processes in ecology and the evolution of plant and animal species. The "hybrid vigor" of interdisciplines and the "symbiosis" of an integrated curriculum demonstrate its synergistic character. The ultimate trump card is the assertion of "natural" place. Organicism and spatiality do not constitute another dichotomy. They coexist. *Ecology*, Michael Winter (1996) recalls, derives from a Greek word meaning household or settlement. The verbs associated with *oikeos* suggest inhabiting, settling, governing, controlling, managing, and other activities in a complex interweaving of fields of social action. Hence, spatial dynamics of place and organic dynamics of production occur simultaneously. Spatial and organic models may even be combined to form a third type, highlighting interactions between social groups and their environments. Organism and environment imply one another mutually. Both are territorial, competitive, and expansionist. The underlying idea is to make and reinforce jurisdictional claims, analogous to the territorial claims that humans and animals make in ecological niches. Organism and environment, Winter adds, also exploit resources to produce new life forms and settlements.

The twined dynamics of location and generation are evident in the hybrid character of interdisciplinary activity. Hybridization is a biological metaphor connoting the formation of new animals, plants, or individuals and groups. Hybrids emerge from interaction or cross-breeding of heterogeneous elements, translated in organizational theory to mean tasks at the boundaries and in the spaces between systems and subsystems (Gibbons et al., 1994, p. 37). Intersections are accommodated in a variety of hybrid communities, from centers and programs to projects, networks, invisible colleges, and matrix structures superimposed on organizations dominated by disciplines. Observing an increase in the number of hybrid fields, Dogan and Pahre (1990) attribute their development to a process of *specialization-fragmentation-hybridization*. When the first stage of specialization reaches a point of density, they argue, disciplines fragment and innovative scholars recombine specialties. There are two kinds of hybrids. The first kind becomes institutionalized as a subfield of a discipline or a permanent cross-disciplinary program. The second kind remains informal, and hybrids will often form as well in the gaps between subfields (pp. 63, 66, 72).

Dogan and Pahre (1990) concede that the core-density relationship is more complicated than their focus on innovations and margins allows. The distance from center to border varies from one discipline to another. In a more recent alternative model, Bruun, Hukkinen, Huutoniemi, and Klein (2005) liken knowledge production to a rhizome. In

botany, a rhizome is a rootlike and often horizontal stem that sends up shoots. A rhizomic model of knowledge calls attention to decentralization and heterogeneity. Any point might be connected to any other, linkages may occur between points, and they may be drivers of development. The system is horizontally organized, without hierarchical differentiation between core and periphery, and there are multiple entryways and dynamic flows of information and knowledge. Interdisciplinarity, in turn, is not limited to integration between static disciplinary essences. It makes connections across perceived boundaries. Disciplinary rules still operate, but they change historically, and modes of practice pluralize even in the same field. Diverse factors are driving change, including complex problems and societal needs; generic instrumentation, models, and theories; mobility between disciplines and informal networks; educational and research projects, programs, institutes, and centers; and interdisciplinary conferences, seminars, and books and journals. The locus of power also shifts, from highly formalized institutions to blurred constellations of actors and institutions with a shared interest in breaking up existing orders of knowledge (pp. 45–59).

A new way of thinking about boundaries follows from the rhizomic model, comparable to the shift from "either/or" to "both/and" thinking in women's studies and the porosity of boundaries in American studies. One of the oft-cited explanations for interdisciplinary work in science is specialty migration to work on problems or questions, regardless of disciplinary affiliations. Yet the metaphor of "migration" implies boundedness when in reality specialties possess no inherent boundaries. They are defined by relative concentrations of interests. Most migration occurs because research areas are in constant reformulation. Boundaries shift and overlap because ideas and techniques do not exist in fixed places. Researchers carry them through multiple groups (Becher, 1990, p. 344; Chubin, 1976, p. 464). Another popular metaphor—"frontier"—is also a dubious signifier. The image of a frontier connotes expansion into uncharted domains and "the cutting edge." Interdisciplinarity is often associated with pathbreaking ideas, discoveries, and new lines of investigation. Yet the space of interdisciplinary work is not just *out* there. It also occurs *within* the heart of disciplinary practice. In some areas, moreover, knowledge production is no longer occurring strictly within disciplinary boundaries, in, for example, the Human Genome Project, biotechnology, molecular biology, risk assessment, and technology assessment (Gibbons et al., 1994, pp. 138, 147).

Boundaries, Greenblatt and Gunn (1992) conclude in a book on literary studies, *Redrawing the Boundaries*, "can be crossed, confused, consolidated, and collapsed; they can also be revised, reconceived, redesigned, and replaced." They cannot, however, be entirely abolished. Furthermore, they differ. Boundary lines are drawn in bold, unbroken strokes and as a series of intermittent, irregular dashes. They cross, overlap, or converge at different places and in different degrees (p. 4). Multiple boundaries are at stake simultaneously—not only disciplinary and interdisciplinary demarcations but also national and geographical, historical and generational, racial and ethnic, social and political, ethical and religious lines. Only by mapping situated practices can we fully understand interdisciplinarity. Generalizing about "its" nature, Thomas Reese (1995) warns, is dangerous. A closer look at the relative permeabilities of boundaries in different settings is required. If disciplinary structures are strong and boundaries fixed, strategies for interdisciplinarity require force and are considered transgressive. If structures are weak, they are assumed to be natural and permitted excursions (p. 544).

NOMENCLATURE AND SCHEMATIC CLAIMS

"Basically," Kenneth Burke (1966) wrote, "there are two kinds of terms: terms that put things together, and terms that take things apart." Furthermore, "we *must* use terministic screens, since we can't say anything without the use of terms" (p. 50). The choices we make constitute an additional kind of screen that directs attention to one field or another, and even within a single field further screens direct attention while shaping the range of observations implicit in particular words. Terminology is not simply a reflection of reality. It is also a selection and deflection of reality. All terminology also embodies, whether implicitly or explicitly, principles of continuity or discontinuity. Even continuing terms, as McKeon also pointed out, assume new meanings in new applications.

A host of adjectives distinguish types of interdisciplinary activity, from *indiscriminate* and *auxiliary* to *free-range* and *cosmological* forms. The earliest uses of the keyword date to the opening decades of the 20th century. The most prominent sites were the new general education movement and social science research. Other terms appeared, though. In education and in humanities, *integration, synthesis, unity*, and *holism* were used; in etymological study of social sciences, Roberta Frank (1988) found the word *cooperative* and, in books published between 1925 and 1930, *interrelation, mutual interdependence, interpenetration, interactions* of disciplines, *border areas*, and *borderlands* between disciplines. At the Social Science Research Council, however, the keyword was used during the early 1920s as shorthand for research that crossed more than one of the seven societies with the aim of producing empirical and social, problem-oriented applied research. By the early 1930s, *inter-discipline* and *interdisciplinary* were appearing more widely. By midcentury, the keyword was common coin in social sciences and during the late 1960s and 1970s grew into a "kind of weather" (pp. 91–96).

The most widely used schematization derives from a typology presented at the first international conference on interdisciplinary research and teaching in 1970, cosponsored by the Organisation for Economic Cooperation and Development (OECD, 1972). Some have tired of debates on terminology, considering them tedious exercises in disputed meanings. Others dictate the prescriptive use of labels, insisting that they are essential for separating "false" from "true" forms. Amid a sometimes confusing array of jargon, the three most widely used terms in the OECD typology are rhetorical signposts of the boundary work of nomenclature. The distinction between the first two terms—*multidisciplinary* and *interdisciplinary*—is widely recognized. The precise meanings of *interdisciplinary* and *transdisciplinary*, however, are disputed. The differences are not minor, since they screen attention toward certain purposes and activities, legitimating them while excluding or subordinating others and remaking the meaning of continuing keywords. (For a fuller analysis of terminology, see Klein, forthcoming.)

> **Multidisciplinary approaches** juxtapose disciplinary/professional perspectives, adding breadth and available knowledge, information, and methods. They speak as separate voices, in encyclopedic alignment.

The consensus meaning of multidisciplinary approaches highlights juxtaposition and encyclopedic alignment of disciplines, fostering breadth of knowledge through a greater number of inputs. Yet the status quo of disciplines is not interrogated, and they retain their original identities. In research projects, a problem or a question is explored

from multiple viewpoints. However, they are not integrated. In education, disciplines or school subjects may be correlated in a parallel sequence. Yet even when a theme, a problem, or a question creates a shared framework for separate content and methods, students do not necessarily experience integrative seminars or projects. Even when team teaching occurs, individuals present their disciplinary perspectives separately in "turn" or "tag" teaching. Many purportedly interdisciplinary programs, to use Messer-Davidow's (2002) term, also turn out to be a "multidisciplinary mélange" of courses in disciplinary departments (p. 158). Likewise, members of a teaching research team do not work collaboratively, and they file separate reports, even if their activities occur within a coordinated sequence. In both cases, integrative focus, direction, goals, and objectives are diminished.

> **Interdisciplinary approaches** integrate separate disciplinary data, methods, tools, concepts, and theories to create a holistic view or common understanding of a complex issue, question, or problem.

Interdisciplinary approaches entail a more conscious effort to bring together disciplinary approaches. In collaborative research, members of a team engage in joint definition of the goals of a project, the core problem and questions, and a framework for coordinated inputs with ongoing communication and interaction. Mutual learning and progressive sharing of empirical and theoretical work occur through iteration and joint activities. New knowledge emerges as novel insights are generated, disciplinary relationships redefined, and integrative constructs developed. In education, content is revised through acts of focusing, linking, blending, and integrating separate approaches to a core theme, problem, or issue. Team teaching may also occur. Core seminars, theses or projects, and theory courses are crucial sites for developing shared vocabulary and assumptions. At a more formal level of development, a new community of knowers with a hybrid interlanguage may emerge.

All forms and purposes are not the same, however. The Nuffield Foundation (1975) proposed two basic metaphors for interdisciplinary work—bridge building and restructuring. Bridge building occurs between complete and firm disciplines. Restructuring detaches parts of several disciplines to form a new coherent whole, often with an implicit criticism of the state of those disciplines (pp. 43–45). Bridge building often occurs in theme-based general education programs and in the daily borrowings of methods, tools, concepts, and theories. Borrowings may be only auxiliary to routine practice, or they may lead to long-term changes in practice and in some cases the formation of new hybrid domains based on new categories of knowledge.

In the latter decades of the 20th century, a new rhetoric of interdisciplinarity arose, challenging older forms while staking claims for new subject matters. The older conceptual vocabulary of *unity* and *universality* was replaced by *plurality* and *heterogeneity*. *Interrogation* and *intervention* supplanted *resolution* and *harmony* and *holism*. Even the underlying assumption that "integration" of disciplines is the "litmus test" of interdisciplinarity was disputed, along with the premise that disciplinary grounding is the necessary basis for interdisciplinary work (Lattuca, 2001, pp. 78, 109). The language of the new rhetoric signaled the evolution of a form of "critical interdisciplinarity" already witnessed in women's studies and in the "critical turn" in American studies (Klein, 2005, pp. 35–36). In humanities and other interdisciplinary fields

forged in critique, the new rhetoric highlighted the difference between what Joe Moran (2002) calls a "retrospectively interdisciplinary" model of an organic society of the past in which culture and society were joined and a "prospectively interdisciplinary" vision of a future society in which divisions between culture and history no longer exist (p. 132). It also reinforced the belief that interdisciplinarity has an inherent political agenda.

"Critical interdisciplinarity" draws two boundaries, between limited forms of interaction and more radical transformations and between "instrumental" and "critical" practices. The difference between instrumentality and critique is a major fault line in the political economy of interdisciplinarity. Instrumental forms motivated by "strategic," "pragmatic," or "opportunistic" goals are prominent in economic, technological, and scientific problem solving, without regard for questions of epistemology or institutional structure. Critical forms interrogate disciplines and institutional structures with the aim of transforming them. As a result of conflicting purposes, the same word may appear in both forms with different connotations. *Innovation*, for instance, is a prime value in instrumental forms with the aim of commercial product development and improved sociotechnical systems. In educational reform and many interdisciplinary fields, *innovation* stands for new ways of performing research and education. Echoing Salter and Hearn (1996) in a collection of research stories from the Canadian academy, interdisciplinarity is construed as a dynamic striving for change. It is the necessary "churn in the system."

Strategic and critical forms are not always separate. Research on problems of the environment and on health often combines critique and problem solving. Nonetheless, a clear division appears in the classification of motivations. Observing trends in the medical curriculum, Bryan Turner (1990) affirmed that when interdisciplinarity is conceived as a short-term solution to economic and technological problems, pragmatic questions of reliability, efficiency, and commercial value take center stage. In contrast, interdisciplinarity emerged as an epistemological goal within social medicine and sociology of health. Researchers focused on the complex causality of illness and disease. Psychological, social, and ethical factors missing from the hierarchical biomedical model are factored into a holistic biosocial or biopsychosocial model.

Comparable to the shift in meaning that "critical interdisciplinarity" fostered, the recent expansion of transdisciplinarity also reformulates a continuing term for new purposes.

TRANSDISCIPLINARY NEGOTIATIONS

The term *transdisciplinarity* is traced conventionally to the OECD typology. It originally connoted a set of common axioms that transcends the narrow scope of disciplinary worldviews through an overarching synthesis, such as anthropology conceived as a comprehensive science of humans (OECD, 1972, p. 26). Characteristic of the time, the most prominent conceptual vocabularies in the OECD conference were general systems theory, structuralism, and cybernetics. The term had limited circulation at first, but it proliferated in the final decades of the 20th century. *Transdisciplinary* now appears as a descriptor of broad fields and synoptic disciplines, a team-based holistic approach to health care, a general ethos, and a comprehensive integrative curriculum design. In a defining essay on the multilingual international electronic network, the td-net Web site, Christoff Küffer (2001) reports that transdisciplinary research has developed in different contexts, fostering differing types and goals (www.transdisciplinarity.ch/bibliographie/Transdis_e.html). Four major trend lines appear at present.

The first trend line is an extension of the OECD connotation of new synthetic frameworks. The Nuffield Foundation (1975) anticipated this development in recognizing a third possibility beyond bridge building and reconstruction. Integration also occurs when a new overarching concept or theory subsumes the theories and concepts of several existing disciplines (p. 47). Miller (1982) defined transdisciplinarity as "articulated conceptual frameworks" that transcend the narrow scope of disciplinary worldviews. Holistic in intent, these frameworks propose to reorganize the structure of knowledge (p. 21). General systems, structuralism, Marxism, policy sciences, feminism, ecology, and sociobiology became leading examples. More recently, a parallel notion of "transdisciplinary [TD] science" has emerged in broad areas such as cancer research. This development stakes its etymological claim, though, to Patricia Rosenfield's (1992) call for a "transcendent interdisciplinary research" that fosters systematic theoretical frameworks for analyzing social, economic, political, environmental, and institutional factors in human health and well-being. Transdisciplinary team science is fostering new forms of collaborative research, methodologies, training programs, and career development outcomes that are being legitimated by efforts to institutionalize the concept in the U.S. National Cancer Institute (Rosenfield, 1992; Stokols, Taylor, Hall, & Moser, 2006).

A second trend line heightens the transgressive claims prioritized in critical interdisciplinarities. In the past, *transdisciplinarity* was not commonly used in humanities, but in the 1990s, it began appearing more often as a label for knowledge formations imbued with a critical imperative. Michael Peters (1999) associated the term with creating new theoretical paradigms, questions, and knowledge that cannot be taken up within the boundaries of existing disciplines. Ronald Schleifer (2002) linked "the new interdisciplinarity" with theory and transdisciplinary or cultural study of large social and intellectual formations that have breached canons of wholeness and the simplicity of the Kantian architecture of knowledge and art. The transdisciplinary operation of cultural studies, Douglas Kellner (1995) specified, draws on a range of fields to theorize the complexity and contradictions of media/culture/communications. It moves from text to contexts, pushing boundaries of class, gender, race, ethnicity, and other identities (pp. 27–28). In women's and gender studies, Dölling and Hark (2000) aligned transdisciplinarity with critical evaluation of terms, concepts, and methods that transgress disciplinary boundaries (pp. 1196–1197). And in Canadian studies, Jill Vickers (1997) grouped trans- and antidisciplinarity with movements that reject disciplinarity in whole or in part while raising questions of sociopolitical justice (p. 41).

The third trend line is the contemporary version of the ancient quest for systematic integration of knowledge. This quest spans ancient Greek philosophy, the medieval Christian summa, the Enlightenment ambition of universal reason, transcendentalism, Umberto Eco's speculation on a perfect language, the Unity of Science movement, the search for unification theories in physics, and E. O. Wilson's theory of consilience. Reviewing the history of this terministic screen, the philosopher Joseph Kockelmans (1979) concluded that it has tended to center on educational and philosophical dimensions of sciences. The search for unity today does not follow automatically from a pregiven, presupposed order of things. It must be continually "brought about" through critical, philosophical, and suprascientific reflection. It also accepts plurality and diversity, a value prominent in the work of the Centre International de Recherches et Études Transdisciplinaire (CIRET). CIRET is a virtual meeting space where a new universality of thought and type of education are being developed. This form of transdisciplinary vision

replaces reductionism with a new principle of relativity that is transcultural and transnational and encompasses ethics, spirituality, and creativity (http://perso.club-internet.fr/nicol/ciret). Informed by the conceptual vocabulary of complexity, this trend line is also prominent in Latin America.

The fourth and increasingly influential trend line is more prominent in Europe than North America and is gaining influence in Latin America in the context of local governance. The core premise of this trend line is that problems in the *Lebenswelt*—the life world—are needed to frame research questions and practices, not problems in the disciplines (Häberli et al., 2001, pp. 10–11). The emergence of a new form of *transdisciplinarity* was anticipated in 1982, when the OECD concluded that *exogenous interdisciplinarity* now has priority over *endogenous interdisciplinarity*. The *endogenous* originates within science and still carries the aim of realizing a unity of science. The *exogenous* originates in "real problems of the community" and the demand that universities perform their pragmatic social mission (OECD, 1982, p. 130). A further progression was evident in the late 1980s and early 1990s in German and Swiss contexts of environmental research that involved the participation of stakeholders in society. By 2000, at a major international conference on transdisciplinarity, case studies of trans-sector transdisciplinary research (TDR) were reported in all fields of human interaction with natural systems and technical innovations as well as in the development context (Klein, Grossenbacher-Mansuy, Scholz, & Welti, 2001).

Not all problems are the same, however. One strand of trans-sector TDR centers on collaborations between academic researchers and the industrial and private sectors for the purpose of product and technology development. Another strand focuses on democratic solutions to controversial social, environmental, and political problems.

Theoretical warrants for one strand have even been marshaled for the other. In 1994, Gibbons et al. proposed that a new mode of knowledge production is fostering a reconfiguration and recontextualization of knowledge. Mode 1, the traditional form, is primarily academic, homogeneous, hierarchical, and dominated by disciplinary boundary work. Mode 2 is nonhierarchical. It is characterized by complexity, hybridity, nonlinearity, reflexivity, heterogeneity, and transdisciplinarity. New configurations of research work are being generated continuously, and a new social distribution of knowledge is occurring. Gibbons et al. initially highlighted instrumental contexts, such as aircraft design, pharmaceutics, and electronics. In 2001, Nowotny, Scott, and Gibbons extended Mode 2 theory to argue that contextualization of problems requires participation in the *agora* of public debate, a claim that is also advanced in some fields of critical interdisciplinarity. When lay perspective and alternative knowledges are recognized, a shift occurs from *reliable scientific knowledge* to inclusion of *socially robust knowledge*. This transgressive way of thinking about science has been further linked with the concept of "postnormal science."

Peter Weingart (2000) identified a common topos among claims for new modes of knowledge production, postnormal and postmodern science, and newer forms of interdisciplinary and transdisciplinary research. They are all oscillating between empirical and normative statements, positing more democratic and participatory modes, while resounding the same theme that triggered the escalation of interdisciplinarity in the context of higher-education reform in the 1960s. Today, however, claims are often framed in the context of application and involvement of stakeholders in systems that are too complex for limited disciplinary modes portrayed as too linear and narrow for "real"-world problem solving. New transdisciplinary and parallel interdisciplinary forms are not without their

own "blind spots," though. They fail to recognize the opportunistic dimensions of both presumably "internal" academic science and strategic research for nonscientific goals (pp. 36, 38).

In an analysis of forms of interdisciplinary explanation, Mark Kann (1979) identified three political positions. Conservative elites want to solve social and economic problems, without concern for epistemological questions. Liberal academics demand accommodation but maintain a base in the existing structure, in the middle ground of harmonious interaction. Radical dissidents challenge the existing structure of knowledge, demanding that interdisciplinarity respond to the needs and problems of oppressed and marginalized groups to achieve greater equality (pp. 197–198). Within humanities, Giles Gunn (1992) adds, the radical response calls for a revolt against not only disciplinary boundaries but all institutional hierarchies. The left interdisciplinary project is more militant than the liberal one, which preserves the distinction between the academy and the world with the aim of reforming the way that knowledge is produced within the academy. The radical project exposes the political nature of the distinction, with the aim of transforming not only academic structure but also the larger structure of social articulations (pp. 187–188).

The escalation of transdisciplinarity and critical interdisciplinarity signals a new phase in the history of the keyword. Framed initially by ancient warrants of unity and universality, the underlying concept evolved over the course of a century to serve multiple and conflicting purposes, pluralizing the discourse and introducing new thematics of critique, complexity, collaboration, and problem solving. Hearkening back to McKeon (1971), both rhetoric and interdisciplinarity are architectonic arts that have been instruments of continuity and change, tradition and revolution. The rhetorical device of schematization has structured new interdisciplinary subject matters and conceptual vocabularies to address unmet needs. The terministic screens of inter-disciplinarity are all prompted by the inadequacy of conventional schematizations for addressing the pressing problems and questions of our time. They do not agree, however, on priorities.

REFERENCES

Addelson, K. P., & Potter, E. (1991). Making knowledge. In J. Hartman & E. Messer-Davidow (Eds.), *(En)Gendering knowledge: Feminists in academe* (pp. 259–277). Knoxville: University of Tennessee Press.

Allen, P. G. (1992). The intersection of gender and color. In J. Gibaldi (Ed.), *Introduction to scholarship in modern languages and literatures* (pp. 303–319). New York: Modern Language Association.

Armstrong, C., & Fontaine, S. I. (1989). The power of naming: Names that create and define the discipline. *WPA: Writing Program Administration, 13*(1/2), 5–14.

Association of American Colleges and Universities. (1990). Women's studies. In *Reports from the fields* (pp. 207–224). Washington, DC: Author.

Becher, T. (1990). The counter-culture of specialization. *European Journal of Education, 15*(1), 333–346.

Bennett, D. (1997). Innovation in the liberal arts and sciences. In R. Orrill (Ed.), *Education and democracy: Re-imagining liberal learning in America* (pp. 131–149). New York: College Board.

Boxer, M. J. (1982). For and about women: The theory and practice of women's studies in the United States. *Signs, 7*(3), 661–695.

Bruun, H., Hukkinen, J., Huutoniemi, K., & Klein, J. T. (2005). *Promoting interdisciplinary research: The case of the Academy of Finland* (Publications of the Academy of Finland, Series 8/05). Helsinki, Finland: Academy of Finland.

Burke, K. (1966). *Language as symbolic action: Essays on life, literature, and method.* Berkeley: University of California Press.

Caldwell, L. K. (1983). Environmental studies: Discipline or metadiscipline? *Environmental Professional, 5,* 247–259.

Campbell, D. (1969). Ethnocentrism of disciplines and the fish-scale model of omniscience. In M. Sherif & C. Sherif (Eds.), *Interdisciplinary relationships in social sciences* (pp. 328–348). Chicago: Aldine.

Campbell, N., & Kean, A. (1997). *American cultural studies: An introduction to American culture.* London: Routledge.

Chubin, D. (1976). The conceptualization of scientific specialties. *Sociological Quarterly, 17,* 448–476.

Cornwall, G., & Stoddard, E. (2001). Toward an interdisciplinary epistemology: Faculty culture and institutional change. In B. L. Smith & J. McCann (Eds.), *Reinventing ourselves: Interdiscipinary education, collaborative learning, and experimentation in higher education* (pp. 162–178). Bolton, MA: Anker.

Coyner, S. (1991). Women's studies. *National Women's Studies Association Journal, 3*(3), 349–354.

DeSoto, A. M. (2001). Chicanos. In Kurian, G. T., Butler, J., Mechling, J., & Orvell, M. (Eds.), *Encyclopedia of American studies* (Vol. 1, pp. 299–304). New York: Grolier Educational.

Dogan, M., & Pahre, R. (1990). *Creative marginality: Innovation at the intersections of social sciences.* Boulder, CO: Westview Press.

Dölling, I., & Hark, S. (2000). She who speaks shadow speaks truth: Transdisciplinarity in women's and gender studies. *Signs, 25*(4), 1195–1198.

Elam, D. (1990). Ms. en abyme: Deconstruction and feminism. *Social Epistemology, 4*(3), 293–308.

Elam, D. (2002). Taking account of women's studies. In R. Wiegman (Ed.), *Women's studies on its own: A next wave reader in institutional change* (pp. 218–223). Durham, NC: Duke University Press.

Elliott, M. J. S. (2001a). Chicano literature. In Kurian, G. T., Butler, J., Mechling, J., & Orvell, M. (Eds.), *Encyclopedia of American studies* (Vol. 1, pp. 304–308). New York: Grolier Educational.

Elliott, M. J. S. (2001b). Mestiza consciousness. In Kurian, G. T., Butler, J., Mechling, J., &

Orvell, M. (Eds.), *Encyclopedia of American studies* (Vol. 3, pp. 106–107). New York: Grolier Educational.

Fisher, D. (1993). *Fundamental development of the social sciences: Rockefeller philanthropy and the United States Social Science Research Council.* Ann Arbor: University of Michigan Press.

Frank, R. (1988). "Interdisciplinary": The first half-century. In E. G. Stanley & T. F. Hoad (Eds.), *WORDS: For Robert Burchfield's sixty-fifth birthday* (pp. 91–101). Cambridge, UK: D. S. Brewer.

Friedman, S. S. (2001). Academic feminism and interdisciplinarity. *Feminist Studies, 27*(2), 499–531.

Garber, M. (2001). *Academic instincts.* Princeton, NJ: Princeton University Press.

Gibbons, M., Limoges, C., Nowotny, H., Schwartzman, S., Scott, P., & Trow, M. (1994). *The new production of knowledge: The dynamics of science and research in contemporary societies.* London: Sage.

Goldman, H. (1995). Innovation and change in the production of knowledge. *Social Epistemology, 9*(3), 211–232.

Greenblatt, S., & Gunn, G. (1992). Introduction. In S. Greenblatt & G. Gunn (Eds.), *Redrawing the boundaries: The transformation of English and American literary studies* (pp. 1–11). New York: Modern Language Association.

Gunn, G. (1992). *Thinking across the American grain: Ideology, intellect and the new pragmatism.* Chicago: University of Chicago Press.

Häberli, R., Bill, A., Grossenbacher-Mansuy, W., Klein, J. T., Scholz, R., & Welti, M. (2001). Synthesis. In J. T. Klein, W. Grossenbacher-Mansuy, R. Scholz, & M. Welti, M. (Eds.), *Transdisciplinarity: Joint problem solving among science, technology, and society* (pp. 6–22). Basel, Switzerland: Birkhäuser.

Hartman, J., & Messer-Davidow, E. (1991). Introduction: A position statement. In J. Hartman & E. Messer-Davidow (Eds.), *(En)Gendering knowledge: Feminists in academe* (pp. 1–7). Knoxville: University of Tennessee Press.

Henderson, M. H. (1995). Introduction: Borders, boundaries, and frame(work)s. In M. Henderson (Ed.), *Borders, boundaries, and*

frames: Cultural criticism and cultural studies (pp. 2–30). New York: Routledge.

Kann, M. (1979). The political culture of interdisciplinary explanation. *Humanities in Society, 2*(3), 185–200.

Katz, S. (1996, June 17). *Beyond the disciplines.* An address at a meeting on "The Role of the New American College in the Past, Present, and Future of American Higher Education," Saint Mary's College of California, Moraga.

Kearney, M. (1991). Borders and boundaries of state and self at the end of empire. *Journal of Historical Sociology, 4*(1), 52–74.

Kellner, D. (1995). *Media culture: Cultural studies, identity, and politics between the modern and the postmodern.* London: Routledge.

Klein, J. T. (1990). *Interdisciplinarity: History, theory, and practice.* Detroit, MI: Wayne State University Press.

Klein, J. T. (1996). *Crossing boundaries: Knowledge, disciplinarities, and interdisciplinarities.* Charlottesville: University Press of Virginia.

Klein, J. T. (2005). *Humanities, culture, and interdisciplinarity: The changing American academy.* Albany: State University of New York Press.

Klein, J. T. (forthcoming). Interdisciplinarity and its types. In R. Frodeman, J. T. Klein, & C. Mitcham (Eds.), *The Oxford handbook of interdisciplinarity.* Oxford, UK: Oxford University Press.

Klein, J. T., Grossenbacher-Mansuy, W., Scholz, R., & Welti, M. (Eds.). (2001). *Transdisciplinarity: Joint problem solving among science, technology, and society.* Basel, Switzerland: Birkhäuser.

Kockelmans, J. J. (1979). Why interdisciplinarity? In J. Kockelmans (Ed.), *Interdisciplinarity and higher education* (pp. 123–160). University Park: Pennsylvania University Press.

Kolodny, A. (1980). Dancing through the minefield: Some observations on the theory, practice, and politics of a feminist literary criticism. *Feminist Studies, 6,* 1–25.

Küffer, C. (2001). *About the bibliography transdisciplinarity.* Retrieved August 5, 2007, from www.transdisciplinarity.ch/bibliographie/Transdis_e.html

Lattuca, L. (2001). *Creating interdisciplinarity: Interdisciplinary research and teaching among college and university faculty.* Nashville, TN: Vanderbilt University Press.

Lauter, P. (2001). *From Walden Pond to Jurassic Park: Activism, culture, and American studies.* Durham, NC: Duke University Press.

Limerick, P. (1997). Insiders and outsiders: The borders of the USA and the limits of the ASA. *American Quarterly, 49*(3), 449–469.

Lipsitz, G. (2002). "Sent for you yesterday, here you come today": American studies scholarship and the new social movements. In D. E. Pease & R. Wiegman (Eds.), *The futures of American studies* (pp. 441–460). Durham, NC: Duke University Press.

McKeon, R. (1987). The uses of rhetoric in a technological age: Architectonic productive arts. In M. Backman (Ed.), *Rhetoric: Essays in invention and discovery* (pp. 1–24). Woodbridge. CT: Ox Bow Press.

McLaughlin, T. (1990). Figurative language. In F. Lentricchia & T. McLaughlin (Eds.), *Critical terms for literary studies* (pp. 80–90). Chicago: University of Chicago Press.

Messer-Davidow, E. (2002). *Disciplining feminism: From social activism to academic discourse.* Durham, NC: Duke University Press.

Messer-Davidow, E., Shumway, D., & Sylvan, D. (1993). Preface. In E. Messer-Davidow, D. Shumway, & D. Sylvan (Eds.), *Knowledges: Historical and cultural studies in disciplinarity* (pp. vii–viii). Charlottesville: University Press of Virginia.

Miller, R. (1982). Varieties of interdisciplinary approaches in the social sciences. *Issues in Integrative Studies, 1,* 1–37.

Moran, J. (2002). *Interdisciplinarity.* London: Routledge.

Nowotny, H., Scott, P., & Gibbons, M. (2001). *Re-thinking science. Knowledge and the public in an age of uncertainty.* Cambridge, UK: Polity Press.

Nuffield Foundation. (1975). *Interdisciplinarity: A report by the Group for Research and Innovation in Higher Education.* London: Author.

Organisation for Economic Cooperation and Development. (1972). *Interdisciplinarity: Problems of teaching and research in universities.* Paris: Author.

Organisation for Economic Cooperation and Development. (1982). *The university and the community: The problems of changing relationships.* Paris: Author.

Ostriker, J., & Kuh, C. V. (Eds.). (2003). *Assessing research-doctorate programs: A methodology study.* Washington, DC: National Academies Press.

Peck, J. (1989). There's no place like home? Remapping the topography of German studies. *German Quarterly, 62*(2), 178–187.

Peters, M. (1999). Preface. In M. Peters (Ed.), *After the disciplines: The emergence of cultural studies* (pp. xi–xiii). Westport, CT: Bergin & Garvey.

Reese, T. F. (1995). Mapping interdisciplinarity. *Art Bulletin, 77*(4), 544–549.

Rosenfield, P. L. (1992). The potential of transdisciplinary research for sustaining and extending linkages between the health and social sciences. *Social Science and Medicine, 35*(11), 1343–1357.

Salter, L., & Hearn, A. (Eds.). (1996). *Outside the lines: Issues in interdisciplinary research.* Montreal, Ontario, Canada: McGill-Queen's University Press.

Schleifer, R. (2002). A new kind of work: Publishing, theory, and cultural studies. In D. Shumway & C. Dionne (Eds.), *Disciplining English: Alternative histories, critical perspectives* (pp. 179–194). Albany: State University of New York Press.

Scott, R. L. (1979). Personal and institutional problems encountered in being interdisciplinary. In J. Kockelmans (Ed.), *Interdisciplinarity and higher education* (pp. 306–327). University Park: Pennsylvania State University Press.

Star, S., & Griesemer, J. (1989). Institutional ecology, "translations," and boundary objects: Amateurs and professionals in Berkeley's Museum of Vertebrate Biology. *Social Studies of Science, 19*(3), 387–420.

Stokols, D., Taylor, B., Hall, K., & Moser, R. (Co-Chairs). (2006, October 30–31). Introduction. In *NCI conference on the science of team science: Assessing the value of transdisciplinary research.* Bethesda, MD: National Cancer Institute.

Turner, B. (1990). The interdisciplinary curriculum: From social medicine to post-modernism. *Sociology of Health and Illness, 12,* 1–23.

Vickers, J. (1997). [Un]framed in open, unmapped fields: Teaching and the practice of interdisciplinarity. *Arachne: An Interdisciplinary Journal of the Humanities, 4*(2), 11–42.

Weingart, P. (2000). Interdisciplinarity: The paradoxical discourse. In P. Weingart & N. Stehr (Eds.), *Practicing interdisciplinarity* (pp. 25–41). Toronto, Ontario, Canada: University of Toronto Press.

Wiegman, R. (2002). Introduction: On location. In R. Wiegman (Ed.), *Women's studies on its own: A next wave reader in institutional change* (pp. 1–44). Durham, NC: Duke University Press.

Winter, M. (1996). Specialization, territoriality, and jurisdiction in librarianship. *Library Trends, 45*(2), 343–363.

Wise, G. (1978). Some elementary axioms for an American culture studies. *Prospects: The Annual of American Cultural Studies, 4,* 517–547.

Wise, G. (1979). Paradigm dramas in American studies. *American Quarterly, 31*(3), 293–337.

Women's studies. (1990). Women's studies. In *Reports from the fields* (pp. 207–224). Washington, DC: Association of American Colleges and Universities.

PART III

Rhetoric and Pedagogy

Rhetoric as Pedagogy

CHERYL GLENN

MARTÍN CARCASSON

Isocrates was famous in his own day, and for many centuries to come, for his program of education (paideia), which stressed above all the teaching of eloquence. His own works . . . were the vehicles for his notion of the true "philosophy," for him a wisdom in civic affairs emphasizing moral responsibility and equated with mastery of rhetorical technique.

—Thomas Conley

Rhetoric has always been a teaching tradition, the pedagogical pursuit of good speaking and writing. When Homer's Achilles, "a rhetor of speech and a doer of deeds," used language purposefully, persuasively, and eloquently, his voice sparked a rhetorical consciousness in the early Greeks (trans. 1938, *Iliad* 9.443) that was carried into the private sphere by Sappho and then into the public sphere by the Greeks and Romans, who made pedagogy the heart of the rhetorical tradition. To that end, competing theories and practices of rhetoric were displayed and put to the test in the Greek academies of Gorgias, Isocrates, Aspasia, Plato, and Aristotle. Later it flourished as the centerpiece of the Roman educational system made famous by such rhetorical greats as Cicero and Quintilian.

More than 2,000 years later, the pedagogy of rhetoric played a key role in the early universities of the United States. During the 18th century, for instance, "rhetoric was treated as the most important subject in the curriculum" (Halloran, 1982). It was not until the 20th century that the importance of rhetoric to the cultivation of citizens both began to wane in the shadow of higher education's shift in focus from the development of rhetorical expertise to that of disciplinary knowledge. Despite this shift, the foundational rhetorical theories, practices, and pedagogies developed by the ancients survived, even thrived, as they continued to guide rhetorical studies, whether those studies inhabit English or Communication departments.

Thus, rhetoric is the grandparent of both English and Speech (communication) departments, as William Riley Parker, former secretary of the Modern Language Association (MLA), so easily explains. In an essay first published in 1967, he writes,

> English was born about 100 years ago. Its mother, the eldest daughter of Rhetoric, was Oratory—or what we now prefer to call public speaking or, simply, speech. Its father was Philology or what we now call linguistics. Their marriage [Oratory and Philology's] . . . was short-lived. . . . I date the break with the mother, however, not from the disgraceful affair she had with Elocution, but rather from the founding of the [National Association of Academic Teachers of Public Speaking] Speech Association of America in 1914, which brought, as was hoped, the creation of many departments of speech. I date the break with the father, not from his happy marriage to Anthropology, but from the founding of the Linguistic Society of America in 1924, and the developing hostility of literary scholars to non-prescriptive grammar, new terminology, and the rigors of language study. Splinter groups form when their founders feel their interests neglected, and English teachers, absorbed in what they considered more important business, were indeed neglecting speech by 1914 and losing all vital concern with linguistics by 1924. (1981, p. 6)

As half siblings often do, English and Speech developed individual interests, with English concentrating on literature and theory (how to read literature) and Speech eventually broadening its focus from one of oral delivery to the wide science of communication. Despite their divergences, however, English and Speech both carried the genetic influence of their shared grandparent: Both disciplines remained in the same department, tethered to rhetoric. And rhetoric has always been a teaching tradition, no matter where it has resided.

AN INSTITUTIONAL HISTORY OF RHETORICAL PEDAGOGY IN THE UNITED STATES

"Not to know what happened before one was born is always to be a child."

—Cicero

The MLA, disciplinary home of English literary studies (as well as modern language studies), was established in 1883, in part, as a way to resist the hegemony of classics in the college curriculum but, more obviously, as a way to "strengthen the study and teaching of language and literature" (www.mla.org/about). By the end of the 19th century, Yale, Harvard, and Johns Hopkins were among the many American colleges and universities reconfiguring their courses and methods in such a way as to slip the yoke of the clergy, who had traditionally held a near monopoly on a curriculum of theology, classics, and languages, and, instead, to harness themselves to the model of the German research university, where truth, rather than being passed down, was to be pursued disinterestedly. In 1874, James Morgan Hart, who received his Ph.D. at the University of Göttingen, wrote in unqualified praise of the German university system, saying that even the laziest of German students has forgotten twice as much as the idler of American, the industrious student knows twice as much as the industrious under-graduate, and the future scholar of Germany is a man of whom we in America have no conception. He is a man who could not exist under our system, he would be choked by recitations and grades. What he studies, he studies with the devotion of a poet and the trained skill of a scientist. (p. 303)

By that time, Hart had moved from the University of Cincinnati, Ohio, where he also served as the president of the MLA of Ohio, to Cornell University, where he became president of the national MLA in 1895. The MLA soon paved the way for an emphasis on research in literary and language studies, its inception professionalizing English studies as well as the teaching of English and public speaking. Not 30 years later, in an attempt to thwart the curricular impositions of colleges on high schools, 65 high school and college teachers came together to establish the National Council of Teachers of English (NCTE) in 1911. Like the MLA, they, too, linked English studies with teaching, including the teaching of public speaking. And they, too, soon began to promote the research necessary for improving the teaching of English and public speaking as well as the material conditions for teachers. Given the complementary interests of the two organizations, many college teachers of English have held membership in both the MLA and NCTE.

All during this time of early professionalization, college teachers of public speaking were members of English departments, but they were not the half siblings of literature and composition teachers that Parker refers to; rather they were the poor cousins. In an attempt to carve out an academic discipline for themselves and their work, a small group of public-speaking teachers (17 to be exact) broke away from NCTE in 1914 to form the National Association of Academic Teachers of Public Speaking. These "Seventeen Who Made History" espoused disciplinary research as their priority (Weaver, 1959), but their scientific learnings seem to have had more to do with gaining academic respectability within the research university than with striving for a scientific approach to the successful teaching of public speaking. By 1935, more than 200 American college and university catalogs listed a separate department of speech (Griffin, 1997, para. 7). The name of their organization was changed to the Speech Association of America (SAA) in 1950, Speech Communication Association (SCA) in 1970, and the National Communication Association (NCA) in 1997—name changes that reflect the ever-broadening interests of their discipline.

During these early years of disciplinary formation, English teachers were occupied with teaching literature, grammar, composition—and some oral rhetoric. But the study of literature dominated the study of rhetoric. And after speech established its autonomy in terms of departmental status, teachers of public speaking offered courses in public address, oral interpretation of literature, radio announcing, drama, debate, and roundtable discussions. But soon social scientists began to establish themselves in speech communication departments, their numbers and influence often marginalizing more traditional rhetorical studies.

Still, the "rhetorical turn" toward scientific communication and decision science at the expense of rhetorics of deliberation has, in many ways (and ironically), elevated the status of the discipline of rhetoric in the modern university, with colleagues from across camps recognizing the value and importance of rhetorical studies, whether analysis, deliberation, oration, or composition. Graduate rhetoric programs at the University of Iowa, Penn State University, University of Minnesota, Northwestern University, and University of Maryland are among the universities enjoying a renaissance, what with thriving interdisciplinary programs, successful graduate student placements, and, on the undergraduate level, close connections with undergraduate writing programs (e.g., Stanford University, University of Denver, University of Colorado, University of

Memphis). Whether the actual teaching of rhetoric and the delivery of rhetorical education are also enjoying similar renewal is debatable.

Certainly, some would argue that it is not. David Fleming (1998), for example, laments the "simultaneous rise of rhetorical theory and continued decline of rhetorical education" (p. 169). Despite the rise in graduate rhetoric programs, the decline in rhetorical education, per se, is, indeed, a different issue. According to Walter Beale (1990),

> Rhetorical education is an attempt to shape a certain kind of character capable of using language effectively to carry on the practical and moral business of a polity. It is based implicitly or explicitly on ideas of individual competence and political well-being. Its dual purposes are the cultivation of the individual and the success of a culture. (p. 626)

Little wonder, then, that Thomas Miller (2004) was so dismayed by the results of his research, which revealed how very little rhetorical education undergraduate students are currently receiving. Miller surveyed the course requirements and electives for English and Communication majors at 100 four-year institutions, a survey that revealed a paucity of undergraduate courses focused exclusively on rhetoric, whether rhetorical history, theory, or practice. So despite rhetoric's long link with pedagogy, the teaching of rhetoric, especially the teaching of undergraduates, appears to suffer from low status, in particular at the prestigious high-research institutions. Status for professors (rhetoric professors and otherwise) remains linked to their scholarship (i.e., their publications and research agenda), rarely to the quality of their teaching.

In *The Vocation of a Teacher* (1988), Wayne Booth captures the tension between the importance of rhetorical scholarship relative to rhetorical pedagogy by raising the fact that most undergraduate students take only one or maybe two rhetoric courses, or courses that can be even loosely related to a rhetorical education: first-year writing and public speaking, which, in many colleges and universities, hardly qualify as exposure to the rhetorical tradition. Even more dispiriting to Booth is the fact that these two courses, courses that could invite students into rhetorical education and rhetorical studies, are most often taught by

> underpaid part-timers, our exploited TAs (many of them just out of college themselves), at best our assistant professors, who are told, sometimes without even an effort at euphemism, that the road to promotion is not to teach well but to get that book out fast. (p. 23)

Were these courses taught by rhetorical scholars, the courses might look markedly different. They might serve as a venue for rhetorical scholars to pass on rhetorical traditions to the vast majority of college students who will not major in either English or Communication, thereby invigorating the rhetorical education of many more college students. As it is, undergraduate teaching is rarely rewarded and often passed on to the untenured or untenurable teachers to whom Booth alluded, most of whom have little or no training in rhetoric.

More recently, however, there seems to be morphic resonance across the country for emphasizing the pedagogy of rhetoric and rhetorical education. The impetus for this emphasis has come from inside departments of English and Communication as well as from the greater community. From the outside, for example, there has been a growing call for the revitalization of the civic mission of universities, a call that appears to be inherently tied to the pedagogy of rhetoric.

Having identified the lack of any civic focus in higher education, various foundations and associations have published reports addressing that lack and offering recommendations, among them the Carnegie Foundation for the Advancement of Teaching (*Educating Citizens*) (Colby, 2003); the Association of American Colleges and Universities (*Greater Expectations: A New Vision for Learning as a Nation Goes to College*) (Association of American Colleges and Universities, 2002); the National Association of State Universities and Land-Grant Colleges (*Returning to Our Roots: The Engaged Institution*) (Kellogg Commission on the Future of State and Land-Grant Universities, 1999); and a coalition of the University of Michigan, Campus Compact, the Ford Foundation, the Johnson Foundation, and the W. K. Kellogg Foundation (*Wingspread Declaration on Renewing the Civic Mission of the American Research University*) (Boyte & Hollander, 1999). These calls to citizenship education, which is rhetorical education, go beyond the need for more voting, civic engagement, and service learning; rather, they consist of the importance of reexamining the purpose of higher education and the responsibility of college graduates. These calls often highlight the importance of "21st-century skills" such as critical thinking, innovative problem solving, deliberation, and judgment—skills, most rhetorical scholars would argue, that are part and parcel of the pedagogy of rhetoric.

In addition to the call for rhetorical, citizenship education, the rise of the "deliberative democracy movement" (Gastil & Levine, 2005), a movement based outside the walls of academia, is providing additional support for the growing focus on the need for universities, as well as public education in general, to do a better job of producing able citizens equipped for the 21st century. To paraphrase Gerard Hauser (2004), perhaps universities have finally begun to understand the importance of balancing the needs of Berlin (disciplinary knowledge production) and Athens (the cultivation of citizens).

The recent pedagogical push has also emanated from within English and Communication departments. Indeed, a number of prominent rhetoricians have recently joined this broader call to action. The 2003 Evanston, Illinois, conference sponsored by the Alliance of Rhetoric Societies (ARS) resulted in a number of eloquent statements concerning the importance of rhetorical pedagogy. In his impassioned summary of the discussions that took place in Evanston, Gerard Hauser (2004) focused on the pedagogical ones, admonishing his readers that "capacitating students to be competent citizens is our birthright. It has been ours since antiquity. Modern education has stripped us of it. We need to reclaim it" (p. 52; see also Hauser, 2002). One of the offshoots of the ARS meeting was the inaugural biennial Rhetoric Society of America (RSA) summer institute, held on the Kent State University campus in Kent, Ohio. An extension of the summer institute, with its various workshops and short seminars, was the inaugural week-long seminar for graduate students and junior faculty, which, led by Michael Leff and Cheryl Glenn, focused on "Rhetoric as a Teaching Tradition."

But the ARS, the RSA, and Hauser are not the only entities to call for enriching rhetorical education in America. Rosa Eberly (2000, 2002) has made similar pleas, as well as Hart (1993), Miller (2004), Denman (2004), Haskins (2006), and Walker (2006), among others. Two recent anthologies have also taken up the cause of specifically examining rhetorical pedagogy and rhetorical education in America (Petraglia & Bahri, 2003; Glenn, Lyday, & Sharer, 2004). Clearly, interest in rhetorical pedagogy has significantly increased in important ways in the past 10 years.

Indeed, we would argue that a primary source for the recent collaborations between rhetorical scholars in English and Communication, evidenced by RSA, ARS, and this very volume, is the common ground all of us share by being teachers of rhetoric. Regardless of whether we are in the midst of a "pedagogical turn"—the phrase Andrea Lunsford used to summarize her perceptions of the ARS conference (Leff & Lunsford, 2004, p. 61)—all rhetorical scholars need to consider a twofold critical question. Given this recent surge of interest in both rhetoric and the teaching of citizenship (or rhetorical education), what are the necessary tools of citizenship in the 21st century, and how might rhetorical scholars work to help develop them?

If rhetoric renews its commitment to "cultivating citizens," what should those citizens be taught? What should they be taught to do? To know how to do? The chapters in this section seek to address these questions by considering key issues and questions relevant to the contemporary pedagogy of rhetoric. These chapters also describe the material conditions in which the teaching of rhetoric takes place. To those ends, this section considers three distinct levels of rhetorical instruction, according to what audience is being educated. The first level consists of the introductory courses in English (first-year writing) and Communication (public speaking) departments that, as mentioned above, often provide the only exposure to rhetoric, however minor it may be, to the thousands of students in majors other than English or Communication. A second level consists of those sparse but valuable upper-level undergraduate courses in rhetoric that are populated primarily by English and Communication majors. In these upper-level courses, rhetorical scholars have the opportunity to expand students' exposure to and understanding of the rhetorical tradition in its many guises (from rhetorical history and theory to rhetorics of specific disciplines or practices). A third level goes beyond the university classroom to consider the role of rhetorical scholars in educating communities. Were we to include a fourth level, it would surely focus on graduate education, but graduate courses in rhetoric, whether in English or Communication departments, usually concentrate on scholarship and theory rather than pedagogy. Therefore, the chapters in this section range across these three levels in different ways, with some chapters focusing on the basic courses (Horner and Lu, Chapter 16), some on upper-level concepts (Ott and Dickinson, Chapter 21; Young and Kendall, Chapter 18; Middleton, Chapter 19; Mountford, Chapter 22), and some on extra-curricular endeavors (Atchison and Panetta, Chapter 17; Sharer, Chapter 20). Still each of the essays in this section seeks to inform rhetorical pedagogy across all the levels.

In Chapter 16, Horner and Lu analyze the phrase "rhetoric and composition" as a means of reviewing the history of attempts to stabilize the field's meaning. Focusing specifically on composition and its contextualization within universities, the authors argue that the field of rhetoric and composition is ideally situated to take advantage of a variety of learning experiences that are unrecognized in official university channels. Thus, the flexibility of the phrase "rhetoric and composition" ultimately facilitates the particular goal of attending to the diverse needs of composition students.

In Chapter 17, Atchison and Panetta examine the critical role intercollegiate debate has served in rhetorical pedagogy throughout the 20th century and into the 21st century. Involvement in debate programs was the entry point for many of the field's preeminent rhetoricians, particularly within speech communication, and debate continues to provide a particularly public face for rhetorical studies for many outside English and Communication departments. Atchison and Panetta describe debate's evolution from its early days within literary societies to freestanding academic units and also examine some of the key concerns faced by contemporary debate programs. They conclude with suggestions for reform to the practice.

By tracing the development of several major narratives of literacy in rhetorical scholarship, Young and Kendall (Chapter 18) show that literacy is not only a rhetorical artifact but also a form of persuasion: The stories we tell about the importance of literacy reveal the priorities and biases of our cultural situations. Beginning with the Great Divide literacy theorists of the mid-20th century, Young and Kendall trace literacy studies' development from a view of literacy as an autonomous talent, to a socially constructed practice, to a globally minded method of engagement. The tensions inherent in these different narratives of literacy play out, as Young and Kendall observe, in classroom situations—through standardized tests, placement programs, and government-mandated standards that lack nuanced attention to the contextual nature of literacy practices. Throughout these developments, literacy plays an important persuasive role for those attempting to shape education and establish cultural capital.

Looking back on Walter Ong's *Orality and Literacy,* Middleton (Chapter 19) describes the development and deployment of orality theory with an overview of significant publications in that field. She begins with a description of historical privileging of literacy and moves on to recover a variety of primary and secondary oral practices, arguing that increased attention to such practices can and should rescue our field from exclusive, and narrow-sighted, attention to written literacy. Middleton ends with a series of questions that hope to "broaden the range of inquiry on orality theory."

Sharer (Chapter 20) examines the long-standing and sometimes tenuous relationship between the teaching of rhetoric and civic engagement. Tracing this connection from the roots of rhetorical theory to the modern university, she observes that modern rhetorical instruction often neglects its civic origins. Sharer turns to progressive and radical educators, as well as political, historical, and ethnographic researchers, to argue that civic engagement should be reintegrated into our pedagogies via critical reading and writing, service learning, and cross-disciplinary movements. Such reintegration would not only better prepare our students to be knowledgeable and participating citizens but would also emphasize the practical importance of rhetorical education.

Ott and Dickinson (Chapter 21) examine the rhetorical response to the "pictorial turn" and the "rise of image," as well as how visual rhetoric has been incorporated into the classroom. They review, synthesize, and comment on the principal conceptions of visual rhetoric and outline an approach to teaching (with) visual rhetoric. In addition, they connect the pedagogy of visual rhetoric to the notion of critical citizenship, arguing that students must learn to interrogate and evaluate visual forms of rhetoric.

In the final chapter in this section, Mountford (Chapter 22) examines the relationship between composition and speech communication and argues that for the gap between the two disciplines to be bridged, concerned scholars must be familiar with the historical legacy of separation that they are attempting to overcome. The split between composition and speech communication came at a time when the educative philosophies of each discipline clashed: Scholars of composition criticized the mass media focus of communication in favor of the more traditional objects of study within communication. Recent attempts to bridge this gap have not recognized the historical reasons for separation. Mountford's historical narrative and suggestions about the possibility of unity through feminist work point toward how composition and communication could again unify rhetoric's disciplinary standing.

REFERENCES

Association of American Colleges and Universities. (2002). *Greater expectations: A new vision for learning as a nation goes to college.* Washington, DC: Author.

Beale, W. H. (1990). Richard M. Weaver: Philosophical rhetoric, cultural criticism, and the first rhetorical awakening. *College English, 52*(6), 626–640.

Booth, W. (1988). *The vocation of a teacher: Rhetorical occasions 1967–1988.* Chicago: University of Chicago Press.

Boyte, H., & Hollander, E. (Eds.). (1999). *Wingspread Declaration on renewing the civic mission of the American Research University.* Ann Arbor, MI: Campus Compact.

Colby, A., Ehrlich, T., Beaumont, E., & Stephens, J. (2003). *Educating citizens: Preparing America's under-graduates for lives of moral and civic responsibility*. San Francisco: Jossey-Bass.

Denman, W. N. (2004). Rhetoric, the "citizen-orator," and the revitalization of civic discourse in American life. In C. Glenn, M. Lyday, & W. Sharer (Eds.), *Rhetorical education in America* (pp. 3–17). Tuscaloosa: University of Alabama Press.

Eberly, R. (2000). *Citizen critics: Literary public spheres*. Urbana: University of Illinois Press.

Eberly, R. (2002). Rhetoric and the anti-logos doughball: Teaching deliberating bodies the practices of participatory democracy. *Rhetoric & Public Affairs, 5*, 287–300.

Fleming, D. (1998). Rhetoric as a course of study. *College English, 61*, 169–191.

Gastil, J., & Levine, P. (Eds.). (2005). *The deliberative democracy handbook: Strategies for effective civic engagement in the 21st century*. San Francisco: Jossey-Bass.

Glenn, C., Lyday, M., & Sharer, W. (Eds.). (2004). *Rhetorical education in America*. Tuscaloosa: University of Alabama Press.

Griffin, E. (1997). *A first look at communication* (3rd ed.). New York: McGraw-Hill. Retrieved November 9, 2006, from http://www.afirstlook.com/archive/talkabout.cfm?source=archther

Halloran, M. (1982). Rhetoric in the American college curriculum. *Pre/Text, 3*, 245–269.

Hart, J. M. (1874). *German universities*. New York.

Hart, R. P. (1993). Why communication? Why education? Toward a politics of teaching. *Communication Education, 41*, 97–105.

Haskins, E. (2006). Choosing between Isocrates and Aristotle: Disciplinary assumptions and pedagogical implications. *Rhetoric Society Quarterly, 36*, 191–201.

Hauser, G. A. (2002). Rhetorical democracy and civic engagement. In G. A. Hauser & A. Grim (Eds.), *Rhetorical democracy: Discursive practices of civic engagement* (pp. 1–14). Selected papers from the 2002 conference of Rhetoric Society of America. Mahwah, NJ: Lawrence Erlbaum Associates.

Hauser, G. (2004). Teaching rhetoric. Or why rhetoric isn't just another kind of philosophy or literary criticism. *Rhetoric Society Quarterly, 34*(3), 39–53.

Homer. (1938). *The Iliad* (W. H. D. Rouse, Trans.). New York: Mentor-New American Library.

Kellogg Commission on the Future of State and Land-Grant Universities. (1999). *Returning to our roots: The engaged institution*. Washington, DC: National Association of State Universities and Land-Grant Colleges.

Leff, M., & Lunsford, A. A. (2004). Afterwards: A dialogue. *Rhetoric Society Quarterly, 34*(3), 55–67.

Miller, T. P. (2004). How rhetorical are English and communications majors? *Rhetoric Society Quarterly, 35*, 91–113.

Parker, W. R. (1981). Where do English departments come from? In G. Tate & E. P. J. Corbett (Eds.), *The writing teacher's sourcebook* (pp. 3–19). New York: Oxford University Press. (Original work published 1967)

Petraglia, J., & Bahri, D. (Eds.). (2003). *The realms of rhetoric: The prospects for rhetoric education*. Albany: State University of New York Press.

Walker, J. (2006). What a difference a definition makes, or, William Dean Howells and the Sophist's shoes. *Rhetoric Society Quarterly, 36*, 143–153.

Weaver, A. T. (1959). Seventeen who made history: The founders of the association. *Quarterly Journal of Speech, 45*, 195–199.

16

Rhetoric and (?) Composition

BRUCE HORNER

MIN-ZHAN LU

Despite the current prevalence of the phrase *rhetoric and composition* in academic discourse to name an academic program, field, or subject, there is a tension among many of those who might be identified as working in the field called "rhetoric and composition" about the appropriateness of that phrase to name what they do. That tension, embedded in the conjoining of *rhetoric* and *composition*, provides the frame for our overview of "rhetoric and composition."[1] We will not, in this chapter, attempt to resolve the tensions regarding rhetoric, composition, and the relationship between the two. We reject the possibility of stabilizing either rhetoric or composition, let alone any putative stabilizing of the relationship of either to either. Instead, we review the problems produced by past and arising from current efforts to stabilize the function and meaning of *and* in the phrase *rhetoric and*

composition while remaining alert to the opportunities arising from such efforts.

We begin by delineating both the pervasiveness and the peculiar character of practices conjoining *rhetoric* and *composition* into *rhetoric and composition*. The peculiar character of such practices, as well as the differences among them, can be explained as resulting in part from differences in how each term is defined: Different views on the relationship between "rhetoric" and "composition" arise in part from different understandings of what each term refers to. But those different understandings, we argue, represent both differences in the ideological positionings of those engaged in rhetoric and in composition and, more generally, an index of (as well as a response to) the perduringly uncertain status of a body of work that does not easily fit under the rubric "rhetoric." We examine how the differences in naming that body of work might help us to delineate the contours of the current shape, and past and future directions, of the field's work and to map the contingent character of what is sometimes called "rhetoric and composition."

RHETORIC AND/OR COMPOSITION: WHAT'S IN A NAME?

We can get a sense of the current tensions and assumptions regarding the relationship between rhetoric and composition from a recent posting on the WPA Listserv by Bruce McComiskey (2006):

> I recently had a colleague tell me that she is a composition specialist and I'm a rhetoric specialist—the implication was that we don't think the same way and we don't do the same things. Honestly, I didn't even understand the comment. How can anyone be one (a composition specialist) and not the other (a rhetoric specialist)? Are rhetoric and composition separate again? Can we teach composition without teaching rhetoric? Do we have to add rhetoric to composition now? Is this problem (if it even exists) stemming from the textbook industry? Is the distinction present in some textbooks and forcing us to find new ways to re-integrate what should already be integrated? The history of our discipline tells us that the separation of composition from rhetoric was, at least in part, one cause of the downfall and subsequent denigration of composition. Are we heading back in that direction?

Read as, well, "rhetorical," the questions in McComiskey's post would suggest that rhetoric and composition are inseparable. But read as nonrhetorical, his questions arise from his discovery that, however incomprehensibly to him, others in fact see the two as not only separable but separate: His erstwhile colleague, he finds, does not share his own sense of their common disciplinary identity.

That some believe one cannot separate rhetoric from composition, or at least composition from rhetoric, is not surprising given the prevalence of using the two terms for some time now to name a single academic disciplinary field, as well as course work, textbooks, and scholarship. For example, the 2007 MLA Job Information List uses the category "composition and rhetoric" [*sic*] to help its users search for positions at schools that advertise for people to direct "writing programs" and "composition programs" and/or for people who can teach or have scholarly expertise in the areas of "composition"; "advanced composition"; "basic writing"; "developmental writing through advanced writing, technical and/or scientific writing, and professional writing"; "international technical communication and comparative rhetoric"; successful college teaching in technical writing/communication and/or rhetoric and composition"; as well as "visual and/or digital rhetorics, literacy, minority rhetorics, teacher preparation, and mixed/multiple genres" (Association of Departments of English, 2006). Those taking such positions are likely to attend conferences on "rhetoric and composition" (e.g., the Penn State Conference on Rhetoric and Composition and the Watson Conference on Rhetoric and Composition), and if they teach graduate courses, there's a good chance that they will be in programs deemed "rhetoric and composition." Courses with composition titles frequently require students to purchase textbooks that have *rhetoric* in their titles, and even when those textbooks don't use the term *rhetoric*, they are routinely referred to as "rhetorics." Thus, individuals who can claim expertise in either composition or rhetoric commonly apply for positions in either or in both, in which they will be expected to teach courses in either or in both, including courses called "composition" that employ texts called "rhetorics." To judge from these practices, rhetoric and composition are inseparable:

Composition is synonymous with rhetoric, and the conjoining of the two in the phrase *rhetoric and composition* is simply a way to confirm that synonymy.

At the same time, there are other features of these practices that suggest that the relationship between rhetoric and composition is more conflicted. First, the two terms operate differently in job and course descriptions and in texts, particularly in relation to two other terms: *writing* and *English*. While candidates might well apply for positions in "rhetoric and composition," they typically find those positions in Web sites sponsored by organizations of English departments (e.g., the Association of Departments of English), and any administrative duties that they are expected to take on typically involve not "rhetoric" but either "writing" or "composition": They may be appointed to positions as "directors of composition" or expected to direct a "writing program" or a "writing center," but they are almost never appointed to positions as directors of rhetoric, rhetoric programs, or rhetoric centers. The listserv on which McComiskey posted his response is the *WPA Listserv*—the listserv of *writing* program administrators, not an organization of *rhetoric* program administrators. The courses in these writing and/or composition programs that WPAs administer are most commonly called "first-year writing," "first-year composition" (a.k.a. "FYC"), or "Freshman English."

That the relationship between rhetoric and composition is more conflicted is suggested not only by the language of jobs and job advertisements but also by the repeated attempts to argue for the inseparability of rhetoric and composition, and especially for the relevance of the former to the latter. These arguments implicitly acknowledge at least the possibility of the contrary, pointing to some kind of fissure in the relationship between the two. James Murphy (1982), for example, has argued that composition needs rhetoric, warning that in abandoning a tradition of

rhetorical education, "we may well have thrown out the baby of literacy with the rhetorical bathwater" (p. 9). The title of W. Ross Winterowd's *Composition/Rhetoric: A Synthesis* (1986) implies a need for synthesizing. More recent work (Alliance of Rhetoric Societies, 2003; Coleman & Goodman, 2003, 2004; Mulderig, 1999; Swearingen, 2002) addresses the possible fissuring of the relationship between rhetoric and composition explicitly.

One way to account for this diversity of positions on the relationship between rhetoric and composition is to assume that those adopting each position are defining each of the two terms differently than those adopting other positions, with the consequence that the relationship between the two is likewise seen as different. We ourselves discern at least nine different ways of defining each term operating in the debates over rhetoric's relationship to composition:

1. The production of discourse

2. The study of discourse production

3. A tradition of such study

4. The teaching of discourse production

5. The study of that teaching

6. An academic institutional unit (e.g., a department or a program)

7. A university course intended for, and often required of, most first-year undergraduates

8. A textbook used in such a course

9. A profession, manifested in formal and informal organizations, for sustaining points 2 to 5[2]

How we define either affects the relationship posited between the two. For example, if rhetoric is understood as referring to a tradition of studying discourse production (3) and composition is understood as the production of one kind of discourse—say, student themes—then composition (1) might well be seen as being subsumed by rhetoric. Conversely, if rhetoric is understood as the study of discourse production (2) and composition is understood as a tradition of studying discursive production (3) that draws on a range of disciplines, including cognitive psychology, literary theory, literacy studies, and rhetoric, then rhetoric can be understood as subsumed within the tradition of composition as one of its many branches.

But while distinguishing among different definitions of rhetoric and composition can help explain in part disputes about the relationships between the two, we do not suppose that clearer definitions of these terms will resolve these disputes. First, contrary to what our numbering of the definitions above might suggest, the different senses of *rhetoric* overlap, as do those of *composition* and as do definitions of each. For example, the study and teaching of discourse production overlap in both rhetoric and composition, and there is significant overlap in the professional organizations associated with both. Moreover, how one defines or inflects either, and thus the relationship between the two, is an ideological as much as a conceptual matter, shaped by one's professional interests, commitments, and history. Those with training and scholarship in a tradition of rhetorical study (3) might be invested in foregrounding the link between their work in "rhetoric" and their work in and commitment to teaching courses titled "composition" within a composition curriculum. Those who affiliate more with composition as an academic unit (6), as a teaching practice (4), and as a profession (9) might view colleagues' claims to a lineage with the tradition of rhetorical study (3) as deeply suspect, even a betrayal of trench comradeship through spurious claims to an ostensibly more academically "respectable" ancestry (see Miller, 1991a). These differences manifest themselves in ways obvious and not so obvious: in research methodology and foci,

administrative strategy, teaching commitments, and pedagogy. Furthermore, they carry political weight; one's research methodology, administrative strategy, teaching commitments, and pedagogy speak both to one's social positioning and how one positions oneself.

Our own position is aligned with definitions of composition highlighting its commitment to the teaching of first-year undergraduate writing, especially to "nontraditional" students; with a tradition of studying student writing and the teaching of writing in terms of power relations between teachers and students and readers and writers and the politics of literacy that draws on both the immediate experience of teaching writing and work in cultural-materialist, feminist, postcolonial, and critical-race theory; and with a recognition of and resistance to the marginalization of student writers and composition teachers, and the study of composition and its teaching resulting from its character as what Harris (1997) has called a "teaching subject." That positioning leads us to see pedagogy as the focal point of intersection between the body of work one might designate "composition" and work that might be designated "rhetoric" to constitute what we would call "rhetoric and composition." That is, from our perspective, the best work in the singular field of "rhetoric and composition" is that which draws on "composition's" commitment to student writing and "rhetoric's" commitment to historicizing the rhetorical traditions and practices of differently situated individuals and collectives to inform teaching practice as well as the institutional academic status of composition as an administrative unit (6). Our definition of "rhetoric and composition" in terms of pedagogical commitment is thus contingent on particular definitions of each (e.g., rhetoric's concern with delineating various "rhetorical traditions" and composition's concern with teaching marginalized students).

At the same time, we recognize that the addition of the qualifier "and composition" to "rhetoric" more commonly serves to give a particular inflection to composition rather than to rhetoric, a practice signaling the problematic, even tenuous, academic institutional and disciplinary identity, status, and history of composition as distinct from rhetoric (which as a tradition of study [3] can and has survived without composition [1–9]). Consequently, we devote the remainder of this chapter to mapping some of the questions and relations concerning definitions of composition, putting aside conflicting definitions of rhetoric. Because of composition's problematic disciplinary and institutional status, the "normal" ongoing questioning of disciplinary definition, commitment, and focus that takes place in already legitimized academic fields carries, in composition, the burden of working toward disciplinary and institutional legitimation. Each of the various ways of defining composition presented above is one locus for the playing out of uncertainty about such legitimation, often in ways that do not merely resonate but intersect with and are contingent on uncertainty over other loci. To grasp the work of "rhetoric and composition," then, requires proceeding not through definitions but questions of definition, and questions of relations between definitions, of composition alone.

In keeping with this, in what follows, we examine questions of definition to map the interdependent, contingent character of work in composition, sometimes also identified as work in "rhetoric and composition," as well as to delineate the contours of the current shape and past and future directions of that work. In doing so, we focus on the following questions: What is the tradition (3) of composition study? What is a composition, and what is involved in its production (1–2)? What is, or should be, a composition program? What is, or should be, a compositionist (6, 7, 9)? How does one teach composition (4–5)? We do so, it should be clear by now, from the perspective of those in "rhetoric and composition," defining that

singular field in terms of a pedagogical commitment. The contours we delineate, in other words, say as much about our position and the conceptual horizon it imposes as it does about that which we delineate.

WHAT IS "THE TRADITION" OF COMPOSITION STUDY?

Raymond Williams (1977) has warned that "tradition is in practice the most evident expression of the dominant and hegemonic pressures and limits," noting that

> what we have to see is not just "a tradition" but . . . an intentionally selective version of a shaping past and a pre-shaped present, which is then powerfully operative in the process of social and cultural definition and identification. . . . [by offering] a sense of *predisposed continuity*. (pp. 115–116)

The "rhetoric and composition" label, by linking current practices of composition teaching and theories about the production and teaching of composition with a posited tradition extending back to ancient Greece, offers a sense of continuity by overlooking significant differences and gaps in the "handing down" or "handing over" of that tradition (*tradition* from the Latin *tradere*, "to hand over, surrender, deliver; to betray; to hand down, bequeath, transmit, pass on; to relate, recount; to teach"). Insofar as there are significant differences between any posited rhetorical tradition and present-day practices in the teaching and study of composition, these must be glossed over in arguments positing continuity, or, alternatively, they must be identified as "betrayals" of that tradition, betrayal being one of the possible outcomes of and dangers inherent in the process of a tradition's transmission.

As a historical question, it would seem, however, that while one might argue for the relevance of a rhetorical tradition (3) to the teaching and study of composition, as is commonplace, arguments for the institution of composition as a historical continuation of that tradition are more difficult to make. In other words, if by *rhetorical tradition* one means an academic (and predominantly Western male) dialogue extending from ancient Greece to the present, from Isocrates to Kenneth Burke and beyond, and if by *composition* one means an equivalent, if much shorter, academic area of research on what composing involves, then one could argue at best that the (syntactically and chronologically) latter has at times drawn on the former as one resource among many in attempting to understand what composition involves (e.g., invention). If, however, by *composition* one means the history and practice of teaching and administering courses in postsecondary writing in the United States (4–6), then the connection of (that) composition to any rhetorical tradition seems tenuous in the extreme (see Crowley, 2003).

That the definition of composition as above all an academic institutional practice of teaching writing should dominate discussions of the identity of the field is one of the characteristics that distinguish it from rhetoric and most other fields of academic study, except perhaps education, a field with which composition is closely allied in the public imagination and with which, many would argue, it has far more direct genealogical ties than with rhetoric. That is, whereas most fields of disciplinary study begin with a "subject"—a canonical national literature, the social, history, physical matter—knowledge about which is taught, composition is routinely characterized as a "teaching subject" (Harris, 1997), beginning, and often ending, with the question of what to do with the students who have appeared in one's required first-year composition course. Even most of the "subdisciplines" of composition are defined largely in terms of the site or means or forms of instruction: "basic writing," "advanced composition," "writing centers," WAC (writing across the curriculum) and WID (writing in the disciplines), ESL (English as a Second Language), "service-learning," "teaching in the two-year college," "computers and composition."

Thus, whatever scholarly research in composition may lead to, it is the teaching situation that serves as immediate exigence (to borrow a term from rhetoric [3]) for that research and, maddeningly to some, the criterion against which the research will often be judged, as in "How will this help me and my composition students?" As Scott (1991) has observed, composition is a "mission-centered field" (p. 81). While some who identify themselves as compositionists have strained against what has become known as the "pedagogical imperative" in composition (see Dobrin, 1997; Olson, 1991; Worsham, 1991), or see the move from the immediate exigencies of classroom teaching to research as necessary for the emergence of composition as an academic discipline (Nystrand, Greene, & Wiemelt, 1993), it remains a characteristic that historically has defined composition and continues to dominate it, and it is a characteristic that has strong defenders.

Furthermore, insofar as composition remains a relatively "young" field, the personal experience of those participating in it and attempting to define it inexorably ties composition to teaching. For, at the personal level, most of those who would currently identify themselves with composition as a field of study have typically come to such an identification through the experience of teaching composition. Like Shaughnessy, a towering figure in composition, and the teachers that Shaughnessy (1976) has described, they then pursue research to make sense of their students and their writing and better understand how to teach them. As Lunsford (1991) has observed, even the conflicts animating composition studies are prompted because of commitments "to link the scholarly and the pedagogical and the practical at every turn; and to make students and learning the heart of our endeavors" (pp. 5–6).

One paradoxical manifestation of composition's characteristic concern with teaching is that much work in composition involves attempts to delineate the implications and relevance of work ostensibly belonging to other fields for composition teaching. These fields include not just rhetoric (3) but also literacy studies, social and political theory, education, anthropology/ethnography, psychology, philosophy, feminist theory, Marxist theory, literary critical theory, cultural studies, and linguistics. Furthermore, much work in composition draws on the methodologies of these other fields. That is, working in a "teaching subject" drives composition's practitioners to seek help not just wherever but also however they may find it: Composition seems not to have, or be defined in terms of, either a subject or a methodology of its own and is instead defined by that absence. That absence not only distinguishes it from other fields but also contributes to its low academic institutional status as a site merely for the "application" of these other fields' findings.

A further consequence of the at best peculiar nature of composition's (teaching) subject, interdisciplinary research approaches, and low academic institutional status is that a significant area of work "in" composition is "on" composition—that is, like this chapter itself, work about the difficulty of defining, defending, and improving the field and protecting those working in that field from denigration within the academy, a kind of metadiscourse within composition on the difficulties of the field as a field.[3] Much of this work is concerned first and foremost with the operation of power relations on the field, usually to maintain the subjugated status of both tenure-line and contingent composition faculty within the academy generally and in English departments specifically, and also with the operation of power relations among these faculty, between instructors and students, and, more generally, in the larger social realm of (mostly) the United States.

This metadiscursive literature on the difficulties of composition has been complemented by work "introducing" readers to composition (or "composition studies"). In some versions of this literature, composition is treated primarily as a teaching (or learning) activity rather than as a subject of scholarly inquiry. Irmscher (1979), for example, cites no specific scholarship for the advice he gives in *Teaching Expository Writing*, instead choosing merely to include, in a "coda," "a limited number of sources that will help someone find a direction" (p. 187). In contrast, Lindemann's (1982) *A Rhetoric for Writing Teachers* includes citations of composition (and other) scholarship throughout, in addition to providing a selected bibliography and a lengthy list of "works consulted," and the subtitle of Foster's (1983) *A Primer for Writing Teachers: Theories, Theorists, Issues, Problems* makes clear the importance of locating teaching practice in theories. There is a similar split in texts intended for courses training new composition teachers. These range from collections of reprints of scholarly texts to texts consisting almost entirely of direct advice to novice teachers.

Between these are texts that negotiate the relationship between scholarship and teaching in more self-conscious ways. Donovan and McClelland's (1980) *Eight Approaches to Teaching Composition*, for example, presents accounts of teaching composition, each of which articulates the assumptions about writing, writers, and knowledge on which the approach is based. And Bartholomae and Petrosky's (1986) *Facts, Artifacts, and Counterfacts: Theory and Method for a Reading and Writing Course* presents accounts of teaching a 6-hour college "basic reading and writing" course that mix reproductions of the writing assignments and student papers and revisions and tutoring transcripts from the course with highly theoretical analyses of the teaching and learning activities represented by such artifacts.

These two texts differ from both those offering direct advice on teaching and those introducing readers to scholarship on composition teaching in how they represent the relationship between teaching and scholarship. For while the titles of these two texts might suggest that they were intended to provide answers to how (and what) to teach in a composition course, the authors of both caution against such a view. Donovan and McClelland (1980) describe the approaches presented in their collection as "enactments of a sort. . . . [that] simply invite us to reconsider our own teaching, our own enactment of theory and practice in the classroom" (p. xv). And Bartholomae and Petrosky (1986) warn, "The purpose of [the essays in *Facts, Artifacts, and Counterfacts*] is *not* [italics added] to defend or explain a curriculum" (Preface).

As Horner (1994b) has argued, these cautions continue, in a very real sense of "tradition," a practice—also seen in Coles's *Teaching Composing* (1974) and *The Plural I*—(1978b) of resisting, in books on writing and its teaching, the temptation to prescribe to others how to teach. Paradoxically, such cautions and reluctance are a reminder of the importance of teaching as a defining characteristic of the field: Prescriptive teaching, whether in the classroom or the text, has largely been rejected in composition, even in teaching that takes the form of writing about teaching. This is exemplified in Coles's (1978a) warning to his fellow compositionists, issued at a point in the history of composition (4) Coles identified as a time when "we have begun again to have a discipline, a profession to refer to" that could speak of "'how much there is we do not know yet'" (p. 4):

> The other side of placing the premium we do on the substantive knowledge we are all so busily in pursuit of, is to seem to suggest that the mastery of substantive knowledge *itself* will be enough to produce teachers of writing and enable such teachers to produce writers. It is to seem to suggest that when

we *do* come to know enough, that *that* will be enough; that mastery of some body of substantive knowledge will do *for* prospective teachers of writing what in fact such people, if they are ever to become effective teachers of writing, will have to be left to do for themselves. Nor will the mechanical solution of requiring courses in methodology or teaching techniques be other than to offer as a solution what is but another form of the problem. (p. 6)

While Coles's assumptions about the relationship between "substantive knowledge" and teaching have been disputed (see, e.g., Young, 1980), it is clear that the usefulness of that knowledge for effective teaching of writing is the criterion against which it is to be judged for its value to the "discipline" and "profession." The "tradition" of composition study, then, is marked by a commitment to teaching that produces ambivalence not toward knowledge per se as traditionally understood but toward claims to the value of such knowledge outside composition as a teaching subject.

WHAT IS A COMPOSITION, AND WHAT IS INVOLVED IN ITS PRODUCTION?

As the quotation from Coles (1978a) above suggests, the ambivalence toward the use of knowledge in traditions of composition study has not precluded pursuits of that knowledge, though it may have shaped the nature of the pursuits. Not surprisingly, to the extent that those engaged in such pursuits are motivated by what they encounter in their teaching, those pursuits have included questions about both the very nature of what it is they are asking students to produce and how students are to produce it. To put it in more general terms, composition scholars have asked, What is a text? How do we account for the forms texts take? Who and what is responsible for textual production? Who and what is responsible for the reception of these texts? Though, put this way, there is clear overlap between these concerns and the concerns of literary critical theory and, even more clearly, rhetorical theory, particularly regarding voice, audience, genre, and invention, pursuit of these questions in composition has been distinguished by a focus on *composition*, here a term used to distinguish student writing from all other writing (see Crowley, 1985)—as in "Write a composition of 500 words on the theme of work"—and to delimit the production processes to be investigated. Thus, while Emig's (1971) landmark study *The Composing Processes of Twelfth Graders* makes reference to what might be learned about composing processes from reading accounts by and about established writers of literature, her primary focus remains on writing—compositions—produced by students in and for composition courses.

At the same time, those very delimitations have troubled composition researchers, leading to questions about either the legitimacy of the writing investigated or the validity of the "findings" about that writing insofar as "composition" is, in fact, distinct from writing produced by others or under other conditions. It has been unclear whether student writing/composition produced in composition courses merits the term *writing* at all, or, even if it does, what relation it can be said to have to other writing by other students and to other writing altogether. Scholarship attempting to address this trouble has vacillated between attributing what makes student writing different to the students themselves or to the institutional setting of the course and the school. Scholarship attributing this difference to the students has focused on students' degree or level of cognitive development, their specific composing processes, their language inheritance, and/or their cultural background. The question for these scholars and teachers then becomes what the course can do to bridge this difference—how to prompt greater cognitive development, say, or change the

students' composing processes, or address (read "overcome") language or cultural differences. Scholarship attributing this difference to the institutional setting of the course and the school has focused on the effects of placement, writing program and course and assignment design, genre, and pedagogy on the writing produced. Those adopting this perspective then pursue the question of how these might be revised in response to limitations in the writing produced—how, for example, we might change placement procedures or the curriculum, the kind of writing that is assigned, or our style of teaching.

In the past 30 years, there has been a shift in understanding student composing from approaches attributing writing performance to levels and forms of cognition to approaches attending more closely to the effect of the context of student composing on written production, and from seeing student composition as an instance of "general writing" (the title of the first composition course the authors of this chapter taught) to seeing it as a particular kind of writing shaped by contexts of schooling, pedagogy, and personal and sociocultural history, including contexts of race, class, gender, age, professional aspiration, religion, and sexual orientation.

Responses to recognizing these particularities of student composing have taken at least two quite different turns. At its best, such recognition has led to studies that bridge what's come to be known as the "social-cognitive divide," to consider how spheres officially designated academic, cognitive, and abstract intersect with spheres officially designated nonacademic, personal, social, and particular in the production of student writing. Increasingly drawing on scholarship in "situated learning" that focuses on the interdependence of cognition and situation, and rejecting attempts to locate in any particular instance of writing the operation of general cognitive skills and ability or to see composition as the occasion for teaching "general writing skills," these studies claim composition as a site for students and teachers to both investigate and revise, as "social," academic literacy practices. Responding to Street's (1984) call for an "ideological" model of literacy attending to "the contexts and the ideologies in which a set of particular literacy practices are embedded," these studies treat the literacies acquired in school, like all literacies, as social practices, taking into consideration "the social contexts within which any literacy event is occurring, and . . . the meanings that are produced for individuals who are engaged in any process of reading and writing" (Lea, 1999, p. 105). Typically, these studies take the form of fine-grained analyses of individual students' engagement and difficulties with academic literacy practices and their revision of those through their writing.[4] Rather than invoking abstractions of "academic" discourse or, for that matter, "personal" or "political" discourse, they consider how the "academic," "social," and "personal" are necessarily reconstituted in writing by students as well as other writers. In so doing, they grant a purpose to the work of student composition and the teaching of composition beyond preparation for predetermined, predesigned, and predesignated futures.

But for those who see the purpose of composition teaching to be largely preparatory for subsequent academic and workplace writing, recognizing student compositions as particular kinds of writing shaped by immediate contexts has led to questioning the legitimacy of teaching "composition" at all. These have led to calls for a variety of changes, including eliminating first-year composition courses altogether for teaching a bogus set of "general writing skills" (Petraglia, 1995a); developing writing across the curriculum (WAC) programs (see Maimon, 1994; Walvoord, 1996) and writing through service-learning opportunities (Adler-Kassner, Cross, & Waters, 1997); and changes to the media, genre, form, and purpose of texts to be assigned (Bridwell-Bowles, 1992; George,

2002; Yancey, 2004) as well as changes in how writing is to be "taught."

WHAT IS/SHOULD BE A COMPOSITION PROGRAM, AND WHAT IS/SHOULD BE A "COMPOSITIONIST"?

Arguments to abolish required first-year college composition instruction arise not only from its questionable role in preparing students for subsequent writing tasks but also from the poor status and working conditions of those involved in such instruction. These are commonly viewed as an inevitable consequence of composition's association with "precollege" and "service" work, its distinction from traditional academic disciplinary fields as at best a "teaching subject," and its traditionally subordinate administrative institutional location within departments of English (Crowley, 1995). To address these issues, an entire subfield of composition has emerged—writing program administration (with its own journal, annual conference, and listserv)—for which there are few parallels in other, more well-established academic disciplines. But the long-standing and ongoing history of composition teachers enduring poor working conditions (Connors, 1991), a history with which almost all those associated with composition have at least some personal experience, has made those conditions a concern for all in composition and has given a particular cast to all the work in composition.

The institutional marginalization of those assigned to teach basic writing, for example, has led them to identify strongly with the marginal academic status of their students and to reject the value system governing most academic institutions that is responsible for that marginalization. As Shaughnessy (1980a) reported, "As writing instruction is presently organized, the teacher who wishes to give his best energies to the instruction of ill-prepared freshmen must be ready to forego many of the rewards and privileges of his profession" (p. 95). But as she also reported (1980b), insofar as this experience has led teachers to "come to know, through [their] students, what it means to be an outsider in academia," it has "pedagogically radicalized" them, leading them to "reject in [their] bones the traditional meritocratic model of a college" (p. 114).

Particularly in many Research I institutions, that traditional meritocratic model has devalued the teaching of composition and any scholarship associated with that teaching, and it has assigned composition instruction to non-tenure-line instructors and graduate teaching assistants assigned heavy teaching loads for little pay, thereby undermining the means by which these instructors might engage in scholarship on teaching. Nonetheless, while some instructors have responded to such treatment by aligning themselves with those who denigrate composition instruction as somehow inherently inferior work, inevitably "horrifying" and something that "is—or should be—a matter of rudimentary drill, dull and dulling" (O'Dair, 2000, p. 51), many others have attempted to make sense of their students and their writing, as well as their own situation as composition teachers, and to improve it. Attempts to understand and improve the situation of composition teaching have taken four, often overlapping, forms: historical studies, moves to "professionalize" the work of composition, moves to organize instructors and engage in collective bargaining, and moves to improve writing program administration.

Historical studies have repeatedly drawn correlations between the poor working conditions and status of composition teachers, the low social and academic institutional status of those they teach, and composition's ostensible origins in the development of Harvard's freshman-year required composition course and its commitment to daily "themes." The relegation of composition teaching to first-year students, particularly students from socially marginalized groups, has reinforced its low, remedial rather than "college-level" status, and those teaching it have been assigned less than college status—as feminized "handmaidens" (or worse) to the more masculine pursuit of literature (Miller, 1991a; Tuell, 1992). Such correlations have led to calls for changes to at least one of these features: to change the status of composition instructors (say, by assigning only tenure-line faculty to teach); to spread writing instruction throughout the under-graduate years; to make writing instruction not required but elective (Crowley, 1995); or to change the composition curriculum to one focused on something more seemingly sub-stantial than students' rendering of personal observation and experience, either by changing what students are asked to write or by giving composition a "subject" more traditionally recognized as "content" (Crowley, 2003; Miller, 1991b; Petraglia, 1995b).

Most of these recommendations have proved, for most schools, DOA. While the occasional small and wealthy school with a strong teaching tradition might succeed in hiring sufficient tenure-line faculty to teach first-year composition responsibly, in persuading faculty across the curriculum to incorporate writing substantially into their courses, or in persuading them that no first-year composition requirement is necessary, the ideologies and attendant economies prevalent at most schools, and especially state-supported schools, preclude such radical changes. Attempts to make student writing more "transitive" (Miller, 1991b), and therefore more substantial in effect, have led either to attacks on the courses for becoming "politicized" (Brodkey, 1994) or to more administrative demands, such as those imposed in courses with substantial "service-learning" "components."

Attempts to "professionalize" composition have worked at odds with attempts to organize instructors to pursue collective bargaining for improved working conditions. The former are directed at improving the status of composition instructors within the "traditional meritocratic model" of colleges and universities. These take the form of developing graduate programs in "rhetoric and composition"; encouraging the production of traditionally recognized forms of scholarship along with traditionally recognized forums for the distribution of such scholarship (e.g., conferences; scholarly, "blind-reviewed" journals; university-press book series; edited collections; and handbooks such as the one in which this chapter appears); explicitly aligning composition with already academically recognized scholarly work in fields such as rhetoric, philosophy, and feminist studies; and maintaining professional organizations to support all these (see Council of Writing Program Administrators, 2006; National Council of Teachers of English, 2006) and, where appropriate, to support the recognition of nontraditional criteria for evaluating the work of the profession's members (Council of Writing Program Administrators, 1998).

At least one of the motives behind these attempts is the conviction that insofar as the "field" of composition appears to have a body of scholarship worthy of graduate and postgraduate work and insofar as composition teachers can meet the standards of other tenure-line faculty through developing a record of scholarship as well as teaching and service, those in composition will be accorded the status and rewards granted these other faculty. However, others who also identify themselves as being somehow "in" composition view these attempts to "professionalize" with skepticism. To the extent that such attempts might succeed, they argue, composition will lose what makes it distinctive and worth doing at all, producing "the composition specialist who never teaches composition" with "a career that has everything to do with status and identity in English and little to do with the organization, management, and evaluation of student writing, except perhaps as an administrative problem" (Bartholomae, 1996, p. 23). Any attempt to secure for composition the status of a "discipline" in the

prevailing academic sense of that term is either doomed to failure or will succeed by transforming it into something other than composition—a discipline that is not concerned with students and learning (Slevin, 1996).

In this sense, professionalizing composition can be viewed as a betrayal of a tradition of composition with roots in and commitment to the work of teaching composition (Gunner, 1992). Those taking this perspective have drawn especially on feminist analyses of labor relations to identify and contend with the ideologies devaluing such work. Composition is viewed as "feminized" in its association with teaching students, particularly first-year students, and because the seemingly personal, physical, emotional, maternal, nurturing nature of that work is seen as (therefore) not "real" (read masculine, impersonal, abstract, disinterested, objective) academic work, as not traditional scholarship.

Rather than buying into the ideologies that appear to support the denigration of such feminized work or abandoning it for work more valued by dominant ideologies, at least some compositionists have advocated pursuit of collective action as a strategy to improve the conditions for composition teaching. Much of this literature is taken up with documenting colleges' and universities' growing reliance on a contingent labor force to teach composition and speculating or polemicizing about how best to respond to the poor working conditions of these teachers (Schell & Stock, 2001, p. 28). There are relatively few studies of actual examples of unionizing and unionized composition teachers and even fewer studies of the relationship between such cases and the longer history of teacher unionizing.

Working between and within these different attempts at improving teaching conditions is a burgeoning literature on writing program administration. The WPA is typically responsible for mediating the competing demands of school administrators (deans and higher), students, faculty groups, English departments, composition teachers and other institutions, and his or her own sense of what the teaching of composition should entail. The WPA has been identified as the academic institution's "icon" of and for writing instruction (Bartholomae, 1989) and the "glue" that holds the disparate elements and constituencies together (Cambridge & McClelland, 1995, p. 157). In responding to complaints about the teachers they hire (and/or supervise) and their students and in attempting to ensure a sufficient number of sections of their school's required composition courses for students and a sufficient number of teachers to staff these sections, WPAs perforce confront questions about not only curriculum but also class size, teacher qualifications, teaching load, clerical support, and supplies (photocopying, office space, computers, paper, telephones, classrooms, chalk). Much of the WPA literature addresses just such quotidian matters and the challenges of handling all of them, or at least handling as many as possible while retaining some semblance of sanity and a life (see George, 1999).

But in addition to offering survival advice to novice WPAs, at least some WPA literature is directed at ways to improve, or at least ameliorate, the conditions for teaching and learning composition, often through reports of WPAs' struggles in their own institutions. Given the mediating position of WPAs, much of this literature addresses the difficulties of power: Contrary to what some have claimed, the number of responsibilities assigned WPAs far surpasses any power they are granted as "icons" for writing at their schools. Consequently, WPAs have found themselves looking for ways to increase or use more strategically what little power they are able to muster. In so doing, however, they tend toward arguments that, at least to some of those pursuing the strategy of collective action, have seemed paternalistic or worse. And insofar as WPA positions are increasingly assigned to tenured or at least tenure-line faculty with records of traditionally recognized scholarship as well as teaching and administrative experience, and

insofar as WPAs are expected to supervise primarily non-tenure-track, contingent instructors, the move to "professionalize" composition has come to be associated with the creation and maintenance of a two-tiered workforce within composition of *Tenured Bosses and Disposable Teachers*, as the title of Bousquet, Scott, and Parascondola's edited collection (2004) has it, with WPAs as the "boss compositionists" (Sledd, 1991) engulfed in and supporting a "managerial" discourse that, in the name of those "managed," denies them voice and agency. At its worst, this debate recapitulates long-standing antagonisms among compositionists between "theory" and "practice," scholarship and teaching and is often inflected in terms of the struggle between capital and labor understood in monolithic terms, with commitment to teaching pitted against scholarship (and vice versa), the questioning of specific pedagogies seen as a rejection of the dignity of labor, theorizing viewed as elitist, and the questioning of the usefulness of theory a manifestation of anti-intellectual "theory phobia." In light of the association of composition with teaching, this has tended in at least some debates to render the "rhetoric" part of "rhetoric and composition" into a cipher for "theory" and the "composition" part into a cipher for "practice," with the burden of all the associated suspicions that the relationship between these other sets of terms have come to accrue: rhetoric imagined as "merely rhetoric" and "merely theoretical," practice treated either as somehow more "practical" and "real" or as unthinking, unreflective droid work.

HOW DOES ONE TEACH COMPOSITION?

It may seem curious that in a chapter on "rhetoric and composition" within this *Handbook*'s section on "Pedagogy," we have given so little attention to the question of pedagogy. Our apparent neglect of this question should not be taken as evidence of composition's disinterest in pedagogy: As a "teaching subject," composition has been profoundly concerned with teaching. But how compositionists respond to questions of what to teach and how to teach it depends on how they define a composition and composing as well as the conditions in which they find themselves as teachers—the degree to which they are free to make these decisions, for example; the number and nature of the students they're to teach on any given day and semester; and the material resources to which they have access to teach these.

Available material resources and conditions shape but do not entirely determine teaching. For example, it's sometimes assumed that one can get an idea of composition teaching by considering the textbooks most commonly assigned in composition courses (Connors, 1986). However, as Miller (1982) has observed, histories of composition teaching based on the publishing history of its textbooks "inadvertently imply that composition pedagogy, classroom practices and methods, and writing courses in general have slavishly followed textbooks and that the way to change the teaching and learning of composition necessarily depends on changes in composition textbooks" (p. 22). In other words, as Coles (1978a) argued in the passage quoted above, whatever "knowledge" might be represented in the textbooks does not in itself determine what is learned or made of that knowledge by teachers and students through their work with it. Those adopting this perspective have examined archives of student papers, teacher comments and assignments, and course syllabi and have interviewed teachers and students about their experience to determine what indeed has been learned or made of such knowledge.[5]

But to determine "what is learned" requires, as well, a sense of how "learning" is defined. Young (1980) has distinguished between those he calls the "new romantics" (borrowing from D'Angelo, 1975) and the "new classicists" in terms of whether knowledge about composition

is understood as something that can be explicitly "taught" or must be "learned"— often through a kind of apprenticeship model. For example, the new classicists, Young (1980) maintains, attempt to teach "heuristics"— procedures for intelligent guessing and invention—"and the appropriate occasions for their use" (p. 57). The new romantics, in contrast, might be viewed as engaged in situated learning in which any explicit teaching would constitute an intrusion by an alien, "banking" practice that removes both responsibility and agency from the learners and, it can be argued, undermines the effectiveness of pedagogy by rendering what is to be learned into a commodity (Freire, 1970). In other words, different theories of learning, as well as of what is to be learned, can lead to quite different pedagogies.

As the reference to Freire (1970) indicates, for a discipline in which teaching is the subject, theories of learning are not politically innocent. Not only do questions of what is to be taught and how quickly become intermingled, but power relations operating in teaching-learning also quickly come to the fore. One's stance on pedagogy, in short, is as much a matter of ideology as it is a matter of "objective" knowledge.

While much of the scholarship on composition pedagogy might be categorized in terms of the specific set of power relations on which the scholarship focuses—relations between student and teacher, say; the institutional politics of composition programs in relation to other "units" within the schools; or the relation of composition courses and larger social spheres (the "body politic" of the community, region, and nation)—the best of it examines how these different sites of power interrelate (Fox, 1995). For example, in teaching students how to address what is commonly called "error" in their writing— deviations from conventional spelling, wording, syntax, and punctuation—arguments have attended not only to the challenges of teaching proofreading but also to the politics of declaring some notational and syntactic practices matters of stylistic choice and others matters of correctness, and they have attended to such politics not only in light of the power relations operating between teacher and student in their institutional roles as teacher and student but also in light of the situation of the teacher as contingent laborer and in light of societal power relations operating between various groups—men and women, blacks and whites, young and old, and so on—and conflicting ideologies (Fox, 1990; Lu, 1994; Williams, 1981).

There is a now common move to finesse such matters by acknowledging the inherently "rhetorical" nature of stylistic decisions—what's "appropriate" is determined by one's purpose and audience (see Fulkerson, 1990). However, insofar as this move defers the question of what student writers' purposes and audiences are or ought to be, it is vulnerable to the charge of simply occluding the inherently political nature of decisions about and evaluations of composing. The issue is sometimes framed in terms of competing notions of what writing purposes and audiences composition courses should address (and thereby validate): whether or not the composition course should help prepare students to produce writing demanded by other disciplines, say; help prepare them to meet the demands of future employers; or help them meet the demands of responsible citizenship in their communities and the nation and the world. Those arguing that composition should aim to prepare students to meet the demands of other disciplines or future employers typically ascribe the desire for such preparation to students, conceived of in monolithic terms (e.g., Smith, 1997). In these arguments, pedagogies aimed at helping students challenge the legitimacy of dominant notions of workplace and academic writing are rejected as elitist impositions of teacher ideologies (Hairston, 1992). In reply, others

make three arguments: (1) Students have a multiplicity of fluctuating desires beyond those officially recognized (Chase, 1988; Horner, 1994a); (2) students cannot in fact truly learn conventional forms of writing without questioning these (Lu, 1994); and (3) the types of writing "demanded" by academics and the workplace fluctuate, hence claims that students can be taught to produce the writing "on demand" are false advertising (Kells, 1999). While it may be true that "the subject of a writing course is writing" (David, Gordon, & Pollard, 1995, p. 525), it is also true that one cannot extricate writing from the immediate and larger contexts of its production in determining what is taught as writing and how it is taught.

Those accepting writing's imbrication in such contexts have focused especially on the relation of questions of what to teach and how to teach composition to questions of identity and relations of race, gender, class, ethnicity, and sexual orientation, exploring how these matters operate in the interactions between students and teachers (and between teachers and administrators), as well as in the "rhetorics" of the writing assigned and produced—the "politics" of language used in the scene of composition teaching. While composition's marginal institutional status gives a particular inflection to the politics of teacher-student interactions—"feminized" instructors teaching courses assigned a "remediating" function and required of all first-year undergraduate students face different challenges from those faced by, say, a tenured full professor teaching a graduate seminar—composition can and has drawn effectively on more general work in the politics of education, mostly from feminist and Marxian perspectives, to address the particular concerns of its teachers. Scholarship on the politics of language in teaching composition deals with how teachers should address such politics in the kind of writing they assign and in the way they respond to that writing: the politics, for example, of responding to writing that appears to bear features of what is sometimes referred to as African American Vernacular English; the relationship between feminist ideology and traditional forms of style and argumentation; whether the ethos encouraged in composition textbooks is not just middle class but classist; the epistemologies we are asking students to adopt, and abandon, if we insist on their maintaining a traditionally academic rhetorical stance; oppositional and resistant rhetorics among disenfranchised groups; and the rhetorics of teacherly responsiveness and intervention.[6] Answers to such questions must take into account both the immediate institutional and the larger social-historical contexts in which the teaching occurs. How an instructor answers any of them has much do with the instructor's professional institutional status as well as social positioning; the status and social positioning of the students; the institutional status of the course and program; and the current political and social climate at the local community, regional, national, and international levels.

REDEFINING RHETORIC AND COMPOSITION

Historically, composition or "rhetoric and composition" (though not rhetoric), tied as it is to the first-year college composition course, has been a purely U.S. phenomenon. With few exceptions, composition scholars have until recently ignored writing instruction outside the United States. Furthermore, again until recently, composition scholars have ignored writing instruction in languages other than English, despite the longstanding multilingual history of the U.S. population (Horner & Trimbur, 2002) and the existence of writing in languages other than English outside the United States and of second-language writing in and outside the United States. While U.S. colleges and universities have accepted

students for whom English is not their first language, typically these students have been assumed to be international students, whatever their actual citizenship, and they have been quarantined in ESL and ESL-composition courses and programs (Matsuda, 2006). While there is a substantial body of research and teaching on ESL and ESL composition, this, too, has been largely kept separate from "composition studies" proper through a "disciplinary division of labor" (Matsuda, 1999). In short, historically, composition has restricted its purview to the teaching of writing in English and to U.S. (born) students assumed to be monolingual English speakers. The teaching of writing in other languages and outside the United States, the writing of translations or of multilingual texts, and the writing of students other than U.S. students has been ignored.

In the past 10 years, this has begun to change. While a tacit policy of monolingualism and a U.S.-centric focus remain the norm for composition programs, housed as they mostly are in departments of "English" in U.S. colleges and universities, a growing number of scholars from inside and outside the United States are challenging these norms and the teaching and research practices they mandate.[7] Scholars are beginning to examine the practices of teaching writing outside the United States and in languages other than English. U.S.-located instructors are increasingly hypothesizing ways to not simply acknowledge but also make use of the multilingual character of their students. And there is a growing examination of the role U.S. composition-teaching practices play in response to the pressures of a globalizing economy to standardize "English" (Lu, 2004, 2006; Lu & Horner, 2008).

These changes represent compositionists' recognition of several developments. First, partly as a result of changes in U.S. immigration patterns, it has become increasingly difficult to categorize students by either nationality or language (Harklau, Losey, & Siegal, 1999). A student might, for example, regularly migrate between Mexico and the United States and speak and write in several languages (Frodesen & Starna, 1999). Second, the "globalization" of English has removed control over what constitutes English from the United States and the United Kingdom: There are now a variety of "Englishes," each with their own (contested and fluctuating) standards and conventions, with which the varieties of English used in the United States and the United Kingdom must contend (Kachru, 1990). Third, despite the globalization of English, the increase in international communication has in fact increased the frequency of interlanguage contact, making a belief in linguistic homogeneity as the cultural norm increasingly difficult to sustain.

The growing challenges to composition's monolingualism have a parallel in challenges to standard conceptions of academic discourse. There is a long tradition of composition invoking academic discourse as a monolith and, in reaction both to the perceived power of that monolith and to composition's own marginal academic status, seeking alternatives in what is known as "personal" or "committed" or "experimental" writing. Increasingly, however, scholars examining actual academic literacy practices are complicating this monolithic view, tending instead to recognize a plethora of practices and radical fluctuations in these (Lea & Street, 1998; Schroeder, Fox, & Bizzell, 2002). In line with this, and more broadly, compositionists are increasingly complicating the dominant binaries of self/institution and personal/social used to label writing and to grasp their own situation, finding instead ways in which these dominant categories fail to address the possibilities of what might fall under any one of them and learning, as well, to recognize the role power relations play in the invocation of these categories to police writing and limit their work.

Composition is only beginning to pursue the questions of how and why to respond to language difference in composing in the current context of global relations. Neither its organizations nor many of its publications pretend to be international, let alone interlingual, in scope. Likewise, its battles over issues of working conditions for composition teachers tend to remain resolutely local, fixed on immediate institutional conditions and uninformed by the global contexts responsible for producing and exacerbating those conditions. And in its attempts to work past standard definitions of the academic and the nonacademic, the social and the personal, the institutional and the individual, composition all too often gets caught up in championing dominant definitions of the ostensibly weaker of each pair, pursuing not resistance and transformation but escape. This is both predictable and understandable in light of the conditions in which many of those who teach composition find themselves—"global" perspectives, for example, are not readily available to those working in the trenches.

At the same time, insofar as conditions in the composition "trenches"—the shifting language resources of the students, their lack of time and consequent impatience, the pressure to commodify writing "skills," the reliance on a contingent and "flexible" (read cheap and disposable) workforce—are of a piece with neoliberal economic globalizing, all those in "rhetoric and composition" whose work involves and has been informed by composition teaching, study, programs, and organizations are well positioned to work with their students in identifying and finding ways to resist these conditions in their daily work; and they must perforce learn to find ways past the binaries limiting their sense of what it is possible for them to do and be. Composition's "marginal" institutional status, and the central role played in composition by students of equally marginal academic status, positions all of us in "rhetoric and composition" who are committed to the teaching and learning of writing at the undergraduate level at a point where (now more than ever) the resources of difference and different experiences unrecognized by official categories become manifest. As a site for the work of finding ways to negotiate and make use of these resources, rhetoric and composition's placement on the "margins" puts it, potentially, on the leading edge of change.

NOTES

1. Following Kopelson (in press), we insert "(?)" between "rhetoric" and "composition" in our title to signal this tension.

2. For an earlier analysis along these lines, see Gage (1991).

3. See, for example, Bloom, Daiker, and White (1996, 2003), Ede (2004), Faigley (1992), Harkin and Schilb (1991), Horner (2000), Lu (2004), Miller (1991b), North (1987), Phelps (1988), Slevin (2001), and Trimbur, Bullock, and Schuster (1991).

4. See, for example, Ivanič (1998), Jones, Turner, and Street (1999), and Lillis (2001).

5. See, for example, Hollis (2004), Kates (2000), Masters (2004), Schneider (2006), Varnum (1996), and Wible (2006).

6. See Agnew and McLaughlin (2001), Balester (1992, 1993), Bloom (1996), Brody (1993), Gilyard and Richardson (2001), Jarratt (1991), Johnson (1994), Jung (2005), Lamb (1991), Lindquist (1999), Lu (1991), Ratcliffe (1999), Smitherman (1994), Sternglass (1974), Wallace & Bell (1999), Wallace and Ewald (2000), and Worsham (1991).

7. See Canagarajah (1999, 2002a, 2002b, 2006a, 2006b), Foster and Russell (2002), Jones et al. (1999), Lunsford and Ouzgane (2004), Muchiri, Mulamba, Myers, and Ndoloi (1995), and Severino, Guerra, and Butler (1997).

REFERENCES

Adler-Kassner, L., Cross, R., & Waters, A. (Eds.). (1997). *Writing the community: Concepts and models for service-learning in composition.* Urbana, IL: National Council of Teachers of English.

Agnew, E., & McLaughlin, M. (2001). Those crazy gates and how they swing: Tracking the system that tracks African-American students. In G. McNenny (Ed.), *Mainstreaming basic writers: Politics and pedagogies of access* (pp. 85–100). Mahwah, NJ: Erlbaum.

Alliance of Rhetoric Societies. (2003). *Conference on the status and future of rhetorical studies.* Retrieved January 4, 2007, from www.comm.umn.edu/ARS

Association of Departments of English. (2006). *Job information list.* Retrieved November 30, 2006, from www.ade.org/jil/index.htm

Balester, V. (1992). A reexamination of attitudes towards Black English Vernacular. In M. Secor & D. Charney (Eds.), *Constructing rhetorical education* (pp. 63–85). Carbondale: Southern Illinois University Press.

Balester, V. (1993). *Cultural divide: A study of African-American college-level writers.* Portsmouth, NH: Boynton/Cook.

Bartholomae, D. (1989). *Plenary speech.* Annual conference of the Council of Writing Program Administrators, Oxford, OH.

Bartholomae, D. (1996). What is composition and (if you know what that is) why do we teach it? In L. Bloom, D. Daiker, & E. White (Eds.), *Composition in the twenty-first century: Crisis and change* (pp. 11–28). Carbondale: Southern Illinois University Press.

Bartholomae, D., & Petrosky, A. (1986). *Facts, artifacts, and counterfacts: Theory and method for a reading and writing course.* Upper Montclair, NJ: Boynton/Cook.

Bloom, L. (1996). Freshman composition as a middle-class enterprise. *College English, 58,* 654–675.

Bloom, L., Daiker, D., & White, E. (Eds.). (1996). *Composition in the twenty-first century: Crisis and change.* Carbondale: Southern Illinois University Press.

Bloom, L., Daiker, D., & White, E. (Eds.). (2003). *Composition studies in the new millennium: Rereading the past, rewriting the future.* Carbondale: Southern Illinois University Press.

Bousquet, M., Scott, T., & Parascondola, L. (Eds.). (2004). *Tenured bosses and disposable teachers: Writing instruction in the managed university.* Carbondale: Southern Illinois University Press.

Bridwell-Bowles, L. (1992). Discourse and diversity: Experimental writing within the academy.

College Composition and Communication, 43, 349–368.

Brodkey, L. (1994). Making a federal case out of difference: The politics of pedagogy, publicity, and postponement. In J. Clifford & J. Schilb (Eds.), *Writing theory and critical theory* (pp. 236–261). New York: Modern Language Association.

Brody, M. (1993). *Manly writing: Gender, rhetoric, and the rise of composition.* Carbondale: Southern Illinois University Press.

Cambridge, B., & McClelland, B. (1995). From icon to partner: Repositioning the writing program administrator. In J. Janangelo & K. Hansen (Eds.), *Resituating writing: Constructing and administering writing programs* (pp. 151–159). Portsmouth, NH: Boynton/Cook Heinemann.

Canagarajah, A. S. (1999). *Resisting linguistic imperialism in English teaching.* Oxford, UK: Oxford University Press.

Canagarajah, A. S. (2002a). *Critical academic writing and multilingual students.* Ann Arbor: University of Michigan Press.

Canagarajah, A. S. (2002b). *A geopolitics of academic writing.* Pittsburgh, PA: University of Pittsburgh Press.

Canagarajah, A. S. (2006a). The place of world Englishes in composition: Pluralization continued. *College Composition and Communication, 57,* 586–619.

Canagarajah, A. S. (2006b). Toward a writing pedagogy of shuttling between languages: Learning from multilingual writers. *College English, 68,* 589–604.

Chase, G. (1988). Accommodation, resistance, and the politics of student writing. *College Composition and Communication, 39,* 13–22.

Coleman, L., & Goodman, L. (2003). Rhetoric/composition: Intersections/impasses/differends, Part 1. *Enculturation, 5*(1). Retrieved November 30, 2006, from http://enculturation.gmu.edu/5_1/index51.html

Coleman, L., & Goodman, L. (2004). Rhetoric/composition: Intersections/impasses/differends, Part 2. *Enculturation, 5*(2). Retrieved November 30, 2006, from http://enculturation.gmu.edu/5_2/index52.html

Coles, W. (1974). *Teaching composing: A guide to teaching writing as a self-creating process.* Rochelle Park, NJ: Hayden Press.

Coles, W. (1978a). New presbyters as old priests: A forewarning. *CEA Critic, 41*(1), 3–9.

Coles, W. (1978b). *The plural I: The teaching of writing.* Chicago: Holt, Rinehart, & Winston.

Connors, R. (1986). Textbooks and the evolution of the discipline. *College Composition and Communication, 37,* 178–194.

Connors, R. (1991). Rhetoric in the modern university: The creation of an underclass. In J. Trimbur, R. Bullock, & C. Schuster (Eds.), *The politics of writing instruction: Postsecondary* (pp. 55–84). Portsmouth, NH: Boynton/Cook.

Crowley, S. (1985). writing and Writing. In D. Atkins & M. L. Johnson (Eds.), *Writing and reading differently: Deconstruction and the teaching of composition and literature* (pp. 93–100). Lawrence: University Press of Kansas.

Crowley, S. (1995). Composition's ethic of service, the universal requirement, and the discourse of student need. *Journal of Advanced Composition, 15,* 227–239.

Crowley, S. (2003). Composition is not rhetoric. *Enculturation, 5*(1). Retrieved November 30, 2006, from http://enculturation.gmu.edu/5_1/crowley.html

Council of Writing Program Administrators. (1998). *Evaluating the intellectual work of writing administration.* Retrieved November 30, 2006, from http://wpacouncil.org/positions/intellectualwork.html

Council of Writing Program Administrators. (2006). *Web page about the Council of Writing Program Administrators.* Retrieved November 30, 2006, from http://wpacouncil.org/about

D'Angelo, F. (1975). *A conceptual theory of rhetoric.* Cambridge, MA: Winthrop.

David, D., Gordon, B., & Pollard, R. (1995). Seeking common ground: Guiding assumptions for writing courses. *College Composition and Communication, 46,* 522–532.

Donovan, T. R., & McClelland, B. W. (Eds.). (1980). *Eight approaches to teaching composition.* Urbana, IL: National Council of Teachers of English.

Dobrin, S. (1997). *Constructing knowledges: The politics of theory-building and pedagogy in composition.* Albany: State University of New York Press.

Ede, L. (2004). *Situating composition: Composition studies and the politics of location.* Carbondale: Southern Illinois University Press.

Emig, J. (1971). *The composing processes of twelfth graders.* Urbana, IL: National Council of Teachers of English.

Faigley, L. (1992). *Fragments of rationality: Postmodernity and the subject of composition.* Pittsburgh, PA: University of Pittsburgh Press.

Foster, D. (1983). *A primer for writing teachers: Theories, theorists, issues, problems.* Portsmouth, NH: Boynton/Cook.

Foster, D., & Russell, D. R. (Eds.). (2002). *Writing and learning in cross-national perspective: Transitions from secondary to higher education.* Urbana, IL: National Council of Teachers of English.

Fox, T. (1990). *The social uses of writing.* Norwood, NJ: Ablex.

Fox, T. (1995). Proceeding with caution: Composition in the 90s. *College Composition and Communication, 46,* 566–578.

Freire, P. (1970). *Pedagogy of the oppressed* (M. B. Ramos, Trans.). New York: Continuum.

Frodesen, J., & Starna, N. (1999). Distinguishing incipient and functional bilingual writers: Assessment and instructional insights gained through second-language writer profiles. In L. Harklau, K. M. Losey, & M. Siegal (Eds.), *Generation 1.5 meets college composition: Issues in the teaching of writing to U.S.-educated learners of ESL* (pp. 61–79). Mahwah, NJ: Lawrence Erlbaum.

Fulkerson, R. (1990). Composition theory in the eighties: Axiological consensus and paradigmatic diversity. *College Composition and Communication, 41,* 409–429.

Gage, J. T. (1991). On "rhetoric" and "composition." In E. Lindemann & G. Tate (Eds.), *An introduction to composition studies* (pp. 15–32). New York: Oxford University Press.

George, D. (Ed.). (1999). *Kitchen cooks, plate twirlers, & troubadours: Writing program administrators tell their stories.* Portsmouth, NH: Boynton/Cook.

George, D. (2002). From analysis to design: Visual communication in the teaching of writing. *College Composition and Communication, 54,* 11–39.

Gilyard, K., & Richardson, E. (2001). Students' right to possibility: Basic writing and African American rhetoric. In A. Greenbaum (Ed.), *Insurrections: Approaches to resistance in composition studies* (pp. 37–52). Albany: State University of New York Press.

Gunner, J. (1992). The fate of the Wyoming Resolution: A history of professional seduction. In S. Fontaine and S. Hunter (Eds.), *Writing ourselves into the story: Unheard voices from composition studies* (pp. 107–122). Carbondale: Southern Illinois University Press.

Hairston, M. (1992). Diversity, ideology, and teaching writing. *College Composition and Communication, 43,* 179–193.

Harkin, P., & Schilb, J. (Eds.). (1991). *Contending with words: Composition and rhetoric in a postmodern age.* New York: Modern Language Association.

Harklau, L., Losey, K. M., & Siegal, M. (Eds.). (1999). *Generation 1.5 meets college composition: Issues in the teaching of writing to U.S.-educated learners of ESL.* Mahwah, NJ: Erlbaum.

Harris, J. (1997). *A teaching subject: Composition since 1966.* Upper Saddle River, NJ: Prentice Hall.

Hollis, K. (2004). *Liberating voices: Writing at the Bryn Mawr Summer School for Women Workers.* Carbondale: Southern Illinois University Press.

Horner, B. (1994a). Mapping errors and expectations for basic writing: From the "frontier field" to "border country." *English Education, 26,* 29–51.

Horner, B. (1994b). Resisting traditions in composing composition. *Journal of Advanced Composition, 14,* 495–519.

Horner, B. (2000). *Terms of work for composition: A materialist critique.* Albany: State University of New York Press.

Horner, B., & Trimbur, J. (2002). English only and U.S. college composition. *College Composition and Communication, 53,* 594–630.

Irmscher, W. (1979). *Teaching expository writing.* New York: Holt, Rinehart, & Winston.

Ivanič, R. (1998). *Writing and identity: The discoursal construction of identity in academic writing.* Amsterdam: John Benjamins.

Jarratt, S. (1991). Feminism and composition: The case for conflict. In P. Harkin & J. Schilb (Eds.), *Contending with words: Composition and rhetoric in a postmodern age* (pp. 105–123). New York: Modern Language Association.

Johnson, C. (1994). Participatory rhetoric and the teacher as racial/gendered subject. *College English 56*, 409–419.

Jones, C., Turner, J., & Street, B. (Eds.). (1999). *Students writing in the university: Cultural and epistemological issues*. Philadelphia: John Benjamins.

Jung, J. (2005). *Revisionary rhetoric, feminist pedagogy, and multigenre texts*. Carbondale: Southern Illinois University Press.

Kachru, B. (1990). *The alchemy of English: The spread, functions, and models of non-native Englishes*. Urbana: University of Illinois Press.

Kates, S. (2000). *Activist rhetorics and American higher education, 1885–1937*. Carbondale: Southern Illinois University Press.

Kells, M. (1999). Leveling the linguistic playing field in first-year composition. In M. Kells & V. Balester (Eds.), *Attending to the margins: Writing, researching, and teaching on the front lines*. Portsmouth, NH: Heinemann-Boynton/ Cook.

Kopelson, K. (in press). Sp(l)itting images: Or, back to the future of (rhetoric and?) composition. *College Composition and Communication*.

Lamb, C. (1991). Beyond argument in feminist composition. *College Composition and Communication, 42*, 11–24.

Lea, M. (1999). Academic literacies and learning in higher education: Constructing knowledge through texts and experience. In C. Jones, J. Turner, & B. Street (Eds.), *Students writing in the university: Cultural and epistemological issues* (pp. 103–124). Philadelphia: John Benjamins.

Lea, M., & Street, B. (1998). Student writing in higher education: An academic literacies approach. *Studies in Higher Education, 23*, 157–172.

Lillis, T. (2001). *Student writing: Access, regulation, desire*. London: Routledge.

Lindemann, E. (1982). *A rhetoric for writing teachers*. New York: Oxford University Press.

Lindquist, J. (1999). Class ethos and the politics of inquiry: What the barroom can teach us about the classroom. *College Composition and Communication, 51*, 225–247.

Lu, M. (1991). Redefining the legacy of Mina Shaughnessy: A critique of the politics of linguistic innocence. *Journal of Basic Writing, 10*(1), 26–40.

Lu, M. (1994). Professing multiculturalism: The politics of style in the contact zone. *College Composition and Communication, 45*, 442–458.

Lu, M. (2004). An essay on the work of composition: Composing English against the order of fast capitalism. *College Composition and Communication, 56*, 16–50.

Lu, M. (2006). Living-English work. *College English, 68*, 605–618.

Lu, M.-Z., & Horner, B. (2008). *Writing conventions*. New York: Longman.

Lunsford, A. (1991). The nature of composition studies. In E. Lindemann & G. Tate (Eds.), *An introduction to composition studies* (pp. 3–14). New York: Oxford University Press.

Lunsford, A., & Ouzgane, L. (Eds.). (2004). *Crossing borderlands: Composition and postcolonial studies*. Pittsburgh, PA: University of Pittsburgh Press.

Maimon, E. (1994). Writing across the curriculum: History and future. In C. Schryer & L. Steven (Eds.), *Contextual literacy: Writing across the curriculum* (pp. 12–20). Winnipeg, Manitoba, Canada: Inkshed.

Masters, T. (2004). *Practicing writing: The postwar discourse of freshman English*. Pittsburgh, PA: University of Pittsburgh Press.

Matsuda, P. (1999). Composition studies and ESL writing: A disciplinary division of labor. *College Composition and Communication, 50*, 699–721.

Matsuda, P. (2006). The myth of linguistic homogeneity in U.S. college composition. *College English, 68*, 637–651.

McComiskey, B. (2006, November 8). Re: Teaching rhetoric. Message posted to https://lists.asu.edu/cgi-bin/wa?A2=ind0611&L=WPA-L&T=0&F=&S=&P+21625. Retrieved May 27, 2008.

Miller, S. (1982). Is there a text in this class? *Freshman English News, 11*, 20–24.

Miller, S. (1991a). The feminization of composition. In J. Trimbur, R. Bullock, & C. Schuster (Eds.), *The politics of writing instruction: Postsecondary* (pp. 39–54). Portsmouth, NH: Boynton/Cook.

Miller, S. (1991b). *Textual carnivals: The politics of composition.* Carbondale: Southern Illinois University Press.

Muchiri, M. N., Mulamba, N. G., Myers, G., & Ndoloi, D. B. (1995). Importing composition: Teaching and researching academic writing beyond North America. *College Composition and Communication, 46,* 175–198.

Mulderig, G. (1999). Is there still a place for rhetorical history in composition studies? In M. Rosner, B. Boehm, & D. Journet (Eds.), *History, reflection, and narrative: The professionalization of composition, 1963–1983* (pp. 163–176). Stamford, CT: Ablex.

Murphy, J. (1982). Rhetorical history as a guide to the salvation of American reading and writing: A plea for curricular courage. In J. Murphy (Ed.), *The rhetorical tradition and modern writing* (pp. 3–12). New York: Modern Language Association.

National Council of Teachers of English. (2006). *CCCC mission statement.* Retrieved January 4, 2007, from www.ncte.org/cccc/about

North, S. (1987). *The making of knowledge in composition: Portrait of an emerging field.* Portsmouth, NH: Boynton/Cook.

Nystrand, M., Greene, S., & Wiemelt, J. (1993). Where did composition studies come from? An intellectual history. *Written Communication, 10,* 267–333.

O'Dair, S. (2000). Stars, tenure, and the death of ambition. In P. Herman (Ed.), *Day late, dollar short: The next generation and the new academy* (pp. 45–61). Albany: State University of New York Press.

Olson, G. (1991). The role of theory in composition scholarship. *Freshman English News 19,* 4–5.

Petraglia, J. (Ed.). (1995a). *Reconceiving writing, rethinking writing instruction.* Mahwah, NJ: Lawrence Erlbaum.

Petraglia, J. (1995b). Writing as an unnatural act. In J. Petraglia (Ed.), *Reconceiving writing, rethinking writing instruction* (pp. 79–100). Mahwah, NJ: Lawrence Erlbaum.

Phelps, L. W. (1988). *Composition as a human science: Contributions to the self-understanding of a discipline.* New York: Oxford University Press.

Ratcliffe, K. (1999). Rhetorical listening: A trope for interpretive invention and a "code of cross-cultural conduct." *College Composition and Communication, 51,* 195–224.

Schell, E., & Stock, P. (Eds.). (2001). *Moving a mountain: Transforming the role of contingent faculty in composition studies and higher education.* Urbana, IL: National Council of Teachers of English.

Schneider, S. (2006). Freedom schooling: Stokely Carmichael and critical rhetorical education. *College Composition and Communication, 58,* 46–69.

Schroeder, C. L., Fox, H., & Bizzell, P. (2002). *ALT DIS: Alternative discourses and the academy.* Portsmouth, NH: Boynton/Cook.

Scott, P. (1991). Bibliographical resources and problems. In E. Lindemann & G. Tate (Eds.), *An introduction to composition studies* (pp. 72–93). New York: Oxford University Press.

Severino, C., Guerra, J., & Butler, J. (Eds.). (1997). *Writing in multicultural settings.* New York: Modern Language Association.

Shaughnessy, M. (1976). Diving in: An introduction to basic writing. *College Composition and Communication, 27,* 234–239.

Shaughnessy, M. (1980a). The English professor's malady. *Journal of Basic Writing, 3*(1), 91–97.

Shaughnessy, M. (1980b). The miserable truth. *Journal of Basic Writing, 3*(1), 109–114.

Sledd, J. (1991). Why the Wyoming Resolution had to be emasculated: A history and a quixoticism. *JAC, 11,* 269–281.

Slevin, J. (1996). Disciplining students: Whom should composition teach and what should they know? In L. Bloom, D. Daiker, & E. White (Eds.), *Composition in the twenty-first century: Crisis and change* (pp. 153–165). Carbondale: Southern Illinois University Press.

Slevin, J. (2001). *Introducing English: Essays in the intellectual work of composition.* Pittsburgh, PA: University of Pittsburgh Press.

Smith, J. (1997). Students' goals, gatekeeping, and some questions of ethics. *College English, 59,* 299–320.

Smitherman, G. (1994). "The blacker the berry, the sweeter the juice": African American student writers and the national assessment of educational progress. In A. Dyson & C. Genishi (Eds.), *The need for story* (pp. 80–101). Urbana, IL: National Council of Teachers of English.

Sternglass, M. (1974). Close similarities in dialect features of black and white college students in remedial composition classes. *TESOL Quarterly, 8,* 271–283.

Street, B. (1984). *Literacy in theory and practice.* New York: Cambridge University Press.

Swearingen, C. J. (2002). Rhetoric and composition as a coherent intellectual discipline: A meditation. In G. Olson (Ed.), *Rhetoric and composition as intellectual work* (pp. 12–22). Carbondale: Southern Illinois University Press.

Trimbur, J., Bullock, R., & Schuster, C. (Eds.). (1991). *The politics of writing instruction: Postsecondary.* Portsmouth, NH: Boynton/ Cook.

Tuell, C. (1992). Composition teaching as "women's work": Daughters, handmaids, whores, and mothers. In S. Fontaine & S. Hunter (Eds.), *Writing ourselves into the story: Unheard voices from composition studies* (pp. 123–139). Carbondale: Southern Illinois University Press.

Varnum, R. (1996). *Fencing with words: A history of writing instruction at Amherst College during the era of Theodore Baird, 1938–1966.* Urbana, IL: National Council of Teachers of English.

Wallace, D. L., & Bell, A. (1999). Being black in a predominantly white university. *College English, 61,* 307–327.

Wallace, D. L., & Ewald, H. (2000). *Mutuality in the rhetoric and composition classroom.* Carbondale: Southern Illinois University Press.

Walvoord, B. (1996). The future of WAC. *College English, 58,* 58–79.

Wible, S. (2006). Pedagogies of the "Students' Right" era: The Language Curriculum Research Group's project for linguistic diversity. *College Composition and Communication, 57,* 442–478.

Williams, J. (1981). The phenomenology of error. *College Composition and Communication, 32,* 152–168.

Williams, R. (1977). *Marxism and literature.* New York: Oxford University Press.

Winterowd, W. (1986). *Composition/rhetoric: A synthesis.* Carbondale: Southern Illinois University Press.

Worsham, L. (1991). Writing against writing: The predicament of écriture feminine in composition studies. In P. Harkin & J. Schilb (Eds.), *Contending with words: Composition and rhetoric in a postmodern age* (pp. 67–95). New York: Modern Language Association.

Yancey, K. (2004). Made not only in words: Composition in a new key. *College Composition and Communication, 56,* 297–328.

Young, R. (1980). Arts, crafts, gifts and knacks: Some disharmonies in the new rhetoric. In A. Freedman & I. Pringle (Eds.), *Reinventing the rhetorical tradition* (pp. 53–60). Ottawa, Ontario, Canada: Canadian Council of Teachers of English.

17

Intercollegiate Debate and Speech Communication

Historical Developments and Issues for the Future

JARROD ATCHISON

EDWARD PANETTA

Competitive intercollegiate debate is a uniquely American institution that evolved from the lyceum movement of the 19th century, the university literary societies, and interscholastic speaking competitions in New England preparatory schools.[1] The initial controversial nature of competitive debate was chronicled by the founders of the communication discipline in the early issues of the *Quarterly Journal of Public Speaking*. For example, a 1916 article proclaimed that debating was under fire because it cultivated insincerity and discouraged the advocacy of genuine opinions (Davis, 1916). No one, except a true debate devotee, explained Davis, could be expected to listen to the crass conclusive arguments delivered with technical jargon in a flippant fashion in many debates.

Looking back to the controversy over debate at the beginning of the 20th century, one quickly comes to the conclusion that debate continues to struggle with some of the same issues to this very day. The problems that confront the debate community include determining who should be judging debates and what skills they should possess, finding ways to make the activity more inclusive, finding a pedagogically defensible role for coaches who work with debaters, and finally, balancing the interests in competitive success with the notion that debate should fulfill a civic obligation for society at large.

Specifically, in this chapter, we describe the 19th-century predecessors to intercollegiate debate, sketch debate's evolution from an activity housed in literary societies to freestanding academic units, and outline the emergence of debate at the turn of the 20th century. The parallel set of concerns, judging standards and individual access to participation in debate, that are identifiable at the turn of both the 20th and 21st centuries will be fleshed out and some suggestions for reforms in the practice of debate will be suggested at the end of the chapter.

THE FOUNDATIONS OF INTERCOLLEGIATE DEBATE

The practice of debate in the United States has its roots in the English parliamentary system. Robert Branham (1991) notes that parliamentary debate was prevalent in the colonies and was a foundational concept in the creation of the Congress, where representatives were chosen "as debating gladiators for their constituents" (p. 15). Although the parallels between the deliberative systems of government are easily identifiable, Branham also identifies a powerful role for debate in American society outside the traditional political structures: "As early as 1631, the citizens of Dorchester, Massachusetts, organized a system of town meetings at which problems facing the community could be discussed by its residents and support for solutions could be forged" (p. 16). The English Parliamentary model provided citizens a forum for discussing community problems, but it was the educational benefits of debate that helped give momentum to the activity through the lyceum movement.

Originally conceived of as a method to educate lower-class white men who could not attend colleges and universities, lyceums quickly became forums for discussion and debate throughout America. As Angela Ray (2006) notes, "Since the 1840s lyceum lecturers had traveled the new rail lines as they spread across the country, delivering lectures

in town after town, and by 1860 'lecturer' had become a recognized occupation" (p. 184). The early lyceums were conceived of as evening study groups, but they later developed into public speaking and debate forums. Major political figures and scholars were invited to speak at lyceums across the nation, providing people with a public forum for debating the important questions of the day. Throughout the lyceum movement, public debate was understood as a method of discovery and education. Participation in lyceums, however, was not open to everyone.

Despite the fact that the institution of slavery was the major topic of debate during most of the 19th century, there were few opportunities for African Americans to speak in public. Similarly, the period included early discussions of women's suffrage, but there were often strong prohibitions against women speaking in public. The lyceum movement, however, provided an access point for African Americans and women to gain exposure in the public realm (Ray, 2005). Although participation varied across location and time, lyceums provided limited opportunities for abolitionists such as Maria Stewart and Angelina Grimké to debate in public (Branham, 1991). The limited participation of women and minorities in public debate is a problem that persists even today. Although the explicit prohibitions against public speaking have been removed, some communities, including the intercollegiate debate community, continue to struggle with strategies for improving the diversity of its participants.

The lyceum movement helped bolster the importance of debate in American society. The original goal of providing white middle-class men with increased access to public lectures and debate resulted in an important set of public forums that encouraged discussion of community and national problems. While the lyceum movement was designed to provide public education to people outside the academy, universities developed literary debating societies to train their students in the art of public deliberation, setting the foundation for intercollegiate debate.

Before fraternities and athletics, college students passed their time by participating in literary debate societies. Literary societies were an important part of university social and intellectual life. James Emerson (1931) notes,

> The literary society, indeed, was in those days the end-of-the-week diversion of hosts of young men and women in colleges, the thing they looked forward to through the humdrum of study and recitation, the dessert to the intellectual meal, the frosting on the delectable cake of sociability. (p. 363)

The first half of the society meetings normally included devotionals, speeches on topics of interest, short skits, and the society paper. The second half of the meetings was dedicated to a debate and the judge's response (Emerson, 1931). The meetings were jovial social events that provided comradery and intellectual development.

The societies debated a wide range of policy and value propositions. For example, in 1882 at Wake Forest University, the Euzelian and Philomathesian literary societies debated the question, "Is the system of universal suffrage conducive to the best interests of the Republic?" The student newspaper described the event as follows:

> In the great desert of college life there are occasional oases which refresh the weary, drooping student, as with a foretaste of the Elysian fields. Such an occasion was the forty-seventh anniversary of the Euzelian and Philomathesian Societies . . . The forces of nature had combined to make the occasion one of rejoicing, and when at 2 1/2 o'clock p.m., to the music of the Raleigh string band, the representatives of the two Societies marched down the aisle of the new-chapel, an appreciative audience had already assembled to enjoy the feast of reason so shortly to be set before them. (In and About College, 1882, para. 1)

As the newspaper description demonstrates, the public debates between literary societies drew much attention and fanfare at colleges across the nation. By the early 20th century, however, the literary societies were in sharp decline. In 1931, Emerson argued, "We know of course that such societies existed in great numbers a generation ago; indeed I doubt if there was a college or university in the Untied States 50 years ago without one or more of them" (p. 365). However, he continued,

> I believe that I am safe in saying that since those early days there has been a great decline in the number and strength of these societies, and that nothing of a like nature has come to take their place. (p. 365)

There are several theories of the decline of the literary societies, including the creation of intercollegiate debate squads, the increased prominence of fraternities and college athletics, and the institutionalization of public speaking courses (Emerson, 1931). Whether or not it is causal evidence or simply correlation, one thing is certain, as the literary societies wilted, intercollegiate debate teams flourished across the nation.

Harvard and Yale participated in the first intercollegiate debate in 1892 over the proposition, "Resolved: That a young man casting his first ballot in 1892 should vote for the nominee of the Democratic Party" (Ringwalt, 1897, p. 633). Within 3 years, the practice of intercollegiate debate had spread throughout universities on the east coast and in the Midwest. Iowa and Minnesota met in debates in 1893 and Princeton visited Yale. By 1895, Bates, Boston University, Chicago, Cornell, Dartmouth, Pennsylvania, Stanford, Wesleyan, Williams, and Western Reserve had fielded debate teams. Over the course of the next few years, the number of participating colleges skyrocketed, and new approaches to competition emerged.

Ralph Ringwalt (1897) argues that intercollegiate debate "arose in a natural reaction against the lax conditions of the literary societies and against the lack of genuine interest in any form of public speaking which for many years existed at Harvard and Yale" (p. 633). Ringwalt's outline of the lax conditions in the literary societies is supplemented by Egbert Nichols's (1936) description of the literary society debates:

> It was a desultory discussion in which opinion rather than evidence ruled, hasty inference rather than research was prominent, the subjects discussed were often inconsequential and arbitrary, and the art of rebuttal was comparatively unknown. Humor and satire, indulgence in personalities, rash generalizations, ad hominem appeal . . . were prevalent. (p. 215)

Ringwalt (1897) notes that the Harvard students who agitated for intercollegiate debate had experience in joint debating from their preparatory schools around Boston and pushed for a more rigorous debate structure when they arrived on campus. Participants tinkered with issues of topic selection, length and order of speeches in a debate, and judge selection, but the basic concept of intercollegiate debate was here to stay.

The enthusiasm for debate was due, in part, to the perception that it was an intellectual sport (Cowperthwaite & Baird, 1954). It was an activity governed by rules and guidelines that were crafted to validate a victory in the contest. Wake Forest University, which participated in its first intercollegiate debate in 1897, celebrated the success of the intercollegiate debate team with the same enthusiasm as the literary societies. A description of the debaters' return from a 1909 debate against Randolph Macon demonstrates how important a successful intercollegiate debate team had become to campus life:

> Luggage in hand, two young men left their seats and prepared to get off the train. They were Elbert N. Johnson and Henry B. Jones, and they had just returned from Virginia . . . Jones and Johnson started to descent [sic] from the train; but their feet never touched the ground. Both young students

were lifted in the air on the shoulders of husky athletes. Before them, all the way to Wingate Hall stretched a line of bonfires illuminating the night. Cheers and shouts rent the night air as the two young men took a free ride to Wingate. Then the celebration in their honor began. (Pate, 1955)

The appeal of debate, as a form of intellectual sport, has often stood in opposition to the pedagogical approach taken by some teachers who focus on learning rather than wins and losses. The tension between winning debates and teaching students about debate had surfaced from time to time in a variety of colleges. At the turn of the 20th century, it was not uncommon for participants to engage in advertising that resulted in capacity crowds at the debates. And the crowd was there to see a decisive win by the home team.

While there were not trained coaches until the second decade of the 20th century, faculty found themselves advising debaters in the 1890s. Textbooks were produced that provided models of famous arguments and recipes to produce winning appeals. George Pierce Baker's *Principles of Argumentation* (1895) and *Specimens of Argumentation* (1897) were perhaps the most influential texts of this genre. They provided suggestions for research, argument construction, and fundamentals of refutation for the prospective debater. The Baker textbooks, and others of that era, worked from the assumption that debate was a method of inquiry that could be used to find the correct or true outcome of a controversy. The early debate texts forwarded a strand of scholarship that permeated the field for the first half of the 20th century; some arguments generated conviction while others were intended to persuade the masses (Cox, 1982). The duality of logic and emotion appeals was detailed in the plethora of debate texts written between World War I and World War II. For argumentation to be truly effective, the debater was required to appeal to both the truth of a proposition and human motives. The effective argument was required to contain both logical and emotive elements (Baird, 1928). The capacity to identify both forms of argument and deploy them effectively was at the core of not only the practice of debate but also of the evolving field of public argument between the great wars (Cox, 1982).

The pressures to service a large number of interested students in an ever-growing circle of competitive programs led to changes in formats, including the establishment of debate leagues. The leagues required a school to bring both an affirmative and a negative team to the competitions. The result was that more students from those programs were afforded the chance to compete for their institution. For example, the universities of Georgia, Virginia, North Carolina, Tulane, and Vanderbilt had a league in the south for their interested students and interest in the activity was increased on those campuses (Cowperthwaite & Baird, 1954). As the activity became increasingly popular, it moved from its traditional linkage with literary societies to a more formalized relationship with university faculty who worked with their institution's debaters.

With a substantial demand for intercollegiate debate by the 1920s, debate found itself suffering from a lack of financial support at many colleges and universities (Cowperthwaite & Baird, 1954). In some cases, it was difficult to schedule more than one or two debates a year because of competing demands for other student-based programs. These financial pressures served as another reason that debate programs split from literary societies on some campuses. With the advent of university-imposed student activity fees and the emergence of speech programs, debate programs looked beyond the literary society for support.

As always seems to be the case, this shift in allegiances did not completely solve the financial concerns for some programs. A significant development that served to stretch debate budgets in the 1920s was the advent of the modern intercollegiate debate tournament. The ability to hold several debates over the course of a few days greatly enhanced the ability of programs to service a greater number of students at a relatively low cost.

In addition to lowering costs, the tournament format brought profound changes to the practice of debate. The time limits for speeches were shortened to allow for more debates over the course of the weekend. Eventually, there would be a relatively uniform set of speaking limits in most competitions. The demand for time efficiency ultimately made uniform the two-person team in place of the three- or four-person team that was employed in some debate leagues. The tournament setting also served as the impetus to identify national topics that would allow students to debate at competitions throughout the country. And, most important, the tournament model altered the audience-centered notion of debate and exacerbated the problems that some associated with the game-based conception of debate. The intercollegiate debate tournaments often took place without a public audience, and coaches and debaters focused increasingly on the need to win the tournament.

While lamented by some, the tournament model brought an even larger number of very bright students to contest debating. From its inception at the end of the 19th century, intercollegiate debate has served some of the brightest university students. The value of the activity has been chronicled in a variety of journal essays. In the 1998 annual report of the Georgetown Philodemic Debate Society, Jeff Parcher chronicles the enhanced listening, oral communication, and research skills that are the result of participation in debate. Parcher provides an extended list of people who participated in intercollegiate debate before affecting society at large. That list includes Jimmy Carter, Bill Clinton, Harry Connick Jr., Lee Iacocca, Barbara Jordan, John Kennedy, Richard Nixon, Ann Richards, Franklin Roosevelt, Antonin Scalia, and Nadine Strossen. In addition to generating important agents of change, intercollegiate debate has a close connection to Speech Communication.

INTERCOLLEGIATE DEBATE AND THE DEVELOPMENT OF SPEECH COMMUNICATION

For a burgeoning discipline, intercollegiate debate provided an early justification for specialized training in speech communication. The case in support of trained critics, for example, provided a rationale for teachers trained in speech communication. The discipline was emerging at the turn of the century and communication scholars were struggling to find respect in the academy. William Keith outlined the vagabond nature of the profession in the 19th century in his recently published text, *Democracy as Discussion: Civic Education and the American Forum Movement* (2007). Debate instructors, such as Herbert Wilchens, were alienated from their colleagues in English departments; consequently, they were in search of some academic status. The popularity of debate, while insufficient to garner academic status, did provide the instructor with proof of student demand to secure a place in the academy. An important element that perpetuated demand for debate instruction was that specialized training was required to coach debate.

A quick review of the early issues of the *Quarterly Journal of Public Speaking,* which was later renamed the *Quarterly Journal of Speech,* demonstrates the importance of intercollegiate debate to the early disciplinary identity. During the first 5 years of publication, the journal published a variety of essays on the practice of intercollegiate debate. Everett Lee Hunt (1915) warned of the excesses associated with undue attention to competitive success in his essay "Debating and College Advertising." Frank H. Lane (1915) of the University of Pittsburgh raised the question, "How much help should a coach provide a student who is competing in an intercollegiate contest?" In the same issue of the journal, Howard Woodward (1915) followed with an essay titled "Debating Without Judges." In this piece, he outlined the potential advantages associated with moving debate away from the model of competition that is judged to one that reflected a decision-less discussion. Prodded by critics of debate who published essays in a variety of public outlets, the most prominent of whom was Theodore Roosevelt, William Davis (1916) outlined the negative consequences of debate devolving to nothing more than a competitive game in the essay "Is Debating Primarily a Game?"

In addition to supplementing the disciplinary identity, intercollegiate debate brought some of the leading rhetorical critics of the 20th century to the discipline through their participation in debate. A. Craig Baird, Edwin Black, Celeste Condit, Douglas Ehninger, Thomas Goodnight, Michael McGee, Robert Newman, Marie Nichols, David Zarefsky, and many more of our critics who came to the field through participation in debate. Many Ph.D. programs continue to provide assistantships to graduate students who coach debate, continuing the vital connection between intercollegiate debate and speech communication scholarship.

EARLY ISSUES IN INTERCOLLEGIATE DEBATE

While issues that focused on the positive and negative implications of forensic competition were prevalent in the early *Quarterly Journal of Speech* essays, no subject garnered more attention than issues related to judging debates. Most of the essays worked with an assumption that debates would be juried events. And the recurrent question seemed to be what are the qualities of a good judge? Hugh Wells and J. M. O'Neill (1918) engaged in an exchange that described the choice as one between the skills a debater learns from coaches and then executes in debates or the capacity of the debater to find the best argument and express correct thought. The capacity to reward debate tactics and strategies, thereby privileging the abilities of contestants, was seen by some as a practice that conflicted

with evaluating the strengths of particular res-
olutions. Often, students who relied on technique failed to address the evolving nature of
an argument during the course of a debate.
O'Neill celebrated the attention to using the
skills of debating and asserted that rewarding
the use of tactics was not something that
lacked moral integrity. Rather, judges should
be found that reward debate tactics without
privileging dishonesty.

These concerns were especially controversial
at the time, given the nature of debate in that
era. Unlike the extemporaneous evidence
model of debate that has dominated the debate
community since the 1960s, competitive
debate at the beginning of the 20th century
was dominated by the practice of delivering
scripted speeches that, in many cases, did not
clash with the arguments of an opponent. The
dependence on well-crafted initial speeches
tended to privilege the hands-on coaching style
that led some coaches to help students draft
speeches. As has been exhibited through
multiple generations of coaches, scripting
arguments for students can create a
dependency that deters the student from
engaging arguments that do not relate to the
prepared script.

The issues of the skills privileged by debates
and the judges required to critique those
debates surfaced in other essays, including a
1917 article by Lew Sarett:

> The problem of securing competent judges
> of debate is always with us. Who of us has
> not suffered, or imagined that [he] suffered
> from decisions of incompetent, inexpert
> judges? We have all paid toll to the "promi-
> nent man" judge who lacks a definite stan-
> dard and who bases his vote upon
> non-essentials, petty prejudices, superior
> glibness of tongue, or upon the merits of the
> question rather than upon the merits of the
> debate. (pp. 135–139)

This statement reflects a struggle that has
persisted for generations in the intercollegiate
debate community. A judge is considered, by

some, to be incompetent if he or she cannot
use the standards of argument that are established by professionally trained critics. The
field-dependent standards, established for
competitive debate, had the effect of highlighting argument practices that differ from civic
argument. Since its inception, competitive
debate has used a set of procedural arguments
that are not found in public settings.
Topicality, extratopicality, justification, and
inherency are but a few of the procedural
roadblocks that have been used to win debates
throughout the history of the activity. The
people who have determined the outcome of
debates have been coded as lay judges, stock
issues judges, and argument critics by participants in an effort to match a typology of arguments to a particular judge.

The opposing viewpoint on the role that
judges/coaches should play in debate is that
coaches should be using debate as a laboratory
to enrich the quality of civic argument. This
perspective calls into question the value of
procedural arguments and specialized language
that often permeate a competitive debate. Using
this model, the students should reject the field-
specific language and logic of debate and polish
skills that can be used in the public arena. The
desire to facilitate accessible discourse is one of
the reasons that some turned away from
intercollegiate debate and embraced discussion
and public forums (Keith, 2007). In the effort to
refine specialized argument techniques that
would both win competitive debates and serve
the students later in life, some believe that
intercollegiate debate had crossed a line and
was no longer serving the public good. Debate
had become primarily a game and lost sight of
its larger goal. The contention was that when
debate becomes a contest—that is, a vehicle to
enhance the visibility or status of a college, it
loses its public character and serves merely as a
publicity device for the private interests of that
college (Hunt, 1915).

Unsurprisingly, the essays published at the
turn of the 20th century reflect a tacit
assumption that intercollegiate debate served

to educate young (white) men. While the lyceum movement had the benefit of, at least in a limited sense, increasing opportunities for African Americans and women outside the academy, the exclusive nature of higher education throughout the 19th and early 20th centuries did not create a diverse set of participants in intercollegiate debate. It was not until the early 1920s that women were included on intercollegiate debate teams. Women found themselves debating with men by 1923 (Keith, 2007). In some southern colleges, African Americans were not active debaters until well after *Brown v. Board* (1954) was enforced by the federal government. With hindsight, we can assess that some of the early problems with diversity were closely connected to the relative inaccessibility of higher education, but it is also important to remember that the first intercollegiate debaters were elite white young men who had received prior training at preparatory schools on their way to Ivy League institutions.

Some of the early issues in intercollegiate debate, such as the need to change the format to fit tournament schedules, were the natural results of growth and institutional restraints. Other issues, however, were closely connected to the nature of the activity. The balance between the competitive and educational goals of the activity, the roles of judges and coaches, and the diversity of the participants all represent tensions within the debate community that are negotiated from generation to generation. In the next section, we will assess the current issues facing intercollegiate debate and make recommendations about how to make the tensions as productive for our students as possible.

CURRENT ISSUES IN INTERCOLLEGIATE DEBATE

The educational benefits of debate are often in contest with the productive benefits of competition. In the early years, this tension generated two perspectives that framed the issues facing

the debate community. From one perspective, debate was simply a competitive game with educational benefits. From the other perspective, debate was a training ground for civic-minded students, and competition was the reward for learning the skills necessary for civic engagement. Despite the fact that some issues facing the debate community have evolved over the course of time, the two perspectives on debate persist even today.

Intercollegiate debate continues, in our opinion, to struggle with a variety of community problems. Some of the problems include the poor representation of women and minorities, increased travel and resource demands, the resource disparity between large and small debate programs, and the role of coaches in the production of evidence. In our opinion, the tension between education and competition continues to frame the issues challenging the debate community, but the major difference between the current issues and the early issues has been the introduction of community problems into debate competitions.

Debaters have begun to use the individual debates as a forum for articulating community problems while simultaneously arguing that the judge should vote for them in an effort to help reconcile the community problem. The justifications for winning the debates have included the increased attention to the community problem that comes with winning, rewarding the debaters or debate program for taking measures outside the competitive forum to alleviate the problem, and to encourage their opponents (or their debate program) to consider how they may be contributing to the community problem. From our perspective, the introduction of community problems into the debate competition represents a modern manifestation of the education versus competition tension that has been a part of the debate community from the beginning. The tension has once again produced two perspectives on the form and purpose of intercollegiate debate.

The two dominant perspectives that have emerged from the education versus competition tension depart from one another over the perceived insulation of individual debates and the debate community. The first perspective, which we label "debate as innovation," calls for participants to view individual debate competitions as insulated from other intellectual communities. In the same way that the early proponents of the "debate is simply a game" perspective defended a specialized debate vocabulary and trained judging, the new "debate as innovation" perspective argues that participants should be free to engage in any behavior as long as it makes an argument that a judge might reward with a win. No person is held accountable for anything that they say or do within an individual debate because it is seen as a unique site of experimentation and not a site of civic engagement.

The second perspective, which we label "debate as activism," calls for participants to view individual debates as discussions with no insulation. In the same way that the earlier proponents of the "debate as civic engagement" argued for a vocabulary and style that would increase community accessibility and untrained judges, the new "debate as activism" perspective argues that individual debates are a focal point for change within the debate community and/or society at large. The judge is asked to determine the winner based on what would be best for the debate community or society at large, rather than which team best defended an answer to the question posed by the resolution. Accountability, within this perspective, extends beyond the individual debates to questions regarding squad policies, recruiting, coach interactions, and overall participation within the debate community, to name but a few.

From our perspective, there are problems with both extremes, and the rest of this chapter is dedicated to outlining the deficiencies of the current perspectives and suggesting a supplemental strategy of tournament experimentation to begin the process of using the method debate offers to resolve community problems outside the individual debate competitions. Tournaments provide unique sites for innovation and experimentation that might provide a forum for participants, coaches, and other communities to discuss better the goals and objectives of intercollegiate debate.

Debate as an Insulated Game

As the descriptions of the campuswide celebrations suggest, for much of its existence, intercollegiate debate has had a strong focus on competition. The benefits that students derive from participating in debate are amplified under intense competition. The traditional thought has been that students learn more, work harder, and get more from the activity when they are motivated to succeed. With this focus on competition came an emphasis on debaters' skills that subverted the importance of the argument that they were defending. Indeed, the true mark of a successful traditional debater is the ability to persuade a judge to vote for him or her on both sides of a topic. Switching the sides of a debate has been deemed important to forcing students to consider both sides of an issue and also preserve the focus on fair competition. With an emphasis on competitive success and skill, debaters have chosen to use a wide array of arguments that they may not believe in but that had strategic benefits.

A quick glance through most squads' research files reveals arguments that might sound ridiculous to the average person, but have won debates. Why has the debate community been tolerant of arguments that are rarely persuasive to audiences outside debate? The answer to that question is that for much of its existence, the debate community has had a strong norm against censoring arguments while simultaneously presuming a strong insulation from the communities that support it. The debate community has been quick to defend the use of controversial arguments on the grounds that every idea should undergo rigorous testing, and if the idea is truly flawed, then it should be easily defeated. Although this approach to intercollegiate debate arguments has been accepted for many years, the recent push trend toward alternative argument approaches warrants reconsideration of intercollegiate debate's status as an insulated activity.

In an era of tightened budgets, directors are increasingly pressured to defend the benefits of intercollegiate debate. This is occurring at a time when debate is becoming more and more publicized. The three College Sports Television documentaries produced on the National Debate Tournament along with the increased use of video and audio recording by debate programs challenge the presumption that debate is an insulated activity. Arguments presented by debaters, on the other hand, have moved further and further toward the exotic. The norm against restricting arguments has expanded to include actions that performance artists have deemed resistance but that would not be covered by even liberal interpretations of academic freedom. The presumption of insulation, however, has remained the same. Some people still believe that what takes place in an individual debate has no bearing on anyone else inside or outside the debate community. There has been little communitywide response that demonstrates that directors, coaches, or debaters are concerned that argument choices may negatively influence their or other programs. The norm of argument freedom has become so strong that the threshold for acceptance is whether or not a behavior can be said to be making an argument. It does not take a very experienced argument scholar to recognize that there are few behaviors that cannot be construed as making an argument. From our perspective, the combination of intentionally provocative argument choices and the increased politicization of debate risks the continued institutional support of intercollegiate debate (Atchison & Panetta, 2006).

The "debate as innovation" perspective, outlined here, developed out of an intense focus on competition that rewarded debaters' skills. The natural outgrowth of a competitive focus was for people to celebrate debaters' wins with less concern over the arguments used to achieve the win. The presumption that individual debates had little to no affect on any other community fostered a vision of debate as a community that was willing to put any idea through the rigorous test of debate. The problem with this perspective, however, is threefold. First, the debate community is not as insulated as the proponents assume. Second, the norm of protecting freedom for arguments has allowed debaters to put the community at risk with behaviors that many administrators would find objectionable. Third, there is not a sufficient forum for discussing issues that affect the debate community as a whole. In the next section, we turn to examining the other end of the spectrum that presumes that every individual debate is a place for community change.

Debates as Sites of Community Change

The debate community has become more self-reflexive and increasingly invested in attempting to address the problems that have plagued the community from the start. The degrees to which things are considered problems and the appropriateness of different solutions to the problems have been hotly contested, but some fundamental issues, such as diversity and accessibility, have received considerable attention in recent years. This section will address the "debate as activism" perspective that argues that the appropriate site for addressing community problems is individual debates. In contrast to the "debate as innovation" perspective, which assumes that the activity is an isolated game with educational benefits, proponents of the "debate as activism" perspective argue that individual debates have the potential to create change in the debate community and society at large. If the first approach assumed that debate was completely insulated, this perspective assumes that there is no substantive insulation between individual debates and the community at large.

From our perspective, using individual debates to create community change is an insufficient strategy for three reasons. First, individual debates *are,* for the most part, insulated from the community at large. Second, individual debates limit the conversation to the immediate participants and the judge, excluding many important contributors to the debate community. Third, locating the discussion within the confines of a competition diminishes the additional potential for collaboration, consensus, and coalition building.

The first problem that we isolate is the difficulty of any individual debate to generate community change. Although any debate has the potential to create problems for the community (videotapes of objectionable behavior, etc.), rarely does any one debate have the power to create communitywide change. We attribute this ineffectiveness to the structural problems inherent in individual debates and the collective forgetfulness of the debate community. The structural problems stem from the current tournament format that has remained relatively consistent for the past 30 years. Debaters engage in preliminary debates in rooms that are rarely populated by anyone other than the judge. Judges are instructed to vote for the team that does the best debating, but the ballot is rarely seen by anyone outside the tabulation room. Given the limited number of debates in which a judge actually writes meaningful comments, there is little documentation of what actually transpired during the debate round. During the period when judges interact with the debaters, there are often external pressures (filing evidence, preparing for the next debate, etc.) that restrict the ability of anyone outside the debate to pay attention to the judges' justification for their decision. Elimination debates do not provide for a much better audience because debates still occur simultaneously, and travel schedules dictate that most of the participants have left by the later elimination rounds. It is difficult for anyone to substantiate the claim that asking a judge to vote to solve a community problem in an individual debate with so few participants is the best strategy for addressing important problems.

In addition to the structural problems, the collective forgetfulness of the debate community reduces the impact that individual debates have on the community. The debate community is largely made up of participants who debate and then move on to successful careers. The coaches and directors that make up the backbone of the community are the people with the longest cultural memory, but they are also a small minority of the community when considering the number of debaters involved in the activity. This is not meant to suggest that the activity is reinvented every year—certainly there are conventions that are passed down from coaches to debaters and from debaters to debaters. However, the basic fact remains that there are virtually no transcriptions available for the community to read, and, therefore, it is difficult to substantiate the claim that the debate community can remember any one individual debate over the course of several generations of debaters. Additionally, given the focus on competition and individual skill, the community is more likely to remember the accomplishments and talents of debaters rather than a specific winning argument. The debate community does not have the necessary components in place for a strong collective memory of individual debates. The combination of the structures of debate and the collective forgetfulness means that any strategy for creating community change that is premised on winning individual debates is less effective than seeking a larger community dialogue that is recorded and/or transcribed.

A second problem with attempting to create community change in individual debates is that the debate community is comprised of more individuals than the four debaters and one judge that are present in every round. Coaches and directors have very little space for engaging in a discussion about community issues. This is especially true for coaches and directors who are not preferred judges and, therefore, do not have access to many debates. Coaches and directors should have a public forum to engage in a community conversation with debaters instead of attempting to take on their opponents through the wins and losses of their own debaters.

In addition to coaches and debaters, there are many people who might want to contribute to a community conversation, but are not directly involved in competition. For instance, most debate tournaments take place at an academic institution that plays host to the rest of the community. For that institution to host everyone, they must make tremendous sacrifices. It would be beneficial to the debate community to have some of the administrators who make decisions about supporting debate come to a public forum and discuss what types of information they need when they make decisions about program funding. Directors and coaches would benefit from having administrators explain to the community how they evaluate the educational benefits of debate. Additionally, every institution has unique scholars who work in some area and who could be of benefit to the debate community. The input of scholars who study argument, communication, race, gender, sexuality, economics, and the various other academic interests could provide valuable advice to the debate community. For example, a business professor could suggest how to set up a collective bargaining agreement to reduce the costs associated with travel. Attempting to create an insulated community that has all the answers ignores the potential to create very powerful allies within academic institutions that could help the debate community. After all, debate is not the first community to have problems associated with finances, diversity, and competition. These resources, however, are not available for individual debates. The debate community is broader than the individual participants and can achieve better reform through public dialogue than individual debates.

The final problem with an individual debate round focus is the role of competition. Creating community change through individual debate rounds sacrifices the "community" portion of the change. Many teams that promote activist strategies in debates profess that they are more interested in creating change than winning debates. What is clear, however, is that the vast majority of teams that are not promoting community change are very interested in winning debates. The tension that is generated from the clash of these opposing forces is tremendous. Unfortunately, this is rarely a productive tension. Forcing teams to consider their purpose in debating, their style in debates, and their approach to evidence are all critical aspects of being participants in the community. However, the dismissal of the proposed resolution that the debaters have spent countless hours preparing for, in the name of a community problem that the debaters often have little control over, does little to engender coalitions of the willing. Should a debate team lose because its director or coach has been ineffective at recruiting minority participants? Should a debate team lose because its coach or director holds political positions that are in opposition to the activist program? Competition has been a critical component of the interest in intercollegiate debate from the beginning, and it does not help further the goals of the debate community to dismiss competition in the name of community change.

The larger problem with locating the "debate as activism" perspective within the competitive framework is that it overlooks the communal nature of the community problem. If each individual debate is a decision about how the debate community should approach a problem, then the losing debaters become collateral damage in the activist strategy dedicated toward creating community change. One frustrating example of this type of argument might include a judge voting for an activist team in an effort to help them reach elimination rounds to generate a community discussion about the problem. Under this scenario, the losing team serves as a sacrificial lamb on the altar of community change.

Downplaying the important role of competition and treating opponents as scapegoats for the failures of the community may increase the profile of the winning team and the community problem, but it does little to generate the critical coalitions necessary to address the community problem, because the competitive focus encourages teams to concentrate on how to beat the strategy with little regard for addressing the community problem. There is no role for competition when a judge decides that it is important to accentuate the publicity of a community problem. An extreme example might include a team arguing that their opponents' academic institution had a legacy of civil rights abuses and that the judge should not vote for them because that would be a community endorsement of a problematic institution. This scenario is a bit more outlandish but not unreasonable if one assumes that each debate should be about what is best for promoting solutions to diversity problems in the debate community.

If the debate community is serious about generating community change, then it is more likely to occur outside a traditional competitive debate. When a team loses a debate because the judge decides that it is better for the community for the other team to win, then they have sacrificed two potential advocates for change within the community. Creating change through wins generates backlash through losses. Some proponents are comfortable with generating backlash and argue that the reaction is evidence that the issue is being discussed. From our perspective, the discussion that results from these hostile situations is not a productive one where participants seek to work together for a common goal. Instead of giving up on hope for change and agitating for wins regardless of who is left behind, it seems more reasonable that the debate community should try the method of public argument that we teach in an effort to generate a discussion of necessary community changes. Simply put, debate competitions do not represent the best environment for community change because it

is a competition for a win and only one team can win any given debate, whereas addressing systemic century-long community problems requires a tremendous effort by a great number of people.

The "debate as innovation" perspective views each debate in a vacuum with little to no consequences on any other community. The "debate as activism" perspective views each debate as a site of resistance where the debate community can confront problems in an effort to change. Both extremes replicate the education versus competition tension that has been a part of the debate community ever since the move away from the literary societies. In the final section of this chapter, we outline a potential solution to the divergent perspectives that is based on tournament experimentation. Our goal is to outline a blueprint for a community dialogue that could be replicated week in and week out at regional and national tournaments throughout the country.

Tournaments: Sites for Change

The earliest debaters figured out that there is nothing like the experience of attending an intercollegiate debate tournament. In their modern manifestations, tournaments are rigorous tests of mental acuity and perseverance. From our perspective, there is no other college activity that provides students with an opportunity to engage in such an intense and powerful academic exchange with fellow students from across the country, representing a wide diversity of institutions. What is more impressive is that debaters travel to tournaments several times a semester while maintaining their academic responsibilities. In our experience, few academic conferences produce the same level of rigorous conversation that happens at one college debate tournament. That being said, one thing that is missing from modern college debate tournaments is a forum for discussing community concerns. Debate historians have argued correctly that this was not always the case. In the distant past, tournaments held after-dinner speeches where debaters would address their community about a wide range of topics. In the recent past, tournaments such as Northwestern held forums where coaches, directors, and debaters offered community proposals for discussion. In fact, according to one version of the story, the Northwestern forum was the place where Ross Smith argued that the National Debate Tournament community should seriously consider adopting the Cross Examination Debate Association resolution—precipitating the merger of the two debate communities. Unfortunately, we are not aware of these forums at any of the regional or major national tournaments today. In this final section, we propose experimenting with tournament scheduling to create a period of time for a community forum.

Technology has improved tremendously today's tournament schedules. In the past, pairing a single round of debate required an extensive tab room staff with experience and patience. Today, computer programs have drastically reduced the amount of time necessary to pair debates. Additionally, the community has gotten better about starting debates on time and turning in ballots in a timely fashion. As a result of these innovations, debate tournaments have more flexible time for participants. There are at least three scenarios that a tournament could adopt in an effort to generate public discussions. Much like tournament structure was used to reform debate in the 1920s, debate can look to the weekend competitions as a forum to address the recurrent problems of contest debating.

Scenario One: Tournaments With Banquets

Tournaments that already have banquets scheduled present an easy opportunity for the beginnings of community discussion. The majority of these tournaments have banquets after the end of the preliminary rounds. Traditionally, the banquets serve as a place for announcing speaker awards and teams

clearing to the elimination debates. It would be difficult to use this time for a community discussion because debaters are tired after two strenuous days of debate. Those debaters who are clearing to the elimination rounds are often concerned about getting enough sleep and preparing for their potential opponents. Tournaments, however, that already have allocated resources for having a banquet could consider moving the banquet to the end of the first day of preliminary debates.

There are two primary advantages to moving the banquet to the end of the first day. First, because most tournaments use preset pairings on the first day of preliminary debates, the day ends much earlier. The second day requires more time to pair a tournament, and the judges often require more time to decide debates. Moving the banquet would mean that debaters and directors would have more time to enjoy the meal and engage in a community discussion. As currently scheduled, banquets are put on hold while tabulation rooms attempt to determine speaker awards and teams clearing to the elimination rounds. Moving the banquet means that debaters can get to bed earlier on the second night after the preliminary debates are finished. Second, by moving the banquet and centering it on a forum for community concerns, the tournament increases the people who are exposed to the discussion. Most people attend the banquets for a variety of different reasons; having the community discussion over prepaid food increases the participation of the entire community. Hosting a voluntary forum would be less likely to attract as many participants as having the discussion at the banquet.

Using tournaments with banquets for a community forum is the easiest scenario because the money and time have been set aside already for everyone to gather together. Under our proposal, the banquet would mean more than eating and finding out the results of the preliminary debates. The banquet would be a place forum for a variety of potential topics, including invited speakers, public debates, or just public discussions of community concerns. We suggest moving the banquet, but tournaments may prefer to start small and test the idea of the forum first.

Scenario Two: Voluntary Meeting Time

Tournaments have the opportunity to schedule a voluntary meeting time that is announced to all the participants in advance of the tournament.[2] The major advantage to this type of voluntary forum is that the people who attend are generally motivated to try and make a difference in the community. The major disadvantage to this type of voluntary forum is that the people who do not attend are not exposed to the concerns about their community. However, some form of community discussion is better than not attempting anything at all. The lessons learned from the past meetings are that it is important to publicize the forum well in advance, find a space that is large enough to accommodate the audience, and set aside enough time for people to have dinner before coming to the forum.

Scenario Three: Public Debates

After the events of September 11, 2001, the Wake Forest Shirley Classic experimented with changing the eight-round preliminary debates to a six-round tournament. The final two debates became a series of public debates concerning the issues in the war on terrorism. This type of tournament experimentation could be replicated with public debates over issues of concern in the community. As a debate community, we should put a greater emphasis on public deliberation as a method for resolving problems.

Public debates have several advantages. First, they are more accessible to everyone in and out of the debate community. Although people not directly involved in the activity might be uninterested in some of the topics, our community problems might be similar enough

to other groups' concerns that the public might be interested. Second, public debates allow for a structured interaction that sometimes breaks down in open-ended public forums. Having a set topic to discuss along with time limits and speech orders can be helpful in directing a conversation in a more manageable way than public forums. Finally, we are a community of debaters who value seeing the method of challenging ideas in action. It might be difficult to attract people to come to a public forum for a discussion about community problems. A debate between two prominent members of the community, on the other hand, could generate stronger community participation.

The central problem with this scenario is that many debate participants would object to the elimination of two preliminary debates. Moving to a six-round tournament means that a higher percentage of teams with winning records would be unable to participate in the elimination rounds. However, there are a fair number of tournaments that already use a six-round schedule and could easily rearrange the debates to enable a series of public debates for the community to watch and participate in.

Alternately, tournament hosts could experiment with the format of contest debate to enhance civic involvement. In addition to the well-documented formatting changes that resulted from changing time limits at the Franklin R. Shirley Classic, the Owen Coon tournament instituted a judge cross-examination experiment in the late 1970s in an effort to improve the quality of debates. Our position is that the value of lay audiences could be better discussed by the community if it is a shared experience. We could keep an eight-round format and include two debates for lay audiences into the formula. To ensure that point disparities in these debates did not affect participants, we could simply record wins and losses, using the points from the six preliminary debates judged by "trained judges" to determine seeding. Incorporating these "pseudo-public" debates into a tournament with a banquet discussion session would serve to maximize a shared community experience for the debaters.

CONCLUSION

Intercollegiate debate has been a critical educational tool in the development of an informed citizenry. Countless students have had the opportunity to travel and test ideas under the rigors of competition against some of the smartest students in the nation. History suggests that America understands the importance of deliberation and the consequences of uninformed decisions. Intercollegiate debate grew out of the American spirit of deliberation and flourished in the academy through the support of Speech Communication departments. The result has been a wide variety of successful citizens who have used the skills that debate teaches to make the world a better place.

History also suggests, however, that the more things change, the more they stay the same. The legacy of debate in America includes elitism and a careful balance between competition and education. While the early debaters struggled with inclusion, judge qualifications, roles for coaches, and tournament formats, the current debate community struggles with similar issues surrounding diversity, judge qualifications, roles for coaches, and competitive goals. We have argued that the core of these issues is the balance between the educational benefits of debate and the competitive focus of the activity. From our perspective, there are currently two divergent approaches to addressing this tension. One approach emphasizes competition over all other goals. The other approach emphasizes changing the debate community to enhance its educational opportunities over all other goals. Fundamental to this tension are the same questions that riddled the earliest scholarship in speech communication. Who is debate supposed to benefit? Should debates be accessible to other communities? What role should coaches play in the competitive

process? Although, we do not propose a simple answer to any of these questions, we argue that a return to our roots provides a method of addressing community problems. In short, the debate community needs to return to an earlier model of debate to discuss our community problems. We have proposed three scenarios for tournament experimentation that we believe preserve the competitive benefits of debate while providing opportunities for a wide array of participants to engage in a community forum.

NOTES

1. Portions of this chapter were presented at the 2005 National Communication Association Conference in Boston, Massachusetts.

2. The 1998 Wake Forest Shirley Classic tournament held a public forum dedicated to addressing diversity in debate. Organized by Emma Filstrup, the forum took place at the end of the first day of preliminary debates and was well attended. The momentum of having this forum did not carry into future tournaments, but it demonstrated the potential for having a time set aside for people to attend a forum.

REFERENCES

Atchison, J., & Panetta, E. (2006). Raising a stink: An assessment of argument presentation and effects on secondary audiences. In R. Patricia (Ed.), *Engaging argument* (pp. 512–517). Washington: National Communication Association.

Baird, A. C. (1928). *Public discussion and debate.* New York: Ginn.

Baker, G. P. (1895). *The principles of argumentation.* New York: Ginn.

Baker, G. P. (1897). *Specimens of argumentation* (2nd ed.). New York: H. Holt.

Branham, R. (1991). *Debate and critical analysis: The harmony of conflict.* Hillsdale, NJ: Lawrence Erlbaum.

Brown v. the Board of Education, 347 US 483 (1954).

Cowperthwaite, L., & Baird, C. (1954). Intercollegiate debating. In K. Wallace (Ed.), *History of speech education in America* (pp. 259–276). New York: Appleton-Century Crofts.

Cox, R. (1982). Introduction: The field of argumentation. In J. R. Cox & C. Willard (Eds.), *Advances in argumentation theory and research* (pp. xiii–xlvii). Carbondale: Southern Illinois University Press.

Davis, W. (1916). Is debating primarily a game? *Quarterly Journal of Public Speaking, 2,* 171–179.

Emerson, J. (1931). The old debating society. *Quarterly Journal of Speech, 17,* 363.

Hunt, E. (1915). Debating and college advertising. *Quarterly Journal of Public Speaking, 1,* 272–275.

In and About the College. (1882, March). *The Wake Forest Student, March,* 144–147. Retrieved June 2, 2008, from http://groups.wfu.edu/debate/HistoryPages/1882AnniversaryDebate.htm

Keith, W. (2007). *Democracy as discussion: Civic education and the American forum movement.* Lanham, MD: Lexington Books.

Lane, F. (1915). Faculty help in intercollegiate contests. *Quarterly Journal of Public Speaking, 1,* 9–16.

Nichols, E. (1936). A historical sketch of intercollegiate debating: I. *Quarterly Journal of Speech, 22,* 215.

Parcher, J. (1998). *Report of the Philodemic Debate Society,* Georgetown University, Washington, DC. Retrieved June 2, 2008, from www.tmsdebate.org/main/forensics/snfl/debate_just2.htm

Pate, W. (1955). Changing times: Debaters won, rode athletes' shoulders in 1909. *Old Gold & Black,* February 21. Retrieved June 2, 2008, http://groups.wfu.edu/debate/HistoryPages/1910RMvictory.html

Ray, A. (2005). *The lyceum and public culture in the nineteenth-century United States.* East Lansing: Michigan State University Press.

Ray, A. (2006). What hath she wrought? Woman's rights and the nineteenth-century lyceum. *Rhetoric and Public Affairs, 9*(2), 184.

Ringwalt, R. (1897). Intercollegiate debating. *Forum, 22,* 633.

Sarett, L. (1917). The expert judge of debate. *Quarterly Journal of Public Speaking, 3,* 135–139.

Wells, H., & O'Neill, J. M. (1918). Judging debates. *Quarterly Journal of Public Speaking, 4,* 76–92.

Woodward, H. (1915). Debating without judges. *Quarterly Journal of Public Speaking, 1,* 229–233.

18

The Consequences of Rhetoric and Literacy

Power, Persuasion, and Pedagogical Implications

MORRIS YOUNG

CONNIE KENDALL

While discourses about rhetoric throughout history often have shifted between suspicions about the manipulation of truth and knowledge through language and the development of truth and knowledge by argument and persuasion through language, discourses about literacy have tended to be singular in the belief that literacy (however defined) is a significant cognitive and social achievement. This belief has been so overwhelming at times that threats to literacy often have been seen as threats to society, whether to economic or educational development, safety and security, health and welfare, or even art and culture. Thus, the idea of a "literacy crisis" often conjures more than just concern about the level and quality of reading and writing expected of individuals and a society.

Whether it is the 1975 *Newsweek* story by Sheils, "Why Johnny Can't Write," the 1983 report *A Nation at Risk*, or the No Child Left Behind Act of 2001, the invocation of a literacy crisis serves to provide, as John Trimbur (1991) argues, an explanation for events and conditions that have shaken the confidence of a nation, especially in difficult economic times, a way to conflate various issues that may or may not bear direct relationships with one another in the service of a particular ideological standpoint (p. 281). Perhaps more to the point, Trimbur argues that to think of literacy crises as ideological events is to think rhetorically—to see literacy crises conjuncturally, as strategic pretexts for educational and cultural change that renegotiate the terms of cultural hegemony, the relations between classes and groups, and the meaning and use of literacy. (p. 281)

Talking about literacy is thus an always complicated and sometimes frustrating experience because the term *literacy* itself is just as ambiguous as it is powerful and tends to create or reinforce beliefs already at hand. While literacy most often denotes the skills of reading and writing, it also connotes a standard or quality of cultural capital in the modern, Western nation, manifested, perhaps most visibly, in its educational institutions and in other social institutions as well. Literacy becomes a marker of membership, and those who can demonstrate this membership gain both access to and privilege in the dominant structures of power. Those without membership often face economic and political disadvantage, limiting their participation in the community in various ways. The implications of literacy, then, are always greater than just acquiring reading and writing abilities and a defined body of knowledge that meet a community's "standards": While literacy facilitates participation in society, the legitimacy it confers extends beyond the benefits of national citizenship, community membership, or even basic human rights. The incentive to be identified as literate is great; for anyone to question literacy is a great risk.

Given the complexities of literacy, then, in this chapter we examine the interrelatedness of literacy and rhetoric, or what might be called the "rhetoricity" of literacy, the notion that literacy itself is rhetorical and not merely a precondition for rhetorical action. John Duffy (2004) argues that

to see literacy as rhetorical is to consider the influence of a particular rhetoric on what writers choose to say, the genres they elect

to write in, the words and phrases they use to communicate their messages, and the audience they imagine while writing. (p. 227)

In a similar sense, Juan Guerra (1998) suggests that "orality and literacy are interpreted by [community] members as rhetorical practices involving the representation of self and culture in conventional and inventive terms" (p. 61). With these understandings of the connection between rhetoric and literacy, we unpack, in Beth Daniell's (1999) terms, the grand narratives and the little narratives of literacy and then consider how these narratives ("grand" or "little") have functioned rhetorically whether for individuals, self-defined groups, culturally/socially defined groups, or institutions (p. 394). We begin with one grand narrative, The Great Divide, which has structured discussions of literacy by focusing on developmental models of literacy and binaries of oral and literate, primitive and civilized cultures. We then turn to another grand narrative, the social turn in literacy, and its subsequent, alternative "little narratives" that have become prevalent in current approaches to the study of literacy (Cushman, Kintgen, Kroll, & Rose, 2001, p. 3). By mapping these narratives, we also hope to highlight the rhetorical function of these narratives and the way literacy practices enact the construction of identity, community, and texts through persuasion. Finally, we consider the implications of rhetoric and literacy in pedagogical contexts, examining in particular how specific constructions of literacy affect policies and practices both inside and outside the classroom.

LITERACY: DIVIDES, DICHOTOMIES, AND LEAPS

In their essay "The Consequences of Literacy," Jack Goody and Ian Watt (1963/1988) confirmed what many people in the West had long believed: The roots of democracy as we know it are, in fact, traceable to ancient Greece and, in particular, to the invention of alphabetic literacy in the fifth century BCE.[1] A bold assertion, to be sure, Goody and Watt based their argument on an equally bold theoretical premise about the causal connections between the advent of written literacy some 2,500 years ago and the actual restructuring of basic human thought processes. In short, Goody and Watt hypothesize that the Greeks' development of an alphabetic script brought about a fundamental change in human cognition that, in turn, helped set the social and political conditions within which literacy could flourish and from which other critical cultural advancements, such as the establishment of a democratic form of social rule, would eventually or (in the strong version of the theory) even naturally arise. Not surprisingly, the implications of Goody and Watt's claims about the consequences of literacy have been very far-reaching. For, in ascribing to literacy the power to determine the course and fate of a given society, their ideas worked not only to privilege certain ways of using language over and above all other modes of communication but also to justify some troubling beliefs about the intrinsic value and historical significance of certain kinds of people—those who have acquired alphabetic or "written" literacy—over and above those who have not.

From Goody and Watt's (1963/1988) perspective, the invention of the Greek alphabet, which uniquely revised the existing syllabary to include the graphic representation of all five vowels, not only constitutes an event unprecedented in the ancient world but also represents the defining moment in the history and development of modern society. And on this point, Goody and Watt were certainly not alone. In fact, their arguments in "The Consequences of Literacy" became the basis for a powerful explanatory model known generally as the Great Divide model of literacy, which indicates the ways in which written

literacy is presumed to demarcate the boundary between "traditional" (read primarily oral) cultures and their more "modern" counterparts. Other researchers, principally Eric Havelock (1976, 1982) and Walter Ong (1982), joined Goody and Watt in their efforts to theorize the social and psychological consequences of literacy. Collectively, this group is referred to as the Great Divide theorists.[2]

Despite the four decades that have passed since Goody and Watt (1963/1988) first claimed for literacy the power to forge a "great divide" and despite the flood of criticism that their claims have drawn in the intervening years, this early model of literacy has been extraordinarily resilient. Part of our work as we see it, then, is to examine the foundational claims on which the Great Divide model is built, in an effort to complicate the seemingly simple formula it champions—namely, that the forward progress of a given society and, by extension, the relative value and worth attached to the accomplishments of its people, is both dependent on and determined by the level and kind of literacy achieved. Left out of this neat equation, or perhaps merely hidden by it, is a complex of factors that contemporary researchers have sought to make more visible—issues of access and power (Cushman, 1998; Horner & Trimbur, 2002; Rose, 1989), of cultural and linguistic bias (Crawford, 1992; Farr, 1994; Villanueva, 1993), and of the historical and institutional influences that have shaped the meaning of literacy in the modern era (Brandt, 2001; Gee, 1996; Hull, 1993).

The other goal for this discussion is to inquire into the "legacies of literacy," to borrow from Harvey Graff (1987), by asking a different set of questions. What are the real-world consequences of conceptualizing literacy as the precondition for social progress and intellectual development? How does linking the invention of alphabetic literacy with the rise and influence of Western society privilege certain cultural traditions, institutions, and ideals while marginalizing others? And perhaps most important, how does our faith in literacy as both a public and a private "good," a central means for the unification of society and the empowerment of personal lives, serve also as a means to stratify, differentiate, and far too often justify the success or failure of individuals, communities, or cultures at large? On the cumulative effects of our willingness to view language as the primary source of difference, our tendency to seek contrasts and think in dichotomies, James Paul Gee (1996) wryly remarks, "If language is what makes us human, literacy, it seems, is what makes us civilized" (p. 26). The expectation that literacy functions as a "civilizing" force in the world is a key claim of the Great Divide theorists and a belief resonant with modern U.S. society and mainstream institutions; as such, it provides a good place for us to begin.

PRIMITIVE/CIVILIZED, ORALITY/LITERACY: A RHETORIC OF DICHOTOMIES AND CONTRASTS

In the vernacular, the phrase *to civilize* is often used and understood pejoratively, an attitude supported by its definition, which reads "to bring out of a condition of savagery or barbarism and instruct in the ways of advanced society" (*Webster's Unabridged*). For social anthropologists such as Goody and Watt (1963/1988), however, whose work is traditionally associated with the study of "primitive" cultures, the term *civilized* admits a decidedly less pejorative (though certainly not neutral) meaning: "advanced in social organization and the arts and sciences" (*Webster's Unabridged*). Shades of one meaning have a way of impinging on others, and it would be safe to say that Gee's (1996) remark quoted above aims to remind us of the dangers resulting from this sort of definitional slippage, of assuming that *civilized* simply means "advanced" or, in the reverse, that *primitive* simply means "a condition of savagery or barbarism." Gee's observation that

language—the hallmark of humankind—differs from literacy—the trademark of civility—bears importantly on this discussion as well. For, in spite of our tendency to think of the two terms together, "language" and "literacy" are not interchangeable.

On the difference between language and literacy, Roz Ivanic (1998) suggests that

> literacy is both *less,* and *more* than language. It is less, in the sense that language is a superordinate term, encompassing both spoken and written language, while literacy makes written language its focus. It is more, in the sense that "literacy" is a different sort of word than "language" and refers to more than language itself. (p. 57)

Ivanic's distinction is subtle but crucial, especially if we consider the two terms from a linguistic standpoint. Unlike *literacy,* which has an opposite in both theoretical and everyday usage (i.e., *illiteracy*), *language* has no oppositional counterpart. The very existence of the word *illiteracy,* Ivanic (1998) explains, draws our attention to the fact that literacy "is concerned with people's use of a semiotic system, rather than with the semiotic system itself" (p. 58). And it is the way in which literacy is conceptually and materially linked with a society's ideas about the proper/improper, authorized/unauthorized, desirable/undesirable *uses* of public language that not only fixes the modern hierarchical relationship between literacy and illiteracy but also works to affirm our long-standing belief in literacy's power to tell us something significant about the people who manage to acquire it, as well as those who don't.

The sharply imagined contrasts between "primitive" and "civilized" cultures and people claim a vexed history, most of which lies outside the range of our discussion. And while the terms themselves do not figure explicitly in contemporary literacy studies theory, the spirit of this dichotomy, so prominent in the 20th-century debates shaping the field of modern social anthropology, nevertheless persists. Historically, the primitive/ civilized dichotomy has served as a kind of disciplinary dividing line between anthropology and sociology. And while both disciplines emerged in the mid-19th century and each is centrally concerned with the study of human social behavior, the two fields importantly differ with regard to their analytical focus: Anthropologists study "primitive" societies, and sociologists study "advanced" or "civilized" ones.[3] Moreover, primary modes of communication always have figured in the division between "primitive" and "civilized" cultures, as well. Primitive cultures—the province of anthropology—are typically characterized as often isolated and usually small, homogeneous and highly personalized groups of people, where social relations are regulated by face-to-face encounters and group solidarity relies on oral traditions and storytelling. In contrast, civilized cultures—the province of sociology—are generally defined as large, urban groupings of diverse populations, where social relations tend to be more impersonal and where literacy, technology, and cultural pursuits in the arts and sciences flourish.

No matter how well drawn, disciplinary boundaries are never quite as stable as we might imagine. Throughout the 20th century, a number of researchers working within and across the fields of cultural and social anthropology, ethnography, sociology, and linguistics challenged what they rightly viewed as an ethnocentric bias underwriting the strict separation between primitive and civilized societies, which had, in turn, fostered all kinds of misperceptions about the "primitive mind."[4] In particular, these researchers refuted the grand assumption that "primitive" people were ipso facto "mystical and prelogical" beings (Levi-Bruhl cited in Gee, 1996, p. 47), steeped in myth and doxa, without a sense of history or, worse, incapable of "abstract" thought. Their refutation brought significant pressure to bear on the primitive/civilized dichotomy that had traditionally separated the methodologies and interests of anthropologists

and sociologists. The result was a noticeable blurring of these disciplinary boundaries, setting the stage for what we call the "social turn" in literacy research and theory—that is, the examination of literacy as a social act that occurs within social situations—a subject we will return to later in this chapter.

Despite its weakened theoretical currency, the primitive/civilized dichotomy is resurrected in Goody and Watt's (1963/1988) essay, although its force is somewhat couched by their new emphasis on literacy. They acknowledge that the field

> can no longer accept the view that anthropologists have as their objective the study of primitive man, who is characterized by a "primitive mind," while sociologists, on the other hand, concern themselves with civilized man, whose activities are guided by "rational thought." (p. 4)

They, nevertheless, reject the collapse of the primitive/civilized dichotomy as a foregone conclusion. Instead, their arguments for the unrivaled achievements of classical Greece will work to recast the primitive/civilized dichotomy in new and, to some, more palatable terms: orality versus literacy. In effect, the new orality/literacy dichotomy will enact a "collapse" of its own, one where all cultural, political, historical, and ideological distinctions between "traditional" (read primitive) and "modern" (read civilized) societies can be retheorized as accruing to just one essential, and essentializing, difference—the widespread acquisition and use of written literacy.

A STUPEFYING LEAP: THE SIGNIFICANCE OF GREEK LITERACY FOR THE MODERN ERA

The notion of representing a sound by a graphic symbol is itself so stupefying a leap of the imagination that what is remarkable is not so much that it happened relatively late in human history, but rather that it ever happened at all.

—Jack Goody and Ian Watt
(1963/1988, p. 9)

The desire to express ideas in graphic form is arguably as old as humankind itself. Prehistoric cave paintings, the pictographs of the ancient Plains Indians, Egyptian hieroglyphics, and Chinese logograms all predate, however, the period that most interests the Great Divide theorists—roughly, from 1500 to 1000 BCE, when the Near Eastern syllabaries were developed, to 5th-century BCE Greece, when the final version of the alphabet was adopted for official use in Athens. Deemed "too clumsy and complicated to foster widespread literacy" by Goody and Watt (1963/1988, p. 7), all these earlier and non-Western writing systems were dismissed as either "protoliterate" or, worse, "oligoliterate," a judgment that not only evinces an ethnocentric bias but also suggests that what we're calling the "human desire to express ideas in graphic form" and what actually "counts" as literacy for the Great Divide theorists are not one and the same.[5]

According to the Great Divide theorists, "true" writing systems—the sort that will lead to widespread or "popular" literacy—are those that include phonetic devices, that is, systems where speech sounds are represented by graphic symbols. And while the Great Divide theorists generally considered the Near Eastern syllabaries, which use written characters to represent spoken syllables, an improvement over the older logographic writing systems, which use characters or signs to represent words or ideas, it was the Greeks' invention of a fully phonetic script—an alphabet—that would come to be seen as their greatest achievement.

In "The Coming of Literate Communication to Western Culture," Eric Havelock (1988) notes that the "problem with [syllabaries] was

that the sounds symbolized were the possible syllables of words, not the components of the syllables" (p. 129). And it was this oversight—the need to graphically represent the individual components of a syllable, which when combined produce a particular speech sound—that the Greeks rightly anticipated in their creation of an alphabet. Unlike the existing syllabaries (i.e., indices that assigned a single symbol to sets of syllables arranged according to their initial consonants but lacked adequate symbolization of vowels), the Greek alphabet included symbols for consonants and, for the first time, symbols for all five vowels. The result was a writing system that proved to be more accurate and more economical than the previous syllabaries; for, by adding the five vowels, the Greek alphabet actually worked to reduce the overall number of graphic signs necessary for the adequate—and more accurate—symbolization of speech sounds (i.e., syllables as they are pronounced). This unprecedented act of intellectual ingenuity is the "stupefying leap of the imagination" to which Goody and Watt (1963/1988) refer in the epigraph above. The reduction in the number of symbols needed to accurately transcribe speech into writing meant that it could be more easily taught, acquired, and used by the majority of people in a society. In this way, the Greek invention of the alphabet created the possibility of a popular literacy, an *autonomous* mode of communication based on a set of discrete skills, easily taught and highly transferable to any number of contexts by any number of people.

The invention of alphabetic script surely stands as a significant event in the ancient world, and just as surely holds implications for the development of traditions, values, and sociopolitical institutions characteristically associated with Western cultures.[6] Whether or not the advent of alphabetic literacy actually provoked fundamental changes in the way people think—that is, literacy as a kind of psychological precondition for intellectual "progress," especially the development of higher-order reasoning skills—is another matter altogether. Critics of the Great Divide theorists have endeavored to point out that their jointly held expectations for the social and cognitive consequences of literacy not only derive from a shared perspective on the nature and function of language in society but also imply a mutual ideological investment in the superiority of written communication over and above any other mode of communication.[7]

The guiding premise that language, in any mode, is the most direct and comprehensive expression of any group's collective cultural experience—or what Goody and Watt (1963/1988) call the *Weltanschauung* of a society—sets the basic terms for the Great Divide model of literacy.[8] The overarching claim, in essence, boils down to just this: Writing—as a permanent and portable record of a society's *Weltanschauung*—facilitates and ensures the reliable transmission of a group's cultural heritage across time and space, something that a nonliterate or primarily oral society, whose cultural heritage is presumably held in memory, simply cannot do as well. The theory underpinning this broad claim suggests that the very act of writing—physically setting words to page, separating them from the context in which they were written and thus making them available to be read and reread, interpreted and re-interpreted by any other literate person—establishes a different kind of relationship between a word and its referent than can obtain in oral communication, one that is "more general and more abstract, and less closely connected with the particularities of person, place and time" (p. 13)—that is, a linguistic environment where words can accumulate "successive layers of historically validated meanings" (p. 5).

In contrast, primary orality "makes for a directness of relationship between symbol and referent," which, in turn, creates a linguistic environment where words cannot accumulate these "successive layers of historically validated

meanings" over time because oral communication is constrained by the "concrete" or present situation—that is, the verbal exchange as it is happening, where meaning is "particularized both in specific denotation and in accepted connotative usages" (Goody & Watt, 1963/1988, p. 5). In other words, oral communication is inextricably bound to time and place: It cannot operate "autonomously" and thus does not encourage the sort of generalizable, "abstract" thinking written literacy provokes. Unable to transcend the circumstances of its own production/reception, orality relegates the inhabitants of nonliterate cultures to a life circumscribed by the concrete, the particular, or, as Oswald Spengler puts it, the "tyranny of the present" (cited in Goody & Watt, 1963/1988, p. 7). Thus, whereas logic, objectivity, skepticism, and a kind of historical consciousness are understood as uniformly accruing to individuals in societies that have managed to successfully acquire literacy, such cognitive consequences are theorized as patently unavailable to those living in primarily oral cultures. In these ways, the aptly named Great Divide theory not only defines the differences between literate and nonliterate societies but also concomitantly defines the very people who populate these two disparate worlds—the literate and the "illiterate," a critical and, for many, especially dangerous outcome of our belief in and expectations for the so-called consequences of literacy.

Whether or not Goody and Watt (1963/1988) foresaw the ways their 1963 inquiry into the "traditional dichotomy" between oral and literate societies would influence successive generations of researchers, their claims about the causal connections between the advent of writing and the rise and influence of Western culture have served as a primary source for contemporary theories on literacy, both in its role as a sociopolitical "good" and in its definition as a set of discrete—and therefore measurable—skills. Of the various legacies left behind by the "grand narrative" of the Great Divide, the autonomous view of literacy is arguably the most prominent, yet dominating the landscape of educational policy making, perhaps most visibly in the recent implementation of "high-stakes" testing practices. And while later 20th-century historical and ethnographic studies put into serious question the notion that literacy can in any way be separated from the various social, institutional, and/or ideological ends it serves (Clanchy, 1979; Cressy, 1980; Graff, 1979, 1987; Scollon & Scollon, 1981; Scribner & Cole, 1981; Street, 1984), undermining the authority of the autonomous view of literacy remains a central challenge for today's researchers and teachers.

CROSSING THE GREAT DIVIDE: LITERACY AS A RHETORICAL ACT

While the Great Divide has functioned as one grand narrative of literacy, another grand narrative of literacy has followed the "social turn" made in many of the human sciences, a shift that foregrounds the social construction of knowledge, situates individual subjectivity within broader social contexts and actions, and opens truth and knowledge to interpretation. Work by scholars such as Harvey Graff, Paulo Freire, Brian Street, Shirley Brice Heath, and the aforementioned Roz Ivanic has had significant influence in subsequent studies on the teaching of literacy. The social turn in the study of literacy has helped us understand more explicitly that literate practices, such as reading and writing, are culturally shaped social practices and not merely sets of discrete and transferable skills that can be either acquired or employed in isolation. In other words, literacy is by its very nature embedded in context(s), to include not only the actual concrete settings wherein "literate" communicative exchanges occur but also the individuals' social relationships and purposes as well as the (often) competing values, norms, and

conventions of language use circulating in a given society and its institutions.

Regarded as a social practice, then, literacy has been recast productively as an individual's ways of using written language. Stressing its contextualized nature, Ivanic (1998) argues that "literacy (in the sense of 'using written language') serves some specific social purpose: it is used in order to respond to some particular life demand, not practised for its own sake" (p. 61). The importance of Ivanic's reformulation should not be overlooked, for it not only acknowledges that literacy is an always situated practice (i.e., purposeful, aimed, and responsive to perceived exigencies) but also presumes that the individual language user, as a social being likewise situated within culture, is an always "knowing subject" (i.e., an agent), putting his or her literacy into action toward specific ends. This revised perspective on literacy is a decidedly rhetorical one that informs much of contemporary literacy research and theory.

LITERACY'S SOCIAL TURN: HISTORIES, POLITICS, AND PRACTICES

In his examination of literacy within and across historical periods in Western society, Harvey Graff has focused on how literacy has been used in the interests of Western culture and society and its consequences. Unlike Goody and Watt or Havelock, who extol the virtues of literacy in the building of Western society and culture, Graff offers a more critical and sometimes skeptical view of the benefits of literacy. He argues that the "literacy myth" (1979) and the "legacies of literacy" (1987) have often promised more than literacy itself can deliver, whether it is a belief that there is an objective, quantifiable standard of literacy that can be measured and used unproblematically to compare individuals or groups; a direct connection between literacy and material, political, or moral capital; or a growing belief in multiple literacies as a way to describe more accurately the uses and meanings of literacy (1995, pp. 320–321). To examine the myths and legacies of literacy, Graff (1995) turns to the history of literacy because "historical interpretation offers potentially innovative approaches . . . to reforming questions and problems, understanding, criticism, and alternative conceptualizations and perspectives" (p. 320).

Graff's historical narrative provides a useful long view of the ways literacy has functioned in Western society. Rather than placing literacy in the province of individuals or viewing literacy as a mark of social development for groups, Graff's work allows for a structural analysis of the uses of literacy in historical contexts, from the uses of the Sumerian syllabary through the modernity of the late 20th century. This broad historical scope has allowed Graff to search for "continuities and contradictions" in the history of literacy, creating more complex and nuanced understandings of literacy by looking beyond its promise and examining how literacy is more often a concomitant of social and individual change than it is the origin of such change. However, his own grand historical narrative perhaps is subject to question as well for its institutionalization as a counternarrative to Great Divide theories about literacy, illustrating the point made by Ellen Cushman and colleagues in their introduction to *Literacy: A Critical Sourcebook* (2001) that "recent scholars have become increasingly suspicious of comprehensive historical narratives," moving to studies that focus on specific and diverse literacy practices (p. 7).

If Graff has provided a grand sociohistorical, critical narrative that historicizes literacy and its meanings and values within specific contexts, Paulo Freire has provided a grand political narrative of the emancipatory power of literacy. Freire's *Pedagogy of the Oppressed* (1970) has served as both an important theoretical and a political text. His conceptualization of critical literacy and pedagogy as a means for liberating people from economic and political oppression has helped shape research and pedagogical practice. His Marxist analysis of systems of education as a means of reinforcing particular social relations to support the State cast literacy and its promulgation as ideological and politically interested and no longer neutral or unquestionably positive. This analysis combined with liberation theology resulted in a theorization of pedagogy to empower those who have been disempowered systematically.

When Freire (1970) suggests that the "oppressed" are not "marginal" because they are *already* located in a dominant culture, he looks to activate an agency of the oppressed, or for our purposes to resituate the rhetor. The oppressed are already potentially active members of the community, capable of doing cultural work, although this work may take different forms and represent diverse interests. The challenge, then, is to overcome the various systems of oppression that have maintained marginalized subjects and to dismantle those structures that act to keep cultural control either through simple dominance or through the more subtle hegemonic acts of educational and cultural production. For Freire, the way to do this is to acquire critical literacy, take control of one's own education, and, to borrow an Aristotelean concept, find the available means of persuasion. While aspects of Freire's liberatory pedagogy are problematic because it perhaps maintains a binary of "oppressed" and "liberated" and suggests that acquisition of literacy (even if a critical literacy) may be enough to be transformative, his move to have the oppressed become "beings for themselves" is an attractive alternative narrative of development and achievement. The oppressed not only lift themselves up from oppression but also determine their own course of action and, perhaps most important, determine their own identities not simply located in the dominant culture, or in opposition to it, but as continually being constructed in the conflicts, as Gerald Graff (1992) might describe it.

While Freire's (1970) work uses literacy as a means for political action and offers an important theoretical model of literacy and its purposes, Brian Street (1995) provides a framework in his theoretical models of literacy that describes ideological forces that shape specific beliefs about and purposes for literacy. Moving away from a strong text or autonomous model of literacy that privileges the decoding of texts as an unbiased, cognitive action outside the social context, Street offers an ideological model of literacy that views literacy as embedded within cultural and power structures that affect the ways literacy is perceived and used. For Street, literacy, or more precisely literacy practices, "refers to both behaviour and the social and cultural conceptualizations that give meaning to the uses of reading and/or writing" (p. 2).

An "autonomous" model of literacy, Street (1993) argues, conceptualizes literacy "in technical terms, treating it as independent of social context, an autonomous variable whose consequences for society and cognition can be derived from its intrinsic character" (p. 5). In comparison, an "ideological" model of literacy is an approach that "signals quite explicitly that literacy practices are aspects not only of 'culture' but also of power structures" (p. 7). In addition to providing a method for the structural analysis of literacy practices, what makes Street's focus on ideology and literacy practices especially useful is the attention to specific contexts and the forces that shape these contexts. By turning to specific contexts and the actions within these contexts, the "little narratives" of literacy increasingly became the subjects of studies about literacy, especially as told through ethnography, narrative, and story in a variety of media.

While ethnographic studies of literacy in the early 1980s (e.g., Scribner & Cole, 1981) began to move away from the totalizing narratives of cognitive and social development that characterized the work of Goody and Watt and others to examining language and literacy

practices in specific contexts, it was work by Shirley Brice Heath that highlighted the ways culture and community inform the development and adaptation of these practices by individuals and communities. The significance of Heath's *Ways With Words* (1983) is its focus on the literacy practices of two rural communities within the contexts of these two communities rather than in comparison with some abstraction of literacy and levels of educational achievement. Heath argues that the purposes and forms of literacy can look very different from what we commonly expect in the various uses emphasized and privileged in school (i.e., essayist, literary, critical, or informational). The rich texture of a study like Heath's provides depth to studies about literacy, which is often lost when grand conclusions about the consequences and power of literacy become more significant than understanding actual practices.

Building on the work of Graff, Freire, Street, and Heath, recent studies of literacy have continued in the vein of the social turn but have been formulated as "little narratives," studies that have clearly defined social and historical contexts and seek to examine the uses of literacy by specific groups for specific purposes. For example, work by Anne Haas Dyson is especially useful in rethinking the grand narratives of literacy and illustrating the complex uses and practices of literacy as she examines children's literacy practices within the spaces of the classroom but looks broadly at how these literacy practices cross between school and larger social and cultural networks. In *Writing Superheroes: Contemporary Childhood, Popular Culture, and Classroom Literacy* (1997) and *The Brothers and Sisters Learn to Write: Popular Literacies in Childhood and School Cultures* (2003), Dyson examines how children use the tools of literacy (reading and writing), the dynamics of culture, and the power of their imaginations to create stories, negotiate meaning, and provide opportunities for expression. Other little narratives broaden a complex understanding of social relations whether across larger communities, social organizations, or even racial and cultural groups. In *Literacy in American Lives* (2001), Deborah Brandt documents and analyzes how a cross-section of Wisconsin residents have defined, used, and reshaped the meaning of literacy. Through the development of the concepts "sponsors of literacy" and the "accumulation" of literacy, Brandt illustrates how these "ordinary" Americans come to acquire and put to use reading and writing, as well as accumulate literacy as a resource that they can draw on. In *Intimate Practices: Literacy and Cultural Work in U.S. Women's Clubs, 1880–1920* (1997), Anne Ruggles Gere examines women's clubs of the late 19th through early 20th centuries, arguing that important cultural work through reading and writing took place. Whether it was taking up the political issues of the day or considering matters that were closer to home, Gere argues that women of diverse backgrounds did use literacy for multiple purposes in extracurricular contexts and not simply as extensions of schooled literacy or for personal matters. In *Traces of a Stream: Literacy and Social Change Among African American Women* (2000), Jacquelyn Jones Royster focuses on the literacy and rhetorical practices of 19th-century African American women. However, in unpacking and examining these practices and histories, Royster also theorizes and unpacks her own ideologies, examining the complex matrix of race, gender, and culture and the histories that have shaped her own position as scholar and teacher.

What we see in the emerging little narratives of literacy are emergent scholarly practices, theorizing, and analysis that complicate the grand narratives of literacy, which often still structure the discourses and beliefs about literacy in our culture. These are just a few of the growing number of studies about literacy that have sought to examine literacy in its multidimensional contexts as opposed to understanding literacy as a standard that can be used to measure differences among individuals, groups, and/or whole cultures.

LITERACY OR LITERACY IN ENGLISH?

Studies of literacy have often been conducted in specific cultural and cross-cultural contexts, examining how literacy functions within both monolingual and multilingual settings. Work by Marcia Farr (1994), Juan Guerra (1998), and Ralph Cintron (1997) examines literacy in transnational Latino communities, while Elaine Richardson (2003), Keith Gilyard (1991, 1996), and Geneva Smitherman (1986, 2000) have studied literacy and language practices in African American communities. Despite these and other studies of literacy in multiple contexts, literacy in the U.S. context often has been conflated with Standard English and attendant constructions of culture. While literacy itself is already a complex process and practice, it becomes even more so when placed in the context of bilingual education, ESL education, or even language immersion programs whether for English, French, or Hawaiian. What we find in these negotiations between native and nonnative languages are also negotiations between primary and secondary discourses. As Gee (1996) has argued, literacy is "mastery of, or fluent control over, a secondary Discourse," and those seeking to acquire literacy in a second language are also in the process of acquiring literacy in their primary language (p. 153). Thus, critiques of bilingual education, for example, are not necessarily accounting for the process of literacy acquisition but rather conflate learning English with learning literacy.

Thus, in the United States, being literate often assumes or insists on literacy in English, though the history of the United States shows that this has not always been the case. For example, French- and German-language education was encouraged during the early days of the republic, the status of Spanish as an important language was recognized in varying degrees across the Southwest and California, and the 1917 Immigration Act required literacy in any language more as a bar to the "feeble minded" than as a bar to non-English speakers. However, despite these acknowledgements of a multilingual heritage, throughout the history of the United States there has also been a conflation of literacy, English, and culture, whether it has been a proposal for an English-language academy by John Adams or Noah Webster's appeal for "establishing a national language, and of giving it uniformity and perspicuity" (Webster, 1992, p. 36). The Americanization movement of the early 20th century, which advocated for English, became "a mask for racial, economic, and political hostility toward users of other tongues" and "transform[ed] language from a shield against linguistic chaos into a sword against supposed *nonlinguistic* differences as well—even when those supposed differences were arguably beyond the reach of legitimate public debate" (Leibowicz, 1992, p. 107).

While present-day discussions about literacy are perhaps not as violent or inflammatory as the era described by Leibowicz (1992), we still see discussions about literacy easily become proxies for English-only campaigns or for discourses that challenge the validity of bilingual and second-language education or the validity and value of alternative discourses. As we have discussed earlier in this chapter, the social meanings attached to literacy are ideologically loaded and often yoke together issues of social difference with literacy levels. This perhaps becomes most apparent when literacy in English becomes a primary focus in arguments about English as the official or national language, the efficacy of bilingual education, or even the incorporation of nonstandard or alternative forms of language such as Ebonics or Hawai'i Creole and Pidgin as a pedagogical practice for learning standard English. Implied in these arguments that attempt to impose a particular meaning of

literacy and resist alternative meanings and practices are larger concerns and anxieties about the implications and consequences of a reconceptualized idea of literacy. In many ways, our discussions about literacy or language have become discussions about citizenship, race and ethnicity, social class, and other categories of social difference. As Geoffrey Nunberg (1992) argues,

> Even if the official-language movement is really an "official-culture movement," it could not have been formulated in such terms. . . . It is only when the issues are cast in terms of language that they become amenable to direct political action, and that culture can be made an official component of American identity. (p. 494)

Nunberg's analysis is especially apt given the growing global pressures that have focused attention on the United States and its relationship to the rest of the world. While globalization, geopolitical tensions, and a now constant discourse on war and terrorism have made the world a seemingly smaller place, this also has renewed cultural anxiety within the United States as it continues to stave off "threats" from outside its borders and hold on to a sense of itself within its border.

Of course, the effects of globalization cuts both ways, and as a global language, English is increasingly reaching across the rest of the world. The tensions of global English in this context are focused, then, on the ideological power of the prestige varieties of English— British and American, or, to use A. Suresh Canagarajah's term, *Metropolitan Englishes*— against World Englishes, those varieties that may reflect local and specific purposes but are also a standardized English (Canagarajah, 2006, pp. 588–589). What we see in this case is a challenge to the metropole from the periphery in the metropole's own language, further complicating the question of literacy and confirming that literacy has often been used as a synecdoche for identity (whether racial, cultural, social, or gender).

Notable scholars such as Horner and Trimbur (2002) and Canagarajah (2006) have begun the important work of deterritorializing literacy by historicizing literacy practices and policies and by examining, for example, the development of U.S. composition programs that have reinforced academic literacy in English and created a "tacit language policy of unidirectional English monolingualism" that remains underexamined (Horner & Trimbur, 2002, p. 594). As Trimbur (2006) points out, writing studies has traditionally asked "how cross-language relations inhibit or facilitate students' mastery of academic literacy in English" (p. 586). However, for Trimbur, this question needs to be reformulated to ask "how such available linguistic resources can be tapped to promote biliteracy and multilingualism," and to imagine English as the "linking language in multilingual writing programs, multilingual universities, and a multilingual polity" (p. 586). As a way to enact this practice of drawing on linguistic resources, Canagarajah (2006) argues for the pluralizing of academic discourse through varieties of English, genres, and forms, even to the "'deep structure' of grammar" (p. 613). What we see in the deterritorializing of literacy is a continued examination and unpacking of a grand narrative that has constructed literacy as a state of being (whether by anointment or practice) that is equated with power. In the case of bilingualism or multilingualism in the U.S. context, the prestige of Metropolitan English will still insist that literacy be an enterprise undertaken in English despite the educational levels of speakers and writers of other languages that would define them as "literate."

RHETORIC AND LITERACY: PEDAGOGICAL IMPLICATIONS AND TENSIONS

While many of the researchers and theorists we have discussed thus far have examined literacy in a variety of social and cultural contexts, perhaps the study of literacy and the implications for literacy have been most overdetermined in the context of schooling. For obvious reasons, the classroom has become an important site for both examining and applying theories of literacy. However, just as we have seen tensions in different theories and beliefs about literacy in broader social contexts, we see these tensions played out in educational settings and practices as well.

For some, the classroom has been constructed too often as a site for ideological reproduction: Students are trained in standard academic discourses; they deploy these discourses as part of required practice; they become participants in a community, often reproducing the practices of that community. The call by E. D. Hirsch (1987), Allan Bloom (1987), and William Bennett (1988) in the 1980s to "return" to a romantic conception of education as the discovery of Truth and Knowledge is explicit in its belief that there is a core body of knowledge that separates the literate from the illiterate; Truth and Knowledge necessarily connote a single cultural standard. Sometimes even "progressive" practices within educational institutions that allow for change in curriculum and pedagogy provide only an appearance of educational reform. As C. H. Knoblauch (1990) argues, educational and social reproduction is still present when we locate reform in "personal growth" and "American citizens will accommodate some liberalization of outmoded curricula and an improved quality of life for the less privileged as long as the fundamental political and economic interests are not jeopardized" (p. 78).

One way to ensure that students meet the cultural requirements and language standards of the nation is to install standardized tests of literacy, and this practice claims a long and troubling history in the United States. From the turn of the 20th century, when Second Wave immigrants faced deportation on account of their "illiteracy," to midcentury, when African Americans had to prove their literacy before casting a vote, to today's classrooms, where a single test determines whether or not a student will receive a high school diploma, the conceptual and material connections between acquiring the rights and privileges of citizenship and proving that one is literate are deeply forged. At the heart of these connections is the selfsame expectation for literacy promulgated by the Great Divide theorists—namely, that the fate and course of any society depend on the kind and level of literacy its citizenry achieves. That literacy is believed to be a sociopolitical necessity is made clear in the National Commission on Excellence in Education's (1983) pronounce-ment that the rising rates of "illiteracy" were putting the nation "at risk." And the idea that the nation's literacy is "in crisis" yet circulates powerfully today, resonant in the legislative action that installs "high-stakes" testing practices in an effort to allay the public fear that failing public schools are leaving our children behind. Perhaps unsurprisingly, the "autonomous" model of literacy, though compellingly critiqued in the scholarship, is the model of choice for the newly fashioned standardized tests. Literacy yet imagined as disconnected from its contexts, as without rhetorical purpose or constraint, as something transparently acquired and simply put into practice is, by and large, the kind of precept guiding the recent resurgence of the Standards Movement.

Moreover, there still remains much resistance to conceptualizing literacy as a situated social practice, especially within the context of schooling and testing. Curricular movements to understand and teach literacy as a social practice have come under attack often for being too contextually bound, ignoring specific standards, and lacking content. For example, the Whole Language Movement has been criticized for the use of invented spelling and emphasis on text production, which seem unrelated to conventional or traditional reading comprehension exercises or decontextualized worksheets. When the International Reading Association (IRA) and the National Council of Teachers of English (NCTE) issued their "Standards for the English Language Arts" in 1996, the document received much criticism for outlining a range of abilities, experiences, and genres of texts that students from kindergarten through Grade 12 should engage rather than naming specific content knowledge and "standardized" skill levels that can be used to benchmark students and educational systems against each other despite what may be very different communities with very different needs. While the NCTE and IRA argued that their guidelines allowed for individual communities to determine and implement the criteria and content appropriate for their state- and district-mandated standards, the public criticism of this document reflects the continued conflict between the Great Divide and the social turn in conceptualizing literacy.

What is often misunderstood about conceptualizing literacy as a social practice is that it is not a rejection or a dismissal of "knowledge" or "skills." Rather, this conce-ptualization recognizes social relationships and the ways literacy and language function for individuals and groups: to construct themselves, to construct culture, and to situate themselves within this culture. Literacy in this sense is rhetorical and requires the recon-ceptualization of those spaces where literacy takes place, whether the classroom, the workplace, or the home. To think of literacy in this sense is to recognize what Mary Louise Pratt (1991) has called a "contact zone," those "social spaces where cultures meet, clash, and grapple with each other" (p. 34).

As Jack Goody and Ian Watt (1963/1988) argued more than 40 years ago, the con-sequences of literacy have been great in the development of society. However, the question of exactly what those consequences are, and for whom they have had the most benefit, remains a complicated issue. What is clear, however, is that the rhetoric of literacy has been used to construct and define individuals and communities. In some instances, literacy has functioned to divide people, to mark difference as a way to acquire and sustain cultural capital. In other instances, literacy has been used by people to challenge those in power, whether to install political change, to question the imposition of others' beliefs, or to recognize the value of alternative practices. But in all these contexts, literacy provides a means of social interaction and allows for the available means of persuasion to be called upon in the hope of creating conversation.

NOTES

1. For Goody and Watt (1963/1988), the term *alphabetic literacy* means a writing system based exclusively and systematically on phonetic principles, which can be easily taught and learned, and thus used by a majority of people in a given society.

2. David R. Olson is also often included in this set of theorists. Olson's "From Utterance to Text" (1977) is frequently cited in contemporary literacy scholarship.

3. Anthropology emerged alongside other "new" sciences of the period, including biology, linguistics, psychology, and archaeology. Sociology developed into an independent disciplinary endeavor when the concept of "society" was divested of its strict connections with the State, a shift urged by theorists such as Auguste Comte, Herbert Spencer, and Karl Marx and further refined by philosophers such as Émile Durkheim and Max Weber.

4. Among this cohort of researchers are Margaret Mead (*Coming of Age in Samoa*, 1928); Ruth Benedict (*Patterns of Culture*, 1934/1959); E. E. Evans-Pritchard (*Witchcraft, Oracles and Magic Amongst the Azande*, 1937); Edward Sapir (*Language: An Introduction to the Study of Speech*, 1921); and Claude Levi-Strauss (*Tristes Tropiques*, 1955/1975; *The Savage Mind*, 1966).

5. Goody and Watt (1963/1988) use the descriptors *protoliterate* and *oligoliterate* to highlight what they judged as the socially restrictive nature of these earlier writing systems. The authors reason that

in Chinese writing, a minimum of three thousand characters have to be learned before one can be reasonably literate, and with a repertoire of some fifty thousand characters to be mastered, it normally takes about twenty years to reach full literate proficiency. China, therefore, stands as an extreme example of how, when a virtually nonphonetic system of writing becomes sufficiently developed to express a large number of meanings explicitly, only a small and specifically trained professional group in the total society can master it, and partake of the literate culture. (p. 8)

Conversely, Goody and Watt regard the alphabet as a "democratic script" (p. 10) for its ability to promote widespread or "popular" literacy.

6. More than merely coterminus events, Goody and Watt (1963/1988) theorize a causal relationship between the advent of alphabetic literacy and the social and political advancements of classical Greece reasoning:

The fact that the essential basis both of writing systems and many characteristic cultural institutions of the Western tradition as a whole derived from Greece, and that they both arose there simultaneously, seem[s] to justify the present attempt to outline the possible relationships between the writing system and those cultural innovations of early Greece which are common to all alphabetically literate societies. (p. 12)

7. See especially David Barton (1994), Scribner and Cole (1981), and Street (1984).

8. Goody and Watt (1963/1988) borrow the term *Weltanschauung* from Durkheim; loosely defined, the Weltanschauung of any cultural group includes their customary behaviors, generalized goals and aspirations, and authorized forms of knowledge.

REFERENCES

Barton, D. (1994). *Literacy: An introduction to the ecology of written language*. Oxford, UK: Blackwell.

Benedict, R. (1959). *Patterns of culture*. Boston: Houghton Mifflin. (Original work published 1934)

Bennett, W. J. (1988). *Our children and our country: Improving America's schools and affirming the common culture*. New York: Simon & Schuster.

Bloom, A. (1987). *The closing of the American mind*. New York: Simon & Schuster.

Brandt, D. (2001). *Literacy in American lives*. Cambridge, UK: Cambridge University Press.

Canagarajah, A. S. (2006). The place of world Englishes in composition: Pluralization continued. *College Composition and Communication, 57*(4), 586–619.

Cintron, R. (1997). *Angel's town: Chero ways, gang life, and rhetorics of the everyday*. Boston: Beacon Press.

Clanchy, M. T. (1979). *From memory to written record*. Oxford, UK: Blackwell.

Crawford, J. (Ed.). (1992). *Language loyalties: A sourcebook on the official English controversy*. Chicago: University of Chicago Press.

Cressy, D. (1980). *Literacy and the social order: Reading and writing in Tudor and Stuart England*. Cambridge, UK: Cambridge University Press.

Cushman, E. (1998). *The struggle and the tools: Oral and literate strategies in an inner-city community*. Albany: State University of New York Press.

Cushman, E., Kintgen, R. Kroll, B. M., & Rose, M. (Eds.). (2001). *Literacy: A critical sourcebook*. Boston: Bedford.

Daniell, B. (1999). Narratives of literacy: Connecting composition to culture. *College Composition and Communication, 50*(2), 393–410.

Duffy, J. (2004). Letters from the Fair City: A rhetorical conception of literacy. *College Composition and Communication, 56*(2), 223–250.

Dyson, A. H. (1997). *Writing superheroes: Contemporary childhood, popular culture, and classroom literacy*. New York: Teachers College Press.

Dyson, A. H. (2003). *The brothers and sisters learn to write: Popular literacies in childhood and school cultures*. New York: Teachers College Press.

Evans-Pritchard, E. E. (1937). *Witchcraft, oracles and magic amongst the Azande*. Oxford, UK: Clarendon Press.

Farr, M. (1994). En Los Dos Idiomas: Literacy practices among Chicago Mexicanos. In Moss, B. (Ed.), *Literacy across communities* (pp. 9–47). Cresskill, NJ: Hampton Press.

Freire, P. (1970). *Pedagogy of the oppressed* (M. Bergman Ramos, Trans.). New York: Continuum.

Gee, J. P. (1996). *Social linguistics and literacies: Ideology in discourses* (2nd ed.). London: Falmer Press.

Gere, A. R. (1997). *Intimate practices: Literacy and cultural work in U.S. women's clubs, 1880–1920*. Urbana: University of Illinois Press.

Gilyard, K. (1991). *Voices of the self: A study of language competence*. Detroit, MI: Wayne State University Press.

Gilyard, K. (1996). *Let's flip the script: An African American discourse on language, literature, and learning*. Detroit, MI: Wayne State University Press.

Goody, J., & Watt, I. P. (1988). The consequences of literacy. In E. Kintgen, B. M. Kroll, & M. Rose (Eds.), *Perspectives on literacy* (pp. 3–27). Carbondale: Southern Illinois University Press. (Original work published 1963)

Graff, G. (1992). *Beyond the culture wars: How teaching the conflicts can revitalize American education*. New York: W. W. Norton.

Graff, H. (1979). *The literacy myth: Literacy and social structure in the nineteenth-century city*. New York: Academic Press.

Graff, H. (1987). *The legacies of literacy: Continuities and contradictions in Western culture and society*. Bloomington: Indiana University Press.

Graff, H. (1995). *The labyrinths of literacy: Reflections on literacy past and present*. Pittsburgh, PA: University of Pittsburgh Press.

Guerra, J. C. (1998). *Close to home: Oral and literate practices in a transnational Mexicano community*. New York: Teachers College Press.

Havelock, E. (1976). *Origins of Western literacy*. Toronto, Ontario, Canada: Ontario Institute for Studies in Education.

Havelock, E. (1982). *The literate revolution in Greece and its cultural consequences*. Princeton, NJ: Princeton University Press.

Havelock, E. (1988). The coming of literate communication to Western culture. In E. Kintgen, B. M. Kroll, & M. Rose (Eds.), *Perspectives on literacy* (pp. 127–134). Carbondale: Southern Illinois University Press.

Heath, S. B. (1983). *Ways with words: Language, life, and work in communities and classrooms*. Cambridge, UK: Cambridge University Press.

Hirsch, E. D., Jr. (1987). *Cultural literacy: What every American needs to know.* New York: Vintage Books.

Horner, B., & Trimbur, J. (2002). English only and US college composition. *College Composition and Communication, 53*(4), 594–630.

Hull, G. (1993). Hearing other voices: A critical assessment of popular views on literacy and work. *Harvard Education Review, 63*(1), 21–49.

International Reading Association and National Council of Teachers of English. (1996). *Standards for the English language arts.* Urbana, IL: National Council of Teachers of English.

Ivanic, R. (1998). *Writing and identity: The discoursal construction of identity in academic writing.* Amsterdam: John Benjamins.

Knoblauch, C. H. (1990). Literacy and the politics of education. In A. A. Lunsford, H. Moglen, & J. Slevin (Eds.), *The right to literacy* (pp. 74–80). New York: Modern Language Association.

Leibowicz, J. (1992). Official English: Another Americanization campaign? In J. Crawford (Ed.), *Language loyalties: A sourcebook on the official English controversy* (pp. 101–111). Chicago: University of Chicago Press.

Levi-Strauss, C. (1966). *The savage mind.* Chicago: University of Chicago Press.

Levi-Strauss, C. (1975). *Tristes tropiques.* New York: Athenaeum. (Original work published 1955)

Mead, M. (1928). *Coming of age in Samoa.* New York: Morrow.

National Commission on Excellence in Education. (1983). *A nation at risk: The imperative for educational reform: A report to the Nation and the Secretary of Education, United States Department of Education.* Washington, DC: Government Printing Office.

No Child Left Behind Act of 2001, Pub. L. No. 107–110 (2001). Washington, DC: Government Printing Office.

Nunberg, G. (1992). Afterword: The official English movement: Reimagining America. In J. Crawford (Ed.), *Language loyalties: A sourcebook on the official English controversy* (pp. 479–494). Chicago: University of Chicago Press.

Olson, D. R. (1977). From utterance to text: The bias of language in speech and writing. *Harvard Education Review, 47*(3), 257–281.

Ong, W. J. (1982). *Orality and literacy: The technologizing of the word.* London: Methuen.

Pratt, M. L. (1991). Arts of the contact zone. *Profession, 91,* 33–40.

Richardson, E. (2003). *African American literacies.* New York: Routledge.

Rose, M. (1989). *Lives on the boundary.* New York: Penguin.

Royster, J. J. (2000). *Traces of a stream: Literacy and social change among African American women.* Pittsburgh, PA: University of Pittsburgh Press.

Sapir, E. (1921). *Language: An introduction to the study of speech.* San Diego, CA: Harcourt, Brace, Jovanovich.

Scollon, R., & Scollon, S. W. (1981). *Narrative, literacy, and face in interethnic communication.* Norwood, NJ: Ablex.

Scribner, S., & Cole, M. (1981). *The psychology of literacy.* Cambridge, MA: Harvard University Press.

Sheils, M. (1975, December 8). Why Johnny can't write. *Newsweek.*

Smitherman, G. (1986). *Talkin and testifyin: The language of black America.* Detroit, MI: Wayne State University Press.

Smitherman, G. (2000). *Talkin that talk: Language, culture, and education in African America.* New York: Routledge.

Street, B. V. (1984). *Literacy in theory and practice.* Cambridge, UK: Cambridge University Press.

Street, B. V. (1993). (Ed.). *Cross-cultural approaches to literacy.* Cambridge, UK: Cambridge University Press.

Street, B. V. (1995). *Social literacies: Critical approaches to literacy in development, ethnography, and education.* London: Longman.

Trimbur, J. (1991). Literacy and the discourse of crisis. In R. Bullock & J. Trimbur (Eds.), *The politics of writing instruction: Postsecondary* (pp. 277–295). Portsmouth, NH: Boynton/Cook.

Trimbur, J. (2006). Linguistic memory and the politics of U.S. English. *College English, 68*(6), 575–588.

Villanueva, V. (1993). *Bootstraps: From an American academic of color.* Urbana, IL: National Council of Teachers of English.

Webster, N. (1992). Declaration of linguistic independence. In J. Crawford (Ed.), *Language loyalties: A sourcebook on the official English controversy* (pp. 33–36). Chicago: University of Chicago Press.

19

Echoes From the Past

Learning How to Listen, Again

JOYCE IRENE MIDDLETON

When I tell you a story, do you see it, or do you just write it down?

—A Mayan storyteller

Walter Ong's little book, *Orality and Literacy: The Technologizing of the Word*, is usually the first title that most scholars in rhetoric and composition studies cite when asked to think about the meaning and significance of orality theory. First published in 1982 and translated into at least 11 languages, Ong's book has had enormous scholarly influence across disciplines. Despite or perhaps because of the extraordinary breadth of its scholarly influence, *Orality and Literacy* provoked a very strong opposition to some of its claims in the eighties, and rightfully so. The book's 25-year anniversary serves as a propitious moment for reexamining Ong's arguments on orality and literacy, especially in light of contemporary interdisciplinary scholarship that not only helps us reread historical texts but also challenges us to reconsider the power and range of orality theory in our time. This chapter reviews many of the defining issues, critical arguments, and debates since the publication of *Orality and Literacy*, but the greater part of my discussion puts recent interdisciplinary scholarship in a conversation about the implications of *orality, aurality, secondary orality,* and *changing literacies* in the early 21st century.

ORALITY THEORY AND
ITS EARLY RECEPTION

Many misreadings, misinterpretations, and misconceptions about orality theory are due, in part, to Ong's rather slippery use of seemingly interchangeable terms that very diverse audiences of readers interpret in various ways. For example, *orality* is not the opposite of *literacy*, and yet many debates about orality are rooted in oppositional values (e.g., Daniell, 1995; Farrell, 1983; Goody & Watt, 1968; Havelock, 1963, 1978; Ong, 1982; Street, 1995; see also Swearingen, 1986). In addition, orality was not "replaced" by literacy: Orality is permanent—we have always and will continue to always use human speech arts in our various forms of communication, even as we now witness changes in our personal and professional uses of alphabetic forms of literacy in a number of ways.

So what is orality, or as I choose to describe it, *orality theory?* In contemporary discussions, I describe orality theory as a form of composition that relies, essentially, on word-of-mouth transmission that is shaped or created for acoustic reception and retention. Obviously, this definition must shift and change in relation to a society's reliance on (and pleasure from) acoustics or the seduction of sound; consider, for example, that Shakespeare's audiences went to "hear" a play, not to see one, even though writing played a significant role in Renaissance society (Donawerth, 1984; Middleton, 2004); or consider how much speaking and the body were closely associated with rhetoric and systems of memory in the 18th century (Harrington, 2007); in addition, medieval reading habits of ancient texts were "profoundly oral . . . [the] oralization, which the ancients savored aesthetically, provided mnemonic compensation (through enhanced short-term aural recall) for the difficulty of gaining access to the meaning of unseparated text [*scriptura continua*]" (Saenger, 2005, p. 11). Ong describes a historical continuum

from primary orality to residual orality and then to secondary orality, a description that helps readers trace the relationships among alphabetic literacy, technology, and discourse. (I write about this important focus on technology, rhetoric, and language use when I discuss secondary orality, later in this chapter.)

My description and use of the term *orality* relies significantly on Eric Havelock's classical scholarship, especially *The Muse Learns to Write* (1986a). This book helped me understand many of the complex arguments about orality theory because Havelock relies only on written records of literary texts to make inferences about a Greek theory of primary orality; in fact, he carefully excludes any records that are attributed to Socrates because of his special focus on written documentation as evidence. (With this move, Havelock avoids the errors that many earlier critics and enthusiasts of orality theory have made, including Farrell's infamous *CCC* essay, "IQ and Standard English," 1983.) Importantly, Ong also introduces *Orality and Literacy* with a reference to this literary emphasis as the origin of debates about orality theory:

> The greatest awakening to the contrast between oral modes of thought and expression and written modes took place not in linguistics, descriptive or cultural, but in literary studies, beginning clearly with the work of Milman Parry (1902–35) on the text of the *Iliad* and the *Odyssey,* brought to completion after Parry's untimely death by Albert B. Lord, and supplemented by later work of Eric A. Havelock and others. (Ong, 1982, p. 6)

Then, Ong asks "why the [white, male, Western] scholarly world had to reawaken to the oral character of language" (p. 6), when, as Havelock reminds us, "[t]he history of European literature begins with the poems of Homer and Hesiod" (1986a, p. 19)—that is, with epic literature.

The modern Western bias for alphabetic literacy as a superior form of communication and storage of knowledge faced a major challenge from the early work on orality theory by Parry and Lord. In modern Euro-American studies, Homer's *Illiad* and *Odyssey* have been studied as "literature," for which writing is considered the basic form of language (Ong, 1982, p. 5). Orality theory helped Havelock reread Homer's work (and other early "oral" Greek texts) within its own historical Greek context, where Havelock discovered that the *Iliad* and the *Odyssey* were not works of "great literature" in their own time; instead, they were what Havelock (1978) called a "Homeric, versified, or oral encyclopedia," preserving the Greek *nomos* or cultural knowledge (p. 29).

But this early groundbreaking scholarship on orality theory provides a cautionary note to modern Euro-American historians about reading the ancient past, even a European past, through a contemporary lens with its various, associated, cultural ideologies and biases. In rhetoric studies, for instance, Kathleen E. Welch's "Who Made Aristotle White?" (2005) raises critically challenging questions about rhetoric, race, and reception histories. From a different but related point of view in "'Just Like Us': Cultural Constructions of Sexuality and Race in Roman Art," art historian John Clarke (2002) writes,

> If the Romans seem to be in all things so much like "us," it is because "we" [he describes "we" as the white, male elite of Euro-American culture, the dominant voice in traditional classical scholarship] have colonized their time in history. . . . We have appropriated their world to fit the needs of our ideology. (p. 13)

In an example of this kind of misreading that compares well with our thinking about orality theory, Clarke contrasts the ways traditional, contemporary scholars have interpreted an illustrated Roman wall painting of a bedroom as a "private space"—since "we associate a bedroom with sleeping and sexual

intimacy"—with the ways historical Romans of the period would have understood it. Clarke points out that the bedroom during this time was not about "'privacy'—a concept that does not exist in Roman language or thought—but about high status" (p. 15). Clarke's poignant observation about the psychological concept of privacy during this historical Roman period provides an insight into orality theory since, as Ong and others have argued, the concept of privacy increases with the evolution and interiority of literacy in Western culture.

As for our long history of interiorized, silent reading—reflecting on reading and thinking—in our own time, literary critic and editor Sven Birkerts (1994) in *The Gutenberg Elegies* asserts personal, knowledgeable, and pedagogical arguments that ask readers to consider how the eroding value of interiorized, alphabetic literacy will influence the future of reading as we have known it (though I wonder how a more racially diverse or multicultural representation of texts might inform his decisions about his canon of the most valuable reading, see Birkerts, 2007):

> Reading, because we control it, is adaptable to our needs and rhythms. We are free to indulge our subjective associative impulse; the term I coin for this is *deep reading*: the slow and meditative possession of a book. We don't just read the words, we dream our lives in their vicinity. (p. 146)

A critic of the shifting discourse values for reading, primarily because of the fast-paced influences of secondary orality and electronic technologies (contrasting with the slow pace of reading a book), Birkert's arguments parallel those of Alcibiades who also spoke against the powerful cultural momentum of the new technology of alphabetic literacy and writing that he saw as threatening the ancient Greek primary oral culture. Like the audiences and speakers who preceded us, we modern literates face an unknowable future for the role of books and alphabetic literacy in academic and critical thinking (Elbow, 1985; Fernandez, 2007). With regard to the alleged cultural erosion of reading (and writing), I often wonder about Ong's claim that a literate (reading) culture, compared with an oral culture, produces the huge expansive range of a culture's vocabulary (p. 107). As a teacher of rhetoric and writing, I ask myself whether our students' vocabularies will shrink or expand even more in our age of secondary orality.

LESSONS FROM ORALITY THEORY

Studying orality theory as a theory of literature gives contemporary scholars many advantages, and even Havelock (1986a) emphasizes that his reading of Greek orality relied on evidence from texts rather than on "loose speculation" (p. 4). Based on theoretical research of oral composition, Parry, Lord, Havelock, and later, Ong, make comparative inferences about the psychology and the social and ethical values of a Greek culture that created compositions in a language-to-be-heard (because there was no writing to review or to study) compared with later texts composed in a language-to-be-seen. Havelock confidently asserts that "acoustic laws of composition" may be observed in these ancient Greek, orally composed texts that reveal distinct syntactical and rhetorical differences from later texts that were composed after the Egyptians introduced alphabetic literacy (again, a new writing technology) to the Greek culture (p. 12).

The following linguistic features or behaviors have been clearly observed and defined in written records of orally composed texts designed for a listening audience—that is, in works composed for the ear—"didactically for oral memorization" (Havelock, 1986a, p. 15). First, ancient oralism was essentially an exercise in poetic memorization; the introduction of literacy gradually transformed the practice of oral memory and the dominance of the older poetic culture into a prose culture. Since composing for the ear appealed to the human oral memory, these texts were designed to aid the listening process and "hold the attention of the ear" with an "acoustic flow of language" (p. 13): forms of repetition, for example, formulaic epithets; ritualized utterances, scenes, situations, and performance; an improvisational behavior; a dependence on the use of rhythm, dance, and melody; and an activist narrative syntax.

In addition, the oral poetry of this period should not be misperceived as "talking books." (In fact, are we imposing our own literate bias on this Western historical period by using the metaphor of the book?) Instead, the view of a "speaking picture" or a "cinematic image" would give us a more accurate view of oral poetry during the historical period of Western primary orality (Havelock, 1986a, p. 108; see also, Minchin, 2001). Havelock describes a brief passage from one of the *Homeric Hymns* to illustrate the paradoxical "visuality" of aural poetry (aurality's appeal to the ear too often inhibits discussions about aurality's visual appeal—to the mind's eye) and its oral compositional techniques. Then, he illustrates the contrastive differences in syntax by examining a later historical passage, written for readers, from Callimachus's *Hymn to Zeus*. This passage he describes not as cinema (like the oral syntax illustrates in the *Homeric Hymns*), but as a "still-life portrait" or a "writer's portraiture" (1986a, pp. 107–109): "The Muse has learned to write and in doing so tries to sing in the language of Aristotle" (p. 108).

ORALITY THEORY BEFORE ONG'S *ORALITY AND LITERACY*

The literary bias of traditional Homeric scholars sustained a strong critical debate on the excessive use and placement of similes in the Homeric epics. But in his book *The Oral Nature of the Homeric Similes* (1974), William C. Scott illustrates the problem of the Western literate bias by introducing his subject with a bit of humor (p. 1). Comparing one of Homer's similes to a sample of prose from William Strunk's (and later E. B. White's) *The Elements of Style* (1920), Scott distinguishes the advice of a writer from the advice of an oral poet on the rules of composition. He focuses on the technology available to each of them: "E. B. White has the freedom of the blank page and the eraser. . . . If Homer made a mistake or a slip in taste, there was no second chance and no eraser" (p. 2). The significance of creating a written or oral record cannot be understated here, and Scott's commentary underscores the relationship between language, technology, and cultural memory. Now, in our age of secondary orality with its strong visuality and technological influences, even Strunk and White's *The Elements of Style* has been newly released with images in addition to its prose in an illustrated hardcover edition (2005).

It is more than simply interesting or coincidental to discover many parallel ideas, arguments, and writings by 20th-century European scholars (Scott is one of them) who, like Ong, Havelock, and others, have observed oral and alphabetic literate "behaviors" in thinking processes and Western language use as literary genres and technologies have evolved from oral epic literature. In *The Theory of the Novel*, G. Lukacs (1920/1989) raised questions about some philosophical, oppositional differences between the historical (oral) epic literature and the (highly literate) novel. On the topic of the hero as a character in the historical epic, for example, he observes that "the epic hero is, strictly speaking, never an individual. It is traditionally thought that one of the essential characteristics of the epic is the fact that its theme is not a personal destiny but the destiny of a community" (p. 67). Ong does not cite Lukacs's work in his book, but this description of the oral epic hero follows Ong's (and other early orality theorists') arguments about identity and the participatory relationship between the hero and the community (pp. 69–71). Furthermore, Lukacs observes that

the "way Homer's epics begin in the middle and do not finish at the end is a reflexion of the truly epic mentality's total indifference to any form of architectural construction" (p. 67). Orality theory enhances Lukacs's observation, moving readers to think about the in medias res introduction as a highly appealing feature of the oral epic with its episodic, poetic, and associative rather than a linear appeal, in prose, to its audiences.

Like Lukacs in the 1920s, Walter Benjamin in the 1940s also reflects on epic literature, and specifically, on oral storytelling or "the art of repeating stories" (1968, p. 93). He laments that this art was, in his own time, "in its decline" (p. 83). In *Illuminations* (1968), Benjamin famously muses on many of the characteristics that create and sustain an oral tradition and the life of a storyteller, making wonderful observations on the storyteller and the listener that closely align with Havelock's own commentary on the Greek oral epic, its discourse, and its strategic acoustic appeal to the human memory:

> It has seldom been realized that the listener's naïve relationship to the storyteller is controlled by his interest in retaining what he is told. The cardinal point for the unaffected listener is to assure himself of the possibility of reproducing the story. Memory is the epic faculty *par excellence*. Only by virtue of a comprehensive memory can epic writing absorb the course of events on the one hand and, with the passing of these, make its peace with death on the other. (p. 97)

The greatest of the storytellers, Benjamin goes on to describe, will have "the most encyclopedic memory at his command" (p. 97; see also, Havelock, 1986a, pp. 29, 58). Although Benjamin had read Lukacs's earlier work on the philosophical differences between epic literature and the novel, *Illuminations* focused on the evolutionary differences between storytelling, as an oral performance art, and the novel, as a book. This evolution, he writes, has made oral storytelling obsolete, for the book is dependent on isolated, private readers rather than on a community of listeners.

Havelock (1986a) is careful to distinguish his observations on "Greek theories of orality" from modern discoveries of orality. Nonetheless, his earlier claims about the shifting Greek consciousness from orality to literacy—his "oral-literate continuum"—formed the basis for ample disagreement about what orality theory actually tells us about its relationship to alphabetic literacy and the evolution of logical thinking (e.g., Havelock, 1963). Challenges to the evidence, and more important, to the inferences about differing intellectual values (a changed consciousness) that may be attributed to the shift from orality to literacy—from primitive to civilized—formed a hotly debated scholarly forum for more than a decade after the publication of Ong's book. This academic debate, commonly called the "Great Divide Theory," is still smoldering or simply dismissed (one might ask, for example, if Ong's description of the discourse in primary oral culture as "conservative and traditionalist" (1982, p. 41), is any more conservative or traditional than that of the 21st century's literate culture's response to the new diverse discourses of secondary oral culture). Nonetheless, readers should appreciate that these early oppositional views on orality and literacy have actually served to broaden the ways that scholars have reframed their research questions in the 21st century about valuable historical perspectives on orality theory, and perhaps more important, perspectives on cross-cultural orality theory. Much of the earlier scholarly opposition reflected a powerful response to literate, conservative, cultural biases, as well as racism—even the very word *orality* is a bad (and avoidable) word for some writers of color who wish to avoid its negative, pathetic appeal.

French Canadian scholar Paul Zumthor (1990) identifies an inherent problem in European-Western scholars' theorizing orality

about other people's cultures. He reminds us that orality is not simply speech and should not be "reduced to vocal action. Indeed, it implies everything in us that is addressed to the other, be it a mute gesture, a look. . . . Body movements are thus integrated into a poetics" in his *Oral Poetry* (p. 153). Zumthor's observations help articulate the cultural conflicts that many Western orality theorists have either ignored (intentionally or not) or have been unable to observe due to their own textual or alphabetic, literate biases. It is this kind of ignorance, unconcern, or lack of bodily participation that provoked the query in the epigraph to this chapter from the Mayan storyteller (quoted in Zumthor, p. 188), which questions whether the listener is truly engaged or simply a detached observer. Elaborating on bodily presence in orality studies, Zumthor further observed that

> the oral poetic text, insofar as it engages a body through the voice that carries it, rejects any analysis that would dissociate it from its social function and from its socially accorded place—more than a written text would. Likewise, it rejects dissociation from the tradition that it can explicitly or implicitly claim as its own, from those circumstances in which it makes itself heard. (p. 28)

Zumthor shares his cautionary, social observations, but he simultaneously acknowledges the importance of a cross-cultural orality theory. His commentary on orality and African American blues music, for example, highlights the aesthetics and inventiveness that the blues gave to American music (p. 47; see also Ellison, 2001).

ORALITY THEORY IN THE 21st CENTURY

The new, exciting research on orality theory in the United States and global cultures greatly expands our earlier perspectives on rhetoric, cultural discourse, and technology. This new scholarship includes studies on new rhetorical canons and practices—rooted in aurality/orality; rereadings of medieval texts and historical views on residual orality; the acoustic world of early America; the role of oral/aural rhetoric, democracy, and identity in early America; regendered histories of rhetoric; ocularity versus aurality in American cultural rhetoric and racialized communities; and finally, implications for further research on orality/aurality in our time.

Rereading the Greek Theory of Orality

Ekaterina V. Haskins's *Logos and Power in Isocrates and Aristotle* (2004) bridges my introductory, historical overview with some newer rereadings on orality theory. Haskins argues for a rereading of Isocrates as a rhetorical theorist who, in his own time, embraced both the emergent prose tradition of writing (a well-known fact in rhetoric studies), and historical orality, preserving the older Greek cultural *mythos* and its essential relationship to rhetorical invention. In her chapter titled "Between Orality and Literacy," Haskins assumes a postessentialist view of orality and literacy—a stance found in many of the newer studies on orality theory—and focuses on what she describes as the "gray area" between them. Moving beyond the problematic determinism that earlier orality theorists asserted, Haskins's work provides an excellent rereading of the cultural, intellectual, and inevitable momentum that the invention of alphabetic literacy introduced to a culture in which discourse had been formerly governed by the laws of acoustic composition and aural appeal: where "the culture of poets and prophets conceived of speech as an aesthetically potent, almost magic, social event that activated in the listeners' commonly held truths" (p. 13). In this Greek oral culture, Haskins tells us, philosophers "had to compete for the audience's minds by appealing to their ears" (p. 13).

For Haskins (2004), Aristotle and Isocrates represent "two divergent literate logics and two dissimilar visions of discourses" (p. 30). Isocrates taught that there need not be a separation of poetic performance from political discourse in his theory of a *logos politikos*. But by separating text from context and asserting a political (and intellectual) position on disinterested knowledge, Aristotle separates performance from rhetorical discourse, or *logos*, from human agency (p. 28). Thus, the idea of the citizen-rhetor with its "performance-oriented conception of eloquence" cannot be overstated in emphasizing the oppositional thinking about how the new writing technology could influence the future of literacy and discourse in Greek culture. Clearly, at the center of this fascinating cultural debate was the sensory shift from a language composed for the ear to the new composition for the eye. Haskins tells us that "the privileging of seeing acquires a new layer of significance. It asserts the ocularcentric rationality over the phonocentric. The critical eye now dominates the easily seduced ear" (p. 23). But this cultural and intellectual shift toward the decontextualized (abstract), nonperformance-oriented visuality—which clearly won the debate—poses ethical problems for rhetorical teaching in cultural and cross-cultural communities (Havelock, 1986b).

From Silent Reading to Natural Soundscapes

While the evolution of silent reading is not a new subject for rhetoric, literacy, and composition scholars, Paul Saenger's book *Space Between Words: The Origins of Silent Reading* (2005), not only revisits the medieval research on this event in the history of reading, but it also links his historical research to the physiology of reading, pedagogy, and its contemporary cross-cultural implications (p. 2). For example, Saenger analyzes the cognitive skills that are required for decoding and deciphering written texts according to the kinds of grapholects and writing systems that a culture uses:

> The differing ways in which oral or silent reading depends on the duration of cognitive activity required by differing transcription systems in different cultures appear most clearly in modern languages as differences in language pedagogy. . . . Graphic systems that eliminate or reduce the need for a cognitive process prior to lexical access facilitate the early adaptation of young readers to silent reading, while written languages that are more ambiguous necessitate the oral manipulation of phonetic components to construct words. . . .
>
> Chinese graphic tradition provides optimal conditions for rapid lexical access and allows Chinese children to develop silent reading at an earlier age than in Burma or in the West. As a consequence, many skilled Chinese readers are able to achieve a proficiency in rapid, silent reading perhaps unequaled in modern occidental languages. (p. 2)

Saenger's attention to the Chinese graphic tradition provides an excellent illustration of how historical, medieval research on reading informs contemporary cross-cultural research. In addition, Saenger's research also details the empowerment of the vernacular movement at the end of the Middle Ages in medieval France, Italy, and England. This historical period shows the birth of personal expression, as well as silent, private reading, which, by inference, provides interesting questions for thinking about rhetoric and today's vernacular movements and practices (pp. 256–276).

Following new works on orality theory from Europe to early America should lead readers to Richard Cullen Rath's excellent book *How Early America Sounded* (2004). Unlike other contemporary contributions to orality theory, Rath emphasizes the problematic "Great Divide Theory," but mostly because "both sides" of the debate are, themselves,

centered in sounds that are governed by an alphabet. Rath inquires about the world of sound that cannot be recorded by an alphabetic script, such as thunder, howling, groans, moans, cries, ranting, and other sounds that also contributed to human perceptions and interpretations of the world. He is also interested in the ways that ocularity and a literate bias have literally eclipsed our historical views on the early American aural imagination.

Specifically, Rath (2004) focuses on the distinctive soundways of European Americans, Native Americans, and African Americans "in regard to the natural world" and the "colonizing" of these natural soundscapes. The early American soundways, according to Rath, give contemporary scholars a more accurate perception of the highly contested notions of American identity:

> African American drumming, so troublesome to whites, was a means of creating a covert space that served as a public for African Americans. Bell-ringing to protest British policies before the Revolution was dissonant to loyalist ears but harmonious to those with patriotic leanings. (p. 176)

Although Rath does not focus on rhetoric or the impending 19th-century American oratorical culture, his scholarship holds import for those fields. This early American culture, when print culture and aural culture were not so strongly competitive, empowered American slaves, as for example, Frederick Douglass's *Narrative* reports, to gain access to a limited "shared ethos" in America's literate culture (Bingham & Blight, 1998; Douglass, 2001). Despite Rath's inattention to oratory, he comments frequently on the impending impact of the print and visual culture on a world previously governed by speech, soundscapes, and public acoustic spaces. "Grappling with the full complexity of early American communication networks," especially "contested, pluralistic, polyvocal soundscapes" (Rath, 2004, p. 179), will bring those of us who study rhetoric and democracy closer to understanding American identities as *e pluribus pluribum*, which Rath argues, "makes more sense than the myth of *e pluribus unum*" (p. 176).

Orality, Democracy, and Human Agency

Rath's arguments about the fierce cultural contests in purging the early formation of American identity should move contemporary thinkers to consider the vital role of orality in the struggle for democracy, especially in view of the culture of oratory and its value for a participatory democracy. I would also emphasize here the value for cultural and oral rhetorical memory. Indeed, in spite of slave culture and the oppression of women, Sojourner Truth gave American audiences a way to perceive the human voice as a primary means of personal agency and as a source of participating in American democratic political culture. Shirley Wilson Logan's (1999) research shows us that these "nineteenth-century African American women were full participants in the verbal warfare for human dignity" (p. 1). This tradition of speech and participatory rhetoric creates a cultural, textual inheritance for future African American women speakers. For example, Jacqueline Jones Royster's analysis of Alice Walker's practices of literacy and storytelling examines early Western and African American connected interests in orality. Royster (2000) writes that

> Walker consistently uses classical arrangements that historically are attributable in the African American community to oral practices rather than to literate ones. . . . [C]oincidentally or not, in African American communities, classical rhetoric has been most vibrantly internalized in community practices through oratory, such as preaching. (p. 30)

It is this focus on orality and human agency that Hazel Carby (1986) also addresses when she raised questions about formulating theories of black feminist literary criticism that

ignore the orality of the black women's blues culture and lyricism (p. 12). In addition, Harryette Mullen's (1992) description of black women as "ear witnesses" to America's writing culture is poignant (p. 251). The orality of African culture—its concept of circular time, interiorized epistemological constructions, associative thinking, verbal indirection, signification, and spiritual expression beyond the use of words—becomes a form of clear cultural markers in African American expression and identity (Middleton, 1995; Mullen, 1992, pp. 244–264; see also Mullen, 1996).

These varied readings on African American women, rhetoric, and the role of orality in empowering personal human agency should enable contemporary rhetoric scholars to view the crucial relationship between orality and rhetoric in the early academy and in the participatory democracy in the United States. Therefore, I propose that new rhetorical studies must analyze the important role of orality, especially cultural orality, in their attention to new rhetorical histories and practices. Rhetorical studies in the 21st century that omit any attention to orality theory may give us excellent research, but an implicit bias for literacy and ocularity may also be apparent. Thus, these studies give us only a narrow, partial view of the much larger performative, cultural, regendered, and reraced practices of classical rhetoric that Welch (1999) strongly urged new researchers to integrate into their work (see, e.g., Rabinovitz & Geil, 2004, on memory; Sipiora & Baumlin, 2002, on kairos). I voice this concern in view of what may be misperceived as a loss of the integral role of orality in rhetoric studies as we theorize discourse practices in our secondary oral culture today. Recently, John L. Locke expressed both a scholarly and personal concern about this loss in *The De-voicing of Society* (1998), which examines how electronic technology has transformed and normalized this loss of voice (see also Stephen Miller's masculinist lament in his *Conversation: A History of a Declining Art,* 2006). The increasing number of reports on human feelings of social isolation and loneliness in the United States seem related to Locke's scholarly inquiry.

NEW RHETORICAL PRACTICES: LESSONS FROM LISTENING

As Havelock (1986a) suggests, renewed intellectual interest in rhetoric begins with the new technology of the radio in the early 20th century, which gave Americans (and many nations around the world) an experience that was "shared by the writer and the thinker and the scholar and the common man alike" (p. 30). This shared American and global ethos reflects one of the earliest examples of secondary orality, "a forced marriage or remarriage, between the resources of the written word and of the spoken" (p. 33). Throughout her career, Toni Morrison has emphasized the influence of the radio on her imagination as a storyteller and writer. In an article in *O Magazine,* for example, Morrison (2006) tells her readers,

> Not *only* was I a radio child who grew up in the decades when radio was paramount, when being mesmerized by the dramas and reenactments from a speaker box was commonplace, I was also surrounded by adults who told stories, reshaped and solicited them from each other as well as their children. (p. 175)

Morrison's interest in the radio culture is both aesthetic and rhetorical. In a racially segregated America in the 1930s, 1940s, and 1950s, the radio (as an early form of secondary orality) collapses the abstract, artificial, constructed racial boundaries and creates possibilities for a humanized "shared cultural ethos."

A wonderful recent illustration of this shared cultural public sphere of the radio can be seen in the film *Good Night and Good Luck*. The scene shows an African American female jazz singer in the 1950s (Dianne Reeves) performing the jazz standard "How High the Moon" when the main characters, Fred Friendly and Edward R. Murrow (George Clooney and David Strathairn), learn that a valuable colleague, Don Hollenbeck (Ray Wise), has committed suicide. More than simple background music, the performance of this jazz standard underscores the epideictic moment in this scene, and the camera movement, very effectively, balances its dual gazing on the lament of the main characters and the sublime beauty of Reeves's voice and her lyrical phrasing—the performance captures the adhesiveness of this humanizing moment between the emotional expression of the lyrics and oral memory. Of course, the film also heightens the rhetorical listening experience of its viewing audience.

The inarguable value that links Havelock's cultural observations about the radio and rhetoric with Morrison's reflections on the radio is the power of listening, or, as Royster (1996) and Krista Ratcliffe (2005) would describe it, rhetorical listening and its potential as a "code of cross-cultural conduct" (pp. 34–41). Interestingly, Duane Roen's edited collection of CCCC Chairs' Addresses moves our disciplinary community to think about the power and roles of the fourth and fifth canons for CCCC members as an audience (2006). Every new reader will certainly have his or her own personal sense of "listening" and engagement with these written records of the speeches. In the anecdotal commentary by each chair, Roen provides a glimpse of each of these rhetors' preparation for engagement with their CCCC listening audiences. But, happily, Roen also captures a bit of the kairos of those special speeches by including some "real time" memories from various members of the audiences for these powerful and moving talks (pp. 17–41).

The acoustic metaphors in Ratcliffe's *Rhetorical Listening: Identification, Gender, Whiteness* (2005)—including "discordant notes," "harmonics," "dissonance," "recitatif," and other "h(ear)ing metaphors"—extend or overlap rather seamlessly with music as inventive and interpretive. Victor Villaneuva's (1993) definition of rhetoric helps amplify Ratcliffe's meaning of the term *rhetoric* in rhetorical listening:

> Language used consciously, a matter of rhetoric, is a principal means—perhaps *the* means—by which change can take place. . . . Rhetoric, after all, is how ideologies are carried, how hegemonies are maintained. Rhetoric, then, would be the means by which hegemonies could be countered. (p. 121)

Indeed, countering hegemonies is exactly what rhetorical listening makes possible. In a passage that may remind us of Mark Twain's understanding of cultural discourse in the 19th century (see, e.g. Fishkin, 1993) or Morrison's (1984) rhetorical practices of cultural discourse in the 20th century, Ratcliffe (2005) writes that "we may not always choose or control the discourses that socialize us; neither may we choose or control our unconscious responses to them" (p. 30). Perhaps our neglect of studying the impact of the world of sound on the way that language shapes us reveals a huge vulnerability in our civic practices and our personal human agency. But Ratcliffe recognizes how this vulnerability may be bolstered into a rhetorical strength: "We can, to a limited degree, articulate our conscious identifications and choose to respond to them (or not); in this way, we become responsible for our words, our attitudes, our actions" (p. 30). The responsibility logic that Ratcliffe suggests is not only closely related to ethical behavior, but it also helps us become honestly engaged listeners, negotiating our way through differences and the meaning-making process.

In addition, and related to the ethics and the hard work of negotiating meaning, Wayne Booth describes a "listening rhetoric" or "LR" in *The Rhetoric of Rhetoric: The Quest for*

Effective Communication (2004). As Ratcliffe focuses on the traditional, problematic goals of rhetoric, without rhetorical listening—such as preserving the status quo or authorial intent—so too does Booth urge his readers "to engage in genuine listening" with the end of a listening rhetoric as "pursuing not just victory but a new reality, a new agreement about what is real" (pp. 46–47). "All good rhetoric," Booth emphasizes,

> depends on the rhetor's *listening to and thinking about the character and welfare of the audience,* and moderating what is said to meet what has been heard . . . the good rhetor answers the audience's questions before they're asked. (p. 54)

Given her very provocative study on the history of rhetoric and Isocrates's *logos politikos,* Haskins might ask us to reconsider Aristotle's writing about the rhetorical audience. Part of the problem of the diminished role of the listening audience that both Ratcliffe and Booth want to resolve actually lies in Aristotle's thinking about audience in his *Rhetoric,* written, ironically, when orality was still a powerful practice of Greek cultural discourse. Although Aristotle's rhetoric was rooted in civic performance, his rhetorical instruction gravitates toward stability, for example, with essentialized genres and a fixed vision of the rhetorical audience (Haskins, 2004, pp. 3–8). Aristotle "justifies a restricted participation in politics by the *demos*" and reifies rhetorical knowledge by reducing "the functions of the rhetor and the audience . . . respectively to repetition and recognition of rhetorical knowledge embedded in enthymemes" (p. 9). Haskins argues that Aristotle's rhetoric, associated with a visual, materialized discourse and the influence of alphabetic literacy, begins to teach a decontextualized discourse that separates context (performance) from content (propositions). Effectively, Haskins argues that this separation points to the inherent problems with today's perspectives on teaching writing in the 21st century and on the students as audience in today's classroom (pp. 130–136).

Making similar observations, Havelock (1986b) also expressed concerns about a decontextualized rhetoric from ethics, orality (culture), and literacy. In "Orality, Literacy, and Star Wars," he analyzes the dichotomous oral and written responses to the explosion of the Challenger Space shuttle. Literacy, he observes, has the potential to silence the personal honesty and directness of oral language use (because of its hierarchical relationship to orality) and, relatedly, may represent a depersonalized, conceptualized, decontexualized "misuse of conceptual thinking and a degrading of language" (pp. 129–130). But Havelock also observes that, despite the abstract thinking that literacy may dangerously promote, the power of oral language use (due to its strong appeal to oral memory) frequently becomes the stronger, more memorable concept in popular culture. Thus, the "Strategic Defense Initiative" (announced shortly after the Challenger explosion and discussed in the same article) becomes "Star Wars," renaming and dominating the memory of the new initiative as ordinary people would think of it in popular culture (pp. 131–132). With regard to rhetoric and teaching, Havelock advocates that more time in writing classes should be devoted to speech and orality as well as to writing and that we should question the outcome of an education, including college level instruction, that advocates the speedy acquisition of literacy, reading, and writing, at the expense of a loss of oral language training (pp. 126–127).

The ethical relationship between orality and rhetoric, more often than not, empowers human agency and participatory democratic rhetoric beyond artificially constructed racial and ethnic boundaries of difference. Danielle Allen's (2002) excellent book *Talking to Strangers: Anxieties of Citizenship Since* Brown v. Board of Education, addresses these "fossilized boundaries of difference" rooted in interracial distrust (p. xiii). She argues that an Aristotelian rhetoric should enable Americans to "find methods of generating mutual benefit despite differences of position, experience, and perspective" (p. xix) because Aristotle's rhetoric is essentially a "treatise on talking to strangers" (p. 143), and rhetorical listening is crucial to this participatory democracy. Calling for a politics of friendship (not an emotion but a practice), Allen observes that "we are all always awash in each other's lives, and for most of us that shared life, recorded as history, will be the only artifact we leave behind" (pp. xxi–xxii).

Given their similar visions of a participatory democracy, rhetoric, and discourse, I can only speculate on an imaginary conversation between Haskins, Allen, and their oppositional views on Aristotle's work that supports each of their seemingly shared visions. Haskins and Allen would find common ground, I think, in arguing for the need for rhetoric to help citizens in a democracy learn from otherness to promote personal human agency and citizenly conduct. Both writers are also interested in dismantling the rhetoric of otherness—for Haskins, the "barbarians as the Greek 'other'" and for Allen, nonwhite people before the *Brown v. Board of Education* Supreme Court decision. Indeed, Allen's argument that rhetoric provides the manual for discovering the basis for political friendship reflects the hard work of negotiating and the rhetorical listening that Ratcliffe, Booth, and Royster move us to practice.

Perhaps Aristotle's textbook on rhetoric necessarily reflects orality (e.g., Haskins describes the enthymeme as "an unspoken oral premise"). But Allen's (2002) analysis assumes that Aristotle's *Rhetoric* addresses an audience of democratic equals—thus she describes his work as a manual on "the art of talking to strangers as equals and of proving that one has also their good at heart" (p. 156)—which it most emphatically does not. Perhaps it is Isocrates's "rhetorical theory" that would enable the democratic process that Allen envisions (despite his own elitism), since he promoted an "expansive rather than a generically constrained notion of audience" (Haskins, 2004, p. 8). The role of orality in reconstituting the boundaries of inclusion in American democracy emphasizes a continuity that reflects America's earliest struggles over identity that Rath observes in his book on America's contestatory soundways. But Allen's arguments about Aristotle's rhetoric may remind many of us of Martin Luther King, Jr.'s oral arguments for freedom and equality that were rooted in the *Declaration of Independence,* despite the founding framers' exclusion of nonwhites and women in the conception of that document.

ORALITY THEORY, RHETORIC, AND MEMORY LOSS

My earliest interest in orality theory began with a focus on rhetorical oral memory, a topic that is closely related to Havelock's argument about teaching orality together with writing, poetry together with prose, at the college level. The academic rediscovery of rhetoric in the 1960s did not include much of an interest in the fourth or fifth canons of rhetoric, as Edward P. J. Corbett notes in his *Classical Rhetoric for the Modern Student* (1965). Yet these two canons probably contribute the most to any understanding of a cultural and cross-cultural rhetoric, especially rhetorical memory and its relation to invention. Unlike historical traditions of rhetorical studies, memory receives little attention in schooling today, and unfortunately the subject has largely been given over by English and rhetoric departments to biology and psychology studies (Glenn, 2007, p. A14; Schacter, 1996). Thus, I was intrigued to discover Thomas Butler's interest in a nonbiological, nonpsychological, or nonscientific oral memory in his edited collection of essays, *Memory: History, Culture and the Mind*

(1989). On the "operations of memory," he writes,

> We have learned to process experience so quickly, that we usually are not even conscious of what we are doing. And we encode information according to some schema of which we are often unaware. If it be professional data we are more conscious of what we are doing, filing it with other material of the same category, updating when necessary. As for everyday life experiences, we most often have no filing system at all, leaving their later recollection to chance. (p. 14)

Surely oral memory underscores the sense of personal agency and the struggle over culture and American identities that Rath describes in his argument about *e pluribus pluribum.* Quoting Cicero, and describing history as social memory, cultural historian Peter Burke (1989) describes the construction and reconstruction of social memory and social amnesia. Like Havelock's argument about orality and "Star Wars," Burke's essay emphasizes the uninstructed power of orality (oral memory) in a literate, democratic culture:

> Given the multiplicity of social identities, and the coexistence of rival memories, alternative memories (family memories, local memories, class memories, national memories, and so on), it is surely more fruitful to think in pluralistic terms about the uses of memories to different social groups, who may well have different views about what is significant or "worthy of memory" (p. 107)

If we were to recall just a few examples of differing American racialized memories, for example, that Thomas Jefferson was sexually involved with his slave, Sally Hemmings; or that Strom Thurmond, a staunch racial segregationist, fathered an African American daughter during the American Jim Crow era, we can certainly begin to recognize the essential and powerful role of oral memory and orality in the African American community that was very different from the literate "master narrative," and that was passed on as personal, family, and community histories, side by side with the master narrative of American history.

But the renewed interest in rhetorical memory and the power of orality seems to be moving more white Americans to also question and challenge the master narrative as the only memory and history of America's past. Edward Ball, in *Slaves in the Family* (1998), for example, shifts the gaze of his personal family history to successfully challenge his inherited assumptions about race, family, and American identity. Or more recently, Tim Tyson's *Blood Done Sign My Name* (2004) illustrates a powerful challenge to the racialized master narrative of his small community in Oxford, North Carolina. His book investigates and affirms a racial lynching that he clearly remembered as a child (and that he could recollect in his oral memory) but that barely existed, anywhere, in written historical records in his community. These books serve as excellent markers of the power of our secondary oral culture, where oral memory and the "heard" story works in a partnership with—or as a lever against—the dominance of literacy and the written texts (see also Prendergast, 1998). Together these oral and written narratives support the cultural and cross-cultural, democratizing effect of a participatory, oral rhetoric and democracy. I am sure that many unique and interesting American texts could be added to this discussion and this kind of historical American and global research that examines orality and literacy together.

SOUNDWAYS, SOUNDSCAPES, AND LISTENING FOR A DEMOCRATIC FUTURE

Immediately following the American tragedy in the aftermath of Hurricane Katrina in August 2005, Wynton Marsalis, jazz musician and native son of New Orleans, created his

own media storm not only to respond to the American citizens who suffered from this disaster, but also, like Danielle Allen, to talk about the failure, once again, of American democracy to rise to the call of all its citizens, beyond its "fossilized boundaries of difference" (reflecting a lack of response to both race and class). In an interview with Charlie Rose (Vega, 2006), Marsalis first recounted the history and repetition of these kinds of American failures regarding race and class:

> Americans [are] good in a crisis. . . . The problem we're going to have is after that. We rose in the Civil War. We rose in both World Wars. We rose in [the] Civil Rights movement and changed a lot of legislation that was destructive. . . . But when [the moment of crisis] has passed, we fall back again.

Marsalis emphasizes that these kinds of American heroic narratives never become "a part of the national mythology," and, for him, "that's why we are doomed to repeat the same kind of mistakes (just like what happens in [our] personal lives)." The aftermath of Hurricane Katrina, Marsalis tells Rose, exposes how far we have fallen, once again, from upholding fundamental American principles. Marsalis's commentary on the tragedy in New Orleans reveals a strong violation of his understanding as a jazz musician—steeped in the improvisational values of a cultural orality and aurality—of a participatory democracy. In a previously published interview with scholar and cultural critic Cornel West (1999), Marsalis defined the relationship between democracy and jazz, which frames his view of the tragedy in New Orleans:

> Jazz is an art form that was created to codify democratic experience and give us a model for it. Jazz music was invented to let us know how to listen to each other, how to negotiate. Because when you're playing on a bandstand, you might hate what somebody else is playing, but you've got to play along.

. . . And you've got to listen to people. Because if you aren't listening to them, you can't play with them. And you're forced to play with them because you're on that bandstand with them. (p. 136)

Relatedly, Bernice Reagon in *Sweet Honey in the Rock: Raise Your Voice* (directed by Stanley Nelson, 2005), also reminds us of the rhetorical, counterhegemonic power of orality, aurality, and music in the Civil Rights era of the 1960s and 1970s, especially in music's ability to break down barriers and to help people develop a true sense of community *in the moment*. A member of the Albany Singing Movement in the 1960s, Reagon "thought that [the singing voice] would be the way to connect different communities of protesters. In order to speak across social divides, song became a way, particularly when people were arrested, for folks to come together." Rhetoric scholars Thurmon Garner and Carolyn Calloway-Thomas (2003) would certainly note Reagon's emphasis on community in their research on defining African American orality; their collaborative essay concludes that a truly "shared knowledge is cultural knowledge" (p. 54; see also Bernard Hibbitts, 1994, on orality/aurality, diversity, and legal discourse).

It would seem that the politically polarizing discourses that dominate the American public sphere today, too often resembling the cultural divisiveness of prior historical moments of civil war and unrest in this country, reflect the low esteem, neglect, and lost value for cultural orality and rhetorical listening. Perhaps Marsalis and Reagon would agree. But recently, much of the new illuminating work to regender the history of rhetoric is also rooted in values of orality and helps us broaden our understanding of human communication, personal expression, cultural ways of knowing, and a participatory democracy. Jane Donaworth's research, for example, in *Rhetorical Theory by Women Before 1900* (2002) shows how much women's substantial contributions to rhetorical theory focus on the importance of listening to

the process of negotiating meaning. Donaworth infers that "women theorists bring a model of communication based on conversation, collaboration, and dialogue to our understanding of the history of rhetoric" (p. xl), and these may be compared to music and performance. In addition, Cheryl Glenn's (2005) book *Unspoken*, an argument on silence as a form of rhetorical delivery, is both provocative and useful in fostering honest cultural and personal human engagement: "A rhetorical silence of careful listening can transform the interactional goal of rhetoric, which has traditionally been one of persuasion to one of understanding" (p. 156). If "soundways give us new ways to think about pluralism and American identities," as Rath (2004) eloquently argues (p. 184), then perhaps our wounded democracy will find a new, critical, and rhetorical value in sounds and speaking pictures, not simply in talking books, and will exploit the opportunity to "chant a new world into being" (p. 173)—a world that truly embraces the improvisational goal of *e pluribus pluribum* for ourselves and our posterity.

CONCLUSION: SOME THOUGHTS ON FUTURE LESSONS

If Ong's provocative book promised to open new areas of research on orality theory when it was published in the 1980s, then certainly the research by Allen, Haskins, Saenger, Ratcliffe, Glenn, or Fernandez show the huge contributions that this research gives to those of us who think about human communication as well as the future of alphabetic literacy. The final chapter in Ong's book, titled "Some Theorems," encouraged us to think about the largely "unfinished business" of his widely cited research. He encouraged new inquiries in various disciplinary areas: rhetoric, women's studies, literary history, linguistics, philosophy, and biblical studies. Although many of today's scholars equate orality and literacy studies with media, Ong (1982) emphasized his avoidance of that term throughout his book because it conveys "a false impression of the nature of verbal communication" (p. 175). Human communication differs from the medium model because it "demands anticipated feedback in order to take place at all" (p. 176). "It is never one-way [which media is]. . . . [Human communication] not only calls for response but is shaped in its very form and content by anticipated response" (p. 176).

It would appear that Ong's work carefully anticipated much of the scholarly attention that it has received in the works that I have briefly analyzed with an eye toward encouraging further research on secondary oral culture. Recently, Luke Fernandez (2007) pointed out that Ong's work appeared "before the advent of the Web, podcasting, and wikis, but his observations remain valid today" (p. B27). In a very brief conclusion to my own chapter, I suggest not theorems, but a few questions for future research that not only help broaden the range of inquiry on orality theory in the 21st century but also illustrate how exciting it is to observe and question aspects of literate orality and its complexities from our everyday conversations and global cultural experiences.

1. Ong writes that early women's traditions worked primarily outside of an oral, rhetorical tradition. But by the end of the 17th century, literacy empowered a greater number of women's voices and participation in the Western public sphere, especially in the novel. In what ways has secondary orality reasserted a new masculine dominance in the public sphere, especially in popular culture, music, and film, which limits women's expression, once again, in the Western public sphere?

2. Haskins (2004) acknowledges the difficulty of teaching models of civic excellence and discursive education "in the face of the sheer volume and diversity of discourses" in today's classrooms (p. 135). How can orality theory, especially with a focus on performance, offer ways for thinking about discourse, ideology, consumerism, cultural diversity, democracy, and discursive education in American pedagogy and in our critical responses to the public sphere of popular culture?

3. In what ways should we address the devoicing of society in this age of secondary orality? How does the devoicing of society both limit and empower global rhetorics in Anglo culture (e.g., in the rhetoric and discourse of foreign films)? How should orality theory, as well as newly articulated rhetorical practices (e.g., rhetorical listening and silence), address the loss of voice in the current rhetorical research on memory and delivery in the 21st century? Or, relatedly, in our age of iPods, MP3 players, cell phones, and portable video games—products of secondary oral culture—how should we think about the increasing impact of noise-induced hearing loss (also described as a "loss of intimacy," Van Buskirk, 2006), both in today's youth culture and in our academic practices?

4. In our image-saturated society, how can we explore more teaching and rhetorical subjects to help today's students think critically about the relationships between the visual and the oral/aural as complementary rather than simply as a competing means of perceiving the human world, for example, in the visuality of music in pop culture (and music videos); the power of literate orality and memory in Def Poetry or Classic Jazz music (jazz standards and jazz photography); the shifting of radio sports, such as baseball or hockey, to televised sports, or the oral/aural and visual assimilation practices of U.S. immigrant cultures to the dominant American culture (Roediger, 2005), or even in the future of online teaching and academic discourses?

5. Havelock and others have argued that the radio reasserted the power of rhetoric in U.S. culture. How did the radio transmit American rhetoric to non-Anglo, global

cultures, and how did the American secondary oral culture influence audiences for other global rhetorics via the radio?

Admiring the "detachment and reflection that are hallmarks of print culture," and annoyed by the "quick emotional response and the focus on the present that are typical of oral cultures," Fernandez (2007) ends his essay on a hopeful note, that "academe will always keep a privileged place for writing" (p. B27). Without hearing more of his context for that argument, I'm not sure that I agree with his idea of writing and privilege. But I do believe that new studies on orality in writing will move more students, teachers, scholars, editors, and publishers not only to recover and preserve the best of our past for the future, but also to become better listeners in our present.

REFERENCES

Allen, D. (2002). *Talking to strangers: Anxieties of citizenship since* Brown v. Board of Education. Chicago: University of Chicago Press.

Ball, E. P. (1998). *Slaves in the family*. New York: Random House.

Benjamin, W. (1968). *Illuminations: Essays and reflections*. New York: Harcourt Brace.

Bingham, C., & Blight, D. (1998). *The Columbian orator*. New York: New York University Press.

Birkerts, S. (1994). *The Gutenberg elegies: The fate of reading in an electronic age*. Winchester, MA: Faber & Faber.

Birkerts, S. (2007). *Reading life: Books for the ages*. St. Paul, MN: Graywolf.

Booth, W. (2004). *A rhetoric of rhetoric: The quest for effective communication*. Malden, MA: Blackwell.

Burke, P. (1989). History as social memory. In T. Butler (Ed.), *Memory: History, culture and the mind* (pp. 97–113). Oxford, UK: Basil Blackwell.

Butler, T. (Ed.). (1989). *Memory: History, culture and the mind*. Oxford, UK: Basil Blackwell.

Carby, H. (1986). "It jus be's dat way sometime": The sexual politics of women's blues. *Radical America, 20,* 9–24.

Clarke, J. R. (2002). Just like us: Cultural constructions of sexuality and race in roman art. In K. N. Pinder (Ed.), *Race-ing art history: Critical readings in race and art history* (pp. 13–30). New York: Routledge.

Corbett, E. (1965). *Classical rhetoric for the modern student*. New York: Oxford University Press.

Daniell, B. (1995). Narratives of literacy: Connecting composition to culture. *CCC, 50,* 393–410.

Donawerth, J. (Ed). (1984). *Shakespeare and the sixteenth-century study of language*. Urbana: University of Illinois Press.

Donawerth, J. (Ed). (2002). *Rhetorical theory by women before 1900*. New York: Rowman & Littlefield.

Douglass, F. (2001). *Narrative of the life of Frederick Douglass, an American slave, written by himself*. J. Blassingame, J. R. McKivigan, & P. P. Hinks (Eds.). New Haven, CT: Yale University Press.

Elbow, P. (1985). The shifting relationships between speech and writing. *CCC, 36,* 283–303.

Ellison, R. (2001). *Living with music: Ralph Ellison's jazz writings*. Robert G. O'Meally. (Ed.). New York: Random House.

Farrell, T. B. (1983). I.Q. and black English. *CCC, 34,* 470–484.

Fernandez, L. (2007, January 5). I upload audio, therefore I teach. *The Chronicle of Higher Education*, p. B27.

Fishkin, S. F. (1993). *Was Huck black?* New York: Oxford University Press.

Garner, T., & Calloway-Thomas, C. (2003). African American orality: Expanding rhetoric. In R. Jackson & E. Richardson (Eds.), *Understanding African-American rhetoric: Classical origins to contemporary innovations* (pp. 43–55). Carbondale: Southern Illinois University Press.

Glenn, C. (2005). *Unspoken: A rhetoric of silence*. Carbondale: Southern Illinois University Press.

Glenn, D. (2007, June 8). You will be tested on this. *The Chronicle of Higher Education*, p. A14.

Goody, J., & Watt, I. (1968). The consequences of literacy. In J. Goody (Ed.), *Literacy in traditional societies* (pp. 27–68). New York: Cambridge University Press.

Harrington, D. (2007). *Remembering the body: Corporeal practices and eighteenth-century elocution*. Unpublished manuscript.

Haskins, E. (2004). *Logos and power in Isocrates and Aristotle.* Columbia: University of South Carolina Press.

Havelock, E. (1963). *Preface to Plato.* Cambridge, MA: Harvard University Press.

Havelock, E. (1978). *The Greek concept of justice: From its shadow in Homer to its substance in Plato.* Cambridge, MA: Harvard University Press.

Havelock, E. (1986a). *The Muse learns to write.* New Haven, CT: Yale University Press.

Havelock, E. (1986b). Orality, literacy, and star wars. *Pre/Text, 7,* 123–132.

Hibbitts, B. (1994). Making sense of metaphors: Visuality, aurality, and the reconfiguration of American legal discourse. *Cardozo Law Review, 16,* 229–356.

Locke, J. L. (1998). *The de-voicing of society: Why we don't talk to each other anymore.* New York: Simon & Schuster.

Logan, S. W. (1999). *We are coming: The persuasive discourse of nineteenth-century African American women.* Carbondale: Southern Illinois University Press.

Lukacs, G. (1989). *The theory of the novel: A historico-philosophical essay on the forms of great epic literature.* Boston: MIT Press. (Original work published 1920)

Middleton, J. I. (1995). Confronting the "master narrative": The privilege of orality in Toni Morrison's *The Bluest Eye. Cultural Studies, 9*(2), 301–317.

Middleton, J. I. (2004). "Both print and oral" and "talking about race": Transforming Toni Morrison's language issues into teaching issues. In E. Richardson & R. Jackson (Eds.), *African American rhetoric(s): Interdisciplinary perspectives* (pp. 242–258). Carbondale: Southern Illinois University Press.

Miller, S. (2006). *Conversation: A history of a declining art.* New Haven, CT: Yale University Press.

Minchin, E. (2001). Similes in Homer: Image, mind's eye, and memory. In J. Watson (Ed.), *Speaking volumes: Orality and literacy in the Greek and Roman world* (pp. 25–52). Boston: Brill.

Morrison, T. (1984). Rootedness: The ancestor as foundation. In M. Evans (Ed.), *Black women writers, 1950–1980* (pp. 339–345). New York: Anchor Press.

Morrison, T. (2006, July). The reader as artist. *O Magazine,* p. 175.

Mullen, H. (1992). Runaway tongue: Resistant orality in *Uncle Tom's cabin, Our Nig, Incidents in the life of a slave girl,* and *Beloved.* In S. Samuels (Ed.), *The culture of sentiment: race, gender, and sentimentality in nineteenth-century America* (pp. 244–264). New York: Oxford University Press.

Mullen, H. (1996). African signs and spirit writing. *Callaloo, 19,* 670–689.

Nelson, S. (Director). (2005). *Sweet honey in the rock: Raise your voice* [American Masters]. New York: Public Broadcasting Service.

Ong, W. (1982). *Orality and literacy: The technologizing of the word.* New York: Methuen Press.

Prendergast, C. (1998). Race the absent presence in composition studies. *CCC, 50*(1), 36–53.

Rabinovitz, L., & Geil, A. (Eds.). (2004). *Memory bytes: History, technology, and digital culture.* Durham, NC: Duke University Press.

Ratcliffe, K. (2005). *Rhetorical listening: Identification, gender, whiteness.* Carbondale: Southern Illinois University Press.

Rath, R. C. (2004). *How early America sounded.* Ithaca, NY: Cornell University Press.

Roediger, D. (2005). *Working toward whiteness: How America's immigrants become white.* New York: Basic Books.

Roen, D. (2006). *Views from the center: The CCCC chairs' addresses, 1977–2005.* New York: Bedford/St. Martin's.

Royster, J. J. (1996). When the first voice you hear is not your own. *CCC, 47,* 29–40.

Royster, J. J. (2000). *Traces of a stream: Literacy and social change among African American women.* Pittsburgh, PA: University of Pittsburgh Press.

Saenger, P. (2005). *Space between words: The origins of silent reading.* Stanford, CA: Stanford University Press.

Schacter, D. L. (1996). *Searching for memory: The brain, the mind, and the past.* New York: Basic Books.

Scott, W. C. (1974). *The oral nature of the Homeric simile.* Leiden, the Netherlands: Lugduni Batavorum: E. J. Brill.

Sipiora, P., & Baumlin, J. S. (Eds.). (2002). *Rhetoric and kairos: Essays in history, theory, and praxis.* Albany: State University of New York.

Street, B. V. (1995). *Social literacies: Critical approaches to literacy development, ethnography and education.* New York: Longman Group.

Strunk, W., Jr. (1920). *The elements of style.* New York: Harcourt, Brace.

Strunk, W., Jr., & White, E. B. (2005). *The elements of style* (Illustrated). New York: Penguin Books.

Swearingen, C. J. (Ed.). (1986). The literacy/orality wars [Special ed.]. *Pre/Text, 7,* 115–218.

Tyson, T. B. (2004). *Blood done sign my name: A true story.* New York: Crown.

Van Buskirk, E. (2006, March 20). How to prevent hearing loss. *Wired Magazine,* Online commentary. Retrieved July 18, 2007, from www.wired.com/entertainment/music/commentary/listeningpost/2006/03/70434

Vega, Y. (Executive Producer). (2006, February 7). Interview with Wynton Marsalis. *The Charlie Rose Show* [Television Broadcast]. New York: Public Broadcasting Service.

Villaneuva, V. (1993). *Bootstraps: From an American academic of color.* Urbana, IL: National Council of Teachers of English.

Welch, K. E. (1999). *Electric rhetoric: Classical rhetoric, oralism, and a new literacy.* Cambridge, MA: MIT Press.

Welch, K. E. (2005). Who made Aristotle white? In T. Kennedy, J. I. Middleton, & K. Ratcliffe (Eds.), Symposium on Whiteness Studies. *Rhetoric Review, 24*(4), 359–402.

West, C. (1999). Wynton Marsalis. In *Restoring hope: Conversations on the future of black America* (pp. 113–140). New York: Beacon.

Zumthor, P. (1990). *Oral poetry.* (K. Murphy-Judy, Trans.). Minneapolis: University of Minnesota Press.

20

Civic Participation and the Undergraduate Curriculum

WENDY B. SHARER

Rhetoric's role in civic education . . . is not just in the public performance of political discourse but in the education of young minds that prepares them to perform their citizenship. Free societies require rhetorically competent citizens. Without rhetorical competence, citizens are disabled in the public arenas of citizen exchange . . . and democracy turns to a ruse disguising the reality of oligarchic power.

—Gerard Hauser

Many scholars have argued that when we talk about a curriculum in rhetoric, we implicitly mean (or at least ought to mean) a curriculum that promotes and incorporates civic engagement. The connection between rhetoric and civic engagement, many have argued, has roots in the very origins of rhetorical study. As William Denman (2004) notes,

The ancient links between rhetoric, civic life, and democracy are a part of the European heritage of rhetorical thought and practice. The history of rhetoric makes clear that the teaching of rhetoric was an instrumental part of the development of the civic persona, the 'citizen orator,' whose skills were at the service of the community. (p. 3)

Similarly, Michael Halloran (1982) has explained that classical Roman rhetoric—through figures such as Quintilian's good man speaking well and Cicero's notion of a "learned speaker"—linked rhetorical education and participation in public arenas.

Somewhere along the developmental path of American higher education, however, rhetoric and civic engagement fell by the wayside. The historical reasons for this decline are several. On the one hand, economic and cultural changes in American society during the 19th century created a climate in which academic priority was given to limiting, rather than expanding, influence in public arenas. According to Halloran (1982), while American teachers and scholars in the 18th century took up classical rhetoric and gave "emphasis to communication on public problems, problems that arise from our life in political communities," the rise of capitalism and a growing popular fear of the political and economic "threat" of immigration in the 19th century led to a shift in curricular priorities. To maintain the class distinctions essential to capitalism, popular education was made to focus less on preparing the vast populace for community and political involvement and more on preparing distinct, hierarchically specialized groups of workers and leaders. Value, in other words, was placed less on public problems and more on separating the elite from the unwashed. As a result, the early 20th century saw the rise of what historians of rhetoric and composition commonly refer to as "current traditional" rhetoric: teacher-centered instruction that focused primarily on static, academic modes, and literary "taste."[1]

The emphases on specialization, research, and professional training that emerged with the German model of higher education in the 19th century also diminished the amount of attention paid to the preparation of active citizens in college and university curricula. Under these emphases, the rhetoric curriculum atrophied, essentially becoming training in communicative competence for the sake of transmitting specialized research or for furthering professional success. Rhetoric—as a fundamentally pedagogical endeavor—further lost prominence in the university because research is the sine qua non of the German university model. According to Hauser and others, a true rhetoric curriculum, which draws on the civic-focused goals of rhetoric's Athenian roots, all but disappeared from higher education by the early decades of the 20th century.

Whatever the historical reasons for the movement away from civic engagement in the undergraduate rhetoric curriculum, the past two decades have witnessed numerous calls to revitalize this area of instruction. Many scholars fear an emaciated public sphere that has been famished by "superficiality of public argument and inattention to sustained discussion" (Zarefsky, 2004, p. 31). The popular understanding of argument in an emaciated public sphere runs the risk of being reduced to televised representatives of diametrically opposed "sides" yelling their assertions at one another. The confluence of advertising and politics, as argued by scholars such as Kathleen Hall Jamieson (1993), has severely constricted civic discourse, but, some argue, rhetorical education is a means to counter trends toward brevity and one-sidedness in public discussion. Others have long criticized the power imbalance built into the civic sphere, an imbalance that results in privilege for the wealthy and the "dominant machinery" of Western culture (Zarefsky, p. 31). Capitalistic influence on civic culture, many have suggested, has made participation and efficacy in the civic arena extremely difficult. In the face of these—and many other—concerns about the decline of public discourse, numerous scholars and teachers of rhetoric have made civic engagement a central concern of their research and teaching.

This chapter provides an overview of some of the central theories of civic participation as they relate to the undergraduate rhetoric curriculum, a discussion of some of the many pedagogical methods employed to foster civic participation in the rhetoric curriculum, and some suggestions for where research and practice in this vital area might go next.

THEORIES OF CIVIC PARTICIPATION IN THE UNDERGRADUATE RHETORIC CURRICULUM

The term *civic* in American rhetoric after the Revolutionary War initially referred to "the kind of discourse common to speeches, printed addresses, essays, pamphlets, and tracts . . . a discourse that was preoccupied with matters of government and governance" (Eldred & Mortensen, 2002, p. 1). Many scholars and teachers today, however, take a more expansive view of the term, using "civic" to indicate rhetorical activity taken in "the service of the community" (Denman, 2004, p. 1). In this broader understanding, rhetorical education for civic participation focuses on providing what Denman calls the "ability to function effectively in democratic life" (p. 1). Rhetoric as a course of study in civic engagement, in other words, connects students with the world around them in ways that promote democracy.

Based on this broader understanding of "civic," the overarching goals of rhetorical education for civic engagement can be summarized—in a highly simplified way—thus:

- To foster critical thinking about public issues
- To help students develop rhetorical efficacy in public arenas
- To foster in students a sense of agency—a belief that they can, and indeed should, use rhetoric to improve the worlds around them

Of course, not all scholars and teachers who favor the promotion of civic engagement in the undergraduate curriculum strive to reach all of these goals in a given course; nonetheless, these characteristics distinguish contemporary rhetorical education for civic engagement from rhetorical education that focuses solely on providing training in academic and/or professional discourse.

To understand the specific practices enacted by teachers of rhetoric who wish to prepare students for civic participation, it is necessary to understand some of the political and educational theories that inform their thinking. One major influence on these teachers has been the work of early-20th-century progressive educator John Dewey. Critiquing educational systems in the early 20th century, Dewey (1916) lamented that schools had severed knowledge from application, thus inhibiting learning that might occur through direct, day-to-day experience. Knowledge Dewey stressed, is active; it involves "bringing some of our dispositions to consciousness with a view to straightening out a perplexity, by conceiving the connection between ourselves and the world in which we live" (p. 344). In a Deweyan curriculum, assignments should arise from the difficulties that students face in their daily lives. A rhetoric course employing Dewey's educational theory might, for instance, ask students to research a problem they have encountered on campus and write a proposal or compose a persuasive speech that suggests a way to solve the problem.[2]

Dewey's political theory has also been highly influential for teachers who promote civic participation in their rhetoric courses. Many of these instructors agree with Dewey's claims about the centrality of communication—written and spoken—to a democratic civic arena, and thus see instruction in rhetoric as an essential part of an undergraduate curriculum that promotes democracy. Dewey (1954) argues that

> if the Great Society is to become a Great Community; a society in which the ever-expanding and intricately ramifying consequences of associated activities shall be known in the full sense of that word, so that an organized, articulate Public comes into being . . . a subtle, delicate, vivid, and responsive art of communication must take possession of the physical machinery of transmission and circulation and breathe life into it. (p. 112)

"The essential need," Dewey continues, "is the improvement of the methods and conditions of debate, discussion, and persuasion"

(1954, p. 208). Dewey's construction of democracy puts a premium on rhetorical education—the rhetorical curriculum is "the essential need" for democracy.

Understandings of civic participation within rhetorical education have also been influenced by the work of political theorists of the public such as Jurgen Habermas (1991), Nancy Fraser (1989, 1992), and Oskar Negt and Alexander Kluge (1993). Political theories of the public provide scholars of rhetoric with various frameworks for envisioning the conflicts and alliances at work in the contemporary civic arena. In his *The Structural Transformation of the Public Sphere*, Habermas (1991) describes the evolution of a bourgeois public sphere—a space in which rational discussion among equals took place in the interest of the common good. As many critics have pointed out, Habermas's discussion is drawn from a limited historical study of public discourses as they circulated in middle-class institutions such as coffee houses, literary societies, voluntary associations, and small presses of Europe in the 18th century. Negt and Kluge (1993), for instance, critique Habermas's original conception of the public sphere by pointing out the class stratification on which it relied. In response, Negt and Kluge promote the development of a proletarian counterpublic—a public sphere in which members of the working classes can meet to discuss ideas for social betterment and from which they might challenge and critique the bourgeois sphere that has been constructed to efface their concerns.

Political theorist Nancy Fraser further complicates Habermas's model of the public sphere by explaining that there has never been one, unified public sphere; rather, there is always a "plurality of competing publics," each with distinct concerns and discursive practices (1989, p. 116). Publics can be differentiated according to the power each holds. The most powerful publics are "large, authoritative, and able to set the terms of

debate for many of the rest." These "leading publics," Fraser notes, "usually have a heavy hand in defining what is political. . . . They can politicize an issue simply by entertaining contestation about it" (1992, p. 167). Or, they can depoliticize something by ignoring or minimizing it. To contest and critique these powerful publics, Fraser suggests, "subaltern counterpublics"—"parallel discursive arenas where members of subordinated social groups [such as women, workers, and peoples of color] invent and circulate counterdiscourses, which in turn permit them to formulate oppositional interpretations of their identities, interests, and needs"—arise (1989, p. 67). These subaltern publics "challenge, modify and/or displace hegemonic elements of the means of interpretation and communication," particularly as those elements affect what gets widespread acknowledgement as politically important (1992, p. 171).

Another prominent group of theorists who have spurred teachers of rhetoric to bolster the role of civic participation in their courses are the so-called radical educationists. These theorists and teachers question the structures of the traditional academic classrooms in which teachers operate because these classrooms do little or nothing to empower students for social change or civic activism. As Weisser (2002) explains,

> Radical educationists have attempted to change teachers from oppressive figures working for the maintenance of the status quo into critical intellectuals struggling to make society more equal and democratic. . . . Their inquiry into the role of the teachers' authority is not confined to discourse in the classroom but is associated with their interest in political equality and social justice in society. (p. 25)

Many radical educationists have been influenced by the work of Brazilian educator Paulo Freire. According to Freire, educators should aim "to create a public sphere of citizens who are able to exercise power over their own lives, and especially over the conditions of knowledge production and acquisition" (1993, p. viii). Freirian pedagogy emphasizes that classroom instruction should not operate via a "banking concept" in which students are viewed as receptacles to be filled with the teacher's knowledge. Instead, Freire argues in his well-known works—such as *Pedagogy of the Oppressed* (1970/1993), *Education for Critical Consciousness* (1974), and *The Politics of Education: Culture, Power, and Liberation* (1984)—that pedagogy should engage students in reading, writing, and speaking processes that they can use to improve the conditions of social reality.[3]

Other important perspectives on the intersections between civic participation and rhetorical education have come from historical and ethnographic research. Feminist historians in particular have looked to the past for examples of how women have used writing and speaking to intervene in civic arenas. In *Traces of a Stream: Literacy and Social Change Among African American Women*, Jacqueline Jones Royster (2000) studies several 19th-century African American women writers who used nonfiction prose to promote social change. Royster explores how a group of predominantly elite black women came to acquire their practices of reading and writing, articulates the traditions of literacy within which these women located their work, and outlines a methodology for similar historical recovery work. The women whose rhetoric Royster studies are not simply historically interesting; rather, they provide examples of how literacy and literacy instruction can be used in the civic arena:

> These speaking/writing women have lived and worked in and for their communities, doing what they do, using their speaking and writing abilities in schools, in churches, in other community organizations, in various walks of life, with whatever impact they can manage to achieve. (p. 231)

Royster (2000) also connects her research in the historical work of community activist women to her work as a teacher. She explains in the final chapter of her book that her research helped her develop teaching strategies that "were designed to enhance the literate resources of young African American women who would potentially join the stream of their rhetorically productive ancestors" (p. 265).

Similar links between historical research and contemporary pedagogical practice have been made by scholars such as Susan Kates (2000), Shirley Wilson Logan (1995, 2004), Karyn Hollis (2004), Carol Mattingly (1999), Rosa Eberly (2000), and Wendy Sharer (2004), to name but a few. In her book *Activist Rhetorics and American Higher Education 1885–1937*, Kates (2000) looks at several historical sites where pedagogy focused on cultivating rhetorical skills of activism among disempowered groups. Exploring rhetorical education for women at Smith College, elocutionary course work for the African America community from Hallie Quinn Brown at Wilbeforce University, and the rhetorical curriculum for working-class students at Brookwood Labor College, Kates argues that history has a lot to offer contemporary scholars and practitioners of what she calls "activist education," or "rhetorical study that pursues the relationship between language and identity, makes civic issues a theme in the rhetoric classroom, and emphasizes the responsibility of community service as part of the writing and speaking curriculum" (p. xi). Hollis (2004) also presents a historical example of how curricula in rhetoric have been structured to encourage critical literacy and social activism. Hollis studies the liberatory rhetorical pedagogy enacted at the Bryn Mawr Summer School for Women Workers. Through the education that women workers received at this summer institution, in genres such as newsletters, statistical studies of economic conditions, visual aids, poetry, and critical autobiography, they "built collective solidarity; they issued inspirational calls to action; they boosted morale and found the courage and conviction needed to fight for justice on the shop floor and the picket line" (p. 167).

Other researchers have focused on how rhetorical education for civic engagement has come through channels outside the university. Carol Mattingly (1999), for instance, considers the Women's Christian Temperance Union as a site of rhetorical education for women activists in the 19th century. Sharer's (2004) work also emphasizes the potential benefits of studying the curricular innovations enacted within women's organizations. Her book, *Vote and Voice: Women's Organizations and Political Literacy, 1915–1930*, explores the rhetorical tactics practiced and taught within the League of Women Voters and the Women's International League for Peace and Freedom in the early decades of the 20th century.

Scholarly research into the rhetorical practices of contemporary disempowered groups has also reinforced connections between rhetoric and civic engagement. Scholars such as Ellen Cushman, Ralph Cintron, and Gwendolyn Pough have contributed to understandings of how contemporary counterpublics use rhetorical practices to intervene in dominant publics. Cushman (1998) and Cintron (1998) use ethnography to study the rhetorical practices that specific disempowered publics use every day. In *Angel's Town: Chero Ways, Gang Life, and Rhetorics of the Everyday*, Cintron considers how various members of a Mexican American community in the Chicago area use commonplace rhetorical practices—from displays of posters and pictures on bedroom walls to gang-related graffiti on city surfaces—to confront economic and social hardships. Cushman's book, *The Struggle and the Tools*, presents a detailed study of rhetorical practices used to navigate and critique bureaucratic assistance systems in an inner-city African American community. Pough (2004) connects the lyrical work of groundbreaking women musicians such as Queen Latifah, Missy Elliot, and Lil' Kim to traditions of African American

women's activism in abolition and civil rights. Furthermore, Pough identifies ways in which, despite the oppressive, hypersexualized nature of contemporary popular images of black womanhood, young black women today can use rap music to construct empowering identities for themselves.

EXAMPLES FROM THE CLASSROOM: TEACHING RHETORIC FOR CIVIC PARTICIPATION

So what have teachers of rhetoric done in the classroom in response to theories and research about the connection between rhetoric and civic participation? In short, quite a bit. One of the most common means of enabling civic participation in the rhetoric classroom is through the teaching of critical reading and response strategies. As Wayne Booth (2004) has explained, rhetoric can be used to better the public good, but it can also be used to deceive through "rhetrickery." Activism and efficacy in the public sphere thus require the ability to understand and critique the rhetorical techniques used in the civic arena to empower some groups of people while disempowering others.

To cultivate awareness of the rhetorical features of public controversy, Weisser (2002) suggests, instructors should help students understand the economic, political, and cultural forces that determine what counts as "public" rhetoric. As part of a curriculum to foster civic engagement, Weisser explains, "We should highlight the ways in which material forces shape what gets said, who gets heard, and how those forces have structured public discourse throughout history" (p. 98). An advanced undergraduate course I taught recently employed such an approach. I asked students to gather popular media texts (print, electronic, broadcast, etc.) that covered a political controversy. One group of students, for example, collected news coverage of the policies of the United States in Central America during the 1980s. After carefully analyzing these media coverage samples, students were asked to delve into nonmainstream, "counterpublic" sources of information about this controversial foreign policy. Students located and reviewed the publications of several Central American Peace activist organizations, including the Sanctuary Movement and Witness for Peace, two church-based American groups that actively assisted Central American communities and refugees uprooted by often corrupt and brutal U.S.-supported regimes. To supplement their understanding of public discourse surrounding the Central American policy of the United States during the 1980s, students conducted secondary research using scholarly texts such as Christian Smith's (1996) *Resisting Reagan: The U.S. Central America Peace Movement.* Another group in this class examined press coverage of the internment of Japanese Americans during World War II, contrasting popular press coverage with details from narratives written by those who were interned. Based on their collection of mainstream and counterpublic-based texts, students in the class then composed detailed critiques of the discourses surrounding the public controversy they had selected.

Agreeing with Hauser's (2004) claim that rhetorical pedagogy "may encourage reflection, but ultimately . . . it asks students to be political agents; it asks them to understand and accept agency" (p. 46), teachers of rhetoric often supplement critical analysis of public texts with assignments that ask students to investigate and argue about the larger causes of public problems. Many instructors, for example, use service-learning assignments to engage students directly with public problems. In *Writing Partnerships,* Thomas Deans (2000) identifies three major categories of service learning in the rhetoric classroom— "Writing *about* the Community," "Writing *for* the Community," and "Writing *with* the Community." Courses that employ a "Writing *about* the Community" model typically ask students to participate in community service of some kind and then to write critically about those experiences, often using traditional academic genres to analyze the causes of problems encountered in their volunteer work and to propose ways to address those problems. Students might, for example, tutor in a local elementary school and, drawing on their experiences, write a persuasive essay or speech that addresses inadequacies in the public education system.

While many instructors incorporate civic participation into instruction in traditional academic genres (e.g., essays and class presentations), interest in service-learning and civic participation in the undergraduate curriculum has led a number of instructors to incorporate instruction in "nontraditional" rhetorical genres. The other two varieties of service-learning pedagogy identified by Deans ask students to produce at least one major assignment in a "nonacademic" genre.[4] In both "Writing *for* the Community" and "Writing *with* the Community" approaches, traditional academic assignments, produced primarily for an instructor, are supplemented with, or replaced entirely by, scenarios in which the end product is not an "original scholarly essay," but a text that serves a purpose within communities beyond the academy. "Writing *for* the Community" courses frequently ask students to produce a text in conjunction with a community agency as part of that agency's service to the community. For example, in a junior-level business writing course, I have linked student writing groups with a local nonprofit organization through an assignment that asks students to discover a rhetorical need within the organization and to collaborate with representatives of that organization to produce a document or series of documents to address that need. One group in this class, for instance, worked with a local Habitat for Humanity chapter to design and compose a brochure for potential volunteers.

Similarly, classes that employ a "Writing *with* the Community" approach involve students, teachers, and community members in a collaborative attempt to produce texts that will effect social change. Rhetorical needs identified by the community members, rather than a scenario provided by a course instructor or textbook writer, determine the texts the students produce. Community members often collaborate with students in producing these texts. Cooperative textual production, Wayne Peck, Linda Flower, and Lorraine Higgins (1995) suggest in their discussion of the community literacy center project at Carnegie Mellon University, encourages social change through "intercultural conversation" among community members, students, and university faculty. Intercultural conversation is a process through which members of the community meet with university students and instructors to identify public issues that need to be addressed and to determine the most effective rhetorical means for effecting change. Because intercultural conversation joins community members and university students and faculty in the processes of identifying a problem and determining a rhetorical response to that problem, it cultivates among members of the university and the local community a generative "willingness to create hybrid texts" based on what will be most rhetorically effective in a real-world rhetorical situation (p. 211). As part of their rhetoric curriculum, for instance, students from Carnegie Mellon have collaborated with teens in inner-city Pittsburgh to produce pamphlets and newsletters for various inner-city communities; to develop scripts, story boards, and videos on teen issues; to compose handbooks on various housing and neighborhood issues for Pittsburgh residents; and to compose myriad rhetorical resources for community betterment (Community Literacy Center).

Other teachers of rhetoric have brought new genres and extra-academic audiences[5] into their curricula through the teaching of so-called personal narrative to effect social change. Higgins and Brush (2006), for example, set up an "educational forum to develop and teach a set of rhetorical strategies" for political efficacy to a group of eight current and former welfare recipients. This educational forum involved Higgins, Brush, and several other writing instructors helping these welfare recipients narrate their experiences with welfare reform policies in ways that might influence public policy and public understanding of welfare reform. While the resulting booklet of narratives, Higgins and Brush admit, "will not produce revolutionary change, overturn current time limits for welfare recipiency, or convert those who oppose welfare on principle," the educational process carried out in the project illustrates how "activist rhetoricians can study and intervene in the creative work necessary" to employ the rhetorics of personal experience for social change (p. 700). Working from this initial booklet of narratives, the women involved in the project and others like them, Higgins and Brush suggest, might build stronger arguments for social change.

Another increasingly popular way to incorporate rhetorical practices of civic engagement into the undergraduate rhetoric curriculum is through assignments that ask students to "translate" academic argument into public argument. These kinds of assignments teach the rhetorical processes of recasting the messages of academic or specialized discourse so that they can have an impact beyond the university. Bruce Herzberg (2000a) has used such assignments in an upper-division, service-learning course in which students produce both a researched academic argument on a public policy issue and "a version of the same argument suitable for public presentation as a speech, letter, Web posting, pamphlet, newspaper or journal article, or other form of public expression." Students benefit from this translation of experience in many ways, Herzberg explains. They "see the value of bringing solid academic research to the public forum" and they gain some expertise as civic rhetors: "Their use of sources, evidence, logic, and refutation in even the shortest 'going public' arguments make them very powerful persuaders" (para. 6).

In addition to their usefulness in teaching public rhetoric, "translation" assignments respond to concerns about the responsibilities teachers of rhetoric and composition have to uphold the mission of the universities in which we teach. Herzberg (2000b), drawing on the work of James Berlin and Michael Halloran, points out that the modern university is largely specialized and professional in nature—organized to prepare students for work and expertise within particular fields of study. While we may wish to challenge or complicate this mission, we cannot simply ignore it. Students, administrators, teachers in other disciplines, and even future employers of our students all expect that we will prepare them to communicate effectively in the academy and the workplace. A big part of our jobs, Herzberg reminds us, "is to teach the conventions of academic discourse and the strategies of college writing [and speaking] in lower-division courses and professional writing [and speaking] in the upper-division ones." However, if we add the responsibility of teaching rhetoric for civic engagement, how do we do it all? As Herzberg asks, "If we claim that civic discourse is now the focus of rhetorical education, are we abandoning our proper role?" (2000a, para. 4). Thanks to assignments that incorporate both specialized, academic rhetoric and genres of popular discourse, we do not have to.

Scholars and teachers of rhetoric are also investigating ways to link courses across disciplines to teach students about the importance of rhetoric to civic endeavors. Rhetorical studies, Steven Mailloux (2003) points out, already take place across academic departments: "In contrast to departmentalized disciplines such as history, sociology, and

biology, rhetorical studies is today an *inter*discipline located in fragmented pieces as subfields in various departments, primarily English and Communication, which have their own independent, professional disciplinary identities" (pp. 129–130). These "fragmented pieces" of rhetorical study might be brought together in efforts to provide instruction in the rhetorical practices of active citizenship. Particular attention has been paid of late to integrating instruction in the oral skills of spoken rhetoric and the written skills of printed and electronic rhetoric. In practice, the written and the spoken, the verbal and the visual, and the word and the sound work together to achieve rhetorical purposes. This is certainly the case in efforts to engender social change. For example, lengthy campaigns aimed at changing legislation inevitably require rhetorical skill in both speaking and writing, with both modes of communication working to reinforce the other. Royster (2000) makes a similar point in her study of African American women activists, leading her to suggest that when we examine "literate practices . . . as behavior of events within social and cultural context, dichotomies between literacy and orality blur, and so do hierarchies" (p. 44).

Scholars and teachers of written and spoken rhetoric are attempting to reflect this productive blurring of boundaries through participation in cross-disciplinary coalitions such as the Alliance of Rhetoric Societies (ARS), an organization that brings together scholars studying rhetoric in English departments, Communications departments, and freestanding Rhetoric or Writing programs. One of the many goals of this organization is to promote "dialogue across traditions" to "reclaim rhetoric's role in civic education" (Hauser, 2004, p. 48). How might such cross-disciplinary approaches work? The efforts of educators in composition and speech communication might be coordinated in a curriculum that links instruction in public speaking and community writing or that offers rhetorical instruction in practices of democratic discussion via written (including electronic) and spoken means. For example, overlapping assignments in speech and composition courses might ask students to put together a public issue campaign—a combination of verbal, visual, and oral texts in support of a public policy change. Through such coordination of assignments, students gain facility in multimodal rhetoric and experience in focused, extended civic participation.

Teachers and scholars of rhetoric within English and Communications departments might also work together to advocate for broader undergraduate programs in which rhetorical education for citizenship plays a central role. Responsibility for teaching the rhetorical practices of political engagement should not rest entirely on the shoulders of specialists in Communications or English departments; rather, it should be the concern of all departments. Beyond the obvious fact that one or two required courses in writing or public speaking cannot possibly expose students to the immense variety of persuasive skills needed for political engagement, responsibility for civic involvement should be an interdisciplinary concern because it involves participation in an array of symbolic systems other than writing and speaking. According to David Barton and Mary Hamilton (2000), when participating in literacy events, whether those events are in the political realm or elsewhere, "people use written language in an integrated way as part of a range of semiotic systems: these semiotic systems include mathematical systems, musical notation, maps, and other non-text-based images" (pp. 8–9). Given the variety of semiotic systems involved in civic rhetoric, we might work to develop linked courses in which students combine what they learn in an economics course, for example, with the persuasive skills for public participation that they learn in their composition and speech courses. Through all three courses, a student might develop a powerful series of

arguments in support of a public economic issue, such as welfare reform or public school funding. Instruction in dramatic methods, music, and artwork from colleagues in other departments might also supplement the rhetorical education provided by Communications and English departments, thus expanding the means of delivery through which students can contribute to civic conversations. As Stewart, Smith, and Denton (2001) have explained, music and art have played prominent roles in major social movements; thus, it makes sense to combine instruction in these areas with our larger efforts to promote civic participation in the undergraduate rhetoric curriculum. Through such interdisciplinary efforts, we can encourage students to think of writing and speaking not in terms of producing isolated papers or speeches but as part of larger semiotic campaigns to achieve political and social goals.

Scholars and teachers who wish to see a civic element again pervade rhetorical education must also work to popularize a vision of rhetoric as essential to civic engagement. As David Zarefsky (2004) has noted, rhetoric's image in the public eye is "murky":

> Eloquence and rhetorical leadership are expected, particularly in times of crisis; yet rhetoric is disdained as posturing and bluster. . . . Rhetoric is seen as a path to civic engagement but is also viewed as a deterrent to civic participation. Training in argument and advocacy is seen as essential preparation for civic life and yet also as a means of camouflage for heartfelt personal conviction. (p. 29)

Thus, our work to promote civic participation in the rhetoric curriculum must involve public relations. Part of this effort to change the public image of rhetoric, Zarefsky (2004) argues, might involve scholars and teachers of rhetoric going public with their expertise:

> Rhetoricians should engage in activities that respond to public issues and promote

productive exchanges of ideas and participation in public discourse. These might include organizing and participating in town meetings, facilitating community-based deliberative groups . . . giving talks and writing essays on public issues, [and] analyzing significant rhetorical texts or occasions for the benefit of public audiences, and policy-making bodies. (p. 36)

If scholars of rhetoric can convince those outside the academy of the value of rhetoric to civic life through modeling and teaching what we study, we are much more likely to witness the success of our curricular attempts to integrate rhetorical and civic education.

WHERE DO WE GO FROM HERE? THE FUTURE OF CIVIC ENGAGEMENT RESEARCH AND PEDAGOGY

In addition to public relations efforts aimed at changing popular perceptions of rhetoric, what else needs to happen if, in the near future, rhetoric and civic participation are to be at the center of undergraduate education? What key issues and questions must scholars and teachers address as they consider how to make civic participation one of their goals in the rhetoric classroom?

One important issue involves prioritizing goals and time management: How much curricular time can and should specialists in rhetoric devote to academic discourse? To civic discourse? How much time should undergraduate courses, particularly required courses, devote to engaging students outside the academy? Those of us who teach required classes in writing or public speaking are all too familiar with institutional expectations that our classes will teach proper, error-free academic discourse, not attempt to familiarize our students with genres of local government or civic activity. What are educators who share Bruce Herzberg's (2000b) desire to honor both "the goals of education for democracy" and

"the current academic mission and our current students' needs and expectations" to do? As many teachers of rhetoric are already aware, simply focusing on academic discourse easily fills a semester—how do we also teach civic discourse?

Teachers of rhetoric for civic engagement must also continue to be wary of the potential for elitist, partisan, or paternalistic endeavors to be carried out under the banner of teaching civic participation. Educational work done in the spirit of promoting change should not be constructed or construed as some sort of rescue effort for the underprivileged outside the halls of academe. Even the term *service*, as used in the name of service learning, Deans (2000) explains, "evokes not only the specter of unequal server-served relations . . . but also a gendered history in which women, both within and outside the academy, have been enculturated to submerge their selves in service to others" (p. 23). A related danger attending civic engagement initiatives in rhetoric and composition courses is the risk that these courses will be perceived as a service to local governments, community agencies, or political groups in much the same way that such courses have been viewed in the past as "service courses" for other academic disciplines. The rhetoric classroom should not become a volunteer center or a site for indoctrinating students in particular kinds of political organizations.

Incorporating civic participation into the undergraduate curriculum can also be very risky because of ongoing partisan resistance faced by the university. Conservative pundits have made a habit of critiquing the "liberal bias" of the academy, and both students and their parents have offered resistance to the notion of teaching civic participation, choosing to see this as a politically motivated curriculum. As Elizabeth Ervin (2006) puts it,

> Curricular initiatives that emphasize public intellectualism, community literacy, service learning, advocacy, activism, and the like

are monitored and evaluated with suspicion (if not outright cynicism) by many of the taxpayers, granting agencies, families, and students who pay the tuition and fees and enroll in the courses that make possible our livelihoods. (p. 410)

Linda Brodkey's (1996) experience at the University of Texas in the early 1990s—during which her proposed writing curriculum focused on "Writing About Difference" was abandoned after conservative media outlets generated a public outcry against the supposed liberal bias of the course—is a powerful example of public suspicion and the detrimental results of such suspicion. If our efforts are cast as subversive political plotting, we may encounter heavy pressure from those who determine our financial situation.

Other resistance to civic participation as a goal in the rhetoric classroom results from disconnects between our priorities and those of our students. Some students, while not vehemently opposed to the attitudes and practices we might ask them to take up in a civic engagement curriculum, may resist the curriculum because it is simply not a priority for them—they see higher education as a way to improve their own situations in life, not as a place to cultivate their contributions to the larger public. As Ervin (2006) explains,

> Many of them are in college precisely and unabashedly to transcend membership in "the public" in favor of joining the ranks of those who can afford private services, pursue private interests, and in general separate themselves from the inconveniences and stigma associated with the public. (pp. 414–415)

Professional and financial success, in other words, are their goals for college, and they eschew what they see as "'required' public uplift" (p. 414).

How might we change perception of liberal bias and work with, rather than against, the goals of some of our more career-focused

students? Ervin (2006) proposes a pedagogical shift from an emphasis on "public issues" in the rhetoric curriculum to the teaching of "publicist rhetorical strategies," or the rhetorical practices needed to effectively promote change, regardless of the specific nature of that change (pp. 412, 415). Rather than taking up politicized issues such as health care reform, homelessness, or educational inequities, Ervin suggests, teachers should organize their curriculum around the processes that any rhetor would need to go through to achieve change. The processes of "branding, framing, coalition building, and agitation," she argues, are essential to public participation, regardless of the issue(s) to which they are applied. "Branding" involves "the role of language, logos, and other symbols or images in creating an identity for a company, a product, or even a person" (p. 416), and is essential for the promoters of a particular cause to develop a public ethos. "Framing," Ervin explains, involves identifying the values influencing a particular stand on a public issue and developing a set of facts, articulating a series of consequences, and building a body of arguments based on these values. "Coalition building," as the name suggests, involves the rhetorical practices of recruiting activists to support a particular cause, and "agitation" refers to the rhetorical tactics of raising public awareness of a problem and public desire for change (pp. 416–419). Through a curriculum based on these various rhetorical strategies, students would develop the tools to participate in public discussions on issues that they choose rather than participating in discussions of public issues that we identify and that, Ervin explains, often "carry counterproductive partisan connotations" (p. 419).

While a shift in focus to rhetorical techniques of publicity responds to criticisms leveled against instructors who require students to participate in the rhetoric of politically charged issues, such a shift does not address what instructors of rhetoric are to do when students wish to publicize a change or position that goes against our moral convictions. What do we do, for instance, if a student wants to promote a campus rule that student organizations *can* discriminate on the basis of sexual preference? Do we continue ahead, helping that student develop the rhetorical skills to publicize this notion? As work in civic participation in the undergraduate rhetoric curriculum continues to develop, scholars and teachers will need to face such ethical questions and find a balance between respecting students' political agendas and countering oppressive discourses.

Even if students are not opposed to assignments that foster civic engagement—either because they see those assignments as detracting from the financial/career ends of education or because they see those assignments as partisan endeavors—it is often still a challenge to engage them in civic rhetoric projects. Many times, students do not feel empowered when it comes to communicating in the civic arena. Their ideas and their rhetoric, they sense, will not be heard. To a certain extent, their perceptions are accurate—it is indeed very difficult to have one's voice heard without money and the access to corporatized media channels that money can buy. However, there are pedagogical practices that can help students develop a sense of agency in the civic arena. One such practice involves ensuring that students write for a real audience about a real concern in their immediate lives rather than asking them to focus on enormous, far-reaching problems. The rhetoric and writing curriculum, Paul Collins (2001) argues in his textbook *Community Writing,* has been dominated by curricula tied to essay-based textbook readers that have "spooned out preselected 'important social issues' like cod liver oil, without bothering to ask whether students would have a reason to care about them" (p. xi). Engaging students in issues faced by local and/or regional citizens might be more effective in developing a sense of rhetorical power in students. As

Mortensen (1998) has argued, "If composition teacher-researchers are to stand as public intellectuals . . . they must also speak to the ethical concerns of the local—the community, the commonwealth, the region" (p. 163). More effective assignments to promote civic participation might ask students to investigate community or campus security concerns, controversial local ordinances, specific city or state laws, local election campaign issues, problematic campus policies and procedures, or any number of issues that have a direct, identifiable impact on the students' day-to-day environments.

Others suggest that integrating civic engagement into the curriculum entails altering the scope of who we traditionally consider as the students served by that curriculum. The "community literacy" project articulated and implemented by Peck et al. (1995) at the University of Pittsburgh is one such example of this expansive notion of "university students." In collaborative service-learning projects such as those at the CLC in Pittsburgh, both the enrolled students and the community members those students work with learn and practice strategies of civic engagement. Through such collaborations of students (enrolled and extra-academic), civic engagement is not just the subject of study, it is enacted. Similarly, Ellen Cushman (1996) stresses that civic engagement can become part of the undergraduate curriculum through the instruction that scholars of rhetoric might provide to underserved populations in the communities around the university. As Henry Giroux (1995) argues,

> Public intellectuals . . . need to define higher education as a public resource vital to the moral life of the nation and open to working people and communities that are often viewed as marginal to such institutions and their diverse resources of knowledge and skills. (p. 250)

At the same time that civic engagement in the rhetoric curriculum seems to rely on local audiences and issues, the notion of civic engagement has become more complex due to the increased globalization of politics, economics, and religion. Preparing students for civic participation, in other words, increasingly means preparing students on a global level because civic issues are often intricately connected to global concerns. Margaret Himley (2003) has addressed the need for internationalized instruction in rhetoric and composition. According to Himley, the current context of globalization in communication—a situation made more apparent and accessible to us and to our students through the Web—suggests that our curricula ought to include courses that prepare students to read, critique, and contribute to information in a global context. Globalization, Himley points out, "depends on the circulation of texts, technology, and e-space." To prepare students for critical participation in this global context, she argues, "Students need to acquire an understanding . . . of the ways texts move through production, distribution, and circulation" (p. 60). Furthermore, she continues, "Students can access information instantaneously from around the globe, and need the geopolitical knowledge to assess that information, to frame it, and to challenge and critique it" (p. 61).

In a similar vein, John Trimbur and Bruce Horner (2002) assert that international perspectives ought to have greater prominence in the undergraduate rhetoric curriculum. They suggest several means by which we might advance an internationalist perspective in rhetoric and composition. We might design assignments that encourage students to think about language privileges; we might rethink the institutional, pedagogical, and research relationships among composition, English as a Second Language (ESL), and other languages in the academy; and we might develop stronger relationships between writing programs and writing instruction in other languages (pp. 621–622). As the push for civic education and the scope of globalization grows, teachers

of rhetoric will need to respond to the seemingly contradictory imperatives to focus locally to strengthen students' sense of efficacy and to focus globally to emphasize the complex reality of civic issues.

Developing effective approaches to teaching rhetoric and civic participation will also require vigilant review of the roles that the Internet can and should play in a curriculum aimed at encouraging civic participation. Several years ago, the Internet seemed like a promising venue for engaging students in civic discourse, even on an international scale. But time and the growing commercialization of the Internet have given cause for great concern. As Lester Faigley (1997) warned several years ago in his Chair's address to the Conference on College Composition and Communication, "Providing venues for the discussion of public issues does not necessarily lead to a more informed public, increased civic engagement, or enhanced democracy" (p. 42). For one thing, Faigley points out, much of the technology (software and hardware) that is used to access and navigate the Internet is owned by large corporations. The "cyberdemocracy" of the Internet is restricted by the material conditions that determine which groups of people— nationally and internationally—get their voices heard. Selfe (1999) has expressed similar concerns about access to the Web in her book *Technology and Literacy in the 21st Century: The Importance of Paying Attention.* Irene Ward (1997), too, questions the viability of the Internet as a place to promote public rhetoric because of the economic limitations that affect both basic access to the Internet and the ability to design and publish Web sites. Despite these limitations, the relative ease with which Internet-based research, discussion, and publication can be integrated into undergraduate courses makes the Web very appealing as a means through which students can address real audiences and as a venue through which they can engage and debate public issues. The trick will be for instructors to integrate the

Internet in a way that balances caution and optimism.

If an instructor can negotiate all these complexities of teaching rhetoric for civic engagement, he or she is still faced with a very complicated task: assessing the strengths and weaknesses of her pedagogy. As more scholars and teachers of rhetoric embrace the idea of civic engagement in undergraduate courses, we, as a field, need to identify outcomes. We need to determine and describe the rhetorical abilities we want students to have as a result of an undergraduate curriculum that integrates rhetoric and civic engagement. Hauser (2004), reflecting on the ARS conference, suggests that beyond the fairly standard outcomes of communicative competence in first-year writing and speaking courses, individual teachers and first-year programs might devise and promote a set of outcomes statements that helps students "learn the attributes of civic ethos," that "promotes the development of *deliberative skills* in forums inside and outside academia . . . [and that] develops heightened awareness of the *consequences* of rhetorical performance in and outside of the classroom" (p. 49). Beyond outcomes statements that we may use to assess the performance of individual students and classes, rhetoric teachers need long-term studies to determine the effect that those efforts will have on both the students and the communities we attempt to engage.

NOTES

1. Thomas Miller (2000) has also charted the desiccation of civic rhetoric within the university curriculum. According to Miller, the latter half of the 18th century saw a rift develop between moral philosophy and rhetoric, with specialists in the former lecturing on topics such as psychology, sociology, and political economy; while the latter "moved away from the civic tradition to subordinate the composition of public discourse to commentaries on tasteful responses" (p. 33).

2. For more detail about the relationship between Deweyan educational theory and recent writing pedagogy, see Tom Deans's (2000) book *Writing Partnerships*.

3. Radical pedagogues have also been influenced by the more recent work of critical educational theorists such as Henry Giroux. Giroux and coauthor Susan Searls (2004) argue in *Take Back Higher Education* that "higher education should be an institution that offers students the opportunity to involve themselves in the deepest problems of society and to acquire the knowledge, skills, and ethical vocabularies necessary for critical dialogue and broadened civic participation" (p. 279). Involvement, Giroux and Searls stress, does not just mean studying the texts involved in civic activity in the relative insularity of the classroom; rather,

> students need to cross the boundary that separates colleges and universities from the larger world . . . to use their knowledge and skills to engage in community service, organize partnerships between schools and nonprofits, or protest racism and poverty by actually challenging their manifestations within the larger community and social order. (p. 277)

In addition, in *Schooling and the Struggle for Public Life,* Giroux (1988a) urges that teachers be trained to understand the relationship between power and language in educational practice. If teachers understand how language can construct an oppressive student-teacher dynamic in the traditional classroom, those teachers will be better equipped to subvert that dynamic and thus empower students as civic participants.

4. Several scholars who teach rhetoric through writing instruction have proffered critiques of "essayistic" writing, pointing to its elitism and distance from the rhetorical genres of the everyday. See Crowley (1998), Flannery (1995), Weisser (2002), and Reynolds (1998). Despite these critiques of the academic essay genre, many service-learning practitioners argue that traditional academic essay forms can be usefully incorporated into service-learning projects. The critical analysis skills students can hone through techniques of academic literacy can serve them well in assessing and actively contributing to the goals and tactics of the communities they engage in as part of service-learning courses. See, for example, Horner (2001).

5. Both "Writing *for* the Community" and "Writing *with* the Community" models of service learning in the undergraduate rhetoric curriculum have the advantage of connecting students to audiences beyond the academy, another central goal of rhetorical instruction for civic participation. Teaching rhetoric for civic participation also requires that we locate, or help our students locate, real audiences for their writing—someone other than the teacher. As Susan Wells (1996) has argued, we must discover or construct public spaces in which our students' work will be read or heard by others, otherwise "public writing . . . means 'writing for no audience at all" (p. 328). Only by creating scenarios in which students' literate practices will be received by a broader audience can we hope to teach them to anticipate responses that are more substantial and perhaps more meaningful than our individual comments and grades. Incorporating the search for or construction of spaces to address "real" audiences into the undergraduate classroom also helps students become more aware of the subtle distinctions among groups, breaking down the myth of the "general public" audience and reinforcing the insights of theorists such as Fraser (1989, 1992), who posits the existence of myriad, and often competing, public spheres.

REFERENCES

Barton, D., & Hamilton, M. (2000). Literacy practices. In D. Barton, M. Hamilton, & R. Ivanic (Eds.), *Situated literacies: Reading and writing in context* (pp. 7–15). New York: Routledge.

Booth, W. (2004). *The rhetoric of rhetoric: The quest for effective communication*. Malden, MA: Blackwell.

Brodkey, L. (1996). *Writing permitted in designated areas only*. Minneapolis: University of Minnesota Press.

Cintron, R. (1998). *Angels' town: Chero ways, gang life, and the rhetorics of the everyday*. Boston: Beacon Press.

Collins, P. (2001). *Community writing*. Mahwah, NJ: Erlbaum.

Community Literacy Center. (n.d.). *Hands on community literacy: Backfiles 1986–1996 from the Community Literacy Center*. Retrieved June 13, 2007, from http://english.cmu.edu/research/clc/default.html

Crowley, S. (1998). *Composition in the university: Historical and polemical essays*. Pittsburgh, PA: University of Pittsburgh Press.

Cushman, E. (1996). The rhetorician as an agent of social change. *College Composition and Communication, 47*, 7–28.

Cushman, E. (1998). *The struggle and the tools: Oral and literate strategies in an inner city community*. Albany: State University of New York Press.

Deans, T. (2000). *Writing partnerships: Service learning in composition*. Urbana, IL: NCTE.

Denman, W. (2004). Rhetoric, the "Citizen-Orator," and the revitalization of civic discourse in American life. In C. Glenn, M. Lyday, & W. Sharer (Eds.), *Rhetorical education in America* (pp. 3–17). Tuscaloosa: University of Alabama Press.

Dewey, J. (1916). *Democracy and education*. New York: Free Press.

Dewey, J. (1954). *The public and its problems*. Chicago: Swallow Press.

Eberly, R. (2000). *Citizen critics: Literary public spheres*. Urbana: University of Illinois Press.

Eldred, J. C., & Mortensen, P. (2002). *Imagining rhetoric: Composing women of the early republic*. Pittsburgh, PA: University of Pittsburgh Press.

Ervin, E. (2006). Teaching public literacy: The partisanship problem. *College English, 68*, 407–421.

Faigley, L. (1997). Literacy after the revolution, 1996. CCCC Chair's Address. *College Composition and Communication, 48*, 30–43.

Flannery, K. T. (1995). *The emperor's new clothes: Literature, literacy, and the ideology of style*. Pittsburgh, PA: University of Pittsburgh Press.

Fraser, N. (1989). *Unruly practices: Power, discourse and gender in contemporary social theory*. Minneapolis: University of Minnesota Press.

Fraser, N. (1992). Rethinking the public sphere: A contribution to the critique of actually existing democracy. In C. Calhoun (Ed.), *Habermas and the public sphere* (pp. 109–142). Cambridge, MA: MIT Press.

Freire, P. (1974). *Education for critical consciousness*. New York: Crossroad.

Freire, P. (1984). *The politics of education: Culture, power, and liberation*. Westport, CT: Bergin & Garvey.

Freire, P. (1993). *Pedagogy of the oppressed* (M. B. Ramos, Trans.). New York: Continuum. (Original work published 1970)

Giroux, H. A. (1988a). *Schooling and the struggle for public life: Democracy's promise and education's challenge.* Minneapolis: University of Minnesota Press.

Giroux, H. A. (1995). Beyond the ivory tower: Public intellectuals and the crisis of higher education. In M. Bérubé & C. Nelson (Eds.), *Higher education under fire: Politics, economics, and the crisis of the humanities* (pp. 238–258). New York: Routledge.

Giroux, H. A., & Searls, S. (2004). *Take back higher education.* New York: Palgrave.

Habermas, J. (1991). *The structural transformation of the public sphere.* Boston: MIT Press.

Halloran, S. M. (1982). Rhetoric in the American college curriculum: The decline of public discourse. *PRE/TEXT, 3,* 245–269.

Hauser, G. (2004). Teaching rhetoric: Or why rhetoric isn't just another kind of philosophy or literary criticism. *Rhetoric Society Quarterly, 34*(3), 39–54.

Herzberg, B. (2000a). Civic literacy and service learning. In L. K. Shamoon, R. M. Howard, S. Jamieson, & R. A. Schwegler (Eds.), *Coming of age: The advanced writing curriculum* (pp. 123 and CD-ROM). Portsmouth, NH: Boynton/Cook.

Herzberg, B. (2000b). Service learning and public discourse. *JAC, 20,* 391–404.

Higgins, L., & Brush, L. (2006). Personal experience narrative and public debate: Writing the wrongs of welfare. *College Composition and Communication, 57*(4), 694–729.

Himley, M. (2003). Writing programs and pedagogies in a globalized landscape. *WPA: Writing Program Administration, 26,* 49–66.

Hollis, K. (2004). *Liberating voices: Writing at the Bryn Mawr summer school for women workers.* Carbondale: Southern Illinois University Press.

Horner, B. (2001). Resisting academics. In A. Greenbaum (Ed.), *Insurrections: Approaches to resistance in composition studies* (pp. 169–184). Albany: State University of New York Press.

Jamieson, K. H. (1993). *Dirty politics: Deception, distraction, and democracy.* New York: Oxford University Press.

Kates, S. (2000). *Activist rhetorics and American higher education, 1885–1937.* Carbondale: Southern Illinois University Press.

Logan, S. W. (1995). *We are coming: The persuasive discourse of nineteenth-century black women.* Carbondale: Southern Illinois University Press.

Logan, S. W. (2004). "To get an education and teach my people": Rhetoric for social change. In C. Glenn, M. Lyday, & W. Sharer (Eds.), *Rhetorical education in America* (pp. 36–54). Tuscaloosa: University of Alabama Press.

Mailloux, S. (2003). Practices, theories, and traditions: Further thoughts on the disciplinary identities of English and communication studies. *Rhetoric Society Quarterly, 33*(1), 129–138.

Mattingly, C. (1999). *Well-tempered women: Nineteenth-century temperance rhetoric.* Carbondale: Southern Illinois University Press.

Miller, T. (2000). Rhetoric within and without composition: Reimagining the Civic. In L. K. Shamoon, R. M. Howard, S. Jamieson, & R. A. Schwegler (Eds.), *Coming of age: The advanced writing curriculum* (pp. 32–41). Portsmouth, NH: Boynton/Cook.

Mortensen, P. (1998). Going public. *College Composition and Communication, 50,* 182–205.

Negt, O., & Kluge, A. (1993). *Public sphere and experience: Analysis of the bourgeois and proletarian public sphere.* Minneapolis: University of Minnesota Press.

Peck, W. C., Flower, L., & Higgins, L. (1995). Community literacy. *College Composition and Communication, 46,* 199–222.

Pough, G. (2004). *Check it while I wreck it: Black women, hip hop culture, and the public sphere.* Boston: Northeastern.

Reynolds, N. (1998). Interrupting our way to agency: Feminist cultural studies and composition. In S. Jarratt & L. Worsham (Eds.), *Feminism and composition studies: In other words* (pp. 58–73). New York: MLA.

Royster, J. (2000). *Traces of a stream: Literacy and social change among African American women.* Pittsburgh, PA: University of Pittsburgh Press.

Selfe, C. L. (1999). *Technology and literacy in the twenty-first century: The importance of paying attention.* Carbondale: Southern Illinois University Press.

Sharer, W. (2004). *Vote and voice: Women's organizations and political literacy, 1915–1930.*

Carbondale: Southern Illinois University Press.

Smith, C. (1996). *Resisting Reagan: The U.S. Central America peace movement.* Chicago: University of Chicago Press.

Stewart, C. J., Smith, C. A., & Denton, R. E. (2001). *Persuasion and social movements* (4th ed.). Prospect Heights, IL: Waveland Press.

Trimbur, J., & Horner, B. (2002). English only and U.S. college composition. *College Composition and Communication, 53,* 594–630.

Ward, I. (1997). How democratic can we get? The Internet, the public sphere, and public discourse. *JAC, 17,* 365–380.

Weisser, C. (2002). *Moving beyond academic discourse: Composition studies and the public sphere.* Carbondale: Southern Illinois University Press.

Wells, S. (1996). Rogue cops and health care: What do we want from public writing? *College Composition and Communication, 43,* 325–341.

Zarefsky, D. (2004). Institutional and social goals for rhetoric. *Rhetoric Society Quarterly 34*(3), 27–38.

21

Visual Rhetoric and/as Critical Pedagogy

BRIAN L. OTT

GREG DICKINSON

Once again a complexly related transformation is occurring in [the] disciplines of the human sciences and the sphere of public culture. I want to call this shift "the pictorial turn."

—Mitchell (1994, p. 11)

Some meanings are better communicated pictorially than verbally. . . . Images also can wield great power—religious, tribal, romantic, pedagogic.

—Stephens (1998, pp. 59, 62)

For the last 40 years now, the Western world has been undergoing a seismic, even paradigmatic, shift—the transition from modernity to postmodernity. Like all paradigm shifts, this one is driven, at least in part, by advances and changes in communication technologies. Just as the invention and development of the printing press gave rise to modernity, spreading literacy along with scientific rationalism, the comparatively recent development of electronic and digital media technologies has fueled the endless production of spectacle, styles, and images that typify the "postmodern condition." While what has been described as "the pictorial turn" or "the rise of the image" has certainly not eliminated the printed word—just as mass printing did not eliminate the spoken word—the visual is quickly coming to displace the linguistic in social importance. To the extent that images are structured and function differently than language, the proliferation of visual imagery in contemporary life is (re)orienting our sense of ourselves and our world. Images are increasingly coming to shape both what we think and how we think. The growing centrality and significance of visuality in society has spawned a new, interdisciplinary field of research—variously termed visual rhetoric, visual argument, visual communication, visual culture, and visual studies—that draws on the disparate literatures in art history, aesthetics, communication, English, sociology, philosophy, psychology, and cognitive science among others (Elkins, 2003, pp. 1–7; Finnegan, 2004b, p. 234). The intellectual energy around visual rhetoric is evident in the sheer number of introductory texts and readers that have emerged in the last few years (Elkins, 2003; Fuery & Fuery, 2003; Hill & Helmers, 2004; Mirzoeff, 1998; Rose, 2001; Schirato & Webb, 2004; Smith, Moriarty, Barbatsis, & Kenney, 2005; Sturken & Cartwright, 2001).

As a field, visual rhetoric is broadly interested in the pedagogical character of images—in the way visual imagery *teaches* us to participate in "sense making." In addition to being a *mode* of pedagogy, images can also be a *tool for* and *subject of* classroom pedagogy. To use this tool or teach this subject effectively requires an understanding of the unique character of images themselves. Thus, the goal of this essay is twofold: To review, synthesize, and comment on the principal conceptions of visual rhetoric and to outline an approach to teaching (with) visual rhetoric. In doing so, this chapter maps the multifaceted terrain and territory of visual rhetoric. Like all maps, its specific signposts and markers are the product of its cartographers and, subsequently, neither comprehensive nor objective. For example, a roadmap of the United States visually represents the borders of the nation, the internal spatial relations among cities and states, and the highways and roads that connect these individual places, and, if it is an AAA map, designates some roads as particularly beautiful. At the same time, the map will necessarily ignore other important aspects of the nation's geography, passing over, for example, detailed

representation of land ownership or altitude change. Maps, then, are at best guides—instruments for orienting oneself spatially. Whatever its limitations, we believe that *mapping* is an especially appropriate method for taking up the field of visual studies, whose central object of analysis—the image—is itself a spatial mode of communication.

CONCEPTUALIZING VISUAL RHETORIC

There is little consensus about what visual rhetoric is or what it does. So let us begin by identifying the few principles about which there appears to be agreement. (1) Visual rhetoric is a *meaningful* set of visible signs and therefore a mode of communication. But as with other modes of communication, visual imagery does not have to be meaningful to everyone to function as rhetoric. Visual signs in one culture may have little or no significance in another. (2) Visual rhetoric is rooted in looking, seeing, and visualizing. It is fundamentally an optical process, although that process is registered viscerally by the body as well as symbolically by the mind. (3) While the forms of visual rhetoric vary widely, from paintings and photographs to sculptures and buildings to films and television, they are human constructions and indulgences. Thus, while landscapes and distant stars can both be seen, they are meaningless outside of human affairs. They are imbued with meaning by their (re)production in visual imagery.

It is with regard to meaning making that visual imagery is most clearly like other modes of rhetoric such as speech and writing. The difficulty, of course, is that the rhetorical tradition privileges the word by focusing on how spoken and written language persuades. But paintings, photographs, buildings, television, and films convey meaning largely without words. Indeed, the force of these messages exists not only in spite of language's absence but also frequently *because* of language's absence. Such texts appeal to different cognitive structures, to different modes of understandings, and to different emotional possibilities. And so visual rhetoric, while clearly rhetorical in the sense that its messages engage us in questions of belief, value, and action, is *not* simply rhetoric as it has been theorized and taught for more than 2,000 years.

The struggle for teachers of visual rhetoric, then, is to draw on the rhetorical tradition to illuminate visual texts while, at the same time, recognizing the very real limitations of traditional rhetorical theory, criticism, and pedagogy in accounting for the unique rhetorical power of visual imagery. Rhetorical theorists and critics have, we maintain, addressed these concurrent themes in three key ways: (1) One group of scholars has applied the tools of public address scholarship to evaluate the civic role of public images; (2) a second group has turned to theories of everyday life to explore the visual framing of everydayness; and (3) a third group has sought to identify the unique logic fostered by visual imagery. In the next section, we will review and assess each of these perspectives on visual rhetoric. As a way of helping readers understand the differences among these perspectives, we will also conduct a concise analysis of one image in relationship to each of the perspectives we discuss.

Before turning to the individual perspectives, however, we wish to briefly introduce and contextualize the image that will serve as our running example. Tourists traveling to or coming from Yellowstone National Park are likely to visit the Buffalo Bill Historical Center (BBHC) in Cody, Wyoming. The BBHC is an impressive complex that houses five separate, though related, museums: the Buffalo Bill Museum, the Cody Firearms Museum, the Whitney Gallery of Western Art, the Plains Indian Museum, and the Draper Museum of Natural History. On entering the complex, visitors are greeted by a large bronze statue of William "Buffalo Bill" Cody, who became famous first through his appearance in dime store novels about the "Old West" and later through his traveling Wild West show. Our running example is a photograph that we took of that statue while studying the BBHC (see

Figure 21.1   The Statue of William "Buffalo Bill" Cody at the Entrance to the Buffalo Bill Historical Center in Cody, Wyoming

SOURCE: Photograph by Brian L. Ott.

Figure 21.1). Raised above visitors on a dais, Cody stands in a relaxed pose, his hat off as if welcoming guests and his gun resting gently at his side. He is clothed in his familiar show costume and looks every bit the dramatic figure that history and popular memory story him to have been. As we return to this image throughout the chapter, it is important to remember that we will be reflecting on the rhetoric of the photograph, not that of the actual statue or the Center and its museums (though they are all clearly instances of visual rhetoric in their own right).

Visual Rhetoric as Public Address

Key concepts: public address, persuasion, argument, representation, aesthetics, semiotics

Key figures: Foss, Barthes, Olson, Finnegan, Hariman, Lucaites, DeLuca

One common approach to the study of visual rhetoric draws its inspiration from the traditional public address model. From this perspective, imagery is treated as a visual mode of address strategically produced to persuade an audience. The roots of this perspective can be traced back to Aristotle, who defined rhetoric as "an ability, in each [particular] case, to see the available means of persuasion" (Aristotle, trans. 1991, p. 36). Scholars who adopt this outlook treat visual rhetoric as a "communicative artifact" (Foss, 2004, p. 304; 2005, p. 143). The assumptions underlying this perspective are most explicit in the work of Sonja Foss, who has repeatedly argued for the need to develop a rhetorical schema for evaluating images. Despite Foss's (1994) claims to offer an alternative approach to linguistic models as well as to aesthetic and semiotic approaches to imagery (p. 214), her schema is closely tied to nearly all the key assumptions of these approaches.

In concert with traditional public address scholarship, Foss is concerned with how visual imagery "evokes a response" (1982, p. 55) and "influence[s] viewers" (1992, p. 85). By focusing on the rhetorical "effects" of images, Foss simply replaces the sender-message-receiver model of language with a creator-image-viewer model of visual imagery. Although Foss's (1994) stance is anti-intentionalist (p. 215) and privileges the autonomy of the text over the creator's intended meaning, it nevertheless situates the viewer as a receiver who is addressed or acted on by a finished product. Indeed, it is the autonomous or "independent" nature of the text that connects Foss's approach to aesthetics. Aesthetics, which is inherited from idealist philosophy, involves identifying "those textual properties which can be said to render it [art] beautiful" (O'Sullivan, Hartley, Saunders, Montgomery, & Fiske, 1994, p. 6). While Foss (1994) is not concerned with judging the beauty of images, her approach is concerned with judgment (p. 215). And like aesthetics, judgment is rooted in the structural elements of the text—"the physical data of the image" (p. 216). Moreover, it is this structuralist view of images that locates Foss's schema within what Roland Barthes (1977) calls "the semiology of images" (p. 32). In his landmark essays, "The Photographic Message" and "Rhetoric of the Image," Barthes charts the unique analogical codes of images and how those codes convey meaning (pp. 15, 17, 32). Although Foss rarely, if ever, cites Barthes in her work on visual imagery, her approach could scarcely be more indebted to his insights.

The public address model of visual rhetoric is built, then, on structuralist principles and a symbolic or representational understanding of images. For Lester Olson (2004), rhetoric is "an aspect of symbolic action in general, not verbal language in particular" (p. xii). While expanding the field of rhetorical action to include the visual, his perspective reinforces an understanding of rhetoric as exclusively symbolic and, thus, fits neatly within non-controversial 20th-century notions of rhetoric (Blair, 1999, p. 18). Even as Olson (2004) broadens the *category* of rhetoric to accommodate forms other than speech and writing, he employs an explicitly Aristotelian *view* of rhetoric in which messages (in this case, visual messages) are symbolic assertions that aim to convince audiences about justice, expediency, or values (p. 16). Visual rhetoric scholars who draw on traditional rhetorical theory often recognize, however, that imposing linguistic theories of persuasion directly onto visual images stretches the traditional terms. Although Edwards and Winkler (1997) suggest that metaphor can be used in the analysis of visual rhetoric, for instance, they concede that it is simply not up to the task of explaining the rhetorical workings of at least some images.

Lacking an alternative vocabulary or perspective, public address studies of visuality often reinforce traditional goals of rhetorical theory and criticism by demonstrating that visual rhetoric is a central component of civic discourse. Cara Finnegan (2004a) argues that one goal of visual rhetoric inquiry "might be the construction of a rhetorical history that accounts systematically for the ways in which images become inventional resources in the public sphere" (p. 198). For example, Finnegan (2001) argues that photographs in the 1930s "documenting" the effects of the Depression and the drought "carry with them a profoundly influential but often unrecognized argumentative resource: Their perceived relationship to nature" (p. 135). Finnegan (2001) argues that photographs of cattle skulls on the dust bowl's vast wastelands offer a "naturalistic enthymeme," engaging viewers in public arguments about Depression-era policies (p. 135). Visual images not only make public arguments but also become part of the dialogue itself. This view has led many scholars to trace the rhetorical legacies of particular images. Lester Olson (2004), for example, examines how images created by Benjamin Franklin were taken up, resisted, reprinted, and circulated.[1] Finnegan's (2003) work on the FSA (Farm Security Administration) photographs of poverty during the Depression follows a similar logic, as does much of the work of Hariman and Lucaites (2002, 2003). But public address studies of visual rhetoric are about more than simply the history and circulation of images.

More important, these studies detail the ways in which images make demands on audiences and foster particular forms of civic engagement. In a case study of iconic photography, Hariman and Lucaites (2002) argue that the image of the flag raising on Iwo Jima "provides performative resolution of the tension between liberalism and democracy in U.S. post-war public culture" (p. 364). Elsewhere, Hariman and Lucaites (2003) contend that visual images appeal to "the public through an act of common spectatorship. When the event shown is itself part of national life, the public seems to see itself, and to see itself in terms of a particular conception of civic identity" (p. 36). These studies assert that visual

imagery influences audiences on matters of public policy such as poverty (Finnegan, 2003) and the environment (DeLuca, 1999; DeLuca & Demo, 2000), as well as on broad political issues such as U.S. American middle-class identities (Smith, 1999) and a nascent vision of U.S. national identity (Olson, 2004).

Studies of visual rhetoric as public address, then, draw their critical vocabulary from traditional rhetorical theory. More important, however, this scholarship details the ways visual communication is a central part of civic and political life. From the public address perspective, visual rhetoric is simply another form of rhetoric. As such, it demands a (modest) rethinking of some rhetorical terms, since the classic terms do not always translate neatly to the images under investigation. At the same time, the public address vision of visual rhetoric maintains a quite traditional view of rhetoric as symbolic action designed to address and persuade audiences. The contribution of the public address model to rhetorical studies has more to do with *what* counts as rhetoric than with *how* visual rhetoric functions.

If one were to evaluate the photograph of the Buffalo Bill statue outside the BBHC from this perspective, she or he would likely begin by noting the symbolic and thus suasory character of the image. The statue occupies the center of the photograph, suggesting its importance within the frame. Moreover, as the statue is shot nearly straight on—the viewers' gaze meeting Cody's, the image invites a sense of comfort and identification. Cody is welcoming us into his home as though we are friends. The second depiction of Cody within the photograph is on a banner that hangs in the background. This Cody is more active but also more distant and blurry, evoking a sense of the past. The photograph proffers two central messages, then. Through the banner, it communicates that Cody was a historical figure who lived in the Old West and was "amazing." But it also communicates, through the statue, that he was warm, gracious, and accessible. The photograph urges viewers to envision two Codys—one who is the adventurer and cowboy that history remembers and one who in some ways is still quite like us. Perhaps a deeper meaning lies in their juxtaposition—that the cowboy of the Old West, while fading, is still with and in us today, that the "cowboy spirit" is part of what it means to be "American."

Visual Rhetoric as Everyday Life

Key concepts: everyday life, materiality, space, culture, interpellation, ideology

Key figures: Blair, Dickinson, Clark, Fuery and Fuery, Sturken and Cartwright

If visual rhetoric as public address draws its inspiration from traditional rhetorical theory and structuralist semiotics, visual rhetoric as everyday life is far more likely to invoke critical cultural studies and post-structuralist theory. Scholars such as Michele de Certeau (1984) and Henri Lefebvre (1958/1991) resist unidirectional understandings of communication, arguing instead (though in different ways) for a vision of culture and subjectivity in which each is implicated in and constitutive of the other. For both de Certeau and Lefebvre, these mutual relations adhere in the interstices of everyday life and are enacted within the banalities of daily living. Drawing on this understanding of the relation between culture and subjectivity, scholars of everyday treat visuality not as a mode of expression that addresses a particular, preexisting and constituted audience but as the warp and woof of daily life. As Victor Burgin (1996) explains, visual *"representations cannot be simply tested against reality, as reality is itself constituted through the agency of representations"* (p. 238). Visual rhetoric, in this view, is a fundamental grounding for reality, not simply a mimetic representation of reality.

This "agency of representations" suggests that images proffer the symbolic and material resources through which individuals, groups, and nations constitute themselves (Berlant, 1997, pp. 29–53). Within this model, the endless array of images that circulate as part of everyday life function to interpellate or hail viewers as subjects. Building on Louis Althusser's understanding of ideology, the visual rhetoric as everyday life perspective sees images as material articulations of ideological State apparatuses such as education, religion, family, and media. To paraphrase Althusser (2001), ideology is a visual representation of the imaginary relationship of individuals to their real conditions of existence (p. 109). From this perspective, visual imagery—be it films and photographs or street signs and architecture—constitutes concrete individuals as concrete subjects. In other words, in addition to symbolically conveying cultural beliefs and practices, visual rhetoric also materially limits and shapes cultural beliefs and practices through the interpellation of subjects.

The material grounding of subjectivity through visuality can function at both individual and collective levels. In engaging visual texts, individuals begin to negotiate their way through the "semiotic excess" that characterizes postmodernity (Collins, 1995, pp. 4–9). Burgin (1996) notes that in today's image-saturated mediascape, for example, an individual's memory not only is the storehouse of actual past events filtered through the scrim of psychodynamics but is also infused with all the images an individual has engaged. For example, when asked to recount life in Nazi-occupied France, French survivors used movie scenes to fill in memory gaps (Burgin, 1996, p. 226). It becomes possible for individuals to "fill in" the gaps of memory with (often mediated) visual imagery in ways that allows them to narrate their personal stories as a quilt of events, images, and fantasies (pp. 194, 211, 226). Imaging what a suburb or a city ought to look like depends not only on an individual's experience with suburbs and cities but also on the vast array of images of suburbs and cities, including television shows and nightly news, films, advertising, and the like (Burgin, 1996; Kenyon, 2004; Macek, 2006). Individual uses of, resistances to, and engagement with visual texts is, of course, limited by the available images. So, while subjectivity is a personal performance of memory images, it is a performance that relies on the cultural products of a specific sociohistorical matrix. These cultural products include not only the images on our television, movie, and computer screens but also our broader built environment.

Individuals apprehend buildings visually, for instance. As concrete, material structures, the visual experience of buildings is an embodied one that necessarily shapes what is possible and impossible in daily life. The varying designs of buildings, communities, and whole cities (i.e., our built environment) interpellate us as particular types of ideological subjects, such as patrons, consumers, parishioners, and citizens. Studies of material spaces such as Old Pasadena, Starbucks, Wild Oats, Yellowstone, and Las Vegas (Clark, 2004; Dickinson, 1997, 2002; Dickinson & Maugh, 2004; Wood, 2005) all trace the intersections among visual culture, space, and everyday life. These studies contend that sites are places where subjects are hailed (literally by police officers but also by the sites/sights themselves) and where individuals stake their own claims to identity. Wood (2005), for example, argues that visitors to Las Vegas are well aware that the Eiffel Tower on the strip is not "the real thing." This awareness of in-authenticity allows for, indeed fosters, a playfulness that Wood (2005) suggests may be "the most radical choice one can make" (p. 328). These spaces—each embedded in postmodern consumer culture—are part of the ideological project of post-Fordist informationalism. Each draws on the hyper-real, mediated images of postmodernity, and each is available to its users for embodied enactments of agency.

The intersection of visual and material culture suggests implications beyond individual

subjectivity, however. Particularly important are the ways in which everyday visuality engages questions of collective identity and nationhood. A number of scholars who are interested in the issues of civic engagement and nation building have taken to studying the rhetorical force of memorials and museums. In nearly every case, this scholarship explores the ways particular memory sites engage visitors in what it means to be members of a larger, often national, community. In their study of Mount Rushmore, Carole Blair and Neil Michael (2004) contend, for instance, that the monument "is important . . . because it nominates for us a particular 'consensual' mirror of the American past and present. It marks out a particular image of the national *ethos*" (p. 159). This "image" is, of course, fashioned by attendant sites. In another essay, Blair and Michael (1999) note that the rhetorical force of the Astronauts Memorial is mitigated by the surrounding tourist landscapes of Orlando, Florida. What these essays, and a range of other essays on memorials and museums, indicate are the ways in which visualized landscapes create and resist both literal and figurative visions of nationhood (Armada, 1998; Blair, Jeppeson, & Pucci, 1991; Dickinson, Ott, & Aoki, 2005, 2006; Gallagher, 1995, 1999; Katriel, 1994).

The work we have mapped in this section has two important implications. First, visual rhetoric in everyday life is not *merely* visual; it is not only an effect of the eye or a consequence of cognition. The visual is a constitutive part of subjectivity and an embodied understanding of rhetoric. The turn to the body in rhetorical scholarship (Dickinson, 1997, 2002; Blair, 1999) serves to undercut the primacy of the symbol. Visual rhetoric as everyday life sees the visual not only as partly symbolic but also as working directly and in nonsymbolic ways on the body. Mount Rushmore encases its visitors in a deeply embodied and emplaced sense of national identity, while Starbucks sutures the whole person into its rhetoric of authenticity.

A second implication is that visuality is always contextual. From the everyday perspective, images do not appear in a vacuum, and they are not engaged a-historically or a-spatially. Instead, images appear somewhere and are taken up by somebody. Space, however, is not just the site of the appearance of visual images but is itself a set of visual images. The city, the suburb, the coffee shop, and the memorial or museum both present images and are themselves images—images that hail subjects. The visual rhetoric as everyday life perspective moves us well beyond the visual rhetoric as public address model by suggesting that visuality is material, spatial, and constitutive. In doing so, this perspective not only alters the pedagogical dimensions of visual rhetoric, it also realigns our understanding of the function and force of rhetoric itself.

Unlike our reading of the Cody photograph from a public address perspective, which focused almost exclusively on the symbolic content of the image (or "text") itself, approaching the photograph from an everyday life perspective, one might begin by asking, In what embodied context has one encountered the image and why does that matter? It is not inconsequential, for instance, that most viewers will see this photograph in an encyclopedic book on rhetoric. If one is reading such a book when he or she comes on the Cody statue image, then one has already been hailed and responded to, at least in part, as a student of rhetoric. The meaning of the image is no longer a product solely of its contents; it is also a product of its material context. While the symbolic content of the image is far from irrelevant, the critic cannot ignore the photograph's appearance in an academic book, as opposed to say in a private photo album. In this context, the image is understood, even if only unconsciously, as a teaching aid rather than a vacation photo. From this perspective, Cody may be viewed as a teacher himself and the photograph an invitation to learn about the Old West by entering the museum. The

everyday life perspective would take seriously how the photograph constitutes one as a student of visual rhetoric, history, and perhaps the life of Buffalo Bill.

Visual Rhetoric as Logic

Key concepts: logic, looking, perception, cognition, spatial intelligence

Key figures: Berger, Elkins, Arnheim, Hoffman, Mitchell, de Bono, Gardner, van Alphen

Whereas the first perspective conceives of visual rhetoric as a way of *doing*—of situated, prudential action—and the second perspective approaches visual rhetoric as a way of *being* or *becoming*—of creating ideological subjects, the third perspective treats visual rhetoric as a way of *knowing*. From this perspective, visual rhetorics are "not merely . . . devices of persuasion but . . . underlying forms that make thought possible" (Benson, 1993, p. xvii). The visual rhetoric as logic perspective is premised on the idea that images operate according to their own unique codes, syntax, and grammar. As such, images shape not only *what* we see but also *how* we see, by training the brain to employ a particular pattern-making system (de Bono, 1970, pp. 26–27). Scholarship on the logic of images is rooted in studies of perception and cognition. Although this research is diverse, ranging from the work of art scholars such as Rudolf Arnheim to that of cognitive scientists such as Donald Hoffman, there are four basic tenets on which scholars largely agree.

1. *Seeing is creative:* The practice of looking is not merely a physiological process of involving stimulus and response. Rather, seeing is a psychological process involving desire and the unconscious; it is a subjective mode of organization, alteration, and ultimately construction (Hoffman, 1998, p. 1; Sewall, 1999, p. 22). As John Berger (1972) explains in *Ways of Seeing*, "The way we see things is affected by what we know and by what we believe"

(p. 8). Because every observer brings different values, beliefs, and experiences to looking, "No two people will see [precisely] the same object" (Elkins, 1996, p. 41). Seeing, then, is an act of active production rather than passive consumption. "By looking at and engaging with images in the world," explain Sturken and Cartwright (2001), "we influence the meanings and uses assigned to . . . images" (p. 42). While seeing is a highly constructive process, it is not an unstructured or unlimited process. As Rudolf Arnheim has demonstrated in *Art and Visual Perception* (1954) and *Visual Thinking* (1969), aesthetic aspects of images, such as shape, form, space, light, and color, limit the way our minds organize and process material.

2. *Seeing is selective:* Often as important as what we see when we look at images or the world is what we do not see—what we unconsciously filter out (Schirato & Webb, 2004, p. 14). "There are things we don't see, even when we are looking straight at them," writes James Elkins (1996), for "a great deal of vision is unconscious: We are blind to certain things and blind to our blindness" (pp. 12, 13). The selectivity of perception evolved as part of humans' instinct for self-preservation (Arnheim, 1969, p. 19). Since not all things we see are of equal importance, the capacity to filter out less important visual material can literally be life saving. If one is about to be struck by a car, it is far more important that one be able to quickly process the vehicle's direction and velocity than be able to discern how a passerby is dressed. As such, when we look, we are constantly, if unconsciously, screening out those things we believe to be less important (Sewall, 1999, pp. 66–71). The end result is that seeing is decidedly partial.

3. *Seeing is contextual:* When and where we see something shapes what we see. Seeing is deeply connected to time and timing—to the cultural and historical moment of observation. As Barthes (1977) explains, "Thanks to its code of connotation the reading of the photograph is thus always historical" (p. 28). Because cultural values, beliefs, and practices change over time, so too do the ways viewers see and interpret images (Sturken & Cartwright, 2001, p. 25). Seeing is also a matter of place and placement, of the social and material spaces in which looking occurs. The ground on which we engage with images influences the way we interpret them (Mitchell, 1994, p. 31). As Susan Sontag (2003) observes,

> Even those ultimate images whose gravity, whose emotional power, seems fixed for all time, the concentration camp photographs from 1945, weigh differently when seen in a photography museum; in a gallery of contemporary art in a museum catalogue; on television; in the pages of *The New York Times;* in the pages of *Rolling Stone;* in a book. . . . Every picture is seen in some setting. (pp. 119–120)

And the setting, the very stage itself, "*produces* [italics added] certain ways of looking" (Dorst, 1999, p. 167).

4. *Seeing is spatial:* Visual signs differ from linguistic signs in, at least, two fundamental ways. First, whereas linguistic signs—be they spoken or written—are arranged temporally and thus processed sequentially, visual signs are arranged spatially and thus processed simultaneously. So, while it is quite impossible to utter two distinct words at the same time, one can easily view multiple images concurrently. Commenting on the unique spatial character of looking, Arnheim (1954) notes, "No object is perceived as unique or isolated. Seeing something involves assigning it a place in the whole: A location in space" (p. 11; see also Elkins, 1996, p. 35). Second, while linguistic signs are entirely arbitrary (Saussure, 1983, p. 67), visual signs are typically analogical. Images are meaningful because they look like the things to which they refer, while language is meaningful purely because of social convention and agreement.

These four basic premises about looking, perception, and cognition are foundational to the ways we process and make sense of visual imagery. The belief that our minds function differently when confronted with images than when confronted with language began to take hold in the 1970s. In *Lateral Thinking*, for instance, Edward de Bono contends that linear, analytical logic, which he refers to as vertical thinking, is quite distinct from lateral thinking, which entails side-by-side patterns rather than step-by-step patterns (1970, pp. 39–45). This basic distinction would later be refined by Howard Gardner in his book *Frames of Mind: The Theory of Multiple Intelligences*. According to Gardner (1983), spatial intelligence, which is visually based, differs from linguistic intelligence because it privileges juxtaposition, association, and resemblance over sequence, causality, and linearity. More recently, scholars (Hoffman, 1998; Stephens, 1998; van Alphen, 2005) have explored how images work on an emotional-corporeal level to arouse, move, and mobilize us. The visual rhetoric as logic perspective, then, questions whether traditional, rationalist models of language and discourse can be used to interpret, understand, or assess visual imagery, positing that images operate according to their own logic.

If one were to approach the Cody statue photograph from a logic perspective, he or she would be more concerned with the mode or medium than the message. How is a photograph of the statue different from a verbal or written representation of it? How is it different from the statue itself? Photographs train our consciousness to process information in very particular ways. Unlike speech, which is decidedly linear (i.e., it is quite impossible to utter two distinct words simultaneously), a photograph can convey a plethora of information all at once. A photograph is not forced, as is a speaker, in representing the statue to "say" one thing first, then another, and so on. Thus, when one engages the Cody statue photograph, one takes it in as a whole, not as a sequential set of signifiers. Nor do any two viewers see the same whole, for what each viewer sees is a consequence of her or his experiences, background, and predispositions. Whereas a child might become fixated on the gun, not even noticing that the statue is located outside a museum, an adult may be drawn to the intersecting elements of the building, the banner, and the statue, thinking the site depicted to be an interesting tourist destination. The important question to consider from this perspective is, Why does it matter that this information comes to the viewer in the form of a photograph?

Teaching (With) Visual Rhetoric

Key concepts: simulation, critical pedagogy, citizenship, visual literacy

Key figures: Baudrillard, McLuhan, Giroux, Messaris, Lewis, Jhally

As visual rhetoric has come to occupy and play a more central role in our daily lives, its importance *to* and *in* education has grown as well. The challenge for educators within this new cultural landscape is to take up visual rhetoric in productive pedagogical ways. This challenge is complicated, however, by the fact that students, like the public more generally, have integrated visual imagery into their everyday lives without reflecting on the implications or consequences of having done so. While the uncritical reception and adoption of images is likely the result of a complex array of forces, two factors suggest themselves as particularly salient. First, the sheer speed with which the new information technologies invaded our lives, thereby fueling a dramatic proliferation of images, happened so rapidly that society scarcely had time to reflect on, let alone consciously assess and adjust to, this shift (see Ott, 2007). Second, the changing role of the image itself—from representation of a basic reality to pure simulacrum (Baudrillard,

1983)—has contributed to a felt sense of the image as unmediated reality. These intersecting forces have severely short-circuited critical judgment, leading to the unreflective use of images in college classrooms. Frequently, visual rhetoric is integrated into the curriculum as nothing more than a set of aesthetic principles in advertising and public relations courses, as a presentational device in business communication courses (see Brumberger, 2005), or as a form of entertainment designed to momentarily engage today's seemingly disinterested and inattentive students.

But such a practice misses, we believe, the crucial pedagogical role that visual rhetoric can and should play in education. Visual rhetoric cannot simply be added to course catalogs and inserted into existing classes with the intent of increasing their student appeal and relevance in 21st-century education without taking seriously the social roles and functions of visual imagery. Given the persuasive, constitutive, and epistemological dimensions of visual rhetoric, it must be incorporated into the classroom as part of a broader critical pedagogy designed to foster *critical citizenship*. Students must learn to interrogate and evaluate visual forms of rhetoric in a manner that expands the opportunities for democratic participation in public spheres, illuminates social networks of power/knowledge, and provides patterns for processing information in meaningful, pragmatic ways. Ultimately, a critical pedagogy equips individuals with intellectual tools and interpretive skills to enhance the quality of public life for both themselves and others. It invites students to be insistently aware of how their own beliefs, choices, actions, and discourses both reflect and contribute to a social structure that works ideologically to value and legitimate some voices while denigrating and excluding others (Giroux, 1991, pp. 47–55). Toward that end, the remainder of this section recommends three specific tactics for treating visual rhetoric as critical pedagogy.

1. *Exercise visual literacy:* It is not simply enough to "use" images in the classroom; educators must strive to promote visual literacy by teaching students how images do their work. Visual literacy describes a "viewer's awareness of the conventions through which the meanings of visual images are created and understood" (Messaris & Moriarty, 2004, p. 481; see also Messaris, 1998, p. 70). Given its long-standing connection to the print paradigm, and hence to reading and writing, *literacy* may seem an unlikely term to use with regard to images. But as no comparable concept has emerged in the field of visual rhetoric to challenge it, we regard it as a suitable term to describe an understanding of and facility with the unique character of images. The goal of teaching visual literacy is not solely to make students skeptical or critical of images. Rather, "literacy should be about helping people to become sophisticated citizens rather than sophisticated consumers" (Lewis & Jhally, 1998, p. 109). Ideally, visual literacy equips students with an understanding of images that allows them to engage in the political process in informed and responsible ways. Minimally, this would entail teaching students to think critically about the rhetorical implications of visual elements such as composition (dominance, unity, variety, rhythm, balance), framing, perspective, depth, light, color (hue, intensity, value), genre, and medium or technology. Students might be asked, for instance, to think carefully about how the aesthetic elements of the Cody statue photograph encourage particular views of masculinity, the West, and "Americanism."

2. *Problematize visual imagery:* Images cannot be added to existing curricular materials without social and political implications. All images—be they PowerPoint slides, photographs, or film clips—make demands on viewers. Thus, their inclusion as teaching aids cannot be seen or treated as apolitical. The decision to illustrate a concept, a principle, or a theory using a visual example *frames* the

very way students understand (i.e., *see*) the material they are studying. Examples make abstract ideas concrete, and visual examples make abstract ideas visually concrete. This is no small matter. Because visual messages are typically high density, they contain more data or information than purely linguistic messages. This density discrepancy is obvious when one compares the relative file size of an image with that of a written document (even a lengthy one). The high density of images can have numerous unintended consequences. While linguistic examples invite us to fill in the gaps based on imagination or previous experience and knowledge, visual examples often fill in the gaps for us. As such, a visual example may actually provide a more narrow or finished understanding of a concept than a linguistic example, by requiring less involvement from the message recipient. Thus, students must be encouraged both to take images seriously and to reflect seriously on the consequences for perception and cognition when engaging visual imagery. If, for example, a teacher used the photograph of the Cody statue to show students what cowboys looked like at the turn of the century, the image would significantly limit how students perceive "coyboyness" by filtering it through the lens of Whiteness.

3. *Contextualize visual rhetoric:* Each of the perspectives on visual rhetoric discussed in the first section of this essay provides a particular way of understanding what images do. As such, it is vital that students be taught to reflect on the assumptions and implications of conceptualizing visual rhetoric in the model of public address, everyday life, or logic. In our view, each of the three approaches to visual rhetoric offers insights as well as limitations. Furthermore, while the perspectives are not wholly compatible, neither are they wholly exclusive. Indeed, teaching students to reflect on the various ways in which visual rhetoric has been conceptualized may lead to new and innovative understandings. In thinking about visual

rhetoric in terms of doing, being, or knowing, one could inquire into the relations among perspectives. For instance, if visual rhetoric is seen to shape who we are (being) and how we think (knowing), then one could ask, How does the spatial way of processing information fostered by images limit the possible subjectivities we come to enact or perform? Or one might ask, How does the fact that visual rhetoric can be used to persuade others (doing) limit the way we think (knowing)? The point is that the very diversity of perspectives on visual rhetoric makes the field an exciting and dynamic one. As an analysis of the Cody statue photograph illustrates, what one asks of an image alters what one concludes an image is doing.

These same basic strategies for incorporating visual rhetoric into existing classes could also be used to design a stand-alone course on visual rhetoric. In a course whose central subject matter is visual rhetoric, we would proffer one additional pedagogical strategy. Time permitting, such a class, we maintain, ought to incorporate applied assignments. In addition to equipping students with visual literacy and teaching them to critically interrogate the social and political significance of images, we advocate getting students behind the camera. Providing opportunities for students to become producers, as opposed to just consumers, of visual rhetoric has two key benefits. First, it assists students in understanding the broad array of decisions that go into the creation of visual messages. Asking students to fulfill an assignment in which they have to make such decisions heightens their critical sensitivity to the syntax, codes, and grammar of images. A second benefit of applied assignments is that it decenters the social production of visual material. In most universities today, media production classes and critical theory classes are separate. The problem with *production-only* classes is that, lacking a *critical* understanding of images, students tend to imitate the well-worn formulas of media. In the process, they unwittingly reproduce the structures of domination and hegemonic ideologies characteristic of mainstream media. Blending critical understanding with production, however, opens the door for alternative, more progressive images. Toward this end, we recommend that students demonstrate their understanding of visual rhetoric by taking photographs and shooting short films.

If, for example, students were each asked to photograph the Cody statue, they would begin to realize that there are radically different ways of (re)presenting the same object. They would learn that the sculpture does not have a singular, fixed meaning and that photographs do not (re)produce "objective" visions of the world. If the students were then asked to create short documentaries about Buffalo Bill's Wild West, they could become even more aware of the ways visual texts are shot through with choices that embody ways of doing, being, and knowing. In short, students would begin to develop crucial critical citizenship tools to help them analyze, use, and produce visual texts in a visual world.

As society has undergone paradigmatic change, so too have our primary communication modes and hence our processes of learning. In particular, the recent social upheaval has been marked by the proliferation and centrality of images in our daily lives. Consequently, scholars have increasingly taken up visual rhetoric as an important object and means of investigation. Early in the chapter, we suggested that the scholarship on visual rhetoric, while diverse, can generally be classified into one of three models or approaches: public address, everyday life, and logic. Each of these approaches brings its own assumptions and thus helps us understand the role of images in social life somewhat differently. But all of them point to the need for educators to take visual imagery seriously. In an effort to make visual rhetoric's addition to and integration into the curriculum a profitable one, we have proposed three pedagogical strategies. We contend that

by teaching students to exercise visual literacy, problematize visual imagery, and contextualize the study of visual rhetoric, the current generation of students will come to engage images not as passive consumers but as critical citizens.

NOTE

1. Olson (2004) focuses on three particular important Revolutionary images by Benjamin Franklin: the 1754 JOIN or DIE, the 1776 Magna Britannia: Her Colonies Reduc'd, and the 1782 Libertas Americana.

REFERENCES

Althusser, L. (2001). *Lenin and philosophy and other essays* (B. Brewster, Trans.). New York: Monthly Review Press.

Aristotle. (1991). *On rhetoric: A theory of civic discourse* (G. A. Kennedy, Trans.). New York: Oxford University Press.

Armada, B. (1998). Memorial agon: An interpretive tour of the National Civil Rights Museum. *Southern Communication Journal, 63,* 235–243.

Arnheim, R. (1954). *Art and visual perception: A psychology of the creative eye.* Berkeley: University of California Press.

Arnheim, R. (1969). *Visual thinking.* Berkeley: University of California Press.

Barthes, R. (1977). *Image, music, text* (S. Heath, Trans.). New York: Hill & Wang.

Baudrillard, J. (1983). *Simulations* (P. Foss, P. Patton, & P. Beitchman, Trans.). New York: Semiotext(e).

Benson, T. (1993). Beacons and boundary-markers: Landmarks in rhetorical criticism. In T. Benson (Ed.), *Landmark essay on rhetorical criticism* (pp. xi–xxii). Davis, CA: Hermagoras Press.

Berger, J. (1972). *Ways of seeing.* New York: Viking Press.

Berlant, L. (1997). *The queen of America goes to Washington City: Essays on sex and citizenship.* Durham, NC: Duke University Press.

Blair, C. (1999). Contemporary U.S. memorial sites as exemplars of rhetoric's materiality. In J. Selzer & S. Crowley (Eds.), *Rhetorical bodies* (pp. 16–57). Madison: University of Wisconsin Press.

Blair, C., & Michael, N. (1999). Commemorating in the theme park zone: Reading the astronauts memorial. In T. Rosteck (Ed.), *At the intersection: Cultural studies and rhetorical studies* (pp. 29–83). New York: Guilford Press.

Blair, C., & Michael, N. (2004). The Rushmore Effect: Ethos and national collective identity. In M. J. Hyde (Ed.), *The ethos of rhetoric* (pp. 156–196). Columbia: University of South Carolina Press.

Blair, C., Jeppeson, M., & Pucci, E. (1991). Public memorializing in postmodernity: The Vietnam Veterans Memorial as prototype. *Quarterly Journal of Speech, 77*, 263–288.

Brumberger, E. R. (2005). Visual rhetoric in the curriculum: Pedagogy for a multimodal workplace. *Business Communication Quarterly, 68*, 318–333.

Burgin, V. (1996). *In/different spaces: Place and memory in visual culture.* Berkeley: University of California Press.

Clark, G. (2004). *Rhetorical landscapes in America: Variations on a theme from Kenneth Burke.* Columbia: University of South Carolina Press.

Collins, J. (1995). *Architectures of excess: Cultural life in the information age.* New York: Routledge.

de Bono, E. (1970). *Lateral thinking: Creativity step by step.* New York: Harper & Row.

de Certeau, M. (1984). *The practice of everyday life* (S. Randall, Trans.). Berkeley: University of California Press.

DeLuca, K. M. (1999). *Image politics: The new rhetoric of environmental activism.* New York: Guilford Press.

DeLuca, K. M., & Demo, A. (2000). Imaging nature: Watkins, Yosemite, and the birth of environmentalism. *Critical Studies in Media Communication, 17*, 241–260.

Dickinson, G. (1997). Memories for sale: Nostalgia and the construction of identity in Old Pasadena. *Quarterly Journal of Speech, 83*, 1–27.

Dickinson, G. (2002). Joe's rhetoric: Starbucks and the spatial rhetoric of authenticity. *Rhetoric Society Quarterly, 32*, 5–28.

Dickinson, G., & Maugh, C. M. (2004). Placing visual rhetoric: Finding material comforts in Wild Oats Marketplace. In C. A. Hill & M. Helmers (Eds.), *Defining visual rhetorics* (pp. 259–275). New York: Lawrence Erlbaum.

Dickinson, G., Ott, B., & Aoki, E. (2005). Memory and myth at the Buffalo Bill Museum. *Western Journal of Communication, 69*(2), 85–108.

Dickinson, G., Ott, B., & Aoki, E. (2006). Spaces of remembering and forgetting: The reverent eye/I at the Plains Indian Museum. *Communication and Critical/Cultural Studies, 3*(1), 27–47.

Dorst, J. D. (1999). *Looking West.* Philadelphia: University of Pennsylvania Press.

Edwards, J. L., & Winkler, C. K. (1997). Representative form and the visual ideograph: The Iwo Jima image in editorial cartoons. *Quarterly Journal of Speech, 83*, 289–310.

Elkins, J. (1996). *The object stares back: On the nature of seeing.* New York: Harcourt.

Elkins, J. (2003). *Visual studies: A skeptical introduction.* New York: Routledge.

Finnegan, C. A. (2001). The naturalistic enthymeme and visual argument: Photographic representation in the "skull controversy." *Argumentation and Advocacy, 37*, 133–149.

Finnegan, C. A. (2003). *Picturing poverty: Print culture and FSA photographs.* Washington, DC.: Smithsonian Books.

Finnegan, C. A. (2004a). Doing rhetorical history of the visual: The photograph and the archive. *Defining visual rhetorics.* In C. Hill & M. Helmers (Eds.), *Defining visual rhetorics* (pp. 195–214). Mahwah, NJ: Lawrence Erlbaum.

Finnegan, C. A. (2004b). Visual studies and visual rhetoric. *Quarterly Journal of Speech, 90*, 231–248.

Foss, S. (1982). Rhetoric and the visual image: A resource unit. *Communication Education, 31*, 55–66.

Foss, S. (1992). Visual imagery as communication. *Text and Performance Quarterly, 12*, 85–96.

Foss, S. (1994). A rhetorical scheme for the evaluation of visual imagery. *Communication Studies, 45*, 213–234.

Foss, S. (2004). Framing the study of visual rhetoric: Toward a transformation of rhetorical theory. In C. Hill & M. Helmers (Eds.), *Defining visual rhetorics* (pp. 303–313). Mahwah, NJ: Lawrence Erlbaum.

Foss, S. (2005). Theory of visual rhetoric. In K. Smith, S. Moriarty, G. Barbatsis, & K. Kenney (Eds.), *Handbook of visual communication: Theory, methods, and media* (pp. 141–152). Mahwah, NJ: Lawrence Erlbaum.

Fuery, P., & Fuery, K. (2003). *Visual cultures and critical theory.* New York: Arnold.

Gallagher, V. (1995). Remembering together: Rhetorical integration and the case of the Martin Luther King, Jr. Memorial. *Southern Communication Journal, 60,* 109–119.

Gallagher, V. (1999). Memory and reconciliation in the Birmingham Civil Rights Institute. *Rhetoric and Public Affairs, 2,* 303–320.

Gardner, H. (1983). *Frames of mind: The theory of multiple intelligences.* New York: Basic Books.

Giroux, H. (1991). Introduction. In H. Giroux (Ed.), *Postmodernism, feminism, and cultural politics: Redrawing educational boundaries* (pp. 1–59). Albany: State University of New York Press.

Hariman, R., & Lucaites, J. L. (2002). Performing civic identity: The iconic photograph of the flag raising on Iwo Jima. *Quarterly Journal of Speech, 88,* 363–392.

Hariman, R., & Lucaites, J. L. (2003). Public identity and collective memory in U.S. iconic photography: The image of "accidental napalm." *Critical Studies in Media Communication, 20,* 35–66.

Hill, C., & Helmers, M. (Eds.). (2004). *Defining visual rhetorics.* Mahwah, NJ: Lawrence Erlbaum.

Hoffman, D. (1998). *Visual intelligence: How we create what we see.* New York: W. W. Norton.

Katriel, T. (1994). Sites of memory: Discourses of the past in Israeli pioneering settlement museums. *Quarterly Journal of Speech, 80,* 1–20.

Kenyon, A. M. (2004). *Dreaming suburbia: Detroit and the production of postwar space and culture.* Detroit, MI: Wayne State University Press.

Lefebvre, H. (1991). *Critique of everyday life: Vol. 1* (J. Moore, Trans.). London: Verso. (Original work published 1958)

Lewis, J., & Jhally, S. (1998). The struggle over media literacy. *Journal of Communication, 48*(1), 109–121.

Macek, S. (2006). *Urban nightmares: The media, the right, and the moral panic over the city.* Minneapolis: University of Minnesota Press.

Messaris, P. (1998). Visual aspects of media literacy. *Journal of Communication, 48*(1), 70–80.

Messaris, P., & Moriarty, S. (2004). Visual literacy theory. In K. Smith, S. Moriarty, G. Barbatsis,

& K. Kenney (Eds.), *Handbook of visual communication theory* (pp. 479–502). Mahwah, NJ: Lawrence Erlbaum.

Mirzoeff, N. (Ed.). (1998). *The visual culture reader.* New York: Routledge.

Mitchell, W. J. T. (1994). *Picture theory: Essays on verbal and visual representation.* Chicago: University of Chicago Press.

Olson, L. C. (2004). *Benjamin Franklin's vision of American community: A study in rhetorical iconology.* Columbia: University of South Carolina Press.

O'Sullivan, T., Hartley, J., Saunders, D., Montgomery, M., & Fiske, J. (1994). *Key concepts in communication and cultural studies* (2nd ed.). New York: Routledge.

Ott, B. (2007). *The small screen: How television equips us to live in the information age.* Malden, MA: Blackwell.

Rose, G. (2001). *Visual methodologies: An introduction to the interpretation of visual materials.* Thousand Oaks, CA: Sage.

Saussure, F. (1983). *Course in general linguistics* (R. Harris, Trans.). Chicago: Open Court.

Schirato, T., & Webb, J. (2004). *Understanding the visual.* Thousand Oaks, CA: Sage.

Sewall, L. (1999). *Sight and sensibility: The ecopsychology of perception.* New York: Tarcher/Putnam.

Smith, K., Moriarty, S., Barbatsis, G., & Kenney, K. (Eds.). (2005). *Handbook of visual communication: Theory, methods, and media.* Mahwah, NJ: Lawrence Erlbaum.

Smith, S. M. (1999). *American archives: Gender, race, and class in visual culture.* Princeton: Princeton University Press.

Sontag, S. (2003). *Regarding the pain of others.* New York: Farrar, Straus & Giroux.

Stephens, M. (1998). *The rise of the image the fall of the word.* New York: Oxford University Press.

Sturken, M., & Cartwright, L. (2001). *Practices of looking: An introduction to visual culture.* Oxford University Press.

van Alphen, E. (2005). *Art in mind: How contemporary images shape thought.* Chicago: University of Chicago Press.

Wood, A. F. (2005). "What happens [in Vegas]": Performing the post-tourist *flâneur* in "New York" and "Paris." *Text and Performance Quarterly, 25,* 315–333.

22

A Century After the Divorce

Challenges to a Rapprochement Between Speech Communication and English

ROXANNE MOUNTFORD

In retrospect, the connection between composition and communication, still codi-
fied in the title of our leading journal and professional association, looks like a ves-
tige of the late 1940s and 1950s—a brief affair, characterized by mutual attractions
and misgivings, that proved unable to imagine a future for itself.

—Diana George and John Trimbur (1999, p. 682)

Crossing disciplinary boundaries is never easy, and if we are to succeed, we must not
only continue the conversation but must also listen carefully and learn much more
about the aspirations, idiosyncrasies, and anxieties of our rhetorical neighbors.

—Michael Leff (2000b, p. 92)

Author's Note: I am deeply grateful for the feedback of Cheryl Glenn, Patrica A. Malesh, and Thomas Miller in the development of this essay and for a helpful suggestion from Michelle Ballif. Any errors or infelicities that remain are of my own making.

Between January 25 and 27, 1970, a small group of scholars met at the Wingspread Conference Center in Racine, Wisconsin, to discuss the future of rhetoric. The fields of English, speech communication, philosophy, and sociology were all represented, with Richard McKeon, Henry Johnstone, Wayne Booth, and Chaim Perelman among the speakers. Edward P. J. Corbett (1971) pointed out that the conference was the first in his reckoning in which scholars across the disciplines came together to discuss rhetoric (p. 166). Participants agreed that rhetoric is "the process by which symbols and systems of symbols have influence upon beliefs, values, attitudes, and actions" and that the methodologies for rhetorical study are fundamentally interdisciplinary—"philosophical, historical, critical, empirical, creative, or pedagogical" (Ehninger et al., 1971, p. 208). Reading the pages of *The Prospect of Rhetoric*, the conference proceedings for Wingspread, one is struck by the great optimism of the participants for their newfound interdisciplinary mission.

Only Corbett (1971) offered a note of caution. Tempering the enthusiasm so evident in his fellow participants' papers, he pointed out that participants had long been used to "talking about a specialized subject over a long period of time only with [their] colleagues," and as a result, the goal of the conference— finding a suitable definition of rhetoric and a common goal for future study suitable for interdisciplinary alliances—would be difficult. But even if they succeeded, Corbett warned, the real benefit of the conference for future scholars would be lost if participants at the Wingspread Conference chose to ignore the perspective of rhetoricians from other disciplines. "It will be interesting to see whether this cross-fertilization bears fruit," he intoned. "If it does not, the deliberations of this conference may come to be referred to as Murmurings from the Wax Museum" (p. 167). As I argue in this essay, Corbett's concerns about disciplinary entrenchment are, sadly, prescient.

Rather than optimism over the tremendous interdisciplinary potential of rhetoric, rhetoricians at the turn of 21st century have instead noted the erosion of their influence in English and speech communication, their disciplinary homes. At the 2000 Conference on College Composition and Communication (CCCC), Nan Johnson stood at the Coalition of Women Scholars in the History of Rhetoric meeting and exclaimed, "WHERE are the panels on the history of rhetoric?" (Cited in Ratcliffe, 2003, p. 1). Two months later, rhetoricians from speech communication and English met at the Rhetoric Society of America (RSA) to consider "the difficulties involved in promoting rhetorical studies within institutions and associations" such as the National Communication Association and CCCCs (Leff, 2000a). Their conversations led to the formation of the Alliance of Rhetoric Societies (ARS). "An experience of loss and mourning pervades discussions among rhetoricians," James Arnt Aune said at the 2003 meeting of the newly formed ARS, "a feeling-tone perhaps unique in the modern university" (p. 8). Returning to the model of Wingspread, participants at ARS pledged to mark out the joint territories shared by rhetoricians in English and speech communication and to begin anew to define cross-disciplinary coalitions.

This work depends on a renewed sense of collaboration between speech communication and English. However, a rapprochement between scholars in these disciplines is troubled by their long disciplinary estrangement, in which English has been the more powerful and privileged of the two. As Min-Zhan Lu (2004) points out, one of the marks of privilege and power in colonial relationships is a one-way system of knowledge. In such a system, the colonized group is expected to learn about those in power, whereas the powerful group assumes that there is nothing important to learn from its subordinates. For example, "postcolonial specialists in English departments often join other literature faculty in making public confessions of their ignorance of composition theory," Lu points out, "using that professed ignorance as an excuse for exempting themselves from having occasionally to teach a composition course" (p. 11). The irony, Lu writes, is that they are never held accountable by their profession or departments for their ignorance, because knowledge of composition holds little cultural capital in English studies. Drawing on the economy of gift exchange in colonial relationships, Lu argues that scholarship in literature is a "gift" that postcolonial scholars in composition simply cannot refuse.

Similarly, though speech communication became the caretaker of rhetoric throughout much of the 20th century, knowledge of the work in this field is surprisingly limited among rhetoric and composition scholars in English. When rhetoric was revived in the 1960s, it served the cause of teaching writing, and so work in speech communication held limited value.[1] The vibrant work of rhetoricians in speech communication before and after Wingspread is not well-known in English, including some of the more interesting studies of rhetorical practice in everyday life. As I argue in this essay, this ambivalence over work in speech communication by the field of rhetoric and composition suggests the ongoing legacy of domination that forced the exit of speech teachers from English in 1914. If the efforts of rapprochement are finally to succeed, this legacy must be addressed.

A BRIEF HISTORY OF THE DIVORCE

There is broad agreement that, by the turn of the 20th century, not only had rhetoric lost its place of honor in the classical system of education that dominated American colleges and universities until the 19th century, but also that it was being dismantled as a holistic art of communication. By 1900, the triumph of literature over all other objects of study was almost

completed, despite the best efforts of Fred Newton Scott (1980) and other visionaries. By 1903, the Modern Language Association had turned so ardently toward philology and literary criticism as the central foci of English studies that it divested itself of its own Pedagogical Section. As president of this defunct group, Scott had tried to garner interest in reviving a fuller curriculum of rhetoric instruction at the graduate and undergraduate level (Mead, 1900, 1901); in the wake of the MLA's abandonment of pedagogy, he moved his leadership to the newly founded National Council of Teachers of English (NCTE). Scott's NCTE offered shelter for two groups of teachers: those who taught public speaking and those who taught literature and composition (after 1910, MLA and its journal, *Publications of the Modern Language Association of America* [PMLA], offered no papers on pedagogy) (Goggin, 2000, p. 22). But NCTE reflected many of the prejudices of the MLA, associating rhetoric only with first-year writing instruction and privileging the teaching of literature. And so, in 1914, 17 speech teachers left NCTE to form the National Association of Academic Teachers of Speech (now the National Communication Association) and to found a little journal called *The Quarterly Journal,* which eventually became the widely respected *Quarterly Journal of Speech (QJS).* By 1916, so many independent speech departments had been founded in colleges and universities nationwide to house disaffected speech teachers that the editor of *The Quarterly Journal* called for a discussion of department names to unify the new field (Cohen, 1994, p. 18). Separated by divorce, the arts of rhetoric moved into disciplinary homes that focused only on one modality of reception and production—oral discourse in speech communication, written discourse in English, and soon, pulled along by different academic forces, they grew separate identities and interests.

The history of the revival of rhetoric and its role in enriching composition instruction in the

1960s is well known. James Kinneavy (1990) characterizes English teachers as somnolent formalists who awakened from "their dogmatic slumbers" in the 1960s only because of the "massive increases in college registrations" of students who "were only marginally literate" (p. 188). For most of the century, English teachers taught a modified form of Alexander Bain's rhetoric, focusing on modes of discourse, grammar, and style rather than invention and arrangement. In 1965, Corbett, then an 18th-century literary scholar, published *Classical Rhetoric for the Modern Student,* a foundational textbook in rhetoric and composition history—the first major publication in the revival of rhetoric for the purpose of composition instruction. To be sure, prior to this revival, literary theorists produced important theories that broadened the purview of rhetoric. In his history of speech communication, Herman Cohen (1994) acknowledges that "the really interesting and innovative work [of the 1940s] in rhetoric was being done by literary, not speech scholars," including Kenneth Burke, I. A. Richards, Wayne C. Booth, Richard McKeon, and Richard Weaver (p. 168). Their theories drove later work in rhetorical criticism.[2] But within English studies, such theory was rare (new criticism dominated the 20th century, despite the best efforts of Burke, 1953b). Speech communication scholars knew what to do with "the new rhetoric" long before scholars in English studies did, in part, because the concerns articulated by Burke and others connected rhetoric with the public sphere, where speech communication scholars located the exigencies for their field. With the exception of these few theorists, English scholars were more interested in the private sphere, with reading and the development of taste (including correctness of expression).[3]

In English studies, the poverty of the current-traditional paradigm came into focus for composition teachers around the time of the Wingspread Conference. In 1972, Donald Murray published "Teach Writing as a Process Not a Product," shifting the emphasis from student production of the tired four modes of current-traditional pedagogy (exposition, description, narration, and argument) in grammatically correct, five-paragraph themes to students exploring their own ideas, in their own language, in as many drafts as necessary. As a result of libratory efforts such as Murray's, a new field within English studies began to form—rhetoric and composition—and two objects of study identified—the student writer and the writing process. Two primary disciplines contributed to the new field: English education, which supplied new empirical paradigms of study, and rhetoric, which enlarged the foundation for teaching and research on writing. A few of the early scholars recognized that drawing on the rhetorical tradition would mean locating students in the broader worlds of communication in which they moved and had their being (see especially Young, Becker, & Pike's *Rhetoric: Discovery and Change* [1970], which is primarily remembered for the complex heuristic method developed by Pike). However, this broader view of rhetoric did not prevail in English departments (Crowley, 2004, p. 90).

Much of the work of rhetoricians in English in the first two decades of the field was historical in nature and focused on concepts that would be useful to composition instruction. Indeed, until the mid-1990s, books on rhetoric by rhetoric and composition scholars often ended with a chapter on the teaching of writing, even when to do so was a stretch.[4] As John Schilb put it wryly in 1993, the field was producing "historians of rhetoric because we have more people anxious to legitimize the teaching of writing as a serious affair" (p. 237). Today, rhetoricians in English still primarily do historical research, while composition scholars are more likely to employ a range of research methods focused on literacy and composition pedagogy.[5] Rhetoricians in English such as

Elizabeth C. Britt (2001) and Ralph Cintron (1997), who employ field research and criticism to study "the rhetoric of the everyday," are relatively rare.[6]

Speech communication took a different path. As Cohen (1994) recounts, "Oral English" was a "fairly standard component of the English curriculum" at the turn of the 20th century (p. ix). Its formation "by testimony of its founders, came into being, primarily, to escape the domination of English departments, where the teachers of Oral English occupied a place below the teachers of Literature and English Composition" (p. ix–x). The split occurred at an important moment in the history of American universities, when research and doctoral training were gaining momentum. In order to establish separate departments of speech communication, the fledgling discipline had to begin a program of research, and many faculty had to return for a doctorate (p. x). According to Cohen (1994), the field developed four primary scholarly foci: rhetorical theory, rhetorical criticism, scientific study of communication, and pedagogy. In fact, the early essays in *The Quarterly Journal* are pedagogical in nature, not surprising for a group that splintered from the NCTE. Over time, the primary tension in speech communication scholarship grew between the rhetoricians and the social scientists; Cohen (1994) points out that the tensions between these two groups, repeated "with almost monotonous frequency" in the 20th century, were present in the fledgling field's first year (1915) in the debates among Charles Woolbert, James Winans, Herbert Wichelns (considered the founder of the "Cornell School" of rhetoric), and others (p. ix). While rhetoricians in speech worry that their influence in the field is now waning, throughout the 20th century, they were a dominant force at Cornell and throughout much of the Midwest (Leff, 2000b, p. 86). Their achievements during this period should be of particular interest to rhetoricians in English, a point I explore in the following pages.

During the 1940s, the United States Army engaged several universities in the training of Army officers in basic communication as part of their preparation for leadership in World War II. After reviewing what passed as composition instruction in English departments—the reading of literature and emphasis on form and correctness of writing, the Army decided that teachers of speech communication and English needed to work together to produce a more holistic approach to communication for its officers. Remarkably, the Army refused to allow an infusion of literature into the course, believing it to be useless for the kind of training they wanted, and required that reading, writing, listening, and speaking skills be taught together. The CCCC was founded in 1949 to provide a location for instructors of the new communication course (which included speech teachers) and instructors of composition courses to meet to explore their mutual interests. For a brief period, the fields were reunited in service of a common cause. But the reunion would be short-lived—quashed, once again, by English teachers.

THE RISE AND FALL OF THE FOURTH "C"

There are several histories of the communication course, the most prominent by Arthur Applebee (1974), James Berlin (1987), Diana George and John Trimbur (1999), and Sharon Crowley (2004). They, in turn, draw on essays published in *College English* and *College Composition and Communication* (CCC) in the 1940s and 1950s on the communication course and course descriptions gleaned from some of the programs. However, with the exception of Crowley (2004), there is very little discussion of the contributions that the field of speech communication made to this collaboration. Beginning with Applebee (1974), the primary interest of composition historians has been with the role the communication course played in the later development of composition.

From Berlin's (1987) point of view, the Army Specialized Training Personnel (ASTP) program's emphasis on English was important because it provided employment for many English teachers, and because it required a unified approach to a holistic set of communication skills that led to a number of innovations in the teaching of writing. Such courses were geared to the individual student's needs; reading, writing, speaking, and listening were taught as one integrated process; literary reading and modes of writing were specifically excluded; and the relationship of the individual to the larger society was emphasized (pp. 97–104). More than 200 universities had established such a course by 1948; even more were established in the 1950s (Berlin, 1987, p. 96).

The innovations made in the communication course to pedagogy cannot be underestimated. One of the more progressive courses, established at the University of Denver, provided writing clinics that helped students overcome their fear of writing and see themselves as writers, using Rogerian techniques (Berlin, 1987, p. 100). The "clinicians" were graduate students from speech communication and English departments; they were supported in their work by a full-time psychiatrist. The psychiatrist's help was needed occasionally for the first quarter of work in the writing course, which focused on a long autobiography that was to explore themes of the students' adjustment to the social world around them (pp. 102–103). The second quarter focused on the development of the research paper. In the third quarter, students explored their own interests and produced a piece of writing that could be delivered as a talk via radio, a drama on stage, or a publication (p. 103). Although Berlin doesn't acknowledge it, the influence of John Dewey (1938) here is clear, particularly in the emphasis on the individual's relationship to the social world and the development of tasks that would involve students in defining the path of their own learning. Most important, those who taught the courses exhibited a deep commitment to students, arguing that they must be treated with "respect and consideration" (Berlin, 1987, p. 104). Despite some of the "false turns" in some programs, Berlin concludes that "overall, the communications course . . . encouraged a fresh and worthy set of ideas in composition and finally made a substantial contribution to the development of writing instruction in colleges" (p. 104). However, with the exception of tantalizing clues about the presence of speech teachers, such as the fact that they were employed in Denver's precursor to a writing center, the collaboration that the ASTP mandated between speech and English is simply invisible.

What is clear in Berlin's (1987) account and others is the prolonged resistance that English departments offered to the communication course. In his politically astute way, Berlin suggests that the communication course posed a challenge to "departmental autonomy and academic specialization" and that the key evidence of this fact is that "the alternative to them commonly proffered by the English department was writing about literature" (p. 104).[7] Proponents of the communication course protected themselves from creeping current-traditionalism by establishing separate departments where their more progressive teaching methods could flourish. In his discussion of the Written and Spoken English course at Michigan State College, Frederic Reeve (1949) argues that separation from the English department "[made] possible the encouragement of good teaching, the incentive to study . . . communication as a large problem worthy of much independent work and research, and the possibility of rewarding effective work with rank and salary" (p. 85). In other words, the English department at Michigan State could not be counted on to support the study and teaching of holistic arts of rhetoric.

However, the group that finally ended the communication course was not made up of current-traditionalists but of early process-oriented composition scholars. Their resistance of the course can be measured through the programs of the CCCC and in its journal, *College Composition and Communication*. For the first decade of its history, the CCCC's program contained separate sessions for teachers of the communication course (George & Trimbur, 1999, p. 685). But by 1959, there were no separate sections, and by 1961, reference to the communication course had disappeared. Most students of composition history know that in 1963, the twin strands of rhetoric and composition studies were the theme of the CCCC's program for the first time: composing and the reemergence of rhetoric. Booth, Corbett, Francis Christensen, Josephine Miles, and Gary Tate were some of the more famous speakers. When Ken Macrorie took over the journal *College Composition and Communication* in 1962, articles associated with the communication course "virtually disappeared," including articles on "mass media, propaganda analysis, and general semantics" (George & Trimbur, 1999, p. 685). In 1962, Francis Bowman declared in a *CCC* essay that "the 'communication' battle was over" (p. 55), effectively declaring the fourth "C" dead, despite the stated goal of the original CCCC Constitution and Bylaws: "to unite teachers of college composition and communication" (p. 682).

What was this battle about, and why did composition scholars reject the role of communication in their courses? As George and Trimbur (1999) argue, the teachers of the communication course were progressive educational reformers, and their methods were repugnant to humanist English teachers, even those who were most responsive to their students' needs. George and Trimbur write,

For the "generation of composition" (with its roots presumably in the liberal culture of

embattled humanists and its affiliations to English departments and *belles lettres*), the "generation of communication" must have seemed to be the heralds of social utility and "life adjustment" skills without the redeeming connection to language and literature sponsored by English studies. (p. 688)

The progressive reformers were an embattled group that eventually lost ground to the emerging process movement, which was deeply suspicious of a holistic model of communication.

In 1960, Ken Macrorie published an article in *CCC* that offered a parody of the communication course. The article featured two fictitious characters—Ed, a technical writer who George and Trimbur (1999) argue is the mouthpiece for the communication movement (p. 689); and George, a beleaguered teacher of writing and Macrorie's spokesperson for the process movement (p. 690). Macrorie's 1960 essay, titled "Writing's Dying," satirized the communication course's focus on mass media. The dialogue begins with Ed exclaiming, "Electronics are taking over. Pictures. Sounds. Words in the air" (p. 206). "Writing," he says, "is outnumbered by sounds and pictures" and "outvolumed by the electronic stream" (p. 207). Horrified, George offers his own profession as a way to turn back the invading hoard of visuals: "My God!" he replies, "The first line of the war for the mind may be the freshman writing course" (p. 208).

Macrorie spoke for his generation. In 1960, the Executive Committee of CCCC published a report calling for the establishment of an academic discipline focused on writing—not communication (George & Trimbur, 1999, p. 691). The communication course was, above all, about the development of students as communicators in the world—in short, it was far more akin to a course in rhetoric than one in composition, foreshadowing the revival of rhetoric, a point one of its proponents, John C. Gerber, maintained throughout his life

(Crowley, 1998, p. 183). In contrast, Macrorie effectively established the new discipline through the pages of *CCC* by promoting "a view of 'composition as art,' an expressive and epistemic activity that resisted the notion of writing as a medium of social communication" (George & Trimbur, 1999, p. 693).[8] This turn away from writing as a medium of social engagement is an important source of the enduring tensions between rhetoricians and composition scholars in English.[9]

But where did this attention to the world beyond the student, to the emerging force of new media on the rhetorical situation, and to progressive education come from? These histories make clear that it did not come from English departments. Indeed, English departments (including the emerging field of rhetoric and composition), fought the communication course vigorously and sought to reassert their dominance over language instruction whenever possible. That most historians of composition are so deeply uninterested in the origins of the communication course is a sign that something is under erasure. And in this case, what is under erasure—or rather who—are speech communication teachers.

Even before the founding of their profession, speech communication scholars and teachers embraced the rhetorical tradition, including the study and teaching of public address. The influence of the elocutionists was waning by the turn of the century, and the rhetoricians and social scientists of communication lay the brickwork for the profession. In 1901, Brander Matthews insisted that "an oration or a drama, shall be judged not as literature only, but also in accordance with the principles of its own art" (p. 218), for "nothing ought to be clearer than the distinction between the written word and the spoken—between the literature which is addressed to the eye alone and that which is intended primarily for the ear and only secondarily for the eye" (p. 219). By 1925, Wichelns answered Matthews's call for a new criticism of public

address, drawing on Aristotle to elaborate a rhetorical criticism that evaluated a speech for its social effect. "Effect" was not understood in the one-dimensional terms that it is often taught in composition—that is, the effect on a few classmates. Rather, this criticism evaluated the way in which the speaker drew on the entire tradition and rhetorical situation for materials, invented arguments that would bring multiple audiences into sympathy with his or her views, delivered the address (and under what circumstances), and influenced the democratic process. (I say "his or her" because while most work in this period focused on male orators, Doris G. Yoakam used this criticism in 1937 to evaluate pioneer women orators.) Wichelns's approach became known as "Neo-Aristotelian criticism," and it dominated the study of public address until around 1970. Thereafter, just as English departments began embracing Aristotle's *On Rhetoric* as an answer to moribund pedagogies, scholars in speech communication were exploring theories of genre, dramatism, feminism, and social movements and rejecting Aristotle's tome as the primary basis of understanding rhetoric.[10] The first person to recognize the importance of Kenneth Burke's theories of rhetoric was not in English, though that was Burke's home discipline; the first person was Marie Hochmuth Nichols, who published on dramatism in *QJS* in 1952. Burke (1952a, 1952b, 1953a) responded to Nichols with a series of essays on rhetoric in the same journal. Meanwhile, in English, the new critics dominated the study and teaching of literature, effectively closing down any consideration of social context in the analysis of texts.

In contrast, speech communication teachers committed themselves to viewing their students as beings in the world and saw pedagogy as contributing to their development as individuals and as citizens. Speech communication was always open to the social sciences, particularly psychology, and during the 1920s, speech teachers embraced Dewey's theory of social adjustment and other new theories of personality (Cohen, 1994, p. 119). Many speech teachers believed that their job was to help students identify limitations in their personality and grow beyond them during a public speaking class. Drawing on Dewey's famous definition of education—"to adjust society to the child and the child to society"—speech teachers such as Earl Emery Fleischman (1941) argued that teaching public speaking was "at its core . . . concerned with human relations and the attitudes and behaviors of the individual which affect his measure of success or failure as a human being in a social world" (Cohen, 1994, p. 132). Fleischman (1941) and others believed that students' personalities were revealed in a public speaking class in ways that they were not elsewhere in the curriculum. Some of the attitudes and behaviors that Fleischman hoped to inspire in his students included pragmatism, open-mindedness, lack of sentimentality, social cooperation, directness, and the ability to negotiate with difficult people (pp. 513–514). To the extent that the full range of an individual's personality (including attitudinal predilections) was potentially on display during a speech, Fleischman and others hoped to find ways to intervene to improve the chance for a student's future success. Teachers used personality inventories to identify students' tendencies and used role-playing and other exercises to help them develop a fuller range of behaviors (e.g., by assigning shy students to aggressive roles and more assertive students to more passive roles). Some of the "excesses" of the communication course cited by Applebee (1974), Berlin (1987), and Crowley (2004)—including extensive testing and "tracking" of students—come directly from speech communication teachers' efforts to enact Dewey's pedagogy, using tools from psychology.[11]

Despite these problematic forays into "adjustment" of students, the impulse of speech teachers to find ways to help their students succeed beyond the classroom ultimately grew out of a deeper and more long-standing sense of the moral and ethical obligations of the profession. Those obligations, for many, were social in nature. For example, in his article "Public Speaking and Social Obligations," Angelo Pellegrini (1934) attacked the idea that public speaking courses were meant primarily to put power in the hands of individuals "for leadership and service to one's community," exposing these goals as potentially exploitative (pp. 346–347). Instead, he argued that public speaking

> must refuse to serve such unsocial ends. It must cease to be an instrument for exploitation and become an instrument for social regeneration. It must no longer serve purely personal ends; it must devote itself to the realization of our social needs. (p. 348)

To accomplish this goal, he argued that student speeches should be honest, reasoned, and intellectually and socially worthy, and that all students should be taught to avoid and actively oppose "charlatanism and demagoguery . . . wherever found" (p. 350). As Cohen (1994) put it, while others "had sought to use the public speaking classroom as the locus for the improvement of personality and mental hygiene, Pellegrini saw the classroom as the arena for the inculcation of ethical responsibility" (p. 144).

The rhetoricians in speech communication were especially vocal in their view that training in forensics played a central role in a democracy. For example, Wichelns (1935) located a key social problem in the increasingly polarized debate between the political right ("the conservatives see Red and impose oaths of allegiance") and the left ("the radicals hold that education should prepare the next generation to remake the world") in the pre–World War II period. He argued that speech communication needed to "re-think and re-state the rationale of discussion in the educational system of a democracy" to respond to these trends (p. 560). Such a system would

> demand that the citizen shall be schooled in habits of cooperation, made aware of his place in various groups as well as in the larger community, more inclined to see his own life related to that of his group or class, better disposed to mass action. (p. 558)

Speech teachers should focus their energies, then, on "increased socialization" and "an expansion of speech activities, . . . in the direction of discussion" (Wichelns, 1935, p. 558). Similar statements were made by both Donald C. Bryant and A. Craig Baird in 1938. Cohen notes that the pages of the *QJS* were filled with concern for how to make students better citizens, and, as the world watched Italy, Germany, Japan, and the Soviet Union occupy sovereign nations in Africa, Asia, and Europe, concern was growing about the prospects for democracy. "Essays in *The Quarterly Journal of Speech* reflected the national unease in a way which has not since been duplicated," Cohen writes. "It is to the credit of the profession that it manifested such a strong social conscience about its own activity" (p. 146).

By 1941, when the communication course was commissioned by the Army, these twin goals—the development of students' personalities and their ability to participate as citizens in the democratic process—were transported from speech communication into the experimental programs. Even programs founded after the war embraced these goals. For example, when Michigan State founded its Department of Written and Spoken English in 1945, Paul D. Bagwell included among the department's pedagogical goals "an appreciation of the role that speaking and writing play in a democracy" (cited in Cohen, 1994, p. 156). To be sure, speech communication did not hold on to such values as the 20th century wore on. Cohen concludes his chapter on the early essays on ethics and democracy in *QJS* with a lament that "the high moral tone of the profession and the importance that was

attached to the responsibility of ensuring that the teaching of speech measured up to scrupulous standards" is missing in the scholarship of speech journals. "Some of us may even regret that not even in the pages of *Communication Education* are such issues raised today," he writes, admitting "warm nostalgic feelings for the idealism of early writers" (p. 157). Yet how remarkable to read those earlier statements now, given the current arguments in the pages of the *Rhetoric Society Quarterly* (*RSQ*) for a renewal of a rhetorical education that links skills of speaking and writing to the larger social and political world (see Crowley, 2004; Hauser, 2004; Jackson, 2007; Miller, 2001; see also Glenn, Lyday, & Sharer, 2004). For a time, speech communication teachers led English teachers in preparing students for a world in which reading, writing, listening, and speaking had something to do with their work as citizens and social beings—not only as future professionals. Their idealism—though sobered by so much loss of disciplinary ground—seems to be renewed by contemporary dialogue in *RSQ*.

RECENT EFFORTS AT RAPPROCHEMENT

In an attempt to establish a bridge between rhetoricians in speech communication and English, Steve Mailloux (2000) published "Disciplinary Identities: Rhetorical Paths between English and Communication Studies" in *RSQ*. In it, he seeks to establish a history of the separate paths English studies (including composition) and speech communication took in the 20th century and to discover a way to unite them. In his account, speech communication teachers split off from English to establish a "speech science" at a time when American universities were increasingly promoting research and graduate education. "Again and again in the earliest discussions," Mailloux writes, "teachers of public speaking argued for developing their field as a scientific discipline, and it was through such a development that Speech distinguished itself clearly and decisively from English Studies" (p. 6). In this essay and in his recent book, *Disciplinary Identities* (2006), Mailloux argues that English studies instead chose to develop a scholarly identity firmly in the humanistic tradition. The history of speech communication, for him, is the history of the science of communication. Their problem can be identified as an issue of disciplinary identity—English is the humanities, whereas speech communication is science.

There are more than a few problems with this history, as William Keith (2000) and Michael Leff (2000b) point out. For one thing, it seems to ignore a great deal of scholarship in speech communication and rhetoric and composition. As Keith (2000) argues,

> Mailloux's basic thesis is that once upon a time Speech Communication rhetoricians sought to remake rhetoric as a science (Woolbert's attempt to integrate rhetoric with the evolving social science of "speech"), while in the meantime science itself became rhetorical (demonstrated by Kuhn, Gadamer and Perelman); the moral of the story, presumably, is that if Speech Communication rhetoricians awoke from their scientific slumbers, they would see their common cause with English department rhetoricians. . . . Both sides of the chiasmus "From rhetoric as science to science as rhetoric" are flawed, since they are inconsistent with history and assumptions that underlie much of the Speech Communication tradition in rhetoric. (p. 95)

In short, Keith (2000) accuses Mailloux (2000) of creating a fictional history. Leff (2000b) is more charitable, calling Mailloux's history a "a useful and creative misreading" (p. 87), while at the same time suggesting his "story has many gaps and disquieting leaps of inference," one of which was treating "Woolbert as though he were the only founding presence in the discipline" (p. 86). Leff (2000b) corrects Mailloux's historiography by pointing to rhetorical critics in speech communication who "invoked the humanistic tradition and decried efforts to reduce rhetoric

to 'impersonal knowledge'" (p. 86). Importantly, Leff (2000b) argues, "Hudson and Wichelns invoked and refurbished pre-modern rhetorical lore *more than forty years before the revival of rhetoric that Mailloux applauds* [italics added]" (p. 86). In a later essay, Martin Nystrand (2001) points out the scientific influence on composition studies, which Mailloux (2000) oddly overlooks. Instead, Mailloux (2000) argues that composition emerged after Kuhn and founded itself on a humanistic "rhetorical hermeneutic" that he hopes to promote.

In his *Disciplinary Identities*, Mailloux (2006) repeats this flawed history. However, the book makes clear that he hopes to establish a bridge between speech communication and English studies based on his own theory of rhetorical hermeneutics. What is it that speech communication lacks that English has to offer? In Mailloux's view, it is interpretation. Linking production with theories of reception, he draws heavily on Gadamer to offer a perspective of rhetoric that he hopes will provide a way for the fields to begin participating in greater interdisciplinary cooperation. But his bridge allows traffic to flow in only one direction: from literary theory to speech communication. He has been a lone voice among literary scholars who wish for rhetoric to become a greater bridge between literature and composition. His struggles at Syracuse are legendary, and those of us who have known him since those days deeply admire his work. Nevertheless, his own disciplinary expertise is in the interpretation of texts, and his theoretical base is literary theory. He offers rhetorical hermeneutics as a gift to speech communication, without acknowledgment that rhetoricians and social scientists in speech communication might have something to offer English.

Despite his reservations, Leff (2000b) acknowledges that Mailloux's (2000) history may be of some use to speech communication, which has become more of a social science in recent years. Yet despite Leff's gracious acceptance of Mailloux's gift, one might ask if he may well be an "ungrateful receiver" of ideas the larger and more powerful English studies offers—and which cannot be refused.[12] If so, Leff is not alone. Lu (2004) writes,

> Composition has been assigned the role of a grateful recipient: an ideal "laboratory for articulating the pedagogical implications" of the theoretical and scholarly advances in diverse theories housed in the literature wing of English (R. Miller p. 168). The intellectual work of composition, as that work is evidenced in both the teaching of composition and in composition scholarship, continues to escape notice. (p. 10)

Indeed, Nystrand (2001) makes the point that Mailloux (2000) seems unfamiliar with the history of composition scholarship, or he could not have escaped the influence of science on composition. While Mailloux's perspective is helpful to the ongoing development of bridges between speech communication and English, his misconceptions of the history of rhetoric and composition and speech communication are perplexing, calling forth the specter of his discipline's colonialist history, whether intended or not.

Speech communication does have its own interpretative history. It is called rhetorical criticism. The Cornell School's past and present influence on scholarship in rhetoric should be part of the shared knowledge of the disciplines, a commonplace for anyone writing a disciplinary history of English and speech communication. And yet, Mailloux's study suggests that this scholarship is not well-known in English. He is not alone. By and large, rhetoric and composition scholars have earned their disciplinary educations in English departments, so when they have need of an interpretative tradition, they have turned to literary studies. As Thomas Miller points out, the work of literary critics in cultural studies can make this a productive relationship for composition (p. 110), but it does create some strange

situations. For example, in his overview of research paradigms in rhetoric and composition, Stephen North (1987) argues that "Rhetoric can be defined as an art to be mastered . . . But there is not . . . any inherently Rhetorical mode of inquiry" (p. 64). He underscores his scholarly innocence of rhetorical criticism later, when describing his efforts to analyze student essays, using "essentially the same critical methodology [he] would use were it a study of Whitman, Thoreau, and Emerson, or any other trio of 'major' figures" (p. 118). In other words, North draws on literary criticism to analyze student essays, exploring those texts not as examples of rhetoric—because for him there is no such analytic procedure—but rather as literature. Mailloux (2000) writes that it may be tempting "to single out Literary Studies as being the most awe-inspiring in its total obliviousness to the work in both Composition and Speech communication," but that to do so would be "counterproductive" (p. 23). Perhaps he is right. However, the absence of any acknowledgment of rhetorical criticism in North's work and his own suggest a disturbing continuity within English studies—one that echoes through the 20th century to the present day.

THE PROSPECTS OF RAPPROCHEMENT

There are few scholars who can read and digest most literatures that pertain to their project—McKeon, one of the Wingspread visionaries, was one of the very few. And so most scholars allow their disciplines to help them limit the scope of their work. Sediments of power relations inform their interpretations of what it means to be a member of their discipline. Scholars know whom to read and quote to ensure publication in their own field; they know whom they can routinely exclude. How many rhetoric and composition scholars were perplexed when Jane Tompkins (1996) "discovered" the struggles of her students, with no recognition whatsoever that an entire group of scholars in her own discipline might have done some interesting work in pedagogy? Apparently, for her, scholarship in rhetoric and composition studies simply escaped her notice. The MLA's dissolving of its Pedagogical Section in 1903 informs her of her scholarly identity.

One group of scholars routinely marginalized in English studies and speech communication are feminists. In fact, only Crowley (2004) has participated in the recent Mailloux debate on finding bridges between English studies and speech communication, and while Jacqueline Jones Royster gave a keynote address at the first Alliance of Rhetoric Societies meeting, the subsequent reports have been dominated by men.[13] Women were not included in the all-male world of Wingspan, and feminist rhetoricians continue to speak primarily to themselves, though their work is broadly applicable in their fields. Their frustration with being routinely overlooked in discussions of the future of rhetoric is crystallized in Martha Cooper's (1997) paper at the 1996 meeting of the RSA, in which she laments,

> It seems to me that one quite viable face for the critical rhetorician is that of the feminist communication scholar who engages in ongoing struggle either to critique the grand narrative of patriarchy or to expose the operation of power in those smaller discourses that promise freedom. (p. 102)

For Cooper, the work of feminists in rhetoric offers us a model for "how to create a new discursive space that allows for both diversity and community" (pp. 104–105). She suggests that "feminist scholarship reminds us that rhetoric can be both critical and creative, both suspicious and affirming, both resistant and renewing" (p. 105). I would add that this literature is deeply invested in the kind of "fieldwork" in the communities—rhetoric on the ground—that so many admire (e.g., see Miller, 2001, p. 115). It has always tended to join production and reception theory, and efforts

of feminists to listen carefully to one another across differences has sparked innovative research that has pushed the study of rhetoric in interesting new directions (see recent work by Glenn, 2004; Johnson, 2002; and Ratcliffe, 2005). Finally, feminist rhetoricians in English studies and speech communication have a history of reading one another's work—and citing it, because their object of study so frequently overlaps, and because their subaltern position makes interdisciplinary alliances more attractive. They offer a model for rhetoricians looking for greater rapprochement between speech and English.

In the responses to Mailloux, we hear the distant echo of Corbett (1971), murmuring from Wingspread's Wax Museum. Leff (2000b), for example, pleads for English and speech communication to "listen carefully and learn much more about the aspirations, idiosyncrasies, and anxieties of our rhetorical neighbors" (p. 92). One way to do so is to learn about the *histories, theories, and practices* of our neighbors so that we may more fully—and respectfully—collaborate with them. When rhetoricians are trained in programs that teach an interdisciplinary approach, the fruits of rapprochement are great: For example, graduates of Rensselaer's Rhetoric and Communication Ph.D. program are responsible for the 1996 RSA Program celebrating the scholarly legacy of the Wingspread Conference (Carolyn Miller) and editorial policies at *RSQ* that have deepened the dialogue between rhetoricians in speech and English (Gregory D. Clark).[14] ARS recommendations for further collaboration among speech and English scholars and teachers offer an important opportunity to deepen rapprochement between our fields in a way that was not really possible in the 1940s and 1950s (see especially Hauser, 2004; Leff & Lunsford, 2004; Zarefsky, 2004). But to do so, we must recognize that gifts have already flowed in both directions in the century since Oral and Written English filed for divorce.

NOTES

1. Corbett collaborated with speech communication historian James Golden (Golden & Corbett, 1968). But until recently, such alliances have been relatively uncommon.

2. "In fact, a case can be made," Cohen (1994) continues, "that literary, not rhetorical critics were primarily responsible for bringing about the shift away from Neo-Aristotelian criticism" (p. 168).

3. Crowley (1998) makes this point repeatedly.

4. See, for example, Susan Jarratt (1991) and Krista Ratcliffe (1996). For a discussion of the problems of rhetoric scholarship yoking itself too tightly with the teaching of writing, see Mountford and Reynolds (1996).

5. Rhetoricians of science and professional writing also employ a wide range of methods.

6. Historical and theoretical work in rhetoric and composition by feminists has been responsible for broadening the scope of scholarship, as I explain elsewhere (Mountford, 2003, pp. 3–4). Literacy scholars have also broadened the scope of the field. See Moss (1994) for an especially rich view of the range of research possible in this area.

7. As Crowley (1998) argues, the vestigial presence of literature in composition courses to this day reflects the continued dominance of literature over the more progressive practices in composition studies (p. 87). In many universities, rhetoric and composition programs have split off into separate programs and departments to protect themselves from the literature faculty.

8. Despite the invisibility of the fourth C, George and Trimbur (1999) argue that its presence pulls composition—reluctantly, it seems—"toward the worldly, the actual, the material" as opposed to writing as "simply . . . the mental activity of composing" (p. 697).

9. The perceived resistance of composition studies to the idea of a rhetorical education forms an important backdrop to Crowley's work and the work of the ARS. In her review of the history of the communication course, Crowley (1998) puts it succinctly, "Communication skills . . . was sympathetic to the notion that language was only meaningful in social contexts, whereas current-traditionalism was not" (p. 183). She finds strong evidence in composition textbooks that current-traditionalism is still

not dead and indeed is deeply compatible with the process movement that Murray and others ushered into being in the 1970s (pp. 211–213). Therefore, though Crowley (1998) finds some problems with the communication course, she finds it to be superior to the conservative and humanistic bent of some composition pedagogies.

10. I like to point out to my graduate students that in 1965, Corbett introduced Aristotle's theories of rhetoric to composition in *Classical Rhetoric for the Modern Student*, and in the same year, Edwin Black effectively ended the use of those same theories for speech communication in *Rhetorical Criticism: A Study in Method*.

11. Indeed, citing one lone study of the period that sought to link students' speaking ability and social traits with environmental factors rather than personality, Cohen (1994) wryly notes, "Unsurprisingly, the best speakers were students from cities; with parents in professions; and who were regular church goers" (p. 123).

12. In his epilogue, Cohen (1994) argues that English is now the dominant force in rhetoric studies (p. 326).

13. Jacqueline Jones Royster focused her plenary address on pedagogy, drawing on the example of Anna Julia Cooper and other African American women. Andrea Lunsford cited this address in her dialogue with Michael Leff (2000b), pointing out that "renewed commitments to rhetorical education must take care to avoid racism and sexism" (p. 66).

14. Without a rhetorical approach to the study of texts, artifacts, and communicative events, I could not properly train graduate students in my doctoral program; to do so, I teach a course in rhetorical criticism—with scholarship drawn from both speech communication and rhetoric and composition. I thank S. Michael Halloran at Rensselaer, where graduate students successfully train for careers in both speech and English, for spurring me to develop such a course. This experience raised my awareness of the soft disciplinary divide between speech and English.

REFERENCES

Applebee, A. N. (1974). *Tradition and reform in the teaching of English*. Urbana, IL: National Council of Teachers of English.

Aune, J. A. (2003). *The politics of rhetorical studies.* Retrieved June 2, 2008, from www.rhetoricsociety .org/ARS/pdf/auneresponse1.pdf

Baird, A. C. (1938). The educational philosophy of the teacher of speech. *Quarterly Journal of Speech, 24,* 545–553.

Berlin, J. A. (1987). *Rhetoric and reality: Writing instruction in American colleges, 1900–1985.* Carbondale: Southern Illinois University Press.

Black, E. (1965). *Rhetorical criticism: A study in method.* New York: Macmillan.

Bowman, F. (1962). The chairman retires. *College Composition and Communication, 13,* 55–56.

Britt, E. C. (2001). *Conceiving normalcy: Rhetoric, law, and the double-binds of infertility.* Tuscaloosa: University of Alabama.

Bryant, D. C. (1938). Speech for teachers. *Quarterly Journal of Speech, 24,* 538–541.

Burke, K. (1952a). A dramatistic view of the origins of language: Part one. *Quarterly Journal of Speech, 38*(1), 251–265.

Burke, K. (1952b). A dramatistic view of the origins of language: Part two. *Quarterly Journal of Speech, 38*(4), 446–461.

Burke, K. (1953a). A dramatistic view of the origins of language: Part three. *Quarterly Journal of Speech, 39*(1), 79–92.

Burke, K. (1953b). *Counter-statement.* Los Altos, CA: Hermes.

Cintron, R. (1997). *Angels' town: Chero ways, gang life, and rhetorics of the everyday.* Boston: Beacon.

Cohen, H. (1994). *The history of speech communication: The emergence of a discipline, 1914–1945.* Annandale, VA: Speech Communication Association.

Cooper, M. (1997). A feminist glance at critical rhetoric. In T. Enos & R. McNabb (Eds.), *Making and unmaking the prospects for rhetoric: Selected papers from the 1996 Rhetoric Society of America Conference* (pp. 99–108). Mahwah, NJ: Lawrence Erlbaum.

Corbett, E. P. J. (1965). *Classical rhetoric for the modern student.* New York: Oxford University Press.

Corbett, E. P. J. (1971). Rhetoric in search of a past, present, and future. In L. F. Bitzer & E. Black (Eds.), *The prospect of rhetoric: Report of the national development project* (pp. 166–178). Englewood Cliffs, NJ: Prentice Hall.

Crowley, S. (1998). *Composition in the university: Historical and polemical essays.* Pittsburgh, PA: University of Pittsburgh Press.

Crowley, S. (2004). Communication skills and a brief rapprochement of rhetoricians. *Rhetoric Society Quarterly, 34*(1), 89–103.

Dewey, J. (1938). *Experience and education.* New York: Macmillan.

Ehninger, D., Benson, T. W., Ettlich, E. E., Fisher, W., Kerr, H. P., Larson, R. L. et. al. (1971). Report of the committee on the scope of rhetoric and the place of rhetorical studies in higher education. In L. F. Bitzer & E. Black (Eds.), *The prospect of rhetoric: Report of the national development project* (pp. 208–219). Englewood Cliffs, NJ: Prentice Hall.

Fleischman, E. E. (1941). Speech and progressive education. *Quarterly Journal of Speech, 27,* 511–517.

George, D., & Trimbur, J. (1999). The "communication battle," or, whatever happened to the 4th C? *College Composition and Communication, 50*(4), 682–698.

Glenn, C. (2004). *Unspoken: A rhetoric of silence.* Carbondale: Southern Illinois University Press.

Glenn, C., Lyday, M. M., & Sharer, W. B. (Eds.). (2004). *Rhetorical education in America.* Tuscaloosa: University of Alabama Press.

Goggin, M. D. (2000). *Authoring a discipline: Scholarly journals and the post-World War II emergence of rhetoric and composition.* Mahwah, NJ: Lawrence Erlbaum.

Golden, J., & Corbett, P. J. (1968). *The rhetoric of Blair, Campbell, and Whately.* New York: Holt.

Hauser, G. A. (2004). Teaching rhetoric: Or why rhetoric isn't just another kind of philosophy or literary criticism. *Rhetoric Society Quarterly, 34*(3), 39–53.

Jackson, B. (2007). Cultivating paideweyan pedagogy: Rhetoric education in English and communication studies. *Rhetoric Society Quarterly, 37*(2), 181–201.

Jarratt, S. C. (1991). *Rereading the sophists: Classical rhetoric refigured.* Carbondale: Southern Illinois University Press.

Johnson, N. (2002). *Gender and rhetorical space in American life, 1866–1910.* Carbondale: Southern Illinois University Press.

Keith, W. (2000). Identity, rhetoric and myth: A response to Mailloux and Leff. *Rhetoric Society Quarterly, 30*(4), 95–106.

Kinneavy, J. L. (1990). Contemporary rhetoric. In W. B. Horner (Ed.), *The present state of* scholarship in historical and contemporary rhetoric (pp. 186–246). Columbia: University of Missouri Press.

Leff, M. (2000a, June 30). *Is fragmentation bad?* Online post to H-Rhetor. Retrieved June 2, 2008, from H-rhetor@h-net.msu.edu.

Leff, M. (2000b). Rhetorical disciplines and rhetorical disciplinarity: A response to Mailloux. *Rhetoric Society Quarterly, 30*(4), 83–93.

Leff, M., & Lunsford, A. A. (2004). Afterwords: A dialogue. *Rhetoric Society Quarterly, 34*(3), 55–67.

Lu, M. (2004). Composing postcolonial studies. In A. A. Lunsford & L. Ourzgane (Eds.), *Cross borderlands: Composition and postcolonial studies* (pp. 9–32). Pittsburgh, PA: University of Pittsburgh Press.

Macrorie, K. (1960). Writing's dying. *College Composition and Communication, 11*(4), 206–210.

Mailloux, S. (2000). Disciplinary identities: On the rhetorical paths between English and communication studies. *Rhetoric Society Quarterly, 30*(2), 5–29.

Mailloux, S. (2006). *Disciplinary identities: Rhetorical paths of English, speech, and composition.* New York: Modern Language Association.

Matthews, B. (1901). *The historical novel and other essays.* New York: Scribner.

Mead, W. E. (1900). The graduate study of rhetoric. *PMLA, 15*, xix–xxxii.

Mead, W. E. (1901). The undergraduate study of rhetoric. *PMLA, 16*, x–xxiv.

Miller, T. (2001). Disciplinary identifications/public identities: A response to Mailloux, Leff, and Keith. *Rhetoric Society Quarterly, 31*(3), 105–117.

Moss, B. J. (Ed.). (1994). *Literacy across communities.* Cresskill, NJ: Hampton Press.

Mountford, R. (2003). *The gendered pulpit: Preaching in American protestant spaces.* Carbondale: Southern Illinois University Press.

Mountford, R., & Reynolds, N. (1996). Rhetoric and graduate studies: Teaching in a postmodern age. *Rhetoric Review, 15*(1), 192–214.

Murray, D. (1972). Teach writing as a process not a product. *The Leaflet,* 11–14.

Nichols, M. H. (1952). Kenneth Burke and the "new rhetoric." *Quarterly Journal of Speech, 38*(2), 133–144.

North, S. M. (1987). *The making of knowledge in composition: Portrait of an emerging field.* Upper Montclair, NJ: Boynton/Cook.

Nystrand, M. (2001). Distinguishing formative and receptive contexts in the disciplinary formation of composition studies: A response to Mailloux. *Rhetoric Society Quarterly, 31*(3), 93–103.

Pellegrini, A. (1934). Public speaking and social obligations. *Quarterly Journal of Speech, 20*, 345–351.

Ratcliffe, K. (1996). *Anglo-American feminist challenges to the rhetorical traditions: Virginia Woolf, Mary Daly, and Adrienne Rich.* Carbondale: Southern Illinois University Press.

Ratcliffe, K. (2003). The current state of Composition scholar/teachers: Is rhetoric gone or just hiding out? *Enculturation, 5*(1). Retrieved April 6, 2007, from http://enculturation.gmu.edu/5_1/ratcliffe.html

Ratcliffe, K. (2005). *Rhetorical listening: Identification, gender, whiteness.* Carbondale: Southern Illinois University Press.

Reeve, F. (1949). Basic communication at Michigan State College. In E. J. McGrath (Ed.), *Communication in general education* (pp. 33–36). Dubuque, IA: Wm. C. Brown.

Schilb, J. (1993). The history of rhetoric and the rhetoric of history. In V. Vitanza (Ed.), *Pre/text: The first decade* (pp. 237–262). Pittsburgh, PA: University of Pittsburgh Press.

Scott, F. N. (1980). Rhetoric rediviva. 1909 address to the Modern Language Association. *College Composition and Communication, 31*(4), 413–419.

Tompkins, J. (1996). *A life in school: What the teacher learned.* Reading, MA: Addison-Wesley.

Wichelns, H. A. (1925). The literary criticism of oratory. In A. M. Dummond (Ed.), *Studies in rhetoric and public speaking in honor of James A. Winans* (pp. 181–216). New York: Century.

Wichelns, H. A. (1935). Speech and the educational scene: Notes on the future. *Quarterly Journal of Speech, 21*, 557–560.

Yoakam, D. G. (1937). Pioneer women orators of America. *Quarterly Journal of Speech, 23*, 251–259.

Young, R., Becker, A., & Pike, K. (1970). *Rhetoric: Discovery and change.* New York: Harcourt, Brace, & World.

Zarefsky, D. (2004). Institutional and social goals for rhetoric. *Rhetoric Society Quarterly, 34*(3), 27–38.

PART IV

Rhetoric and Public Discourse

The Common Goods of Public Discourse

KIRT H. WILSON

ROSA A. EBERLY

Any approach to the study of rhetoric is incomplete unless it recognizes the scope and functions of critical practice. Since its inception, rhetorical inquiry has entailed three creative dimensions: the invention and performance of rhetoric, the construction of theoretical principles concerning rhetoric, and the analysis of rhetorical practices. The study of rhetorical objects, most often labeled "rhetorical criticism" in the modern academy, has such a rich history that its full breadth is beyond the scope of this section. Indeed, rhetorical criticism—and especially case-study analysis—has dominated rhetorical inquiry in communication studies. In English studies, rhetorical criticism has assumed different forms; the trajectory of Wayne C. Booth's work, for instance, reflects that range, from the rhetorical criticism of fiction (Booth, 1961, 1983) to an explicitly political and interdisciplinary approach to rhetoric (Booth, 2004). Nevertheless, the analysis of discursive products and practices—as well as instruction in not only academic but also public composition and communication—have shaped the disciplinary histories of English and composition studies as well as that of speech and communication studies (see Connors, 1997; Mailloux, 2006).

Rather than addressing rhetorical criticism in general, this section focuses on historical, critical, and theoretical approaches to public discourse. This focus is intended to narrow the section's content toward studies of rhetorical production that explicitly relate to "the public sphere," variously defined. Public discourse, we argue, is more than a specific area of study in particular disciplines, subdisciplines, and interdisciplines. Public discourse is—and should be—among the most common of topics. As Chapter 23 by David Zarefsky avers, public discourse is the glue that holds—or fails to hold—a democratic polity together. Consequently, its study and practice place in stark relief the reflexive relationship between academic inquiry and the lived experiences of individuals, communities, and institutions. Robert McChesney (2000) has observed that democracy requires critical publicity, particularly about the media themselves. We make a similar observation about public discourse: To the extent that public discourse is neither studied nor made *topos* for publicity and common concern, our shared worlds suffer.

This introduction first establishes the theoretical and critical warrants for this section and then prepares readers to anticipate the contributions of the chapters that follow. A section devoted to the analysis of public discourse must first establish its exigency by addressing specific conceptual questions. What is "public"? "Public sphere"? "Public discourse"? What are the limitations of various perspectives for examining public discourse? How might the critical habits and practices of different disciplines be compared—and perhaps combined—in scholarship about and through public discourse? This introduction will proceed by addressing each of these questions in turn and concluding with brief summaries of each chapter.

CONCEPTUAL CLAIMS AND LIMITING ASSUMPTIONS

We draw on two large bodies of criticism and theory to ground this section: public address and publics theory. While the translation into English of Jürgen Habermas's *Structural Transformation of the Public Sphere: An Inquiry Into a Category of Bourgeois Society* in 1989 generated intense scholarly interest in publics and public spheres across the social sciences and humanities, rhetoricians and public address scholars have been conducting critical and theoretical studies of public discourse since the early decades of the 20th century. Generating a shared space for empirical and critical studies of public discourse—particularly given an increasing concern for the sustainability of democracy itself—remains a central and abiding enterprise of rhetorical studies in the early 21st century.

Habermas's (1962/1989) narrative of structural transformation suggests that the bourgeois public sphere grew out of the 18th-century public sphere in the world of letters, where the reading and writing practices of individuals at home—writing letters and reading novels out loud to each other—allowed people to form what he called "audience-oriented subjectivities." That literary public sphere, Habermas argues, was the structural predecessor to the bourgeois public sphere: "The public sphere in the political realm evolved from the public sphere in the world of letters; through the vehicle of public opinion it put the state in touch with the needs of society" (pp. 30–31). The public sphere, for Habermas, consisted of "public discussion among private individuals" (p. 55), or "private people engaged in public rational-critical debate" (p. 160). While Habermas's account has been roundly and productively critiqued, his seven definitions of "public"—what he describes as a "syndrome of meanings"—are helpful as starting places for this section: (1) "We call events and occasions 'public' when they are open to all, in contrast to closed or exclusive affairs—as when we speak of public places or public houses" (p. 1). (2) "'Public buildings' simply house state institutions and as such are 'public.'" "Public" also describes such occasions when (3) "a powerful display of representation is staged whose 'publicity' contains an element of public recognition" and (4) "when we say someone has made a name for himself, has a public reputation." What Habermas calls the most common usage is (5) "the public as carrier of public opinion; its function as a critical judge is precisely what makes the public character of proceedings—in court, for instance—meaningful." Hence Habermas's final two definitions are (6) "the public sphere itself . . . as a separate domain—the public domain versus the private" and

(7) "the public . . . simply as that sector of public opinion that happens to be opposed to the authorities." Linguistic differences between German and English enable this "syndrome of meanings" (see also Habermas, 1964/1974).

Then, with a brief reference to Arendt's *The Human Condition* (1958), Habermas (1989) notes that "notions of what is 'public' and what is not—that is, what is "private"—however, can be traced much further back into the past." Habermas proceeds to distinguish the *polis* and the category of "what is common" (*koine*) from the *oikos* and what is not common, what is particular to each individual (*idia*). He adds that "since the Renaissance this model of the Hellenic public sphere, as handed down to us in the stylized form of Greek self-interpretation, has shared with everything else considered 'classical' a peculiarly normative power" (p. 4). Though Habermas's account historicizes the public sphere in 18th-century Europe and England rather than in Greek antiquity, the normative similarities between Habermas's project and fundamental concerns of speech communication since its inception are clear. Commentators on and criticisms of Habermas are interdisciplinary and legion (e.g., Benhabib, 1993; Berlant, 1997; Black Public Sphere Collective, 1995; Cvetkovich, 2003; Fraser, 1993; Schudson, 1993; Warner, 2002a, 2002b).

For the purposes of this section, "public discourse" refers to rhetorical processes and products articulated, circulated or performed, deliberated, and rearticulated in the public sphere by private people come together as publics or movements. Whether or not a public sphere exists and whether it serves only the interests of white, bourgeois males are matters of serious and sustained scholarly contention (see, e.g., Goodnight & Hingstman, 1997). We acknowledge these concerns, but believe, with Gerard A. Hauser (1998), that the public sphere does have a particular material expression that implicates social and intellectual histories as well as definable discursive practices. Furthermore, we agree that publics and public spheres—even as counterfactual norms—themselves establish the possibility of democratic processes and practices. We contend that, despite or even perhaps because of its contingent nature, the public sphere perdures—as do the continuously evolving and increasingly threatened practices that warrant its critical relevance.

With Hauser (1998) we posit that the "public sphere" is "a discursive space in which individuals and groups associate to discuss matters of mutual interest and, where possible, to reach a common judgment about them. It is the locus of emergence for rhetorically salient meanings" (p. 21). We extend this position by recognizing Michael Warner's (2002a, 2002b) point that the public in the public sphere is organized through its own discursive habits. Furthermore, multiple publics exist at any one time, and sometimes these publics express different interests, competing claims, and diverse rhetorical cultures. A single public provides meaning for adherents not via individual or personal logics alone, but largely through a collaborative and intersubjective rhetoric that simultaneously involves and extends beyond the identity of individuals. Finally, one of the most important dimensions of the public sphere is that its discursive constitution enables alternative expressions that challenge existing norms and, thereby, relational and institutional configurations within the public sphere. Whether or not such challenges can lead to significant political transformation remains a point of scholarly debate (see, e.g., Deem, 2002).

The authors within this section have been encouraged to move beyond what Dilip Gaonkar (2002) argues is the dominant understanding of rhetorical criticism: the critique of political oratory. Our decision to use the terms *public discourse* as well as *public address* indicates our commitment, first, to a broad object domain, and, second, to the interdisciplinary field that is contemporary public discourse studies. When we do use the term *public address* (see, e.g., Darsey and Ritter below), we do so to indicate a specific and venerable nearly century-old subdiscipline of speech communication studies. Indeed, each chapter in this section considers scholarship that moves beyond public speeches. Laura Gurak and Smiljana Antonijevic's chapter, for example, focuses explicitly on studies of digital rhetoric (Chapter 26), while Stephen Browne's survey of research on the U.S. Revolution and early Republic juxtaposes sermons with public letters and visual icons (Chapter 27). Each author in this section also has tried to include work that cuts across English and communication studies, and, in some cases, across political science, American studies, and gender studies. Angela Ray (Chapter 28), for example, performed a systematic survey of interdisciplinary journals and university presses to identify trends in the study of late-19th-century public discourse.

It is important, however, to recognize the limits of this section: It certainly does not cover the totality of public discourse or social movement scholarship, nor does it dwell on public memory (see, e.g., Browne, 1995; Phillips, 2004), public scholarship (see, e.g., Eberly & Cohen, 2004), public intellectuals (see, e.g., Hauser, 2006), or public culture more widely. Some will agree with Gaonkar (2002) that the broadening scope of rhetorical objects and the pluralism in methods evinced in this section have not led to conceptually dense and innovative theory (p. 411). Indeed, the research discussed in this section is mostly case oriented. Yet while the editors believe that future scholarship in rhetorical studies must combine the act of criticism with more robust theoretical development, public discourse studies has begun to consider situated practices longitudinally, comparatively, and transhistorically (see Jasinski, 2001, pp. 136–141). Others will recognize a bias toward rhetoric from the United States, on discourses of elites rather than subalterns, and on the habits and practices of communication studies rather than interdisciplinary rhetoric or composition studies. Despite our belief that transnational analysis (see Medhurst, 2001, p. 508) and interdisciplinary collaboration are the future of public discourse studies, the past is dominated by Anglo-American work, and, until recently, by one discipline. Steven Mailloux's (2006) history of English and speech communication explains how and why a certain type of rhetorical criticism flourished in speech but not in English departments. Mailloux contends that rhetoric played only a minor, background role in English until the 1960s, when the work of Thomas Kuhn, Hans-Georg Gadamer, Chaim Perelman, and Lucie Olbrechts-Tyteca provided a theoretical vocabulary and renewed pedagogical functions for rhetorical study (pp. 16–26). Wayne Booth (2001) complicates and extends Mailloux's characterization:

> According to the broader definitions of rhetoric—not mere oratory or argument but all modes of persuasion—literary critics have never been able to avoid practicing some form of rhetorical criticism. According to narrower and more popular definitions, however, rhetoric had almost completely disappeared from the literary scene by the end of the eighteenth century. (p. 182; see also Clark & Halloran, 1993)

For both pragmatic and historical reasons, then, this section's editors have chosen a narrow conceptualization of rhetorical criticism. Put differently, we perceive the origins of public discourse studies as generally concerning the study of speeches rather than literature; although this research has fortunately evolved beyond the oral tradition, its oratorical origins have shaped its intellectual history in unavoidable ways. We contend that the most expeditious way to proceed is to focus on scholarship that self-consciously travels under the signs of rhetorical studies, public address or public discourse studies, or social movement rhetoric. Given this approach, the work of scholars in communication studies plays a significant role in this section.

SECTION ORGANIZATION

This section is divided into two subsections. In the first, we asked authors to address the section title from theoretical, disciplinary, and interdisciplinary points of departure. The first two chapters, for example, work through the same history to offer related yet distinct narratives about the evolution of public discourse studies from the early 20th century onward. Read together, Chapter 23 by Zarefsky and Chapter 24 by Campbell and Keremidchieva present a robust account of how the study of public discourse, while always concerned with issues of deliberation, democracy, and public policy, also struggled with issues of equity, identity, and difference. Chapter 25 by Hauser and Hegbloom theorizes a rapproachment between rhetoric and critical theory through public discourse and deliberation, while Chapter 26 by Gurak and Antonijevic reflects on the social, political, and discursive transformations brought about by digital technology.

For the second subsection, we asked authors to address specific discourse practices, focusing on kinds of public discourse or delineated periods of practice. The goal throughout the section is to present a state-of-the-art view of work in rhetorical studies and then to argue for how scholars of rhetoric might best address understudied areas. Three chapters examine the historical periods that are most often the focus of intellectual scrutiny: The U.S. Revolution and early Republic (Chapter 27 by Browne), 1860 to 1900 (Chapter 28 by Ray), and the first half of the 20th century (Chapter 29 by Benson). In each instance, the author has analyzed an enormous amount of literature. That said, omissions are inevitable. Most particularly, the editors did not commission essays that addressed 1830 to 1860 or 1950 to 2007. This is not to suggest that research about these periods is absent from the section, however. Studies of these periods appear in three topically oriented chapters: Darsey and Ritter's study of U.S. religious rhetoric (Chapter 30), Cox and Foust's review of social movement studies (Chapter 32), and Beasley's consideration of contemporary political rhetoric (Chapter 31). By combining chapters that focus explicitly on three often-studied historical periods and three broader themes, this subsection demonstrates both the breadth and diversity of public discourse studies. It not only speaks to our enduring concerns, but it also identifies the field's historic strengths and opportunities for future growth.

CHAPTER SUMMARIES

David Zarefsky, "History of Public Discourse Studies"

Zarefsky defines public discourse studies as the analysis of situated moments of rhetorical practice. In the 19th century, claims Zarefsky, rhetoric sustained public interest because of its presumed connection to historically significant events and its inherent artistry. Speech anthologies were published and purchased, facilitating the growth of academic research and a stable mode of inquiry Zarefsky terms the "rhetorical biography." Studies of great orators and their rhetoric, he explains, served the theoretical and pedagogical needs of young speech departments well into the 1950s, when new rhetoric scholars, social scientists, rhetoric instructors, and movement scholars began to question the rhetorical biography's efficacy. According to Zarefsky, 1965 marks the tipping point when the largely homogeneous study of public discourse fragmented into an increasingly pluralistic set of methods, perspectives, and paradigms. Although Zarefsky notes the enormous benefits that plurality has provided, he concludes with a challenge: Can public discourse studies survive as a coherent and identifiable subfield in the face of so much contemporary diversity?

Karlyn Kohrs Campbell and Zornitsa D. Keremidchieva, "Race, Sex, and Class in Rhetorical Criticism"

Campbell and Keremidchieva extend and complicate Zarefsky's narrative by arguing that the rhetorical biographies that comprised the first stage of public discourse research aligned critical practice with "the interests of cultural establishments, political power, and the value of social cohesion." The impulse to legitimize criticism in established forms of traditional authority was ironic, they contend, because these same scholars were marked by difference and felt marginalized in departments of English. Campbell and Keremidchieva highlight this irony by interpreting the performance of rhetorical criticism as a regular cycle of recognizing and incorporating difference within a generally conservative framework of intellectual inquiry. Only in the last decade, they conclude, have scholars of public discourse begun to understand difference as productive, as a process of identity construction that need not be identified with Anglo-American masculinity.

Gerard A. Hauser and Maria T. Hegbloom, "Rhetoric and Critical Theory: Possibilities for Rapprochement in Public Deliberation"

Hauser and Hegbloom explore the prospects for a theoretical accommodation between rhetoric and critical theory in a milieu of fragmentation and assess the realistic possibilities for such an accommodation to address the challenges facing public deliberation. They argue that the prevailing politics of rational choice, with its instrumental focus on personal gain, undermines democratic action, while public deliberation, with its discursive focus on the public good, offers a competing model that seeks to recuperate democratic action. They contend that a rapprochement between Habermas's construction of critical theory and a rhetorical understanding of public deliberation offers a possibility for refiguring public deliberation in a way capable of addressing relations of mutual dependency in a world of increasing cultural and ideological fragmentation.

Laura J. Gurak and Smiljana Antonijevic, "Digital Rhetoric and Public Discourse"

Gurak and Antonijevic begin their chapter with a statement that is accurate, yet challenging: "We have reached a time where the phrase 'digital rhetoric' is redundant." Their chapter proceeds by detailing the ubiquitous presence of technology not only in rhetoric's current production but also in its historical preservation. They establish, further, how studies of computer-mediated communication (CMC) evolved into the robust field of Internet studies. Unfortunately, their literature review indicates that while scholars occasionally consider technology as a means of rhetoric's distribution, there are few studies that consider the "rhetorical dynamics of the case study's digital component to help explain the rest of the case." What is needed, they argue, is a recognition that digitized forms of public discourse are shaped by a different canon—speed, reach, anonymity, interactivity, *kairos,* and collaborative community. The traditional rhetorical canon is still relevant, but they conclude that the new canon must be incorporated into our research if public discourse analysis is going to account for the majority of rhetoric produced in the 21st century.

Stephen Howard Browne, "Arts of Address in Revolutionary America"

Browne investigates how students of rhetoric have and might best continue "to offer their distinctive insights to the growing body of work on the nation's founding" and early history. The chapter offers an overview of resources and then discusses and performs the state of the art in rhetorical criticism where rhetorical studies of this period might best focus. Browne argues for revitalized interest in rhetorical form—defined as modes of address that function in distinctive but not exclusive manners. The chapter focuses on three genres: the sermon, the public letter, and the visual icon. The sermon, Browne argues, functions as oral critique; the public letter as community formation; and the visual icon as instilling the drama of resistance into public memory. Though genre studies may have fallen on hard times, Browne argues that scholars of rhetoric who want to focus on this period would do well to help revitalize studies of rhetorical forms.

Angela G. Ray, "Explosive Words and Glimmers of Hope: U.S. Public Discourse, 1860–1900"

Ray's chapter balances a reflexive appreciation of her own professional evolution within public discourse studies and a systematic survey of journals and presses that publish 19th-century rhetorical criticism. The personal perspective she brings to bear on this literature not only establishes an organizational structure for the enormous amount of literature she identifies, but it also provides unique insights into both the strengths and weaknesses of 1860–1900 public discourse research. She notes, for example, that the scholarship seems to gravitate toward rhetoric that is either emotionally transformative or symbolic of large social conflict, or both simultaneously. While this has led to a great deal of exciting and progressive work on the late 19th century, especially in the analysis of marginalized voices, it may also explain the surprising absence of studies that consider economic development, "particularly relations of labor and capital" during the Gilded Age.

Thomas W. Benson, "For the Common Good: Rhetoric and Discourse Practices in the United States, 1900–1950"

Benson opens his chapter, a systematic review of interdisciplinary work on this period, by reflecting on similarities between "the turbulent first half of the 20th century" and the present. For instance, studies of the Progressive and New Deal eras, he writes,

> seem to have taken on a new urgency and edge . . . as key administration leaders openly announce their ambition to repeal the New Deal; some even boast of returning to an America that existed before the reforms of the Progressive Era.

Benson argues that while public address studies is "thriving," it remains focused on the lives and texts of various elites:

> Implicitly, our discipline celebrates public rhetoric that is discursive, democratic, decisive, deliberative, and diverse. In practice, no subset of the discipline has cultivated a full historical account of the public practices that might meet such an ideal, nor even a coherent history of the various practices that act as substitutes, deferrals, approximations, or corruptions of such practices.

Benson concludes that, despite the quality and quantity of scholarship, "the rhetorical agendas of the period are unfinished, and our scholarship is painfully incomplete."

James Darsey and Joshua R. Ritter, "Religious Voices in American Public Discourse"

In their survey of scholarship on religious public discourse in the United States, Darsey and Ritter describe existing work "as a mass of tessera waiting to be assembled into a mosaic, wanting an inventory of the missing pieces." Though focusing on public address scholarship, they address interdisciplinary literatures as well,

> in an effort to piece together something of the story of religious rhetoric in the United States, to provide a sense of its parameters and its trajectory, and to identify opportunities for rhetorical scholars to extend our understandings of this fundamental of American public discourse.

The chapter is structured both chronologically and topically; it features new rhetorical criticism on Jonathan Edwards's "Sinners" as representative anecdote; and it culminates by weighing in on controversies surrounding a fifth great awakening and postmodernity. "Only by suggesting the essential coherence of the story," write Darsey and Ritter,

> can we make a compelling case that the study of religious discourses in the United States ought to be more than a sideshow, a rare look at what are too often imagined as rhetorical oddities at the margins of public life, removed from the realm of reason and evidentiary obligations.

Vanessa B. Beasley, "Between Touchstones and Touch Screens: What Counts as Contemporary Political Rhetoric"

Beasley addresses the strange paradox that although, in public opinion, the quality of U.S. political rhetoric has declined, its study has never been more robust. The study of political communication is so widespread, she argues, that two distinct subfields have developed within the academy. The first and oldest is represented by the "public address" tradition and is most often located in speech and communication departments. The second subfield is more frequently characterized by its method than through a consistently applied label; it involves the social scientific analysis of political communication's effects. Although the two subfields have existed for almost 30 years, Beasley argues that new media innovations are beginning to transform the practice and study of political rhetoric, perhaps even complicating distinctions between the two subfields. In particular, she notes that "visual rhetorics," photography, film, television imagery, and Internet video, have become essential components of political communication and its study. She anticipates that as the impact of digitized media is better recognized, scholars may find themselves in new territory as they struggle to understand the changing terrain of contemporary political rhetoric.

Robert Cox and Christina R. Foust, "Social Movement Rhetoric"

Perhaps more than any other kind of work in rhetorical studies, scholarship on social movements has embraced critical and theoretical pluralism and moved from studies of individual leaders, individual texts, and individual movements into wider studies of social change. Cox and Foust argue that studies of social movements have themselves "broadened rhetorical theory and criticism by bringing uninstitutionalized, nonnormative, and incongruous voices into conversation with public discourse scholarship." The chapter reviews five major trajectories in scholarship on social movement rhetoric (SMR): early studies; refigurations of social movements into "new social movements" and counterpublics; resistance performed by bodies, through images, and on public screens; democracy, representation, and new modalities of social dissent; and continuing challenges for social movement scholarship. Cox and Foust conclude their chapter and, appropriately, this section by articulating rhetoric with the question of efficacy:

> In the end, we believe, a robust theory of the efficacy or impact of rhetorical acts in oppositional struggles holds the greatest promise for continued development and contribution of SMR scholarship. For beyond simple accounts of "resistance" lies the possibility of understanding the relationships among discursive acts, power, and the sources of social and political transformation.

REFERENCES

Arendt, H. (1958). *The human condition.* Chicago: University of Chicago Press.

Benhabib, S. (1993). Models of public space: Hannah Arendt, the liberal tradition, and Jürgen Habermas. In C. Calhoun (Ed.), *Habermas and the public sphere* (pp. 73–98). Cambridge, MA: MIT Press.

Berlant, L. (1997). *The queen of America goes to Washington City: Essays on sex and citizenship.* Durham, NC: Duke University Press.

Black Public Sphere Collective. (Ed.). (1995). *The black public sphere.* Chicago: University of Chicago Press.

Booth, W. C. (1961). *The rhetoric of fiction.* Chicago: University of Chicago Press.

Booth, W. C. (1983). *The rhetoric of fiction* (2nd ed.). Chicago: University of Chicago Press.

Booth, W. C. (2001). Criticism. In T. O. Slone (Ed.), *Encyclopedia of rhetoric* (pp. 181–190). New York: Oxford University Press.

Booth, W. C. (2004). *The rhetoric of rhetoric.* Oxford, UK: Blackwell.

Browne, S. H. (1995). Reading, rhetoric, and the texture of public memory. *Quarterly Journal of Speech, 81,* 237–250.

Clark, G., & Halloran, S. M. (Eds.). (1993). *Oratorical culture in 19th-century America: Transformations in the theory and practice of rhetoric.* Carbondale: Southern Illinois University Press.

Connors, R. (1997). *Composition-rhetoric: Backgrounds, theory, pedagogy.* Pittsburgh, PA: University of Pittsburgh Press.

Cvetkovich, A. (2003). *An archive of feelings: Trauma, sexuality, and lesbian public cultures.* Durham, NC: Duke University Press.

Deem, M. (2002). Stranger sociability, public hope, and the limits of political transformation. *Quarterly Journal of Speech, 88,* 444–454.

Eberly, R. A., & J. Cohen (Eds.). (2004). *A laboratory for public scholarship and democracy.* San Francisco: Wiley.

Fraser, N. (1993). Rethinking the public sphere: A contribution to the critique of actually existing democracy. In C. Calhoun (Ed.), *Habermas and the public sphere* (pp. 109–142). Cambridge: MIT Press.

Gaonkar, D. P. (2002). Publics and counterpublics: Introduction. *Quarterly Journal of Speech, 83,* 410–412.

Goodnight, G. T., & Hingstman, D. B. (1997). Studies in the public sphere. *Quarterly Journal of Speech, 83,* 351–399.

Habermas, J. (1974). The public sphere: An encyclopedia article (S. Lennox & F. Lennox, Trans.). *New German Critique, 3,* 49–55. (Original work published 1964)

Habermas, J. (1989). *Structural transformation of the public sphere: An inquiry into a category of bourgeois society* (T. Burger, Trans.). Cambridge, MA: MIT Press. (Original work published 1962)

Hauser, G. A. (1998). Civil society and the principle of the public sphere. *Philosophy and Rhetoric, 31,* 19–40.

Hauser, G. A. (Ed.). (2006). Forum: The nature and function of public intellectuals. *Philosophy and Rhetoric, 39,* 125–156.

Jasinski, J. (2001). Criticism in contemporary rhetorical studies. In *Sourcebook on rhetoric: Key concepts in contemporary rhetorical studies* (pp. 125–144). Thousand Oaks, CA: Sage.

McChesney, R. (2000). *Rich media, poor democracy: Communication politics in dubious times.* Urbana: University of Illinois Press.

Medhurst, M. J. (2001). The contemporary study of public address: Renewal, recovery, and reconfiguration. *Rhetoric & Public Affairs, 4,* 495–514.

Mailloux, S. (2006). *Disciplinary identities: Rhetorical paths of English, speech, and composition.* New York: Modern Language Association.

Phillips, K. (Ed.). (2004). *Framing public memory.* Tuscaloosa: University of Alabama Press.

Schudson, M. (1993). Was there ever a public sphere? If so, when? Reflections on the American case. In C. Calhoun (Ed.), *Habermas and the public sphere* (pp. 143–163). Cambridge, MA: MIT Press.

Warner, M. (2002a). *Publics and counterpublics.* New York: Zone Books.

Warner, M. (2002b). Publics and counterpublics (abbreviated version). *Quarterly Journal of Speech, 83,* 413–425.

23

History of Public Discourse Studies

DAVID ZAREFSKY

Public discourse is situated rhetorical practice. It is the product of a rhetorical transaction in the context of a particular situation. The situation is a set of circumstances presenting opportunities and constraints, and the discourse exhibits the ways in which rhetors and audiences respond to them.

Public discourse is both the result of rhetorical creativity and the object of rhetorical analysis. The tradition of oratorical performance can be traced back to the ancients, notably featuring (in the West) the orations of Demosthenes and Cicero. Each of the genres identified by Aristotle—deliberative, forensic, and epideictic—embodies a strong tradition of performance. Texts most likely to be preserved today are sermons and speeches about public issues. Although examples of public discourse can be found in every society and culture, vibrant discourse traditions are most likely to be found in democratic societies, because democracies depend, always in theory and

usually in practice, on explicit or implicit consent of the people. Consent is necessary not only for legitimacy but also for a democracy's effective functioning. Discursive interaction between leaders and led is typically the means for obtaining consent and making decisions about public issues. It is the decision-making procedure that most clearly recognizes human fallibility by providing for the continual testing and reexamination of beliefs (see Thorson, 1962). The most thoroughly developed and preserved traditions of public discourse are in Great Britain and the United States. More recent work has sought to recover discourse traditions of non-English-speaking and non-Western cultures.

EARLY STUDIES OF PUBLIC DISCOURSE

For centuries, the paradigm case of public discourse was the oration, and the primary mode of its appreciation was through collection and personal edification. By the middle of the 19th century, anthologies of speeches were published. The most notable in Britain was Goodrich (1852). In the United States, landmark collections were those edited by Depew (1902) and Reed (1900, 1903). Anthologies were sometimes arranged alphabetically by author, sometimes chronologically, and sometimes by the genre of the discourse. These multivolume collections were of interest, not only to scholars but also to the general public. The speech texts were read for their own sake, whether because their delivery constituted historically significant events, they displayed the artistry of their creators, or they were models that others might seek to emulate. The tradition of anthologizing speeches continues today. Most have been composed of speeches delivered in the United States. Recent examples include Safire (1997) and Torricelli (1999), both intended for a broad reading audience, and Andrews and Zarefsky (1989, 1992) and R. Reid and Klumpp (2005), whose collections are intended for students. More specialized anthologies are also available, such as Holland (1971), which is a collection of sermons; Wrage and Baskerville (1960, 1962), focusing on competing perspectives on public issues; Foner and Branham (1998), containing an extensive collection of speeches by 19th-century African Americans; K. Campbell (1989b) and Sarkela, Ross, and Lowe (2003) featuring speeches by U.S. women; and Houck and Dixon (2006), a collection of Southern sermons on civil rights and race relations. Online speech collections are easily available, including american rhetoric.com, presidentialrhetoric.com, and voicesofdemocracy.com.

If the performance of public discourse has occurred for centuries, the study and analysis of public discourse is of much more recent origin. It is a phenomenon of the 20th century that has taken place largely in the United States. Studying public discourse serves historical,

critical, and theoretical purposes. Historically, it permits assessment of discourse as a causal force by examining texts that make a difference. Since causality usually is elusive, it is often more productive to use public discourse as an interpretive lens, a way to explain or account for historical events. Critically, studying public discourse makes it possible to evaluate rhetorical acts, instrumentally in regard to their effectiveness and also in terms of their significance and quality. It also permits an understanding of history as a series of rhetorical problems, situations that call for public persuasion to reach collective decisions (see Zarefsky, 1998).

With respect to theory, studying public discourse helps illuminate what has taken place in a particular rhetorical transaction so that the scholar may offer a "theory of the case." Studies of public discourse also may suggest hypotheses for more systematic study under controlled conditions in the manner proposed by Bowers (1968). More commonly, however, studies of discourse will apply theories to cases, demonstrating either the broad reach of the theory or the limiting conditions that it confronts in actual practice.

The earliest works of public address criticism were pedagogical in orientation. Students were expected to appreciate and imitate great orations. Representative of these early works is Shaw (1928), a collection of 21 great speeches by great American speakers, ranging chronologically from Patrick Henry to Woodrow Wilson. Beyond an anthology, however, it places the orators and their speeches within the context of the issues and historical forces of the time. Each chapter describes orators of the period, provides biographical information, sketches the setting of the speech, and suggests collateral studies. The collection is limited, almost completely, to speakers on political themes; the few exceptions such as Rufus Choate and Theodore Parker are justified because these speakers did not limit themselves to their own expertise but addressed the broad social and political questions of the day. All were white males. Collateral studies, exercises, and appendices are designed to help students develop the rhetorical skills that Shaw finds exhibited in the individual speeches.

Shaw's (1928) work appeared toward the end of the period that emphasized primarily the pedagogical utility of public discourse studies. Albeit slowly, scholars saw their goal as explaining and evaluating, more than imitating, the public discourse they studied. The landmark essay setting out the rationale for this project was Wichelns (1925). Arguing that oratory should be seen as a genre of discourse distinct from literature, he maintained that its goal was not permanence or beauty, but effect. "The literary criticism of oratory," then, should focus on how public discourses achieve their effects. Significantly, Wichelns was not calling for an empirical demonstration of a speech's effects, nor even suggesting that most single speeches could have recognizable effects, though some of the work that would cite his article as justification sought to do precisely that. Rather, Wichelns was suggesting that analysis and criticism of oratory should focus on how, and how well, it is designed to achieve effects. Wichelns's essay launched the subfield of rhetorical criticism, often thought synonymous with "public address" because that was the principal object to which criticism would be applied.

The slightly more than 80 years since the publication of Wichelns's (1925) article witnessed the slow start and then rapid growth of public discourse studies, culminating in what Lucas (1988) has characterized as a "rhetorical renaissance." For the period from 1925 to about 1965, despite occasional calls for broader perspective, there was a standard method for studying public discourse and a generally accepted view of its subject matter. In subsequent years, almost geometrically, there has been an expansion in what counts as public discourse, in the kinds of rhetors

studied, in the approaches taken to such studies, in their audiences, and in their purposes. Scholars have not abandoned earlier foci but have transformed them so that they are more robust and insightful. Throughout the expansions, moreover, public discourse studies have wrestled with dialectical tensions that, for the most part, have been productive of strong scholarship. For these reasons, the year 1965 serves as a convenient dividing point in the review that follows.

PUBLIC DISCOURSE STUDIES TO 1965

For most of the 40 years following Wichelns's (1925) essay, public discourse was understood primarily, if not exclusively, as oratory. Yet, ironically, the focus of scholarship was not on *oratory* but on *orators*. As Medhurst (1993) has noted, the first article devoted to a single speech text did not appear until 1937—a contemporary analysis of Franklin D. Roosevelt's second inaugural address. The subjects of study were well-known historical figures such as Abraham Lincoln, Woodrow Wilson, John Bright, Lyman Beecher, John C. Calhoun, and Daniel Webster. Religion and politics were the fields in which they achieved fame. The assumption was that at least part of their historical achievement could be credited to their practice of public address. The task for the student of public discourse, as Hochmuth (1955a) wrote about criticism, was one of "evaluating human effort as it manifests itself in the making of speeches" (p. 2). By understanding and evaluating the components of the speaking situation, the analyst could judge the orator as an agent in history.

Public discourse studies, then, were a special kind of rhetorical biography. Most were confined to the length of an essay or journal article, although there are exceptions. Brigance (1934) produced a book-length analysis of the rhetorical career of Jeremiah Sullivan Black, and Aly (1941/1965) devoted a book to the rhetoric of Alexander Hamilton. These were among the first scholarly books to come from the new field of speech.

The biographical essays followed a fairly standard format, discussing various constituents of the rhetorical act. A common pattern was to comment on the speaker's use of the three genres of oratory identified by Aristotle (forensic, deliberative, and epideictic), the five canons of rhetoric (invention, arrangement, style, memory, and delivery), and the three modes of proof (logos, ethos, and pathos). Examples would be offered from several of the orator's speeches. To provide context, the writer usually included a biographical background, discussion of the orator's rhetorical training and speaking experience, and an overview of the times and the issues. The danger always was that this background material, usually drawn from secondary sources, would eclipse the actual analysis. Because of its debt to Aristotle's *Rhetoric,* this category system retrospectively was called neo-Aristotelianism, a moniker pejoratively bestowed by Black (1965), although it is far from certain that Aristotle would have endorsed it. As Medhurst (1993) explains, it is "a bastardized form of Aristotelianism, static in its category system and devoted largely to establishing that the categories could be made to fit the speaking career of almost every orator."

The crowning achievement of this early period was the publication of a three-volume anthology, *A History and Criticism of American Public Address,* with the first two volumes under the editorship of William Norwood Brigance (1943), and the third edited by Marie Hochmuth (1955b). The three volumes were published under the auspices of the forerunner to the National Communication Association.

Although the method of neo-Aristotelianism was regarded as "historical-critical," the Brigance (1943) volumes distinguish between historical and critical studies. Five chapters present overviews of the colonial, early national,

and later national periods, a discussion of "woman's introduction to the American platform" (even though all the individual studies are of men), and a discussion of the teaching of rhetoric during the early years of the United States. There follow 40 individual chapters, each devoted to the public discourse of a historically prominent person. These are grouped according to fields of practice, including religion, reform, law, general culture, education, labor, and statecraft (the largest single category). The third volume, under Hochmuth's (1955b) editorship, follows the same general orientation. There are only 12 essays (including Hochmuth's introduction), so more extensive treatment of each orator is possible. The table of contents is not divided by field, but the same overall approach is maintained. Volume 3 is the first in the multivolume series to examine the speaking of a woman, Susan B. Anthony.

During the decade after 1955, studies of individual orators continued to be the mainstream of scholarship in public discourse. Both historical and contemporary speakers were the subjects of analysis, but occasionally, scholars found other organizing principles besides the biographical. For example, two symposia (Boase, 1960; Miller, 1960) considered keynote speeches at political conventions, and speaking during the presidential campaign, but each symposium consisted of essays on individual speeches. Another essay (Gunderson, 1961) explored not speech but silence, the refusal by Abraham Lincoln to deliver substantive speeches between his election in 1860 and his inauguration. This period also included one of the few treatments of an orator outside the United States, the South Korean president Syngman Rhee (Oliver, 1962).

So widespread was the approach of neo-Aristotelianism, that it was codified by Thonssen and Baird (1948) as the basic approach to studies of public discourse. But voices were raised challenging its seeming hegemony. Aly (1943) urged a broadening of research questions beyond the biographical, and L. Reid (1944) distinguished between reporting and criticism, arguing that neo-Aristotelianism was doing the former under the guise of the latter. In Reid's view, the historical work was "second-hand," rather than relying on primary sources, and the critical apparatus was in reality the mechanical application of categories drawn from an overly restricted conception of rhetorical theory.

Moreover, these same years witnessed at least a few examples of public discourse studies using organizing principles other than the biographical and critical methods of the neo-Aristotelian. Even Thonssen and Baird (1948), usually understood to be the canonical textbook on neo-Aristotelian methodology, took an expansive view of the critical object. It could be a single speech, or the complete speaking career of an individual, or what they called a "speaking movement" (a group of speakers advocating social change over a period of time) or a particular historical period in the development of speaking. In later years, the exclusive focus on oral delivery would be relaxed, and the study of public discourse would include other forms of overtly persuasive discourse—pamphlets, broadsides, tracts, editorials, and other essays.

A more fundamental challenge to the reigning paradigm was proposed by Crandell (1947), who questioned the focus on individual "great speakers." Rather than accepting that history was primarily the record of orations of great men, he instead emphasized the role of social movements and broad intellectual forces. Although few scholars immediately took up this call, one who soon did was Leland Griffin (1952), who offered a general orientation to the study of historical movements. He followed with an example: a robust analysis of the rhetorical structure of the anti-Masonic movement of the 1820s and 1830s (Griffin, 1958), which had

been the focus of his doctoral dissertation. This emphasis on social movements offered a potential linkage between rhetoric and sociology, as well as history. Tyler's (1944/1962) *Freedom's Ferment* is a study of antebellum reform movements in the United States that significantly emphasizes public communication. Later scholars such as Gusfield (1970) and Laraña, Johnston, and Gusfield (1994) concerned themselves mostly with contemporary movements.

Wrage (1947) articulated another challenge to the dominant paradigm. Instead of emphasizing biographical characteristics of speakers, he focused on the content of the speech, believing that it offered unique insight into how ideas are modified in the process of transmission to an audience. Like others of his time, he saw public discourse studies as contributing to the understanding of history, but for him it was a branch of both social and intellectual history. Since he examined ideas in conflict, he was inclined to view the controversy rather than the speaker as the basic unit of analysis. In the two-volume anthology of speeches he coedited with Baskerville (Wrage & Baskerville, 1960, 1962), he selected speeches that represented opposing positions in major controversies such as the locus of sovereignty, the merits of slavery, women's suffrage, and the clash between modernism and fundamentalism in religion. These were not necessarily the best known speakers or speeches. Nor did Wrage and Baskerville always provide full texts; they edited to focus readers' attention on the passages that most clearly revealed the main ideas. Wrage's approach inspired the work of a generation of students, but little of it saw publication until after Wrage's untimely death in 1965. A collection of essays, many embodying Wrage's approach, is Holland's (1973) *America in Controversy: History of American Public Address.*

Meanwhile, other scholars called into question the exclusive reliance on Aristotle as the theoretical anchor for public discourse studies. Not only were studies of the classical tradition bringing other works to the attention of public discourse scholars, but even more influential was contemporary scholarship across the humanities with strong implications for understanding public discourse. Hochmuth (1952) first introduced the speech discipline to the work of Kenneth Burke, whose theories of human life as drama would have at least as much impact on late-20th-century studies as would the writing of Aristotle. Other theorists whose work would influence public discourse studies in later years, some of whom were first brought to the attention of contemporary scholars during the 1950s, included I. A. Richards, Stephen Toulmin, Chaim Perelman, Richard Weaver, and Michel Foucault.

Parrish (1954) went so far as to question the dominance of the effect standard in the analysis of public discourse, arguing instead that speeches had intrinsic qualities unrelated to their actual effects. What Parrish actually was challenging was the reduction of "effect" to a purely empirical question. Not only was it usually unanswerable, but it also diverted attention from the recognition, appreciation, and evaluation of a speech's artistry. The implication of Parrish's argument was that scholarly attention should be devoted more to critical study of specific speech texts than to identifying their effects. Regarding the text as the main object of study rather than merely a source of examples of a speaker's use of various techniques would not become commonplace for another 30 or 40 years, but the touchstone for such activity was provided during the 1950s.

A synthesis of the scholarship in public discourse during this period was offered by Oliver (1965), who undertook the ambitious task of writing a history of public speaking in the United States. It is largely a study of selected speakers from various historical periods. The speakers are chosen for their historical prominence, and the analysis reveals more about their biographies and the historical context than about their speaking or speeches. It does bring together a large number of issues and speakers, and it symbolized the state of public discourse studies at the time. That condition would be drastically altered by forces of social change sweeping the 1960s and beyond, and the scholarship of the ensuing 40 years in some respects would be drastically different from that of the 40 years prior to 1965.

THE SCOPE OF PUBLIC DISCOURSE STUDIES SINCE 1965

The years since 1965 have witnessed both considerable enlargement in what counts as "public discourse" for study and substantial reconsideration of issues related to methods and approaches to such study. The former transformation has moved studies far beyond a focus on only individual speeches and orators; the latter has heralded pluralism in critical approaches and a wider audience for studies of public discourse.

A brief review of some of the major trends will suggest how public discourse has been construed far more broadly than just oratory. It has come to designate not discourse of a certain *form* but discourse with a certain *purpose*— calling together and addressing a public.

Movement Studies

Studies of historical and social movements, for which Crandell and Griffin had called, flourished in the decades after 1965. They focused not on individual speakers, but on the mobilization of masses of people, usually lacking in institutional power, in support of a cause. Sometimes, these were studies of historical movements. For example, Lucas (1976) studied the successful efforts to influence middle-class Philadelphians to support independence two centuries earlier. Andrews (1967) examined the early pacifist movement in Britain.

For the most part, though, contemporary social movements were the objects of study, and the selection of movements undoubtedly was influenced by the social turmoil sweeping the country at the time. Griffin (1964) himself led the way with a magisterial study of the contemporary New Left. Several scholars, such as Burgess (1968), Gregg, McCormack, and Pedersen (1969), and Stewart (1997), trained their lenses on the Black Power Movement, which at the time, not only complicated Americans' understanding of the civil rights struggle and race relations but also complicated scholars' understanding of political persuasion. As the Civil Rights Movement developed, it inspired a resurgence of concern about the rights of women. First Hancock (1972) and then K. Campbell (1973) examined oxymoronic elements of rhetoric in behalf of women's rights. Campbell, in particular, followed this early work with a substantial research program devoted to recovery and analysis of speeches of U.S. women, many of whom had to fight for access to the public forum as well as for the merits of the causes that they espoused. (For examples of her work see Campbell, 1980, 1995, 2005.)

Simons (1970) theorized that social movements had distinctive requirements, problems, and strategies for successful persuasion. This was so, he maintained, because they were uninstitutionalized collectivities operating from a position of relative weakness in a struggle with elite leaders or organizations. A special issue of *Central States Speech Journal* in 1980 was devoted to movement studies, even including skeptical essays by McGee (1980a) and Zarefsky (1980), who argued that movements were interesting sociologically but had no distinctive rhetorical form or dynamics.

For largely unknown reasons, movement studies (which had been written frequently during the 1960s and 1970s) largely passed from the scene after the mid-1980s. Subsequent studies remain in the tradition of social protest, however. Morris and Browne (2006) anthologize essays on protest rhetoric, including several published during the 1990s. DeLuca and Peeples (2002) investigate protest during the 1999 meeting of the World Trade Organization in Seatttle. And in her recent study of 19th-century women's rights petitions, Zaeske (2002) locates some of her work in the tradition of social movement studies. Cox and Foust (Chapter 32, this volume) consider the development of social movement rhetoric and its criticism.

Discourse as a Means of Empowerment

Not just movement studies, but other studies of public discourse also focused on those in a subordinate position within hierarchies of power, for whom rhetoric provided a means to offset the power disadvantage. Many of these studies had both a scholarly and an emancipatory purpose. As mentioned, K. Campbell (1989a, 1989b) extended her research program on women's rhetoric, focusing, in part, on how 19th-century U.S. feminists used public discourse to gain attention and elicit support for their causes. Often, they needed to establish their right to speak in light of their assumed subordinate status and then used public discourse to contest the very basis of that subordination.

Scott and Smith (1969) looked more generally at the rhetoric of confrontation, circumstances in which people's profound moral convictions required them to place their bodies on the line to dramatize the immorality of the regime in power or to force a stark moral choice on the part of their audiences. Using the disturbances at Columbia University in 1968 as his case study, Andrews (1969) explored confrontation in the university environment, warning against what he called "coercive rhetoric." Conversely, Haiman (1967) focused on public confrontation through techniques such as rallies, parades, marches, and picketing—techniques that he referred to as "the rhetoric of the streets." There was little doubt that Haiman's study, in the language of the day was "relevant." Some historical ballast for studies of confrontation was found in Fletcher (1968), which examined the draft riots in New York City following the beginning of conscription during the Civil War.

Goodman and Gorden (1971) studied the symbolism, and hence the rhetorical dimension, of desecration of a society's sacred objects. The principal example in those years was the desecration of the U.S. flag, the topic of several Supreme Court decisions. Probably the verbal analogue for the physical act of desecration was the diatribe, studied by Windt (1972), a rhetorical form whose roots were in the classics and which was understood to be the last resort of an advocate for change who had failed in earlier efforts to puncture the resistance of the dominant society.

Expanding the Definition of "Text"

The years since 1965 have seen the notion of what counts as a "text" expand considerably beyond the earlier preoccupation with oratory. Perhaps the most obvious expansion is to include pamphlets, tracts, and other forms of persuasive written discourse. Illustrative studies are those by Burgchardt (1980) on the pamphlets from two different periods in the history of American communism and by Diffley (1988) examining the 1854 *Appeal of the Independent Democrats.* For these scholars and others with similar projects, what distinguishes the rhetorical text is not the oral mode of its delivery but, rather, its persuasiveness.

The natural next extension of textuality would encompass formal written documents. Here, the exemplar is a series of works by Stephen E. Lucas (1989) on the rhetorical dynamics of the Declaration of Independence. Beyond formal documents, textual studies have also been conducted of conversation and informal interaction. Philipsen (1975) studied the speaking practices of a Chicago neighborhood that he called Teamsterville, and

Stanback and Pearce (1981) examined the communication strategies of those in subordinate social groups. The most fully developed study of these informal communications is Hauser's (1999) *Vernacular Voices: The Rhetoric of Publics and Public Spheres,* an investigation of "vernacular voices" such as citizens' letters to the president during the Franklin D. Roosevelt administration.

Of course, these artifacts share with oratory an emphasis on verbal discourse. Yet the concept of rhetorical textuality has been extended to encompass nonverbal and visual modes of interaction as well. There have been numerous studies of the persuasiveness of popular music. For example, Branham and Hartnett (2002) trace the development and the persuasiveness of "My Country 'Tis of Thee." A number of projects, such as Brummett's (1991) *Rhetorical Dimensions of Popular Culture,* identify rhetorical dimensions of popular culture, which often achieve persuasiveness while ostensibly providing nothing more than entertainment, so that audience members' defenses against being persuaded are down. Although there are exceptions, most of the analyses of popular culture's persuasive dimension rely on contemporary rather than historical case studies.

Visual expression also has been the subject of rhetorical study. For example, Finnegan (2003) examined documentary photographs of the 1930s Depression as rhetorical texts. Hariman and Lucaites (2007), in a series of essays and in a book, study what they call "iconic photographs," those that so clearly embody cultural meanings and convey persuasive messages that "no caption [is] needed." Meanwhile, Edwards and Winkler (1997) analyze how cartoons constitute a form of public discourse. L. Olson (2004) gives a historical dimension to the treatment of cartoons by considering pictorial motifs by Benjamin Franklin as visual representations of arguments that he was making on behalf of colonial unity.

Hay (1969) studied the liberty tree as a visual symbol, exemplifying the claim that physical objects can be so invested with meaning and symbolic significance as to constitute a form of public discourse. The same can be said of public memorials. In a series of essays (e.g., Blair, Jeppeson, & Pucci, 1991), Blair and her collaborators have understood commemorative memorials as, at least in part, a discourse in which society publicly defines and reinforces its shared values. This was also a principal focus of Blair's (2006) Carroll C. Arnold Lecture at the National Communication Association. With specific attention to memorials commemorating the Civil Rights movement, Gallagher (1999, 2004) also has interpreted commemorative memorials and other visual forms (Gallagher & Zagacki, 2005) as a kind of epideictic public discourse.

Other examples of studies of visual discourse are the several essays by Rushing or by Rushing and Frentz that explicate the rhetorical messages of popular film (e.g., Rushing & Frentz, 1980), as well as studies finding public messages in the physical act of massing bodies for demonstrations and protests (e.g., Haiman, 1967, 1969). A good synthesis and assessment of scholarship in visual discourse is L. Olson (2008).

So thoroughly did rhetorical studies embrace this broader understanding of what constitutes a text that, as early as 1970, the National Developmental Project on Rhetoric regarded as appropriate for rhetorical study "any human act, process, product, or artifact which, in the critic's view, may formulate, sustain, or modify attention, perception, attitudes, or behavior" (Sloan, 1971). This is a far cry from equating public discourse with the literary criticism of oratory.

Studying Society and Culture

In a provocative book, sociologist Richard Harvey Brown (1987) regards social structure and social practices as "enacted texts" that convey meaning and influence. Following similar lines of reasoning, numerous scholars have investigated specific cultural rituals and social practices. Schudson (1998) addresses the meaning and symbolism of voting in different eras of U.S. history. Garner (1983) focuses on the communicative ritual of "playing the dozens" in African American communities. More recently, Ray (2005) explores the 19th-century lyceum as a site for the generation and transmission of public discourse. She focuses not only on individual speakers but also on the cultural significance and meaning of the lyceum as an institution.

A second aspect of cultural practice that has been studied as public discourse is the formation of collective, or public, memory. The aforementioned studies on ritual commemoration are pertinent here, as are studies by K. Olson (1989), which explicated the entirety of President Reagan's visit to Bitburg and the controversy surrounding it as a collective act of remembering and forgetting. Biesecker (2002) explores Americans' collective memory of World War II. Perhaps the most extensive studies of public memory relate to Abraham Lincoln. Both M. Peterson (1994) and Schwartz (2000) examine how succeeding generations, eager to align Lincoln's commitments with their own, have drawn on one or another aspect of the Lincoln record to shape collective understanding through an ongoing public discourse.

Reflecting the belief that social reality is not "given" but is constructed through discourse, scholars have explored the "public culture" that discourse creates and sustains. The 19th-century United States has been especially well studied in this regard, through works of Cmiel (1990), Robertson (1995), and Hartnett (2002). Each of these writers considers how the evolution of democracy and dissent were both achieved by, and reflected in, public discourse. Andrews (1971) attempted the even more formidable task of finding reflections of an enduring national character in American public discourse. In one of the few attempts to study the construction of social reality outside the United States, Andrews (1973) investigated the creation of radical consciousness and its influence on the British pacifist movement.

Renewal of Textual Studies

The emphasis so far on the multiplication of objects of study might lead one to the mistaken conclusion that studying traditional texts became passé and was supplanted by investigations of movements, genres, public culture, and the like. Nothing would be further from the truth. The years since 1965 have also been characterized by a renewed interest in studying oratorical texts. Indeed, many of the textual studies of the past 40 years are far more solid in their historical foundation, far more penetrating in their analysis, and far more rich heuristically than were many of their predecessors.

The unit of analysis in textual studies has varied. Following the lead of McGee (1980b), some scholars have focused on "ideographs," words or phrases that convey ideological content although the ideology often is ill defined. Probably, the most thorough of these works is Condit and Lucaites's (1993) *Crafting Equality: America's Anglo-African Word,* a historical analysis of the term *equality* and the different interests in whose service the term has been invoked.

Far more common, however, have been article-length studies of particular speeches or similar rhetorical texts. For the most part, these studies have examined texts already well recognized for their historical significance, most of them from the political realm. The articles often trace the history of the text's creation, but they spend far more space in setting the text in its context and showing how it helped in both shaping and reflecting the context. Illustrative of the many examples of this work are Underhill's (1966) "Fulton's Finest Hour," a study of Winston Churchill's "Iron Curtain" speech; Lucas's (1973) "The

Man With the Muck Rake: A Reinterpretation," which offers a fresh perspective on Theodore Roosevelt's 1906 speech, "The Man with the Muckrake"; the close analysis of Lincoln's Cooper Union speech offered in Leff and Mohrmann (1974); and a perspective by Ryan (1979) on President Franklin D. Roosevelt's First Inaugural Address.

Recent years have seen not only article-length studies of specific texts, but also a growing number of book-length treatments. Again, it seems that Lincoln has been an especially inviting subject. Holzer (2004) is devoted to the creation, reception, and analysis of the Cooper Union address of 1860. Both Wills (1992) and Boritt (2006) explore the Gettysburg Address, and both White (2002) and Tackach (2002) have written books on the Second Inaugural Address. Book-length studies of more recent texts include Tofel's (2005) *Sounding the Trumpet* on John F. Kennedy's Inaugural Address and Hansen's (2003) *The Dream* on "I Have a Dream," the most famous speech by Martin Luther King, Jr. Under the imprint of Texas A&M University Press, the newly launched series Library of Presidential Rhetoric eventually may include some 50 volumes, each devoted to a particular presidential speech. Among the volumes that have appeared so far are Houck's (2002) *FDR and Fear Itself* on Franklin D. Roosevelt's First Inaugural, Benson's (2004) *Writing JFK* on Kennedy's speaking after the Bay of Pigs crisis, Chernus's (2002) *Eisenhower's Atoms for Peace* on Eisenhower's "Atoms for Peace" speech, Browne's (2003) *Jefferson's Call for Nationhood* on Jefferson's First Inaugural Address, Hogan's (2006) *Woodrow Wilson's Western Tour* on Woodrow Wilson's Western speaking tour, Pauley's (2007) *LBJ's American Promise* on Lyndon B. Johnson's 1965 voting rights address, Stuckey's (2006) *Slipping the Surly Bonds* on Reagan's speech in response to the explosion of the spaceship *Challenger* in 1986, Jensen's (2007) *Reagan at Bergen-Belsen and Bitburg* on Reagan's 1985 visit to the

Bergen-Belsen concentration camp and the German cemetery at Bitburg, and Kiewe's (2007) *FDR's First Fireside Chat* on Franklin D. Roosevelt's initial "Fireside Chat."

Especially valuable as critical models are studies in which the same text is explored from multiple, probably competing, points of view. Two such examples are noteworthy. President Richard Nixon's address of November 3, 1969, on Vietnam was the subject of essays by Newman (1970), Stelzner (1971), Hill (1972), and K. Campbell (1972), some of which stimulated rejoinders. A collection of essays on Lincoln's Second Inaugural Address by Zarefsky (1990a), Leff (1990), Aune (1990), Carpenter (1990), and Solomon (1988) appeared in the first issue of *Communication Reports* and has been reprinted in Andrews (1990). Reading textual studies comparatively enables one both to fill in elements of historical understanding and to test the utility of alternative critical approaches and methods.

Another sort of comparative study is the examination of multiple texts by the same rhetor. The culmination of specific studies enables the reader to identify continuities and trends in a person's rhetorical development. Once again, Lincoln is the subject of perhaps the most extensive study. Both D. Wilson (2006) and Briggs (2005) focus primarily on the pre-presidential period, whereas White (2005) is concerned with Lincoln's presidential speeches and writings.

New Rhetorical Biographies

Closely related to textual studies are biographies that trace the rhetorical career of a speaker or writer. These might be seen as the closest descendants of the pre-1965 studies, although they are far less monistic in the materials studied or the methods used. In the 1960s, for example, Jones (1968) published an article-length rhetorical biography of Alfred E. Smith, and Fisher (1965) published on John Bright. Other examples of article-length

rhetorical biographies can be found in three anthologies that serve as reference works: Duffy and Ryan's (1987a) *American Orators Before 1900* on American orators of the 19th century, and Duffy and Ryan's (1987b) *American Orators of the Twentieth Century* and Duffy and Leeman's (2005) *American Voices* on 20th-century American orators. More recently, however, book-length rhetorical biography has become the norm. Illustrative examples include books by Terrill (2004) on Malcolm X, Lampe (1998) on Frederick Douglass, Browne (1999) on Angelina Grimké, and G. Olson (1995) on Senator Mike Mansfield. One of the few examples not focused on American rhetoric is Bytwerk (1983), a study of Nazi propagandist Julius Streicher.

Institutional Discourses

Reflecting the fact that in a complex society, most public discourse is mediated through institutions, a growing number of studies have examined institutional discourse. For example, scholars such as Crable and Vibbert (1983) and Benoit and Lindsey (1987) have inquired into the discourse of corporations as they seek to enhance their credibility or to repair their public image in the aftermath of crisis. There are obvious similarities to the *apologia* of individual rhetors, but the discourse is also affected by the institutional context of its production. Benoit (1995) offers a general theory of such apologetic rhetoric.

In keeping with the general emphasis of public discourse studies, however, most institutional studies are concerned with the political realm. An overview of political communication research is offered by Beasley (Chapter 31, this volume). The most-studied institution is the U.S. presidency. Tulis (1987) argued that 20th-century presidents, needing more resources of power to manage a complex society than are contained in the Constitution, overlaid a rhetorical presidency on the Constitutional one, using the ability to mobilize public opinion on behalf of their agenda as a resource to sway Congress and other elite decision makers. Tulis is critical of this development, which he says was foreshadowed by Theodore Roosevelt and pursued vigorously by Woodrow Wilson. In turn, his thesis has been criticized, especially on the basis that the rhetorical presidency was not a uniquely 20th-century development (e.g., Ellis, 1998; Zarefsky, 2002). But most scholars argue that the public discourse of the presidency has emerged as one of the key defining features of the office. Some maintain that the president's public discourse plays a strong role in defining American identity (e.g., Beasley, 2004; Stuckey, 2004). Others focus, not on the presidency as an institution, but on the discourse that it produces. A series of volumes generated by conferences at Texas A&M University examines presidential public discourse on foreign policy (Medhurst & Brands, 2000), civil rights (Aune & Rigsby, 2005), the environment (Peterson, 2004), and rhetorical leadership (Dorsey, 2002), among other topics. So important is public discourse to the modern presidency that Medhurst (2006) maintains that even such a seemingly nonrhetorical figure as George H. W. Bush ultimately was judged, in part, on the quality of his administration's public discourse. There are many examples of excellent studies of messages by individual presidents; this body of scholarship is so robust that there are far too many examples to list.

There have been very few studies, however, devoted to particular genres of presidential discourse. K. Campbell and Jamieson (1990, 2008) explore inaugural addresses, State of the Union messages, war rhetoric, the discourse of presidential leave taking, and other categories. Some of these categories also have furnished the data for content-analytic studies of presidential discourse. One of the few studies of presidential press conferences is by Orr (1980). While there are many studies of individual election campaigns, a small number of studies address campaigning itself as a kind

of discourse. Trent (1978) examines the ritual that she calls "surfacing," by which candidates try to establish their viability in the early primaries. Farrell (1978) explored the modern political convention as a legitimation ritual. More generally, McBath and Fisher (1969) synthesized the role of communication in presidential campaigning.

While the presidency has been the focus of a rich tradition of scholarship, far less attention has been focused on other branches of government. Vatz and Windt (1974) explored the Senate's rejection of Clement Haynsworth and G. Harrold Carswell, both nominated by Richard Nixon to the U.S. Supreme Court. More generally, Parry-Giles (2006) investigates the process of seeking confirmation of Supreme Court justices from the perspective of public discourse. He ranges across 20th-century nomination struggles for his case studies. There are few, if any, studies of congressional hearings and floor debates, or of other forms of legislative deliberation, other than studies of individual cases. Judicial discourse fares only slightly better. Wasby, D'Amato, and Metrailer (1976) consider the nature of oral argument, Dicks (1981) identifies discursive strategies in the courtroom, and Bennett (1979) focuses on the rhetorical dimension of criminal trials. There have been few studies of the judicial decision as a form of public discourse, except for those addressing specific landmark cases. Hariman (1990) reviews several famous trials. Rountree (2007) offers an incisive analysis of the Supreme Court's decision in *Bush v. Gore* and the events that preceded it; this case was also the focus of an essay by Prosise and Smith (2001).

Scholars have begun to explore the public discourse of scientists. Moving beyond arguments about whether or not science is inherently rhetorical (e.g., Gross, 1990), Ceccarelli (2001) investigates how the writing of three major scientists of the 20th century is inflected by rhetorical considerations. This line of inquiry was anticipated by J. Campbell's several studies of Charles Darwin (e.g., Campbell, 1975). Nevertheless, this brief review suggests the opportunity for studies of public discourse by and about other social institutions—science and medicine, education, trade and commerce, and social services, for example—as well as for deepening what is known about corporate communication and the discourse of political institutions.

Public Affairs and Public Policy Studies

A growing body of scholarship is devoted to the connections between public discourse and public policy. Sometimes, the approach has been to examine discourse devoted to a specific issue or policy; sometimes, it has been to explain choices of policies or their outcomes by reference to considerations of public discourse. In these studies, the unit of analysis is the *controversy* rather than either the rhetor or the text. Studies of public affairs typically encompass a variety of rhetors and media over time and attempt to account for the development or resolution of a public issue.

Jasinski (2003), for instance, examines the controversies about the American Revolution, ratification of the U.S. Constitution, and slavery to see how different dimensions of prudence were manifested. Many scholars have explored issues regarding slavery and race relations in the United States; examples include Zarefsky (1990b) on the Lincoln-Douglas debates, Pfau (2005) on the use of conspiracy rhetoric before the Civil War, K. Wilson (2002) on the proposed civil rights legislation during Reconstruction, and Pauley (2001) on how modern presidents have addressed the issue of civil rights. There are a few studies of public discourse on economic policy issues, including Houck's (2001) *Rhetoric as Currency* on economic discourse during the Depression era and Murphy's (2004) "The Language of the Liberal Consensus" on President Kennedy's attempt to consider economic issues as largely technical questions about the management of a complex economy. Welfare policy has been addressed in books by Zarefsky (1986) on the Johnson administration's war on poverty and by Asen (2002) on the images of poverty that are evident in more recent welfare debates. At this writing, Asen is at work on a book-length study of public discourse regarding the Social Security program. Among complex domestic social issues, the abortion controversy has received attention in scholarly essays and a book by Condit (1990) examining what the author regards as the codes embedded in this discourse.

A growing number of studies have addressed public discourse about defense and foreign policy. Hogan (1994) provides a detailed study of the nuclear freeze controversy of the early 1960s. Mitchell (2000) examines the sometimes arcane controversies over defense policies, especially the attempts by the Reagan and George W. Bush administrations to develop strategic missile defenses. In the aftermath of the September 11, 2001, terrorist attacks, several scholars examine how terrorism and means to counter it can be understood as types of public discourse; including Ivie (2005), Hartnett and Stengrim (2006), and Winkler (2006).

This brief survey can only suggest the range of scholarship at the nexus of public discourse and public affairs. The formation in 1998 of the journal *Rhetoric & Public Affairs* provided an important publication outlet for scholarship of this type. So great has been the interest in this area of studies that the journal's editor, Medhurst (2001), maintains that scholars who used to identify their object of study as *public address* now understand themselves to be scholars of *public affairs*.

Discourses of Identity

Like other fields across the humanities, public discourse studies in recent years have paid increasing attention to issues of identity, especially those arising from explicit consideration of gender, race, and class. One approach is to focus on the recovery of discourse traditions previously neglected: speeches by women, the oral culture of African Americans, and the vernacular discourses of labor and of the economic middle and lower classes, for example. This literature is growing and exemplars have been mentioned in other sections of this chapter.

Another approach, however, is to hypothesize that questions of identity inflect public discourse in fundamental ways. There is now a large literature articulating feminist perspectives on rhetoric; examples include many of the essays published since 1981 in the journal *Women's Studies in Communication.* The development of discourse on gay liberation is traced in Darsey's (1991) "From 'Gay Is Good' to the Scourge of AIDS." Morris's (2007) *Queering Public Address* is a collection of essays that broaden the focus from gender to sexual identity. A landmark work moving the study of race beyond the binary of black and white and beyond the discourse of particular African Americans is Nakayama and Krizek's (1995) "Whiteness: A Strategic Rhetoric." Not as much attention has been devoted to the discourse of class, although the previously mentioned scholarship by Philipsen (1975) and Hauser (1999) is relevant here. Tonn's (1996) "Militant Motherhood" is also illustrative of class-based scholarship.

If broad trends in humanistic scholarship have predictive power for public discourse studies, it is likely that questions of identity will loom larger in coming years.

Public Discourse as Pedagogy

The original rationale for studying histories of public discourse—that it would provide models for emulation by would-be orators—has returned with an interesting twist. In recent years, the focus has been more on the training of *audiences* rather than *speakers,* reflecting the fact that people spend far more time as consumers than as producers of public discourse. Illustrative of this work is Eberly and Cohen's (2006) *A laboratory for public scholarship and democracy,* which maintains that studying public discourse enables students to be more critical consumers. Beyond this emphasis on critical pedagogy, some recent studies touch on a pedagogical dimension in specific cases of public discourse. Antczak (1985) examines the movement for popular education during the early 19th century, and the aforementioned study by Ray (2005) considers how the lyceum, among its other functions, served as a principal means of informal adult education during the same time period.

Summary

The years since 1965 have seen a flowering of public discourse studies that could only be imagined and wished for in earlier times. While the focus usually remained on the United States, the scope of what counts as "public discourse" has been broadened considerably. The traditional focus on oratorical texts has been sustained and invigorated by more sophisticated scholarship. But public discourse also has been understood to embrace a variety of other textual forms as well as social, institutional, and cultural practices that can be understood as somewhat analogous to traditionally rhetorical texts.

A representative example of the richness of current public discourse studies is the February 2007 issue of the *Quarterly Journal of Speech.* The function of this journal has changed over the years, but it now is regarded as the communication discipline's "flagship" for rhetorical scholarship. Included in this fairly typical issue are four major essays. One examines voting by women during the 1870s as public performance (Ray, 2007). A second is a close reading of Henry Highland Garnet's 1843 "Address to the Slaves" that focused on the constitution of African American identity (Jasinski, 2007). The third essay considers a debate that took place on the pages of a newspaper, *Freedom's Journal* (Bacon, 2007). Finally, one essay addresses the use of irony in newspaper essays from 1790 dealing with relationships between the sexes (Galewski, 2007). Although the temporal emphasis of these essays is less contemporary than is the norm—all relate to the 18th or 19th century—the nature and range of the textual sources and the varied questions asked of them exemplify the multiple foci of contemporary scholarship. Individually, each essay illustrates sophisticated scholarship that illumines an important example of public discourse. Taken together, they show both the range and the richness of current study.

CHANGES IN SCHOLARLY PERSPECTIVES SINCE 1965

Paralleling the changes since 1965, in the scope of public discourse studies, is an expansion in the methods for conducting such studies, the infrastructure for reporting results, and the disciplinary apparatus for the conduct of scholarship. Several of the most significant changes are highlighted here.

Interdisciplinarity

Public discourse studies began as a subset of rhetoric within the communication discipline. That remains an intellectual center of strength, but scholars in multiple disciplines now investigate public discourse. The scholars whose work is cited above come from English, history, politics, composition studies, and other academic fields. Furthermore, while communication scholars still draw more on work in other disciplines than scholars in those disciplines draw on communication scholarship, the imbalance of trade has narrowed. Regardless of their own field, scholars generally want to cite the best work

available, and this desire enables scholarship in communication to receive increased disciplinary attention.

Mode of Publication

For many years, public discourse studies were primarily an "article" field. Early examples of book publication were as notable as they were rare. In recent years, though, far more of the publication has been in book form. Series devoted to the study of public discourse have emerged from such university presses as South Carolina, Alabama, Michigan State, Southern Illinois, and Texas A&M, as well as individual works published by Illinois, Chicago, Oxford, and Harvard, and commercial publishers such as Rowman & Littlefield and Peter Lang. Publishing books is not inherently better than publishing articles; much nonsense can be placed between two covers. But book-length publication permits the sustained development and testing of an argument, allows a scholar the opportunity to provide supporting evidence and to trace out the implications of the idea, and makes it easier to enter into a professional conversation with scholars in other fields who happen not regularly to read the communication journals but who do read books and book reviews. The growing expectation of book publishing has raised the quality of public discourse studies to the next level.

The Concept of "The Public"

For much of the past century, the term *the public* has been unproblematic, referring either to a broad and undifferentiated general audience or to the audience for a particular rhetorical act. Recently, however, the concept of "the public" has undergone scrutiny. For some scholars, it has offered the basis for a set of norms against which to assess actual public discourse. The "universal audience" of Chaim Perelman and Olbrechts-Tyteca (trans. 1969) and the "ideal speech situation" of Jürgen Habermas (1979) are examples. On other occasions, the term *the public* is used to designate a sphere of discourse open to participation by anyone without preconditions. Goodnight (1982), for example, distinguishes among personal, technical, and public spheres of argument on this basis and explains how determining what sphere a given discourse is in is a matter, at least in part, of strategic choice. In his focus on vernacular rhetorics, Hauser (1999) likewise regards "the public" as an audience that might not be swayed by claims to special expertise. The revival of this view of "the public" owes much to the work of John Dewey (1927), who took issue with the view expressed by Walter Lippmann (1922, 1925) that in a complex society, ordinary individuals were not competent to address issues of consequence; these would be assigned to subject matter experts. Dewey (1927), in contrast, maintained that a public was called into being through deliberation in moments of rhetorical crisis and that individuals could be taught to act as representatives of this deliberating public. This view implied that public discourse studies belonged within the ambit of liberal education as a means of cultivating articulate citizens.

Recently, Dewey's (1927) concept has been rendered problematic by scholars arguing that the Enlightenment notion of the public was in practice limited to educated white males. To think of the public sphere in that way, they insist, would reproduce the exclusion of underrepresented minorities from the public forum. This line of inquiry drew on thinking by Fraser (1992) in her critique of democracy's potential and actuality. It led to an emphasis on counterpublics as well as the public. Counterpublics have the same attributes as a public—they engage in collective decision making on matters of widespread interest to their constituencies, but they stand in opposition to the commitments of the presumed mainstream public. Theorists of counterpublics include especially Warner (2002) and Asen and Brouwer (2001). Relationships between publics and counterpublics, as well as the vitality of the public sphere, are topics of disputation within contemporary public discourse studies. Timmerman and McDorman (2008) assemble a collection of essays reappraising the relationship between rhetoric and democracy.

Methodological Pluralism

Probably the most notable of trends in public discourse studies since 1965 is the enlargement of available methods of analysis, an expansion that matches the widening scope of the term *public address* itself. Not only are there many alternatives to the neo-Aristotelianism of the past but neo-Aristotelianism is now very hard to find. Currently, there is no predetermined method; rather, the scholar's approach is seen as arising from the nature of the subject matter and the scholarly purpose.

For example, the revival of interest in textual studies has been aided by the approach of close textual analysis (Leff, 1986). Scholars oriented to the study of life as a social drama employ dramatistic criticism, exemplified by Tonn, Endress, and Diamond (1993). Bormann (1972) drew on studies of small groups, in which collective fantasies often emerge, to study how fantasy themes chain out in public discourse. Reflecting the assumption that there are a finite number of genres of discourse, other scholars have explored specific genres such as apologia (Ware & Linkugel, 1973) or inaugural addresses (Campbell & Jamieson, 1990, 2008). The premise that people by nature are storytellers has encouraged a "narrative paradigm" for the study of public discourse (Fisher, 1987), in which narrative coherence and fidelity to what already is known are the key tests of effectiveness; examples include Fisher (1984) and Simons (2007). Metaphorical analysis, as its name suggests, emphasizes the work that metaphors do in constructing social reality.

Exemplary studies are those by Osborn (1967) concerning the metaphors of light and darkness, Ivie (1982) on metaphors in war rhetoric, and Black (1970) on the metaphor of communism as a cancer.

These approaches certainly do not exhaust the perspectives currently employed. Nor are all approaches new. The orientation underlying traditional historical-critical methods is still valid, and studies that reflect it can yield valuable insight. But contemporary historical-critical methods, relying increasingly on primary sources, archival research, and sophisticated historical analysis, are far richer than those of the discipline's early years. And in any event, the field of public discourse studies has moved beyond the methodological monism characteristic of these studies before 1965. A contemporary analogue to Thonssen and Baird (1948) would be both more pluralistic and less formulaic. Rather than endorsing or employing a single method or perspective, it would reflect the advice attributed to Kenneth Burke, that the student of discourse should use all that is there to use. Examples of such counsel can be found in the Summer 2001 issue of the *Western Journal of Communication*, that journal's most recent decennial survey of the state of the field.

The methodological pluralism of the years since 1965 is often associated with Black, whose influential *Rhetorical Criticism: A Study in Method* was published in that year. This book, an outgrowth of Black's doctoral dissertation, is a trenchant critique of neo-Aristotelianism. Rather than offering new perspective on rhetorical texts, he believed that, all too often, studies within this paradigm proved only that a text could be made to fit into the neo-Aristotelian categories—which, since they were all-purpose categories, was hardly surprising. In trying to illustrate possible alternatives, Black forecast the development of psychological criticism and of generic analysis.

Black's strong critique of neo-Aristotelianism may well have contributed to its demise. But he did not single-handedly call into being the methodological pluralism that has marked the years since 1965. Calls for alternative approaches had been voiced at least since the 1940s. More likely, Black's work codified and reflected trends underway at the same time he wrote. In retrospect, his book can be taken as the intellectual justification for a significant broadening of perspectives and approaches that occurred simultaneously and continues to the present day.

CURRENT ISSUES AND CONCERNS

To complete this survey of the history of public discourse studies, brief reflection on five current issues and trends is in order.

1. What is meant by "public address"? Both words in this term have been rendered problematic. Is anything that is accessible by others therefore rendered "public"? Or must *public* address be that of matters addressed to citizens in their collective capacity? Is it restricted to matters of governance and civic deliberation? Does public address stand in opposition to personal and technical discourses? Does a strong tradition of public address require a healthy public sphere?

Similarly, what does it mean to refer to public *address?* Is there such a thing as a rhetorical text that is *not* "addressed"? Or does any text imply a notion of its audience? Does addressing presuppose intentionality, or do texts work in the world without regard to the wishes of their creators? And what is encompassed by the term *text?* Does it designate only verbal discourse, or does it extend to any kind of social practice that can be understood symbolically as a means of communication, or is there some middle ground between these two options?

The breadth of these questions moves thought about public discourse far beyond its original identification with oratory, but that still is what the term means to many. Since the culture has diminished, though not eliminated, the significance of this mode of interaction, "public address" can be too easily dismissed as narrowly antiquarian. To be sure, the study of oratory remains a vital intellectual tradition, but it is only part of what is embraced by the term *public address* or *public discourse*. Understanding public discourse as situated rhetorical practice places the object of study where text and context, theory and practice, rhetorical situation, and rhetorical artifact all meet.

2. What are the priorities for study? Granted a very broad conception of public discourse, one cannot study everything. Any scholar must determine priorities based on his or her interests and the questions for which answers are sought. Sometimes, however, the justification given for undertaking a particular study involves denigration of other approaches. For instance, it sometimes is said that the voiceless and disempowered should be studied because we already have extensive studies of the privileged and powerful, especially white male preachers and politicians. There are many good reasons to study the voiceless and disempowered, but this is not one of them. It simply is not true that traditional elites have been overstudied. Even the canonical orations of the American past have, in most cases, received very little attention from scholars of public discourse.

The drawback of the "thousand flowers" approach is that it spreads a discipline too thin. There are simply not enough critics of public discourse to cover everything. On any given subject, the available expertise may be only one or two scholars deep, without a scholarly "critical mass." This concern is true enough, but the simple answer is that research is not so easily corralled; intellectual curiosity will lead scholars where it will. Rhetorical studies remain in Toulmin's (1972) term "a diffuse discipline". One hopes that in the fullness of time, the seemingly random courses of interest and curiosity will yield a body of scholarship that will support increasingly robust claims.

3. What assumptions should be made about human agency? As societies become more typically the working of complex systems, the power of human agency can be called into question. People's experience is more likely to be seen as the result of large social and political forces than as the products of human choice. Yet the study of public discourse is grounded in faith in human agency: in the beliefs that individuals make rhetorical choices and that these choices make a difference. Reality is somewhere between these competing assumptions about agency, and this was probably as true in earlier eras as it is in our own. Rather than making a priori assumptions, public discourse scholars must be sensitive in individual cases to the extent and limits of human agency, so that they neither fault rhetors for failing to make choices that were not realistically available to them nor absolve them by assuming that the course of events was predetermined. Like so much else in humanistic scholarship, this topic emphasizes the necessity for prudential judgment.

4. How can parochialism in the study of public discourse best be overcome? As noted above, much of the extant public discourse scholarship is conducted within and focuses on the United States. Certainly, there is much still to be done to articulate American traditions of public discourse. But just as certainly, the United States is not the only or necessarily the paradigm case. Once-strong traditions in the study of British public discourse and classical public discourse should be revived. But even more, scholars must become sensitive to, and familiar with, the rich non-Western traditions of public discourse. For too long, the origin story has been limited to ancient Greece, and the current story, to the democracies of the West. There are large knowledge gaps to be filled if the ultimate

goal is to understand public discourse in all its variety and multiplicity.

5. How does public discourse have effects? Studies often make assertions about effects that are unencumbered by either explanation or evidence. In recent years, some political scientists, particularly George Edwards (1996, 2003) have put this proposition to the test and found it wanting. Edwards assembles voluminous and impressive evidence to cast doubt on the claim that U.S. presidential rhetoric affects citizens' attitudes or behavior. And a fortiori, if presidential rhetoric makes little difference, how much less so will the public discourse of individuals who lack the president's rhetorical resources. Of course, almost *no* one-shot effort at persuasion will have much effect. But if public discourse does not make a difference in the most obvious way, then how *does* it make a difference, and how do we know? Studies of public discourse will make more of a difference in the scholarly world if we can explain how public discourse itself makes a difference in the world of human affairs.

Public discourse, as noted, is situated rhetorical practice. Although before (about) 1965 it was studied within a narrow framework of topics, methods, and approaches, in the years since 1965 the paths to scholarship have multiplied almost beyond belief. The result has been to give rise to a body of scholarship growing steadily in quality and dazzling in its diversity, but at the risk of so fragmenting a scholarly community that any sense of a common core might be lost. How scholarship confronts this quandary and resolves the five critical questions above will determine, to a large degree, the future of scholarship in public discourse.

REFERENCES

Aly, B. (1943). The history of American public address as a research field. *Quarterly Journal of Speech, 29*, 308–314.

Aly, B. (1965). *The rhetoric of Alexander Hamilton*. New York: Russell & Russell. (Original work published 1941)

Andrews, J. R. (1967). The ethos of pacifism: The problem of image in the early British peace movement. *Quarterly Journal of Speech, 53*, 28–33.

Andrews, J. R. (1969). Confrontation at Columbia: A case study in coercive rhetoric. *Quarterly Journal of Speech, 55*, 9–16.

Andrews, J. R. (1971). Reflections of the national character in American rhetoric. *Quarterly Journal of Speech, 57*, 316–324.

Andrews, J. R. (1973). The passionate negation: The chartist movement in rhetorical perspective. *Quarterly Journal of Speech, 59*, 196–208.

Andrews, J. R. (1990). *The practice of rhetorical criticism*. New York: Longman.

Andrews, J. R., & Zarefsky, D. (Eds.). (1989). *American voices: Significant speeches in American history, 1640–1945*. New York: Longman.

Andrews, J. R., & Zarefsky, D. (Eds.). (1992). *Contemporary American voices: Significant speeches in American history, 1945-present*. New York: Longman.

Antczak, F. J. (1985). *Thought and character: The rhetoric of democratic education*. Ames: Iowa State University Press.

Asen, R. (2002). *Visions of poverty: Welfare policy and political imagination*. East Lansing: Michigan State University Press.

Asen, R., & Brouwer, D. C. (Eds.). (2001). *Counterpublics and the state*. Albany: State University of New York Press.

Aune, J. A. (1990). Lincoln and the American sublime. In J. R. Andrews (Ed.), *The practice of rhetorical criticism* (2nd ed. pp. 70–75). New York: Longman.

Aune, J. A., & Rigsby, E. D. (Eds.). (2005). *Civil rights rhetoric and the American presidency*. College Station: Texas A&M University Press.

Bacon, J. (2007). "Acting as freemen": Rhetoric, race, and reform in the debate over colonization in *Freedom's Journal*, 1827–1828. *Quarterly Journal of Speech, 93*, 58–83.

Beasley, V. B. (2004). *You the people: American national identity in presidential rhetoric*. College Station: Texas A&M University Press.

Bennett, W. L. (1979). Rhetorical transformation of evidence in criminal trials: Creating grounds for legal judgment. *Quarterly Journal of Speech, 65,* 311–323.

Benoit, W. L. (1995). *Accounts, excuses, and apologies: A theory of image restoration strategies.* Albany: State University of New York Press.

Benoit, W. L., & Lindsey, J. J. (1987). Argument strategies: Antidote to Tylenol's poisoned image. *Argumentation and Advocacy, 23,* 136–146.

Benson, T. W. (2004). *Writing JFK: Presidential rhetoric and the press in the Bay of Pigs crisis.* College Station: Texas A&M University Press.

Biesecker, B. A. (2002). Remembering World War II: The rhetoric and politics of national commemoration at the turn of the 21st century. *Quarterly Journal of Speech, 88,* 393–409.

Black, E. (1965). *Rhetorical criticism: A study in method.* New York: Macmillan.

Black, E. (1970). The second persona. *Quarterly Journal of Speech, 56,* 109–119.

Blair, C. (2006, November 16). Civil rights/civil sites: " . . . Until justice rolls down like waters." In *The Carroll C. Arnold lecture, National Communication Association.* Boston: Allyn & Bacon.

Blair, C., Jeppeson, M. S., & Pucci, E., Jr. (1991). Public memorializing in postmodernity: The Vietnam Veterans Memorial as prototype. *Quarterly Journal of Speech, 77,* 289–308.

Boase, P. H. (Ed.). (1960). Presidential campaign 1960: A symposium (Part I): Pre-convention speaking. *Quarterly Journal of Speech, 46,* 239–252.

Boritt, G. (2006). *The Gettysburg gospel: The Lincoln speech that nobody knows.* New York: Simon & Schuster.

Bormann, E. G. (1972). Fantasy and rhetorical vision: The rhetorical criticism of social reality. *Quarterly Journal of Speech, 58,* 396–407.

Bowers, J. W. (1968). The pre-scientific function of rhetorical criticism. In T. R. Nilsen (Ed.), *Essays on rhetorical criticism* (pp. 126–145). New York: Random House.

Branham, R. J., & Hartnett, S. J. (2002). *Sweet freedom's song: "My country 'tis of thee" and democracy in America.* New York: Oxford University Press.

Brigance, W. N. (1934). *Jeremiah Sullivan Black, a defender of the constitution and the ten commandments.* Philadelphia: University of Pennsylvania Press.

Brigance, W. N. (Ed.). (1943). *History and criticism of American public address* (Vols. 1 and 2). New York: McGraw-Hill.

Briggs, J. C. (2005). *Lincoln's speeches reconsidered.* Baltimore: Johns Hopkins University Press.

Brown, R. H. (1987). *Society as text: Essays on rhetoric, reason, and reality.* Chicago: University of Chicago Press.

Browne, S. H. (1999). *Angelina Grimké: Rhetoric, identity, and the radical imagination.* East Lansing: Michigan State University Press.

Browne, S. H. (2003). *Jefferson's call for nationhood: The first inaugural address.* College Station: Texas A&M University Press.

Brummett, B. (1991). *Rhetorical dimensions of popular culture.* Tuscaloosa: University of Alabama Press.

Burgchardt, C. R. (1980). Two faces of American communism: Pamphlet rhetoric of the third period and the popular front. *Quarterly Journal of Speech, 66,* 375–391.

Burgess, P. G. (1968). The rhetoric of black power: A moral demand? *Quarterly Journal of Speech, 54,* 122–133.

Bytwerk, R. L. (1983). *Julius Streicher: The man who persuaded a nation to hate Jews.* New York: Stein & Day.

Campbell, J. A. (1975). The polemical Mr. Darwin. *Quarterly Journal of Speech, 61,* 375–390.

Campbell, K. K. (Ed.). (1972). An exercise in the rhetoric of mythical America. In *Critiques of contemporary rhetoric* (pp. 50–57). Belmont, CA: Wadsworth.

Campbell, K. K. (1973). The rhetoric of women's liberation: An oxymoron. *Quarterly Journal of Speech, 59,* 74–86.

Campbell, K. K. (1980). Stanton's "The solitude of self": A rationale for feminism. *Quarterly Journal of Speech, 66,* 304–312.

Campbell, K. K. (Ed.). (1989a). *Man cannot speak for her. A critical study of early feminist rhetoric* (Vol. 1). New York: Praeger.

Campbell, K. K. (Ed.). (1989b). *Man cannot speak for her. Key texts of the early feminists* (Vol. 2). New York: Praeger.

Campbell, K. K. (1995). Gender and genre: Loci of invention and contradiction in the earliest speeches by U.S. women. *Quarterly Journal of Speech, 81,* 479–495.

Campbell, K. K. (2005). Agency: Promiscuous and protean. *Communication and Critical/Cultural Studies, 2,* 1–19.

Campbell, K. K., & Jamieson, K. H. (1990). *Deeds done in words: Presidential rhetoric and the genres of governance.* Chicago: University of Chicago Press.

Campbell, K. K., & Jamieson, K. H. (2008). *Presidents creating the presidency: Deeds done in words.* Chicago: University of Chicago Press.

Carpenter, R. H. (1990). In not-so-trivial pursuit of rhetorical wedgies: An historical approach to Lincoln's second inaugural address. In J. R. Andrews, *The practice of rhetorical criticism* (2nd ed., pp. 75–80). New York: Longman.

Ceccarelli, L. (2001). *Shaping science with rhetoric: The cases of Dobzhansky, Schrödinger, and Wilson.* Chicago: University of Chicago Press.

Chernus, I. (2002). *Eisenhower's atoms for peace.* College Station: Texas A&M University Press.

Cmiel, K. (1990). *Democratic eloquence: The fight over popular speech in nineteenth-century America.* New York: Morrow.

Condit, C. M. (1990). *Decoding abortion rhetoric: Communicating social change.* Urbana: University of Illinois Press.

Condit, C. M., & Lucaites, J. L. (1993). *Crafting equality: America's Anglo-African word.* Chicago: University of Chicago Press.

Crable, R. E., & Vibbert, S. L. (1983). Mobil's epideictic advocacy: "Observations" of Prometheus bound. *Communication Monographs, 50,* 380–394.

Crandell, S. J. (1947). The beginnings of a methodology for social control studies in public address. *Quarterly Journal of Speech, 33,* 36–39.

Darsey, J. (1991). From "gay is good" to the scourge of AIDS: The evolution of gay liberation rhetoric, 1977–1990. *Communication Studies, 42,* 43–66.

DeLuca, K. M., & Peeples, J. (2002). From public sphere to public screen: Democracy, activism, and the "violence" of Seattle. *Critical Studies in Media Communication, 19,* 125–151.

Depew, C. M. (Ed.). (1902). *The library of oratory* (Vols. 1–15). New York: DuMont.

Dewey, J. (1927). *The public and its problems.* New York: Henry Holt.

Dicks, V. I. (1981). Courtroom rhetorical strategies: Forensic and deliberative perspectives. *Quarterly Journal of Speech, 67,* 178–192.

Diffley, K. (1988). "Erecting anew the standard of freedom": Salmon P. Chase's "Appeal of the independent Democrats" and the rise of the Republican party. *Quarterly Journal of Speech, 74,* 401–415.

Dorsey, L. G. (Ed.). (2002). *The presidency and rhetorical leadership.* College Station: Texas A&M University Press.

Duffy, B. K., & Leeman, R. W. (Eds.). (2005). *American voices: An encyclopedia of contemporary orators.* Westport, CT: Greenwood Press.

Duffy, B. K., & Ryan, H. R. (Eds.). (1987a). *American orators before 1900: Critical studies and sources.* New York: Greenwood Press.

Duffy, B. K., & Ryan, H. R. (Eds.). (1987b). *American orators of the twentieth century: Critical studies and sources.* New York: Greenwood Press.

Eberly, R. A., & Cohen, J. (Eds.). (2006). *A laboratory for public scholarship and democracy.* San Francisco: Jossey-Bass.

Edwards, G. C., III. (1996). Presidential rhetoric: What difference does it make? In M. J. Medhurst (Ed.), *Beyond the rhetorical presidency* (pp. 199–217). College Station: Texas A&M University Press.

Edwards, G. C., III. (2003). *On deaf ears.* New Haven, CT: Yale University Press.

Edwards, J. L., & Winkler, C. K. (1997). Representative form and the visual ideograph: The Iwo Jima image in editorial cartoons. *Quarterly Journal of Speech, 83,* 289–310.

Ellis, R. J. (Ed.). (1998). *Speaking to the people: The rhetorical presidency in historical perspective.* Amherst: University of Massachusetts Press.

Farrell, T. B. (1978). Political conventions as legitimation ritual. *Communication Monographs, 45,* 293–305.

Finnegan, C. A. (2003). *Picturing poverty: Print culture and FSA photographs.* Washington: Smithsonian Books.

Fisher, W. R. (1965). John Bright: "Hawker of holy things." *Quarterly Journal of Speech, 51,* 157–163.

Fisher, W. R. (1984). Narration as a human communication paradigm: The case of public moral argument. *Communication Monographs, 51,* 1–22.

Fisher, W. R. (1987). *Human communication as narration.* Columbia: University of South Carolina Press.

Fletcher, W. L. (1968). Speechmaking of the New York draft riots of 1863. *Quarterly Journal of Speech, 54,* 134–159.

Foner, P. S., & Branham, R. J. (Ed.). (1998). *Lift every voice: African-American oratory, 1787–1900.* Tuscaloosa: University of Alabama Press.

Fraser, N. (1992). Rethinking the public sphere: A contribution to the critique of actually existing democracy. In C. Calhoun (Ed.), *Habermas and the public sphere* (pp. 109–142). Cambridge, MA: MIT Press.

Galewski, E. (2007). The strange case for women's capacity to reason: Judith Sargent Murray's use of irony in "On the Equality of the Sexes" (1790). *Quarterly Journal of Speech, 93,* 84–108.

Gallagher, V. J. (1999). Memory and reconciliation in the Birmingham Civil Rights Institute. *Rhetoric & Public Affairs, 2,* 303–320.

Gallagher, V. J. (2004). Memory in social action: Cultural projections and generic form in civil rights memorials. In P. A. Sullivan & S. R. Goldzwig (Eds.), *New approaches to rhetoric* (pp. 149–171). Thousand Oaks, CA: Sage.

Gallagher, V. J., & Zagacki, K. S. (2005). Visibility and rhetoric: The power of visual images in Norman Rockwell's depictions of civil rights. *Quarterly Journal of Speech, 91,* 175–200.

Garner, T. (1983). Playing the dozens: Folklore as strategies for living. *Quarterly Journal of Speech, 69,* 47–57.

Goodman, R. J., & Gorden, W. I. (1971). The rhetoric of desecration. *Quarterly Journal of Speech, 57,* 23–31.

Goodnight, G. T. (1982). The personal, technical, and public spheres of argument: A speculative inquiry into the art of public deliberation. *Argumentation and Advocacy, 18,* 214–227.

Goodrich, C. A. (Ed.). (1852). *Select British eloquence.* New York: Harper.

Gregg, R. B., McCormack, A. J., & Pederson, D. J. (1969). The rhetoric of black power: A street-level interpretation. *Quarterly Journal of Speech, 55,* 151–160.

Griffin, L. M. (1952). The rhetoric of historical movements. *Quarterly Journal of Speech, 38,* 184–188.

Griffin, L. M. (1958). The rhetorical structure of the antimasonic movement. In D. C. Bryant (Ed.), *The rhetorical idiom* (pp. 145–159). Ithaca, NY: Cornell University Press.

Griffin, L. M. (1964). The rhetorical structure of the "new left" movement: Part I. *Quarterly Journal of Speech, 50,* 113–135.

Gross, A. G. (1990). *The rhetoric of science.* Cambridge, MA: Harvard University Press.

Gunderson, R. G. (1961). Lincoln and the policy of eloquent silence: November, 1860 to March, 1861. *Quarterly Journal of Speech, 47,* 1–9.

Gusfield, J. R. (Ed.). (1970). *Protest, reform, and revolt: A reader in social movements.* New York: Wiley.

Habermas, J. (1979). *Communication and the evolution of society.* Boston: Beacon Press.

Haiman, F. S. (1967). The rhetoric of the streets: Some legal and ethical considerations. *Quarterly Journal of Speech, 53,* 99–114.

Haiman, F. S. (1969). The rhetoric of 1968: A farewell to rational discourse. In W. A. Linkugel, R. R. Allen, & R. L. Johannesen (Eds.), *Contemporary American speeches* (2nd ed., pp. 153–167). Belmont, CA: Wadsworth.

Hancock, B. R. (1972). Affirmation by negation in the women's liberation movement. *Quarterly Journal of Speech, 58,* 264–271.

Hansen, D. D. (2003). *The dream: Martin Luther King, Jr. and the speech that inspired a nation.* New York: HarperCollins.

Hariman, R. (Ed). (1990). *Popular trials: Rhetoric, mass media, and the law.* Tuscaloosa: University of Alabama Press.

Hariman, R., & Lucaites, J. L. (2007). *No caption needed: Iconic photographs, public culture, and liberal democracy.* Chicago: University of Chicago Press.

Hartnett, S. J. (2002). *Democratic dissent and the cultural fictions of antebellum America.* Urbana: University of Illinois Press.

Hartnett, S. J., & Stengrim, L. A. (2006). *Globalization and empire: The U.S. invasion of Iraq, free markets, and the twilight of democracy.* Tuscaloosa: University of Alabama Press.

Hauser, G. A. (1999). *Vernacular voices: The rhetoric of publics and public spheres.* Columbia: University of South Carolina Press.

Hay, R. P. (1969). The liberty tree: A symbol for American patriots. *Quarterly Journal of Speech, 55,* 414–424.

Hill, F. I. (1972). Conventional wisdom; traditional form: The president's message of November 3, 1969. *Quarterly Journal of Speech, 58,* 373–386.

Hochmuth, M. K. (1952). Kenneth Burke and the new rhetoric. *Quarterly Journal of Speech, 38,* 133–141.

Hochmuth, M. K. (Ed.). (1955a). The criticism of rhetoric. In *History and criticism of American public address* (Vol. 3, pp. 1–23). New York: Russell & Russell.

Hochmuth, M. K. (Ed). (1955b). *History and criticism of American public address* (Vol. 3). New York: Russell & Russell.

Hogan, J. M. (1994). *The nuclear freeze campaign: Rhetoric and foreign policy in the telepolitical age.* East Lansing: Michigan State University Press.

Hogan, J. M. (2006). *Woodrow Wilson's western tour: Rhetoric, public opinion, and the League of Nations.* College Station: Texas A&M University Press.

Holland, D. (Ed.). (1971). *Sermons in American history: Selected issues in the American pulpit, 1630–1967.* Nashville, TN: Abingdon.

Holland, D. (Ed.). (1973). *America in controversy: History of American public address.* Dubuque, IA: Wm. C. Brown.

Holzer, H. (2004). *Lincoln at Cooper Union: The speech that made Abraham Lincoln president.* New York: Simon & Schuster.

Houck, D. W. (2001). *Rhetoric as currency: Hoover, Roosevelt, and the Great Depression.* College Station: Texas A&M University Press.

Houck, D. W. (2002). *FDR and fear itself: The first inaugural address.* College Station: Texas A&M University Press.

Houck, D. W., & Dixon, D. E. (Eds.). (2006). *Rhetoric, religion, and the civil rights movement, 1954–1965.* Waco, TX: Baylor University Press.

Ivie, R. L. (1982). The metaphor of force in prowar discourse: The case of 1812. *Quarterly Journal of Speech, 68,* 240–253.

Ivie, R. L. (2005). *Democracy and America's war on terror.* Tuscaloosa: University of Alabama Press.

Jasinski, J. (2003). Idioms of prudence in three antebellum controversies: Revolution, constitution, and slavery. In R. Hariman (Ed.), *Prudence: Classical virtue, postmodern practice* (pp. 168–176). University Park: Pennsylvania State University Press.

Jasinski, J. (2007). Constituting antebellum African American identity: Resistance, violence, and masculinity in Henry Highland Garnet's 1843 "Address to the slaves." *Quarterly Journal of Speech, 93,* 27–57.

Jensen, R. J. (2007). *Reagan at Bergen-Belsen and Bitburg.* College Station: Texas A&M University Press.

Jones, J. L. (1968). Alfred E. Smith, political debater. *Quarterly Journal of Speech, 54,* 363–372.

Kiewe, A. (2007). *FDR's first fireside chat: Public confidence and the banking crisis.* College Station: Texas A&M University Press.

Lampe, G. P. (1998). *Frederick Douglass: Freedom's voice, 1818–1845.* East Lansing: Michigan State University Press.

Laraña, E., Johnston, H., & Gusfield, J. R. (Eds.). (1994). *New social movements: From ideology to identity.* Philadelphia: Temple University Press.

Leff, M. C. (1986). Textual criticism: The legacy of G. P. Mohrmann. *Quarterly Journal of Speech, 72,* 377–389.

Leff, M. C. (1990). Dimensions of temporality in Lincoln's second inaugural address. In J. R. Andrews (Ed.), *The practice of rhetorical criticism* (2nd ed., pp. 80–85). New York: Longman.

Leff, M. C., & Mohrmann, G. P. (1974). Lincoln at Cooper Union: A rhetorical analysis of the text. *Quarterly Journal of Speech, 60,* 346–358.

Lippmann, W. (1922). *Public opinion.* New York: Harcourt, Brace.

Lippmann, W. (1925). *The phantom public.* New York: Harcourt, Brace.

Lucas, S. E. (1973). The man with the muck rake: A reinterpretation. *Quarterly Journal of Speech, 59,* 452–462.

Lucas, S. E. (1976). *Portents of rebellion: Rhetoric and revolution in Philadelphia, 1765–1776.* Philadelphia: Temple University Press.

Lucas, S. E. (1988). The renaissance of American public address: Text and context in rhetorical criticism. *Quarterly Journal of Speech, 74,* 241–260.

Lucas, S. E. (1989). Justifying America: The Declaration of Independence as a rhetorical document. In T. W. Benson (Ed.), *American rhetoric: Context and criticism* (pp. 67–130). Carbondale: Southern Illinois University Press.

McBath, J. H., & Fisher, W. R. (1969). Persuasion in presidential campaign communication. *Quarterly Journal of Speech, 55,* 17–25.

McGee, M. C. (1980a). "Social movement": Phenomenon or meaning? *Central States Speech Journal, 31,* 233–244.

McGee, M. C. (1980b). The "ideograph": A link between rhetoric and ideology. *Quarterly Journal of Speech, 66,* 1–16.

Medhurst, M. J. (Ed.). (1993). The academic study of public address: A tradition in transition. In *Landmark essays on American public address* (pp. 9–13). Davis, CA: Hermagoras Press.

Medhurst, M. J. (2001). The contemporary study of public address: Renewal, recovery, and reconfiguration. *Rhetoric & Public Affairs, 4,* 495–511.

Medhurst, M. J. (Ed). (2006). *The rhetorical presidency of George H. W. Bush.* College Station: Texas A&M University Press.

Medhurst, M. J., & Brands, H. W. (Eds.). (2000). *Critical reflections on the cold war: Linking rhetoric and history.* College Station: Texas A&M University Press.

Miller, N. E. (Ed.). (1960). Presidential campaign 1960: A symposium (Part II): Contest for the presidency. *Quarterly Journal of Speech, 46,* 355–364.

Mitchell, G. R. (2000). *Strategic deception: Rhetoric, science, and politics in missile defense advocacy.* East Lansing: Michigan State University Press.

Morris, C. E., III. (Ed.). (2007). *Queering public address: Sexualities in American historical discourse.* Columbia: University of South Carolina Press.

Morris, C. E., III., & Browne, S. H. (Eds.). (2006). *Readings on the rhetoric of social protest* (2nd ed.). State College, PA: Strata.

Murphy, J. M. (2004). The language of the liberal consensus: John F. Kennedy, technical reason, and the "new economics" at Yale University. *Quarterly Journal of Speech, 90,* 133–162.

Nakayama, T. K., & Krizek, R. (1995). Whiteness: A strategic rhetoric. *Quarterly Journal of Speech, 81,* 291–309.

Newman, R. P. (1970). Under the veneer: Nixon's Vietnam speech of November 3, 1969. *Quarterly Journal of Speech, 56,* 168–178.

Oliver, R. T. (1962). Syngman Rhee: A case study in transnational oratory. *Quarterly Journal of Speech, 48,* 115–127.

Oliver, R. T. (1965). *History of public speaking in America.* Boston: Allyn & Bacon.

Olson, G. A. (1995). *Mansfield and Vietnam: A study in rhetorical adaptation.* East Lansing: Michigan State University Press.

Olson, K. M. (1989). The controversy over President Reagan's visit to Bitburg: Strategies of definition and redefinition. *Quarterly Journal of Speech, 75,* 129–151.

Olson, L. C. (2004). *Benjamin Franklin's vision of American community: A study in rhetorical iconology.* Columbia: University of South Carolina Press.

Olson, L. C. (2008). Intellectual and conceptual resources for visual rhetoric: A reexamination of scholarship since 1950. In D. Zarefsky & E. Benacka (Eds.), *Sizing up rhetoric* (pp. 118–137). Long Grove, IL: Waveland Press.

Orr, C. J. (1980). Reporters confront the president: Sustaining a counterpoised situation. *Quarterly Journal of Speech, 66,* 17–32.

Osborn, M. (1967). Archetypal metaphor in rhetoric: The light-dark family. *Quarterly Journal of Speech, 53,* 115–126.

Parrish, W. M. (1954). The study of speeches. In W. M. Parrish & M. K. Hochmuth (Eds.), *American speeches* (pp. 1–20). New York: Longman.

Parry-Giles, T. (2006). *The character of justice: Rhetoric, law, and politics in the Supreme Court confirmation process.* East Lansing: Michigan State University Press.

Pauley, G. E. (2001). *The modern presidency & civil rights: Rhetoric on race from Roosevelt to Nixon.* College Station: Texas A&M University Press.

Pauley, G. E. (2007). *LBJ's American promise: The 1965 voting rights address.* College Station: Texas A&M University Press.

Perelman, C., & Olbrechts-Tyteca, L. (1969). *The new rhetoric: A treatise on argumentation* (J. Wilkinson & P. Weaver, Trans.). Notre Dame,

IN: University of Notre Dame Press. (Original work published 1958)

Peterson, M. D. (1994). *Lincoln in American memory.* New York: Oxford University Press.

Peterson, T. R. (Ed.). (2004). *Green talk in the White House: The rhetorical presidency encounters ecology.* College Station: Texas A&M University Press.

Pfau, M. W. (2005). *The political style of conspiracy: Chase, Sumner, and Lincoln.* East Lansing: Michigan State University Press.

Philipsen, G. (1975). Speaking "like a man" in Teamsterville: Culture patterns of role enactment in an urban neighborhood. *Quarterly Journal of Speech, 61,* 13–22.

Prosise, T. O., & Smith, C. R. (2001). The Supreme Court's ruling in *Bush v. Gore:* A rhetoric of inconsistency. *Rhetoric & Public Affairs, 4,* 605–632.

Ray, A. G. (2005). *The lyceum and public culture in the nineteenth-century United States.* East Lansing: Michigan State University Press.

Ray, A. G. (2007). The rhetorical ritual of citizenship: Women's voting as public performance, 1868–1875. *Quarterly Journal of Speech, 93,* 1–26.

Reed, T. B. (Ed.). (1900). *Modern eloquence* (Vols. 1–10). Philadelphia: Morris.

Reed, T. B. (Ed.). (1903). *Modern eloquence* (Vols. 11–15). Philadelphia: Morris.

Reid, L. D. (1944). The perils of rhetorical criticism. *Quarterly Journal of Speech, 30,* 416–422.

Reid, R. F., & Klumpp, J. F. (Eds.). (2005). *American rhetorical discourse.* Long Grove, IL: Waveland Press.

Robertson, A. W. (1995). *The language of democracy: Political rhetoric in the United States and Britain, 1790–1900.* Ithaca, NY: Cornell University Press.

Rountree, C. (2007). *Judging the Supreme Court: Constructions of motives in* Bush v. Gore. East Lansing: Michigan State University Press.

Rushing, J. H., & Frentz, T. S. (1980). "The deer hunter": Rhetoric of the warrior. *Quarterly Journal of Speech, 66,* 392–406.

Ryan, H. R. (1979). Roosevelt's first inaugural: A study of technique. *Quarterly Journal of Speech, 65,* 137–149.

Safire, W. (Ed.). (1997). *Lend me your ears: Great speeches in history.* New York: Norton.

Sarkela, S. J., Ross, S. M., & Lowe, M. A. (Eds.). (2003). *From megaphones to microphones: Speeches of American women, 1920–1960.* Westport, CT: Praeger.

Schudson, M. (1998). *The good citizen: A history of American civic life.* New York: Free Press.

Schwartz, B. (2000). *Abraham Lincoln and the forge of national memory.* Chicago: University of Chicago Press.

Scott, R. L., & Smith, D. K. (1969). The rhetoric of confrontation. *Quarterly Journal of Speech, 55,* 1–8.

Shaw, W. C. (1928). *History of American oratory.* Indianapolis, IN: Bobbs-Merrill.

Simons, H. W. (1970). Requirements, problems, and strategies: A theory of persuasion for social movements. *Quarterly Journal of Speech, 56,* 1–11.

Simons, H. W. (2007). Rhetoric's role in context: Beginning with 9/11. *Rhetoric & Public Affairs, 10,* 183–194.

Sloan, T. O. (1971). Report of the committee on the advancement and refinement of rhetorical criticism. In L. F. Bitzer & E. Black (Eds.), *The prospect of rhetoric: Report of the national developmental project* (pp. 220–227). Englewood Cliffs, NJ: Prentice Hall.

Solomon, M. (1990). "With firmness in the right": The creation of moral hegemony in Lincoln's second inaugural. In J. R. Andrews (Ed.), *The practice of rhetorical criticism* (2nd ed., pp. 85–90). New York: Longman.

Stanback, M. H., & Pearce, W. B. (1981). Talking to "the man": Some communication strategies used by members of "subordinate" social groups. *Quarterly Journal of Speech, 67,* 21–30.

Stelzner, H. G. (1971). The quest story and Nixon's November 3, 1969 address. *Quarterly Journal of Speech, 57,* 163–172.

Stewart, C. J. (1997). The evolution of a revolution: Stokely Carmichael and the rhetoric of black power. *Quarterly Journal of Speech, 83,* 429–446.

Stuckey, M. E. (2004). *Defining Americans: The presidency and national identity.* Lawrence: University Press of Kansas.

Stuckey, M. E. (2006). *Slipping the surly bonds: Reagan's Challenger Address.* College Station: Texas A&M University Press.

Tackach, J. (2002). *Lincoln's moral vision: The second inaugural address.* Jackson: University Press of Mississippi.

Terrill, R. E. (2004). *Malcolm X: Inventing radical judgment.* East Lansing: Michigan State University Press.

Thonssen, L., & Baird, A. C. (1948). *Speech criticism.* New York: Ronald.

Thorson, T. L. (1962). *The logic of democracy.* New York: Holt, Rinehart, & Winston.

Timmerman, D., & McDorman, T. (Eds.). (2008). *Rhetoric and democracy: Studies in the tradition of William Norwood Brigance.* East Lansing: Michigan State University Press.

Tofel, R. J. (2005). *Sounding the trumpet: The making of John F. Kennedy's inaugural address.* Chicago: Ivan R. Dee.

Tonn, M. B. (1996). Militant motherhood: Labor's Mary Harris "Mother" Jones. *Quarterly Journal of Speech, 82,* 1–21.

Tonn, M. B., Endress, V. A., & Diamond, J. N. (1993). Hunting and heritage on trial: A dramatistic debate over tragedy, tradition, and territory. *Quarterly Journal of Speech, 59,* 165–181.

Torricelli, R. (1999). *In our own words: Extraordinary speeches of the American century.* New York: Kodansha.

Toulmin, S. (1972). *Human understanding: The collective use and evolution of concepts.* Princeton, NJ: Princeton University Press.

Trent, J. S. (1978). Presidential surfacing: The ritualistic and crucial first act. *Communication Monographs, 45,* 281–292.

Tulis, J. K. (1987). *The rhetorical presidency.* Princeton, NJ: Princeton University Press.

Tyler, A. F. (1962). *Freedom's ferment: Phases of American social history from the colonial period to the outbreak of the Civil War.* New York: Harper & Row. (Original work published 1944)

Underhill, W. R. (1966). Fulton's finest hour. *Quarterly Journal of Speech, 52,* 155–163.

Vatz, R. E., & Windt, T. O., Jr. (1974). The defeats of Judges Haynsworth and Carswell: Rejection of Supreme Court nominees. *Quarterly Journal of Speech, 60,* 477–488.

Ware, B. L., Jr., & Linkugel, W. A. (1973). They spoke in defense of themselves: On the generic criticism of apologia. *Quarterly Journal of Speech, 59,* 273–283.

Warner, M. (2002). *Publics and counterpublics.* New York: Zone Books.

Wasby, S. L., D'Amato, A. A., & Metrailer, R. (1976). The functions of oral argument in the U.S. Supreme Court. *Quarterly Journal of Speech, 62,* 410–422.

White, R. C., Jr. (2002). *Lincoln's greatest speech: The second inaugural.* New York: Simon & Schuster.

White, R. C., Jr. (2005). *The eloquent president: A portrait of Lincoln through his words.* New York: Random House.

Wichelns, H. A. (1925). The literary criticism of oratory. In A. M. Drummond (Ed.), *Studies in rhetoric and public speaking in honor of James Albert Winans* (pp. 181–216). New York: Century.

Wills, G. (1992). *Lincoln at Gettysburg: The words that remade America.* New York: Simon & Schuster.

Wilson, D. L. (2006). *Lincoln's sword: The presidency and the power of words.* New York: Knopf.

Wilson, K. H. (2002). *The reconstruction desegregation debate: The politics of equality and the rhetoric of place, 1870–1875.* East Lansing: Michigan State University Press.

Windt, T. O., Jr. (1972). The diatribe: Last resort for protest. *Quarterly Journal of Speech, 58,* 1–14.

Winkler, C. K. (2006). *In the name of terrorism.* Albany: State University of New York Press.

Wrage, E. J. (1947). Public address: A study in social and intellectual history. *Quarterly Journal of Speech, 33,* 451–457.

Wrage, E. J., & Baskerville, B. (Eds.). (1960). *American forum: Speeches on historic issues, 1788–1900.* New York: Harper & Row.

Wrage, E. J., & Baskerville, B. (Eds.). (1962). *Contemporary forum: American speeches on twentieth-century issues.* New York: Harper & Row.

Zaeske, S. (2002). Signatures of citizenship: The rhetoric of women's antislavery petitions. *Quarterly Journal of Speech, 88,* 147–168.

Zarefsky, D. (1980). A skeptical view of movement studies. *Central States Speech Journal, 31,* 245–254.

Zarefsky, D. (1986). *President Johnson's war on poverty: Rhetoric and history.* Tuscaloosa: University of Alabama Press.

Zarefsky, D. (1990a). Approaching Lincoln's second inaugural address. In J. R. Andrews, *The practice of rhetorical criticism* (2nd ed., pp. 66–70). New York: Longman.

Zarefsky, D. (1990b). *Lincoln, Douglas, and slavery: In the crucible of public debate.* Chicago: University of Chicago Press.

Zarefsky, D. (1998). Four senses of rhetorical history. In K. J. Turner (Ed.), *Doing rhetorical history: Concepts and cases* (pp. 19–32). Tuscaloosa: University of Alabama Press.

Zarefsky, D. (2002). The presidency has always been a place for rhetorical leadership. In L. G. Dorsey (Ed.), *The presidency and rhetorical leadership* (pp. 20–41). College Station: Texas A&M University Press.

24

Race, Sex, and Class in Rhetorical Criticism

KARLYN KOHRS CAMPBELL

ZORNITSA D. KEREMIDCHIEVA

The study of rhetoric and communication began with an argument over difference, distinction, and equity. What difference did it make if or how public discourse was taught and studied? The written exchanges over the course of the first year of publication of the *Quarterly Journal of Speech* put forth various visions with respect to this question. For example, bothered by the low repute of public-speaking teachers within the university structure, J. A. Winans (1915) advocated a reformulation of the profession's goals. Scholarship, he suggested, would bring about "the recognition we demand" (p. 17); he argued that "by scholarship which is the product of research the standing of our work in the academic world will be improved. It will make us orthodox. Research is the standard way into the sheepfold" (p. 17). The object of the discipline,

according to Winans, was to discover and determine the truth about "how an idea is planted in a human mind and brought to fruition" (p. 19). A commitment to truth and standards, in this view, was evidence of academic and social standing and distinction; and a methodical, scholarly approach to the subject of public address was the means to achieving higher class standing within the academy.

Resisting Winans's fervor for scientific standardization, Everett Lee Hunt (1915) proposed a more grounded vision of disciplinary identity and located the status of the discipline within a larger political field. Pointing to the traditional goal of public speaking teachers to understand broadly "all that contributes to the making of a 'good man,' skilled in speaking" (p. 185), Hunt warned that "no man who attempts to make oratory exclusively a scholastic pursuit upon the shaded porches of the philosophers will himself be a power as an orator or will develop that power in others" (p. 188). Besides being hopelessly reductive, a purely scholastic and impartial approach to rhetoric was dangerous for Hunt, because it would disconnect the discipline from its true mission "to send out from our colleges active, enthusiastic, intelligent men, confident in their own powers . . . We want men who are to be leaders of men, who will have an active share in all public affairs" (pp. 191–192). The point of rhetorical scholarship, according to Hunt, was "never [to] exalt learning above sincerity, academic recognition above service, or logic above life" (p. 193). Rhetoric was not a simple phenomenon that could be reduced to discrete elements and skills; for Hunt it was invariably a means "for some social or political reform" (p. 189).

The Winans-Hunt debate offers an early glimpse into the complex motives and considerations that have driven rhetorical scholarship over its nearly 100-year history in U.S. communication departments. Concerns over the value of intellectual labor, within and outside the academy, would continuously affect how rhetorical scholars conceived their purpose, methods, and objects of study. Consequently, the purpose of this chapter is to trace and examine the historical development of U.S. rhetorical scholarship with attention to the ways in which concerns about difference, distinction, and equity have shaped the discipline's conception of the practice and scholarship of public discourse and its role in a democracy. Specifically, this chapter narrates the history of public discourse studies with an eye on the following questions: how conceptions of the field's academic and cultural value have affected notions about who gets to do scholarship in rhetorical studies, what are the proper objects and methods of rhetorical studies, and ultimately, to whom is the field of rhetorical studies accountable. The last question refers to the ongoing debate as to whether or not, and if so how, rhetorical work should respond to political and cultural developments outside academia.

THE EARLY YEARS: A QUEST FOR CULTURAL AUTHORITY

Within 10 years from the inception of the field of speech communication in 1914, the study of public address was beginning to take distinctive shape, consciously driven, in part, by the struggle to differentiate its approach to rhetoric from the field of English to establish its own place and rank within the academy (Hudson, 1923; Wichelns, 1923). Hoyt H. Hudson (1923) sought to establish the field's credibility by framing rhetoric as an analytic field, a "pure science," "the science of discourse" (p. 168), to differentiate it from composition that he considered an applied art. In 1925, Herbert A. Wichelns asserted the discipline's value and identity by pointing to its relevance to the world outside academia. Although he recognized that oratory was now less revered than in the past, he asserted that "the conditions of democracy necessitate . . . the study of the art" (p. 4). For Wichelns (1925) oratory was "the art of influencing men [sic] in some concrete situation," and the orator was "a public man whose function it is to exert influence by speech" (p. 21). These comments helped define distinctively disciplinary scholarship: rhetorical criticism, which "regards a speech as a communication to a specific audience, and holds its business to be the analysis and appreciation of the orator's method of imparting his ideas to his hearers" (Wichelns, 1925, p. 22). As Wichelns argued,

Rhetorical criticism lies at the boundary of politics (in the broadest sense) and literature; its atmosphere is that of the public life, its tools are those of literature, its concern is with the ideas of the people as influenced by their leaders. (p. 26)

Notably, this conception of rhetoric derived the discipline's cultural authority through an alignment with the interests of cultural establishments, political power, and the value of social cohesion. Wichelns (1925) established the discipline's identity by orienting it to a proper object of study: the practice of political communication by which leaders influence the citizenry. The criterion of excellence was the successful persuasion of the immediate audience, a conception suggested much earlier by Winans's definition of persuasion as "the process of inducing others to give fair, favorable, or undivided attention to propositions" (as cited in Brigance, 1935, p. 20). This conception of rhetoric as a form of persuasion aiming to enhance social cohesion was adopted even if, based on their readings of the classics, scholars were mindful of rhetoric's bad reputation as a bag of tricks and embellishments (Hudson, 1923; Hunt, 1920). Rhetoric was allocated to a public sphere in which elite male citizens deliberated about great issues, and through public argument, discovered the most prudent and expedient ways to resolve conflicts and solve problems and celebrated the values that unified the community. In defense of public oratory, these norms privileged logical argument, deliberation, prudence, and decorum, values that tended to disparage those who disrupted established institutions and procedures.

This early disciplinary alignment with the interests of established political powers remained mainstream for nearly 50 years. For example, in 1934, under the sponsorship of the national organization, the Committee on Joint Research in the History of American Oratory began its work and subsequently published *History and Criticism of American Public Address* in three volumes under the editorship of W. N. Brigance (1943) and Marie Hochmuth (1955). Brigance insisted that social

stature and influence, not artistry, guided the selection of speakers, who were "men who have used words to direct the course of American history" (1943, vol. 1, p. vii). He added "that public address may have permanence and aesthetic excellence is not denied, nor is it ignored; but final judgment is here based on effect instead of beauty, on influence instead of appeal to the imagination" (1943, vol. 1, p. viii). Consistent with that philosophy, the speakers whose oratory was examined in Brigance's collection were leaders in the fields of politics, law, and religion.

What constituted discourse worthy of study was reflected in public address anthologies. Ernest Wrage and Barnet Baskerville (Baskerville, 1979; Wrage & Baskerville, 1960, 1962) defended the study of select national leaders on the basis of their representative character: "From the speeches given by many men, it is possible to observe the reflections of prevailing social ideas and attitudes" (Wrage, 1947, pp. 455–456). When Marie Hochmuth Nichols (1963) surveyed early anthologies of American orations in *Rhetoric and Criticism,* she revealed that the express purpose of these collections was "to exemplify the substance of statecraft, inspire patriotism, implant ideals, ethical and political, convey information about the growth of the state, show oratory to be connected to the game of politics," as well as to preserve exemplary works of the genre of oratory and to showcase its development (pp. 57–58).

Although they sought to establish the prestige and credibility of the discipline within academic and political circles, these criteria for selecting proper objects of study resulted in a gap between what rhetorical practices were accomplishing outside and the image of rhetoric inside academia. Not all leaders could represent the sentiment of the people, and not all people were represented by their leaders. A speech by Eugene V. Debs was the only example of rhetoric by a labor leader noted in the discipline's preeminent anthology (Wrage & Baskerville, 1962, pp. 13–26), although

Gunderson (1940) and Lomas's (1955) somewhat humorous and somewhat sympathetic portrayals of workingmen speakers should be noted. Women's presence on the public platform and the national impact of women's organizations was largely ignored in the first 50 years of the discipline, except for three essays and a book (Donaldson, 1951; O'Connor, 1954; Yoakam, 1937, 1943). African Americans were also notably absent in the scholarship of this period, except when mentioned as a curiosity, such as in two articles about black vernacular preaching (Honan, 1956; Pipes, 1945) or as an exception to the rule (Wallace, 1943). Booker T. Washington was the single African American to receive separate treatment in Brigance's (1943) collection (vol. 1, pp. 407–433). His inclusion was justified because he was praised for his adaptation to white audiences, for speeches "in tune with all classes of listeners; in line with their desires and attitudes, he selects his ideas and arguments . . . to recommend and amplify his program of Negro advancement and racial understanding" (Wallace, 1943, p. 408).

Thus, even if methodologically the field remained diverse (Baird & Thonssen, 1947), by the late 1950s the discipline had achieved a level of coherence through the discovery and defense of certain types of public address as a proper and significant—politically, culturally, and academically—object of study. That the discipline was consciously and explicitly deriving its cultural authority and distinction from an alignment with the interests of political leadership was evident from its selection of appropriate texts for study and its expressed goals of analysis: to explain how a speaker may achieve "a desired effect upon the hearers" in a given situation (Thonssen & Baird, 1948, p. vi). Speeches were evaluated with respect to how they propagated norms of decorum, ideals of national identity, and class unity. In this perspective, dissent could only be conceived as negativism and a "cult of antirationalism" (Baskerville, 1979, pp. 222–223). Thus, the

defense of "proper rhetoric" was a means to defend the study of rhetoric as a proper intellectual, scholarly practice.

THE 1960s AND 1970s: A QUEST FOR CONTEMPORARY RELEVANCE

The social upheavals of the 1960s prompted a reevaluation of rhetorical studies' purpose to register and analyze rhetoric's role in public life. While some decried the way social unrest was spilling into classrooms as a "tyranny of relevance" (Nichols, 1970), others, such as R. L. Scott and D. K. Smith (1969), pointed to the incongruity between what was happening inside and outside the academia and called for reexamining the assumptions and principles of public discourse scholarship which had guided the discipline so far:

> Since the time of Aristotle, academic rhetorics have been for the most part instruments of established society, presupposing the "goods" of order, civility, reason, decorum, and civil or theocratic law. . . . Even if the presuppositions of civility and rationality underlying the old rhetoric are sound, they can no longer be treated as self-evident. A rhetorical theory suitable to our age must take into account the charge that civility and decorum are masks for the preservation of injustice, that they condemn the dispossessed to nonbeing, and that as transmitted in a technological society they become the instrumentalities of power for those who "have." (pp. 7–8)

Rhetoric could no longer be conceived of as a benign tool for creating an unassuming vision of social cohesion. For Robert Scott and Bernard Brock (1972), the field was facing a crisis of relevance which was not solely due to the discipline's limited scope of objects of study; rather it was also a methodological and, ultimately, a political, crisis of disciplinary identity. In what Greene calls "the aesthetic turn"

(1998), the discipline was adopting a view of reality that increasingly appreciated the contingency of human motivations and perception, and their manifestations in human actions and discourse. Kenneth Burke's dramatistic theory of motives and linguistic action (Burke, 1952a, 1952b, 1953a, 1953b; Hochmuth, 1952; Holland, 1953), Edwin Black's (1965) attention to the creative and artistic dimensions of rhetoric, and R. L. Scott's (1967) influential essay "On Viewing Rhetoric as Epistemic" were distinctive in driving the theoretical turn-around of the discipline. Collectively, the epistemic turn was a radical departure from prior theoretical grounds, which had posed rhetoric as the effective communication of truth (especially the truth as leaders saw it). Instead, the epistemic turn oriented rhetorical studies to a notion of truth as an effect of discourse, rather than its precondition. The significance of this move cannot be underestimated: It meant that any social truth was the result of symbolization, that any social truth could be contested, but also that any solution to a conflict would entail a rhetorical strategy. Rhetorical studies could become involved and help nurture the solution to peace.

The epistemic turn enabled an active reevaluation of the discipline's imagination about what rhetoric and rhetorical scholarship could be doing and should be doing in the world. Rhetorical studies could now be armed with a new sense of relevance and augmented by a new ethical imperative, but the field was only slowly starting to change gear. For example, the report of the Wingspread conference broadened the appropriate subjects for analysis by asserting that "rhetorical criticism may be applied to any human act, process, product, or artifact which, in the critic's view, may formulate, sustain, or modify attention, perceptions, attitudes, or behavior" (Bitzer & Black, 1971, p. 220). Yet despite the emphasis on the importance of studying contemporary rhetorical actions, on examining the transactional nature of rhetorical actions, and on

expanding the range of objects for rhetorical analysis rhetoric, the conference itself seemed to replicate the deepening divisions of the social field. As Marie Nichols (Nebergall & Nichols, 1972) observed, "one wonders if a sufficient amount of consensus existed among conferees about the reality of the present and of the possibilities of rhetoric for transforming it" (p. 96). Against a powerful presumption that favored mainstream notions of truth and propriety, the powers of symbolization would be noted most vividly in rhetorics of dissent, confrontation, and difference. Thus, while the epistemic turn did not lead to or sanction alternative discourses to mitigate the use of force by the political establishment, it did provide the discipline with a new capacity for vision, a sight that illuminated the margins of political and social existence.

The "rhetoric of confrontation," as Scott and Smith (1969) termed it, produced a body of research that examined many aspects of the role of rhetoric in ongoing social conflicts and political activism related to racial justice, sex equity, workers' rights, and peace activism. Although aided with new theories and ethical focus, much of this work became social movements research, an established tradition (Bryant, 1937; Grandell, 1947; Griffin, 1950, 1952). Informed by Burkean theory (Griffin, 1964; Rueckert, 1969) and persuasion theory (Simons, 1970, 1972), social movement studies approached the contemporary civil rights movements as "an effort to establish communication between two dissonant groups: the haves and have-nots," and they were particularly interested in the way the civil rights discourses could activate "the sacred documents of America's heritage" as a means to bridge the political divide (Smith, 1966, p. 1). To understand the roots of confrontation, the field's attention turned to new voices entering the political landscape; consequently, such studies focused primarily on the rhetoric of the dissenters, and only on few occasions examined the resistant assumptions of the mainstream culture (King, 1976; Scott, 1973; Scott & Brockriede, 1969; Wander, 1971). Thus, the rhetoric of confrontation and dissent, inadvertently perhaps, became almost exclusively a study of the movement rhetoric representing African Americans and other subjugated groups.

THE RHETORIC OF RACIAL CONFLICT

The ongoing racial conflicts of the civil rights era seemed to make the biggest impression on the discipline. Early essays in journals, however, tended to be more descriptive than analytical, and resisted expressing a political motive, for example, report of Dr. Martin Luther King Jr.'s first speech as head of the Montgomery Improvement Association (Smith, 1968), or brief, traditional comments on Stokely Carmichael's speeches (Jefferson, 1967; Phifer & Taylor, 1967; Pollock, 1971). With resolution of the racial conflicts nowhere in sight, however, a number of more analytical studies on the rhetoric of Black Power initiated the discipline's critical investment in the rhetoric of confrontation (Brockriede & Scott, 1968; Scott, 1968a, 1968b; Scott & Brockriede, 1966; Scott & Smith, 1969). Arthur L. Smith (Molefi Asante)'s *Rhetoric of Black Revolution* (1969) was a particularly extended and nuanced study of revolutionary voices, which included historical background, sophisticated rhetorical analysis, materials from interviews, an excellent bibliography, and some speech texts.

In *The Rhetoric of Black Power*, R. L. Scott and Wayne Brockriede (1969) combined their critical essays published in 1966 and 1968 with essays by the Rev. Dr. Martin Luther King Jr., James Comer, and Charles Hamilton and speech texts by Vice President Hubert Humphrey, Stokely Carmichael, and Dr. Martin Luther King Jr. The collection attempted to give a more comprehensive picture of the views of advocates, the struggle over nonviolence and direct action, and the

ways in which these conflicts emerged in speeches and essays. As analyzed by Scott and Brockriede (1969), media coverage and liberal response converged in undeserved condemnation of Black Power advocates. An alternative response, they argued, might have challenged white liberals "to search for new ways of achieving power rather than being threatened to fear riots" and to hear Carmichael's claims, made repeatedly, that "Negroes are acting in self-defense" (p. 129). Thus, Scott and Brockriede (1969) placed a substantial share of responsibility on whites, especially white liberals, who reacted quickly and thoughtlessly to the distorted images and partial messages in journalistic reports.

The rhetoric of confrontation over racial justice challenged the discipline to look beyond the ethical implications of demands made on the white majority, and to rethink the political implications of the deliberative process. Parke Burgess was among the first to grapple with the challenges that Black Power's contestation of the democratic process posed for critics. In an attempt to reframe the issue, and to suggest the legitimacy of dissent both as a practice and as an object of study, Burgess (1968) wrote, "Neither the culture at large nor its leadership takes pains to distinguish sharply between the violence of deeds and the violence of words" (p. 122). And further, he asked, "Are most American citizens and institutions so intolerant of conflict as to lack toleration for the democratic motive itself?" (p. 318).

Possibly the answer to the above question was yes, as few essays concerned primarily with the challenges posed by its nontraditional rhetorical forms appeared in the 1970s (Campbell, 1971, 1972a; Heath, 1973; Kennicott & Page, 1971; Larson, 1970). Richard Fulkerson's 1979 study was the first critical analysis of a work by Martin Luther King Jr., other than the essay by Scott and Brockriede (1969). No other analyses of King's rhetoric would appear until the mid-1980s (Snow, 1985). One plausible explanation, based on disciplinary history and the issues raised by Brockriede and Scott (1968), Burgess (1968, 1969), Scott and Smith (1969), Smith/Asante (1969), and K. K. Campbell (1971), is that traditional methods were not well suited to the analysis of this discourse. Moreover, to discredit the activism of Martin Luther King Jr., and of civil rights activism generally, the FBI and Southern white organizations spread the allegation that King was a Communist or under the influence of Communists or their sympathizers (Roberts & Klibanoff, 2006), thus perhaps stifling the scholars' academic freedom. If critics adopted patriotic norms, then the rhetoric of confrontation was off-limits.

Even if the field was turning away from the rhetoric of confrontation, however, an effort was under way to inaugurate a recovery project, in which African Americans' rhetoric could be redeemed and the racial conflict could be provided with context. For example, critics reexamined the rhetoric of the antislavery movement (Hammerback, 1971; Weaver, 1971) and the role of African Americans in it (Fulkerson, 1972; Kennicott, 1970; Smith, 1970b). Other critics turned their attention to recovering African American speakers and leaders (King, 1974). Others examined the culture of black audiences (King, 1971; Smith, 1970a). Arthur L. Smith's (1972) collection *Language, Communication and Rhetoric in Black America* was a unique compilation of arguments and observations about the discursive foundations of race relations. Scholars also began to pay attention to the racial divide as a communication problem (Bloch & Pitts, 1975; Gregg & McCormack, 1968; Gregg, McCormack, & Pedersen, 1970; Hurt & Weaver, 1972; Rich, 1971). What began as an urgent call to pay attention to the rhetorical and political challenges of racial dissent was now morphing into a scholarly tradition that would develop along with, yet parallel to, the mainstream field of rhetorical studies.

THE RHETORIC OF WOMEN'S LIBERATION

Second-wave feminism posed still other problems for rhetorical critics in the late 1960s. Newspapers and network television were slow to report women's liberation activities, and much early coverage dismissed movement leaders as "loonies, lesbians or sex-crazed libbers" (Simpson, 1999/2000; also Dow, 1999). This is not surprising, as Janet Brown (1978) observed, because feminism was "not only a political movement, but also a gradual alteration of the states of mind of many individuals" (p. 138). Consequently, although early scholarship focused on the second wave of feminism as a social movement (Campbell, 1973; Foss, 1979; Hancock, 1972; Hope, 1975; Solomon, 1979), traditional methods of rhetorical criticism proved just as inadequate for analyzing second-wave feminism as they were for analyzing the Black Power movement. According to Campbell (1973), feminism too defied traditional concepts of persuasion because what appeared to be standard arguments for natural rights, when demanded by women, were seen as and became attacks on fundamental social values; the style of consciousness raising, whether in small groups or in public rhetoric, violated discursive norms to adapt to the problem of constituting women as an audience and creating new identities for them. Finally, movement rejection of traditional notions of leadership required critics to examine dispersed examples emanating from widely varied sources that used confrontational strategies to violate the reality structure and prompt moments of identification and realization. In other words, critical methods had to be adapted to the particular character of different bodies of rhetoric.

Thus, the activities of the women's liberation movement of the 1960s and 1970s, especially the most unconventional and provoking ones (Bosmajian, 1974; Deem, 2003), remained largely shielded from view in the rhetorical scholarship on feminism, and perhaps contributed to the field's increasing preference for historical scholarship rather than criticism of current events. Meanwhile, the question of what constituted feminist criticism posed further challenges. Brown (1978) anticipated and critiqued at least five approaches to criticism that could be termed feminist: (1) any criticism written by a woman, regardless of the subject; (2) any criticism written by a woman that analyzes a man's book from a "political" or "feminist" perspective; (3) any criticism by a woman about a woman's text; (4) any analysis of texts extracting signs of a universal "feminine consciousness;" or (5) any compensatory activity that attempted to make up for all that was previously omitted. These approaches made evident the effect of the absence of women in the field: Any action by a woman, be it speaking or writing, could potentially amount to a feminist, and therefore political, act. Once seen as political, it could be deemed unnatural, mischievous, and transgressive, and therefore subject to disciplinary censorship (Blair, Brown, & Baxter, 1994).

THE RHETORIC OF PEACE ACTIVISM

Finally, the antiwar protests too added fuel the study of the rhetoric of confrontation and dissent in the 1960s even if they received more scattered attention. The earlier attempt by Leland M. Griffin (1964) to account for the rhetorical structure of the "New Left" movement as a coherent social formation was followed by a few studies that focused on more specific manifestations of the peace activism of the civil rights era (Benson & Johnson, 1968; Gustainis, 1983). Others turned to historical precedent as a way to elucidate the current situation (Sillars, 1972). Only one study provided a more extended perspective on U.S. peace activism, but it firmly embraced a social movement perspective (Cox, 1974). Still, the academic debates prompted by the Vietnam War left a mark on the field. As evidenced by

the Campbell-Hill debate (Campbell, 1972a, 1972b; Hill 1972a, 1972b), rhetorical criticism was no longer the expression of academic interest alone. It invariably became an expression of the critics' political affinities as well. Did that realization prompt a radical reconsideration of the purposes of criticism? In one sense it did, as the study of alternative political discourses itself became an alternative and political form of scholarship. On the other hand, the lessons from studying the rhetoric of protests did not necessarily subvert, but instead seemed to affirm, the discipline's presumption that public address in a democracy was an essential enactment of citizenship. After examining the challenges and strategies of the anti–Vietnam War protesters, Robert Cox (1974) noted that despite the proliferation of studies of the rhetoric of movements, "the arduous task of outlining the bases for *theory* is still before us" (p. 268).

AFTER THE CIVIL RIGHTS ERA: RECOVERY, IDENTITY, INTERSECTIONALITY, AND THE CHALLENGES OF CRITICAL RHETORIC

Despite its relative isolation in the overall map of the field, the criticism of the rhetoric of the civil rights protests shifted scholarship toward two critical concepts: identity and power. The protests of the 1960s and the 1970s dramatized conceptions of difference as they solidified notions of identity, as the rhetoric of protest came to represent in the discipline's imagination all those populations that were not otherwise represented among its ranks. In 1964, Roy L. Hill had compiled and commented on speeches by African Americans addressing African American audiences. In his introduction, Hill noted that the act of publishing these speeches "at a time when we are attempting to emphasize integration" was important because they represented an otherwise lost tradition, and he argued that "if one knows what contribution he or his people have made, it gives him a firm base from which he can make further progress. It gives him dignity" (p. i).

Thus, against continuing mainstream norms and publication standards (Blair et al., 1994), the study of alternative rhetoric became framed as an alternative tradition of scholarship. The idea that choosing nonmainstream speakers and speech acts as objects of study was politically transformative became the political and institutional subtext of the discipline. Inspired by the women's liberation movement, the publication and study of the historical discourses of women and members of racial minorities would be understood as acts of consciousness raising and political mobilization against the mainstream mass institution of education described by King (1978). Thus, the project of recovering the rhetorical acts of women and other subjugated groups for the historical record became a scholarly and a political act aiming to constitute, mobilize, and legitimate alternative identities.

The recovery of the rhetorical activities of nonwhite, nonmale, nonelite speakers soon became a prolific strand of scholarship in the field. For example, the canon of elite white male orators was challenged in the 1980s and 1990s by rhetorical criticisms, which illuminated outstanding works by women speakers of the past such as Elizabeth Cady Stanton (Campbell, 1980) and Angelina Grimké (Daughton, 1995; Japp, 1985), Susan B. Anthony (Campbell, 1983), Ida B. Wells, Mary Church Terrell, and Sojourner Truth (Campbell, 1986), and Emma Goldman (Solomon, 1988), Anna E. Dickinson (Campbell, 1989a), and Anna Howard Shaw (Linkugel & Solomon, 1991), among others. Alternative anthologies of women's and African Americans' rhetorical texts were published (Campbell, 1989b; Donawerth, 2002; Logan, 1995, 1999; Ritchie & Ronald, 2001; Walker, 1992. Anthologies of speeches by early women activists appeared (Anderson, 1984; Kennedy & O'Shields, 1983). In 1989, the two volumes of *Man Cannot Speak for Her* offered critical analysis of movement rhetoric and speech texts

from the 1830s to 1925 (Campbell, 1989b). An important study of the woman suffrage press appeared in 1991 (Solomon, 1991). Along with a flurry of articles in journals, essays on women and African American rhetorics were collected in edited anthologies (Gray-Rosendale & Gruber, 2001; Jackson & Richardson, 2003; Lunsford, 1995; Miller & Bridwell-Bowles, 2005; Wertheimer, 1997). The rhetorical circumstances of immigrants, workers, and the poor as well as the rhetoric of their leaders were examined (Burkholder, 1989; Cloud, 1999; Mattina, 1994; Tonn, 1986). Book-length historical studies of the rhetorical activities of disenfranchised individuals and groups began to appear as well (Bacon, 2002; Hammerback, Jensen, & Gutierrez, 1985; Logan, 1995; Peterson, 1995; Triece, 2007; Zaeske, 2003). Finally, the search was on for theoretical postulations that could stem from and embrace the specific experiences and subject positions of various groups (Asante, 2004; Blake, 1997; Foss, Griffin, & Foss, 1997; Hamlet, 1998). Perhaps, characterizing these research efforts as recovery is an oxymoron. Collectively, these studies did not recover dissenting and subjugated rhetorics in a simple sense, because the act of recovery was an act of making a difference.

Much of the research on recovering alternative rhetorics adhered to a persuasion model of rhetorical action in which power and identity were often at odds with each other. The persuasion model conceived the social field as a site of contestation in which persuasive discourses competed for the assent of audiences. According to King (1978), rhetoric was a means to power, as it recruited and mobilized subjects as constituents united in consciousness, beliefs, and aspirations. Furthermore, rhetoric solidified power by endowing the mass institutions—military, political, educational, and so on, with ideological orientation, legitimacy, and mission. Working within the persuasion model of rhetoric, the rhetorical criticism of alternative voices aimed to emancipate individuals and populations from the shackles of institutionalized cultural norms. And so the recovery efforts often joined forces with ideological criticisms (McKerrow, 1983, 1989; Wander, 1983) that aimed to reveal the interests lurking behind dominant discourses and their negative effects on disenfranchised groups. Thus, the persuasion model allocated its notion of power to the mainstream norms and institutions and celebrated the ability of otherwise disenfranchised subjects to transcend and redirect such relations of power. Embracing the pluralism of alternative identities and traditions was understood as a safeguard against the power of the established institutions described by King (1978), and the critic's job was to highlight the ways groups and individuals were able to push forward their agendas despite obstacles. Thus, the ethical force of the persuasion model invoked a disciplinary narrative of transgression, overcoming, and redemption.

Eventually, however, identity-centered recovery efforts that adhered to the persuasion model were put to the test by questions about the intersectionality of categories such as sex, race, ethnicity, and class (Flores, 1996; Houston & Davis, 2002; Mao, 2004; Turner, 1998). Intersectionality debates called attention to the difficulty in isolating the complex discursive contexts framing speakers' experiences both with regard to their audiences and their self-understanding. Scholars also began to point to and examine critically the essentializing effects of scholarship that took perceived difference as a sufficient criterion in selecting objects of study and treated difference as an empirical, rather than a discursive, reality (Allen, 2002; Buzzanell, 2000; McPhail, 1991, 2002). Scholars extended the scope of rhetorical struggles with attention to transnational and international inequities (Hasian, 2001; Shome, 2006; Shome & Hegde, 2002). Furthermore, scholars critically examined the political implications of changing the disciplinary canon of exemplary speakers (Biesecker, 1992).

As rhetorical studies began to appreciate more fully how social identities were embedded in relations of power and discourse, the possibility of a stronger version of constitutive rhetoric became possible and along with it, a different version of critical public discourse studies. This perspective, which can be characterized as critical cultural rhetoric, expanded and nuanced the concept of power as a constructive, and not only an oppressive, force of cultural production. Scholars who embraced this perspective have paid attention to the discursive production of subjectivities and subjects (Charland, 1987); they have interrogated the performative, not just the instrumental, dimensions of rhetoric (Deem, 1995; Wilson, 2003); they have construed matter as a discursive production rather than as substance outside discourse (Stormer, 2004); and they have embraced a reflexive mode, as the act of theorizing difference itself became interrogated as a historically, culturally, and institutionally situated impulse (Crenshaw, 1991; Dow, 1995). Furthermore, studies in this tradition do not take the body-in-difference as transparent text, but as a manifestation of regimes of visibility (Dow, 2001; Sloop, 2004). They allocate citational, political authority to regimes of publicity and publicness (Deem, 2002; Parry-Giles, 1998). Finally, public discourse scholarship within the critical cultural tradition has traced and critically examined the role of institutions—political, educational, and others—and their discourses in circulating and perpetuating notions of difference, identity, and authority (Brookey, 2002; Condit & Lucaites, 1993; Greene, 1993; Wilson, 2002).

REINVENTING RHETORICAL SCHOLARSHIP FOR THE 21ST CENTURY: CHALLENGES AND CONTINUITIES

In the end, what difference has it made that public discourse studies have engaged difference—rhetorical, social, or political? The seeming theoretical impasse between approaches that find rhetoric at work at the moments when subjects use symbols and approaches that find rhetoric at work when subjectivities emerge from symbolic systems does not necessarily bring rhetorical studies to a tragic halt. On the contrary, such theoretical differences have energized the field's involvement with the challenges of political and social differences.

The field's approaches to difference have emerged through the interplay between quests for theoretical novelty and habits of thought. As Greene (1998) observed, the persuasion and the constitutive models of rhetorical effectivity have continued to operate in the field alongside each other, and each has contributed a notion of ethics and power. A critical cultural approach to public discourse does not deny, but rather attempts to explain when, how, and why, persuasion is conceivable. The rhetorical and biographical study of historic speakers has pointed our attention to the cultural practices and educational and other institutions that have historically produced the very capacity for rhetoricity that we embrace in public discourse studies. Among these institutional practices, we should locate our disciplinary pedagogy and publication practices, as they too attune our senses to finding rhetoric at work in the world. Finally, seemingly incongruent theoretical affinities may have affected our conceptions of agency and emancipation, but they have not canceled our orientation to politics at large, not the least because, to reiterate Scott and Smith's (1969) observation, confrontation still "crackles menacingly from every issue in our country . . . hemisphere . . . and globe" (p. 2). Thus, the problematics of difference continue to energize public discourse studies, both with regards to our contribution to scholarship and rhetorical praxis at large and to our evolving conceptions of disciplinary identity.

REFERENCES

Allen, B. J. (2002). Goals for emancipatory communication research on black men. In M. Houston & O. I. Davis (Eds.), *Centering ourselves: African American feminist and womanist studies of discourse* (pp. 21–34). Cresskill, NJ: Hampton Press.

Anderson, J. (1984). *Outspoken women: Speeches by American women reformers, 1635–1935.* Dubuque, IA: Kendall/Hunt.

Asante, M. K. (2004). The Afrocentric idea. In R. L. Jackson II (Ed.), *African American communication & identities: Essential readings* (pp.16–28): Thousand Oaks, CA: Sage.

Bacon, J. (2002). *The humblest may stand forth: Rhetoric, empowerment, and abolition.* Columbia: University of South Carolina Press.

Baird, A. C., & Thonssen, L. (1947). Methodology in the criticism of public address. *Quarterly Journal of Speech, 33,* 134–138.

Baskerville, B. (1979). *The people's voice: The orator in American society.* Lexington: University Press of Kentucky.

Benson, T., & Johnson, B. (1968). The rhetoric of resistance: Confrontation with the warmakers. *Today's Speech, 16,* 35–42.

Biesecker, B. (1992). Coming to terms with recent attempt to write women into the history of rhetoric. *Philosophy & Rhetoric, 25,* 140–161.

Bitzer, L. F., & Black, E. (Eds.). (1971). The prospect of rhetoric: Report of the national developmental project, sponsored by Speech Communication Association. Englewood Cliffs, NJ: Prentice Hall.

Black, E. (1965). *Rhetorical criticism: A study in method.* New York: Macmillan.

Blair, C., Brown, J. R., & Baxter, L. A. (1994). Disciplining the feminine. *Quarterly Journal of Speech, 80,* 383–409.

Blake, C. (1997). Afrocentric tokens: Afrocentric methodology in rhetorical analysis. *Howard Journal of Communications, 8,* 1–14.

Bloch, E. H., & Pitts, J. H. (1975). The effects of three levels of Black dialect on perceived speaker image. *Speech Teacher, 24,* 218–225.

Bosmajian, H. A. (1974). The abrogation of the suffragists' First Amendment rights. *Western Speech, 38,* 218–232.

Brigance, W. N. (1935). Can we redefine the James-Winans theory of persuasion? *Quarterly Journal of Speech, 21,* 19–26.

Brigance, W. N. (1943). *History and criticism of American public address* (2 vols.). New York: McGraw-Hill.

Brockriede, W. E., & Scott, R. L. (1969). *The rhetoric of black power.* New York: Harper & Row.

Brockriede, W. E., & Scott, R. L. (1968). Stokely Carmichael: Two speeches on Black Power. *Central States Speech Journal, 19,* 3–13.

Brookey, R. A. (2002). *Reinventing the male homosexual: The rhetoric and power of the gay gene.* Bloomington: Indiana University Press.

Brown, J. (1978). Kenneth Burke and "The Mod Donna": The dramatistic method applied to feminist criticism. *Central States Speech Journal, 29,* 138–144.

Bryant, D. C. (1937). Some problems of scope and method in rhetorical scholarship. *Quarterly Journal of Speech, 23,* 187–188.

Burgess, P. G. (1968). The rhetoric of Black Power: A moral demand? *Quarterly Journal of Speech, 54,* 122–133.

Burgess, P. G. (1969). The racial crisis: Intolerable conflict versus democratic violence. *Quarterly Journal of Speech, 55,* 318–324.

Burke, K. (1952a). A dramatistic view of the origins of language. *Quarterly Journal of Speech, 38,* 251–264.

Burke, K. (1952b). A dramatistic view of the origins of language. *Quarterly Journal of Speech, 38,* 446–460.

Burke, K. (1953a). A dramatistic view of the origins of language. *Quarterly Journal of Speech, 39,* 79–92.

Burke, K. (1953b). Postscripts on the negative. *Quarterly Journal of Speech, 39,* 209–216.

Burkholder, T. R. (1989). Kansas populism, woman's suffrage, and the agrarian myth: A case study in the limits of transcendence. *Communication Studies, 40,* 292–307.

Buzzanell, P. M. (2000). Commentary about Aimee M. Carillo Rowe's "Locating feminism's subject: The paradox of white femininity and the struggle to form feminist alliances." *Communication Theory, 10,* 81–89.

Campbell, K. K. (1971). The rhetoric of radical black nationalism. *Central States Speech Journal, 22,* 151–160.

Campbell, K. K. (1972a). *Critiques of contemporary rhetoric.* Belmont, CA: Wadsworth.

Campbell, K. K. (1972b). "Conventional wisdom—traditional form:" A rejoinder. *Quarterly Journal of Speech, 58,* 451–455.

Campbell, K. K. (1973). The rhetoric of women's liberation: An oxymoron. *Quarterly Journal of Speech, 59,* 74–86.

Campbell, K. K. (1980). Stanton's "The Solitude of Self": A rationale for feminism. *Quarterly Journal of Speech, 66,* 304–312.

Campbell, K. K. (1983). Contemporary rhetorical criticism: Genres, analogs and Susan B. Anthony," In J. I. Sisco (Ed.), *The Jensen lectures* (pp. 117–132). Tampa: University of South Florida.

Campbell, K. K. (1986). Style and content in the rhetoric of early Afro-American feminists. *Quarterly Journal of Speech, 72,* 434–445.

Campbell, K. K. (1989a). *La Pucelle d'Orleans* becomes an American girl: Anna E. Dickinson's "Jeanne d'Arc." In M. C. Leff & F. J. Kauffeld (Eds.), *Texts in context: Critical dialogues on significant episodes in American political rhetoric* (pp. 91–111). Davis, CA: Hermagoras Press.

Campbell, K. K. (1989b). *Man cannot speak for her* (2 vols.). New York: Greenwood Press.

Charland, M. (1987). Constitutive rhetoric: The case of the "Peuple Quebecois." *Quarterly Journal of Speech, 73,* 133–150.

Cloud, D. (1999). The null persona: Race and the rhetoric of silence in the uprising of '34. *Rhetoric & Public Affairs, 2,* 177–209.

Condit, C. M., & Lucaites, J. L. (1993). *Crafting equality: America's Anglo-African word.* Chicago: University of Chicago Press.

Cox, R. J. (1974). Perspectives on the rhetorical criticism of movements: Antiwar dissent, 1964–1970. *Western Journal of Speech Communication, 38,* 254–268.

Crenshaw, C. (1991). Mapping the margins: Intersectionality, identity politics, and violence against women of color. *Stanford Law Review, 43,* 1241–1299.

Daughton, S. M. (1995). The fine texture of enactment: Iconicity as empowerment in Angelina Grimké's Pennsylvania Hall address. *Women's Studies in Communication, 18,* 19–43.

Deem, M. (1995, August). Decorum: The flight from the rhetorical. In *Argumentation & Values: Proceedings of the Alta Conference on Argumentation* (pp. 226–229). Washington, DC: National Communication Association/American Forensic Association.

Deem, M. (2002). Stranger sociability, public hope, and the limits of political transformation. *Quarterly Journal of Speech, 88,* 444–455.

Deem, M. (2003). Disrupting the nuptials at the Town Hall debate: Feminism and the politics of cultural memory in the USA. *Cultural Studies, 17,* 615–647.

Donaldson, A. (1951). Women emerge as political speakers. *Speech Monographs, 18,* 54–61.

Donawerth, J. (2002). *Rhetorical theory by women before 1900: An anthology.* Lanham, MD: Rowman & Littlefield.

Dow, B. (1995). Feminism, difference(s), and rhetorical studies. *Communication Studies, 46,* 106–117.

Dow, B. (1999). Fixing feminism: Women's liberation and the rhetoric of TV documentary. *Quarterly Journal of Speech, 90,* 53–80.

Dow, B. J. (2001). *Ellen,* television, and the politics of gay and lesbian visibility. *Critical Studies in Media Communication, 18,* 123–140.

Flores, L. A. (1996). Creating discursive space through a rhetoric of difference: Chicana feminists craft a homeland. *Quarterly Journal of Speech, 82,* 142–156.

Foss, S. (1979). Equal rights amendment controversy: Two worlds in conflict. *Quarterly Journal of Speech, 65,* 275–88.

Foss, S. K., Griffin, C. L., & Foss, K. A. (1997). Transforming rhetoric through feminist reconstruction: A response to the gender diversity perspective. *Women's Studies in Communication, 20,* 117–135.

Fulkerson, G. (1972). Frederick Douglass and the Kansas-Nebraska Act: A case study in agitational versatility. *Central States Speech Journal, 23,* 261–269.

Fulkerson, R. P. (1979). The public letter as rhetorical form: Structure, logic, and style in King's "Letter from Birmingham Jail." *Quarterly Journal of Speech, 65,* 121–136.

Grandell, S. J. (1947). The beginnings of a methodology for social control studies in public address. *Quarterly Journal of Speech, 33,* 36–39.

Gray-Rosendale, L., & Gruber, S. (Ed.). (2001). *Alternative rhetorics: Challenges to the rhetorical tradition.* New York: State University of New York Press.

Gregg, R. B., & McCormack, A. J. (1968). "Whitey" goes to the ghetto: A personal chronicle of a communication experience with black youths. *Today's Speech, 16,* 25–30.

Gregg, R. B., McCormack, S. J., & Pedersen, D. (1970). A description of the interaction between black youth and white teachers in a ghetto speech class. *Speech Teacher, 19,* 1–8.

Greene, R. W. (1993). Argumentation and the aporias of state formation: The Palestinian Declaration of Independence. *Argumentation & Advocacy, 29,* 124–137.

Greene, R. W. (1998). The aesthetic turn and the rhetorical perspective on argumentation. *Argumentation and Advocacy, 35,* 19–30.

Griffin, L. M. (1950). *The antimasonic persuasion: A study of public address in the American antimasonic movement, 1826–1838.* Unpublished doctoral dissertation, Cornell University, Ithaca, NY.

Griffin, L. M. (1952). The rhetoric of historical movements. *Quarterly Journal of Speech, 38,* 185–188.

Griffin, L. M. (1964). The rhetorical structure of the "New Left" movement: Part I. *Quarterly Journal of Speech, 50,* 113–135.

Gunderson, R. (1940). The calamity howlers. *Quarterly Journal of Speech, 26,* 401–411.

Gustainis, J. J. (1983). The Catholic ultra-resistance: Rhetorical strategies of anti-war protest. *Communicator, 13,* 37–50.

Hamlet, J. D. (Ed.). (1998). *Afrocentric visions: Studies in culture and communication.* Thousand Oaks, CA: Sage.

Hammerback, J. C. (1971). The rhetoric of a righteous reform: George Washington Julian's 1852 campaign against slavery. *Central States Speech Journal, 22,* 85–93.

Hammerback, J. C., Jensen, R. J., & Gutierrez, J. A. (1985). *A war of words: Chicano protest in the 1960s and 1970s.* Westport, CT: Greenwood Press.

Hancock, B. R. (1972). Affirmation by negation in the women's liberation movement." *Quarterly Journal of Speech, 58,* 264–271.

Hasian, M., Jr. (2001). Rhetorical studies and the future of postcolonial theories and practices. *Rhetoric Review, 20,* 22–27.

Heath, R. L. (1973). Dialectical confrontation: A strategy of black radicalism. *Central States Speech Journal, 24,* 168–177.

Hill, R. L. (1964). *The rhetoric of racial revolt.* Denver, CO: Golden Bell Press.

Hill, F. (1972a). Conventional wisdom—traditional form: The president's message of November 3,

1969. *Quarterly Journal of Speech, 58,* 373–387.

Hill, F. (1972b). Reply to Professor Campbell. *Quarterly Journal of Speech, 58,* 454–461.

Hochmuth, M. K. (1952). Kenneth Burke and the "New Rhetoric." *Quarterly Journal of Speech, 38,* 134–144.

Hochmuth, M. K. (1955). *History and criticism of American public address* (Vol. 3). New York: Longmans, Green.

Holland, V. (1953). Rhetorical criticism: A Burkean method. *Quarterly Journal of Speech, 39,* 444–450.

Honan, W. H. (1956). John Jaspers and the sermon that moved the sun. *Speech Monographs, 23,* 255–261.

Hope, D. S. (1975). Redefinition of self: A comparison of the rhetoric of the women's liberation and black liberation movements. *Communication Quarterly, 23,* 17–25.

Houston, M., & Davis, O. I. (2002). Introduction: A black woman's angle of vision on communication studies. In M. Houston & O. I. Davis (Eds.), *Centering ourselves: African American feminist and womanist studies of discourse* (pp. 1–18). Cresskill, NJ: Hampton Press.

Hudson, H. H. (1923). The field of rhetoric. *Quarterly Journal of Speech, 9,* 167–180.

Hunt, E. L. (1915). The scientific spirit in public speaking. *Quarterly Journal of Speech, 1,* 185–193.

Hunt, E. L. (1920). Plato on rhetoric and rhetoricians. *Quarterly Journal of Speech, 6,* 35–56.

Hurt, H. T., & Weaver, C. H. (1972). Negro dialect, ethnocentrism, and the distortion of information in the communicative process. *Central States Speech Journal, 33,* 118–125.

Jackson, R. L., & Richardson, E. B. (Eds.). (2003). *Understanding African American rhetoric: Classical origins to contemporary innovations.* New York: Routledge.

Japp, P. (1985). Esther or Isaiah? The abolitionist-feminist rhetoric of Angelina Grimké. *Quarterly Journal of Speech, 71,* 335–348.

Jefferson, P. (1967). The magnificent barbarian at Nashville," *Southern Communication Journal, 33,* 77–87.

Kennedy, P. S., & O'Shields, G. H. (1983). *We shall be heard: Women speakers in America.* Dubuque, IA: Kendall/Hunt.

Kennicott, P. C. (1970). Black persuaders in the antislavery movement. *Speech Monographs, 37,* 15–25.

Kennicott, P. C., & Page, W. E. (1971). H. Rap Brown: The Cambridge Incident. *Quarterly Journal of Speech, 57,* 325–354.

King, A. A. (1971). The rhetorical legacy of the black church. *Central States Speech Journal, 22,* 179–185.

King, A. A. (1974). Booker T. Washington and the myth of heroic materialism. *Quarterly Journal of Speech, 60,* 323–328.

King, A. A. (1976). The rhetoric of power maintenance: Elites at the precipice. *Quarterly Journal of Speech, 62,* 127–134.

King, A. A. (1978). Power: The rhetoric of mobilization. *Central States Speech Journal, 29,* 147–154.

Larson, C. U. (1970). The trust establishing function of the rhetoric of Black Power. *Central States Speech Journal, 21,* 52–56.

Linkugel, W. A., & Solomon, M. (1991). *Anna Howard Shaw: Suffrage orator and social reformer.* New York: Greenwood Press.

Logan, S. W. (1995). *With pen and voice: A critical anthology of nineteenth-century African American women.* Carbondale: Southern Illinois University Press.

Logan, S. W. (1999). *"We are coming:" The persuasive discourse of nineteenth-century black women.* Carbondale: Southern Illinois University Press.

Lomas, C. W. (1955). Deannis Kearney: Case study in demagoguery. *Quarterly Journal of Speech, 41,* 234–242.

Lunsford, A. A. (Ed.). (1995). *Reclaiming rhetorica: Women in the rhetorical tradition.* Pittsburgh, PA: University of Pittsburgh Press.

Mao, L. (2004). Uniqueness or borderlands? The making of Asian-American rhetorics. In K. Giliard & V. Nunley (Eds.), *Rhetoric and ethnicity* (pp. 46–55). Portsmouth, NH: Boynton/Cook.

Mattina, A. F. (1994). "Rights as well as duties": The rhetoric of Leonora O'Reilly. *Communication Quarterly, 42,* 196–205.

McKerrow, R. E. (1983). Marxism and a rhetorical conception of ideology. *Quarterly Journal of Speech, 69,* 192–205.

McKerrow, R. E. (1989). Critical rhetoric: Theory and praxis. *Communication Monographs, 56,* 91–111.

McPhail, M. L. (1991). Complicity: The theory of negative difference. *Howard Journal of Communications, 3,* 1–13.

McPhail, M. L. (2002). *The rhetoric of racism revisited: Reparations or separation?* Lanham, MD: Rowman & Littlefield.

Miller, H., & Bridwell-Bowles, L. (Eds.). (2005). *Rhetorical women: Roles and representations.* Tuscaloosa: University of Alabama Press.

Nebergall, R. E., & Nichols, M. H. (1972). Two windows on "The prospect of rhetoric." *Quarterly Journal of Speech, 58,* 88–96.

Nichols, M. H. (1963). *Rhetoric and criticism.* Baton Rouge: Louisiana University Press.

Nichols, M. H. (1970). The tyranny of relevance. *Spectra, 6*(1), 9–10.

O'Connor, L. (1954). *Pioneer women orators.* New York: Columbia University Press.

Parry-Giles, S. J. (1998). Image based politics, feminism, and the consequences of their convergence. *Critical Studies in Mass Communication, 15,* 460–468.

Peterson, C. L. (1995). *Doers of the word: African-American women speakers and writers in the North, 1830–1880.* New York: Oxford University Press.

Phifer, E. F., & Taylor, D. R. (1967). Carmichael in Tallahassee. *Southern Communication Journal, 33,* 88–92.

Pipes, W. H. (1945). Old-time Negro preaching: An interpretative study. *Quarterly Journal of Speech, 31,* 15–21.

Pollock, A. (1971). Stokely Carmichael's new black rhetoric. *Southern Communication Journal, 37,* 92–94.

Rich, A. L. (1971). Some problems in interracial communication: An interracial group case study. *Central States Speech Journal, 22,* 228–235.

Ritchie, J., & Ronald, K. (Eds.). (2001). *Available means: An anthology of women's rhetoric(s).* Pittsburgh, PA: University of Pittsburgh Press.

Roberts, G., & Klibanoff, H. (2006). *The race beat: The press, the civil rights struggle, and the awakening of a nation.* New York: Alfred A. Knopf.

Rueckert, W. H. (Ed.). (1969). *Critical responses to Kenneth Burke, 1924–1966.* Minneapolis: University of Minnesota Press.

Scott, R. L. (1967). On viewing rhetoric as epistemic. *Central States Speech Journal, 18,* 9–16.

Scott, R. L. (1968a). Justifying violence: The rhetoric of militant Black Power. *Central States Speech Journal, 19,* 96–104.

Scott, R. L. (1968b). Black Power bends Martin Luther King. *The Speaker and Gavel, 5,* 80–86.

Scott, R. L. (1973). The conservative voice in radical rhetoric: A common response to division. *Speech Monographs, 40,* 123–135.

Scott, R. L., & Brock, B. (1972). *Methods of rhetorical criticism.* New York: Harper & Row.

Scott, R. L., & Brockriede, W. E. (1966). Hubert Humphrey faces the "Black Power" issue. *The Speaker and Gavel, 4,* 11–17.

Scott, R. L., & Brockriede, W. E. (1969). *The rhetoric of black power.* New York: Harper & Row.

Scott, R. L., & Smith, D. K. (1969). The rhetoric of confrontation. *Quarterly Journal of Speech, 55,* 1–8.

Shome, R. S. (2006). Transnational feminism and communication studies. *Communication Review, 9,* 255–267.

Shome, R., & Hegde, R. S. (2002). Culture, communication, and the challenge of globalization. *Critical Studies in Media Communication, 19,* 172–189.

Sillars, M. O. (1972). The rhetoric of petition in boots. *Speech Monographs, 39,* 92–105.

Simons, H. W. (1970). Requirements, problems, and strategies: A theory of persuasion for social movements. *Quarterly Journal of Speech, 56,* 1–11.

Simons, H. W. (1972). Persuasion in social conflicts: A critique of prevailing conceptions and a framework for future research. *Speech Monographs, 39,* 227–247.

Simpson, P. A. (1999/2000). Covering the women's movement. *Nieman Reports, 53/54,* 1–14. Retrieved on October 18, 2006, from www.nieman.harvard.edu/reports/99-4_00–1NR/Simpson_Covering.html

Sloop, J. M. (2004). *Disciplining gender: Rhetorics of sex and identity in contemporary U.S. culture.* Amherst: University of Massachusetts Press.

Smith, A. L. [Molefi Asante]. (1969). *Rhetoric of black revolution.* Boston: Beacon Press.

Smith, A. L. (1970a). Some characteristics of the black religious audience. *Speech Monographs, 37,* 207–210.

Smith, A. L. (1970b). Henry Highland Garnet: Black revolutionary in sheep's vestments. *Control States Speech Journal, 21,* 93–98.

Smith, A. L. (1972). *Language, communication, and rhetoric in black America.* New York: Harper & Row.

Smith, D. H. (1966). Civil rights: A problem in communication. *Spectra, 2*(1–2), 4, 8.

Smith, D. H. (1968). Martin Luther King, Jr.: In the beginning at Montgomery. *Southern Communication Journal, 34,* 8–17.

Snow, M. (1985). Martin Luther King's "Letter from Birmingham Jail" as Pauline Epistle. *Quarterly Journal of Speech, 71,* 318–334.

Solomon, M. (1979). The "positive woman's" journey: A mythic analysis of the rhetoric of STOP ERA. *Quarterly Journal of Speech, 65,* 262–274.

Solomon, M. (1988). Ideology as rhetorical constraint: The anarchist agitation of "Red Emma" Goldman. *Quarterly Journal of Speech, 74,* 184–200.

Solomon, M. (Ed.). (1991). *A voice of their own: The woman suffrage press, 1840–1910.* Tuscaloosa: University of Alabama Press.

Stormer, N. (2004). Articulation: A working paper on rhetoric and taxis. *Quarterly Journal of Speech, 90,* 257–284.

Thonssen. L., & Baird, A. C. (1948). *Speech criticism: The development of standards for rhetorical appraisal.* New York: Ronald Press.

Tonn, M. B. (1986). Militant motherhood: Labor's Marry Harris "Mother" Jones. *Quarterly Journal of Speech, 82,* 1–21.

Triece, M. E. (2007). *On the picket line: Strategies of working-class women during the depression.* Urbana: University of Illinois Press.

Turner, K. J. (1998). Rhetorical studies in the twenty-first century: Envisioning the possibilities. *Southern Communication Journal, 63,* 330–336.

Walker, R. J. (1992). *The rhetoric of struggle: Public address by African American women.* New York: Garland.

Wallace, K. (1943). Booker T. Washington. In W. N. Brigance (Ed.), *History and criticism of American public address* (Vol. 1, pp. 407–433). New York: McGraw-Hill.

Wander, P. C. (1971). Salvation through separation: The image of the Negro in the American colonization society. *Quarterly Journal of Speech, 57,* 57–67.

Wander, P. (1983). The ideological turn in modern criticism. *Central States Speech Journal, 34,* 1–18.

Weaver, R. L. (1971). The negro issue: Agitation in the Michigan lyceum. *Central States Speech Journal, 22,* 196–201.

Wertheimer, M. M. (Ed.). (1997). *Listening to their voices: The rhetorical activities of historical women.* Columbia: University of South Carolina Press.

Wichelns, H. A. (1923). Our hidden aims. *Quarterly Journal of Speech, 9,* 315–323.

Wichelns, H. A. (1925). The literary criticism of oratory. In A. M. Drummond (Ed.), *Studies in Rhetoric and Public Speaking in Honor of James Albert Winans* (pp. 181–216). New York: Century Books.

Wilson, K. (2002). *The reconstruction desegregation debate: The politics of equality and the rhetoric of place, 1870–1875.* East Lansing: Michigan State University Press.

Wilson, K. (2003). The racial politics of imitation in the nineteenth century. *Quarterly Journal of Speech, 89,* 89–108.

Winans, J. A. (1915). The need for research. *Quarterly Journal of Speech, 1,* 17–23.

Wrage, E. J. (1947). Public address: A study in social and intellectual history. *Quarterly Journal of Speech, 33,* 451–457.

Wrage, E. J., & Baskerville, B. (1960). *American forum: Speeches on historic issues, 1788–1900.* New York: Harper.

Wrage, E. J., & Baskerville, B. (1962). *Contemporary forum: American speeches on twentieth-century issues.* Seattle: University of Washington Press.

Yoakam, D. G. (1937). Pioneer women orators of America. *Quarterly Journal of Speech, 23,* 251–259.

Yoakam, D. G. (1943). Woman's introduction to the American platform. In W. N. Brigance (Ed.), *History and Criticism of American Public Address* (Vol. 1, pp. 153–192). New York: McGraw-Hill.

Zaeske, S. (2003). *Signatures of citizenship: Petition, antislavery, and women's political identity.* Chapel Hill: University of North Carolina Press.

25

Rhetoric and Critical Theory

Possibilities for Rapprochement in Public Deliberation

GERARD A. HAUSER

MARIA T. HEGBLOOM

Globally, a new dynamic is shaping public deliberation. This dynamic is defined by social fragmentation, rapid change, rapid circulation of information, and networks of interdependence. Increasingly, since World War I, divergent perspectives have led to differences in how people experience and understand public problems. Changing conditions have given rise to new problems that place groups and nations in novel and often unstable networks of relationship. Rapid dissemination of competing desires and tactics for appropriating the means of goal satisfaction have further complicated these changes. At the same time, goal satisfaction often rests on partnerships of mutual dependency in ongoing negotiation over proper action and interaction. In this new dynamic,

can public deliberation play more than a nominal role in theory and praxis?

In this chapter, we explore the challenges to public deliberation presented by a milieu of cultural and ideological fragmentation. We discuss the prospects for a theoretical accommodation between rhetoric and critical theory and assess the realistic possibilities for such an accommodation to address the challenges facing public deliberation. We begin with a consideration of the challenges to public deliberation posed by relations of mutual dependency in a political context controlled by elites. We argue, first, that the prevailing politics of rational choice, with its instrumental focus on personal gain, undermines democratic action, while public deliberation, with its discursive focus on the public good, offers a competing model that seeks to recuperate democratic action. However, we also argue that this goal is imperiled. Elites buffer ordinary citizens from decision-making processes at all but local levels, thereby effectively making public deliberation, as traditionally understood, an idle practice. Beyond local arenas, public deliberation capable of reaching accord on practices and policies often must invent arguments in newly defined reference worlds of identity and aspirations. We thus discuss how identity differences among interdependent partners challenge assumptions about rhetoric as a productive art; we also outline the major challenges to the orthodoxies of common ground, arguments based on audience assumptions, and consensus. We contend that a rapprochement between Habermas's (1974) construction of critical theory and a rhetorical understanding of public deliberation offers a possibility for refiguring public deliberation in a way capable of addressing relations of mutual dependency in a world of increasing cultural and ideological fragmentation. We conclude with a brief discussion of the prospects for public moral arguments in the contemporary context of lived democracy.

THE PROBLEM OF FRAGMENTATION AND MUTUAL DEPENDENCY

The ideal of public deliberation is in trouble. Beyond the local level, citizens have experienced an increasing distance between themselves and those with the authority to act. At the same time, the ability of citizens' voices to influence public policy has declined. Special interests, the economically privileged, knowledge and moral elites, positions of status, ideological control of legislatures, and academics have displaced citizen involvement as a guiding force in the political process. Vested interests not only have well-financed and powerful lobbies but also actually write legislation to protect or advance their concerns, while

meaningful citizen engagement has receded to the point where there is a serious question whether public deliberation among citizens matters. Public deliberation no longer occurs, if it ever did, on a level playing field.

This is not news (see, e.g., Bohman, 2000; Gastil, 1992; Hicks, 2002; Ono & Sloop, 1995). Observations on the perilous state of American politics have been with us since at least the post–World War I era, when Walter Lippmann (1922/1965) and John Dewey (1927/1954) had their seminal exchange on the prospects of the public. At that time, the prospect of a public forming, much less participating with, informed voices in public deliberation was already thought to be fading over the horizon of industrialization, modern modes of transportation, and mass communication (Dewey, 1927/1954; Lippmann, 1922/1965). Thirty years later, C. Wright Mills (1956) considered post–World War II America to have fallen into a deeper and more dangerous political chasm. In Mills's view, the ideals of public deliberation, assumed to guide the political process in a representative democracy, had become idle. Even then an assumed narrative continued to rationalize public deliberation as the method for citizen participation in a liberal democracy: publics consisting of a community of citizens who share common ends, values, and procedures and a deliberative process that protects the rights of all interested parties while discovering public opinion that has traction for public policy.

Whether these assumptions ever prevailed in practice is questionable. The dictum that the people are sovereign while the elite rule was certainly true during the periods of populism in the 19th-century America, when voter turnout was often a function of clienteles fostered by big-city party machines that preyed on the tribal loyalties of ethnic communities (Piven & Cloward, 1988, pp. 35–41). Later, at the turn of the 20th century, regional absence of party competition spurred internal oligarchy within the parties and made large voter turnout unnecessary for the party to retain power or posed the threat of voters who could not be controlled. Low-wage workers, immigrants, and black citizens were systematically thinned out from voter roles by residency, literacy, and property tax requirements for voter registration (Piven & Cloward, 1988, pp. 64–95). In neither case were liberal democratic ideals guiding political practice.

Half a century later, on different grounds, President Kennedy echoed Lippmann's (1922/1965) concerns. Kennedy thought that public problems had migrated from the public to the technical sphere, which favored the technical language and mathematical logic of knowledge elites while marginalizing the ordinary citizens. At a May 1962 press conference, Kennedy stated,

> Most of us are conditioned for many years to have a political viewpoint—Republican or democratic, liberal, conservative, or moderate. The fact of the matter is that most of the problems . . . we now face are technical problems. They are very sophisticated judgments, which do not lend themselves to the great sort of passionate movements which have stirred this country so often in the past. [They] deal with questions which are now beyond the comprehension of most men. (Quoted in Lasch, 1978, p. 77)

Kennedy thought that commonsense language—the language of intersubjective meaning that intelligent but not technically trained citizens share and use to deliberate public problems—was no longer able to express a "sophisticated judgment" on public issues. Requiring competence in information sciences plus technical expertise for participation in discussions on public problems renders the average citizen a befuddled observer dealt out of the game (Hauser, 1987).

This narrative of rule by elites is reproduced in models of political action predicated on advancing personal interests and a logic of rational choice as guiding political decisions,

where the rational choice is whatever option advances personal interests (Hardin, 1999; Mansbridge, 1993; Page & Shapiro, 1993). A politics of rational choice reflects the instrumental logic of governance by political elites, who act much as autonomous economic actors free to choose preferences that maximize private wealth and adopt strategies to accomplish this end, such as concealing preferences from trading partners or minimizing regret should conditions not develop as anticipated. Discourse is treated as equally instrumental, of value only insofar as it encourages ordinary citizens to make choices portrayed as advancing special interests rather than the public good. Discourse is understood as having little to do with the rhetorical valences that may constitute deliberative activity and more to do with the quantifiable elements, such as polling data on citizen susceptibilities, which link persuasive appeals to self-interested choice (Hauser & Benoit-Barne, 2002).

More fundamentally from the perspective of deliberation, however, the rational choice model violates a long-held understanding of democratic politics: that deliberation must be a public activity open to all and distinct from the private preferences expressed in commercial transactions. Furthermore, while a democracy recognizes the equal worth of each individual citizen and therefore the citizen's autonomy with respect to exercising his or her political right to participate in the political process, the point of a democracy is not to maximize satisfaction of individual preferences but to maximize the common good. Over and against self-interest, democracy has an abiding concern with justice.

PUBLIC DELIBERATION AND THE REDEMPTION OF DEMOCRACY

In the past century, rhetoric scholars and some political and social theorists attempted to redeem the political efficacy of discourse on which a democracy that is more than nominal depends. Some regarded education in rhetorical skills suited to democratic deliberation as enabling citizens to deliberate in a climate of difference. In the 1920s and 1930s, Dewey's *How We Think* (1910) gave rise to the introduction of small-group discussion in the speech curriculum. Group discussion provided an alternative to debate as a mode of increasing citizen participation in public deliberation. William Keith (2002) summarized this movement's rationale as follows:

> For democracy to be renewed, we have to have a sense of democratic argument/communication outside of legislative or parliamentary contexts, and even in those, debate seems a tool of interests, rather than a genuine method. Hence, a more appropriate mode is one that is less grossly political, and more capable of export to various contexts. Discussion is something anybody can do and hence participate in the democratic process. Discussion was as much an attitude or approach as a specific technique. (p. 315)

Framing public deliberation as group discussion conceptualized rhetorical skills as extending beyond the podium. Even today, advocates of group discussion as a mode of democratic deliberation (Gastil, 1992; Gastil & Dillard, 1999) contend that interaction in problem-oriented discussion is the common context in which most citizens encounter public problems and difference. Moreover, scholars outside communication have highlighted the positive consequences of group deliberation. James Fishkin (1995), using his method of "deliberative polling," found that citizens who are informed on an issue are more likely to reach consensus, and Robert Putnam's (1993) longitudinal study of regional politics in Italy found that citizens who engage in informed group discussion are more trusting and more likely to participate in the political process.

These studies also issued a call for structures that facilitate public deliberation. Town, union, and Grange Hall meetings, forensics tournaments, issue forums, talk radio, and blogs are a few examples of the places where public problems are deliberated and skills at deliberation honed. Eberly (2002), writing about this expanse of possibilities for citizen engagement, underscored the importance of public speaking, writing, small-group discussion, and other courses in secondary and undergraduate curricula that allow the classroom to function as a deliberative forum:

> Teaching the praxis of rhetoric as a productive and practical art can be a radically democratic act, and . . . teaching the praxis of rhetoric in classrooms understood as protopublic spaces can serve a more important cultural function than training students how to use Powerpoint or Pagemill. (p. 290)

Others, such as Ivie (2002), emphasized rhetorical theory's millennial position that public deliberation is necessarily agonistic—a claim also advanced by political theorists such as Young (1997) and Mouffe (1993). Ivie argued that "rowdy democracy," the ability to live together without sacrificing key differences, embraced the messiness of pluralistic politics. "Pluralistic politics . . . is foremost a matter of figuring out how a necessarily conflicted polity can bridge its divisions sufficiently for people to live together without sacrificing a healthy degree of diversity" (p. 277).

Thomas Farrell (1993) and Thomas Goodnight (1982) moved the argument for public deliberation in a different theoretical direction, as each sought rapprochement with Jürgen Habermas's (1987) theories of communicative action and the public sphere, respectively, to support the requirement of open public deliberation in which procedural norms of participation obtain. These normative characteristics that underwrite the rationality of rhetorical practices, they argued, are inescapably strategic—a claim we consider in greater detail below.

Regardless of their approach, rhetoric scholars generally agree that for democratic processes to be politically functional in a mass society composed of myriad identities and competing interests, citizens must learn to engage difference in a way that recognizes individuals as subjects (Aune, 1994; Touraine, 1997). This is to say that while democracy may be unruly, public deliberation can still be reasonable. Insofar as issues involve relations of mutual dependence, solutions to common problems call for public deliberation to foster cooperation among linked partners who recognize differences and include those differences in their deliberations. Rhetoricians hold that this engagement of difference requires rhetorical skills.

PUBLIC DELIBERATION IN A WORLD OF STRANGERS

In addition to the instrumental character of a politics in which elites reign while citizens are atomized actors whose political decisions favor attaining personal goals over public goods, public deliberation faces a second major problem. At least since the end of World War II, a reference world of shared values and beliefs has been receding. A spreading network of intertwined relationships, from the local to the global, has created the challenge of achieving coordinated social action among individuals and groups who, in many respects, are strangers. This is perhaps the greatest challenge public deliberation must address. Complex societies, mass media, globalization of economic and political resources, and proliferation of new media pose the problem of ongoing deliberation among partners who are personally unknown to each other, often geographically distant; have varying degrees of cultural difference; are bound in relations of mutual dependency; and have instant information about and access to one another and their respective actions. While it is possible and at times attractive to make partisan strategic choices in order to maximize personal and group gain, networks of nested interdependencies make that a risky strategy. Going it alone

is seldom a viable option. Apart from force or violence to gain compliance, goal satisfaction requires cooperation among partners with divergent identities and shifting affiliations.

At all but the local level, mutual accord must function in newly defined reference worlds of identity and aspirations. A common world of just laws, fair marketplace conditions, equity in access to and distribution of social resources, and guarantees of human rights and the like requires tolerance of differences and acknowledgment of each other's goals as legitimate and relevant to deliberation over common problems. Pluralism and fragmentation both require representative discourse capable of forging agreements that serve multiple and even different ends and that can be justified from multiple perspectives. Awareness of cultural, economic, social, and political differences, of concerns and positions of other groups and nations, and instant communication about issues and actions inflected by difference does not make this an easy accomplishment.

This heightened sense of fragmentation intensifies the threat of difference and challenges pluralism. This consciousness also enables the power elites we discussed above—special interests; ideologically inscribed legislatures; epistemic, moral and economic elites; and academics—to exert undue influence on public perceptions and policy decisions. Elites have easy access to, if not a monopoly on, mass media and decision-making processes. Elites' capacity to control information and participate in official forums of public deliberation limits the field of contestants for ownership of public issues (Gusfield, 1981). Elites' concentrated control of a problem's definition, salient issues, relevant evidence, and access to the deliberative process can be decisive; it distorts both public perception of issues and representation of public opinion.

Here, we must qualify our analysis to note that ordinary citizens are neither without resources nor as apathetic as they are commonly portrayed (see Gamson, 1992; Noelle-Neumann, 1993). Furthermore, we do not mean to suggest that meaningful dialogue and deliberation are impossible or always without consequence. The work of Ono and Sloop (1995), Hauser (1999), Eberly (2002), Tracy and Standerfer (2003), Asen (2004), and Tracy and Dimock (2004), not to mention the legion of studies on the power of public deliberation in bringing about changes in civil rights and social policies, points to counter-examples where citizen discourse has proven to be consequential. Still, for ordinary citizens, the nature and viability of public deliberation are open to question.

Specifically, citizens' engagement can have significant traction in local deliberative forums and on major national issues where evidence of citizen support is essential to legitimate public policy. Outside of these conditions, public deliberations are of significantly less consequence. In the United States, for example, legislation and policy during the administration of George W. Bush have served corporate interests in areas such as the environment, tax rates, and universal health insurance. Meanwhile, as most New Deal social legislation is being dismantled, counter-balancing corporate versions of social programs are being eliminated. These developments testify to the extent to which power elites remain the principal determiners of social policy.

This problem is not confined to U.S. domestic politics. Innocent civilians in the Middle East find their lives threatened by feuding religious and militant factions; European governments ignore private-sector arms deals with paramilitary organizations and governments that support them (Deutsche, 2002); the U.S. government awards contracts to private firms without putting projects out for bid (National Public Radio, 2005); Argentinian politicians accept bribes from oil companies in return for votes on favorable laws (Brown, 2000); the French government bans Muslim schoolgirls from wearing hijabs as part of its policy of not allowing religious symbols in school (Esfandiari, 2006). Each of these is an image in a collage of fragmentation challenging the efficacy of public deliberation.

Confronted by these circumstances, ordinary citizens have circumscribed options: Focus on public deliberation at the local level, join the deliberative process within a political party, or engage in deliberation in a counterpublic sphere. These arenas do not necessarily represent a retreat; they may be the locus of direct engagement of and détente with difference. Public deliberation in these arenas questions the lifeworld through a discourse about proper action and interaction in arenas where fundamental commitments to openness, justice, truth, sincerity, and autonomy of action emerge.[1] Put differently, under conditions of pluralism and fragmentation, three universal commitments are necessary to counter these power imbalances: (1) recognition of the human subject's autonomy (Touraine, 1997), (2) inclusion of free citizens in the political community, and (3) guarantee of a public sphere independent of the state and private interests (Habermas, 1974). The third of these requirements is essential for realization of the first two.

THE CENTRALITY OF THE PUBLIC SPHERE

In the face of fading opportunities for citizens to engage their government in meaningful deliberation about their collective fate, the ongoing exchanges within civil society's public sphere offer a possibility, however challenging, for reviving the hope that public deliberation might matter (Cohen, 1999; Cohen & Arato, 1992). Habermas's theory of communicative action (1987), often critiqued as decoupled from the lived practices of democracy (Benhabib, 1992; Fraser, 1989, 1990; Hauser, 1999; Robbins, 1993), still may be read as pointing to formal theoretical conditions that are useful for rethinking the rhetorical face of public deliberation within the context of mutual dependencies we have been discussing.

The rhetorical character of public deliberation requires, at some level, integrating discursive processes into the processual norms set forth in Habermas's *Structural Transformation of the Public Sphere* (1968/1989). Habermas's norms, necessary to rationalize public deliberation, help chart the problems facing contemporary public opinion formation; furthermore, those norms highlight the critical possibilities for a space in which public deliberation could function in the process of a democratic creation of society. Habermas's (1974) historical contextualization of this possibility with the rise of a bourgeois public sphere is not intended to make it the ultimate realization of an ideal. Instead, it is an illustration of the advent of critical impulses that continue to provide a glimmer of hope for future prospects.

The important function of the public sphere[2] is discursive; it stands as the discursive space for public discussion and deliberation to act as the vehicle through which common interests are sought and public opinion is formed. It is the realm in which private individuals form a public capable of critically assessing problems and issues so that a rational consensus is possible. This space requires the normative claim to publicity—that is, the claim that proceedings and information be accessible to the public, so that public opinion can be brought into play as a critical authority. Furthermore, the public sphere, if it is to have any traction, must operate in a way that has some bearing on policy formation. Ideally, public opinion, as a critical assessment of problems, issues, and solutions, should stand as a court of appeal to which political decisions must be subject.

This understanding of the public sphere theorizes it as an arena in which individual differences could be negotiated rationally and democratically. However, Habermas (1974) points out that to fulfill this function, the public sphere would require a form of public deliberation meeting certain procedural standards. Open participation and equal access to information as well as the ability to call into question other positions are necessary if public deliberation is to result in a *genuine* public opinion and not a pseudolegitimation of predetermined outcomes. While these procedural norms remain counterfactual, they act as tools for assessing the current state of public deliberation and the public sphere. As such, they guide both inquiry and practice.

While this view of the public sphere is an ideal—a potential rarely if ever actualized—it faces ever greater challenges in contemporary society. Whereas the publicity principle[3] was once invoked critically to assess political decisions, it now legitimates a pseudopublic sphere geared to mold public opinion in the service of special interests and entrenched power elites. Given this situation, a return to some ideal public sphere where citizens face one another as individuals to determine common interests and come to rational agreements on pressing issues seems an unrealistic aspiration. However, the critical impulses that fueled the public sphere are not completely absent even today.

Given contemporary social and political formations, any hope for a public sphere requires a commitment by various rival organizations that mediate relations between individuals to the procedural norms of public deliberation, both in their internal structure and in relation to one another and the state. Such public deliberation in the public sphere would be conducted along the lines of organized individuals rather than private ones. This prospect for a public sphere shares some qualities with a rhetorical perspective, although this is not stressed in Habermas (1974). In turn, the hope for the public to influence policy decisions is not lost as long as political officials still appeal to the public for legitimation of their decisions and plans of action. Only when violence is accepted as a means to political ends will all hope be lost for public deliberation in the shaping of a shared world. The possibility for some kind of public sphere remains as long as an appeal to the public is made, however disingenuous this appeal may be. Habermas's foundational statement has been adapted by rhetoricians to suit the conditions of public deliberation as it is experienced in actually existing democracies.

Rhetorical theory generally agrees with critical theory that encountering difference in ways that have traction on common problems, albeit not necessarily commonly defined, requires a public sphere as a distinctively discursive realm in which issues are defined; views are explored through discussion, deliberation, and persuasion; common interests are sought; and public opinion is formed—ideally to a body that is empowered to set policy and act and that is responsive to public opinion (Hauser, 1999). Furthermore, Habermas (1968/1989) has made a convincing case that procedural standards are a prerequisite for public deliberation to be more than a cover for pseudolegitimation of predetermined outcomes. These standards rationalize the deliberative process by which social actors form *genuine* public opinions that can carry weight in public policy decisions. They also are counterfactual norms, and as such a theoretical fiction that, from a certain perspective, rhetoric and critical theory share. That is to say, although rhetoric and critical theory diverge in their understanding of what constitutes reasonableness, the legitimacy of emotion, and the role of strategic communication or persuasion, they share a critical stance in their mutual recognition that not all parties have equal access to information, media of dissemination, or public forums in which political voice is manifest. Insofar as such access is lacking, public deliberation is distorted, sometimes systematically so.

Regardless of their counterfactual character, these norms set parameters for public spheres capable of accommodating public deliberation under conditions of fragmentation and interdependency. While rhetoric takes from Habermas (1974) this understanding of the public sphere, it seeks to find ways to accentuate the plural character of public deliberation. In this, the idea of public spheres is offered in place of *a* public sphere to account for the plurality of identities, commitments, and aspirations in contemporary deliberation. In turn, the notion of counterpublic spheres (Asen & Brouwer, 2001) is given space in rhetorical treatments of public deliberation to account for those arenas in which the excluded, marginalized, and silenced reform themselves as a deliberative community.[4] This move helps not only to reconstruct the notion of the public sphere in light of actually existing democracies but also to point to continued possibilities for public deliberation in contemporary society.

In light of the continually diminished possibilities for a well-functioning public sphere, public deliberation in the service of critical assessment of public interests has found some life in counterpublic spheres. The problem here, however, lies in the possibilities for these counterpublics to influence policy formation and political decision-making processes. For these publics to be viable forces in society, they must not remain enclaves of deliberation but must seek some relation to the state and other publics.

REFIGURING PUBLIC DELIBERATION

Taking account of plurality, which rhetorical treatments of public spheres seek to accommodate, helps make sense of contemporary conditions of public deliberation. However, it also draws attention to problems in public deliberation that traditional treatments of rhetoric have failed to theorize adequately. The orthodoxy of common ground as a first principle for the solution to common problems, the appeal to shared audience assumptions, and the ideal of consensus as the ultimate outcome of public deliberation are problematized when plurality is taken into consideration as a key condition of public deliberation beyond the local level. As such, both rhetorical and critical theories that hope adequately to address contemporary prospects for public deliberation must contend with these problems.

While these problems are not addressed in exactly the same manner by critical and rhetorical theory, they nevertheless point to common considerations. Highlighting these commonalities allows for understanding of the ways in which rhetorical theory and critical theory meet on issues addressing the prospects for public deliberation in contemporary society. To consider in a meaningful way the possibility of public deliberation in a fragmented but mutually dependent world, issues of trust, competence, and process must be addressed. The problem of common ground requires the possibility for questions of trust to be raised and redeemed in public deliberation. The problem of shared assumptions—or better the absence of such assumptions—requires reconsidering what competence is necessary for making relevant judgments. Finally, the problem of consensus points to the need for commitment to the process of public deliberation over and beyond any particular product.

Conditions of public deliberation problematize the orthodoxy of common ground as a first principle on which a rhetorically constituted solution to common problems could be justified. From antiquity, the rhetorical tradition has advised rhetors to base their arguments on premises that they and their audiences could endorse. Although inter-dependency has always involved relations among partners whose cultural and value systems diverged, they were resolvable by reference to a hierarchical system of beliefs, such as religion, a legal code, or mutual ends. However, since at least the end of World War II, the availability of shared premises on which decisions could be justified has receded. Cultural differences have eclipsed those of class as defining conditions of

mutual dependency. Furthermore, solutions to common problems have been complicated by commitments to identity. Common ground as the basis for efficacious public argument faces serious challenges in these contexts.

Among the most serious of the challenges arising from the absence of common ground is establishing a basis for trust (Seligman, 1997). Historically shared systems of beliefs and values offered some security that participants in deliberation were mutually oriented to common ends. This common ground accentuated the mutual dependency of interlocutors such that the sincerity of participants was not rendered problematic. In practices of local democracy, such as town hall meetings, which were the basis for Dewey's (1927/1954) envisioned "great community," the proximity of individuals who shared a common everyday existence made questions of sincerity less central. Although Dewey was alarmed by the consequences of increased mobility, he regarded the flexibility required of ordinary citizens who belonged to many intersecting groups and who had to continue to share a common physical environment as a model for a revived public at the core of a democratic state. However, as conditions of mutual dependency enlarge to include participants who were distant not only physically but also in core principles, trust and sincerity become significant problems for public deliberation. The commonsense perspective that sees all public officials as untrustworthy[5]—and the derogatory way in which the adjective *political* is used to call into question the sincerity of even everyday citizens who participate in deliberations about local issues—points to just how serious the question of trust has become for contemporary democracy.

Habermas (1976) acknowledges this absence of trust as "the" realm of strategic action. It is in strategic action that the validity claim to truthfulness is suspended. Although this may be necessary at certain times, as a general state of public discourse the absence of trust renders obsolete the question of sincerity such that it is no longer even granted status as a valid question. Any agreement is suspect because sound judgment is impossible. Are interlocutors sincerely engaging in an effort toward mutual understanding? Or are they simply feigning communicative action in an effort to win favor for their position? Any hope for the revitalization of a public sphere would require raising questions of sincerity and the necessity of their redemption through future action as well as systems of accountability (see Hauser & Benoit-Barne, 2002). On the other hand, the problem of trust and its relationship to a viable democracy and public deliberation can be overcome, as is illustrated in South Africa's Truth and Reconciliation hearings following the dismantling of apartheid, as Erik Doxtader (2000, 2001; Doxtader & Villa-Vicencio, 2004) has demonstrated.

Conditions of fragmentation and mutual dependency problematize the orthodoxy of building arguments on audience assumptions. Rhetoric's traditional centering of enthymematic argument assumes common meanings that will focus public deliberation on means to common ends. However, different aspirations for the resolution of common problems present serious challenges to a means-ends logic. Here, critical theory and rhetoric converge in ways that make them compatible, even if somewhat different in their approach to the problem, by grounding public deliberation in the participants' common reference world or lifeworld.

Habermas (1987) offers his reconstruction of universal pragmatics to explain the invariant structures of communicative action but also recognizes the dependence of this process on particular situational contexts that constitute the lifeworld. The lifeworld marks "the horizon within which communicative actions are 'always already' moving." It is that shared social world that acts as "a background

of mutual intelligibility" (p. 119), without which communication itself could not occur.

On this point, critical theory and rhetorical theory have complementary perspectives even though their emphases differ. In theory, Habermas (1987) holds, everyday communicative action renews and develops a shared background consensus that stands as the resource for mutual understanding, social action, and identity formation. This background consensus pertains to those interpretations of situations, problems, and reasons that are taken for granted among participants in interaction. The lifeworld helps explain the communicative basis of a shared social reality.

When issues of validity go unthematized, this background consensus remains intact. However, by raising validity claims, specific taken-for-granted aspects of the lifeworld are made available for reflection. To be sure, this happens more frequently in a world marked by difference and fragmentation. However, these encounters specifically allow for the possibility of a reflective redefinition not only of social problems but also of a shared social world. Maintaining a communicative orientation rather than resorting to covert strategic action or breaking off communication altogether offers the possibility of a rational reconstruction of otherwise untheorized aspects of a shared lifeworld.

This political practice of negotiating a background understanding that spans differences is no less problematic for a rhetorical perspective toward public deliberation. Fragmentation introduces the complication of political actors having divergent ends, which problematizes rhetoric's means-ends logic—a logic that rests on a shared understanding of what constitutes social goals. The lack of common ends decenters arguments that rely on premises rooted in shared values and beliefs; it transforms the central rhetorical problem of public deliberation from (1) inventing instrumental appeals to realize common ends to (2) inventing appeals that can reinterpret and constitute a shared lifeworld. This is an inventional and interpretive problem.

The realities of a lifeworld are not scientific facts but practices. Desires that give impulse to engage in deliberation are bound to culture and identity; each has a language that influences interpretations of experience. When problematic situations are defined by differences of identity rather than shared social realities, engaged groups must constitute what counts as public deliberation. This is no easy task. Contemporary conditions of deliberation are seldom dialogic and more often multilogic. Consequently, intersubjective meaning, which constitutes the prevailing conditions of deliberation, exists at the level of praxis. It is at this level, where actions follow symbolic exchanges, that salient rhetorical meaning emerges. That is, public deliberation depends on an intersubjective praxis that invents rhetorically salient meanings on which common understanding relies.

Public deliberation must remain open to inventive possibilities. Even when there appear to be irreconcilable differences, public deliberation holds promise for accentuating relevant mutual dependencies among those who are contesting for ownership of a public problem and offers the opportunity to create common meanings that underwrite common understanding. Genuine public deliberation is first and foremost procedural. Engaging in bilateral exchange (Johnstone, 1982) enables the invention of not only common meanings with respect to action and interaction in the future but also common reference worlds of mutual accountability. These inventions, in turn, must themselves be accountable to the conditions of mutual dependency and respectful of difference as valid considerations—even when disagreements get rowdy. These inventions must insist on and protect the rights of individuals and groups to be recognized as subjects (Touraine, 1997). Members of a community may hold diametrically opposed

commitments, and consensus may be beyond hope. Yet, at the same time, norms of accountability that allow agreement on the terms of engagement must be followed. Though deliberators may abhor each others' views, they may agree to refrain from acts that will tear the fabric of their community, for example, or disrupt friendships among their children. When they do, they affirm that deliberation, at heart, is the process of continuing to find a rational basis for forging agreements. Public deliberation that embodies openness to inventive possibilities in its encounters with difference requires communicative and rhetorical competence. The need to find a basis for forging agreements that have mutual rationality speaks to the issue of competence in that it requires a reformulation of the terms by which participants can make judgments on relevant arguments. Pluralism makes problematic appeals to common systems of beliefs and values. Public deliberation in a pluralistic society has to reconsider alternatives to arrive at common understandings. Both critical theory and rhetoric turn to a notion of competence to address this issue. Furthermore, both democratize competence by locating it within the processes of everyday communication. Both view competence as a possibility of everyday practice and not as the attribute of an elite and educated class. Still, the ability to use this capacity requires structural and performative elements. These undergird the relevance of communicative competence to questions of judgment, which always bear on the development of a shared social reality.

Habermas's (1987) theory of communicative action is grounded on a notion of communicative competence, which is necessary for any possibility of using language with communicative intent. Communicative competence, for Habermas, is not a specialized skill that one must acquire. Rather, this competence is acquired by virtue of learning a language. To engage in communication, one must have mastered not only the linguistic rules of a language but also the intersubjective expectations of role behavior. This includes the possibility of propositionally differentiating between a world of shared objects, of private feelings and impressions, and of intersubjective norms. Additionally, communicative competence also requires the mutual recognition of subjects and the ability to conduct oneself reciprocally toward another's expectations (Habermas, 1970). This means that by virtue of learning a language, individuals are already capable of identifying moments of understanding and what it means to come to an understanding with another, as well as recognition of communicative failure. In this sense, communicative competence means mastery of the ideal speech situation.

Unlike strategic or purposive-rational action, mastery of the ideal speech situation, which is the basis of competent communication, articulates expectations that participants engaging in communicative action already anticipate prior to any communicative situation. The possibility of being questioned and of questioning, as well as the responsibility of offering intersubjectively acceptable arguments, defines the performative potential of mutual understanding. This potential translates into the mutual exchange of arguments and reasons that have the capacity to forge understanding.

While the performative aspect of communicative competence stands as an anticipation of the ideal speech situation, this situation is still unrealizable without social structures that provide a space for its utilization. Habermas's (1974) work on the public sphere illuminates the structural necessities required for its functioning. The critical ideals that defined the bourgeois public sphere, however imperfectly realized, articulated the possibility of a form of public deliberation in which the force of the better argument could be actualized. Furthermore, as an intermediary between civil society and the state, the public sphere allowed for a discursive realm freed from the immediacy of the intimate but also capable of informing public policy. It is only in this kind of discourse made possible by certain structural possibilities in society that communicative competence could be fully realized.

Rhetorical competence, like the mutual exchange of arguments and reasons, requires a capacity to advance and defend ideas. Competence to advocate, refute, and rebut refutations is a fundamental skill on which meaningful public deliberation depends. Going beyond assertions of wants to the reasons why these claims have validity tames the threat of difference. Advocating and defending views to an audience that does not necessarily share one's starting points or one's goals and aspirations denies the option of insisting on the rightness of one's own norms. Rhetorical competence requires a capacity to translate arguments from one perspective into frameworks that make different assumptions. At the same time, public deliberation requires skill at listening so that real differences can be more clearly detected and apparent differences can be resolved. Reasoned agreements with partners who do not share the same assumptions rest on each understanding how the other regards the problem that led them to engage in public deliberation. They must seek to experience the other side's arguments, to engage in representative and reflective thinking (Arendt, 1968/1977) in order to understand the world of the other side(s) from its (their) perspective(s). The need for representative and reflective thinking also highlights the centrality of tolerance for a reasonable pluralism (Cohen, 1997) that does not disqualify individuals and groups from the deliberative process based on markers of difference. Tolerance for reasonable pluralism often leads to focusing public arguments on agreements about future actions rather than on mutually acceptable justifications for why deliberating partners will collaborate.

The focus on competence as the performative possibility of rational debate and argument differs for critical theory and rhetoric regarding the commitment to mutually acceptable justifications for deliberation or agreement on future action. Despite this difference, however, these competencies reflect a commitment to process over product for both critical theory and rhetoric. The very act of public deliberation is a process of political learning. Participating in genuine public deliberation offers the possibility of grasping not only the range of difference but also the mediating grounds of similarity that make civic community and collaborative relations possible. Civic community does not require that citizens think alike, or even that they subscribe to views that underwrite consensus. Consensus, in fact, is not to be expected when issues inflame partisan biases and alternative historicities (Taylor, 1971; Touraine, 1981). At the same time, public deliberation is undermined by the insistence that its primary purpose is strong expression of different interests and narrow fulfillment of partisan interests. Without gainsaying the importance of partisan arguments, civic community requires citizens capable of participating in the deliberative interactions of civic conversation and who trust this conversation to prove consequential for policies eventually enacted in response to public problems.

Conditions of fragmentation and mutual dependency problematize the orthodoxy of consensus on the rationale for action as the goal of public deliberation. Public deliberation presupposes a well-functioning public sphere as a space of appearance for social actors whose interests are at stake in a public problem. A viable public sphere may include institutional sites where deliberation occurs and require institutional guarantees for its emergent opinion to have traction on public policies. However, a public sphere is defined not by its place but rather by its discursive activity of open deliberation in which communication is a self-regulating process of opinion formation. Its dominant characteristic is the procedural status of the discursive means to forge public understanding. Public deliberation requires the structural characteristics of a well-functioning public sphere: inclusion of all relevant perspectives, which affords individuals and groups the right to speak and be heard; availability of relevant information to all participants in public deliberation, which requires open dissemination of information and arguments to those in its discursive arenas; and rights to refute and rebut opposing arguments. At the same time, critical theory and rhetoric have different perspectives on the role of consensus in the deliberative process as it occurs within the milieu of interdependent partners who have common or intersecting problems but whose identities, interests, and ends are divergent.

The recognition of fragmentation and mutual dependency suggests a commitment to the *process* of deliberation that supersedes a commitment to its end result. Ideally, a commitment to the process should result in an equal commitment to the product of public deliberation to the extent that a shared definition of the situation and common reasons and justifications allow for the development of consensus. However, in an increasingly fragmented society, this result stands much more as a counterfactual than an empirical reality. Different cultural values and aspirations require qualifying the ideal of consensus on justification with one that reflects tolerance for these differences. The need always to recognize the fallibility of any agreement requires self-regulation for overcoming difference. Public deliberation as a rhetorical performance of democracy and communicative action emphasizes *processes* of public deliberation as the hope for ensuring democratic outcomes. Both critical theory and rhetoric agree that a commitment to processes of deliberation over any particular outcome helps define and defend democratic possibilities.

For Habermas (1987), consensus is not simply the outcome of a process of deliberation. Rather, it is part of the fundamental understanding of what it means to use language communicatively. The distinction between communicative and strategic action marks a difference in orientation from communication to control (McLuskie, 1993). In social inter-action in which one takes an orientation to control, one is already precluding the possibility for rational deliberation in which subjects are given room for both the autonomous questioning of claims as well as the responsibility for their discursive justification. This disallows the rational functioning of communication in which an orientation toward understanding is given room to help reshape a shared social world.

An orientation to mutual understanding assumes that, in principle, interlocutors can arrive at an agreement about anything. When deliberators engage seriously in an attempt to understand one another and to be understood, they do so assuming they could and in fact can agree. Habermas (1987) regards failure to engage this presupposition as already a denial of the possibility for communicative action. This failure to entertain the possibility of agreement necessarily suggests an attempt to control the situation, to bring about already determined ends, and to disallow the possibility of inventive descriptions or interpretations of the problem at hand. Given this, the commit-ment to consensus is not simply a choice among others for social coordination; it is the very possibility for communicative action and a democratic orientation to the other.

While this stands as an ideal, it nonetheless helps make sense of the possibility of distinguishing between democratic interaction and other forms of social action. Habermas (1987) acknowledges that communicative action is counterfactual; it cannot always be expected to be the way social interaction takes place. While communicative action is the preferred method, and the only route to social action that ensures a rational outcome preserving the autonomy and freedom of the involved participants, in everyday situations strategic action is often necessary for actualizing results. When "commonality cannot be presupposed, the actors have to draw upon the means of strategic action . . . so

as to bring about a common definition of the situation or to negotiate one directly" (p. 121). Habermas qualifies this by suggesting that even in this use of strategic action an orientation toward mutual understanding is necessary. Without this orientation, the alternative is simple means-ends rationality, which values success rather than democratic interaction among participants.

The commitments expressed in Habermas's assertion of consensus as the normative goal for communicative action express the conditions of possibility for a rhetorical understanding of meaningful public deliberation.[6] Certainly there are circumstances when communities come together to deliberate over what is best for their locality. For these deliberations to overcome differences, especially when they are profound, framing of issues in ways that allow the various perspectives to view their engagement in terms of commitment to a shared goal focuses their considerations on the efficacy of means justified by shared beliefs and values. However, as with impasses resulting from identity politics or legislative assemblies dominated by the ideology of the majority, the basic conditions are absent for the emergence of consensus justified by common beliefs and commitments. Rather than consensus, where individuals and groups come to agreement based on shared values and beliefs, public deliberation takes on a new cast. On the one hand, public opinion may emerge from the engaged public's perceptions of the better arguments insofar as they satisfy desired outcomes that may have quite different justifications. Here, emphasis on mutual dependency matters less than the coalescing of different views to form a majority. On the other hand, deliberation may focus on interdependency, in which continued relations of mutuality are essential for goal satisfaction and a commitment to compromise and cooperation to invent new realities of relationship and praxis (Buckley, 1970; McKeon, 1957).

In either event, there must be a commitment to process over product, to deliberation as not only meaningful but also essential for resolving differences on grounds that have mutual validity. Asymmetries of power may result in asymmetries of goal satisfaction, and the various interdependent partners likely will find the outcome of deliberation to be materially suboptimal. But commitment to the deliberative process will allow relations to continue and possibly produce greater mutual understanding as well as bonds of trust that are essential to sustaining a common reference world.

Rhetoric's commitment to process over product recognizes that the terms of engagement for public deliberation reflect ongoing political learning about differences as well as similarities. Public deliberation decenters public eloquence to include discourse within manifestations of public spheres across society's reticulate fabric (Hauser, 1999). It embraces vernacular exchange among ordinary citizens in the multiple venues of factory floors, classrooms, and letters to the editor; public displays of sympathy and affiliation; and digitally mediated interactions on blogs, in chat rooms, and through other new media. It requires interaction between vernacular and official voices in town hall discussions, public debates, op-eds, and the like. These venues dialogize difference and engender trust through performances of public deliberation rationalized against the backdrop of an overarching aspiration for consensus on building a commonwealth of and through coordinated social action.

CONCLUSIONS

This chapter has sought a rapprochement between rhetoric and critical theory in an effort to conceptualize possibilities for public deliberation in contemporary society. In a way, this rapprochement is not only a theoretical investigation but also a practice in the spirit of deliberation itself. The encounter between critical theory and rhetoric can be drawn in such a way that the differences seem unbridgeable. To be certain, these two perspectives stem from different traditions that emphasize different concerns and values. However, it is in their shared commitment to public discourse and possibilities for the democratic creation of society that these differences become a bridge for conversation rather than a means for its suppression.

A shared commitment to public deliberation means that both critical theory and rhetoric must face the issues present in contemporary society that stand as challenges to realizing the possibility of public deliberation. Fragmentation and mutual dependency characterize the plural world(s) in which public deliberation now takes place. As such, traditional ways of conceptualizing public discourse are insufficient, and new paths must be considered. This chapter considers such directions. When brought together, critical theory and rhetoric converge in ways that offer important suggestions for the possibility of public deliberation in a world of fragmentation and mutual dependency.

First, the issue of trust and the need to find ways of building it through systems of accountability becomes a central concern in a world in which "community" can no longer be counted on as the defining center of public deliberation. Without trust in one another to engage sincerely in attempts at resolving problems that mutually affect us, processes of deliberation will remain hollow and inconsequential. Second, those interested in public deliberation as a means for the democratic creation of society must recognize the importance of communicative and rhetorical competence as the capacity for everyday citizens to come to judgment on relevant issues. When shared assumptions and premises no longer guide the means by which arguments are determined, other means for critical assessment are necessary. This suggests not only that participants must be able to engage performatively in forms of communication that encourage the capacity for competent judgment but also that social structures must be created and maintained where participants can be free to do so. Finally, the rapprochement between critical theory and rhetoric draws attention to the need to focus attention on the process of public deliberation rather than on particular outcomes. The fragmentation that makes public deliberation difficult in the first place colors the outcomes as well. There is no guarantee that the final decision will always be acceptable to all. However, commitment to the process ensures that, regardless of any particular outcome, participants will continue to orient to one another in a way that keeps open the possibility for revision and change.

Habermas (1987) is primarily concerned with the possibility of mutual understanding made possible through communicative action. Rhetoric, on the other hand, is oriented toward problem solving (McKeon, 1957); rhetoric's concern lies in the realm of action more than justification. Offered as extremes, these perspectives seem to occupy completely different spaces—with Habermas living in the ideal world of theory and rhetoric in the practical world of actually existing democracy. Yet these perspectives can inform one another as well: Rhetoric's concern with the functioning of existing democracies pushes conceptualizations of public deliberation to take seriously the realities that participants face in contemporary society, including the possible need for strategic action and compromise. Habermas (1987) urges rhetorical treatments of public deliberation to be continually alert to the normative dimensions of communicative interaction that mark distinctions between democratic orientations and those of control, especially in contexts of divergent cultural and ideological commitments.

Neither rhetoric nor critical theory is able to redeem decision-making processes where valences of power and the reign of elites discount public deliberation. On the other hand, when public issues engage citizen awareness at a fundamental level and policy decisions require overt legitimation—social security, minimum wage, universal health care, and climate change are recent examples—the prospects improve for public deliberation to make headway against the hegemony of elites. In such cases, public deliberation that exemplifies the traits of trust, communicative and rhetorical competence, and commitment to process over product provides opportunities for redemocratizing policy formation by modeling citizen participation.

NOTES

1. For a discussion of how these commitments explicitly guided deliberation among citizens opposed to the totalitarian Polish state during the 1970s, see Schell's (1985) introduction to Adam Michnik's prison writings.

2. We use the singular "public" and "public sphere" to refer to the principle of each, unless otherwise indicated as a specific public or public sphere.

3. The publicity principle holds that there are reasons to doubt that representatives, on average, are wiser or more committed to the common good than the ordinary citizen. Luban (1996) explains as follows:

The empirical validity of the publicity principle turns not on whether the Many are ignorant or wrong-headed, but on whether their leaders are less ignorant or less wrong-headed. No doubt the Wise are few; and the leaders are few; but it hardly follows that the leaders are wise. Before we reject the publicity principle because the leaders know best, we must have reason to believe that the leaders know better. And to find that out, we must look carefully at the variety of mechanisms by which decision-making elites are actually selected. If actual selection mechanisms choose randomly between the Many and the Wise, or affirmatively disfavor the Wise, then the foolishness of the many is irrelevant: the Few in official positions have no reason to suppose that their policy brainstorms are any less foolish. (p. 193)

4. We are mindful of distinctions drawn between subaltern and counterpublic spheres. For purposes of this discussion, we are fusing them under the concept of the counterpublic sphere since this distinction is not critical to our argument.

5. A 2006 *Washington Post: ABC News poll* reported that respondents to the question "Would you rate the level of ethics and honesty of members of Congress as excellent, good, not so good, or poor?" gave them a low grade, with 71% answering "not so good" or "poor" (q. 33). However, when asked, "Would you rate the level of ethics and honesty of your own representative to the U.S. House of Representatives in Congress as excellent, good, not so good or poor?" 69% gave their representative a rating of "excellent" or "good" (q. 34). This difference mirrors answers to earlier questions (11 and 12) that asked whether respondents approved/disapproved of how the U.S. Congress and their own representatives were performing, with 67% disapproving of Congress's performance while 62% approved of their own representatives. These data suggest that the farther removed a representative is from a local district and local issues, considerations such as bad behavior (e.g., Rep. Foley's indecent e-mails to high school students who worked in Congress), ideological wrangling vis-à-vis representing personal values, perceived lack of interest in personal needs, and so forth reinforce an impression that Congress acts to advance special interests and the representatives' personal gain over those of the average citizen. Congress as a whole cannot be held accountable, but citizens' own representatives can.

6. We recognize that there are situations in which power asymmetries—such as those that exist in authoritarian states, where citizens are ignored or excluded from the official public sphere as administratively irrelevant—may render a search for consensus neither possible nor desirable (see Michnik, 1985).

REFERENCES

Arendt, H. (1977). *Between past and future: Eight exercises in political thought* (Enl. ed.). Baltimore: Penguin Books. (Original work published in 1968)

Asen, R. (2004). A discourse theory of citizenship. *Quarterly Journal of Speech, 90,* 189–211.

Asen, R., & Brouwer, D. (Eds.). (2001). *Counterpublics and the state.* Albany: State University of New York Press.

Aune, J. (1994). *Marxism and rhetoric.* Boulder, CO: Westview Press.

Benhabib, S. (1992). Models of public space: Hannah Arendt, the liberal tradition, and Jürgen Habermas. In C. Calhoun (Ed.), *Habermas and the public sphere* (pp. 73–98). Cambridge, MA: MIT Press.

Bohman, J. (2000). Public deliberation: Pluralism, complexity, and democracy. Cambridge, MA: MIT Press.

Brown, S. (2000, September 21). New bribe scandal hits Argentina's "murky" senate. *CNN.* Retrieved February 28, 2007, from http://archives.cnn.com/2000/WORLD/americas/09/21/argentina.bribes.reut

Buckley, M. J. (1970). Philosophic method in Cicero. *Journal of the History of Philosophy, 8,* 143–154.

Cohen, J. (1997). Procedure and substance in deliberative democracy. In J. Bohman & W. Rehig (Eds.), *Deliberative democracy: Essays on reason and politics* (pp. 408–437). Cambridge, MA: MIT Press.

Cohen, J. (1999). Trust, voluntary association, and workable democracy: The contemporary American discourse of civil society. In M. E. Warren (Ed.), *Democracy and trust* (pp. 208–248). New York: Cambridge University Press.

Cohen, J. L., & Arato, A. (1992). *Civil society and political theory.* Cambridge, MA: MIT Press.

Deutsche, W. (2002, December 17). *Iraqi report could prove damaging to Germany.* Retrieved January 28, 2007, from www.dw-world.de/dw/article/0,,716376,00.html

Dewey, J. (1910). *How we think.* Boston: D. C. Heath.

Dewey, J. (1954). *The public and its problems.* Chicago: Swallow Press. (Original work published 1927)

Doxtader, E. W. (2000). Characters in the middle of public life: Consensus, dissent, and ethos. *Philosophy and Rhetoric, 33,* 336–369.

Doxtader, E. W. (2001). Making rhetorical history in a time of transition: The occasion, constitution, and representation of South African reconciliation. *Rhetoric and Public Affairs, 4,* 223–260.

Doxtader, E. W., & Villa-Vicencio, C. (2004). To repair the irreparable: Reparation and reconstruction in South Africa. Cape Town: David Philip.

Eberly, R. A. (2002). Rhetoric and the anti-logos doughball: Teaching deliberating bodies the practices of participatory democracy. *Rhetoric & Public Affairs, 5,* 287–300.

Esfandiari, P. (2006). Hajib [*sic*] hijacked: Politics of the veil. *BlogHer.* Retrieved February 28, 2007, from http://blogher.org/node/11971

Farrell, T. B. (1993). *Norms of rhetorical culture.* New Haven, CT: Yale University Press.

Fishkin, J. S. (1995). *The voice of the people: Public opinion and democracy.* New Haven, CT: Yale University Press.

Fraser, N. (1989). Unruly practices: Power, discourse, and gender in contemporary social theory. Minneapolis: University of Minnesota Press.

Fraser, N. (1990). Rethinking the public sphere: A contribution to the critique of actually existing democracy. *Social Text, 25/26,* 56–80.

Gamson, W. A. (1992). *Talking politics.* New York: Cambridge University Press.

Gastil, J. (1992). Undemocratic discourse: A review of theory and research on political discourse. *Discourse & Society, 3,* 469–500.

Gastil, J., & Dillard, J. P. (1999). The aims, methods, and effects of deliberative civic education through the National Issues Forums. *Communication Education, 48,* 179–192.

Goodnight, G. T. (1982). The personal, technical, and public spheres of argument: A speculative inquiry into the art of public deliberation. *Journal of the American Forensic Association, 18,* 214–227.

Gusfield, J. R. (1981). *The culture of public problem: Drinking-driving and the symbolic order.* Chicago: University of Chicago Press.

Habermas, J. (1970). Towards a theory of communicative competence. *Inquiry, 13,* 360–375.

Habermas, J. (1974). The public sphere. *New German Critique, 3,* 49–55.

Habermas, J. (1976). *Communication and the evolution of society* (T. McCarthy, Trans.). Boston: Beacon Press.

Habermas, J. (1987). *The theory of communicative action* (2 vols; T. McCarthy, Trans.). Boston: Beacon Press.

Habermas, J. (1989). *The structural transformation of the public sphere: An inquiry into a category of bourgeois society* (T. Burger, Trans., with F. Lawrence). Cambridge, MA: MIT Press. (Original work published 1968)

Hardin, R. (1999). Do we want trust in government? In M. E. Warren (Ed.), *Democracy and trust* (pp. 22–41). New York: Cambridge University Press.

Hauser, G. A. (1987). Features of the public sphere. *Critical Studies in Mass Communication, 4,* 437–441.

Hauser, G. A. (1999). *Vernacular voices: The rhetoric of publics and public spheres.* Columbia: University of South Carolina Press.

Hauser, G. A., & Benoit-Barne, C. (2002). Reflections on rhetoric, deliberative democracy, civil society, and trust. *Rhetoric & Public Affairs, 5,* 261–275.

Hicks, D. (2002). The promise(s) of deliberative democracy. *Rhetoric and Public Affairs, 5,* 223–260.

Ivie, R. L. (2002). Rhetorical deliberation and democratic politics in the here and now. *Rhetoric & Public Affairs, 5,* 277–285.

Johnstone, H. (1982). Bilaterality in argument. In J. R. Cox & C. A. Willard (Eds.), *Advances in argumentation theory and research* (pp. 95–102). Carbondale: Southern Illinois University Press.

Keith, W. (2002). Democratic revival and the promise of cyberspace: Lessons from the forum movement. *Rhetoric & Public Affairs, 5,* 311–326.

Lasch, C. (1978). The culture of narcissism: American life in an age of diminishing expectations. New York: W. W. Norton.

Lippmann, W. (1965). *Public opinion.* New York: Free Press. (Original work published 1922)

Luban, D. (1996). The principle of publicity. In R. E. Goodin (Eds.), *The theory of institutional design* (pp. 154–198). Cambridge, UK: Cambridge University Press.

Mansbridge, J. (1993). Self-interest and political transformation. In G. E. Marcus & R. L. Hanson (Eds.), *Reconsidering the democratic public* (pp. 91–109). University Park: Pennsylvania State University Press.

McKeon, R. (1957). Communication, truth, and society. *Ethics, 67,* 89–99.

McLuskie, E. (1993). Against transformation of communication into control: Continuities in the critical theory of Jürgen Habermas. *Journal of Communication, 43*(1), 154–165.

Michnik, A. (1985). *Letters from prison and other essays* (M. Latynski, Trans.). Berkeley: University of California Press.

Mills, C. W. (1956). *The power elite.* New York: Oxford University Press.

Mouffe, C. (1993). *The return of the political.* New York: Verso.

National Public Radio. (2005, August 15). Private, no-bid contractors doing Iraq jobs. *News & Notes.* Retrieved February 28, 2007, from www.npr.org/templates/story/story.php?storyI d=4800207

Noelle-Neumann, E. (1993). *The spiral of silence: Public opinion, our social skin.* Chicago: University of Chicago Press.

Ono, K., & Sloop, J. (1995). The critique of vernacular rhetoric. Communication *Monographs, 62,* 19–46.

Page B. I., & Shapiro, R. (1993). The rational public and democracy. In G. E. Marcus & R. L. Hanson (Eds.), *Reconsidering the democratic public* (pp. 35–64). University Park: Pennsylvania State University Press.

Piven, F. F., & Cloward, R. A. (1988). *Why Americans don't vote.* New York: Pantheon Books.

Putnam, R. D. (with Leonardi, R., & Nanetti, R. Y.). (1993). *Making democracy work: Civic*

traditions in modern Italy. Princeton, NJ: Princeton University Press.

Robbins, B. (Ed.). (1993). *The phantom public sphere.* Minneapolis: University of Minnesota Press.

Schell, J. (1985). Introduction. In A. Michnik (Ed.), *Letters from prison and other essays* (M. Latynski, Trans.; pp. xvii–xlii). Berkeley: University of California Press.

Seligman, A. B. (1997). *The problem of trust.* Princeton, NJ: Princeton University Press.

Taylor, C. (1971). Interpretation and the sciences of man. *Review of Metaphysics, 25,* 3–51.

Touraine, A. (1981). *The voice and the eye: An analysis of social movements* (A. Duff, Trans.). New York: Cambridge University Press.

Touraine, A. (1997). *What is democracy?* (D. Macey, Trans.). Boulder, CO: Westview Press.

Tracy, K., & Dimock, A. (2004). Meetings: Discursive sites for building and fragmenting community. In P. J. Kabfleich (Ed.), *Communication yearbook* (Vol. 28, pp. 127–165). Mahwah, NJ: Lawrence J. Erlbaum.

Tracy, K., & Standerfer, C. (2003). Selecting a school superintendent: Interactional sensitivities in the deliberative process. In L. R. Frey (Ed.), *Group communication in context: Studies of bona fide groups* (2nd ed., pp. 109–134). Mahwah, NJ: Lawrence Erlbaum.

Washington Post: ABC News poll. (2006, October 9). *The Washington Post.* Retrieved February 28, 2007, from www.washingtonpost.com/ wp-srv/politics/polls/postpoll_100906.htm

Young, I. M. (1997). Intersecting voices: Dilemmas of gender, political philosophy, and policy. Princeton, NJ: Princeton University Press.

26

Digital Rhetoric and Public Discourse

LAURA J. GURAK

SMILJANA ANTONIJEVIC

We have now reached a time when the phrase "digital rhetoric" is redundant. Even public speech—for millennia the mode that separated public address from all the other fixed, more stable forms of writing and visual imagery—is no longer beyond the realm of the digital. Speeches are recorded; sliced and diced and mixed; uploaded to Facebook and YouTube; streamed in chunks or snippets on news sites and blogs; and bounced on waves via broadcasts or satellites. Conversations, too, can rarely escape being digitized: Cell phones capture our winged words; hidden Webcams increasingly record our every public move.

What are the implications of these innovations for the study and teaching of persuasive discourse—the art of rhetoric—in our ubiquitous digital age? How can we blend the teaching of the ancient canons with the new practices and principles that are staring at

us from the screens surrounding our everyday lives? Given that digital technology is, at the start of the 21st century, as common as any kitchen appliance, now is the time for rhetorical scholars—and especially public discourse scholars—to assert interdisciplinary rhetoric as an appropriate and useful way to understand the persuasive functions of digital communication.

DIGITAL COMMUNICATION: FROM CMC TO INTERNET STUDIES

Depending on how far back one wants to look, the roots of the contemporary field of study that David Silver (2004) wittily terms "Internet/cyberculture/digital culture/newmedia/ fill-in-the-blank studies" can be traced to the late, mid, or even early 20th century. Steve Jones (2005) suggests that the development of Internet studies should be recognized as part of a multidisciplinary scientific endeavor in the analyses of media and communication throughout the past 100 years. Jones notes,

> This project has been ongoing primarily since the early part of the 20th century and has engaged scholars in numerous fields, including scientific, social scientific, and humanistic, who have sought to understand the shifts in media and communication since the advent of electronic communication. (p. 234)

The origin of the field can similarly be sought in the work of a "dark hero of the Information Age," Norbert Wiener (compare Conway & Siegelman, 2004), and/or related to technological developments such as Defense Advanced Research Projects Administration (DARPANet) and the World Wide Web. Still, from Wiener's "smart machines" to contemporary humanlike agents, from DARPANet to YouTube, certain aspects of the ever-evolving digital technologies have remained sufficiently stable so that we can recognize them in every new digital form. For instance, the observations that Hiltz and Turoff made in their groundbreaking 1978 book *The Network Nation* still ring true and provide a basis for understanding the functions of digital communication. Among many other points, Hiltz and Turoff noted the use of pen names and anonymity online (p. 94), as well as the insertion of gestures and other forms of spoken discourse, which they called "written vocalization" (p. 90), and which would later come to be considered an example of "secondary orality" based on the work of Walter Ong (2002).

Another important publication was the now classic 1984 paper by Kiesler, Siegel, and McGuire in *American Psychologist,* which coined the phrase "computer-mediated communication" (CMC). This paper brought the social and language-based features of CMC to the attention of many scholars and put a concise face on the major linguistic and social-psychological features of digital communication. At the same time, Sherry Turkle's book *The Second Self,* published in 1984, and her *Life on the Screen,* which appeared in 1995, raised the important question of how we should consider the concept of identity in a digital age. In these texts, Turkle asked the reader to rethink her or his postmodern world, where one person can have many screen identities.

Throughout the mid- to late 1990s, the concept of community emerged as an important topic of study in CMC. Howard Rheingold's (1993) book *The Virtual Community* painted an optimistic picture of online groups, while Steven Doheny-Farina argued in *The Wired Neighborhood* (1996) that virtual communities might come at the expense of knowing one's physical neighbors. The study *Persuasion and Privacy in Cyberspace* (Gurak, 1997) used rhetorical analysis and case study methods to document the first two social actions of communities in cyberspace. Nancy Baym's (1999) work on Usenet news and soap opera fan clubs provided additional research-based evidence for the power of online community.

Two additional subjects emerged as significant research topics in CMC: the relationship of the Internet to democracy and politics (see, e.g., Hacker & van Dijk, 2000; Stromer-Galley, 2000), and the problems and potentials of intellectual property and privacy online. The work of Dan Burk (2005) is illustrative of questions raised by a technology that appears built to challenge copyright but is increasingly being subject to such laws, such as the Digital Millennium Copyright Act, that reinforce copyright. Other issues that have been important to the development of Internet studies include questions about the digital divide (see, e.g., Hawkins & Oblinger, 2005); cross-cultural issues and online communication (see, e.g., Ess & Sudweeks, 2005); and the use of the Internet for increasingly mainstream issues such as medicine (see, e.g., Gurak & Hudson, 2006) and education (see, e.g., Benbunan-Fich & Hiltz, 1999).

As the World Wide Web became "the 'new normal' in the American way of life" (Pew,

2005), and as Web sites came to cover everything from news to college courses to recipes, it has become evident that online communication cannot be perceived and analyzed as *one thing* and one thing only. Therefore, one of the most fundamental shifts in CMC studies involved a move away from trying to generalize about *all* online behavior to focusing on contextualized analyses of specific segments and cases of digital communication. One can trace this shift, roughly, to the late 1990s. The establishment of the Association of Internet Researchers (www.aoir.org) in 2000 provided the professional visibility necessary to make clear the shift from CMC studies to Internet studies.

This shift has not only helped correct early studies that overgeneralized about specific CMC practices, but has also opened the door to new areas of inquiry that focus narrowly, but not exclusively, on particular patterns of communicative practice. For instance, early work such as the seminal paper by Kiesler et al. (1984) speaks in general terms about the social-psychological behaviors in online communication, noting behaviors such as changes in turn taking and a lack of "computer etiquette." As the Internet and digital communication technologies permeated into the general population, it became more difficult to generalize about users; thus, more recent studies have focused more on specific contexts. For instance, in 1997, Garton, Haythornwaite, and Wellman advocated a more focused approach when studying online social networks, noting that it is important "to examine what specific kinds of exchanges define the [specific] groups." Today, Internet research is highly case based, and relatively few attempts are made at generalizing all user behavior in all online settings.

A second major shift has been the realization that any one discipline—whether rhetoric, communication, psychology, political science, law, human-computer interaction—is insufficient to address the challenging questions raised by the ubiquitous use of the Internet. Various Internet research activities characterized by diverse disciplinary, theoretical, and methodological approaches have started to merge into a recognizable line of work, and the field of CMC studies has gradually evolved into the field of Internet studies. The Annual Association of Internet Researchers Conference provides an excellent illustration of this broad disciplinary range. Still, within such a novel and multidisciplinary effort, the potential impact of established disciplines—most prominently, in this context, rhetoric—remains promising for addressing important questions of the digital age. To achieve this goal, however, disciplines need to reconceptualize some of their key terms within the context of the digital domain.

DIGITAL RHETORIC: A NEW CANON, KEY TERMS, AND REVISED APPEALS

Digital rhetoric must assert a new canon, drawing on prior rhetorical constructs but recognizing also that our current era is much changed from the 2,000-year-old tradition that constitutes the field of Western rhetoric. We must consider what Kathleen Welch (1999) calls "screen rhetorics" not as some interesting sidebar to the field of public discourse and public address studies but rather as the center of what rhetorical theorists and critics should attend to. What follows is a description of the key concepts in digital rhetoric.[1]

Speed. The primary feature of digital discourse is speed. The Internet allows text, photographs, sound, video, artwork, and the synthesis of various multimedia objects to be circulated around the world with previously unimaginable speed. One keystroke distributes information almost instantaneously. When combined with the other features discussed below, speed becomes the predominant feature in the digital rhetorical canon. Indeed, the speed of this communicative medium has had a dramatic effect on the content and practice of rhetoric. People spend far less time inventing arguments and far more time distributing short bits of information, as rapidly as possible, to an extremely wide audience. Further implications include a tendency toward a blended (oral and written) register (looking and sounding much like Ong's secondary orality), casualness in tone and style, and both a redundant and repetitive quality. An excellent example of this last element is evident in e-mail messages that contain the whole or excerpted parts of previous messages. Speed subsumes the traditional canon of delivery; as Welch (1990) has noted, "electronic technology has made the fifth canon of delivery (medium) take on the urgency of simultaneous communication" (p. 26).

Reach. Along with speed, reach is a powerful feature of digital discourse. Extending on this concept from Kaufer and Carley's (1994) work on the history of printed texts, reach in a digital environment means that thousands or even millions of people can receive the same information. Combined with speed, the spiderlike reach of nonhierarchical distribution that is the key architectural feature of the Internet means that instead of spending time carefully arranging the structure and logical flow of the message or argument, many rhetors in the digital age focus on sheer quantity, achieving the widest reach possible as quickly as possible. The need to persuade specific audiences becomes far less important than the ability to reach many audiences. Reach inspires characteristics such as globalness (the Internet easily allows border crossings), a diminished ability to gatekeep information, and the ability to create wide networks of online communities, spanning distance and time. This topic will be addressed again later under the heading of social networking.

Anonymity. It is simple in a digital environment to create multiple identities and to speak and write with a powerful sense of anonymity. Hiding behind a digital screen means that the speaker/author/creator of information may make claims or invoke a style that he or she might otherwise avoid. This "lack of social cues" model (Sproull & Kiesler, 1986; cited widely by others) means that some linguistic and rhetorical norms, such as politeness, are set aside for more aggressive, abrupt styles. Often called "flaming" in the CMC literature, this behavior has been linked to various attributes of online technology, from the lack of social cues to gender (Herring, 1993) to the speedy nature of online communication (Gurak, 2001). Anonymity also evokes other communicative behaviors of interest to rhetoricians, including the ability to mask one's gender, nationality, economic status, or other social features. We can no longer take for granted that the speaker/rhetor is who she or he says she or he is. Finally, anonymity may result in a somewhat contingent sense of what is (and is not) an appropriate, polite, professional, or otherwise suitable tone for a particular communicative moment.

Interactivity. Unlike television, which until recently has been unidirectional and noninteractive, the Internet and its associated technologies were created with interactivity as a central component. This feature not only allows for but also often demands an active two-way exchange, ending forever the Aristotelian, managed approach to keeping audiences in line with the persuasive intent. Internet users are expected to interact with information, even to transform texts, visuals, photographs, videos, until the final product no longer resembles the original. While this feature may not pertain to many highly commercial, controlled Web sites, it is nevertheless a key feature of digital communication that present and future rhetorical scholars must consider.

What, then, are the appeals, the ways in which rhetorical messages capture and hold an audience? Here, we find some concepts from the classical tradition that have stood the test of time. *Ethos* is still a powerful explanatory and heuristic device in the digital age. In the case of

Lotus MarketPlace, Gurak (1997) describes how the credibility and character of a typed, nonvisual, rather simple e-mail message became the hub for the first online protest. In digital rhetoric, it is the ethos of the message in its entirety—not just the author but the power of the visuals, the sound and style of the text, the speed with which it was delivered, the people to which it was sent, the connection it may have to others who have credible online reputations—that is the key element. Online ethos is often created in community sites such as blogs or discussion boards. Here, we might evoke Halloran's (1982) definition of an "image of people gathering together in a public place, sharing experiences and ideas" (p. 61). This feature is particularly noticeable in online sites that provide users with the ability to connect to others sharing a medical condition or seeking health or medical information.

This is not to say that the traditional appeals of logos and pathos are absent in cyberspace. Digital information, since it covers almost any category, can be easily considered logos based (e.g., a legal brief that is posted on a Web site). However, for the majority of online information—everyday information—ethos is simply the most powerful and important of the classical appeals, the one that holds up best and is most explanatory of the bulk of digital rhetoric. Even in the case of the medical field, which one might assume to be dominated by scientific, logically based appeals, audiences often select online medical information based on how the site looks, what other people have to say about it, and whether the information seems credible to the user (Gurak & Hudson, 2006).

Kairos. While not normally considered one of the traditional rhetorical canons, opportune moments in digital space are in fact one of the psychological characteristics that can be used, intentionally or inadvertently, to create interest and action around a topic. Digitally, opportune moments come and go very quickly. The speedy, broad, and specialized reach of digital communication, combined with the way users interact with and create their own forums and messages, provides a powerful means to mobilize and organize issues. From the two cases documented by Gurak (1997, 2001) to many others, we daily and readily create and react to these opportune moments in digital space. Even a simple e-mail message, sent out at work about a controversial topic, can inspire several days' worth of continued conversation, argument, lobbying, and organized response. Digital exigencies may arise where the same topics might not have otherwise inspired such response, in part due to the features of speed, reach, and interactivity described earlier.

Collaboration and community. Another powerful appeal in digital rhetoric is collaboration and community. From the early cases of Lotus MarketPlace and the Clipper chip to blogs, wikis, YouTube, and other social networking sites, users judge ideas and arguments as credible and make great leaps across the Internet if they are part of a social network. There is a new public sphere for rhetoricians to be concerned about (see, e.g., Warnick, 2001), and it exists across time zones, countries, and cultures. While some (Doheny-Farina, 1996) have expressed concern over how digital communication tends to isolate people into narrow bandwidth interest groups, it is also true that the public sphere has been enriched and widened by citizen access to the kind of interaction and information that only the Internet makes possible.

DIGITAL DELIVERY: A NEW CHALLENGE IN DIGITAL RHETORIC

In addition to revised appeals and key terms, yet another challenge emerges in the study and teaching of persuasive public discourse in digital age. It is the challenge of digital delivery. Delivery (Latin: *actio*), described by Cicero as "eloquence of the body" and by Quintilian as the "language of gesture," was the fifth canon in traditional rhetoric, and it has been part of the rhetorical framework for more than 2,000 years. Aristotle viewed this canon as a rather simple matter involving volume, change of pitch, and rhythm (1404a), while Roman rhetoricians paid more attention to *actio* (Graf, 1991). Ancient theorizing focused on the role of delivery in regard to ethos and pathos as well as on cultural differences in nonverbal expression and the possibility of this type of communication overcoming the language barriers by serving as a "universal" (see, e.g., Corbeill, 2004; Fögen, 2001; Fredal, 2001). In the 18th century, teachers and theorists of oratory expanded on the fifth canon, using the scientific reasoning of their time to theorize about the importance of delivery for an effective and believable speech. Teachers of elocution, especially Sheridan, believed that "tones and gestures" were the devices on which "all that is pleasurable, of affecting in elocution, chiefly depend" (Sheridan, 1796/1991, p. 129). Today, digital technologies provide new rhetorical forums, where speaker and audience come together without regard for physical distance. Still, delivery does not disappear in cyberspace but rather changes form, developing into digital delivery. Therefore, digital technologies force a reexamination of rhetoric's fifth canon, especially in relation to public discourse. Consider, for example, the number of political candidates who reach voters by using real-time video (such as town hall forums) streamed over the Internet, and three-dimensional (3D) virtual environments such as Second Life. For instance, all major contenders in France's 2007 presidential race, as well as some 2008 U.S. presidential candidates (e.g., Barack Obama and John Edwards) established campaign headquarters in Second Life. These synchronous, visual forms of digital public discourse will continue to grow in popularity, as video, sound, and 3D virtual environments become more accessible to users. Therefore, a shift from earlier, text-based forms of CMC to contemporary, multimodal forms of digital communication warrants further discussion,

especially with regard to digital delivery as the form of nonverbal expression and persuasion in online settings.

In text-based CMC, nonverbal expression is limited to written descriptions, the use of emoticons, and/or the use of discursive strategies. This lack of nonverbal cues has been an important area of investigation since the early days of CMC research. For instance, in *The Network Nation*, Hiltz and Turoff (1978) assert that for novice users the experience of CMC could be a kind of culture shock "in which all of the very complex 'rules' for combining the various kinds of communications channels . . . do not work, because the nonverbal channels are missing" (p. 81). In further research, two main lines of thought have been developed with regard to nonverbal communication in text-based CMC. One is the "cues-filtered-out" approach, which posits that the lack of nonverbal cues in CMC results in reduced social presence and in narrowing of communicative abilities of online interactants. For example, in the analysis of CMC at the workplace, Kiesler et al. (1984) argue that "computer communication might weaken social influence by the absence of such nonverbal behavior as taking the head seat, speaking loudly, staring, touching, and gesturing" (p. 1125). Contrary to this, the social information processing theory argues that "[online] communicators deploy whatever communication system they have at their disposal" so that "when most nonverbal cues are unavailable . . . users adapt their language, style, and other cues to such purposes" (Walther, Loh, & Granka, 2005, p. 37).

Again, the emergence of multiuser 3D virtual environments such as Second Life, There, and Active Worlds has brought a significant departure from text-based CMC to online communication that includes both textual and nonverbal discourse. Multiuser 3D virtual environments are desktop-based, nonimmersive virtual reality settings that enable synchronous online interaction. In those environments, a user's presence is achieved through his or her graphic representation, that is, an avatar. An avatar has several important functions, such as to indicate a user's presence in the environment, to convey his or her online identity, and to specify one's physical location in a given virtual area (Benford, Bowers, Fahlen, Greenhalgh, & Snowdon, 1995). As a person's virtual body, an avatar also enables a user's physical movement and nonverbal expression online. Using the cursor keys or some other device, a person moves through a 3D environment placing his or her avatar in position to other avatars and objects in the setting. An avatar can walk, run, fly, wave, shift the direction of gaze, point toward someone or something; in other words, an avatar can render user's motion online. In this way, communicative and persuasive capacities of nonverbal discourse become available to online interactants. In multiuser 3D virtual environments, users can also communicate through the use of predefined nonverbal acts. However, the user neither deliberately performs nor individually encodes those predefined acts. Instead, the computer system generates and models the user's movement. For example, if the user makes a pause in his or her textual exchange with other users, the system detects this keyboard inactivity, and automatically sets the user's virtual body to a spectator posture. It is the system—not the user—that generates a change in the user's body stance, and it is the system that selects a spectator posture as a nonverbal indicator of the user's inactivity. Very similar to predefined nonverbal acts are blended nonverbal cues, which can also be identified in multiuser 3D virtual environments (see, e.g., Antonijevic, 2008). Blended cues refer to nonverbal acts that are user selected and system encoded. For example, the user can select to take a seat; but once he or she has done it, the system will model the user's sitting posture. If the user selects to sit on an animated object, the system will generate his or her avatar's predefined nonverbal behavior.

For instance, if the user sits on a "flirt bench," the system will animate his or her avatar to perform forward lean, head nods, and similar nonverbal acts precoded as nonverbal cues associated with the concept of flirting.

These predefined nonverbal features of 3D virtual environments are strikingly similar to the hand and body movements so carefully mapped out by Gilbert Austin (1806/1966) in *Chironomia*. In fact, the parallel use of a mechanical system of nonverbal behavior by both computer scientists and elocutionists deserves some attention here. Austin, following on the work of other elocutionists of the time, is best known for his *Chironomia*, a treatise that attempted both an overview of the history of the fifth canon up until his time and a notation system of delivery that speakers could follow. The purpose of the *Chironomia*, he states, is to "contribute [his] share of labour towards the completion of the rules for the better study and acquisition of rhetorical delivery" (p. x). To indicate or invoke a particular emotion in a speech, for example, one would employ one of Austin's nonverbal acts. This act, if employed properly and in combination with other features of proper rhetorical delivery (such as language use), would have the desired impact on the audience. Similarly, to create a desired interaction in a virtual environment, a virtual reality participant must also employ a specific set of avatar body movements. In both 18th-century rhetoric and early-21st-century virtual reality, prescribed nonverbal acts are intended to invoke common meaning with a given audience (live or virtual). In 18th-century rhetoric, however, the speaker was supposed to master *Chironomia* and its rules of proper rhetorical delivery, disciplining his body to perform appropriate nonverbal acts that would bring about a positive response on the part of the audience. In our age, digital technology, with its database of predefined nonverbal acts, takes on the role of *Chironomia*, transforming this 18th-century rhetorical apparatus into a system of delivery that speakers *must* follow.

For instance, Second Life users communicating in Virtual Capitol Hill have no obligation, but neither have they the choice, to master the appropriate manners of standing or sitting in this virtual replica of the House of Representatives. The Second Life system "disciplines" users' virtual bodies to perform the nonverbal acts built into the computer script as elements of proper delivery, thus transforming those digital rhetors into perfect elocutionists Austin only could have dreamed of creating.

In this way, digital technologies act as a catalyst whereby humans reexperience what were thought of, prior to the technology, as constant, fixed aspects of living. Digital technologies challenge rhetorical theorists, linguists, psychologists, and others to explore the ways in which nonverbal discourse, inherent to human communication, is manifesting itself in virtual environments. If we are to understand how we might communicate in the coming decades, we must review the current movement from oral delivery to what can be characterized as electronic elocution. Considering a rapidly developing use of 3D virtual environments for educational, commercial, political, religious, and other purposes, digital delivery suddenly moves into the theoretical and practical foreground. Multiuser 3D virtual environments provide new rhetorical forums where speaker and audience come together without regard for physical distance; but, in those environments, speaker and audience still come together with regard to the communicative aspects of virtual bodies and, hence, with an increased regard to digital delivery. Thomas Sheridan, Gilbert Austin, and the other elocutionists of the 18th century would be pleased to see this return to a focus on elocution, although they might be puzzled to see its new virtual form.

In addition to 3D virtual environments, video production and mass dissemination via YouTube and other sites provides an entirely new, open, and inexpensive way for people to create powerful video messages that are accessible to millions. Public discourse is no longer controlled by television stations; even video that is originally distributed over television channels shows up on YouTube. Regular citizens, possessing nothing more than a cheap video camera (or just a cell phone or computer cam) can have a significant impact on an election, a public debate, a business controversy, or any other form of public issue. The power of the visual, combined with the speed and reach of the Internet, highlight the importance of digital delivery in this way.

Given how pervasive digital technologies have become in public discourse, we must add digital delivery to the list of rhetorical features that need to be considered as we teach and theorize digital public discourse.

CONCLUSION: RHETORIC, TECHNOLOGY, AND PUBLIC DISCOURSE STUDIES

What is digital rhetoric? It is everything we consider rhetorical in nature. Text, sounds, visuals, nonverbal cues, material, and virtual spaces—all these have blurred together, and all are digitized. To study, practice, and teach the art and science of persuasive communication, we must consider a new canon. The speedy nature of digital discourse, in combination with wide reach, anonymous rhetors, and a nonpassive, highly interactive "audience" are the four key features. Ethos, kairos, and community/collaboration are at the heart of the digital rhetorical system. Delivery takes on different forms in digital settings. The next question to ask is about the future of rhetoric, technology, and public discourse studies. Given the pervasiveness of digital communication technologies, and given that this trend will only increase for the foreseeable future, what is a useful agenda for further research, teaching, and scholarship?

To begin, we must continue to move away from the study of rhetoric qua rhetoric.

Instead, rhetorical constructs and concepts must be considered and put to use in the context of the people, politics, cases, and settings that surround us. Public discourse studies have been and continue to be highly contextual, and digital technologies are now at the heart of public discourse. Public discourse studies should therefore draw on the literature and research in CMC and Internet studies and lead the way in helping us understand how these new rhetorical concepts offer both heuristic and explanatory power in how we understand public discourse. The power of publics to engage in deliberation through blogs, e-mail, and Web postings is unprecedented. Public discourse studies, as a field, is perfectly poised to engage this area. Such studies are most useful when conducted as case-based research, both single case studies and cross-case studies and analysis.

Every case study of public discourse has a potential digital component. Furthermore, some studies should, because of their specific details, be based entirely on analysis of digital communication. Until recently, the "digital component" of a case study would be set aside as a separate section of an article or separate chapter of the dissertation or book. Yet in many cases, if the scholar expanded the rhetorical dynamics of the case study's digital component to help explain the rest of the case, or if the focus were entirely on the digital component, it would yield a far more rich, contemporary, and important conclusion. Why? Because we have 100 years or more of literature of public address and discourse, but we have little research on public discourse in digital settings. What we do have is 25 years worth of literature in Internet studies that could be used effectively for rhetorical analyses of digital settings.

Take, for example, the tobacco trials in the State of Minnesota, which concluded in 1998. According to the Hennepin County Public Library's Web site (1998), there are more than 39,000 documents associated with this case,

totaling 26 million pages. Traditionally, a scholar of public discourse might pose a research question about the legal language in these documents and how these ideas were translated or understood in public settings (trials, news media, and so on). Yet even back in 1998, the Internet must have played a role here. Is there another avenue to study, one that would inform us about the role of digital technologies, at that time but with implications for today, in this most significant public debate? Indeed, there is a wealth of Web sites that one finds simply by running a Google search on "tobacco trials." Many of these sites make it hard to determine if they are neutral sources of information or if they are advocacy sites. For instance, the first site to appear in our search was "tobacco.org." This site simply labels itself "tobacco news and information." There are hundreds of others just like this, and we know that this is the way most Americans do research and look for information. What kind of public discourse, debate, and rhetorical devices are employed in this arena? Is the discussion ongoing? What is the role of speed and reach, for example, in these sites? Do sites with similar points of view all link to each other, and what are the implications for public debate? After the Minnesota trials, other states followed, and what we see today is a wealth of blogs and other Web sites about, for instance, the Florida tobacco trials. Some of these sites take excerpts from the legal documents and interpret these for the public.

It is easy to agree with Rosa Eberly (2001) when she states that "communication without rhetoric . . . cannot generate the discursive conditions for any notion of public discourse or public address to proceed in practice" (p. 533). We would add that rhetoric without digital communication at its core cannot provide adequate explanatory or heuristic tools in the 21st century and that public discourse studies is precisely the area to lead the way, by acknowledging that digital discourse is at the heart of all public address and by welcoming the new rhetorical canons to mix it up with the ancient ones. Such work will have immediate relevance for our students and for the long-term success of learning about how various publics understand and engage with the key issues of our day.

NOTE

1. Many of these concepts are described in more detail in Gurak (2001).

REFERENCES

Antonijevic, S. (2008). From text to gesture online: A microethnographic analysis of nonverbal communication in the Second Life virtual environment. *Information, Communication, and Society, 11*(2), 221–238.

Austin, G. (1966). *Chironomia, or a treatise on rhetorical delivery.* Carbondale: Southern Illinois University Press. (Original work published 1806)

Baym, N. (1999). *Tune in, log on: Soaps, fandom, and online community.* Thousand Oaks, CA: Sage.

Benbunan-Fich, R., & Hiltz, S. R. (1999, March). Educational applications of CMCS: Solving case studies through asynchronous learning networks [Electronic version]. *Journal of Computer Mediated Communication, 4.3.* Retrieved June 4, 2008, from http://jcmc.indiana.edu/v014/issue3/benbunan-fich.html

Benford, S., Bowers, J., Fahlen, L. E, Greenhalgh, C., & Snowdon, D. (1995). User embodiment in collaborative virtual environments. In *Proceedings of the ACM conference on Human Factors in Computing Systems* (CHI'95) (pp. 242–249). New York: ACM Press.

Burk, D. L. (2005). Expression, selection, abstraction: Copyright's golden braid. *Syracuse Law Review, 55,* 593. Retrieved June 4, 2008, from http://ssrn.com/abstract=699541

Conway, F., & Siegelman, J. (2004). *Dark hero of the information age: In search of Norbert Wiener the father of cybernetics.* New York: Basic Books.

Corbeill, A. (2004). *Nature embodied: Gesture in ancient Rome.* Princeton, NJ: Princeton University Press.

Doheny-Farina, S. (1996). *The wired neighborhood.* New Haven, CT: Yale University Press.

Eberly, R. A. (2001). Public making and public doing: Rhetoric's productive and practical powers. *Rhetoric & Public Affairs, 4*(3), 532–534.

Ess, C., & Sudweeks, F. (Eds.). (2005). Special theme: Culture and computer-mediated communication [Electronic version]. *Journal of Computer-Mediated Communication, 11*(1). Retrieved June 4, 2008, from http://jcmc.indiana.edu/v0111/issue1/ess.html

Fögen, T. (2001) Ancient theorizing on nonverbal communication. In R. M. Brend, A. K. Melby, &. A. R. Lommel (Eds.), *LACUS Forum XXVII: Speaking and Comprehending* (pp. 203–216). Fullerton, CA: Linguistic Association of Canada and the United States.

Fredal, J. (2001). The language of delivery and the presentation of character: Rhetorical action in Demosthenes' Against Meidias. *Rhetoric Review, 20*(3/4), 251–267.

Garton, L., Haythornwaite, C., & Wellman, B. (1997, June). Studying online social networks [Electronic version]. *Journal of Computer-Mediated Communication 3.1.* Retrieved June 8, 2008, from http://jcmc.indiana.edu/v013/issue1/garton.html

Graf, F. (1991). Gestures and conventions: The gestures of Roman actors and orators. In J. Bremer & H. Roodenberg (Eds.), *Cultural history of gesture from antiquity to the present day.* Cambridge, UK: Blackwell/Polity. Retrieved March 26, 2008, from http://theol.eldoc.ub.rug.nl/FILES/root/BremmerJN/1997/586/titlecon.pdf

Gurak, L. J. (1997). *Persuasion and privacy in cyberspace: The online protests over Lotus market place and the clipper chip.* New Haven, CT: Yale University Press.

Gurak, L. J. (2001). *Cyberliteracy: Navigating the Internet with awareness.* New Haven, CT: Yale University Press.

Gurak, L. J., & Hudson, B. (2006). E-health: Beyond Internet searches. In M. Murero, & R. Rice (Eds.), *The Internet and health care* (pp. 29–48). Mahwah, NJ: Erlbaum.

Hacker, K. L., & van Dijk, J. (Eds.). (2000). *Digital democracy: Issues of theory and practice.* London: Sage.

Halloran, S. M. (1982). Aristotle's concept of ethos, or if not his somebody else's. *Rhetoric Review, 1*(1), 58–63.

Hawkins, B. L., & Oblinger, D. G. (2005, July/August). The myth about the digital divide [Electronic version]. *Educause Review, 41.4.* Retrieved December 12, 2007, from http://connect.educause.edu/Library/EDUCAUSE+Review/TheMythabouttheDigitalDiv/40646

Hennepin County Public Library. (1998). *Fugitive fact file: Minnesota tobacco trial documents.* Retrieved July 17, 2007, from www.hennepin.lib.mn.us/pub/search/fff/FullDisplay.cfm?ID=1143

Herring, S. (1993). Gender and democracy in computer-mediated communication [Electronic version]. *Electronic Journal of Communication, 3*(2). Retrieved December 12, 2007, from http://ella.slis.indiana.edu/~herring/ejc.txt

Hiltz, S. R., & Turoff, M. (1978). *The network nation: Human communication via computer.* Reading, MA: Addison-Wesley.

Jones, S. (2005). Fizz in the field: Toward a basis for an emergent Internet studies. *The Information Society, 21*(4), 233–237.

Kaufer, D., & Carley, K. (1994). Some concepts and axioms about communication: Proximate and at a distance. *Written Communication, 11*(1), 8–42.

Kiesler, S., Siegel, J., & McGuire, T. W. (1984). Social and psychological aspects of computer-mediated communication. *American Psychologist, 39*(10), 1123–1134.

Ong, W. (2002). *Orality and literacy: The technologizing of the word* (2nd ed.). London: Routledge.

Pew Internet & American Life Project. (2005). *Internet: The mainstreaming of online life.*

January 25, 2005. Retrieved June 27, 2007, from www.pewinternet.org/pdfs/Internet_Status_2005.pdf

Rheingold, H. (1993). *The virtual community: Homesteading on the electronic frontier.* New York: Harper Collins.

Sheridan, T. (1991). *A course of lectures on elocution.* Delmar, New York: Scholars' Facsimiles & Reprints. (Original work published 1796)

Silver, D. (2004). Internet/cyberculture/digital culture/new media/fill-in-the-blank-studies. *New Media & Society, 6*(1), 55–64.

Sproull, L., & Kiesler, S. (1986). Reducing social context cues: Electronic mail in organizational communication. *Management Science, 32*(11), 1492–1512.

Stromer-Galley, J. (2000). Online interaction and why candidates avoid it. *Journal of Communication, 50*(4), 111–132.

Turkle, S. (1984). *The second self: Computers and the human spirit.* New York: Simon & Schuster.

Turkle, S. (1995). *Life on the screen: Identity in the age of the Internet.* New York: Simon & Schuster.

Walther, J. B., Loh, T., & Granka, L. (2005). Let me count the ways: The interchange of verbal and nonverbal cues in computer-mediated and face-to-face affinity. *Journal of Language and Social Psychology, 24,* 36–65.

Warnick, B. (2001). *Critical literacy in a digital era.* Mahwah, NJ: Erlbaum Press.

Welch, K. (1990). Electrifying classical rhetoric: Ancient media, modern technology, and contemporary composition. *Journal of Advanced Composition, 10*(1), 22–38.

Welch, K. (1999). *Electric rhetoric: Classical rhetoric, oralism, and a new literacy.* Cambridge, MA: MIT Press.

27

Arts of Address in Revolutionary America

STEPHEN HOWARD BROWNE

The renaissance of studies in the American Revolution continues apace. Historians of the subject have effected important shifts in methods of analysis; expanded their scope to include trans-Atlantic, racial, and market dynamics; and revisited old issues with new and productive questions. Popular biographies of the founders are featured routinely on national bestseller lists, while television and film air dramatic versions of the personalities and events that shaped the era. Inevitably, such enthusiasm has generated mixed results, controversies, and no small amount of skepticism; at the same time, no one would now doubt that this surge of interest has been anything but salutary. Now would seem an ideal time, therefore, to consider, again, ways in which students of rhetoric might offer their distinctive insights to the growing body of work on the nation's founding.

I hope to suggest in this chapter that we, in fact, have established already a firm foundation of scholarship on the subject, and that we are in a unique position to push forward our understanding of the role of rhetoric in revolutionary America. To this end, I propose that we revitalize our interest in rhetorical form, defined here as persistently available modes of address that function in a distinctive though not exclusive manner. More specifically, we will examine how three such forms—the sermon, the public letter, and the visual icon—may be said to bear the weight of revolutionary ambitions. The sermon is taken here to exemplify the task of oral critique; the public letter, the work of community formation; and the visual icon, the need to install the drama of resistance into public memory. By attending to the constitutive function of these forms, we arrive at a deeper understanding of what might be called the rhetorical texture of the revolutionary era.

THE SERMON AS REVOLUTIONARY FORM

The role of religion and of religious discourse in the events leading up to armed rebellion has never been judged as anything except crucial. Indeed, from well before the actual outbreak of hostilities, critics and supporters of the clergy alike understood that religious sentiment was intractably part of the source, meaning, and consequence of revolutionary action. Then as now, of course, opinion varied widely as to the nature of this relationship: Peter Oliver raged against the "black regiment" for inciting revolt and for having otherwise "distinguished their-selves [*sic*] in encouraging Seditions and Riots" (Adair & Schutz, 1967, p. 43). The Rev. Nathaniel Niles, on the other hand, confidently assured his parishioners that such was "the kindness of God that, humanly speaking, it is in the power of America to save both herself and Great Britain" (Stout, 1986, p. 297). Scholars and other commentators continue to debate the relevance and details of religious activity during the period, and no effort is made here to referee competing interpretations. The most we can assume, in any case, is that, in the words of Robert Ferguson (1997), "there is no chance of understanding the early American scene, either of the colonies or the early Republic, without assessing the inter-play between religion and politics as a source of liberty" (p. 45).

One key source for exploring this interplay is of course the sermon, and for this historians and critics of rhetoric are singularly well equipped. A substantial body of work has attended to the origins and development of the form, although rather more as a product of earlier Puritan culture than to its role in the revolutionary age. It is not too much to claim, indeed, that sermons provide us with the single most pervasive, detailed, and richest body of

texts from the migrations of the 17th century to the advent of nationhood. In sheer number and scope, in oral performance and published tract, from every colony and parish, sermons dwarf all other textual media of the age. It is scarcely a reach, then, to suspect that they have a great deal to teach us about the rhetorical texture of revolutionary America.[1]

For modern readers, the sermon may well seem an unlikely source for revolutionary sentiment. They were, after all, vehicles of explicitly religious thought, summoned from the moral imaginations of divines, composed within tightly bounded logics of scripture and creed, and addressed to audiences habituated to the form. Because I wish to stress their revolutionary character, it will be necessary to review briefly the rhetorical origins and development of the sermon as a discursive type. We may then be in a position to observe its contributions to late-18th-century political events. The point here is to first establish the case that sermons in fact carried, at least potentially, highly charged political energies, and to prepare us for a closer reading of a characteristic text of the revolutionary era.

The early modern sermon was a product of the Reformation. As such, it announced to English and Continental congregations that the new church was reclaiming an old commitment to the Word. Over and above popish adoration of the sacraments, the sermon was designed to reset the coordinates whereby a people and their God were to behold one another. The effort to place preachers before the devout is itself part of the struggle and achievement of Protestant hegemony; in the end, so successful was the effort that, in the words of one caustic observer, "preaching had almost justled [*sic*] out of the church all other parts of public divine worship; the people relishing nothing besides a sermon, as being withal the cheapest way of serving God" (Hill, 2003, p. 43). The interminable twists and turns that preaching took in the early Reformed church cannot detain us here; but it is worth stressing that from the outset, the practice of rendering sermons was inescapably caught up in the political give and take of the age. Indeed, the very style and structure of the form were themselves conspicuous: Ramistic in design, they eschewed the alleged excesses of the old order and professed a manner of speaking consistent with scriptural injunctions to be clear, simple, and directly accessible to the gathered.[2]

Small wonder, then, that those who chose to pursue their godly commonwealth on these distant shores should take with them a deep and abiding commitment to the sermon. Again, it is useful to remind ourselves that the early European immigrants conceived of no distinction between civic and religious modes of collective life; such a disjunction as is familiar to us would literally have been meaningless in the context of their shared reality. As Perry Miller, Sacvan Bercovitch, and Andrew Delbanco have demonstrated, the sermon under these conditions reached its most impressive heights in the form of the jeremiad. Here the rhetorical function is explicit: to call the people together into a collective acknowledgment of sins committed, to remind them of their covenanted obligation to make good on God's promise, and to strengthen resolve for the arduous task ahead. Such a practice was bound to fuse the secular and the sacred, with implications for future generations that were to be profound. We need not, as some scholars have essayed, to draw a neat causal line between Puritan and Revolutionary cultures to recognize the persistence of the sermonic form and function. Bercovitch (1978) states the case precisely:

> Despite their allegiance to theocracy, the emigrant Puritans were part of the movement toward the future. Their rhetoric and vision facilitated the process of colonial growth. And in sustaining that rhetoric and vision, the later-day Jeremiahs effectually forged a powerful vehicle of middle-class ideology . . . a "civil religion" for a people

chosen to spring fully formed into the modern world. (p. 28)[3]

Taken together, more sermons were published than any other genre of letters before the modern era. The selection of any particular subgenre is thus bound to be, if not arbitrary, at least a reminder to be cautious when making generalizations. Still, we have an especially illustrative type of sermonizing during the era that will go far toward explaining our subject. Election Day sermons represented an enduring tradition of address, in which a local divine was expected to reflect on the duties and dangers attendant on the election of the governor and other officials. The practice was widespread and dates back to the early years of the colonial occupation. Read singly or en masse, the sermons are impressive not so much for their reflections, but for their rather pointed message. None are notably deferential; indeed the tone and content can seem surprisingly bold. This is especially the case as the cultural climate heats up in the 1760s and after. The Election Day sermons are accordingly a rich, even indispensable resource for understanding the texture of revolutionary rhetoric; as Ferguson (1997) has observed, the "belief required for independence literally is born in these sermons" (p. 66).

Several characteristics may be noted by way of general overview. In the main, Election Day sermons were devoted to recalling, Jeremiah-like, the people back to their covenanted ideals. We are a blessed race, congregants were reminded, a chosen people, bound by word and deed to act in accord with their sacred and singular duties. Typically, the speaker would invoke one or several biblical leaders as models of proper governance, often Moses or David. This much a Bernard or a Pownall might expect as an annual ritual, a relatively benign summons to just dealing. But as tensions mounted between colonies and mother country, the sermons took on a decidedly more aggressive air and frequently included admonitions against aping such allegedly British habits of luxury, pride, and imperiousness. More pointedly, the sermons began to ratchet up the pressure on the elected, who were now subjected to sometimes-prolix lectures on the terms of their leadership. Thus, John Barnard acknowledged that governors possessed certain prerogatives by virtue of their station; still, he insisted, it is

> the demand of righteousness that these powers and privileges be preserved in their proper channels, without the use of any secret craft or open violence to dam up the current or divert its course another way. That is to say that rulers are to govern according to law. (Stout, 1986, p. 171)

Thus, events colluded in such a way as to render concrete the more general and abstract proscription against unjust rule. And what were once sermons directed at the colonists themselves, now took up explicitly imperial issues at contest. Increasingly, then, the Election Day sermons became direct calls to action against British depredations. Colonists, Isaac Backus thus declared, "have just a right, before God and man, to oppose King, ministry, Lords, and Commons of England, when they violate their rights as Americans, as they have to oppose any foreign enemy" (Sandoz, 1991, p. 330).

We now turn to a specific example to illustrate the critical force of the Election Day sermon. On May 26, 1773, Charles Turner, pastor of the Duxbury flock near Boston, preached such a sermon before Thomas Hutchinson, his council, and members of the House of Representatives (Turner, 1773). The relief of the Dartmouth, Eleanor, and Beaver of their tea into the waters of Massachusetts Bay was still a half year away, but no one could be unmindful of the current political climate. Orators annually dinned into the ears of their fellow Bostonians the "horrid massacre" of March 5, 1770, the governor had recently moved to receive his salary from the Crown, and not long before, testy Rhode

Islanders had torched the Gaspee, a revenue vessel of the Royal Navy. In the event, recalled the dyspeptic Oliver, colonists'

> demands increased, and their Insult on the British Legislature increased with them; they openly disclaimed any Authority, but their own Government. They complained that they had no Representation in the British Parliament, therefore could not be taxed by them, and in the same Breath declared, that they could not be represented there, and disavowed their Inclination to it. (Adair & Schutz, 1967, p. 100)

Within this environment, the Reverend Turner (1773) approached the beleaguered governor and his accompanying train of officials. The sermon that followed was of standard length, about 45 pages as published, and took as its text Romans 13.4: "He is the minister of God to thee for good." In the manner of most 18th-century sermons, the language is fulsome, the allusions wide ranging, and the argument a long variation on a single theme. Turner makes no pretenses to theological novelty, nor does he seek to introduce the striking political insight. Consistent with the genre, rather, he seeks to marshal from scripture and history the common sense of the matter, and this matter has everything to do with the boundaries placed on those in whom power has been entrusted. For all his troubles, many of which but not all were brought on himself, Governor Hutchinson was a very astute student of power, and it would be virtually impossible for him to miss Pastor Turner's message. Indeed, there is nothing coded or oblique about it. Without rehearsing that message in detail, we can nonetheless gain considerable insight into the critical stance of the sermon by noting several of its chief points.

Why, asks Turner, did God make provision for civil leaders such as those seated before him? Not to benefit God—for He has no need of such; not to enslave others, for no one has that right; and certainly not to enrich themselves. "He never designed, mediately or immediately, to appoint rulers over the people, in state or church, so as to debar them from the privilege of choosing their own officers," Turner (1773) notes, "and they, who attempt to deprive the people of such a privilege, oppose themselves equally, to the will of Good, and to the rights of mankind" (p. 7). Hence the meaning and application of the text from Romans: as with the Christian minister, the political leader is raised to eminence so "that the one should do good in religion, the other in civil respects, to the world" (p. 7).

Here Turner invokes a longstanding tradition of commenting on the character of the good ruler native to the genre of election sermons. Since the late 17th century, such performances were ritualized reminders that governors ruled by virtue of God's design and the people's will. And if guidance could be found for the former in scripture, then the former could well be discerned in the body of law and precedent embodied in the colonial constitutions. Neither the people nor the rulers were to abrogate that law without due appeal to the amendment process. In any case, Turner (1773) stresses,

A Constitution being settled by the public consent, the magistrate, awed by that Sovereignty which God has been pleased to invest the people with in the case, ought ever to maintain a sacred respect for such constitution, in every instance of government legislative or executive. (p. 18)

After a decade rocked by political crises ranging from the Stamp Act revolt, the Townshend Act troubles, and the Boston Massacre, such reminders unquestionably took on a political charge well beyond their routine expression. It is thus important to observe a conspicuous tendency in these election sermons toward comment on the behavior and responsibilities of the magistrate. While we note some discussion of the obligation incumbent on the citizens to obey rightful authority, the rhetorical pressure clearly shifts: Increasingly, the language stresses the duty of

a free people to assert *their* rightful authority. The following passage, because it so well captures this key development, is quoted in full:

The people ought to have the end of government, the publick good, as heart, as well as the magistrate; and therefore, to yield all loyal subjection to well regulated government, in opposition to every thing of a factious nature or complexion: and, for the same reason, it is not only their privilege, but it is also their duty, properly to assert their freedom, and take all rational and necessary methods for the publick security and happiness, when constitutional boundaries are broken over, and so their rights are invaded. This affirmation supposes, the people have a right to judge of the conduct of government, and its tendency; and this again supposes them capable of judging in things of such a nature. (Turner, 1773, pp. 28–29)

By the end of the 18th century, Election Day sermons had been largely given over to other rituals of public affirmation. But in the course of events leading to armed rebellion, they served a vital and instructive function: to reassert the terms of proper governance, to recall before elected officials the duties attendant to office and the right—indeed moral responsibility—of the citizenry to judge their performance accordingly. Turner and the many other ministerial figures who stood before their leaders thus played an important role is the process whereby ritual becomes active critique, religion a resource for political engagement, and where, ultimately, revolution discovers its moral rationale.

PUBLIC LETTERS AND THE CONSTRUCTION OF POLITICAL COMMUNITY

From its origins in Western antiquity, the public letter has remained a vital resource for those seeking to give private voice to communal aspirations. Although Plato and other pre-Christian thinkers exploited its literary and philosophical potential, we typically think of the evangelist Paul as the first great practitioner of the genre. His epistles to the Corinthians, Galatians, Romans, Hebrews, and Philippians constitute the single most impressive body of such writing, the influence of which can still be found in our time. Thus, we readily see in Martin Luther King's "Letter from Birmingham Jail," for instance, the basic ordering of the text into the Pauline sequence of salutation, thanksgiving, analysis, exhortation, and pious conclusion. Certain of its elements shift in emphasis and function, of course, as the form is deployed in various contexts, but the public letter has retained a remarkable coherence for more than 2,000 years. It should not come as a great surprise, then, that American colonists discovered in the tradition a rich set of possibilities for effecting their ends; and although it is surprising that the genre has been so little studied in this context, we can quickly identify why resistance to British rule so effectively expressed itself in and through the public letter.[4]

At first glance, the very concept of a "public letter" appears to be an oxymoron. Public discourse takes those forms appropriate to its needs—the oration, or sermon, or broadside; private discourse, likewise, assumes its familiar shapes in correspondence and conversation. But the concept is perforce a conceit, a linguistic device whose precise function it is to collapse these two realms of discourse into each other and, from that collapsing, to exploit the rhetorical potential of both. By its very nature, then, the public letter seeks to have it both ways even as it retains an explicable identity. In its public aspect, the form grants entree into the shared world of politics, social issues, and collective sensibility; in its private aspect, the form invokes and capitalizes on the resources of tone, stance, and style associated with more intimate relationships. When effective—and this much is a matter of considerable artistic complexity—the public letter can be a powerful catalyst for organizing opinion and securing social cohesion. Because it was mobilized in just this way during the revolutionary era, some further elaboration will prove useful.

Who, we might ask, is the "author" of a public letter? The answer must be complicated by several factors. First, to the extent that such texts are conspicuously artful—that is, the product of strategic invention—then we must be mindful not to conflate the flesh-and-bones source with the persona thus created. Public letters work, when they work, because they successfully produce an *image* of the author. Historically, this image has taken any number of forms, contingent on the circumstances that called a given production into being. But if there is at least one constant at work, it is the image of sound judgment at work: reflective but attuned to the world; rational but engaged; possessed of a distinctive voice but not eccentric to the social order; above all, a private citizen acting only because the common good demands it. A second complicating factor consists in the fact that, especially in the 18th century, so many public letters were offered pseudonymously. We will turn to several of these below, but here it is worth noting that this additional conceit serves certain rhetorical purposes as well: clearly, it helps "name" the "author" in specific and strategic ways. "Cato," "Americanus," "Farmer," and numerous other such designations encouraged readers to see not so much the isolated opinions of individuals but classical types, representatives of shared and longstanding sentiment. The author of a public letter, then, was understood to be acting from motives consistent with the demand for civic virtue, expressing himself with republican simplicity, mature judgment, and in ways deeply informed by the best traditions of political thought.[5]

And who, we might also ask, is the "audience" for the public letter? Again, the answer needs to take into account several considerations. Just as the author is a textual production, so too we can think of the intended audience as, in Edwin Black's (1970) phrase, a "second persona" (pp. 109–119), an image of what the author would have his readers become. Here too, the distinctive function of the genre is illustrative, for to be a reader of such a text is clearly not to occupy the same status as one listening to a sermon, or reading a headline from the *Boston Gazette*. Because the public letter plays the private off the public, it necessarily aligns the reader in a particular manner, as if one were either looking over the shoulder of the author while composing or opening a post from a respected but distant friend with issues of mutual concern. There is, in short, a degree of intimacy secured by the form itself, at once authenticated by virtue of its privacy and generalized into a shared reality. This trait is central to the rhetorical function of the public letter during times of crisis, and is nowhere more evident than during the decade preceding war. The oft-remarked puzzle as to how 13 widely dispersed colonies managed to finally come together in mutual resolve finds its answer, in part, by the rhetorical media through which their inhabitants communicated to each other from afar; and the public letter was instrumental to this process.

Late-18th-century epistolary practice proved to be a golden age. Colonists in need of a model needed only to look to the mother country for inspiration; for there, in the traditions of Sir Roger de Coverly, Swift, Pope, and others could be found a rich fictive and polemical storehouse of arguments, appeals, and imagery. In the main, these productions are marked by a conspicuous civility, and thus set themselves off from the more heated exchanges found in press and Parliament. This kind of rhetorical decorum is not to be overlooked: it alerts us to the constructive uses to which political dissent could be put, and suggests something of the community-building functions of the genre. Their aim was to unite, not simply divide; to calm readers in the face of danger and uncertainty; and to insist on a mutual groundwork for solving problems of genuine complexity. Again, the tone is almost

always rational, the style intimate (though seldom informal). The result is a form of collective reassurance, as if the genre were designed specifically to remind each party that the aim was a return to norms momentarily unsettled by exiguous events.[6] The following passage, though not exceptional, captures these qualities perfectly. The loyalist Daniel Leonard, writing as "Massachusettensis" in the *Gazette* and *Boston Post-Boy* in 1774, opens one of his 17 letters to John Adams ("Novanglus") thus:

> I endeavored last week to convince you of our real danger, not to render you desperate, but to induce you to seek immediately some effectual remedy. Our case is not yet remediless, as we have to deal with a nation not less generous and humane, than powerful and brace; just, indeed, but not vindictive. (Jensen, 1978, p. 278)

As for Adams, the stance is equally irenic:

> There may be occasion, to say some very severe things, before I have finished what I propose, in opposition to this writer, but there ought to be no reviling. *Rem ipsam dic, mitte mal loqui*, which may be justly translated, speak out the whole truth boldly, but use no bad language. (Jensen, 1978, pp. 296–297)

No other text from the revolutionary era so well exemplifies this rhetorical decorum as John Dickinson's *Letters From a Farmer In Pennsylvania to the Inhabitants of the British Colonies*. Initially published in the *Pennsylvania Chronicle* in 1767–1768, and afterward by virtually every newspaper in the colonies, the Letters achieved instant fame both in the American colonies and abroad. The 12 letters were composed as a direct attack on the newly passed Townshend Acts; but though pointed, and covering the entire range of colonial grievances, the Letters are notable for their restraint, deliberation, and shared goodwill. No other production, in any case, so captured the colonial imagination until Paine's *Common Sense* almost a decade later. Needless to say, the later text achieved by different means, and to different ends, unity of another kind. "The Farmer," in any case, became the single most influential source of public argument in the late 1760s and early 1770s, and we have much to learn from its collective appeal.[7]

For purposes of economy, we will attend to the first letter only. Here we will find an exquisitely wrought effort to construct a voice, at once authoritative and benign, actuated by events but not overwhelmed by them, decorous but unmistakably critical. If there is a dominant style to which Dickinson recourses, it is pastoral: at some remove from the bumptious scenes of town life; marked by learning and reflection; conspicuously reasonable and motivated only by the public good. Rhetorically, the text works, in large part, by painting a compelling image, not so much of what his fellow colonists and reader actually were, but of what was best expected of them. Hence, the unity of the text's first and second personae: Each sees, as in a mirrored reflection, an ideal visage of the other and of themselves. Disposed into 11 relatively brief paragraphs, the letter can be read as a virtual handbook of classical and republican rhetorical style: The composition is artful yet simple; dignified but accessible to a broad range of literate readers; and informed without being pedantic. Above all, it is a model of republican reasoning, so uniting style and content that the two cannot be meaningfully separated; indeed, the former assists the latter so effectively that to acknowledge the efficacy of the one is to necessarily grant the same to the other. We will not treat in similar detail every paragraph, but the opening lines are so illustrative as to bear close examination.

> I am a Farmer, settled, after a variety of fortunes, near the banks of the river Delaware, in the province of Pennsylvania. I received a liberal education, and have been engaged in the busy scenes of life; but

am now convinced, that a man may be as happy without bustle, as with it. My farm is small; my servants are few, and good; I have a little money at interest; I wish for no more; my employment in my own affairs is easy; and with a contented, grateful mind, undisturbed by worldly hopes or fears, relating to myself, I am completing the number of days allotted to me by divine goodness. (Jensen, 1978, p. 128)

The passage is notable both for its economy and its symbolic resonance. In three sentences, the author has established a widely recognizable presence in the shape of the farmer; invoked an appropriate and appealing scene from which the figure might give voice to his sentiments; and has in effect assured his readers that such a voice is to be heard as intended—that is, as free from self-interest or partisan ambition. In the image of the farmer, Dickinson hits on a construct ideal for his purposes; within the rhetorical culture of the day, it suggested values associated with what we might now label the landed elite. But more pointedly, the "farmer" here organizes a set of appeals to character, place, and time that extends the message well beyond the favored few. He has, it is true, been blessed by life, but not passively or undeservedly. He has had his ups and downs, and survived both; has known both the library and the city street; is now at ease with the modest means and amiable support that occupy his quiet life. The reader might well note what the farmer is not: not on the make, not given to alarm; certainly not an agitator. His message, we may anticipate, is rather to be more avuncular than demanding, the counsel of one who has lived life and lived it well; learned much; and wishes only to secure for others what he has so long enjoyed—the blessings of freedom.

The issue at hand is Parliament's decision to suspend the legislature of New York for refusing to fully comply with the provisions of the Townshend Act. The farmer professes himself surprised that others have not leapt so quickly as they might to the defense of colonial rights. In truth, he notes, the New Yorkers probably should have acquiesced: "But my dislike of their conduct in that instance, has not blinded me so much, that I cannot plainly perceive, that they have been punished in a manner pernicious to American freedom, and justly alarming to all the colonies" (Jensen, 1978, p. 130). The ocular image here is suggestive, underscoring as it does the quality of insight—of judgment—we expect of a person thus situated. The farmer has held his peace until events demanded that he speak; and because of his exemplary status, he may be seen here as acting as he would have others act. The Letter is in this sense a model of sorts, wherein the reader may discern an example and guide to appropriate civic engagement.

The ensuing paragraphs undertake a brief but incisive analysis of the issue. Our farmer subjects Parliament's position to a rigorous application of logic, the tone and style of which is wholly consistent with the ethos of the Letter generally. There are no exclamation marks, no emboldened type; the matter is one to be gauged by reason and mature judgment. The following is typical:

> The matter being this stated, the assembly of New-York either had, or had not, a right to refuse submission to that act. If they had, and I imagine no American will say they had not, then the parliament had no right to compel them to execute it. If they had not that right, they had no right to punish them for not executing it; and therefore no right to suspend their legislation, which is a punishment. (Jensen, 1978, p. 131)

This deft interplay of disjunctive, hypothetical, and universal syllogisms remains arguable at the level of both major and minor premises, to be sure, but rhetorically the effect is convincing to the sympathetic reader. There is no need, in short, for passionate harangues where reason can lay bare the relevant fault lines. It is worth keeping in mind the historical moment in which

this text appears; its rhetorical efficacy is very much a function of its timing, for Dickinson's appeal to reasoned decorum is perfectly suited to that moment. Only several years before his publication, violent and pervasive resistance to the Stamp Act had rocked the colonies. Those outbursts announced in no uncertain terms the extent and pitch of colonial anger, and brought a quick end to the hated measures; at the same time, however, their very intensity stunned a number of leaders otherwise sympathetic to popular resistance. Mass displays and the burning of effigies were one thing; reducing the governor of Massachusetts' house to rubble was quite another. The destruction was, moreover, largely an urban phenomenon, spearheaded by anonymous individuals as effected by combustible mobs. Was this the form political dissent was fated to take?

Dickinson and other moderate leaders certainly hoped not, and thus sought to chart a path to reform that would prove successful but not corrosive of the social order. To this end, the Letter was clearly designed to offer to the people an example of what protest ought to look and sound like. The farmer was adamant on the point. Disappointed that so far two legislatures had recently sat without voicing concern about the New York suspension, he nevertheless insists,

> It may perhaps be asked, what would have been proper for them to do? I am by no means fond of inflammatory measures; I detest them. I should be sorry that anything should be done, which might justly displease our sovereign, or our mother country: But a firm, modest exertion of a free spirit, should never be wanting on public occasions. (Jensen, 1978, p. 132)

We might expect as much from Dickinson, whose very moderation stayed his hand when the time came for signing the declaration of independence. But we ought not to forget that the Letters were in fact enormously popular in their day, and continued to be for years to come. In time, other voices—more strident, less modest—were to be heard and acted on throughout the colonies. But for the moment, when no one was calling for independence and most wanted only to repair a strong fabric merely rent, the farmer spoke to Americans as they wished to be spoken to: as fellow subjects endowed with historical rights, aggrieved but loyal members of the imperial family. The steady tones, the reassuring style, and controlled reason of the Letters projected an image of the colonists—however dispersed geographically—as a people joined by mutual convictions, shared values, and a collective desire for the public good. To be thus addressed is not to be incited to revolution, it is true, but it is to create the conditions under which revolution can be imagined.

THE IMAGE OF REVOLUTION

The two modes of address thus far considered suggest ways in which colonists exploited the resources of language as such. The written word unquestionably provided the readiest and most pervasive instrument for expressing the complex range of principles and emotions underwriting the movement toward war. But this was scarcely the only rhetorical resource available; indeed, a quick survey of the period gives evidence aplenty of a rich and diverse repertoire of symbolic materials. Liberty trees, parades, funerals, flags, music, theater, exhibits, and other forms of expression were routinely employed for the cause, and if they seldom reached the heights of artistic merit, they nonetheless served an important role in giving collective voice to colonial aspirations. Recent historians have come to understand with greater clarity than ever before the centrality of such symbolic forms and rituals to channeling public sentiment; far from being mere epiphenomena to material forces at work, they may be said to have performed resistance every bit as much as the spoken or written word.[8]

Still, a good deal of labor remains. We now know a great deal more about the cultural work of revolutionary America, and rhetorical critics and historians have assisted in this area to genuine effect.[9] One particularly challenging but necessary concern has to do with the visual discourse of the period, specifically painting, and a subject that has received very little in the way of systematic inquiry. Reasons for this lacuna range from scholarly habits to uncertainty about what kind of critical vocabulary is appropriate to the task. Here, we can only approach the subject in an introductory fashion, but it may prove instructive to take up painting, so to speak, and ask what role it played, why it matters, and what the artists themselves had to say through their medium. After providing a brief context, I will turn then to John Trumbull's *The Battle of Bunker's Hill* as a case study in the rhetoric of visual art. Specifically, I wish to suggest in this final section that painting was instrumental to the process of installing the revolution into the public memory of the early republic. That such a process is itself part of the story of the revolution is attested by a growing number of scholars who are attending closely to the cultural work required to keep a new people— a new nation—mindful of its past. Given the iconic status of the revolution in our time, it may seem a given that the events of 1775–1783 would, of course, remain fresh to their immediate heirs. Two levels of analysis indicate that the issue is not so obviously tendered.

First, those who lived through and participated in the revolution were demonstrably anxious that its lessons not be forgotten; indeed they instituted rituals of remembrance precisely because they feared the forces of amnesia: hence the tradition of Fourth of July orations, commencement speeches, and celebrations of Washington's birthday. The question was not so much whether the revolution as such would be forgotten, but whether the principles thought to animate it might dissipate in a climate of unprecedented prosperity, unbridled individualism, and commercial enterprise. Would the demands of civic virtue—the shared willingness to put the public weal above private gain—prove too much to sustain? Would the generation following Washington's lapse into a kind of ideological stupor, forgetting that the war was a beginning, not an end to national greatness? Such questions plagued the early republic, which, for all its boasted claims on the future, was in fact profoundly uncertain as to its prospects.[10]

Second, students of public memory teach us that collective remembrance is vital to the health of all nations, most of all to new ones. So important is it that a people will virtually invent traditions to serve as bulwarks of national identity. In short, a country that can claim no past of its own does not long remain a country. In this sense, the past is never allowed to remain only the past but is ritually and episodically summoned to present and future purposes; we have only to think of the modern calendar and its interminable series of special days for the remembrance of this figure or that event. And because these acts of recollection are public, they are perforce political, and therefore, about power. The past is thus understood as a vast medium for passing on shared values, maintaining convictions, and cultivating an endless progression of new and worthy heirs to the revolutionary tradition. There can be no mistaking the rhetorical character of this process, and we thus find warrant for asking after the relationship between remembrance and the visual arts.[11]

The profession of painting in the years prior to war was in the main devoted to portraiture. Colonists who found themselves with a bit of discretionary income frequently employed the services of a local or, as often, an itinerant artist, who in turn asked for a modest sum for typically modest productions. The craft did not pay well, required much travel, and often involved much arm-twisting for the agreed-on compensation. But there was a market for such portraiture, and a certain amount of cultural status associated with it; indeed most

of the painters who achieved renown later in their careers started off in this manner. The results, nonetheless, are bound to disappoint the modern eye: stiffly rendered, sober to a fault, bound by genre and by habit to a uniformly drab set of artistic norms.[12]

Art and human nature being what they are, however, much of this was to change in the revolutionary era. A new generation of painters, including Benjamin West, Charles Wilson Peale, John Copley, Gilbert Stuart, and John Trumbull, many of whom had sharpened their skills in England and the Continent, found themselves faced with new, compelling, and open canvasses. This much is not to say that colonial artists were all patriots or even much interested in the political events of the day; but many were, and some of them represent the best of their generation. These "cultural nationalists," as Kenneth Silverman (1976) labels them, quickly captured the popular admiration. "While we boast a Washington, as the great master of the art of war," wrote the *Massachusetts Centinel*,

> a Franklin the chief of Philosophers–an Adams, and an infinitude of others, as statesmen and politicians whose abilities have been acknowledged throughout the civilized world; America may pride herself in giving birth to the most celebrated Artists of the present age. (p. 454)

The preferred medium for this much-heralded group was the historical painting. English tradition had it that such renderings were to capture historic and mythic events in all their sublimity and heroic grandeur. The Americans, however, added an important twist: Instead of invoking distant images of gods and classical lore, they sought to depict current events, as if in this way they might infuse the present with a heroism of its own. The didactic and rhetorical purposes of this innovation were not far to seek: As Peale explained it, he, like his compatriots, was

> ever fond of perpetuating the Remembrance of the Worthies of my Time, as I conceive it

will be a means of exciting an Emulation in our Posterity . . . and mankind will receive an advantage thereby, the Likeness being added to the Historic page giving it more force and the Reader more pleasure. (Ellis, 1979, p. 49)

Thus, what Benjamin West had done for the English with *The Death of General Wolfe* (1770) the American painters hoped to do for America: to impart maximal symbolic and graphic charge to the otherwise abstract principles of liberty, valor, and virtue. To this end, the cultural nationalists bent their labors in America and abroad, assiduously preparing themselves for the moment when they might leave the master's studio, strike out on their own, and contribute their mite to the birth of a new nation.

The times, it seemed, were summoning the artist as well as the soldier and orator. As war ended and the nation began, there emerged a collective apprehension that America, if it was to survive, needed a pantheon of its own. Poets and historians, panegyricists, and musicians put themselves to the task to demonstrated effect. But the painters, too, contributed measurably to constructing this "usable past," and none more dramatically than John Trumbull. "The great object of my wishes," he declared in 1784, "is to take up the History of Our Country, and paint the principle Events particularly of the late War" (Silverman, 1976, p. 465). To this end, he availed himself of Benjamin West's hospitality in London, and 2 years later completed *The Battle of Bunker's Hill* (oil on canvas, 25 × 37 in.). The artist admitted to no small amount of satisfaction with his effort, and West deemed it "the best picture of a modern battle that has been painted" (Silverman, 1976, p. 465).

That may or may not be the case, but the painting will be as instantly recognizable now as it was on first exhibit. Indeed, so imposing is its image that we struggle to think of such battle scenes other than of the type depicted here. The clash of armies at close range, the storm-hurried

skies, the conjoined pathos of valor and death: Are these not touchstones on which our imaginations depend? Hence, the ineluctable bond between the visual and mnemonic; the former is uniquely equipped to effect the latter by virtue of its dramatic efficiency and emotional precision. The historical painting is, by its very nature, designed to capture the maximum amount of symbolic energy within the least amount of space; and while this trait may be said to drastically simplify the informational content of the scene rendered, it imparts to the painting a certain promise to endure in the collective mind of future generations. On first impression, however, a question immediately poses itself. Why Bunker Hill? If the artist's aspiration is to commemorate the past, to excite "emulation in our posterity," why take as one's subject an inconclusive battle featuring no particularly ingenious martial exploits? Trumbull does not tell us explicitly, but some hints might be taken from the genre itself. Our search for them will take us to a more detailed examination of the painting proper.

To answer the question with a question: if this painting is offered as a means to remember, then what, precisely, is the viewer being asked to remember? (See Figure 27.1). What are we looking at? The painting is not large (Trumbull suffered from impairment in one eye, and thought it best to keep his productions within fairly restrained dimensions), but the scene depicted is busy, anxious, and violent. To the left, we see American troops reeling under British assault. Col. Israel Putman stands, holding a musket, over the expiring body of the much-loved Gen. Joseph Warren. Not far away loom Sir William Howe and Sir Henry Clinton, leading their charge even as a British soldier readies his bayonet for its final, fatal plunge. Above, smoke and clouds are made indistinguishable; below, carnage. The three featured Americans—Putman, Warren, and the kneeling soldier hopelessly shielding the fallen hero—appear swathed in light, dressed without ornament, and firmly standing their tentative position.

Figure 27.1 John Trumbull, *The Death of General Warren at The Battle of Bunker's Hill.*
SOURCE: Yale University Art Gallery.

The British, in contrast, are aggressively moving forward, some on horseback, all bedecked in official uniforms but muted by darker hues. American or British, the faces are each expressive, but together they convey the unmistakable shock of the moment, as if events were at once intensely personal and yet abstract; that is, the actors impress us as taking part in a drama of world-historical significance. They are not therefore to be taken as merely tokens of greater forces—they are after all engaged in a death match of their own making; there are no victims here, at least in the conventional sense. But the scene, in general, registers both locally and universally, and this much may be a plausible key to the painting's message. As types, the figures are to be taken as exemplars, embodying at once the immediate drama of the moment and the more archetypal significance of the battle. And this is why it does

not especially matter whether the particular battle ended in victory, loss, or stalemate. At the time of its viewing, Americans would have known the future, as it were, of the event depicted, indeed were able to now assimilate it into their own collective memory.

The Battle of Bunker's Hill was destined to take its place beside the artist's other famed works, including *The Signing of the Declaration of Independence* and *Death of General Montgomery.* As with each of his historical paintings, it trades in historical and artistic verities—it is unmistakably of a genre. But the rhetorical achievement it represents rests not only in exploiting conventions but also in giving to them a new place, in applying them at once to the here-and-now and to an imagined future. *The Battle of Bunker's Hill* may thus be taken as one example of a revolutionary effort to secure that future by rendering the recent past into optimally productive and didactic images, to coach the memory, so to speak, of those liable to forget the lessons of American valor, fortitude, virtue, and the collective quest for liberty. Even as Trumbull was laboring in his London studio, Thomas Paine reminded his weary compatriots that "we see with other eyes; we hear with other ears; and think with other thoughts, that those we formerly used." Trumbull and his fellow artists, we may now say, gave able assistance in that strange but enduring transformation where a new people come to see themselves with different eyes.

CONCLUSION

Genre studies have fallen on difficult times. For several decades now, the assumptions alleged to underwrite such work have been subject to withering critique, typically involving unease over formalism, topologies, and lurking neoplatonism. To the extent that genre critics have in fact committed themselves to unreflective and uncontextualized reliance on discursive forms, then such criticism would seem justified. Students of rhetoric, however, ignore genre to their disadvantage, if only because it remains patently evident that practitioners—producers and consumers of language—remain very much indebted to the persuasive resources organized by generic traditions and expectations. I have tried in this brief chapter to suggest several ways in which the arts of address in revolutionary America were thus organized, specifically with reference to the sermon, the public letter, and the historical painting. Genres persist for a reason, and they persist as rhetorical instruments because those who work within their constraints, and those who become audiences to them, recognize their power to shape human perceptions and guide purposeful public action. Here we have seen how the sermon, for example, offered itself up as rich means for advancing ideological arguments against unwarranted authority; how the public letter

worked to create and sustain a sense of rational community; and how the historical painting promised to install the meaning and significance of the revolution into collective memory. Other such persistent forms abound, of course, and they await further exploration. Our work will be the better as we take seriously the place of genre in crafting the arts of address in our time as well as historically.

NOTES

1. Notable scholarship concerning the role of sermons in the formation of American thought includes Bloch (1985), Bonomi (1985), Hatch (1977), and Stout (1986).

2. For authoritative treatments of the sermon as rhetorical type, see also Miller (1954) and Howell (1961).

3. For detailed examinations of the Jeremiad, see Miller (1953, pp. 27–39) and Bercovitch (1978).

4. For the epistle in early Christian contexts, see Goulder (1987, pp. 479–502).

5. These themes are treated at greater length in Browne (1990).

6. See Hariman (1997) for a more comprehensive exploration of these issues.

7. For biographical and publication history of the Letters, see Jacobson (1965).

8. Particularly informative on these subjects are Waldstreicher (1997), Newman (1997), and Dennis (2001).

9. A notable recent contribution is Olsen (2004).

10. On the theme of uncertainty in the postwar era, see especially Elkins and McKitrick (1993, pp. 31–75).

11. The standard on this subject is Hobsbawm and Ranger (1983).

12. The following review relies on Silverman (1976, pp. 437–468).

REFERENCES

Adair, D., & Schutz, J. A. (Eds.). (1967). *Peter Oliver's origin and progress of the American revolution.* Stanford, CA: Stanford University Press.

Bercovitch, S. (1978). *The American jeremiad.* Madison: University of Wisconsin Press.

Black, E. (1970). The second persona. *Quarterly Journal of Speech, 56,* 109–119.

Bloch, R. H. (1985). *Visionary republic: Millennial themes in American thought, 1756–1800.* Cambridge, UK: Cambridge University Press.

Bonomi, P. U. (1985). Under the cope of heaven: Religion, society, and politics in colonial America. New York: Oxford University Press.

Browne, S. H. (1990). The pastoral voice in John Dickinson's first letter from a farmer in Pennsylvania. *Quarterly Journal of Speech, 9,* 46–57.

Dennis, M. (2001). *Red, white, and blue letter days: Identity, public memory, and the American calendar.* Ithaca, NY: Cornell University Press.

Elkins, S., & McKitrick, E. (Eds.). (1993). *The age of federalism: The early American republic, 1788–1800.* New York: Oxford University Press.

Ellis, J. J. (1979). *After the revolution: Profiles of early American culture.* New York: Norton.

Ferguson, R. (1997). *The American enlightenment, 1750–1820.* Cambridge, MA: Harvard University Press.

Goulder, M. (1987). The Pauline epistles. In R. Alter, & F. Kermode (Eds.), *The literary guide to the Bible* (pp. 479–502). Cambridge, MA: Harvard University Press.

Hariman, R. (1997). *Political style: The artistry of power.* Chicago: University of Chicago Press.

Hatch, N. O. (1977). *The sacred cause of liberty: Republican thought and the millennium in revolutionary New England.* New Haven, CT: Yale University Press.

Hill, C. (2003). *Society and puritanism in pre-revolutionary England.* London: Pimlico.

Hobsbawm, E., & Ranger, T. (Eds.). (1983). *The invention of tradition.* Cambridge, UK: Cambridge University Press.

Howell, W. S. (1961). *Logic and rhetoric in England, 1500–1700.* New York: Russell & Russell.

Jacobson, D. L. (1965). *John Dickinson and the revolution in Pennsylvania.* Berkeley: University of California Press.

Jensen, M. (Ed.). (1978). *Tracts of the American Revolution, 1763–1776.* Indianapolis, IN: Bobbs-Merrill.

Miller, P. (1953). *The New England mind: From colony to province.* Cambridge, MA: Harvard University Press.

Miller, P. (1954). *The New England mind: The seventeenth century.* Cambridge, MA: Harvard University Press.

Newman, S. P. (1997). *Parades and politics of the street: Festive culture in the early republic.* Philadelphia: University of Pennsylvania Press.

Olsen, L. C. (2004). *Benjamin Franklin's vision of American community: A study in iconography.* Columbia: University of South Carolina Press.

Sandoz, E. (Ed.). (1991). *Political sermons of the American founding era, 1730–1805.* Indianapolis, IN: Liberty Press.

Silverman, K. (1976). *A cultural history of the American Revolution.* New York: Thomas Y. Crowell.

Stout, H. (1986). *The New England soul: Preaching and religious culture in colonial New England.* New York: Oxford University Press.

Turner, C. (1773). *A sermon preached before his Excellency.* Boston: Draper.

West, B. (1770). *The death of General Wolfe.* Ottawa, Ontario, Canada: National Gallery of Canada.

Waldstreicher, D. (1997). *"In the midst of perpetual fetes": The making of American nationalism, 1776–1820.* Chapel Hill: University of North Carolina Press.

28

Explosive Words and Glimmers of Hope

U.S. Public Discourse, 1860–1900

ANGELA G. RAY

Scene 1. On the evening of May 4, 1886, workers and labor leaders promoting an 8-hour day gather in Chicago's Haymarket Square to protest police action against strikers. As the meeting is breaking up, police arrive and demand that the crowd disperse. A bomb, which anarchist Voltairine de Cleyre in 1897 would call the Vengeance, arcs through the night sky, killing one policeman outright. Shots are fired, and the death toll among police and workers rises. The following year, a Chicago jury convicts eight anarchists and labor activists of conspiracy. Four are hanged. In 2003, chemical tests show similarities between surviving bombshells and printers' type, implying a rejection of words for deeds (Messer-Kruse, Eckert, Burckel, & Dunn, 2005). A *New Yorker* article about a new book on Haymarket is titled "The Terror Last Time" (Crain, 2006).

Scene 2. In the fall of 1997, I enroll as a doctoral student in Karlyn Kohrs Campbell's course at the University of Minnesota on the rhetoric of woman's rights and woman suffrage. In November, we read Elizabeth Cady Stanton's "Solitude of Self" (1892/2000). I meet this text for the first time alone in my apartment in St. Paul, and it is a revelation. In class, Campbell's teaching of the speech is passionate and inspired. By mid-2007, I have taught "Solitude" to 10 groups of students in four different courses, and it never fails to elicit initial emotive responses: "This is the most depressing thing I've ever read!" exclaims one student. "I thought it was beautiful," says another. "It reminded me of my life." The text serves various pedagogical functions—to demonstrate the invention of a fresh approach to a familiar subject, to illustrate a humanistic strand of suffragist philosophy, or to represent

U.S. reform discourse of the 1890s. As I prepare for class, however, my first thoughts are not about what the speech will illustrate. I read it aloud to myself, and Stanton's ringing peroration produces visceral recognition: "And yet, there is a solitude which each and every one of us has always carried with him, more inaccessible than the ice-cold mountains, more profound than the midnight sea" (Campbell, 1989c, p. 384).

Scene 3. Beginning her 2004 essay that exposes the use of images of Afghan people, particularly women, in justifying the U.S. war in Afghanistan, Dana Cloud sets part of Rudyard Kipling's 1899 poem "The White Man's Burden" against a description of U.S. war rhetoric from the *Seattle Post-Intelligencer* of 2002. Later in the essay, Cloud makes explicit the connections among Kipling's poem, U.S. imperialist expansion in the wake of the Spanish-American War, and the continuing resonance of the idea of the "white man's burden," what Cloud calls "a core element in the belief in a clash between white, Western societies and inferior Others requiring policing and rescue" (Cloud, 2004, pp. 286, 301 fn. 7).

Scene 4. Concluding a discussion of the discourses of reform presented on commercial lyceum platforms in the 1860s and 1870s, I write,

> Yet if stabilizing meaning is impossible, . . . this is not a motive for despair. The instability of meaning, the experience of constantly creating and reforming and reshaping communities, cultures, and characters—the rhetorical nature of human experience—is also a promise of hope. (Ray, 2005, p. 188)

In the charge to which this chapter is the reply, Wilson and Eberly ask, "How do you locate yourself within the research covered in your chapter?" These four scenes enact a response to their query: I locate myself as a student of the 19th century, as a teacher of its

rhetorics, as a participant in a scholarly community that perceives homologies between 19th-century rhetoric and contemporary public questions, and as a researcher of popular discourse that illustrates the limitations and the transformational potentials of rhetorical performance. Partly, I study the 19th century because it furnishes a usable history to explain the present by illuminating the past and, sometimes, to provide models of argument and expression that still resonate today. The deeply conflictual period that includes the Civil War and its consequences, as well as the phenomenal transformations of the Second Industrial Revolution, offers ample material for scholarly investigation that highlights the potentials and limitations of rhetorical action. Partly, I study the 19th century because, like others, I can identify moments of hope—often hope that was later dashed—when the future could have been made better and lives might have changed. What if legal segregation had ended in the 1870s with the Civil Rights Bill? What if the aftermath of Haymarket had not entrenched the power of employers and fomented further fear of immigrants? What if the ideal of democratic self-determination had been readily extended to Puerto Rico, Guam, and the Philippines? What if the law and common sense could have comprehended women as full human beings? These are not nostalgic counterfactuals. None of this was unthinkable at the time. Indeed, such goals were available as rhetorical resources and conveyed as imagined possibilities. Students and scholars of the later 19th century, thus, can create historical patterns, at local and at global scales, which provide a fresh perspective on the present and the future. As this chapter demonstrates, many scholars of public discourse share my belief that a historically informed vision can revise current understandings and even motivate action toward political and social goals.

In addition to lessons learned, the discourse of the later 19th century sometimes provides models of rhetorical eloquence, in language that sings and performances of courage and recognizable truth, creating heritages much richer than previously imagined. Cultural mores can explain reception, but linguistic beauty, or the creative dynamism of inventive rhetorical performances, does provide inspiration. I have seen this response in myself, I have seen it in the work and the energetic involvement of students, and I have read the resonant words of Jacqueline Jones Royster (2000) in *Traces of a Stream* as she describes scholarly respect for the words and lives of her subjects. Indeed, in the relatively short time since I joined the community of rhetorical inquiry, I have seen scholars' passion for certain texts and subjects. This occasionally emerges in textual form, as in Royster's compelling book, but I have seen it most often in performance, as anyone can attest who has witnessed Campbell discussing Stanton's "Solitude," or Kirt Wilson presenting about Douglass's 1876 address at the dedication of the Freedmen's Monument, or Michael Leff teaching Lincoln's Second Inaugural. A scholarly practice that invites emotional commitment, that performatively ignores a distinction between mind and spirit, seems to me a salient feature of contemporary rhetorical study of U.S. public discourse of 1860–1900. It is possible to love what you do and to live it as a key to your own identity, and that energy can spark the imaginations of others in turn. Scene 2 marks the observation that scholarly passion, an appreciation for beauty and for bravery, regularly reanimates discourses of the past in the spaces of classrooms and the pages of scholarship, in ways that embody hope for the efficacy of critical practice and hope for human potential. Scene 4 locates this hope in the power and uncertainties of rhetorical practice.

This chapter seeks to delineate the "state of the art" of contemporary rhetorical scholarship on U.S. public discourse of the later 19th century, characterizing its scope and its central concerns, identifying strengths and gaps in the literature, and suggesting avenues and resources for future inquiry. A review of the current literature on the 1860–1900 period simultaneously demonstrates that much inventive work is being done and that the possibilities for future scholarship are vast. Whereas rhetorical scholars of U.S. public discourse have invested more energy on the discourses of the nation's founding and on the controversies leading up to the Civil War, the later 19th century is receiving growing attention, especially from researchers concerned with the changing dynamics of race and gender in a tumultuous time. Although many areas could be identified as ripe for further study, one that seems most surprisingly overlooked is economics, particularly relations of labor and capital. There is a shortage of current scholarship on the discourse of industrial capital, the gospel of wealth, as well as the rhetoric of the labor movement, the industrial and trades unions, the farmers' alliances, the rise of U.S. socialism and anarchism, and the campaigns for workplace reforms and altered working conditions. Likewise, additional study of the discourses of imperialism and colonialism in the 1890s— from the perspectives of U.S. governmental authorities and of affected parties around the world—would better illuminate the globalization of manifest destiny. Scenes 1 and 3 above gesture toward these two significant bodies of public discourse.

This chapter, however, is primarily about existing rather than potential scholarship. The section that follows provisionally defines "U.S. public discourse" and the scope of the literature reviewed. Then the section "Rhetorical Forms, Critical Themes" characterizes the themes, approaches, and conceptual/theoretical contributions of recent rhetorical scholarship.

DEFINITIONS AND SCOPE

Any review of a literature is bounded by authorial assumptions about terminology, temporal scope, and appropriate sources. In this section, I attempt to make my assumptions as transparent as possible.

This chapter employs a broad definition of "U.S. public discourse," as human-created symbolic phenomena that characterize or affect the identity or development of U.S. culture and that have the potential to be addressed to—that is, the potential to be interpreted by—other people. "U.S." signals phenomena produced in the United States, produced by self-identified citizens or residents, or produced as an effect of or an appeal to political or popular culture of the country or its regions. "Public" in rhetorical scholarship typically is matched with "political," and here I assume that the two terms resonate with each other. Comprehending these terms in a broad way, however, allows for the inclusion of scholarship on topics such as the creation of culturally accepted norms and challenges to them, on the rhetorical education of individuals via conduct or success manuals as well as in formal institutional settings, and on the commemoration of past events via museums, collections, or the production of domestic objects. "Discourse," broadly understood, comprises written and verbal texts, as well as visual images and cultural performances. It embraces relatively bounded objects such as an antilynching speech or pamphlet of Ida B. Wells, or a photograph of Yosemite by Carleton Watkins, as well as relatively dispersed objects such as statements or silences about civil rights of the late-19th-century presidents or the preservation of body parts as trophies of the Sand Creek Massacre.

When preparing undergraduate course syllabi on "U.S. public discourse," or, more usually, "U.S. rhetorical history," I rarely comprehend the term in such a broad way, tending instead to emphasize written and verbal texts that represent direct articulations of or challenges to legislative, judicial, religious, or corporate ideologies and power. But as a researcher and as a participant in the community of rhetorical scholars, I note that a broadening of the parameters of "public discourse" has been under way for some time,

certainly much longer than my habitation in the field. I regard this expansion of rhetorical interests as salutary at the same time that I value the study of written and verbal texts and critical practices of their interpretation. Indeed, disciplinary conflicts over object domains surprised me as a graduate student, and more often than not, I see my own cohort and my current graduate students seeking ways to blend insights and approaches from multiple strands of rhetorical theory and critical practice, innovating from traditions.

To render a snapshot of current research on U.S. public discourse of the 1860–1900 period, I examined scholarship in outlets that most often publish the work of researchers working in the disciplinary traditions of rhetoric in communication and rhetoric in English (although some authors whose work is included in the sample are employed in fields such as journalism or cultural studies). I did not expand the scope of the chapter to include scholarship by historians, although books such as Kenneth Cmiel's (1990) *Democratic Eloquence* are certainly important for scholars of 19th-century discourse. Rhetorical scholars publish books at various academic presses, and regular series in rhetoric are maintained at university presses such as Alabama, Baylor, Michigan State, Pittsburgh, South Carolina, Southern Illinois, the State University of New York, and Texas A&M. For this chapter, my selections of "current" books ranged back in time as far as the late 1980s, on the grounds that several of these have had considerable impact in the field. Books, however, were chosen less systematically than journal articles.

Although no journals are devoted to 19th-century public discourse, scholarship on U.S. rhetoric of the 1860–1900 era appears periodically in many academic journals. For this chapter, I surveyed the contents of a dozen years' worth of 14 journals that regularly publish rhetorical criticism and theory: *Communication and Critical/Cultural Studies, Communication Quarterly, Communication*

Studies, Critical Studies in Media Communication (*Critical Studies in Mass Communication* through 1999), *Howard Journal of Communications, Philosophy and Rhetoric, Quarterly Journal of Speech, Rhetoric and Public Affairs, Rhetoric Review, Rhetoric Society Quarterly, Southern Communication Journal, Text and Performance Quarterly, Western Journal of Communication,* and *Women's Studies in Communication.* Two of the journals (*Communication and Critical/ Cultural Studies* and *Rhetoric and Public Affairs*) began publication during the period studied. My survey encompassed all issues of these 14 journals published between January 1996 and December 1, 2007. Most of the journals had published all their 2007 issues by this time.

The selection of journals limits the purview of this chapter in distinctive ways, notably because the list is heavily weighted toward journals from my own field of communication. Most of these journals have an interdisciplinary mission, but since 1996, rhetorical scholars from English departments have most often published in *Philosophy and Rhetoric, Rhetoric Review,* and *Rhetoric Society Quarterly,* among the journals surveyed. The narrowed disciplinary focus is counterbalanced, I hope, by breadth in other areas: the group of journals showcases recent scholarship published in national and regional journals, in independent journals and journals funded by professional associations, and in journals that typically publish case studies in public address and journals that more often emphasize rhetorical theory, contemporary media, or social scientific approaches to communication inquiry. Current rhetorical research on 19th-century discourse is thus set in several different contexts. Since 1996, essays that take some aspect of later 19th-century U.S. public discourse as their main subjects of study have appeared most frequently in the following journals (in order): *Rhetoric and Public Affairs, Rhetoric Review,*

and *Rhetoric Society Quarterly.* Yet the inclusion of journals such as *Critical Studies in Media Communication* and *Text and Performance Quarterly* better ensures that the representation offered here encompasses discursive and nondiscursive artifacts and a breadth of conceptual/theoretical and methodological approaches.

Periodization is a key issue in selecting books and articles for inclusion. The temporal parameters of the subject field for this chapter (1860–1900) do not neatly mesh with either historical conventions or rhetorical critical practice. Common historical terms describe only portions of this period: Civil War, Reconstruction, Gilded Age, *fin de siècle.* The broader term Second Industrial Revolution, often identified with the period 1860–1920, is the closest approximation to this chapter's focal era. Those of us who study public discourse from 1860 to the end of the century choose temporal dimensions for our projects to suit our own rhetorical purposes. We carve out a narrow time frame, or we range back into earlier eras or extend forward in time as these choices help us to answer our research questions. Since 1996, it has been usual for authors of rhetorical histories that cover all or part of the 1860–1900 period to frame our work as studies of "19th-century" discourse, a term that regularly appears in titles.

In selecting sources for this chapter based on temporal scope, I tended toward inclusion rather than exclusion. I considered books and essays that substantively examine U.S. public discourse that was created, performed, or published between 1860 and 1900, whether or not the scholarship primarily emphasizes rhetorical practices from that period. On the other hand, I did not include scholarship whose sole focus is rhetoric of the antebellum era or the early 20th century even if the producers of that discourse were significant rhetorical actors in 1860–1900 or if the discourse foreshadowed or reflected important attributes of later 19th-century culture—unless scholars highlight these connections. For example, although many scholars have studied rhetoric produced by Abraham Lincoln and, to a lesser extent, Frederick Douglass, I omitted from my sample those works—the preponderance of them, in both cases—that focus solely on these rhetors' prewar discourse. Likewise, I omitted Browne's fine reading of W. E. B. Du Bois's (1906) *Souls of Black Folk* in an edited collection (Hogan, 1998), although I included Wilson's (1999a) essay that reads *Souls* specifically as a creative, antiracist rhetorical response to 19th-century biological determinism, as well as Wells's (2002) comparison of the concept of double consciousness in *Souls* and in S. Weir Mitchell's 1888 presentation of a medical case history. Choosing the literature sample was an art rather than a science, and I am humbled by the certainty of important omissions.

A primary task of this chapter is to elucidate the features of current scholarship on a content area, rather than, say, an area distinguished by commitments to theoretical, methodological, or political projects. In keeping with the emphasis on critical foci, the following section surveys the rhetorical forms and the themes and topics emphasized in current research. Theoretical, methodological, and political commonalities and tensions in the work are also elaborated.

RHETORICAL FORMS, CRITICAL THEMES

A broad definition of U.S. public discourse produces a corresponding breadth of critical foci in the literature. Much current scholarship, however, draws on disciplinary heritages of object selection, even as it expands the purview of primary sources and critical approaches. Some scholarship, for example, situates extant texts of public speeches and their contexts as primary subjects of investigation (e.g., Beasley, 2001, 2004; Darsey, 1997; Engbers, 2007; Gayle & Griffin, 1998; German, 1998; Gross, 2004; Hansen, 2004; Harpine, 2001, 2005; Hogan &

Hogan, 2003; Huxman, 2000; Kimble, 2007; Leff, 1997; Logan, 1997, 1999; Miller, 1999; Ray, 2002, 2005, 2006; Selzer, 1997; Slagell, 2001; Stormer, 1999; Strange, 2002; Towns, 1998; Wilson, 1999b, 2000; Zarefsky, 2000), whereas other research emphasizes the reception history of speeches, such as Ceccarelli's (1998, pp. 399–404) study of reports on Lincoln's Second Inaugural in Northern and Southern newspapers. Scholars also investigate the public oration as a performative event, as in Mattingly's (1999, 2002) studies of the dress of women public speakers or Behling's (2002) work on the "exhibition" of Fannie Barrier Williams, Anna Julia Cooper, and Frances Jackson Coppin at the 1893 World's Columbian Exposition in Chicago. Texts originally presented as written documents also form a notable focus for contemporary scholars. Current research examines books from the period, whether histories, autobiographies, scholarly treatises, textbooks, or conduct manuals (e.g., Browne, 2000; Donawerth, 2002; Dorsey & Harlow, 2003; Elder, 2002; Gunn, 2005, pp. 56–78; Johnson, 2000, 2002; Logue & Miller, 1998; Pittman, 2007; Skinner, 2007; Vivian, 1999; Watson, 1999; Wells, 2002; Whitburn, 2004; Wilson, 1999a), and essays provide a focus for other scholarship (e.g., McMillan, 2002; Royster, 2000). Newspapers and journals of the period receive regular critical attention (e.g., Ceccarelli, 1998; Cramer, 2003; Domke, 1996; Prioleau, 2003; Ray, 2003, 2007; Rodríguez, 1998), with published letters sometimes emphasized (e.g., Berkowitz & Lewis, 1998; Finnegan, 2005; Hoffman, 2002; Stormer, 2001). Debates are also represented as explicit subjects of study in current scholarship, whether occurring in print media or in face-to-face legislative encounters (e.g., Berkowitz & Lewis, 1998; Campbell, 1998b; Stormer, 2001; Wilson, 1998, 2002).

Recent scholarship has highlighted forensic discourse of the later 19th century, as well as the origins of legal doctrines pertinent to the period (Harris, 2004; Hasian, 2000; Hasian,

Condit, & Lucaites, 1996; Hasian & Klinger, 2002; Ray & Richards, 2007). The dynamics of religious discourse receive scholarly treatment (e.g., Bizzell, 2006; Brekus, 1998; Cramer, 2003; Fehler, 2005; Haywood, 2003; Hobbs, 1997), and several contemporary scholars emphasize educational practices, particularly as they affected pedagogy in rhetoric and composition (e.g., Bradway-Hesse, 1998; Carr, Carr, & Schultz, 2005; Johnson, 1991; Kates, 2001; Mastrangelo, 1999; Rothermel, 2002; Salvatori, 2003). Commemorative activity memorializing 19th-century people and events is a focal interest for several current scholars (Dickinson, Ott, & Aoki, 2005, 2006; Hill, 1997; Mandziuk, 2003; Mandziuk & Fitch, 2001; Rohan, 2004). Other objects of study include photographs and their reception (DeLuca & Demo, 2000; Finnegan, 2005), public behaviors or silences (Hoffman, 2002; Parry-Giles & Blair, 2002; Wilson, 2005), medical discourse (Skinner, 2007; Stormer, 2001, 2002), plays (MacKay, 1997), diaries (Harrison, 2003), songs (Harpine, 2004, 2005; Hobbs, 1997; Hurner, 2006), citation systems (Connors, 1998), and student compositions (Zenger, 2004).

In short, the scope of object domains in current scholarship reflects interests in rhetorical inquiry as a whole, as rhetorical scholars develop and re-form traditional strengths of the field and as rhetorical and media studies continue to blend. Visual images and other nonverbal cultural performances of the 1860–1900 period have received less attention from rhetorical scholars than they seem likely to attain in the future, given the trajectory of interests among newer generations of scholars. Finnegan's (2005) essay "Recognizing Lincoln" offers an excellent example of scholarship that meshes traditional interests among rhetorical historians of the 19th century—the life and work of Lincoln—with reception studies and theories of visuality. Providing a reading of letters to *McClure's*

about an 1895 publication of a photograph of the young Lincoln, Finnegan persuasively adduces evidence of ways of seeing—what she calls "image vernaculars"—among viewers in the fin de siècle.

Finnegan's (2005) essay illustrates the assumption that all history is contemporary, in the sense that scholars write from their own historical moments in ways that speak to their own concerns. Thus, observations about any research in a content area lead inevitably to observations about the animating concerns of producing scholars. Object selection tells us a good deal about current practices of rhetorical inquiry, but categorizing the materials by theme or topic is especially revealing. Four broad topic areas describe most current work in rhetorical scholarship on the 1860–1900 period: Scholars place particular emphasis on rhetorics of gender, race, governmental institutions, and education. The most vibrant areas of inquiry are in studies of gender and race, especially the construction of—and challenges to—identities of women of various races, and African American women and men. It is striking that for almost 20 years, most first editions of anthologies produced by rhetorical scholars that include documents from the 1860–1900 period are collections of texts by women, primarily African Americans and European Americans. Continuing the recovery project that emerged in the U.S. academy as part of the mid-20th-century feminist movement, such anthologies provide improved access to important materials (e.g., Campbell, 1989c; Fitch & Mandziuk, 1997; Gifford & Slagell, 2007; Logan, 1995; Ritchie & Ronald, 2001; Royster, 1997). These collections augment and challenge popular classroom anthologies (e.g., Reid & Klumpp, 2005). Additional resources for students and scholars of gender and race can be found in Campbell's (1993) and Leeman's (1996) edited "sourcebooks," which offer biographical and critical articles on women and African American public speakers.

Considerations about women's "coming to voice," of creating identities and selfhoods rhetorically, have been of interest to scholars of women's discourse for several decades, and these remain a key concern of rhetorical critics (e.g., Bizzell, 2006; Harrison, 2003; Hurner, 2006; Logan, 1999; Lunsford, 1995; Pittman, 2007; Royster, 2000; Wagner, 1995; Watson, 1999; Wertheimer, 1997). Women's public advocacy for social change is the area of inquiry in which most recent work on gender is situated. Building on scholarship pioneered by Campbell (1973, 1980, 1989a, 1989b, 1989c, 1993), a substantial body of rhetorical research addresses the various forms of women's advocacy as manifested in the 1860–1900 period. Several studies focus on the woman's rights and woman suffrage movements, illuminating women's direct efforts to challenge social conventions about restrictive gender roles, to gain control of their bodies and their children, to secure access to educational institutions and economic opportunities, and to change political conditions that restrained their participation (e.g., Behling, 2002; Conway, 1995; Engbers, 2007; Fitch & Mandziuk, 1997; Heider, 2005; Huxman, 2000; Johnson, 2000; Lipscomb, 1995; Logan, 1997, 1999; Miller, 1999; Peterson, 1995; Ray, 2003, 2006, 2007; Ray & Richards, 2007; Royster, 1995, 2000; Slagell, 2001; Stormer, 1999, 2001, 2002; Strange, 2002; Watson, 1991). Activist women's work for cognate reform causes, including African American civil rights, temperance, and labor, also gains attention from contemporary critics (e.g., Bizzell, 2006; Campbell, 1998b; Fiesta, 2006; Fitch & Mandziuk, 1997; Heider, 2005; Leff, 1997; Lipscomb, 1995; Logan, 1997, 1999; Mattingly, 1998; McMillan, 2002; Peterson, 1995; Royster, 1995, 2000; Slagell, 2001). Some studies focus on women's advocacy in legislative, judicial, and other institutional arenas, and some highlight activist women's efforts to alter public opinion in other ways. For example, current scholars are explicating the

rhetorical power of women's costume (Mattingly, 1999, 2002; Strange, 2002; Torrens, 1997), and recent work examines the reform discourses of women who were popular lecturers, emphasizing the opportunities and constraints of the commercial medium in which these rhetors worked (Gayle & Griffin, 1998; Hogan & Hogan, 2003; Ray, 2005, 2006; Strange, 2002).

Recognizing that biological sex and its cultural dimension, gender, do not constitute discrete variables in either human experience or rhetorical inquiry, current scholars highlight the dynamics of gender as they interact with other attributes. To date, the intersections of gender and race have received the most consistent attention in rhetorical scholarship of the 19th century, led by important books on African American women speakers and essayists: Logan's (1999) *We Are Coming,* Peterson's (1995) *Doers of the Word,* and Royster's (2000) *Traces of a Stream.* Since 1996, a number of other scholarly works have investigated the experiences and the rhetorics of African American women of the later 19th century, including Harriet Jacobs, Mary Church Terrell, Sojourner Truth, and Frances Ellen Watkins Harper (e.g., Behling, 2002; Campbell, 1998a, 1998b; Fitch & Mandziuk, 1997; Haywood, 2003; Lipscomb, 1995; Logan, 1995, 1997; Logue & Miller, 1998; Pittman, 2007; Royster, 1995, 1997; Watson, 1999). In addition, scholarship on the rhetorical dimensions of race, racism, and antiracist rhetorics of the later 19th century, whether or not they are explicitly connected to dimensions of gender, is burgeoning (see also Campbell, 1998b; Domke, 1996; Fiesta 2006; Forbes, 2003; Gordon, 2003; Prioleau, 2003; Ray, 2002, 2005; Wilson, 1998, 1999a, 1999b, 2000, 2002, 2003, 2005). The rhetoric of Frederick Douglass is of particular interest to scholars of the later 19th century, as it is to scholars of the antebellum era (see, e.g., Prioleau, 2003; Ray, 2002, 2005; Wilson, 2000, 2003). Wilson, the rhetorical scholar currently most active in the study of later

19th-century rhetorics of race, examines the internal and contextual dynamics of African American activist discourse, showing how rhetors shaped and responded to their lived political, economic, and social cultures and how their rhetorical practices complicate theoretical concepts such as prudence and mimesis.

In the early 21st century, I anticipate increasing scholarly attention to the complex interplay among dynamics of gender, race, class, ethnicity, sexuality, region, and religion. It seems likely that studies of rhetorics by and about American Indians of the later 19th century will continue to increase (see, e.g., Black, 2007; German, 1998; Hill, 1997; Miller, 2005; Stromberg, 2006), as well as studies emphasizing immigration and nationality (e.g., Beasley, 2006; Rodríguez, 1998). Furthermore, it seems likely that more research will examine masculinity as a rhetorical category of gender (see Elder, 2002), study the complexities of sexuality (Sloop, 2007), and investigate whiteness as a performed racial category (Campbell, 1998b; Cramer, 2003; Johnson, 2000; Zenger, 2004). Interrogating the terms *gender* and *race* is not the only task of practicing rhetorical critics who study these cultural constructions, however. There still remain relatively few studies of rhetorical action by women of any race or by persons of color of the later 19th century, and the current burgeoning of scholarship on the rhetorics of gender and race in the 1860–1900 period should not mask the fact that this is still a young area of inquiry.

Scholars increasingly seek not only to recover previously ignored histories but also to examine the interplay among marginalized discourses and discourses of elite power. Wilson's work, for example, blends the study of African American activism with the study of the rhetorics of governmental institutions, as he examines the responses of African American rhetors to Lincoln's wartime Emancipation Proclamation (Wilson, 2000), as well as congressional debates on the 1874–1875 Civil

Rights Bill (1998, 2002) and the discourse—and silence—of U.S. presidents on the subject of civil rights for African Americans between 1875 and 1901 (2005). Indeed, the dynamics of power between institutions and marginalized groups are beginning to spark greater rhetorical interest in the late-19th-century presidency, as Beasley's work on the presidency and immigration attests (2004, 2006). Until recently, it has been unusual for rhetorical scholars to study the presidencies of the 1860–1900 period, with the obvious exception of Lincoln's administration. Ryan's (1995) sourcebook on U.S. presidents as orators skips from Lincoln to Theodore Roosevelt, although Campbell and Jamieson (1990) cover the later 19th-century presidencies in their study of genres of governance. Now, in addition to the recent work of Beasley and Wilson, Harpine's scholarship (2000, 2001, 2004, 2005) offers extensive treatment of the 1896 presidential campaign, and recent research reexamines the rhetoric of Lincoln's presidency (Kimble, 2007; Leff, 2000), the reception of Lincoln's discourse and the memory of his image (Ceccarelli, 1998; Finnegan, 2005), the rhetorical performances of Cleveland (Hoffman, 2002), the myth-making writing of Theodore Roosevelt before his presidency (Dorsey & Harlow, 2003), and the changing role of the 19th-century first lady as advisor and volunteer (Parry-Giles & Blair, 2002). Legislatures of the later 19th century have received relatively little recent treatment by rhetorical scholars (but see Wilson, 1998, 2002). Recent studies of national juridical practice have focused on the evolution of the "separate but equal" doctrine (Hasian, 2000; Hasian et al., 1996; Hasian & Klinger, 2002), on rhetorics justifying military tribunals (Hasian, 2005), and on the interplay between the law and women's reform discourses (Ray & Richards, 2007). Few studies of state-level legislative or judicial rhetorics have been published in recent years (but see Harris, 2004). Indeed, institutional power structures at local, state, and national levels offer a fruitful research field, because scholars recognize, theoretically, that these structures shaped and promoted cultural assumptions about gender, race, labor, region, health, the land and the environment, changing technologies, and the place of the United States in the world.

Finally, current rhetorical scholars exhibit a compelling interest in processes of learning. Sometimes these are construed as cultural myth-making processes affected by reading or viewing (e.g., Browne, 2000; DeLuca & Demo, 2000; Domke, 1996; Donawerth, 2002; Dorsey & Harlow, 2003; Elder, 2002; Johnson, 2002; Rodríguez, 1998; Royster, 1995; Vivian, 1999; Wilson, 2003), by absorbing elite discourses (Beasley, 2001, 2004; Broaddus, 1999; Connors, 1998; DeLuca, 2001; Fehler, 2005; Wilson, 2002), or by participating in cultural performances (Behling, 2002; Clark, 2004; Dickinson et al., 2005, 2006; Hill, 1997; Hogan & Hogan, 2003; Horner & Brewin, 2007; Lauer, 2007; MacKay, 1997; Mandziuk, 2003; Mandziuk & Fitch, 2001; Marvin & Simonson, 2004; Miller, 2005; Ray, 2005, 2006, 2007; Strange, 2002). In other research, learning is framed as the result of participating in formal processes of education within families or organizations, including schools and colleges. Rhetorical scholars study practices of teaching and learning, textbooks and their production, and the politics of writing (e.g., Berlin, 1984; Bradway-Hesse, 1998; Carr et al., 2005; Clark & Halloran, 1993; Conway, 1995; Gere, 1997; Johnson, 1991; Kates, 2001; Mastrangelo, 1999; Robbins, 2004; Rothermel, 2002; Whitburn, 2004; Zenger 2004).

These broad and intersecting themes—gender, race, governmental power, and educational practices—encompass most recent research on U.S. public discourse of the later 19th century. The theoretical and political projects that engage current scholars are quite diverse. For example, some scholars marshal evidence from the 1860–1900 period to help explain myths of U.S. national identity (e.g., Beasley, 2004; Dorsey & Harlow, 2003; Ray,

2005; Wilson, 2002), and others study 19th-century rhetorical practices for illumination of present-day beliefs or for models of alternative rhetorics (e.g., Campbell & Meyer, 2003; DeLuca, 2001; Mastrangelo, 1999; McMillan, 2002; Vivian, 1999). Almost all current rhetorical studies of the later 19th century are concerned with explaining the processes of conservation and change. Indeed, the number of research projects that illustrate the simultaneous operations of social conventions and rhetorics of challenge is conspicuous. I hope that we will find ways to thicken our understanding of the complexities of "dominant" and "resistant" discourses, to seek the fissures in our models of elite power, and to confront the uncomfortable paradoxes in rhetorics promoting change. The history of the later 19th century offers compelling cases of public conflict, along nearly every axis one can imagine, and our increasing corpus of case studies should help us make some provisional generalizations about the ways that Americans made sense of an especially tumultuous time. As we continue to select topics for case studies, we should pay more attention to economic issues and to U.S. rhetorics within a global context. In addition, I would wish for us to engage in more comparative projects, to forge links among our various research programs, and to create usable histories of later 19th-century U.S. cultures that more readily allow for the illumination of similarities and differences across cases. Finally, building a community among scholars of the mid- to late 19th century—not only by topical specialty—would enrich our work.

The work remaining to be done can be measured in lifetimes. Current scholars of the rhetorics of the later 19th century, however, have predecessors, colleagues, and publishing outlets. And there is urgency. Historical studies can contribute to rhetorical scholarship and to the public culture of our own time, illuminating the past to offer ways to understand the present, by analogy and by contrast. The challenge of a vast gulf between wealth and poverty, the promise and the perils of new technologies, the changes in patterns of work and leisure, the oppression of assumptions of gender, race, class, region, nationality, sexuality, and physical ability, as well as the results of hope and despair—these are issues to which rhetorical scholars of the later 19th century can speak.

REFERENCES

Beasley, V. B. (2001, February). Making diversity safe for democracy: American pluralism and the presidential local address, 1885–1992. *Quarterly Journal of Speech, 87,* 25–40.

Beasley, V. B. (2004). *You, the people: American national identity in presidential rhetoric.* College Station: Texas A&M University Press.

Beasley, V. B. (Ed.). (2006). *Who belongs in America? Presidents, rhetoric, and immigration.* College Station: Texas A&M University Press.

Behling, L. L. (2002). Reification and resistance: The rhetoric of black womanhood at the Columbian exposition, 1893. *Women's Studies in Communication, 25,* 173–196.

Berkowitz, S. J., & Lewis, A. C. (1998, Fall). Debating anti-Semitism: Ernestine Rose v. Horace Seaver in the *Boston Investigator,* 1863–1864. *Communication Quarterly, 46,* 457–471.

Berlin, J. A. (1984). *Writing instruction in nineteenth-century American colleges.* Carbondale: Southern Illinois University Press.

Bizzell, P. (2006, Fall). Frances Willard, Phoebe Palmer, and the ethos of the Methodist woman preacher. *Rhetoric Society Quarterly, 36,* 377–398.

Black, J. E. (2007, April/June). Remembrances of removal: Native resistance to allotment and the unmasking of paternal benevolence. *Southern Communication Journal, 72,* 185–203.

Bradway-Hesse, B. (1998, Autumn). Midwestern literary societies, with a particular look at a university for the "farmer and the poor." *Rhetoric Review, 17,* 50–73.

Brekus, C. A. (1998). *Strangers and pilgrims: Female preaching in America, 1740–1845.* Chapel Hill: University of North Carolina Press.

Broaddus, D. C. (1999). *Genteel rhetoric: Writing high culture in nineteenth-century Boston.* Columbia: University of South Carolina Press.

Browne, S. H. (2000, Summer). Counter-science: African American historians and the critique of ethnology in nineteenth-century America. *Western Journal of Communication, 64,* 268–284.

Campbell, J. A., & Meyer, S. C. (Eds.). (2003). *Darwinism, design, and public education.* East Lansing: Michigan State University Press.

Campbell, K. K. (1973, February). The rhetoric of women's liberation: An oxymoron. *Quarterly Journal of Speech, 59,* 74–86.

Campbell, K. K. (1980, October). Stanton's "The solitude of self": A rationale for feminism. *Quarterly Journal of Speech, 66,* 304–312.

Campbell, K. K. (1989a). La pucelle d'Orléans becomes an American girl: Anna Dickinson's "Jeanne d'Arc." In M. C. Leff & F. J. Kauffeld (Eds.), *Texts in context: Critical dialogues on significant episodes in American political rhetoric* (pp. 91–111). Davis, CA: Hermagoras Press.

Campbell, K. K. (1989b). *Man cannot speak for her* (Vol. 1). *A critical study of early feminist rhetoric.* New York: Praeger.

Campbell, K. K. (Comp.). (1989c). *Man cannot speak for her* (Vol. 2). *Key texts of the early feminists.* New York: Praeger.

Campbell, K. K. (Ed.). (1993). *Women public speakers in the United States, 1800–1925: A biocritical sourcebook.* Westport, CT: Greenwood Press.

Campbell, K. K. (1998a, Fall). Inventing women: From Amaterasu to Virginia Woolf. *Women's Studies in Communication, 21,* 111–126.

Campbell, K. K. (1998b). The power of hegemony: Capitalism and racism in the "nadir of Negro history." In J. M. Hogan (Ed.), *Rhetoric and community: Studies in unity and fragmentation* (pp. 36–61). Columbia: University of South Carolina Press.

Campbell, K. K., & Jamieson, K. H. (1990). *Deeds done in words: Presidential rhetoric and the genres of governance.* Chicago: University of Chicago Press.

Carr, J. F., Carr, S. L., & Schultz, L. M. (2005). *Archives of instruction: Nineteenth-century rhetorics, readers, and composition books in the United States.* Carbondale: Southern Illinois University Press.

Ceccarelli, L. (1998, November). Polysemy: Multiple meanings in rhetorical criticism. *Quarterly Journal of Speech, 84,* 395–415.

Clark, G. (2004). *Rhetorical landscapes in America: Variations on a theme from Kenneth Burke.* Columbia: University of South Carolina Press.

Clark, G., & Halloran, S. M. (Eds.). (1993). *Oratorical culture in nineteenth-century America: Transformations in the theory and practice of rhetoric.* Carbondale: Southern Illinois University Press.

Cloud, D. L. (2004, August). "To veil the threat of terror": Afghan women and the <clash of civilizations> in the imagery of the U.S. war on terrorism. *Quarterly Journal of Speech, 90,* 285–306.

Cmiel, K. (1990). *Democratic eloquence: The fight over popular speech in nineteenth-century America.* New York: Morrow.

Connors, R. J. (1998, Autumn). The rhetoric of citation systems, Part I: The development of annotation structures from the Renaissance to 1900. *Rhetoric Review, 17,* 6–48.

Conway, K. M. (1995). Woman suffrage and the history of rhetoric at the Seven Sisters colleges, 1865–1919. In A. A. Lunsford (Ed.), *Reclaiming Rhetorica: Women in the rhetorical tradition* (pp. 203–226). Pittsburgh, PA: University of Pittsburgh Press.

Crain, C. (2006, March 13). The terror last time. *New Yorker,* pp. 82–89.

Cramer, J. M. (2003, October/December). White womanhood and religion: Colonial discourse in the U.S. women's missionary press, 1869–1904. *Howard Journal of Communications, 14,* 209–224.

Darsey, J. F. (1997). *The prophetic tradition and radical rhetoric in America.* New York: New York University Press.

DeLuca, K. M. (2001, Winter). Trains in the wilderness: The corporate roots of environmentalism. *Rhetoric and Public Affairs, 4,* 633–652.

DeLuca, K. M., & Demo, A. T. (2000, September). Imaging nature: Watkins, Yosemite, and the birth of environmentalism. *Critical Studies in Media Communication, 17,* 241–260.

Dickinson, G., Ott, B. L., & Aoki, E. (2005, April). Memory and myth at the Buffalo Bill museum. *Western Journal of Communication, 69,* 85–108.

Dickinson, G., Ott, B. L., & Aoki, E. (2006, March). Space of remembering and forgetting: The reverent eye/I at the Plains Indian museum. *Communication and Critical/Cultural Studies, 3,* 27–47.

Domke, D. (1996, September). The press and "delusive theories of equality and fraternity" in the age of emancipation. *Critical Studies in Mass Communication, 13,* 228–250.

Donawerth, J. (2002). Nineteenth-century United States conduct book rhetoric by women. *Rhetoric Review, 21,* 5–21.

Dorsey, L. G., & Harlow, R. M. (2003, Spring). "We want Americans pure and simple": Theodore Roosevelt and the myth of Americanism. *Rhetoric and Public Affairs, 6,* 55–78.

Elder, D. C. (2002). A rhetoric of etiquette for the "true man" of the Gilded Age. *Rhetoric Review, 21,* 150–169.

Engbers, S. K. (2007, Summer). With great sympathy: Elizabeth Cady Stanton's innovative appeals to emotion. *Rhetoric Society Quarterly, 37,* 307–332.

Fehler, B. (2005). Classicism and the church: Nineteenth-century Calvinism and the rhetoric of oratorical culture. *Rhetoric Review, 24,* 133–149.

Fiesta, M. (2006). Homeplaces in Lydia Maria Child's abolitionist rhetoric, 1833–1879. *Rhetoric Review, 25,* 260–274.

Finnegan, C. A. (2005, Spring). Recognizing Lincoln: Image vernaculars in nineteenth-century visual culture. *Rhetoric and Public Affairs, 8,* 31–57.

Fitch, S. P., & Mandziuk, R. M. (1997). *Sojourner Truth as orator: Wit, story, and song.* Westport, CT: Greenwood Press.

Forbes, E. (2003). Every man fights for his freedom: The rhetoric of African American resistance in the mid-nineteenth century. In R. L. Jackson II & E. B. Richardson (Eds.), *Understanding African American rhetoric: Classical origins to contemporary innovations* (pp. 155–170). New York: Routledge.

Gayle, B. M., & Griffin, C. L. (1998, Spring). Mary Ashton Rice Livermore's relational feminist discourse: A rhetorically successful feminist model. *Women's Studies in Communication, 21,* 55–76.

Gere, A. R. (1997). *Intimate practices: Literacy and cultural work in U.S. women's clubs, 1880–1920*. Urbana: University of Illinois Press.

German, K. (1998, January/March). Figurative language in Native American oratory, 1609–1912. *Howard Journal of Communications, 9*, 29–40.

Gifford, C. D., & Slagell, A. R. (Eds.). (2007). *Let something good be said: Speeches and writings of Frances E. Willard*. Urbana: University of Illinois Press.

Gordon, D. B. (2003). *Black identity: Rhetoric, ideology, and nineteenth-century black nationalism*. Carbondale: Southern Illinois University Press.

Gross, A. G. (2004, Summer). Lincoln's use of constitutive metaphors. *Rhetoric and Public Affairs, 7*, 173–189.

Gunn, J. (2005). *Modern occult rhetoric: Mass media and the drama of secrecy in the twentieth century*. Tuscaloosa: University of Alabama Press.

Hansen, A. C. (2004). Dimensions of agency in Lincoln's Second Inaugural. *Philosophy and Rhetoric, 37*, 223–254.

Harpine, W. D. (2000, Summer). Playing to the press in McKinley's front porch campaign: The early weeks of a nineteenth-century pseudo-event. *Rhetoric Society Quarterly, 30*, 73–90.

Harpine, W. D. (2001, August). Bryan's "A cross of gold": The rhetoric of polarization at the 1896 Democratic convention. *Quarterly Journal of Speech, 87*, 291–304.

Harpine, W. D. (2004, Winter). "We want yer, McKinley": Epideictic rhetoric in songs from the 1896 presidential campaign. *Rhetoric Society Quarterly, 34*, 73–88.

Harpine, W. D. (2005). *From the front porch to the front page: McKinley and Bryan in the 1896 presidential campaign*. College Station: Texas A&M University Press.

Harris, L. J. (2004, Winter). The court, child custody, and social change: The rhetorical role of precedent in a 19th century child custody decision. *Rhetoric Society Quarterly, 34*, 29–45.

Harrison, K. (2003). Rhetorical rehearsals: The construction of ethos in Confederate women's Civil War diaries. *Rhetoric Review, 22*, 243–263.

Hasian, M. A., Jr. (2000). *Legal memories and amnesias in America's rhetorical culture*. Boulder, CO: Westview Press.

Hasian, M. A., Jr. (2005). *In the name of necessity: Military tribunals and the loss of American civil liberties*. Tuscaloosa: University of Alabama Press.

Hasian, M. A., Jr., Condit, C. M., & Lucaites, J. L. (1996, November). The rhetorical boundaries of "the law": A consideration of the rhetorical culture of legal practice and the case of the "separate but equal" doctrine. *Quarterly Journal of Speech, 82*, 323–342.

Hasian, M. A., Jr., & Klinger, G. D. (2002, Fall). Sarah Roberts and the early history of the "separate but equal" doctrine: A study in rhetoric, law, and social change. *Communication Studies, 53*, 269–283.

Haywood, C. M. (2003). *Prophesying daughters: Black women preachers and the word, 1823–1913*. Columbia: University of Missouri Press.

Heider, C. (2005, Spring). Suffrage, self-determination, and the Women's Christian Temperance Union in Nebraska, 1879–1882. *Rhetoric and Public Affairs, 8*, 85–107.

Hill, R. T. G. (1997, July). Performance and the "political anatomy" of pioneer Colorado. *Text and Performance Quarterly, 17*, 236–255.

Hobbs, J. H. (1997). *"I sing for I cannot be silent": The feminization of American hymnody, 1870–1920*. Pittsburgh, PA: University of Pittsburgh Press.

Hoffman, K. S. (2002, Spring). "Going public" in the 19th century: Grover Cleveland's repeal of the Sherman Silver Purchase Act. *Rhetoric and Public Affairs, 5*, 57–77.

Hogan, J. M. (Ed.). (1998). *Rhetoric and community: Studies in unity and fragmentation*. Columbia: University of South Carolina Press.

Hogan, L. S., & Hogan, J. M. (2003, Fall). Feminine virtue and practical wisdom: Elizabeth Cady Stanton's "Our boys." *Rhetoric and Public Affairs, 6*, 415–435.

Horner, J. R., & Brewin, M. (2007, March). The Salt River ticket, Democratic discourse, and nineteenth-century American politics. *Critical Studies in Media Communication, 24*, 1–20.

Hurner, S. (2006, July). Discursive identity formation of suffrage women: Reframing the "cult of true womanhood" through song. *Western Journal of Communication, 70*, 234–260.

Huxman, S. S. (2000, Fall). Perfecting the rhetorical vision of woman's rights: Elizabeth Cady Stanton, Anna Howard Shaw, and Carrie Chapman Catt. *Women's Studies in Communication, 23,* 307–336.

Johnson, N. (1991). *Nineteenth-century rhetoric in North America.* Carbondale: Southern Illinois University Press.

Johnson, N. (2000). Reigning in the court of silence: Women and rhetorical space in post-bellum America. *Philosophy and Rhetoric, 33,* 221–242.

Johnson, N. (2002). *Gender and rhetorical space in American life, 1866–1910.* Carbondale: Southern Illinois University Press.

Kates, S. (2001). *Activist rhetorics and American higher education, 1885–1937.* Carbondale: Southern Illinois University Press.

Kimble, J. J. (2007, January/March). My enemy, my brother: The paradox of peace and war in Abraham Lincoln's rhetoric of conciliation. *Southern Communication Journal, 72,* 55–70.

Lauer, J. (2007, April). Traces of the real: Autographomania and the cult of the Signers in nineteenth-century America. *Text and Performance Quarterly, 27,* 143–163.

Leeman, R. W. (Ed.). (1996). *African-American orators: A bio-critical sourcebook.* Westport, CT: Greenwood Press.

Leff, M. C. (1997). Lincoln among the nineteenth-century orators. In T. W. Benson (Ed.), *Rhetoric and political culture in nineteenth-century America* (pp. 131–155). East Lansing: Michigan State University Press.

Leff, M. C. (Ed.). (2000, Spring). Lincoln's rhetorical leadership [Special issue]. *Rhetoric and Public Affairs, 3.*

Lipscomb, D. R. (1995). Sojourner Truth: A practical public discourse. In A. A. Lunsford (Ed.), *Reclaiming Rhetorica: Women in the rhetorical tradition* (pp. 227–245). Pittsburgh, PA: University of Pittsburgh Press.

Logan, S. W. (Ed.). (1995). *With pen and voice: A critical anthology of nineteenth-century African-American women.* Carbondale: Southern Illinois University Press.

Logan, S. W. (1997). Black women on the speaker's platform (1832–1899). In M. M. Wertheimer (Ed.), *Listening to their voices: The rhetorical activities of historical women* (pp. 150–173). Columbia: University of South Carolina Press.

Logan, S. W. (1999). *"We are coming": The persuasive discourse of nineteenth-century black women.* Carbondale: Southern Illinois University Press.

Logue, C. M., & Miller, E. F. (1998, Spring). Communicative interaction and rhetorical status in Harriet Ann Jacobs' slave narrative. *Southern Communication Journal, 63,* 182–198.

Lunsford, A. A. (Ed.). (1995). *Reclaiming Rhetorica: Women in the rhetorical tradition.* Pittsburgh, PA: University of Pittsburgh Press.

MacKay, C. H. (1997, October). "Both sides of the curtain": Elizabeth Robins, synaesthesia, and the subjective correlative. *Text and Performance Quarterly, 17,* 299–316.

Mandziuk, R. M. (2003, Summer). Commemorating Sojourner Truth: Negotiating the politics of race and gender in the spaces of public memory. *Western Journal of Communication, 67,* 271–291.

Mandziuk, R. M., & Fitch, S. P. (2001, Winter). The rhetorical construction of Sojourner Truth. *Southern Communication Journal, 66,* 120–138.

Marvin, C., & Simonson, P. (2004, June). Voting alone: The decline of bodily mass communication and public sensationalism in presidential elections. *Communication and Critical/ Cultural Studies, 1,* 127–150.

Mastrangelo, L. S. (1999, Autumn). Learning from the past: Rhetoric, composition, and debate at Mount Holyoke College. *Rhetoric Review, 18,* 46–64.

Mattingly, C. (1998). *Well-tempered women: Nineteenth-century temperance rhetoric.* Carbondale: Southern Illinois University Press.

Mattingly, C. (1999, Summer). Friendly dress: A disciplined use. *Rhetoric Society Quarterly, 29,* 25–45.

Mattingly, C. (2002). *Appropriate[ing] dress: Women's rhetorical style in nineteenth-century America.* Carbondale: Southern Illinois University Press.

McMillan, G. (2002, Summer). Keeping the conversation going: Jane Addams' rhetorical situation in "A modern Lear." *Rhetoric Society Quarterly, 32,* 61–75.

Messer-Kruse, T., Eckert, J. O., Jr., Burckel, P., & Dunn, J. (2005, Summer). The Haymarket bomb: Reassessing the evidence. *Labor: Studies in Working-Class History of the Americas, 2,* 39–51.

Miller, D. H. (1999, Fall). From one voice a chorus: Elizabeth Cady Stanton's 1860 address to the New York state legislature. *Women's Studies in Communication, 22,* 152–189.

Miller, J. B. (2005, July). Coyote's tale on the old Oregon Trail: Challenging cultural memory through narrative at the Tamástslikt Cultural Institute. *Text and Performance Quarterly, 25,* 220–238.

Parry-Giles, S. J., & Blair, D. M. (2002, Winter). The rise of the rhetorical first lady: Politics, gender ideology, and women's voice, 1789–2002. *Rhetoric and Public Affairs, 5,* 565–599.

Peterson, C. (1995). *"Doers of the word": African-American women speakers and writers in the North, 1830–1880.* New York: Oxford.

Pittman, C. (2007, Winter). Black women writers and the trouble with *ethos:* Harriet Jacobs, Billie Holiday, and Sister Souljah. *Rhetoric Society Quarterly, 37,* 43–70.

Prioleau, R. C. (2003, July/September). Frederick Douglass: Abolitionist and humanist. *Howard Journal of Communications, 14,* 177–190.

Ray, A. G. (2002, Winter). Frederick Douglass on the lyceum circuit: Social assimilation, social transformation? *Rhetoric and Public Affairs, 5,* 625–647.

Ray, A. G. (2003, Spring). Representing the working class in early U.S. feminist media: The case of Hester Vaughn. *Women's Studies in Communication, 26,* 1–26.

Ray, A. G. (2005). *The lyceum and public culture in the nineteenth-century United States.* East Lansing: Michigan State University Press.

Ray, A. G. (2006, Summer). What hath she wrought? Woman's rights and the nineteenth-century lyceum. *Rhetoric and Public Affairs, 9,* 183–214.

Ray, A. G. (2007, February). The rhetorical ritual of citizenship: Women's voting as public performance, 1868–1875. *Quarterly Journal of Speech, 93,* 1–26.

Ray, A. G., & Richards, C. K. (2007, November). Inventing citizens, imagining gender justice: The suffrage rhetoric of Virginia and Francis Minor. *Quarterly Journal of Speech, 93,* 375–402.

Reid, R. F., & Klumpp, J. F. (Eds.). (2005). *American rhetorical discourse* (3rd ed.). Long Grove, IL: Waveland Press.

Ritchie, J., & Ronald, K. (Eds.). (2001). *Available means: An anthology of women's rhetoric(s).* Pittsburgh, PA: University of Pittsburgh Press.

Robbins, S. (2004). *Managing literacy, mothering America.* Pittsburgh, PA: University of Pittsburgh Press.

Rodríguez, I. (1998, October/December). News reporting and colonial discourse: The representation of Puerto Ricans in U.S. press coverage of the Spanish-American War. *Howard Journal of Communications, 9,* 283–301.

Rohan, L. (2004). I remember Mamma: Material rhetoric, mnemonic activity, and one woman's turn-of-the-twentieth-century quilt. *Rhetoric Review, 23,* 368–387.

Rothermel, B. A. (2002, Winter). A sphere of noble action: Gender, rhetoric, and influence at a nineteenth-century Massachusetts state normal school. *Rhetoric Society Quarterly, 33,* 35–64.

Royster, J. J. (1995). To call a thing by its true name: The rhetoric of Ida B. Wells. In A. A. Lunsford (Ed.), *Reclaiming Rhetorica: Women in the rhetorical tradition* (pp. 167–184). Pittsburgh, PA: University of Pittsburgh Press.

Royster, J. J. (Ed.). (1997). *Southern horrors and other writings: The anti-lynching campaign of Ida B. Wells, 1892–1900.* Boston: Bedford Books.

Royster, J. J. (2000). *Traces of a stream: Literacy and social change among African American women.* Pittsburgh, PA: University of Pittsburgh Press.

Ryan, H. R. (Ed.). (1995). *U.S. presidents as orators: A bio-critical sourcebook.* Westport, CT: Greenwood Press.

Salvatori, M. R. (Ed.). (2003). *Pedagogy: Disturbing history, 1820–1930.* Pittsburgh, PA: University of Pittsburgh Press.

Selzer, L. (1997, Autumn). Historicizing Lincoln: Garry Wills and the canonization of the "Gettysburg Address." *Rhetoric Review, 16,* 120–137.

Skinner, C. (2007). "The purity of truth": Nineteenth-century American women physicians write about delicate topics. *Rhetoric Review, 26,* 103–119.

Slagell, A. R. (2001, Spring). The rhetorical structure of Frances E. Willard's campaign for woman suffrage, 1876–1896. *Rhetoric and Public Affairs, 4,* 1–23.

Sloop, J. M. (2007). Lucy Lobdell's queer circumstances. In C. E. Morris III (Ed.),

Queering public address: Sexualities in American historical discourse (pp. 149–173). Columbia: University of South Carolina Press.

Stanton, E. C. (1892, January 23). The solitude of self. *Woman's Journal*, pp. 25, 32.

Stormer, N. (1999). Embodied humanism: Performative argument for natural rights in "The solitude of self." *Argumentation and Advocacy, 36*, 51–64.

Stormer, N. (2001, Spring). *Why not?* Memory and counter-memory in 19th-century abortion rhetoric. *Women's Studies in Communication, 24*, 1–29.

Stormer, N. (2002). *Articulating life's memory: U.S. medical rhetoric about abortion in the nineteenth century.* Lanham, MD: Lexington Books.

Strange, L. S. (2002, Fall). Dress reform and the feminine ideal: Elizabeth Cady Stanton and the "Coming girl." *Southern Communication Journal, 68*, 1–13.

Stromberg, E. (Ed.). (2006). *American Indian rhetorics of survivance: Word medicine, word magic.* Pittsburgh, PA: University of Pittsburgh Press.

Torrens, K. M. (1997, Fall). All dressed up with no place to go: Rhetorical dimensions of the nineteenth century dress reform movement. *Women's Studies in Communication, 20*, 189–210.

Towns, W. S. (1998). *Oratory and rhetoric in the nineteenth-century South: A rhetoric of defense.* Westport, CT: Greenwood Press.

Vivian, B. (1999, Winter). The art of forgetting: John W. Draper and the rhetorical dimensions of history. *Rhetoric and Public Affairs, 2*, 551–572.

Wagner, J. (1995). "Intelligent members or restless disturbers": Women's rhetorical styles, 1880–1920. In A. A. Lunsford (Ed.), *Reclaiming Rhetorica: Women in the rhetorical tradition* (pp. 185–202). Pittsburgh, PA: University of Pittsburgh Press.

Watson, M. (Ed.). (1991). *A voice of their own: The woman suffrage press, 1840–1910.* Tuscaloosa: University of Alabama Press.

Watson, M. (1999). *Lives of their own: Rhetorical dimensions in autobiographies of women activists.* Columbia: University of South Carolina Press.

Wells, S. (2002). Discursive mobility and double consciousness in S. Weir Mitchell and W. E. B. Du Bois. *Philosophy and Rhetoric, 35*, 120–137.

Wertheimer, M. M. (Ed.). (1997). *Listening to their voices: The rhetorical activities of historical women.* Columbia: University of South Carolina Press.

Whitburn, M. D. (2004, Fall). Rhetorical theory in Yale's graduate schools in the late nineteenth century: The example of William C. Robinson's *Forensic oratory. Rhetoric Society Quarterly, 34*, 55–70.

Wilson, K. H. (1998, May). The contested space of prudence in the 1874–1875 civil rights debate. *Quarterly Journal of Speech, 84*, 131–149.

Wilson, K. H. (1999a, Spring). Toward a discursive theory of racial identity: *The Souls of Black Folk* as a response to nineteenth-century biological determinism. *Western Journal of Communication, 63*, 193–215.

Wilson, K. H. (1999b, Fall). Emerson, transcendental prudence, and the legacy of Senator Charles Sumner. *Rhetoric and Public Affairs, 2*, 453–479.

Wilson, K. H. (2000, Spring). The paradox of Lincoln's rhetorical leadership. *Rhetoric and Public Affairs, 3*, 15–32.

Wilson, K. H. (2002). *The Reconstruction desegregation debate: The politics of equality and the rhetoric of place, 1870–1875.* East Lansing: Michigan State University Press.

Wilson, K. H. (2003, May). The racial politics of imitation in the nineteenth century. *Quarterly Journal of Speech, 89*, 89–108.

Wilson, K. H. (2005). The politics of place and presidential rhetoric in the United States, 1875–1901. In J. A. Aune & E. D. Rigsby (Eds.), *Civil rights rhetoric and the American presidency* (pp. 16–40). College Station: Texas A&M University Press.

Zarefsky, D. (2000, Spring). Lincoln's 1862 annual message: A paradigm of rhetorical leadership. *Rhetoric and Public Affairs, 3*, 5–14.

Zenger, A. A. (2004). Race, composition, and "our English": Performing the mother tongue in a daily theme assignment at Harvard, 1886–87. *Rhetoric Review, 23*, 332–349.

29

For the Common Good

*Rhetoric and Discourse Practices
in the United States, 1900–1950*

THOMAS W. BENSON

The first half of the 20th century witnessed enormous changes in the technologies, practices, teaching, and study of communication in the United States. And yet it must be admitted at the beginning of this attempt to characterize scholarship on early 20th-century American discourse practices that despite a vast amount of scholarly literature, the period is not generally regarded as a unified area of scholarly specialization for rhetorical scholars, it is not represented by a taken-for-granted canon of discursive works, and departments of rhetoric in English, Speech, and Communication typically do not offer separate courses in the period as a unit. Furthermore, rhetorical scholarship and criticism typically proceed in a case-by-case approach, which emulates the situated, contingent action of the rhetors under study. Hence, any representation of this literature is bound to be a misrepresentation, selecting and squeezing individual works into recognizable categories, and so should be regarded as at best a partial introduction. This chapter, while it attempts to bring together for the serious student some of the resources and leading lines of research, may inadvertently suggest the existence of a coherent body of work that is in fact better thought of as a series of significant achievements, separate conversations, unfinished business, forgotten controversies, and unfulfilled potential. A review of some of those conversations may contribute to renewed interest in the period and a fresh commitment to study it as a unit—not separate from what came before or after, or elsewhere, but as a time and place of immense interest and crucial importance to our own understandings of rhetoric and discourse practices. The basic materials are in place to support courses centered on the period, and the scholarship is sufficiently rich—and yet sufficiently incomplete—that it is a potentially rich area of scholarly investigation, especially since the problems encountered in the turbulent first half of the 20th century have so much in common with our own times.

In this chapter, I have no particular theory to offer about the period or about our scholarship on the period—that is not how rhetorical knowledge accumulates in the history and criticism of public address. Rather, I attempt to bring together a preliminary survey of the rich literature on the period, the essential scaffolding for research and teaching. The materials now exist in our literature for graduate and undergraduate courses in the public discourse of the early-20th-century United States, and there is important unfinished business in our scholarship, which is rapidly expanding, diversifying, and deepening.

Implicitly, our discipline celebrates public rhetoric that is discursive, democratic, decisive, deliberative, and diverse. In practice, no subset of the discipline has cultivated a full historical account of the public practices that might meet such an ideal, nor even a coherent history of the various practices that act as substitutes, deferrals, approximations, or corruptions of such practices. However frenzied our turf wars, however conservative our curricula, and however rigid our gatekeeping, our scholarly practices are, to a large degree, anarchic, depending on the enterprise of individual scholars to shape the literature of the discipline.

By the turn of the 21st century, many (certainly not all) rhetoric graduate students in departments of Communication and English had come to accept more or less as a given that, in the words of T. V. Reed (1992), their work should be centered not only in literature or speeches but also in "that vast social text we call the world," (p. xi) and "that their work is unavoidably political and needs to become more attuned to radically democratic social movements" (p. xi). The road to the politicizing of rhetorical studies is itself the result of historical events and scholarly arguments that can, in part, be discerned in 20th-century rhetorical scholarship about early 20th-century discursive practices. Early 20th-century rhetorical scholars would more likely have claimed that the discipline of English studies was not political, and that the discipline of speech was political only in the sense that it trained young people for civic participation. A powerful current in rhetorical studies at the beginning of the 21st century suggests a synthesis, such as that suggested by Rosa Eberly, who in *Citizen Critics* (2000) places more emphasis on democratizing than on radicalizing; Eberly writes that "cultural texts have some role to play in reinvigorating participatory democratic practice" (p. 1).

Current scholarly understanding of early 20th-century American public discourse is shaped by two great historical ideals—the Progressive Era and the New Deal—interrupted by a conservative interregnum that acts as a sort of rhetorical pause, allowing the dominance for a time of countervailing suspicion of government activism, a consolidation of progressive gains, and a reshaping of the debate.

The published scholarship of the earliest days in the discipline of "speech" focused more on the theory and pedagogy of public speaking than on the discursive practices of particular speakers or the society in general, but the pedagogy of public speaking was typically grounded in claims that it is a central tool of democratic society. Though the terms *discursive practices* or the more general *discourse practices* did not exist in the literature in the first half of the century, these early scholars would have said that their discussions of public speaking education and writing instruction were precisely directed at understanding and improving the practice of American discourse.[1] Gradually, pedagogical scholarship was joined to theoretical, critical, and historical scholarship. The *Quarterly Journal of Speech,* first published in 1915, began as early as 1927 to publish extended scholarship on early-20th-century discourse with V. E. Simrell's "H. L. Mencken the Rhetorician" (1927) and Gladys Murphy Graham's "Concerning the Speech Power of Woodrow Wilson" (1927). Implicitly, the scholars of the 20th century regarded rhetorical practice as part of a long tradition and an underlying psychological predisposition. Study of ancient Greek and Roman rhetoric and oratory, and of the speeches of 18th- and 19th-century American orators, was justified not only as a mode of historical investigation but also as a search for theoretical continuities and practical wisdom that guided the classroom teaching of public speaking. In this special sense, the whole history of rhetorical practice and theorizing was regarded as relevant to—and continuous with—contemporary practice and classroom instruction. On the other hand, a century of scholarship in speech and communication has gradually produced a separation between public speaking pedagogy and historical-critical-theoretical scholarship, a development very different from what happened with writing instruction and rhetorical scholarship in departments of English.

This review of the literature takes as its domain primarily public discourse and limits its first search to journals and books in speech, communication, and English. A search of journals in these fields yielded 295 historical and critical articles about public address, 1900–1950, broadly conceived, published in

the period 1926–2006. The following table indicates the numbers by journal.

Journal	Articles
Quarterly Journal of Speech	146
Southern Communication Journal	41
Communication Monographs	36
Western Journal of Communication	32
Rhetoric & Public Affairs	21
Communication Quarterly	13
Rhetoric Society Quarterly	6
Total	295

The totals are in some ways misleading, since these journals began publication decades apart. My search indicates that public-address studies, though a small field, is thriving. In the journals searched, the period since 1995 has produced some 81 articles on the period (see the table below)—more than 27% of the journal articles published since 1927. The figure is even more impressive when to these totals are added the many books and book chapters published in the past 20 or so years in communication, English, and related fields.

Year	Articles
1995	5
1996	4
1997	7
1998	10
1999	5
2000	3
2001	13
2002	11
2003	9
2004	9
2005	5
Total	81

But although there is a steady production of high-quality articles, chapters, and books, it must be admitted that the production is so small that we are far from having either a general or a detailed picture of public discourse in early 20th-century America. Some trends are evident—the literature does follow the conventional historical understandings of chronological periods, and it divides primarily between elite, mostly presidential, discourse on the one hand and variously marginal or radical discourse on the other. Even the radical discourse we study tends to identify well-known public figures, so it might be more accurate to say that we study primarily the establishment elite and the radical or marginal elite—most of whom are contenders for a place in an informal canon. The vast middle ground of everyday civic discourse—the domain in which our students in public speaking or composition courses will participate, if they participate at all—is virtually ignored in our historical and critical literature, as is the quasi-elite domain of local and state officialdom, whether legislative, legal, bureaucratic, commercial, or ceremonial. Overwhelmingly, our research is text based. We have tended to study single rhetorical acts or acts clustered in a career, a genre, a theoretical set, or a social movement. We have not, for the most part, studied general discursive practices—the material conditions of speaking, the spaces and times, the formal rules, the institutional settings—except briefly and often at second hand in the context of text-centered studies.

THE PROGRESSIVE ERA

The Progressive Era straddles the end of the 19th century and the first two decades of the 20th century. Wiebe (1967) dates the era to the years 1877–1920. McGerr (2003) starts earlier but ends in the same year, dating the Progressive Era in the years 1870–1920. Both Wiebe and McGerr describe the collapse of an old order in the years following the Civil War, with migration and immigration to American cities, expanding industrialization, the completion of transcontinental railways, the rise of a middle class, and a series of depressions that took place in the context of financial and corporate abuse. An impulse to reform, rationalize, and regulate a society that felt itself torn from old ways, not knowing how to go forward to a new order or back to an old one, provided the context for what came to be called the Progressive Era, which came in retrospect to frame the words and actions of Americans who were often strongly at odds with each other and whose values sometimes seem, in retrospect, contradictory. As a general proposition, the Progressive Era appears to be characterized by a faith that Americans could use their government to accomplish great reforms, both by limiting the abuses of corporate monopolies and by providing services beyond the scope of the private sphere.

In his introduction to *Rhetoric and Reform in the Progressive Era,* a useful starting point for the student of rhetoric interested in the period, J. Michael Hogan (2003) writes that despite the difficulty of defining its historical contours with precision, "there may be something more that distinguishes the Progressive Era: a *Rhetorical Renaissance* that changed how Americans *talked* about politics and society" (p. x). Divided as they may have been about policy, Progressives "above all else . . . looked for answers in a revitalized public sphere. Progressives had faith that a democratic public, properly educated and deliberating freely, provided the best hope for the future of the American democracy" (p. x). That faith was also reflected in the founding of the discipline of Speech/Communication (Benson, 1985, 2003; Cohen, 1994; Wallace, 1954). But the "renaissance" of interest in rhetoric was sometimes seen as partly a last glimmer of the old order. Kraig (2003) writes that Theodore Roosevelt, Woodrow Wilson, and a few others in this "second oratorical renaissance" were the last of their kind in American rhetoric.

> The oratorical tradition Wilson so admired was more than a cultural style. It was at base an ethical tradition that required its adherents to live up to an exalted code of conduct. In an age dominated by the standards and practices of public relations and advertising, this connection between eloquence and character has atrophied. (p. 32)

Hogan (2003) and his collaborators identify a range of speakers, issues, and movements that, when amplified by other work in the discipline, provides a snapshot of studies in the rhetoric of the era.

The two outstanding presidents of the era, Theodore Roosevelt and Woodrow Wilson, are identified as the inventors of what Jeffrey Tulis (1987) terms the "rhetorical presidency" (Ceaser, Thurow, Tulis, & Bessette, 1981; Medhurst, 1996). According to the theory of the rhetorical presidency, Roosevelt and Wilson initiated a practice of going to the people, over the heads of Congress, with enduring Constitutional distortions. Medhurst (1996) and others have countered that the presidency is always and inherently a rhetorical institution. Dorsey finds in Theodore Roosevelt not so much a Constitutional or even legislative leader but rather a "rhetorical progressive," whose seemingly contradictory advocacy of domestic progressivism and foreign wars was reconciled by his interpretation of these matters as moral questions:

> Domestically, Roosevelt's "rhetorical progressivism" exposed the evils corrupting civilization. He condemned the greedy who elevated material gain above all else and the reformers who, out of envy, overzealously condemned the rich. He wrote and spoke prolifically on the need for every American to embrace both virtue and the "strenuous life" necessary to uphold it. In foreign affairs, he likewise reduced great controversies and even wars to simple questions of

character. (p. 76; see also Behl, 1945, 1947; Buehler, 1998; Dorsey, 1995, 1997; Dorsey & Harlow, 2003; Lucas, 1973; Paulson, 2002)

Woodrow Wilson has been of interest to rhetorical historian-critics since the earliest days of the discipline. In 1927, Gladys Murphy Graham speculated about Wilson's rhetorical mastery as his public papers began to make systematic study possible. She identified many themes that were worked out in more detail in the coming decades—the Constitutional propriety of Wilson's rhetorical relations with Congress and the people, the inferiority of his League of Nations speeches, the deep intellectual mastery combined with what Wilson called "the sword of penetrating speech" (p. 414). Scholars studied Wilson's preparation, sources, and background (McKean, 1930a; Wagner, 1929); his international rhetoric (Benjamin, 1979; Flanagan, 2004; Henderlider, 1946; Paget, 1929); his style (McKean, 1930b; Runion, 1935); his rhetorical career (Craig, 1952; Osborn, 1956); and his influence (Stuckey, 2003; Wilson, 1957).

The Progressive Era witnessed the emergence of a new generation of African American rhetorics and rhetors, yet at the same time the perfection of a system of segregation whose echoes and effects are still present. In a cluster of brilliant essays, Browne (1998), Darsey (1998), and Terrill & Watts (2002) examine the powers and limits of W. E. B. Du Bois's concept of "double consciousness" (see also Wilson, 1999). McGee, on the other hand, writes that "far from being a time of progress for African Americans, the Progressive Era marked the worst period for race relations since the Civil War" (McGee, 2003, p. 312; see also McGee, 1998, 2000; Ware & Linkugel, 1982; Watts, 2001, 2002; White, 1944, 1946).

The Progressive Era was marked by the official closing in 1890 of the U.S. frontier, and by changing attitudes about the interaction of science, nature, and public culture. Christine

Oravec (2003) writes that in the progressive conservation movement, "rhetorical discourse both constructed a social movement grounded in progressivism and also positioned the people of the United States as constituents of a progressivist public culture" (p. 87; see also Buehler, 1998; Dorsey, 1995; Oravec, 1984).

The end of the Progressive Era witnessed the success of a movement for equal rights that had begun long before the Progressives came on the scene. In 1848, the first woman's rights convention, in Seneca Falls, New York, passed a resolution for equal rights—including the right to vote—that was proposed by Elizabeth Cady Stanton. Only in 1920, with ratification by Tennessee, did the Woman Suffrage Movement gain the 19th Amendment to the U.S. Constitution, granting women the right to vote. Karlyn Kohrs Campbell has written foundational studies in women's rhetoric that have, in many ways, inspired and set the agenda for later generations of feminist rhetorical historians (see, e.g., Campbell, 1986, 1989, 1993). Jennifer Borda (2002) studies the contrasting rhetorics of three leaders who sparked a renewal of the suffrage movement in the period from 1890 to 1920—Carrie Chapman Catt, Alice Paul, and Harriot Stanton Blatch (on woman's suffrage, see also Beasley, 2002; Borda, 2002; Croy, 1998; Maddux, 2004; Palczewski, 2005; Ramsey, 2000). Rhetorical historians remind us that there is more to woman's rhetoric than the suffrage campaign. Carl R. Burgchardt (2003) describes Jane Addams's "rhetoric of pacifism." Judith A. Allen (1999) writes of the long progressive career of Charlotte Perkins Gilman (see also Cuklanz, 1995; Kerber, 1988; Solomon, 1988).

THE NEW DEAL ERA

Historians generally mark the year 1920 as the end of the Progressive Era. World War I ended in 1918. By 1920, Woodrow Wilson's presidency ended; he was succeeded by three Republicans—Warren G. Harding, Calvin Coolidge, and Herbert Hoover (Houck, 2001; Wilson, 1962). The 1920s were a time of stock market boom and bust, of the Jazz Age, the Harlem Renaissance, the coming of sound film and the radio, the rapid spread of the automobile and the airplane—all of which contributed to the transformation of American culture and communication. Harding appealed for a return to "normalcy." The 1920s ended with the Great Depression and the emergence of Franklin Delano Roosevelt (FDR), who was elected to the presidency in 1932—and then in 1936, 1940, and 1944: an unprecedented four terms. Roosevelt died in office on April 12, 1945, after guiding the longest and one of the most far-reaching governing reformations in the nation's history, and leading the nation through World War II, from which the United States emerged as the most powerful of all the democracies (Benson, 2006; Kennedy, 1999; Schlesinger, 1958, 1960, 1963).

FDR dominated the rhetorical culture of his day, and rhetorical scholars have emphasized Roosevelt in their treatment of the era. Early scholarship focused on FDR's education and practices as an orator, including Crowell's (1950) study of speechwriting practices (see also Behl, 1945, 1947; Braden & Brandenburg, 1955; Brandenburg, 1949a, 1949b; Brandenburg & Braden, 1952, 1955; Cowperthwaite, 1952; Crowell, 1950, 1952, 1955, 1958; Gravlee, 1963, 1965; King, 1937; Oliver, 1945; Shipman, 1948; Voelker, 1936; Zelko, 1942). More detailed studies of particular speeches emerged in the scholarship of the past four decades (Benson, 1969, 2002; Buehler, 1998; Daughton, 1993; Hasian, 2003a; Kiewe, 2004; Lim, 2003; Ryan, 1979, 1981, 1988).

This chapter is being written during the presidency of George W. Bush, when key administration leaders openly announce their ambition to repeal the New Deal; some even boast of returning to an America that existed before the reforms of the Progressive Era. Changing political times prompt us to renew our memories of the rhetoric of these periods, to reassess the period from our own vantage points, and to discover rhetorical resources that might be used in solving our own problems. Studies of the New Deal Era and of FDR seem to have taken on a new urgency and edge. Recent scholarship presents a range of views about Roosevelt's rhetoric, sometimes with a more nuanced appreciation of his rhetorical genius and sometimes with a revisionist suspicion of his dominant rhetorical reputation. In a study of the fireside chats, Daughton (2006) traces metaphors of FDR as the physician, and speculates that though the image is one of benevolence, it also has the potential to short-circuit discourse. Houck and Nocosian (2006), in their investigation of FDR's first inaugural address, press the claims of Raymond Moley as principal author, investigate audience response as demonstrated in letters to FDR, and argue that although Roosevelt was successful in restoring hope by an appeal to action, his solutions may not have been very different from those of Herbert Hoover. Beasley and Smith-Howell (2006) argue that FDR invented a version of the rhetorical presidency that advanced democratic practices while limiting the potential abuses of later rhetorical presidents.

Though Roosevelt dominated his era, he also attracted a wide variety of active supporters and rivals. Labor leader John L. Lewis, radical Catholic priest Father Charles Coughlin, and the Kingfish—Louisiana's Huey Long—at various stages each supported Franklin Roosevelt and then broke from him over policy or personal ambition (Abernathy, 1955; Bormann, 1954, 1957; Brinkley, 1982; Carpenter, 2006; Dorgan, 1971; Gallagher, 1961; Gaske, 1992; Hogan & Williams, 2004; Iltis, 2006; Jensen, 2006; Lee & Lee, 1939). From within the administration, Eleanor Roosevelt and Frances Perkins, the first woman cabinet member, provided significant rhetorical leadership (Atkinson, 2006; Blair, 2001; Waggenspack, 2006).

In the Progressive and New Deal Eras, the United States grew its government and adapted its rhetorical practices through unprecedented prosperity, the Great Depression, and two World Wars. Movies, radio, photojournalism, television, political spectacle, and the mass and popular arts became powerful rhetorical instruments (Becker, 1961; Benson, 1998; Borda, 2002; Bormann, 1957; Carter, 1980; Curtis, 1989; Daniel, Foresta, Stange, & Stein, 1987; Dorsey, 1997; Edwards & Winkler, 1997; Finnegan, 2001a, 2001b, 2003; German, 1990; Medhurst & Benson, 1981; Merritt, 1975; Mohrmann & Scott, 1976; Muscio, 1997; Natanson, 1992; Olson, 1983; Smiley, 1968; Smith, 1970; Spalding, 1959; Stott, 1973; Summers, 1948). In the Progressive and New Deal movements, Americans worked, always in vigorous debate and often with mixed results, to create new mechanisms of government and communication, groping for ways to preserve the best of the old while struggling with racism, social injustice, inequality, insecurity, and war. The rhetorical agendas of the period are unfinished, and our scholarship is painfully incomplete. The dynamic rhetoric of the period has produced some of our finest scholarship in rhetorical history and criticism, well worth the attention of today's students. There is much to be done.

NOTE

1. The term *discourse practice,* adopted from the writings of Michel Foucault, did not enter the discipline of speech communication until the 1980s. In one of the earliest articles on the subject, Foss and Gill (1987) write,

Of primary importance in Foucault's theory of rhetoric as epistemic is discursive practices. By "discursive practices" Foucault does not mean the speech acts of our daily lives. Rather, he is concerned with discourse that, because it follows particular rules or has passed the appropriate tests, is understood to be true in a culture. (p. 387)

And yet in the past 20 years, the term has lost some of the special sense in which Foucault defined it and has come to refer to patterns of discourse (including nonverbal forms, which Foucault also included in the term) more generally.

REFERENCES

Abernathy, E. (1955). Huey Long: Oratorical "wealth sharing." *Southern Communication Journal, 21,* 87–102.

Allen, J. A. (1999). Reconfiguring vice: Charlotte Perkins Gilman, prostitution, and frontier sexual contracts. In J. Rudd & V. Gough (Eds.), *Charlotte Perkins Gilman: Optimist reformer* (pp. 173–199). Iowa City: University of Iowa Press.

Atkinson, A. (2006). The rhetoric of social security and conservative backlash: Frances Perkins as Secretary of Labor. In T. W. Benson (Ed.), *American rhetoric in the New Deal Era, 1932–1945* (pp. 211–243). East Lansing: Michigan State University Press.

Beasley, V. B. (2002). Engendering democratic change: How three U.S. presidents discussed female suffrage. *Rhetoric & Public Affairs, 5,* 79–103.

Beasley, V. B., & Smith-Howell, D. (2006). No ordinary rhetorical President? FDR's speechmaking and leadership, 1933–1945. In T. W. Benson (Ed.), *American rhetoric in the New Deal Era, 1932–1945* (pp. 1–32). East Lansing: Michigan State University Press.

Becker, S. L. (1961). Presidential power: The influence of broadcasting. *Quarterly Journal of Speech, 47,* 10–18.

Behl, W. A. (1945). Theodore Roosevelt's principles of speech preparation and delivery. *Communication Monographs, 12,* 112–122.

Behl, W. A. (1947). Theodore Roosevelt's principles of invention. *Communication Monographs, 14,* 93–110.

Benjamin, J. (1979). Rhetorical and diplomatic errors in Woodrow Wilson's war message. *Communication, 8,* 1–7.

Benson, T. W. (1969). Inaugurating peace: Franklin D. Roosevelt's last speech. *Speech Monographs, 36,* 138–147.

Benson, T. W. (Ed.). (1985). *Speech communication in the 20th century.* Carbondale: Southern Illinois University Press.

Benson, T. W. (1998). Thinking through film: Hollywood remembers the blacklist. In J. M. Hogan (Ed.), *Rhetoric and community* (pp. 218–255). Columbia: University of South Carolina Press.

Benson, T. W. (2002). FDR at Gettysburg: The New Deal and the rhetoric of presidential leadership. In L. G. Dorsey (Ed.), *The presidency and rhetorical leadership* (pp. 145–183). College Station: Texas A&M University Press.

Benson, T. W. (2003). The Cornell school of rhetoric: Idiom and institution. *Communication Quarterly, 51,* 1–56.

Benson, T. W. (Ed.). (2006). *American rhetoric in the New Deal Era.* East Lansing: Michigan State University Press.

Blair, D. M. (2001). No ordinary time: Eleanor Roosevelt's address to the 1940 Democratic National Convention. *Rhetoric & Public Affairs, 4,* 203–222.

Borda, J. L. (2002). The woman suffrage parades of 1910–1913: Possibilities and limitations of an early feminist rhetorical strategy. *Western Journal of Communication, 66,* 25–52.

Bormann, E. G. (1954). Huey Long: Analysis of a demagogue. *Communication Quarterly, 2,* 16–19.

Bormann, E. G. (1957). A rhetorical analysis of the national radio broadcasts of Senator Huey Pierce Long. *Communication Monographs, 24,* 244–257.

Braden, W. W., & Brandenburg, E. (1955). Roosevelt's fireside chats. *Speech Monographs, 22,* 290–302.

Brandenburg, E. (1949a). The preparation of Franklin D. Roosevelt's speeches. *Quarterly Journal of Speech, 35,* 214–221.

Brandenburg, E. (1949b). Franklin D. Roosevelt's international speeches: 1939–1941. *Communication Monographs, 16,* 21–40.

Brandenburg, E., & Braden, W. W. (1952). Franklin D. Roosevelt's voice and pronunciation. *Quarterly Journal of Speech, 38,* 23–30.

Brandenburg, E., & Braden, W. W. (1955). Franklin Delano Roosevelt. In M. K. Hochmuth (Ed.), *A history and criticism of American public address* (Vol. 3, pp. 458–530). New York: Longmans, Green.

Brinkley, A. (1982). *Voices of protest: Huey Long, Father Coughlin, and the Great Depression.* New York: Knopf.

Browne, S. H. (1998). Du Bois, double-consciousness, and the modern city. In J. M. Hogan (Ed.), *Rhetoric and community: Studies in unity and fragmentation* (pp. 75–92). Columbia: South Carolina University Press.

Buehler, D. O. (1998). Permanence and change in Theodore Roosevelt's conservation jeremiad. *Western Journal of Communication, 62,* 439–458.

Burgchardt, C. R. (2003). From Hull House to The Hague: Jane Addams's rhetoric of pacifism, 1898–1917. In J. M. Hogan (Ed.), *Rhetoric and reform in the progressive era* (pp. 387–389). East Lansing: Michigan State University Press.

Campbell, K. K. (1986). Style and content in rhetoric of early Afro-American feminists. *Quarterly Journal of Speech, 72,* 434–445.

Campbell, K. K. (1989). *Man cannot speak for her* (Vol. 1). New York: Greenwood Press.

Campbell, K. K. (1993). *Women public speakers in the United States, 1800–1925: A bio-critical sourcebook.* Westport, CT: Greenwood Press.

Carpenter, R. H. (2006). Father Charles E. Coughlin: Delivery, style in discourse, and opinion leadership. In T. W. Benson (Ed.), *American rhetoric in the New Deal Era, 1932–1945* (pp. 315–367). East Lansing: Michigan State University Press.

Carter, D. A. (1980). The industrial workers of the world and the rhetoric of song. *Quarterly Journal of Speech, 66,* 365–374.

Ceaser, J. W., Thurow, G. E., Tulis, J., & Bessette, J. (1981). The rise of the rhetorical Presidency. *Presidential Studies Quarterly, 11,* 158–171.

Cohen, H. (1994). *The history of speech communication: The emergence of a discipline, 1914–1945.* Annandale, VA: Speech Communication Association.

Cowperthwaite, L. L. (1952). Franklin D. Roosevelt at Harvard. *Quarterly Journal of Speech, 38,* 37–41.

Craig, H. (1952). Woodrow Wilson as an orator. *Quarterly Journal of Speech, 38,* 145–148.

Crowell, L. (1950). Franklin D. Roosevelt's audience persuasion in the 1936 campaign. *Communication Monographs, 17,* 48–64.

Crowell, L. (1952). Roosevelt the Grotonian. *Quarterly Journal of Speech, 38,* 31–36.

Crowell, L. (1955). The building of the 'Four Freedoms' speech. *Speech Monographs, 22,* 266–283.

Crowell, L. (1958). Word changes introduced *ad libitum* in five speeches by Franklin Delano Roosevelt. *Communication Monographs, 25,* 229–242.

Croy, T. D. (1998). The crisis: A complete critical edition of Carrie Chapman Catt's 1916 presidential address to the National American Woman Suffrage Association. *Rhetoric Society Quarterly, 28,* 49–73.

Cuklanz, L. M. (1995). "Shrill squawk" or strategic innovation: A rhetorical reassessment of Margaret Sanger's woman rebel. *Communication Quarterly, 43,* 1–19.

Curtis, J. (1989). *Mind's eye, mind's truth: FSA photography reconsidered.* Philadelphia: Temple University Press.

Daniel, P., Foresta, M., Stange, M., & Stein, S. (1987). *Official images: New deal photography.* Washington, DC: Smithsonian Institute.

Darsey, J. (1998). "The Voice of Exile": W. E. B. Du Bois and the quest for culture. In J. M. Hogan (Ed.), *Rhetoric and community: Studies in unity and fragmentation* (pp. 93–110). Columbia: South Carolina University Press.

Daughton, S. M. (1993). Metaphorical transcendence: Images of the holy war in Franklin Roosevelt's first inaugural. *Quarterly Journal of Speech, 79,* 427–446.

Daughton, S. M. (2006). FDR as family doctor: Medical metaphors and the role of physician in the Fireside Chats. In T. W. Benson (Ed.), *American rhetoric in the New Deal Era, 1932–1945* (pp. 33–82). East Lansing: Michigan State University Press.

Dorgan, H. (1971). Gerald L. K. Smith and the Huey P. Long funeral oration. *Southern Communication Journal, 36,* 378–389.

Dorsey, L. G. (1995). The frontier myth in presidential rhetoric: Theodore Roosevelt's campaign for conservation. *Western Journal of Communication, 59,* 1–19.

Dorsey, L. G. (1997). Sailing into the "Wondrous Now": The myth of the American navy's world cruise. *Quarterly Journal of Speech, 83,* 447–465.

Dorsey, L. G., & Harlow, R. M. (2003). "We want Americans pure and simple": Theodore Roosevelt and the myth of Americanism. *Rhetoric & Public Affairs, 6,* 55–78.

Eberly, R. A. (2000). *Citizen critics: Literary public spheres.* Urbana: University of Illinois Press.

Edwards, J. L., & Winkler, C. K. (1997). Representative form and the visual ideograph: The Iwo Jima image in editorial cartoons. *Quarterly Journal of Speech, 83,* 289–310.

Finnegan, C. A. (2001a). Documentary as art in *U. S. Camera. Rhetoric Society Quarterly, 31,* 37–68.

Finnegan, C. A. (2001b). The naturalistic enthymeme and visual argument: Photographic representation in the "Skull Controversy." *Argumentation and Advocacy, 37,* 133–149.

Finnegan, C. A. (2003). *Picturing poverty: Print culture and FSA photographs.* Washington, DC: Smithsonian Books.

Flanagan, J. C. (2004). Woodrow Wilson's "Rhetorical Restructuring": The transformation of the American self and the construction of the German enemy. *Rhetoric & Public Affairs, 7,* 115–148.

Foss, S. K., & Gill, A. (1987). Michel Foucault's theory of rhetoric as epistemic. *Western Journal of Speech Communication, 51,* 384–401.

Gallagher, M. B. (1961). John L. Lewis: The oratory of pity and indignation. *Today's Speech, 9,* 15–16, 29.

Gaske, P. C. (1992). The analysis of demagogic discourse: Huey Long's "Every Man a King" Address. In H. R. Ryan (Ed.), *Contemporary American public discourse: A collection of speeches and critical essays* (3rd ed., pp. 47–65). Prospect Heights, IL: Waveland Press.

German, K. M. (1990). Frank Capra's *Why We Fight* series and the American audience. *Western Journal of Communication, 54,* 237–248.

Graham, G. M. (1927). Concerning the speech power of Woodrow Wilson. *Quarterly Journal of Speech, 13,* 412–424.

Gravlee, J. (1963). Stephen T. Early: The "Advance Man." *Communication Monographs, 30,* 41–49.

Gravlee, J. (1965). Franklin D. Roosevelt's speech preparation during his first national campaign. *Communication Monographs, 31,* 437–460.

Hasian, M. A., Jr. (2003a). Franklin D. Roosevelt, The Holocaust, and modernity's rescue rhetorics. *Communication Quarterly, 51*(2), 154–173.

Hasian, M. A., Jr. (2003b). Franklin D. Roosevelt, wartime anxieties, and the saboteurs' case. *Rhetoric & Public Affairs, 6,* 233–260.

Henderlider, C. R. (1946). Woodrow Wilson's speeches on the League of Nations, September 4–25, 1919. *Communication Monographs, 13*(1), 23–34.

Hogan, J. M. (Ed.). (2003). *Rhetoric and reform in the Progressive Era.* East Lansing: Michigan State University Press.

Hogan, J. M., & Williams, G. (2004). The rusticity and religiosity of Huey P. Long. *Rhetoric & Public Affairs, 7,* 149–171.

Houck, D. W. (2001). *Rhetoric as currency: Hoover, Roosevelt and the Great Depression.* College Station: Texas A&M University Press.

Houck, D. W., & Nocasian, M. (2006). Dictator, savior, and the return of confidence: Text, context, and reception in FDR's first inaugural address. In T. W. Benson (Ed.), *American rhetoric in the New Deal Era, 1932–1945* (pp. 83–114). East Lansing: Michigan State University Press.

Iltis, R. S. (2006). Reconsidering the demagoguery of Huey Long. In T. W. Benson (Ed.), *American rhetoric in the New Deal Era, 1932–1945* (pp. 369–417). East Lansing: Michigan State University Press.

Jensen, R. J. (2006). The thundering voice of John L. Lewis. In T. W. Benson (Ed.), *American rhetoric in the New Deal Era, 1932–1945* (pp. 279–314). East Lansing: Michigan State University Press.

Kennedy, D. M. (1999). *Freedom from fear: The American people in depression and war, 1929–1945.* New York: Oxford University Press.

Kerber, L. K. (1988). Separate spheres, female worlds, woman's place: The rhetoric of women's history. *Journal of American History, 75,* 9–39.

Kiewe, A. (2004). Whither bound? Franklin D. Roosevelt's Quo Vadis. *Southern Communication Journal, 70,* 56–71.

King, R. D. (1937). Franklin D. Roosevelt's second inaugural address. *Quarterly Journal of Speech, 23,* 439–444.

Kraig, R. A. (2003). The second oratorical renaissance. In J. M. Hogan (Ed.), *Rhetoric and reform in the Progressive Era* (pp. 1–48). East Lansing: Michigan State University Press.

Lee, A. M., & Lee, E. B. (1939). *The fine art of propaganda: A study of Father Coughlin's speeches.* New York: Harcourt, Brace.

Lim, E. T. (2003). The lion and the lamb: De-mythologizing Franklin Roosevelt's fireside chats. *Rhetoric & Public Affairs, 6,* 437–464.

Lucas, S. E. (1973). The man with the muck rake: A reinterpretation. *Quarterly Journal of Speech, 59,* 452–462.

Maddux, K. (2004). When patriots protest: The anti-suffrage discursive transformation of 1917. *Rhetoric & Public Affairs, 7,* 283–310.

McGee, B. (1998). Speaking about the other: W. E. B. Du Bois responds to the Klan. *Southern Communication Journal, 63,* 208–219.

McGee, B. (2000). Thomas Dixon's *The clansman:* Radicals, reactionaries, and the anticipated utopia. *Southern Communication Journal, 65,* 300–316.

McGee, B. (2003). Rhetoric and race in the Progressive era: Imperialism, reform, and the Ku Klux Klan. In J. M. Hogan (Ed.), *Rhetoric and community: Studies in unity and fragmentation* (pp. 311–338). Columbia: South Carolina University Press.

McGerr, M. (2003). A fierce discontent: The rise and fall of the progressive movement in America, 1870–1920. New York: Oxford University Press.

McKean, D. D. (1930a). Woodrow Wilson as a debate coach. *Quarterly Journal of Speech, 16,* 458–463.

McKean, D. D. (1930b). Notes on Woodrow Wilson's speeches. *Quarterly Journal of Speech, 16,* 176–184.

Medhurst, M. J. (Ed.). (1996). *Beyond the rhetorical presidency.* College Station: Texas A&M University Press.

Medhurst, M. J., & Benson, T. W. (1981). The city: The rhetoric of rhythm. *Communication Monographs, 48,* 54–72.

Merritt, R. L. (1975). The bashful hero in American film of the nineteen forties. *Quarterly Journal of Speech, 61,* 129–139.

Mohrmann, G. P., & Scott, F. E. (1976). Popular music and World War II: The rhetoric of continuation. *Quarterly Journal of Speech, 62,* 145–156.

Muscio, G. (1997). *Hollywood's new deal.* Philadelphia: Temple University Press.

Natanson, N. (1992). *The black image in the new deal: The politics of FSA photography.* Knoxville: University of Tennessee Press.

Oliver, R. T. (1945). The speech that established Roosevelt's reputation. *Quarterly Journal of Speech, 31,* 274–282.

Olson, L. C. (1983). Portraits in praise of a people: A rhetorical analysis of Norman Rockwell's icons in Franklin D. Roosevelt's "Four Freedoms" campaign. *Quarterly Journal of Speech, 69,* 15–24.

Oravec, C. (1984). Conservationism vs. preservationism: The "public interest" in the Hetch Hetchy controversy. *Quarterly Journal of Speech, 70,* 444–458.

Oravec, C. (2003). Science, public policy, and the "Spirit of the People": The rhetoric of progressive conservation. In J. M. Hogan (Ed.), *Rhetoric and reform in the Progressive era* (Vol. 6, pp. 85–112). East Lansing: Michigan State University Press.

Osborn, G. C. (1956). Woodrow Wilson as a speaker. *Southern Communication Journal, 22,* 61–72.

Paget, E. (1929). Woodrow Wilson: International rhetorician. *Quarterly Journal of Speech, 15,* 15–24.

Palczewski, C. H. (2005). The male Madonna and the feminine uncle Sam: Visual argument, icons, and ideographs in 1909 anti-woman suffrage postcards. *Quarterly Journal of Speech, 2005,* 365–394.

Paulson, J. (2002). Theodore Roosevelt and the rhetoric of citizenship: On tour in New England, 1902. *Communication Quarterly, 50,* 123–134.

Ramsey, E. M. (2000). Inventing citizens during World War I: Suffrage cartoons in *The Woman Citizen. Western Journal of Communication, 64,* 113–147.

Reed, T. V. (1992). *Fifteen jugglers, five believers: Literary politics and the poetics of American social movements.* Berkeley: University of California Press.

Runion, H. L. (1935). An objective study of the speech style of Woodrow Wilson. *Communication Monographs, 2,* 75–94.

Ryan, H. R. (1979). Roosevelt's first inaugural address: A study of technique. *Quarterly Journal of Speech, 65,* 137–149.

Ryan, H. R. (1981). Roosevelt's fourth inaugural address: A study of its composition. *Quarterly Journal of Speech, 67,* 157–166.

Ryan, H. R. (1988). *Franklin D. Roosevelt's rhetorical presidency.* New York: Greenwood Press.

Schlesinger, A. M., Jr. (1958). *The coming of the new deal.* Boston: Houghton Mifflin.

Schlesinger, A. M., Jr. (1960). *The politics of upheaval.* Boston: Houghton Mifflin.

Schlesinger, A. M., Jr. (1963). *The politics of hope.* Boston: Houghton Mifflin.

Shipman, F. W. (1948). The Roosevelt papers. *Quarterly Journal of Speech, 34,* 137–142.

Simrell, V. E. (1927). H. L. Mencken the rhetorician. *Quarterly Journal of Speech, 13,* 399–412.

Smiley, S. (1968). Rhetoric on stage in living newspapers. *Quarterly Journal of Speech, 54,* 29–36.

Smith, R. R. (1970). Raymond Swing's broadcasts "In the name of sanity." *Quarterly Journal of Speech, 56,* 369–377.

Solomon, M. (1988). Ideology as rhetorical constraint: The anarchist agitation of "Red Emma" Goldman. *Quarterly Journal of Speech, 74,* 184–200.

Spalding, J. W. (1959). The radio speaking of William John Cameron. *Communication Monographs, 26,* 47–55.

Stott, W. (1973). *Documentary expression and thirties America.* New Haven, CT: Yale University Press.

Stuckey, M. E. (2003). "The Domain of Public Conscience": Woodrow Wilson and the establishment of a transcendent political order. *Rhetoric & Public Affairs, 6,* 1–23.

Summers, H. B. (1948). Radio in the 1948 campaign. *Quarterly Journal of Speech, 34,* 432–438.

Terrill, R. E., & Watts, E. (2002). W. E. B. Du Bois, double consciousness, and pan Africanism in the progressive era. In M. J. Hogan (Ed.), *A rhetorical history of the United States: Vol 6. Rhetoric and reform in the progressive era* (pp. 269–309). East Lansing, MI: Michigan State University Press.

Tulis, J. K. (1987). *The rhetorical presidency.* Princeton, NJ: Princeton University Press.

Voelker, C. H. (1936). A phonetic study of Roosevelt. *Quarterly Journal of Speech, 22,* 366–368.

Waggenspack, B. M. (2006). Eleanor Roosevelt: Social conscience for the new deal. In T. W. Benson (Ed.), *American rhetoric in the New Deal Era, 1932–1945* (pp. 157–209). East Lansing: Michigan State University Press.

Wagner, R. H. (1929). Wilson and his sources. *Quarterly Journal of Speech, 15,* 525–537.

Wallace, K. (Ed.). (1954). *A history of speech education in America.* New York: Appleton-Century-Crofts.

Ware, B. L., & Linkugel, W. A. (1982). The rhetorical *persona:* Marcus Garvey as Black Moses. *Communication Monographs, 49,* 50–62.

Watts, E. K. (2001). Cultivating a black public voice: W. E. B. Du Bois and the "Criteria of Negro Art." *Rhetoric & Public Affairs, 4,* 181–201.

Watts, E. K. (2002). African American ethos and hermeneutical rhetoric: An exploration of Alain Locke's *The new negro. Quarterly Journal of Speech, 88,* 19–32.

White, E. E. (1944). Anti-racial agitation as a campaign device: James K. Vardaman in the Mississippi gubernatorial campaign of 1903. *Southern Communication Journal, 10,* 49–56.

White, E. E. (1946). Mississippi's great white chief: James K. Vardaman. *Quarterly Journal of Speech, 32,* 442–446.

Wiebe, R. H. (1967). *The search for order: 1877–1920.* New York: Hill & Wang.

Wiley, E. W. (1943). The rhetoric of the American democracy. *Quarterly Journal of Speech, 29,* 157–163.

Wilson, J. F. (1957). Rhetorical echoes of a Wilsonian idea. *Quarterly Journal of Speech, 43,* 271–277.

Wilson, J. F. (1962). Harding's rhetoric of normalcy. *Quarterly Journal of Speech, 38,* 406–411.

Wilson, K. H. (1999). Towards a discursive theory of racial identity: The souls of black folk as a response to nineteenth-century biological determinism. *Western Journal of Communication, 63,* 193–215.

Zelko, H. P. (1942). Franklin D. Roosevelt's rhythm in rhetorical style. *Quarterly Journal of Speech, 28,* 138–141.

30

Religious Voices in American Public Discourse

JAMES DARSEY

JOSHUA R. RITTER

Religion lies close to the core of America's genetic code; religious discourse is elemental to our national talk. The sermon of John Winthrop, first governor of the Massachusetts Bay Colony, given aboard the *Arabella* prior to stepping onto the shores of the New World, sounded a chord that defined the key signature for much of American public rhetoric to follow:

> The lord make it like that of New England: for wee must Consider that wee shall be as a Citty upon a Hill, the eies of all people are uppon us; soe that if wee shall deale falsely with our god in this worke wee have undertaken and soe cause him to withdrawe his present help from us, wee shall be made a story and a by-word through the world, wee shall open the mouthes of enemies to speake evill of the wayes of god and all professours

for Gods sake; wee shall shame the faces of many of gods worthy servants, and cause theire prayers to be turned into Cursses upon us till wee be consumed out of the good land whether wee are goeing. (Winthrop, 1965, p. 93)

Stephen Browne argues that Winthrop's "Modell of Christian Charity" exercises an "enduring claim on debates over national identity" (Browne, 2007, p. 2). The resonances of Winthrop's sermon have proved so perdurable that the most celebrated line—"We shall be as a city upon a hill," a line in which Winthrop alludes to Matthew's (5:14) account of the Sermon on the Mount—becomes a theme in Ronald Reagan's bid for a second term as president of the United States almost three and a half centuries after Winthrop's sermon was delivered.

The harmonics are more complex than Reagan's quotations and allusions might indicate. The metaphor of the city on the hill is surrounded, in both Winthrop's and Reagan's versions, by issues of heritage and lineage; and the attention devoted, in "A Model of Christian Charity," to questions of borrowing, lending, and economic benevolence suggests the wisdom of reading even "Reaganomics" as a manifestation of Winthrop's influence (Kiewe & Houck, 1991). Many presidents and presidential aspirants, even to the present day, have voiced some version of what Robert Bellah has identified as the "exemplary impulse" in the American civil religion (Bellah & Hammond, 1980; Shogan, 2006), that vision captured in Winthrop's application of the biblical metaphor: John Kennedy's inaugural address, George H. W. Bush's "thousand points of light," Bill Clinton's "new covenant." During his run for the U.S. presidency, Gen. Wesley Clark, speaking to the Council on Foreign Relations, concluded his remarks with the charge, "America should always be a beacon of hope and freedom" (Clark, 2007). The representation of the United States as "the City on a Hill" is such a pervasive feature of our public talk that Browne refers to it as a "resonant though promiscuous commonplace in our political culture" (Browne, 2007, p. 2; see also Fitzgerald, 1987; Kincaid, 1971).

Winthrop's 1630 sermon is one of those formative discourses described by James Andrews (2007) as "rhetorical expressions—largely religious in nature—that made deep and lasting impressions on constructions of such potent intangibles as 'American identity,' the 'American character,' and the 'American Dream'" (p. xvi) and, as such, is part of the rhetorical DNA of the United States. The centrality of religious discourse to the American identity notwithstanding, the existence of a Religious Communication Association and the *Journal of Communication and Religion,* despite the occasional call to make

religious rhetoric the subject of sustained and systematic study (Sillars, 1981), and despite a long history of crossovers of scholars from schools of divinity to departments of communication, religious rhetoric has rarely been at the center of studies in American public address. The first two volumes of *A History and Criticism of American Public Address,* sponsored by the Speech Association of America (now the National Communication Association) and edited by William Norwood Brigance (1943), helped set the agenda for scholarship in American public address studies for at least the two decades following their publication. Even after the neo-Aristotelian approach that characterized most of this work was pushed aside, the pride of place enjoyed by studies of the rhetoric of "statecraft" (fourteen essays in the Brigance volumes) continued unchallenged while concerns with other arenas, "reform" and "religion," for example (four entries each in the Brigance volumes), languished in the margins.

Although C. Jan Swearingen (2002) and others have noted signs of a revival of interest in the relationship between rhetoric and religion, the scholarship on religious discourse in America exists as a mass of tessera waiting to be assembled into a mosaic, wanting an inventory of the missing pieces. It is our admittedly ambitious aim in this essay to provide a rough survey of the literature in an effort to piece together something of the story of religious rhetoric in the United States, to provide a sense of its parameters and its trajectory, and to identify opportunities for rhetorical scholars to extend our understandings of this fundamental of American public discourse. Only through a careful inventory of what we know as measured against the likely boundaries can we discover what pieces of the puzzle are missing and where the contested territories are located. Most important, only by suggesting the essential coherence of the story can we make a compelling case that the study of religious discourses in the United

States ought to be more than a sideshow, a rare look at what are too often imagined as rhetorical oddities at the margins of public life, removed from the realm of reason and evidentiary obligations.

WHAT IS RELIGIOUS RHETORIC?

We may legitimately debate what constitutes religious discourse, what distinguishes religious discourse from discourse that is not religious (Boyle, 2001; Garver, 1990; Kirkwood, 1994; Lantz, 1955; Montesano, 1995; Ohlhauser, 1996; O'Rourke, 2001; Ricoeur, 1980, 1995; Sullivan, 1992; Tukey, 1990, 1995). Some contemporary theologians and communication scholars, including David S. Cunningham and Stephen H. Webb (Cunningham, 1991; Webb, 1991, 1993; see also Tracy, 1987, 1990; Van Beeck, 1979; Wilder, 1976.), have explicated theology itself as a rhetorical enterprise, strongly implying that the reverse may also be true. Wayne C. Booth (1991) has argued that rhetoric and religion are "inextricably wedded," which would make the quest to isolate a religious rhetoric futile, and Wendy Farley's (2005) definition of theology as "a kind of desire that employs thought as a religious practice" makes the "weddedness" of rhetoric and religion inescapable (p. xii). When Peter Jackson (2006) suggests that the metaphorical inscription of gesture in religious discourse reflects the very notion of religion, his work resonates with both current trends toward tropological analysis and with St. Augustine's emphasis, in *De Doctrina Christiana,* on the figurative.

Religious rhetoric is thoroughly grounded, on the one hand, in the material realities that situate rhetorical endeavors; yet it lays claim, on the other hand, to the supernal. As Kenneth Burke might have it, *religious* rhetoric is also religious *rhetoric.* Logologically, the study of all rhetoric reveals religious undertones and a hierarchical structure of order and sacrifice that is continually and necessarily transgressed in order for rhetoric to continue to function at

all. Borrowing from Kenneth Burke, Mircea Eliade, and others, we define religious rhetoric as rhetoric in which the process of invention is ultimately both constrained and authorized by the mystical sacred, by a severe obligation to the realm of things beyond human capacity to alter, a realm not accessible through our pedestrian methodologies or logic, by a connection to and a desire for the supernatural (Appel, 1993; Burke, 1970; Eliade, 1959; Jamieson, 1973; Jost & Olmsted, 2000; Klemm, 1987; Lessl, 1993; Pernot, 2006; Porter, 1990). *Inventio* in religious rhetoric suggests, as it did for the ancient Greeks, a process more akin to discovery than to creation; it exists in the lacuna—a symptom of our separation from the divine—between the ontologically certain and nonnegotiable and the epistemologically apprehensible, the space occupied by faith (as *fiducia*), a way of learning to trust one's way of being in the world. Out of this *agon* rises religious discourse, which is basically rhetorico-theological in its creative constructions of various conceptions and models of the supernatural and how that realm interacts with material reality. In Burke's terms, the "supernatural" provides the element of "transcendence," the fourth order beyond the natural, the sociopolitical, and the symbolic, that is distinctive to religious rhetoric (Burke, 1970, pp. 14–15, *passim;* see also Rowland & Jones, 2006, on the fault line between what they term the *moral* and the *pragmatic* in Reagan's address at the Brandenburg Gate).

For the purposes of this survey, we are restricting our consideration to rhetoric that engages the holy; "God stuff," Roderick Hart (1977) called it in his classic work on religious rhetoric and the American presidency, though even "God stuff" does not quite capture the essence of the subject. In 1965, in the case *U.S. v. Seeger,* the Supreme Court of the United States ruled unanimously that belief "in a Supreme Being" was not necessary to claim a religious basis for objection to participation in the military. Justice William O. Douglas's opinion in the case allowed that a person who had "a sincere belief, which in his life fills the same place as a belief in God in the life of an orthodox religionist," could legitimately claim religious grounds for exemption from military service (Gaustad & Schmidt, 2004, pp. 54–55). Religion without a God: It is difficult, in this context, to determine what might be meant by the surviving phrase "by reason of religious training and belief." Rhetorical scholars have in this episode a fallow site for excavation (Heinemann, 1997; Ramsey, 1997).

Theoretical debates over the essence of religious discourse are ongoing and unresolved, but this does not enjoin us from circumscribing our topic so as to provide needed limits, though in so doing, we unhappily exclude consideration of what Robert Bellah has termed America's *civil religion* (Bellah, 1975, 1976; Bellah & Hammond, 1980; Hart, 1977, from a rhetorical perspective, raises important questions about Bellah's idea of "civil religion." On the debate between Bellah and Hart, see Hart, 2002; Lee, 2002; Marvin, 2002). Including civil religion would require us to look at the Declaration of Independence, possibly the Federalist Papers, and certainly the Constitution of the United States as sacred texts; to examine many federal appellate court decisions as examples of exegesis of sacred texts; and to consider the myriad appeals to the beatified figures of George Washington, Thomas Jefferson, Benjamin Franklin—any of the Founding Fathers, really—and Abraham Lincoln, to name only the most obvious and least controversial.

It is also worth noting that the overwhelming preponderance of what we know about religious rhetoric in the United States is about Christian rhetoric, indeed, largely and specifically Protestant rhetoric. Catholic rhetoric has garnered scant attention and usually in the context of work on reform or demagoguery (Appel, 1987a, 1987b; Chandler, 1989; see work on Dorothy Day and on Charles Coughlin below). Jewish rhetoric has received even less attention, though noteworthy exceptions do exist (see Frank, 2003, 2004; Friedenberg, 1983, 1984; Tauber, 1969), and the rhetorics of Buddhism, Hinduism, Islam (excepting Merriam, 1974), or any of the other world religions as those rhetorics have been practiced in an American context, virtually none at all (excepting Chapel, 1989). The national history that produced both Mormonism and Christian Science has failed to give either its rhetorical due (for exceptions, see Flake, 2004; Chapel & Jensen, 2000; Pearce, 2000), and there is almost nothing on religious cults, aside from the context of looking at apocalyptic discourse, though Joshua Gunn's work on occult rhetoric is a notable exception (Gunn, 2005).

THE GENRES OF RELIGIOUS RHETORIC IN THE UNITED STATES

While recognizing that there are highly specialized forms of religious discourse in the history of American public address that have received attention from rhetorical scholars, including pastoral letters and prayer (Adler, 1995; Bland, 1990; Hogan, 1989; Jablonski, 1989; Kari, 2004; Lindsay, 1997; Lynch, 2005; Medhurst, 1977), a review of scholarship reveals four broad genres under which religious rhetoric most commonly manifests itself in the United States.

The Sermon

The sermon is the most prevalent of these, both in terms of its occurrence and in terms of scholarly attention. Robert Oliver (1965), in his sweeping, single-volume 1965 survey of the history of American public address, declared that "with the exception of schoolteaching, the most frequent and perhaps the most influential public speaking in America has been in the pulpit" (p. 358). Thomas D. Clark, 30 years ago, did the analysis to establish the Christian sermon, as it existed at the time, as a genre (Clark, 1977), but long before Clark's analysis, scholars had treated the sermon as a group of discourses that "share substantive, stylistic, and situational characteristics" and in which forms recur "*together* [italics added] in constellation" (Campbell & Jamieson, 1978, p. 20).

Among the most prominent projects to assume a generic kinship among sermons are the two volumes edited by DeWitte Holland, *Preaching in American History* (1969) and *Sermons in American History* (1971). These volumes were produced under the imprimatur of the then Speech Association of America on the model of the *History and Criticism of American Public Address* volumes, individual studies by multiple authors. Holland's first volume was greeted with multiple reviews in the journals and hailed on publication as a "landmark" contribution (Hance, 1970, p. 86). The essays in *Preaching in American History* addressed many of the key questions still with us, including the nature of religious authority and its claims (Collins, 1969; Miller, 1969; White, 1969), the relationship of church and state (Bailey, 1969; Camp, 1969; Stewart, 1969), the relationship of religious rhetoric to reform in the United States (Boase, 1969; Bos & Faries, 1969; Leathers, 1969; Pinson, 1969; Stewart, 1969; Taylor & Schwartz, 1969), and the challenges posed to the grounds of religious discourse in a pluralistic world (Carlton, 1969; Davis, 1969). Kenneth Hance (1970) celebrated *Preaching in American History* for demonstrating "the value of a research program sometimes overlooked in a preoccupation with the communication process *per se*" (p. 85), but there was, even in the celebration, the sense of a line of scholarship whose moment had passed. By the time the second volume appeared 2 years later, there was no fanfare, no notice at all that we can find in the communication journals. The volumes failed to inspire a new generation of scholars, brought up in the secular sixties, to focus on pulpit oratory and homiletics as public address. Though Holland followed in 1980 with a volume on the history of the preaching tradition, this book seems to have found an audience primarily among preachers.

Studies of the sermon by scholars of public address have typically followed either a Wragean model, reading specific sermons or looking at the rhetorical behavior of specific preachers as symptomatic of a historical moment (e.g., Jones, 1993; Larson, 1971; MacVaugh, 1932; McCall, 1953). Or such studies have provided insights, on the neo-Aristotelian model, into the practice of individual preachers (e.g., Chandler, 1982; Chesebrough, 2001; Crocker, 1933, 1936; Mattis, 1929; Nau, 1954; White & Henderlider, 1954; Williams, 1948), assuming the continuities and contiguities necessary to speak of "the sermon" or "sermons," but rarely interrogating this assumption and almost never looking toward any broad conclusions about the genre or its role in American history (Griffin, 1998; exceptions include Abernathy, 1943; Bosley, 1969; Browne, 1992; Hart, 1971; Jackson, 2007; Longaker, 2006; McGee, 1970; Reid, 1998, 1999; Reid, Bullock, and Fleer, 1995; White, 1972). A very few studies have attempted to use preaching as a case study to enlarge our understanding of rhetorical theory or of critical practice (e.g., Appel, 1987a, 1987b; Conrad, 1983; White, 1972; Yarbrough & Adams, 1993). A significant number of rhetorical studies of preaching and homiletics have exhibited a practical orientation, providing advice to preachers on rhetorical strategies (e.g., Bachman, 1959; Bailey, 1980; Holland, 1964; McGlon et al., 1954). In rare cases, scholars have used religious discourse as a case study for methodological or theoretical ends (Casey, 2004; Hostetler, 1997; Houck & Dixon, 2006; Lewis, 2007; Mahaffey, 2007; Minnick, 1971; Selby, 2008; Tell, 2003).

African American preaching has been recognized in the scholarship as a subgenre of preaching; consequently, there exist, in addition to the studies of individual black preachers and sermons, a number of studies that work to explicate the general characteristics of African

American preaching, especially inasmuch as those characteristics point to distinctions between the pulpit practices of black and white preachers (Evans, 2006; Pipes, 1945; Pitts, 1989). Studies of African American preaching have also focused on how oratorical skills, honed in the pulpit, have manifested themselves in the political arena (Bacon & McClish, 2006; Brownlow, 1972; Leeman, 2006b; Miller, 1989; Slanger, 1995). Less attention has been paid to the spiritual journeys made by individual leaders in the black community (Jensen & Hammerback, 1986) or to the influence of non-Christian religions on the struggle for civil rights.

Occasionally, subgenres of the sermon are suggested on the basis of a common subject matter (Minnick, 1968; Quimby, 1964). A limited amount of work has been done on preaching within particular denominations or sects (Casey, 2004; Huebner, 1991; Medhurst, 2004; Pullum, 2001; Quimby & Billigmeier, 1959; Reid, 2004; White, 1972; Wiethoff, 1977), and of this work, the most promising direction for future research seems to be at the intersection of work on preaching practices and a renascent interest in regional studies (Conser, 1997; Dorgan, 1987; Enholm, Skaggs, & Welsh, 1987; Hudson, 1958).

The Jeremiad

If preaching is the most obvious site for scholarship in religious rhetoric, Em Griffin's (1998) helpful review of scholarship in the *Journal of Communication and Religion* reminds us that "preaching is only one form of religious communication, and probably not the one that is most influential" (p. 130). Though sermons have been relatively popular in public address studies, scholars need not restrict themselves to preaching or the sermon.

In 1978, Sacvan Bercovitch refocused attention on religious dimensions of public discourse with the publication of what was to become an important work in American

studies, literary criticism, and rhetorical studies. Bercovitch's book *The American Jeremiad* goaded rhetoricians to look at what Bercovitch termed *political sermons,* discourses that attempted, in ways peculiar to the American context, to "fuse sacred and profane" (Bercovitch, 1978, pp. xiv, 29, 79). Bercovitch's study begins in the colonial pulpit—John Winthrop, John Cotton, Samuel Danforth, Cotton Mather, Jonathan Edwards—but his real purpose was to focus our attention on the genre itself, to trace the trajectory of the jeremiad out of the pulpit and to follow its transformation into "a powerful vehicle of middle-class ideology: a ritual of progress through consensus, a system of sacred-secular symbols for a laissez-faire creed, a 'civil religion' for a people chosen to spring fully formed into the modern world" (Bercovitch, 1978, p. 28). Bercovitch's book inspired significant activity among rhetorical critics and students of American public address (Johannesen, 1985; Jones & Rowland, 2005; Lattin & Underhill, 2006; Mitchell & Phipps, 1985).

Prophetic Rhetoric

Though the study of the jeremiad takes us into the sphere of civil religion, the jeremiad's eponym, the Old Testament prophet Jeremiah, suggests a genre of religious discourse that is distinctly not sermonic but still focused on the ineffable and transcendent. James Darsey has argued that the model of the Old Testament prophets provides a compelling explanation for the shape of radical discourse in the United States, discourse that has often vexed rhetorical critics because of its stridency, its tendency to excoriate rather than conciliate or seek common ground, its offensiveness, its violation of the most fundamental tenets of Western rhetorical theory (Darsey, 1988, 1997). Old Testament prophets presented themselves—and to the extent they had any impact, were seen (or heard) by a significant enough number of their audience to make the prophet a threat—as sent by God to carry His message of judgment on a people that had fallen away from the covenant. The terms of the covenant in the prophetic message are immutable; the message is inexorable. The message, given the exigence that produced it, is necessarily unpleasant, and the prophetic configuration of the communication situation effectively turns the Graeco-Roman model of discourse on its side, making the divine message rather than adaptation to audience the generative principle. Analyses that acknowledge prophetic elements in American public address are now relatively common (e.g., Baxter, 2004; Browne, 1999; Campbell, 2003; Hogan & Williams, 2004; Huxman & Biesecker-Mast, 2004; Kaveny, 2006; Kurtz, 2004; Leeman, 2006b; McGee, 1998; Pauley, 1998; Shogan, 2006; Simonson, 2003; Swatos & Wellman, 1999; Tell, 2003; Terrill, 2001; Timmerman, 2005; Vail, 2006; Verkruyse, 2005; Wood, 1999).

Apocalyptic Rhetoric

More extreme even than prophetic rhetoric is the genre of apocalypticism. Though the terms are too often used indiscriminately and interchangeably, prophecy and apocalypticism are distinct genres. There is an enormous and well-defined literature on apocalypticism, both within rhetorical studies and without. Perhaps because of its status as a biblical genre, perhaps because it is a perennial feature in history (Jasinski, 2001, p. 17), apocalypticism is highly theorized in terms of its socio-psychological motives (Cohn, 1993; Collins, McGinn, & Stein, 2000; McGinn, Collins, & Stein, 2003); its history and place in American history (Boklund, 1967; Hanson, 1975; Heald, 1975; Longenbach, 1989; Moorhead, 1984, 1987; Valeri & Wilson, 1985; Wojcik, 1997; Zamora, 1982); and, compared with more pervasive genres such as the sermon, as a rhetorical form (Mavrodes, 1968; Mixon & Hopkins, 1988; Wilder, 1971). It is clear that

apocalypticism, though it is an extreme response to a moment of crisis, is continuous with sermons and prophecy as they have historically operated in American thought: highlighting our anointed relationship to the divine, both reassuring us of our election and magnifying our shortcomings, and recalling us to the terms of the covenant.

Easily the two most prominent theorists of apocalyptic rhetoric are Barry Brummett (1984, 1988, 1991, 1994) and Stephen O'Leary (O'Leary & McFarland, 1989; O'Leary, 1994). In his 1994 book, *Arguing the Apocalypse,* O'Leary explicitly challenges the ideas of apocalyptic discourse forwarded by Brummett and by Ronald Reid (1983). James Jasinski aptly characterizes thse debate between Brummett and O'Leary as "formism" (Brummett) versus a situational, evolutionary approach that allows for "an appreciation of both the enduring and the dynamic features of apocalyptic discourse" (O'Leary) (Jasinski, 2001, p. 18).

There has been a significant amount of productive criticism of American public address focused on apocalyptic dimensions (Apple & Messner, 2001; Biesecker-Mast, 2007; Bobbitt & Mixon, 1994; Caliendo, 1999; Nixon, 1989). In addition to critical work done by Brummett, O'Leary, and Reid as part of theory-building projects, G. Thomas Goodnight (1986, 1988) and J. Michael Hogan (1987) have produced analyses of American public discourses as inflected by potential nuclear annihilation. One of the recurring features emerging from both theories and criticism of apocalypticism is the connection between apocalypticism and myth (e.g., Rowland, 1990).

CHARISMA AND RELIGIOUS ETHOS

In addition to the three broad genres of religious rhetoric, there have been, in rhetorical studies, fitful and sporadic attempts to engage the concept of charisma, a form of ethos that lays claim to the transcendent and ineffable. In Max Weber's definition, charisma is a certain quality of an individual personality by virtue of which he is set apart from ordinary men and treated as endowed with supernatural, superhuman, or at least specifically exceptional powers or qualities. These are such as not to be accessible to the ordinary person, but are regarded as of divine origin or as exemplary, and on the basis of them the individual is treated as a leader. (Eldridge, 1971, p. 229)

Though it is the nature of the ineffable to avoid definition, rhetorical scholars have, confronted with so powerful a form of *ethos*, attempted to articulate its properties and the principles by which it operates in persuasion (Boss, 1976; Hirst, 1995; Keyes, 1982; King, Sawyer, & Benke, 1998; Sequeira, 1994; Sevitch, 1996; Smith, 1993).

Related to charisma, sometimes an element of it, the rhetorical representation of religious conversion has been given some attention by rhetorical scholars (Darsey, 1988; McGee, 1998; McLennan, 1996; Spencer, 1995). Yet considering the significant psychological power "conversion experiences" wield over audiences as well as the vast resources religious scholars have developed over the years in regard to religious conversion that could be drawn on by rhetorical scholars, it is surprising that more work in our field has not been done on the phenomenon.

GENDERED SPACES AND RELIGIOUS RHETORIC

Deserving special attention in the consideration of religious rhetoric is the complex relationship of religion and gender in the United States (Bineham, 1993; Campbell, 2001; Jablonski, 1988; Johnson, 2002; Lynch, 1997; Mountford, 2005). On the one hand, institutional religion can be an oppressive force, as Elizabeth Cady Stanton's (1999) "Introduction" to *The Woman's Bible* makes clear:

[The Bible] has been used to hold [woman] in the "divinely ordained sphere," prescribed in the Old and New Testaments. The canon and civil law; church and state; priests and legislators; all political parties and religious denominations have alike taught that woman was made after man, of man, and for man, an inferior being, subject to man. (p. 7)

Thus, it is not surprising that there is considerable scholarship addressing the oppressive effects of institutional religion on women (Abbott, 2006, 2007; Sillars, 1995).

At the same time, religious institutions were among the first to make spaces for women to speak in public in the United States, and women in the 19th century and beyond have used a putatively superior feminine moral instinct to extend "woman's sphere" to political issues. Debates over the forced removal of Native Americans from their traditional lands, slavery, and regulation and sale of alcoholic beverages in the United States were all profoundly colored by women's voices insisting on their authority with respect to moral issues in the public sphere, but as recent work by Alisse Portnoy and others reveals, our understanding of women's participation is still incomplete (Bacon, 1999a; Portnoy, 2005).

AT THE "WALL OF SEPARATION": RELIGIOUS RHETORIC AND POLITICS IN THE UNITED STATES

While we must exclude from our consideration the rhetoric of civil religion, we would be remiss not to acknowledge the degree to which "God stuff" often penetrates the fabric of our putatively secular political life. Its place in the U.S. Constitution taken by huge numbers of Americans as a matter of faith, the "wall of separation" is actually Thomas Jefferson's phrase from a public letter of 1802 (Gaustad, 2003, p. 35). The difficulty of separating religion and politics is often found at Jefferson's wall, which on close inspection, turns out to be more screen door than rampart. Rhetorical scholars have attended to some of the perennial debates over the "establishment clause" and the "free exercise clause" of the First Amendment, beginning in the Revolutionary era (Sewell, 1975) and continuing to the present day (Aune, 1999; Bosmajian, 1985).

In practice, U.S. politicians often make explicit appeals to religious, even Christian, values; they often court religious constituencies, seek advice from religious leaders, and invoke the name of "God" for suasory effect (Adams, 1989; Dionne, 2004; Noll, 1988; Noll & Harlow, 2007; Shogan, 2006; Wills, 1990), but the tenor of those appeals changes over time. It would not be unreasonable to suggest that the history of political rhetoric in the United States could be written as an account of the vicissitudinous relationship of God and Mammon. In 2007, Mitt Romney's much heralded "Mormon speech" at Texas A&M University was widely compared—and the selection of Texas as a site for the speech invited such comparisons—with John F. Kennedy's speech to the Greater Houston Ministerial Association 47 years earlier. Though Kennedy, in his speech, expressed his belief in an America in which "the separation of church and state is absolute," Romney was insistent that "the founders proscribed the establishment of a state religion, but they did not countenance the elimination of religion from the public square. We are a nation 'Under God' and in God, we do indeed trust" (Romney, 2007).

RELIGION AND THE RHETORIC OF REFORM IN THE UNITED STATES

Religious rhetoric is hardly confined to institutional politics in the United States. Many reform movements in U.S. history have built their cases largely on the authority of moral law. Sociologists, recovering from their long intoxication with materialist explanations of social movements, are recognizing ideological,

even religious, motives at the root of many reforms, what Rhys Williams (1999) characterizes as "the religious roots of American political culture." William McLoughlin's (1978) *Revivals, Awakenings and Reform: An Essay on Religion and Social Change in America, 1607–1977* provides a sweeping survey of the interplay of religion and reform in U.S. history (see also Sandeen, 1982). There exist a number of studies of the role of U.S. clergy in movements for social reform, especially during the 1960s (Yoder, 1969; Wilson, 2005). Other movements that feature religious premises prominently include the Social Gospel Movement; the Sunday School Movement; the Abolitionist Movement; the Civil Rights Movement; the farm workers movement (Zompetti, 2006); movements concerned with abortion, sex education, birth control (Lake, 1984), and gay and lesbian rights (Caliendo, 1999; Chávez, 2004); and the antinuclear movement (Brand, 1997).

Still, rhetorical studies of social movements tend to be focused largely on connections to the social movements' literature in sociology, including the literature on the nature of social movements, identity movements, and strategies. Evidence of the strong moral tenor in the rhetoric of many rhetorics of reform would suggest that connecting rhetorical scholarship more closely to scholarship on the nature and power of religious argument could be fruitful.

A SERIES OF AWAKENINGS

The idea that the story of religious rhetoric in the United States can best be told as a cycle in which Americans, both blessed and burdened by our exceptionalism, have ardently committed to follow the terms of our covenant with God, have repeatedly fallen away from that covenant, and have predictably returned to "a strickt performance of the Articles contained in it" with revivalistic fervor in order to avoid the "wrathe against us [by which God is] revenged of such a perjured people and make us knowe the price of the breache of such a Covenant" (Winthrop, 1630), only to fall away again when the fear has passed, is not without basis (Bailyn, 1970; Becker, 1932; Davis, 1973, McLoughlin, 1973; Wilson, 1983) but not without controversy either (Barkun, 1985). Religious profession and activity in the United States has ebbed and flowed over the course of our history, the American people coming together in a renewal of shared commitment to common values, then dispersing into sects, factions, and ethnic identities. These flows and ebbs correspond closely to the alternation of times of anxiety and uncertainty with periods of relative confidence and complacency or, perhaps perversely, with periods of such intense crisis (e.g., wars) that we fail to fear in the moment.

This narrative structure need not signal commitment to a cyclical view of U.S. history. There are iterative patterns, to be sure, but the loops in the spiral grow larger over time, suggesting a diminishing capacity to perform that most essential function of *religio*, to bind. It is an open question whether or not Americans in postmodernity will be able to continue to find the center that holds, a basis for common renewal.

The First Great Awakening

Surprisingly, given the increasing tendency of public address studies toward the contemporary, we know more about the role of religious discourse in colonial America and about the individual practitioners of that discourse than about religious discourse in any other period of American history. Among historians and historians of rhetoric, there is almost universal consensus with respect to the broad outlines of a story of the pulpit in the British colonies of the 17th and 18th centuries. The fundamentals of that story include the idea that the colonists, settling in a new, unspoiled, unsullied, virginal world, had been

elected to wipe clean the sinful slate and begin again. This status of the colonists as children of the "New Israel" conveyed special privileges and protections and special obligations. God's new chosen people were expected to create a "(shining) city on the hill," which, by its purity and strict adherence to the terms of the divine covenant, would set forth an example, recalling the rest of the world to God's holy will. Given this exemplary station, any failing of the elect was magnified.

As might be expected, the obligation to occupy the hilltop, standing in the unremitting gaze not only of God, but of the rest of the world, created great anxiety among the colonists, who became increasingly obsessed with their own shortcomings. At such an altitude, every stumble has the potential to become a tragic fall. As the great Cotton Mather put it to an audience gathered in Boston on Lecture Day, April 7, 1698:

> We are a very Unpardonable Town, if, after all the *Help* which our God has given us, we do no ingenuously Enquire, *What shall we Render to the Lord, for all His Benefits?* Render! Oh! Let us our selves thus answer the Enquiry: *Lord, we will Render all possible, and Filial Obedience unto thee, because Hitheto thou hast Helped us; Only do thou also Help us, to Render that Obedience!* (Potter & Gordon, 1970, pp. 404–405)

Historian of American religion William McLoughlin (1978) finds in the First Great Awakening "the beginnings of a distinctly American identity" (p. 112), and the critical role of religion in fomenting the American Revolution is well established (Bailyn, 1970; Becker, 1932; Davis, 1994; Stout, 1977).

As is true of the rhetorical study of sermons and preaching generally, most of the studies we have of the First Great Awakening are studies of individual sermons and preachers (Berens, 1977; Boase, 1954; Evans, 1987; Golden, 1961; Larson, 1971, 1978; Lazenby, 1971; White, 1948, 1950a, 1950b, 1953).

The most famous sermon of this era, arguably the most famous sermon in American history, is Jonathan Edwards's "Sinners in the Hands of an Angry God." John Adams and Stephen Yarbrough have, over the course of almost two decades, turned their attentions to Edwards and to the sermon with which he is so closely identified (Adams & Yarbrough, 1997, 2007; Yarbrough & Adams, 1993). Adams and Yarbrough have labored to relate Edwards's ideas to their roots in a complex theology born of European thought and Christian and Enlightenment discourses, yet even such sustained scrutiny accompanied by solid scholarship may have missed other contexts, more intimate to "Sinners" and, by virtue of that intimacy, less susceptible to analysis—the context of Edwards's own *oeuvre*. Where Adams and Yarbrough appear to read "Sinners" as continuous with Edwards's other works, the product of techniques arrived not "all at once . . . but over a period of time" (Adams & Yarbrough, 2007, p. 276) and as exemplary of Puritan rhetoric "substantively shaped by the predestinarian doctrines of original sin and the sovereignty of God championed by Edwards and his Puritan predecessors" (Adams & Yarbrough, 2007, p. 286), current scholarship in Edwards studies and religious studies opens this position to interrogation. Religious historian H. Leon McBeth (1987) is among those who assert that "Sinners" is decidedly *atypical* among Edwards's sermons (p. 202), and Douglas Winiarski (2005) notes that while literary and rhetorical critics have devoted much time and effort in the analysis of "Sinners," theologians and intellectual historians "frequently have dismissed *Sinners* altogether. Repeatedly branded an anomaly within Edwards's homiletical writings, it remains oddly disconnected from studies of his Awakening era theological treatises" (pp. 686–687).

Adams and Yarbrough are right to insist on the complexity of Edwards's thought and even on the continuing influence of his intellectual

trajectory—William Frankena suggests that Edwards "was perhaps the outstanding American theologian and certainly the ablest American philosopher to write before the great period of Peirce, James, Royce, Dewey, and Santayana" (quoted in Wilson & Porter, 2003, p. 183)—which is all the more reason to give Edwards his due, to give full hearing to the differing interpretations of the man and his work, and to extend scholarship that no one holds to be complete.

We highlight this controversy over Edwards because of his prominence and because of the relative wealth of scholarship on his work, but the lesson is generalizable: We have yet to develop in rhetorical studies a literature rich and multivocal enough to reveal competing interpretations of the same rhetorical phenomena. This is true in the case of major figures, such as Edwards; major rhetorical eras, such as the First Great Awakening; major genres of discourse, such as preaching; and modes of public rhetoric as central to American history as religious rhetoric itself. Though many of the studies of religious public address in the colonial period are studies of individual rhetors or orations and sermons in the literary tradition of Herbert Wichelns, few attempt to use the analysis of religious rhetoric to read large cultural trends. Wade Williams (2000), in an analysis of some of the medical lectures and political reform essays by that preeminent physician of the American Revolution, Benjamin Rush, draws together contemporary attention to the intersections of religion and science; a large view of what might be susceptible to rhetorical analysis, moving beyond oratory to medical lectures as well as political essays; and a Wragean commitment to exploring "the cultural uses of rhetoric, the ways that individuals encountered, synthesized, and utilized assumptions about language to fashion identities at specific historical moments" (p. 55).

What is surprising about this era is how much has been left unexamined. There is little rhetorical scholarship exploring the influence of John Wesley (Golden, 1961) or even of John Calvin (Fehler, 2007; Rountree, 1994) in the New World, though the influence of both men is momentous, and there is nothing on the important debates between Wesleyan Arminianism and Augustinian/Calvinist predestination. Barbara Larson has given some attention to Samuel Davies and the "New Lights" (Larson, 1971, 1978), but Samuel Hopkins, Joseph Bellamy, Theodore J. Frelinghuysen, Charles Chauncy, the Tennents (father and sons), and Hezekiah Smith have been completely neglected.

The Second Great Awakening

For those who came of age in the early decades of the 19th century, the American Revolution stood as a towering moral achievement (Gabriel, 1950; Maclear, 1971; Noble, 1968; Wagenknecht, 1972). Standing in the shadow of such greatness, Americans in the early republican period were anxious about their abilities to find a vocation of significance (Appleby, 2000; Scott, 1979). As John Kincaid (1971) has put the issue with respect to the idea of vocation generally:

> The meaning of nationhood is found in purposes that transcend daily life. For Americans this intentional collective identity goes beyond the record of the past, based as it is on a sense of vocation—a concrete faith in the future of new beginnings which will mediate the limitations of the past and fulfill the promises of the fathers to their children. The vocation is fulfilled in the present as long as the people are on the way toward its fulfillment, but it is also locked in a dynamic tension between the immanent and the imminent because it poses ideals which are usually just beyond reach. (p. 115)

There is much during this period for rhetorical scholars to explore. Highly significant religious movements developed during this time: the quite radical notion of denominationalism, the social phenomenon of the camp meeting that swept across the entire nation, the rise of

the premillennial dispensationalists, the establishment of a truly "American religion" by Joseph Smith, the emergence of Unitarianism, the essential development of voluntarism and its impact on religion and the nation, the Sunday School Movement, and the growing popularity of ecumenism (mixed with a portion of empire). These movements, and the often colorful characters associated with them, including Nathaniel W. Taylor, Charles G. Finney, William Ellery Channing, Henry Ward Beecher, and Theodore Parker, have received some attention from rhetoricians (Bjerga, 2001; Chesebrough, 1999, 2001; Heisey, 1992; Ryan, 1990), but far less than what might be expected given such profound and far reaching developments with deeply rhetorical dimensions.

The response of the New England transcendentalists to the anxieties of the age created an intellectual tradition and an accompanying rhetoric that has rivaled that of their Puritan forebears. Among the prominent transcendentalists, Ralph Waldo Emerson alone was an ordained minister, but the rhetoric fits our criteria for consideration as religious rhetoric, and the transcendentalist school and its individual proponents have been the subjects of a number of rhetorical studies (Azarnoff, 1961; Chandler, 1991; Funk, 1972; Johnstone, 1974; Kurtz, 2001; Lawton, 1968; Oliver, 1960; Ray, 1974; Tompkins, 1976). But much remains to be done.

Perhaps the most prominent 19th-century reform movement to be fueled by the Second Great Awakening was abolitionism. Historical scholarship has consistently featured the religious foundations of abolitionist argument (Mintz & Stauffer, 2007), and rhetorical scholarship has recognized the featuring of moral premises in these debates, including the presentation of arguments, pros and cons, from the pulpit (Burke, 1996; Chesebrough, 1991, 1996; Dill, 1988) as well as those voices beyond the pulpit (Bacon, 1999b; Bacon & McClish, 2006; Browne, 1996, 1999; Conser, 1997; Dick, 1964; Japp, 1985; Kennicott, 1970;

McClish, 2005; Prioleau, 2003; Ray, 1998, 2006; Selby, 2002; Slanger, 1995). Other, more focused movements, fanned by the excitement of the revival as well, included the "Female Moral Reform Movement," which focused on the abolition of sexual vice and the promotion of sexual abstinence among the young as they entered the marriage market (Wright, 2006). Together with the moral reform societies, the number of newspapers in the 19th century that self-consciously identified as vehicles of "moral reform," including *The Vanguard: A Journal of Moral Reform* (v.1, n. 1, 1893), is astonishing, and little rhetorical analysis has been done (Bell, 1958).

The Third Great Awakening

The period following the Civil War saw, predictably, another crisis of conscience. The war was hardly over when the country began to obsess over its moral failings. Unlike the Revolution, which towered over the succeeding generation as a pinnacle of moral achievement, the Civil War, despite Lincoln's famous framing of it in his second inaugural address, had only marginally been waged for moral reasons and was less a great moral victory than a case of *occasus interruptus*. Many of the reform efforts of the last half of the 19th century were not new causes but continuations of movements that had begun before the war, not new initiatives but evidence of persistent shortcomings. Anxiety surrounding key elements of the American ideal, especially the freedom-slavery dialectic and its relationship to "virtue," steadily increased; potential shackles were omnipresent: alcohol, sex, even one's own passions. In 1891, William Dougherty captured the tenor of the times with his tract titled "The Lights and Shadows of Society: An Attempt to Show the Deplorable Condition of American Society, Socially and Politically." The situation was dire: "These are terrible times—savage times—times lacking every vestige of respect for honesty and manliness," wrote Otto Peltzer (1887):

> Virility is at a discount, flabby aestheticism is mistaken for refinement, delicate points of honor are met with derision, trusts are broken, and faith is wanting in every station. Slum journalism, vilely-illustrated prints and the dime novel, like immoral epidemics, are sapping the morals of our youth. (p. 11)

Thomas Acheson's (1900) perfervid insistence on "The Moral Personality of the Nation," published by the National Reform Association as part of its Studies in Christian Citizenship series, was part of the reaction to an attack on religion itself from some quarters—in England Thomas Huxley and in the United States Robert Ingersoll emerged as powerful spokespersons against received religion (Jensen, 1965; Towne, 1962). Furthermore, the rise of modern science, including Darwinian evolutionary theory, presented a threat to common conceptions of God and God's creation. The Third Great Awakening might even be said to end with the Scopes trial.

As with its antecedents, much of the energy that drove the Third Great Awakening was the desire to recover a sense of ourselves that had been lost, and many of rhetorical studies of the Third Great Awakening are studies of its most celebrated characters, including Aimee Semple McPherson (Bartow, 1997; Ebeling, 1957; Schuetz, 1986), Billy Sunday (Davis, 1966; Quimby & Billigmeier, 1959), and Dwight L. Moody (Huber, 1952; Quimby, 1954, 1957; Quimby & Billigmeier, 1959; Taylor & Schwartz, 1969; Willey & Hume, 2004). Some attention has been paid to significant orators of the time who, while not preachers, entered into public debates on moral issues of the day and who made their arguments on morals grounds. Most notable among these spokespersons was William Jennings Bryan who, in his later years, campaigned vigorously for Prohibition and against the teaching of evolution in the schools and liberal biblical criticism (Barrett, 1962, 1968; Hostetler, 1998; Mills, 1949).

There is no little irony in the fact that two of the most prominent reformers of this era featured their Roman Catholic faith as the basis for their reform efforts but found themselves at very different places on the political spectrum. Dorothy Day of the Catholic Worker Movement and Father Charles Coughlin have both been subjects of rhetorical analysis, though there is certainly more to be done (Anderson, 1982; Jablonski, 2000). It is perhaps unfair to include Father Charles Coughlin as part of the Third Great Awakening, but he is a figure who has received a remarkable level of attention from rhetorical scholars, though most have begun their analyses with the fact of Coughlin's extraordinary power rather than probing the sources of that power and its possible connections to Coughlin's status as a Roman Catholic priest (Carpenter, 1998; Casey & Rowe, 1996; Sayer, 1987). The juxtaposition of Day and Coughlin itself points to an unsolved mystery with respect to religious rhetoric: How can shared sacred premises lead to such divergent conclusions?

The impact of the Third Great Awakening on politics and public policy was profound. The period between 1865 and 1920 saw not only the enactment of the United States's most famous attempt at the legislation of morality, the 18th Amendment to the Constitution, prohibiting "the manufacture, sale, or transportation of intoxicating liquors within, the importation thereof into, or the exportation thereof from the United States and all territory subject to the jurisdiction thereof for beverage purposes," but Congress, Gaines Foster reminds us, urged on by a "Christian lobby" passed laws to regulate or proscribe obscenity; forms of sexual behavior, including polygamy and prostitution; divorce; gambling; prizefighting; and narcotics (Foster, 2002; see also Parker, 1997). These changes and the rhetoric that helped fuel them have received little attention from rhetoricians.

The range of concerns of this "Christian lobby" provides a lesson in contextual reading to scholars of public discourse. Contrary to our own time, when religion tends to be viewed as the province of the political right, the *fin de siècle* in the United States saw religious principles invoked on behalf of progressive as well as conservative causes. In fact, it is not at all clear that our contemporary distinctions are applicable. Was Prohibition a conservative cause? It was supported by many whom we would otherwise today hold to be "leftists." Much of what passed under the banner of "the Social Gospel" or "Christian Socialism" was of this nature, calling attention to the rootedness of genuine radicalism (Boase, 1980). There are a number of rhetorical studies of prominent exponents of the Social Gospel, most following the basic models we have already reviewed: studies of individual rhetors or texts (Alexander, 1989; Anderson, 1982). Less obvious and even less well explored are the evangelical roots of muckraking (Evensen, 1989).

Newspapers were to the Third Great Awakening what radio and television would be to later generations. Newspapers helped create and fuel debate on the issues and helped make national spokespersons out of some of the most prominent rhetors of the period (Evensen, 2001, 2002). Yet we know relatively little about the modes of dissemination of some of the great sermons and speeches delivered on the burning causes of the day, nor do we well understand the seemingly contradictory ascension of print as the main vehicle for mass communication at the moment of the zenith of grand American oratory.

The Fourth Great Awakening

The idea of a Fourth Great Awakening in the United States does not claim the consensus enjoyed by the first three. The historian of American religion William McLoughlin has been a major exponent of the idea of a "Fourth Great Awakening" in U.S. history

(McLoughlin, 1978, 1983). McLoughlin argues that the Fourth Great Awakening began ca. 1960 and finds evidence for his characterization in the evident desire for a revitalization in American culture during the 1960s, 1970s, and 1980s (McLoughlin, 1983, pp. 105, 110, 113). The economic historian Robert Fogel (2002) has also argued for a Fourth Great Awakening, a phenomenon that he identifies with the late 1960s and early 1970s. Fogel's concatenation of the religious behaviors of this period with those of the First, Second, and Third Great Awakenings has created controversy and has not been widely accepted.

We propose that the period immediately following the Second World War and extending through much of the 1950s has much greater kinship with the first three Great Awakenings than do the decades proposed by McLoughlin or Fogel. In the period following World War II, Americans had to reckon with a dramatically changed world. The Soviet Union, our ally during the war, was now our archrival, especially after it usurped our monopoly on atomic weapons and was the first to put a satellite in outer space. Germany and Japan, who had been our enemies, were now our friends and the beneficiaries of our aid. America's special relationship with God was subject to question. The very existence of God was an open question. Harvey Cox presented his secularization thesis (Cox, 1965), and Thomas Altizer proposed "Christian atheism" (Altizer, 1966, 1970; Altizer & Hamilton, 1966); everyone now knew that a previously obscure philosopher, Friedrich Nietzsche, had proclaimed the death of God.

It is precisely in these moments of crisis, moments in which the world threatens to descend into meaninglessness, that the claims of faith can be most welcomed. We do not really want to be free of God, Nietzsche reminds us; His death is, for most, no cause for celebration. The 1950s saw a renewed enthusiasm for religion similar to that seen during the first three great awakenings. Some

of the major figures to emerge during the 1950s and early 1960s to lead us out of the wilderness were Billy James Hargis, Carl McIntire, Frederick Schwarz, and Oral Roberts (Baskerville, 1963; Horne, 1990), but surely the most important religious spokesperson to emerge during this period was Billy Graham. Beginning in the 1950s, Graham laid the foundations for influence at the very highest levels of American politics, gaining the ear as advisor and confessor to 11 presidents, a feat rivaled only by Bernard Baruch a generation earlier, and establishing himself as the country's senior pastor. His rhetorical significance notwithstanding, Graham has received only scant attention from scholars of the U.S. public discourse. Scholars of public address have taken note of books about Graham by journalists and scholars in other disciplines; we have acknowledged the availability of the archives at the Billy Graham Center at Wheaton College; we have looked at Graham as part of a sample of revivalistic preaching in American Protestant evangelism (Quimby & Billigmeier, 1959); we have acknowledged Graham's status as a legendary orator of the 20th century (Duffy & Leeman, 2005); but there have been no studies looking exclusively at Graham's rhetorical practices.

If the religious fervor of the 1950s seemed to subside in the 1960s, it was really the locus of religious discourse that changed. Though the continuing role of the Christian church in the Civil Rights Movement is well documented, and rhetoricians such as Parke Burgess called us to recognize the moral essence of black power rhetoric (Burgess, 1968), the innocent utopian strains in "The Port Huron Statement" are often overlooked in our memories of what the Students for a Democratic Society became. Too little attention has been paid to the moral grounding of much of the political activity on the left during the 1960s, perhaps because not all of it enjoyed the benison of the church. Children of the sixties made the pilgrimage to Tibet; explored Buddhism, Hinduism, Taoism;

sought themselves in sweat lodges and in the books of Carlos Casteneda; and flirted with paganism. Thomas Merton attempted to bridge the gap between Christianity and other philosophies such as Zen Buddhism, but only one rhetorical scholar has done any work on this influential Cistercian monk whose influence is still being explored today (Horne, 1988). Cults became a prominent feature of the American scene and were viewed not as alternative religions, but as threats to religion. For all the rhetoric spent in attempting to disarm these pretenders, these snakes in the garden, very little attention has been paid to either the cults themselves or to their opponents (Howard, 2005).

A Fifth Great Awakening?

As the messy 1960s drew to an untidy close, characteristically spilling over into the 1970s, the decade that had brought us protests, acts of rebellion, riots, psychedelic drugs, a general celebration of nonconformity, nudity in the theatre, the sexual revolution, and the Yippies attempted to leave its legacy. Coercive prayer in schools had been banned by the U.S. Supreme Court in 1963. In 1973, as the United States was finally extricating itself from Vietnam, the U.S. Supreme Court abdicated on the question of defining obscenity (*Miller v. California*) and effectively repudiated most federal and state restrictions on abortion (*Roe v. Wade*). In that same year, the American Psychological Association began the process that would remove homosexuality as a pathology in its *Diagnostic and Statistical Manual of Mental Disorders*.

Christian fundamentalists, and in truth many Americans, saw in events the ascendancy of chaos over order, the divine covenant in tatters. The theme song "Those Were the Days," composed for the television series *All in the Family* (which premiered in 1971), parodied the longing for a renewed sense of definition felt by many. "And you knew who you were then. Girls were girls, and men were men," the song affirmed. In 1977, provoked by the decision of the Dade County (Florida) Commission to extend nondiscrimination in housing, employment, and public accommodations to homosexuals, Anita Bryant spearheaded a religiously based campaign, first, to overturn the Dade County decision, then to turn back other gay rights ordinances across the country and to prevent still others from being passed. In 1979, Jerry Falwell created a more permanent, more broadly focused vehicle for the new Christian Right when he founded the Moral Majority (Appel, 1987b; Biesecker-Mast, 2007; Brown, 1991; Mitchell & Phipps, 1985).

In the 1970s, the foundations were being laid for the "culture wars," and key theaters involved prayer in schools, abortion, gay rights, and the teaching of scientific evolution. In each case, the arguments engaged in profound ways questions of morality, religion, and the role of religion in a secular society (Hudson, 1972; Servin-Gonzalez & Torres-Reyna, 1999; Smith & Windes, 1997; Vanderford, 1989).

Barnet Pearce and his colleagues (1987) suggested that the discursive intensity of the culture wars emanated from incompatible and incommensurable moral premises, resulting in what these scholars called a "reciprocated diatribe." The lines in the culture wars lie not, as superficial treatments might have it, between the religious and the nonreligious. A shattered window would be a better representation: complex, fragmented, crazing religions and rupturing denominational bonds. The period from the 1980s to the present has probably witnessed more intra-denominational, internecine conflict than any time since the Civil War. Few studies have been done on how argumentative territories are divided among members of the same ideological or theological family, various parties claiming the same principles and warrants (Huebner, 1991).

One of the critical elements in these new religious debates was a shift in media. The Moral Majority and its progeny proved to be very sophisticated users of electronic media, especially television (Appel, 1987b; Schultze, 1988). Pat Robertson, Oral Roberts, Jimmy Swaggart (Pullum, 1990), Jim and Tammy Faye Baker, John Hagee—these and others created the role of the televangelist, often creating substantial independent broadcasting empires in the process. The rise of televangelism, the effects of the new medium on the message and of the message on the medium, have received considerable attention from rhetorical and media scholars (Fore, 2007; Frankl, 1987; Hadden & Swann, 1981; Stout & Buddenbaum, 1996; Turner, 2007; White, 2007). There have also been a number of traditional studies of the rhetorical practices of individual televangelists, studies that focus on individual sermons or speeches and aspects of *inventio, dispositio, elecutio,* and *actio* without reference to mediation (Detwiler, 1988).

The urge, in the 1970s and 1980s, to recover a center that would hold was not confined to the Christian right. Mainstream politics found various ways to reconnect with religion, and the trend attracted the attention of political scientists, sociologists, historians, and scholars of communication and public address (Hollander, 2006; Pierard, 1985). The presidencies of Jimmy Carter (Boase, 1989; Erickson, 1980; Hahn, 1980; Johnstone, 1978; Lee, 1995; Patton, 1977; Porter, 1990), Ronald Reagan (Boase, 1989; Coe & Domke, 2006; Glenn, 1988; Goodnight, 1986; Jones & Rowland, 2005; Porter, 1990; Willhite, 1989), and both presidents Bush, including the elder Bush's invocation of the just war doctrine to justify the 1991 military intervention by the United States in the Persian Gulf (Coe & Domke, 2006; Gunn, 2004; Pearce & Fedely, 1993; Spielvogel, 2005), have particularly been highlighted in rhetorical scholarship.

When Jimmy Carter was elected in 1976, he was the first born-again president of the United States. When Carter ran for reelection in 1980, he had new company with respect to public professions of private faith. The ubiquity of overtly religious appeals in the election of 1980 made that election one of special interest to students of religion and U.S. politics, including students of American political rhetoric (Miller & Wattenberg, 1984; Porter, 1990). The election of 1984 continued the trend (Glenn, 1988). In 1988, Pat Robertson, whose political base was his ministry, made a bid for the Republican nomination for president. O'Leary and McFarland (1989) examined how Robertson's rhetoric shifted from premillennialism to a blend of pre- and postmillennialism in order to appeal to moderates and provide a plan of action. While in office, Bill Clinton used religious rhetoric to disarm criticism and mobilize support (Ofulue, 2002), though Joe Lieberman's experience in the presidential campaign of 2000 demonstrated that such personal professions of faith, designed to be galvanizing, unifying appeals, may, when the electoral core is incoherent, prove fissiparous (Hostetler, 2002; see also Layman, 1997; Powell & Neiva, 2006).

The relationship between religion and politics in America is one that is continually shifting, perpetually redefining itself. We need broad, longitudinal studies of this amorphous nexus, this dance in which the steps are always changing. In order to have those broad longitudinal studies, we need more case studies of individual instantiations of this relationship. This relationship promises to become only more complicated in the future as the nation's leaders struggle to find acceptable appeals for calling the plurality into being as one people.

A POSTMODERN UNRAVELING AND THE FUTURE OF RELIGIOUS RHETORIC

If the public profession of religion, especially on the model presented by classical theism, long the dominant model in America, depends on an immutable authority, what happens when that authority fractures? Our long historical commitment to religious pluralism notwithstanding, religion in the United States has, for most of our history, occupied a relatively narrow band on the theological spectrum. While respecting the felt differences that resulted in the removal of Roger Williams and Anne Hutchinson from the Massachusetts colony; the differences that gave rise to the anti-Catholic movement of the early 19th century; the differences that split denominations during and following the Civil War; the differences that continue to split denominations today over, for example, homosexuality; while acknowledging the unbridgeable chasm seen by Mary Doren of Iowa when confronted with the prospect of voting for Mitt Romney, a Mormon, for president of the United States—"I'm a Christian. I don't think a Mormon or a Catholic is a Christian" (Winker, 2007)—we must nonetheless recognize that America's religious pluralism has, until very recently, exhibited a very limited range. No president before George H. W. Bush had to pay any significant rhetorical attention to Islam, for example.

Our essential agreement on religious issues has helped mask the role of religion in politics—the virtual hegemony of Christianity in the history of the United States has predictably served to obscure its ideological functions—but recent decades have seen an increase in the number of Americans whose faith is other than Christian, even other than "Judeo-Christian," and this increase in numbers has been accompanied by an increased adamancy that the United States has to live up to its profession as a pluralist and secular state. These demands have been met by an equally adamant response that, as a nation, we should return to our Christian roots. The veil has been rent; the religious basis of many policies and practices has been exposed, and the nature and limits of tolerance as a social bond have been interrogated (Clark & Corcoran, 2000).

Case studies of the religious themes and motifs in the rhetoric of particular political figures contribute to larger debates about the propriety of religious influences in American politics and the appropriate place of religion in the public square and in public discourse (Dunn, 1983; Johnson, 1985; Leeman, 2006a). Ancient questions regarding the division between the public and the private have achieved renewed salience (Beyer, 1990). The United States is divided over religious tests for public officials; over creationism, intelligent design, and what ought to be taught in the public schools (Campbell & Meyer, 2004; Johnson, 1998; Lessl, 2003); over genetic engineering, with all its possibilities, and over stem cell research (Harris, Parrott, & Dorgan, 2004); over the validity and meaning of the repeated assertion that, at our core, we are a "Judeo-Christian culture" (Hartmann, Zhang, & Wischstadt, 2005). The very existence of the divine has, through the vehicle of several bestselling books, assumed an extraordinarily central place in public debate (Longaker, 2006).

The debate has escalated in recent years; a need really to wrestle with the demands of pluralism seems to be at the center of the storm, and the locus has shifted from a chronicling or analysis of present practice to prescriptive studies arguing about the proper place of religion in the public square (Audi, 2000; Badaracco, 1992; Boxx & Quinlivan, 1995; Cortese, 2004; D'Costa, 2005; Demerath, Diamond, Mapes, & Wedam, 2005; Dionne, 2004; Diiulio & Carlson-Thies, 2001; Gaddy, 2005; Heclo & McClay, 2003; Licht, Mittleman, & Sarna, 2002; Sears & Carper, 1998; Thiemann, 1996; Wander, 1985; Wolterstorff & Audi, 1996).

In response to this dissolution, Steven Goldzwig (1987) has gone so far as to propose a rhetoric of public theology, as opposed to a rhetoric of civic piety. This public theology includes a partisan god with clear, simple mandates on pressing policy problems, presented to the public through action rituals. Bryan Turner's (2006, 2007) work has focused on the possibility of religious rhetoric—rhetoric that binds us, rhetoric that commits us—in an age in which authority has disintegrated and the divine has been eclipsed by the objective. Though the problem of authority in a democratic culture is not unique to postmodernity (Marsden, 1982), there is in postmodernity a fundamental shift of presumption, a shift that makes it difficult to credit claims on the divine, to share a collective faith, or to be engaged by grand mythic narratives—Michael Harrington (1985) saw in our dissolute state "the spiritual crisis of Western culture." James Darsey (1997), concluding his survey of prophetic rhetoric in the United States, suggests that we may have reached the end of our "cycle of awakenings." Other scholars, though, see different possibilities.

Bekerman and Neuman (2001) have argued that fundamentalism, at least in a postmodern age, is not at all what we assume it to be, dependent on an invariant truth embedded in a fixed and sacred tradition, but that fundamentalism has the power to adapt itself to a new era by incorporating a modern/postmodern dialogue; Lewis Snyder (1999) has argued for a "holographic post-postmodernism" as the basis for a new apologetics in the 21st century; John O'Neill (1988) has examined the urge for a renewal of religious symbolism in the work of Daniel Bell and Frederic Jameson; and Eric Rothenbuhler (1989) has suggested ostensibly secular social rituals as a source of *religio* in a world in which competing gods have been neutralized by pluralism.

DIRECTIONS FOR FUTURE RESEARCH

Even a survey as brief as this makes clear the enormous amount of work there is to be done on religion in U.S. public discourse and the great need for that work. In a world that seems increasingly fractured, people look for common ground, for the bonds that religion has traditionally supplied. Yet our theories of religious discourse are anemic; we have little sense of the power of religious discourse, of the sources of its claims on our consent, or of what distinguishes it from more pedestrian discourses. The religious ethos, especially when it manifests itself charismatically, remains largely a mystery. In examining the religious ethos in America, we need to decode its complicated relationship to gender. We need, in addition to refining our understanding of the forms we have identified, to expand our repertoire of religious forms and to follow recent trends in rhetorical studies in expanding the range of symbolic behaviors that might be considered texts for analysis. We need more attention to the conditions that seem to bring religious discourse into prominence and continued attention to the ever-shifting relationship between religion and politics in the United States.

In all of these efforts, we need more and richer historical accounts of religious rhetorics in America. Our attempt here to sketch a broad narrative of religion in American public discourse is presented as a kind of working hypothesis, an exercise in primitive cartography, the value of which will be found in its explanatory power, in its capacity to provide coherence to the mass of data that is religious public address in the United States. Our preliminary survey has pointed to some fine but often neglected scholarship, and even more often to the want of scholarship, though the significance of the territory is without question. The refinement and emendation of this map depend on more detail, more case studies, more scrupulous attention to the individual plats that constitute the whole than we have currently provided. In addition to refining (or contesting or replacing) the map that we have proposed here, we must remember that, just as there are political maps, engineering maps, cadastral maps, forestry maps, flood control maps, geologic maps, we may produce different maps of the same territory for different purposes. There are other broad accounts of religious rhetoric in the United States that need to be told. Recent work by Robbie Goh (2006) suggests a literal interpretation of this cartographic metaphor. Goh, who sees a conflict between the localization of religious sites and the significance invested in the accoutrement of their location versus the urge to transcendence in most religious thought, has called for studies of religious sites as a supplement to the study of religion.

Nor will it be enough to map the historical and existing terrain. The landscape of religious rhetoric is shifting. The recognition of the legitimacy of plural religions, the spaces shared by religion and science, the possibilities for a religious rhetoric in the absence of God—all these issues and others that we cannot see deserve the attention of rhetorical scholars, for as Burke would remind us, communication is a form of communion. In the early 21st century, we are as the people of Babel, confounded in language and unable to understand one another's speech (Genesis 11:7). In a world in which consequences may be global, but understandings remain fiercely provincial, we need to find the language of a common faith, if not to a universal deity, at least a faith in our own mutual goodwill and common fate.

REFERENCES

Abbott, J. Y. (2006). Religion and gender in the news: The case of promise keepers, feminists, and the "Stand in the Gap" rally. *Journal of Communication & Religion, 29*(2), 224–261.

Abbott, J. Y. (2007). The positive functions of "negative" rhetoric: Feminists' expository campaign against the promise keepers. *Women's Studies in Communication, 30*(1), 1–33.

Abernathy, E. (1943). Trends in American homiletic theory since 1860. *Speech Monographs, 10*(1), 68.

Acheson, T. H. (1900). *The moral personality of the nation (studies in Christian citizenship)*. Warrenton, VA: National Reform Association.

Adams, D. (1989). The imperative to volunteer: Religious themes in public pronouncements of American presidents, Hoover to Reagan. In *Philanthropy and the religious tradition: Working papers* (pp. 291–303). Washington, DC: Independent Sector and United Way.

Adams, J. C., & Yarbrough, S. R. (1997). "Sinners" in the hands of an angry God, saints in the hands of their father. *Journal of Communication & Religion, 20*(1), 25–35.

Adams, J. C., & Yarbrough, S. R. (2007). Jonathan Edwards, the Great Awakening, and "Sinners in the Hands of an Angry God." In J. R. Andrews (Ed.), *Rhetoric, religion, and the roots of identity in British colonial America* (pp. 275–296). East Lansing: Michigan State University Press.

Adler, B. J. (1995). Building and maintaining church identity: Rhetorical strategies found in letters from two Lutheran leaders. *Journal of Communication & Religion, 18*(2), 29–39.

Alexander, J. C., Jr. (1989). George D. Herron: The man and his rhetoric. *Journal of Communication & Religion, 12*(1), 7–13.

Altizer, T. (1966). *The gospel of Christian atheism*. Philadelphia: Westminster Press.

Altizer, T. (1970). *Descent into hell: A study of the radical reversal of the Christian consciousness*. Philadelphia: J. B. Lippincott Company.

Altizer, T., & Hamilton, W. (1966). *Radical theology and the death of God*. Indianapolis: Bobbs-Merrill.

Anderson, R. D. (1982). Dorothy Day's last speech: A culmination of her life's journey. *Religious Communication Today, 5*, 30–34.

Andrews, J. R. (2007). Roots of an "American" rhetoric. In J. R. Andrews (Ed.), *Rhetoric, religion, and the roots of identity in British colonial America* (pp. xv–xxvii). East Lansing: Michigan State University Press.

Appel, E. C. (1987a). The tragic-symbol preaching of the Rev. Dr. Wallace E. Fisher. *Journal of Communication & Religion, 10*(1), 34–43.

Appel, E. C. (1987b). The perfected drama of Reverend Jerry Falwell. *Communication Quarterly, 35*(1), 26–38.

Appel, E. C. (1993). Kenneth Burke: Coy theologian. *Journal of Communication & Religion, 16*(2), 99–110.

Apple, A. L., & Messner, B. A. (2001). Paranoia and paradox: The apocalyptic rhetoric of Christian identity. *Western Journal of Communication, 65*(2), 206.

Appleby, J. (2000). *Inheriting the revolution: The first generation of Americans.* Cambridge, MA: Belknap Press.

Audi, R. (2000). *Religious commitment and secular reason.* Cambridge, UK: Cambridge University Press.

Aune, J. A. (1999). Three justices in search of historical truth: Romance and tragedy in the rhetoric of establishment clause jurisprudence. *Rhetoric & Public Affairs, 2*, 573–597.

Azarnoff, R. S. (1961). Walt Whitman's concept of the oratorical ideal. *Quarterly Journal of Speech, 47*(2), 169.

Bachman, J. V. (1959). Rhetoric in the ministry. *Today's Speech, 7*(3), 3–5.

Bacon, J. (1999a). "God and a woman": Women abolitionists, biblical authority, and social activism. *Journal of Communication & Religion, 22*(1), 1–39.

Bacon, J. (1999b). Taking liberty, taking literacy: Signifying in the rhetoric of African-American abolitionists. *Southern Communication Journal, 64*(4), 271.

Bacon, J., & McClish, G. (2006). Descendents of Africa, sons of '76: Exploring early African-American rhetoric. *Rhetoric Society Quarterly, 36*(1), 1–29.

Badaracco, C. (1992). Religious lobbyists in the public square. *Public Relations Quarterly, 37*(1), 30–36.

Bailey, R. (1969). Building men for citizenship. In D. Holland (Ed.), *Preaching in American history* (pp. 135–149). Nashville, TN: Abingdon Press.

Bailey, R. E. (1980). A rhetorical perspective on pastoral leadership. *Religious Communication Today, 3*, 15–18.

Bailyn, B. (1970). Religion and revolution: Three biographical studies. *Perspectives in American History, 4*, 85–169.

Barkun, M. (1985). The awakening-cycle controversy. *Sociological Analysis, 46*(4), 425–443.

Barrett, H. (1962). Scott of the Oregonian vs. William Jennings Bryan. *Quarterly Journal of Speech, 48*(2), 169.

Barrett, H. (1968). The rhetoric of a "possible infidel." *Western Speech, 32*(1), 4–10.

Bartow, C. L. (1997). Just now: Aimee Semple McPherson's performance and preaching of Jesus. *Journal of Communication & Religion, 20*(1), 71–79.

Baskerville, B. (1963). The cross and the flag: Evangelists of the far right. *Western Speech, 27*(4), 197–206.

Baxter, T. (2004). *Frederick Douglass's curious audiences: Ethos in the age of the consumable subject.* New York: Routledge.

Becker, C. (1932). *The heavenly city of the eighteenth-century philosophers.* New Haven, CT: Yale University Press.

Bekerman, Z., & Neuman, Y. (2001). Joining their betters rather than their own: The modern/postmodern rhetoric of Jewish fundamentalist preachers. *Journal of Communication Inquiry, 25*(2), 184–199.

Bell, H. H. (1958). *The American Moral Reform Society, 1836–1841.* Houston: Texas Southern University.

Bellah, R. N. (1975). *The broken covenant: American civil religion in time of trial.* New York: Seabury Press.

Bellah, R. N. (1976). The revolution and the civil religion. In J. C. Brauer (Ed.), *Religion and the American Revolution.* (pp. 55–73). Philadelphia: Fortress Press.

Bellah, R. N., & Hammond, P. E. (1980). *Varieties of civil religion.* San Francisco: Harper & Row.

Bercovitch, S. (1978). *The American jeremiad.* Madison: University of Wisconsin Press.

Berens, J. F. (1977). 'Like a prophetic spirit': Samuel Davies, American eulogists, and the deification of George Washington. *Quarterly Journal of Speech, 63*(3), 290.

Beyer, P. F. (1990). Privatization and the public influence of religion in global society. *Theory, Culture & Society, 7*(2/3), 373–395.

Biesecker-Mast, S. (2007). Fundamental gaffes. *Communication & Critical/Cultural Studies, 4*(1), 98–101.

Bineham, J. L. (1993). Theological hegemony and oppositional interpretive codes: The case of evangelical Christian feminism. *Western Journal of Communication, 57*(4), 519–529.

Bjerga, A. (2001). Trials of faith: Discussion of religion and the Beecher adultery scandal, 1870–1880. *American Journalism, 18,* 73–94–22p.

Bland, D. (1990). Patterns of spontaneous rhetoric: Ways of praying among the charismatic Bible temple community. *Journal of Communication & Religion, 13*(1), 1–11.

Boase, P. H. (1954). The education of a circuit rider. *Quarterly Journal of Speech, 40*(2), 130.

Boase, P. H. (1969). *The rhetoric of Christian socialism.* New York: Random House.

Boase, P. H. (1980). *The rhetoric of protest and reform, 1878–1898.* Athens: Ohio University Press.

Boase, P. H. (1989). Moving the mercy seat into the White House. *Journal of Communication & Religion, 12*(2), 1–9.

Bobbitt, D., & Mixon, H. (1994). Prophecy and apocalypse in the rhetoric of Martin Luther King, Jr. *Journal of Communication & Religion, 17*(1), 27–38.

Boklund, G. (1967). Time must have a stop: Apocalyptic thought and expression in the twentieth century. *Denver Quarterly, 2,* 69–98.

Booth, W. C. (1991). Rhetoric and religion: Are they essentially wedded? In W. G. Jeanrond (Ed.), *Radical pluralism and truth: David Tracy and the hermeneutics of religion* (pp. 62–80). New York: Crossroad.

Bos, W., & Faries, C. (1969). The social gospel: Preaching reform, 1875–1915. In D. Holland (Ed.), *Preaching in American history* (pp. 223–238). Nashville, TN: Abingdon Press.

Bosley, H. A. (1969). The role of preaching in American history. In D. Holland (Ed.), *Preaching in American history* (pp. 17–35). Nashville, TN: Abingdon Press.

Bosmajian, H. (1985). The "Wall of Separation": Metaphor in Supreme Court Church-State decisions. *Religious Communication Today, 8,* 1–7.

Boss, G. P. (1976). Essential attributes of the concept of charisma. *Southern Speech Communication Journal, 41,* 300–313.

Boxx, T. W., & Quinlivan, G. M. (1995). *Policy reform and moral grounding.* Washington, DC: Center for Economic and Policy Education.

Boyle, M. O. (2001). Religion. In T. O. Sloane (Ed.). *Encyclopedia of rhetoric* (pp. 662–672). New York: Oxford University Press.

Brand, J. D. (1997). Protest as prayer. *Journal of Communication & Religion, 20*(2), 41–52.

Brigance, W. N. (Ed.). (1943). *History and criticism of American public address.* New York: Russell & Russell.

Brown, G. (1991). Jerry Falwell and the PTL: The rhetoric of apologia. *Journal of Communication & Religion, 14*(1), 9–18.

Browne, S. H. (1992). Samuel Danforth's errand into the wilderness and the discourse of arrival in early American culture. *Communication Quarterly, 40*(2), 91–101.

Browne, S. H. (1996). Encountering Angelina Grimké: Violence, identity, and the creation of radical community. *Quarterly Journal of Speech, 82*(1), 55–74.

Browne, S. H. (1999). Remembering Crispus Attucks: Race, rhetoric, and the politics of commemoration. *Quarterly Journal of Speech, 85*(2), 169.

Browne, S. H. (2007). Errand into mercy: Rhetoric, identity, and community in John Winthrop's "Model of Chirstian Charity." In J. R. Andrews (Ed.), *Rhetoric, religion, and the roots of identity in British colonial America* (pp. 1–35). East Lansing: Michigan State University Press.

Brownlow, P. C. (1972). The pulpit and Black America: 1865–1877. *Quarterly Journal of Speech, 58*(4), 431.

Brummett, B. (1984). Premillennial apocalytpic as a rhetorical genre. *Central States Speech Journal, 35,* 84–93.

Brummett, B. (1988). Using apocalyptic discourse to exploit audience commitments through "transfer." *Southern Speech Communication Journal, 54,* 58–73.

Brummett, B. (1991). *Contemporary apocalyptic rhetoric.* New York: Praeger.

Brummett, B. (1994). Arguing the apocalypse: A theory of millennial rhetoric. *Rhetoric Society Quarterly, 24*(1/2), 132–134.

Burgess, P. G. (1968). The rhetoric of black power: A moral demand? *Quarterly Journal of Speech, 54*(2), 122–134.

Burke, K. (1970). *The rhetoric of religion: Studies in logology.* Berkeley and Los Angeles: University of California Press.

Burke, R. K. (1996). Samuel Ringgold Ward and black abolitionism: Rhetoric of assimilated

Christology. *Journal of Communication & Religion, 19*(1), 61–71.

Caliendo, G. G. (1999). Behind the political rhetoric of the Colorado family values coalition: The paranoid and the apocalyptic styles. *Journal of the Northwest Communication Association, 27,* 53–64.

Camp, L. R. (1969). Man and his government: Roger Williams vs. the Massachusetts oligarchy. In D. Holland (Ed.), *Preaching in American history* (pp. 74–97). Nashville, TN: Abingdon Press.

Campbell, J. A. (2003). Evil as the allure of perfection. *Rhetoric & Public Affairs, 6,* 523–530.

Campbell, J. A., & Meyer, S. C. (Eds.). (2004). *Darwinism, design, and public education.* East Lansing: Michigan State University Press.

Campbell, K. K. (2001). Religious women rhetors. *Review of Communication, 1*(2), 194–198.

Campbell, K. K., & Jamieson, K. H. (1978). Form and genre in rhetorical criticism: An introduction. In K. K. Campbell & K. H. Jamieson (Eds.), *Form and genre: Shaping rhetorical action* (pp. 9–32). Falls Church, VA: The Speech Communication Association.

Carlton, J. W. (1969). The ecumenical movement. In D. Holland (Ed.). *Preaching in American history* (pp. 292–309). Nashville, TN: Abingdon Press.

Carpenter, R. H. (1998). Father Charles E. Coughlin: Surrogate spokesman for the disaffected. Westport, CT: Greenwood Press.

Casey, M., & Rowe, A. (1996). "Driving out the money changers": Radio priest Charles E. Coughlin's rhetorical vision. *Journal of Communication & Religion, 19*(1), 37–47.

Casey, M. W. (2004). "Come let us reason together": The heritage of the churches of Christ as a source for rhetorical invention. *Rhetoric & Public Affairs, 7,* 487–498.

Chandler, D. R. (1982). Harry Emerson Fosdick: Spokesman for the Modernist Movement. *Religious Communication Today, 5,* 1–4.

Chandler, D. R. (1989). The rhetorical synthesis of William Laurence Sullivan. *Journal of Communication & Religion, 12*(1), 28–37.

Chandler, D. R. (1991). A comparison of the Bhagavad Gita with Henry David Thoreau's Walden. *Journal of Communication & Religion, 14*(1), 19–39.

Chapel, G. W. (1989). Synthesizing Eastern and Western religious traditions: The rhetoric of

Japan's Seicho-No-Ie Movement. *Journal of Communication & Religion, 12*(1), 14–21.

Chapel, G. W., & Jensen, R. (2000). Synthesizing Jamesian pragmatism and Platonic idealism in nineteenth-century America: The discourse of Mary Baker Eddys Christian Science. *Journal of Communication & Religion, 23*(2), 95–122.

Chávez, K. R. (2004). Beyond complicity: Coherence, queer theory, and the rhetoric of the "Gay Christian Movement." *Text & Performance Quarterly, 24*(3/4), 255–275.

Chesebrough, D. B. (1991). *"God ordained this war": Sermons on the sectional crisis, 180–1865.* Columbia: University of South Carolina Press.

Chesebrough, D. B. (1996). *Clergy dissent in the Old South, 1830–1865.* Carbondale: Southern Illinois University Press.

Chesebrough, D. B. (1999). *Theodore Parker: Orator of superior ideas.* Westport, CT: Greenwood Press.

Chesebrough, D. B. (2001). *Phillips Brooks: Pulpit eloquence.* Westport, CT: Greenwood Press.

Clark, K. J., & Corcoran, K. (2000). Pluralism, secularism, and tolerance. *Rhetoric & Public Affairs, 3,* 627–639.

Clark, T. D. (1977). An exploration of generic aspects of contemporary American Christian sermons. *Quarterly Journal of Speech, 63*(4), 384–395.

Clark, W. K. (2007). *Remarks on restoring America's alliances.* Retrieved August 7, 2007, from http://clark04.com/speeches/012/

Coe, K., & Domke, D. (2006). Petitioners or prophets? Presidential discourse, God, and the ascendancy of religious conservatives. *Journal of Communication, 56*(2), 309–330.

Cohn, N. (1993). *Cosmos, chaos, and the world to come: The ancient roots of apocalyptic faith.* New Haven, CT: Yale University Press.

Collins, E. M. (1969). The rhetoric of sensation challenges the rhetoric of the intellect: An eighteenth-century controversy. In D. Holland (Ed.), *Preaching in American history* (pp. 98–117). Nashville, TN: Abingdon Press.

Collins, J. J., McGinn, B., & Stein, S. J. (2000). *The encyclopedia of apocalypticism: Vol. 1. The origins of apocalypticism in Judaism and Christianity.* New York: Continuum International.

Conrad, C. (1983). The rhetoric of the moral majority: An analysis of romantic form. *Quarterly Journal of Speech, 69,* 159–170.

Conser, W. H., Jr. (1997). Political rhetoric, religious sensibilities, and the Southern discourse on slavery. *Journal of Communication & Religion, 20*(1), 15–24.

Cortese, A. J. P. (2004). *Walls and bridges: Social justice and public policy.* Albany: State University of New York Press.

Cox, H. (1965). The secular city: Secularization and urbanization in theological perspective. New York: Macmillan.

Crocker, L. (1933). The rhetorical training of Henry Ward Beecher. *Quarterly Journal of Speech, 19*(1), 18.

Crocker, L. (1936). The rhetorical theory of Harry Emerson Fosdick. *Quarterly Journal of Speech, 22*(2), 207.

Cunningham, D. S. (1991). *Faithful persuasion: In aid of a rhetoric of Christian theology.* Notre Dame, IN: University of Notre Dame Press.

Darsey, J. (1988). The legend of Eugene Debs: Prophetic ethos as radical argument. *Quarterly Journal of Speech, 74*(4), 434.

Darsey, J. (1997). *The prophetic tradition and radical rhetoric in America.* New York: New York University Press.

Davis, D. H. (1994). Religion and the American Revolution. *Journal of Church & State, 36*(4), 709.

Davis, L. (1969). Popular vs. experimental religion. In D. Holland (Ed.), *Preaching in American history* (pp. 333–351). Nashville, TN: Abingdon Press.

Davis, R. E. (1966). Billy Sunday: Preacher-showman. *Southern Speech Journal, 32,* 83–97.

D'Costa, G. (2005). *Theology in the public square: Church, academy and nation.* Oxford, UK: Blackwell.

Demerath, N. J., Diamond, E., Mapes, M. L., & Wedam, E. (2005). *Sacred circles, public squares: The multicentering of American religion.* Bloomington: Indiana University Press.

Detwiler, T. (1988). Viewing Robertson's rhetoric in an Augustinian mirror. *Journal of Communication & Religion, 11*(1), 22–31.

Dick, R. C. (1964). Negro oratory in the anti-slavery societies: 1830–1860. *Western Speech, 28*(1), 5–14.

Diiulio, J. J., & Carlson-Thies, S. W. (Eds.). (2001). Religion and the public square in the 21st century. In *Proceedings from the conference, The Future of Government Partnerships with the Faith Community.* Washington, DC: Hudson Institute.

Dill, R. P. (1988). An analysis of stasis in James H. Thornwell's sermon, "The rights and duties of masters." *Journal of Communication & Religion, 11*(2), 19–24.

Dionne, E. J., Jr. (Ed.). (2004). *One electorate under God? A dialogue on religion and American politics.* Washington, DC: Brookings Institution Press.

Dorgan, H. (1987). "Ol time way" exhortation: Preaching in the old regular Baptist Church. *Journal of Communication & Religion, 10*(2), 24–30.

Dougherty, W. J. (1891). *The lights and shadows of society: An attempt to show the deplorable condition of American society, socially and politically. The philosophy of crime and the possibility of moral reform.* New York: Author.

Duffy, B. K., & Leeman, R. W. (Eds.). (2005). *American voices: An encyclopedia of contemporary orators.* Westport, CT: Greenwood Press.

Dunn, C. W. (1983). Theology and American public policy. *Humanities in Society, 6,* 53–70.

Ebeling, H. (1957). Aimee S. McPherson: Evangelist of the city. *Western Speech, 21*(3), 153–159.

Eldridge, J. E. T. (Ed.). (1971). *Max Weber: The interpretation of social reality.* New York: Scribner.

Eliade, M. (1959). *The sacred and the profane: The nature of religion* (W. R. Trask, Trans.). New York: Harcourt, Brace & World.

Enholm, D. K., Skaggs, D. C., & Welsh, W. J. (1987). Origins of the Southern mind: The parochial sermons of Thomas Cradock of Maryland, 1744–1770. *Quarterly Journal of Speech, 73*(2), 200.

Erickson, K. V. (1980). Jimmy Carter: The rhetoric of private and civic piety. *Western Journal of Speech Communication, 44*(3), 221–235.

Evans, J. N. (2006). *African American sacred rhetoric: An African American homiletic style informed by Western tradition* (Dissertation). Ann Arbor, MI: ProQuest Information and Learning.

Evans, V. N. (1987). Benjamin Colman and compromise: An analysis of transitional Puritan preaching. *Journal of Communication & Religion, 10*(1), 1–8.

Evensen, B. J. (1989). Evangelical origins of the Muckrakers. *American Journalism, 6*, 5–29.

Evensen, B. J. (2001). "Saucepan journalism" in an age of indifference. *Journalism History, 27*(4), 165–77.

Evensen, B. J. (2002). "The greatest day that our city has ever seen": Moody, Medill, and Chicago's Gilded Age revival. *Journal of Media & Religion, 1*(4), 231–249.

Farley, W. (2005). *The wounding and healing of desire: Weaving heaven and earth.* Louisville, KY: Westminster John Knox Press.

Fehler, B. (2007). *Calvinist rhetoric in nineteenth-century America: The Bartlet professors of sacred rhetoric of Andover seminary.* New York: Edwin Mellen Press.

Fitzgerald, F. (1987). *Cities on a hill: A brilliant exploration of visionary communities remaking the American dream.* New York: Simon & Schuster.

Flake, K. (2004). *The politics of American religious identity: The seating of Senator Reed Smoot, Mormon apostle.* Chapel Hill: The University of North Carolina Press.

Fogel, R. W. (2002). *The fourth great awakening and the future of egalitarianism.* Chicago: University of Chicago Press.

Fore, W. F. (2007). The unknown history of televangelism. *Media Development, 54*, 45–48.

Foster, G. M. (2002). *Moral reconstruction: Christian lobbyists and the federal legislation of morality, 1865–1920.* Durham: University of North Carolina Press.

Frank, D. A. (2003). The Jewish countermodel: Talmudic argumentation, the New Rhetoric Project, and the classical tradition of rhetoric. *Journal of Communication & Religion, 26*(2), 163–194.

Frank, D. A. (2004). Arguing with God, Talmudic discourse, and the Jewish countermodel: Implications for the study of argumentation. *Argumentation & Advocacy, 41*(2), 71–86.

Frankl, R. (1987). *Televangelism: The marketing of popular religion.* Carbondale: Southern Illinois University Press.

Friedenberg, R. V. (1983). Isaac Leeser: Pioneer preacher of American Judaism. *Religious Communication Today, 6*, 22–27.

Friedenberg, R. V. (1984). Rabbi Isaac Mayer Wise and American Judaism's rhetorical indebtedness to the Reverend Hugh Blair. *Religious Communication Today, 7*, 12–18.

Funk, A. A. (1972). Henry David Thoreau's "Slavery in Massachusetts." *Western Speech, 36*(3), 159–168.

Gabriel, R. (1950). Evangelical religion and popular romanticism in early nineteenth century America. *Church History, 19*, 34–47.

Gaddy, C. W. (2005). God talk in the public square. In C. H. Badaracco (Ed.), *Quoting God: How media shape ideas about religion and culture* (pp. 43–58). Waco, TX: Baylor University Press.

Garver, E. (1990). Essentially contested concepts: The ethics and tactics of arguments. *Philosophy & Rhetoric, 23*(4), 251–270.

Gaustad, E. S. (2003). *Proclaim liberty throughout all the land: A history of Church and State in America.* New York: Oxford University Press.

Gaustad, E. S., & Schmidt, L. (2004). *The religious history of America: The heart of the American story from colonial times to today.* San Francisco: HarperOne.

Glenn, G. D. (1988). Rhetoric and religion in the 1984 campaign. *Political Communication & Persuasion, 5*, 1–13.

Goh, R. B. H. (2006). Religious sites. *Theory, Culture & Society, 23*, 450–452.

Golden, J. L. (1961). John Wesley on rhetoric and belles lettres. *Speech Monographs, 28*(4), 250.

Goldzwig, S. (1987). A rhetoric of public theology: The religious rhetor and public policy. *Southern Speech Communication Journal, 52*, 128–150.

Goodnight, G. T. (1986). Ronald Reagan's reformulation of the rhetoric of war: Analysis of the "Zero Option," "Evil Empire," and "Star Wars" addresses. *Quarterly Journal of Speech, 72*(4), 390.

Goodnight, G. T. (1988). Argumentation in the nuclear age. *Journal of the American Forensic Association, 24*, 141–143.

Griffin, E. (1998). Journal of communication and religion: A state-of-the-art critical review. *Journal of Communication & Religion, 21*(2), 108–140.

Gunn, J. (2004). The rhetoric of exorcism: George W. Bush and the return of political demonology. *Western Journal of Communication, 68*(1), 1–23.

Gunn, J. (2005). *Modern occult rhetoric: Mass media and the drama of secrecy in the twentieth century.* Tuscaloosa: University of Alabama Press.

Hadden, J. K., & Swann, C. E. (1981). *Prime time preachers: The rising power of televangelism.* Reading, MA: Addison-Wesley.

Hahn, D. F. (1980). One's reborn every minute: Carter's religious appeal in 1976. *Communication Quarterly, 28*(3), 56–62.

Hance, K. G. (1970). Preaching in American history. *Speech Teacher, 19*(1), 85–86.

Hanson, P. D. (1975). *The dawn of apocalyptic.* Philadelphia: Fortress Press.

Harrington, M. (1985). *The politics at God's funeral: The spiritual crisis of Western civilization.* New York: Penguin Books.

Harris, T. M., Parrott, R., & Dorgan, K. A. (2004). Talking about human genetics within religious frameworks. *Health Communication, 16,* 105–116.

Hart, R. P. (1971). The rhetoric of the true believer. *Speech Monographs, 38*(4), 249.

Hart, R. P. (1977). *The political pulpit.* West Lafayette, IN: Purdue University Press.

Hart, R. P. (2002). God, country, and a world of words. *Journal of Communication & Religion, 25*(1), 136–147.

Hartmann, D., Zhang, X., & Wischstadt, W. (2005). One (multicultural) nation under God? Changing uses and meanings of the term "Judeo-Christian" in the American media. *Journal of Media & Religion, 4,* 207–234.

Heald, J. C. (1975). Apocalyptic rhetoric: Agents of the antichrist from the French to the British. *Today's Speech, 23,* 33–37.

Heclo, H., & McClay, W. M. (Eds.). (2003). *Religion returns to the public square: Faith and policy in America.* Washington, DC: Johns Hopkins University Press.

Heinemann, R. L. (1997). Secular spirituality and the evangelical search for rhetorical ground. *Journal of Communication & Religion, 20*(2), 53–65.

Heisey, D. R. (1992). Horace Bushnell's rhetorical training. *Journal of Communication & Religion, 15*(1), 55–69.

Hirst, R. (1995). The sixth canon of sacred rhetoric: Inspiration in nineteenth-century homiletic theory. *Rhetoric Society Quarterly, 25,* 69–90.

Hogan, J. M. (1987). Apocalyptic pornography and the nuclear freeze: A defense of the public. In J. M. Wenzel (Ed.), *Argument and critical practices: Proceedings of the Fifth SCA/AFA Conference on Argumentation* (pp. 541–548). Annandale, VA: Speech Communication Association.

Hogan, J. M. (1989). Managing dissent in the Catholic church: A reinterpretation of the pastoral letter on war and peace. *Quarterly Journal of Speech, 75*(4), 400.

Hogan, J. M., & Williams, G. (2004). The rusticity and religiosity of Huey P. Long. *Rhetoric & Public Affairs, 7,* 149–173.

Holland, D. T. (1964). Humor in the pulpit. *Today's Speech, 12*(4), 17–18.

Holland, D. T. (Ed.). (1969). *Preaching in American history.* Nashville, TN: Abingdon Press.

Holland, D. T. (Ed.). (1971). *Sermons in American history.* Nashville, TN: Abingdon Press.

Hollander, B. (2006). Religion as a chronically accessible construct. *Journal of Media & Religion, 5,* 233–244.

Horne, J. (1988). The sacramental rhetoric of Thomas Merton. *Journal of Communication & Religion, 11*(1), 1–9.

Horne, J. S. (1990). Visions and voices: The last temptation of Oral Roberts. *Journal of Communication & Religion, 13*(2), 15–23.

Hostetler, M. J. (1997). Rethinking the war metaphor in religious rhetoric: Burke, Black, and Berrigan's "Glimmer of Light." *Journal of Communication & Religion, 20*(1), 49–60.

Hostetler, M. J. (1998). William Jennings Bryan as Demosthenes: The Scopes Trial. *Western Journal of Communication, 62*(2), 165–180.

Hostetler, M. J. (2002). Joe Lieberman at Fellowship Chapel: Civil religion meets self-disclosure. *Journal of Communication & Religion, 25*(2), 148–165.

Houck, D. W., & Dixon, D. E. (2006). *Rhetoric, religion and the civil rights movement 1954–1965.* Waco, TX: Baylor University Press.

Howard, R. G. (2005). Sustainability and radical rhetorical closure: The case of the 1996 "Heaven's Gate" Newsffroun Camnaien. *Journal of Communication & Religion, 28*(1), 99–130.

Huber, R. B. (1952). Dwight L. Moody: Master of audience psychology. *Southern Speech Journal, 17,* 265–271.

Hudson, L. (1972). Belting the Bible: Madalyn Murray O'Hair vs. fundamentalism. *Western Speech, 36,* 233–240.

Hudson, R. F. (1958). Rhetorical invention in colonial New England. *Speech Monographs, 25*(3), 215.

Huebner, T. M., Jr. (1991). A house divided: Heresy and orthodoxy in the Southern Baptist convention. *Journal of Communication & Religion, 14*(2), 34–43.

Huxman, S. S., & Biesecker-Mast, G. (2004). In the world but not of it: Mennonite traditions as resources for rhetorical invention. *Rhetoric & Public Affairs, 7*(4), 539–554.

Jablonski, C. J. (1988). Rhetoric, paradox, and the movement for women's ordination in the Roman Catholic Church. *Quarterly Journal of Speech, 74*(2), 164.

Jablonski, C. J. (1989). Aggiornamento and the American Catholic bishops: A rhetoric of institutional continuity and change. *Quarterly Journal of Speech, 75*(4), 416.

Jablonski, C. J. (2000). Dorothy Day's contested legacy: "Humble Irony" as a constraint on memory. *Journal of Communication & Religion, 23*(1), 29–49.

Jackson, B. (2007). Jonathan Edwards goes to hell (House): Fear appeals in American evangelism. *Rhetoric Review, 26*(1), 42–59.

Jackson, P. (2006). The literal and metaphorical inscription of gesture in religious discourse. *Gesture, 6,* 215–222.

Jamieson, K. M. (1973). Generic constraints and the rhetorical situation. *Philosophy & Rhetoric, 6*(3), 162–170.

Japp, P. M. (1985). Esther or Isaiah? The abolitionist-feminist rhetoric of Angelina Grimké. *Quarterly Journal of Speech, 71*(3), 335.

Jasinski, J. (2001). *Sourcebook on rhetoric: Key concepts in contemporary rhetorical studies.* Thousand Oaks: Sage.

Jensen, J. V. (1965). The rhetorical strategy of Thomas H. Huxley and Robert G. Ingersoll: Agnostics and roadblock removers. *Speech Monographs, 32*(1), 59.

Jensen, R. J., & Hammerback, J. C. (1986). From Muslim to Mormon: Eldridge Cleaver's rhetorical crusade. *Communication Quarterly, 34*(1), 24–40.

Johannesen, R. L. (1985). The Jeremiad and Jenkin Lloyd Jones. *Communication Monographs, 52*(2), 156.

Johnson, J. T. (Ed.). (1985). *The Bible in American law, politics, and political rhetoric.* Philadelphia: Fortress Press.

Johnson, N. (2002). *Gender and rhetorical space in American life, 1866–1910.* Carbondale: Southern Illinois University.

Johnson, P. E. (1998). Rhetorical problem of intelligent design. *Rhetoric & Public Affairs, 1,* 587–591.

Johnstone, C. L. (1974). Thoreau and civil disobedience: A rhetorical paradox. *Quarterly Journal of Speech, 60*(3), 313.

Johnstone, C. L. (1978). Electing ourselves in 1976: Jimmy Carter and the American faith. *Western Journal of Speech Communication, 42,* 241–249.

Jones, J., & Rowland, R. (2005). A covenant-affirming jeremiad: The post-presidential ideological appeals of Ronald Wilson Reagan. *Communication Studies, 56*(2), 157–174.

Jones, S. G. (1993). A value analysis of Brigham Young's ascension to latter-day Saint leadership. *Journal of Communication & Religion, 16*(1), 23–39.

Jost, W., & Olmsted, W. (2000). *Rhetorical invention and religious inquiry: New perspectives.* New Haven, CT: Yale University Press.

Kari, C. J. (2004). *Public witness: The pastoral letters of the American Catholic Bishops.* Collegeville, PA: Liturgical Press.

Kaveny, M. C. (2006). Prophecy and casuistry: Abortion, torture and moral discourse. *Villanova Law Review, 51,* 499–579.

Kennicott, P. C. (1970). Black persuaders in the Antislavery Movement. *Speech Monographs, 37*(1), 15.

Keyes, C. F. (1982). Charisma: From social life to sacred biography. *Journal of the American Academy of Religion Thematic Studies, 48,* 1–22.

Kiewe, A., & Houck, D. W. (1991). *A shining city on a hill: Ronald Regan's economic rhetoric, 1951–1981.* Westport, CT: Praeger.

Kincaid, J. (1971). The American vocation and its contemporary discontents. *Publius, 1,* 115–140.

King, P. E., Sawyer, C. R., & Benke, R. R. (1998). A case study of the Weberian leadership of

Joseph Smith. *Journal of Communication & Religion, 21*(1), 1–21.

Kirkwood, W. G. (1994). Studying communication about spirituality and the spiritual consequences of communication. *Journal of Communication & Religion, 17*(1), 13–26.

Klemm, D. E. (1987). The rhetoric of theological argument. In J. S. Nelson, A. Megill, & D. M. McCloskey (Eds.), *The rhetoric of the human sciences* (pp. 276–297). Madison: University of Wisconsin Press.

Kurtz, J. B. (2001). Condemning Webster: Judgment and audience in Emerson's "Fugitive Slave Law." *Quarterly Journal of Speech, 87*(3), 278.

Kurtz, J. B. (2004). "They were days delirious with belief": Public moral rhetoric, biography, and our democratic fortunes. *Review of Communication, 4,* 265–277.

Lake, R. A. (1984). Order and disorder in anti-abortion rhetoric: A logological view. *Quarterly Journal of Speech, 70*(4), 425.

Lantz, W. C. (1955). Rhetoric and theology—Incompatible? *Western Speech, 19*(2), 77–82.

Larson, B. A. (1971). Samuel Davies and the rhetoric of the new light. *Speech Monographs, 38*(3), 207.

Larson, B. A. (1978). *Prologue to revolution: The war sermons of the Reverend Samuel Davies.* Falls Church, VA: Speech Communication Association.

Lattin, B. D., & Underhill, S. (2006). The soul of politics: The Reverend Jim Wallis's attempt to transcend the religious/secular left and the religious right. *Journal of Communication & Religion, 29,* 205–223.

Lawton, C. W. (1968). Thoreau and the rhetoric of dissent. *Today's Speech, 16,* 23–25.

Layman, G. C. (1997). Religion and political behavior in the United States. *Public Opinion Quarterly, 61*(2), 288–316.

Lazenby, W. (1971). Exhortation as exorcism: Cotton Mather's sermons to murderers. *Quarterly Journal of Speech, 57*(1), 50.

Leathers, D. (1969). The thrust of the radical right. In D. Holland (Ed.), *Preaching in American history* (pp. 310–332). Nashville, TN: Abingdon Press.

Lee, R. (1995). Electoral politics and visions of community: Jimmy Carter, virtue, and the small town myth. *Western Journal of Communication, 59*(1), 39–60.

Lee, R. (2002). The force of religion in the public square. *Journal of Communication & Religion, 25*(1), 6–20.

Leeman, M. A. (2006a). A house divided against itself cannot stand: Problematizing public and private in organized religion. *Communication Studies, 57,* 5–23.

Leeman, M. A. (2006b). Speaking as Jeremiah: Henry McNeal Turner's I claim the rights of a man. *Howard Journal of Communications, 17*(3), 223–243.

Lessl, T. M. (1993). Toward a definition of religious communication: Scientific and religious uses of evolution. *Journal of Communication & Religion, 16*(2), 127–138.

Lessl, T. M. (2003). Scientific rhetoric as religious advocacy: Origins in the public schools. *Journal of Communication & Religion, 26,* 1–27.

Lewis, C. K. (2007). Romancing the difference: Kenneth Burke, Bob Jones University, and the rhetoric of religious fundamentalism. Waco, TX: Baylor University Press.

Licht, R., Mittleman, A., & Sarna, J. D. (2002). *Jews and the American public square: Debating religion and republic.* Lanham, MD: Rowman & Littlefield.

Lindsay, S. A. (1997). Prayer as proto-rhetoric. *Journal of Communication & Religion, 20*(2), 31–40.

Longaker, M. G. (2006). Idealism and early-American rhetoric. *Rhetoric Society Quarterly, 36*(3), 281–308.

Longenbach, J. (1989). Matthew Arnold and the modern apocalypse. *Quarterly Journal of Speech, 104,* 844–855.

Lynch, C. (1997). Our lady of television: Bishop Sheen's television rhetoric of womanhood. *Journal of Communication & Religion, 20*(2), 81–91.

Lynch, J. (2005). Institution and imprimatur: Institutional rhetoric and the failure of the Catholic Church's pastoral letter on homosexuality. *Rhetoric & Public Affairs, 8,* 383–393.

MacVaugh, G. S. (1932). Structural analysis of the sermons of Dr. Harry Emerson Fosdick. *Quarterly Journal of Speech, 18*(4), 531.

Maclear, J. F. (1971). The republic and the millennium. In E. A. Smith (Ed.), *The religion of the republic* (pp. 183–216). Philadelphia: Fortress Press.

Mahaffey, J. D. (2007). *Preaching politics: The religious rhetoric of George Whitefield and the founding of a new nation.* Waco, TX: Baylor University Press.

Marsden, G. (1982). Everyone one's own interpreter? The Bible, science, and authority in mid-nineteenth-century America. In N. O. Hatch & M. Noll (Eds.), *The Bible in America: Essays in cultural history* (pp. 79–100). New York: Oxford University Press.

Marvin, C. (2002). A new scholarly dispensation for civil religion. *Journal of Communication & Religion, 25*(1), 21–33.

Mattis, N. (1929). Robert South. *Quarterly Journal of Speech, 15*(4), 537.

Mavrodes, G. (1968). The problem of evil as a rhetoric problem. *Philosophy and Rhetoric, 1,* 91–102.

McBeth, H. L. (1987). *The Baptist heritage: Four centuries of Baptist witness.* Nashville, TN: Broadman Press.

McCall, R. C. (1953). Harry Emerson Fosdick: Paragon and paradox. *Quarterly Journal of Speech, 39*(3), 283.

McClish, G. (2005). William G. Allen's "Orators and Oratory": Inventional amalgamation, pathos, and the characterization of violence in African-American abolitionist rhetoric. *Rhetoric Society Quarterly, 35*(1), 47–72.

McGee, B. R. (1998). Witnessing and ethos: The evangelical conversion of David Luke. *Western Journal of Communication, 62*(3), 217–243.

McGee, M. C. (1970). Thematic reduplication in Christian rhetoric. *Quarterly Journal of Speech, 56*(2), 196–204.

McGinn, B., Collins, J. J., & Stein, S. J. (2003). *Continuum history of apocalypticism.* New York: Continuum International.

McGlon, C. A., Fosdick, H. E., Dawson, J. M., Sockman, R., Flynn, V. J., Rauch, J., et al. (1954). How I prepare my sermons: A symposium. *Quarterly Journal of Speech, 40*(1), 49.

McLennan, D. B. (1996). Rhetoric and the legitimation process: The rebirth of Charles Colson. *Journal of Communication & Religion, 19*(1), 5–12.

McLoughlin, W. G. (1973). The role of religion in the Revolution: Liberty of conscience and cultural cohesion in the new nation. In S. G. Kurtz & J. H. Hutson (Eds.), *Essays on the American Revolution.* (pp. 197–255). Chapel Hill: University of North Carolina Press for the Institute of Early American History and Culture.

McLoughlin, W. G. (1978). *Revivals, awakenings and reform: An essay on religion and social change in America, 1607–1977.* Chicago: University of Chicago Press.

McLoughlin, W. G. (1983). Faith. *American Quarterly, 35,* 101–115.

Medhurst, M. J. (1977). American cosmology and the rhetoric of inaugural prayer. *Central States Speech Journal, 28,* 272–283.

Medhurst, M. J. (2004). Filled with the spirit: Rhetorical invention and the Pentecostal tradition. *Rhetoric & Public Affairs, 7*(4), 555–572.

Merriam, A. H. (1974). Rhetoric and the Islamic tradition. *Today's Speech, 22*(1), 43–49.

Miller, A. H., & Wattenberg, M. P. (1984). Politics from the pulpit: Religiosity and the 1980s elections. *Public Opinion Quarterly, 48*(1B), 301–317.

Miller, H. (1969). The voice of God: Natural or supernatural. In D. Holland (Ed.), *Preaching in American history* (pp. 206–222). Nashville, TN: Abingdon Press.

Miller, K. D. (1989). Voice merging and self-making: The epistemology of "I have a dream." *Rhetoric Society Quarterly, 19*(1), 23–31.

Mills, J. (1949). The speaking of William Jennings Bryan in Florida, 1915–1925. *Southern Speech Journal, 14,* 137–169.

Minnick, W. C. (1968). The New England execution sermon, 1639–1800. *Speech Monographs, 35*(1), 77.

Minnick, W. C. (1971). A case study in persuasive effect: Lyman Beecher on duelling. *Speech Monographs, 38*(4), 262.

Mintz, S., & Stauffer, J. (Eds.). (2007). *The problem of evil: Slavery, freedom, and the ambiguities of American Reform.* Amherst: University of Massachusetts Press.

Mitchell, N. E., & Phipps, K. S. (1985). The Jeremiad in contemporary fundamentalism: Jerry Falwell's listen America. *Religious Communication Today, 8,* 54–62.

Mixon, H., & Hopkins, M. F. (1988). Apocalypticism in secular public discourse: A proposed theory. *Central States Speech Journal, 39,* 244–257.

Montesano, M. (1995). Karios and kerygma: The rhetoric of Christian proclamation. *Rhetoric Society Quarterly, 25,* 164–179.

Moorhead, J. H. (1984). Between progress and apocalypse: A reassessment of millennialism in

American religious thought, 1800–1880. *Journal of American History, 71,* 524–542.

Moorhead, J. H. (1987). Searching for the millennium in American. *Princeton Seminary Bulletin, 8,* 17–33.

Mountford, R. (2005). *The gendered pulpit: Preaching in American Protestant spaces.* Carbondale: Southern Illinois University Press.

Nau, E. M. S. (1954). George H. Atkinson, Oregon missionary and speaker. *Western Speech, 18,* 223–230.

Nixon, H. (1989). "A city upon a hill": John Cotton's apocalyptic rhetoric and the fifth monarchy movement in puritan New England. *Journal of Communication & Religion, 12*(1), 1–6.

Noble, D. W. (1968). *The eternal Adam and the New World garden: The central myth in the American novel since 1830.* New York: George Braziller.

Noll, M. A. (1988). *One nation under God: Christian faith and political action in America.* New York: HarperCollins.

Noll, M. A., & Harlow, L. E. (2007). *Religion and American politics: From the colonial period to the present* (2nd ed.). Oxford, UK: Oxford University Press.

O'Leary, S. D. (1994). *Arguing the apocalypse: A theory of millennial rhetoric.* New York: Oxford University Press.

O'Leary, S. D., & McFarland, M. (1989). The political use of mythic discourse: Prophetic interpretation in Pat Robertson's presidential campaign. *Quarterly Journal of Speech, 75,* 433–452.

O'Neill, J. (1988). Religion and postmodernism: The Durkheimian bond in Bell and Jameson. *Theory, Culture & Society, 5*(2/3), 493–508.

Ofulue, N. I. (2002). President Clinton and the White House prayer breakfast. *Journal of Communication & Religion, 25,* 49–63.

Ohlhauser, J. B. (1996). Human rhetoric: Accounting for spiritual intervention. *Howard Journal of Communications, 7*(4), 339–349.

Oliver, E. S. (1960). Emerson's almost perfect orator: Edward Taylor. *Today's Speech, 8*(2), 20–22.

Oliver, R. T. (1965). *History of public speaking in America.* Needham Heights, MA: Allyn & Bacon.

O'Rourke, B. M. (2001). Religion. In T. O. Sloane (Ed.), *Encyclopedia of rhetoric* (pp. 662–672). Oxford, UK: Oxford University Press.

Parker, A. M. (1997). *Purifying America: Women, cultural reform, and pro-censorship activism, 1873–1933 (Women in American History).* Urbana: University of Illinois Press.

Patton, J. H. (1977). A government as good as its people: Jimmy Carter and the restoration of transcendence to politics. *Quarterly Journal of Speech, 63,* 249–257.

Pauley, J. L. (1998). Reshaping public persona and the prophetic ethos: Louis Farrakhan at the Million Man March. *Western Journal of Communication, 62*(4), 512–536.

Pearce, K. C. (2000). Rhetorical polysemy in Mary Baker Eddy's "Christian Science in Tremont Temple." *Journal of Communication & Religion, 23*(2), 73–94.

Pearce, K. C., & Fedely, D. (1993). George Bush's "Just War" rhetoric: Paradigm of universal morality. *Journal of Communication & Religion, 16*(2), 139–152.

Pearce, W. B., Littlejohn, S. W., & Alexander, A. (1987). The new Christian Right and the humanist response: Reciprocated diatribe. *Communication Quarterly, 35*(2), 171–192.

Peltzer, O. (1887). *The moralist and the theatre: A series of articles which originally appeared in "Music and drama," embracing a brief history of the stage, its relation to the Church, its present condition and needed reform.* Chicago: D. Fraser.

Pernot, L. (2006). The rhetoric of religion. *Rhetorica, 24,* 235–254.

Pierard, R. V. (1985). Religion and the 1984 election campaign. *Review of Religious Research, 27,* 98–114.

Pinson, W. (1969). The pulpit and race relations, 1954–1966. In D. Holland (Ed.), *Preaching in American history* (pp. 375–390). Nashville, TN: Abingdon Press.

Pipes, W. H. (1945). Old-time Negro preaching: An interpretative study. *Quarterly Journal of Speech, 31*(1), 15.

Pitts, W. (1989). West African poetics in the Black teaching style. *American Speech, 64*(2), 137.

Porter, L. W. (1990). Religion and politics: Protestant beliefs in the presidential campaign of 1980. *Journal of Communication & Religion, 13*(2), 24–39.

Portnoy, A. (2005). *Their right to speak: Women's activism in the Indian and slave debates.* Cambridge, MA: Harvard University Press.

Potter, D., & Gordon, T. L. (Eds.). (1970). *The colonial idiom.* Carbondale: Southern Illinois University Press.

Powell, L., & Neiva, E. (2006). The Pharisee effect: When religious appeals in politics go too far. *Journal of Communication & Religion, 29*(1), 70–102.

Prioleau, R. C. (2003). Frederick Douglass: Abolitionist and humanist. *Howard Journal of Communications, 14*(3), 177.

Pullum, S. J. (1990). The mass appeal of Jimmy Swaggart: Pentecostal media star. *Journal of Communication & Religion, 13*(1), 39–54.

Pullum, S. J. (2001). Southern Baptist Rhetoric. *Review of Communication, 1*(1), 144–148.

Quimby, R. W. (1954). The Western campaigns of Dwight L Moody. *Western Speech, 18*(2), 83–90.

Quimby, R. W. (1957). How D. L. Moody held attention. *Quarterly Journal of Speech, 43*(3), 278.

Quimby, R. W. (1964). Recurrent themes and purposes in the sermons of the Union Army chaplains. *Speech Monographs, 31*(4), 425.

Quimby, R. W., & Billigmeier, R. H. (1959). The varying role of revivalist preaching in American protestant evangelism. *Speech Monographs, 26*(3), 217.

Ramsey, E. R. (1997). Communication and eschatology: The work of waiting, an ethics of relief, and areligious religiosity. *Communication Theory, 7,* 343–361.

Ray, A. G. (1998). "In my own hand writing": Benjamin Banneker addresses the slaveholder of Monticello. *Rhetoric & Public Affairs, 1*(3), 387–405.

Ray, A. G. (2006). What hath she wrought?: Woman's rights and the nineteenth-century lyceum. *Rhetoric & Public Affairs, 9*(2), 183–213.

Ray, R. K. (1974). The role of the orator in the philosophy of Ralph Waldo Emerson. *Speech Monographs, 41*(3), 215–225.

Reid, R. F. (1983). Apocalypticism and typology: Rhetorical dimensions of a symbolic reality. *Quarterly Journal of Speech, 69,* 229–248.

Reid, R. S. (1998). Faithful preaching: Preaching epistemes, faith stages, and rhetorical practice. *Journal of Communication & Religion, 21*(2), 164–199.

Reid, R. S. (1999). Corrections to faithful preaching: Preaching epistemes, faith stages, and rhetorical practice. *Journal of Communication & Religion, 22*(1), 121–123.

Reid, R. S. (2004). Being Baptist. *Rhetoric & Public Affairs, 7*(4), 587–601.

Reid, R. S., Bullock, J., & Fleer, D. (1995). Preaching as the creation of an experience: The not-so-rational revolution of the new homiletic. *Journal of Communication & Religion, 18*(1), 1–9.

Ricoeur, P. (1980). *Essays on biblical interpretation.* Philadelphia: Fortress Press.

Ricoeur, P. (1995). *Figuring the sacred: Religion, narrative, and imagination* (D. Pellauer, Trans.). Minneapolis: Augsburg Fortress.

Romney, M. (2007). *Speech at Texas A&M University.* College Station: Texas A&M University.

Rothenbuhler, E. W. (1989). Values and symbols in orientations to the Olympics. *Critical Studies in Mass Communication, 6*(2), 138–158.

Rountree, J. C., III. (1994). Charles Haddon Spurgeon's Calvinist rhetoric of election: Consulting an elect. *Journal of Communication & Religion, 17*(2), 33–48.

Rowland, R. C. (1990). On mythic criticism. *Communication Studies, 41,* 101–116.

Rowland, R. C., & Jones, J. M. (2006). Reagan at the Brandenburg Gate: Moral clarity tempered by pragmatism. *Rhetoric & Public Affairs, 9*(1), 21–50.

Ryan, H. R. (1990). *Henry Ward Beecher: Peripatetic preacher.* Westport, CT: Greenwood Press.

Sandeen, E. R. (Ed.). (1982). *The Bible and social reform.* Philadelphia: Fortress Press.

Sayer, J. E. (1987). Father Charles Coughlin: Ideologue and demagogue of the depression. *Journal of the Northwest Communication Association, 15*(1), 17–30.

Schuetz, J. (1986). Storytelling and preaching: A case study of Aimee Semple McPherson. *Religious Communication Today, 9,* 28–36.

Schultze, Q. J. (1988). Researching televangelism. *Critical Studies in Mass Communication, 5,* 271–275.

Scott, D. M. (1979). Abolition as a sacred vocation. In L. Perry & M. Fellman (Eds.), *Antislavery reconsidered: New perspectives on the abolitionists* (pp. 51–74). Baton Rouge: Louisiana State University Press.

Sears, J. T., & Carper, J. C. (1998). *Curriculum, religion, and public education: Conversations for an enlarging public square.* New York: Teachers College Press.

Selby, G. S. (2002). Mocking the sacred: Frederick Douglass's "Slaveholder's Sermon" and the antebellum debate over religion and slavery. *Quarterly Journal of Speech, 88*(3), 326–342.

Selby, G. S. (2008). *Martin Luther King and the rhetoric of freedom: The exodus narrative in America's struggle for civil rights.* Waco, TX: Baylor University Press.

Sequeira, D.-L. (1994). Gifts of tongues and healing: The performance of charismatic renewal. *Text & Performance Quarterly, 14*(2), 126.

Servin-Gonzalez, M., & Torres-Reyna, O. (1999). Religion and politics. *Public Opinion Quarterly, 63*(4), 592–621.

Sevitch, B. (1996). When black gods preached on earth: The heavenly appeals of Prophet Cherry, Daddy Grace, and Father Divine. *Journal of Communication & Religion, 19*(1), 26–36.

Sewell, E. H., Jr. (1975). Isaac Backus' plea for religious freedom, 1770–1776. *Today's Speech, 23*(2), 39–47.

Shogan, C. J. (2006). *The moral rhetoric of American Presidents.* College Station: Texas A&M University Press.

Sillars, M. O. (1981). Investigating religious argument as a field. In G. Ziegelmueller & J. Rhodes (Eds.), *Dimensions of argument: Proceedings of the second summer conference on argument* (pp. 143–151). Annandale, VA: Speech Communication Association.

Sillars, M. O. (1995). From romantic idealism to enlightenment rationalism: Lucretia Coffin Mott responds to Richard Henry Dana, Sr. *Rhetoric Society Quarterly, 25*, 47–55.

Simonson, P. (2003). A rhetoric for polytheistic democracy: Walt Whitman's "Poem of Many in One." *Philosophy & Rhetoric, 36*(4), 353–375.

Slanger, K. L. (1995). Slave resistance and rhetorical self-definition: Spirituals as a strategy. *Western Journal of Communication, 59*(3), 177–192.

Smith, C. R. (1993). The problem with writing on rhetorical charisma, power, and spirituality. *Journal of Communication & Religion, 16*(2), 83–97.

Smith, R. R., & Windes, R. R. (1997). The progay and antigay issue culture: Interpretation, influence and dissent. *Quarterly Journal of Speech, 83*, 28–48.

Snyder, L. L. (1999). Apologetics before and after postmodernism. *Journal of Communication & Religion, 22*(2), 237–271.

Spencer, G. H. (1995). The rhetoric of Malcolm Muggeridge's gradual Christian conversion. *Journal of Communication & Religion, 18*(2), 55–64.

Spielvogel, C. (2005). "You Know Where I Stand": Moral framing of the war on terrorism and the Iraq War in the 2004 presidential campaign. *Rhetoric & Public Affairs, 8*(4), 549–569.

Stanton, E. C. (1999). *The Woman's Bible.* Amherst, New York: Prometheus Books.

Stewart, C. (1969). Civil war preaching. In D. Holland (Ed.), *Preaching in American history* (pp. 184–205). Nashville, TN: Abingdon Press.

Stout, D. A., & Buddenbaum, J. M. (Eds.). (1996). *Religion and mass media: Audiences and adaptations.* Thousand Oaks, CA: Sage.

Stout, H. S. (1977). Religion, communication, and the ideological origins of the American revolution. *William and Mary Quarterly, 34*, 519–541.

Sullivan, D. L. (1992). Kairos and the rhetoric of belief. *Quarterly Journal of Speech, 78*(3), 317–333.

Swatos, W. H., & Wellman, J. K. (1999). *The power of religious publics: Staking claims in American society.* Westport, CT: Praeger.

Swearingen, C. J. (2002). Rhetoric and religion: Recent revivals and revisions. *Rhetoric Society Quarterly, 32*, 111–137.

Tauber, A. (1969). Jewish rhetoric. *Today's Speech, 17*(4), 57–67.

Taylor, H. V., & Schwartz, H. (1969). Dwight L. Moody: American evangelist, 1837–1899. *Today's Speech, 17*(4), 73–83.

Tell, D. W. (2003). The man and the message: Timothy Dwight and homiletic authorization. *Journal of Communication & Religion, 26*(1), 83–108.

Terrill, R. E. (2001). Protest, prophecy, and prudence in the rhetoric of Malcolm X. *Rhetoric & Public Affairs, 4*(1), 25–53.

Thiemann, R. F. (1996). *Religion in public life: A dilemma for democracy*. Washington, DC: Georgetown University Press.

Timmerman, D. M. (2005). Christian pacifism and the prophetic voice: Dietrich Bonhoeffer's peace address. *Journal of Communication & Religion, 28*(2), 153–171.

Tompkins, P. K. (1976). On "paradoxes" in the rhetoric of the New England transcendentalists. *Quarterly Journal of Speech, 62*(1), 40.

Towne, R. L. (1962). Robert Green Ingersoll: A case study of free speech. *Today's Speech, 10*(4), 10–29.

Tracy, D. (1987). *Plurality and ambiguity*. San Francisco: Harper & Row.

Tracy, D. (1990). *Dialogue with the other: The inter-religious dialogue*. Louvain, Belgium: Peeters Press.

Tukey, D. D. (1990). Toward a research agenda for a spiritual rhetoric. *Journal of Communication & Religion, 13*(1), 66–76.

Tukey, D. D. (1995). Researching "ultimate" communication: A response to Kirkwood and a research agenda. *Journal of Communication & Religion, 18*(2), 65–72.

Turner, B. S. (2006). Religion. *Theory, Culture & Society, 23*, 437–444.

Turner, B. S. (2007). Religious authority and the new media. *Theory, Culture & Society, 24*, 117–134.

Vail, M. (2006). The "integrative" rhetoric of Martin Luther King Jr.'s "I Have a Dream" Speech. *Rhetoric & Public Affairs, 9*(1), 51–78.

Van Beeck, F. J. (1979). *Christ proclaimed: Christology as rhetoric*. New York: Paulist Press.

Vanderford, M. L. (1989). Vilification and social movements: A case study of pro-life and pro-choice rhetoric. *Quarterly Journal of Speech, 75*(2), 166.

Valeri, M., & Wilson, J. F. (1985). Scripture and society: From reform in the old world to revival in the new. In J. T. Johnson (Ed.), *The Bible in American law, politics, and political rhetoric* (pp. 13–38). Philadelphia: Fortress Press.

Verkruyse, P. A. (2005). *Prophet, pastor, and patriarch: The rhetorical leadership of Alexander Campbell*. Tuscaloosa: University of Alabama Press.

Wagenknecht, E. (1972). *Ambassadors for Christ: Seven American preachers*. New York: Oxford University Press.

Wander, P. (1985). The place of morality in the modern world. In J. R. Cox, M. O. Sillars, & G. B. Walker (Eds.), *Argument and social practice: Proceedings of the fourth SCA/AFA Conference on Argumentation* (pp. 323–339). Annandale, VA: Speech Communication Association.

Webb, S. H. (1991). *Re-figuring theology: The rhetoric of Karl Barth*. Albany: State University of New York Press.

Webb, S. H. (1993). *Blessed excess: Religion and the hyperbolic imagination*. Albany: State University of New York Press.

White, E. E. (1948). The preaching of George Whitefield during the Great Awakening in America. *Speech Monographs, 15*(1), 33.

White, E. E. (1950a). George Whitefield's preaching in Massachusetts and Georgia: A case study in persuasion. *Southern Speech Journal, 15*, 249–262.

White, E. E. (1950b). Whitefield's use of proofs during the Great Awakening in America. *Western Speech, 14*(1), 3–6.

White, E. E. (1953). George Whitefield and the paper war in New England. *Quarterly Journal of Speech, 39*(1), 61.

White, E. E. (1972). *Puritan rhetoric: The issue of emotion in religion*. Carbondale: Southern Illinois University Press.

White, E. E., & Henderlider, C. R. (1954). What Norman Vincent Peale told us about his speaking. *Quarterly Journal of Speech, 40*(4), 407.

White, E. E. (1969). Puritan preaching and the authority of God. In D. Holland (Ed.), *Preaching in American history* (pp. 36–73). Nashville, TN: Abingdon Press.

White, R. A. (2007). The media, culture, and religion perspective. *Communication Research Trends, 26*, 3–24.

Wiethoff, W. (1977). Rhetorical enterprise in the ministry of "Reverend Ike." *Communication Monographs, 44*(1), 52.

Wilder, A. (1971). The rhetoric of ancient and modern apocalyptic. *Interpretation, 25*, 436–453.

Wilder, A. (1976). Theopoetic: Theology and the religious imagination. Philadelphia: Fortress Press.

Willey, S., & Hume, J. (2004). God's man for the gilded age: D. L. Moody and the rise of modern mass evangelicalism [Book review]. *Journalism History, 29*(4), 202.

Willhite, K. (1989). "God and Country" in Ronald Reagan's addresses to the national religious broadcasters: A "Faith" that backslides or perseveres. *Journal of Communication & Religion, 12*(2), 38–42.

Williams, H. M. (1948). David Swing: The voice of music hall. *Speech Monographs, 15*(1), 44.

Williams, R. H. (1999). Visions of the good society and the religious roots of American political culture. *Sociology of Religion, 60*(1), 1–34.

Williams, W. (2000). Religion, science and rhetoric in revolutionary America: The case of Dr. Benjamin Rush. *Rhetoric Society Quarterly, 30*(3), 55–72.

Wills, G. (1990). *Under God: Religion and American politics.* New York: Simon & Schuster.

Wilson, J. F. (1983). Perspectives on the historiography of religious awakenings. *Sociological Analysis, 44*(2), 117–120.

Wilson, K. H. (2005). Interpreting the discursive field of the Montgomery bus boycott: Martin Luther King Jr.'s Holt Street Address. *Rhetoric & Public Affairs, 8*(2), 299–326.

Wilson, S. A., & Porter, J. (2003). Taking the measure of Jonathan Edwards for contemporary religious ethics. *Journal of Religious Ethics, 31*(2), 183–199.

Winiarski, D. L. (2005). Jonathan Edwards, enthusiast? Radical revivalism and the Great Awakening in the Connecticut Valley. *Church History, 74*(4), 683–739.

Winkler, A. (Producer). (2007, July 5). *All things considered* [Radio broadcast]. Washington, DC: National Public Radio.

Winthrop, J. (1630). *A model of Christian charity.* Retrieved June 10, 2008, from www.libertynet .org/edcivic/winthrop.html

Wojcik, D. (1997). *The end of the world as we know it: Faith, fatalism, and apocalypse in America.* New York: New York University Press.

Wolterstorff, N., & Audi, R. (1996). *Religion in the public square: The place of religious convictions in political debate.* New York: Rowman & Littlefield.

Wood, J. E., Jr. (1999). Public religion vis-à-vis the prophetic role of religion. *Journal of Church & State, 41*, 51–76.

Wright, D. S. (2006). *"The first of causes to our sex": The female moral reform movement in the Antebellum Northeast, 1834–1848.* New York: Routledge.

Yarbrough, S. R., & Adams, J. C. (1993). *Delightful conviction: Jonathan Edwards and the rhetoric of conversion.* Westport, CT: Greenwood Press.

Yoder, J. (1969). The protest of the American clergy in opposition to the war in Vietnam. *Today's Speech, 17*(3), 51–59.

Zamora, L. P. (Ed.). (1982). *The apocalyptic vision in America: Interdisciplinary essays on myth and culture.* Bowling Green, OH: Bowling Green University Popular Press.

Zompetti, J. (2006). Caesar Chavez's rhetorical use of religious symbols. *Journal of Communication & Religion, 29*(2), 262–284.

31

Between Touchstones and Touch Screens

What Counts as Contemporary Political Rhetoric?

VANESSA B. BEASLEY

Political rhetoric is not what it used to be. As someone who is not easily given to nostalgia, I nevertheless begin with this claim because it is generally accepted to be true in at least two senses. That is, the *quality* of political rhetoric has declined in the United States over the past 30 to 40 years, even as there has been an increase in its overall *quantity* and *distribution,* especially via new technologies. The conventional wisdom seems to be that we are presently one generation beyond a time when U.S. politics was the breeding ground for stirring and memorable public discourse, "great speeches" that stood beyond the clattering din of most public and private communication by virtue of their eloquence and assumed consequence. According to this narrative, once, America was thrilled by King's "I Have a Dream"; today there is the Howard Dean scream. Or, to make a more direct comparison, while convention delegates in 1896 heard warnings of a "cross of gold" by a speaker (William Jennings Bryan) who aimed to serve "a cause as holy as the cause of liberty," in 2004, delegates heard charges and countercharges about things that may or may not have happened—on a boat in another country—from a group calling itself the Swift Boat Veterans for Truth. It hardly seems the same, does it?

Some may wonder, then, what has happened to the study of contemporary political rhetoric? Rather than going into a parallel decline, it has taken, I argue in this chapter, some fascinating turns. Here, I discuss two emergent lines of inquiry; each suggesting increasingly important questions about how audiences—voters and nonvoters alike—experience contemporary political discourse and thus, arguably, politics itself in the United States. It is not my intent to feature either of these lines simply as exciting new research agendas, although they are surely that even if some of the research within them goes back 20 years. Instead, I mean to emphasize the themes and ideas that these approaches reveal about the enduring characteristics of contemporary U.S. politics and its evolution since the last third of the 20th century.

Because political rhetoric does not seem to be what it once was, scholars have begun to reconsider fundamental questions about how political messages function and what they are purposed to accomplish. Today, for example, scholars are faced with a recurrent question about the scope of political rhetoric—wildly popular "fake" news shows, the latest polemic by Ann Coulter or Al Franken, instantaneous media coverage of the Supreme Court nomination process, horrific photographic evidence of atrocities committed by U.S. soldiers in Iraq, the invective on talk radio airwaves, feverish Internet blogging on behalf of both the right and the left, and so on. In addition to questions concerning scope, scholars of political rhetoric have been forced to move beyond deliberative models of communication to ask how this discourse plays performative, constitutive, and material roles within U.S. political culture. Many of these concerns are the focus of the most exciting work currently being done within political communication scholarship; nevertheless, even as critics and theorists are asking new sets of questions, there are at least two important paradigms that one must credit with setting the stage for this research: public address scholarship, with its typical emphasis on reading U.S. politics as persuasive efforts intended to shape judgment, and social scientific research on mediated political communication, with its emphasis on voting and/or attitude change as the "bottom line" with which to measure the impact of rhetorical messages. Scholarship from both of these paradigms has

been crucial in establishing the salience and legitimacy of political rhetoric as a subdiscipline within the U.S. academy. To underscore this influence, I have alluded to each of these traditions synecdochically in this chapter's title with "touchstones" standing for public address and "touch screens" for social scientific studies of media effects and voting behavior.

While both of these traditions have contributed much to the academic study of political rhetoric, their implicit biases and inherent terministic screens (Burke, 1966) mean that some questions have not been asked. That is as it should be, as any Kuhnian would tell us, and my point here is not to criticize either tradition. Instead, I hope to provide a broad overview of how many disciplinary foci evolved when the "great speeches" model of public discourse shifted. Having established this context, I then list two emergent areas that I believe are making important contributions to both the theory and criticism of contemporary political communication. In each case, I highlight exemplary scholarship from within each one to demonstrate specific contributions as well as general emphases. This chapter concludes with a discussion of some questions that remain for scholars of contemporary political discourse.

Also, at this point I should note that I will use the terms *political rhetoric*, *political communication*, and, by extension, *politics* in largely traditional ways. My working definition of political communication research includes any project that studies messages designed and/or issued on behalf of electoral candidates, officeholders, or their appointees (e.g., presidential cabinet members) to reach their assumed constituents for ostensible purposes of campaigning or governing as well as any responses to those messages. This definition is meant to limit the purview of this chapter, and limits have implications. First, I am aware of arguments that the terms *rhetoric* and *communication* should not be used to refer to the same phenomenon. Yet for the purposes of this chapter, I use them more or less synonymously, albeit within their disciplinary contexts—that is, humanists tend to be more comfortable talking about rhetoric, while social scientists seem to prefer the term *communication*—to refer to messages with suasory potential. Secondly, I am also aware of the limitations of traditional definitions of both concepts as well as the notion of "politics" as a statist enterprise. My approach here may seem to exclude more transcendent concerns related to the "politics of culture," especially those related to persistent power inequities (e.g., racism, gender bias, heteronormativity, etc.). Nevertheless, given that a central goal of this chapter is to underscore how new perspectives are needed to understand emerging developments in contemporary U.S. electoral politics, I will focus most intensively on phenomena with obvious implications for the role of public discourse within campaigns, governance, legislation, and public policy.

DISCIPLINARY CONTEXTS: ABOUT THOSE TOUCHSTONES AND TOUCH SCREENS

Much of what we know about political discourse in the United States has come from one of two traditions: "public address scholarship" that is grounded in a humanist tradition performed by scholars within speech communication or communication studies departments, and a set of concerns regarding the effects of contemporary political discourse on the social scientific side, with researchers in speech communication, mass communication, and political science. In addition to their differing methodologies and disciplinary homes, a central point of disagreement between these two traditions revolves around what political communication is and, thus, how it should be analyzed and judged. A necessarily oversimplified overview of where these two traditions stand on such matters will enable us to see some stark contrasts.

The public address tradition is based, in part, on the assumption that political communication is inherently worthy of study because it is a form of socially influential rhetoric in the traditional sense of the term—that is, "those discourses, spoken or written, which aim to influence" (Black, 1978, p. 15). The "touchstones" or "great speeches" of U.S. history and contemporary politics fit into this category in obvious ways, and the study of these texts from the past is, in fact, one of the main pillars of public address scholarship. (In fact, some observers might even say that this research has a bias for historical texts and against contemporary discourse.) What exactly makes a text great has been a matter of contention (Black, 1978) and, thus, the significance of a scholar's chosen object must be established early on within an analysis (Campbell, 1995). For my purposes here, however, the more important point is that the object of study—the object that counts as political discourse within this paradigm—is typically a verbal text that (1) has been designed with the intent to persuade, (2) features fairly traditional characteristics of textuality (e.g., allowing for a transcript with a clearly defined beginning and end), and (3) occurs within a rhetorical situation in which at least one set of audience, exigence, and constraints can be identified (Bitzer, 1968; Medhurst, 1996). Not surprisingly, the public address paradigm has also tended to be speaker/source oriented, even as it has generally assumed some level of interaction between speaker and audience (Leff, 2003).

The texts typically studied within this paradigm do not have to be political within a specific institutional or electoral context; they do not have to be campaign speeches, for example. Nevertheless, the great majority of public address scholarship is focused on rhetoric that has been somehow consequential within U.S. social relations. And yet public address scholars are not primarily concerned with documenting the exact nature of this consequence per se. Even if many of them would agree with Aristotle that the end of rhetoric is decision making, these scholars do not define their field of study by its perceived influence. In fact, some of the most pointed arguments against taking such an effects-oriented position have come from scholars who work with overtly political texts—namely, presidential rhetoric. In Martin J. Medhurst's (1996) words, such critics "begin from the premise that rhetoric is an art that has both practical and productive dimensions—dimensions that point inward to principles of operation as well as outward to the accomplishment of certain goals" (p. xiv).

This central notion of rhetoric as an art is one of the similarities between rhetorical criticism and literary criticism, with an appreciation of the rhetor's stylistic, argumentative, and other compositional choices often being a key feature of public address scholarship. From this perspective, political rhetoric, like all rhetoric, should not be judged by what it does but rather for what it is. Medhurst (1996) has explained this distinction:

> The art of rhetoric lies not in whether persuasion actually happens, but in the intellectual powers displayed by the rhetorician in the selection of what to say, how to say it, to whom, under what conditions, and with what apparent outcome. I say "apparent" outcome, because there is no way to discern with certainty that the selections made by the speaker were the causal factors operative in the behavior manifested by the audience, whether that behavior was in line with the intentions of the speaker or whether it was not. (p. xvi)

Without a behavioral or otherwise external barometer to use as a critical yardstick, public address scholars typically conduct interpretive, historical, and/or critical "close readings" of suasive texts (Leff, 2001) to identify signs of "persuasive potency," in Medhurst's (1996) words, within the internal workings of the text itself (p. xvi).

In contrast, there is far less tolerance for mere potency within the social scientific tradition of political communication analysis. There, political communication hardly counts as such unless it has measurable impact on an audience; hence, my previous allusion to the touch screen for electronic voting and other media interfaces as an emblem of this paradigm. Whereas rhetorical discourse per se can sometimes be seen as the province of humanists alone, political communication typically has been the territory of social scientists who tend to think that "what counts" as being worthy of study are those messages with effects that can be identified and measured. As Doris Graber (1993) has explained, "The key element is that the message has a *significant political effect* [italics added] on the thinking, beliefs, and behaviors of individuals, groups, institutions, and whole societies and the environments in which they exist" (p. 305). Given the disciplinary bias in political science toward effects-oriented research, Graber's definition is not surprising. Neither are the most common objects of study for social scientists interested in contemporary political discourse. According to Graber and Smith's (2005) recent review of this literature, the three most popular topics in social scientific research of political communication published in select journals from 2000 to 2003 were election campaigns, new media, and civic engagement (p. 482).

These three topics deal directly with the audience or "user" side of political messages, and Graber and Smith (2005) suggest that there is increasing overlap among them. As an example, they cite recent research into the "use of Internet for campaigning in mayoral elections and for contacting local communities" (p. 483). Such questions fit comfortably within the "voter persuasion paradigm" that Swanson and Nimmo (1990) identified as the driving force behind the majority of traditional social scientific research in political communication. In their words, "the main source of the field's rough-and-ready identity has been the proposition that communication in election campaigns constitutes the field's paradigm case" (p. 8). There is room within this paradigm for many aspects of campaign communication, especially for its coverage via journalism and other forms of new media. Yet even here, most of the emphasis is on determining a relationship between mediated content and its creation of "common knowledge" held by an "active, interpreting, meaning-constructing audience" (Neuman, Just, & Crigler, 1992, pp. 17–18). Consider, for example, the growing use of public opinion polls as a methodological resource for determining "what counts" as a worthy object of study within this tradition as well as others in the social sciences (Norrander & Wilcox, 2002, p. 1).

To this end, empirical and experimental research regarding media effects, particularly the impact of political news stories and campaign advertising, has continued to advance the two arguably most influential theoretical constructs within social scientific political communication: priming and framing. Priming refers to the strategic promotion of certain "standards or criteria that people use to make political evaluations" (Kenski, 1996, p. 72). Framing should be understood as the processes through which "a communication source . . . defines and constructs a political issue or public controversy" (Nelson, Clawson, & Oxley, 1997, p. 567) as well as the outcome of these processes, particularly to the extent that the resulting frame "determines what information is included and what is ignored" by journalists and their audiences (Jamieson & Waldman, 2003, p. xiii). The implications of framing are both numerous and important because frames "define problems . . . diagnose causes . . . make moral judgments . . . and suggest remedies" (Entman, 1993, p. 91).

Interestingly, humanists have embraced framing as a concept and methodological practice as well (Dow, 2004; Spielvogel, 2005;

Tucker, 1998). Yet within the traditional social scientific approach, Graber and Smith (2005) are correct to list both of these theories as part of the general study of "information processing" (p. 485). That characterization is telling, for here again the premium is placed on measuring the ability of political communication to influence the attitudes and/or behaviors of eligible voters. Rather than being evaluated as an art, then, the political communication paradigm tends to evaluate discourse in terms of its efficacy as a stimulus. By this standard, if political discourse happens in a forest and no one hears it, it is hardly political discourse. To borrow a line from George Edwards (2003), unless researchers can demonstrate that the specific instance of communication changed something, it presumably falls "on deaf ears."

Obviously, both of these traditions are much more nuanced than my portrayals here suggest, yet I intentionally risk overgeneralizing to make a point about what their emphases tend to offer: the public address tradition focuses on discrete texts and their authors/ rhetors' assumed intent; the social scientific tradition aims to understand the effect of specific instances of communication on a specific audience for a specific outcome. When we look at these two traditions side by side on these terms, we can see some points of contrast. First, in terms of the classic Shannon-Weaver model of communication, we might assume that one tradition privileges message while the other privileges receiver(s). Second, in terms of more recent debates within rhetorical theory, we might also say that the public address tradition is more likely to emphasize agency (Campbell, 2005) while the social scientific tradition is more likely to feature assumptions that come closer to structuralism, at least in terms of its assumptions about how demographically distinct audiences tend to interpret messages as well as in its bias toward systems and practices that form the basis for institutionalized politics in the United States. Third, in terms of the distinctions between historic and contemporary discourse, we might say that public address scholars seem more comfortable making arguments about the past—for example, the rhetoric of mostly dead, mostly white politicians—while social scientific research has tended to focus on recent events (sometimes looking only as far back as the last election cycle) while also trying to make some descriptive claims about the present (through public opinion research, for example) as well as predictive claims about the future (through designs of communication strategies).

But what of the spaces between message and receiver, between agency and structure, between the past, present, and future? Some observers might say that this is precisely where U.S. citizens find themselves today: awash in a sea of political messages without any certainty or even confidence in the messages' sources or their consequences. Likewise, there is a growing cynicism about the veracity of political messages (Maltese, 1992) as well as doubt about whether politicians are interested in citizens' responses. While both the public address and social scientific paradigms assume a more or less linear relationship between a speaker, his/her message, and a receiver and vice versa, through "feedback" forms of communication, contemporary political discourse is characterized by heightened levels of both intersubjectivity and intertextuality that complicate greatly a message's points of origin, transmission, and ending. In some cases, it is difficult to fathom these points at all, because there are so many voices engaged in political communication through new media. The result of this message explosion is that studies must now consider how political communication is increasingly collaborative, reproduced, and omnipresent. That is, the linear models of production, distribution, and consumption no longer seem adequate to understanding the milieu of political rhetoric.

New media and forms of political discourse are, in fact, major contributing factors in the paradoxical situation I described at this chapter's outset. Even as contemporary political discourse is assumed to be in a state of decline, it also is assumed to be ubiquitous and determinative. This increased amount of discourse is not necessarily healthy for democracy, according to some observers. Bender (2003) has suggested that the rise of mass communication over the second half of the 20th century has resulted in a "thinning" of the political culture. The same time period, especially since the mid-1970s, has been associated with a sharp decline of social capital and civic participation in the United States (Putnam, 2000). Other commentators have raised concerns about the kind of talk that contemporary citizens hear about politics, with charges ranging from a loss of civility (Benson, 1996; Carter, 1998) to a worry that the expansive meaning of the term *political* promotes new levels of informed passivity among citizens (see Hart, Jarvis, Jennings, & Smith-Howell, 2005). In light of these observations, what can recent research on contemporary political communication tell us about what is going on?

The public address tradition can tell us a great deal about the messages that are being issued and the circumstances that surround them. Furthermore, when a piece of oratory comes along that seems remarkable in terms of its artistry (e.g., Barack Obama's keynote address at the 2004 Democratic National Convention and/or many of his presidential campaign speeches in 2008), it can bring this text to our attention and reveal much about both its style and its significance. Likewise, the social scientific tradition can continue to tell us a great deal about how, when, and why messages mobilize voters. Additionally, and importantly, there has been recent research from social scientists on specific practices within news media and political advertising that could have a negative impact on political participation in the United States (Dahlgren, 2001a; Scheufele, 2001). Nevertheless, we still need to know more about the communicative changes that are taking place within U.S. political culture, especially given the consequences of the decline in civic engagement and electoral turnout, and the foundational paradigms alone do not provide a broad enough view of how political discourse functions or even what it has become in the contemporary era. There is reason to believe that contemporary political communication is in fact becoming something different, in terms of both degree and kind, from its historic predecessors. Two particularly exciting lines of research suggest that contemporary political discourse has taken on new properties in terms of its textuality and its channels.

CHANGING TEXTUALITIES: CONTEMPORARY POLITICAL DISCOURSE AS VISUAL IMAGERY

In Kathleen Hall Jamieson's (1988) book *Eloquence in an Electronic Age: The Transformation of Political Speechmaking,* she predicted that "what we traditionally knew as eloquence" within U.S. political discourse "cannot survive . . . intact" in our heavily mediated age (p. ix). Little could she have guessed how prophetic those words were. Since she wrote them, notions about what had traditionally counted as a political text have had to change; now text is no longer "merely" words and rhetor no longer "merely" the speaker alone. Jamieson noted that television in particular placed new demands on the ways politicians should speak in public, and she also suggested television changed the ways the politicians and their environs should try to look on screen. As a "visual medium whose natural grammar is associative," television requires no presentation of stated argument or textual evidence to make a persuasive claim, Jamieson argued (p. 13; see also Foss, 1982, 1992). As a result, Jamieson feared that citizen-viewers would be discouraged from engaging in deep contemplation of such claims.

By 1988, then, Jamieson already was pointing scholars' attention to a set of questions that would later fall under the rubric of "visual rhetoric." Today, visual rhetoric has rapidly grown into its own subdiscipline within the field of speech communication, and such scholars frequently refer to work from other disciplines, especially photography, film, and art criticism, to identify relevant critical methods and theories (Barthes, 1981; Elkins, 2003; Mitchell, 1986, 1994; Sontag, 1977, 2003; Trachtenberg, 1989). For scholars with an interest in U.S. politics, however, two types of photographic and/or filmic texts seem especially worthy of attention: (1) strategic and/or mediated representations of politicians themselves and (2) the mediated depiction of injustices—social, economic, or even physical—experienced by individuals and/or environments.

For her part, Jamieson (1988) discussed both of these types of texts. She credited the televised images of Bull Connor's treatment of African American women and children in Birmingham, Alabama, as being a turning point in public opinion for the civil rights movement in the 1960s. She also implicated Ronald Reagan's use of visual rhetoric as a contributing factor to the triumph of the "moving synoptic moment" over the "eloquent speech" (p. 117). Consider, however, a fundamental difference between the two: one comprises images of an elected official or even a candidate on whose behalf these images themselves were (presumably) manufactured for public consumption, while the other is of circumstances (presumably) far less staged and taken by a camera that is less welcome. Although scholarly attention to both types of images performs an unmasking function long associated with the rhetorical criticism of political discourse, the images themselves differ a great deal with regard to questions of rhetorical agency—especially with regard to authorship—and this difference can have implications for the critic's position.

In the first instance, media-savvy "spin masters" behind specific *mise en scène* within political messages are assumed to be calling the shots, literally, with this team including speechwriters as well as public relations specialists and political advisors. Here the critic of such imagery is perceived to be revealing the "man [*sic*] behind the curtain" and thus enabling readers to better understand the symbolic manipulations that go on "behind the scenes" in politics. Even the metaphors we use here are telling, for they reveal that the critic's role is to engage in the investigation of a Goffmanesque backstage for politics as well as the cultural functions of particular discourses (Goffman, 1956).

Images of particular presidents as well as the presidency in general have often been the object of this sort of study. Referencing Ong's (1982) argument that we live in an age of "secondary orality," Gronbeck (1996) has argued that the presidency is now "electronic," with mediated representations encouraging citizens to think of their nation's chief executive office via a "visual intimacy, a verbal-visual-acoustic construction of a sense of conversation" (p. 35; see also Hart, 1994). Political communication is thus simultaneously ocularentric, verbocentric, and phonocentric. According to Gronbeck (1996), "Political rhetoric in our time is multimediated in that all three codes contain signs that, when taken together or agglutinated, become the political meanings upon which we act" (p. 42). Gronbeck (1995) sees such developments as worrisome, or "especially disruptive to traditional democratic thought," and has called on scholars to fulfill their social responsibility by attending to visual images (p. 216).

Individual presidents, as well as the presidency itself, have been a frequent subject for this type of analysis. For example, Erickson (1998) has provided a specific analysis of images of "political illusionism" within televised portrayals of presidential travel. In other work, Erickson (2000) has also provided a taxonomy through which scholars

might identify and contrast "prudent and imprudent presidential performance" in photographs of chief executives. According to Erickson (1998), in such moments, visual images of the president can function in a variety of ways, with "prudent" enactments maintaining, or at least promoting, the dominant ideology (p. 142–148). Importantly, Erickson (2000) also argues that media images of presidents, as objects of study by critics interested in political texts, fall comfortably within the paradigm of materialist rhetoric. Finnegan (2005) has shown that the analysis of presidential representations need not be limited to the contemporary era through her work on "image vernaculars" circulating around photographs and portraits of President Lincoln at the end of the 19th century. Similarly, Olsen (1983) analyzed Norman Rockwell posters that were used to support the Franklin Roosevelt administration's war efforts. Kiewe (1999) studied the visual cues offered to prospective voters worried about Franklin D. Roosevelt's health during his "dress rehearsal" campaign for governor of New York in 1928. Both the ideological potential and the materialistic features of such images enable critics to read them as texts with some of the same assumptions held within the public address paradigm—namely, that political rhetoric speaks or, rather, shows volumes to the performance of institutional power in the United States.

But what of the less powerful? Increasingly, critics and theorists are turning to visual imagery in order to understand contemporary political discourse by drawing attention to the plights of citizens themselves. In this case, the mediators—presumably the journalists, photojournalists, and sometimes fellow citizens responsible for capturing rather than creating the image—are assumed to possess rhetorical agency to the extent that they decide which images demand exposure to "the public." Some of these decisions hardly seem like decisions at all, of course, with media outlets having little choice but to show the images of the aftermath of Hurricane Katrina, for example. But a growing body of literature examines mediated representations of injustice, crisis, and controversy in American life, and these texts too are undeniably political, if only in the sense that they all take up questions about how information about social issues or events has been disseminated to citizens.

Some authors have looked at visual images of disempowered individuals in U.S. history to argue about political potential(s) of these texts. For Finnegan (2003), this potential can be read at least partially through reception. In *Picturing Poverty: Print Culture and FSA Photographs,* Finnegan argues that while the content of the photographs themselves reveals much about how FSA officials chose to portray rural poverty during the late 1930s, the circulation of these same images can also be viewed as a "decidedly rhetorical process" (p. 224), one which at times literally made a spectacle of poverty for middle- and upper-class American readers of *Life* magazine. Likewise, Harold and DeLuca (2005) have argued that the circulation of photographs of the body of brutally murdered Emmett Till "became a visual trope illustrating the ugliness of white violence and the aggregate power of the black community" (p. 266).

Other scholars have examined the visual rhetoric created by mediated representations of more social protests. Deluca and Peeples's (2002) analysis of the 1999 protests at the World Trade Organization's meetings in Seattle contributes to the critical understanding of the role of visual imagery by advancing the concept of the "public screen," which they offer as a "necessary supplement to the metaphor of the public sphere for understanding today's political scene" especially in light of "technological and cultural changes" (p. 125). Likewise, Dow (2004) and Entman (1990) have examined newscasters' use of visuals in more contemporary coverage of the struggles of U.S. women and racial minorities, while Condit (1990) has studied the usage of images within coverage of abortion protests.

Gurevitch and Kavoori (1992) even went as far as naming "televison spectacles *as* [italics added] politics." In a concise argument for why visual images must be considered by rhetorical critics interested in contemporary politics, they address a variety of televised images—including the Clarence Thomas hearings, the Rodney King beating, and scenes from the 1992 presidential campaign—to suggest that "media spectacles, seen as social texts, should be regarded as playing a role in expanding and configuring what Habermas calls the 'public sphere' or Dewey's notion of democratic community" (p. 415).

Hariman and Lucaites (2003) agree, and yet they argue that the role that visual images can play in differentiating the powerful and the powerless in the United States is more complicated than it might seem. "Photographs," they write, "are capable of aesthetic mediations of political identity that include but also exceed ideological control" (p. 38). Writing about the widely reproduced photograph of the "accidental napalm" victim during the Vietnam War, they question the Habermasian assumption that visual images "subvert" rational discussions of politics (p. 35). They claim that visual images, especially once they become iconic within the culture, "are calls to civic action, sites of controversy, vehicles for ideological control, and sources of rhetorical invention" (p. 54). Indeed, Skow and Dionisopoulos (1997) suggest that journalists themselves can become conscious participants in these processes; in their study of the 1963 photograph of the "burning monk" on a Saigon street and its reproduction in various news outlets across the United States, they argue that "elements of the print media competed with each other to provide the 'correct' interpretation" of this image (p. 394). That visual images could invite such efforts to "manage" meaning is another indication of the new types of questions rhetorical critics must ask as we approach the nature and limits of textuality within suasory discourse in the United States. Likewise, critical openness to such possibilities challenges traditional assumptions about who has the power to control symbols and therefore engage in political rhetoric in the United States.

So far, I have focused on photographs as a common object of study for critics interested in visual forms of political communication. There is, of course, another time-honored form of political rhetoric in the United States: the political cartoon. The persuasive nature of political cartoons is perhaps more obvious than that of photographs: Editorial cartoonists, in particular, are assumed and, indeed, encouraged to engage in social and political critique. Using the term *graphic persuasion* to refer to such efforts, Medhurst and DeSousa (1981) suggest that the "classical canons of rhetoric, slightly modified, provide an adequate superstructure for the production and criticism of graphic discourse" (p. 197). Similarly, DeSousa (1991) analyzed an assortment of U.S. editorial cartoons depicting the Ayatollah Khomeini and found three "commonplaces," another term familiar to public address scholars, with regard to how these representations were offered and assumed to impact viewers' understanding of Iranian politics. Bostdorff (1991) has also applied some of the more traditional tools of rhetorical criticism to her study of patently political cartoons by applying Burkean concepts of "perspective by incongruity, the attitude of the burlesque, and the fusion of form and attitude" (p. 194). As these examples suggest, much of the efforts of public address scholars to understand this form of rhetoric reveal clear roots in that tradition, possibly because political cartoon, like political iconology, is as old as the republic itself (Olsen, 1987).

CHANGING CHANNELS AND URLs: CONTEMPORARY POLITICAL DISCOURSE IN THE ETHER

If studies of cartoons and iconography can remind us that at least these types of visual imagery are perhaps "old news" as forms of political communication in the United States, there is some new news in how rhetorical messages are delivered and, indeed, experienced in the United States as well. The term *new media* generally refers to computer-mediated communication and especially digital media, ranging from more established channels, such as television, to relative newcomers, such as the Internet. Lest this definition seem overly focused on primarily the mechanism of transmission, Flew (2002) has argued that "technology is understood not only as hardware, or the things that we as humans make use of, but also as content or software, and as systems of knowledge and social meaning that accompany their development and use" (p. 2). Dahlgren (2001b) puts it even more succinctly: "Politics no longer exists as a reality taking place outside of media. . . . Rather, politics is increasingly organized as a media phenomenon, planned and executed for and with the cooperation of the media" (p. 85).

In fact, this shift from viewing new technologies as an instrumental process of transmitting political information to a creative and even collusive process through which political information is given social meaning is the entry point for studies of contemporary political discourse. To see the interdependence between hardware, software, and political meanings, however, many scholars have looked closely at television, as we saw in the previous section. Yet whereas the previous observers of visual rhetoric frequently took up questions of how (and, indeed, if) televised images and still photography could function argumentatively within the public sphere to bring attention to candidates or issues, other scholars have been more interested in the overall processes of television viewership, a la Postman (1984), and what these processes might do to civic engagement.

While radio and television were initially touted as having the potential for strengthening democracy by virtue of spreading political information more efficiently among the electorate (Klotz, 2004), this assumption has been repeatedly challenged, especially in the case of television. Most influential is undeniably Putnam's (1995) suggestion that the decline in feelings of trust among the citizens of the United States can be correlated to the increase in hours of their average television viewing. Contrast this negative relationship with the positive one that newspaper reading seems to have on these same feelings, Putnam argues, and we have reason to be suspicious of televisual technology itself; "tuning in" television thus means "tuning out" of civic obligations. Other scholars have also indicted television with even more specific charges regarding the specific negative messages it gives viewers regarding U.S. politics and journalism (Hart, 1994; Patterson, 1993). Television discourages viewers from becoming involved with politics in the traditional sense, these authors argue, and it teaches them to distrust the news media as their main source of political information.

If this group of political communication scholars blames television for declining rates of civic engagement in the United States, perhaps they are merely providing support for McLuhan's (1962, 1964, 1967) arguments that electronic media alter human perception. To examine such possibilities in the most literal sense, some political communication scholars have moved into the realm of the biological science involved in human perception, namely neurophysiology and cognitive psychological research, to learn more about the ways in which televised political advertising taps into existing associative networks within the cognitive schema of likely and/or targeted viewers (Biocca, 1991; Lodge & McGraw, 1995). Even though this type of research is ostensibly as much concerned with "visual rhetoric" as the humanistic studies referenced in the previous section, the unit of analysis here is the brain (receiver) versus the text (stimuli).

An alternative line of research asks about the impact on viewers of a relatively recent development in television content: the increased blurring of the lines between news and entertainment within mainstream media. As Jones (2005) has pointed out, network-broadcast humorous shows with overtly political content such as *Politically Incorrect With Bill Maher* and *The Daily Show With John Stewart* do not employ "the same linguistic or epistemological guidelines that [we] have come to accept as the normative ideal in discussing politics" in the United States (p. ix). Tracing the history of such programming back to the rise of "pundit talk" with the airing of *National Review* in 1966 (pp. 37–38), Jones has coined the phrase "New Political Television" to refer to this genre of contemporary political discourse.

Jones (2005) characterizes this discourse as having several key features, from patently political content delivered in front of live audiences to the host's full-fledged embracing of a "political persona built on his particular type of humor" (p. 58). Importantly, he also notes that the platform "demands a level of sophistication or knowledge about *both* politics and popular culture" from its audience (p. 59); otherwise, viewers cannot get the jokes. Self-perceived identification such as being "in the know" brings to mind related feelings of familiarity and smugness, two of the attitudes that Hart (1994) has suggested are bred by watching television. "To feel clever," Hart writes, "is to become a political methodologist, an expert on the moves and countermoves of the public sphere" (p. 77). Or at least to think one's self as an expert, and perhaps thus "above" politics. Not all scholars agree that new political television necessarily breeds such contemptuous suspicion of politics, however. Jones (2005) argues that, in conjunction with Internet-based forums, these shows give viewers a chance to see connections between politics and their "panoramic view of life in its totality" (p. 185) and therefore can facilitate fans' "general concern for a shared democratic life" (p. 186).

The fact that Jones points to online discussion groups as sites of new forms of civic engagement is important, for the Internet is also increasingly attracting the attention of new media scholars. As Wellman (2004) has noted, many of the first analyses by scholars from multiple disciplines who wrote on the Internet had a noticeably utopian flavor, often with an emphasis on its democratic potential. Some scholars of political communication have also viewed this technology in terms of its possible liberating capacities for citizens (Blumler, 2001; Flanagin, Farinola, & Metzger, 2000; Kahn & Kellner, 2004).

In terms of more specific investigations of the role of the Internet within electoral politics, Klotz (2004) has suggested that while Internet campaigning has unique features that distinguish it from more traditional forms of political campaign communication, such as "low accidental exposure, audience discretion in choosing when and what communication to receive, interactivity on a mass level, and unlimited time and space," all these characteristics have the potential to both help and hurt candidates (p. 64). Klotz points especially to candidates' fear of losing control of their own Web sites by adding more interactive features, such as message boards and blogs that feature comments (p. 70). Likewise, while the major U.S. political parties all view Web sites as central to their communication efforts, Klotz argues that the technology itself seems more likely to work in favor of smaller, "minor" parties, for example, Ralph Nader's online campaign during the 2000 presidential election, in terms of issue awareness and voter mobilization (see also Margolis, Resnick, & Wolfe, 1999). Instead of studying messages that are transmitted or created via the Internet, other political communication scholars have used it as a tool within their own experiments on how voters respond to contemporary political discourse. Iyengar (2001) has advocated strongly for this approach, in which subjects might view online footage of a political advertisement or speech, for example, and then be asked to respond to linguistic or visual manipulations via online surveys.

Whether the research is experimental, historical, or even phenomenological in its approach, the social scientific paradigm tends to ask questions about what contemporary political discourse, in all its emergent forms, *does* to and for its receivers. In contrast, the humanistic tradition is more likely to ask what this discourse *is*, at least in terms of its origin, circulation, and/or textual properties. The preceding pages suggest that we have learned from both approaches, as both the public address and the social scientific paradigms have incubated some important new lines of inquiry that underscore what is new and different about contemporary political rhetoric. To conclude, I will briefly raise three additional sets of questions that might emerge when we ask about even more anticipated changes in both the function and nature of this discourse.

CONCLUSION: NEW RELATIONSHIPS AND NEW QUESTIONS

Earlier, I referred to research by Wellman (2004) that suggested that a large body of the first studies of the Internet remarked on its emancipatory potential for users as citizens. In the same article, Wellman also suggests that the most recent wave of research has focused less on citizenship and more on relationships. In his words, the Internet has created

> sparsely-knit, far-reaching networks, in which people relate to shifting relationships and communities . . . people don't just relate to each other online, they incorporate their computer-mediated communication into their full range of interaction, in-person, phone, fax, and even writings. (p. 123)

If the contemporary era is one in which the hardware of computer-mediated and televisual communication has also become both a frame for understanding politics *and* part of the content of citizens' lives, then we obviously need to know more about both what this discourse is and what it does. What might happen, for instance, if contemporary political discourse becomes, like the Internet, more about relationships than we might have ever imagined?

Here, I do not refer to the classic notion of citizens' relationships with each other in the civic republican tradition. Instead, I am thinking of at least three sets of imagined relationships that I view as being encouraged by contemporary political discourse in all its forms. First, contemporary political discourse invites citizens to imagine that they have personal relationships with U.S. politics. This phenomenon has been described as "feeling intimate" by Hart (1994), who writes about the ways in which soft journalism increasingly means that candidates have to go on "Oprah" or "Dr. Phil." Additionally, however, I think we should also pay attention to the growing personalization of political discourse itself in ways that are not only directed at elected officials (e.g., "Luvya Dubya" bumper stickers) but also toward pundits, including people such as Ann Coulter or Al Franken, and their product-driven personae. Discourse, more than politics, is the pundits' business; no matter who gets elected, such rhetors have to have something to say in order to sell books or stay on the air. What are these folks preaching, the humanist might ask. Do citizens feel politically engaged when they listen to such commentators, the social scientist might inquire. These are good questions, and yet we also need to ask what is happening when these messages are taken *as* politics in the United States. In addition to assuming this shift might mean that mere listening might become a substitute for more traditional forms of political activism, we might also ask what it means when political commentators take on celebrity roles (and vice versa).

Secondly, there is reason to believe that the photograph, as old-fashioned as it may seem, and its counterpart the video clip are increasingly important as "texts" within contemporary political communication. Photographs and short videos are circulating more and more (sometimes via new technologies) to reinforce hegemonic notions of

not just a generalized other, but also of "the enemy," and scholars of visual rhetoric as well as political communication alike need to take more notice of this usage. The best recent examples are undoubtedly the pictures from Abu Ghraib prison that first circulated via public channels in the United States in 2004. What relationship(s) do those images hail their U.S. viewers into—with those who were photographed or with the government who had allowed such activities? Likewise, what feelings—rage, futility, self-righteousness, justification—did both the photographs and the public discourse around it encourage? What messages, if any, were citizens given about what to do with these feelings? And what of the textual properties of the photos themselves; how did those images function for individual citizens?

Third, there is a growing interest in questions about whether or not what was once called "civic culture" (Almond & Verba, 1963) has now morphed into "consumer culture" in the United States (Postrel, 2003). That is, elected politicians and those who seek office increasingly seek to be "branded," like so many consumer goods, in ways that promote public recognition and presumably thus boost the likelihood of votes. Citizens, this theory goes, likewise think of the political world as they would the grocery store: Their job is primarily to make choices among alternatives, and thus, to extend the metaphor, not to clean the aisles, ask questions about the costs or advantages of lowering the freezer temperatures, and so on.

As I mentioned in the first lines of this chapter, I am no fan of nostalgia, and I am aware of the long history of political advertising in the United States. And yet it is possible that cultural conditions have changed in the United States to the extent that even this most predictable type of advertising is not what it used to be. As Lyotard (1979) famously wrote, one of the hallmarks of postmodernity is that knowledge has no value in and of itself; it is instead a commodity whose only value is in its exchange. Political advertising, however, is increasingly concerned with exchange only at the most superficial level. Demands for evidence, nuance, and even counterargument can be viewed as dangerous within such a consumer-driven model of contemporary political discourse—even as these very same demands have traditionally been thought of as crucial for providing high-quality political information to a voting public.

As difficult as it is for scholars to study discourses and conditions that are themselves undergoing rapid change, we must ask some new questions about the texts that invite citizens to also view themselves less and less as citizens and more as something else: as friends of politicians, as spectators of images, or as mere customers in a cafeteria line of political preferences. Within any of these three scenarios, what counts as contemporary political discourse may become increasingly predictable and yet increasingly inconsequential; neither touchstones of eloquence nor the touch screens of voters may be able to turn the tide once political rhetoric seems to be everywhere and yet somehow unimportant at the same time.

REFERENCES

Almond, G., & Verba, S. (1963). *The civic culture: Attitudes and democracy in five nations.* Princeton, NJ: Princeton University Press.

Barthes, R. (1981). *Camera Lucida: Reflections on photography* (1st ed.). New York: Hill & Wang.

Bender, T. (2003). The thinning of American political culture. In J. Rodin & S. P. Steinberg (Eds.), *Public discourse in America* (pp. 27–34). Philadelphia: University of Pennsylvania Press.

Benson, T. W. (1996). Rhetoric, civility, and community: Political debates on computer bulletin boards. *Communication Quarterly, 44,* 359–378.

Biocca, F. (1991). *Signs, codes, and images: Volume two of television and political advertising.* Hillsdale, NJ: Erlbaum.

Bitzer, L. F. (1968). The rhetorical situation. *Philosophy and Rhetoric, 1,* 1–14.

Black, E. (1978). *Rhetorical criticism: A study in method.* Madison: University of Wisconsin Press.

Blumler, J. (2001). The new media and our political communication discontents: Democratizing cyberspace. *Information, communication & society, 4,* 1–13.

Bostdorff, D. (1991). Making light of James Watt: A Burkean approach to the form and attitude of political cartoons. In M. J. Medhurst & Tom W. Benson (Eds.), *Rhetorical dimensions in media: A critical casebook* (pp. 196–215). Dubuque, IA: Kendall Hunt.

Burke, K. (1966). *Language as symbolic action: Essays on life, literature, and method.* Berkeley: University of California Press.

Campbell, K. K. (1995). Pluralism in rhetorical criticism: The case of Lucretia Coffin Mott's "Discourse on Woman." *Rhetoric Society Quarterly, 25,* 1–10.

Campbell, K. K. (2005). Agency: Promiscuous and protean. *Communication and Critical/Cultural Studies, 2,* 1–19.

Carter, S. L. (1998). *Civility: Manners, morals, and the etiquette of democracy.* New York: Basic Books.

Condit, C. M. (1990). *Decoding abortion rhetoric: Communicating social change.* Urbana: University of Illinois Press.

Dahlgren, P. (2001a). The public sphere and the net: Structure, space and communication. In W. L. Bennett & R. M. Entman (Eds.), *Mediated politics: Communication in the future of democracy* (pp. 33–55). Cambridge, UK: Cambridge University Press.

Dahlgren, P. (2001b). The transformation of democracy? In B. Axford & R. Huggins (Eds.), *New Media and Politics* (pp. 64–88). London: Sage.

Deluca, K. M., & Peeples, J. (2002). From public sphere to public screen: Democracy, activism, and the 'violence' of Seattle. *Critical Studies in Mass Communication, 19,* 125–151.

DeSousa, M. (1991). Symbolic action and pretended insight: The Ayatollah Khomeini in U.S. Editorial Cartoons. In M. J. Medhurst & T. Benson (Eds.), *Rhetorical dimensions in media: A critical casebook* (pp. 216–244). Dubuque, IA: Kendall Hunt.

Dow, B. J. (2004). Fixing feminism: Women's liberation and the rhetoric of television documentary. *Quarterly Journal of Speech, 90,* 53–80.

Edwards, G. C. (2003). *On deaf ears: The limits of the bully pulpit.* New Haven, CT: Yale University Press.

Elkins, J. (2003). *Visual studies: A skeptical introduction.* New York: Routledge.

Entman, R. M. (1990). Modern racism and the images of blacks in local television news. *Critical Studies in Mass Communication, 7,* 332–345.

Entman, R. M. (1993). Framing: Toward clarification of a fractured paradigm. *Journal of Communication, 43,* 51–58.

Erickson, K. (1998). Presidential spectacles: Political illusionism and the rhetoric of travel. *Communication Monographs, 65,* 141–153.

Erickson, K. (2000). Presidential rhetoric's visual turn: Performance fragments and the politics of illustration. *Communication Monographs, 67,* 138–157.

Finnegan, C. A. (2003). *Picturing poverty: Print culture and FSA photographs.* Washington, DC: Smithsonian Books.

Finnegan, C. A. (2005). Recognizing Lincoln: Image vernaculars in nineteenth-century visual culture. *Rhetoric & Public Affairs, 8,* 31–57.

Flanagin, A. J., Farinola, W. F., & Metzger, M. J. (2000). The technical code of the Internet/World Wide Web. *Critical Studies in Media Communication, 17,* 409–428.

Flew, T. (2002). *New media: An introduction.* New York: Oxford University Press.

Foss, S. J. (1982). Rhetoric and the visual image: A resource unit. *Communication Education, 31,* 55–66.

Foss, S. J. (1992). Visual imagery as communication. *Text and Performance Quarterly, 12,* 85–96.

Goffman, E. (1956). *The presentation of self in everyday life.* Edinburgh, UK: University of Edinburgh.

Graber, D. A. (1993). Political communication: Scope, progress, promise. In A. W. Finifter (Ed.), *Political science: The state of the discipline* (pp. 305–332). Washington, DC: American Political Science Association.

Graber, D. A., & Smith, J. M. (2005). Political communication faces the 21st century. *Journal of Communication, 55,* 479–507.

Gronbeck, B. E. (1995). Rhetoric, ethics, and telespectacles in the post-everything age. In R. H. Brown (Ed.), *Postmodern representations: Truth, power, and mimesis in the human*

sciences and public culture (pp. 216–238). Urbana: University of Illinois Press.

Gronbeck, B. E. (1996). The presidency in the age of secondary orality. In M. J. Medhurst (Ed.), *Beyond the rhetorical presidency* (pp. 30–49). College Station: Texas A&M University Press.

Gurevitch, M., & Kavoori, A. (1992). Television spectacles as politics. *Communication Monographs, 59,* 415–416.

Hariman, R., & Lucaites, J. (2003). Public identity and collective memory in U.S. iconic photography: The image of 'accidental napalm.' *Critical Studies in Mass Communication, 20,* 35–66.

Harold, C., & DeLuca, K. M. (2005). Behold the corpse: Violent images and the case of Emmett Till. *Rhetoric & Public Address, 8,* 263–285.

Hart, R. P. (1994). *Seducing America: How television charms the modern voter.* New York: Oxford University Press.

Hart, R. P., Jarvis, S. E., Jennings, W. P., & Smith-Howell, D. (2005). *Political keywords: Using language that uses us.* New York: Oxford University Press.

Iyengar, S. (2001). The method is the message: The current state of political communication research. *Political Communication, 18,* 225–229.

Jamieson, K. H. (1988). *Eloquence in an electronic age: The transformation of political speechmaking.* New York: Oxford University Press.

Jamieson, K. H., & Waldman, P. (2003). *The press effect: Politicians, journalists, and the stories that shape the political world.* New York: Oxford University Press.

Jones, J. P. (2005). *Entertaining politics: New political television and civic culture.* Lanham, MD: Rowman & Littlefield.

Kahn, R., & Kellner, D. (2004). New media and Internet activism: From the 'Battle of Seattle' to blogging. *New Media & Society, 6,* 87–95.

Kenski, H. C. (1996). From agenda-setting to priming and framing. In M. E. Stuckey (Ed.), *The theory and practice of political communication research* (pp. 67–83). Albany: State University of New York Press.

Kiewe, A. (1999). A dress rehearsal for a presidential campaign: FDR's embodied "run" for the governorship. *Southern Communication Journal, 64,* 155–167.

Klotz, R. J. (2004). *The politics of Internet communication.* Lanham, MD: Rowman & Littlefield.

Leff, M. C. (2001). Lincoln at Cooper Union: Neoclassical criticism revisited. *Western Journal of Communication, 65,* 232–249.

Leff, M. C. (2003). Tradition and agency in humanistic rhetoric. *Philosophy and Rhetoric, 36,* 135–147.

Lodge, M., & McGraw, K. M. (1995). *Political judgment: Structure and process.* Ann Arbor: University of Michigan Press.

Lyotard, J.-F. (1979). *The postmodern condition.* Minneapolis: University of Minnesota Press.

Maltese, J. A. (1992). *Spin control: The White House Office of Communications and the management of presidential news.* Chapel Hill: University of North Carolina Press.

Margolis, M., Resnick, D., & Wolfe, J. D. (1999). Party competition on the Internet in the United States and Britain. *Harvard International Journal of Press/Politics, 4,* 24–27.

McLuhan, M. (1962). *The Gutenberg galaxy: The making of typographic man.* Toronto, Ontario, Canada: University of Toronto Press.

McLuhan, M. (1964). *Understanding media: The extensions of man.* New York: McGraw-Hill.

McLuhan, M. (1967). *The medium is the message.* New York: Random House.

Medhurst, M. J. (Ed.). (1996). *Beyond the rhetorical presidency.* College Station: Texas A&M University Press.

Medhurst, M. J., & DeSousa, M. (1981). Political cartoons as rhetorical form: A taxonomy of graphic discourse. *Communication Monographs, 48,* 197–236.

Mitchell, W. J. T. (1986). *Iconology: Image, text, and ideology.* Chicago: University of Chicago Press.

Mitchell, W. J. T. (1994). *Picture theory: Essays on verbal and visual representation.* Chicago: University of Chicago Press.

Nelson, T. E., Clawson, R. A., & Oxley, Z. M. (1997). Media framing of a civil liberties conflict and its effect on tolerance. *American Political Science Review, 91,* 567–583.

Neuman, W. R., Just, M. R., & Crigler, A. N. (1992). *Common knowledge: News and the construction of political meaning.* Chicago: University of Chicago Press.

Norrander, B., & Wilcox, C. (Eds.). (2002). *Understanding public opinion.* Washington, DC: CQ Press.

Olson, L. C. (1983). Portraits in praise of a people: A rhetorical analysis of Norman Rockwell's icons in Franklin D. Roosevelt's "Four Freedoms" campaign. *Quarterly Journal of Speech, 69,* 15–24.

Olson, L. C. (1987). Benjamin Franklin's commemorative medal Libertas Americana: A study in rhetorical iconology. *Quarterly Journal of Speech, 9,* 23–45.

Ong, W. J. (1982). *Orality and literacy.* London: Routledge.

Patterson, T. (1993). *Out of order.* New York: Vintage Books.

Postman, N. (1984). *Amusing ourselves to death: Public discourse in an age of show business.* New York: Penguin Books.

Postrel, V. (2003). *The substance of style: How the rise of aesthetic value is remaking commerce, culture, and consciousness.* New York: HarperCollins.

Putnam, R. D. (1995). Tuning in, tuning out: The strange disappearance of social capital in America. *Political Science and Politics, 27,* 664–684.

Putnam, R. D. (2000). *Bowling alone: The collapse and revival of American community.* New York: Simon & Schuster.

Scheufele, D. A. (2001). Democracy for some? How political talk informs and polarizes the electorate. In R. P. Hart & D. Shaw (Eds.), *Communication in U.S. elections: New agendas* (pp. 19–32). Lanham, MD: Rowman & Littlefield.

Skow, L. M., & Dionisopoulos, G. N. (1997). A struggle to contextualize photographic images: American print media and the "burning monk." *Communication Quarterly, 45,* 393–409.

Sontag, S. (1977). *On photography.* New York: Farrar, Straus & Giroux.

Sontag, S. (2003). *Regarding the pain of others.* New York: Farrar, Straus & Giroux.

Spielvogel, C. (2005). "You know where I stand": Moral framing of the war on terrorism and the Iraq war in the 2004 presidential campaign. *Rhetoric and Public Affairs, 8,* 549–569.

Swanson, D. L., & Nimmo, D. (1990). *New directions in political communication.* Newbury Park, CA: Sage.

Trachtenberg, A. (1989). *Reading American photographs: Images as history from Mathew Brady to Walker Evans.* New York: Noonday Press.

Tucker, L. R. (1998). The framing of Calvin Klein: A frame analysis of media and discourse about the August 1995 Calvin Klein jeans advertising campaign. *Critical Studies in Mass Communication, 98,* 141–158.

Wellman, B. (2004). The three ages of Internet studies: Ten, five, and zero years ago. *New Media & Society, 6,* 123–129.

32

Social Movement Rhetoric

ROBERT COX

CHRISTINA R. FOUST

Since 1952, when Leland M. Griffin called on critics to "isolate the *rhetorical* movement" in historical movements, rhetorical study of movements has proved to be both a heuristic and episodic endeavor. In their approach to such studies, critics also have begun to blur the lines between the rhetoric of a discrete "movement" and broader scholarship in public discourse studies. Gaonkar (2002) observed that as scholars have come to view discourse as an "immensely rich and complex" object of analysis, the demand has risen "for a flexible critical practice no longer governed by a single monolithic theoretical perspective" (p. 411).

We believe that a similar critical flexibility has come to characterize recent study of oppositional rhetorics and the discrete acts or practices of movements. Through analysis of "counterpublics" (Asen, 2000; Asen & Brouwer, 2001) and resistant bodies and images (DeLuca, 1999a, 1999b; DeLuca & Peeples, 2002; Harold & DeLuca, 2005), social movement rhetoric (SMR) scholars have offered new protocols for engaging the discourse of those challenging dominant norms and institutions. At the same time, critics are bringing new, more nuanced perspectives to traditional movement texts (e.g., Dr. King's "Letter" from the Birmingham jail) as well as to key figures and discursive practices in the civil rights, women's, and other social movements.[1]

Throughout its growth, the study of movements has broadened rhetorical theory and criticism by bringing uninstitutionalized, nonnormative, and incongruous voices into conversation with public discourse scholarship. We share this desire to inquire broadly into the sources of social transformations as well as the need for critical reflexivity. We have therefore reviewed the major trajectories in SMR scholarship to suggest areas of congruences as well as departures. We survey these developments in five sections: (1) early studies of SMR; (2) rethinking the figure of "social movements": New Social Movements (NSM) and counterpublics; (3) performing resistance: bodies, images, and public screens; (4) democracy, representation, and new modalities of social dissent; and (5) continuing challenges for the study of SMR. Since understandings of theory and critical practice emerge most clearly in engagements with discourse, we have attempted to illustrate these major areas through the work of scholars most closely associated with each period or practice.

EARLY STUDIES OF SOCIAL MOVEMENT RHETORIC

Early SMR scholars distanced themselves from the "great orator" tradition of public address, seeking instead to understand a multiplicity of voices urging changes beyond the judgment of single audiences. Moreover, the vibrant, sometimes confrontational rhetoric of the 1960s occasioned critics to question the fecundity and ethics of traditional theory and to deepen their conceptions of movement discourse. By the 1970s, critics had fashioned a conceptual vocabulary assigning rhetoric a central role in social change. Through rhetorical appeals, leaders could balance competing demands placed on their movements and potentially affect wider change. Influenced by the work of Kenneth Burke, other critics theorized SMR as it took place within dialectical struggles with dominant norms and institutions. By the 1980s, diverse characterizations of movement rhetoric in early studies would give rise to spirited debates on the nature and relevance of the "social movement" figure itself.

Griffin (1952) is widely credited with the first attempt to characterize the rhetoric of movements as a distinct area for rhetorical scholarship. He challenged public address scholars to forego the "clearly demarked" and "conventionalized" study of great orators (p. 184) in favor of analyzing "the pattern of

public discussion, the configuration of discourse, the physiognomy of persuasion" (p. 185) peculiar to a movement. He located such patterns within larger historical movements, or concerted efforts to change the "social, economic, political, religious," (p. 184) or other conditions that people deemed unsatisfying. Anticipating his later Burkean approach (see Griffin, 1969), he encouraged critics to trace this *rhetorical* "pattern" as the movement proceeded through its phases of development, from "a period of inception" through "rhetorical crisis" to "a period of consummation" (Griffin, 1952, p. 186). Nevertheless, the sit-ins, marches, and "confrontational" rhetoric occurring in the 1960s would severely strain Griffin's framework, occasioning critics to rethink neo-Aristotelian standards of rhetoric, reason, and persuasion.

The "Rhetoric of the Streets": 1960s Movement Studies

By the late 1960s, both the message and means of street protests that were associated with struggles for civil rights, Black Power, feminism, peace, and campus democracy shook the foundations of "reasonable" public speech. Skeptics denounced a "climate of anarchy," which they attributed to the "rhetoric of the streets," including draft-card burnings, boycotts, traffic blockades, campus sit-ins, mass marches through segregated neighborhoods, and obscene chants protesting the Vietnam War (Haiman, 1967, p. 100). The new rhetoric exceeded "the bounds of permissible time, place, and manner" (p. 100) and the traditional province of rhetoric as "verbal communication" (p. 99). Most important for rhetorical critics, some charged that the new rhetoric constituted "'persuasion' by a strategy of power and coercion rather than by reason and democratic decision-making" (p. 102).

In a defense of the "Rhetoric of the Streets," Haiman (1967) offered a justification of agitators' "body rhetoric" as a First

Amendment right and an understandable tactic that dramatized the injustice of a law and, in the case of riots, catalyzed the process of institutional reform. Rather than dismissing outright such protests as irrational, he argued that critics should "avoid the blithe presumption that the channels of rational communication are open to any and all who wish to make use of them and attempt, instead, a careful assessment of the power structure of the situation" (p. 114). He thus inaugurated a call for alternative theories of movement rhetorics capable of explaining new modalities of protest and the exigencies inspiring them.

Haiman's call was not always echoed by other critics. Andrews (1969), for example, criticized the militant rhetoric and actions of Students for a Democratic Society. The group had seized an administrative building at Columbia University in May 1968 to protest construction of a gymnasium that affected a nearby Harlem neighborhood. Yet the activists' "physical rhetoric of resistance," Andrews argued, was "coercive" since it limited the audience's choices, and thus fell beyond the canons of rhetoric conceived as "persuasion" (p. 9).

Others such as Burgess (1968) stressed the urgency of reinterpreting the apparently threatening expression of such groups. The confrontational rhetoric of "Black Power," he argued, was not "a call to arms but a call for justice, a call uttered outside law and order," because the institutions that created and enforced order were "racist" (p. 123). Critics who judged such rhetoric through the standards of reasonableness and the inherent morality of democratic institutions were bound to dismiss Black Power as a *coercive* threat. By failing to engage Black Power rhetoric on its own terms, critics could perpetuate a racist status quo under the guises of order, calm, and "business as usual" (p. 130).

Others also took up the challenge posed by the 1960s rhetoric of the streets, questioning

the traditional view of rhetoric as a set of "amoral techniques of manipulating a message to fit various contexts" (Scott & Smith, 1969, p. 2, fn. 2). The most provocative response was Scott and Smith's (1969) assertion that Black Power advocates and leaders of the New Left rejected the common notion that their protests were cries for inclusion within the status quo and its institutions. Radical leaders did not represent "an inert mass hoping to receive what they lack[ed] through action by the 'haves'" (p. 2). In an attempt to understand such rhetoric on its own terms rather than as a cry for "recognition," they urged critics to explore the ways in which unorthodox dissent represented a powerful challenge to dominant norms. They argued, moreover, that confrontation challenged not only the "establishment" but also academic rhetorics that "have been for the most part instruments of established society, presupposing the 'goods' of order, civility, reason, decorum, and civil or theocratic law" (p. 7).

Critics who engaged the radical, material, and symbolic acts of 1960s protests more often than not read these sympathetically by locating their emergence within conditions of social and economic injustice. Early SMR critics also adopted a self-consciously critical stance toward rhetorical theory itself. As Scott and Smith (1969) pointedly insisted,

> A rhetorical theory suitable to our age must take into account the charge that civility and decorum serve as masks for the preservation of injustice, that they condemn the disposed to non-being, and that as transmitted in a technological society they become the instrumentalities of power for those who "have." (p. 8)

Following the work of early SMR critics, two major perspectives emerged that identified social movements as grand undertakings employing an array of strategic choices and rhetorical styles: (1) a leader-centered approach inspired by new sociological theories that identified core "functions" of movements and (2) a Burkean approach that viewed movements as "dramatistic" forms.

The Rhetorical "Functions" of Movements

Simons (1970) laid the foundation for the functional approach to SMR, arguing that the standard tools of rhetorical criticism were "ill-suited for unraveling the complexity of discourse in social movements or for capturing its grand flow" (p. 2). Simons viewed movements as organizations, not unlike corporations or state agencies, whose leaders faced certain "rhetorical requirements": to *"attract and mold workers* (i.e., followers) *into an efficiently organized unit,"* to *"secure adoption of their product by the larger structure* (i.e., the external system, the established order),"* and to *"react to resistance generated by the larger structure"* (pp. 3–4). Stewart (1980) reworked Simons's assumptions, as a "functional approach," positioning rhetoric "as the primary *agency* through which social movements perform necessary *functions* that enable them to come into existence, to meet opposition, and, perhaps, to succeed in bringing about (or resisting) change" (p. 299).

Though the functional approach treated social movements as organizations, it characterized them as "uninstitutionalized collectivit-[ies]" (Simons, 1970, p. 3). As such, leaders faced very difficult rhetorical situations given their movements' status as "outsiders." As Simons noted,

> Shorn of the controls that characterize formal organizations, yet required to perform the same internal functions, harassed from without, yet obligated to adapt to the external system, the leader of a social movement must constantly balance inherently conflicting demands on his [or her] position and on the movement he [or she] represents. (p. 4)

The basis of the functional approach, in Simons's view, was the ability of the leader to craft "strategies" that fulfilled "the requirements of the movement by resolving or reducing rhetorical problems" (p. 2).

The functional approach represented a significant departure from the hermeneutic approach urged by critics of 1960s radical rhetoric. Unlike Burgess (1968, 1970), Scott and Smith (1969), Gregg (1971), Windt (1972), Campbell (1973), and others who sought to understand movements in their own rights, the functional approach seemed like social science, seeking theories that would advance "generalizations" about movement rhetoric (Stewart, 1980, p. 298), and end critics' "preoccup[ation] with explicating the events . . . the people . . . and the strategies . . . that have captured headlines and intruded upon our world" (p. 298). Though functional critics did not claim an ability to predict a movement's course, their approach prioritized efforts to *classify* movement advocates and/or their discourse according to taxonomies of "militant," "moderate," or "intermediate" strategies (Simons, 1970), or as "revivalistic" or "innovative" movements (Stewart, 1980). Thus, while the functional approach provided a vocabulary distinctive to the rhetorical study of movements, it tended to decenter "specific events, speeches, and strategies" (Stewart, 1980, p. 298) in favor of the social movement figure itself. This orientation later proved somewhat limiting since, as we suggest below, the notion of a discrete "movement" would be increasingly questioned.

Movements as Dramatistic Form

Departing from the functional approach, other scholars, influenced by Kenneth Burke, proposed to view social movements as a dialectical form or *movement* in the social arena. Griffin (1969) offered the earliest statement of this approach by extending Burke's idea of the "negative" or conflict as impetus for the "dramatistic" transformations that movements experience. Like the functional critics, Griffin envisioned a grand theory, though it would be based in a view of language itself: As a result of their symbol-creating nature, humans, "moved by the impious dream of a mythic new Order," inevitably experience conflict ("Guilt") and thus are moved "to rise up and cry *No* to the existing order" (p. 460). For Griffin, then, "to study a movement is to study a progress, a rhetorical striving" (p. 461). This rhetorical striving was "a progress from *pathema* through *poiema* to *methema:* from a 'suffering, misfortune, passive condition, state of mind,' through 'a deed, doing, action, act,' to an 'adequate idea; the thing learned'" (p. 461, quoting Burke, 1945, pp. 38–43). In Griffin's view, to study a movement was "to study a drama, an Act of transformation, an Act that ends in transcendence, the achievement of salvation" (p. 462).

The attempt to identify the *rhetorical* form of movements led to efforts by others—similarly influenced by Burke—to specify this form as a distinctive act and therefore the focus of rhetorical study. Chief among these was Cathcart (1972, 1978), who proposed that movements are distinguished by reciprocal acts set off between the movement and the established order, a *"dialectical enjoinment in the moral arena* [italics added]" (1972, p. 87). For Cathcart (1978), this reciprocity was constituted by a radical break with societal norms, "a kind of ritual conflict whose most distinguishing form is *confrontation*" (p. 235). Whereas scholars such as Andrews (1969), Burgess (1968), Scott and Smith (1969), and Simons (1970) had looked at confrontation as an *instrumental* act—a tactic to open channels of communication—Cathcart (1978) now proposed confrontation "as a *consummatory form essential to a movement*" (p. 237). That is, confrontational rhetoric ensures the agonistic ritual that a radical break from the established order calls forth. The rhetoric of such movements thus

differs from the neo-Aristotelian "managerial rhetorics" of reform or status quo movements since those, while disagreeing with a practice or policy, stay "within the value structures of its existing order" and speak "with the same vocabularies of motive as do the conservative elements in the order" (p. 239).

Cathcart's insistence on a dialectical view drew immediate criticism. Critics charged that it was an incomplete account (Wilkinson, 1976) and a "more restrictive usage" having potentially "negative consequences" for rhetorical study of movements (Smith & Windes, 1975, p. 142). Whether for these reasons, or because the fires of social controversies had begun to lessen in the United States by the 1980s, the search for sweeping accounts of the rhetoric of movements ceased by the end of the decade.

CONTESTING THE FIGURE OF "SOCIAL MOVEMENTS": NEW SOCIAL MOVEMENTS AND THE DISCOURSE OF COUNTERPUBLICS

The tensions among the diverse theoretical assumptions in early SMR scholarship became heightened during the 1970s and were fully articulated in the 1980s. Forums such as the *Central States Speech Journal* (*CSSJ*) featured debates about the nature of movements and methodological approaches to the study of their rhetorics. Some skeptics questioned the self-evident figure of a "social movement" itself (McGee, 1980; Sillars, 1980). Others remained committed to views of movements as already-constituted entities with specific rhetorical demands on their leaders (Simons, 1980; Simons, Mechling, & Schreier, 1984; Stewart, 1980). Still others lamented the obsession with theory and urged a return to historical and critical studies of specific movements and texts (Andrews, 1980; Lucas, 1980; Zarefsky, 1980).

The impetus for debates over the study of SMR came from both pedagogical and methodological concerns. Though Griffin

(1980) notably praised the pluralistic study of social movements, others argued that "the lack of consistent methodology" confused students and failed to foster uniquely *rhetorical* scholarship (Hahn & Gonchar, 1971, p. 44). As a consequence of these and other concerns, contributors to special issues of *CSSJ* in 1980 and 1983 addressed a number of pivotal questions: How should theorists conceive of the relationship between rhetoric and its object—the social movement? Are movements identifiable phenomena whose life and success depend on rhetoric? Should scholarship emphasize theory building or historical and critical analysis? Should critics conceive of movements as born of, and engaged in, oppositional struggles with rhetorically defined "enemies?"

A principal focus in these debates was an assumption of early SMR scholars that movements were already-constituted entities, with empirical identities, stages of development, strategies, and so on. Against this, McGee (1980) insisted movements are not observable, knowable "things"; instead, the concept "movement" is "a set of meanings" (p. 233), an *analogy,* "comparing the flow of social facts to physical movements" (pp. 236–237). Positing that movements exist prior to rhetoric, McGee charged, reduces rhetoric to a "passive, reactive . . . facilitator of change, subordinate to and determined by an objective phenomenon" (p. 242). Alternatively, critics should explore "changes in patterns of discourse *directly*" (p. 243), echoing Griffin's (1952) call to analyze changes in the "pattern of public discussion" (p. 185).

In a similar vein, Zarefsky (1980) charged that studies that sought "generalizable claims about patterns of persuasion characteristic of movements as a class" rested on the false premise that "movements comprise a distinct rhetorical genre" (p. 246). For example, movements are not inherently *out*groups, since they are sometimes "sponsored and financed by government" (p. 246). As a result, he

believed that a key premise of the dramatistic model was not above reproach: "Only in a situation of actual revolution . . . could one say that there is no common ground among participants in a controversy" (p. 247) sharing at least some cultural ground with the "enemy." Instead of disputes about conceptual models, Zarefsky argued that the primary contribution of SMR scholarship is historical: Critics should explore how "our understanding of history will be enhanced by attention to [a movement's] rhetorical dimension" (p. 253). Andrews (1980), too, argued that critics should avoid "the imposition of consistency at the expense of complexity" (p. 281) and urged more historical case studies to counter the generalizations of theory-driven criticism.

However, the social movement figure was not without its defenders. Simons (1980) argued that SMR scholarship would suffer if the views of McGee and Zarefsky were "widely accepted, since they transgressed the commonly accepted understanding of movements as recognizable in their struggles for change (p. 307). Rather than bicker over terminology, scholars should focus on locating the "invariant characteristics" of movements (p. 314). Likewise, Stewart (1983) objected, "Regardless of what we call them, [movements] have been major forces for change and resistance to change in American history" (p. 77). McGee (1983), however, sharply delineated the functional and critical viewpoints, arguing that the former reflected "the sterile, preposterous world of logical positivism" (p. 75). Rhetorical critics were not "technicians" (p. 76); instead, urging an "interpretive, critical theory," he proposed that they focus on the movement of human consciousness evident in rhetorical discourse (p. 74).

In many ways, McGee's position reflected the wider "critical turn" occurring in the humanities. Movement scholars in sociology, cultural studies, and rhetoric turned increasingly to the study of marginal voices within (and against) dominant publics. In doing so, they employed a range of critical and interpretive theories beyond the taxonomies of the functional model. Some scholars would find alliances with critics of theorist Jürgen Habermas's concept of a liberal public sphere. Critical studies of "new" social movements and the discourse of "counterpublics" would become dominant trajectories in SMR scholarship.

Rhetoric and New Social Movements

In spite of the vigorous debates in the 1980s, the study of SMR waned during the decade. Lucas (1988) found such scholarship to be "moribund"; it was difficult, he noted, even "to find a glimmer of interest in confrontation as a rhetorical strategy" (p. 243). Although some disputed Lucas's assessment, it was clear that "concern with synthesizing issues of 'definition, form, methodology, and meaning' [had] moved from center stage" (Henry & Jensen, 1991, quoting Griffin, 1980, p. 232). Nevertheless, two developments outside of communication studies would begin to influence SMR scholarship: "New Social Movement" theorists' interest in the role of discourse and a corresponding interest in theorizing "counterpublics" as a mode of critical resistance.

The emergence of so-called New Social Movement (NSM) theory came as social theorists attempted to understand movements that foregrounded issues of identity and a "politics of recognition," in lieu of, or alongside, a "politics of redistribution" (Fraser, 1997b).[2] Originating in European social theory (Habermas, 1981; Melucci, 1985; Offe, 1985), NSM proponents offered a competing model to the rational-actor approach of "resource mobilization" theory (McCarthy & Zald, 1977) to account for the movements emerging in the 1960s and 1970s (civil rights, feminism, gay and lesbian struggles, ecology, etc.). In rhetorical studies, for example, Darsey's (1991)

analysis of "gay liberation rhetoric" in the late 1970s and 1980s attempted to understand the construction of a movement's interests from the discourse of those within the movement itself.

A central insight in NSM theory was the constitutive role of culture, particularly discourse, in the activities and interests of oppositional groups. As Palczewski (2001) observed, instead of seeing a movement as a "unity, to which one attributes goals, choices, interests, decisions," NSM scholars insisted that these features be viewed "as results instead of as points of departure" (p. 166, quoting Melucci, 1985, p. 793). This approach provided considerable impetus for the conceptual shift urged by McGee (1980, 1983), foregrounding the *rhetoric* of social movements rather than a *social movement's* rhetoric.

Though NSM scholarship was relatively limited within the rhetorical study of movements, its focus on the constitutive nature of discourse has been advanced in another thread of rhetorical scholarship: the study of publics and "counterpublic" discourse. Viewing social movements as counterpublics invited critics to appreciate the ability of movements "to function outside the dominant public as a site of critical oppositional force" (Palczewski, 2001, p. 165). As a result, Brouwer (2006) argued that the emergence of counterpublic theory "reinvigorated the study of social movements by shifting the terrain of such studies" (p. 204).

Counterpublics and Social Movement Rhetoric

The term *counterpublic* emerged initially in reaction to Habermas's (1962/1989) description of the bourgeois public sphere as a realm of "common" interests and a socially accessible sphere of rational-critical debate able to mediate state authority. Negt and Kluge (1993), Landes (1988), and others objected that alternative "counterpublics," whose participants

did not share the attributes of a unified, bourgeois public sphere, existed alongside this public in the life of workers and women's roles in
the literary salons of the 18th century.

The work of two social theorists, in
particular, appeared to be influential as
rhetorical scholars elaborated an understanding
of "counterpublic" discourse in constituting
multiple publics. In using the term *subaltern
counterpublics*, Fraser (1992) called attention
to "parallel discursive arenas where members of
subordinated social groups invent and circulate
counterdiscourses to formulate oppositional
interpretations of their identities, interests, and
needs" (p. 123). In addition, Felski (1989)
noted that, unlike the idealistic traits of
Habermas's bourgeois public sphere—notably,
a bracketing of specific interests, and an
assumption of "universal" interests—the discursive labor of counterpublics is "directed toward
an affirmation of specificity in relation to
gender, race, ethnicity, age, sexual preference,
and so on" (p. 166).

Importantly, the affirmation of specific
interests in counterpublic theory is not
exclusively inward, toward a collective
solidarity. For both Fraser and Felski, the
recognition of a dialectic of withdrawal and
engagement with dominant publics is critical.
Fraser argued that counterpublics retain a
publicist orientation: They "aspire to dissem-
inate [their] discourse to ever widening
arenas" (p. 124). As such, counterpublics have
a dual character: "They function as spaces of
withdrawal and regroupment; on the other
hand, they also function as bases and training
grounds for agitational activities directed
toward wider publics" (p. 124). Thus, in both
instances, the discursive practices of counterpublics *matter*; that is, they enable construction
of interests inwardly and "agitational activities"
toward public audiences.

For many scholars of SMR, the dialectical
character of counterpublics signaled a productive
focus in recognizing not only the achievement
of marginal groups in articulating the bases of

their exclusion but also their oppositional or
counterpublicist orientation as they challenged
those norms or discourses sustaining their
exclusion.[3] Brouwer (2006) commented that,
for rhetorical scholars, who are "prone to
thinking in terms of agonistics, eristics, conflict,
dissent, argument, controversy, or social
movement," the "counterpublic's origins in
oppositionality render it familiar and
potentially productive" (p. 198).

Indeed, by the early 21st century, rhetorical
critics had begun to deploy the concept of
"counterpublic" in wide-ranging studies of
oppositional rhetorics. Among these were
studies of the antisuffrage movement (Maddux,
2004); government censorship of the black
press in the early 20th century (Squires, 2001);
struggles for recognition and redress by HIV-
AIDS groups (Brouwer, 2001, 2005) and
women with breast cancer (Pezzullo, 2003a);
opposition to the state (Asen & Brouwer,
2001); and efforts by some to constitute
virtual or "cyber-counterpublics" (McDorman,
2001; Palczewski, 2001).

Still, the term *counterpublic* has not always
been used consistently. Asen and Bouwer
(2001) have pointed out that "scholars
sometimes write about counterpublics with a
frustrating vagueness" (p. 8). And Brouwer
(2006) has noted that scholars have yet to
"systematically interrogate differences between
counterpublics and social movements [italics
added]" (p. 204). In some cases, the term
appears to be used simply for "movement" or
as a synonym for "new social movements,"
while in other cases, "counterpublic" signals
the internal, reflexive discourse of a group's
turn away from dominant publics to focus
inward. Influenced perhaps by Warner's
(2002a) view that counterpublics are "structured
by alternative dispositions or protocols" (p. 56),
some have associated counterpublics with their
*non*public phase of withdrawal. For example,
Maddux (2004) has argued that the evolution
of the antisuffrage movement into an
antiradical movement in 1917 represented a

change "from social movement organizing to counterpublic discursive space" (p. 302). Whereas movements are defined by persuasion directed at external audiences (in Maddux's view), counterpublics are marked by an "internal discursive exchange" (p. 302) and are "further delineated by what Warner calls the 'reflexive circulation of discourse'" (pp. 302–303, quoting Warner, 2002b, p. 420). Others such as Brouwer (2001) invoke *counterpublic* precisely to capture the "oscillation" of groups such as ACT-UP, "'between protected enclaves . . . [and] broader surroundings in which they can test those ideas against the reigning reality'" (p. 89, quoting Mansbridge, 1996, p. 57).

In an attempt to clarify, Asen (2000) and Asen and Brouwer (2001) have posed the question of what is specifically "counter" (and significant) about the discourse of *counter-publics*? Warning against the danger of simple classificatory schemas—the identification of counterpublics along lines of group identity, topics, or spheres as ontological markers—they proposed to foreground "counter" as a *qualifier* of "public," yielding "a rich and varied set of conceptual understandings" (Asen & Brouwer, 2001, p. 9). The point appears to be that the category of counter-public is not meant to be ontologically stable or even distinct from "movement," itself a discursive achievement. Rather, "counter-public" is seen as an analytic category that invites attention to the particular achievements of self-reflexive discourse as it aids in binding identifications and inventing the vocabularies of an opposition. For SMR critics, developments in counterpublic theory thus invited a "move toward multiplicity, the move to loosen borders" (Asen & Brouwer, 2001, p. 17).

In an important sense, critical study of NSMs and counterpublics appears to extend McGee's (1980, 1983) call to decenter the "movement" figure. In counterpublic studies, scholars have departed from leader-centered approaches and the assumption that movements are preconstituted entities. Instead, many critics turned to the self-initiated rhetorical acts of particular activists, street performers, antiapartheid theologians, HIV-AIDS 'zine writers, and others who, through their discursive inventions, position themselves in opposition to dominant publics. Still, as Brouwer (2006) reminds SMR scholars, the "precise contours" of counterpublics "have yet to be thoroughly elaborated" (p. 204). The same might be said of two other major trajectories in recent SMR scholarship—a critical, "performative turn" in understanding the body and its communicability; and emerging studies of "democracy" and new modalities of social protest in global society.

PERFORMING RESISTANCE: BODIES, IMAGES, AND PUBLIC SCREENS

Throughout the 1980s and 1990s, post-structuralist social theory became increasingly influential in scholarly conversations about rhetoric. Theoretical orientations debated by the early SMR scholars faded from research agendas as discourse fragmented and new modalities of protest and communication technologies eclipsed the traditional oration in cultural significance. Instead, SMR critics and rhetorical scholars generally explored texts as they denaturalized ideology, displaced meta-narratives, and disrupted cultural authority, often through pastiche and playfulness. For instance, Blair, Jeppeson, and Pucci (1991) adopted a "postmodern" perspective in reading the Vietnam Veterans Memorial as resisting "a single, signature style" (p. 266) and embodying dissent amid other memorials in Washington, D.C., through its "refusal of unities or universals" (p. 267).

A similar, postmodern perspective encouraged rhetorical critics to attend to the malleability and "polysemy" of texts (Ceccarelli, 1998) and ways in which modernist approaches privileged rationality and propositional rhetorics at the expense of other ways of knowing and acting in the world. Some found alliance with scholars in performance studies who urged recognition of the extrasymbolic, material character of human expression and the embodied and fluid nature of identity (Butler, 1990). Indeed, performance and rhetorical scholars have influenced each other's work in a growing body of scholarship on resistance and social change (e.g., Cohen-Cruz, 1998; Fuoss, 1997; Haedicke & Nellhaus, 2001; Kershaw, 1999; Pezzullo, 2003a, 2003b). Though not always identified with discrete "movements," two related areas have emerged that reflect a "performative turn": studies of bodies and material rhetoric and studies of visual rhetorics and images of the body in resistance.

Performance, Bodies, and Material Rhetoric

Like earlier critics of the "rhetoric of the streets," recent critics of social protest have argued that received frameworks are unable to explain the irrational (or a-rational), material, and embodied appearance of resistance as a public practice. Although rhetoric, since ancient times, has been a "bodily art" (Hawhee, 2004), its corporeal dimensions have been largely deemphasized over the centuries. However, by approaching resistance as *performance* or as *performed,* an emerging group of critics believe that they are better able to understand material and corporeal acts of dissent through their own logics or grammars. Furthermore, by foregrounding rhetorical *acts of resistance,* rather than the *social movement* figure, performance-based criticism has drawn closer to the hermeneutic objectives of some early SMR scholars.

An important marker of such studies is Fuoss's (1997) analysis of Depression-era labor strikes as cultural performances. These events, he argued, were "heightened occasions" (p. 173) that were both strategic and excessive. Strikers scheduled, publicized, and sequenced

their performances; they acknowledged the temporal and spatial contexts that established a stage for their events and constrained their ability to meet political ends. Yet such performances exceeded rhetors' strategic efforts for change, encouraging playfulness and escapism for those involved. By treating resistance (strikes, in this case) as a performance, SMR critics began to read "effects" beyond the strategic goals typically associated with social movements, considering instead the "liminal" state between instrumentality and aesthetics (Bruner, 2005, p. 140).

One site of resistance that has received much attention from both rhetorical and performance critics has been the growing antiglobalization or "global justice" movement against the neoliberal expansion of capital. For example, Bruner (2005) observed that protests at meetings of international capital (World Bank, International Monetary Fund, etc.) often become sites of resistance in which aspects of the "carnivalesque" occur. By carnivalesque, Bruner was referring to the historical experience of festivals that provided common people with opportunities to critique authority and hierarchy as well as experiment with identities and alternative possibilities for communal life. Bruner argued that the carnivalesque involves an embracing of the "fictive" (e.g., the wearing of masks, reversal of binaries, suspension of rank, and other hierarchies) in which the fluidity and "betweenness" of such play may (at times) prove powerful vis-à-vis the "humorless" logic of corrupt states. "The humorless state has a very difficult time dealing with absurdity, symbolic protest, and the curious blending of the fictive and the real," such as when environmentalists performed as sea turtles at the 1999 Seattle protests against the World Trade Organization (WTO) (p. 148). Such suspension of the "real," Bruner argued, enables "a temporary retextualizing of social formations that expose their 'fictive' foundations" (p. 139).

Though not treating resistance as a cultural performance, other scholars have used performance theory to create a more holistic methodology for appreciating acts of resistance beyond their linguistic components. For instance, Feldman's (1991) rich study of the Irish Republican Army (IRA) introduced the notion of a "biosymbolic complex" wherein the human body and its material practices, formations of space, and symbolic narratives intertwine to form a complicated rhetorical palette. Feldman's work with IRA prisoners suggested that the human body itself—not simply the significations that emanate from and surround it in the form of words, clothing, and artifacts—may become a wellspring of resistance.

Similarly, Pezzullo (2003a) foregrounded the display, movements, and disruptions of bodies in her analysis of the San Francisco–based Toxic Links Coalition (TLC) "tour" of agencies and institutions associated with environmental causes of cancer. (TLC is an alliance of women with cancer, cancer survivors, and other health and environmental groups.) By focusing on street performances of participants, Pezzullo attended to "the ways in which the body, affect, and desire disrupt the normative discursive logics of publics" (p. 351, quoting Deem, 2002, p. 448). The assumptions of performativity in work such as Feldman's and Pezzullo's invite critics to explore the rhetorical significance of the body and materiality as these interact with counterpublic narratives or as they stand as rhetorics on their own terms.

Moreover, the nature of some protests themselves has invited rhetorical critics to privilege the non- or extrasymbolic dimensions of protest. DeLuca (1999b), for example, has argued that radical groups such as EarthFirst!, ACT-UP, and Queer Nation "slight formal modes of public argument" and envision the ends of activism beyond "the conventional goals of electoral, legislative, legal, and material gains" (p. 9). Opel and Pompper's

(2003) *Representing Resistance* featured studies of antiglobalization protests that foreground the performative or rhetorical body as a key site of resistance. For example, Vanderford (2003) described the actions of the Italian collective YaBasta! as it ironically appropriated consumer culture to oppose neoliberal trade ideologies. The group transformed recycled trash and other artifacts such as "rubber duckie" inner tubes into symbolic armor to wear at protests. The appearance of activists standing down armed police, protected only by children's flotation devices, aided the public in understanding "on which side lay reason, and who started the violence" (p. 17). Like Bruner, Vanderford argued that "the laughter of carnival overcomes the seriousness of official culture as grotesque and blasphemous bodies displace reverence and dogmatism" (pp. 17–18).

Importantly, such critics insist that bodies are not, in any simple way, "determined or limited by verbal frames. . . . [They] exceed the protocols of deliberative reasoning" (DeLuca, 1999b, p. 12). Extending this critique to an assumption of earlier theory, DeLuca has argued that our understanding of the body cannot be limited to how it serves certain movement "functions": For instance, to treat bodily spectacles (e.g., Julia "Butterfly" Hill's living in an ancient redwood tree for 3 years) as simply "getting attention" diminishes the rhetorical power of the body. Alternatively, he proposed that critics understand the effects of "body rhetoric" in new ways. For instance, the body may materialize or challenge a dominant proposition. Protestors also "translate" their bodies into new signs of identification, such as when a tree sitter "'becomes' the tree" (p. 13). Finally, DeLuca argued that embodied presence may be "a direct response" to authority, a "NO" that impedes authority's ability to act with legitimacy (p. 17).

This last interpretation of the body points to an important, but potentially confounding, assumption in recent scholarship on resistance:

The human body is both symbolic and extrasymbolic, "enmeshed in a turbulent stream of multiple and conflictual discourses that shape what [it] mean[s] in particular contexts" (DeLuca, 1999b, p. 12) and presenting a "force" that makes it both "a sublime and contested site" (p. 17). Put differently, some critics have assumed that the body both represents strategic, linguistic persuasion and exceeds symbolic action through its bare material presence. In the 1960s, this tension between the body as symbolic and the body as material framed the debates over the "rhetoric of the streets," as rhetorical critics questioned whether Black Power or students' corporeal protest was "coercion" or "persuasion."

As rhetorical critics increasingly focus on the body in resistance, difficult questions remain: Is the *physical presence* of protestors "enough" to count as resistance? If we attempt to assess body rhetoric through the grammar of linguistic signs, do we reduce its corporeal power? Finally, can critics craft a conceptual vocabulary that respects the body as both *physis* and *nomos*, as material and symbolic? Similar questions might also be asked of the growing study of visual rhetorics and of mediated images of resistant bodies.

Image Events, Visual Rhetoric, and Public Screens

Like recent criticism of the body in resistance, studies of visual rhetoric depart from traditional interpretive frameworks in accounting for the impact of visually mediated rhetorics. While the former approaches its object of analysis by foregrounding the human body as it performs in concrete space, recent work in visual rhetoric foregrounds the *mediation* of bodies, in photographs, televised or hyperlinked images of resistance. We acknowledge that this distinction appears somewhat arbitrary; the emphasis, however, partly reflects a rupture in some critics' understanding of contemporary media culture

as a basis for understanding the significance of visual resistance. For DeLuca and Peeples (2002), for example, antiglobalization protests in 1999 dramatized a new sociopolitical world in which multinational corporations "eclips[e] the nation-state" and where television screens represent "the contemporary shape of the public sphere" (p. 126).

In this environment, DeLuca and Peeples argued, new conceptual resources become necessary to interpret newer forms of resistance. In particular, the Habermasian concept of the public sphere, grounded in visions of 18th-century salon conversations, privileged face-to-face communication, and embodied voices. As a result, they contended, public sphere scholarship "ignores the social and technological transformations of the 20th century" (p. 131). The advent of television and the Internet has "fundamentally transformed the media matrix that constitutes our social milieu, producing new forms of social organization and new modes of perception" (p. 131). New media, for example, flatten hierarchies and rely on "remediation" (the presence of one medium in another), while "disseminating" a distracting amount of information (p. 132).

Given these shifts, critics face new challenges in appreciating contemporary forms of resistance: "TV places a premium on images over words, emotions over rationality, speed over reflection, distraction over deliberation, slogans over arguments, the glance over the gaze, appearance over truth" (p. 133). With the *public screen*, critics are invited to appreciate, rather than dismiss, ways in which a resistant act "both participates in and punctures the habit of distraction characteristic of the contemporary mode of perception" (p. 145). Like the human body that may exceed and interrupt dominant discourses, images of resistance may "interrupt the flow . . . give pause . . . by making the mundane malevolent, the familiar fantastic" (p. 145).

Separately, DeLuca (1999a) has suggested that a particular form of rhetorical logic is gaining currency within the new media milieu, what he terms "image events." Such events work by "reducing a complex set of issues to [visual] symbols that break people's comfortable equilibrium" (p. 3); they are "mind bombs, that," quoting Manes (1990, p. 77), "work to expand 'the universe of thinkable thoughts'" (DeLuca, 1999a, p. 6). Image events—such as images of Greenpeace activists steering rubber rafts between whaling ships and whales—are typically invented through and with television, privileging the visual over the linguistic and deconstructive logics over propositional logics. DeLuca noted that, in earlier studies, visually mediated events "have tended not to be recognized as rhetorical acts working for social movement" (p. 58). That, however, is not the case in recent scholarship.

Like performance-oriented criticism of the body in resistance, a number of critics have attempted to account for the extralinguistic impacts of visual rhetoric within or surrounding the social movement context. For instance, Harold and DeLuca (2005) revisited the "haunting images" of Emmett Till, the black Chicago teenager who was brutally murdered while visiting his uncle in Money, Mississippi, in 1955. The Till case is remembered as a catalyst for the civil rights movement and remains in America's consciousness in no small part because of the photographs of Till's corpse and open-casket funeral: "The dissemination and reception of this image—of the severely mutilated face of a child—illustrates the rhetorical and political force of images in general and of the body specifically" (p. 266).

Echoing scholarship on the body, Harold and DeLuca argued that the image of Till's corpse "temporarily provokes a physical response that temporarily precedes and exceeds 'sense'" (p. 275). His corpse and its image provided "graphic testimony to the brutal race hatred in the 1950s south in a way that written text could never have done." (p. 274). It provided a point of articulation for

Southern and Northern blacks, and sympathetic whites; the images galvanized a movement. Harold and DeLuca's analysis, we suggest, points to an emerging line of interpretation regarding rhetoric's impact: "We would not suggest that the experience of viewing this body is easily described as an unproblematic *recognition* of one's self (and hence, one's vulnerability) in the corpse, but more of an inability to ignore the witnessing as an event— a rhetorical event that requires a response" (p. 280). In addition to "galvanizing" a movement, the body and its image prompt a form of subjectivity: such rhetoric moves people to witness.

In short, a major trajectory of recent scholarship has begun to explore acts of social protest within a performative context as corporeal, material, and, at times, as mediated resistance. However, we believe that questions remain as scholars continue this line of research: How do individual acts of resistance, such as image events, relate to movements more broadly, if not through function-alist vocabularies of "requirements" or the reconciling of competing "demands" of the movement? What are the effects of material, corporeal performances and mediated visual rhetoric? Are critics unduly isolating such acts of resistance from their discursive contexts or the "social movement" figure itself?

In an important sense, the relationship of discrete acts to broader movements raises questions more generally about the "possibilities of alternative terrains of practice, power, and politics" that increasingly define the experiences of cultural and mediated life in democracy (Best, 2005, p. 232). And, it is here, we believe, that a final, promising line of SMR scholarship is emerging.

DEMOCRACY, REPRESENTATION, AND NEW MODALITIES OF DISSENT

In addition to recent shifts in methods and the objects of study (e.g., bodies, images), there also has emerged scholarship that is rethinking democracy and the role of "representation" via new modalities of dissent within democracies. Much of the impetus for this scholarship derives from Hardt and Negri's (2000) provocative critique of representation in the altered logics of global society. In their ambitious work *Empire*, they argued that the global rise of a post-Fordist economy of "knowledge, information, communication, and affects" (p. 407) is leading to a form of "imperial" sovereignty, which infiltrates and infuses all realms of human life. Within this postmodern milieu, "the economic, political, and cultural increasingly overlap and invest one another" (p. xiii). In their subsequent work, *Multitude*, Hardt and Negri (2004) contend that only nonmodernist forms of resistance, or movements "whose constitution and action is based not on identity or unity" (p. 100), may effectively resist imperial sovereignty.

What implications do Hardt and Negri's theses have for the study of SMR? One that has only begun to be fleshed out, we believe, lies in their claim that resistance does not gain its power from traditional modes of representation—what they sometimes refer to as "mediation"—such as appeals to the nation-state, public sphere, or "identity" (Greene, 2004). Hardt and Negri (2000) propose, alternatively, that a new revolution will begin as the "multitude" (their figure of collective resistance) recovers a kind of *immanence* within *Empire*: "Through the cooperation, the collective existence, and the communicative networks that are formed and reformed within the multitude . . . the multitude reveals labor as the fundamental creative activity that . . . goes beyond any obstacle imposed on it and constantly re-creates the world" (pp. 401–402). Greene (2004) similarly argues that "human innovation and invention" (p. 170), particularly *rhetoric*, powers resistance.

Hardt and Negri's questioning of the "modern legacy of mediation" underwriting traditional ideas of citizenship (Greene, 2004,

p. 170) has opened new inquiry into the modalities of social protest occurring in democracies. Neoliberal orderings of democracies, particularly, are viewed as disempowering for citizenship and critical publicity. Institutions such as the World Bank and WTO, for example, seek "not to expand sites of public deliberation, and not to strengthen local democratic processes, but to accelerate the privatization of state-held assets ranging from telecommunications to mining to energy to water" (Bruner, 2003, p. 694). As the relationships among citizens, nation-states, and channels of dissent undergo change, SMR scholars have begun to broaden the scope of their inquiry by exploring alternative theories of democracy and their implications for social change.

At the forefront of such theories have been efforts to understand the move by contemporary protestors away from modes of representation and the traditional mediations of nation, political party, and identity, and toward new channels through which actors organize and speak. These new communication technologies (NCTs) tend to be more experiential, drawing on "everyday" forms and modes of democratic practices. In particular, NCTs work together to form "the base and the basis for" the activism by antiglobalization and other progressive movements (Kahn & Kellner, 2005, p. 88). For example, the digitized worlds of the blogosphere and Internet, as well as the expanding array of mobile technologies such as cell phones and PDAs (personal data assistants) have helped globalize local issues, form alliances, coordinate resistant actions, and circulate oppositional discourses (Kahn & Kellner, 2005; Russell, 2005).

Interestingly, as Stengrim (2005) suggests of the international Web network of independent media or "Indymedia," the grassroots use of NCTs performatively resists corporate globalization while it enables activists to dissent. Through "a multiplicity of subversive gestures that promote political activism, forward political critique, and take over the vehicles by which knowledge is produced and transferred" (p. 294), Indymedia challenges a growing, corporate monopoly of global media. Although critics should be wary of viewing NCTs as a panacea of democracy, Kahn and Kellner (2005) suggest that the evolving "technoculture make[s] possible . . . a refocusing of politics on everyday life" (p. 93).

Interestingly, contemporary activists not only employ new modalities to communicate and organize; their uses reflect the loose, hyperlinked, and immanent logics implicit in this networked environment (Pickard, 2006). Antiglobalization activists, for example, rely on the communicative fabric and logics of hyperlinks: "Networks are open structures, able to expand without limits, integrating new nodes as long as they are able to communicate within the network, namely as long as they share the same communication codes" (Castells, 1996, p. 470; quoted in Pickard, 2006, p. 319). The important difference for SMR scholars is that network structures diverge from the traditional forms of activism that rely on organization and long-lasting relationships (e.g., top-down or "leader-followers" movement structures). Networks ally, instead, with the fractured, fleeting, distracting environment of DeLuca and Peeples's (2002) "public screen."

In addition to rethinking movement organizing and modes of resistance, some SMR scholars are beginning to rethink "democracy." For instance, in considering the "globalization movement," Best (2005) shifts from a reliance on "New Social Movement" theories for evaluating movements. These, she argues, do not necessarily "further the necessary conditions of democracy, especially in relation to their constitution of public life and public space" (p. 215). Instead, she suggests, critics must first understand "the contemporary experiences and practice of democracy," itself (p. 215). Democracy, she

proposes, is not so much the constitution of a *sphere*, but an "assemblage of modes of material and discursive organizing designed to grant popular power" (p. 215).

Like Kahn and Kellner, Best (2005) believes that a theorization of democracy must begin with the "everyday" practices that make "democracy . . . a way of life" (p. 215, quoting Carey, 1997, p. 233). People increasingly experience democracy through the mediation of NCTs: "Democracy has evolved into an electronic/digital and visceral compound, lived and practiced through individual and collective levels of experience interwoven with mediated resources" (p. 221). Thus, while critics have chastised contemporary movements for failing to "provide for . . . the formation of public space" (p. 223), Best interprets the loosely organized, spectacular protests of the globalization movement as pushing toward democracy-as-practice, rather than democracy-as-space or sphere.

What might these new approaches hold for the study of movement rhetoric? For Best, theories of the everyday and cultural aspects of democracy offer "a map for scrutinizing new routes of power that traverse the daily, individualized, and highly mediated modes of contemporary democratic citizenship, a map [also] for subjecting these pathways of power to more specific and potentially constructive critique and reconstruction" (p. 232). In an important sense, scrutiny of such "new routes of power" invites renewed reflection regarding what constitutes "social movement rhetoric," and what are its relevant agents, modalities, and effects that may be related to social change.

CONTINUING STUDY OF SOCIAL MOVEMENT RHETORIC

In the last four decades, the study of SMR has broadened considerably, both in its modes of analysis and objects of study. The most obvious development has been the steady move from broad or a priori theories of the rhetoric of movements to a "critical pluralism" (Gaonkar, 2002, p. 410) that characterizes public discourse studies more broadly. This move has broadened critics' understanding of complex texts that enable both opponents and supporters of a dominant order to contest or bolster the discursive terms of power. To use Gaonkar's description, rhetorical critics now see the "object domain" of movement or resistance studies—whether a speech to supporters of a bus boycott, dissemination of a photograph, or a street performance—"as immensely rich and complex and almost coextensive with 'discourse' and 'discursivity' that calls for a flexible critical practice" (p. 411).

As SMR study has gained flexibility, the idea of a discrete "social movement" has become somewhat problematic. While not quite abandoning the reference, many critics increasingly are bracketing a focus on large collectivities in favor of specific texts, performative acts, or discursive interventions. In so doing, critics have expanded the field of rhetorical analysis and the conceptual or theoretical categories that inform their understanding of social change. Among the important changes characterizing the study of SMR over the last four decades have been the following:

1. A shift from an emphasis on *SMR* to the *rhetorical acts* or practices related to movements and their opponents. The distinction speaks to the interest of many critics in reading concrete practices in their own right, rather than as signs of a larger movement's "functions" (e.g., "getting attention").

2. An expanded understanding of the *audience(s)* and/or *objectives* of oppositional rhetorics, recognizing the multiple intentions or constitutive forces at work. Such multiple objectives include not only confronting state institutions or reforming laws but also challenging discursive norms that themselves sustain dominance. In addition, counterpublic theories have invited attention to the arenas in which marginal groups "invent and circulate counterdiscourses to formulate oppositional interpretations of their [own] identities, interests, and needs" (Fraser, 1992, p. 123).

3. A rethinking of the concept of *rhetoric* itself, beyond the binary of "reason" versus "coercion" that concerned early SMR scholars. This has led to a wider recognition of the linguistic and *non-* or *extra*linguistic modalities of social protest, including material, bodily, visual, and NCT-mediated rhetorics.

4. An embrace of *plural, critical modes of analysis,* drawing from a wide range of conceptual and theoretical perspectives appropriate to the varied linguistic and extralinguistic forms of dissent.

5. An implicit shift in theorizing the efficacy or *effect* of the rhetorical acts of movements. Because this latter development raises a number of questions for continuing study of movement rhetoric, we return to it below.

We expect the study of SMR will continue to broaden its scope and modes of analysis as groups make use of new communication technologies and other "new routes of power" (Best, 2005). As these studies unfold, we note two challenges for SMR scholars: (1) a more systematic analysis of non-Western movements and perspectives, and (2) an effort to theorize more explicitly the *effects* of social movement or "resistant" rhetorics.

Non-Western Movements and Perspectives

Despite recent interest in "Indymedia" networks and the global justice movement (Best, 2005; Bruner, 2005; Opel & Pompper, 2003; Stengrim, 2005), rhetorical critics have paid slight attention to social movements in other regions of the world. Neither Simons, Mechling, and Schreier's (1984) extensive review of SMR studies nor Morris and Browne's (2006) recently updated collection includes studies of movements in non-Western cultures. The reason may not be hard to discern. Apart from the Chartist and early

British peace movements (Andrews, 1967a, 1967b, 1973), the principal focus of SMR critics in the past four decades has been U.S. movements.[4] Similarly, critics have been slow to appreciate non-Western perspectives for the study of movement discourse. Carabas (2003), for example, noted that rhetorical scholarship on counterpublics "use[s] mostly Western concepts and employ[s] the tools of liberal democracy as the default mode of thinking about the relationship between the state and marginalized communities" (p. 170).[5]

The failure largely to include non-Western case studies and perspectives remains a challenge for the study of SMR. This is particularly relevant in light of controversies surrounding the effects of economic globalization in many Third World nations. For example, Doyle (2005) noted the "profound difference" between U.S. and Philippine environmental movements in his study of resistance in the Philippines against multinational mining companies. The latter, he observed, were "more revolutionary," pursuing radically different strategies of resistance against multinational corporate behaviors (p. 50). Relatedly, Keck and Sikkink (1998) have drawn attention to the emergence of transnational networks of advocates that coordinate their work on human rights, environment, violence against women, and other concerns. Although some communication scholars (Dempsey, 2007; Garrido & Halavais, 2003; Kowal, 2002) have begun to examine this mode, SMR critics—with the exception of anti-globalization networks—have largely ignored such alliances.

Theorizing "Effect" in SMR Studies

Social movements arise ostensibly to effect change—whether to reform unjust laws, throw off an oppressive regime, or rewrite discursive or normative practices. It was inevitable, therefore, that SMR critics would face questions of *efficacy:* How do the rhetorical acts of movements "matter"? In some ways, however, the question of efficacy remains the white elephant in the room as scholars often ignore the conceptual ambiguities in the vocabulary and categories for assessing the consequential nature of movement and, particularly, "resistant" rhetoric. As a result, a number of questions remain: In what ways are the linguistic and extralinguistic acts of activists related to changes (if any) in law, policy, prevailing discourses, activists' identities, or interests? If historical events are overdetermined or the result of multiple and complex causes, can SMR scholars speak intelligibly about "effects" at all? What are the conceptual or theoretical challenges in specifying *rhetorical* effects, instead of external policy or historical effects?

Early SMR scholars seldom raised questions about the conceptual bases for an assessment of "effects." For example, Griffin (1952) set the tone when he invited critics to evaluate the "effectiveness" of a movement's rhetoric simply in terms of "the ends projected by the speakers and writers" and "the theories of rhetoric and public opinion indigenous to the times" (p. 187). In a similar vein, Simons (1970) proposed that the "primary rhetorical test" of a leader and of the strategies chosen was their ability to fulfill the movement's "functional requirements" by resolving or reducing the dilemmas or conflicts among these functions (p. 2).

Early assessments of effect assumed a *strategic* context in which movements or their leaders were seen as achieving or failing to achieve state or other institutional outcomes (civil rights legislation, campus reform, etc.). Yet few, if any, critics provided an account of how rhetorical acts or utterances were articulated to these external events. In their survey of rhetorical studies of movements from 1968 to 1977, Simons et al. (1984) found that although these studies "had little difficulty pronouncing judgments of success or failure, they did not always indicate clearly what they meant by these terms" (p. 845). Perhaps recognizing the complex processes in such outcomes, they observed that "the rhetoric of social movements may sometimes be a necessary condition for social change, but it is never a sufficient condition" (p. 836).

By the 1990s and early 2000s, critics had largely abandoned broad claims about the "effects" of a movement's rhetoric. Instead, SMR critics turned to descriptions of "resistance" or characterized particular discursive acts or performances as "resistant," "destabilizing," "transgressive," or some other attribute. DeLuca (1999b), for example, noted that, within the context of homophobia, "by their very presence at a protest the [gay rights] activists are enacting a defiant rhetoric of resistance" (p. 17). And, in describing street performances protesting a festival's honoring of Andrew Jackson, Schriver and Nudd (2002) explained, "By infiltrating the parade we hoped to destabilize the spectacle of whitewashed history" (p. 213). Although long a theme in cultural theory and media studies (Scott, 1990; Williams, 1977), references to "resistance" and its variants now began to appear in rhetorical and performative accounts of movements (Houston & Kramarae, 1991; Jordan, 2003; Kennedy, 1999; Opel & Pompper, 2003; Sanger, 1995). While this move may promise a more nuanced understanding, few critics have offered an account of actual processes of influence of a "resistant" act. Among the more promising, we believe, is Harold and DeLuca's (2005) account of the "rhetorical force" occasioned by the dissemination and reception of the images of the mutilated corpse of Emmett Till (see above).

Nevertheless, the move to describe oppositional acts or texts as "resistant" or "destabilizing" assumes a theory of effectivity still largely absent from SMR scholarship. As a result, key questions remain for critics: How is "resistance" related to power? In praising "resistant acts" are SMR critics "settling' for cultural raids" (Cloud, 2001, p. 244) while larger systems of dominance remain in place? In what ways are acts of "resistance" articulated to wider discursive codes and/or changes in material or political conditions?

CONCLUSION

As we have seen in this chapter, the scholarship of SMR has developed into a diverse, critically flexible literature driven by the (often) unorthodox voices of social change. As such, SMR scholars have pushed the understanding of rhetoric and public discourse beyond its rational, propositional, and linguistic roots. Through their analyses, rhetoric and public discourse scholars have developed the vocabularies and critical methods offering students and other scholars a means to understand some of the relevant sources of social change. These approaches have shifted the critic's focus from discrete social movement figures to discursive fields (see Wilson, 2005) and arenas (e.g., counterpublics), diverse channels of mediation (e.g., the body, visual images, and NCTs), and performances of democracy in and through which social change occurs. In the end, we believe, a robust theory of the efficacy or impact of rhetorical acts in oppositional struggles holds the greatest promise for continued development and contribution of SMR scholarship. For beyond simple accounts of "resistance" lies the possibility of understanding the relationships among discursive acts, power, and the sources of social and political transformation.

NOTES

1. See the special issues devoted to rhetorical analyses of Dr. King's "Letter" from Birmingham jail (*Rhetoric & Public Affairs*, 7(1), 2004) and the 50th anniversary of the murder of Emmett Till and Rosa Parks' refusal to give up her seat on a Montgomery bus (*Rhetoric & Public Affairs*, 8(2), 2005).

2. Despite the heuristic of Fraser's observation and rise of new struggles around gender, race, sexuality, and other concerns of "recognition," the claim that such movements were "merely cultural," not having economic or material implications, drew sharp criticism, most notably from Judith Butler (1997) (for a response, see Fraser, 1997a).

3. Some rhetorical scholars had called attention earlier to the discursive achievement of marginal groups in articulating their own interests or identities. See, particularly, Gregg's (1971) thesis of an "ego-function" of protest rhetorics, and Lake's (1983, 1991) studies of the "ritual self-address" of Native American rhetorics.

4. Notable exceptions include Doxtader's (2001) analysis of the civil and theological uses of "reconciliation" as forms of resistance against apartheid in South Africa; Fabj's (1993, 1998) studies of the defiance of Italian women against the Mafia and the rhetoric of the Mothers of Plaza De Mayo in Buenos Aires, Argentina; and Cloud's (2001) thesis that the economy and nation-state remain as important sites of struggle in the 1998 revolt in Indonesia.

5. One important exception is the study of ethnic protests within the United States that draw on rhetorical traditions reflecting the cultural or national heritage of these groups (Dicochea, 2004; Hammerback, Jensen, & Gutiérrez, 1985; Lake, 1983, 1991; Wong, 1992). For example, Hammerback and Jensen (1994) draw on traditions of the "proclamation" in Mexican social upheavals to assess Chicano protests and organizing by farm workers in the United States in the 1960s and 1970s.

REFERENCES

Andrews, J. R. (1967a). The ethos of pacifism: The problem of image in the early British peace movement. *Quarterly Journal of Speech, 53,* 28–33.

Andrews, J. R. (1967b). Piety and pragmatism: Rhetorical aspects of the early British peace movement. *Communication Monographs, 34,* 423–436.

Andrews, J. R. (1969). Confrontation at Columbia: A case study in coercive rhetoric. *Quarterly Journal of Speech, 55,* 9–16.

Andrews, J. R. (1973). The passionate negation: The chartist movement in rhetorical perspective. *Quarterly Journal of Speech, 59,* 198–208.

Andrews, J. R. (1980). History and theory in the study of the rhetoric of social movements. *Central States Speech Journal, 31,* 274–281.

Asen, R. (2000). Seeking the "counter" in counterpublics. *Communication Theory, 10,* 424–446.

Asen, R., & Brouwer, D. C. (2001). *Counterpublics and the state.* Albany: State University of New York Press.

Best, K. (2005). Rethinking the globalization movement: Toward a cultural theory of contemporary democracy and communication. *Communication and Critical/Cultural Studies, 2,* 214–237.

Blair, C., Jeppeson, M. S., & Pucci, E., Jr. (1991). Public memorializing in postmodernity: The Vietnam Veterans Memorial as prototype. *Quarterly Journal of Speech, 77,* 263–288.

Brouwer, D. C. (2001). ACT-ing UP in congressional hearings. In R. Asen & D. C. Brouwer (Eds.), *Counterpublics and the state* (pp. 87–109). Albany: State University of New York Press.

Brouwer, D. C. (2005). Counterpublicity and corporeality in HIV/AIDS zines. *Critical Studies in Media Communication, 22,* 351–371.

Brouwer, D. C. (2006). Communication as counterpublic. In G. J. Shepherd, J. St. John, & T. Striphas (Eds.), *Communication as . . . Perspectives on theory* (pp. 195–208). Thousand Oaks, CA: Sage.

Bruner, M. L. (2003). Global governance and the critical public. *Rhetoric & Public Address, 6,* 687–708.

Bruner, M. L. (2005). Carnivalesque protest and the humorless state. *Text and Performance Quarterly, 25,* 136–155.

Burgess, P. G. (1968). The rhetoric of black power: A moral demand? *Quarterly Journal of Speech, 54,* 122–133.

Burgess, P. G. (1970). The rhetoric of moral conflict: Two critical dimensions. *Quarterly Journal of Speech, 56,* 120–130.

Butler, J. (1990). *Gender trouble: Feminism and the subversion of identity.* New York: Routledge.

Butler, J. (1997). Merely cultural. *Social Text, 52–53,* 265–277.

Campbell, K. K. (1973). The rhetoric of women's liberation: An oxymoron. *Quarterly Journal of Speech, 59,* 74–86.

Carabas, T. (2003). Review of "*Counterpublics and the state.*" *Southern Communication Journal, 68,* 169–170.

Castells, M. (1996). *The rise of network society.* Malden, MA: Blackwell.

Cathcart, R. S. (1972). New approaches to the study of movements: Defining movements rhetorically. *Western Speech, 36,* 82–88.

Cathcart, R. S. (1978). Movements: Confrontation as rhetorical form. *Southern Speech Communication Journal, 43,* 233–247.

Ceccarelli, L. (1998). Polysemy: Multiple meanings in rhetorical criticism. *Quarterly Journal of Speech, 84,* 395–406.

Cloud, D. L. (2001). Doing away with Suharto—and the twin myths of globalization and new social movements. In R. Asen & D. C. Brouwer (Eds.), *Counterpublics and the state* (pp. 235–263). Albany: State University of New York Press.

Cohen-Cruz, J. (Ed.). (1998). *Radical street performance: An international anthology.* London: Routledge.

Darsey, J. (1991). From "Gay is good" to the scourge of AIDS: The evolution of gay liberation rhetoric, 1977–1990. *Communication Studies, 42,* 43–66.

Deem, M. (2002). Stranger sociability, public hope, and the limits of political transformation. *Quarterly Journal of Speech, 88,* 444–454.

DeLuca, K. M. (1999a). *Image politics: The new rhetoric of environmental activism.* New York: Guilford Press.

DeLuca, K. M. (1999b, Summer). Unruly arguments: The body rhetoric of Earth First!, Act Up, and Queer Nation. *Argumentation and Advocacy, 36,* 9–21.

DeLuca, K. M., & Peeples, J. (2002). From public sphere to public screen: Democracy, activism, and the "violence" of Seattle. *Critical Studies in Media Communication, 19*(2), 125–151.

Dempsey, S. E. (2007). Towards a critical organizational approach to civil society contexts: A case study of the difficulties of transnational advocacy. In B. J. Allen, L. A. Flores, & M. P. Orbe (Eds.), *The international and intercultural communication annual: Communicating within/across organizations* (Vol. 30, pp. 317–339). Washington, DC: National Communication Association.

Dicochea, P. R. (2004). Chicana critical rhetoric: Recrafting *la causa* in Chicana movement discourse, 1970–1979. *Frontiers: A Journal of Women Studies, 25,* 77–92.

Doxtader, E. (2001). In the name of reconciliation: The faith and works of counterpublicity. In R. Asen & D. C. Brouwer (Eds.), *Counterpublics and the state* (pp. 59–85). Albany: State University of New York Press.

Doyle, T. (2005). *Environmental movements in majority and minority worlds.* New Brunswick, NJ: Rutgers University Press.

Fabj, V. (1993). Motherhood as political voice: The rhetoric of the mothers of Plaza De Mayo. *Communication Studies, 44,* 1–18.

Fabj, V. (1998). Intolerance, forgiveness, and promise in the rhetoric of conversion: Italian women defy the Mafia. *Quarterly Journal of Speech, 84,* 190–208.

Feldman, A. (1991). *Formations of violence: The narrative of the body and political terror in Northern Ireland.* Chicago: University of Chicago Press.

Felski, R. (1989). *Beyond feminist aesthetics: Feminist literature and social change.* Cambridge: Harvard University Press.

Fraser, N. (1992). Rethinking the public sphere: A contribution to the critique of actually existing democracy. In C. Calhoun (Ed.), *Habermas and the public sphere* (pp. 109–142). Cambridge: MIT Press.

Fraser, N. (1997a). Heterosexism, misrecognition, and capitalism: A response to Judith Butler. *Social Text, 52/53,* 279–289.

Fraser, N. (1997b). *Justice interruptus: Critical reflections on the "post-socialist" condition.* New York. Routledge.

Fuoss, K. (1997). *Striking performances/Performing strikes.* Jackson: University Press of Mississippi.

Gaonkar, D. P. (2002). Introduction [The Forum: Public and counterpublics]. *Quarterly Journal of Speech, 88,* 410–412.

Garrido, M., & Halavais, A. (2003). Mapping networks of support for the Zapatista movement: Applying social network analysis to study contemporary social movements. In

M. McCaughey & M. Ayers (Eds.), *Cyberactivism: Critical practices and theories of online activism* (pp. 165–184). Routledge: New York.

Greene, R. (2004). The concept of global citizenship in Michael Hardt and Antonio Negri's *Empire*: A challenge to three ideas of rhetorical mediation. In G. A. Hauser & A. Grim (Eds.), *Rhetorical democracy: Discursive practices of civic engagement* (pp. 165–171). Mahwah, NJ: Lawrence Erlbaum.

Gregg, R. B. (1971). The ego-function of the rhetoric of protest. *Philosophy and Rhetoric, 4,* 71–91.

Griffin, L. M. (1952). The rhetoric of historical movements. *Quarterly Journal of Speech, 38,* 184–188.

Griffin, L. M. (1969). A dramatistic theory of the Rhetoric of movements. In W. H. Rueckert (Ed.), *Critical responses to Kenneth Burke, 1922–1966* (pp. 456–478). Minneapolis: University of Minnesota Press.

Griffin, L. M. (1980). On studying movements. *Central States Speech Journal, 31,* 225–232.

Habermas, J. (1981). New social movements. *Telos, 49,* 33–37.

Habermas, J. (1989). *The structural transformation of the public sphere* (T. Burger, Trans.). Cambridge, MA: MIT Press. (Original work published 1962)

Haedicke, S. C., & Nellhaus, T. (Eds.). (2001). *Performing democracy: International perspectives on urban community-based performance.* Ann Arbor: University of Michigan Press.

Hahn, D. F., & Gonchar, R. M. (1971). Studying social movements: A rhetorical methodology. *Speech Teacher, 20*(1), 44–52.

Haiman, F. S. (1967). The rhetoric of the streets: Some legal and ethical considerations. *Quarterly Journal of Speech, 53,* 99–114.

Hammerback, J. C., & Jensen, R. J. (1994). Ethnic heritage as rhetorical legacy: The plan of Delano. *Quarterly Journal of Speech, 80,* 53–70.

Hammerback, J. C., Jensen, R. J., & Gutiérrez, J. A. (1985). *A war of words: Chicano protest of the 1960s and 1970s.* Westport, CT: Greenwood Press.

Hardt, M., & Negri, A. (2000). *Empire.* Cambridge, MA: Harvard University Press.

Hardt, M. & Negri, A. (2004). *Multitude: War and democracy in the age of empire.* New York: Penguin.

Harold, C., & DeLuca, K. M. (2005). Behold the corpse: Violent images and the case of Emmett Till. *Rhetoric & Public Affairs, 8,* 263–286.

Hawhee, D. (2004). *Bodily arts: Rhetoric and athletics in ancient Greece.* Austin: University of Texas.

Henry, D., & Jensen, R. J. (1991). Social movement criticism and the renaissance of public address. *Communication Studies, 42,* 83–93.

Houston, M., & Kramarae, C. (1991). Speaking from silence: Methods of silencing and of resistance. *Discourse and Society, 2,* 387–399.

Jordan, J. W. (2003). Sabotage or performed compliance? Rhetorics of resistance in temp worker discourse. *Quarterly Journal of Speech, 89,* 19–40.

Kahn, R., & Kellner, D. (2005). Oppositional politics and the Internet: A critical/reconstructive approach. *Cultural Politics: An International Journal, 1,* 75–100.

Keck, M. E., & Sikkink, K. (1998). *Activists beyond borders: Advocacy networks in international politics.* Ithaca, NY: Cornell University Press.

Kennedy, K. (1999). Cynic rhetoric: The ethics and tactics of resistance. *Rhetoric Review, 18,* 26–45.

Kershaw, B. (1999). *The radical in performance: Between Brecht and Baudrillard.* London: Routledge.

Kowal, D. (2002). Digitizing and globalizing indigenous voices: The Zapatista movement. In G. Elmer (Ed.), *Critical perspectives on the Internet* (pp. 105–126). Lanham, MD: Rowman Littlefield.

Lake, R. A. (1983). Enacting red power: The consummatory function in Native American protest rhetoric. *Quarterly Journal of Speech, 69,* 127–142.

Lake, R. A. (1991). Between myth and history: Enacting time in Native American protest rhetoric. *Quarterly Journal of Speech, 77,* 123–151.

Landes, J. (1988). *Women and the public sphere in the age of the French revolution.* Ithaca, NY: Cornell University Press.

Lucas, S. E. (1980). Coming to terms with movement studies. *Central States Communication Journal, 31,* 255–266.

Lucas, S. E. (1988). The renaissance of American public address: Text and context in rhetorical criticism. *Quarterly Journal of Speech, 75,* 241–260.

Maddux, K. (2004). When patriots protest: The anti-suffrage discursive transformation of 1917. *Rhetoric & Public Affairs, 7,* 283–310.

Manes, C. (1990). *Green rage: Radical environmentalism, and the unmaking of civilization.* Boston: Little, Brown.

Mansbridge, J. (1996). Using power/fighting power. In S. Benhabib (Ed.), *Democracy and difference: Contesting the boundaries of the political* (pp. 46–66). Princeton, NJ: Princeton University Press.

McCarthy, J. D., & Zald, M. (1977). Resource mobilization and social movements: A partial theory. *American Journal of Sociology, 82,* 1212–1241.

McDorman, T. F. (2001). Crafting a virtual counterpublic: Right-to-die advocates on the Internet. In R. Asen & D. C. Brouwer (Eds.), *Counterpublics and the state* (pp. 187–209). Albany: State University of New York Press.

McGee, M. C. (1980). "Social movement": Phenomenon or meaning? *Central States Speech Journal, 31,* 233–244.

McGee, M. C. (1983). Social movement as meaning. *Central States Speech Journal, 34,* 74–77.

Melucci, A. (1985). The symbolic challenge of contemporary movements. *Social Research, 52,* 789–815.

Morris, C. E., III, & Browne, S. H. (2006). *Readings on the rhetoric of social protest* (2nd ed.). State College, PA: Strata.

Negt, O., & Kluge, A. (1993). *Public sphere and experience: Towards analysis of the bourgeois and proletarian public sphere* (P. Labanyi, J. O. Daniel, & A. Oksiloff, Trans.). Minneapolis: University of Minnesota Press. (Original work published 1972)

Offe, C. (1985). New social movements: Challenging the boundaries of institutional politics. *Social Research, 52,* 817–868.

Opel, A., & Pompper, D. (Eds.). (2003). *Representing resistance: Media, civil disobedience, and the global justice movement.* Westport, CT: Praeger.

Palczewski, C. H. (2001). Cyber-movements, new social movements, and counter-publics. In D. C. Brouwer & R. Asen (Eds.), *Counterpublics and the state* (pp. 161–186). New York: State University of New York Press.

Pezzullo, P. C. (2003a). Resisting "National Breast Cancer Awareness Month": The rhetoric of counterpublics and their cultural performances. *Quarterly Journal of Speech, 89,* 345–365.

Pezzullo, P. C. (2003b). Touring "cancer alley," Louisiana: Performances of community and memory for environmental justice. *Text and Performance Quarterly, 23,* 226–252.

Pickard, V. W. (2006). United yet autonomous: Indymedia and the struggle to sustain a radical democratic network. *Media, Culture, & Society, 28,* 315–336.

Russell, A. (2005). Myth and the Zapatista movement: Exploring a network identity. *New Media & Society, 17,* 559–577.

Sanger, K. L. (1995). Slave resistance and rhetorical self-definition: Spirituals as a strategy. *Western Journal of Communication, 59,* 177–192.

Schriver, K., & Nudd, D. M. (2002). Mickee Faust Club's performative protest events. *Text & Performance Quarterly, 22,* 196–216.

Scott, J. C. (1990). *Domination and the arts of resistance: Hidden transcripts.* New Haven, CT: Yale University Press.

Scott, R. L., & Smith, D. K. (1969). The rhetoric of confrontation. *Quarterly Journal of Speech, 55,* 1–8.

Sillars, M. O. (1980). Defining movements rhetorically: Casting the widest net. *Southern Speech Communication Journal, 46,* 17–32.

Simons, H. W. (1970). Requirements, problems, and strategies: A theory of persuasion for social movements. *Quarterly Journal of Speech, 56,* 1–11.

Simons, H. W. (1980). On terms, definitions, and theoretical distinctiveness: Comments on papers by McGee and Zarefsky. *Central States Speech Journal, 31,* 306–315.

Simons, H. W., Mechling, E. W., & Schreier, H. N. (1984). The functions of human communication in mobilizing for action from the bottom up: The rhetoric of social movements. In C. C. Arnold & J. W. Bowers (Eds.), *Handbook of rhetoric and communication theory* (pp. 792–867). Boston: Allyn & Bacon.

Smith, R. R., & Windes, R. R. (1975). The innovational movement: A rhetorical theory. *Quarterly Journal of Speech, 61,* 140–153.

Squires, C. (2001). The black press and the state. In R. Asen & D. C. Brouwer (Eds.), *Counterpublics and the state* (pp. 111–136). Albany: State University of New York Press.

Stengrim, L. A. (2005). Negotiating postmodern democracy, political activism, and knowledge production: Indymedia's grassroots and e-savvy answer to media oligopoly. *Communication and Critical/Cultural Studies, 2,* 281–304.

Stewart, C. J. (1980). A functional approach to the rhetoric of social movements. *Central States Speech Journal, 31,* 298–305.

Stewart, C. J. (1983). A functional perspective on the study of social movements. *Central States Speech Journal, 34,* 77–80.

Vanderford, A. (2003). Ya Basta! A mountain of bodies that advances, seeking the least harm possible to itself. In A. Opel & D. Pompper (Eds.), *Representing resistance: Media, civil disobedience, and the global justice movement* (pp. 16–26). Westport, CT: Praeger.

Warner, M. (2002a). *Publics and counterpublics.* New York: Zone Books.

Warner, M. (2002b). Publics and counterpublics (abbreviated version). *Quarterly Journal of Speech, 88,* 413–425.

Wilkinson, C. A. (1976). A rhetorical definition of movements. *Central States Speech Journal, 27,* 88–94.

Williams, R. (1977). *Marxism and literature.* Oxford, UK: Oxford University Press.

Wilson, K. H. (2005). Interpreting the discursive field of the Montgomery bus boycott: Martin Luther King Jr.'s Holt Street address. *Rhetoric & Public Affairs, 8,* 299–326.

Windt, T. O., Jr. (1972). The diatribe: Last resort for protest. *Quarterly Journal of Speech, 72,* 1–14.

Wong, K. (1992). A fitting rhetorical response: Asian American social protest of the 1960s and 1970s. In J. C. Hammerback & P. M. Fitts (Eds.), *Conference in rhetorical criticism, 1990–1991: Addresses of the conference and commended papers* (pp. 12–19). Hayward: California State University.

Zarefsky, D. (1980). A skeptical view of movement studies. *Central States Speech Journal, 31,* 245–254.

Author Index

Author Index

U.S. public discourse, 1860–1900 and, 530, 531,
532, 533, 534
Johnson, R. H., 109, 117
Johnston, H., 437
Johnstone, C. L., 43, 47, 564, 569
Johnstone, H., 408, 487
Jones, C., 256, 310n 4, 310n 7
Jones, J., 142
Jones, J. M., 555, 558, 569
Jones, J. L., 443
Jones, J. P., 597
Jones, S., 497
Jones, S. G., 557
Jordan, J. W., 228, 622
Jordan, M. A., 143
Jordan, M. D., 135n 2
Jost, W., 126, 555
Journet, D., 182
Joyce, J., 218
Judis, J., 96
Jung, J., 147, 310n 6
Just, M. R., 591

Kachru, B., 309
Kahl, M. L., 24
Kahn, R., 598, 618, 619
Kann, M., 279
Kant, I., 85, 86, 259
Kari, C. J., 556
Kastely, J. L., 157, 159, 162n 4
Kates, S., 77
    civic engagement curriculum and, 377
    composition and, 310n 5
    feminist rhetoric and, 145
    historiography and, 21
    U.S. public discourse, 1860–1900 and, 531, 534
Katriel, T., 397
Katula, R. A., 37
Katz, S., 180, 267
Kaufer, D., 500
Kaveny, M. C., 559
Kavoori, A., 595
Kean, A., 271
Kearney, M., 271
Keck, M. E., 249, 621
Keehner, M., 97
Keith, W., 14, 93, 169, 322, 323, 324, 416,
417, 480
Keller, E. F., 181, 186, 235
Kellner, D., 278, 598, 618, 619
Kellner, H., 62
Kells, M., 307
Kempe, M., 41, 57
Kémpton, D., 56
Kendall, A., 183
Kendall, C., 635
Kennedy, D. M., 546
Kennedy, G. A., xxv, 1, 2, 4, 36, 37, 39, 63n 1,
67, 69, 104, 131

comparative rhetoric and, 154, 155, 159, 163n 25
historical rhetoric and, 40
historiography and, 15, 17, 23, 24, 25, 26, 27, 29
Medieval/Renaissance women rhetoricians and, 56
New Testament rhetoric and, 129
women rhetoricians and, 53
Kennedy, J. F., 479
Kennedy, K., 622
Kennedy, P. S., 469
Kenney, K., 392
Kennicott, P. C., 466, 467, 564
Kenski, H. C., 591
Kenyon, A. M., 397
Keränen, L., 228, 232
Kerber, L. K., 546
Keremidchieva, Z. D., 427, 428, 635
Kersey, S. N., 57, 60
Kershaw, B., 614
Kessler, J. H., 186
Keyes, C. F., 560
Khagram, S., 253
Khatami, M., 255
Kidd, J. S., 186
Kidd, R., 186
Kiesler, S., 499, 500, 502
Kiewe, A., 443, 546, 554, 594
Kijak, L., 233
Kimball, B. A., 163n 17
Kimble, J. J., 530, 533
Kincaid, J., 554, 564
King, A. A., 466, 467, 469, 470
King, M. L. Jr.
    historiography and, 21
    Medieval/Renaissance women rhetoricians
        and, 59
    orality theory and, 365
    public discourse and, 442
    racial conflict and, 466, 467
    revolutionary-era public letters and, 514
    social movements and, 605, 622n 1
King, P. E., 560
King, R. D., 546
King, S., 231
Kinneavy, J. L., 40, 130, 410
Kinsella, W. J., 250
Kintgen, R., 336
Kipling, R., 526
Kirkpatrick, A., 162n 6
Kirkpatrick, J. J., 250
Kirkwood, W. G., 555
Kitchin, G. W., 225
Kitzhaber, A. R., 15
Klamer, A., 201, 202
Klein, J. T., 172, 278, 635–636
    interdisciplinary inquiry and, 266, 270, 273,
        275, 276
Klein, R. D., 62
Klemm, D. E., 555
Klibanoff, H., 467

Subject Index

About the Editors

Andrea A. Lunsford is the Louise Hewlett Nixon Professor of English, Director of the Program in Writing and Rhetoric at Stanford University, and a member of the faculty of The Bread Loaf Graduate School of English. She has designed and taught undergraduate and graduate courses in writing history and theory, rhetoric, literacy studies, and intellectual property and is the author or coauthor of many books and articles, including *The Everyday Writer; Essays on Classical Rhetoric and Modern Discourse; Singular Texts/Plural Authors: Perspectives on Collaborative Writing; Reclaiming Rhetorica: Women in the History of Rhetoric; Everything's an Argument; Exploring Borderlands: Composition and Postcolonial Studies,* and *Writing Matters: Rhetoric in Public and Private Lives.*

Kirt H. Wilson is Associate Professor and Director of Graduate Studies in the University of Minnesota's Communication Studies Department. Winner of the National Communication Association's New Investigator Award (2001) and the Karl R. Wallace Memorial Award (2002), he is the author of *The Reconstruction Desegregation Debate.* He is currently working on two book manuscripts— first, a study of the theory and practices of imitation in the 19th century and, second, a study of the sentimental aesthetics in contemporary commemorations of the civil rights movement.

Rosa A. Eberly is Associate Professor in the departments of Communication and English and a Fellow of the Laboratory for Public Scholarship and Democracy at Pennsylvania State University. She is the author of *Citizen Critics: Literary Public Spheres, The Elements of Reasoning,* and studies on rhetoric, civic engagement, and public scholarship in journals such as *Rhetoric and Public Affairs, Rhetoric Review,* and *New Directions for Teaching and Learning.*

About the Contributors

Smiljana Antonijevic is completing her Ph.D. in Rhetoric at the University of Minnesota, specializing in Internet studies. Her research focuses on social aspects of information and communication technologies, virtual ethnography, and nonverbal communication in virtual environments. She is a coeditor of *Into the Blogosphere: Rhetoric, Community, and Culture of Weblogs;* she has published several book chapters and peer-reviewed articles in the field of Internet studies.

Jarrod Atchison is Assistant Professor of Speech Communication and the Director of Debate at Trinity University. His primary research interest concerns 19th-century public address with a focus on the public discourse of Confederate President Jefferson Davis. A secondary research interest stems from his position as Director of Debate, which involves publishing debate theory pieces designed to improve the practice of intercollegiate debate in the United States. His research has been published in the *Quarterly Journal of Speech* and *Women's Studies in Communication.*

James Arnt Aune is Professor of Communication at Texas A&M University. His research focuses on the historical sociology of rhetoric, especially the interaction between rhetoric and the technical discourses of economics and law. He is the author or editor of four books: *Rhetoric and Marxism* (1994), *Selling the Free Market* (2001), *Civil Rights Rhetoric and the American Presidency* (2004),

and *The Prospect of Presidential Rhetoric* (2008). He is also the editor of *Free Speech Yearbook.*

David Beard is Assistant Professor of Writing Studies at the University of Minnesota Duluth. His research approaches rhetoric at the intersection of disciplines of communication, composition, and philosophy. He has published essays in *Philosophy and Rhetoric, Southern Communication Journal, Reference and User Services Quarterly, Quarterly Journal of Speech,* and in several anthologies in rhetoric and composition. He has served as editor of the *International Journal of Listening* and coeditor of the collected edition of *Advances in the History of Rhetoric: The First Six Years* with Richard Enos. He is currently working on a book on I. A. Richards and the Anglo-American roots of the New Rhetoric.

Vanessa B. Beasley (Ph.D., University of Texas) is Associate Professor of Communication Studies at Vanderbilt University. She is the author of *You, the People: American National Identity in Presidential Rhetoric* and editor of *Who Belongs in America: Presidents, Rhetoric and Immigration.* Her research has also been published in *Quarterly Journal of Speech, Rhetoric & Public Affairs, Communication Monographs, Political Communication,* and elsewhere. She teaches courses in political communication, rhetorical criticism, presidential rhetoric, and the history of public address in the United States.

Thomas W. Benson is the Edwin Erle Sparks Professor of Rhetoric at Penn State University. He is the author or editor of 13 books, most recently *Writing JFK: Presidential Rhetoric and the Press in the Bay of Pigs Crisis*; *American Rhetoric in the New Deal Era*; and *The Rhetoric of the New Political Documentary*. He is a former editor of *The Quarterly Journal of Speech, Communication Quarterly,* and *The Review of Communication.*

Don Bialostosky is Professor of English at the University of Pittsburgh. His primary responsibility is in the Composition, Literacy, Pedagogy, and Rhetoric Program, and he also teaches history of criticism and the British romantic poets. He is the author of *Making Tales: The Poetics of Wordsworth's Narrative Experiments* (1984) and *Wordsworth, Dialogics and the Practice of Criticism* (1992) and coeditor with Lawrence Needham of *Rhetorical Traditions and British Romantic Literature* (1995). He has also published widely on the Bakhtin School. He has taught at the Universities of Utah, Washington, and Toledo and at Stony Brook and Pennsylvania State Universities. He is currently finishing a book on rhetoric in the Bakhtin School.

Stephen Howard Browne is Professor of Rhetorical Studies at the Pennsylvania State University. He is the author of *Jefferson's Call for Nationhood* (2003), *Angelina Grimké: Rhetoric, Identity, and the Radical Imagination* (1999), and *Edmund Burke and the Discourse of Virtue* (1993).

Karlyn Kohrs Campbell is Professor of Communication Studies at the University of Minnesota Twin Cities. Her publications include *Critiques of Contemporary Rhetoric; The Rhetorical Act; Man Cannot Speak for Her* (2 vols.); *Interplay of Influence: News, Advertising, Politics,* and *The Mass Media; Deeds Done in Words: Presidential Rhetoric and the Genres of Governance; Form and Genre: Shaping Rhetorical Action.* She has

edited *Women Public Speakers in the United States, 1800–1925: A Bio-Critical Sourcebook, Women Public Speakers in the United States, 1925–1993: A Bio-Critical Sourcebook,* and the *Quarterly Journal of Speech* (2000–2004). Her articles appear in *Philosophy and Rhetoric, Quarterly Journal of Speech, Presidential Studies Quarterly, Communication Studies, Communication Education, Communication and Cultural/Critical Studies,* and *Women's Studies in Communication.*

Martín Carcasson is Assistant Professor in the Speech Communication Department at Colorado State University (CSU) and the founder and director of the CSU Center for Public Deliberation. His research interests are focused on deliberative democracy and rhetoric and public affairs, especially concerning public policy issues such as poverty, education, freedom of speech, and the environment. His essays have appeared in journals such as *Rhetoric & Public Affairs, Quarterly Journal of Speech, Presidential Studies Quarterly,* and the *International Negotiation.*

Edward M. Clift is Associate Professor and Chair of Communication at Woodbury University in Burbank, California. Drawing on research interests that range from rhetoric to communication ethics, he teaches classes on media culture, interpersonal communication, and communication theory. He recently edited *How Language Is Used to Do Business: Essays on the Rhetoric of Economics* (2008). Clift serves as a reviewer for *Vestnick: Theory and Practice of Communication,* an international journal sponsored by the Russian Communication Association (RCA). The undergraduate student government at his university named him Faculty Advisor of the Year in 2006. In mid-2008, he was appointed Director of the School of Media, Culture & Design.

Robert Cox is Professor of Communication Studies and the Ecology Curriculum at the University of North Carolina at Chapel Hill.

His principal areas of research and teaching are rhetorical theory, environmental communication, and the discourse of social change/social movements, including critical studies of civil rights, labor, antiwar, and environmental movements. His current work explores the influence of "crisis disciplines" in the natural sciences and medicine on the emerging scholarship in environmental communication. His 2006 book *Environmental Communication and the Public Sphere* is the recipient of the Christine L. Oravec Award in Environmental Communication. He received his Ph.D. from the University of Pittsburgh (1973). His work has appeared in the *Quarterly Journal of Speech, Environmental Communication: A Journal of Nature and Culture, Communication Monographs, Argumentation and Advocacy,* and the *Journal of Applied Communication.*

James Darsey is Professor of Communication at Georgia State University. His work, concentrating largely on radical rhetorics and the rhetorics of marginalized people and groups, has appeared in the *Quarterly Journal of Speech, Communication Monographs,* the *Western Journal of Communication, Communication Studies,* and in a number of anthologies and reference works. His work has been recognized with the B. Aubrey Fisher Award and the Randy Majors Award, and his 1997 book, *The Prophetic Tradition and Radical Rhetoric in America,* was the recipient of the National Communication Association's Diamond Anniversary and Winans-Wichelns awards and of the Marie Hochmuth Nichols Award from the Public Address Division of NCA. *The Prophetic Tradition and Radical Rhetoric in America* has been widely cited in work in public address. Darsey is presently working on a project on cosmopolitan rhetoric.

Greg Dickinson is Associate Professor in the Department of Speech Communication at

Colorado State University. His research concerns the intersections of rhetoric, place, memory, everyday life, consumer culture, and suburbia. He investigates local built spaces as a mode to understand the ways specific places engage individuals as well as to build a theory about the materiality and spatiality of rhetoric. In 2007, he (along with his coauthors Brian L. Ott and Eric Aoki) won the NCA Visual Communication Division Excellence in Scholarship Award. His essays have appeared in *Communication and Critical/Cultural Studies, Quarterly Journal of Speech, Rhetoric Society Quarterly, Southern Journal of Communication,* and *Western Journal of Communication.*

Richard Leo Enos is Professor and Holder of the Lillian Radford Chair of Rhetoric and Composition at Texas Christian University. His research concentration is in classical rhetoric with an emphasis on the relationship between oral and written discourse. He is the past president of the Rhetoric Society of America and former editor of *Advances in the History of Rhetoric.* In 2006, he was awarded the George E. Yoos Distinguished Service Award by the Rhetoric Society of America (RSA) and was inducted as an RSA Fellow.

Jeanne Fahnestock is a Professor in the Department of English, University of Maryland. She is the author of *Rhetorical Figures in Science* (1999/2002) and coauthor of *A Rhetoric of Argument* (3rd ed., 2004). She has published articles and contributed chapters on rhetorical theory, argument, language analysis, and the rhetoric of science. She served on the Board of Directors of the Rhetoric Society of America and was co-organizer of its conference in 2000. She has directed the Professional Writing Program and the combined University Writing Programs at Maryland.

Christina R. Foust is Assistant Professor in the Department of Human Communication

Studies at the University of Denver. Her research and teaching engage rhetoric, power, and social change in a variety of contexts, including social movements, political discourse, and popular culture. Her current projects focus on retheorizing relationships between resistance and the body, social subjectivity, and collective action in light of global justice activism. She completed her Ph.D. at the University of North Carolina at Chapel Hill with Robert Cox as her dissertation advisor. Her dissertation won the 2005 Gerald R. Miller Outstanding Dissertation award from the National Communication Association; it is currently being revised into a book manuscript. Her work has appeared in the *Western Journal of Communication, Review of Communication,* and *Women's Studies in Communication.*

Lynée Lewis Gaillet is Associate Professor of English at Georgia State University and President of the Coalition of Women Scholars in the History of Rhetoric and Composition. She is the editor of *Scottish Rhetoric and Its Influences* and author of numerous articles and book chapters addressing writing program administration and the history of rhetoric/writing practices. Currently, she is coediting with Winifred Bryan Horner the second edition of *The Present State of Research in the History of Rhetoric.*

Cheryl Glenn is Liberal Arts Research Professor of English and Women's Studies and codirector of the Center for Democratic Deliberation at The Pennsylvania State University. She is also Chair of the Conference on College Composition and Communication. In the summers, she teaches courses in rhetoric and writing at the Bread Loaf School of English, a summer graduate program especially geared to secondary school teachers. Her scholarly work focuses on histories of women's rhetorics and writing practices, processes for the teaching of writing, and inclusionary rhetorical practices and theories.

Her publications include *Rhetoric Retold: Regendering the Tradition From Antiquity Through the Renaissance, Unspoken: A Rhetoric of Silence, Rhetorical Education in America, The St. Martin's Guide to Teaching Writing, The Writer's Harbrace Handbook, Making Sense: A Real-World Rhetorical Reader,* and *The Harbrace Guide to Writing.* With Shirley Wilson Logan, she coedits the Southern Illinois University Press series, "Studies in Rhetorics and Feminisms." Her scholarship has earned fellowships from the National Endowment for the Humanities, the Richard Braddock Best Article of the Year Award from *College Composition and Communication,* and an Outstanding Article Award (shared) from *Rhetoric Review.*

Laura J. Gurak is Professor and Founding Chair of the Department of Writing Studies at the University of Minnesota. She is author of *Cyberliteracy: Navigating the Internet With Awareness* (2001) and *Persuasion and Privacy in Cyberspace: The Online Protests Over Lotus Market Place and the Clipper Chip* (1997), the latter of which was the first book-length study to use rhetoric to study online communication. She is the coeditor of an electronic edited collection, *Into the Blogosphere* (http://blog.lib.umn.edu/blogosphere/), which was published entirely on a blog and explores the communicative features of Weblogs. Her research continues to focus on the rhetorical and social dynamics of digital communication.

Gerard A. Hauser is Professor of Communication and College Professor of Distinction at the University of Colorado at Boulder. He is the editor of *Philosophy and Rhetoric.* His publications include *Introduction to Rhetorical Theory,* second edition (2002) and *Vernacular Voices: The Rhetoric of Publics and Public Spheres* (1999). He is the past president of the Rhetoric Society of America and recipient of its George Yoos Distinguished Service Award. He is an RSA Fellow and an NCA Distinguished Scholar. His current research focuses on vernacular rhetoric as a means of resistance.

Maria T. Hegbloom is a Ph.D. candidate in Communication at the University of Colorado at Boulder. She received her B.A. and M.A. in Communication from Boise State University. Her research is largely focused on the theory and philosophy of communication, with particular emphasis on critical and cultural theories. Her current work is concerned with the relationship between neoliberalism, globalization, and democracy.

Bruce Horner is Endowed Chair in Rhetoric and Composition at the University of Louisville, where he teaches courses in composition, composition pedagogy and theory, and literacy studies. His books include *Writing Conventions* (2008), coauthored with Min-Zhan Lu; *Terms of Work for Composition: A Materialist Critique* (2000), winner of the 2001 W. Ross Winterowd Award for the Most Outstanding Book in Composition Theory; *Key Terms in Popular Music and Culture* (1999), coedited with Thomas Swiss; and *Representing the "Other": Basic Writers and the Teaching of Basic Writing* (1999), coauthored with Min-Zhan Lu. His essays have appeared in journals such as *College Composition and Communication, College English, JAC, Rhetoric Review, English Education,* and the *Journal of Basic Writing.* "English Only and U.S. College Composition," an essay he coauthored with John Trimbur, won the 2002 Richard Braddock Award. His scholarship is frequently cited, and he has been a guest speaker at national and international venues.

Sue Hum is Associate Professor of English at the University of Texas at San Antonio and the coeditor of two anthologies: *Ways of Seeing, Ways of Speaking: The Integration of Rhetoric and Vision in Constructing the Real* (2007) with Kristie S. Fleckenstein and Linda

T. Calendrillo and *Relations, Locations, Positions: Composition Theory for Writing Teachers* (2006) with Peter Vandenberg and Jennifer Clary-Lemon. Her research and teaching interests include postprocess composition theory, multicultural and contrastive rhetoric, and cultural studies. She is completing a manuscript titled "Networked Learning, Learning Networks: The Nature of Students' Literacies in Course Management Software."

Connie Kendall is Assistant Professor of Literacy in the Center for Access and Transition at the University of Cincinnati, where she teaches various courses in developmental reading and writing as well as a graduate seminar in basic writing theory and pedagogy. Her research interests center on the history and politics of literacy testing in U.S. contexts, and she is currently at work on a book project that examines the connections between "high-stakes" tests of literacy and nation building. Her essays appear in *Rhetorical Agendas: Political, Ethical, Spiritual* (2006), *Untenured Faculty as Writing Program Administrators: Institutional Practices and Politics* (2007), and *The Literacy Standard* (in press).

Zornitsa D. Keremidchieva is a visiting Assistant Professor in Communication Studies at Hamline University in Saint Paul, Minnesota. She holds a B.A. from the American University in Bulgaria, two M.A.s from the University of Maine, and a Ph.D. in communication studies with graduate minors in feminist studies and literacy and rhetorical studies from the University of Minnesota. Her research interests are in the areas of feminist rhetorical theory and history, congressional rhetoric, and critical citizenship studies.

Julie Thompson Klein is Professor of Humanities at Wayne State University. She has also held visiting posts in Japan and New Zealand and was a Fulbright professor in

Nepal and Senior Fellow at the Association of American Colleges & Universities. She is an internationally recognized expert on interdisciplinary research, education, and problem solving. She received the Kenneth Boulding Award for outstanding scholarship on interdisciplinarity and has lectured and consulted throughout North America, Europe, Latin America, the South Pacific, and Asia. She has also served on national task forces and advised public and private agencies. Her authored and edited books include *Interdisciplinarity: History, Theory, and Practice* (1990); *Interdisciplinary Studies Today* (1994); *Crossing Boundaries: Knowledge, Disciplinarities, and Interdisciplinarities* (1996); *Mapping Interdisciplinary Studies* (1999); *Transdisciplinarity: Joint Problem Solving Among Science, Technology, and Society* (2001); *Interdisciplinary Education in K–12 and College* (2002); and *Humanities, Culture, and Interdisciplinarity: The Changing American Academy* (2005).

John Lyne is Professor of Communication at the University of Pittsburgh. He also serves on the faculty of the graduate program in Bioethics and is a resident fellow at the Center for Philosophy of Science. His work on philosophical and theoretical issues in rhetoric, argumentation, and rhetoric of science appears in journals and edited volumes both inside and outside the field of communication. He has been editor-in-chief for a book series on Rhetoric and the Human Sciences. A past president of the Association for the Rhetoric of Science and Technology and an active member of the National Communication Association, he has also served as department chair at the University of Iowa and the University of Pittsburgh. He has directed several national award–winning dissertations. He received his Ph.D. from the University of Wisconsin–Madison in 1978.

Min-Zhan Lu is Professor of English and University Scholar at the University of Louisville, where she teaches courses in composition, composition pedagogy and theory, life writing, critical and cultural theory, and theories of languages and literacies. Her books include *Shanghai Quartet: The Crossings of Four Women of China* (2001); *Comp Tales*, coedited with Richard Haswell (2000); and *Writing Conventions* (2008), coauthored with Bruce Horner. Her work is frequently cited and has been reprinted both in general readers and in scholarly collections such as *Feminism and Composition* (2003), *Landmark Essays in Basic Writing* (2001), and *Landmark Essays on Writing Processes* (1994). She is the winner of the Richard Braddock Award (2005) and the Mina Shaughnessy Award (1992), as well as several teaching awards, and she has served as a keynote and featured speaker at national and international venues.

Arabella Lyon is Associate Professor of English at the State University of New York, Buffalo, and is the author of the Ross Winterowd Award winner *Intentions: Negotiated, Contested, and Ignored*. She is currently working on two book-length projects, one on transnationalism and comparative rhetoric and the other on deliberative democracy, human rights, and speech act theory.

Joyce Irene Middleton is Associate Professor of English at East Carolina University. She has published essays on rhetorical memory, orality, and literacy; on pedagogy, race, and gender; and writings by Toni Morrison in journals such as *College English, Journal of Advanced Composition,* and *Cultural Studies;* and in scholarly collections such as *African American Rhetoric(s): Interdisciplinary Perspectives* and the award-winning *Calling Cards: Theory and Practice in the Study of Race, Gender, and Culture.* She was awarded a position in the 2001 NEH Summer Institute for Black Film Studies. She teaches and writes about visual rhetoric in film and film as a form of public pedagogy. She served as a guest coeditor, with Krista Ratcliffe, for a special issue on Whiteness Studies in *Rhetoric Review* (Fall, 2005), and she is a member of the editorial board for the *Rhetoric Society Quarterly*. She is completing a book-length project on race, whiteness, and gender, titled *"Shifting the Gaze": Toni Morrison and "Race Matters" Rhetoric.*

Carolyn R. Miller is SAS Institute Distinguished Professor of Rhetoric and Technical Communication at North Carolina State University. She has published essays on digital rhetoric, rhetorical theory, the rhetoric of science and technology, and technical communication in journals such as *Argumentation, College English,* the *Journal of Business and Technical Communication,* the *Quarterly Journal of Speech, Rhetorica,* and *Rhetoric Society Quarterly,* as well as in many edited volumes. Her publications have received three awards from the National Council of Teachers of English. She has lectured and taught in North America, Europe, and South America. She is a past president of the Rhetoric Society of America and current editor of *Rhetoric Society Quarterly.*

Gordon R. Mitchell is Associate Professor of Communication and Deputy Director of the Ridgway Center for International Security Studies at the University of Pittsburgh. His book *Strategic Deception* (2000) won the National Communication Association's Winans-Wichelns Award for Distinguished Scholarship in Rhetoric and Public Address, while *Hitting First* (coedited in 2006 with William Keller) is the lead title in the University of Pittsburgh's Ridgway-Ford "Security Continuum" book series. His

research has also appeared in journals such as *The Bulletin of the Atomic Scientists; The Fletcher Forum of World Affairs; Science, Technology, and Human Values;* and the *Quarterly Journal of Speech,* while his briefing papers have been published by organizations including the Federation of American Scientists, the International Security Information Service (United Kingdom and Europe), and the Peace Research Institute, Frankfurt. As an intercollegiate debate coach, he has guided teams to two national championships and currently serves as Director of the William Pitt Debating Union.

Roxanne Mountford is Associate Professor of English at the University of Kentucky. She teaches rhetorical history, theory, and criticism; ethnographic research methods; composition pedagogy; and gender issues in communication. She is the author of two books, *The Gendered Pulpit: Preaching in American Protestant Spaces* and *Women's Ways of Making It . . . In Rhetoric and Composition* (with Michelle Ballif and Diane Davis), and numerous articles and book chapters. Her research focuses on rhetorical performance, religious rhetoric, research methodology, the future of the discipline, and feminist issues in rhetoric and composition.

Brian L. Ott is Associate Professor of Media and Rhetorical Studies at Colorado State University. An award-winning scholar and teacher, he has published widely in national and regional journals, including *Critical Studies in Media Communication, Communication and Critical/Cultural Studies, Cultural Studies <=> Critical Methodologies, Rhetoric and Public Affairs, Western Journal of Communication, Southern Communication Journal, Women's Studies in Communication,* and *The Journal of Popular Culture.* He is author of *The Small Screen: How Television*

Equips Us to Live in the Information Age and editor of the *Western Journal of Communication*.

Edward Panetta is Associate Professor of Speech Communication and the Director of Debate at the University of Georgia. His research program is in the area of argumentation. One element of his project is the work associated with the development of a nationally visible intercollegiate debate program. As an outgrowth of working with the Georgia Debate Union, he publishes debate theory pieces that are intended to influence the practice of intercollegiate debate in the United States. A second element of his research is the assessment of argumentation in public movements. He focuses on the impact of economic transformation on religious, environmental, and labor rhetoric. His research has been published in journals such as *Argumentation, Communication Quarterly, Free Speech Yearbook*, and *Argumentation & Advocacy*.

Angela G. Ray is an Assistant Professor in the Department of Communication Studies at Northwestern University. As a rhetorical critic, she studies public discourse of the 19th-century United States, with particular interests in popular education, commercial entertainment, and social reform. Her essays have appeared in *Argumentation and Advocacy*, the *Quarterly Journal of Speech, Rhetoric and Public Affairs*, and *Women's Studies in Communication*. She received awards from the American Forensic Association, the National Communication Association, and the Rhetoric Society of America for her 2005 book, *The Lyceum and Public Culture in the Nineteenth-Century United States*, a study of the development of the popular lecture circuits.

Joshua R. Ritter is a doctoral candidate in Communication at Georgia State University. His main area of interest is rhetoric and religion, and he is currently exploring issues surrounding rhetorical theology and the

various historical and contemporary intersections of rhetoric and religion. An ordained Baptist minister, he has served as a chaplain at the Hillcrest Baptist Medical Center in Waco, Texas, as well as at the Atlanta Medical Center in Atlanta, Georgia, where he began exploring ways in which pastoral care might be approached as a rhetorical process. He received an M.Div. from the McAfee School of Theology at Mercer University.

Kate Ronald is the Roger and Joyce L. Howe Professor of English at Miami University, where she teaches graduate and undergraduate courses in composition and rhetoric and directs the Howe Writing Initiative in the School of Business. Her recent publications include *Reason to Believe: Romanticism, Pragmatism, and the Teaching of Writing*, coauthored with Hephzibah Roskelly (1998), and *Available Means: An Anthology of Women's Rhetoric(s)* (2001) and *Teaching Rhetorica* (2006), both coedited with Joy Ritchie.

Edward Schiappa is Professor and Chair of the Communication Studies Department of the University of Minnesota, where he holds the Paul Frenzel Chair of Liberal Arts. He writes about classical and contemporary rhetorical theory, with particular interests in definitional controversies, theories of interpretation, and the rhetorical work of popular culture. His books include *Protagoras and Logos: A Study in Greek Philosophy & Rhetoric, Landmark Essays on Classical Greek Rhetoric, Warranting Assent: Case Studies in Argument Evaluation, The Beginnings of Rhetorical Theory in Classical Greece, Defining Reality: Definitions and the Politics of Meaning*, and *Beyond Representational Correctness: Rethinking Criticism of Popular Media*. He has published in journals in English, communication, classics, psychology, and philosophy.

Judy Z. Segal is Professor of English at the University of British Columbia, where she teaches rhetorical history and theory rhetoric of science, and rhetoric of health and medicine. Her monograph, *Health and the Rhetoric of Medicine* (Southern Illinois University Press), appeared in 2005. Her recent essays appear in journals such as *Journal of Medical Humanities* and *Health: An Interdisciplinary Journal for the Social Study of Health, Illness, and Medicine*, and in the books *Unfitting Stories: Narrative Approaches to Disease, Disability, and Trauma* (edited by V. Raoul et al., 2007) and *Rhetoric of Healthcare: Essays Toward a New Disciplinary Inquiry* (edited by B. Heifferon and S. Brown, 2007). Her current research project is entitled "Values and Public Persuasion: The Rhetoric of Direct-to-Consumer Advertising for Prescription Pharmaceuticals." From 2003 to 2007, she was a member of the President's International Advisory Committee for the Canadian Institutes of Health Research.

Wendy B. Sharer is Associate Professor of English and Director of Composition at East Carolina University. She is the author of *Vote and Voice: Women's Organizations and Political Literacy, 1915–1930* (2004), coauthor of *1977: A Cultural Moment in Composition* (2007), and coeditor of *Rhetorical Education in America* (2004). Her work has also appeared in *Rhetoric Review* and *Rhetoric Society Quarterly.*

Christine Mason Sutherland was educated at Oxford and McGill and is now Professor of Communication and Culture at the University of Calgary, where she teaches courses in rhetoric and the history of rhetoric, and also the senior seminar in Communications Studies. She has published essays on the rhetoric of St. Augustine of Hippo and on the plain style movement of the 17th century, but her work has mostly been on women in the history of rhetoric. In 1999, she was the principal editor of *The Changing Tradition: Women in the History of Rhetoric*, commissioned by the

International Society for the History of Rhetoric. Her single-authored book, *The Eloquence of Mary Astell*, a study of the theory and practice of an important 17th/18th-century thinker and writer, was published in 2005.

C. Jan Swearingen is Professor of English at Texas A&M University, where she teaches courses in the history and theory of rhetoric, comparative studies in literacy, feminist theory, Chinese rhetorical traditions, the rhetoric of religion, and Colonial American oratory. The author of *Rhetoric and Irony: Western Literacy and Western Lies* and editor of *Rhetoric, the Polis, and the Global Village*, she has served as President of the Rhetoric Society of America and as Chair of the MLA Division on the History and Theory of Rhetoric and Composition and the Division on Language and Society.

Elizabeth Tasker is Assistant Professor of English at Stephen F. Austin State University, where she teaches writing and 18th-century literature. Her research interests include Restoration actresses, 18th-century female authors, historiography, and the rereading of Restoration and 18th-century drama as performative rhetoric. She has published articles on feminist historical rhetoric in *Peitho* and *Rhetoric Review.*

Frans H. van Eemeren is Professor of Speech Communication, Argumentation Theory, and Rhetoric at the University of Amsterdam, Department Head, and Director of the Research Program "Argumentation and Discourse" and the Research Master Program "Rhetoric, Argumentation Theory, and Philosophy" (RAP). He is Distinguished Scholar of the National Communication Association, Fulbright Professor, recipient of various research awards, chairman of the International Society for the Study of Argumentation (ISSA), and editor of the journal *Argumentation* and Springer's Argumentation Library. Together with Rob Grootendorst, he developed the influential pragma-dialectical theory of argumentation. Among his book publications are *Speech Acts in Argumentative Discussions; Argumentation, Communication and Fallacies;* and *A Systematic Theory of Argumentation* (with Grootendorst); *Reconstructing Argumentative Discourse* (with Grootendorst, Jackson, and Jacobs); *Fundamentals of Argumentation Theory* (with other prominent argumentation scholars); *Dialectic and Rhetoric* (with Houtlosser); and *Argumentative Indicators in Discourse* (with Houtlosser and Snoeck Henkemans).

Arthur E. Walzer is Professor in Communication Studies at the University of Minnesota, Twin Cities. He is the author of *George Campbell: Rhetoric in the Age of the Enlightenment* (2003), coeditor (with Richard Graff and Janet Atwill) of *The Viability of the Rhetorical Tradition* (2005), and coeditor (with Alan G. Gross) of *Rereading Aristotle's Rhetoric* (2000). His essays have appeared in *Rhetorica, Quarterly Journal of Speech, Rhetoric Review,* and other periodicals. He is past president of the American Society for the History of Rhetoric and immediate past Board Chair of the Alliance of Rhetoric Societies.

Morris Young is Director of English 100, Associate Professor of English, and faculty affiliate in Asian American Studies at the University of Wisconsin–Madison. He was formerly a faculty member at Miami University in Oxford, Ohio. His research and teaching focus on composition and rhetoric, literacy studies, and Asian American literature and culture. His essays and reviews have appeared in *College English, Journal of Basic Writing, Amerasia* and *Composition Forum,* and he has contributed chapters to many edited collections, including *The Literacy Connection* (1999), *Personal Effects: The Social Character of Scholarly Writing* (2001), *East Main Street: Asian American Popular Culture* (2005), and *Women and Literacy: Local and Global Inquiries for a New*

Century (2007). His book *Minor Re/Visions: Asian American Literacy Narratives as a Rhetoric of Citizenship* (2004) received the 2004 W. Ross Winterowd Award and the 2006 Outstanding Book Award from the Conference on College Composition and Communication. With LuMing Mao, he is coeditor of the collection *Representations: Doing Asian American Rhetoric.*

David Zarefsky is Owen L. Coon Professor of Argumentation and Debate and Professor of Communication Studies at Northwestern University. Among his publications are *President Johnson's War on Poverty: Rhetoric and History* and *Lincoln, Douglas, and Slavery: In the Crucible of Public Debate,* both of which received the Winans-Wichelns Award for distinguished scholarship in rhetoric and public address from the National Communication Association. He also has been named an NCA distinguished scholar. He is a former president of the National Communication Association, the Rhetoric Society of America, and the Central States Communication Association. He wishes to acknowledge especially the assistance of Angela G. Ray and Kirt Wilson.

Margaret D. Zulick is Associate Professor of Communication at Wake Forest University. She now teaches and conducts research in rhetorical theory and criticism, American public discourse, the history of rhetoric, and prophetism in American public discourse. Her recent publications include "The Ethos of Invention: The Dialogue of Ethics and Aesthetics in Kenneth Burke and Mikhail Bakhtin," *The Ethos of Rhetoric* (2004, M. J. Hyde, Ed., pp. 34–55) and "Prophecy and Providence: The Anxiety Over Prophetic Authority," *Journal of Communication and Religion,* 26(2) (2003). Her Ph.D. in Religious Studies (Northwestern University, 1993) concentrated in rhetoric of the Hebrew Bible and was conducted under the auspices of the Garrett/Northwestern Joint Program in Religious Studies.